SHAKESPEARE SURVEY

A Sixty-Year Cumulative Index

ADVISORY BOARD

(1) Shakespeare and his Stage
(2) Shakespearian Production
(3) The Man and the Writer
(4) Interpretation
(5) Textual Criticism
(6) The Histories
(7) Style and Language
(8) The Comedies
(9) *Hamlet*
(10) The Roman Plays
(11) The Last Plays (with an index to *Surveys 1–10*)
(12) The Elizabethan Theatre
(13) *King Lear*
(14) Shakespeare and his Contemporaries
(15) The Poems and Music
(16) Shakespeare in the Modern World
(17) Shakespeare in his Own Age
(18) Shakespeare Then Till Now
(19) *Macbeth*
(20) Shakespearian and Other Tragedy
(21) *Othello* (with an index to *Surveys 11–20*)
(22) Aspects of Shakespearian Comedy
(23) Shakespeare's Language
(24) Shakespeare: Theatre Poet
(25) Shakespeare's Problem Plays
(26) Shakespeare's Jacobean Tragedies
(27) Shakespeare's Early Tragedies
(28) Shakespeare and the Ideas of his Time
(29) Shakespeare's Last Plays
(30) *Henry IV* to *Hamlet*
(31) Shakespeare and the Classical World (with an index to *Surveys 21–30*)
(32) The Middle Comedies
(33) *King Lear*
(34) Characterization in Shakespeare
(35) Shakespeare in the Nineteenth Century
(36) Shakespeare in the Twentieth Century
(37) Shakespeare's Earlier Comedies
(38) Shakespeare and History
(39) Shakespeare on Film and Television
(40) Current Approaches to Shakespeare through Language, Text and Theatre
(41) Shakespearian Stages and Staging (with an index to *Surveys 31–40*)
(42) Shakespeare and the Elizabethans
(43) *The Tempest* and After
(44) Shakespeare and Politics
(45) *Hamlet* and its Afterlife
(46) Shakespeare and Sexuality
(47) Playing Places for Shakespeare
(48) Shakespeare and Cultural Exchange
(49) *Romeo and Juliet* and its Afterlife
(50) Shakespeare and Language
(51) Shakespeare in the Eighteenth Century (with an index to *Surveys 41–50*)
(52) Shakespeare and the Globe
(53) Shakespeare and Narrative
(54) Shakespeare and Religions
(55) *King Lear* and its Afterlife
(56) Shakespeare and Comedy
(57) *Macbeth* and its Afterlife
(58) Writing about Shakespeare
(59) Editing Shakespeare
(60) Theatres for Shakespeare
(61) Shakespeare, Sound and Screen

Aspects of *Macbeth*
Aspects of *Othello*
Aspects of *Hamlet*
Aspects of *King Lear*
Aspects of Shakespeare's 'Problem Plays'

SHAKESPEARE SURVEY

A Sixty-Year Cumulative Index

EDITED BY

PETER HOLLAND

CAMBRIDGE
UNIVERSITY PRESS

CAMBRIDGE UNIVERSITY PRESS
Cambridge, New York, Melbourne, Madrid, Cape Town, Singapore, São Paulo, Delhi

Cambridge University Press
The Edinburgh Building, Cambridge CB2 8RU, UK

Published in the United States of America by Cambridge University Press, New York

www.cambridge.org
Information on this title: www.cambridge.org/9780521517010

First published 2009

Printed in the United Kingdom at the University Press, Cambridge

A catalogue record for this publication is available from the British Library

ISBN 978-0-521-51701-0 hardback

PREFACE

Shakespeare Survey is now sixty years old. Its volumes provide a rich and continuing history of Shakespeare studies, exploring every part of Shakespeare's writing and writing about Shakespeare, detailing the contexts, performances, meanings and possibilities of his works. Since its inception, the series has ensured that each volume contains its own index of names and, where appropriate, individual titles (including, of course, references to each of Shakespeare's plays and poems). Every ten years an index has been added which amalgamates the previous ten. Such decennial indexes currently appear in volumes 11 (published in 1958), 21 (1968), 31 (1978), 41 (1989) and 51 (1998). This year it was decided it would be a great help to the thousands who read and consult *Shakespeare Survey* if one cumulative index was provided to cover the whole sixty years, rather than just the last ten, enabling them to find references across six decades without having to consult six separate indexes. Because of its size, and for ease of use, this sixty-year index has been made separately available as a freestanding volume.

Indexing is a careful art but its styles have changed over the sixty years of work that this volume represents. Some kinds of entry appeared in the first cumulative index in volume 11 that were not continued thereafter. Others start to appear much later but parallel earlier examples were not retrieved. Greater consistency across this volume could only have been achieved if the entire indexing had been started afresh. Thanks to the exceptional work of Caroline Burkitt, we have been able to catch numerous errors and doublings but others undoubtedly remain. I encourage readers to look widely and to forgive us the mistakes that remain.

Peter Holland

INDEX

***Bold** figures indicate a volume number.*

A., H., *Partheneia Sacra* (1633), **12**, 107
Aabel, Per, **11**, 121
Aaron, Stephen, **13**, 134
Aasand, Hardin L., **53**, 344; **54**, 313; **57**, 342; **59**, 157n1, 174
Abartis, Caesarea, **31**, 166
Abate, Corinne S., **57**, 320
Abbado, Claudio, **60**, 189n19
Abbey, Edwin Austin, **37**, 51–2; **49**, 126, 306
Abbot, George, Archbishop of Canterbury, **46**, 26n; **56**, 227
Abbott, Charles D., **36**, 30n
Abbott, Claude Colleer, **55**, 128n, 130n, 135n, 136n, 137n, 138, 140n
Abbott, E. A., **23**, 9n, 11n; **34**, 192; **41**, 236n; **58**, 319, 320
Shakespearian Grammar, **7**, 2, 24n
Abbott, H. Porter, **55**, 157n
Abbott, June, **47**, 216; **49**, 269; **56**, 297
Abbott, Russ, **59**, 341
Abel, Royston, **54**, 290
Abel, Walter, **4**, 124
Abelove, Henry, **46**, 144n; **53**, 80n
Abels-Ludwig, Nele, **56**, 315
Abend, Murray, **5**, 139n
Aberbach, D., **33**, 201–2
Abercrombie, Lascelles, **1**, 14, 118; **4**, 7–8, 21; **6**, 143; **7**, 5; **10**, 135; **16**, 45; **19**, 12, 23n; **22**, 148; **45**, 77n; **55**, 135
Plea for the Liberty of Interpreting, **3**, 9, 137
Aberle, Erich, **16**, 134
Abington, Mrs, **14**, 113; **32**, 28, 33
Abiteboul, Maurice, **39**, 235
Abomell, Charles, **56**, 269
Abraham, Lyndy, **53**, 322
Abrahams, Roger D., **29**, 18n; **46**, 109
Abrams, Meyer, **9**, 100n; **31**, 62n; **51**, 321
Abrams, Richard, **33**, 188; **43**, 70n, 73n, 77n; **50**, 287n; **51**, 326–7; **56**, 72n; **60**, 268
Abrams, W. A., **38**, 88n
Abravanel, E., **34**, 6n
Abulafia, John, **45**, 156
Abusch, Alexander, **48**, 178–80
Accius, **10**, 36
Achebe, Chinua, **39**, 177n
Acherson, Neal, **56**, 244n
Acheson (model maker), **47**, 17
Acheson, A. C., **8**, 6; **10**, 120
Lost Years of Shakespeare, **3**, 2
Shakespeare and the Rival Poet, **3**, 10
Shakespeare's Sonnet Story, **3**, 10
Acheson, Arthur, **38**, 53; **44**, 37
Acheson, Carol, **55**, 172n
Achurch, Janet, **6**, 140
Acker, Paul, **39**, 7
Ackerman, Belinda, **42**, 155
Ackerman, James S., **33**, 145n
Ackerman, Vanessa, **59**, 299
Ackland, Joss, **36**, 153
Ackroyd, Peter, **54**, 34n; **59**, 108n2
Acquart, André, **18**, 122
Act-Division, **1**, 12
Acting
Elizabethan, **2**, 31–2; **5**, 143–4 *and* n; **7**, 27, 82–9
modern, **2**, 6, 11–12, **14**
see also under Productions of Shakespeare's plays; Shakespeare; *and* Theatre, Elizabethan
Acting Funny: Comic Theory and Practice in Shakespeare's Plays (ed. F. Teague), **48**, 245
Acting Shakespeare, **42**, 162
Acton, David, **51**, 246
Acton, H. M., **41**, 34
Acton, J. E. E. D. (Lord Acton), **28**, 21
Acton, Richard, **21**, 98
Actors' companies, *see under* Theatre, Elizabethan, companies
Acuña, José B., **28**, 160; **31**, 175
Adès, Thomas, **59**, 345
Adam, Abigail, **53**, 127; **56**, 130n
Adam, Cornel, **18**, 131
Adam, Ian, **53**, 119n
Adamaitis, R., **39**, 83n
Adamian, Petros, **24**, 169
Adamov, Arthur, **57**, 119
Adams, Barry B., **24**, 162; **32**, 246; **54**, 306
Adams, Beverley, **42**, 154
Adams, Brooks, **24**, 97
Adams, Charles Francis, **24**, 89, 100n, 101
Adams, Clement, **17**, 31

INDEX

Adams, Graham C., **37**, 196; **48**, 264
Ottoneum Theater: An English Survivor from Seventeeth Century Germany, The, **48**, 264
Adams, H. H., *English Domestic or Homiletic Tragedy 1575–1642*, **14**, 3, 65n
Adams, H. M., 'The Shakespeare Collection in Trinity College Library, Cambridge', **5**, 50–4
Adams, Heather, **46**, 90n
Adams, Henry Brooks, **24**, 87–104
Adams, Henry Hitch, **45**, 23n
Adams, John, **41**, 184; **42**, 162; **44**, 233; **46**, 191; **57**, 128, 129, 130, 131; **60**, 321
Adams, John Cranford, **1**, 6, 10, 27, 36n; **2**, 141; **3**, 84, 89; **5**, 143; **6**, 161; **7**, 70, 72–3, 74–5, 79n, 80n, 81n, 144; **9**, 146, 148; **10**, 83–4, 85, 87n, 88n, 89n; **11**, 123, 146; **12**, 4, 13, 143–4; **13**, 114, 119–21, 122–3, 132; **16**, 152; **17**, 200; **29**, 130n, 131; **33**, 47, 49; **36**, 119n, 179; **40**, 217; **41**, 1, 3, 6, 20n; **43**, 149, 167; **52**, 2–8, 11
views on a 'tarras' in the Globe Theatre criticized, **4**, 97–100
Adams, John Quincy, **23**, 126, 175; **24**, 88, 93, 101; **25**, 5n; **26**, 82, 86; **34**, 52n; **41**, 35–6, 106n; **43**, 152; **46**, 248n; **53**, 134, 206n
Adams, Joseph Quincy, **1**, 4, 17, 19, 20, 21, 22, 61, 62, 64, 66–7, 74, 75, 77n; **2**, 134, 147; **3**, 4, 24, 28, 49, 146; **4**, 11, 84; **5**, 25; **6**, 73n; **8**, 109; **9**, 2, 3–4, 8, 9; **10**, 2, 86n; **11**, 115n; **12**, 129n; **13**, 48n, 88n; **14**, 5; **17**, 167n, 200n; **18**, 105; **19**, 1; **26**, 82, 86; **27**, 93, 111n, 112, 113, 118, 121n, 129; **29**, 104; **30**, 167n; **45**, 19n, 20n; **54**, 59n; **59**, 23n13; **60**, 252n3, 256
Life of William Shakespeare, **3**, 8, 27
Adams, Kingsley, **15**, 130n
Adams, Miriam, **50**, 147
Adams, Richard, **15**, 159; **30**, 206n; **41**, 212
Adams, Robert M., **8**, 146; **44**, 20n; **53**, 40n
Adams, Simon, **38**, 21n; **44**, 234; **60**, 4
Adams, W. Bridges, **2**, 10, 15; **45**, 35n
Adams, W. E., **58**, 109, 110, 115
Adamson, Henry, **19**, 62
Adamson, Jane, **35**, 167; **37**, 127n; **42**, 180; **49**, 241n
Adamson, Sylvia, **55**, 183n, 353–4; **57**, 196
Adamson, W. D., **36**, 170
Addams, Jane, **55**, 167
Addison, Joseph, **2**, 3; **8**, 66; **34**, 181; **36**, 139; **37**, 146; **51**, 73, 113; **52**, 149; **55**, 96
Cato, **10**, 30, 38
Adebayo, Dotun, **60**, 167
Adee, David, **58**, 144
Adelman, Janet, **28**, 156, 157; **33**, 101n, 102, 104, 115n, 118, 119n, 185n; **38**, 153; **41**, 85n; **45**, 196; **46**, 3, 74, 92n, 93n, 95n, 96n, 101n, 103, 110n, 151n, 207; **47**, 234; **49**, 206n, 213, 312; **50**, 52n, 55n, 108, 196n, 247; **51**, 279, 284; **52**, 325; **53**, 83n, 303; **55**, 8, 224n, 232n, 233n; **56**, 146, 229, 233, 234; **57**, 1, 40, 191, 312, 339; **58**, 50, 251, 309, 331
Suffocating Mothers: Fantasies of Maternal Origin in Shakespeare's Plays, **46**, 207
Aden, John M., **34**, 93n
Ades, John I., **24**, 168n; **25**, 185
Adlard, John, **30**, 195
Adler, Doris, **38**, 229; **39**, 233
Adler, Gerhard, **21**, 133
Adler, Hermann, **45**, 21
Adler, Jacob, P., **50**, 35; **55**, 115, 125n
Adler, John, **57**, 86, 89
Adler, Luther, **7**, 117
Adler, Max, **35**, 76n
Adler, Steven, **56**, 342–3
Adling, Wilfried, **27**, 179n
Adlington, William, **23**, 61; **31**, 33, 38, 39, 43; **47**, 150; **53**, 56; **57**, 215
Admiral's Men, *see under* Theatre, Elizabethan, companies
Adolphus, John, **51**, 111n
Adorno, Rolena, **51**, 297
Adorno, Theodor W., **55**, 72–3, 75, 77–9, 81, 156; **56**, 139–40; **59**, 291
Adrian, Max, **14**, 129, 130
Adso of Montier-en-Der, **59**, 241, 242n22, 247, 248n67, 249
Adson, John, **19**, 105, 106n
Advance Players, **1**, 103, 104–5
Ady, Endre, **54**, 55
Ælian, **48**, 142
Aebischer, Pascale, **55**, 55n; **57**, 46; **58**, 334, 336, 342; **60**, 229, 355
Aeneid, **50**, 60
Aers, David, **51**, 151n; **55**, 5
Aers, Leslie, **46**, 205, 239; **49**, 142n; **55**, 9n
Shakespeare in the Changing Curriculum, **46**, 205, 239
Aeschylus, **10**, 36; **11**, 36; **19**, 55; **29**, 31; **30**, 104; **32**, 220; **35**, 162–3; **36**, 11–19; **38**, 217; **41**, 125; **45**, 90; **55**, 308; **58**, 211
Agamemnon, **13**, 20
Prometheus Bound, **4**, 31; **13**, 70
Aesop, **15**, 64; **17**, 60; **56**, 225
Aesop's Crow, **15**, 64
Ages of Sin, or Sinnes Birth & groweth, The, **12**, 107, 108n
Fables, **4**, 65; **7**, 23; **10**, 15
Aesopus, actor, **7**, 86, 89n
Æthiopian Historie of Heliodorus, **3**, 54
Afford, Mike, **45**, 130
Africanus, Leo, **52**, 202n, 205, 206n
Agamben, Giorgio, **60**, 125–6, 128
Agar, Ann, **45**, 114
'Agas' Map, **1**, 25–6, 31, 35n, 36n
Agas, Ralph, **33**, 198; **53**, 203n
Agate, James, **2**, 12, 18; **7**, 122; **9**, 18; **10**, 75–6; **32**, 27n; **36**, 81; **48**, 282; **49**, 227, 229, 230, 231; **57**, 81
Agazarri, Alphonsus, **56**, 192, 195
Age of Kings, An, **39**, 9, 9–21, 30–1, 94
Agee, James, **39**, 3
Ager, Mark, **45**, 157
Aggas, E., **28**, 39n
Aggeler, Geoffrey, **42**, 178; **47**, 233; **53**, 320; **55**, 220n
Aggrey, Jah-Man, **51**, 221
Agnew, Gates K., **23**, 143; **42**, 6n, 10n
Agnew, Jean-Christophe, **51**, 147, 148n, 157
Agostini, Lucien, **7**, 110
Agrippa, Henricus Cornelius, of Nettesheim, **25**, 126; **28**, 119; **43**, 3; **54**, 227; **56**, 82n
Of the Vanitie and uncertaintie of Artes and Sciences, **4**, 67n
à Kempis, Thomas, **54**, 118
Ahern, John, **52**, 189n
Ahl, Frederick, **53**, 18, 19
Aho, James, **48**, 93n

INDEX

Ahonen-Mäkelä, Mrs Ritva, **18**, 121
Ahrens, Rüdiger, **37**, 156n; **56**, 314
Ahrenson, Rene, **13**, 131; **57**, 160
Aicard, Jean, adaptation of *Othello*, **3**, 103, 104
Aichele, Klaus, **59**, 247n64
Aiken, R., **18**, 180
Aikin, Judith P., **45**, 159
Aikman, J., **28**, 64n
Aimerito, Lella, **5**, 113
Ainger, Alfred, **6**, 4
Ainley, Henry, **2**, 7; **18**, 73; **41**, 56; **49**, 226; **55**, 129
Ainsle, Scott, **58**, 302
Ainsworth, Kacey, **52**, 229
Airamo, Hemmo, **13**, 126
Aitchison, Nick, **57**, 9, 73, 75
Aithal, K., **19**, 143
Aitken, A. J., **26**, 164n
Aitken, Jonathan, **53**, 268
Aitken, Maria, **43**, 212; **47**, 209
Ajax Flagellifer, **11**, 114n
Ajo, Wali, **41**, 188
Akalaitis, JoAnne, **47**, 3
Akalin, Sahap, **16**, 137
Akbar, Jalaluddin, **32**, 87
Akçan, Yildiz, **9**, 116; **12**, 117; **14**, 123
Ake, Jami, **58**, 325, 331
Akechi Mitsuhide, **12**, 115
Akenside, Mark, **58**, 73
Akerby, Charles, **51**, 47
Akerby, George, **51**, 47n
Akerman, Antony, **52**, 156, 157n
Akesson, Birgit, **16**, 137
Akhmanova, Olga, **31**, 174–5
Akhmeteli, Sandro, **48**, 188–9
Akimov, N. P., **54**, 147–8
Akinbode, Akintayo, **44**, 192; **52**, 261
  Alchemist, The, **52**, 22–3, 26, 68, 120, 143
Akrigg, G. P. V., **13**, 159; **20**, 158; **21**, 148; **23**, 159–60; **25**, 174; **31**, 178; **44**, 77; **54**, 136n
Aksimova-Vulf, I., **13**, 133
Akurgal, Ekrem, **54**, 37n
Akutagawa, Hiroshi, **13**, 130
Akuwudike, Jude, **57**, 282
Alabaster, Rosie, **58**, 280
Alabaster, William, *Roxana*, **1**, 64, 65; **43**, 152, 155, 158, 161–2, 167
  See also under Roxana
Alanus, **20**, 26n
Alarum for London, **12**, 36
'Alasco' (Łaski, Olbracht), **32**, 198
Alasco, Prince Albertus, **4**, 95
Alba, **11**, 114n
Albanese, Denise, **55**, 341
Albany, Duke of (Charles), **55**, 44–5
Al-bassan, Sulayman, **58**, 182; **59**, 339
Albee, Edward, **19**, 24n; **22**, 4, 27, 28, 29, 32; **24**, 19; **32**, 4
Albert Edward, Prince of Wales, **56**, 126
Albert, Archduke, **29**, 22, 27, 28, 30; **33**, 162–3, 165, 168
Albert, Pierre, **24**, 81n; **60**, 218n16
Albert, Prince, **1**, 83; **37**, 47
Albertazzi, Giorgio, **18**, 126
Alberti, L. B., **31**, 19, 22; **35**, 134
Albertini, Edda, **5**, 113
Alberto, Felix, **54**, 285
Albertus Magnus, **2**, 111
Albery, Tim, **44**, 191; **50**, 207–11; **51**, 261
Alboin, **59**, 247n65, 248n67
Albrecht, A., **1**, 10
Albrecht, L., **25**, 7
Albright, A. C., **55**, 240n
Albright, Evelyn May, **6**, 6; **28**, 8, 9
Albright, Victor E., **3**, 84; **4**, 100n; **43**, 149
Albus Ovidius Juventinus, **15**, 98n
Alby, James, **43**, 213
Alcazar, Battle of, **11**, 90
Alcestis, **11**, 40
Alchemist, The, **47**, 121, 124; **50**, 259
Alciatus, Andreas, **1**, 63; **15**, 97n; **17**, 181–2, 185–6; **24**, 66; **40**, 79n; **43**, 246; **56**, 45n, 46–51
Alcibiades, **34**, 34
Alcock, N. W., **56**, 201n
Alcott, Bronson, **53**, 131n
Alcott, Louisa May, **53**, 136, 166n
Alday, James, **11**, 90
Aldee, Edward, **15**, 35
Aldee, John, **14**, 26
Alden, John (theatre company), **10**, 115; **11**, 117; **12**, 109; **13**, 124; **14**, 26
Alden, R. M., **15**, 11, 12, 13, 15, 17
Alden, T., **46**, 214
Alder, Paul, **41**, 189
Aldersey, Laurence, **52**, 101
Aldington, Annie, **47**, 210
Aldington, Richard, **32**, 138n
Aldred, Mike, **51**, 227
Aldrich, Putnam, **23**, 164
Aldrich, Zoë, **52**, 234; **59**, 340
Aldridge, Ira, **3**, 118; **38**, 213; **42**, 162; **48**, 196; **51**, 63
Aldrovandus, U., **15**, 97n, 109n; **54**, 26n
Aldus Manutius, printer, **7**, 35
Aldus, Paul J., **10**, 143; **31**, 170; **39**, 143
Alekseev, M. P., **20**, 159; **54**, 144n
Aleman, Mateo, **16**, 119
Alembert, Jean le Rond d', **60**, 216
Alençon, Duke of, **48**, 40
Aleppo, **11**, 91, 93, 95
Alexander III, Czar, **9**, 66
Alexander III, Pope, **49**, 184
Alexander the Great, **10**, 71; **27**, 72, 75, 78, 79; **30**, 4; **42**, 66; **44**, 61
Alexander, Bill, **38**, 205; **39**, 197; **40**, 173, 180; **41**, 162, 165–6, 179, 187–8, 226; **42**, 139, 142, 150, 154, 160; **43**, 188–90, 200, 250; **44**, 170, 193; **45**, 121, 152, 154; **46**, 173, 175; **47**, 126, 217; **48**, 233; **49**, 279, 306; **50**, 69n, 229; **51**, 200–1; **52**, 249–50, 259; **55**, 282, 309, 333, 345; **56**, 5, 278; **57**, 284, 285; **58**, 31, 206, 290, 306, 353; **59**, 208n47, 340; **60**, 322
Alexander, Bruce, **41**, 166; 42, 140; **44**, 161
Alexander, Catherine M. S., **51**, 1–15; **52**, 291; **53**, 300, 301, 344; **59**, 359–60, 368; **60**, 168n1.6
Alexander, David, **49**, 119n; **59**, 129, 132
Alexander, George, **2**, 5; **4**, 105

INDEX

Alexander, Geraldine, **44**, 202; **51**, 215; **57**, 294
Alexander, Graham, **45**, 149
Alexander, Jennifer, **57**, 236
Alexander, Ken, **46**, 195; **50**, 233
Alexander, Louis C., **54**, 72
Alexander, Maev, **41**, 186
Alexander, Nigel, **22**, 158, 170; **23**, 152; **26**, 23n, 25, 160; **27**, 46n, 59, 54, 55, 56n; **28**, 113n; **29**, 27n; **30**, 101n, 206; **32**, 153; **33**, 201; **36**, 44; **39**, 139, 149n; **57**, 223
'Critical Disagreement about Oedipus and Hamlet', **20**, 33–40
'Thomas Rymer and *Othello*', **21**, 67–77
Studies on Shakespeare's Life, Times and Stage, *reviewed:*
(1971), **25**, 186–93
(1972), **26**, 168–76
(1973), **27**, 172–9
Alexander, Peter, **1**, 12, 131; **3**, 23, 26, 28, 32n; **4**, 6, 7, 60, 66, 67n, 159, 160; **5**, 45, 146, 148; **6**, 5, 6, 8, 147, 164; **7**, 3, 55, 149; **8**, 11, 156, 157; **9**, 5–6, 15, 48, 63, 122, 137–8, 152; **10**, 14, 15, 59n; **12**, 147; **13**; **21**, 4, 27n, 155, 161, 162; **23**, 27n, 49n, 99n, 143, 185; **24**, 156; **25**, 7n, 8, 30n, 200; **26**, 69n, 72n, 95n, 181; **27**, 62n, 119n, 129n, 132n, 135; **28**, 11n, 66n, 76n; **29**, 15n, 24n, 120n, 184; **30**, 1n, 35n, 61n, 86n, 135n; **31**, 23n, 78n; **32**, 51n, 73n, 153, 154n, 158n; **33**, 1, 67n; **35**, 88n, 119n, 183; **36**, 53n, 188; **38**, 12, 101; **39**, 86n, 94; **41**, 211; **43**, 266n, 267; **45**, 7, 91n; **49**, 299, 330n; **50**, 173n; **51**, 142; **53**, 181n, 183; **55**, 18n, 394; **57**, 225; **59**, 3, 7n27, 7n28, 382
The Heritage Shakespeare reviewed, **14**, 144, 157; **15**, 71n; **16**, 88, 173, 181; **18**, 24, 43–4, 131, 177; **19**, 9, 142, 146, 161–2; **20**, 160–1, 175–6
'Restoring Shakespeare: The Modern Editor's Task', **5**, 1–9
Shakespeare's Life and Art, **3**, 8, 24
Shakespeare's 'Henry VI' and 'Richard III', **4**, 58–9
A Shakespeare Primer, reviewed, **6**, 158
Alexander, R. N. (Nigel), **41**, 188; **45**, 10n, 22n, 76n
Alexander, Robert, **47**, 50n; **51**, 290
Alexander, Ryllis Clair, **54**, 48n
Alexander, Sir William, **20**, 18; **21**, 165
Aurora, **7**, 39
Paraenesis, **7**, 39
Tragedie of Darius, **3**, 54; **7**, 39
Alexandro, Alexander ab, **15**, 97n
Alexandrov, Yuri, **56**, 295
Alexejew, Michail Pawlowitsch, **4**, 125; **23**, 158–9
Alexi-Meskhishvili, George, **49**, 275
Alexi-Meskhishvili, Keti, **49**, 275
Alexis, Guillaume, **15**, 97n
Alfar, Cristina León, **57**, 310
Alfield, John, **54**, 95
Alfield, Thomas, **54**, 35n
Alfieri, Vittorio, **5**, 10, 94
Alford, B. W. E., **45**, 101n, 111n
Alford, Henry, **54**, 86
Alfred the Great, King, **49**, 176n
Alfreds, Mike, **52**, 266; **55**, 314; **56**, 264, 288; **57**, 294; **59**, 183
Algan, Ayla, **18**, 130
Alger, Horatio, **24**, 92
al-Hakim, Tawfik, **36**, 1
Alias, Charles, **55**, 110, 111n
Alifantis, Nicu, **46**, 196
All My Sons, **54**, 114
Allam, Roger, **41**, 166, 173; **42**, 134–5, 151, 199; **44**, 171, 172; **45**, 152; **50**, 208, 210; **51**, 261; **53**, 259; **58**, 59
Allam, Rory, **42**, 158
Allde, Edward, **3**, 149; **22**, 182; **24**, 176; **34**, 193; **50**, 276; **55**, 29, 392
Allde, John, **54**, 91
Alleman, Gellert S., **32**, 139n
Allemann, Beda, **40**, 88n
Allen, A. R., **13**, 103n, 105n
Allen, Brian, **49**, 113n; **51**, 10
Allen, Dave, **60**, 207
Allen, Don Cameron, **4**, 141n; **7**, 107; **8**, 110; **23**, 187; **31**, 15; **34**, 85n; **36**, 177; **38**, 52n; **42**, 66n; **44**, 34; **46**, 15n, 19n, 145n; **53**, 30n; **55**, 14n, 220n
Star-Crossed Renaissance, **3**, 7
Studies in Honor of T. W. Baldwin, **13**, 152n; **14**, 88n, 145; **15**, 21, 29, 88n, 109n; **18**, 173
'Some Observations on *The Rape of Lucrece*', **15**, 89–98
Allen, Giles, **45**, 104, 106; **52**, 12
Allen, Graham, **56**, 67
Allen, Hannah, **49**, 303
Allen, James, **47**, 174n
Allen, John A., **22**, 154; **27**, 164; **44**, 99n, 101n
Allen, Margaret V., **53**, 131n
Allen, Michael J. B., **33**, 191–2; **36**, 91n; **37**, 211–12; **47**, 163n; **49**, 21n, 29n; **51**, 315; **53**, 338; **55**, 54n
Allen, Ned B., **23**, 151
'The Two Parts of *Othello*', **21**, 13–29
Allen, P. S., **44**, 61n; **54**, 63n
Allen, Patrick, **14**, 133; **16**, 145; **45**, 61
Allen, Paul, **54**, 170n
Allen, Percy, **3**, 11; **9**, 141; **30**, 110n
Allen, Phyllis, **17**, 71n
Allen, Rachel Jane, **56**, 254
Allen, Rod, **39**, 104n
Allen, Sheila, **38**, 172
Allen, Shirley S., **35**, 9, 12; **38**, 189n; **56**, 130n
Allen, Thomas, **49**, 190
Allen, Viola, **32**, 20, 22, 24
Allen, W. S., **34**, 57n
Allen, Walter, **51**, 28
Allen, William, **54**, 35n, 91n, 94n–95n, 118–19; **56**, 192–3, 195
Allen, William, Cardinal, **17**, 121, 123–4
Allen, Woody, **40**, 8; **43**, 228
Allentuck, Marcia, **31**, 190; **49**, 113n; **51**, 10n
Allerton, Charles, **9**, 56; **11**, 124
Allerton, Patricia, **52**, 297
Alleva, Richard, **52**, 96n
Alleyn, Edward, **2**, 152; **5**, 144n; **6**, 85, 160–1; **7**, 50, 61, 147; **8**, 106–7, 108; **9**, 78, 147; **13**, 111, 112; **15**, 172; **16**, 95–102; **17**, 194; **18**, 182; **24**, 40; **27**, 134; **29**, 127–32; **32**, 194, 196–7; **33**, 140, 149, 156, 159, 160; **36**, 135, 140–1, 144–5, 147, 175; **37**, 193–4; **39**, 227; **40**, 215; **44**, 149n, 151n, 230, 232; **45**, 108, 109; **46**, 231; **47**, 15–19, 22, 24–5, 27, 35, 46, 52, 171–9, 241, 251, 252n; 50, 151, 156, 256; **52**, 73, 77; **53**, 326, 334; **55**, 28, 252, 377; **57**, 232, 233, 341; **58**, 65, 66, 230; **60**, 9, 21, 46n50, 47n59, 49, 50, 52, 53, 54, 55, 57
Diary, **8**, 107n

Petition to Lord Cranfield, **8**, 107
style of acting and reputation discussed, **7**, 82–8 *and* n.
W. P.'s letter to, a conjectural Shakespearian autograph, **8**, 159
Alleyn, Joan (*née* Woodward), **7**, 61; **13**, 112; **33**, 154, 160, 161; **36**, 135; **37**, 217; **44**, 151n; **49**, 19; **60**, 51
Alleyn, William, **56**, 186
Allgood, Sara, **2**, 4
Allies, Wiesia, **43**, 216
Allington, Jane, **53**, 200
Allio, René, **13**, 127; **16**, 133
Allison, A. F., **24**, 72n; **29**, 21n; **54**, 95n; **56**, 189
Allison, Jonathan, **52**, 286
Allman, Eileen Jorge, **35**, 169
Allombert, Guy, **39**, 80
Allon, Daphna, **32**, 115
Allot, Robert, **9**, 84
Allott, R., **56**, 230n
Allridge, Mark, **42**, 155
Allsopp, Ric, **55**, 343
Alma-Tadema, Sir Lawrence, **26**, 142; **29**, 176
Almaçik, Gulsen, **16**, 137
Almagor, Dan, **54**, 182
Almeida, Barbara Heliodora Carneiro de Mendonça, F. de (*see also* Mendonça, B. H. C. de), **19**, 134; **22**, 175n
'Shakespeare in Brazil', **20**, 121–4
Almereyda, Michael, **54**, 124n; **57**, 194; **58**, 187, 189, 191, 195, 196, 340; **60**, 354–5
Almodóvar, Pedro, **60**, 332
Almond, **2**, 26
Aloes, **54**, 152
Alonso, Dámaso, **23**, 82n
Alpers, Paul J., **33**, 4, 10; **35**, 79n; **53**, 30n; **58**, 317, 331
Alpers, Svetlana Leontief, **31**, 16n, 19n
Al-Shetawi, Mahmoud F., **44**, 242
Alsloot, van, Dennis, painting of The Triumph of Isabella, **12**, 31
Alsop, Bernard, printer, **17**, 206
Alston, L., **28**, 63n; **29**, 93n
al-Subair, Shayk, **36**, 2, 3, 8, 10
Alswang, Ralph, **5**, 116
Altenloh, Emilie, **45**, 45n
Alter, André, **12**, 111
Alter, Iska, **43**, 230; **54**, 312; **55**, 116n
Alterman, Nathan, **5**, 113; **13**, 129
Altham, Sir James, **38**, 33
Altham, Joan, **38**, 33
Althusser, Louis, **44**, 70; **49**, 88, 89, 90, 91n, 92n; **51**, 272; **54**, 323
Altick, Richard D., **2**, 136; **4**, 20; **5**, 86, 88; **6**, 11, 35n; **9**, 137, 138; **18**, 19, 20; **24**, 41; **32**, 16n; **49**, 111n, 119n, 123n; **56**, 130
Altieri, Joanne, **28**, 162; **35**, 155–6; **36**, 178; **38**, 9
Altman, George, **9**, 146n
Altman, Joel B., **40**, 97; **52**, 113, 117; **43**, 6n; **45**, 164; **48**, 85, 97n, 243; **49**, 55
Altman, Leah, **55**, 333
Altman, Robert, **34**, 41; **58**, 195
Alton, R. E., **4**, 95; **35**, 130n
Alty, Charles, **44**, 198
Alulis, Joseph, **51**, 282
Alvarez, A., **10**, 142; **15**, 27, 30n, 99, 104, 107, 108n, 109n
Alvis, John E., **36**, 164; **45**, 161; **56**, 222n, 225n
Alyoshin, Samuel, **58**, 138
Amadis de Gaule, **14**, 27
Amaghlobeli, Sergó, **48**, 189
Ambler, Chris, **45**, 154
Ambrocio, Rafael, **54**, 160n
America Play, The, **52**, 33
America, *see* U.S.A.
Americans on Shakespeare, **54**, 302
Ames, William, **27**, 90; **43**, 61
Ames, Winthrop, **32**, 19–23
Amherst College, **1**, 57, 59
Amiel, H. F., **28**, 44
Amin, Idi, **46**, 238
Aminoff, Marianne, **14**, 123
Amiot, Jacques, **29**, 103
Amirthanayagan, Guy, **55**, 180n
Amman, Joost, **43**, 161; **50**, 159
Amner, John, *Sacred Hymnes*, **1**, 69
Amnéus, Daniel A., **16**, 175; **27**, 90
Amneus, David, **40**, 231
Amory, Mark, **36**, 28n
Amphitheatre, the projected, **2**, 24–35
Amphitruo, **54**, 202
Amphlett, H., *Who was Shakespeare? A New Enquiry* reviewed, **10**, 143
Amram, David, **45**, 172
Amuki-Bird, Nikki, **58**, 335
Amyot, Jacques, **12**, 138; **19**, 147; **46**, 96, 106; **53**, 74n; **56**, 42n, 44
translation of Plutarch's *Lives*, **10**, 50–3, 56, 57
Amyot, Thomas, **1**, 83, 88n
Anabaptists, **2**, 69
Anatol, Constantin, **20**, 126
Anaxagoras, **48**, 30; **60**, 126, 127
And, Metin, **19**, 145
Anderegg, Michael, **59**, 63n2, 67n13
Anders, H. R. D., **4**, 9, 68n; **6**, 3; **10**, 14, 15
Shakespeare's Books, **3**, 5, 21n, 54
Andersen, Hans Christian, **29**, 145, 146; **35**, 12n; **56**, 158
Andersen, Ludwig, **13**, 125
Anderson, Abigail, **50**, 226; **59**, 344
Anderson, Benedict, **51**, 17; **52**, 55–6
Anderson, Clive, **41**, 185
Anderson, Donald K., Jr, **18**, 180–1; **34**, 196; **55**, 84n
Anderson, Fiona, **12**, 120
Anderson, Inger Marie, **11**, 121
Anderson, J. J., **26**, 153
'The Morality of *Love's Labour's Lost*', **24**, 55–62
Anderson, James, **16**, 104; **43**, 180; **51**, 55
Anderson, Jennifer, **60**, 269n4
Anderson, John, **20**, 111
Anderson, John Jr., **55**, 388
Anderson, Dame Judith, **52**, 178n
Anderson, Judith H., **39**, 219n; **41**, 210; **43**, 50, 60n; **60**, 67n17
Anderson, Keith Alayre, **33**, 190
Anderson, Kevin, **39**, 189
Anderson, Laurie, **54**, 292
Anderson, Linda, **42**, 173
Anderson, M. D., **26**, 73n, 75n, 76n
Anderson, Mary, **32**, 24; **49**, 116n, 128; **56**, 134
Anderson, Maxwell, *Winterset*, **8**, 109
Anderson, Melville B., **56**, 206n

INDEX

Anderson, Meryle, **45**, 150
Anderson, Miles, **37**, 164–5; **43**, 209; **44**, 195
Anderson, Perry, **49**, 203; **59**, 151n16
Anderson, Peter S., **41**, 210
Anderson, Ruth L., **4**, 11; **6**, 9; **18**, 168; **19**, 126; **29**, 82
Anderson, Stewart, **53**, 54n
Anderson, Thomas P., **60**, 358, 360
Anderson, Tom, **55**, 311
Anderson, V. H., **4**, 141n
Anderson, W. S., **39**, 126n, 167n
Andersson, Bibi, **16**, 137
Andersson, Hans, **7**, 114
Andjelinović, D., **4**, 118; **15**, 142; **18**, 134
Andoh, Anjou, **42**, 152
Andre, Martin, **54**, 288
Andreadis, A. Harriette, **29**, 174
Andreas, James R., **47**, 232; **49**, 142; **54**, 311; **55**, 346; **56**, 157n
Andreoni, Maria A., **5**, 113
Andresen-Thom, Martha, **33**, 198
Andreu, Mariano, **40**, 16
Andrew (of Wyntoun), **57**, 77
Andrew, Doreen, **50**, 206
Andrew, Dudley, **52**, 193
Andrew, Paul, **48**, 227
Andrewes, John, **55**, 84n; **57**, 241
Andrewes, Lancelot, **17**, 119; **23**, 84, 167; **33**, 93–4, 96; **34**, 182; **55**, 230; **57**, 239, 242; **58**, 12
Andrewes, Richard, **60**, 21
Andrews, Allen, **56**, 127n
Andrews, Becs, **58**, 278
Andrews, Harry, **1**, 106; **3**, 122; **4**, 137; **6**, 132, 135; **7**, 126, 127; **10**, 132–3; **12**, 122, 124–6
Andrews, John F., **27**, 185; **30**, 207; **35**, 163–4; **40**, 211; **42**, 188; **43**, 2n; **47**, 235; **49**, 88n, 96n, 142; **56**, 169n; **57**, 321; **59**, 55n17
Andrews, Keith, **13**, 80n; **17**, 21n, 22n, 23n, 26n, 27, 27n, 29; **47**, 99, 106
Andrews, Mark Edwin, **27**, 95, 98, 104
Andrews, Michael Cameron, **17**, 39n; **23**, 171n; **25**, 182; **28**, 155; **32**, 236; **33**, 186; **44**, 237–8; **51**, 183, 184n
Andrews, Nigel, **39**, 85n
Andrews, Paul, **48**, 235; **49**, 273; **50**, 228
Andrews, Richard, **46**, 240n; **47**, 254; **55**, 247; **59**, 361
Andrews, Simeon, **47**, 214
Andrews, Sophie, **59**, 338
Andrews, Thomas, **11**, 73
Andriessen, Juriaan, **7**, 113; **45**, 172
Andro, Christabell, **49**, 193
Androboros, **55**, 93
Andronicus, **48**, 33
Androver, Karine, **51**, 239
Androzzi, Fulvio, **29**, 21
Aneau, Barthélemy, **36**, 166
Anet, Daniel, **5**, 115
Angel, Louisa, **32**, 33
Angell, Edward, **58**, 243
Angellier, Auguste, **2**, 119
Anger, Kenneth, **56**, 7
Anglade, C., **15**, 98n
Anglerius, Peter Martyr, **17**, 31, 41n, 51n
Anglicus, Bartholomaeus, **17**, 39
Anglo, Sydney, **43**, 4n; **45**, 182; **54**, 124n, 194, 195n; **60**, 59n3, 60n7
Angus, William, **21**, 156
Anikst, Alexander, **12**, 118; **13**, 133; **15**, 140; **16**, 15, 139; **20**, 127; **21**, 131; **23**, 165, 168n, 174n, 175n, 176n; **39**, 85n
Animated Shakespeare, The, **52**, 289–90
Anjou, Duke of, **3**, 24
Ankers, Kathleen, **1**, 100
Anna of Cleve, Queen of England, **60**, 75
Anna, wife of Sigismund III of Poland, **36**, 145
Anna-Maria, **12**, 114
Anna-Sophia, wife of Frederick Ulric of Wolfenbüttel, **36**, 139
Annals of Great Brittaine, The, see Chester, Robert, *Loves Martyr*
Annals, Michael, **42**, 162
Annas, Julia, **46**, 145n, 154, 156
Anne of Denmark, Queen (wife of James I), **1**, 32; **7**, 61; **11**, 76; **12**, 143; **27**, 172; **30**, 162, 165; **33**, 162–3, 165, 168; **36**, 139–40, 142, 147; **38**, 51; **60**, 58
  Queen Anne's Men, *see under* Theatre, Elizabethan, companies
Anne, Queen, **29**, 4; **43**, 55–6; **44**, 154; **45**, 110; **46**, 106; **50**, 142–5; **53**, 201; **54**, 197; **57**, 70, 74
Annesley, Brian, **9**, 141; **13**, 30; **55**, 7, 39n
Annis, Francesca, **30**, 175, 176; **49**, 239; **57**, 147, 148, 151, 153
anonymous works, **59**, 338
  Alphonsus Emperor of Germany, **59**, 73, 75
  Arden of Faversham, **59**, 5n12, 6, 75
  Beowulf, **59**, 240
  Brut, Brute Chronicle, **59**, 243, 246n55, 246–7n60, 379–80
  Charlemagne, **59**, 73
  Chronicles of England, **59**, 243, 244n38, 246, 246n58, 251
  De origine gigantium, **59**, 243, 244, 251
  A Declaration of Great Troubles Pretended Against the Realm (1591), **59**, 246n59
  Des Grantz Geanz, **59**, 242–3
  Every Woman in Her Humour, **59**, 71
  First Book of Homilies, **60**, 73n4
  Fouke Fitz Waryn, **59**, 245n44
  Gnomic Verses, Old English, **59**, 240
  God's Warning to His People of England (1607), **59**, 252
  1 Sir John Oldcastle, **60**, 266, 266n42
  Jack Straw, **59**, 74, 77
  King Leir, **59**, 73, 74, 77, 78
  A Knack to Know a Knave, **59**, 71
  Liber Albus, **59**, 245
  Liber Regalis, **60**, 113
  Little Device for Henry VII, **60**, 112n42, 113n44
  Look About You, **59**, 73; **60**, 105
  Lust's Dominion, **59**, 74
  Mary Magdalene (Digby), **60**, 81n39
  Mask of Proteus, **60**, 64
  Nobody and Somebody, **59**, 73
  A Poore Knight his Pallace of Priuate Pleasures, **60**, 272n13
  Respublica, **59**, 248
  Soliman and Perseda, **59**, 73
  A Survey of History: or, A Nursery for Gentry, **60**, 275n30
  The Birth of Hercules, **59**, 74
  The Judd Marriage (painting), **60**, 226
  The Pilgrimage to Parnassus, **59**, 72
  The Return from Parnassus, **59**, 71, 75
  The Ruin, **59**, 240
  The Second Shepherd's Play, **60**, 108

INDEX

The Taming of A Shrew, **59**, 7, 74; **60**, 73n6, 204
The Tragical History, Admirable Atchievements and various events of Guy earl of Warwick, **60**, 342–3
The True Chronicle History of King Leir, **60**, 253
The True Tragedy of Richard III, **59**, 72, 77
The Wanderer, **59**, 240
A Warning for Fair Women, **59**, 71, 74, 75, 78
The Weakest Goeth to the Wall, **59**, 73, 75, 78
Timon, **59**, 72, 77
Wily Beguilde, **60**, 272n14
Woodstock, **59**, 11, 73
see also 'W. S.', **59**, 11, 73
Anouilh, Jean, **6**, 140; **8**, 38; **11**, 138; **15**, 133; **16**, 19; **18**, 123, 171; **34**, 3; **57**, 114, 119, 122
The Lark, **12**, 1
adaptation of *Twelfth Night*, **12**, 112
Anouilh, Nicole, **15**, 133
Anoun, Abd el-Ouahed ben Messaoued ben Mohammed, **11**, 89–97; **60**, 164, 168n3.9
Anozie, Nonso, **56**, 284, 285; **58**, 285; **59**, 343
Anrieu, Paul, **8**, 118
Ansari, A. A., **49**, 131n
Anschütz, Heinrich, **35**, 21, 24–5; **37**, 199n
Anscombe, G. E. M., **36**, 22n; **46**, 146n
Ansell, John, **45**, 104
Anselm, Pseudo-, **59**, 248n67
Ansen, David, **52**, 91n
Anson, John, **21**, 132; **31**, 10n
Ansorge, Peter, **24**, 122n, 132n
Anstee, Mark, **45**, 145
Anthony, Francis, **17**, 160
Antiochus IV Epiphanes, **29**, 24, 25, 26–7
Antipodes, The, **50**, 255; **52**, 80; **54**, 263
Antoine, André, **2**, 2; **14**, 119; **16**, 54; **47**, 2, 3
Anton, George, **58**, 263, 300
Antonetti, Charles, **12**, 112
Antoni, Bob, **37**, 217
Antonio and Mellida, **52**, 297; **46**, 227
Antonio's Revenge, **52**, 297; **46**, 227; **54**, 224
Antonioni, Michelangelo, **40**, 148n
Antwerp, festival of 1561, **12**, 5
Aoike, Yasuko, **60**, 133n13
Aoki, Keiji, **28**, 159; **38**, 15; **41**, 212
Aoyama, Sugisaku, **12**, 115
Apfelbaum, Roger, **50**, 280n; **53**, 294
Aphthonius, **10**, 146; **18**, 166
Apocryphal plays, **9**, 84
Apollinaire, Guillaume, **45**, 44
Apollonio, Mario, **1**, 8
Apollonius of Tyrus, **29**, 30; **30**, 6
Apollonius' *Conics*, **17**, 66
Appelbaum, Robert, **52**, 93n, 280
Appelles, **31**, 18
Appia, Adolphe, **2**, 5, 10; **10**, 149; **29**, 176; **35**, 1; **45**, 66, 67
Appiah, Antony, **52**, 163n, 164
Appian, **14**, 153; **31**, 9
Civil Wars (Henry Bynnemann's translation), **10**, 4, 30, 31
Appius and Virginia, **20**, 19–20, 24, 120n; **55**, 358
Appleton, Elizabeth, **39**, 224
Appleton, Peter, **41**, 188
Appleton, William W., **35**, 10; **42**, 85n; **57**, 87
Beaumont and Fletcher, **14**, 12
Appleyard, **7**, 116
Apsion, Annabelle, **46**, 164
Apuleius, *Metamorphoses sen de Asino Aureo*, translated by W. Aldington, *The Golden Asse* (1566), **11**, 71; **12**, 90–1, 93, 94 and n.; **14**, 154; **15**, 29; **19**, 57, 59
Apuleius, Lucius, of Madura, **22**, 5; **23**, 61, 62; **31**, 33–43; **36**, 175; **40**, 69; **47**, 150n; **52**, 185
Aquaviva, Jesuit General, **17**, 127
Aquilano, Serafino, **7**, 100, 101
Aquinas, St Thomas, **10**, 136; **14**, 154; **19**, 121; **23**, 86; **24**, 91n, 140; **29**, 80, 88; **33**, 94; **50**, 239; **55**, 213
Aquino, Deborah T. Curren, **39**, 43n
Arab, Ronda A., **55**, 377
Arac, Jonathan, **53**, 110
Aragon, Catherine of, **38**, 25; **54**, 242–3
Arambam, Lokendra, **52**, 258
Arambam, Somorendra, **52**, 258
Arany, János, **3**, 117; **12**, 113; **18**, 125; **59**, 126
Aratama, Michiyo, **15**, 137
Aratus, **55**, 206
Arbeau, **55**, 244
Arber, Edward, **29**, 29; **36**, 142n; **51**, 95n, 179n; **54**, 94n, 230n; **55**, 267; **56**, 34n
Transcripts of the Stationers' Register, **11**, 153; **17**, 31n, 68n
Arbman, Sigvard, **9**, 116
Arbus, David, **51**, 260
Arbusow, Leonid, **34**, 103
Arc Dance Company, **58**, 300
Arch, Joseph, **58**, 109, 111
Archbishop of Armagh, **54**, 75
Archdall Manuscript, **36**, 110, 113
Archdeaconry Court of London, **11**, 105n
Archenholz, Johann Wilhelm von, **9**, 98, 100n
Archer, Ian W., **49**, 301; **55**, 374
Archer, J. W., **1**, 83
Archer, John, **56**, 34n
Archer, John Michael, **50**, 65, 199n; **51**, 279; **57**, 14, 20
Archer, Robert, **33**, 168
Archer, Sir Simon, **17**, 118n
Archer, Thomas, **60**, 369
Archer, William, **1**, 3; **4**, 12, 18; **7**, 80n; **9**, 16, 17; **12**, 9, 11; **20**, 130; **32**, 18; **34**, 9, 190; **35**, 6, 43, 55n; **37**, 14, 21; **42**, 104; **43**, 112n; **47**, 108; **52**, 31; **57**, 94; **59**, 149–50, 287
Archers, The (cast of), **56**, 244
Archibald, Lady, **56**, 135n
Archimedes, **17**, 66; **52**, 185
Archipropheta, **54**, 62n
Arden of Faversham, **3**, 48, 110, 112; **4**, 92; **7**, 95; **9**, 84; **12**, 41; **20**, 130; **47**, 219; **48**, 277; **50**, 258; **55**, 21
Arden, Agnes, **21**, 148; **37**, 187
Arden, Annabel, **46**, 169, 173; **47**, 218; **59**, 372
Arden, Edward, **47**, 255n; **54**, 116, 118
Arden, Forest of, **17**, 15
Arden, Jane, **44**, 200
Arden, John, **22**, 28; **28**, 141; **55**, 160; **56**, 246; **58**, 1
Arden, Mary, **17**, 14, 117, 170; **21**, 148; **53**, 85; **54**, 74, 116; **56**, 201
Arden, Mary: house at Wilmcote, **1**, 86
Arden, Robert, **21**, 148; **38**, 227; **40**, 220; **54**, 116
Ardener, Shirley, **46**, 110n

INDEX

Ardens, N. N., **5**, 105n
Arditti, Michael, **56**, 236, 239
Arditti, Paul, **57**, 274
Arendt, Hannah, **39**, 53n; **40**, 47; **45**, 134n; **53**, 91; **56**, 140n
Arens, J. C., **23**, 186
Arestad, Sverre, **43**, 115n
Aretino, Frederico, **15**, 95, 98n; **20**, 166
Aretino, Pietro, **35**, 175; **53**, 32n; **56**, 34n
Argan, Giulio Carlo, **15**, 136
Argens, Jean-Baptiste de Boyer, Marquis d', **60**, 215
Argensola, Bartolemé Leonardo de, **52**, 211–12
Argenterius, Johannes, **38**, 182n, 183
Arghezi, Tudor, **20**, 125, 127
Ariès, Philippe, **56**, 2n; **60**, 230–1, 232, 233, 233n58, 235
Ariosto, M. Ludovico, **1**, 63; **3**, 15; **7**, 95, 96; **14**, 100; **16**, 170; **22**, 51; **31**, 18; **35**, 111–12, 189; **46**, 10, 12n, 14, 15, 18, 19; **47**, 130n, 165–6, 274; **52**, 274
I Suppositi, **1**, 53
Aris's Birmingham Gazette, **7**, 90
Aristophanes, **10**, 135; **22**, 1, 3, 4, 5, 8, 36; **33**, 34; **39**, 155; **49**, 61; **50**, 144; **57**, 213
Aristotle, **4**, 93; **5**, 86; **6**, 154; **7**, 95; **8**, 1, 41; **9**, 10, 59, 93, 97, 99, 122, 123, 138; **10**, 11, 40, 48, 58, 59n; **11**, 137–8; **12**, 28, 151; **16**, 12, 45, 88, 125; **17**, 64, 86, 139, 146; **18**, 36, 122; **19**, 121; **20**, 4, 20, 26n, 33–4; **21**, 67, 68, 69, 74, 130; **22**, 1, 4; **23**, 147, 148; **24**, 79, 139, 140; **26**, 167; **27**, 78, 160; **28**, 29, 57, 63; **29**, 7, 99, 134, 162; **30**, 19, 103, 135, 192; **31**, 7, 14; **33**, 23; **34**, 16, 34, 73; **36**, 17, 28; **37**, 13, 14, 141, 144, 146, 148, 152, 207, 217; **38**, 178; **39**, 149n, 220, 234; **40**, 33, 40, 47, 79n; **41**, 121; **42**, 89; **44**, 1, 210; **46**, 38, 55, 65, 82n, 88, 114n, 123, 133n, 153; **47**, 227; **48**, 26, 30, 42, 141n; **49**, 137, 169, 193, 211; **50**, 71n, 144, 239, 245, 246; **51**, 114; **53**, 21, 39, 40, 221–2; **54**, 3, 29, 39, 128n, 223, 226, 230, 232, 297, 306; **55**, 48, 63, 205, 219n; **56**, 5n, 232; **57**, 318; **59**, 228, 229, 230, 290, 293, 365; **60**, 126
his view of tragedy, **3**, 58, 62, 65
Poetics, **5**, 130
Arkwright, G. E. P., **15**, 4
Årlin, Georg, **11**, 122; **18**, 128
Arlidge, Anthony, **57**, 202
Armada, The, **11**, 90, 91; **17**, 21, 21n, 22, 24, 26, 34, 123, 127
Armada, The Spanish (1588), allusion to it in Shakespeare's *Sonnets*, **4**, 148, 154–5; **5**, 138, 149
Armatrading, Tony, **44**, 202
Armfield, Constance, **17**, 172
Armin, Robert, **1**, 46; **3**, 28; **5**, 122, 123; **8**, 73; **10**, 150; **15**, 5, 8, 10; **17**, 195; **18**, 166; **25**, 161, 167; **27**, 163, 178; **28**, 177; **29**, 178; **30**, 194; **31**, 187; **32**, 6, 238; **33**, 69; **34**, 185; **37**, 198; **41**, 39, 127, 218; **42**, 187; **52**, 148n; **53**, 71n; **54**, 196; **55**, 247, 250; **56**, 95, 97; **58**, 63, 69; **60**, 358
Two Maids of Moreclacke, **10**, 146
Nest of Ninnies, **15**, 2
Armitage, David, **41**, 133n, 137
Armitage, Fay, **42**, 156
Armstrong, Alun, **37**, 39n, 167; **39**, 205
Armstrong, C. A. J., **44**, 57n
Armstrong, C. E., **17**, 34n
Armstrong, Edward A., **4**, 19; **5**, 88; **6**, 43–4; **10**, 139; **23**, 99; **29**, 180; **32**, 155n; **37**, 182; **54**, 207
Shakespeare's Imagination, **11**, 54, 57, 58; **12**, 149; **15**, 28; **18**, 54, 55; **20**, 87
Shakespeare's Imagination reviewed, **1**, 119, 121–2
Armstrong, Gareth, **41**, 191; **42**, 156; **53**, 279; **59**, 341
Armstrong, Gavin, **54**, 284
Armstrong, Isobel, **43**, 180–1, 224; **58**, 83
Armstrong, Julie, **45**, 154
Armstrong, Louis, **13**, 142
Armstrong, Nancy, **51**, 20; **52**, 303; **53**, 16n
Armstrong, Neil, **52**, 192
Armstrong, Philip, **48**, 252; **50**, 249; **55**, 9, 68; **56**, 306
Armstrong, Richard, **54**, 288
Armstrong, William A., **1**, 121, 126; **2**, 142; **4**, 142n; **6**, 9; **9**, 147; **12**, 144; **15**, 8; **16**, 95–6, 99–100, 166; **18**, 182, 184–5; **19**, 8, 148; **20**, 24n, 72n, 73n, 162; **22**, 116n, 117n; **26**, 40n; **27**, 23n, 31n, 179; **43**, 3n; **47**, 176n; **54**, 248
The Elizabethan Private Theatre, **14**, 13
'Shakespeare and the acting of Edward Alleyn', **7**, 82–9
Arnatt, John, **7**, 125
Arne, Mrs Cecilia, **51**, 82, 83, 84, 89
Arne, Thomas, **15**, 173; **18**, 96, 97, 98, 99, 100; **49**, 111; **51**, 6, 82–6, 88–93; **54**, 50
'Actors and Theatres', **17**, 191–204
Arneberg, Urda, **14**, 122
Arnfield, Jane, **55**, 314–15
Arnisenko, Valery, **51**, 261
Arnold, Aerol, **9**, 137; **11**, 140; **27**, 26n
Arnold, Andy, **51**, 263; **55**, 328
Arnold, Arthur, **26**, 176n
Arnold, Dominic, **48**, 237
Arnold, Janet, **59**, 176
Arnold, Matthew, **2**, 42; **4**, 1; **10**, 23; **13**, 63, 68; **14**, 140; **18**, 114; **24**, 127, 134; **40**, 29; **41**, 103n; **44**, 136n; **45**, 6; **56**, 327; **59**, 149, 264
Arnold, Paul, *Ésotérisme de Shakespeare* reviewed, **10**, 143
Arnold, Dr Samuel, composer, **18**, 99
Arnold, Thomas, **54**, 83
Arnold, Dr Thomas, **56**, 242–3, 245
Arnott, J. F., **44**, 244
Arnott, Peter, **57**, 297
Aronson, Alex, **12**, 136; **25**, 186; **27**, 171
Arpe, Verner, **29**, 176
Arrindell, Clive, **41**, 187; **43**, 210, 217
Arroyo, Bronson, **60**, 144–5
Arroyo, José, **52**, 94, 96n
Art Imitates Business: Commercial and Political Influences in Elizabethan Theatre, **48**, 291
Art of Living, The, **46**, 218
Artaud, Antonin, **18**, 61, 149; **40**, 5; **45**, 66, 67, 69; **47**, 111; **50**, 246; **52**, 161–2; **56**, 346; **57**, 33, 119, 149; **60**, 164Fig.27
Artemidorus, **53**, 79, 80n
Arthos, John, **2**, 139n; **8**, 144; **10**, 136; **13**, 151; **20**, 156–7; **22**, 168; **25**, 3n; **26**, 166; **27**, 163; **29**, 8; **31**, 12n; **43**, 135n; **47**, 112
Arthur, H. H. G., **13**, 105n
Arthur, King, **16**, 9
Arthur, Prince, **52**, 177–9
Arthur, Robert, **52**, 29
Arts Council, The, **1**, 103, 112; **4**, 106; **11**, 118, 129
Hamlet and *Othello*, **1**, 115

INDEX

Arumugam, Vaneshran, **60**, 289–90, 291, 292
Arundel House, **1**, 30
Arundel, Earl of (Philip Howard), **54**, 91, 96
Arundel, Earl of (Thomas Howard), **60**, 54
Arundel, Earl of, **1**, 34; **18**, 192; **47**, 18
Arundel, Thomas (Archbishop of Canterbury), **54**, 102–5
Arundell, Dennis, **12**, 111
Arvide, Juan Carlos, **54**, 152n, 160, 162–3
Arvidsson, Gun, **18**, 128
Arvirargus, **11**, 44, 46
Asals, H., **28**, 163
Asami, Rei, **60**, 304
Ascensius, **38**, 42n
Ascham, Roger, **17**, 53, 61; **22**, 169; **33**, 22; **35**, 115; **37**, 180; **39**, 214; **43**, 238; **49**, 195n; **56**, 227
  Toxophilus, **1**, 70; **7**, 19
Asche, Oscar, **2**, 5; **8**, 78; **32**, 19, 20
Ascoli, Albert Russell, **51**, 184n
Ascroft, Elizabeth, **43**, 209; **45**, 145; **54**, 268; **55**, 322; **59**, 299
Ash, Sarah Jane, **43**, 211
Ashbee, William, **59**, 149
Ashbourne portrait of Shakespeare, *see under* Shakespeare, portraits
Ashbourne, Jayne, **53**, 260, 282, 284
Ashby Folville Manor, Leicestershire, **12**, 99
Ashby, A. W., **8**, 27n
Ashby, John, **44**, 201
Ashcroft, Bill, **48**, 157n
Ashcroft, Dame Peggy, **5**, 123–4; **7**, 125–6; **11**, 134; **12**, 114; **16**, 20, 22, 23, 27; **18**, 147, 152–3; **19**, 115, 116, 154; **23**, 131; **24**, 43; **26**, 147; **27**, 142; **28**, 171; **31**, 149; **32**, 29, 31; **36**, 149–50; **39**, 95n; **40**, 11n, 14, 15, 17, 18; **45**, 189; **46**, 162; **49**, 3, 14, 128, 136; **50**, 149; **51**, 144; **52**, 322; **56**, 181, 245; **57**, 260, 339; **58**, 164; **60**, 78, 79, 80
Ashcroft, Liz, **48**, 237; **51**, 264
Ashcroft, Richard, **48**, 233
Ashe, Geoffrey, **5**, 142
Ashe, Graham, **41**, 191
Ashe, Thomas, **23**, 102; **27**, 97
Asher, Lyell, **55**, 361
Ashhurst, Richard L., **59**, 86
Ashizo, Kaori, **53**, 293
Ashley Library, *see under* Libraries
Ashley, Anthony, third Earl of Shaftesbury, **9**, 94, 97, 98; **18**, 36; **53**, 92
Ashley, Maurice, **57**, 73
Ashley, Robert, **45**, 168
  Of Honour, **6**, 60
Ashley, Tim, **57**, 116
Ashmore, Catherine, **59**, 308, 324, 326
Ashton, Alison, **46**, 194
Ashton, Beth, **42**, 158
Ashton, E. B., **55**, 72
Ashton, Frederick, **56**, 294; **60**, 325
Ashton, Geoffrey, **49**, 114n, 115n, 118n, 119n, 123n, 125n, 126n, 128n; **51**, 11
Ashton, J. W., **8**, 105n
Ashton, Richard, **42**, 158
Ashton, Robert, **44**, 12n; **56**, 217n, 218n, 219n, 220n, 221n
Ashwin, A. E., **28**, 119n
Aske, Robert, **48**, 71
Askew, Anne, **53**, 319
Aslan, Raoul, **2**, 126
Asp, Carolyn, **26**, 155; **33**, 202; **36**, 166; **41**, 69, 74; **45**, 167
Asper, Helmut G., **29**, 175
Aspinall, Dana E., **60**, 84n2, 88n8, 92n29, 97n36
Aspley, William, **1**, 57; **33**, 208; **52**, 304
Asquith, Ros, **41**, 75
Asseo, Abraham, **5**, 120
Assheton, William, **57**, 70
Astangov, M., **12**, 118
Astington, John H., **35**, 174; **37**, 196, 198; **40**, 218; **41**, 221; **44**, 147n; **46**, 110n, 231, 232; **47**, 37n, 172n, 237, 252n; **50**, 242; **52**, 7, 275; **53**, 326; **55**, 44n, 45n, 242n; **60**, 17n46, 40n16
Astle, Thomas, **59**, 122n54
Astley, Joan, **6**, 66
Astley, Sir John, **26**, 173; **42**, 188–9; **47**, 249n
Astley, Neil, **56**, 243n
Astley, Philip, **49**, 277
Aston, Elaine, **45**, 44n
Aston, Lucy, **44**, 195
Aston, Margaret, **52**, 57, 60n, 61; **54**, 20n
Aston, Sir Thomas, **60**, 226
Astrana Marín, Luis, **54**, 154n, 155, 156
Asture, Gui, **57**, 234
Atah, Risah, **50**, 234
Atalay, Turgut, **18**, 130
Atchlow, **6**, 74n
Athenaeus, **14**, 61
Atherton, David, **60**, 192n25
Atkins, Eileen, **27**, 149
Atkins, G. Douglas, **55**, 4n
Atkins, J., **38**, 71
Atkins, Rachel, **45**, 155
Atkins, Robert, **2**, 10, 12; **5**, 119, 120; **8**, 124; **10**, 124; **13**, 134; **14**, 127, 128; **15**, 145, 146; **28**, 148, 171; **32**, 31, 35n; **47**, 90; **54**, 265; **59**, 198
Atkinson, Brooks, **8**, 122
Atkinson, Dorothy F., **8**, 4
Atkinson, Geoffroy, **17**, 39, 40, 40n
Atkinson, James B., **51**, 177
Atkinson, Kate, **56**, 302
Atkinson, Margaret E., **16**, 63; **48**, 4n, 5n
Atkinson, Rosalind, **12**, 124
Atkinson, Rowan, **56**, 117
Atmore, Antony, **52**, 160n
Attenborough, Michael, **51**, 269; **52**, 247, 263; **53**, 255; **54**, 274, 277–80, 290; **55**, 286, 324; **56**, 256, 276, 282, 289, 290; **57**, 290; **58**, 156; **59**, 183, 190
Attey, John, *First Book of Ayres*, **1**, 69
Attingham Park, Shropshire, **12**, 130n
Attlee, Richard, **45**, 150
Attree, John, **7**, 67n
Attridge, Derek, **46**, 96n; **53**, 21
Attwater, Donald, **54**, 92n
Atwood, Margaret, **56**, 103
Auberlen, Eckhard, **23**, 121; **38**, 16
Aubrey, James R., **47**, 233, 258; **51**, 189n
Aubrey, John, **3**, 5; **4**, 86, 88; **6**, 159; **7**, 86; **10**, 13; **16**, 165; **17**, 195; **18**, 187; **19**, 57, 60; **29**, 135; **37**, 189; **44**, 231; **54**, 58; **55**, 82, 83n; **56**, 78, 242n

INDEX

Aubrey, Karen, **49**, 290
Auchincloss, Louis, **24**, 138
Auden, W. H., **15**, 61; **19**, 139; **21**, 3, 10n, 11n; **22**, 10, 14n, 48, 51; **25**, 153; **28**, 75; **29**, 93, 180; **32**, 51n; **34**, 36; **35**, 160; **36**, 29–37; **37**, 123n, 177; **41**, 201; **42**, 183; **49**, 95n, 227; **51**, 162n; **52**, 268, 309, 319; **53**, 144, 150; **55**, 343; **56**, 309; **59**, 225, 227, 236
Audi, Robert, **59**, 228n6
Audiberti, Jacques, French adaptation of *The Taming of the Shrew* (1957), **12**, 111
Audiences at Elizabethan plays, *see under* Theatre, Elizabethan
Audley, Hugh, **28**, 19
Audley, Maxine, **6**, 146; **9**, 131; **16**, 24
Audran, E., **18**, 76
Auer, Erich, **6**, 117
Auerbach, Erich, **26**, 53; **37**, 72n; **60**, 214–15
Auerbach, Nina, **42**, 49n; **49**, 133, 136n; **53**, 110n, 125n; **56**, 136; **58**, 85, 96
Aughterson, Kate, **50**, 256; **53**, 36n
Augier, Emile, **9**, 62
Augustin, Alexander, **23**, 118
Augustine of Hippo, St, **1**, 67; **10**, 136; **15**, 90, 91, 94, 97; **20**, 26; **31**, 8, 15, 189; **40**, 75; **42**, 195; **54**, 33, 36, 40, 80; **55**, 221, 228; **57**, 3; **59**, 241n18, 251n88, 263
Augustine, Aurelius, **48**, 73
Augustus, **11**, 46
Aulen, Gustaf, **57**, 242, 245
Aulotte, Robert, **56**, 44n
Ault, Norman, **32**, 42n; **51**, 15n
Ault, Tyler, **55**, 166n
Aulularia, **54**, 194n
Aum Shinrikyo, **60**, 139
Aurelius, Emperor Marcus, *Meditations*, **10**, 31
Ausonius, **42**, 66
Austen, Jane, **6**, 152; **19**, 13; **23**, 40; **51**, 17n; **55**, 141–3; **56**, 122; **58**, 83, 84, 91
  Mansfield Park, **8**, 58
Austin, John L., **28**, 65; **50**, 19n, 26; **53**, 310n; **57**, 308; **60**, 155–6
Austin, Warren B., **10**, 144; **26**, 182, 184; **27**, 130n
Australia, report on Shakespeare in, **1**, 112; **6**, 117; **7**, 107; **10**, 115
Austria, **1**, 115
  report on Shakespeare in, **3**, 116; **4**, 128; **5**, 111; **6**, 117; **7**, 107–8; **8**, 118; **11**, 117; **12**, 109; **13**, 124; **14**, 116; **15**, 131; **16**, 132; **18**, 119–20
Authorship problems in Shakespeare's plays, *see under* Shakespeare
Autran, Paulo, **20**, 123
Autrand, Françoise, **4**, 57n
Avci, Esin, **15**, 138
Aveling, Edward, **35**, 66n
Avens, Sally, **56**, 168n
Averell, William, **38**, 185–6; **50**, 188n
  Mervailous Combat of Contrarieties, **8**, 147
Avermaete, Roger, **18**, 120
Averroes, **40**, 79n
Avery, Alex, **59**, 299, 346
Avery, E. L., **32**, 37n
Avery, Emmett L., **11**, 147; **43**, 88n, 96n, 101n; **51**, 3, 56n, 79n; **53**, 217n
Avery, Gillian, **56**, 2n
Avery, Susan, **25**, 137n
Avey, Wayne, **39**, 76n
Avianus, **4**, 65
  see also Aesop's *Fables*
Avicenna, **17**, 147–8
Avilov, Victor, **42**, 150
Avilova, Lydia, **48**, 117
Avinoam, Reuben, **5**, 113; **8**, 120; **9**, 114; **10**, 119; **12**, 114; **14**, 121
Avoin, Don, **52**, 192n
Awdeley, John, **38**, 27; **44**, 21; **55**, 82, 83
  Fraternitie of Vacabondes, **1**, 70
Axelrad, A. José, **9**, 138; **14**, 11; **16**, 133
  'Shakespeare's Impact Today in France', **16**, 53–6
Axton, Marie, **42**, 46n, 50n; **43**, 3n, 235; **47**, 113n; **50**, 45n; **55**, 40n; **60**, 59n3, 60n7
Ayckbourn, Alan, **45**, 152; **53**, 5, 288
Ayckbourn, Philip, **51**, 268; **52**, 257
Aycock, Roy E., **26**, 175
Aycock, Wendell M., **42**, 34n
Aydelotte, Frank, **17**, 83n; **52**, 125n
Ayer, Miles, **25**, 144
Ayers, Lemuel, **7**, 117
Ayers, P. K., **48**, 250
Aylesbury, Sir Thomas, **2**, 32
Ayliff, H. K., **8**, 78; **11**, 124
Aylmer, John, Bishop, **17**, 122
Aylward, J. D., **42**, 115n
Ayola, Rakie, **47**, 214; **52**, 250; **55**, 310, 333
Ayre, John, **54**, 69n
Ayrer, Jakob, **21**, 153
  Opus Theatricum, **1**, 64
Ayres, H. M., **10**, 4; **40**, 75n
Ayres, Philip J., **24**, 163n; **54**, 36n
Ayrton, Randle, **36**, 73–4, 78–9
Ayscough, Samuel, **18**, 17, 108; **57**, 341; **59**, 159–60
Azevedo, Marcos, **52**, 265
Azzuz, al Caid, **11**, 90, 91

B., R. Gent., *Greene's Funerals*, **4**, 63, 64, 67n; **10**, 144
Bab, Julius, **35**, 26n, 27n; **48**, 10n
Babakitis, Peter, **58**, 185; **60**, 355
Babb, Lawrence, **1**, 127; **12**, 135; **17**, 258; **25**, 189; **29**, 82; **45**, 20
  The Elizabethan Malady, **6**, 154–5
  'Elizabethan Psychological Literature', **2**, 142–3
Babbitt, Irving, **48**, 65
Babcock, Barbara A., **46**, 18n, 131n
Babcock, R. W., **3**, 25; **7**, 128; **34**, 12n, 181; **37**, 149n; **51**, 6, 14
Babham, Christopher **58**, 235
Babington conspiracy, **17**, 123
Babington, Anthony, **23**, 41
Babington, Gervaise, **42**, 77
Babits, Mihály, **3**, 117; **12**, 114
Babler, O. F., **9**, 110n; **12**, 145
Babrius, **4**, 65
  see also Aesop's *Fables*
Babula, William, **29**, 166; **32**, 219; **38**, 15
  'Whatever Happened to Prince Hal? An Essay on *Henry V*', **30**, 47–59
Babych, Mark, **53**, 277; **59**, 345
Bacci, Paola, **15**, 136
Bach, Alexander, **9**, 102, 107
Bach, J. S., **36**, 74; **41**, 160

INDEX

Bach, Rebecca Ann, **51**, 278
Bachchan, H. R., **14**, 120
Bachchielli, Rolando **58**, 358
Bache, William B., **10**, 146; **19**, 137; **32**, 8; **51**, 282
Bachelet, Th., *see* Dezorry, Charles
Bachrach, A. G. H., **12**, 146 and n.; **18**, 126; **40**, 215
Bachtík, Josef, **18**, 121
Back, Guy, **25**, 178
Backer, Fr. de, **5**, 109
Backhouse, Carolyn, **42**, 155
Backscheider, Paula R., **51**, 45n
Backus, Edythe N., **6**, 55
Bacon, Alan, **54**, 86n
Bacon, Lady Anne, **57**, 200, 201, 205
Bacon, Anthony, **14**, 102, 103, 104, 107, 108n; **16**, 165; **57**, 200, 201, 207
Bacon, Craig, **56**, 297; **59**, 340
Bacon, Delia, **14**, 153; **18**, 107, 111–12; **54**, 303
Bacon, Sir Francis, **2**, 108–9, 111, 118; **3**, 17, 134; **4**, 25, 30, 146; **6**, 148; **7**, 18, 35, 61; **9**, 2, 144; **10**, 11, 33, 59n; **15**, 16; **16**, 7, 11, 158; **17**, 50, 56–7, 80–1, 85, 118, 126–7, 132, 142; **18**, 176; **21**, 128; **22**, 172; **23**, 49, 58; **24**, 153, 157; **26**, 37, 44; **27**, 95; **28**, 6, 9, 13, 15, 16, 19, 20–1, 170; **29**, 87; **33**, 22; **34**, 144; **35**, 79, 165; **37**, 115, 134; **38**, 20, 61, 122; **39**, 131; **40**, 49, 195; **42**, 192; **43**, 3, 160, 238; **44**, 62, 63n, 138, 232; **45**, 19; **46**, 98; **48**, 48n, 161; **50**, 43, 72, 74, 79; **51**, 297; **53**, 298, 319; **54**, 74–6, 78–9, 82, 229n, 303; **56**, 44, 91, 145, 216, 232, 324; **57**, 20, 25, 200, 202, 207; **58**, 137, 140, 144; **59**, 256
  Advancement of Learning, **2**, 109
  Essays, **8**, 66
  Novum Organum, **2**, 109
Bacon, Matthew, **9**, 141
Bacon, Sir Nicholas, **1**, 126; **13**, 104n; **47**, 173
Bacon, Roger, **32**, 110
Bacon, W. A., **4**, 147; **10**, 138, 147
'Baconian' theory, **3**, 6, 11; **9**, 106, 141
Baconians, American, **18**, 111–15
Bacquet, Paul, **32**, 218
Bacster, William, **1**, 64
Badalić, H., **4**, 117
Badaracco, Claire, **39**, 247–8
Badawi, M. M., **34**, 52n; **36**, 2
  Euphemism and Circumlocution in 'Macbeth', **15**, reviewed, 164
Baddeley, Angela, **13**, 141
Baddeley, Mrs, **51**, 89
Baddeley, Robert, **51**, 121
Baddeley, Sophia, **51**, 121
Badel, Alan, **10**, 130; **16**, 23; **18**, 166; **39**, 81n; **57**, 147
Baden Powell, Revd Professor, **54**, 84
Badenhausen, Rolf, **29**, 176
Badger, George, **1**, 80; **60**, 12n35
Badham, Ann, **25**, 148–9
Badham, John, **25** 148
Badiou, Alain, **60**, 345–6; **59**, 353
Bady, David, **40**, 197n
Baer, Ann, **30**, 202
Baer, Marc, **51**, 4
Baeske, Wilhelm, **6**, 4; **38**, 94; **48**, 74n
Bagchi, Jasodhara, **21**, 131; **22**, 158
Bage, Kirk **59**, 343, 344
Bagehot, Walter, **56**, 127n, 209, 210
Bagford, John, **1**, 28; **53**, 201
Baggs, A. P., **47**, 21n
Bagshaw, Christopher, **21**, 72, 73, 74, 75, 76
Bagwell, William, **17**, 95n
Bahanet, al Hage, **11**, 91
Bahti, Timothy, **51**, 126n
Baigent, Harold, **6**, 122; **7**, 113
Baildon, H. Bellyse, **10**, 1–2
Baildon, Joseph, **18**, 99
Baildon, W. P., **33**, 147n; **49**, 196n
Bailey, Benjamin, **13**, 62, 64; **24**, 114; **41**, 103n
Bailey, Bryan, **12**, 119; **14**, 126
Bailey, Derrick S., **32**, 132n, 135n
Bailey, F. A., **13**, 104n
Bailey, Helen Phelps, **45**, 2n
Bailey, Ian, **41**, 178
Bailey, James, **5**, 115
Bailey, John, **4**, 5; **6**, 3, 12, 13; **19**, 5
Bailey, Lucy, **51**, 215–16; **52**, 216, 221; **53**, 274; **56**, 256, 264, 266; **57**, 268, 294; **58**, 307; **59**, 207–8, 211, 306; **60**, 307–9
Bailey, Mark, **51**, 262; **56**, 291
Bailey, Nathaniel, **24**, 175; **59**, 165, 166
Bailey, Robin, **7**, 124; **47**, 191
Baillie, William W., **43**, 53n, 55n, 59n
Bain, Allister, **42**, 155
Bain, Donald, **14**, 127
Baines, Barbara J., **34**, 170; **50**, 42n
Baines, Helen, **48**, 236
Baines, Paul, **59**, 110, 110n7
Baines, Richard, **14**, 87; **37**, 189
Baines, Thomas, **42**, 83n
Bains, Yashdip Singh, **46**, 255; **51**, 322–3
Bainton, Roland, **48**, 88n
Baird, John D., **54**, 46n
Baird, William, **53**, 5n
Bajic, Brana, **49**, 266
Bajić, S., **18**, 134
Bak, Janos M., **54**, 126n
Bakare, Ariyon, **60**, 304–5
Ba-Kathir, Ali Ahmad, **36**, 1, 10
Bakeless, John, **7**, 88n; **14**, 9, 44n; **50**, 46n
Baker, Arthur E., **7**, 3; **13**, 44, 47n
Baker, D. C., **23**, 168
Baker, D. S., 'Shakespeare in Ghana', **16**, 77–82
Baker, David J., **46**, 215; **52**, 286; **53**, 323–4; **59**, 360
Baker, Eliot, **48**, 60
Baker, Ernest, **13**, 104n
Baker, George Pierce, **1**, 13; **4**, 11–12; **6**, 2; **8**, 5, 7; **10**, 2; **29**, 152; **47**, 87n
Baker, Herschel, **26**, 163n; **28**, 174; **29**, 81; **32**, 73n; **34**, 132; **35**, 8–9, 45n, 54; **38**, 11, 63; **41**, 145n; **42**, 39; **56**, 178n
Baker, Howard, **10**, 2–3, 40, 49n
Baker, Iain, **46**, 198
Baker, J. H., **29**, 94n, 96n, 97n; **49**, 193n; **55**, 38n
Baker, Dame Janet, **41**, 113; **55**, 313
Baker, Michael, **32**, 25
Baker, Mrs, **14**, 112, 113
Baker, Oliver, **39**, 223; **54**, 120
  Shakespeare's Warwickshire and the Unknown Years, **3**, 2

INDEX

Baker, Sir Richard, **7**, 84; **30**, 10n; **47**, 213
Chronicle of the Kings of England, **6**, 57
Baker, Robert, **17**, 31
Baker, Sean, **39**, 203; **41**, 173; **42**, 134, 153; **44**, 199
Baker, Steven, **41**, 211
Baker, Stewart A., **24**, 146
Baker, Susan, **46**, 208, 211
Baker-Smith, Dominic, **33**, 92n
Baker, Will, **16**, 118–20
Bakhtin, Mikhail, **40**, 77, 78n, 187–8, 193; **42**, 166, 196; **44**, 69n, 85, 89; **46**, 17, 18n, 55, 56; **49**, 70–2, 74–5, 77–8, 287, 301; **50**, 250, 257; **51**, 148n, 150, 151, 271, 285; **52**, 274, 298; **53**, 132, 311; **54**, 323–4; **55**, 240; **56**, 102; **57**, 196, 197; **59**, 362
Bakst, Léon, **47**, 93
Balanchine, George, **53**, 280; **54**, 289
Balavoine, C. **57**, 213
Balazs, Bela, **39**, 1n
Bald, R. C., **2**, 142, 153; **3**, 3, 30–1; **4**, 25n; **6**, 5, 161; **7**, 75; **8**, 104n; **9**, 69, 72; **11**, 153; **14**, 12; **21**, 146; **25**, 37n; **27**, 178; **36**, 110; **42**, 119; **44**, 126n, 127; **59**, 25n23, 25n26, 93, 276n23, 281n45
'*The Booke of Sir Thomas More* and its Problems', **2**, 44–61; **11**, 78
Balderstone, Peter **57**, 47
Baldi, Sergio, **22**, 165
Baldick, Chris, **44**, 111n
Baldini, Gabriele, **4**, 128; **7**, 113; **8**, 120; **9**, 114; **10**, 3, 120; **12**, 114; **13**, 130; **16**, 136; **18**, 125–6
John Webster e il linguaggio della tragedia reviewed, **8**, 150
Baldo, Jonathan, **48**, 253; **49**, 287; **50**, 251; **51**, 272–3, 293
Baldwin, Anna, **48**, 260; **56**, 305
Baldwin, C. S., **6**, 3; **31**, 18n
Baldwin, Frances Elizabeth, **55**, 46n
Baldwin, John, **3**, 56
Baldwin, Michael, **45**, 156
Baldwin, Thomas W., **1**, 4, 8, 12; **2**, 108, 134; **3**, 3, 24, 25, 31; **4**, 8–9, 148; **5**, 143; **6**, 155; **7**, 6–7, 132–3, 149; **8**, 2, 7, 11–12, 36; **9**, 34n; **10**, 5, 14, 15, 25n, 43, 49n, 142; **11**, 21, 30n, 136; **12**, 141 and n; **13**, 89n; **15**, 8, 10, 12–14, 17, 19, 26, 29, 60, 61n, 63, 71n, 72n, 94, 100, 108n, 110n; **17**, 59 and n.; **18**, 159, 177, 179, 181; **19**, 93n, 94n, 101, 103–4, 105n, 162; **22**, 113; **23**, 69, 71, 73, 74, 143, 161; **25**, 9, 82, 83; **27**, 59n, 105, 106n, 127n, 129, 132n, 134n; **28**, 71n; **29**, 22n, 104n; **30**, 61n, 89; **31**, 5, 33n; **32**, 78n, 171n, 175n; **34**, 98n; **35**, 79n, 119, 128; **36**, 85n, 92n; **38**, 41n, 42, 44n, 45n, 116n; **39**, 124n, 160n, 168n; **41**, 138n; **42**, 1n, 39n, 53n, 54, 58n, 67n, 75n; **44**, 114n; **46**, 45n; **47**, 131n, 258; **50**, 82n; **53**, 20, 78n, 155n; **54**, 16, 97, 224n; **56**, 31n, 33n, 56n, 60n, 61n, 62n
On the Literary Genetics of Shakspere's Poems and Sonnets reviewed, **5**, 137–8
Shakspere's Small Latine & Lesse Greeke, **3**, 5, 15, 21n
Shakspere's Petty School, **3**, 5
William Shakespeare's Five-Act Structure, **2**, 149–50 reviewed, **1**, 126
Baldwin, William, **28**, 1, 41; **32**, 163, 169n; **48**, 257
A Marvellous History entitled, Beware the Cat, **15**, 64
Moral Philosophy, **3**, 19
Bale, Bishop, **28**, 138, 141
Bale, John, **12**, 21n; **16**, 169; **17**, 46; **21**, 59, 61; **36**, 171; **38**, 93–5, 99, 133, 143; **42**, 26; **48**, 257; **54**, 9, 62, 100, 102–7; **57**, 239; **59**, 248, 250, 250n83, 251, 261n17
Kyng Johan, **2**, 139; **6**, 60
The Temptation of Christ, **4**, 9
Bales, Peter, *Brachygraphie*, **5**, 151
Balfe, Michael William, **18**, 81; **45**, 173; **56**, 130n
Balfoort, Maurits, **5**, 108; **12**, 110
Balibar, Etienne, **52**, 203, 205
Ball, Martin, **44**, 192
Ball, Robert Hamilton, **7**, 145n; **8**, 12; **23**, 174; **28**, 171n, 172; **39**, 4, 53n, 77n; **45**, 43n, 63n, 64n
Ballads, **3**, 54, 55
Ballagh, Robert, **46**, 198; **47**, 210
Ballard, Henry, **26**, 184
Ballard, J. G., **53**, 164n, 169, 173, 174
Ballard, John, **19**, 104, 107n
Ballard, Richard, **19**, 104
Ballaster, Ros, **51**, 293
Ballet Comique de la Reine (1581), **12**, 21n
Balls, Alphonso, **19**, 105, 107n
Balls, Richard, **19**, 104–5, 107n
Balme, Christopher, **60**, 128n31
Balsen, Ewald, **6**, 117; **11**, 117, 118
Baltazarini, **22**, 168
Balten, Pieter, **12**, 32
Balthus, **15**, 132
Balzac, Honoré de, **15**, 143; **16**, 10; **34**, 33; **49**, 285; **53**, 110, 111; **55**, 143, 145, 147
Bamber, David, **53**, 257–9, 268–70; **54**, 293
Bamber, Linda, **37**, 179n; **42**, 108; **44**, 42n; **54**, 312
Bamborough, J. B., **4**, 140n; **51**, 59n
Bamford, Karen, **55**, 358–9
Bamford, Nick, **45**, 153
Bamford, Samuel, **58**, 108
Bampton Classical Opera, **58**, 303
Banbury, Frith, **9**, 121
Bancroft, Richard, Archbishop, **17**, 126; **54**, 43, 170; **57**, 247
Bancroft, Sir Squire and Lady, **10**, 75; **31**, 188; **35**, 16, 18n, 19; **41**, 23, 25
Bandel, Betty, **18**, 131; **24**, 168
Bandello, Matteo, **1**, 63; **3**, 54, 55; **11**, 144; **15**, 29, 170; **16**, 170; **26**, 172; **27**, 172; **34**, 185; **45**, 184; **47**, 161, 164, 166; **49**, 1, 45, 47; **55**, 204
Bandinel, Bulkeley, **4**, 81
Bandmann-Palmer, Mrs, **45**, 43
Banergee, A., **47**, 232
Banerje, Srikumar, **21**, 140
Bang, W., **14**, 6, 7; **26**, 4
Bángyörgyi, Károly, **18**, 125
Banham, Martin, **39**, 96n; **43**, 249
Banham, Simon, **42**, 160; **43**, 206; **47**, 214
Banham, Teresa, **45**, 138
Banionis, D., **39**, 83n
Banister, John, **11**, 65; **17**, 154; **18**, 94; **38**, 180
Banke, Cécile de, **7**, 144
Bankes, T. H., **55**, 86n
Bankes-Jones, Bill, **45**, 147, 153
Banks, Carol, **56**, 320, 347
Banks, Evangeline, **47**, 97
Banks, Nigel, **49**, 270

Bannen, Ian, **16**, 23, 27
Bannerman, W. Bruce, **60**, 53n21
Bannister, Charles, **49**, 113n
Bannister, John, **51**, 80, 92
Bañuelos, Juan, **54**, 157–60
Banville, John, **49**, 105n
Baptista, Mantuanus, **17**, 61
Bara, Theda, **54**, 312
Barák, J., **9**, 108
Barale, Michèle Aina, **53**, 80n
Barasch, Frances, **54**, 322
Barasch, Sy, **55**, 124
Barash, M., **55**, 238n
Barba, Eugenio, **52**, 162–3
Barbarina, **49**, 249
Barbaro, Daniele, **35**, 137; **47**, 20
Barbarossa, Frederick, **16**, 9
Barbary Company, **11**, 89–97
Barbauld, Anna Laetitia, **55**, 108, 109n
Barbeito, Mañuel, **44**, 42n; **53**, 303
Barbensi, G., **7**, 113
Barber, C. L., **14**, 4, 146–7; **15**, 113, 122; **20**, 153; **21**, 130; **22**, 9, 31, 35, 154; **23**, 137, 147; **24**, 150; **25**, 108, 109, 110, 111, 158; **28**, 160; **31**, 130; **32**, 3, 4, 7, 47n, 50n, 68n, 70; **33**, 126; **34**, 111, 112n, 113, 117; **35**, 72n, 83, 96; **37**, 2, 3, 5, 7, 9, 66n; **38**, 8; **40**, 188; **41**, 193, 203; **42**, 9n, 191, 196; **44**, 42, 208; **46**, 33n, 92n, 111n, 208; **47**, 226; **49**, 69; **50**, 246; **51**, 145, 170n; **52**, 61n, 275; **56**, 65n, 71, 310; **58**, 212, 319, 320; **60**, 114n50, 117n66
  Shakespeare's Festive World: Elizabethan Seasonal Entertainment and the Professional Stage, **46**, 209
  '"Thou that beget'st him that did thee beget": Transformation in *Pericles* and *The Winter's Tale*', **22**, 59–67
Barber, Charles, **19**, 151
Barber, Frances, **42**, 160; **43**, 209; **51**, 61; **60**, 306, 307
Barber, Jamie, **57**, 291, 292
Barber, John, **24**, 126n
Barber, Lester E., **25**, 178
Barber, Paul, **43**, 208; **44**, 199
Barber, Peter, **56**, 337
Barber, Richard, **28**, 76n; **51**, 176n; **59**, 243n32
Barber, Samuel, **24**, 5, 8
Barbieri, Richard, E., **29**, 175
Barbour, Evelyn, **54**, 291
Barckley, Sir Richard, *Discourse of the Felicitie of Man*, **9**, 32
Barcklow, Brigitte, **37**, 160n
Barclay, Alexander, **32**, 165n, 169
  (tr.), **17**, 49n
Barclay, Bishop, **24**, 60
Barclay, John, **56**, 217
  The Mirrour of Mindes, **4**, 27
Bardskier, Hanns, **22**, 123
Bardsley, Julia, **48**, 230; **49**, 270
Bareham, T., **25**, 178
Barentz, William, **32**, 86–7
Barfield, Owen, **7**, 4
Barfoot, C. C., **42**, 180; **45**, 85n
Bargagli, Scipione, **17**, 183
Bargains with Fate, **46**, 215
Barge, Gillian, **39**, 86n, 87
Bargent, Harold, **14**, 116
Barham, James, **45**, 150
Baring, Maurice **58**, 140
Barish, Jonas A., **13**, 152; **14**, 11, 14n; **20**, 155; **24**, 165; **25**, 193; **27**, 171; **28**, 161; **32**, 6; **34**, 145n; **38**, 8; **39**, 233; **44**, 66; **46**, 98n, 106n; **55**, 154; **57**, 33, 116
Bark-Jones, David, **52**, 249
Barkan, Leonard, **32**, 219; **36**, 167, 175–6; **38**, 232; **41**, 133n; **47**, 143n; **54**, 15n, 29; **56**, 35, 82n, 83n, 84n
Barker, A., **48**, 141n
Barker, Andrew, **17**, 32
Barker, Christopher, **50**, 142
Barker, Cicely M., **40**, 173
Barker, Clive, **39**, 234; **48**, 177
Barker, Deborah, **45**, 44n
Barker, Ernest, **11**, 136
Barker, Felix, **27**, 34n
Barker, Francis, **40**, 64n; **43**, 1n, 15; **46**, 71; **48**, 130–1, 240, 250; **51**, 274, 278; **52**, 285; **55**, 7, 54n, 73, 80, 340; **60**, 235
Barker, H. A., **20**, 108, 111n
Barker, Harley Granville, **52**, 290; **60**, 187–8, 189n17
Barker, Howard, **44**, 194; **55**, 132; **57**, 291; **58**, 358
Barker, J., **53**, 226n
Barker, Joseph, **58**, 108
Barker, Kathleen M. D., **26**, 175; **30**, 196; **41**, 225
Barker, R. H., **14**, 11
Barker, Robert, **26**, 37, 42n; **55**, 44n
Barker, Sean, **45**, 156
Barker, T. C., **45**, 101n, 111n
Barker-Benfield, B. C., **59**, 114n27
Barkham, Sir Edward, **44**, 115, 127
Barkstead, William, **49**, 99n; **58**, 232
Barlaeus, Caspar, **48**, 26n
Barlow, Andrew, **51**, 13n
Barlow, Frank, **54**, 125n; **57**, 30
Barlow, Graham F., **42**, 194; **50**, 165
Barlow, James, **44**, 191
Barlow, Patrick, **52**, 266; **56**, 124
Barlow, Rich, **60**, 177–8
Barlow, Bishop Thomas, **4**, 93
Barlow, Tim, **52**, 257
Barlow, William, *see* Lavater, Ludwig
Barlowe, Arthur, **17**, 32
Barnard, E. A. B., **5**, 140
  New Links with Shakespeare, **3**, 2
Barnard, Sir John, **5**, 56; **33**, 187
Barnard, Lady, **1**, 80; **47**, 91
Barnay, Ludwig, **35**, 14, 15, 19
Barne, George, **32**, 90n
Barnes, Barnabe, **26**, 173; **42**, 70, 71; **47**, 133n; **52**, 7, 143; **56**, 217, 218; **60**, 105
  The Devil's Charter, **4**, 42, 47n; **7**, 78; **12**, 44, 45, 46; **13**, 118; **17**, 201, 203
  Parthenophil and Parthenope, **15**, 42
Barnes, Charlotte, **44**, 241
Barnes, E. C., **10**, 75
Barnes, Jonathan, **46**, 145n, 154, 156
Barnes, Joseph, **48**, 135n
Barnes, Julian, **52**, 317
Barnes, Mr, **14**, 112
Barnes, Peter, **28**, 139, 140; **56**, 299; **58**, 154
Barnes, Richard, **25**, 149

Barnes, Robert, **54**, 4
Barnes, W., **24**, 177n
Barnestrawe, Captain, **17**, 29
Barnet, Robbie, **47**, 211
Barnet, Sylvan, **9**, 136; **10**, 137, 143; **12**, 138, 139; **23**, 144; **26**, 154; **27**, 16n; **29**, 89; **32**, 9; **35**, 119n; **59**, 40, 41
Barnett, Howard B., **23**, 164
Barney, Hazel, **52**, 263
Barney, Stephen A., **55**, 198
Barnfield, Richard, **26**, 103; **34**, 87; **46**, 248; **60**, 87n7, 256–8, 259–60; **57**, 224
Encomion of Lady Pecunia, **4**, 87
The Shepherde's Confession (MS.), **1**, 71
Barnhill, Paul **58**, 279
Barnstaple, interlude at, **12**, 19, 21n
Baron, Richard, **49**, 270; **55**, 329; **59**, 345
Baron, Wendy, **49**, 129n
Barr, Gordon, **58**, 303; **59**, 342, 344
Barradas, Sebastian, **3**, 15
Barratt, Mark, **44**, 198
Barrault, Jean-Louis, **2**, 123; **7**, 108, 115; **9**, 67; **10**, 118, 138; **14**, 119; **15**, 132, 133; **16**, 54; **18**, 122, 185; **20**, 121; **40**, 2; **48**, 6n
Barrault, Madeleine, **7**, 115
Barre, Renatus Laurent de la, **15**, 97n
Barret, Alan, **44**, 203
Barret, David, **44**, 242
Barret, Robert, **58**, 37
Barrett, Bob, **59**, 318, 319
Barrett, C. R. B., **17**, 69 and n.
Barrett, Daniel, **38**, 236
Barrett, Felix, **58**, 302
Barrett, John, **58**, 240, 243
Barrett, Pete, **52**, 257
Barrett, Wilson, **9**, 56–7; **11**, 124; **29**, 176; **35**, 16; **40**, 37
Barrey, David, **17**, 80
Barrie, Alistair, **51**, 262
Barrie, Frank, **41**, 190; **45**, 148
Barrie, Sir James M., **8**, 131; **53**, 150n; **55**, 328, 329, 343; **56**, 10
Barrie, Robert, **56**, 97n
Barrington, Lady Joan, **38**, 31, 32n, 33n
Barrington, Sir Thomas, **38**, 31
Barrit, Desmond, **42**, 147–8; **44**, 176–8, 202; **45**, 146; **48**, 204–6; **49**, 275, 280; **52**, 261; **54**, 278–9; **55**, 313, 324; **56**, 4n, 248, 289, 290; **57**, 266, 281; **58**, 302; **60**, 328
Barroll, J. Leeds, **13**, 155; **19**, 148, 162–3; **25**, 175, 199n; **26**, 182n; **27**, 31n, 160; **28**, 152; **29**, 171, 172; **34**, 23n; **38**, 228; **39**, 218; **40**, 218; **41**, 5n, 36n; **44**, 154; **45**, 240–1; **46**, 106n; **50**, 19n, 21, 22n, 25n, 257; **51**, 157, 291; **52**, 74n, 135n; **53**, 71, 72n; **54**, 198n; **55**, 13n, 220n, 226n, 356; **56**, 317; **57**, 5, 13; **59**, 220, 354; **60**, 54–5, 56n32
Barron, Caroline M., **53**, 203n
Barron, Dennis, **46**, 43n
Barron, John, **42**, 159
Barrow, Andrew, **46**, 193; **47**, 213; **55**, 329
Barrow, Henry, **54**, 96
Barry, Bruce, **13**, 124
Barry, Cora Masters, **57**, 136
Barry, E. M., **1**, 85
Barry, Mrs Elizabeth, **14**, 113
Barry, J. G., **28**, 153
Barry, James, **13**, 75, 76; **51**, 119–20; **53**, 109; **59**, 131n47
Barry, Lodovic, **32**, 94
Barry, Lording, **59**, 72, 74
Barry, Spranger, **14**, 113; **36**, 180; **49**, 114, 116; **51**, 58, 64, 108, 120; **53**, 292; **57**, 86
Barrymore, John, **2**, 10; **9**, 18–19; **18**, 71; **35**, 2; **40**, 16; **43**, 252; **45**, 54; **49**, 153–4, 271; **52**, 292; **59**, 66
Barrymore, William, **53**, 226n, 327
Barsacq, André, **15**, 133
Barsanti, Jane, **37**, 44–5
Barshavit, Shlomo, **6**, 12; **10**, 119
Bartels, Emily C., **50**, 199n; **52**, 202n, 206n; **60**, 348
Bartenschlager, Klaus, **25**, 177–8; **30**, 210; **31**, 189; **32**, 244; **43**, 268n
Barthelemy, Anthony G. **52**, 204n, 207n, 213n; **55**, 347; **59**, 361
Barthelemy, Nicholas, *Christus Xylonicus*, **20**, 25n
Barthes, Roland, **10**, 118; **34**, 33–4; **37**, 164, 180; **40**, 186; **43**, 25; **44**, 66; **46**, 58; **48**, 118; **52**, 287; **53**, 39, 40n, 41, 42, 117n, 120, 153, 311, 325; **54**, 306; **55**, 348; **56**, 8, 67, 140; **60**, 72n2, 77n27, 79, 155, 155n5, 176
Bartholomaeus Anglicus, **37**, 86
Bartholomeusz, Dennis, **23**, 173; **26**, 81, 84–6; **35**, 10–11; **37**, 199; **50**, 114n; **54**, 41n; **57**, 56, 59, 87; **59**, 369–70, 375
Bartholomew Fair (Jonson), **48**, 259; **49**, 291, 304; **52**, 68, 81, 84, 136; **54**, 14, 58, 333
Bartholomew, Ian, **54**, 249; **56**, 266, 293
Bartington, Master, **53**, 240
Bartini, Gari, **13**, 129
Bartkowiak, Andrzej, **55**, 332
Bartlet, Keith, **42**, 136–7, 153
Bartlett Karen, **44**, 200
Bartlett, Henrietta C., **3**, 47, 54; **4**, 84; **5**, 53; **6**, 57–8; **9**, 83
Bartlett, John, **13**, 44; **23**, 176, 177–8; **25**, 76n, 94; **28**, 177, 178; **56**, 221n
Concordance to Shakespeare, **5**, 86
Bartlett, Keith, **55**, 289
Bartlett, Neil, **49**, 240–2, 253; **50**, 233; **57**, 273; **58**, 304
Bartlett, Phyllis Brooks, **52**, 111n
Bartlett, Robert, **52**, 205, 206n, 214n
Bartley, Eva, **57**, 296
Bartley, Jim, **44**, 192
Bartolommeo, Fra, **26**, 54
Bartolovich, Crystal, **50**, 199n; **55**, 341, 344
Bartolozzi, Francesco, **49**, 119
Barton (Righter, Roesen), Anne, **22**, 35, 178n; **23**, 132; **24**, 54, 124; **25**, 7, 107; **26**, 16, 165; **27**, 44, 152, 165; **28**, 156, 174; **29**, 6, 7, 42; **30**, 14, 125, 171; **31**, 81n, 118n, 147; **32**, 7, 9, 10, 48, 109n, 177n, 178n, 179n, 207; **33**, 198; **34**, 125, 152, 164; **35**, 117n, 178, 182–3; **36**, 117n, 178; **37**, 3, 17n, 24n; **38**, 6, 7, 9, 226, 229–30; **39**, 75n, 133n, 230; **40**, 83n, 109, 120, 216; **41**, 103n, 120, 122; **42**, 6n, 12n; **43**, 19, 21n, 22n, 109, 132, 138n, 243; **44**, 8n, 72, 210, 232; **45**, 128; **46**, 76n, 104n; **48**, 245, 255; **50**, 44, 80, 128; **51**, 145; **52**, 190, 311; **53**, 167n, 306; **54**, 22n; **55**, 213n; **56**, 147n, 304, 329; **57**, 209, 320; **58**, 50, 52, 202, 204; **59**, 47; **60**, 88n9
Essays Mainly Shakespearian, **48**, 255
'Shakespeare and the Limits of Language', **24**, 19–30
Barton, J. L., **29**, 93n, 97n
Barton, James, **54**, 292

Barton, John, **5**, 120; **8**, 124; **9**, 120; **14**, 129; **15**, 145; **18**, 149; **19**, 113, 117, Pl. XXIIB; **20**, 134, 135; **22**, 137, 138, 140, 142–4; **23**, 132, 133, 134, 135; **24**, 117, 122, 123, 124, 125, 129, 130, 131, 177; **25**, 45n, 48, 51n, 58n, 158, 164, 167; **26**, 175; **27**, 141, 144, 151, 152, 153; **28**, 103n, 138, 139, 140, 141, 142, 143; **29**, 180; **30**, 171–2, 173, 174–6; **31**, 141–2, 149, 152–3; **32**, 17, 201, 204–5, 208–9; **33**, 82; **34**, 151–3; **35**, 141–4, 149; **36**, 160; **37**, 115; **38**, 17, 50, 226, 237–8; **39**, 13n, 47, 105, 188, 240; **40**, 19, 223–4; **41**, 46, 57, 67, 166, 244–5; **42**, 37, 137, 200; **43**, 171–2, 176, 191; **44**, 163, 192, 243; **45**, 121; **46**, 242; **47**, 11, 197n; **49**, 13, 226; **50**, 49, 66, 69n; **51**, 238; **53**, 231–2; **54**, 274; **55**, 280, 293, 308; **56**, 5, 96, 246n; **57**, 292, 298, 329; **58**, 47, 50, 206; **59**, 208n47; **60**, 78, 79, 310, 329
Barton, Richard (vicar of Stratford), **55**, 328; **60**, 11
Barton, Robert, **52**, 233
Bartoshevich, A., **23**, 168
Bartra, Roger, **52**, 204n
Barwick, Humphry, **58**, 36
Barzilai, Shuli, **53**, 304–5
Bascombe, G. E. M. **57**, 107
Baseggio, Cesco, **6**, 121
Basil, Simon, **35**, 132–3; **45**, 109–11; **47**, 17, 21n
Basile, Giambattista, **7**, 105
Basilicon Doron (James I), **48**, 259
Basing House, **1**, 34
Baskervile, Francis, **7**, 61, 62, 67n
Baskervile, James, **7**, 61, 62, 63, 65, 67n
Baskervile, Susan (Browne and Greene by earlier marriages; *see also* Worth, Ellis), her share in the finances of Queen Anne's Men described, **7**, 57–68
Baskervill, Charles Read, **1**, 8; **13**, 123n; **15**, 71n; **54**, 193n, 196n; **55**, 193n, 196n; **56**, 62n, 63n, 64n
Baskerville, Heledd, **59**, 345
Baskerville, J., **18**, 17
Baskerville, Romy, **44**, 192
Baskin, Judith, **55**, 119n
Basore, John W., **32**, 89n
Basque folk-stage, **3**, 85
Bass, Alan, **39**, 147n; **44**, 68n; **55**, 284n
Bassano family of musicians, **7**, 139
Bassano, Anselm, **42**, 187
Bassano, Emilia, **32**, 228
Basse, Thomas, actor, **7**, 58, 62, 64, 65, 67n
Basse, William, **3**, 53; **59**, 267–83
Bassett, Margery, **17**, 233
Bassi, Shaul, **54**, 302
Bassnett (McGuire), Susan, **42**, 103n; **48**, 244
Shakespeare: The Elizabethan Plays, **48**, 244
Bastard, Thomas, **17**, 131
Básti, Lajos, **18**, 125
Basu, Kajal, **21**, 132
Bataille, Georges, **49**, 63n; **50**, 243
Batchelor, John, **53**, 178n; **55**, 107n, 181n; **58**, 155
Bate, Jonathan, **37**, 219; **39**, 133n; **40**, 200, 206; **41**, 103n; **44**, 42n, 109n, 206, 207; **47**, 253–4, 256; **48**, 51n, 152n, 153, 248; **49**, 9n, 42n, 63n, 310–12, 316–18; **50**, 82n, 85n, 89n, 262; **51**, 2–3, 9, 18n, 67n, 125–31, 176, 190n, 300, 324; **52**, 269; **53**, 34, 106, 164n, 219, 220n, 236n, 237, 293, 296; **54**, 15n, 22n, 34n, 225; **55**, 3n, 107n, 200n, 203n, 208n, 257, 271n, 280n, 381; **56**, 9n, 14, 23n, 25, 41n, 123n, 131, 204n, 206n, 210n; **57**, 3, 6, 331, 335; **58**, 75; **59**, 30–1, 112n19, 168, 299; **60**, 185, 366
Bate, Walter Jackson, **9**, 90
Bateman, Ellen, **7**, 92
Bateman, Kate, **7**, 92
Bateman, Kate and Isobel, **38**, 193
Bateman, Stephen, **51**, 183n; **54**, 92, 93n
Bates, Alan, **43**, 183; **44**, 198; **46**, 193; **53**, 248; **56**, 247
Bates, Catherine, **54**, 297–8, 319
Bates, Django, **54**, 272; **55**, 335
Bates, E. S., **15**, 15
Bates, Paul A., **22**, 165; **32**, 214; **33**, 199
Bates, Ronald, **9**, 135; **10**, 141; **15**, 28
Bateson, David, **44**, 197
Bateson, F. W., **5**, 138, 149n; **7**, 4; **9**, 135; **11**, 138; **12**, 137n; **13**, 168n; **15**, 138; **18**, 189; **43**, 233
Bateson, Thomas, *Second Set of Madrigals*, **1**, 70
Bath, *for* Theatre Royal, Bath, *see under* Theatres
Bath, Marquis of, *see* Thynne, Henry
Bath, Michael, **41**, 223; **43**, 247
Batho, E. C., **28**, 120n
Batho, G. R., **11**, 148n
Bathory, Dennis, **51**, 282
Batley, E. M., **26**, 167; **56**, 151n
Batman, John, **35**, 31
Batman, Stephen, **17**, 39; **26**, 111n; **28**, 121; **32**, 87n, 89, 90
Battenhouse, Roy W., **2**, 66, 71; **3**, 68; **4**, 22; **6**, 156–7; **7**, 7; **8**, 12, 16, 27n, 141; **9**, 8, 138; **10**, 138; **12**, 134, 136; **14**, 10; **15**, 115; **18**, 169–70; **19**, 120; **24**, 139–40, 143; **25**, 6, 183; **26**, 16n, 127n, 161; **28**, 158; **29**, 88n, 161; **30**, 185; **31**, 13n, 15, 180; **32**, 231; **33**, 89; **34**, 85n; **35**, 157n; **36**, 177; **37**, 88n; **38**, 9, 14; **45**, 21, 22; **50**, 102n; **54**, 61n, 123n, 124n; **57**, 244; **60**, 103n9
'The Relation of Henry V to Tamburlaine', **27**, 71–9
Battersby, Roy, **14**, 128
Battestine, Martin, **42**, 100n
Batteux, Abbé, **20**, 34, 35
Battistella, Antonio, **12**, 114
Battle of Alcazar, The (plot of), **3**, 52; **9**, 41
Battle of Alcazar, The, **17**, 51; **50**, 288
Battles, Ford Lewis, **54**, 139; **55**, 229n; **57**, 237
Batusic, S., **18**, 134
Baty, Gaston, **1**, 114; **2**, 123; **14**, 119; **40**, 2
Baudelaire, Charles Pierre, **43**, 223; **45**, 2
Baudiš, J., **9**, 104, 110n
Baudissin, Count Wolf von, **6**, 124; **13**, 124; **16**, 132
see also under Schlegel, A. W. von
Baudoin, J., **48**, 144n
Baudrillard, Jean, **52**, 198n; **58**, 187
Bauduin, J., **25**, 180
Bauer, Charlotte, **52**, 158n
Bauer, Robert J., **23**, 153; **24**, 158
Bauernfeld, Eduard von, **35**, 23
Baugh, Albert C., **56**, 241n
Baum, Bernard, **8**, 144
Baum, H. W., **14**, 10
Baume, Georges, **15**, 133
Baumgarten, E., **10**, 10, 11
Baumgartner, Balthasar, the younger, **33**, 56
Baumlin, Tita French, **46**, 213; **53**, 38n
Baur, Harry, **39**, 77n

Baur, Lilo, **52**, 219, 225
Bavli, Hillel, **8**, 120
Bawcutt, N. W., **14**, 8, 9; **23**, 169–70; **24**, 158; **32**, 238–9; **36**, 127n; **38**, 227; **43**, 269; **44**, 70; **46**, 245–8; **47**, 249n; **50**, 255; **51**, 291; **52**, 72n, 73n, 81n; **54**, 19n; **55**, 196, 197; **59**, 23n13
  Studies on Shakespeare's Life, Times and Stage, *reviewed:*
    (1974) **28**, 164–72
    (1975) **29**, 168–77
    (1976) **30**, 191–203
Bawcutt, Priscilla, **34**, 196
Bax, Clifford, **58**, 139, 141
Baxandall, Michael, **31**, 19n
Baxendale, Helen, **52**, 259
Baxter, James, **25**, 147
Baxter, John, **20**, 152; **38**, 6; **57**, 16, 17
Baxter, Keith, **39**, 42–3
Baxter, Nathaniel, **54**, 92n; **57**, 209, 216
Baxter, Richard, **7**, 58, 59, 60, 63, 67n; **9**, 147; **23**, 167; **27**, 87n; **36**, 162; **49**, 303; **54**, 59
Baxter, Thomas, **49**, 194
Baxter, William Giles, **43**, 61n; **49**, 128
Bayldon, Geoffrey, **9**, 124
Bayley, John, **21**, 4, 5, 6, 9, 10n; **29**, 162–3; **35**, 165–6; **36**, 48–9; **37**, 127; **41**, 74, 121, 205; **44**, 217; **45**, 59, 60, 166; **49**, 203n, 206, 214n, 215n; **55**, 10–11; **59**, 365; **60**, 194n31
  The Characters of Love reviewed, **15**, 156–8
Baylis, Lilian, **44**, 102; **47**, 238
Baylis, Nadine, **34**, 151; **41**, 184; **54**, 291
Bayliss, Peter, **43**, 188; **44**, 194; **53**, 255
Bayliss, Stanley A., **15**, 7; **60**, 187n12, 189n17
Bayly, Lewis (vicar of Shipston-on-Stour), **60**, 10n25
Bayly, Thomas, **17**, 100
Baynard, John, **55**, 264
Bayne, Peter, **49**, 134, 138n, 140n
Bayne, Ronald, **25**, 127n
Baynham, Sir Edmund, **24**, 157n
Bayreuth, **12**, 1
Baziliwlogia, **11**, 98
Bazin, André, **39**, 3, 39, 52, 91, 93, 95, 96n; **45**, 64
Bazine, Jean, **10**, 118
Beach, Elizabeth, **24**, 154, 155
Beacham, Stephanie, **57**, 298
Beacon, Richard, **52**, 286
Beadle, Nick, **51**, 258
Beadle, Richard, **41**, 114n; **56**, 168n; **57**, 241
Beadle-Blair, Rikki, **41**, 184
Beagley, Lee, **47**, 212; **51**, 259; **53**, 284; **57**, 297
Beal, Peter, **40**, 227n; **59**, 118
Beale, David, **44**, 197
Beale, Dorothea, **55**, 108
Beale, H. G., **55**, 37n
Beale, John, **55**, 263n
Beale, Richard, **53**, 326
Beale, Robert, Clerk to the Council, **17**, 127
Beale, Roger, **60**, 346
Beale, Simon Russell, **44**, 173, 174; **45**, 125, 148, 156; **46**, 163, 164; **47**, 122–3, 200, 202–5, 216; **48**, 115; **49**, 235; **51**, 253–4; **52**, 262; **53**, 192–3, 322; **54**, 258–62; **55**, 292, 297, 323; **56**, 97, 100, 238n, 257, 261–2, 288, 289, 343; **57**, 297, 331; **58**, 268; **59**, 328, 329, 330–3; **60**, 160, 168n4.9, 322, 323
Beales, Kate, **55**, 333
Beam, Marjorie, **31**, 184
Beamish, Mick, **41**, 184
Beamish, Oliver, **47**, 212
Bean, John C., **37**, 6, 33n, 34–6, 39; **60**, 84–5n2, 88n10
Bean, Sean, **41**, 189; **42**, 157; **56**, 257, 280–1; **57**, 293; **58**, 301
Bear-baiting arenas, **3**, 85, 89
Beard, Martin, **54**, 291
Beard, Robert, **39**, 183
Beard, Steven, **43**, 210
Beard, Thomas, **43**, 5n; **44**, 71; **48**, 40
Beardsley, Aubrey, **37**, 53; **55**, 311
Beargarden, The, **1**, 25–37, *passim*; **2**, 21, 22
Bearman, Robert, **48**, 267; **56**, 184–202; **58**, 3, 321; **60**, 1, 2n6, 8n18, 10n24, 10n25, 11n30, 15n41
Bearwish, Mick, **42**, 162; **44**, 192; **47**, 217, 218; **49**, 280; **51**, 264
Beason, Nick, **53**, 275
'Beasts and Gods: Greene's *Groatsworth of Witte* and the Social Purpose of *Venus and Adonis*', **15**, 62–72
Beatles, The, **44**, 177; **56**, 120; **57**, 155, 156
Beaton, Cecil, **55**, 309
Beaton, David, **46**, 199; **47**, 216; **51**, 268
Beaton, Norman, **49**, 272
Beattie, Ian, **49**, 278
Beattie, James, **40**, 72n
Beattie, Maureen, **45**, 154; **49**, 261; **51**, 253–4; **57**, 285
Beatty, A., **15**, 12
Beatty, Bernard, **57**, 109
Beauchamp, Gorman, **39**, 6
Beaujour, Michael, **29**, 14n
Beaulieu, J., **33**, 167
Beauman, Sally, **36**, 73, 74n; **38**, 17; **41**, 59n; **56**, 247n, 249n
Beaumarchais, Pierre Augustin Caron de, **9**, 91; **51**, 41
Beaume, Georges, **11**, 120
Beaumont and Fletcher, **11**, 48, 64, 81, 82; **14**, 6, 8, 12, 15, 77–82, 84, 87; **15**, 6, 8; **17**, 172–3, 175–6, 196, 198, 209; **22**, 1, 114, 164; **23**, 46; **26**, 1, 4, 33, 55, 66, 67, 100
  The Bloody Brother, **18**, 187
  Bonduca, **1**, 46; **3**, 52; **11**, 82, 87n; **14**, 163; **20**, 8
  The Captain, **1**, 46; **9**, 86; **13**, 116; **18**, 187
  Collected Works, **9**, 89n
  Cupid's Revenge, **1**, 45, 48
  The Double Marriage, **12**, 48; **13**, 116
  The Elder Brother (MS.), **3**, 52
  The Faithful Shepherdess, **1**, 45; **11**, 110
  The Fatal Marriage (MS.), **3**, 52
  The Honest Man's Fortune, **11**, 82; **13**, 120
  The Island Princess, **12**, 42; **20**, 11
  A King and No King, **1**, 46, 49, 64; **13**, 119
  The Knight of the Burning Pestle, **1**, 43, 45; **4**, 126; **5**, 4; **7**, 70; **11**, 100, 119; **15**, 5; **18**, 132; **20**, 95, 103n
  The Little French Lawyer, **12**, 48; **15**, 40n
  Love's Changelings' Change (MS.), **3**, 52
  Love's Cure, **4**, 97
  Love's Pilgrimage, **13**, 116
  The Loyal Subject, **12**, 48; **20**, 95, 103n
  The Mad Lover, **20**, 3, 4
  The Maid in the Mill (with Rowley, William), **12**, 42
  The Maid's Tragedy, **1**, 46, 49; **7**, 80n; **20**, 6, 8–9

Monsieur Thomas, **1**, 46; **12**, 48; **20**, 3, 7
Philaster, **1**, 45, 48, 49; **4**, 2; **9**, 151; **13**, 119; **14**, 84
The Prophetess (with Massinger, Philip), **13**, 122; **20**, 95, 103n
Rule a Wife and Have a Wife, **20**, 7
Scornful Lady, **1**, 45
Sea Voyage, **12**, 37
The Second Maiden's Tragedy, **11**, 48, 87n
The Triumph of Death, **20**, 4
The Wild-Goose Chase, **14**, 163
A Wife for a Month, **12**, 48; **20**, 12–13
The Woman-Hater, **18**, 35; **20**, 91
The Woman's Prize, **15**, 126; **20**, 91
Thierry and Theodoret, **11**, 51
Two Noble Kinsmen, **11**, 50–9, 123; **12**, 63n, 149–50; **13**, 38, 157; **14**, 163; **15**, 169, 180; **18**, 54; **19**, 138; **20**, 175
Valentinian, **1**, 46; **14**, 163; **20**, 2–4, 6, 8, 11
Wit at Several Weapons, **13**, 114
Woman Hater, **1**, 45
Beaumont, Count de, **11**, 92
Beaumont, Cyril, **57**, 61
Beaumont, Francis, **1**, 40, 44–6, 48–9, 65; **3**, 44, 45; **6**, 57; **7**, 6, 14, 141, 142; **8**, 52, 55, 66; **10**, 3; **13**, 103; **17**, 79, 175; **18**, 46, 132; **23**, 171; **24**, 159; **28**, 180; **29**, 3, 4, 7; **32**, 93n, 232, 241; **34**, 52, 178; **35**, 185; **36**, 107n, 110, 188; **37**, 42; **39**, 131, 133, 230; **40**, 219; **41**, 7, 61, 92n, 100n; **42**, 109n, 197–8, 208n; **43**, 25, 81n, 84, 87–8; **44**, 126n; **45**, 179, 184, 195; **46**, 29n, 30, 106, 133; **48**, 185n, 259, 260, 269; **50**, 169n; **51**, 101, 135, 206, 215, 289, 309, 317–18; **52**, 26, 43n, 139, 212, 308; **54**, 20, 63, 214; **57**, 69; **58**, 358; **59**, 2, 22, 23–4, 24n20, 71, 72, 73, 75, 76, 77n12, 214, 221, 222, 267, 274; **60**, 270n5, 368
see also under Beaumont and Fletcher *and* Fletcher, John
Poems (1640), **6**, 55
Beaumont, Sir Francis, **55**, 86, 265, 266, 350; **56**, 38, 78, 101
Beaumont, Joseph, **38**, 251
Beaumont, Keith, **57**, 118
Beaumont, Thomas, **21**, 145
Beaune, Colette, **44**, 58n
Beauregard, David, **50**, 239
Beaurline, L. A., **23**, 170; **39**, 133n; **44**, 245, 252; **48**, 37n, 38n; **50**, 71n; **53**, 176n, 178, 181n, 183n
Beauty and Good Properties of Women, The, **4**, 9
Beaven, A. B., *The Aldermen of the City of London*, **11**, 97n
Beavis, Michelle, **46**, 197
Beazley, C. R., **17**, 38n
Bebb, Richard, **24**, 2n
Becanus, Joan Goropius, **56**, 41n
Bechtler, Hildegard, **44**, 183; **45**, 148; **49**, 264; **50**, 232; **53**, 267; **54**, 288; **59**, 321
Beck, Cave, **48**, 32
Beck, Christopher, **52**, 232
Beck, Diane, **54**, 253
Beck, Ervin, **30**, 192
Beck, Jeffrey P., **45**, 162
Beck, Peter, **58**, 300
Beck, R. G., **53**, 196n
Beck, Robert, **48**, 235; **51**, 261
Beck, Rosalie, **23**, 167
Beck, Sydney, **15**, 9
Becker, Ernest, **42**, 6n; **44**, 211
Becker, George, **33**, 190
Becker, Lawrence, **53**, 91
Becker, Maria, **13**, 128; **18**, 129
Beckerman, Bernard, **10**, 88n; **18**, 62, 182; **20**, 170; **22**, 35; **23**, 174n; **25**, 6, 191; **26**, 155; **30**, 17, 197; **32**, 223, 226; **33**, 187, 198; **34**, 119n, 176; **35**, 160n; **36**, 57n, 63, 178; **37**, 38, 40; **39**, 229; **41**, 4, 37, 86; **42**, 86, 87n; **43**, 232, 250; **44**, 152, 243; **45**, 27n, 28n, 29n; **47**, 30n; **55**, 237n, 242n; **59**, 41
Beckerman, Gloria Brim, **55**, 237n
Becket, Thomas à, **26**, 75; **54**, 124–5; **59**, 112
Beckett, Arthur, **56**, 127n
Beckett, Samuel, **12**, 110; **16**, 19, 34, 35, 70, 158; **18**, 61, 156; **22**, 4, 5, 28; **24**, 19; **26**, 93; **30**, 188; **36**, 21–2, 23n, 24–5, 28; **39**, 136; **40**, 210; **41**, 108; **43**, 222, 251; **44**, 210; **48**, 4; **49**, 225, 226, 230; **50**, 19, 120, 121, 289; **53**, 112; **55**, 1, 74, 75, 77, 78, 81, 153–8, 160, 161, 171, 174; **57**, 114, 119, 120, 148
End Game, **16**, 34
Waiting for Godot, **11**, 19; **12**, 1, 2, 7
Beckett, Stephen, **55**, 330
Beckinsale, Kate, **52**, 293
Beckley, Richard, **50**, 41n
Beckley, Tony, **14**, 127
Beckman, Margaret Boerner, **32**, 217
Becks, George, **32**, 21n
Beckwith, Sarah, **54**, 342
Becon, Thomas, **2**, 68, 69; **17**, 54n; **28**, 92
Bede, **57**, 305; **59**, 241, 242n22, 250n87
Bedford (book-binder), **3**, 45
Bedford, Brian, **31**, 147; **34**, 43, 155–9; **36**, 60; **39**, 183
Bedford, Countess of, *see* Russell, Lucy Harrington
Bedford, Duke of, **48**, 53–4, 60
Bedford, Kristina, **56**, 173n
Bedford, R. D., **53**, 306
Bedford, S. K., **49**, 290
Bedford, Thomas, **50**, 194
Bedford, twelfth Duke of, *see* Russell, Hastings
Bedingfield, T., **3**, 21
Bednarz, James, **58**, 200, 202
Bednarz, James P., **38**, 232; **47**, 47n, 233; **55**, 369–70; **60**, 263n34, 252–63, 266n42
Beecham, Richard, **56**, 296; **58**, 307
Beecham, Sir Thomas, **32**, 84
Beecher, Charles, **51**, 3; **53**, 217n
Beecher, D., **54**, 115n
Beechey, Gwilym, **23**, 164
Beeching, H. C, **15**, 11, 12, 15; **18**, 187; **20**, 172
Beehler, Sharon A. **58**, 314, 331
Beer, Gillian, **49**, 104; **53**, 117, 123n; **60**, 186n11
Beer, Tobias, **57**, 296
Beerbohm, Sir Max, **7**, 123; **16**, 109; **29**, 133–44; **31**, 176, 191; **32**, 19n; **35**, 6; **40**, 210; **45**, 44; **53**, 139n; **57**, 82, 95
Beesley, Terence, **44**, 198
Beeston, Christopher, **7**, 58, 59, 64–5, 67n, 68n; **9**, 147; **10**, 13; **30**, 161–3, 166, 167; **33**, 163; **41**, 2, 5; **43**, 162; **44**, 232; **52**, 82; **54**, 120; **58**, 235
Beeston, Robert, **33**, 164
Beeston, William, **3**, 14; **10**, 13; **30**, 167; **42**, 64, 194; **44**, 232; **56**, 60
Beethoven, Ludwig van, **8**, 15; **11**, 31; **13**, 70; **18**, 75; **21**, 3; **22**, 2; **38**, 199; **50**, 3

INDEX

Beeton, Mrs (née Isabella Mary Mayson) **56**, 131n
Beeton, Samuel, **56**, 131
Beevers, Geoffrey, **58**, 278; **60**, 292
Begbeider, Marc, **10**, 118
Begg, Edleen, **6**, 7; **29**, 84
Begg, Robin, **43**, 214
Begley, Kit, **49**, 275
Behaim, Martin, **52**, 184, 187–8
Behn, Aphra, **3**, 44; **49**, 304; **50**, 256; **53**, 27n; **55**, 380; **56**, 107; **60**, 330, 349
The Younger Brother, **4**, 94
Behrens, Ralph, **11**, 141
Behrndt, Synne K., **60**, 155n7
Beier, A. L., **44**, 17n, 24; **52**, 121n, 209n; **54**, 166n, 229n; **55**, 82; **56**, 224n
Beier, Karin, **49**, 278; **50**, 34, 35, 36–40; **52**, 289
Beier, Ulli, **39**, 176n
Beijer, Agne, **12**, 33
Beilin, Elaine, **46**, 17n
Beiner, G., **48**, 245
Shakespeare's Agonistic Comedy: Poetics, Analysis, Criticism, **48**, 245
Beith-Halahmi, Esther Yael, **29**, 174
Bek, J., **7**, 109
Bel Savage Inn, **3**, 16
Belasco, David, **24**, 167; **39**, 75n
Belasco, Sonia, **52**, 92, 93n
Beldam, Joseph, **30**, 165n
Beldoch, Michael, **40**, 104
Belfield, Jane, **34**, 184–5
Belgion, Montgomery, **37**, 107n
Belgium, report on Shakespeare in, **1**, 114; **5**, 106–10, 111; **6**, 117–18; **7**, 108; **8**, 118; **10**, 115; **12**, 110; **13**, 125; **14**, 117; **18**, 120
Belihan, Constance C., **43**, 233
Beliles, David, **54**, 313
Belinsky, V., **2**, 105, 126; **5**, 118; **9**, 118; **16**, 14
Beljame, Alexandre, **2**, 119
Bell Helicopter, **55**, 323
Bell, Alex, **42**, 158
Bell, Arthur H., **26**, 158; **28**, 157; **33**, 101n
Bell, C. F., **1**, 11, 37n
Bell, David, **46**, 199
Bell, Duncan, **42**, 147–8; **51**, 264
Bell, Elizabeth, **45**, 148, 152
Bell, Fiona, **55**, 287–8; **56**, 248, 290
Bell, Ilona, **53**, 323–4; **60**, 351
Bell, J. H., **35**, 73n
Bell, Jeremy, **41**, 187; **42**, 157
Bell, John, **10**, 73; **18**, 17; **36**, 103n, 119n; **41**, 190; **43**, 105; **46**, 143; **49**, 115n, 118; **51**, 88; **53**, 214, 216–18, 225–6, 228, 343; **58**, 59; **59**, 158
Bell, Marie, **6**, 118; **7**, 108
Bell, Mary, **22**, 145; **23**, 50n
'Walter Whiter's Notes on Shakespeare', **20**, 83–94
Bell, Maureen, **59**, 117n37
Bell, Richard, **49**, 184
Bell, Robert, **15**, 61
Bell, Simon, **53**, 275, 279
Bell, Stanley, **49**, 226
Bell, Suzy, **52**, 158n
Bell, Tony, **57**, 265; **59**, 318
Bellaguet, L. F., **44**, 57n
Bellamy and Robarts, **13**, 76
Bellamy, Alastair, **54**, 136n
Bellamy, John, **52**, 172n, 173–4
Bellamy, Madeline, **41**, 184
Bellamy, Mrs George Anne, **48**, 59; **49**, 114–15
Bellan, Le Sr de, **52**, 212n
Bellard-Thomson, Carol, **46**, 11n
Bellarmine, Cardinal Robert, **17**, 121; **54**, 44; **59**, 250, 252n92
Bellecourt, (Jean Claude Gilles Colson), **9**, 91
Belleforest, François de, **1**, 63; **9**, 29; **10**, 99; **14**, 45; **15**, 29, 170; **20**, 98, 103; **21**, 152; **27**, 172; **29**, 171; **35**, 184; **40**, 10; **43**, 267; **44**, 240; **45**, 7, 42; **47**, 164
The hystorie of Hamblet, **5**, 53
Bellenden, John, **28**, 120; **57**, 70
Bellette, A. F., **33**, 191
Bellini, Giovanni, **56**, 45, 47, 296
Bellini, Vincenzo, **18**, 75, 80, 81; **19**, 70; **49**, 4, 285; **54**, 291; **58**, 305
Bellman, Gina, **49**, 236–7, 271
Belloc, Hillaire, **55**, 345
Bellori, Giovanni Petro, **36**, 85
Bellow, Saul, **36**, 49; **55**, 357
Bellringer, A. W., **24**, 147; **40**, 81, 82n
Belott, Stephen, **3**, 11–12, 13; **25**, 138–9, 141, 147; **57**, 234
Belott-Mountjoy, **42**, 123, 126
Belsey, Catherine, **27**, 159; **30**, 192; **34**, 170; **40**, 187, 191; **42**, 107, 168; **43**, 100n; **44**, 48n, 89, 226; **46**, 6, 71, 220; **47**, 8n; **49**, 58n, 60n, 64n, 91n, 213, 295; **51**, 150n, 274, 286; **53**, 234n, 236–7, 239, 329; **54**, 298, 300, 321, 323; **56**, 73, 330; **57**, 99, 312, 315; **60**, 167, 169n9.2
Belson, Louise, **48**, 232
Belsye, Anna, **23**, **42**
Belte, Thomas, **58**, 230, 231
Belton, Cathy, **48**, 234
Belton, Ellen R., **40**, 209
Belton, Fred, **56**, 126n
Belvoir Castle, **3**, 4
Belyakovich, Valery, **42**, 150
Bembo, Cardinal, **25**, 103, 104; **33**, 164; **42**, 68; **49**, 61
Bemrose, J. M., **18**, 180
Ben Hur, **10**, 38
Ben-Ami, Issachar, **48**, 56n
Benassi, Memo, **5**, 113; **9**, 114
Benbow, R. Mark, **55**, 86n
Benchettrit, Paul, **11**, 147
'*Hamlet* at the Comédie Française: 1769–1896', **9**, 59–68
Benchley, Robert, **34**, 164
Benckendorf, Count A. von, **5**, 99
Bencomb, Marcia, **49**, 140n
Benda, Jiři (Georg) Antonin, **9**, 107; **18**, 78
Bendall, Ernest, **55**, 134
Bender, John, **34**, 184
Bendikson, Lodowyk, **6**, 55
Bendokat, Margit, **40**, 56
Benedek, Marcell, **13**, 129
Benedetti, Jean, **56**, 173n; **57**, 86; **59**, 288n19, 292
Benedict, Claire, **43**, 208; **44**, 196; **45**, 153; **46**, 182
Benedict, Peter, **43**, 211; **44**, 200; **45**, 156; **50**, 235
Benedict, Ruth, **15**, 117

Beneke, Jürgen, **37**, 158n
Benese, Richard, **33**, 143n
Benet, Tony, **48**, 230
Benfield, Robert, **58**, 233
Benham, W., **1**, 35n
Benigne of Fleury, **15**, 98n
Benison, Ben, **46**, 160; **47**, 211; **50**, 226; **53**, 277
Benivieni, Girolamo, **34**, 96
Benjamin, Christopher, **44**, 198; **49**, 251–2; **50**, 228; **58**, 268; **59**, 314, 339
Benjamin, Ivor, **44**, 195
Benjamin, Jessica, **49**, 65n
Benjamin, Walter, **39**, 53; **45**, 134n, 137; **50**, 250; **51**, 126; **54**, 138, 163n; **56**, 10, 77, 140; **59**, 150–1; **60**, 79n32
Benn, Ernest, **14**, 87
Bennent, David, **45**, 155
Bennet, Paul E., **11**, 141
Bennett, Alan, **53**, 268; **54**, 249, 319; **55**, 174
Bennett, Andrew, **55**, 69n
Bennett, Bruce, **55**, 174n
Bennett, H. S., **1**, 7; **3**, 7; **14**, 8; **32**, 137n; **51**, 142
  'Shakespeare's Stage and Audience' reviewed, **3**, 140
Bennett, H. S. and Rylands, George, 'Stratford Productions', **1**, 107–11
Bennett, J. A. W., **54**, 61n
Bennett, Jonathan, **36**, 23n, 24, 25n
Bennett, Josephine Waters, **7**, 135; **11**, 139; **12**, 136n; **14**, 33n; 17, 39; **18**, 165; **21**, 52n, 134; **22**, 160, 182; **25**, 4, 7, 29; **28**, 89n; **34**, 97n; **37**, 99n; **46**, 36n; **52**, 133; **54**, 90n; **56**, 215n; **59**, 41
Bennett, Kenneth C., **35**, 158
Bennett, Laurie, **51**, 269
Bennett, Ned, **51**, 264
Bennett, Paul E., **10**, 2, 70n, 146n; **36**, 173
Bennett, Robert B., **31**, 165
Bennett, Rodney, **39**, 100; **45**, 53, 59, 60
Bennett, Stuart, **55**, 267
Bennett, Susan, **51**, 272, 276; **59**, 285n3; **60**, 360
Bennett, Vivienne, **36**, 82; **47**, 96; **60**, 78
Bennewitz, Fritz, **32**, 217
Bennington, Geoff, **46**, 96n
Bennison, Ben, **52**, 260
Bennison, Ishia, **47**, 185–6, **48**, 199, 200, 203; **49**, 253, 275, 276; **51**, 266; **56**, 252
Benny, Jack, **35**, 154n
Bennytt, William, **25**, 144
Benoît, Jean-Louis, **54**, 285; **58**, 339
Benrath, Martin, **48**, 229
Bensley, Robert, **7**, 26; **9**, 136; **10**, 73; **53**, 223
Benson, Lady Constance, **25**, 115n; **35**, 19n; **41**, 221
Benson, F. R. (Sir Frank), **2**, 1, 2, 3, 14, 16; **4**, 105; **6**, 49, 119; **7**, 29, 121, 146; **8**, 76, 152; **9**, 19, 57; **18**, 72; **25**, 1, 114–15, 117, 118, 122; **29**, 136, 137, 143; **35**, 10; **36**, 74; **44**, 106, 110n; **47**, 92, 94; **52**, 290; **59**, 150, 198n4; **60**, 188
Benson, George, **4**, 133
Benson, John, **9**, 85; **15**, 11, 12, 13; **22**, 182; **23**, 158; **46**, 35, 36, 37, 41, 48, 238; **50**, 140, 278; **52**, 324; **60**, 253, 254–5, 266, 281
  edition of Shakespeare's poems (1640), **4**, 153–4
Benson, Larry D., **43**, 71n; **53**, 29n; **54**, 25n; **57**, 150
Benson, Mrs, **29**, 141
Benson, Nick, **45**, 155; **46**, 202
Benson, Peter, **39**, 106
Benson, Susan, **31**, 143; **39**, 185
Benstock, Shari, **60**, 76n22
Benston, Alice N., **34**, 177; **37**, 59n
Bent, J. Theodore, **52**, 207n
Bentall, Paul, **49**, 252, 260
Benthall, Michael, **1**, 109; **4**, 123; **5**, 115; **8**, 125, 132, 134, 136, 138; **9**, 22, 119, 120, 123, 124, 127, 129; **10**, 123, 124, 125, 130; **11**, 128, 129, 131; **12**, 120, 121; **48**, 109
  production of *Antony and Cleopatra* reviewed, **6**, 140–2, 143, 145
  production of *Henry* VIII, **13**, 134, 135; **16**, 22, 27
Benthall, Paul, **51**, 240
Bentham, Jeremy, **60**, 225, 227n25
Bentinck, G. Cavendish, **54**, 125n
Bentivoglio, Hercole, **35**, 110
Bentley, Eric, **22**, 28; **26**, 143; **35**, 163n; **37**, 35; **50**, 41n; **58**, 136
Bentley, Gerald Eades, **1**, 4, 8; **6**, 163; **7**, 60; **10**, 144; **11**, 30n, 108, 115n; **12**, 65; **13**, 123n; **14**, 1, 10, 77, 88n; **15**, 8; **18**, 36, 177; **19**, 101, 103, 104, 105n, 145, 152–3; **20**, 81n, 160; **21**, 146; **22**, 174; **23**, 126, 127, 172n; **24**, 53; **25**; 200; **26**, 5, 9, 98, 168, 169, 170; **28**, 167, 169; **29**, 30, 161n, 163n, 167; **31**, 185; **33**, 165n; **34**, 118n, 131n, 178; **35**, 4, 130n; **36**, 135n, 136n, 137; **38**, 85n, 90n, 91n; **40**, 204, 212; **41**, 5–9, 21n, 40n, 91n, 92n, 214; **42**, 39n, 47n, 86, 99n, 106n, 107n; **43**, 149n, 152n, 243; **45**, 185; **46**, 231n; **47**, 16n, 49, 50, 60n, 172n, 175n; **50**, 261; **51**, 144, 317; **52**, 71n, 82n; **53**, 196, 197n, 206n; **54**, 19n, 62; **55**, 44n; **58**, 224, 226, 233, 234, 237, 238, 239, 242; **59**, 23n13, 41, 213; **60**, 1n2, 270n6
  'Shakespeare and the Blackfriars Theatre', **1**, 38–50
Bentley, Greg, **49**, 96n
Bentley, John, **6**, 74n; **58**, 62; **60**, 4, 21–2
Bentley, Richard, seventeenth-century publisher, **3**, 48; **5**, 2; **9**, 84; **51**, 129, 130, 131n, 133, 321; **55**, 263n
Bentley, Thomas, **32**, 97; **59**, 223–4
Benveniste, **54**, 323
Bercovitch, Sacvan, **23**, 161n; **24**, 162n, 169; **28**, 49n
Bereblock, John, **35**, 131n; **42**, 117
Berek, Peter, **36**, 167; **37**, 191; **42**, 1n; **43**, 230; **52**, 101n, 209; **55**, 29
Berenson, B., **14**, 149
Beresford, Katie, **45**, 145
Beresford, Stephen, **58**, 277; **59**, 345
Berg, James, **54**, 321
Berg, O. van den, **14**, 122
Bergbusch, Matt, **55**, 346
Bergemann, Otto, **9**, 138
Berger, André, **3**, 104–5; **5**, 111; **6**, 118; **8**, 118
Berger, David, **55**, 122n
Berger, Harry Jr, **25**, 177; **40**, 190, 195; **41**, 223; **43**, 16n, 31n, 38n, 219, 238; **44**, 244; **47**, 30n; **48**, 88; **51**, 277; **52**, 146, 270, 274, 280; **53**, 91; **54**, 226n, 227n, 322; **55**, 10; **56**, 84n; **57**, 29, 188; **58**, 30, 317; **60**, 107n26, 114n51
Berger, John, **50**, 135
Berger, Karol, **43**, 12n
Berger, Ludwig, **13**, 128; **16**, 134; **23**, 122
Berger, Sarah, **37**, 164–5

INDEX

Berger, Thomas L., **29**, 180; **33**, 209; **34**, 196; **35**, 181, 189n; **36**, 194n; **39**, 75n; **42**, 208n, 212; **44**, 256; **45**, 198; **46**, 241n; **49**, 107n; **50**, 141n, 275; **53**, 331n, 332, 339–40; **54**, 14n, 23n, 346; **55**, 194n, 257n, 258, 389; **57**, 337; **59**, 20n4, 43–4
Bergeron, David M., **23**, 172; **24**, 163; **26**, 38n, 39n, 45n, 160; **27**, 166; **29**, 177; **30**, 199; **32**, 225–6; **33**, 188; **34**, 183; **37**, 198; **41**, 4; **43**, 45n, 53n, 240; **45**, 170; **46**, 76; **49**, 25n; **50**, 240–1; **54**, 41n; **55**, 4n; **60**, 268n3, 368, 369
Berggren, Paula S., **38**, 232; **46**, 6
Berggren, Tommy, **16**, 137
Berghaus, Gunter, **54**, 194n
Berghaus, Ruth, **48**, 175
Bergin, Thomas G., **9**, 152
Bergman, Eva, **53**, 327–8
Bergman, Ingemar, **5**, 114; **19**, 5; **24**, 13; **36**, 65–72, 165; **38**, 234, 237; **41**, 223; **42**, 150; **44**, 94; **48**, 15; **50**, 37, 248; **51**, 199; **54**, 124n; **56**, 3, 5, 6n
Bergmann, Frederick Lois, **43**, 105n; **48**, 51n; **51**, 23n; **54**, 49n; **57**, 59
Bergner, Elisabeth, **18**, 73; **40**, 4
Bergom-Larsson, Maria, **36**, 69n
Bergomensis, Jacobus, **15**, 97n
Bergson, Henri Louis, **8**, 1; **22**, 1, 9, 16, 36; **35**, 68; **36**, 27; **37**, 36; **40**, 94; **57**, 122; **58**, 42
Bergstrand, Allan, **10**, 121
Beria, Laurentia, **48**, 189
Berio, Luciano, **44**, 201
Berkeley, Busby, **52**, 90
Berkeley, David, **19**, 129; **22**, 186
Berkeley, David Shelley, **44**, 221; **46**, 125n
Berkeley, George, **24**, 97
Berkeley, Sir Lennox, **45**, 173
Berkeley, Sir William, **43**, 270n
Berkely, Busby, **43**, 211
Berkely, Thomas, **41**, 220
Berkes, Randall, **29**, 33n
Berkin, Sandra, **45**, 145
Berkley, Thomas, **3**, 26
Berkoff, Steven, **48**, 192; **50**, 226; **51**, 258; **52**, 255; **53**, 285–6; **56**, 289; **58**, 307; **60**, 321, 326
Berkovec, Jiři, **18**, 121
Berkowitz, Joel, **50**, 35n
Berkowitz, Steven, **47**, 245
Berlin, Sir Isaiah, **33**, 181; **56**, 203n
Berlin, Normand, **28**, 171n; **36**, 21n; **39**, 79n; **57**, 145
Berlioz, Harriet Smithson, **37**, 200–1
see also Smithson
Berlioz, Hector, **3**, 102; **9**, 108; **18**, 75, 77, 85; **19**, 151; **20**, 164; **21**, 80; **35**, 12; **37**, 200–1; **45**, 172–3; **49**, 4, 6, 12, 285; **56**, 295, 296; **57**, 115
Berman, Antoine, **50**, 128n
Berman, Ed, **36**, 26
Berman, R. S., **18**, 169; **20**, 155, 163; **22**, 155, 161, 165; **26**, 163; **27**, 24n, 159; **30**, 47n; **38**, 16, 49n, 141n; **40**, 75n; **43**, 44n
'Anarchy and Order in *Richard* III and *King John*', **20**, 51–60
Bermann, Sandra L., **43**, 228
Bermondsey Church, *see under* London
Bernadin, Mike, **60**, 328
Bernal, Martin, **52**, 207n
Bernard, Anthony, **36**, 82
Bernard, Eliza, **14**, 114
Bernard, G. W., **44**, 234
Bernard, John D., **33**, 192
Bernard, M. A., **18**, 168
Bernard, Richard, **3**, 52; **19**, 58; **43**, 64
Bernard, St, **20**, 26n
Bernardy, Michel, **15**, 147
Bernasconi, R., **46**, 82n
Bernau, Anke, **59**, 244n37
Bernbeimer, Richard, **52**, 204n
Berne, Joseph, **55**, 123
Berners, Lord, **17**, 238; **28**, 3
Bernhardt, Sarah, **2**, 116; **3**, 103, 113; **9**, 57, 63, 64, 67; **11**, 124; **20**, 121; **29**, 143; **41**, 225; **45**, 43–5; **48**, 1, 11; **51**, 300; **52**, 185n; **53**, 327
Bernhardt, W. W., **23**, 150; **24**, 166
Bernhays, Michael, **9**, 100n
Bernheimer, Richard, **13**, 159; **20**, 167; **28**, 117, 118
Bernhere, Thomas, **11**, 91–2
Bernini, **26**, 116n
Bernstein, Charles, **60**, 142
Bernstein, J. M., **55**, 75–7; **56**, 139
Bernstein, Leonard, **49**, 153, 240, 285
Bernstein, Melvin H. **59**, 141n14
Bernthal, Craig A., **41**, 208; **45**, 163–4
Berr, Georges, **9**, 66
Berret, Anthony J., **48**, 261
Mark Twain and Shakespeare: A Cultural Legacy, **48**, 261
Berrigan, Joseph R., **42**, 21n
Berrong, Richard M., **49**, 70n
Berry, Cicely, **41**, 184; **43**, 208; **51**, 276–7; **53**, 325; **55**, 183, 280; **56**, 173n, 247n, 343
Berry, Sir Edward, **31**, 168; **34**, 176, 184; **35**, 158; **38**, 4, 141n, 145n; **39**, 212; **41**, 202; **42**, 30; **43**, 9n, 45n, 48n, 49n, 52n, 67n; **46**, 10n, 208; **49**, 203n, 204n; **56**, 219n; **57**, 30; **60**, 114n49
Berry, Eric, **1**, 102; **15**, 139
Berry, Francis, **13**, 152; **20**, 49n, 158–9; **25**, 83–4; **29**, 172; **32**, 4, 9; **44**, 212
Berry, Herbert, **20**, 168; **21**, 154, 155; **23**, 128, 172; **26**, 170; **28**, 169; **33**, 161; **34**, 118n, 179; **36**, 178–9; **38**, 228; **40**, 214–15; **41**, 1, 5; **43**, 236; **44**, 146, 147n, 153; **47**, 16n; **53**, 197n, 326; **55**, 377; **56**, 335, 337; **60**, 41n18, 44n33, 45n41, 47n60
Berry, Lloyd E., **32**, 167n; **48**, 40n, 41n, 43n, 85n; **49**, 165n; **50**, 81n, 197n; **51**, 186n; **57**, 209
Berry, Mary, **46**, 240n
Berry, Philippa, **54**, 301; **55**, 8, 9; **58**, 312, 333
Berry, Ralph, **24**, 55n, 61n, 149; **25**, 180; **26**, 154, 162, 167, 174; **27**, 162; **28**, 157; **29**, 165, 176; **30**, 188; **31**, 4n, 54, 152, 166; **32**, 1, 9, 64n, 212; **34**, 62n, 178, 184; **35**, 2n, 12, 170–1, 175; **36**, 159–60, 169, 180–1; **37**, 6, 7, 13n, 39n; **38**, 236; **39**, 215; **40**, 204, 212; **41**, 167–8, 224; **42**, 49n; **43**, 227, 250; **44**, 212; **45**, 139; **46**, 29n, 184n; **47**, 236–7; **53**, 232n, 236n; **57**, 210; **58**, 50
'The Words of Mercury', **22**, 69–77
'"To Say One": an Essay on *Hamlet*', **28**, 107–15
Berry, William, **41**, 113n
Berryman, John, **1**, 131; **8**, 148
Bersani, Leo, **53**, 300
Bert, Edmund, **44**, 139n, 140n

Berteau, Marcel, **7**, 108
Berthoz, Alain, **60**, 144n11
Bertini, Gari, **10**, 119
Bertish, Suzanne, **53**, 252; **60**, 204
Bertram, Anthony, **55**, 128n, 135n, 136n, 137n
Bertram, Paul, **15**, 180; **20**, 175; **21**, 146; **36**, 108n, 188–9; **38**, 16; **40**, 224, 235; **46**, 254n; **52**, 312; **59**, 98n10, 157, 159, 160, 163n19
Bérubé, Michael, **60**, 151
Beruthrum, Dorothy, **59**, 242n23
Berwińska, Krystyna, **9**, 114–15; **11**, 121
Besant, Walter, **1**, 35n; **6**, 73n; **17**, 45n, 46n, 49n
Besch, Anthony, **5**, 120
Besekow, Sam, **2**, 128
Besnault, Marie-Hélène, **56**, 307
Besoiu, Ion, **45**, 146
Bess, Henrietta, **44**, 203
Bessenyei, Ferenc, **12**, 113; **13**, 129; **18**, 125
Besser, Gretchen, **55**, 145n
Besson, Benno, **40**, 2; **48**, 174, 182, 183
Besson, Claude, **15**, 133
Best, Eve, **56**, 292
Best, George, **17**, 31, 32; **52**, 208n
Best, John, **30**, 161, 163, 164n, 165, 166
Best, Jonathan, **55**, 313
Best, Michael R., **23**, 169
Best, Susanna, **46**, 202
Best, Revd Thomas, **54**, 80
Beste, George, **32**, 88n, 89n
Besterman, Kirsty, **56**, 284, 285
Besterman, Theodore, **37**, 146n; **60**, 215n3
Beston, David, **51**, 261
Beston, John P., **55**, 172n
Bestrafte Brudermord, Der, **1**, 114; **9**, 1, 5, 6
Betera, Caroline, **43**, 217; **44**, 192
Bethell, S. L., **2**, 104, 139; **4**, 10, 11–12, 16, 23; **5**, 85, 143–4; **7**, 5, 7, 9, 130, 133; **8**, 21, 34, 117n; **10**, 10, 106; **11**, 31–2, 34–8, 39–40, 41n; **12**, 57; **13**, 148; **17**, 41n; **18**, 57n; **19**, 11, 33n, 129; **20**, 73n; **21**, 62; **23**, 61n, 67n; **24**, 42; **25**, 10n; **29**, 88n; **30**, 112; **31**, 9n, 62n; **32**, 153, 154n; **33**, 5, 6, 126n; **36**, 101n; **38**, 8, 11, 56; **42**, 104n
  'The Diabolic Images in *Othello*', **5**, 62–80
Bethmann-Hollweg, Theobald von, **44**, 108
Betken, William T., **37**, 162n
Bett, John, **43**, 209; **44**, 196
Bettelheim, Bruno, **44**, 45; **50**, 243
Bettenson, Henry, **53**, 25n
Betteridge, Thomas, **54**, 9n; **59**, 352–3, 368
Betterton, Thomas, **3**, 1; **7**, 28; **8**, 152; **9**, 54; **10**, 13, 76n, 150; **13**, 113; **17**, 197; **18**, 35, 36; **30**, 200; **32**, 240; **43**, 81, 89; **45**, 35; **51**, 108; **52**, 149; **53**, 327; **55**, 308, 376; **57**, 56, 60, 82, 84; **58**, 40, 243
  adaptation of *1 Henry IV*, **9**, 85n
Betterton, William, **58**, 243
Bettinger, Peter, **37**, 160n
Betts, Hannah, **52**, 114
Betts, John H., **32**, 230; **38**, 45
Betty and Boaby's Macbeth, **43**, 208
Betty, Henry, **9**, 56
Betty, Master William Henry West, **9**, 55
Beutler, Ernst, **9**, 97–8, 100n
Bevan, Elinor, **21**, 143
Bevan, Elway, **3**, 56
Bevan, Gillian, **44**, 162, 192
Bevell, Sir Robert, **38**, 33
Beveney, Nicholas, **52**, 232
Beveridge, Amanda, **59**, 342
Beveridge, Henry, **33**, 89n
Beverley Sisters, The, **9**, 125
Beverley, William, **10**, 75; **41**, 24
Beverly, Peter, *History of Adriodanto and Ieneura*, **8**, 4
Beves, Donald, **5**, 120
Bevington, David M., **17**, 192; **18**, 181, 182; **20**, 23, 26n; **21**, 131; **23**, 168; **26**, 100n; **27**, 72, 165; **29**, 90; **30**, 39, 47n, 198; **32**, 174n; **33**, 2n, 28n, 181n, 208n; **34**, 94n, 111n; **36**, 31n, 122n; **38**, 11, 37n, 53, 131n, 155n; **39**, 56n, 247; **40**, 77n, 198; **41**, 8n, 19n, 21n, 83n, 85n, 231n, 237, 242–3; **42**, 2n, 38n; **43**, 5n, 9n, 265n, 266; **44**, 2n; **45** 193n, 194, 196–7; **46**, 101n, 112n, 227; **47**, 47n; **48**, 71n, 75n, 281, 282; **49**, 24, 204n; **50**, 3, 51n, 254; **51**, 181n, 305–6, 314, 335; **52**, 305–7, 320; **53**, 86n, 341n, 343; **54**, 58, 67, 100n, 122n, 196n, 197n, 307, 310, 331–2, 350; **55**, 2n, 3, 40n, 65n, 182n, 240n, 241n, 242n, 243n, 389; **56**, 352, 353; **57**, 238; **58**, 132, 201, 206, 355, 356; **59**, 3, 89n34, 170, 376, 376n3, 378, 381, 383; **60**, 191n22, 192, 194n30, 253, 350, 352
Bew, William, **54**, 58n
Beydts, Louis, **7**, 111
Beyer, Edvard, **11**, 141; **12**, 139 and n.
Beyer, Manfred, **42**, 214
Beyer, Simon, **60**, 327
Beylie, Claude, **39**, 3
Bèze, T. de, **32**, 174n; **54**, 129, 139; **59**, 113n22
Bezzola Lambert, Ladina, **58**, 333
Bhabha, Homi, **54**, 305; **59**, 364, 369; **60**, 332
Bharracharji, Amal, **21**, 138
Bhasker, **44**, 192
Bhatt, Yogesh, **48**, 237
Bhattarcharjee, Jyotsna, **21**, 150
Bhattarcharjee, Paul, **53**, 267; **58**, 278; **59**, 345
Bhavnani, Dakshu, **16**, 135
Bhuchar, Sudha, **43**, 214
Bianchi, Francesco Saverio Maria, **56**, 188
Bianchi, Rosemary, **53**, 277
Bianchini, Pietro, **9**, 65
Biberti, Léopold, **3**, 105, 106
Bible, The, **2**, 67, 68; **3**, 18, 19; **4**, 9, 24, 28; **5**, 54, 63, 73, 87; **6**, 75, 76; **7**, 6; **9**, 81; **17**, 38, 108, 111; **18**, 49; **19**, 3, 59, 62, 66; **59**, 230, 235, 252n93; **60**, 268–9
  Authorized Version, **7**, 37, 38
  Baruch **59**, 239n3
  Ecclesiasticus **59**, 239n3
  Editions in the Huntington Library, **6**, 56, 59
  Exodus, **8**, 17; **59**, 237
  Ezekiel **59**, 235, 241
  Genesis **59**, 239, 241n13; **60**, 117n66
  Job, **4**, 31; **8**, 24, 25; **11**, 60; **59**, 238
  John **59**, 237
  Matthew **59**, 358
  Psalm xix, **4**, 55n
  Psalms **59**, 251n88
  Revelation, **10**, 5, 140, 145–6; **59**, 241, 241n18

Bible, The (*cont.*)
see also under Shakespeare, William, religion
Song of Songs **59**, 251n88
Wisdom **59**, 239n3
see also Paul, St **59**, 239n3
Bibliographical Society, *see* London Bibliographical Society
Bicat, Nick, **42**, 152
Bichon, Guillaume, **15**, 105
Bickersteth, G. L., **33**, 6–7
'Golden World of *King Lear*', reviewed, **1**, 119
Bickham, George, **47**, 27n
Bidaux, Jerome, **59**, 343
Biddle, Hester, **49**, 303
Biddles, Adelaide Ellen, **41**, 24
Bieito, Calixto, **57**, 286; **58**, 262, 300, 302
Bielmann, J., **29**, 29n
Biese, Y. M., **23**, 13n
Bietenholz, Peter G., **54**, 63n
Bieto, Calixto, **60**, 287
Big Brother, **55**, 75n
Big Chill, The, **55**, 296
Bigges, Walter, **17**, 32n
Biggins, Dennis, **20**, 150; **33**, 136n
Biggs, Murray, **28**, 84n; **45**, 61n, 190n; **46**, 228
'A Neurotic Portia', **25**, 153–9
Bigsby, C. W. E., **36**, 21n, 23n
Biko, Steve, **55**, 275, 279
Biller, J., **23**, 171n
Billigheimer, Rachel V., **44**, 221
Billings, W., **26**, 157
Billington, Kevin, **48**, 265
Billington, Michael, **30**, 174n; **38**, 209; **40**, 178; **43**, 189; **45**, 121; **46**, 177; **47**, 194, 201; **48**, 1, 219; **49**, 11, 232n, 242, 261; **50**, 69n; **52**, 317; **57**, 331; **58**, 135; **60**, 203
Billington, Sandra, **32**, 233; **45**, 178–9, 185–6; **60**, 104n10, 105n14
Bilson, Thomas, Bishop, **2**, 70; **17**, 106, 112–13; **57**, 238
Bilton, Peter, **23**, 158; **29**, 159; **40**, 205; **49**, 328; **50**, 169n
Binder, Anton, **55**, 333
Binder, R., **10**, 8
Bindoff, S. T., **17**, 127
Bing, Rudolph, **50**, 29
Bing, Suzanne, **2**, 121; **7**, 108, 110; **8**, 118; **10**, 118; **12**, 112; **14**, 119
Bingham, Caroline, **57**, 73
Bingham, Madeleine, **34**, 115n; **35**, 9–10
Bingo, **43**, 222
Binnie, Jean, **47**, 214; **51**, 262
Binnie, Patricia, **55**, 30n
Binns, J. W., **32**, 69, 70n; **37**, 218; **42**, 54n; **55**, 219n
Binns, Simon, **41**, 184
Binstock, Lynn, **56**, 292
Binyon, Laurence, **55**, 79, 80
Bion, **15**, 20, 29, 81, 85
Birch, Christopher, **42**, 155
Birch, George, **58**, 232
Birch, Peter, **42**, 151
Birch, T., *and* Oldys, W., **27**, 56
Birch, Thomas, **14**, 102; **47**, 18n; **54**, 136n; **57**, 201
Bircher, Martin, **23**, 154; **28**, 172
Bird, J., **54**, 124n
Bird, Nikki Amuka, **59**, 345
Bird, Theophilus, **42**, 107n; **58**, 236–7, 240
Bird, William, **3**, 150; **4**, 71; **33**, 158; **40**, 219
Birdwhistel, Ray, **40**, 38
Birje-Patil, J., **25**, 176; **32**, 130n
Birkett, Jack, **45**, 63n, 73
Birkett, Michael, **39**, 79, 81
Birkin, Jane, **60**, 321
Birkinshaw, Philip, **13**, 131
Birkoff, Steven, **24**, 13n
Birley, Robert, **6**, 120
Birmingham Public Library, *see under* Libraries
Birmingham Reference Library, *see under* Libraries
Birmingham Shakespeare Memorial Library, *see under* Libraries
Biron, Marshal, **38**, 49n, 52
Birrell, Augustine, **6**, 13
Birringer, Johannes H., **38**, 229; **40**, 207
Birth of Hercules, **3**, 52
Birth of Merlin, The, **44**, 203; **48**, 277
Birtwistle, Harrison, **39**, 193; **42**, 145; **43**, 206, 215
Bischoff, Ferdinand, **36**, 142
Bishop, Henry Rowley, **18**, 98, 99, 100; **20**, 107; **45**, 172
Bishop, T. G., **50**, 245; **54**, 29
Bishop, Tom, **55**, 240; **58**, 321
Bishop, W. W., **1**, 69
Biswanger, Raymond S., Jr., **10**, 144n.
Biswas, D. C., **25**, 188; **34**, 163
Bitot, Michel, **53**, 25n
Bitskey, T., **14**, 120
Bitterli, Dieter, **57**, 221
Bixby, Jerome, **53**, 170n
Bizet, Alexandre César Léopold (Georges), **45**, 173; **53**, 287
Bizzarri, Carla, **5**, 113
Bjelland, Karen, **50**, 277
Bjerke, Adolf, **10**, 120
Bjerke, André, **13**, 130; **14**, 122
Bjiork, Lennart A., **49**, 134n
Björkman, Stig, **36**, 68n
Björnson, Maria, **28**, 146; **36**, 154; **46**, 196
Björnstrand, Gunnar, **11**, 122
Blacher, Boris, **8**, 119; **18**, 87
Black Book, The, **54**, 13
Black Star, **42**, 162
Black, Don, **57**, 296
Black, Eugene R., **18**, 133
Black, J., **28**, 159, 162; **29**, 164
Black, J. B., **35**, 65–6; **48**, 72n
'The Unfolding of *Measure for Measure*', **26**, 119–28
Black, James, **31**, 95; **33**, 190; **35**, 166; **38**, 13, 14, 161n; **48**, 86n; **49**, 85; **53**, 43; **55**, 96n, 130n
Black, Jennifer, **54**, 287
Black, Jeremy, **51**, 55n
Black, John, **37**, 152n; **42**, 113n
Black, Lucy, **56**, 292
Black, M. H., **50**, 142n
Black, Matthew Wilson, **2**, 140; **3**, 18, 26; **6**, 11, 171; **11**, 152, 153; **18**, 175; **28**, 2n; **32**, 237; **50**, 51n, 52n, 53n; **55**, 259–60, 262; **59**, 124n2; **60**, 270n6, 275n27
New Variorum edition of *Richard II* reviewed, **10**, 151
Problems in the Editing of Shakespeare, **3**, 143

Black, Pauline, **44**, 191
Black, Scott, **57**, 186
Black, Stewart, **54**, 289
Black, W. H., **4**, 88
Blackall, E. A., **18**, 174
Blackborne, William, **45**, 107, 108
Blackburn, Ruth, **54**, 57n
Blackburn, Thomas, **39**, 169
Blackfriars, *see under* London
Blackfriars Theatre, *see under* Theatres, Elizabethan
Blackman, Maurice, **58**, 306
Blackmur, R. P., **30**, 137; **31**, 127n, 128, 135–7
Blackstone, Sir William, **60**, 93
Blackwood, Robert, **33**, 163, 164n
Blackwood, Tilly, **49**, 255
Blagden, Cyprian, **17**, 68n
Blagrave, William, **3**, 51; **58**, 235
Blague, Thomas, **2**, 70
Blahník, V. K., **9**, 110n
Blaho, J., **7**, 109
Blaine, David, **59**, 211
Blair, Hugh, **18**, 16; **58**, 78, 82
Blair, Isla, **42**, 152; **51**, 259
Blair, Lionel, **42**, 149
Blair, Paul, **59**, 340
Blair, Tony, **51**, 238; **54**, 246, 252; **55**, 296, 393; **56**, 93, 282
Blair, Wilfrid, **58**, 140
Blaisdell, Charmarie J., **54**, 92n
Blake, Anne, **53**, 296; **57**, 312; **58**, 314, 331
Blake, Jo, **59**, 343
Blake, N. F., **43**, 18n; **45**, 203; **46**, 105n; **53**, 154n; **56**, 173n; **59**, 193
Blake, Norman, **56**, 168, 173n, 310; **58**, 319, 331
Blake, Paul, **43**, 208
Blake, Simon, **49**, 279
Blake, William, **7**, 30; **11**, 140; **12**, 125; **13**, 76; **16**, 171; **19**, 79, 80; **23**, 93n; **24**, 107; **36**, 78; **40**, 42, 200–1; **41**, 224; **43**, 121; **44**, 213; **49**, 121–2; **51**, 11; **55**, 149; **59**, 131; **60**, 354
Blakeley, Claudie, **53**, 267; **58**, 270, 271, 298
Blakely, Colin, **26**, 149–50; **34**, 156; **39**, 89n, 90
Blakemore, Michael, **56**, 297
Blakeney, Annabel, **46**, 193
Blakeway, M. G., **24**, 157
Blakiston, Caroline, **48**, 216, 221
Blamey, Kathleen, **44**, 68n
Blamires, Alcouin, **60**, 81n39
Blanc, Anne Marie, **5**, 114
Blanc, Pauline, **56**, 306, 307
Blanchot, Maurice, **55**, 67, 71n, 76, 77
Blanco-White, José Maria, *see* Crespo, José María Blanco
Bland, D. G., **15**, 124n
Bland, D. S., **7**, 5, 137; **19**, 100n; **20**, 164; **23**, 164n; **24**, 156; **27**, 118n; **32**, 235; **57**, 202
'Shakespeare and the "Ordinary" Word', **4**, 49–55
'Shakespeare at Street Level', **19**, 95–100
Bland, Marjorie, **31**, 143; **32**, 205
Blane, Sue, **43**, 207; **44**, 198; **46**, 184; **47**, 209
Blaney, John, **7**, 58, 63
Blaney, Peter, **56**, 34n
Blank, Paula, **52**, 280
Blanpied, John W., **29**, 160; **38**, 7; **39**, 211–12
Blatch, Helen, **44**, 168
Blatcher, M., **17**, 84n
Blatchley, John, **1**, 109; **8**, 123; **13**, 127
Blatherwick, Simon, **47**, 84n, 179n; **52**, 12n, 13n; **60**, 44n36
Blau, Herbert, **55**, 153–4, 281; **60**, 72n1, 78n28; **57**, 82
Blaydes, Sophia B., **40**, 222
Blayney, G. H., **25**, 149n; **29**, 35n; **32**, 138n
Blayney, Peter W. M., **26**, 183; **27**, 185; **30**, 206, 207; **31**, 193–4; **33**, 28n, 34n; **35**, 179n; **37**, 210–11; **38**, 101–2, 107, 155n; **40**, 150, 152; **44**, 153n; **45**, 195; **46**, 252, 253; **47**, 260; **48**, 269, 280–1; **49**, 220, 333–5; **50**, 288; **51**, 313; **52**, 69, 87, 304; **53**, 337; **54**, 92n, 356; **55**, 2n, 28, 29n, 55n, 375, 386, 393; **58**, 350; **59**, 1, 7n30, 14, 25n22, 83–4, 89, 90, 105n19, 114n24, 162
Bleach, Julian, **47**, 213; **60**, 315, 316
Blecua, J., **20**, 98, 105n
Bleeck, Peter van, **13**, 74
Bleibtreu, K., **43**, 112n
Blench, J. W., **23**, 84
Blenerhasset, Thomas, **6**, 57
Blenkinsop, Sarah, **54**, 292
Blessed, Brian, **38**, 207, 209; **44**, 194; **48**, 233; **52**, 259; **58**, 191
Blessed Jew of Morocco, The, **17**, 50
Blethyn, Brenda, **39**, 86n, 87
Blewett, David W., **38**, 227
Blin, Roger, **55**, 157
Blincoe, Noel R., **43**, 258n; **50**, 289; **51**, 310
Blinn, Hansjürgen, **37**, 156n
Blish, James, **53**, 170n
Bliss, Carey S., **6**, 63n
Bliss, L., **29**, 165
Bliss, Lee, **38**, 16, 135n, 140n; **40**, 219; **43**, 45, 47n, 49, 50n, 53n, 67n; **45**, 184; **52**, 167n, 316; **54**, 354–5; **56**, 171n; **59**, 24n20
Bliss, Leslie E., **6**, 55, 63n
Bliss, William, **5**, 92n, 139n; **7**, 96
The Real Shakespeare reviewed, **1**, 123–4; **3**, 9
Blissett, William, **14**, 145; **19**, 11; **22**, 163; **23**, 170; **26**, 163; **29**, 7; **34**, 138n
Blistein, Elmer M., **24**, 143n; **32**, 5
Blits, Jan H., **51**, 283; **55**, 223n; **57**, 29, 32
Blitzstein, Marc, **5**, 116
Blixen, Karen, **43**, 110n; **53**, 111
Bloch, Eduard, **13**, 80n; **18**, 75, 86–7; **19**, 151
Bloch, Ernst, **7**, 113; **45**, 173
Bloch, Howard R., **46**, 91n, 98, 122n
Block, E. A., **14**, 143
Block, Giles, **53**, 244, 246; **54**, 262; **55**, 323; **56**, 99; **60**, 328; **59**, 320
Block, Haskell, M., **15**, 116, 123n
Block, K. S., **21**, 65n
Blocksidge, Martin, **58**, 331, 333
Blodek, **9**, 108
Blok, Alexander, **16**, 15; **21**, 129
Blom, Benjamin, **23**, 173
Bloom, Adi, **60**, 159
Bloom, Allan D., **15**, 165; **36**, 164; **55**, 355–6
Bloom, Burckhardt, **15**, 165
Bloom, Claire, **8**, 132, 135–6; **34**, 176; **39**, 105, 108; **45**, 61
Bloom, Edward A., **19**, 119n; **33**, 53n; **41**, 145n; **51**, 5n; **55**, 58n

INDEX

Bloom, Harold, **37**, 164; **40**, 70, 190; **41**, 212; **42**, 65–76; **43**, 109; **45**, 186; **46**, 62n, 105n; **51**, 2, 159n, 164n, 271; **52**, 93n, 102n; **53**, 18n, 91, 116, 287, 294, 312; **54**, 10, 11, 12n, 88n; **55**, 10; **56**, 204, 205n, 349; **57**, 23, 238, 241, 331; **59**, 352, 355; **60**, 159, 168n1.8
Bloom, Lilian D., **51**, 5n
Blostein, David A., **54**, 15n
Blount, Charles, Eighth Baron Mountjoy, **6**, 84; **9**, 24, 25, 26, 33n, 155; **11**, 138; **54**, 171
Blount, Sir Christopher, **21**, 100; **38**, 22n
Blount, Edward, **1**, 57; **3**, 140, 151; **5**, 26; **11**, 154; **13**, 165; **24**, 170; **26**, 181; **44**, 113, 114; **53**, 78n; **60**, 263, 266, 358
Blount, Thomas, **52**, 187
Blow, John, **23**, 164; **52**, 215
Blow, Suzanne, **27**, 176
Blower, Ian, **42**, 155
Blower, Patrick, **56**, 94
Bloxam, John Francis, **53**, 137–40, 143, 150n
Bluestone, Max, **24**, 161; **29**, 169–70; **31**, 54n
Blum, Abbe, **45**, 160
Blum-Kulka, Shoshana, **59**, 193n4
Blume, Friedrich, **23**, 164
Blumenau, Colin, **53**, 281
Blumenthal, John, **39**, 6
Blumenthal, Pinchas, **20**, 153
Blunden, Edmund, **4**, 9
Blundeville, Thomas, **32**, 165n; **42**, 55n; **53**, 22n, 23n
Blunt, Anthony, **31**, 18n
Blunt, Edward, **57**, 222, 223
Blunt, Emily, **57**, 296
Blunt, Sir Walter, **19**, 152
Bluthal, John, **42**, 145, 152
Bly, Mary, **53**, 326; **55**, 378–9; **60**, 277
Blythe, David, **32**, 235, 244; **34**, 186; **36**, 194
Blythe, Domini, **31**, 144; **39**, 186, 188
Blythe, Joan Heiges, **32**, 235
Blythe, Peter, **45**, 147; **57**, 280, 283
Blythe, Robert, **57**, 282
Boaden, James, **9**, 100n; **10**, 73; **11**, 124; **51**, 58–9, 115; **57**, 61, 87, 88
Boadicea, **42**, 26
Boaistuau, Pierre, **20**, 96, 98, 99, 100, 101, 103; **49**, 1, 45–7; **50**, 190n, 194n
Boal, Augusto, **53**, 305; **55**, 272; **57**, 327
Boar's Head playhouse, **52**, 11
Boar's Head Theatre, *see under* Theatre, Elizabethan
Boas, Conrad Van Emde, **6**, 160 *and* n.; **10**, 143
Shakespeare's Sonnetten en hun Verband met de Travesti-Double Spelen reviewed, **10**, 141
Boas, Frederick Samuel, **4**, 144; **5**, 132, 138, 149; **6**, 162; **9**, 33n; **10**, 4, 6; **14**, 3, 7, 8, 9, 12, 89n; **17**, 220n; **18**, 39; **24**, 160; **25**, 2; **26**, 6; **35**, 130n; **37**, 69n; **41**, 64, 68; **42**, 33, 83n; **43**, 155, 158n; **56**, 29n, 30n
Boas, Guy, **9**, 147; **10**, 123; **12**, 119; **17**, 41n; **29**, 80; **35**, 161n
Boase, T. S. R., **3**, 141n; **10**, 76n; **37**, 41, 42n
Boccaccio, Giovanni, **1**, 68; **4**, 93; **10**, 17; **11**, 45, 46, 144; **15**, 95; **18**, 85; **22**, 85, 91; **25**, 3, 45, 46, 48, 51, 52, 53, 56, 59, 61; **29**, 169; **31**, 25n; **32**, 137; **33**, 199; **37**, 99; **40**, 10; **50**, 23; **51**, 309; **59**, 265
Decameron, **3**, 15–16, 55; **8**, 10; **9**, 142
Filocopo, **1**, 69
Bocchi, Giulio, **17**, 182, 184
Boccki, Achille, **49**, 73n
Bochner, Lloyd, **9**, 111; **10**, 116
Böcking, E., **48**, 5n
Bodart, Anne and Roger, French adaptation of *Hamlet*, **12**, 110
Bode, Emile, **33**, 16n
Boden, Nicholas, **18**, 17
Bodenham, John, **60**, 260n28
Belvedére, **3**, 54
Bodenheimer, Rosemarie, **53**, 116
Bodichon, Barbara, **49**, 133
Bodin, Jean, **28**, 119, 121; **41**, 197; **43**, 238; **44**, 62n, 213; **52**, 205
Six Books of the Commonweale (1606), **12**, 144; **16**, 38; **17**, 65, 128, 141, 215 and n.
Bodinetz, Gemma, **54**, 284; **57**, 291
Bodio, Stephen, **44**, 131n, 134n, 141n
Bodkin, Maud, **5**, 91n; **6**, 152; **15**, 119; **21**, 9, 62
Bodleian Library, The, *see under* Libraries
Bodley, Donald, **15**, 144
Bodley, Sir Thomas, **4**, 78, 92, 94; **11**, 107; **26**, 168; **35**, 130n
Bodmeier, C., **47**, 107
Bodmer, Johann Jakob, **59**, 131
Bodmer, Martin, **26**, 177; **52**, 304
collection of Shakespeariana, **7**, 115
see also under Libraries
Bodtke, Richard, **27**, 177
Boe, John, **40**, 217; **54**, 44n
Boece, Hector, **4**, 35, 39, 40; **28**, 120; **50**, 14n; **57**, 70, 71, 72, 73, 77, 80, 126
Boecker, Alexander, **7**, 96; **10**, 5
Boehme, Jakob, **59**, 228, 236
Boehrer, Bruce Thomas, **48**, 246; **51**, 69n, 167n, 292; **54**, 315; **57**, 304
Boesky, Amy, **51**, 297
Boethius, Anicius, **15**, 174; **17**, 64; **20**, 26n; **24**, 151; **32**, 166; **33**, 202; **49**, 73, 172, 176
Boettcher, Henry, **6**, 124
Boettinger, C. A., **37**, 46
Bogard, John, **29**, 28
Bogard, Travis, **9**, 137; **14**, 11; **38**, 8
Bogatyrev, Petr, **60**, 228
Bogdan, Robert, **50**, 199n
Bogdanov, Michael, **32**, 201–2; **39**, 13n; **40**, 178; **41**, 159, 160–1, 178, 185, 189; **42**, 129, 157, 161; **43**, 171, 173, 175, 181, 183–4, 224, 250; **44**, 213; **45**, 130, 132, 134, 146, 156; **46**, 81, 85, 202; **47**, 111, 212, 218–19; **48**, 21, 234; **49**, 2–4, 6, 7, 11, 12, 14, 96, 151, 257; **51**, 262, 299; **52**, 98, 232–3, 250–3, 260, 265; **53**, 274, 278, 304; **54**, 274, 290, 293; **56**, 248n; **57**, 46, 279, 294; **58**, 186, 193, 302, 307; **59**, 186–7, 338, 345; **60**, 78, 196–13, 292, 321
Bogdanović, M., **4**, 117, 118, 119, 121
Bogey, John, **25**, 149
Bögholm, Niels, **3**, 109
Boguet, Henry, **28**, 121
Böhm, Otto Hans, **18**, 119
Böhm, Rainer, **42**, 159
Böhm, Rudolf, **22**, 166; **23**, 115
Bohr, Nils, **22**, 147
Bohringer, Romane, **45**, 155
Boiardo, M. M., **29**, 104
Boileau, Nicolas, **5**, 98; **20**, 7

Boillet, D., **52**, 122n
Boillot, Joseph, **47**, 24
Boissise, Count de, **11**, 94
Boitani, Piero, **44**, 217
Boitard, François, **37**, 42; **49**, 112–13; **59**, 131
Boito, Arrigo, **18**, 83–4, 85; **21**, 87–94; **57**, 116
Bok, G., **44**, 6n
Bok, Sissela, **50**, 71n
Boklund, Gunnar, **14**, 11, 50, 55n; **18**, 128; **20**, 148; **23**, 145; **24**, 164; **26**, 8
Bolam, James, **44**, 196; **51**, 264
Bolchi, Sandro, **14**, 121
Bolen, Frances, **28**, 48n
Boleyn, Anne, **26**, 41; **36**, 176; **38**, 25; **43**, 50, 54, 57; **52**, 169–71, 175, 177, 179, 181–2; **54**, 242–3
Boleyn, Mary, **52**, 170, 177
Bolgar, R. R., **31**, 4, 7
Bolger, Stephen G., **25**, 174
Boling, Ronald J., **55**, 242n
Bolitho, Hectar, **8**, 149
Bollas, Christopher, **60**, 146n18
Bolle, Roberto, **53**, 282
Bolt, Ranjit, **60**, 317
Bolte, J., **22**, 119; **32**, 192n, 193n, 194n, 196n, 197n; **33**, 166n; **36**, 137n, 141n, 143n
Bolton, Edmund, **17**, 68–70; **20**, 28; **58**, 21
Bolton, J. L., **38**, 205
Bolton, Joseph S. G., **10**, 2, 157; **15**, 180; **27**, 191; **38**, 248n
Bolton, W. F., **27**, 191; **30**, 204; **46**, 215; **56**, 217n
Boltum, Thomas, **22**, 121–3
Boltz, Ingeborg, **41**, 245n
Bonaparte, Marie, **7**, 97
Bonaventure, S. M., **19**, 139
Bonaventure, Saint, **54**, 128n
Bonazza, Blaze O., **22**, 152; **42**, 1n
Bond, Chris, **42**, 153
Bond, E. A. (ed.), **17**, 22n
Bond, Edward, **25**, 182; **26**, 176; **28**, 146; **29**, 175; **36**, 2, 28, 152, 158; **38**, 129; **40**, 6, 210; **41**, 199; **43**, 222; **54**, 78; **55**, 131, 159–69; **56**, 246; **58**, 50, 140, 145, 146, 158, 260; **60**, 323
Bond, James, **40**, 169
Bond, Jilly, **41**, 186; **42**, 152
Bond, Jonathan, **52**, 224; **59**, 207
Bond, R. Warwick, **1**, 11; **8**, 3; **11**, 77n; **14**, 7, 18; **23**, 180; **27**, 111n, 112, 113, 119; **28**, 39; **29**, 104n, 108, 111n; **30**, 125, 127; **34**, 30n; **42**, in, 2n, 106n; **43**, 5n; **44**, 50n; **46**, 57n; **55**, 25n, 207n; **56**, 45n; **59**, 272; **60**, 77n25, 99n39
Bond, Richard, **23**, 44
Bond, Ronald B., **33**, 189
Bond, Samantha, **41**, 189; **42**, 132; **43**, 212; **46**, 7, 174, 178, 179; **47**, 209, 219; **55**, 313; **56**, 257, 280; **57**, 293; **58**, 301
Bondarenko, F., **13**, 133
Bonde, Thomas, **58**, 224
Bondy, Luc, **54**, 288
Bone, Jane, **51**, 260
Bone, Kate, **47**, 212; **51**, 266
Bonenfant, Paul, **44**, 56n, 57n
Bones, Ken, **40**, 173; **45**, 157, 47, 215; **53**, 263, 265; **60**, 298
Bonfield, Lloyd, **55**, 37n, 38n, 39n
Bonham-Carter, Helena, **46**, 193; **51**, 268; **54**, 267
Bonheim, Helmut, **37**, 191; **53**, 3n
Bonheim, Jean, **22**, 155; **55**, 20n
and Bonheim, Helmut, **26**, 156; **27**, 24n
Bonian, Richard, **11**, 154; **21**, 161; **25**, 7; **26**, 33n; **60**, 369
A Booke of Christian Prayers (*Queen Elizabeth's Prayer-Book*), **60**, 226n18
A brefe and a playne declaratyon of the dewty of maried folks, **60**, 89, 89n14, 90n23, 91
Bonifacio, Giovanni, **48**, 31
Bonito, Eduardo, **52**, 265
Bonjour, Adrien, **5**, 114; **7**, 136; **9**, 138; **13**, 131, 132, 147; **18**, 129, 167 173; **19**, 125, 129, 133, 135; **20**, 154; **23**, 156; **38**, 12
'From Shakespeare's Venus to Cleopatra's Cupids', **15**, 73–80
Bonnamy, Yvonne, **16**, 148
Bonnar, Mark, **57**, 268; **59**, 343
Bonnard, Georges A., **2**, 128; **4**, 141n; **6**, 164; **7**, 107, 133; **8**, 121; **9**, 116, 143; **10**, 121; **11**, 122, 137; **12**, 117; **13**, 164; **15**, 27, 28; **27**, 112, 113, 119; **28**, 46n; **29**, 111n
'Shakespeare in the Bibliotheca Bodmeriana', **9**, 81–5
'Suggestions Towards an Edition of Shakespeare for Continental Readers', **5**, 10–15
Bonnefoy, Claude, **57**, 118, 120
Bonnefoy, Yves, **15**, 132; **16**, 75; **18**, 122; **40**, 207; **50**, 129, 132; **58**, 314, 331; **59**, 363–4, 368
Bonner sisters, **29**, 35, 36
Bonner, Bathsuba, **29**, 34, 37
Bonner, Duncan, **47**, 212
Bonner, Edmund, Bishop, **15**, 64; **17**, 89
Bonner, John, **25**, 142, 146, 147; **29**, 34, 35, 36, 37–9
Bonner, Thomas, **29**, 35, 36, 37–8
Bonnet, Charles, **9**, 91
Bonneville, Richard, **43**, 214; **45**, 127; **46**, 202; **47**, 182
Bonnie and Clyde, **52**, 90
Bono, Barbara J., **49**, 289
Bontoux, G., **15**, 7; **17**, 220n
Book of Common Prayer, **7**, 38; **59**, 252n91
Booke of Sir Thomas More
date, **2**, 52–4
description of MS., **2**, 45–7
deterioration of MS., **2**, 44
editions, **2**, 44
handwritings, **2**, 45–7, 52–8
history of owners, **2**, 44
nature of censorship, **2**, 51–4
previous discussions, **2**, 44–5
spellings, **2**, 52–8
style and thought, **2**, 58–60
theatrical companies concerned, **2**, 51–4
transcript of 'Shakespearian' portion, **2**, 62–5
see also 'Sir Thomas More'
Boon, Richard, **58**, 358
Boone, Joseph, **46**, 4
Boone, Messrs, **3**, 45
Boorde, Dr Andrew, **17**, 154
Boorman, Neil, **44**, 203
Boorman, S. C., **42**, 174
Boose, Lynda E., **37**, 125n; **44**, 226; **45**, 169, 178; **46**, 3, 130; **48**, 241; **49**, 207n, 210n; **50**, 254; **51**, 172n; **52**, 197n 202n, 203, 289, 290; **53**, 15n, 16; **55**, 273n; **56**, 34n, 335; **57**, 194; **58**, 334, 342; **60**, 84n2, 85, 138n28

Booth, Abraham, **47**, 42; **52**, 15; **53**, 196, 201
Booth, Anita, **59**, 314
Booth, Barton, **32**, 42; **58**, 40
Booth, Conny, **56**, 118
Booth, Edmund, **22**, 133
Booth, Edwin, **1**, 61; **6**, 163; **8**, 152; **9**, 57; **11**, 124; **24**, 100; **25**, 192; **27**, 34n; **30**, 199; **35**, 31–2; **40**, 38; **41**, 129; **42**, 199; **45**, 32, 34n; **49**, 126; **52**, 292; **53**, 327; **56**, 100, 111; **57**, 127, 253, 254; **58**, 42, 43; **59**, 374; **60**, 116n60
Booth, Junius Brutus, **16**, 104; **18**, 104, 106–7; **24**, 100; **47**, 62, 66
Booth, Lionel, **23**, 1n
Booth, Matthew, **56**, 238
Booth, Michael R., **31**, 187; **35**, 1n, 6, 8, 10n; **37**, 199; **38**, 188n; **41**, 224; **47**, 3n; **52**, 24n, 104–5
Booth, Roy, **54**, 315
Booth, Sarah, **49**, 123
Booth, Stephen, **23**, 157–8; **24**, 144, 161; **31**, 53n, 128, 168; **32**, 214–15; **34**, 39; **38**, 156n, 161n, 164n, 165n, 235; **39**, 136, 208–9, 212; **41**, 242; **42**, 67n; **43**, 20; **45**, 79n; **46**, 36n, 44n, 46n, 47n, 129n; **48**, 271; **49**, 141n; **50**, 58n; **52**, 281, 304–5; **53**, 295, 311; **54**, 28n; **55**, 10–11, 69n, 220, 233n; **57**, 198, 318; **59**, 53–4n12, 237, 360; **60**, 124–5
Booth, Thomas, **11**, 98
Booth, Wayne C. **59**, 31n54
Booth, William James, **53**, 100
Bootle, Raymond, **47**, 210
Boots, Wessel, **60**, 240, 251
Booty, John E., **41**, 148n; **49**, 182n
Boquet, Louis René, **10**, 72
Bor, Matej, **13**, 140; **15**, 141, 142, 143
Bora, Oğuz, **18**, 130
Borchardt, Frank L., **44**, 233
Borcherdt, Hans Heinrich, **1**, 11; **10**, 150; **57**, 63
Borde, Andrew, *Introduction of Knowledge*, **10**, 146
Bordinant, Philip, **40**, 222
Bordman, Gerald, **57**, 256
Bordon Hill, *see* Shottery
Bordone, Paris, **56**, 45, 46
Borel, Petrus, **15**, 136
Boreland, Anne, **43**, 208
Borew, Jurij, **22**, 36
Borgeaud, Nelly, **12**, 111
Borgerhoff, J.-L., **21**, 86n
Borges, Jean Louis, **58**, 149
Borges, Jorge Luis, **34**, 161; **53**, 165; **59**, 285–6, 293, 295, 297
Borgia, Caesar, **37**, 96; **49**, 195n; **56**, 208
Borgwardt, Ralph, **40**, 57
Borinski, Ludwig, **7**, 107; **8**, 68n; **10**, 8, 136, 142; **14**, 156; **24**, 153, 157; **32**, 6; **35**, 87n
'Shakespeare's Comic Prose', **8**, 57–68
Borisch, Frank, **40**, 53n
Börjesson, Karl, **43**, 113n
Borman, Thomas D., **14**, 143–4
Born, Anne, **43**, 117n
Born, Hanspeter, **25**, 187; **29**, 173; **38**, 12
Born, Lester K., **30**, 61n; **32**, 167n; **56**, 215n
Borne, Theophilus *see* Bird, Theophilus
Bornstein, Diane, **42**, 34; **56**, 43n
Bornstein, George, **54**, 30n; **57**, 136
Borough, William, **17**, 27–8, 28n
Borowsky, David, **44**, 193
Borowy, W., **3**, 118
Borromeo, Charles, **56**, 188, 191, 192, 194–8, 200
Borromeo, Saint Charles **1**, 123
Borromeo, Frederico, **56**, 195
Borsos, Miklos, **18**, 125
Borthwick, Ginny, **44**, 195
Borthwick, Kate, **49**, 270
Boryaskaya, Elizabeta, **60**, 313Fig.57
Borza, Mario, **54**, 287
Bosch, Hieronymus, **22**, 141; **37**, 50; **56**, 138, 232
Bosch, Jerome, **8**, 150
Bose, Analendu, **22**, 153
Bose, Kalidas, **22**, 165
Böse, Peter, **23**, 118
Bose, Tirthankar, **21**, 146
Bosgrave, George, **19**, 103
Bosman, Anston, **54**, 321
Bosseley, Edward, **19**, 103
Bossuet, Jacques, **33**, 22
Bossy, John, **54**, 126
Boswell, Eleanor, **42**, 117n
Boswell, J. (ed.), **16**, 32
Boswell, James, the elder, **15**, 1, 2; **18**, 37; **21**, 10n, 68; **24**, 37; **30**, 3; **34**, 13; **46**, 39, 40, 41n; **51**, 5, 42; **54**, 50, 51, 52; **56**, 187n; **58**, 76; **59**, 112, 287, 297
The Life of Samuel Johnson, **7**, 4, 66n
Boswell, James, the younger, **4**, 80; **47**, 256; **59**, 32, 122n54
Boswell, Laurence, **42**, 153; **53**, 252–3; **54**, 284
Boswell, Simon, **54**, 289
Boswell-Stone, W. G., **6**, 1, 3; **11**, 43, 49n; **23**, 160; **26**, 82n, 87n; **60**, 106n22
Botbol, Albert, **20**, 130
Botello, Leonard, **38**, 183
Botha, P. W., **55**, 272
Bothwell, Candace, **39**, 75n
Bothwell, Earl of, **43**, 57
Bothwell, James Hepburn, Earl of, **9**, 12
Bott, William, **31**, 177; **33**, 203
Botticelli, Sandro, **8**, 72; **15**, 19; **27**, 139; **37**, 175; **48**, 168; **49**, 157; **50**, 63; **53**, 30
Bottom of the Garden and Other Twisted Tales, **43**, 210
Bottomley, Emily, **55**, 138
Bottomley, Gordon, **53**, 110; **55**, 128–41
Bottom's Dream, **43**, 210
Bottoms, Janet, **58**, 84
Bouchage, Henri, Comte de, **7**, 105n
Boucher, François, **37**, 43
Boucicault, Nina, **56**, 9n, 132–3
Boudessin, Graf, **48**, 3
Boughner, Daniel C., **6**, 15n; **8**, 3; **9**, 143; **24**, 150; **35**, 109n, 110; **48**, 123
Boughton, Edward, **12**, 98
Boulter, John, **12**, 115
Boulter, Russell, **48**, 192; **49**, 271
Boulton, James T., **46**, 256
Bourbon, Charles de, **15**, 105
Bourchier, Arthur, **18**, 72; **39**, 7
Bourchier, Sir Henry, **3**, 53; **38**, 86
Bourdichon, Jean, **6**, 59

INDEX

Bourdieu, Pierre, **46**, 45; **50**, 91–9; **51**, 153; **53**, 311; **55**, 40n, 248n, 341, 356; **57**, 26, 170, 172, 176, 177, 200; **59**, 369; **60**, 333
Bourgeoise, Derek, **42**, 152
Bourgoin, Marie-Thérèse-Etiennette, **3**, 101
Bourgy, Victor, **26**, 171; **35**, 87n, 176; **47**, 230; **52**, 323
Bourke, Charon, **44**, 196
Bourke, Major-General Sir Richard, **22**, 126
Bourne, Bette, **57**, 273; **60**, 302
Bourne, Betty, **47**, 209
Bourne, William, **17**, 28, 143; **40**, 219; **43**, 152
Bourneuf, Philip, **7**, 116
Bournonville, A. A., **29**, 146
Boustead, Alan, **18**, 183
Bousyguina, Anastasia, **50**, 38
Bouton, James, **28**, 171
Bouts, Thierry, **56**, 232
Bouwsma, William J., **48**, 130n; **54**, 20n
Bovell, Brian, **42**, 156
Bovell, Susan, **42**, 159
Bovillus, Carolus, **60**, 126, 127
Bovino, Jim, **60**, 170–2, 177, 180
Bowden, H. S., **54**, 116n
Bowden, Nina, **51**, 266
Bowden, William R., **10**, 150; **12**, 133; **15**, 8; **18**, 170; **21**, 132; **25**, 177
Bowdler, Henrietta Maria, **20**, 163; **46**, 137, 138, 141, 143, 144
Bowdler, Thomas, **12**, 140; **14**, 86; **18**, 18–19; **20**, 163; **29**, 183; **46**, 137, 138, 141, 143, 144; **47**, 257; **49**, 131
Bowe, John, **34**, 150; **36**, 129n
Bowen, Barbara, **55**, 341
Bowen, Catherine Drinker, **27**, 100n; **38**, 33n
Bowen, David, **42**, 154
Bowen, Philip, **42**, 161; **48**, 234
Bower, Dallas, **52**, 193–4
Bowerbank, Sylvia, **39**, 231
Bowers, A. Robin, **34**, 174; **36**, 170, 177
Bowers, Frederick, **23**, 164n
Bowers, Fredson T., **3**, 148; **4**, 163; **6**, 171; **7**, 8, 142, 150–1; **9**, 7, 48n, 149–50, 153; **10**, 3, 138, 152n, 155–6; **14**, 12, 140, 164; **15**, 138; **16**, 6, 179; **17**, 208–9, 210 nn; **18**, 44, 131–2, 165, 189; **19**, 123–4, 154–9; **20**, 173–4, 177; **21**, 52n, 141, 143, 150, 155n, 160–1, 162; **23**, 148; **24**, 151, 172, 174, 176, 177; **25**, 195, 198n; **26**, 4–5, 39n, 180; **28**, 180; **30**, 207, 208; **32**, 11, 93n, 174n, 238, 241; **33**, 204–6; **34**, 191–3; **35**, 185–7; **36**, 188; **37**, 211; **38**, 78n, 251; **39**, 131n, 236, 247–8; **40**, 233; **41**, 61n, 64n, 91n, 92, 234–5; **42**, 100n, 187n, 188, 208, 210n; **43**, 81n, 264; **44**, 216, 233; **45**, 16, 17, 18n, 19, 24, 194, 197–8; **46**, 226, 243; **47**, 275; **49**, 99n, 325; **50**, 153, 289; **53**, 338, 343; **54**, 15n, 17n, 25n, 68n, 214n; **55**, 25n, 85n; **57**, 217; **58**, 356; **59**, 10–11, 28–9n38, 30, 31n53, 31n54, 40, 45n6, 47, 80, 84–5, 86, 88, 98, 214
The Bibliographical Way, **14**, reviewed, 159–60
(ed.) *The Dramatic Works of Thomas Dekker*, **14**, 9
Elizabethan Proofing, **2**, 152
Elizabethan Revenge Tragedy 1587–1642, **14**, 3, 55n
'Hamlet's "Sullied" or "Solid" Flesh: a bibliographical case-history', **9**, 44–8
On Editing Shakespeare, **14**, 6
Principles of Bibliographical Description, **14**, 6
'Proof Correction in *Lear*', **2**, 152–3
(ed.) *Studies in Bibliography*, **14**, 6
Textual and Literary Criticism, **14**, 6, 157; reviewed, 160–1
Bowers, Gary, **51**, 84n, 129
Bowers, John M., **38**, 231
Bowers, R. H., **15**, 172; **19**, 138
Bowers, Rick, **56**, 335
Bowers, Robert, **40**, 97n
Bowers, Roger, **54**, 342; **55**, 377, 389; **56**, 335
Bowers, T., **27**, 45n
Bowie, David, **56**, 8
Bowker, Judy, **57**, 295
Bowler, Dom Hugh, **11**, 105n
Bowles, **15**, 9
Bowles, Jessica, **41**, 187; **43**, 214
Bowles, Peter, **56**, 247
Bowling, Lawrence E., **19**, 130
Bowman, J., **13**, 113
Bowman, James, **35**, 145
Bowman, Jim, **41**, 190
Bowman, Robert, **50**, 217; **52**, 235–6; **56**, 343
Bowman, William, **31**, 177
Bowmer, Angus, **31**, 173
Bowring, Sir John, **9**, 102
Bowsher, Julian M. C., **47**, 84n, 179n; **60**, 25n8, 31n27, 32n30, 36n2, 36, 37n4, 37n5, 40n12, 47n60
Boxall, Rosalind, **7**, 125
Boxer, Amanda, **42**, 155; **57**, 293
Boxer, Stephen, **43**, 207; **46**, 164; **48**, 218–19; **52**, 237, 241–2
Boxus, Louis, **7**, 108; **8**, 118; **12**, 110
Boyadjiev, G., **54**, 148n
Boyce, Benjamin, **4**, 147; **18**, 95, 96, 97, 98
Boyce, Todd, **53**, 252
Boyce, William, **15**, 173; **49**, 111; **51**, 88
Boyd, Brian, **50**, 288; **51**, 324; **53**, 178n, 181n
Boyd, Elizabeth, **58**, 140
Boyd, M. C, **15**, 7
Boyd, Michael, **48**, 230; **51**, 230–1, 265; **52**, 241–2; **53**, 259–61, 271–3, 284; **54**, 255–8 274, 289; **55**, 286–9, 331; **56**, 257, 260, 271–2, 274, 276, 279, 281, 290, 295, 296; **57**, 258, 296; **58**, 268, 295, 337; **59**, 190, 191, 313–14, 339, 373; **60**, 284, 305, 328
Boydell Shakespeare Gallery, **59**, 131, 132
Boydell, Alderman John, **18**, 18; **37**, 45–8; **39**, 77; **49**, 114, 119–22, 126; **51**, 8, 9, 300; **53**, 109n; **59**, 112
Boydell, Josiah, **6**, 61; **7**, 92; **10**, 73; **51**, 9, 13
Boyer, Alan D., **54**, 97n
Boyes, Georgina, **60**, 186, 186n6, 187
Boyette, Purvis, **50**, 42n
Boyle, Harry H., **25**, 188
Boyle, Nicholas, **53**, 167n
Boyle, Robert R., **10**, 140
Boyle, Roger, Earl of Orrery, **43**, 93
Henry the Fifth, **1**, 66; **4**, 94
Mustapha, **1**, 66; **4**, 94
Tryphon, **4**, 94
Boyne, John, **38**, 71
Boys' companies, *see under* Theatre, Elizabethan, companies
Bozanich, Robert, **34**, 185
Bozzoli, Belinda, **57**, 159

Brabander, Gerard den, **14**, 122
Brabbins, Martyn, **41**, 191
Bracebridge, Amanda, **47**, 212
Bracey, W., **25**, 200
Bracher, Mark, **39**, 210n
Brack, O. M., Jr, **24**, 177n; **34**, 197
Brackley, Viscount, Second Earl of Bridgewater, **12**, 107
Brackman, W. L., **40**, 215
Bracton, Henry de, **17**, 112; **37**, 192
Bracy, William, *The Merry Wives of Windsor: The History and Transmission of Shakespeare's Text* reviewed, **6**, 169
Bradbrook, Frank W., **9**, 143n; **12**, 137
Bradbrook, Muriel C., **1**, 4; **4**, 11–12, 15–16, 22; **5**, 135–6; **6**, 14, 48n; **7**, 142; **8**, 4, 9, 11, 12; **9**, 110n, 134; **10**, 3, 39, 42, 47, 49n, 141; **11**, 49n; **13**, 153, 158; **14**, 4; **15**, 24, 28; **16**, 3, 4; **18**, 180; **19**, 144, 150; **21**, 138, 139, 142, 143, 152; **22**, 7, 69, 79, 80, 85, 89, 90, 153; **23**, 49; **24**, 15, 19, 41, 45–6, 47; **25**, 3, 6, 9, 52n, 57, 64, 174; **26**, 3–4, 26n, 47; **27**, 11n, 89–90, 91n, 113–14, 115, 116–17, 118, 119, 122, 127, 130n; **28**, 86n; **29**, 109, 111n; **31**, 13, 14, 29n, 30, 62n, 63n, 178; **32**, 6, 52n, 63n; **33**, 195; **34**, 5, 106n, 164, 174; **35**, 160n, 174; **36**, 195; **37**, 8, 30, 184; **38**, 49n, 238; **40**, 212; **41**, 9, 127n; **42**, 3n; **43**, 70n, 230; **44**, 37, 49n; **45**, 114n; **46**, 64; **47**, 107–16, 142; **48**, 43n; **50**, 54n; **53**, 30n; **55**, 24n; **56**, 34; **59**, 77n11, 215
  'Fifty Years of the Criticism of Shakespeare's Style', **7**, 1–11
  Shakespeare and Elizabethan Poetry, **15**, 21, 88n
  Shakespeare and Elizabethan Poetry reviewed, **6**, 155
  The Growth and Structure of Elizabethan Comedy, **14**, 3
  The Growth and Structure of Elizabethan Comedy reviewed, **10**, 137
  The Rise of the Common Player, **20**, 72n
  '*The Sources of Macbeth*', **4**, 35–48; **19**, 3, 45, 63, 67n, 91
  Themes and Conventions of Elizabethan Tragedy, **14**, 3, 55n; **16**, 35, 40n
Bradbury, M. and Palmer, D. J., **27**, 162n, 163n, 164n, 165n, 167n, 170n
Bradbury, Malcolm, **32**, 5, 7, 48n; **34**, 35n, 125n; **37**, 6, 20n, 59n; **38**, 54n; **39**, 217n; **40**, 81n; **41**, 127n; **42**, 11n; **47**, 139n; **48**, 163; **53**, 2n; **58**, 159
Bradby, David, **35**, 12n
Bradby, G. F., **9**, 11
Braddy, Haldeen, **11**, 143
Braden, Gordon, **42**, 53n; **55**, 350; **56**, 29, 55n
Bradford, Alan Taylor, **29**, 171, 175; **30**, 195
Bradford, Gamaliel, **51**, 96n, 103n
Bradford, Gamaliel, Jr., **43**, 82n
Bradford, Robin, **55**, 183n
Bradford, William C., **53**, 339; **54**, 14n
Bradford, William C., Jr, **29**, 180; **35**, 189n; **36**, 194n
Bradley, A. C., **1**, 14, 120; **2**, 9, 19, 108, 119; **3**, 9, 16, 130, 131; **4**, 10, 12, 16, 17, 18, 21, 23, 44, 141; **5**, 75; **6**, 2; **7**, 127, 129, 133; **8**, 26n; **9**, 2–4, 8, 9, 15, 138; **10**, 1, 6, 98, 137; **11**, 59 and n.; **12**, 132, 134, 136, 149; **13**, 1, 2, 4–5, 10n, 11, 14, 17, 18n, 19n, 33, 45, 69; **14**, 66–7, 72–4, 75n; **15**, 5, 123, 157, 160–1; **16**, 43–4, 58, 155; **18**, 5, 9, 40, 44, 55; **19**, 4–6, 9–10, 12, 50, 62–3; **20**, 14, 76, 160; **21**, 1, 2, 3–4, 5, 8, 9, 16, 27n, 28n, 39, 45, 61, 134, 138; **22**, 148, 157, 163; **23**, 31, 36, 37, 149, 151; **24**, 1, 37, 93, 99, 139; **25**, 2, 111, 192; **26**, 13–14, 151, 167; **27**, 72, 156, 157, 160; **28**, 89, 152; **29**, 82; **30**, 35, 98n, 189; **31**, 48; **32**, 60n, 221, 226; **33**, 4, 6, 8, 11, 27n, 28n, 43, 46, 53, 59, 89, 94, 120, 182, 195; **34**, 1–2, 9, 17, 68, 105–7, 109; **35**, 1, 33, 95, 101, 161, 165, 171; **36**, 43, 53, 56n, 78, 151–2; **37**, 143n, 146n, 147, 149, 150n; **38**, 87; **39**, 59, 63, 135n, 245; **40**, 24, 185–6; **41**, 147–8, 153, 155n, 157, 194, 218; **44**, 75, 217; **45**, 6, 19, 20, 21, 23, 65, 76n; **46**, 61, 132; **47**, 71–80, 159; **49**, 151, 201–3, 212–16; **50**, 102, 105, 180, 181, 185n; **51**, 284; **52**, 270, 324; **53**, 92, 94–5, 184, 287, 305; **54**, 306, 312–13, 318, 324; **55**, 4, 68, 140, 150, 340, 356, 361; **56**, 130, 205–6, 210–14, 302; **57**, 85, 128, 172, 176; **58**, 141; **59**, 153, 348; **60**, 185, 194, 354
  influence on Shakespeare criticism, **4**, 3–5
  interpretation of Falstaff, **6**, 12–13
  Miscellany, **4**, 4
  Oxford Lectures on Poetry, **3**, 7; **4**, 4
  Shakespearean Tragedy, **4**, 3–4
Bradley, David, **39**, 198; **41**, 166; **42**, 142, 150; **44**, 185, 186, 188; **45**, 116, 119, 143, 148, 153; **46**, 228–31; **47**, 183–4, 201, 204–5; **48**, 271, 272n; **50**, 223; **52**, 84; **56**, 260; **57**, 284; **59**, 323–4; **60**, 9n20, 322
Bradley, Efron, **40**, 228
Bradley, Frank, **43**, 217
Bradley, Henry, **7**, 1, 2, 5; **52**, 186n
Bradley, Jesse Franklin, **54**, 59n
Bradley, William, **17**, 88
Bradshaig, Lady, **51**, 28, 35
Bradshaigh family, **13**, 92–8, 104n
Bradshaw, Cathryn, **45**, 146; **54**, 260
Bradshaw, Christopher Brooke, **54**, 7n, 323; **58**, 146
Bradshaw, Fanny, **18**, 133
Bradshaw, George, **41**, 23n
Bradshaw, Graham, **42**, 172–3, 180; **43**, 226; **46**, 145n, 152n; **48**, 237, 239, 240, 249; **49**, 206n, 208n; **50**, 186n; **52**, 108, 110; **53**, 8n, 53, 293; **55**, 231, 232n; **56**, 310; **58**, 333; **59**, 162, 370–1, 375
  Misrepresentations: Shakespeare and the Materialists, **48**, 239
  Shakespeare's Scepticism, **48**, 239
Bradshaw, Jon, **36**, 27n, 28n
Bradshaw, Oliver, **59**, 339
Bradshaw, Thomas, **31**, 46
Bradstreet, John, **33**, 153–4, 157
Brady, Frank, **54**, 51n; **59**, 67n13
Brady, Ian, **57**, 43
Brady, Jennifer, **45**, 186n; **51**, 292
Brady, Leo, **13**, 125
Brady, William E., **25**, 181
Brae, Andrew, **23**, 103, 104, 105, 111; **27**, 107, 108
Braekman, W., **24**, 156
Bragg, Billy, **54**, 281
Bragg, Melvyn, **45**, 57n
Brahe, Tycho, **17**, 138, 142, 143, 145–6, 145n
Brahms, J., **18**, 100
Braid, Hilda, **28**, 139
Brailow, David G., **36**, 170n
Brailsford, Liz, **43**, 211
Brainerd, Barron, **29**, 183; **41**, 232
Braines, W. W., **1**, 6, 30, 34, 36n; **60**, 44n35, 46
Braithwait, Richard, **55**, 84n
Braithwaite, Edward Kamau, **48**, 155–62
Braithwaite, Richard, **43**, 162; **58**, 62

Brake, Patricia, **44**, 198
Bräker, Ulrich, **18**, 129, 174
Brambach, Heide, **40**, 55n
Bramelo, Prudence, **23**, 44
Bramley, Kate, **54**, 291
Bramley, Peter, **60**, 327
Branagh, Joyce, **59**, 345
Branagh, Kenneth, **38**, 205; **41**, 189; **42**, 129, 130, 133, 160, 199; **43**, 183, 205–6, 212, 251; **44**, 194; **45**, 151; **46**, 184, 186; **47**, 10, 181–5, 192, 210, 211, 258; **48**, 85, 208, 233, 250, 263; **49**, 13, 308; **50**, 256, 264; **51**, 259, 265, 299; **52**, 89, 108–9, 117, 211n, 279–80, 289; **53**, 294; **54**, 124n, 306, 311; **55**, 325, 341, 382–4; **56**, 3, 95, 98, 112, 257, 276–7, 317, 347–8; **57**, 282, 295, 330, 331, 339; **58**, 38, 47, 185, 187, 188, 189, 190, 191, 192, 193, 195, 334, 342; **59**, 198–9n4, 199n8; **60**, 160, 225, 230n41, 354, 355
Branch, Lady Helen, **34**, 87, 89
Brand, John, **17**, 174 and n.
Brand, Sir Matthew, **36**, 179n
Brand, Neil, **51**, 268
Brand, Peter, **33**, 153n, 156–7, 162; **36**, 135
Brandenburg, Christian Wilhelm, **32**, 195
Brandenburg, Elector of, **36**, 147
Brandes, George, **3**, 9, 110, 113; **4**, 1; **7**, 96; **10**, 6; **12**, 138; **27**, 106n; **43**, 112, 113n, 114–7; **48**, 3, 116; **56**, 312; **58**, 121, 313
  William Shakespeare, **3**, 1, 8, 107–8, 109, 111
Brandimarte, Anna, **14**, 121
Brandl, Alois, **3**, 7; **21**, 53, 57; **26**, 44; **28**, 39n; **44**, 108n, 111n
Brando, Marlon, **18**, 74; **40**, 57
Brandon, Charles (Duke of Suffolk), **60**, 68, 69–70
Brandon, Samuel, **59**, 72, 75
Brandow, Elizabeth S. C., **43**, 172n, 175n, 176n
Brandreth, Gyles, **60**, 328
Brandstrup, Kim, **48**, 229; **58**, 300
Brandt, Philippe, **43**, 211
Brandt, Sebastian, **1**, 68; **17**, 49n
  Ship of Folys, **1**, 67
Branston, John, **55**, 323
Brant, Damian, **47**, 210
Brantôme, **30**, 201, 202
Branwell, John, **48**, 201; **56**, 237, 251
Brasch, Thomas, **60**, 317
Brashear, Lucy, **31**, 198; **36**, 194n
Brashear, M., **18**, 118n
Brashear, William R., **40**, 82n
Brasseur, Pierre, **12**, 111
Brassington, Jill, **43**, 212; **45**, 145
Brassington, William Salt, **52**, 119
Bratchell, D. F., **44**, 207
Bratcher, T., **21**, 152
Brathwait, Frances (*née* Lawson), **60**, 278–82
Brathwaite, Richard, **46**, 114n, 115n, **50**, 71; **60**, 268
  Whimsies, or A New Cast of Characters, **13**, 114; **17**, 175, 203
Bratton, Jacky, **41**, 224–5; **53**, 104, 108n; **55**, 96n; **59**, 170, 201, 202, 202n24, 212n63
Braudel, Fernand, **47**, 111
Braun and Hohenberg, **1**, 26, 30, 31
  Civitates Orbis Terrarum, **1**, 26
Braun, Erich, **23**, 120
Braun, Georg, **53**, 198, 203n, 212n
Braun, Hans, **10**, 150n; **12**, 139
Braun, Margareta, **23**, 116
Braun, Volker, **48**, 178
Brauneck, Manfred, **36**, 143n
Braunmuller, Albert R., **39**, 217, 230; **41**, 204n; **42**, 46n, 169, 192; **43**, 255–7; **45**, 184; **46**, 241n; **49**, 312; **50**, 141; **51**, 310–12, 330, 331; **52**, 185n; **53**, 99–100, 331n, 333; **54**, 58n; **56**, 105n; **57**, 39, 43, 58, 69, 81, 90, 91, 95, 146, 341; **59**, 71n9, 169; **60**, 105n17, 115n58
Braunschweig, Stéphane, **49**, 280; **51**, 224, 226; **52**, 259
Brawne, Fanny, **8**, 32
Bray, Alan, **44**, 228; **46**, 4, 41, 48; **48**, 254; **56**, 72n
Bray, Denys, **15**, 11, 13, 17
Bray, Neil, **42**, 150
Bray, William G. **57**, 138
Brayne, Ellen, **45**, 101
Brayne, John, **38**, 227n, 228; **43**, 236; **44**, 146, 147; **45**, 103; **53**, 179
Brayne, Thomas, **45**, 101
Brayton, Dan, **58**, 21
Brayton, Lily, **32**, 20, 24
Brazil, report on Shakespeare in, **10**, 115; **20**, 121–4
Bready, Catherine, **51**, 262
Brecht, Bertolt, **10**, 118; **12**, 1, 79; **22**, 3, 175; **26**, 94; **31**, 63, 184; **32**, 223; **36**, 2; **37**, 161, 170–1; **38**, 9, 222; **39**, 81–2, 85, 169; **40**, 6, 53, 187, 202–3; **41**, 199, 223; **42**, 22, 103, 104, 109, 181; **43**, 251; **44**, 89, 160, 186, 223; **45**, 9, 92n, 100, 132–4, 143; **46**, 64, 213; **48**, 8, 9, 11, 12, 16, 173–7, 181; **50**, 41, 55, 130, 246, 250; **52**, 49, 156, 273, 283; **53**, 305; **54**, 110, 276, 340; **55**, 160, 161, 168, 180n, 282, 346; **56**, 346; **57**, 119, 313; **58**, 130; **59**, 209–10, 373; **60**, 174
  Berliner Ensemble, **13**, 127; **15**, 88n; **16**, 133–4; **18**, 61, 122; **19**, 23n; **20**, 117, 118, 120n
Bredemeyer, Reiner, **40**, 52n
Breen, Miles, **58**, 264
Breen, Robert, **3**, 114
  production of *Hamlet*, **4**, 124–5
Breight, Curtis, **44**, 222, 224n, 226; **51**, 278
Breitenberg, Mark, **50**, 244; **56**, 233
Breitholtz, L., **18**, 129
Breitinger, Johann, **59**, 131
Brekle, H. E., **23**, 23n
Bremer Shakespeare Company, **58**, 299
Bremer, F., **54**, 172n
Bremmer, Richard, **53**, 244–5
Bremner, Jan, **48**, 37n; **55**, 241n
Bremond, Claude, **53**, 11, 40n
Brenher, Matthew, **43**, 214; **55**, 322, 324
Brennan, Anthony, **40**, 195–6; **44**, 212; **47**, 231; **52**, 112
Brennan, Brid, **50**, 208
Brennan, Dennis, **6**, 119
Brennan, Elizabeth M., **42**, 3n; **48**, 37n; **60**, 232n53
Brennan, Liam, **43**, 214; **53**, 277; **56**, 288; **57**, 276; **58**, 277, 304; **59**, 341, 343
Brennan, Michael G., **42**, 188–9; **43**, 244
Brennan, Paul, **42**, 161
Brennecke, Ernest, **7**, 135; **15**, 7, 9
Brennen, Paul, **51**, 224–5; **52**, 259; **55**, 304–5
Brenner, Gerry, **36**, 169
Brent, Damien, **46**, 193
Brenton, Howard, **54**, 288

Brenton, Kyle, **60**, 168n3.3
Brereton, Austin, **35**, 19
Brereton, Geoffrey, **23**, 147–8, 149
Brereton, Georgine, **59**, 242n25
Bresslaw, Bernard, **41**, 187; **43**, 217; **44**, 202; **47**, 212; **49**, 306
Breton, Nicholas, **22**, 112; **23**, 165; **25**, 188; **46**, 224; **60**, 272n12
Fantasticks, **11**, 98; **17**, 17
Melancholic Humours, **15**, 104
Brett, David, **50**, 235; **52**, 232
Brett, Philip, **55**, 198
Brett-James, Norman, **30**, 161
Brett-Smith, H. F. B., **30**, 202
Brettle, R. E., **11**, 105n
Breuer, Horst, **29**, 175; **30**, 188; **41**, 221; **44**, 211; **51**, 333
Breuer, Lee, **45**, 51
Breuer, Rolf, **37**, 159
Breughel, Pieter, the elder, **8**, 150; **37**, 136–7; **49**, 80, 81, 85
Breughel, Pieter, the younger, **12**, 32
Breuning, P. S., **1**, 23
Brewer, Antony, **17**, 51n
Brewer, Derek S., **6**, 157; **10**, 9; **23**, 85n; **46**, 212; **48**, 261; **56**, 325
Brewer, Ellie, **46**, 197
Brewer, John S., **12**, 20n, 21n; **51**, 2, 17n; **54**, 18n
Brewer, Mark, **46**, 197
Brewer, Thomas, **15**, 126; **55**, 84n
Brewis, Peter, **51**, 257
Brewster, C., **9**, 84
Brewster, E., seventeenth-century publisher, **3**, 48; 5, 51
Brewster, Paul G., **14**, 156
Brewster, Yvonne, **46**, 197; **48**, 196–7; **49**, 272; **52**, 262
Breyer, Bernard, **22**, 111, 117n
Brezhnev, Leonid, **54**, 151
Brian, G. **57**, 232
Bricker, Herschel L., **6**, 124
Brickman, Mark, **45**, 154; **46**, 191
Bridal, David, **53**, 283
Bridenbaugh, Carl, **40**, 136n
Bridenthal, Renate, **46**, 134n
Brideoake, Ralph, **54**, 58n
Bridewell Dock, *see under* London
Bridge, Sir Frederick, **13**, 111n; **18**, 100n
Bridge, J. F., **15**, 3
Bridge, Simon, **42**, 156
Bridge, Tony Van, **13**, 126
Bridges, Alan, **7**, 125
Bridges, Robert, **1**, 7; **4**, 2–3, 16; **6**, 143–4; **9**, 70; **10**, 98, 99, 103, 106n; **18**, 22n; **24**, 37, 39, 46; **26**, 165; **29**, 137; **56**, 244
Bridges-Adams, William, **20**, 77; **32**, 29, 31; **36**, 75; **41**, 57–8, 62; **47**, 81, 90; **59**, 206–7
Bridgewater, second Earl of, *see* Egerton, Sir John
Bridgewater, *see under* Libraries
Bridgmont, Andrew, **51**, 215
Bridgwater, Patrick, **56**, 213n
Bridlington, Maria, **53**, 263
Brie, F., **8**, 4
Brief and True Report, A, **52**, 111
Brief Postil, **2**, 67, 69
Brien, Alan, **45**, 9n
Brierley, David, **47**, 117
Brierley, Tim, **33**, 174
Briers, Richard, **42**, 160; **44**, 194; **45**, 151; **46**, 184, 187; **48**, 233; **54**, 284; **56**, 98, 274; **57**, 297
Briggs, Asa, **29**, 183n; **41**, 23
Briggs, Henry, **17**, 71–2, 144; **43**, 152
Briggs, Henry Perronet, **49**, 123, 126
Briggs, Julia, **37**, 88; **48**, 247; **54**, 314; **56**, 2n; **58**, 118
Briggs, K. M., **34**, 182; **37**, 9
The Anatomy of Puck, **14**, 24n
Pale Hecate's Team, **19**, 60, 66n, 77
Briggs, Stephen, **60**, 324
Briggs, William Dinsmore, **6**, 3; **29**, 79; **50**, 46n
Bright, B. H., **4**, 86
Bright, Kellie, **52**, 263
Bright, Thomas, **38**, 180, 183
Bright, Timothy, **7**, 36; **9**, 11; **13**, 38, 40n; **17**, 160; **19**, 56, 66; **22**, 168; **24**, 71; **29**, 82; **40**, 81
Characterie, **5**, 151
Treatise on Melancholy, **4**, 11
Brightwell, Paul, **47**, 214
Brignone, Lilla, **11**, 121
Briley, John, **40**, 215
'Of Stake and Stage', **8**, 106–8
Brill, Leslie W., **33**, 187
Brimble, Nicholas, **32**, 85n
Brimble, Vincent, **51**, 210
Brimer, Alan, **49**, 285
Brimilcombe, Liz, **52**, 262
Brimson-Lewis, Stephen, **60**, 293–4
Brindley, D. J., **19**, 126
Brining, James, **45**, 150; **53**, 281; **54**, 286
Brink, André, **51**, 281
Brink, C. O. **59**, 289n24
Brink, J. R. **57**, 126, 188
Brinkman, Mark, **41**, 184
Brinkmann, Karl, **11**, 121; **12**, 113, 145; **23**, 174n; **26**, 176
Brinsley, John, **17**, 53, 62; **42**, 54n, 58n; **56**, 56n, 57n
Briquet, C. M., **7**, 56n
Brisman, Leslie, **27**, 192
Brissenden, Alan, **27**, 172; **33**, 203, 210; **35**, 176, 178, 189; **36**, 161; **37**, 9; **38**, 49n, 55n; **40**, 203; **42**, 111, 118n; **47**, 273–5; **54**, 198n; **55**, 243n, 255, 382; **56**, 80n, 170n; **59**, 48
Brissoni, Alessandro, **13**, 129
Bristol, Michael D., **44**, 20n, 205; **45**, 170; **46**, 209; **48**, 241; **49**, 70n, 203; **51**, 1, 14, 271–2, 278, 285, 290; **52**, 114, 269; **54**, 310; **55**, 92n, 339–40; **56**, 203, 204n, 342; **57**, 129; **58**, 349; **59**, 27n33, 28n36; **60**, 166, 168n2.2
Bristow, E. J., **51**, 73n, 74n, 77n
Bristow, James, **58**, 229
Britain, Ian, **59**, 149n10
British Broadcasting Corporation, The, **7**, 92; **11**, 105, 129
British Council, The, **7**, 92
British Museum, *see under* Libraries
British Youth Opera, **58**, 303
Brittain, Edward, **45**, 152
Brittaine, William, **45**, 102
Britten, Benjamin, Lord, **6**, 123; **14**, 152; **16**, 134; **18**, 75, 87; **19**, 151; **21**, 87; **35**, 144–6; **36**, 161; **39**, 219; **41**, 113–14; **45**, 173; **49**, 275, 307; **54**, 289; **56**, 123, 294; **58**, 303; **59**, 342; **60**, 325
Britten, Tony, **42**, 158

Brittin, Norman A., **11**, 137
Britton, Chris, **59**, 346
Britton, Jasper, **46**, 182; **50**, 232; **53**, 259, 282; **54**, 263–5, 293; **55**, 305, 332, 334; **56**, 292; **57**, 259, 260, 261; **59**, 344–5; **60**, 292, 293
Britton, John, **53**, 208n
Britton, Mike, **59**, 303, 314
Britton, Tim, **59**, 346
Britton, Tony, **42**, 152; **48**, 207–8; **58**, 305
Brizard, Jean-Baptiste, **9**, 91
Brkić, S., **18**, 134
Broad, John, **51**, 52
Broadbent, Jim, **42**, 160; **60**, 329
Broby-Johansen, R., **23**, 165n
Brock, D. Heyward, **37**, 189
Brock, Susan, **47**, 242; **55**, 37n; **56**, 184n
Brock-Sulzer, Elizabeth, **18**, 185
Brockbank, J. Philip, **13**, 149; **15**, 179; **16**, 161; **18**, 175; **21**, 140; **26**, 163; **29**, 3, 5, 8, 87; **30**, 203–4; **32**, 220, 247; **33**, 201; **34**, 189; **35**, 113, 117n; **38**, 4, 115n, 217, 238n; **39**, 170n, 233; **40**, 230; **41**, 57n, 121n; **42**, 199; **43**, 11n, 185; **44**, 213; **45**, 89n, 162; **46**, 83n, 93n, 256; **48**, 66; **51**, 145–6; **53**, 85n; **55**, 261n; **56**, 171n
'Hamlet the Bonesetter', **30**, 103–15
'History and Histrionics in *Cymbeline*', **11**, 42–49
'*Pericles*' and the Dream of Immortality', **24**, 105–16
'Shakespeare and the Fashion of these Times', **16**, 30–41
Brocklebank, Daniel, **57**, 285
Brockman, B. A., **31**, 176
Brockman, Robin, **44**, 194
Brockmann, Johann F. H., **35**, 23
Broderick, Alan Houghton, **47**, 179n
Brodmeier, Carl, **1**, 3
Brogan, T. V. F. **57**, 251
Broggi, Luigi, **12**, 114
Brogi, Giulio, **15**, 136
Brohan, Augustine, **9**, 63
Broich, Ulrich, **38**, 225
Broida, E., **9**, 114
Broitman, Jeff, **60**, 181, 182
Broke, Matilda, **49**, 186
Broke, Thomas, **17**, 233–4
Brolly, Tristan, **58**, 299
Bromberg, Murray, **4**, 149
Brome, Alexander, **54**, 70n; **55**, 264–5
Brome, Paul, **44**, 24
Brome, Richard, *The Antipodes*, **3**, 45; **12**, 55n; **16**, 101; **17**, 194, 196–8; **22**, 174; **32**, 93–4; **41**, 5; **46**, 31; **51**, 291; **52**, 80, 296; **53**, 324; **54**, 263; **55**, 85, 262–4, 268; **59**, 200n15, 206n41; **60**, 109
Late Lancashire Witches (with Heywood, Thomas), **13**, 114, 120
Bromham, A. A., **46**, 233–5
Bromley, David, **44**, 192; 45, 155
Bromley, George, **45**, 107
Bromley, J. S., **28**, 24n; **57**, 74
Bromley, J., **54**, 82
Bromley, John, **27**, 72n; **38**, 4
Bromly, J. C., **26**, 155–6
Bron, Eleanor, **48**, 228
Brönniman-Egger, Werner, **40**, 211n; **41**, 245n; **58**, 313, 331; **59**, 196
Bronson, Bertrand H., **23**, 175; **42**, 19n; **46**, 108n
Bronstein, Herbert, **23**, 144
Brontë, Charlotte, **44**, 206, 241; **48**, 7, 261
Brontë, Emily, **49**, 67; **53**, 106n; **60**, 330
Bronzino, Agnolo, **11**, 36; **26**, 50, 56–7; **60**, 103n6
Brook family, descendants of Sir John Oldcastle, **8**, 158
Brook, Arthur, **25**, 127
Brook, D., **7**, 88n
Brook, G. L., **41**, 156n
Brook, Irina, **51**, 222–3; **52**, 254
Brook, Meril, **42**, 162
Brook, Peter, **1**, 107, 108, 110; **2**, 19; **4**, 129; **5**, 119; **8**, 80; **10**, 124, 125, 126–9, 134; **11**, 39, 128, 134, 135; **12**, 78, 85, 86, 120; **13**, 70; **15**, 151, 152; **16**, 20, 22, 24; **18**, 67, 120, 125, 149; **19**, 111; **20**, 130; **23**, 132; **24**, 60n, 118, 119, 125, 126, 128, 131, 132–4; **25**, 27–35, 158n; **26**, 175; **27**, 143, 145, 167; **28**, 144; **29**, 151; **30**, 21; **31**, 141, 151–2, 173, 187; **32**, 201; **33**, 34, 45, 50, 177–8; **35**, 12; **36**, 60, 74, 79, 80, 83, 160; **37**, 5, 9, 162, 184; **38**, 50, 232, 237; **39**, 4, 6, 7, 9, 39, 79, 80, 81, 83, 85–6, 235, 241; **40**, 1, 2, 8, 52, 54, 58; **41**, 179; **42**, 199; **43**, 110, 117, 200, 251; **44**, 75, 79, 80, 179, 213; **45**, 4n, 9, 63–5, 67, 73, 115, 137, 155; **46**, 121, 188; **47**, 90, 101, 112, 201; **48**, 14n, 15, 109, 175–6, 201–3, 263, 282; **49**, 3, 6, 11, 14, 226, 232, 306, 319; **50**, 30, 33, 37–9, 128, 249, 263; **51**, 193–4, 259; **52**, 114, 162–3, 260, 270, 285, 287, 290, 309; **53**, 233, 306; **54**, 152, 164, 304, 348; **55**, 57, 153, 159, 161, 174, 292–3, 301–3, 313–14; **56**, 5, 9, 10, 19, 63n, 97, 99, 247–8, 289, 345–6, 348; **57**, 114, 145, 147, 150, 265; **58**, 56, 57, 300; **59**, 203; **60**, 295
production of *Measure for Measure*, **4**, 135–8
production of *The Winter's Tale* reviewed, **6**, 142–5
Brooke, Arthur, **31**, 182; **34**, 99n, 103–4, 196; **38**, 242; **42**, 196; **47**, 147; **49**, 1, 6, 45–9, 57, 63, 66, 73, 80, 83, 85, 87, 93n, 137, 163–6, 167n, 170–4; **53**, 42n, 44n; **58**, 143
Romeus and Juliet, **3**, 25, 54; **4**, 87; **6**, 58; **7**, 104; **10**, 21; **11**, 143; **12**, 70, 141; **14**, 44n; **15**, 153; **20**, 18, 96, 97, 98, 99, 100, 101, 104n
Brooke, C. F. Tucker, **1**, 76; **2**, 78, 153; **4**, 8; **6**, 3, 6, 14, 39, 58; **9**, 152; **10**, 4, 33, 59n; **11**, 153; **15**, 8, 11; **22**, 180; **27**, 98n, 99n, 112n, 119; **29**, 111n, 180; **38**, 132n; **39**, 143n; **42**, 56n; **44**, 83n; **49**, 100n; **55**, 65n
Essays on Shakespeare, **2**, 134–5, 145
Life of Marlowe, **14**, 9
Shakespeare Apocrypha, **2**, 44; **9**, 84
Shakespeare of Stratford, **3**, 1
(ed.) *The Shakespeare Apocrypha*, **14**, 7
Brooke, Christopher, **27**, 120; **60**, 283
Brooke, G. L., **45**, 82n
Brooke, Gustavus, **9**, 56; **16**, 104; **35**, 32–7
Brooke, Sir Henry, 8th Lord Cobham, **38**, 86, 90n, 91, 97–8, 100; **41**, 217
Brooke, Sir John, Lord Cobham, **34**, 183
Brooke, Kate, **50**, 228
Brooke, Lord, **11**, 115n; **17**, 66
Brooke, Nicholas, **16**, 167–8; **19**, 119, 127; **20**, 155; **23**, 142; **27**, 1n, 31n, 34, 35, 40n; **28**, 11n; **29**, 89; **32**, 217; **33**, 5, 10–11, 35, 38, 53; **34**, 93–4, 103, 164; **38**, 4, 5, 8, 165n; **40**, 75n, 85n, 86n, 88; **41**, 123, 145n; **44**, 245–8; **47**, 153n, 240, 241; **48**, 283; **49**, 48n, 49, 50; **50**, 54n, 101n, 104–6, 109n; **51**, 312; **55**, 58n, 153n; **57**, 23, 28, 81; **60**, 126

Brooke, Nicholas (*cont.*)
'Marlowe as Provocative Agent in Shakespeare's Early Plays', **14**, 34–44
'All's Well that Ends Well', **30**, 73–84
Brooke, Paul, **32**, 202, 204
Brooke, Ralph, **1**, 61
Brooke, Rupert, **26**, 2; **55**, 128–9, 135; **58**, 124
John Webster and the Elizabethan Drama, **14**, 11
Brooke, Sian, **59**, 340, 344
Brooke, Stopford Augustus, **4**, 5; **8**, 1; **9**, 3
Brooke, Tucker, **59**, 5
Brooke, Sir William, 7th Lord Cobham, **1**, 128, 130; **16**, 172; **38**, 86, 97–8, 100; **41**, 217; **44**, 248, 249; **54**, 97n, 98n
Brooker, Peter, **53**, 36n
Brookes of Cobham, the, **34**, 182
Brookes, Baldwin (*see also* Hall, Dr John), **4**, 70–1
Brookes, John B., **38**, 229
Brooks, Angela, **55**, 277n
Brooks, Charles, **15**, 172; **39**, 76n
Brooks, Christopher, **55**, 37n
Brooks, Cleanth, **4**, 19; **5**, 85, 86, 87; **7**, 10; **13**, 146; **15**, 27, 123; **16**, 50; **18**, 55, 158; **19**, 6, 45, 46, 47, 54n, 94n; **46**, 88; **57**, 39, 40
Brooks, Douglas A., **53**, 311; **54**, 356–7; **57**, 336; **58**, 66; **59**, 213n4, 381–2, 383
Brooks, Harold F., **9**, 151; **11**, 152; **16**, 159, 161; **18**, 159, 179; **20**, 152; **22**, 18, 26n, 40; **23**, 180; **24**, 177, 178; **25**, 84n, 87, 88; **27**, 191; **34**, 173, 184, 187–9; **35**, 57, 87n, 119n; **37**, 2, 6, 9; **38**, 8, 248n; **39**, 240n, 241–2; **40**, 55n; **41**, 137n; **42**, 53, 60n, 181; **47**, 140–2, 145; **49**, 37n, 310; **50**, 45, 54n; **51**, 179n; **54**, 350; **55**, 21; **56**, 39n, 55n, 69n; **59**, 40, 48; **60**, 272n13
Brooks, Jeremy, **42**, 161
Brooks, Louise, **45**, 44n
Brooks, Mel, **40**, 8
Brooks, Peter, **43**, 25–6; **46**, 92; **53**, 40n, 41n; **58**, 32, 248
Brooks-Davies, Douglas, **43**, 3n; **50**, 63
Brooksbank, Michael, **49**, 277
Broomfield, David, **14**, 127
Brophy, Brigid, **53**, 139, 140, 143n, 149n; **56**, 151n
Brophy, John, *Gentleman of Stratford*, **3**, 9
Brosnan, John, **53**, 168n
Broster, Eric B., **10**, 124
Brotanek, Rudolf, **1**, 11; **44**, 107, 109
Brotherston, Lez, **43**, 211; **46**, 199; **56**, 293
Brotton, Jeremy, **52**, 187, 188n, 202n; **53**, 290; **54**, 233; **55**, 343; **56**, 330
Broude, R., **27**, 159; **29**, 173; **45**, 24n
Brougham, Henry, **38**, 69
Broughton, Pip, **44**, 202; **46**, 195, 197
Brower, Reuben A., **26**, 159; **27**, 173; **30**, 135n; **31**, 7, 10, 12n; **33**, 4n; **40**, 75n, 86n; **41**, 133n; **43**, 16n, 22n; **48**, 6n; **50**, 125n; **54**, 153n
Brown, A. D., J., **46**, 236–7
Brown, Adrian, **42**, 153; **49**, 269
Brown, Alan, **47**, 97
Brown, Amelda, **43**, 211
Brown, Andy, **42**, 156
Brown, Anthony, **42**, 139; **47**, 99
Brown, Arthur, **3**, 13; **6**, 158; **10**, 152–3; **14**, 157 and n.; **15**, 171; **16**, 30, 166–7; **19**, 135; **20**, 177; **26**, 9; **42**, 78n
'Studies in Elizabethan and Jacobean Drama since 1900', **14**, 1–14
'The Printing of Books', **17**, 205–13
'"The Great Variety of Readers"', **18**, 11–22
Brown, Basil, **57**, 202
Brown, Bille, **44**, 195; **48**, 206, 221
Brown, Brian Naper, **44**, 194
Brown, Carleton, **15**, 25, 108n; **21**, 140; **53**, 20n, 23n
Brown, Carlyle, **53**, 282
Brown, Carolyn E., **41**, 197; **43**, 75n; **48**, 247; **51**, 276
Brown, Charles, **24**, 116
Brown, Charles Brockden, **57**, 129, 130, 131, 133, 134, 135, 136
Brown, Christopher, **1**, 28
Brown, Christy L., **41**, 199
Brown, Dave, **43**, 216
Brown, E. H. Phelps, **38**, 26n
Brown, Eluned, **35**, 7n
Brown, Eric C., **53**, 70n; **51**, 175–91
Brown, Ford Madox, **13**, 78, 79; **49**, 125; **55**, 138n
Brown, Geoff, **45**, 62
Brown, Georgia, **56**, 34n
Brown, Gilmore, **7**, 124
Brown, H., **26**, 164
Brown, Horatio F., **7**, 96; **53**, 60n, 62n
Brown, Huntington, **8**, 143; **10**, 8; **18**, 166; **46**, 11n
Brown, Ian, **41**, 183; **42**, 156; **43**, 211; **46**, 195; **56**, 280, 287; **57**, 126, 291; **60**, 328
Brown, Irina, **50**, 233
Brown, Ivor, **2**, 14, 18; **4**, 6; **12**, 126; **19**, 67n; **23**, 159; **32**, 29; **36**, 74n, 82; **44**, 106n
Shakespeare, **3**, 9, 138
Brown, James, **49**, 99, 101n
Brown, Jane K., **55**, 352; **56**, 151n
Brown, Jayson B. **59**, 215n10
Brown, John, **30**, 200; **44**, 158; **51**, 13–14; **58**, 73, 110
Brown, John Mason, **6**, 141
Brown, John Russell, **8**, 151; **9**, 7, 27, 33n, 48n, 132, 145, 153; **10**, 136, 152, 155; **11**, 148n; **12**, 132 and n., 133; **13**, 166; **14**, 14n, 152, 157 and n.; **15**, 145, 177; **16**, 38, 157n, 161; **17**, 208, 210n; **18**, 156, 161, 175, 186; **19**, 5, 125; **20**, 49n, 73n, 134, 170; **21**, 118, 127n, 130, 139–40, 142, 153–4; **22**, 166, 177; **23**, 137; **24**, 145, 154, 161; **25**, 10n, 84n, 93n, 171, 185; **26**, 9, 24n, 140, 141, 176; **27**, 145, 148, 162; **28**, 82n, 150; **29**, 7, 64, 93n, 101, 153, 154; **30**, 148n; **31**, 156n; **32**, 1–7, 11, 139n; **33**, 8n; **34**, 54n, 58n, 103n, 112n, 133n; **35**, 113n, 145; **36**, 50n, 97n, 157–9, 178; **37**, 1, 2, 5, 10, 11, 21, 29n, 56n, 59n, 183n, 184; **38**, 8n, 17, 80n; **39**, 135n, 139n, 145n, 191; **41**, 9, 26n, 57, 67, 83n, 134n; **43**, 10n, 23n, 26n, 230, 250; **44**, 45n, 127n; **45**, 7n; **46**, 101n, 125, 220; **50**, 164n; **51**, 145, 160n, 193–203; **52**, 99n; **53**, 10, 234n, 295, 311–12, 329; **54**, 89n, 98n, 99n, 304, 313, 323; **55**, 25, 231n, 233n, 242n, 381; **56**, 74n, 105n; **57**, 8, 27, 94, 185, 330; **59**, 41, 44, 200–1n16, 201n17, 370, 373, 374; **60**, 156–7
'Acting Shakespeare Today. A review of performances at the Royal Shakespeare Theatre, August 1962', **16**, 143–51
'Free Shakespeare', **24**, 127–35
'The Interpretation of Shakespeare's Comedies: 1900–1953', **8**, 1–13
'S. Franco Zeffirelli's *Romeo and Juliet*, **15**, 147–55
New Arden edition of *The Merchant of Venice* reviewed, **10**, 151

INDEX

'The Royal Shakespeare Company 1965', **19**, 111–18
Stratford-upon-Avon and Edinburgh, **18**, 147–55
'The Study and Practice of Shakespeare Production', **18**, 58–69
'Three Adaptations', **13**, 137–45
'Three Directors: A Review of Recent Productions', **14**, 129–37
'Three kinds of Shakespeare: 1964 Productions at London,
Brown, Jonathan, **57**, 30
Brown, Judith, **58**, 237
Brown, Keith, **23**, 149–50; **26**, 173; **28**, 153; **31**, 179; **36**, 189–90; **38**, 228; **41**, 3n; **58**, 313
' "Form and Cause Conjoined": *Hamlet* and Shakespeare's Workshop', **26**, 11–20
Brown, Laura, **43**, 102n
Brown, Mather, **49**, 119, 121
Brown, Michael N., **42**, 153; **43**, 216; **45**, 150; **47**, 102, 104, 106
Brown, Miss, **51**, 90
Brown, Nick Murray, **53**, 278
Brown, Pamela Allen, **1**, 98; **24**, 3n, 8; **55**, 347; **60**, 357, 360
Brown, Paul, **44**, 191; **54**, 230n; **55**, 316, 323, 328, 330, 332; **56**, 283, 297; **57**, 287
Brown, Paul E., **43**, 1n, 15n, 16
Brown, Penelope, **50**, 98n
Brown, Peter, **54**, 38n, 303
Brown, R., **46**, 43n
Brown, Ralph, **1**, 72; **41**, 186
Brown, Rawdon, **54**, 125n; **60**, 60n4
Brown, Richard, **52**, 286
Brown, S. J., **4**, 18; **5**, 91n; **29**, 164
Brown, Sarah Anne, **49**, 294; **56**, 146–60; **58**, 95; **59**, 366
Brown, Stephen, **18**, 53
Brown, Steve, **44**, 228
Brown, Susan, **58**, 228
Brown, Terry, **41**, 186; **42**, 153
Browne, Anthony, **40**, 230
Browne, Augustyne, **11**, 102
Browne, Coral, **59**, 371
Browne, E. Martin, **11**, 147; **24**, 39; **55**, 132
'English Hamlets of the Twentieth Century', **9**, 16–23
Browne, Edward, **60**, 21
Browne, Gertrude, **7**, 58, 59, 62, 63, 67n
Browne, Jane, **36**, 137
Browne, Jeremy, **42**, 155
Browne, Ned, **52**, 127
Browne, Ray B., **12**, 146; **57**, 250, 255
Browne, Richard, husband of Gertrude Browne, **7**, 58, 59
Browne, Robert (actor), **60**, 21
Browne, Robert (clergyman), **60**, 12n32
Browne, Robert, 'of the Boar's Head', **33**, 160–1; **36**, 135
Browne, Robert, junior, actor, son of Susan Baskervile, **7**, 61, 63; **36**, 135–6
Browne, Robert, senior, actor, husband of Susan Baskervile, **7**, 60, 61, 62, 63, 66, 67n, 68n
Browne, Robert, **32**, 194–7; **33**, 153–66 *passim*; **36**, 135, 137–8, 141–2, 144, 146–7; **40**, 215; **44**, 150; **54**, 191, 193; **58**, 237
Browne, Susan, **33**, 161; **40**, 215
see Baskervile, Susan
Browne, Sir Thomas, **8**, 58; **17**, 175, 181n, 228, 239; **19**, 60; **23**, 167; **32**, 227; **45**, 109n; **48**, 27; **52**, 148n; **55**, 64; **56**, 40n, 92
Browne, William, actor, son of Susan Baskervile, **7**, 58, 61, 62, 63; **21**, 145–6; **47**, 173; **57**, 214; **58**, 224; **60**, 283
Brownell, Morris R., **43**, 103n
Brownes, Robert, **58**, 237
Browning, I. R., **9**, 139; **10**, 11
Browning, Keefe, **48**, 231
Browning, Robert, **7**, 9; **22**, 48; **24**, 39, 43; **34**, 5; **53**, 125, 137n; **56**, 235n
Brownlee, Lewis, **60**, 116n63
Brownlow, F. W., **23**, 165; **32**, 213; **38**, 5; **43**, 248; **47**, 254–5; **58**, 17
Brownson, Orestes Augustus, **53**, 131
Brownstein, Oscar L., **25**, 191; **31**, 186; **34**, 118n, 180; **60**, 44, 47n59
Brownsword, John, **3**, 2
Bruce, Brenda, **22**, 139; **23**, 134; **24**, 122; **34**, 151; **39**, 185; **49**, 261
Bruce, Colin, **40**, 183
Bruce, Deborah, **52**, 263
Bruce, Dorothy H., **8**, 4
Bruce, Dr, **32**, 198n
Bruce, Edward, **54**, 133n, 134n
Bruce, Graham, **49**, 277
Bruce, J., **29**, 173
Bruce, J., (ed.), **17**, 79n
Bruce, John, **54**, 133n
Bruce, Lenny, **57**, 156
Bruce, Susan, **54**, 308
Bruce-Lockhart, Dugald, **59**, 318, 319
Brucher, Richard T., **35**, 154, 155n, 163
Brudenell, Edward, **12**, 101
Brudenell, Jeremy, **51**, 246
Bruegel, Peter, **26**, 49, 54; **53**, 15, 16
Bruggioti, bust of Shakespeare, **9**, 112; **12**, 111
Brugmann, K., **23**, 28n
Bruguière, Antoine, **2**, 116
Brulé, André, **9**, 68n
Bruller, Jean, **57**, 122
Brumm, Dennis, **57**, 138
Brummett, Palmira, **54**, 232n
Brunacci, Giorgio, **8**, 120
Brundage, James A., **49**, 183n; **55**, 36n
Bruneau, J., **19**, 130
Brunelli, Bruno, **5**, 113
Brunges, Harry, **59**, 343
Bruni, Emily, **51**, 233; **53**, 265
Brunkhorst, Martin, **27**, 179; **28**, 172n; **37**, 159n
Brunner, Karl, **1**, 115; **2**, 128; **7**, 107, 140; **8**, 118; **11**, 118; **12**, 113, 132n, 146 and n.
'Middle-Class Attitudes in Shakespeare's Histories', **6**, 36–8
Bruno, Giordano, **9**, 118; **16**, 16; **20**, 167; **33**, 22; **34**, 56–7, 100; **36**, 41n; **38**, 53; **44**, 232; **50**, 239; **54**, 73; **56**, 82; **59**, 228–9
Bruns, Gerald L., **51**, 126, 132
Brunswick-Wolfenbüttel, Henry Julius, Duke of, **33**, 155–6, 166
Brunton, Anne, **49**, 119, 121
Brunton, Miss, **32**, 21, 30, 35n
Brunwand, Jan Harold, **21**, 151, 153; **38**, 239; **46**, 221
Brusberg-Kermeier, Stefani, **56**, 320
Brussels, **12**, 32, 33, 34
Brustein, Robert, **36**, 21n; **57**, 138

Bruster, Douglas, **47**, 245n, 248; **50**, 188n, 199n; **51**, 147; **55**, 339; **56**, 326; **59**, 353, 373–4; **60**, 226, 230, 348
Brut, **11**, 46, 48
Brute, **11**, 43, 44, 46
Bruto, Giovanni, **39**, 225
Brutus, Junius, **44**, 34, 35
Bruzzi, Zara, **46**, 233–5; **52**, 274
Bryan, Sir Francis, **17**, 237
Bryan, George B., **22**, 121; **23**, 175; **32**, 194; **37**, 198; **54**, 193; **60**, 54
Bryan, Graham, **57**, 45
Bryan, Margaret B., **30**, 185; **31**, 10n
Bryan, Marie, **50**, 256
Bryans, Kenny, **47**, 217
Bryanston, Claudette, **51**, 264
Bryant, Edward, **43**, 211
Bryant, J. A. Jr., **9**, 140, 147; **11**, 148n; **12**, 134; **15**, 115; **16**, 171n; **19**, 136; **25**, 108n; **29**, 88n; **33**, 137n, 183; **38**, 6, 14, 15; **41**, 202–3; **48**, 75n
Hippolyta's View, **15**, reviewed, 160; **19**, 7
Bryant, J. H., **18**, 172, 188n
Bryant, Johanna, **43**, 209, 216; **45**, 155; **52**, 261; **56**, 297
Bryant, Mark, **44**, 45n
Bryant, Michael, **34**, 155; **41**, 175, 177; **42**, 145, 147; **43**, 196–7, 215; **44**, 193; **49**, 265; **51**, 251
Bryant, Nigel, **42**, 159; **43**, 209
Bryant, Peter, **22**, 154; **30**, 184
Bryant, W. C, **18**, 103
Bryars, Gavin, **46**, 202
Bryden, Bill, **37**, 168–9; **56**, 240; **60**, 285, 326
Bryden, Ronald, **23**, 131
Brydon, Diana, **54**, 312; **58**, 313, 333
Bryson, Anna, **55**, 240–1
Bryson, Karen, **54**, 266
Bryusov, Valery, **54**, 144
Buazzelli, Tino, **16**, 136
Buc, Sir George, **1**, 44; **9**, 85n; **25**, 188; **32**, 245; **38**, 90n, 227n; **41**, 217, 220; **42**, 189–90; **43**, 242, 249; **44**, 229; **53**, 71; **54**, 62; **57**, 73; **58**, 13; **59**, 22n13
History of Richard III, **3**, 51
Buccleuch, eighth Duke of, *see* Montague-Douglas-Scott, Walter
Bucer, Martin, **2**, 68; **17**, 55n
Buchan, Cynthia, **35**, 145
Buchan, David, Earl of, **51**, 14
Buchan, John, **56**, 119
Buchanan, George, **17**, 40; **19**, 3, 83; **27**, 172; **28**, 64; **30**, 68n; **31**, 40, 42; **41**, 196; **43**, 57; **47**, 245; **54**, 136; **57**, 70, 71, 72, 73, 75, 76, 77, 80, 126; **60**, 340
Buchanan, Jack, **49**, 233
Buchanan, Judith, **55**, 384
Buchell, Arend van, **1**, 23; **10**, 77; **12**, 16, 31; **28**, 128n
Bucher, François, **33**, 143n
Büchler, Klaus, **30**, 197
Buchloh, Paul Gerhard, **23**, 121
Buchman, Lorne M., **41**, 227
Büchner, Georg, **28**, 172; **29**, 175; **37**, 155
Büchner, Ludwig, **40**, 202
Buck, David, **52**, 266
Buck, Eva, **10**, 10
Buck, Sir George, **17**, 70–1, 70n, 80; **52**, 73, 75
Buck, Thomas, **43**, 158
Buckeridge, Corin, **42**, 155; **45**, 150, 152; **48**, 229; **50**, 229; **53**, 281; **55**, 334
Buckhurst, Alison, **46**, 196
Buckhurst, Lord, *see under* Sackville, Thomas
Buckingham, Duke of, *see* Villiers, George, Duke of Buckingham
Buckingham, Duke of, **42**, 189; **43**, 50, 96; **52**, 167–8, 172–7
Buckingham, Edmund Sheffield, Duke of (died *c.* 1736–7), **37**, 198
Buckingham, Edward Stafford, 3rd Duke of, **38**, 25
Buckingham, George Villiers, 1st Duke of, **38**, 23
Buckingham, George Villiers, 2nd duke of, **56**, 119
Buckingham, Marquis of, **54**, 198, 242
Buckingham, Mr, **22**, 131
Buckingham, Nicola, **49**, 278
Buckland, William, **54**, 82
Buckle, Linda, **46**, 240n
Buckley, Christine, **59**, 48
Buckley, G. T., **26**, 171; **30**, 202
Buckley, Keith, **13**, 124
Buckley, Reginald R., **56**, 130
Buckmorss, Susan, **56**, 10n
Bucknell, Peter A., **5**, 120
Bucknill, Sir J. C, **13**, 30, 39n; **17**, 258; **19**, 36, 43n; **30**, 81n; **49**, 232
Buckridge, Patrick, **56**, 335
Buckroyd, Daniel, **45**, 148
Buckton, Florence, **32**, 33
Budd, F. E., **8**, 12
Budde, Fritz, **6**, 163n
Budden, Julian, **57**, 65
Budé, Guillaume, **56**, 44n
Budgen, Frank, **56**, 138n
Budil, V., **9**, 107
Budra, Paul, **49**, 286
Budský, Joseph, **4**, 112–13
Buerger, Gottfried A., **7**, 111
Buether, Miriam, **56**, 289
Buffery, Bill, **41**, 190; **43**, 211; **44**, 203; **46**, 197; **47**, 218; **48**, 235, 237
Buffery, Kate, **38**, 211
Buffery, Mark, **42**, 153
Buffini, Fiona, **59**, 299, 346; **60**, 328
Buffoni, Clayton, **46**, 196
Buggbear, The, **19**, 56, 60
Bugge, Stein, **4**, 128
Bugliosi, Vincent, **57**, 146
Buhler, Stephen M., **49**, 284; **51**, 274
Buic, Jagoda, **53**, 281
Bujnák, P., **4**, 115n
Bukhman, N., **13**, 132
Buland, Mabel, **21**, 27n
Bulgakov, A. Y., **5**, 100
Bulgaria, report on Shakespeare in, **1**, 114; **2**, 127; **3**, 116; **10**, 115–16; **13**, 125
Bulger, James, **57**, 41, 51
Bulgo, Matthew, **58**, 300
Bull-baiting, **3**, 85, 89
Bull, Adrian, **44**, 191
Bull, Francis, **43**, 115n

INDEX

Bull, George, **27**, 46n; **37**, 96n
Bull, John, **51**, 8
Bull, Richard, **6**, 61
Bull, Thomas, **22**, 119–23
Bullard, Alexander, **19**, 104
Bullard, J. E., **11**, 30n
Bullasse, Edith, **45**, 101
Bullasse, Margaret, **45**, 101
Bullasse, Thomas, **45**, 101–2
Bullein, William, **17**, 100
Bullen, A. H., **3**, 21n; **14**, 13, 87; **15**, 109n; **25**, 149n; **30**, 202; **32**, 99n; **43**, 81n; **44**, 120; **49**, 98n, 190n; **57**, 209
Bullen, Mary, **45**, 150
Bullett, Gerald, **53**, 33n
Bullinger, Heinrich, **2**, 75; **15**, 97n; **19**, 63; **32**, 133–4; **60**, 76, 89, 90n20, 91n24
Fiftie Godlie and Learned Sermons, **2**, 70
Bulloch, John, **35**, 189
Bullock, Alan, **48**, 113
Bullock, Christopher, **51**, 45, 47, 48
Bullokar, John, **52**, 187
Bullokar, William, grammarian, **7**, 35, 36
Bullough, Geoffrey, **15**, 179; **18**, 128; **19**, 146, 147; **20**, 164; **21**, 150; **23**, 60n; **24**, 106n; **25**, 7, 9, 41n, 45n, 51, 96n; **26**, 113n, 115; **27**, 16n, 19n, 28n, 112, 172, 173, 174; **28**, 3, 4n, 67n; **29**, 4, 5, 27, 105n, 111, 169; **30**, 69, 125n; **31**, 33n, 35n, 40n, 42n, 58n; **32**, 2, 174n, 228; **33**, 13n, 16–18, 19n, 22, 127n, 194; **34**, 72, 103n, 164, 184; **36**, 86n, 87n, 93n; **37**, 2, 57n; **38**, 18, 29n, 49n, 52n, 53n, 55n, 56n, 61n, 63n, 67n, 93n, 98, 115n, 124n, 127n, 249; **39**, 150n, 159; **40**, 71, 81n; **41**, 85n, 136n, 138n; **42**, 42n, 43n, 46n, 109n; **44**, 19n, 50, 65n; **45**, 85n; **46**, 10n, 12n, 17n, 20n, 94n; 221; **47**, 131n, 164n, 166n, 167n, 169; **48**, 38n, 127n; **49**, 46n, 64n, 71n, 73n, 75n, 80n, 83n, 85n, 163n; **50**, 72n, 138n; **51**, 155n, 175n, 177n, 179n, 335–6; **52**, 120n; **53**, 6n, 42n, 44n, 50n, 60n, 73, 78n, 180n, 338; **54**, 38, 41, 89n, 203n, 357n; **55**, 13–14, 19, 20, 22n; **56**, 100, 222n,.230n; **57**, 69, 76, 77, 241; **59**, 170, 224n40; **60**, 106n22, 111n38
Narrative and Dramatic Sources of Shakespeare, Vol. I, **12**, reviewed, 141–2; **15**, 19, 22; **20**, 104n; *Vol. II*, **13**, reviewed, 157; *Vol. III*, **15** reviewed, 169; *Vol. IV*, **16**, reviewed, 168–9
(ed.) Poems and Dramas of Fulke Greville, **14**, 75
Shakespeare the Elizabethan, **20**, 162, 165
Bulman, James C., **30**, 203; **31**, 182; **40**, 210; **41**, 201–2, 204n; **43**, 252; **45**, 187; **47**, 7n; **48**, 54n; **50**, 262; **51**, 57n; **52**, 62n, 88n, 101, 155n; **53**, 234n, 236n; **54**, 208n; **55**, 172n, 283n; **57**, 330; **59**, 77n11
'The Date and Production of *Timon* Reconsidered', **27**, 111–27
'Shakespeare's Use of the *Timon* Comedy', **30**, 103–16
Bulman, Michael, **31**, 147
Bulmer, Bevis, **17**, 5
Bülow, Eduard von *see* Von Bülow, Eduard
Bülow, Fürst von, **44**, 108
Bülow-Møller, Anne Marie, **29**, 148n
Buloz, F., **9**, 62
Bulwer, John, **10**, 147, 148; **38**, 227; **48**, 29–39, 44, 48n; **50**, 152; **53**, 85
Chirologia, **10**, 147
Chironomia, **10**, 147
Bunburg, Helen William, **49**, 119
Bunbury, Henry William, **59**, 132
Bunce, Stuart, **49**, 241–2; **50**, 23
Bund, J. W. Willis, **17**, 77n
Bundy, Murray W., **6**, 163; **29**, 81, 82
Bunford, Alan Miller, **47**, 106
Bunim, Samuel, **14**, 120
Bunn, Alfred, **54**, 81
Bunnell, Charlene E., **56**, 152n
Bunnett, F. E., **37**, 152; **40**, 72n
Bunsee, Anthony, **44**, 192
Bunselmeyer, J., **31**, 130n
Buntrock, Dietrich, **23**, 118
Bunuel, Luis, **45**, 67
Bunyan, John, **17**, 176; **19**, 56, 67n; **23**, 178; **27**, 91; **34**, 172; **36**, 45; **53**, 115, 121
Pilgrim's Progress, **4**, 30
Bunzi, Geraldine, **53**, 274
Burbage, Alice, **45**, 103n
Burbage, Cuthbert, **1**, 41, 42, 65; **11**, 103; **36**, 136; **45**, 103, 106, 107; **47**, 173
Burbage, Ellen, **45**, 103n, 105
Burbage, James, **3**, 85, 88, 90; **7**, 143; **12**, 31; **24**, 166; **34**, 180; **38**, 228; **41**, 5, 127; **42**, 63, 194; **43**, 236; **44**, 146–8, 151, 155; **45**, 101, 103–7, 110, 113, 183; **47**, 1, 16, 113, 240, 241, 242, 273; **49**, 17, 19; **52**, 12, 15; **53**, 179; **60**, 9, 21, 30, 54
Burbage, Richard, **1**, 8, 25, 38, 39, 41, 42, 43, 46, 50n, 62, 65; **2**, 148; **3**, 4, 11, 53, 74; **4**, 76; **7**, 27, 50, 57, 82, 83, 84–5, 88, 149; **9**, 6, 29, 34n, 147; **10**, 72; **11**, 100, 103, 105; **13**, 116; **14**, 76, 151; **16**, 8, 95, 96, 97, 98, 101; **17**, 185, 191, 196, 198; **22**, 51; **24**, 40, 43; **26**, 26n, 45; **30**, 15, 199; **31**, 16, 177; **33**, 150, 196; **34**, 180; **35**, 101; **37**, 193; **38**, 51–2, 237; **40**, 38, 217; **41**, 35, 38–9, 42, 94; **42**, 114, 194; **44**, 146, 151, 155, 231, 233n, 236, 243; **45**, 106–8, 113; **47**, 175, 241; **49**, 41; **52**, 82–3, 99, 133; **53**, 178, 186–7, 195, 256, 327; **54**, 300; **55**, 56–7, 188, 252; **56**, 64, 97, 111; **58**, 10, 44, 65, 66, 68, 70, 140, 230, 232, 233; **60**, 54
Burbage, Robert, **45**, 103
Burbage, Winifred, **33**, 195
Burbridge, Ernest W. **10**, 115; **11**, 117; **51**, 142
Burbridge, Paul, **51**, 269
Burby, Cuthbert, **25**, 79n; **32**, 109; **49**, 42; **50**, 275; **52**, 310; **57**, 218; **60**, 258, 259, 263
Burchanov, Sh., **13**, 132
Burchfield, R. W., **45**, 2n; **49**, 176n; **56**, 244n
Burchill, S. C., **9**, 152n
Burckhardt, Jakob, **50**, 174; **56**, 207; **60**, 125
Burckhardt, Sigurd, **18**, 161; **21**, 148; **23**, 140; **27**, 83, 91; **30**, 93; **33**, 22; **37**, 11; **38**, 6, 7, 11; **39**, 211; **40**, 85n, 86n; **46**, 108n; **52**, 307; **55**, 355
Burden, Clive, **53**, 196–201
Burden, Dennis H., **42**, 25n
Burden, Howard, **41**, 189
Burden, Philip, **53**, 196–201
Burden, Suzanne, **40**, 175; **41**, 72, 75; **59**, 300
Burdett-Coutts, Baroness, **1**, 59
Burford, E. J., **32**, 103n
Burford, T., **20**, 111n
Burg, B. R., **56**, 73n
Burgainy, Lord, **60**, 69–70

Burge, Barbara, **19**, 123
Burge, Stuart, **9**, 120, 121; **41**, 228; **45**, 63; **60**, 160Fig.23, 168n4.9
Bürger, Gottfried A., **4**, 127; **23**, 122
Burgerdyk, A. L., **18**, 120
Burgersdyk, L. A. J., **5**, 109; **6**, 122; **7**, 108; **10**, 115; **13**, 125; **14**, 117, 122
Burgess, Anthony, **20**, 160; **40**, 212; **48**, 190; **53**, 318; **54**, 73
Burgess, C. F., **51**, 67, 69
Burgess, Glenn, **56**, 216n
Burgess, Guy, **45**, 150
Burgess, John, **42**, 152
Burgess, Mike, **46**, 195
Burgess, Pascale, **57**, 273
Burgh, George *see* Birch, George
Burghe, James, **11**, 116n; **40**, 34n
Burghley, William Cecil, Lord, **13**, 95, 104n; **17**, 16, 78, 115–16, 122–3, 125, 127, 165; **21**, 99; **23**, 41, 44; **27**, 94; **28**, 15n, 20, 21, 23; **32**, 87, 91n; **35**, 72–3, 75, 133n, 178; **38**, 21, 29, 34, 86; **42**, 18; **44**, 1; **47**, 174, 255n; **48**, 76n, 266; **52**, 315; **54**, 95n, 119, 120, 230–1; **55**, 357
Burgundy, Duke of, **44**, 56, 57
Burian, Orhan, **6**, 163n; **9**, 116; **14**, 124; **16**, 137; **18**, 130
Burke, Alfred, **7**, 125; **41**, 170; **48**, 221; **54**, 257, 274
Burke, David, **39**, 106; **51**, 251; **54**, 253
Burke, Edmund, **4**, 80; **51**, 20; **56**, 138, 140; **58**, 89; **59**, 30n48, 122n54, 130–1
Burke, Henry, **10**, 123; **51**, 266
Burke, Joseph, **51**, 60n
Burke, Kate, **43**, 232
Burke, Kenneth, **15**, 119; **21**, 139; **39**, 141n, 145, 234; **40**, 126; **43**, 20n, 28; **46**, 93n; **49**, 205n, 206n, 216; **53**, 304; **56**, 230, 231n
Burke, Kevin, **43**, 209
Burke, Louis, **18**, 128
Burke, Peter, **24**, 158; **44**, 69n, 81n; **52**, 55; **56**, 228n; **59**, 233
Burke, Tom, **59**, 344
Burkert, Walter, **30**, 103n, 115n
Burkhart, Robert E, **28**, 158; **30**, 209; **33**, 198; **40**, 204; **41**, 221; **49**, 27, 28, 42
Burkinshaw, Alison, **41**, 212
Burko, Faina, **55**, 122n
Burleigh, Lord, *see* Cecil, William
Burling, William J., **51**, 45
Burlington, Lord, **43**, 103–4
Burman family of Shottery and Stratford, **12**, 95–106
Burman, Sir John, **12**, 106n
Burn, Michael, **25**, 173
Burnaby, Charles, **35**, 85n
Burnaby, William, **35**, 85; **51**, 48n
Burnacini, Lodovico Ottavio, **10**, 76n
Burnard, Lou, **43**, 264n
Burne-Jones, Sir Edward Coley, **10**, 75
Burnell, Henry, **57**, 338
Burner, Sandra A., **43**, 244–5
Burness, Donald, **52**, 160n
Burness, Edwina, **42**, 195
Burnet, R. A. L., **33**, 203; **34**, 185; **35**, 177; **36**, 176n
Burnett, Cliff, **44**, 196; **46**, 201; **47**, 216; **48**, 230
Burnett, Kate, **41**, 187, 189; **43**, 216; **45**, 149; **55**, 326, 327
Burnett, Mark Thornton, **48**, 246; **50**, 248; **51**, 191n; **52**, 286, 295–6; **55**, 384; **56**, 4, 6n, 97n; **57**, 194; **58**, 115, 185; **59**, 372; **60**, 355–6, 360
Burney, A. L., **28**, 151
Burney, Dr Charles, **3**, 48, 56; **15**, 1; **18**, 78, 96–7; **45**, 172; **51**, 84–6
Burney, Edward Francis, **13**, 75; **59**, 379
Burney, Fanny, **3**, 43; **51**, 5, 21
Burnie, David, **12**, 109
Burnim, Kalman A., **13**, 80n, 159; **49**, 11n, 115n, 116n; **51**, 4, 82n, 109n, 110n, 113n; **53**, 327
Burns, Edward, **54**, 350–2; **59**, 291; **60**, 334, 351–2
Burns, Elizabeth, **55**, 237n
Burns, M. M., **36**, 170
Burns, Margie, **60**, 88n8, 94n30
Burns, Martha, **40**, 161–2, 164, 168
Burns, Raymond S., **49**, 101n
Burns, Robert, **14**, 77; **38**, 73
Burnyeat, Myles, **46**, 145n
Burón, Leopoldo, **54**, 154
Burre, Walter, **60**, 369
Burrell, John, **2**, 18; **9**, 117
Burrell, Margaret D., **9**, 139
Burrell, Michael, **51**, 261; **53**, 286
Burrell, Paul B., **41**, 200n
Burrell, Sheila, **24**, 118
Burrett, Alan, **45**, 144
Burroughs, Josephine L., **36**, 91n
Burrow, Colin, **56**, 349–50; **58**, 26, 27, 30; **59**, 225, 227, 229, 231, 235, 237, 366; **60**, 255n15, 256, 256n17, 257, 265n38
Burrow, J. A. **59**, 263n23
Burrow, J. W., **56**, 207
Burrows, Donald, **56**, 119n
Burrows, John, **49**, 277; **54**, 293
Burrows, Vinie, **18**, 133
Burt, Nicholas, **58**, 241–3, 342
Burt, Richard, **51**, 333; **52**, 197n, 289, 290; **53**, 329–30; **55**, 273n, 346; **56**, 34n, 348; **58**, 334, 340, 341; **60**, 138n28, 151, 360
Burt, Robert, **57**, 194
Burton, Dolores M., **29**, 184; **36**, 171
Burton, Edwin H., **56**, 194n
Burton, Hal, **1**, 107; **60**, 116n62
Burton, Harry, **54**, 265
Burton, John, **45**, 103n
Burton, Jonathan, **52**, 202n; **53**, 290
Burton, Julie, **43**, 234
Burton, Philip, **54**, 72–3
Burton, Richard, **6**, 136–7, 138; **8**, 132; **10**, 130, 133, 134; **18**, 71, 132, 133; **23**, 174; **24**, 3; **30**, 21, 23; **38**, 237; **39**, 86; **40**, 37; **42**, 37; **43**, 252; **45**, 192; **48**, 109; **49**, 230, 231; **52**, 319; **53**, 168; **56**, 111; **57**, 219, 261, 331
Burton, Richard D. E., **43**, 222–3
Burton, Robert, **4**, 79–80, 88, 93, 96n; **9**, 82; **17**, 136; **18**, 112; **19**, 55, 57, 58–9, 63, 64, 66n; **23**, 167; **31**, 105, 112–13; **33**, 96; **34**, 73, 102; **41**, 110; **46**, 118; **47**, 234; **54**, 62n, 65n; **55**, 263; **56**, 232n; **57**, 214, 216, 217; **59**, 350, 351
  Anatomy of Melancholy, **4**, 80
  Philosophaster, **1**, 65
Burton, T. G., **26**, 161
Buruiana, Mariana, **45**, 146
Burwash, D., **17**, 22n

Burwick, Frederick, **51**, 9, 301; **53**, 109n
Bury, John, **18**, 148; **19**, 116; **31**, 158n; **34**, 154; **35**, 145; **39**, 191; **40**, 180; **43**, 172; **54**, 64–5; **56**, 294
Bury, R. G., **55**, 220n
Bury, Shirley, **49**, 190n
Busacker, Klaus, **37**, 160n
Busby, John, **18**, 189
Busby, Olive Mary, **35**, 87
Busch, Ernst, **48**, 173
Busche, A. van den, *see* Sylvain, Le
Bush, Douglas, **10**, 5, 14, 15, 25n, 43, 49n; **15**, 19–20, 21–3, 29, 115, 123n; **21**, 141; **29**, 81; **31**, 29, 46n, 48, 128n, 132; **33**, 22; **46**, 158n; **47**, 127n, 131n; **54**, 14n, 16; **56**, 28n, 34; **57**, 35
Bush, Geoffrey, **11**, 136; **13**, 10n; **29**, 87, 89
Bush, George, **55**, 295
Bushell, Kirsty, **59**, 302
Bushell-Mingo, Josette, **47**, 212; **48**, 235; **50**, 39n; **52**, 265; **59**, 330; **60**, 320
Bushman, Mary Ann, **46**, 208
Bushnell, N. S., **29**, 83
Bushnell, Paul, **55**, 172n
Bushnell, Rebecca, **57**, 79
Busiño, Orazio, **54**, 197–8
Butcher, Justin, **59**, 346
Butcher, Louise, **46**, 68
Butcher, Maud, **46**, 33
Butcher, Philip, **7**, 135
Butdahl, E. M. **57**, 213
Butel, M. H., **15**, 133
Buthelezi, Chief, **52**, 160
Butini, **9**, 91
translation of *Othello*, **3**, 99
Butler, Alan, **56**, 292
Butler, (Bobeler) Nathaniel, **17**, 35 and n
Butler, Charles, **50**, 58n
Principles of Musik, **1**, 70
Butler, Christopher, **19**, 138
Butler, Francelia, **20**, 150, 155; **21**, 138; **29**, 103n
Butler, H. E., **42**, 89n; **53**, 13n; **55**, 219n
Butler, Judith, **50**, 25n; **52**, 293; **53**, 293, 300; **59**, 353; **60**, 148–50, 152, 153
Butler, M., **55**, 108n, 359
Butler, Marilyn, **40**, 194
Butler, Martin, **38**, 228; **45**, 184; **46**, 31n; **48**, 257; **54**, 19n, 323, 331–2; **56**, 217n; **59**, 379–81, 383
Butler, Nathaniel, **3**, 148, 151
Butler, Paul, **49**, 274
Butler, R. A., **40**, 29
Butler, Robert, **56**, 249
Butler, Samuel (1835–1902), **4**, 154; **9**, 135; **15**, 12, 19; **17**, 52; **26**, 165; **46**, 32; **52**, 303; **58**, 123; **60**, 341
Butlin, Martin, **19**, 79; **49**, 123, 125n
Butlin, Roger, **46**, 191; **55**, 334
Butsch, A. F., **43**, 161n
Butsko, Yuri, **44**, 193
Butt, Ronald, **37**, 172n
Butter, Nathaniel, Elizabethan publisher, **5**, 52; **50**, 160; **60**, 253
Butterfield, Herbert, **40**, 195; **41**, 195
Butters, Ronald, **47**, 156n
Butterworth, G. W., **46**, 117n
Butterworth, Tyler, **43**, 211
Buttes, Henry, **56**, 41n, 42
Büttner, R., **10**, 4
Buttrey, John, **39**, 229
Butts, Dr, **11**, 109
Butts, Thomas, **19**, 79
Butts, Sir William, **17**, 157
Buxton Forman, M., **8**, 120
Buxton, John, **18**, 181; **24**, 159; **26**, 174n
Buxton, Judy, **34**, 151
Buzacott, Martin, **46**, 238
Byatt, A. S., **53**, 118n
Byatt, Andrew, **43**, 209
Byers, Kate, **47**, 217
Byfield, Mary, **49**, 79n
Byford, Roy, **36**, 77
Byland (Beeland), Ambrose, **19**, 101–4, 105n, 106n, 107n
Bylebyl, Jerome J., **38**, 183n; **55**, 64n
Byles, Catherine, **53**, 2n
Byles, Joanna, **49**, 287
Bynnemann, Henry, *see under* Appian
Byrd, William, **2**, 29, 31; **5**, 115; **15**, 6, 10n; **40**, 220; **48**, 135n
Mass for Three Voices, **1**, 69
Psalms, Sonnets, Songs, **1**, 70
Songs of Sundrie Natures, **1**, 70
Byrne, Alexander, **42**, 151; **45**, 157
Byrne, Catherine, **43**, 216
Byrne, Geraldine, **53**, 232n
Byrne, Mike, **46**, 201
Byrne, Muriel St Clare, **2**, 51; **3**, 6; **4**, 11, 152; **7**, 79n, 124; **9**, 145; **10**, 11, 149; **12**, 129n, 145; **13**, 160; **14**, 151; **17**, 214–39, 229n; **18**, 184; **19**, 153; **21**, 142; **23**, 39–40, 41, 44; **33**, 34n; **35**, 7, 11, 12n, 18n; **57**, 246; **59**, 359
'Fifty Years of Shakespearian Production: 1898–1948', **2**, 1–20
'The Foundations of Elizabethan Language', **17**, 223–39
'A Stratford Production: *Henry VIII*', **3**, 120–9
Byrne, Patsy, **19**, Pl. VII A
Byrne, Paula, **58**, 91
Byrne, Sister St Geraldine, **24**, 2n
Byron, George Gordon, Lord, 6th Baron, **4**, 65–6; **5**, 93–4, 98, 100, 104; **7**, 115; **9**, 55, 114; **12**, 85; **13**, 49; **14**, 86, 156; **16**, 75; **18**, 125; **19**, 65; **21**, 81; **36**, 49; **38**, 74; **40**, 200–1; **48**, 105; **60**, 227n25
Mazeppa, **5**, 93
The Corsair, **5**, 105n
Byron, H. J., **29**, 136
Byron, John, **5**, 58
Bysryakov, A., **15**, 139
Bysshe, Edward, **59**, 93
Bywater, Ingram, **4**, 93; **46**, 55n; **49**, 193n
Bywater, Isabella, **42**, 159; **47**, 215; **48**, 236, **49**, 280
Bywater, Jim, **50**, 203

'C.T.S.', **27**, 116n
Cabbalero, Katia **57**, 296
Cabot, Michael, **50**, 230
Cabreros Avendaño, Antonio, **60**, 240
Cadden, Michael, **46**, 4
Caddy, William, **13**, 94, 95
Cade, Jack, **44**, 18, 19; **55**, 287

INDEX

Cadell, Pauline, **42**, 159
Cadell, Selina, **48**, 225; **55**, 312; **56**, 261
Cadell, Thomas, **13**, 75, 76; **51**, 6n
Cademan, William, **2**, 148
Cadiz expedition, **3**, 25
Cadiz, raid on, **11**, 90, 91
Cadle, Giles, **56**, 264; **60**, 314
Cadman, Michael, **41**, 163
Cadwallader, **11**, 45
Cady, Joseph, **48**, 254
Cadzow, Julie, **43**, 209
Caesar Interfectus, **9**, 34n
Caesar's Revenge, **9**, 142; **10**, 4; **52**, 308
Caesar, Augustus, **38**, 215–16
Caesar, Bert, **44**, 199
Caesar, Sir Charles, **7**, 61
Caesar, Julius, **11**, 44, 46; **16**, 4, 86; **23**, 36; **38**, 40–1, 116; **44**, 65, 66; **53**, 78–83; **55**, 212
Commentaries, **10**, 37
Caesar, Sir Julius, **60**, 53
Cage, John, **57**, 152
Cagli, Corrado, **18**, 126
Cagney, James, **18**, 73; **52**, 289
Cahan, Abraham, **55**, 124–5
Cahiers du Sud, Les, **2**, 120
Caiger-Smith, A., **26**, 73n, 74n, 75n
Caillous, Roger, **55**, 238
Caimi, Gino, **5**, 113
Cain, H. Edward, **6**, 15n, 24n; **20**, 82n; **30**, 35n; **38**, 14
Cain, Thomas A., **40**, 124n; **49**, 299; **53**, 20n, 178n; **55**, 107n, 181n
Caines, Michael, **58**, 331
Caird, David, **58**, 302
Caird, John, **37**, 163; **38**, 207, 209; **43**, 184, 200, 202; **44**, 161, 192, 198; **45**, 121; **46**, 173, 181, 182, 184; **47**, 11, 209; **50**, 69, 227; **54**, 258–9, 261, 263, 277–8, 333; **55**, 185n, 323; **56**, 97, 257, 288, 289; **57**, 291; **58**, 300; **59**, 330–3; **60**, 306, 323
Cairncross, Andrew S., **3**, 31; **9**, 14; **10**, 145, 156–7; **11**, 142n, 150–1, 152; **11**, ed. of 2 *Henry VI* reviewed, 150–1; **14**, 158; **16**, ed. of 1 *Henry VI* reviewed, 173–4; **19**, 88, 94n, **19**, ed. of 3 *Henry VI* reviewed, 160–1; **23**, 51, 180; **25**, 194; **26**, 69–70, 166, 180–1, 183; **27**, 132n, 135, 181–2, 183, 185; **29**, 174, 181, 185; **30**, 203, 207; **31**, 182; **34**, 194; **36**, 184; **37**, 202; **38**, 1, 42; **42**, 25n; **46**, 251; **48**, 35n; **49**, 313–14, 323; **54**, 352
Cairney, John, **44**, 196
Cairns, Christopher, **54**, 295; **55**, 247n
Cairns, Ellen, **48**, 196; **52**, 262; **59**, 327, 328
Cairns, Huntington, **36**, 85n; **49**, 61n
Cairns, Tom, **42**, 159, 160; **43**, 210
Caius Marius, **49**, 2
Caius, John, Dr, **17**, 150, 155, 157–8, 157n
Cake, Jonathan, **60**, 291
Cakebread, Caroline, **54**, 311–12; **56**, 155n
Calabresi, Bianca F. C. **59**, 382, 383
Calabresi, Paolo, **50**, 38, 39n
Calante, Maria, **44**, 199
Calarco, Joe, **58**, 305; **59**, 344
Calasso, Roberto, **59**, 261
Calbraith, Clare, **56**, 254; **58**, 279; **59**, 341
Calcagnini, Celio, **15**, 98n
Calcutt, David, **59**, 345
Caldecott, Thomas, **3**, 50; **4**, 81; **51**, 5; **59**, 111–12, 113, 117–18, 122, 160
Calder, A., **55**, 143n
Calder, Charles, **54**, 71n
Calder, David, **43**, 178; **44**, 212; **47**, 197–8, 200; **48**, 231; **50**, 227; **52**, 237–8; **53**, 283; **55**, 74
Calder, John, **57**, 66
Calder-Marshall, Anna, **39**, 89n
Calder-Marshall, Arthur, *Havelock Ellis*, **14**, 89n
Calderón de la Barca, Pedro, **5**, 94; **6**, 25, 106; **23**, 82, 84, 85, 86, 88; **24**, 169n; **29**, 3; **35**, 75, 152; **41**, 204; **54**, 87
El médico de su honra, **14**, 144
La vida es Jsueño, **12**, 6; **13**, 129
Calderwood, James L., **18**, 164; **19**, 133; **20**, 153; **21**, 139; **25**, 3n; **26**, 152; **27**, 27n; **30**, 135n, 136n; **33**, 190; **34**, 97n; **35**, 169; **37**, 3, 7, 9; **38**, 7, 12, 55n, 80, 218n; **39**, 136n, 211; **40**, 206; **41**, 206–7; **42**, 105, 172; **44**, 211; **45**, 10; **46**, 63n, 70, 93n, 117n, 211; **47**, 227; **49**, 215n; **55**, 223n; **57**, 241; **60**, 104n12, 105n14
Caldwell, Colin, **51**, 60n
Caldwell, Ellen C., **49**, 287
Caldwell, Finn, **55**, 296, 309
Caldwell, John, **24**, 158; **45**, 162
Caldwell, Zoë, **13**, 124, 142; **24**, 3n; **31**, 145
Calfhill, James, **54**, 62n
Calgari, G., **7**, 115, 137–8
Calhern, Louis, **5**, 115, 116
Calhoon, Kenneth S., **60**, 105n15
Calhoun, Craig, **57**, 26
Calhoun, Eleanor, **56**, 135n
Calhoun, Jean S., **18**, 166–7
Câliman, Câlin, **20**, 131n
Callaghan, Dympna, **43**, 223, 252–4; **46**, 134n; **47**, 228; **49**, 61n, 66, 284; **50**, 247; **51**, 63n, 274, 285; **52**, 108, 293n; **53**, 86n; **54**, 299–300; **55**, 184n, 277, 341; **56**, 27–38, 75n, 204n; **57**, 32, 312, 315; **58**, 325, 331; **60**, 169n5.2
Callanan, Ann, **49**, 273
Callard, Rebecca, **48**, 234; **57**, 267
Callas, Maria, **50**, 246; **57**, 116
Calle, Richard, **32**, 137
Callerghis, Lycurgus, **16**, 134
Callister, David, **43**, 216
Callois, Roger, **55**, 248n
Callot, Jacques, **10**, 72; **43**, 162, 164–5
Balli di Sfessania, **12**, 32
Callow, Simon, **33**, 180; **53**, 276; **56**, 345, 346–7; **59**, 63, 63n2; **60**, 317, 318
Cally, Gilian, **44**, 203
Calore, Michela, **52**, 85n; **55**, 377; **60**, 356, 361
Calve, Eleanor, **56**, 200
Calvert, Charles, **41**, 23–34; **43**, 232; **51**, 299; **57**, 326
Calvert, George, **2**, 27
Calvert, Hugh, **45**, 200
Calvert, Louis, **25**, 119; **37**, 85; **49**, 230
Calvert, Mrs, **41**, 26–8
Calvert, Richard, **41**, 23–34 *passim*
Calvert, Sir William, **44**, 56
Calvete de Estrella, Juan Cristóbal, **23**, 81n, 83, 87
Calvi, Jacques, **12**, 111

Calvin, Jean, **13**, 148; **17**, 60, 103; **53**, 320; **54**, 39n
Calvin, John, **1**, 67; **2**, 67, 68; **4**, 78; **23**, 80, 83, 86, 87; **33**, 89, 91–7; **35**, 164n; **43**, 237; **45**, 23; **46**, 26, 27, 127n; **48**, 73–4, 80, 82; **54**, 19n, 20, 35, 43, 55, 95, 129, 139; **55**, 228–9; **56**, 29; **57**, 237, 242
Calvinism, **5**, 141
Calvino, Italo, **38**, 223; **44**, 201
Camargo, Christian, **51**, 211, 213
Camaso, Claudio, **16**, 136
Camati, Anna Stegh, **57**, 327
Cambridge University, **3**, 74; *see also under* Libraries
  acting in, **17**, 197
  King's College, **11**, 15, 30
  Queens' College, **11**, 20n
  St John's College, **4**, 91
Cambyses (1569), **6**, 72, 74n; **20**, 18, 19, 24, 25n
Camden, Carroll, **1**, 127; **16**, 171; **19**, 124; **22**, 147; **32**, 11
  The Elizabethan Woman reviewed, **7**, 140–1
Camden, William, **3**, 18, 54; **5**, 149; **17**, 63–6; **20**, 28; **28**, 66; **30**, 205; **32**, 198; **33**, 16; **38**, 57n, 185, 229; **42**, 192; **43**, 238, 246–7; **44**, 12n, 62, 227; **48**, 76n; **51**, 135; **56**, 88, 324; **57**, 232; **59**, 250
  Annales, **11**, 96, 97n
  Britannia, **1**, 27; Gough's edition, **1**, 81; **16**, 169
  editions of his works in the Huntington Library, **6**, 57
  Remains, **11**, 144
Came Each Actor on his Ass, **52**, 266
Camerarius, P., **4**, 65; **15**, 97n; *see also* Aesop's *Fables*
Cameron, Elizabeth, **24**, 99n, 102
Cameron, G. M., **39**, 224
Cameron, James, **48**, 121n; **57**, 75
Cameron, John, **55**, 323
Cameron, Mrs, **22**, 128, 131
Cameron, Sarah, **50**, 217–8
Camillo, Giulio, **39**, 140n
Camm, B., **54**, 119n
Cammans, Jean, **7**, 108
Cammarano, Salvatore, **21**, 88; **57**, 64
Cammell, Donald, **57**, 147, 148
Campagnac, E. T., **42**, 54n, 58n; **57**, 197
Campanella, Tommaso, **50**, 239
Campaspe (Lyly), **48**, 259
Campbell, Alexi Kay, **59**, 341
Campbell, Lady Archibald, **56**, 135
Campbell, Beatrix, **57**, 46
Campbell, Cheryl, **36**, 150–1; **46**, 180, 181; **48**, 222
Campbell, Christopher, **41**, 190
Campbell, Douglas, **7**, 124; **10**, 116; **11**, 118; **13**, 125; **14**, 117; **39**, 185
Campbell, Dowling, **56**, 330
Campbell, Gordon, **35**, 178
Campbell, Joseph, **15**, 124n
Campbell, K. T. S., **26**, 164; **36**, 149; **53**, 278
Campbell, Lily B., **1**, 11; **2**, 108; **4**, 3, 11, 14, 147; **6**, 10, 57, 157; **7**, 8, 10; **8**, 144; **9**, 11; **10**, 9; **14**, 55n; **22**, 148; **28**, 1n, 2, 7, 121n; **29**, 82, 83, 85, 88; **30**, 63, 65; **32**, 146n, 147; **33**, 89n; **34**, 1; **38**, 11; **39**, 132n; **45**, 16, 17n, 22n; **48**, 69–70; **55**, 57; **56**, 28n, 32n; **58**, 133
  'Bradley Revisited' reviewed, **1**, 120
  'Polonius: the Tyrant's Ears', **2**, 135
  Shakespeare's 'Histories', **12**, 129n
  Shakespeare's 'Histories' reviewed, **1**, 121, 125–6; **6**, 10
  Shakespeare's Tragic Heroes, **18**, 41, 167; **19**, 2, 3, 9; **20**, 147
Campbell, Marion, **48**, 240; **55**, 174n; **56**, 205n
Campbell, Mrs Patrick, **1**, 92; **29**, 136; **49**, 128
Campbell, Oscar James, **1**, 9; **2**, 108; **3**, 29, 137; **4**, 13–14; **7**, 106n; **8**, 3, 4, 5, 11, 12–13, 28, 31, 36, 37, 45; **9**, 48n, 132; **10**, 10; **11**, 59n, 135; **21**, 141, 151, 159n; **25**, 5n, 6, 9, 67; **26**, 5, 114n; **27**, 120n; **29**, 88n, 103n; **33**, 43n; **41**, 68, 145n; **42**, 1n; **45**, 19n, 192; **55**, 247n; **59**, 81n9
  Comicall Satyre and Shakespeare's Troilus and Cressida, **3**, 11
  'Shakespeare and the "New" Critics', **2**, 136
Campbell, Paul Newell, **39**, 234
Campbell, Thomas, **29**, 149n; **32**, 17; **53**, 137n; **59**, 133
Campbell, W. E., **32**, 173n
Campbell-Moore, Stephen, **56**, 267, 282
Camper, Fred, **60**, 179n16
Campion, Edmund, **14**, 26; **17**, 122–3, 126; **53**, 317; **54**, 15, 35, 90, 92, 94, 96, 120–1; **56**, 184, 192, 194, 195, 199
Campion, Jane, **48**, 24
Campion, Richard, **7**, 113
Campion, Thomas, **3**, 52; **5**, 115; **6**, 60, 156; **13**, 106; **14**, 146; **15**, 8; **21**, 145; **22**, 51; **39**, 131; **40**, 215, 220; **42**, 77; **43**, 248; **44**, 238; **60**, 188, 357
  Ayres, **1**, 70
  Lord Hay's Masque, **15**, 4
  Lords Masque, **1**, 54
  Somerset Masque, **15**, 6
  Songs of Mourning, **1**, 70
Campo, Antoine, **44**, 193
Campos, Edmund, **57**, 186
Camus, Albert, **12**, 110; **18**, 73; **25**, 181; **44**, 145; **56**, 113
Can Grande della Scala, **8**, 17, 26n
Canada Council, **11**, 118
Canada, report on Shakespeare in, **1**, 112; **3**, 116–17; **4**, 125; **6**, 118; **7**, 108–9; **8**, 118–19; **9**, 111; **10**, 116; **11**, 118; **13**, 125; **14**, 117
Canar, Salih, **9**, 116
Canaris, Volker, **37**, 161n; **50**, 34n
Canary, Robert H., **44**, 145n
Cancalon, Elaine D., **53**, 40n
Candido, Joseph, **36**, 169–70; **37**, 191; **38**, 112n, 227; **52**, 276; **59**, 136n1
Candle, Giles, **59**, 307–8
Candoni, Luigi, **6**, 121
Candy, Andrew, **59**, 362
Cane, Andrew, *see* Du Caine
Cane, Gigi, **5**, 113
Canetti, Elias, **40**, 55; **48**, 24n, 30, 286
Canfield, J. Douglas, **48**, 78, 79n
Canham, Neil, **55**, 329
Cankar, J., **4**, 117
Canmore, Malcolm, **57**, 70
Cannadine, D., **54**, 166n
Cannan, Phyllis, **44**, 195
Canning, Heather, **33**, 172
Cannon, Charles Kendrick, **24**, 159; **25**, 182
Cannon, Edmund, priest, **17**, 96
Cannon, Robert, **34**, 180
Canova, Mahir, **7**, 116; **14**, 124; **15**, 138
Cant, Richard, **45**, 128; **51**, 230
Cantalupe, E. B., **18**, 173

Canterbury, *see* Prerogative Court of Canterbury
Canterbury, Convocation of (1529), **17**, 58
Cantor, Paul A., **31**, 8; **35**, 163n; **43**, 22n; **44**, 8n; **49**, 205n; **51**, 282
Cantrell, Paul L., **10**, 155; **11**, 155; **25**, 73n
Canuteson, John, **24**, 164
Canzler, David G., **23**, 168
Capek, Jaroslav, **4**, 120
Capel, Arthur, **17**, 65n
Capell, Edward, **3**, 43, 44, 49; **4**, 87; **5**, 7, 19, 53; **7**, 50; **16**, 180; **18**, 16–17, 23, 24; **19**, 2; **23**, 61n, 185; **26**, 181, 182; **27**, 187; **28**, 37, 38n; **29**, 105n; **30**, 204–5; **32**, 246; **36**, 186; **39**, 153n; **40**, 72n; **42**, 205; **43**, 256; **47**, 88, 257; **49**, 75; **50**, 140, 280; **51**, 7, 8, 129, 133–7, 139, 321; **52**, 303; **53**, 302; **55**, 12, 260, 264n, 388; **59**, 30n46, 32n58, 49, 52, 53, 56–7n20, 57n21, 58, 59–60, 98, 100, 100n12, 114, 159–60; **60**, 364
  collection in Trinity College library, Cambridge, **5**, 50–1, 52, 53
Capella, Francesco, **42**, 199
Capellanus, Andreas, **11**, 144; **46**, 75
Capgrave, John, **6**, 59
Capitolinus, Julius, *Life of the Emperor Pertinax*, **3**, 21n
Caplan, Neil, **17**, 38n; **44**, 198
Capocci, Valentina, **5**, 113; **7**, 106n; **8**, 120
Capodaglio, Wanda, **12**, 114
Capon, William, **6**, 66; **20**, 107
Capp, Bernard, **59**, 250n80
Cappello, Bianca, **7**, 95, 97, 105–6
Capper, Charles, **53**, 127n, 128n, 129
Cappuzo, Marcello, **48**, 257
Capra, Fritjof, **40**, 145, 148, 153; **42**, 208
Caputa, Paul, **48**, 235
Caputi, Anthony, **16**, 163; **20**, 151
Caracalla, Abdul Halim, **48**, 233
Caracalla, Ivan, **48**, 233
Caraher, Brian, **50**, 199n
Caraman, Philip, **54**, 35n, 231n; **59**, 252n92
Caramitru, Ion, **45**, 146; **48**, 119n, 120; **56**, 293
Carandinos, S., **4**, 128
Caravaggio, Michelangelo Merisi da, **14**, 156; **30**, 80, 83; **39**, 100
Carberry, John C., **32**, 132n
Card, James V., **19**, 134
Cardan, Jerome, astrologer **17**, 145; **28**, 40, 41n; **48**, 140n; **54**, 224
  De Consolatione, **3**, 19
Cardboard Citizens Company, **58**, 304
Cardenio, **1**, 47–9; **13**, 157; **15**, 169, 179; **49**, 303; **54**, 314
Cardiff University Library, *see* under Libraries
Cardim, Luiz, **3**, 118
Cardinal's Conspiracy, The, **54**, 18
Cardoso, Sergio, **20**, 122, 123
Cardozo, J. L., **8**, 4, 6
Carducci, J. S., **41**, 211
Cardy, David, **52**, 229
Carew (Cary), Sir George, **3**, 10; **16**, 172; **27**, 99, 101, 103, 104; **29**, 99n; **49**, 42
Carew, George, Earl of Totnes, **21**, 104
Carew, Matthew, **12**, 97
Carew, Richard, **3**, 53; **15**, 97n
Carew, Thomas, **16**, 95, 97; **17**, 184, 198; **21**, 149; **41**, 10; **46**, 227; **50**, 258
Carey family, as patrons of Thomas Nashe, **4**, 60
Carey, Denis, **13**, 125, 126; **41**, 60; **5**, 119, 120; **8**, 123, 124, 125, 126; **9**, 119, 121; **10**, 122
Carey, Edmund, **57**, 88
Carey, Elizabeth, **3**, 26, 31; **8**, 143
Carey, Emily J., **40**, 72n
Carey, Henry (1st Baron Hunsdon), **3**, 150; **49**, 42; **60**, 50, 51
Carey, Professor John, **33**, 192; **34**, 191n; **35**, 164n; **53**, 34n; **54**, 201n; **56**, 206n; **57**, 217; **60**, 342
Carey, Robert, First Earl of Monmouth, **4**, 91; **7**, 68n
Carey, Robin, **26**, 176n
Cargill, Oscar, **54**, 90n
Cariou, Len, **39**, 180–1
Carl, Joseph, **10**, 119
Carlell, Lodowick, **24**, 166; **42**, 188; **58**, 225, 234
Carleton, Sir Dudley, **1**, 44; **4**, 155; **11**, 94; **23**, 44; **52**, 135
Carleton, Mary, **49**, 303
Carleton, R.
  The Concealed Royalty, **4**, 94
  The Martial Queen, **4**, 94
Carley, James P., **59**, 243, 243n31, 243n34
Carlisle, 1st Earl of (James Hay), **60**, 54
Carlisle, Carol Jones, **9**, 140, 148; **22**, 159; **25**, 172; **34**, 175; **35**, 8n, 9, 10, 53n; **41**, 224; **51**, 58; **56**, 134n
Carlisle, Countess of, *see under* Hay, Lucy
Carlisle, John, **35**, 149; **36**, 152; **41**, 163; **42**, 154; **43**, 190, 201, 216; **44**, 193, 198; **45**, 152, 157; **54**, 248
Carlo, Augustin Millares, **48**, 39n
Carlson, Eric Joseph, **49**, 182n; **54**, 171
Carlson, Leland H., **54**, 118n; **60**, 11n31
Carlson, Marvin, **35**, 24n; **40**, 222; **41**, 225; **47**, 1n; **50**, 35n, 37n, 38n; **60**, 155
Carlson, Thomas B. **58**, 24
Carlton, Bob, **44**, 201; **52**, 258; **56**, 297; **58**, 302, 303; **59**, 344; **60**, 320–1
Carlyle, A. J., **44**, 105n
Carlyle, Robert, **45**, 156; **47**, 213
Carlyle, Thomas, **9**, 99; **14**, 85, 153; **16**, 35; **18**, 114; **27**, 21; **44**, 109n; **45**, 38n; **54**, 86; **59**, 369; **60**, 78
  The Nibelungen Lied, **14**, 88n
Carmichael, Charlotte, **19**, 4
Carmichael, Coralie, **1**, 94
Carmichael, Hayley, **51**, 246
Carnegie, Andrew, **1**, 87
Carnegie, David, **38**, 229; **52**, 69n; **60**, 109n33
Carnegy, Patrick, **60**, 161, 168n3.5
Carnicelli, D. D., **49**, 85n
Carnovsky, Morris, **12**, 117; **18**, 132; **20**, 73n; **31**, 173; **39**, 85n
Caro, Sir Anthony, **56**, 239
Caroline, Queen, **38**, 73–4; **51**, 13
Caroso, Fabritio, **55**, 244
Carousos, T., **10**, 119
Carpenter, Christine, **60**, 2n6
Carpenter, F. I., **25**, 138n
Carpenter, Humphrey, **36**, 29n, 37n; **53**, 150n
Carpenter, John, **58**, 189
Carpenter, Nick, **44**, 193
Carpenter, Sarah, **33**, 204; **36**, 180; **44**, 202; **45**, 150; **56**, 338–9
Carr, Andrea, **45**, 153
Carr, Bronwen, **55**, 334
Carr, Caline, **43**, 214

Carr, Comyns, **57**, 93
Carr, H., **13**, 100n
Carr, Jane, **35**, 147
Carr, Jason, **49**, 274; **50**, 232; **51**, 257; **52**, 265; **54**, 283; **55**, 330, 335
Carr, Joan, **33**, 202; **55**, 264
Carr, Kevin, **41**, 184; **43**, 207
Carr, R. H., **10**, 4, 33
Carr, Richard A., **49**, 47n
Carr, Sir Robert, **15**, 168; **55**, 374; **56**, 219, 220
Carr, Virginia M., **27**, 161; **29**, 174; **33**, 200; **38**, 5, 79
Carraci, A. **57**, 215
Carraro, Tino, **12**, 114
Carre, John, **19**, 103
Carrère, Félix, **8**, 142
Carrero, Tonia, **20**, 123
Carrière, Jean-Claude, **45**, 155; **50**, 39
Carrington, Murray, **55**, 135
Carrington, Norman T., **55**, 113n
Carrió, Raquel, **53**, 283
Carrithers, Gale H., **51**, 191n
Carroll, Andrina, **44**, 202; **46**, 201
Carroll, Carleton W., **54**, 92n
Carroll, D. Allen, **26**, 184; **28**, 180; **29**, 175; **32**, 227; **48**, 266
(ed.) *Greene's Groatsworth of Wit, Bought with a Million of Repentence*, **48**, 266
Carroll, David, **53**, 120, 121n
Carroll, Dominic, **60**, 326
Carroll, J., **51**, 28n
Carroll, John, **20**, 107
Carroll, Lewis, **2**, 151; **19**, 143; **46**, 177; **56**, 119, 139
Carroll, Nancy, **54**, 273, 278; **57**, 264
Carroll, Timothy, **47**, 219; **48**, 229; **53**, 261; **55**, 305, 334; **56**, 257, 258, 292; **57**, 276, 297; **58**, 304, 307; **59**, 185, 320, 344; **60**, 327
Carroll, William C., **31**, 164; **32**, 217; **37**, 7, 17n, 18n; **40**, 198; **41**, 133n; **42**, 10n, 194, 210; **44**, 21n; **45**, 164; **46**, 8, 108n; **49**, 105n; **50**, 82n, 259–60; **52**, 311; **55**, 82n, 349; **57**, 9, 69, 73, 199; **58**, 347–8, 357; **59**, 383
Carruthers, Bob, **52**, 259; **57**, 127
Carruthers, Ian, **55**, 385
Carruthers, Liz, **43**, 214
Carson, Christie, **50**, 36n; **59**, 170, 173, 176–7, 201n21
Carson, David L., **20**, 151
Carson, Edward, **56**, 137
Carson, Heather, **55**, 287
Carson, James Robert, **44**, 197; **47**, 209
Carson, Marion S., **16**, 171
Carson, Neil, **26**, 154; **30**, 197–8; **31**, 186; **32**, 233; **33**, 150n; **42**, 190; **43**, 147, 242–3; **44**, 152; **52**, 74n
'The Staircases of the Frame: New Light on the Structure of the Globe', **29**, 127–32
Carstairs, William, **59**, 115n29
Cartari, G., **29**, 109
Cartari, Vincenzo, **26**, 112n; **31**, 47–9, 51; **41**, 207; **46**, 113n, 116n, 117n; **57**, 210, 214
Carte, Eric, **45**, 150
Cartelli, Thomas, **38**, 230; **40**, 208; **42**, 163; **43**, 15n; **49**, 294; **53**, 289, 293
Carter, Albert Howard, 'Punctuation of Shakespeare's *Sonnets*', **2**, 153; **10**, 136
Carter, Alexandra, **55**, 239
Carter, Angela, **48**, 205, 261; **50**, 264; **52**, 273; **53**, 294; **56**, 302; **58**, 83, 84
Carter, David, **55**, 326; **58**, 302
Carter, Elizabeth, **51**, 6; **58**, 72
Carter, Harry, **18**, 64; **55**, 266n; **56**, 170n
Carter, Huntly, **52**, 19n
Carter, John, **53**, 208n
Carter, John, sketches of Trinity Hall, **6**, 69–70, 71, 72n
Carter, Mike, **55**, 330
Carter, Naomi, **50**, 274n
Carter, Stephen J., **50**, 251
Carter, Thomas, **34**, 185; **55**, 111n
Carter, William, **54**, 91, 95
Carteret, Anna, **51**, 248; **52**, 245
Carteret, Sir Edward de, **30**, 163n
Carteret, Sir George, **10**, 15
Cartier, Général, **2**, 118
Cartier, Jacqueline, **20**, 130
Cartier, Jacques, *Two Navigations to New France*, **1**, 69
Cartigny, Jean de, *The Wandering Knight*, **1**, 62
Cartmell, Deborah, **55**, 383; **56**, 316–17
Cartwright, Faith Wotton, **32**, 94n
Cartwright, Kent, **33**, 198; **46**, 217, 218; **49**, 70n; **54**, 329; **55**, 236n, 263n; **57**, 102; **60**, 125n19
Cartwright, Thomas, **12**, 21n; **17**, 109–10, 125, 125n; **54**, 39n, 68, 69n; **60**, 11–12
Cartwright, William, **35**, 130; **43**, 25; **47**, 37; **54**, 58n, 62–3; **56**, 45; **58**, 241
Cartwright, William, *Royal Slave* (MS.), **1**, 65; **3**, 51
Caruth, Cathy, **52**, 63, 65n
Carvel, Bertie, **59**, 340
Carver, Carol, **48**, 237
Carver, Raymond, **58**, 310
Cary, Cecile Williamson, **37**, 193n
Cary, Elizabeth, Lady Falkland, **41**, 220; **46**, 226; **48**, 261, 265, 284; **53**, 323; **54**, 301; **55**, 380; **60**, 349
Cary, George, 2nd Baron Hunsdon, **44**, 249; *see also under* Carey
Cary, George, **59**, 241n14, 241n16
Cary, Lady Elizabeth, **31**, 198; **36**, 194; **37**, 218
Cary, Lord, **35**, 131
Cary, Sir Robert, **36**, 140
Casarès, Maria, **7**, 111; **9**, 113; **10**, 118
Casaubon, Isaac, **17**, 42; **33**, 22; **47**, 26
Casaubon, Meric, **54**, 65n
Case, John, **23**, 164; **37**, 176; **48**, 140
Case, R. H., **8**, 157; **10**, 4, 6; **14**, 8; **49**, 310; **59**, 2
Case, Sue-Ellen, **46**, 6n; **60**, 148n27
Casey, Leslie, **43**, 214
Cashman, Michael, **49**, 274; **51**, 267; **52**, 249
Casimir, Ernest, Count of Orange-Nassau, **33**, 155, 166
Caspar, Horst, **48**, 172
Caspari, Fritz, **17**, 57n
Cass, Deborah, **14**, 117
Cass, Frank, **51**, 5
Casserio, Giulio, **48**, 26
Cassian, Nina, **48**, 119n
Cassibelane, **11**, 44
Cassiodorus, **20**, 26n
Cassirer, Ernst, **10**, 104, 106n; **29**, 91; **33**, 22; **36**, 91n, 94n; **59**, 365; **60**, 126

Cassius, Spurius, **38**, 117
Casson, Ann, **10**, 116; **11**, 118
Casson, Christopher, **6**, 119
Casson, John, **5**, 119
Casson, Philip, **47**, 9
Casson, Sir Lewis, **1**, 106; **2**, 4, 11, 17; **6**, 143; **40**, 223; **41**, 226; **47**, 82n; **52**, 28n
Castaldo, Annalisa, **56**, 348
Castelain, Maurice, **2**, 120
Castell, C. A., **55**, 135
Castellani, Renato, **9**, 114; **45**, 63; **49**, 153, 156–7, 162
Castelletti, Cristoforo, **33**, 18
Castellucci, Romeo, **53**, 276; **54**, 286
Castelnuovo-Tedesco, Mario, **13**, 129; **18**, 87; **45**, 172; **46**, 57n, 123n, 133n; **49**, 61, 62n
Castelvetro, L., **28**, 57; **31**, 18
Castiglione, Baldassare, **1**, 68; **7**, 96; **14**, 93; **25**, 103; **27**, 56, 163; **54**, 106n; **59**, 228, 232–3, 235, 365; **60**, 62
Castiglione, Giovanni Battista da, **31**, 85–91; **34**, 95; **35**, 175; **36**, 172; **40**, 98, 99n; **42**, 88; **43**, 238; **48**, 3, 77, 78n; **50**, 65, 66, 71, 75
Casting Shakespeare's Plays, **46**, 230
Castle of Perseverance, The, **1**, 64; **7**, 70; **12**, 70n, 142; **50**, 53
Castle, Eduard, **9**, 34n; **43**, 82n; **51**, 95n
Castle, John, **42**, 161; **43**, 180, 196
Castle, Terry, **43**, 106n
Castle, Zoe, **49**, 277
Castledine, Annie, **46**, 169
Castleford, *Chronicle of England*, **59**, 243
Castlereagh, Lord, **38**, 74
Castorf, Frank, **48**, 184
Castoriadis, Cornelius, **44**, 68n
Castrop, Helmut, **23**, 121; **42**, 183
Catalini, Angelica, **23**, 109
Cater, Wayne, **55**, 296; **56**, 280; **59**, 345
Catesby, Sir William, **54**, 120
Cathcart, Charles, **59**, 222n36
Cathcart, Mrs Charles, **41**, 24
Cathcart, Fanny, **35**, 32, 35
Cathcart, J. L., **41**, 24
Catiline, **54**, 28
Catlyn, Maliverny, **57**, 15
Cato, Dionysius, **17**, 60
Caton, Juliette, **59**, 341
Cattley, Stephen Reed, **38**, 24n; **43**, 53n
Catuelan, Comte de, **3**, 98; **9**, 92
Catullus, **12**, 142; **37**, 189; **46**, 113n
Cauchi, Simon, **45**, 181
Caulfield, Don, **44**, 193
Caulfield, Holden, **57**, 155
Caulfield, James, first earl of Charlemont, **59**, 120–1
Caulfield, John, **11**, 64, 65, 69n; **15**, 2, 3; **18**, 99; **51**, 89, 92
Caurier, Patrice, **54**, 289; **58**, 300
Causey, Andrew, **55**, 138
Cauthen, I. B. Jr., **4**, 162; **7**, 152; **9**, 137; **11**, 137, 143n; **12**, 142; **25**, 197n; **30**, 207n
Cauvin, Claude, **35**, 176
Cavafy, C. P., **45**, 54
Cavalchini, Mariella, **32**, 183n
Cavanagh, Dermot, **54**, 321; **56**, 317
Cavanagh, John, **44**, 244
Cavanagh, Sean, **41**, 186, 189; **42**, 151, 160, 161; **51**, 269
Cavanagh, Stephen, **58**, 195
Cavanaugh, Jean C., **39**, 231
Cave, Edward, **18**, 16
Cave, Richard Allen, **53**, 321–2; **59**, 200n15, 210n56
Cave, Terence, **42**, 67n, 74; **50**, 81, 82n, 87; **53**, 116n, 120
Cavell, Stanley, **33**, 12; **38**, 153, 155, 164–5; **40**, 102, 103n; **42**, 171–2; **43**, 99n; **44**, 205; **46**, 62n, 70, 93n; **47**, 234; **49**, 206, 208, 214n; **53**, 83n, 91, 294; **54**, 322; **55**, 3n, 71n, 74n, 75, 76, 78, 220, 339; **57**, 22, 23, 105, 108; **58**, 169, 178, 254, 351
Cavendish family, **49**, 20n
Cavendish, George, **31**, 189–90; **43**, 50–1; **52**, 178n, 179, 180n; **60**, 67n17
Life of Cardinal Wolsey, **3**, 53
Cavendish, Lord John, **38**, 71
Cavendish, Lady Margaret, Duchess of Newcastle, **34**, 11; **37**, 141–2; **39**, 231; **49**, 303; **51**, 317; **52**, 271; **55**, 83n, 380; **60**, 336
Cavendish, Thomas, **17**, 28–9, 32, 34n; **32**, 91n
Cavendish, William, Duke of Newcastle, *The Country Captain*, **3**, 52; **36**, 117
Cawarden, Sir Thomas, **28**, 170
Cawardine, Sir Thomas, **1**, 65
Cawdry, Robert, **59**, 165, 166
Cawelti, John G., **24**, 91
Cawley, A. C., **40**, 219; **56**, 242n; **57**, 246
Cawley, R. R., **17**, 33n, 35n, 36, 38n, 39n; **28**, 120n
Caxton, William, **1**, 67; **6**, 56, 63; **8**, 31; **9**, 81; **14**, 153; **21**, 150; **24**, 113n; **35**, 179; **36**, 87n; **37**, 207; **41**, 70; **42**, 28; **47**, 149; **54**, 103n; **55**, 368; **56**, 30, 242; **57**, 123, 314; **59**, 243, 246, 364
Recuyell of the Histories of Troye, **9**, 142
Troy Book, **5**, 53
Cayworth, John, **17**, 39n
Cazaban, Ion, **20**, 131n
Cazalet, Peter, **49**, 271
Cazamian, Louis, **2**, 119; **8**, 9
L'humour de Shakespeare, **2**, 120
Cazenove, Christopher, **46**, 198
Ceaucescu, Elena, **56**, 166
Cecil, Lady Anne, Countess of Northumberland, **11**, 111; **35**, 72, 75
Cecil, Jonathan, **52**, 222–3, 226
Cecil, Lord David, **10**, 10; **29**, 133, 134n
Poets and Story-Tellers, **14**, 11
Cecil, Sir Robert, first Earl of Salisbury (1563–1612), **1**, 43; **3**, 35, 40n; **4**, 154; **11**, 90–6; **16**, 170; **17**, 12, 112, 118, 127; **21**, 99, 100; **27**, 94; **28**, 4, 15, 16, 19, 20, 21, 23, 24–7, 151; **30**, 199; **35**, 104; **38**, 22, 24, 86; **43**, 242; **44**, 155; **46**, 12n; **48**, 131n; **53**, 64, 67; **54**, 98n, 133–4, 170; **56**, 219, 220; **57**, 17
see also Cranborne, Viscount
Cecil, Sir Thomas, **4**, 154; **50**, 152
Cecil, William, *see* Burghley
Cecil, William, Lord Burleigh, **1**, 126; **7**, 105; **9**, 12, 79n; **46**, 18n
Cecill, Thomas, **43**, 160n
Cefalu, Paul, **55**, 342
Čejka, J., **9**, 103
Čelakovský, F. L., **9**, 102

INDEX

Čelakovský, L., **9**, 103
Çelenk, Ali C., **14**, 124
Celi, Adolfo, **20**, 123
Cellan-Jones, James, **42**, 201
Celli, Maria Letizia, **11**, 121
Cellini, Benvenuto, **8**, 120; **14**, 121; **18**, 126
Cellius, Erhard, **54**, 192
Celoria, Francis, **43**, 269
Cenean, Stefania, **52**, 265
Centeno, Augusto, **26**, 90n
Century Dictionary **59**, 158n5, 164
Cerasano, Susan P., **37**, 194; **38**, 227; **39**, 229; **40**, 218–19; **41**, 221; **44**, 152, 230; **46**, 231; **47**, 172n, 173n, 241; **50**, 256; **51**, 29; **53**, 326; **55**, 372, 377; **58**, 311, 331; **60**, 46n50, 49–56, 100n40
Cercignani, Fausto, **26**, 171; **35**, 176; **44**, 252; **47**, 156n
Certaine advertisements out of Ireland, concerning the losses to the Spanish nauie (1588), **17**, 34
Certeau, Michel de, **52**, 91
Cervantes Saavedra, Miguel de, **1**, 68; **5**, 131; **16**, 14; **20**, 95, 103n; **22**, 11, 166; **23**, 83; **26**, 49; **34**, 28n; **35**, 108, 110; **36**, 104; **37**, 189; **40**, 216; **43**, 83; **49**, 72; **51**, 95–105; **53**, 129; **54**, 304, 333; **56**, 40
Don Quixote, **1**, 70; **8**, 67
Césaire, Aimé, **48**, 155, 159–62; **53**, 164; **55**, 167n, 343; **56**, 157; **59**, 364
Cesare, Mario A. Di, **57**, 32
Cesariano, Cesare, **47**, 20, 24
Cespedes, Frank V., **36**, 165; **38**, 16, 131n, 138n, 149n; **43**, 45, 49, 50n, 53n, 54n
Cezzar, Engin, **16**, 137
Chabrol, Claude, **18**, 122
Chaderton, Laurence, **27**, 83n
Chadjiskos, N., **15**, 134
Chadwick, Henry, **55**, 221n
Chadwick, Hubert, **29**, 22n, 29n
Chadwick, Jonathan, **45**, 149
Chadwick, Owen, **54**, 83
Chadwick, Rebecca, **55**, 325
Chadwin, Nick, **41**, 186; **42**, 152, 158; **43**, 217; **45**, 150; **47**, 212; **49**, 275
Chahidi, Paul, **56**, 259; **57**, 274; **60**, 319
Chaillet, de, **18**, 129
Chakravorty, Jagannath, **19**, 141; **21**, 143; **22**, 158; **24**, 142–3; **45**, 167; **46**, 61n
Chakravorty-Spivak, Gayatri, **21**, 141
Chalker, John, **38**, 40n, 41
Challis, John, **55**, 333
Chalmers, Alexander, **37**, 145n; **59**, 124–34
Chalmers, George, **4**, 91; **25**, 7n; **46**, 141, 142; **51**, 5
Chaloner, Sir Thomas, **27**, 59, 60, 61, 62, 63, 65, 66n, 67, 68, 69; **33**, 74n, 77n; **37**, 181; **53**, 71
Chamber Accounts, *see* Stanhope, John, Lord
Chamberlain's (King's) Men, *see under* Theatre, Elizabethan, companies
Chamberlain, Ellie, **16**, 138
Chamberlain, John, **1**, 44; **11**, 94, 97n; **12**, 42; **13**, 110n; **15**, 125, 127; **23**, 44; **30**, 161; **31**, 99–100, 104n; **35**, 130n; **36**, 179; **44**, 154; **47**, 18; **51**, 291; **52**, 135; **54**, 198; **55**, 93; **56**, 2n; **60**, 367
Chamberlain, Martin, **44**, 193
Chamberlain, Paul, **43**, 208
Chamberlain, Dr Peter, **17**, 157n
Chamberlain, Richard, **43**, 252
Chamberlayne, E., **17**, 91n
'Chambers of Rhetoric', **12**, 5
Chambers, Colin, **47**, 3n; **56**, 316; **58**, 334, 336, 342
Chambers, Sir Edmund K., **1**, 3, 4, 5, 9, 10, 17ff., 49n, 54, 55, 80, 129; **2**, 49, 50, 60n, 147; **3**, 4, 11, 13, 146, 151; **4**, 1, 5, 7, 58, 60, 67n, 74n, 160; **5**, 25, 57n; **6**, 14, 39, 73n, 74n, 75, 160, 170; **7**, 6, 11, 24n, 50, 76, 77, 79n, 80n, 81, 86, 88n; **8**, 4, 6, 7, 40, 107n; **9**, 4, 5, 29, 30, 31, 33n, 34n, 72, 78, 85n, 141; **10**, 3, 4, 6, 13, 24n, 25n, 69, 70n, 86n, 153; **11**, 50, 81, 83, 87n, 88n, 104, 105n, 106n, 108, 115n, 144; **12**, 4, 20n, 21n, 54, 55n, 147, 149; **13**, 114, 123n, 156, 159, 160; **14**, 1, 7, 13, 106; **15**, 7, 12, 13, 71n, 112; **16**, 9; **17**, 51n, 167n, 191, 198, 202, 207–8; **19**, 144; **21**, 31; **22**, 119; **24**, 52; **25**, 2, 8, 73n, 110, 186; **26**, 2, 3, 5, 20n, 33n, 74n, 81n, 82; **27**, 1n, 95n, 98n, 106n, 127n, 129n, 132, 134n, 135; **28**, 4, 5n, 6n; **30**, 6, 38; **31**, 100, 104n, 127n; **32**, 49n, 106, 108–9, 195, 196n, 197n, 198; **33**, 153–6, 159–64, 165n; **34**, 11n, 85, 86n, 178; **35**, 4, 129n; **36**, 111n, 135n, 136n, 137, 138n, 141, 142n; **37**, 2, 7, 102, 217; **38**, 51n, 61n, 88n, 90n, 91n, 254; **39**, 223; **40**, 218; **41**, 2, 5–8, 10, 35, 37, 39, 40, 42, 43n, 214, 220; **42**, 16n, 193, 204; **43**, 142; **44**, 122n, 145, 147, 151n, 155; **45**, 175, 185, 186n; **46**, 14n, 224, 225; **47**, 52n, 53, 107, 172n, 175n, 240n; **49**, 27; **50**, 148, 161n, 163, 237, 261; **51**, 95n, 143, 161n; **52**, 1, 3, 16, 75n, 135n, 306, 309; **53**, 187n, 206n; **54**, 13n, 26n, 57n, 98n, 99n, 120, 316; **55**, 17n, 18, 30n, 54n, 249n; **56**, 338; **57**, 69, 229, 237; **58**, 3, 8; **59**, 5, 147–8, 151, 152, 155–6, 280, 367; **60**, 4, 4n7, 7n12, 21, 22, 43n24, 44n37, 44n38, 45, 45n41, 45n44, 45n46, 49–50, 58n2, 60n7, 59–60n3, 62n13, 73n7, 224n9
dating of Shakespeare's plays, **3**, 22–33 *passim*
Sources for a Biography of Shakespeare reviewed, **1**, 122–3
William Shakespeare, A Study of Facts and Problems, **3**, 1, 4, 8, 22
Chambers, Janice Wardle, **56**, 317
Chambers, Janys, **42**, 152; **43**, 207; **45**, 149
Chambers, R. W., **2**, 59, 66; **3**, 3; **4**, 7, 9, 22; **6**, 5, 7, 63n; **8**, 10, 12, 16, 17, 68n; **9**, 77, 78; **10**, 5; **13**, 18n; **25**, 5, 64; **26**, 119n, 170; **27**, 173; **28**, 89n, 120n, 167, 170; **29**, 81, 86n, 168; **31**, 107n; **33**, 6; **40**, 225; **42**, 77n, 119; **43**, 262; **57**, 228, 229, 231, 235; **59**, 76
The Jacobean Shakespeare, **3**, 9
Chambers, Robert, **54**, 40
Chambers, William, **19**, 103, 104
Chambrun, Comtesse Clara de Longworth, **1**, 71, 123; **2**, 118, 120; **3**, 10; **4**, 148, 154–5; **5**, 148; **7**, 97, 106n, 139; **10**, 120; **28**, 38
Giovanni Florio, **3**, 10
Mon Grand Ami Shakespeare (My Shakespeare, Rise!), **3**, 9
Shakespeare Rediscovered, **3**, 4, 10
Champion, Larry S., **19**, 131; **20**, 154; **25**, 178; **26**, 163; **29**, 161; **30**, 187; **32**, 218; **34**, 167–8; **38**, 10; **41**, 145n; **42**, 166, 192; **45**, 163; **47**, 232; **55**, 145, 147
Champness, Samuel Thomas, **51**, 89
Chan, Mary Joiner, **24**, 156; **35**, 175–6
Chance, Carlton, **43**, 213; **60**, 208
Chance, Stephen, **44**, 198
Chancellor, Anna, **54**, 248
Chancellor, Nicholas, **17**, 32

INDEX

Chancellor, Richard, **17**, 27, 31
Chancerel, Léon, **16**, 53
Chancery, Court of, suits relating to Queen Anne's men discussed, **7**, 57–68
Chandler, Frank W., **52**, 125n
Chandler, Raymond, **45**, 7; **53**, 172n
Chandor, Hugo, **51**, 261
Chandos portrait of Shakespeare, *see under* Shakespeare, William, portraits
Chandos's Men, **44**, 150
Chandrashekar, Laxmi, **59**, 370
Chang, Joseph S. M. J., **21**, 144; **22**, 152; **24**, 148; **40**, 75n; **55**, 212n, 215n
Chang, Y. Z., **32**, 85–6, 89n, 93n
'Changeling' and the Years of Crisis, The, **46**, 233
Changeling, The, **52**, 296; **50**, 238
Channing, William Ellery, **53**, 131n, 134
Chantel, Viviane, **7**, 108
Chao's Bridge, a Chinese story, **6**, 112–13
Chap's ballets for *Othello*, **3**, 100
Chaplin, Charlie, **11**, 121; **22**, 4; **56**, 18
Chapman, Alison A. **57**, 305, 315
Chapman, Belinda, **42**, 150
Chapman, Derek, **44**, 192; **45**, 152
Chapman, Duncan, **45**, 152
Chapman, George, **1**, 52, 71; **2**, 54, 56, 57, 59, 60; **3**, 19, 45, 65, 66, 138; **4**, 7, 25, 42, 149; **5**, 139, 140; **6**, 9, 78n, 155, 157, 159; **7**, 6, 7, 11n, 12, 84, 131, 142; **8**, 55, 56, 145; **9**, 10, 24, 137, 144; **10**, 35, 48; **11**, 102, 103; **12**, 144; **14**, 7, 8, 11–13, 31, 82, 87; **15**, 8, 43, 105; **17**, 45, 183, 202, 207; **20**, 1, 3, 27–31, 172; **21**, 146, 147; **22**, 52, 171, 172; **23**, 46, 97, 129, 161, 170; **24**, 156, 159, 161n, 163; **25**, 9, 189; **26**, 1, 3, 5, 6, 8, 9, 34, 55, 168, 173; **27**, 175, 176, 179, 186; **29**, 170; **31**, 6, 33; **32**, 229; **33**, 197; **36**, 93n, 174; **39**, 224, 231; **41**, 7, 115–16, 220; **42**, 187, 212; **43**, 160, 270n; **44**, 6, 36, 37, 153; **45**, 75; **46**, 111, 116, 177n; **48**, 267; **51**, 289, 294, 320, 328; **52**, 111, 296; **53**, 320; **54**, 32, 64n, 301, 357; **55**, 369; **56**, 101, 121, 217; **59**, 2, 71, 72, 73, 75, 77, 213, 214, 216, 219–20, 221–3, 224, 272n13, 366; **60**, 109n33, 337
  All Fools, **15**, 40n
  Blind Beggar of Alexandria, **13**, 167n
  Bussy D'Ambois, **4**, 43; **11**, 73, 74; **17**, 202; **20**, 30
  Caesar and Pompey, **20**, 29–30
  Chabot, **20**, 30
  Charles, Duke of Byron, **11**, 103; **17**, 184; **20**, 30
  Gentleman Usher, **1**, 64
  Lincoln's Inn and Middle Temple Masque, **17**, 184
  Masque of the Middle Temple, **1**, 54, 64
  May Day, **13**, 167n
  Revenge of Bussy D'Ambois, **5**, 132; **12**, 134; **20**, 29, 30
  Shadow of Night, **3**, 10; **4**, 149
  translation of Homer, **9**, 134, 142; **12**, 142; **14**, 80; **15**, 96
  see also under Jonson, Ben, *Eastward Ho!*
Chapman, Gerald W., **25**, 111n; **38**, 10n
Chapman, H., **54**, 124n
Chapman, John Kemble, **47**, 64, 67n; **57**, 214
Chapman, Mark David, **57**, 155
Chapman, R. W., **51**, 18n; **58**, 84
Chapman, Raymond, **4**, 146, 151; **6**, 160; **38**, 233n
Chapman, Robert L., **52**, 103n
Chapman, Spencer, **51**, 266
Chapman–Jonson–Marston, *Eastward Ho*, **11**, 103, 104; **12**, 41; **17**, 203
Chappell, Fred, **19**, 130
Chappell, John, **58**, 222
Chappell, William, **11**, 64, 65, 69n; **15**, 2, 3, 7, 8, 9, 35, 40n; **17**, 219n; **51**, 92n; **55**, 82n, 84, 86, 89n, 92n
Chappuys, Gabriel, **20**, 166; **47**, 164–5, 167
Chapterhouse Theatre Company, **58**, 300, 303, 304, 305
Character as a Subversive Force in Shakespeare, **46**, 215
Charell, Erik, **13**, 45n
Charington, William, **58**, 239
Charisius, **15**, 109n
Charity, A. C., **36**, 16n
Charlemagne, **14**, 152
Charlemagne (MS.), **3**, 51, 52
Charlemont Library, *see under* Libraries
Charlemont, James Caulfield, first earl of, **59**, 120–1
Charles I, King of Great Britain, **2**, 24, 32, 34; **3**, 48; **4**, 80; **6**, 56; **11**, 107–14; **15**, 128; **25**, 48, 166; **28**, 22, 23, 65, 170; **32**, 198; **35**, 130; **38**, 20, 91; **43**, 54; **52**, 81; **54**, 50, 58, 61, 134, 136; **55**, 63–4; **57**, 30, 56, 70, 73
  as Prince Charles, **4**, 91; **7**, 68n; **26**, 36, 40n, 43, 44, 45; **31**, 102; **36**, 147; **56**, 166
  as Prince of Wales, **60**, 54
Charles II, King, **3**, 48; **11**, 74; **13**, 109; **17**, 10, 161; **39**, 229; **42**, 25–31; **43**, 95–7; **44**, 80; **51**, 23, 73; **54**, 134; **55**, 97; **57**, 30, 55
Charles V, Emperor, **42**, 29
Charles VI, King of France, **44**, 57
Charles VII of France, **20**, 25n
Charles of Styria, **36**, 145
Charles Pratt and Co., **1**, 57
Charles, Archduke of Poland, **32**, 196; **36**, 145–6
Charles, Duke of Croy and Aarschot, **33**, 167
Charles, F. W. B., **52**, 12n
Charles, Joseph, **44**, 202
Charles, Keith, **52**, 256
Charles, Michael Ray, **60**, 165, 169n7.9
Charles, Nicholas, **6**, 70
Charles, Prince-Count of Arenberg, **33**, 163–4, 167
Charleson, Ian, **32**, 203; **47**, 209; **56**, 247
Charlewood, John, printer, **17**, 206; **54**, 91, 92, 94, 95; **60**, 266n41
Charlotte, Queen, **3**, 56
Charlton, H. B., **1**, 121; **4**, 5, 23, 43; **6**, 6, 7, 13; **8**, 2, 3, 7, 8, 47; **9**, 4; **10**, 5, 8, 98–9, 100, 106n; **14**, 8; **16**, 47, 78; **18**, 54; **19**, 9, 61, 63, 67n; **20**, 19–20, 25n, 131n; **21**, 31, 137; **22**, 14n; **27**, 25n; **29**, 80; **31**, 18n; **32**, 49n; **34**, 89n, 93, 96n; **37**, 66n, 163; **49**, 88, 93; **51**, 142; **54**, 101
  Shakespearian Comedy, **4**, 4
  Shakespearian Tragedy reviewed, **3**, 130, 131, 132, 136; **4**, 4
Charlton, Orla, **44**, 192; **45**, 152
Charman, Sue, **43**, 211
Charn, Richard, **48**, 236
Charnes, Linda, **44**, 221; **46**, 219; **48**, 256; **51**, 149n, 150, 158n, 284; **55**, 339–40; **60**, 345–6, 347, 352
  Notorious Identity: Materializing the Subject in Shakespeare, **48**, 256

INDEX

Charney, Maurice, **11**, 141; **12**, 138; 14, 142; **15**, 80n; **16**; **21**, 154, 161; **23**, 183; **24**, 144, 162; **26**, 23n; **28**, 113n, 150; **31**, 171; **32**, 98n; **33**, 189; **34**, 58n, 131n, 176; **35**, 154n, 155, 172; **36**, 193; **39**, 95, 138; **40**, 86n, 107n, 212; **41**, 83n; **42**, 179; **43**, 17n, 230, 266n; **44**, 111n; **45**, 80, 166; **46**, 93n, 101n; **49**, 207n; **53**, 165n; **54**, 305–6, 338; **55**, 59n, 247
Shakespeare's Roman Plays reviewed, 162; **18**, 54
Charnock, Nigel, **54**, 288
Charnock, Ralph, **13**, 104n
Charnock, Roger, **13**, 104n
Charon, Jacques, **11**, 120
Charpentier, Gabriel, **45**, 173
Charques, R. D., **36**, 74n
Charron, Pierre, **17**, 43n; **22**, 111, 116n; **29**, 81, 82; **33**, 22
Chartier, Roger, **50**, 78n; **51**, 139
Chase, Richard, **24**, 98
Chasles, Philarète, **2**, 116; **28**, 42
Chassereau, **53**, 206n
Chaste Maid in Cheapside, A, **52**, 43n, 227
Chastel, André, **24**, 158; **34**, 102
Chateaubriand, (François) René, Vicomte de, **60**, 215
Chatelain, M., **9**, 62
Chatman, Seymour, **53**, 153n
Chatterjee, Bhabatosh, **21**, 143n; **22**, 166, 175n
Chatterjee, Sati, **19**, 142
Chatterjee, Sudipto, **54**, 312
Chatterjee, Visvanath, **19**, 125; **29**, 167; **31**, 171; **40**, 211n; **60**, 352
Chatterji, Aruna, **15**, 136
Chatterton, Frederick Balsir, **12**, 117; **44**, 242
Chatterton, Thomas, **4**, 156; **19**, 61; **24**, 108; **29**, 136; **59**, 109–10, 112
Chatwin, Margaret, **32**, 30
Chaucer, Geoffrey, **3**, 15; **4**, 52, 78, 94; **5**, 50, 54; **7**, 19; **8**, 17, 109; **9**, 24, 25, 81; **10**, 17, 20, 36; **11**, 145; **13**, 158; **14**, 97, 99–100, 142, 154; **15**, 23–4, 29, 81, 89, 170; **16**, 157; **17**, 37, 42, 155; **18**, 113; **20**, 20; **21**, 27, 150; **22**, 1, 52, 147, 166, 169; **25**, 9; **27**, 109n; **30**, 193–4, 196; **31**, 3, 4, 15; **32**, 133n, 166n, 229–30; **34**, 188; **35**, 158n; **36**, 87, 89n, 176; **37**, 191, 207; **39**, 150n, 219, 221; **41**, 74, 134n; **42**, 59n, 61n, 63n, 66; **43**, 228; **44**, 42n, 43, 49, 136, 220; **46**, 210; **47**, 139, 142, 144–5, 254; **49**, 73, 176n; **50**, 1, 4n, 138; **51**, 135, 136, 177, 309; **52**, 101; **54**, 8, 25n, 76, 303; **55**, 202, 204, 368; **56**, 30, 49, 50, 57, 64n, 68, 75, 77, 209, 305, 328; **57**, 150, 215, 311, 314, 320; **59**, 244–5, 246–7, 250, 251, 258–9, 259n11, 261, 265, 267, 274, 275–6, 364; **60**, 293
Canterbury Tales, **1**, 67; **6**, 56, 59
The Clerk's Tale, **8**, 18–19
The Friar's Tale, **8**, 24, 25
Legend of Good Women, **10**, 21–3, 25n, 26n
Troilus and Criseyde, **8**, 31, 36; **10**, 21, 25n
Chauchavadze, Ilia, **48**, 186–7
Chaudhuri, Sujata, **21**, 141
Chaudhuri, Sukanta, **35**, 166; **38**, 14; **44**, 238–9; **46**, 10n; **47**, 274; **55**, 220n; **57**, 307
Chaudhuri, Supriya, **41**, 208n
Chaudhuri, Una, **52**, 33
Chauncey, George, **46**, 4n
Chauvet, Tonia, **52**, 223, 226
Chávez, Felipe, **54**, 160n
Cheadle, B. D., **40**, 142n
Cheban, A., **54**, 146
Chedgzoy, Kate, **50**, 264; **53**, 291; **55**, 352; **56**, 155n
Cheeseman, Peter, **41**, 185; **50**, 226; **53**, 283
Cheesmond, Robert, **43**, 210; **44**, 202; **56**, 254
Cheetham, David, **51**, 268
Cheevers, Sarah, **49**, 303
Cheffaud, P. H., **2**, 120
Chegdzoy, Kate, **51**, 293
Cheke, Sir John, **7**, 19; **17**, 53; **36**, 166
Chekhov, Anton, Pavlovich **4**, 104, 120; **12**, 79; **16**, 15, 30, 35; **20**, 35, 40n; **22**, 3; **23**, 176; **24**, 19, 38; **31**, 105; **34**, 2; **35**, 153; **36**, 73; **39**, 94; **40**, 174; **45**, 4, 6; **48**, 108, 115–19; **49**, 47; **50**, 38; **53**, 8, 288, 295, 307; **54**, 142; **55**, 273, 274, 294; **56**, 260
The Three Sisters, **4**, 106
The Seagull, **13**, 151
Chekhov, Mikhail, **54**, 146
Chélard, Hippolyte, **18**, 81
Chelidze, V., **48**, 187
Chellappan, K., **40**, 211n
Chelli, Maurice, **2**, 120; **14**, 12
Chelsom, Peter, **35**, 144, 148
Chelton, Tsilla, **18**, 123
Chen-Hsien, Chang, **12**, 110
'Shakespeare in China', **6**, 112–16
Chenery, Julian, **52**, 263; **54**, 291; **55**, 327; **59**, 341, 342
Cheney, David R., **14**, 141; **22**, 168
Cheney, Patrick, **38**, 230; **56**, 311; **57**, 308; **58**, 358; **59**, 355–6, 359, 368; **60**, 343, 351
Cheng, Vincent John, **39**, 222; **56**, 144n, 145
Cherbonnier, Philippe, **47**, 217
Cherix, Pierre, **5**, 114
Chernaik, Warren, **49**, 304
Chernyshevsky, Nikolay, **16**, 11; **23**, 159
Cherrell, Gwen, **9**, 130
Cherry, Helen, **7**, 124
Cheshire, Richard, **45**, 154
Chester *Play of Antichrist*, **59**, 247
Chester Plays, **6**, 60; **7**, 99; **21**, 55, 57
Chester, Alan G., **11**, 153; **54**, 36n
Chester, Sir Robert, **15**, 25, 27, 99, 100, 102, 103, 105; **21**, 140; **43**, 242; **52**, 285
Loves Martyr, **4**, 85; **6**, 58; **8**, 121; **9**, 135
authorship of, **8**, 48
Chesterton, G. K., **9**, 110n; **12**, 9; **36**, 49, 50n; **39**, 160; **41**, 110; **46**, 257
Chetsingh, Rajan, **14**, 120
Chettle, Henry, **2**, 53; **3**, 11, 50, 150; **4**, 63, 68n, 158; **6**, 159; **7**, 148; **8**, 100; **14**, 97; **16**, 164; **21**, 148; **24**, 176; **26**, 182, 183; **27**, 130n; **32**, 197; **34**, 88; **35**, 190; **36**, 173; **37**, 215; **41**, 216; **42**, 187; **43**, 262; **46**, 16n; **48**, 266; **49**, 105n; **50**, 287; **51**, 334; **55**, 82n, 90; **57**, 233; **59**, 10, 71, 73, 74, 377; **60**, 369
Chettle, Henry and Mundy, Anthony, *Downfall of Robert Earl of Huntingdon, The*, **13**, 107
Hoffman, **12**, 47
Kind Heart's Dream, **2**, 52; **3**, 54; **4**, 59–62, 149, 158; **5**, 140; **11**, 151; **14**, 26; **15**, 63, 66–8, 71, 72n; 20, 64, 72n
share in *Sir Thomas More*, **2**, 46, 47, 51; **9**, 72, 143
Chetwind, Philip, **2**, 148

Chetwood, William Rufus, **14**, 81; **29**, 183; **51**, 54; **53**, 216–18
Chevalley, Sylvie, **24**, 85n
Chevara, Robert, **41**, 184; **54**, 288
Chevigny, Bell Gale, **55**, 156n
Chevreau, Urbain, **15**, 91
Chevreuse, Duchess of, **11**, 113
Chew, Samuel C., **1**, 76; **2**, 143; **17**, 44; **21**, 52n; **48**, 127n; **52**, 102n, 206n, 207n; **60**, 103n5
Chew, Shirley, **56**, 156n
Cheyette, Brian, **47**, 197
Cheyfitz, Eric, **48**, 32n, 155, 160
Cheyney, Edward P., **33**, 147n; **44**, 62n
Chiappelli, Freddi, **43**, 16n; **48**, 150n
Chicago American, The, **59**, 67
Chichester Festival Theatre Company, **58**, 279, 302
Chickering, Howell, **48**, 248
Chidley, John, **17**, 23
Chidley, Samuel, **17**, 91n
Chief Promises of God Unto Man, The, **54**, 62
Chieregato, Francesco, **60**, 60
Chiesa, Norberto, **48**, 233
Chih-mo, Hsu, **6**, 115, 116
Chikamatsu, Montzaemon, **48**, 102, 107; **53**, 329; **54**, 109, 110
Chilcot, Thomas, **18**, 97, 98, 100
Child, Harold, **2**, 7, 15; **12**, 129n; **15**, 4, 8; **25**, 1n; **35**, 9
Children of the Queen's Revels, *see under* Theatre, Elizabethan, companies
Childs, H. E., **18**, 183
Chillington, Carol (*see* Rutter, Carol)
Chillingworth, William, **54**, 6
China, **2**, 128
China, report on Shakespeare in, **12**, 110
Chinard, Gilbert, **17**, 39n, 42
Chinn, Graham, **43**, 211
Chinn, Richard, **57**, 50
Chinoy, Helen Krich, **49**, 158n; **57**, 60
Chinweizu, **39**, 175
Chipperfield, Faith, **53**, 127
Chisholm, Alex, **50**, 232
Chisholm, Cecil, **47**, 93
Chisholm, Jimmy, **52**, 242–3; **57**, 296; **59**, 342
Chisholm, Marie, **60**, 178
Chiswell, R., **9**, 84
Chitty, Alison, **41**, 176; **42**, 152, 162; **43**, 206, 215–16; **45**, 119; **46**, 198; **55**, 292–3, 308; **56**, 288; **57**, 291; **58**, 279; **59**, 333, 336
Cho, Kwang Soon, **52**, 297
Chodowicki, Daniel, **7**, 92
Choe, Jaison, **19**, 140–1
Cholij, Irena, **42**, 199; **51**, 79–94; **53**, 301
Cholmeley, John, **43**, 141; **44**, 230; **60**, 26, 28–30, 31, 44–5
Cholmeley's Players, **54**, 40
Chomsky, Noam, **23**, 11n; **35**, 76n; **53**, 156
Chopra, Vikram, **50**, 242, 248
Chothia, Jean, **47**, 3n; **59**, 170
Choudhury, Serita, **52**, 234–5
Chowdhury, Ajay, **49**, 270
Chramostova, Vlasta, **36**, 26
Chrimes, S. B., **59**, 263n24
Christ, Jesus, **11**, 20, 46; **33**, 99, 105–6, 109–10, 126; **36**, 18, 67, 173
Christensen, Ann, **51**, 284
Christensen, Pelle, **14**, 122
Christian IV, King of Denmark, **2**, 146, 148; **3**, 30, 52; **19**, 2–3; **20**, 165; **37**, 198; **60**, 139
Christian VII, King of Denmark, **3**, 114
Christian Turn'd Turke, A, **52**, 211; **55**, 378–9
Christian, John, **49**, 119n, 125
Christian, King of Denmark, **44**, 247
Christianson, Paul, **43**, 67n
Christie, Bunny, **42**, 149, 160; **46**, 192; **47**, 210; **48**, 228; **49**, 270; **52**, 222; **53**, 274
Christie, Julie, **51**, 259
Christie, Robert, **10**, 116
Christin, Olivier, **54**, 48n
Christmas family, **23**, 172
Christmas, Henry, **54**, 102n
Christodoulidès, Michel, **57**, 119
Christopher Marlowe (T. Healy), **46**, 234; **48**, 259
Christophersen, P., **23**, 13n
Christus Triumphans, **54**, 61–2
Christy, Miller, **52**, 187n
Chronegk, Ludwig, **35**, 13–14
Chu Chin Chow, **9**, 17
Chudoba, F., **9**, 106
Church, Elihu Dwight, his library, **6**, 54
Church, Geoffrey, **42**, 156; **44**, 194
Church, Jonathan, **51**, 263; **53**, 274, 282
Church, Madeleine, **41**, 188
Church, Tony, **20**, 138, 140; **25**, 165; **27**, 148; **30**, 176; **34**, 152; **35**, 149–50; **39**, 233; **41**, 46; **42**, 142
Churchill, Donald, **47**, 97
Churchill, G. B., **6**, 3; **7**, 151
Churchill, Sarah, **47**, 96
Churchill, Sarah, Duchess of Marlborough, **51**, 52n, 53n
Churchill, Winston, **1**, 127; **55**, 135
Churchyard, Thomas, **17**, 30 and n., 32 and n; **38**, 57n; **39**, 228; **42**, 54n
A Sparke of Friendship, **9**, 32, 34n
Chute, Marcette, **5**, 139
Chwalewik, Witold, *Poland in Shakespeare's Hamlet*, **11**, 121
trans. of *Measure for Measure*, **14**, 122; **20**, 164
Cialente, Romano, **4**, 128
Cibber, Colley, **2**, 15; **7**, 28; **10**, 72; **14**, 78, 88n; **15**, 153; **16**, 112; **18**, 36, 77, 102, 184, 185n; **19**, 153; **20**, 110, 169; **22**, 128, 132; **28**, 139n; **29**, 176; **32**, 42–4, 47; **34**, 12n; **39**, 233; **42**, 47, 137; **44**, 242–3; **49**, 41n; **51**, 18n, 54, 111, 113; **55**, 376; **56**, 154–5; **58**, 244
Cibber, Jennie, **51**, 25–6
Cibber, Mrs C., **13**, 74
Cibber, Mrs, **49**, 114–16; **51**, 10,
Cibber, Theophilus, **19**, 153; **37**, 199; **46**, 140n, 141; **49**, 2, 111; **51**, 3, 18n, 22, 25–6, 70, 86, 111, 129; **53**, 301, 323
Cicero, M. Tullius, **7**, 89n; **10**, 31, 36; **11**, 151; **17**, 60–1, 64, 216; **19**, 147; **20**, 26n; **22**, 109, 110, 111; **23**, 36; **24**, 150; **25**, 99; **29**, 100n; **31**, 3, 7, 19n; **32**, 171n, 234; **33**, 14, 23, 77n; **34**, 18n, 23; **35**, 123–4; **37**, 148, 151; **38**, 42; **40**, 75, 78–9; **42**, 68, 69, 88, 89, 90n; **46**, 13, 98; **48**, 31n, 33, 39–41; **50**, 247; **51**, 334; **52**, 185; **54**, 40; **55**, 199n, 201n, 205, 219n, 368; **58**, 61, 62; **59**, 363
Foure Severall Treatises (1577), **1**, 69
De Officiis, **4**, 83

INDEX

Cimarosa, **18**, 85
Cimino, Michael, **57**, 190
Cinthio, Geraldi (Giovanni Battista Giraldi), **1**, 63; **3**, 15, 55; **5**, 71, 72; **7**, 95; **10**, 98–9, 100, 101; **11**, 89; **20**, 166; **21**, 13–15, 16, 17, 19, 20, 24, 27n, 32, 33, 41, 50, 135; **27**, 172; **35**, 101–3, 108, 111; **37**, 119, 145; **39**, 150; **41**, 136n; **45**, 184; **47**, 140, 161, 164–9; **52**, 134; **53**, 9, 184, 190, 191; **60**, 349
Epitia, **7**, 104; **13**, 157
Hecatommithi, **7**, 103, 104; **13**, 88n
Cioni, Fernando, **40**, 205; **55**, 348
Cipolla, Carlo M., **24**, 47n
Cirillo, A. R., **26**, 154
Cirillo, L., **51**, 153n
Cirlot, J. E., **49**, 190n
Ciroma, Adam, **39**, 175
Citron, Pierre, **55**, 143n
City Match, **54**, 62–4
Ciubotariu, Constantin, **49**, 277
Ciulei, Liviu, **20**, 128–9
Civil Idolatry, **46**, 224
Civitas Londini, **1**, 28 ff.
Cixous, Hélène, **46**, 20; **53**, 325; **54**, 323
Claeys, P., **33**, 167
Claffey, Isabel, **58**, 264
Clair, Colin, **55**, 266, 267n
Clair, René, **18**, 73
Clairon (Claire Josèphe Hippolyte Léris de la Tude), **9**, 91
Clamp, Michael, **46**, 240
Clampitt, Amy, **41**, 109n
Clancy, Deirdre, **47**, 206
Clancy, Liam, **51**, 261
Clapp, Henry Austin, **9**, 68n; **35**, 7n
Clapp, Susannah, **60**, 209
Clapp, W. W. Jr., **18**, 117n
Clare, Janet, **38**, 85; **40**, 140n; **41**, 197, 217; **42**, 190; **44**, 229; **51**, 333; **56**, 335–6; **58**, 199
Clare, John, **58**, 113, 260
Clare, Robert, **42**, 152; **49**, 219n, 334; **52**, 325; **55**, 3n; **59**, 15n65
Clarendon, Earl of, **18**, 187; **20**, 30
Claretie, Jules, **9**, 62, 63, 64, 65, 66, 67n
Clariond, Aimé, **3**, 105; **5**, 111, 115
Clark, A. C., **55**, 266
Clark, Andrew, **38**, 249; **56**, 78n
Clark, Anthony, **41**, 187; **45**, 149; **52**, 248, 256; **56**, 279–80; **58**, 299
Clark, Arthur Melville, **2**, 60n; **6**, 74n; **36**, 174; **41**, 91n
Thomas Heywood, **14**, 12
Clark, C. R., **60**, 179
Clark, Charles, **59**, 40, 43
Clark, Cumberland, **6**, 33n; **8**, 7, 110, 111; **20**, 80; **60**, 117n65
Shakespeare and the Supernatural, **3**, 5
Clark, D. L., **6**, 156
Clark, David R., **20**, 166
Clark, G. N., **17**, 113n
Clark, Hannah, **60**, 293
Clark, Herbert H. **58**, 24
Clark, Ira, **51**, 29
Clark, J., **54**, 124n
Clark, J. M., **49**, 79n
Clark, Jonathan, **60**, 1, 15, 15n42, 15–16n44
Clark, Katerina, **40**, 78n
Clark, Sir Kenneth, **26**, 51
Clark, Kjeld, **53**, 262; **56**, 254
Clark, Max Stafford, **60**, 323
Clark, Peter, **54**, 290; **60**, 13, 13n39
Clark, Sandra, **39**, 231; **42**, 181; **50**, 93n
Clark, Simon, **49**, 274; **51**, 269
Clark, Stuart, **43**, 3n, 4n; **59**, 248n69
Clark, Tim, **44**, 197; **45**, 155
Clark, W. G., **19**, 1, 2
Clark, W. G. and Wright, W. Aldis, *see under* Shakespeare, editions
Clark, William, **55**, 388
Clark, William Andrews, **51**, 4
Clark, William George, **52**, 183n; **59**, 160n12
Clark, William Mark, **25**, 107
Clark, Wynne, **3**, 121, 129
Clarke, A. W. Hughes, **25**, 144n
Clarke, Cecil, **9**, 111
Clarke, Charles Cowden, **10**, 20, 25n; **14**, 145n; **19**, 9; **25**, 107; **32**, 17n, 25; **38**, 157n, 187; **41**, 105n
Clarke, Charles W., **6**, 163
Clarke, Charlotte, **51**, 3
Clarke, D. Waldo, **5**, 139
Clarke, George, **4**, 94; **23**, 126
Clarke, Helen Armstrong, **8**, 8; **55**, 391n; **59**, 57n22, 136–45
Clarke, Hugh, **58**, 237, 240
Clarke, Ian, **55**, 238n
Clarke, Jeremiah, **18**, 95
Clarke, Larry R., **45**, 168
Clarke, Laura Dunton, **59**, 340
Clarke, Mary Cowden, **4**, 3; **13**, 77; **32**, 15, 16; **38**, 157n, 187; **41**, 105n; **42**, 37, 47; **51**, 279; **53**, 92, 96; **56**, 127; **57**, 113
Clarke, Norma, **58**, 76
Clarke, Roger, actor, **1**, 28; **7**, 58, 59, 60, 63–4, 67n
Clarke, S., **60**, 11n31
Clarke, Samuel, **51**, 136
Clarke, Stanley, **55**, 332
Clarke, Steve, **53**, 274
Clarke, Thomas, **60**, 21
Clarke, William, **57**, 13
Clarkson, James, **56**, 297
Clary, Frank Nicholas, **53**, 344; **54**, 313; **57**, 343; **59**, 157n1, 174
Claude, Jean, **48**, 6n
Claude, Queen of France, **60**, 61, 70
Claudel, Paul, *L'Echange*, **14**, 119
Portage de Midi, **8**, 109
Soulier de Satin, **12**, 111
Claudian, **14**, 154; **15**, 100, 103, 106, 107, 109n; **55**, 202
Claudius Tiberius Nero, **13**, 121
Clausen, Christoph, **60**, 353, 356, 360; **57**, 313
Clausen, Claus, **13**, 128
Clausen, Iven, *Palace Revolution*, **3**, 114
Clavel, Maurice, **18**, 123
Clavell, John, **58**, 226, 234
Clay, Frederick, **41**, 24
Clay, William Keatinge, **32**, 164n; **54**, 122n; **57**, 241
(ed.), **17**, 48n
Clayton, Desmond, **44**, 195
Clayton, Professor F. W., **56**, 53; **57**, 209, 210, 212, 214, 217
Clayton, James, **54**, 58n
Clayton, Mr, **14**, 114

Clayton, Paul, **49**, 270
Clayton, Thomas, **21**, 134; **22**, 183; **24**, 155; **25**, 199; **28**, 161; **37**, 200n, 209, 217; **38**, 101, 251–2; **41**, 154–5; **42**, 211n; **45**, 80n; **46**, 61n, 254; **48**, 280; **49**, 27n, 43, 214n, 301; **51**, 331; **54**, 306; **59**, 14
Cleaver, Ralph, **52**, 25
Cleaver, Robert, **32**, 134n
Cleese, John, **38**, 240; **56**, 118, 119
Clegg, Cyndia Susan, **51**, 313, 321–2; **52**, 280; **54**, 90n, 91n, 95n; **56**, 217n, 354
Cleland, James, **50**, 66n, 69, 71, 72, 78–80
Cleland, John, **51**, 70
Clemen, Wolfgang H., **3**, 132; **4**, 18, 20, 127; **5**, 81, 92n, 112; **6**, 6, 11; **8**, 8, 68n, 112, 119, 143, 145; **9**, 14, 43n, 113, 137; **10**, 119, 137; **13**, 128–9; **14**, 147–8; **18**, 124, 175; **19**, 143; **20**, 130, 131n, 157; **21**, 7, 144; **22**, 151, 155; **23**, 113–14, 116, 141; **24**, 2n, 145; **26**, 151–2; **27**, 11n, 24n, 25n, 26n, 29n, 32n; **28**, 30, 31–2, 46n, 151n; **31**, 77; **32**, 224; **33**, 4; **34**, 6, 164; **37**, 14, 157; **38**, 7, 10; **42**, 174; **54**, 202n; **55**, 20–1; **58**, 31; **59**, 41, 195
  'Anticipation and Foreboding in Shakespeare's Early Histories', **6**, 25–35
  The Development of Shakespeare's Imagery, **14**, 163n; **16**, 46; **18**, 52, 54–5; **19**, 6, 45
  The Development of Shakespeare's Imagery reviewed, **6**, 150–1
  English Tragedy before Shakespeare, **12**, 70n; **20**, 49n
  Kommentar zu Shakespeares Richard III, **12**, 131 and n.
  'Shakespeare and the Modern World', **16**, 57–62
  Die Tragödie vor Shakespeare reviewed, **10**, 138, 144–5
  work on Shakespeare's imagery, **7**, 8–9
Clement XIV, Pope, **59**, 246n59
Clement, Dan Nicholas, monk, **16**, 53; **17**, 230
Clement, Pope, **54**, 44
Clements, John, **24**, 3n; **27**, 142
Clements, Mark, **50**, 232
Clemons, Harry, **35**, 80n
Clemons, W. H., **29**, 110, 111n
Clerck, Paul de, **60**, 243n32
Clerici, Fabrizio, **18**, 126
Clericus, J., **32**, 163n
Cletten, Gertrud, **22**, 121–2
Cletton, Raf, **22**, 121
Cleveton, **11**, 71
Cliff, Michelle, **49**, 294; **53**, 293
Clifford, Lady Anne, **7**, 140; **56**, 32; **59**, 381–2, 383
Clifford Family, **1**, 71
Clifford, Henry, Earl of Cumberland, **11**, 75; **17**, 29n
Clifford, James, **48**, 13
Clifford, John, **43**, 214; **46**, 195
Clifford, Peter, **23**, 43; **56**, 293
Clifford, Richard, **42**, 129
Clifton, Harry, **46**, 81; **58**, 222
Clifton, Thomas, **58**, 222
Clilverd, Rob, **47**, 211
Climbié, Victoria, **57**, 42
Clint, George, **51**, 118–19
Clinton, Hillary, **57**, 136
Clinton, William (Bill), **52**, 113–14; **57**, 136
Clissold, Roger, **42**, 155
Clitheroe, Margaret, **53**, 319–20; **60**, 357
Clive, John, **47**, 255n
Clive, Kitty, **18**, 63; **51**, 84–6
Clive, Lady Mary, **23**, 167
Clopper, Lawrence M., **47**, 46n; **60**, 19–20
Clopton, Joyce, **21**, 104
Clopton, Sir Hugh, **5**, 55, 56
Clopton, William, **17**, 126
Close, A. J., **24**, 158
Close, Del, **60**, 230
Close, Glenn, **45**, 61; **46**, 193
Closson, Herman, **13**, 125
Clothier, Richard, **57**, 265; **59**, 317, 318
Cloud, Random (McLeod, Randall) **51**, 332–3
Clough, Peter, **33**, 172
Clout, Martin, **52**, 2n
Cloutier, Suzanne, **60**, 167
Clowes, Richard, **36**, 82
Clowes, William, **17**, 25, 150, 154 and n., 158, 164
Clubb, Louis George, **22**, 167; **35**, 177; **40**, 107n; **44**, 239; **55**, 247n
Clubb, Louise, **52**, 276
Clucas, Stephen, **60**, 283n54
Clugston, George A., **55**, 24n
Clun, Walter, **58**, 241
Clunes, Alec, **1**, 115; **3**, 105; **5**, 119, 123, 126, 127; **6**, 138; **10**, 129; **11**, 132, 134; **36**, 82
Clunes, Martin, **45**, 147
Cluny, Alain, **13**, 127
Clurman, Harold, **18**, 160
Clute, John, **53**, 165n
Clutton-Brock, A., **4**, 24; **9**, 14
Clynes, J. R. **58**, 110, 112, 114
Coates, John, **33**, 191; **41**, 210
Coates, Simon, **50**, 217–18
Coates, Susan, **51**, 269
Coates, W., **15**, 7
Coats, Robert, **49**, 123
Cobb, Lee J., **40**, 40
Cobbett, William, **57**, 20
Cobbler of Canterbury, The, **15**, 72n
Cobham family, **3**, 27, 28; **25**, 110, 112; *also see* Brooke
Cobham, Lady Jane, **38**, 98
Cobham, Lord, **21**, 113; **25**, 174; **38**; **57**, 12, 238, 239, 333
  see Sir Henry Brooke, Sir John Brooke, Sir William Brooke, *and* Sir John Oldcastle
Cobham, Thomas, **35**, 50
Cobos, Juan, **39**, 43n, 44n, 50n
Cocayne, William, alderman, **17**, 12
Cochois, Mlle (actress), **60**, 215
Cochran, Jeanetta, **46**, 192, 198
Cochran, Peter, **53**, 161n
Cochrane, Claire, **47**, 91n; **48**, 264
  Shakespeare and the Birmingham Repertory Theatre, **48**, 265
Cochrane, Lydia G., **51**, 139n
Cocieru, Ion, **45**, 146
Cockayne, Oswald, **46**, 112n
Cockcroft, Robert, **58**, 322, 331
Cocke, John, **49**, 185n; **58**, 68, 221
Cockeram, Henry, **23**, 156; **50**, 197n; **52**, 187
Cockerell, Toby, **51**, 211; **53**, 245; **54**, 286
Cockerham, Harry, **48**, 4n
Cockpit Theatre, *see under* Theatres, Elizabethan
Cockshutt, John, **45**, 112

INDEX

Coco, William, **55**, 237n
Cocteau, Jean, **1**, 27; **34**, 3; **49**, 129
adaptation of *Romeo and Juliet*, **12**, 112
Coddon, Karin S., **45**, 166; **47**, 228; **49**, 309; **57**, 28, 34; **60**, 232, 236
Cody, Alan, **44**, 203; **48**, 236
Cody, Richard, **24**, 62; **29**, 91
Coe, Charles Norton, *Shakespeare's Villians*, **12**, 135 and n.
Coe, Peter, **12**, 121; **16**, 153, 154
Coecke, Michael, **60**, 246
Coecke van Aelst, Pieter, **60**, 246
Coertze, L. I., **1**, 112; **5**, 112
Coetzee, J. M., **48**, 50
Cœur de Lion, romance, **6**, 37
Coffey, Denise, **44**, 203; **59**, 204
Coffin, Hayden, **12**, 129n
Coffin, Martyn, **1**, 67
Coghill, Nevill, **3**, 141; **5**, 148; **7**, 107; **8**, 4, 8; **9**, 133, 136; **10**, 124, 136; **12**, 145; **16**, 38; **19**, 152, 162; **20**, 62, 72n, 153, 178; **21**, 134, 155, 161, 162; **22**, 8, 14n, 93–4, 98; **25**, 7, 40n; **26**, 127n; **27**, 82n; **28**, 86n; **29**, 7, 88n; **32**, 6, 8; **36**, 189; **37**, 5, 33n; **38**, 243; **39**, 137n; **41**, 37n, 65n; **46**, 88; **60**, 123n16
'Comic Form in *Measure for Measure*', **8**, 14–27
'Six Points of Stage-craft in *The Winter's Tale*', **11**, 31–41
Coghlan, Charles, **35**, 10
Coghlan, Michael, **45**, 155
Cogswell, Thomas, **54**, 136n
Cohan, Robert, **48**, 233
Cohen, Alan, **46**, 195; **47**, 209; **48**, 233
Cohen, Alexander, **5**, 116
Cohen, David, **56**, 8, 25n
Cohen, Derek, **35**, 153–4; **42**, 32n; **43**, 226; **44**, 238n; **47**, 223–4; **48**, 240; **53**, 290; **58**, 323, 331
The Politics of Shakespeare, **48**, 240
Cohen, Eileen, **34**, 69n; **25**, 184
Cohen, Erik, **50**, 32n
Cohen, G., **19**, 74n
Cohen, Israel, **54**, 182n, 184n, 186n, 188n
Cohen, J. M., **49**, 77n; **51**, 104n
Cohen, Marion, **37**, 219
Cohen, Marshall, **39**, 1n; **57**, 150
Cohen, Michael, **44**, 216; **49**, 269
Cohen, Nadya, **50**, 235
Cohen, Nicholas, **45**, 157; **53**, 283
Cohen, Ralph Alan, **50**, 226; **52**, 324; **53**, 331n; **55**, 194n, 195n
Cohen, Stephen, **55**, 339; **58**, 326, 331
Cohen, Walter, **37**, 186, 187; **42**, 163, 198n; **43**, 15n, 16, 240; **44**, 41n; **45**, 89; **48**, 126; **51**, 150, 158n; **55**, 5, 341–2
Cohn, Albert, **32**, 195, 196n, 197n; **33**, 153, 154, 155, 161; **36**, 138–9, 141n, 146n; **54**, 191n, 192n, 193n, 195n
Cohn, Ruby, **30**, 190; **36**, 23n; **45**, 3n; **55**, 140–1, 154n; **56**, 314; **57**, 112
Cohoon, J. W., **36**, 85n
Cokain, Aston, **12**, 142
Cokayne, G. D., **13**, 103n
Cokayne, G. E., **26**, 36n
Coke, Sir Edmund, **23**, 43–4
Coke, Sir Edward, **11**, 72, 73; **17**, 49, 80–1, 81n, 83, 85, 86, 112; **27**, 95n; **28**, 8, 64, 68; **29**, 95, 96, 98; **38**, 32–3; **42**, 193; **43**, 238; **49**, 183n; **51**, 166–7
Coke, Sir John, **44**, 231
Coke, Robert, 7th Earl of Leicester, **11**, 97n
Colas, Stella, **38**, 192–3
Colbert, Claudette, **54**, 312
Coldewey, John C., **30**, 196; **31**, 186–7; **42**, 184, 212–13
Coldwell, D. F. C., **53**, 20n
Coldwell, Joan, **29**, 177; **35**, 6n
Cole, B., **1**, 81
Cole, Douglas, **35**, 160; **36**, 95n; **49**, 63n
Cole, George Watson, **6**, 54, 55
Cole, Howard C., **20**, 153; **36**, 176–7; **49**, 181n, 196n
Cole, J., **49**, 197n
Cole, John William, **38**, 189n; **40**, 66n, 67n; **41**, 26, 31
Cole, Maria Jansson, **36**, 179
Cole, Miss, **51**, 85n
Cole, Richard, **45**, 154
Cole, Susan, **47**, 218
Cole, Toby, **49**, 158n; **57**, 60
Cole, Wendell, **35**, 14n
Colebrook, Claire, **58**, 172
Coleman, Beau, **52**, 279
Coleman, David, **52**, 157n
Coleman, John, **9**, 55, 58n; **16**, 104; **38**, 194; **53**, 309
Coleman, Peter, **9**, 121
Coleman, William S. E., **43**, 232
Colenso, Bishop, **54**, 80
Coleridge, E. H., **24**, 44
Coleridge, H. N., **45**, 116n
Coleridge, Hartley, **53**, 89, 90
Coleridge, Mrs H. N., **21**, 65n
Coleridge, Samuel Taylor, **2**, 19, 108, 109; **3**, 50; **4**, 1, 3, 144; **6**, 17, 87, 149; **7**, 1, 8, 129; **8**, 26n, 28, 110; **9**, 2, 3, 99; **10**, 39, 49n, 50, 98, 103, 104, 106n, 137; **11**, 59; **12**, 139, 149; **13**, 50, 62, 63, 151; **14**, 79, 83, 84, 85, 88n, 153; **15**, 22, 52, 53; **16**, 4, 33–4, 43, 158; **18**, 2, 5, 9, 38, 39, 50, 103, 104, 108, 109, 112, 113, 114, 117; **19**, 56, 65, 75, 139, 143; **20**, 86, 94n; **21**, 3, 4, 6, 24, 61, 74, 141; **22**, 151; **23**, 97, 101–11, 175; **24**, 6, 44, 127, 153; **25**, 45, 127, 128, 185, 187; **28**, 89; **29**, 87; **30**, 2, 88, 104; **31**, 62, 105, 111–12; **32**, 50n, 51n, 179, 181, 229; **34**, 9, 14, 21, 51–9, 93, 104; **35**, 33, 52, 98; **36**, 53; **37**, 185, 199; **38**, 161, 168; **39**, 139, 175, 215; **40**, 132, 185, 194, 200–1; **41**, 224; **42**, 15n, 113; **43**, 220; **44**, 217; **45**, 5, 6, 8, 10, 15, 16, 18, 75, 76n, 116; **47**, 107; **48**, 282; **49**, 9, 60, 61n, 63, 71, 282, 289; **50**, 101n, 102, 171, 180, 242, 268; **51**, 118; **52**, 275; **53**, 31, 81, 92, 292; **54**, 66n; **55**, 107, 337–8, 356; **56**, 113, 209; **57**, 88, 128; **58**, 10, 85, 93, 127; **59**, 153; **60**, 330
Coles, Jane, **55**, 197
Colet, John, **1**, 68; **17**, 53, 109; **44**, 250
Colet, Louise, **56**, 303
Colette, **3**, 104
Coletti, Teresa, **44**, 151n
Colgrave, Bertram, **41**, 156n
Colicos, John, **16**, 154
Colie, Rosalie L., **21**, 145; **28**, 149; **29**, 52n; **31**, 53n; **32**, 10; **36**, 48n, 104; **37**, 4, 72n; **38**, 162n, 163n, 166n; **40**, 109n, 124; **41**, 145n; **44**, 86n; **45**, 79, 81, 84, 196; **46**, 101, 102n; **55**, 59n
Collections, Vol. XV (Malone Society), **48**, 266
Collé, Charles, **24**, 84n, 85; **60**, 221n25
Collett, Nicholas, **46**, 161

Colletti, Lucio, **35**, 76n
Colley, John Scott, **28**, 163; **31**, 175; **51**, 163n, 164n
Colley, Linda, **48**, 60n; **51**, 2, 17, 20
Collick, John, **45**, 64n, 66, 67, 69; **47**, 62n
Collier, Constance, **1**, 92
Collier, J., **22**, 177
Collier, J. P., **1**, 1, 10, 18, 73, 83; **2**, 24, 32, 35n, 44, 148; **3**, 27, 53; **4**, 88; **5**, 2, 25, 46n; **6**, 58, 60, 63n, 162; **7**, 145
Collier, Jeremy, **46**, 138; **47**, 84, 257, 265n, 272; **56**, 107
Collier, John Dyer, **23**, 102
Collier, John Payne, **12**, 140; **14**, 83; **15**, 2; **16**, 32; **18**, 19–20, 109; **23**, 101–11; **25**, 185, 187, 200; **26**, 81, 82, 85; **29**, 136; **31**, 7n; **32**, 245; **37**, 217; **38**, 168n; **40**, 231; **42**, 186; **43**, 221; **44**, 152; **59**, 87, 88, 122, 125
Collier, Peter, **44**, 44n
Collinder, Björn, **14**, 123; **15**, 138; **16**, 137; **18**, 128; **24**, 162n
Collingbourne, William, **20**, 77
Collings, David, **41**, 191; **55**, 291
Collingwood, R. G., **20**, 27; **36**, 33; **48**, 69; **56**, 208n
Collini, Stefan, **53**, 174n; **56**, 209n, 210n, 211; **57**, 125
Collins, A. J., **4**, 74n
Collins, Arthur, **35**, 19; **38**, 90n
Collins, D. C., **2**, 52
Collins, Edward, **19**, 103
Collins, Forbes, **48**, 231
Collins, Garry, **55**, 331
Collins, H. E., **7**, 3
Collins, J. Churton, **4**, 9; **6**, 3; **7**, 51; **8**, 68n; **10**, 20; **15**, 40n
'Shakespeare as a Classical Scholar', **3**, 5
Collins, Jeffery, **19**, 103
Collins, Joseph B., **56**, 32n
Collins, Marie, **35**, 199
Collins, Michael, **51**, 284
Collins, Michael J., **49**, 284; **51**, 276; **56**, 317; **60**, 84n2
Collins, P. A. W., **12**, 139
Collins, Peter, **45**, 156; **54**, 285
Collins, Philip, **53**, 107n; **56**, 128n
Collins, Randall, **60**, 151
Collins, Rowland L., **19**, 162
Collins, Tom, **43**, 221
Collins, Wilkie, **38**, 190; **58**, 102
Collins, William, **14**, 78
Collinson, Patrick, **17**, 125n; **22**, 169; **40**, 212; **48**, 74n; **51**, 296; **52**, 60; **54**, 1, 7n, 59n, 72n, 123n, 166n, 169n, 170n, 172n; **56**, 28n; **60**, 2, 8n18, 11, 11–12n31, 13
Collinson, Richard, **32**, 88n
Collis, David, **41**, 185, 191; **42**, 159; **51**, 264
Collot d'Herbois, Jean Marie, **9**, 91
Colman, Diana, **18**, 121
Colman, E. A. M., **22**, 163; **32**, 100n, 103n; **33**, 190
Colman, George, **1**, 60; **25**, 192; **34**, 11; **36**, 180; **38**, 73; **51**, 19n, 121; **55**, 96; **57**, 87
Colman, George, the younger, **22**, 128
Colman, Walter, **40**, 215
Colombo, Maria Rosa, **34**, 70n
Colón Semenza, Gregory M., **57**, 316
Colonna, Francesco, **17**, 181
Colored Museum, The, **52**, 34
Colothus, **36**, 85n
Colquhoun, Christopher, **59**, 301
Colquhoun, Robert, **7**, 127; **13**, 79, 80
Colt, Alvin, **8**, 122
Colt-Hoare, Sir Richard, **3**, 55
Coltellacci, Giulio, **4**, 128; **6**, 121; **11**, 121
Colthorpe, Marion, **41**, 219
Coltrane, Robbie, **44**, 194
Columbia, Theatre Museum at, *see under* Libraries
Columbus, Christopher, **17**, 40, 164; **35**, 105
Columbus, Realdus, **48**, 26
Colverd, Susan, **46**, 200; **50**, 230
Colvin, Daniel, **53**, 213n
Colvin, H. M., **35**, 133n; **45**, 111n; **47**, 17, 18n
Colvin, Howard, **53**, 203n
Colvin, Sidney, **1**, 32, 36n; **31**, 15
Colynet, Antony, **38**, 50n 58n
Combe, Don Thomas, **28**, 166
Combe, John, **60**, 283; **57**, 234
Combe, Thomas, **17**, 182; **25**, 188; **29**, 34n
Combe, William, **3**, 35; **53**, 64, 67
Comber, Michael, **44**, 42n
Combes, John, **27**, 99
Combes, Thomas, **27**, 99
Combes, William, **27**, 99
Combre, **10**, 74
Comédie Française, *see under* Theatres
Comensoli, Viviana, **52**, 274
Comes, Natalis, **41**, 143n; **59**, 82n; **57**, 218
Comines, Philippe de, **17**, 65
Comins, Bea, **46**, 201
Comito, Terry, **36**, 170–1
Commedia dell'Arte, **1**, 8–9, 95; **3**, 85; **4**, 133; **7**, 98, 104
Common Law, suit relating to Queen Anne's Men, **7**, 61, 66
Common Prayer, Book of, *see* Book of Common Prayer
Comorovski, C., **29**, 166
Compagnie Mimodram (Georgia) **58**, 300
Companies of Actors, *see* Theatre, Elizabethan, companies
Companion to Shakespeare Studies, A, **4**, 9
Compass Theatre Company, **58**, 307
Complete Works of William Shakespeare, The, **44**, 203
Compton, Edward, **47**, 92
Compton, Fay, **3**, 114; **8**, 133, 134, 135; **9**, 18; **42**, 37
Compton, Lord, **44**, 249
Comte, Auguste, **16**, 30
Comte, Edward S. Le, *see* Le Comte
Conacher, D. J., **36**, 14n; **41**, 209n
Conacher, William, **45**, 156
Conan Doyle, Arthur, **60**, 223
Conati, Marcello, **57**, 65
Concentric Circles Company, **58**, 304
Condell, Henry, **1**, 38, 41, 42, 46; **2**, 31; **3**, 144, 147, 151; **4**, 56, 76, 159; **5**, 145; **7**, 1, 10, 24n, 46, 51, 53–4, 57, 59, 138; **8**, 90; **9**, 76, 155; **10**, 156, 157; **11**, 82, 151; **12**, 148; **13**, 166; **14**, 90, 97; **16**, 8; **18**, 11, 21, 102; **28**, 173, 177; **32**, 108; **33**, 81; **34**, 61; **36**, 174, 191; **37**, 75, 213; **38**, 91–2; **39**, 250; **40**, 231; **41**, 229; **42**, 17, 24, 63; **43**, 43; **44**, 114; **45**, 113; **47**, 175, 240; **48**, 28; **49**, 40, 323; **52**, 76, 82, 144, 306, 320, 322; **53**, 342; **54**, 67; **55**, 264; **56**, 60, 61, 354; **57**, 224; **58**, 10, 74, 237; **59**, 9, 25, 25n26, 27, 382; **60**, 266, 268–9, 270, 277–8, 281, 336, 368–9
Condon, Kerry, **55**, 297, 300
Condron, Aidan, **58**, 264
Conejero, Manuel Angel, **38**, 234

Conger, G. P., **19**, 43n
Congia, Vittorio, **14**, 121
Congress, Library of, *see under* Libraries
Congreve, William, **3**, 45; **4**, 104; **8**, 68, 131; **14**, 78; **17**, 49; **24**, 43; **45**, 58; **47**, 259; **49**, 41; **53**, 5
Coningsby, Sir Thomas, **38**, 49n
Conkie, Rob, **59**, 343; **60**, 154–69, 169
Conklin, Paul S., **18**, 34; **45**, 19n
History of 'Hamlet' Criticism, **2**, 138
Conlon, Declan, **47**, 211; **53**, 255; **54**, 272; **58**, 263
Conlon, Mary, **47**, 213
Conn, Shelley, **58**, 272
Connecticut, American Shakespeare Festival, **12**, 117, 118
Connell, Charles, **36**, 174
Connell, Norrey, **58**, 140, 142, 146
Connell, Norreys, **54**, 76
Connellan, Patrick, **52**, 256; **54**, 289; **56**, 279
Connelly, Maeve, **48**, 235
Connerton, Paul, **52**, 55n, 61, 62n
Connery, Jason, **48**, 235; **52**, 259
Connes, Georges, *Le mystère Shakespearien*, **2**, 118
Connick, Jill, **42**, 153
Connolly, S. J., **54**, 75n
Connor, Peter, **49**, 63n
Conolly, L. W., **48**, 55
Conolly, Patricia, **34**, 159; **39**, 182–3, 189
Conover, James H., **24**, 163
Conquest of Brute (Brute Greenshield), **11**, 49n
Conquest, Charlotte, **56**, 287; **60**, 320; **58**, 302, 306; **59**, 300, 342
Conrad, H., **8**, 4
Conrad, Joseph, **19**, 15; **26**, 8; **34**, 147; **45**, 12; **53**, 297; **54**, 78; **58**, 140
Conrad, Peter, **49**, 285; **53**, 111; **55**, 139–40, 147
Conroy, John, **43**, 211
Cons, Emma, **47**, 238
Consett, Henry, **49**, 192n
Considine, Mary, **50**, 234
Constable, Henry, **9**, 24; **10**, 141; **15**, 42
Sonnets to Diana, **6**, 88
Constantia of Styria, **36**, 145
Constantius, **15**, 94, 97n
Contarini, Gasparo, **11**, 143; **19**, 146; **26**, 172; **48**, 123–4, 125n, 126
Contention betweene the two famous houses Lancaster and Yorke, The Whole, **4**, 84; **5**, 52; **6**, 4–5; **7**, 91; **9**, 83
Contention betwixt the two famous houses of Yorke and Lancaster, The First Part of the, **3**, 23, 47; **4**, 7, 57, 58, 84, 160; **5**, 52; **6**, 4–5, 58, 169; **7**, 147, 148; **9**, 83, 154; **10**, 87n; **11**, 151; **14**, 165, 166; **16**, 173, 176; **20**, 162, 175; **54**, 13
Contested Will, **51**, 269
Conti, Gian Biagio, **40**, 74
Conti, Natalis, **31**, 47; **51**, 180n, 191
Contile, Luca, **17**, 183
Converted Robber, The, **15**, 172
Conville, David, **41**, 187
Conway, Alice, **37**, 189
Conway, Denis, **58**, 261
Conway, Edward (2nd Viscount Conway), **60**, 255–6n16
Conway, Frank, **43**, 216
Conway, Joe, **53**, 279
Conway, Lord, **2**, 24
Conway, Robert, **58**, 241
Conway, William Augustus, **46**, 237
Conybeare, F. C., **25**, 100n
Conyngham, Lady, **38**, 49n
Cook, A. M., **21**, 152
Cook, Albert, **32**, 57n
Cook, Ann Jennalie, **29**, 172; **36**, 170, 179; **40**, 205; **41**, 6, 7, 215; **42**, 39n; **43**, 240; **45**, 176–7; **46**, 69, 74n; **49**, 204n; **55**, 38n; **56**, 313
Cook, Caldwell, **10**, 108
Cook, Carol, **40**, 208; **46**, 7, 151n
Cook, Caroline, **58**, 84
Cook, D., **26**, 157
Cook, David, **11**, 115n; **18**, 169; **60**, 56n35, 56n37
'Timon of Athens', **16**, 83–94
Cook, Dutton, **35**, 7
Cook, Edward, **31**, 16n
Cook, Ginny, **58**, 84
Cook, Hardy M., **47**, 11n
Cook, Ivor R. W., **21**, 155n; **23**, 160
'William Hervey and Shakespeare's Sonnets', **21**, 97–106
Cook, John, **54**, 59n; **56**, 203n
Cook, Judith, **41**, 49; **49**, 136n; **55**, 273n
Cook, Kandis, **47**, 212; **48**, 234; **54**, 277
Cook, Miranda, **58**, 299
Cook, Pat, **56**, 289
Cook, Peter, **57**, 265
Cook, Ron, **39**, 106; **41**, 226; **46**, 180
Cooke, Abel, **11**, 103, 105n; **5**, 119
Cooke, Alexander, **58**, 230, 231, 237
Cooke, Alistair, **18**, 133; **33**, 181; **39**, 81–2
Cooke, Clarenceux, **17**, 117
Cooke, Dominic, **57**, 259, 274, 275, 276; **58**, 287, 299; **59**, 312–13, 340; **60**, 320, 323
Cooke, Edward, **57**, 73, 74
Cooke, George Frederick, **18**, 104; **28**, 171; **35**, 8; **51**, 115, 116, 117–18
Cooke, John, *Epigrammes*, **4**, 87; **17**, 98, 206
Cooke, Juliet, **13**, 138
Cooke, Katherine, **26**, 167; **56**, 205, 206n
Cooke, Liz, **53**, 261, 281; **54**, 283
Cooke, Nigel, **59**, 320
Cooke, T. P., **38**, 189
Cooke, Thomas, **55**, 89; **60**, 21
Cooke, William, **51**, 58, 61n, 64; **53**, 292
Cookman, Anthony, **32**, 35
Cool, Jacob, **15**, 128
Coolidge, John S., **31**, 180; **51**, 170
Coomb, John, **5**, 55
Coomb, Judith, **5**, 55
Coomb, William, **5**, 55
Coon, R. H., **10**, 6
Cooney, Ray, **56**, 118
Cooper and Graham, printers, **59**, 113
Cooper, Adam, **55**, 331
Cooper, C., **36**, 137n
Cooper, C. H., *Annals of Cambridge*, **11**, 108
Cooper, Donald, **59**, 176
Cooper, Sir Duff, *Sergeant Shakespeare* reviewed, **4**, 149–50
Cooper, Helen, **42**, 160; **60**, 342–3; **58**, 328, 331
Cooper, J. R., **25**, 179

Cooper, James, **5**, 119
Cooper, James Fenimore, **60**, 330
Cooper, John, **55**, 86
Funeral Teares, **1**, 70
Cooper, Julie, **46**, 195
Cooper, Karen, **45**, 149
Cooper, Marilyn M., **38**, 240
Cooper, Miriam, **43**, 209
Cooper, Thomas, **19**, 86, 87; **26**, 112n; **32**, 89–90; **38**, 94; **42**, 26, 27, 58, 59, 61, 62; **43**, 5n; **54**, 40, 118; **55**, 25, 205; **56**, 58, 59; **58**, 111–12, 117; **59**, 165, 166; **60**, 356
Cooper, Thomas, bishop, **17**, 124
Cooper, Trevor, **57**, 237
Cooper, William, **25**, 147
Cooperman, Stanley, **20**, 148
Coopman, Hendrick, **5**, 110n
Coorens, Roger, **7**, 108
Coote, Edmund, **17**, 68–9
Cope, Jackson I., **55**, 4
Cope, Sir Walter, **38**, 51; **44**, 155
Copeau, Jean-Jacques, **2**, 121; **4**, 101; **7**, 108, 110; **8**, 118; **10**, 118; **12**, 112; **14**, 119; **15**, 133; **16**, 54; **18**, 123; **40**, 2; **41**, 57–60, 62; **47**, 83
productions of Shakespeare, **2**, 122–3
Copeland, Dolley, **13**, 93
Copeman, W. S. C., **17**, 258
Coperario, Giovanni, (*alias* John Cooper), **15**, 6
Copernicus, Nicolaus, **3**, 7; **4**, 14; **17**, 39, 65–6, 141–3; **20**, 3; **26**, 49; **29**, 85; **40**, 145; **42**, 208; **55**, 63
Copland, Murray, **20**, 158
Copland, R., *The Highway to the Spital-House*, **13**, 103
Copleston, F. C., **37**, 151n
Copley, Anthony, *Witts Fittes*, **13**, 158
Copley, J., **10**, 139; **20**, 158
Copley, Peter, **7**, 123; **49**, 229
Copley, Thomas, **54**, 231
Coppe, Abiezer, **44**, 79
Coppedge, Wendy, **22**, 158
Coppin, George Seth, **35**, 32, 35
Coppin, Johnny, **52**, 254; **53**, 279
Coppleston, F. S., **54**, 128n
Coprario, Giovanni, **3**, 56; **6**, 60
Coquelin, Constant, **59**, 287, 290, 294
Corballis, Richard P., **33**, 197; **35**, 178, 189–90; **36**, 21n; **38**, 231; **40**, 236
Corbet, Richard, **54**, 61
Corbett, J. S., **17**, 22n, 34n
Corbett, M., **43**, 149n, 155n, 158n, 160n, 162n; **50**, 152n
Corbett, Ronnie, **53**, 271
Corbier, Annie, **47**, 211
Corbin, Alain, **49**, 211
Corbin, John, **9**, 9; **55**, 122
Corbin, Peter, **43**, 270n; **46**, 225
Corble, Simon, **48**, 230; **52**, 260
Corder, Jim W., **21**, 152n, 156n
Corder, Michael, **54**, 291
Corderius, **22**, 168
Cordery, Richard, **52**, 248; **57**, 265, 294; **58**, 287; **59**, 314; **60**, 328
Cordier, Mathurin, **17**, 60
Cording, Alastair, **41**, 189; **48**, 231
Cordner, Michael, **48**, 245; **49**, 104n; **51**, 205–17, 276; **54**, 333; **56**, 167–83; **57**, 40, 342
Core, Rebecca, **55**, 325
Corelli, Marie, **51**, 141; **55**, 143
Coriden, James A., **49**, 184n
Corin, Fernand, **14**, 152; **15**, 173
Coriolan, Frei nach Shakespeare, **48**, 8
Coriolanus, Caius Martius, **38**, 115–17, 120, 122–6
Cork, Adam, **59**, 335
Cork, Sir Kenneth, **44**, 101
Corkin, William, **36**, 140
Corkine, William, *Ayres*, **3**, 56
Cormac, James, **41**, 185
Cormican, L. A., **5**, 142; **6**, 156; **7**, 5; **15**, 115
Corneille, Pierre, **5**, 111; **10**, 72; **20**, 11; **24**, 82; **31**, 2; **34**, 16; **35**, 24; **37**, 143; **56**, 162; **60**, 216, 218
Le Cid, **9**, 60
Cinna, **10**, 76n
Horace, **10**, 76n
Cornelis Drebbel ('Cornelius the Dutchman'), **2**, 29, 31
Cornelius Agrippa, **29**, 159
Cornell, Katharine, **2**, 130, 131; **6**, 141
Cornish, Charles J., **54**, 84n
Cornish, William, **17**, 195; **54**, 194
Cornwall, Barry (B. W. Procter), **5**, 101
Cornwall, Duke of (Henry), **55**, 44–5
Cornwallis, Sir Charles, **29**, 23, 24n
Cornwallis, Sir William, **28**, 39; **30**, 63
Cornwell, Charlotte, **31**, 148
Coronado, Celestino, **39**, 77; **45**, 63n, 67, 68, 69, 71
Corpus Christi College Library, Oxford, *see under* Libraries
Corpus Christi Plays, **59**, 364
Corrie, G. E., **48**, 72n
Corrigan, Beatrice, **24**, 161
Corrigan, Kevin, **57**, 187
Corrigan, Robert W., **49**, 164n; **58**, 132
Corrozet, Gilles, **1**, 63; **17**, 182, 187
Corson, Hiram, **59**, 140
Cortejôn, Clemente, **34**, 28n
Cortes, Hernendo, **51**, 184–5
Cortes, Martin, **17**, 28
Corti, Victor, **52**, 161n
Corum, Richard, **54**, 307
Corvin, John, **16**, 144
Corvinus, Antonius, **2**, 68, 69; **28**, 92
Corvo, Baron, *see* Rolfe, F. W.
Hadrian IV, **11**, 26
Coryat, Thomas, **2**, 30; **16**, 119; **30**, 201; **51**, 161n; **54**, 196n
Crudities, **5**, 72
Cosgrave, Frankie, **37**, 169
Cosgrove, S., **55**, 108n
Cosimo, Piero di, **1**, 26, 56; **15**, 19
Coslett, Philippa, **45**, 151
Cosmas Indicopleustes, monk, **17**, 38
Cosneau, E., **44**, 58n
Cossa, Frank, **40**, 224
Costa, C. D. N., **35**, 119n
Costello, Kevin, **45**, 152; **46**, 202
Costenoble, Carl Ludwig, **35**, 24–5
Costigan, Eduard, **53**, 2n
Costigan, George, **52**, 257; **57**, 287

Costume, *see* Theatre, Elizabethan
Cosway portrait of Shakespeare, *see under* Shakespeare, portraits
Cosyn Virginal Book, **3**, 56
Cotarelo y Mori, Emilio, **23**, 79n
Cotes, Richard, **58**, 356
Cotes, Thomas, **22**, 182
Cotgrave, Randle, **17**, 203; **47**, 23, 26; **52**, 125; **53**, 14; **56**, 40, 52; **57**, 218
Cotrubas, Ileana, **35**, 145
Cotta, John, **57**, 21
Cottam, Thomas and John, **17**, 126; **39**, 223; **53**, 317; **54**, 120
Cottis, David, **50**, 235; **54**, 287
Cotton, Alice, **49**, 194
Cotton, John, **2**, 24, 25, 26, 27
Cotton, Oliver, **43**, 174, 177, 180; **51**, 260; **56**, 259
Cotton, Sir Robert, **3**, 53; **11**, 115n; **28**, 170; **38**, 86
Cottrell, Beekman, W., **19**, 138
Cottrell, Grant, **45**, 155
Cottrell, John, **52**, 193
Couchman, G. C., **16**, 168
Coud, Cinal, **55**, 328
Coulette, Yvonne, **7**, 124; **38**, 207
Coulson, Jessie, **55**, 140n
Coulter, Cornelia, **8**, 2
Coulthard, Raymond, **48**, 235; **53**, 258–9, 268
Coulton, G. G., **60**, 76n19
Council, Norman, **27**, 160–1; **28**, 159; **38**, 80, 81n
Counter scuffle, The, **17**, 97
Coupland, Diana, **49**, 258–9
Courant, Kurt, **45**, 43n
Coursen, H. F., **52**, 276–7
Coursen, Herbert Randolph, **18**, 163; **23**, 149, 156, 169; **25**, 179; **26**, 157, 176n; **31**, 171; **38**, 4; **39**, 11; **40**, 192; **43**, 252; **46**, 239n; **47**, 7n, 232; **48**, 263; **49**, 306; **50**, 263; **55**, 383
Court Company, **58**, 299
Court of Chancery, **11**, 72, 73, 102, 103, 107; **12**, 95–106
Court of High Commission, **11**, 72, 109
Court of King's Bench, **11**, 101, 102
Court of Requests, **11**, 100, 101, 102
Court Performances, *see* Theatre, Elizabethan
Court, Mrs, of Stratford-upon-Avon, **14**, 112
Court, Nick, **60**, 315
Court, Richard, of Stratford-upon-Avon, **12**, 105n
Court, the (royal), **17**, 10–12
Court, Thomas, **1**, 80, 82
Courteaux, Willy, **18**, 120
Courtenay (Courtney), James, **21**, 97, 100
Courtenay, Margaret, **12**, 125; **43**, 185
Courtenay, Tom, **18**, 73; **39**, 76; **53**, 276; **54**, 249–50, 254, 286
Courthope, W. J., **6**, 2, 5
Courtier, Karen, **47**, 126n
Courtney, Charles, The Life, apprehension, arraignement, and execution of, **17**, 96n
Courtney, T. P., **6**, 1; **56**, 247
Courts of law, **17**, 7–8, 73–86, 116, 135
Courtyard Theatre Company, **58**, 307
Coury, Simon, **52**, 232; **58**, 262
Cousin, Geraldine, **39**, 235n; **40**, 222; **49**, 305; **52**, 163n
Cousins, A. D., **49**, 295
Couson, Herbert R., Jr, **22** 162
Couturier, Marcel A. J., *L'Ours brun*, **11**, 41n
Covarrubias Horozco, Sebastián de, **56**, 40, 41n
Covell, William, **17**, 128; **34**, 87
Polimanteia, **3**, 26, 54; **4**, 159
Coveney, Alan, **42**, 149
Coveney, Michael, **40**, 174; **52**, 317
Coventry Mystery Plays, **7**, 69–70; **8**, 109
Coventry, Lord, **2**, 24, 31
Coventry, Sir Thomas, **7**, 66
Coverdale, Miles, **1**, 68; **17**, 201, 221–2; **23**, 30; **32**, 134n; **34**, 185; **46**, 11n
Covington, Judy, **41**, 186
Cowan, Alan, **43**, 216
Coward, Sir Noël, **43**, 124; **44**, 195; **51**, 219; **57**, 264
Coward, Rosalind, **49**, 91n
Cowden Clarke, Charles, **55**, 108n, 111n, 112; **58**, 98, 102
Cowden Clarke, Mary, **53**, 110; **55**, 108n, 111n, 112; **58**, 95
Cowel, John, *Law Dictionary*, **11**, 72
Cowell, John, **28**, 65; **29**, 99n; **53**, 69
Cowie, Peter, **39**, 90n
Cowley, Abraham, **39**, 232; **44**, 136n; **50**, 165; **51**, 87; **55**, 268–9; **60**, 253, 267
Cowley, Richard, **1**, 46; **11**, 62; **35**, 87–8, 93, 98; **36**, 147; **42**, 204; **58**, 232
Cowley, William, *Naufragium Joculare*, **14**, 61
Cowling, G. H., **15**, 4; **19**, 104, 107n
Cowling, Jane, **55**, 377
Cownie, Tony, **51**, 225; **56**, 287; **57**, 296
Cowper, F. Cadogan, **37**, 51
Cowper, Francis, **53**, 200n
Cowper, Mary, **46**, 139n
Cowper, William, **54**, 46, 53, 54
Cox, Alan, **46**, 182
Cox, Alex, **44**, 65
Cox, Brian, **31**, 159–60; **41**, 169, 178, 180–1; **42**, 158, 159; **45**, 148, 153; **50**, 232; **56**, 247; **58**, 334
Cox, C. B., **39**, 96n; **40**, 82n
Cox, J. E., **53**, 204n
Cox, Jeffrey, **58**, 172
Cox, John, **43**, 45, 67n; **50**, 143n; **52**, 71n. 81n, 291–2, 304n
Cox, John D., **33**, 200; **38**, 138n; **39**, 221; **51**, 313; **54**, 57n; **55**, 28n, 393, 394–6; **58**, 354, 356
Cox, John F., **32**, 22n; **34**, 173; **56**, 169
Cox, Lee Sheridan, **18**, 160; **23**, 156; **29**, 67, 69; **33**, 132
Cox, Murray, **46**, 238; **48**, 120n; **49**, 308; **59**, 292, 292n41, 292n42, 292n43, 293n44, 293n45, 293n46, 293n47, 294n48, 294n49, 294n50, 294n51, 295n52, 295n53, 295n54, 296n56, 296n57, 296n60, 297n61; **60**, 42n22
Shakespeare comes to Broadmoor, 46, 238
Cox, Robert, **36**, 139; **56**, 121
Cox, Roger L., **21**, 133; **24**, 146; **30**, 185; **46**, 211
Cox, Samuel, **58**, 140
Cox, Reverend Thomas, **53**, 63
Cox, Virginia, **47**, 254
Coxcomb, The, **52**, 25–6, 28n
Coxe, H. O., **4**, 94
Coxe, William, **51**, 86n, 87n
Coy, Jonathan, **51**, 219
Coyle, Martin, **48**, 254; **54**, 308; **55**, 352
Coyne, J. Stirling, **58**, 140
This House to be Sold, **1**, 83
Coyne, Jonathan, **45**, 156; **54**, 252

Cozens, Hardy B., **49**, 185n, 198n
Cozorici, G., **20**, 126
Crabb, A. L., **4**, 31
Crabb, Sally, **42**, 153
Crabbe, George, **7**, 30
Cracherode, Revd, Clayton, **3**, 44, 47; **59**, 122n54
Cradock, John, **46**, 33
Craig, Alexander, *Amorous Songs*, **1**, 69
Craig, D. H., **40**, 37, 204
Craig, Edward Gordon, **14**, 118; **16**, 143; **18**, 67; **31**, 188; **32**, 19, 35n; **37**, 201; **38**, 236; **39**, 5; **52**, 162n; **55**, 138; **56**, 95, 96, 346
Craig, Edy, **53**, 328
Craig, Gordon, **1**, 11, 89; **2**, 5, 8, 10, 14; **8**, 77, 80; **9**, 17, **18**; **10**, 75; **23**, 174; **29**, 141, 142, 144, 176; **41**, 223; **43**, 113; **44**, 102; **45**, 66–8; **47**, 237; **48**, 187, 189; **54**, 142–6, 149, 151
Craig, Hardin, **2**, 134; **3**, 6, 21n, 24, 27, 29, 136, 146, 151–2; **4**, 5, 11, 14, 24, 37, 43, 147, 150; **5**, 43, 44, 140–1; **6**, 4, 8, 11, 156; **7**, 5, 6, 134–5; **8**, 5, 8, 111; **9**, 6, 45, 48n; **11**, 49n; **13**, 42, 47n; **14**, 11, 94; **16**, 155; **17**, 226; **19**, 8, 93n, 123n, 127, 147n; **20**, 49n, 59n; **23**, 141; **26**, 9, 111n; **27**, 96n, 106n; **28**, 40, 107n; **29**, 81, 82, 83n, 88; **30**, 47n; **32**, 158; **34**, 118; **40**, 81n; **44**, 205; **55**, 17, 18n; **59**, 3, 8n32, 81n9
  The Enchanted Glass, **3**, 7
  In Interpretation of Shakespeare, **2**, 133
  'Motivation in Shakespeare's Choice of Materials', **4**, 26–34
  'Trend of Shakespeare Scholarship', **2**, 107–14
  'Shakespeare's Bad Poetry', **1**, 51–6
  A New Look at Shakespeare's Quartos, **16**, reviewed, 176–7
Craig, Hugh, **50**, 186n; **54**, 333, 342; **56**, 310; **57**, 300
Craig, Leon Harold, **56**, 321
Craig, Martha, **35**, 79
Craig, Russell, **46**, 194; **49**, 255; **50**, 233
Craig, W. J., **18**, 20; **23**, 15n; **24**, 55n; **28**, 117n; **31**, 48n; **49**, 310; **59**, 2, 3, 151
Craigie, James, **21**, 48; **57**, 21
Craik, Katharine A. **58**, 26
Craik, T. W., **8**, 143; **24**, 163, 164; **27**, 191; **29**, 171, 177; **30**, 198; **32**, 50n, 64n, 74n; **33**, 147n; **34**, 196; **35**, 80; **39**, 215; **44**, 249–50; **49**, 310, 312–15; **50**, 65n; **51**, 214n; **52**, 6n, 130n; **56**, 174n; **59**, 52n9, 53–4, 57n22
  The Tudor Interlude, **14**, 4
Cranach, Lucas, **18**, 126; **36**, 170; **37**, 176
Cranach, Lucius, **25**, 103
Cranborne, Viscount, **38**, 51n
  see also Cecil, Sir Robert
Crane, D. E. L., **42**, 62n; **60**, 260n29
Crane, David, **52**, 317–19
Crane, Francis, **6**, 54
Crane, Hart, **22**, 55
Crane, Mary Thomas, **42**, 192; **52**, 280; **53**, 306; **60**, 234
Crane, Milton, **7**, 4; **8**, 68n; **9**, 136; **19**, 135; **41**, 78n; **44**, 20n; **52**, 120n
Crane, R. S., **10**, 98, 106n
Crane, Ralph, **1**, 128; **2**, 148; **3**, 29, 51, 52; **6**, 60; **7**, 35, 45; **11**, 82, 87n; **13**, 164; **17**, 209; **20**, 178; **22**, 178; **23**, 182, 183; **27**, 181, 184, 185; **32**, 108; **35**, 185; **36**, 107–20; **37**, 213; **38**, 253; **40**, 230; **41**, 98–9; **44**, 249; **45**, 195; **46**, 231, 242–3, 244n, 246–7; **48**, 266, 272–5; **50**, 282, 284; **52**, 72–3, 76, 322; **53**, 336; **54**, 19n; **55**, 258; **56**, 355; **58**, 233; **59**, 11–12, 16, 92, 93, 97n8, 98–9, 101, 101n14, 102, 103, 104, 105, 380
  transcription of plays, **4**, 91
Crane, William G., **53**, 13n
Cranefield, Paul F., **18**, 180n
Cranfield, G. A., **48**, 53n
Cranfield, Lionel, Earl of Middlesex, **8**, 107
Cranfill and Bruce, **17**, 41n
Cranfill, T. M., **29**, 167
Cranham, Kenneth, **43**, 211
Cranitch, Lorcan, **55**, 332
Cranko, John, **37**, 162
Cranley, Thomas, *Amanda; or the reformed whore*, **17**, 99 and n.
Cranmer, Thomas, **21**, 130; **23**, 79, 81, 162; **38**, 25; **48**, 40–1; **52**, 166–9, 170–2, 182; **54**, 2, 4, 5, 7, 242, 349; **55**, 54n; **59**, 249–50, 252n95; **60**, 118–22
Crashaw, Richard, **11**, 39; **39**, 232; **40**, 227
Crashaw, Thomas, **4**, 93
Crashaw, William, **54**, 231
Crast, Antonio, **7**, 112
Craven, Alan E., **26**, 183; **27**, 186; **29**, 182; **31**, 192; **33**, 206; **36**, 192; **39**, 240n; **47**, 271–2; **59**, 379
Craven, Babette, **29**, 177
Craven, Hawes, **49**, 126
Craven, Michael, **58**, 261
Craven, William Lord, **9**, 84
Crawford, Charles, **3**, 19; **42**, 127
Crawford, Cheryl, **1**, 112
Crawford, Dan, **52**, 263
Crawford, Earls of, *see* Lindsay, Alexander, James *and* David
Crawford, Jane, **22**, 183
Crawford, M. A., **55**, 144n
Crawford, Nicholas, **57**, 304, 305, 308
Crawford, Patricia, **49**, 303
Crawford, Richard, **49**, 270
Crawford, Robert, **59**, 355
Crawfurd, Sir Raymond, **17**, 161
Creaser, John, **45**, 195n
Creasy, Lois, **59**, 342
Creation Theatre Company, **58**, 306
Creed, Thomas, **54**, 94n
Creede, Thomas, printer, **8**, 90, 95–6; **9**, 152; **12**, 149; **25**, 79n; **30**, 210; **50**, 286n; **55**, 29, 30n
Creedy, A., **10**, 123
Creeth, Edmund, **31**, 169; **32**, 230
Creigh, Geoffrey, **23**, 161
Creighton, Charles, **17**, 258; **50**, 19n
Creizenach, Wilhelm M. A., **1**, 11; **7**, 143; **12**, 11; **14**, 1; **36**, 137–8; **39**, 143n
Crellin, David, **48**, 199; **59**, 209
Crerar, Don, **49**, 274
Crespo, José María Blanco, translation of *Hamlet*, **6**, 107–9
Cressonois, Lucien, **9**, 63, 67n
Cressy, David, **50**, 255; **51**, 295–6; **60**, 75n15, 224, 231
Creswell, Jill, **49**, 274
Creswell, Joseph, **29**, 21, 23, 24n, 32
Creswell, Thomas, **19**, 103
Creswick, W., **9**, 56
Cret, Paul Phillipe, **1**, 58
Crew, Francis, *The Shakespeare Newspaper*, **1**, 83
Crewe, Derek, **42**, 155

Crewe, Jonathan V., **40**, 221; **41**, 194, 196; **46**, 216; **48**, 75n; **50**, 254; **56**, 105n, 169
Crewe, Lord, **44**, 106
Crewe, Mrs, **59**, 122n54
Crews, F. C., **26**, 164n; **46**, 76n
Cribb, T. J., **36**, 169; **37**, 152
Crice, H. P., **44**, 215
Crichton-Browne, Sir James, **56**, 246n
Crick, Bernard, **44**, 57n
Crick, John, **32**, 11, 50n, 53n, 60n
Crick, Julia, **59**, 243, 243n31, 243n34
Crier, Andrew, **56**, 238
Crilly, David, **53**, 277; **55**, 323, 327, 328, 331
Crinkley, Richmond, **44**, 243
Crinò, Anna Maria, **5**, 131
Crisp, Quentin, **45**, 63n; **54**, 312
Crispin, Edmund, **50**, 101
Critchley, Simon, **55**, 73, 74n, 75n, 77n, 78, 79n
Croce, Benedetto, **1**, 14; **2**, 110, 111; **5**, 113; **7**, 5, 8, 10; **20**, 127; **58**, 172
Shakespeare, **3**, 130, 132
Crocker, Ben, **50**, 226; **53**, 280; **54**, 291; **55**, 328; **56**, 289; **57**, 296; **60**, 321
Crocker, Pennie, **56**, 293
Crockett, Bryan, **52**, 57n
Croft, Judith, **45**, 151
Croft, Michael, **12**, 119; **13**, 135; **14**, 126; **15**, 145; **18**, 120; **41**, 185
Croft, P. J., **38**, 109; **46**, 19n
Croft, Pauline, **58**, 20
Crofts, J. E. V., **3**, 29
Crofts, Mr, **11**, 113
Croll, Dona, **46**, 191; **51**, 238
Croll, Morris William, **7**, 4; **25**, 193; **33**, 80n
Croll, Oswald, **56**, 84n
Cromek, R. H., **13**, 75
Cromer, Martin, **22**, 168
Crompton, Michael, **49**, 271
Crompton, R., **30**, 69
Crompton, Richard, **46**, 252
Crompton, Richmal, **55**, 131
Cromwell, O., *Thomas Heywood*, **14**, 12
Cromwell, Oliver, **44**, 5
Cromwell, Sir Thomas (Earl of Essex), **17**, 18, 233–5, 237; **28**, 18, 20, 21, 26; **38**, 25; **43**, 54; **45**, 101; **52**, 171, 182; **54**, 8, 242; **60**, 118–22
Thomas Lord Cromwell, **17**, 212
Cron, Evelyn, **40**, 54
Cronin, Anthony, **55**, 157n
Cronin, Michael, **45**, 133; **52**, 229; **58**, 278
Cronin, Peter, **23**, 152; **26**, 162
Cronin, Richard, **56**, 151n
Crooke, Andrew, **43**, 155, 158
Crooke, Frederick, **10**, 130
Crooke, Helkiah, **46**, 114, 118; **48**, 26n; **50**, 73n; **53**, 298; **60**, 241n24
Cropp, Martin, **41**, 209n
Crosby, Joseph, **31**, 190–2; **32**, 241; **40**, 236
Cross, Brenda, **45**, 49n, 55n, 56n
Cross, F. L., **26**, 116n
Cross, Felix, **43**, 213
Cross, George C. **58**, 103
Cross, Gerald, **38**, 14
Cross, Michael, **49**, 275; **51**, 268
Cross, Richard, **48**, 55; **51**, 86
Crossan, Gerard, **48**, 235
Crosse, Gordon, **2**, 5, 6; **32**, 28, 32n; **35**, 2, 7; **36**, 79, 81n, 82, 84
Shakespearean Playgoing 1890–1952 reviewed, **8**, 152
Crosse, Nicholas, **58**, 233
Crosse, Samuel, **6**, 74n
Crosse-Hopkins Diary, The, **1**, 72
Crosswell, Chris, **41**, 188; **42**, 156; **44**, 201
Crotty, Derbhle, **51**, 244; **53**, 268; **54**, 288
Crouch, Anna Maria, **51**, 93
Crouch, J. H., **24**, 168; **26**, 176n
Crouch, Julian, **46**, 201; **52**, 260
Crouch, Mrs, **18**, 97, 98
Crouch, Tim, **47**, 214
Crow, Charles R., **20**, 160
'Chiding the Plays: Then Till Now', **18**, 1–10
Crow, John, **11**, 153; **13**, 146; **15**, 113; **17**, 69n, 210n; **25**, 151n; **29**, 7; **34**, 187–8; **42**, 91n; **50**, 153
Crow, Karen, **51**, 158; **52**, 255; **57**, 294, 297; **58**, 300, 303, 304
Crowden, Graham, **49**, 265
'Crowe sits upon the wall' (ballad), **3**, 54
Crowl, Samuel, **36**, 165; **38**, 18; **39**, 50n, 53n; **47**, 239n; **55**, 383; **56**, 347; **60**, 348, 355
Crowley, Bob, **38**, 202, 204; **39**, 200; **40**, 175; **51**, 249; **55**, 334
Crowley, Dermot, **33**, 180
Crowley, John, **53**, 254; **54**, 287
Crowley, Mart, **56**, 71n
Crowley, Richard C., **31**, 12n
Crowley, Robert, printer and Archdeacon of Hereford, **17**, 104–5; **41**, 170, 183, 186, 190; **42**, 152, 160; **43**, 176, 212, 254; **44**, 20, 187, 199; **45**, 140, 153; **46**, 193; **47**, 12, 118, 182–3, 211; **48**, 230; **52**, 130, 257; **53**, 62; **54**, 5
The Confutation etc., **1**, 70
Crowne, John, **43**, 172; **51**, 3
adaptation of *1* and *2 Henry VI*, **9**, 85n
Crowther, Bosley, **39**, 3; **49**, 157
Crowther, Leslie, **44**, 198
Crowther, Liz, **42**, 153; **43**, 216; **47**, 104
Crowther, William, Keeper of Newgate, **17**, 100
Croxford, Richard, **51**, 263
Croy, Kate, **44**, 41
Crozier, Eric, **1**, 109
Cruddas, Audrey, **9**, 123, 126
Cruden, Damian, **54**, 291; **56**, 294; **60**, 323
Crüger, Johannes, **33**, 159, 163n; **36**, 137n, 138n
Cruickshank, A. H., **11**, 52; **14**, 12
Cruickshank, George, **58**, 40
Cruickshank, Marty, **55**, 299, 300
Cruickshanks, Eveline, **51**, 51n, 55n
Cruikshank, C. G., **33**, 30n
Cruikshank, George, **12**, 14; **44**, 207
Cruikshank, Isaac, **38**, 72–3; **49**, 115
Crumley, J. Clinton, **56**, 321
Crump, Jeremy, **41**, 225
Crumrine, N. R., **55**, 249n
Crunelle-Vanrigh, Anny, **50**, 196n
Crupi, Charles, **23**, 165n
Crusius, Martin, **56**, 227

Crusoe, Robinson, **11**, 130
Crutcher, Bill, **44**, 193; **45**, 146
Crutchley, Rosalie, **1**, 100, 102
Cruttenden, Abigail, **41**, 189
Cruttenden, Alan, **56**, 182n
Cruttwell (of Bath), **18**, 18
Cruttwell, Patrick, **7**, 139; **15**, 16; **16**, 2–3, 163; **18**, 35; **19**, 123; **20**, 36, 40n; **24**, 154; **31**, 127, 130; **38**, 177–8; **44**, 232; **50**, 241
The Shakespearean Moment and its Place in the Poetry of the Seventeenth Century reviewed, **8**, 145
Crutwell, Greg, **44**, 193
Cruz, A. J., **48**, 137n
Cryer, Andrew, **48**, 201; **49**, 253; **56**, 251
Cryer, Bob, **59**, 314, 315
Crystal, Professor David, **56**, 248n; **59**, 376
Csengeri, Karen, **44**, 233
Cubeta, Paul M., **27**, 39n; **32**, 226
Cudworth, Charles, **19**, 151
Cuffe, Henry, **30**, 195; **58**, 222
Cuka, Frances, **59**, 309
Cukor, George, **39**, 2, 77; **49**, 153, 156
Culank, Jenny, **52**, 258
Culbert, T., **14**, 145n
Cullen, Jonathan, **58**, 229
Cullen, Max, **59**, 205
Cullen, Viscount, **17**, 12
Culler, Jonathan, **34**, 33; **53**, 18n, 308; **60**, 156n12
Cullerton, Jim, **50**, 233
Culliford, S. G., **11**, 105n
Cullor, Jonathan, **46**, 104n; **50**, 59n
Culmann, Leonhard, **18**, 176; **39**, 225
Cultural Aesthetics, **46**, 223
Cultural Exchange between European Nations during the Renaissance (ed. G. Sorelius and M. Srigley), **48**, 248
Culture and Politics in Early Stuart England (K. Sharpe and P. Lake), **48**, 257
Culture of Violence, The (F. Barker), **48**, 240
Culver, Roland, **41**, 50
Cumber, John, actor, **7**, 58, 66n, 67n
Cumberland, Earl of, *see under* Clifford, Henry
Cumberland, John, **53**, 216, 228–301
Cumberland, Richard, **32**, 23; **34**, 12, 18n; **51**, 21–2, 24–5; **57**, 61; **58**, 140
Cumming, Alan, **48**, 228; **56**, 4n
cummings, e. e., **28**, 177; **42**, 213
Cummings, R. M., **23**, 164
Cunchillos, Carnelo, **51**, 97n
Cunin, Marcel, **54**, 319
Cunliffe, Barry, **48**, 113n
Cunliffe, Emma, **57**, 268; **60**, 320
Cunliffe, John W., **6**, 12; **8**, 3; **29**, 80; **49**, 79n; **50**, 81n
Early English Classical Tragedies, **14**, 7; **19**, 93n, 20, 17, 18, 19, 20, 21, 24n
Cunnar, Eugene R., **55**, 245n
Cunneen, Paddy, **42**, 157; **43**, 206, 215; **44**, 203; **45**, 146; **46**, 191; **47**, 216; **52**, 262; **53**, 280; **55**, 324
Cunningham, Sir David, **35**, 133
Cunningham, Dolora G., **9**, 139; **10**, 10; **14**, 11; **18**, 168; **43**, 230
Cunningham, F., **14**, 13, 87
Cunningham, Fiona, **48**, 234
Cunningham, Henry, **5**, 148; **19**, 1
Cunningham, J. S., **36**, 121n; **47**, 176n, 177
Cunningham, J. V., **5**, 133; **7**, 137; **9**, 11; **10**, 49n, 142; **15**, 27, 109n; **20**, 153; **34**, 95; **44**, 85n, 86n; **51**, 274–5
Woe or Wonder reviewed, **7**, 129–30
Cunningham, John, **48**, 58–60; **57**, 320
Cunningham, John E., **21**, 143
Cunningham, Karen, **44**, 238
Cunningham, Liam, **50**, 205–6
Cunningham, Neil, **41**, 187
Cunningham, Peter, **1**, 1, 11, 83
Accounts of the Revels at Court, **11**, 115n
Cunnington, C. W. and P., **53**, 201n; **56**, 58n
Cunnison, Ian, **55**, 40n
Cuny, Alain, **10**, 117, 118
Cupid's Cabinet Unlocked, **6**, 58
Cupper, Revd William, **4**, 159
Cura, Jose, **56**, 295
Curicke, Reinhold, **32**, 190
Curle, Walter, **32**, 104n
Curley, Michael J., **51**, 182n
Curling, Henry, **58**, 146
Curll, Edmund, **14**, 81
Curnow, Susan, **46**, 191
Curram, Kay, **59**, 335
Curran, Roland, **43**, 211
Curreli, Mario, **33**, 188n
Curren-Aquino, Deborah T., **43**, 231; **46**, 8
Currey, Anne, **42**, 153, 159
Currie, Emma, **43**, 214
Currie, Gregory, **53**, 95n
Curry, Jack, **60**, 144n13
Curry, John V., *Deception in Elizabethan Comedy*, reviewed, **11**, 136; **14**, 4
Curry, Julian, **52**, 240
Curry, Walter Clyde, **4**, 11; **19**, 4, 24n, 62, 75; **21**, 148; **28**, 117; **29**, 83; **54**, 228n
'Curtesse, Flaminio', **21**, 38
Curtin, Lucy, **46**, 196
Curtis, Anthony, **38**, 50n
Curtis, Ellis, **45**, 107
Curtis, J. R., **28**, 154
Curtis, Jean, **9**, 113
Curtis, M. H., **17**, 53–72, 57n, 63n; **54**, 170n; **56**, 55n, 56n
Curtis, Nela, **53**, 25n
Curtis, Richard, **56**, 117, 138
Curtis, Stephen, **52**, 261
Curtis, Tracy, **56**, 298
Curtius, Ernst Robert, **21**, 144; **32**, 99n; **40**, 124n, 125n
Curtius, Marcus, **38**, 115–16
Cusack sisters, **56**, 247
Cusack, Bridget, **25**, 184; **52**, 299
'Shakespeare and the Tune of the Time', **23**, 1–12
Cusack, Catherine, **51**, 224, 227; **52**, 259
Cusack, Cyril, **39**, 79n; **47**, 210
Cusack, Niall, **41**, 187
Cusack, Niamh, **41**, 189; **42**, 157, 199; **50**, 205–6; **51**, 257; **57**, 266; **58**, 302
Cusack, Sinead, **33**, 141–2; **34**, 150; **36**, 152; **37**, 167; **41**, 170, 186; **42**, 152; **43**, 254; **56**, 256, 282; **57**, 40, 42, 290, 330; **60**, 78, 79

Cushman, Charlotte, **1**, 72; **7**, 92; **18**, 104, 106; **32**, 35n; **42**, 199; **49**, 2, 14, 126; **56**, 134; **57**, 127, 128, 130, 136
Cushman, Mrs Victor N., **1**, 72
Cushman, Robert, **21**, 53, 57; **30**, 169; **36**, 154; **37**, 128n, 168, 170n; **47**, 6
Cushman, Susan, **7**, 92; **49**, 126
Cusick, Henry Ian, **53**, 255, 272
Cust, Lionel, **26**, 74n; **60**, 240n16, 245n36
Cust, Richard, **44**, 75
Custodio, Alvaro, **24**, 169; **25**, 183
Cuthbert, set designer, 1882, **49**, 126
Cutlack (a lost play), **7**, 85
Cutts, E. L., **32**, 109n
Cutts, John P., **11**, 63–4, 65–6, 146; **13**, 157, 161; **15**, 9, 40n, 167, 173; **18**, 160, 165–6, 186–7; **19**, 2, 106n, 152; **22**, 165; **23**, 155, 160; **24**, 141–2; **25**, 180; **29**, 2, 185; **30**, 148n; **32**, 242
  'An Unpublished Contemporary Setting of a Shakespeare Song', **9**, 86–9
  La Musiquc de Scene de la Troupe de Shakespeare, **14**, 152
  'New Findings with regard to the 1624 Protection List', **19**, 101–7
Cutts, Thomas, **25**, 144
Cuvelier, Éliane, **3**, 100; **37**, 194
Cuvier, Georges, **60**, 234
Cynthia's Revels, **50**, 58n
Cyvile and uncyvile life, **17**, 11
Czaplińnski, W., **36**, 147n
Czechoslovakia, *see also under* Slovakia
Czechoslovakia, report on Shakespeare in, **2**, 127; **5**, 111; **6**, 118–19; **7**, 109; **8**, 119; **9**, 111; **10**, 116–17; **11**, 118; **12**, 114; **13**, 126; **14**, 118; **16**, 133; **18**, 120–1
Czinner, Paul, **18**, 73; **39**, 2; **40**, 4; **49**, 153
'Education and Apprenticeship', **17**, 53–72

D., A., **5**, 139n
D., H., **4**, 147
Daalder, Joost, **48**, 28n
Daatter, Jehanne Thygis, **22**, 122
Daatter, Suenndtz, **22**, 122
Dabney, L. E., **15**, 97n
Daborne, Robert, **33**, 203; **37**, 217; **52**, 211; **59**, 10, 71, 75
  Dick of Devonshire, **3**, 52
  Nero, **3**, 52
  Poor Man's Comfort, **3**, 52
Däbritz, Fritz, **30**, 200
Dabydeen, David, **51**, 60, 62n; **56**, 155n; **60**, 167
Dacier, Anne, **58**, 72
Da Costa, Liz, **41**, 190; **44**, 193
Dacqmine, Jacques, **11**, 120
Dacres, Edward, **38**, 122
Da Cunha, Tristão, **20**, 122
Dadd, Joanna, **45**, 150
Dadd, Richard, **37**, 48, 50; **49**, 124, 125
D'Agato d'Ottavi, Stefania, **56**, 309
Daggett, Tim, **60**, 143
D'Agostino, Nemi, **18**, 126
Dahinten, Gisela, *Die Geisterszene in der Tragödie vor Shakespeare*, reviewed, **13**, 155–6
Dahl, Liisa, **24**, 177
Dahlin, Hans, **10**, 121; **12**, 116
Dahlstrom, Daniel O., **57**, 62
Daiches, David, **18**, 170; **27**, 54n; **29**, 183
Daigle, Lennet J., **36**, 169
Daileader, Celia R., **53**, 300; **54**, 13, 30; **60**, 159, 168n1.6, 330–1, 352
Daines, Simon, *Orthoepia Anglicana*, **7**, 35, 42
Dainville, F. de, **17**, 44n
Daish, Charles, **43**, 214
Daixi, Cheng, **45**, 89n
Dal, O., **39**, 83n
Dalberg, Wolfgang Heribert von, **14**, 151
Dalder, Joost, **57**, 122
Dale, Charles, **45**, 145
Dale, James, **32**, 32
Dale, Janet, **39**, 198
Dale, R. W., **54**, 87–8
Dale, Richard, **12**, 96–7, 100
Dale, Sam, **42**, 151
Dale, Thomas, **47**, 57
D'Alembert, Jean Le Rond, **9**, 93–4
d'Alençon, Duc, **42**, 2
Daley, A. Stuart, **38**, 224; **45**, 169
Dali, Salvador, **3**, 118; **44**, 177
Dallam, Thomas, **52**, 207n
Dallas, Meredith, **18**, 132
Dallaway, James, **41**, 113n
Dallmyer, Andrew, **42**, 154
da Longiano, Fausto, **56**, 43n
Dalrymple, David, **54**, 133n
Dalton, Timothy, **27**, 147, 150, 151; **40**, 169, 173, 181–3; **41**, 183, 189
Daly, A. Stewart, **44**, 209–10
Daly, Ann, **55**, 239n
Daly, Augustin, **7**, 29; **8**, 76; **25**, 113, 115–16; **32**, 18, 19, 21, 23n, 25n; **35**, 3, 10n, 12; **40**, 2; **46**, 9; **52**, 288; **60**, 77Fig.14
Daly, Peter M., **32**, 236; **43**, 246–7; **53**, 100
Daly, Peter-Hugo, **47**, 189
Dam, B. A. P. van, **9**, 5
Damant, D. G., **43**, 230
Damassa, J. E., **51**, 261
D'Ambrosi, Dario, **56**, 4n
Dambrowski, Stanislaw, **2**, 128; **3**, 118
Damer, Anne Seymour, **10**, 73
Damianakou, Voula, **58**, 209
Damiani, Luciano, **12**, 114
Damiani, Peter, **26**, 115
Damianov, Krassy, **49**, 273
D'Amico, Jack, **46**, 209; **52**, 204n; **56**, 317–18
Damirale, M. N., **5**, 51
Damler, Artus, **22**, 119–21, 123
Damlos-Kinzel, Christiane, **56**, 314, 317
Damon and Pithias (1571), **1**, 64
Dana, R. H., **18**, 103
Danbury, Marc, **51**, 261
Danby, John F., **2**, 142; **4**, 25, 55n, 142n, 147; **6**, 10; **7**, 135, 136, 137; **10**, 10, 59n; **22**, 62; **23**, 66n; **24**, 112, 155; **26**, 7; **27**, 22n, 31n; **29**, 4, 51n, 86; **31**, 48n; **33**, 5–8, 43n; **40**, 219; **42**, 198; **44**, 2n, 75
  Poets on Fortune's Hill, **14**, 12
  Poets on Fortune's Hill reviewed, **7**, 141

Danby, John F. (*cont.*)
Shakespeare's Doctrine of Nature, **13**, 18n, 47n
Shakespeare's Doctrine of Nature reviewed, **3**, 130, 134, 141n
Dance, Charles, **31**, 147; **44**, 164, 165, 192
Dance, George, **51**, 11
Danchin, Pierre, **51**, 3
Danckerts, Cornelis, **1**, 26
Dancy, Richard, **29**, 34, 35, 36, 37
Dandridge Sisters, The, **13**, 142
Dane, Clemence, **58**, 139, 141, 158
Dane, John, **57**, 292
Dane, Joseph, **50**, 283; **51**, 333
Dane, Rosanna, **42**, 155
Daneau, Lambert, **27**, 190
Danell, David, **60**, 97n36
Daneman, Paul, **9**, 124; **12**, 124; **18**, 70
Danes, Claire, **52**, 94–5, 264; **53**, 96
Danes, Joseph A., **59**, 122n53
Dangerfield, Gay, **5**, 124
Dangeville, Marie Anne Botot, **9**, 91
Daniel, Alexis, **52**, 244
Daniel, Carter A., **43**, 270n
Daniel, George, **1**, 59; **3**, 45; **38**, 86; **40**, 228; **53**, 216
Daniel, P. A., **8**, 98n, 155; **10**, 157; **13**, 48n; **14**, 158; **19**, 156–60; **21**, 16, 27n; **25**, 74n, 198; **44**, 195; **59**, 6
Daniel, Samuel, **1**, 62, 67; **5**, 139n; **6**, 9; **8**, 152; **9**, 24, 143n, 144; **11**, 102–3, 105n, 108, 116n; **13**, 158; **14**, 80, 145–6, 154; **15**, 42–6, 169; **16**, 169; **17**, 129, 183; **18**, 35; **19**, 1–3, 146; **20**, 81n; **21**, 145, 151; **22**, 152, 170; **23**, 74, 97, 166, 167n; **24**, 68; **26**, 33, 35, 39, 41, 43, 45, 47, 48, 107; **27**, 131; **28**, 3, 4, 171, 174; **29**, 4, 171, 174; **30**, 8; **31**, 183; **34**, 87; **35**, 133; **37**, 191; **41**, 87; **42**, 66, 184, 186, 198; **43**, 245; **44**, 6, 8; **45**, 197; **46**, 14n, 40, 41n; **49**, 299; **50**, 51; **51**, 135; **52**, 295; **55**, 263, 361, 368; **58**, 23, 24–6; **59**, 72; **60**, 66, 343
Civil Wars, **3**, 18, 26; **6**, 4, 35n; **10**, 145
Cleopatra, **7**, 145; **10**, 4, 145
its possible reference to Shakespeare's *Antony and Cleopatra*, **6**, 91–3
Complaint of Rosamond, **10**, 145; **20**, 89
Delia, **15**, 42–3, 45
Delia; Delia and Rosamund; Philotas, **1**, 70
Philotas, **11**, 103
The Queenes Arcadia, **4**, 95; **15**, 170
Syr P.S. his Astrophel and Stella, **3**, 54
Tethys Festival, **11**, 108, 116n
Works, **4**, 92
Daniell, David, **44**, 234–5; **54**, 11n, 44n; **55**, 210n, 211–12; **59**, 68n19, 249n76, 251n89
Daniell, Dieter, **41**, 202
Daniell, Gillian, **43**, 209
Daniell, Richard, **25**, 145
Daniels, Barry Vincent, **30**, 200
Daniels, Ben, **54**, 268, 271–2
Daniels, Maurice, **34**, 189; **47**, 6n
Daniels, Phil, **42**, 134; **55**, 319
Daniels, Ray, **44**, 192
Daniels, Robert L., **45**, 50n
Daniels, Ron, **33**, 171–3; **34**, 150–1, 153; **35**, 146–7, 149; **36**, 154; **37**, 172; **38**, 209, 211; **41**, 188; **42**, 156; **43**, 184, 194, 196, 202, 206; **45**, 116, 117, 125, 153; **48**, 120; **51**, 236–7; **52**, 244, 256; **53**, 309; **55**, 345; **56**, 5, 100; **59**, 294
Daniels, Roy, **42**, 159
Danielsson, B., **23**, 11n
d'Angelo, Carlo, **16**, 136
Danks, K. B., **9**, 136, 139; **17**, 92n
Dankworth, Jacqueline, **47**, 215
Dankworth, Johnny, **45**, 175; **59**, 359
Dannenberg, F., **15**, 17
Dannoville, Jacques, **57**, 119
Dans, Augustus Van, **4**, 155
Danson, Lawrence N., **27**, 160; **28**, 155; **29**, 163; **30**, 85n, 93n; **31**, 54n; **32**, 216; **37**, 58n, 195; **38**, 78, 230; **40**, 85n, 86n, 109, 136n; **41**, 202; **44**, 42n, 49n; **46**, 93n; **49**, 209n; **52**, 102–3; **54**, 309
Dante Alighieri, **4**, 28, 93; **6**, 152; **7**, 112; **8**, 4; **9**, 81, 97; **10**, 33; **21**, 81, 83, 128; **22**, 1, 146, 159, 162; **26**, 161; **28**, 31, 60; **29**, 80, 86; **31**, 174, 184; **33**, 99n; **39**, 160; **43**, 123; **45**, 115; **51**, 180n; **54**, 32; **55**, 21; **56**, 87; **59**, 225, 265
Convivio, **8**, 26n
La Divinia Commedia, **8**, 17; **13**, 70; **15**, 114, 143; **19**, 55, 64; **20**, 23
exposition of comedy, **8**, 17–18
Paradiso, **8**, 109
Danter, John, **3**, 145, 149; **4**, 158; **21**, 148; **24**, 176; **27**, 135–6; **32**, 106; **49**, 27, 28, 42, 318–19; **50**, 276; **54**, 94n; **55**, 30n
da Ponte, Lorenzo, **44**, 214
da Porto, Luigi, **49**, 45, 55
Danti, Vincenzo, **26**, 112n
Danyel, John, *Songs for the Lute*, **1**, 70
Danziger, Marlies K., **34**, 168
Daphinoff, Dimiter, **30**, 195
d'Aquili, Eugene D., **55**, 248
Darbyshire, Alfred, **41**, 23–5, 28–9, 34
Darcy, Robert, **58**, 310
Dare, Daphne, **24**, 120
Dares, Phrygius, **36**, 87n
D'Argens, Marquis, **23**, 173
Darie, Alexandru, **45**, 115, 134; **46**, 168, 169, 197; **47**, 215
Dariell, Richard, **29**, 33n
Dark Lady, **43**, 217
Dark, Gregory, **26**, 176n
Darley, George, **14**, 87; **52**, 212n
Darley, Sir Richard, **2**, 34
Darling, Lieut.-General Ralph, **22**, 126
Darlington, Benjamin, **55**, 291
Darlington, W. A., **2**, 10, 11; **22**, 144; **36**, 76
Darlow, T. H., **54**, 6
D'Arnaud, Baculard, **9**, 91; **24**, 85
Darnell, David, **52**, 307–9
Darnley, Henry Stuart, Lord, **9**, 12; **43**, 57
Darnley murder, **1**, 124–5
Darondeau's music for *Othello*, **3**, 100
Darrah, Kelly, **49**, 273
Darrell, John, **26**, 72; **42**, 94; **47**, 254
Darrow, Paul, **47**, 213
Dart, Paul, **44**, 200; **45**, 156; **51**, 227
Dart, Philip, **43**, 216
Dart, R. Thurston, **15**, 6, 7, 8, 9, 10
D'Artagnan, **11**, 119
Darwin, Charles, **18**, 52; **22**, 48; **48**, 119; **54**, 76, 80, 82–4; **55**, 130; **60**, 346
D'Ancenzo Studios, **1**, 59

INDEX

Dasgupta, Arun Kumar, **15**, 165; **21**, 134
Das Gupta, N. K., edition of *Othello* noted, **10**, 139
Das Gupta, R. K., **16**, 168
  'Milton on Shakespeare', **14**, 98–101
Dasent, J. R., **6**, 73n; **53**, 202n; **54**, 94n, 96n
Dasent, J. R. (ed.), **17**, 79n
Dash, Irene G., **26**, 192; **33**, 202, 210; **37**, 33n, 34; **42**, 1n, 32n; **46**, 3, 8, 151n; **51**, 280; **52**, 309; **53**, 343
Da Silva, Naoe Takei, **35**, 160
Dasté, Jean, **7**, 110; **10**, 118
Daste, M.-H., **41**, 58n
Daston, Lorraine J., **50**, 187n, 194n
Datta, K. S., **33**, 64n
da Todi, Jacopone, **56**, 37
Daubeny, Peter, **52**, 155, 157, 258
Daudet, Léon, *Le Voyage de Shakespeare*, **2**, 118
Daugherty, Dr Leo, **36**, 173; **54**, 237n; **60**, 281n50
D'Aulnoy, Marie-Catherine, **57**, 74
Dauphin, the French, **44**, 57–9
Dauphiné, James, **34**, 183
Daus, John, **40**, 47n
D'Avanzo, Mario L., **31**, 190
Davenant, Mrs, **3**, 10
Davenant (D'Avenant), Sir William, **1**, 33; **2**, 148; **3**, 45, 56; **4**, 80; **5**, 53, 148; **6**, 58; **7**, 1; **10**, 14; **11**, 111; **13**, 137–8, 145; **16**, 95, 181; **17**, 197, 198n; **18**, 47, 94; **19**, 58, 65; **20**, 76, 169; **22**, 57, 130, 182; **23**, 126, 173; **24**, 167, 169; **25**, 113; **26**, 81; **30**, 166, 167n, 198, 199; **32**, 38, 93; **34**, 186; **35**, 36, 47; **36**, 114n; **37**, 193; **40**, 222; **41**, 204; **42**, 137; **43**, 81–2, 89, 91, 93–9, 100n, 101–3, 105–6; **45**, 173; **46**, 143n, 237–8; **50**, 262; **51**, 69n, 80, 82, 83, 85n, 86–7, 89, 93, 309; **52**, 143, 148–9, 151–3, 155; **53**, 137n, 149, 171, 217, 323, 336; **54**, 199; **55**, 257–8, 263, 265; **56**, 118; **57**, 55, 56, 57, 58, 59, 60, 63, 65, 68, 69, 76, 83, 84, 326; **60**, 114–15, 214
Davenant's version, **16**, 181
  adaptation of *Macbeth*, **9**, 85n
  Britannia Triumphans, **1**, 33
  Brittania Triumphans, **11**, 111
  The Cruel Brother, **13**, 120
  The Cruelty of the Spaniards in Peru, **13**, 120
  The First Day's Entertainment, **13**, 120
  The Just Italian, **17**, 198n
  Luminalia, or the Festival of Light, **11**, 113
  The Man's the Master, **2**, 34
  The Rivals, **4**, 97
  The Siege of Rhodes, **13**, 120
  The Temple of Love, **11**, 111
  The Unfortunate Lovers, **13**, 120
Davenant–Dryden, *The Tempest*, **11**, 74
Davenport, A., **47**, 130n, 177n
Davenport, Arnold, **8**, 147
Davenport, Bromley, **9**, 19
Davenport, Edwin, **53**, 325
Davenport, Fanny, **32**, 20, 21n
Davenport, James, **56**, 185, 186, 189, 190, 201
Davenport, Johnny Lee, **48**, 234; **52**, 262
Davenport, Mary Ann, **49**, 123
Davenport, Millie, **39**, 40n
Davenport, Mrs, **14**, 111
Davenport, Nigel, **41**, 185
Davenport, Robert, **58**, 238
  A New Trick to Cheat the Devil, **13**, 120
  King John and Matilda, **20**, 162
  The City-Night-Cap, **5**, 142
Davenport, Thomas, *Drinking Academy*, **6**, 60
Davey, Gideon, **50**, 229
Davey, Sarah, **51**, 268; **56**, 297
Davey, Shaun, **45**, 155; **46**, 173; **47**, 219; **48**, 230, 236; **51**, 268; **52**, 266; **55**, 335
David, Alan, **31**, 147; **49**, 262; **51**, 239; **55**, 299; **56**, 97
David, Gerard, **6**, 59
David, Herbert, **56**, 170n
David, Jacques Louis, **10**, 37, 73
David, Jan, **60**, 103n5
David, John, **12**, 20n
David, King, **20**, 26n
David, Lloyd, **54**, 313
David, Richard, **4**, 67n; **5**, 144n; **6**, 148, 163n; **7**, 146n; **8**, 6; **9**, 147; **10**, 149; **11**, 128, 148; **12**, 129n, 136n, 145; **15**, 136; **18**, 181; **24**, 53, 55n; **25**, 4, 28, 29, 30; **26**, 176; **31**, 151; **32**, 105, 108; **33**, 59, 199; **34**, 156n; **35**, 12; **37**, 184; **38**, 17, 49n, 51n, 52n, 53; **41**, 52; **47**, 6n; **49**, 10n, 13; **51**, 142, 145; **56**, 181n
  'Actors and Scholars: A View of Shakespeare in the Modern Theatre', **12**, 76–87
  'Of an Age and for All Time: Shakespeare at Stratford', **25**, 161–70
  'Drams of Eale, A Review of Recent Productions', **10**, 126–34
  edition of *Love's Labour's Lost* reviewed, **6**, 168
  'Plays Pleasant and Plays Unpleasant', **8**, 132–8
  'Shakespeare's Comedies and the Modern Stage', **4**, 129–38
  'Shakespeare's History Plays: Epic or Drama?', **6**, 129–39
  'Shakespeare in the Waterloo Road', **5**, 121–8
  'The Tragic Curve: A Review of two Productions of *Macbeth*', **9**, 122–31
David, Terence, **52**, 255
Davidge, William, **47**, 67
Dàvidházi, Péter, **53**, 318–19; **54**, 46n, 48n
David-Lloyd, Gareth, **58**, 278; **60**, 322
Davidson, Clifford, **23**, 154; **24**, 163; **26**, 161; **37**, 193n; **41**, 195n, 208n; **43**, 247–8; **46**, 93n; **50**, 167; **52**, 59n; **57**, 236; **60**, 226n17
Davidson, F., **18**, 172; **19**, 137
Davidson, Levette J., **7**, 146n
Davidson, Peter J., **50**, 226; **51**, 298; **52**, 14n
Davidson, Revd Principal, **54**, 183n
Davie, Cedric Thorpe, **7**, 109
Davies, Acton, **57**, 255
Davies, Andrew, **56**, 295; **58**, 168; **60**, 165Fig.28
Davies, Anthony, **41**, 227; **43**, 251; **45**, 64; **49**, 153n, 159n, 308; **53**, 329; **55**, 383
Davies, Brenda, **39**, 86n
Davies, C. S. L., **48**, 70n
Davies, C. W., **13**, 151
Davies, Carl, **42**, 151
Davies, D. W., **21**, 42
Davies, Eleanor, **53**, 319
Davies, Geoffrey, **46**, 193; **47**, 211, 213; **53**, 276
Davies, Geraint Wyn, **40**, 156–7, 159; **46**, 193
Davies, Godfrey, **8**, 105n; **52**, 256
  'The Huntington Library', **6**, 53–63

Davies, Gwen Frangçon, **49**, 128
Davies, H. Neville, **35**, 6n; **39**, 230
Davies, Horton, **54**, 27n
Davies, Howard, **36**, 151–2; **37**, 170; **39**, 203; **41**, 67, 69, 71–2, 75–6, 190; **45**, 168; **48**, 265; **55**, 164n, 167; **60**, 67n18
Davies, Jane, **45**, 145
Davies, John, of Hereford, **48**, 285n; **56**, 34n, 60, 61n, 65n; **58**, 63; **60**, 351
Microcosmos, **3**, 54; **14**, 75n; **17**, 43
Davies, Lyndon, **42**, 139
Davies, Malcolm, **57**, 261, 275, 278, 284; **59**, 305, 313
Davies, Margaret C., **17**, 62n, 67
Davies, Meredith, **16**, 134
Davies, Michael, **53**, 25n
Davies, Miranda, **57**, 331
Davies, Natalie, **60**, 231n47
Davies, Norman, **32**, 137n
Davies, Oliver Ford, **57**, 292, 329, 331–2
Davies, Peter Marshall, **45**, 174; **55**, 174
Davies, R. Trevor, **19**, 67n
Davies, Richard, **38**, 99
notes on Shakespeare, **4**, 88
Davies, Robertson, **3**, 116; **6**, 118; **7**, 108; **8**, 5
Davies, Rosalind, **60**, 283n54
Davies, Rowena, **33**, 204
Davies, Rudi, **46**, 202
Davies, Ryland, **35**, 145
Davies, Sir John, **12**, 16; **15**, 103; **32**, 86n; **34**, 23; **40**, 79, 80; **44**, 69; **46**, 16n; **54**, 196; **57**, 206, 208;
A Contention betwixt a Wife, a Widow, and a Maid, **15**, 103
Epigrams, **17**, 130–2, 135
'Ignoto', **16**, 165
Epigrammes and Elegies, **8**, 107n
Hymnes of Astraea, **1**, 70
signature, **2**, 54
Orchestra, **11**, 60
Davies, Stevie, **60**, 126n23
Davies, Terry, **44**, 166, 192; **55**, 329
Davies, Thomas, **20**, 78; **34**, 14, 16n; **37**, 85n; **51**, 22n; **57**, 60, 61, 85
Davies, Timothy, **44**, 197; **49**, 255
Davies, W., **51**, 6n
Davies, Sir William Llewelyn, **17**, 100n
Davies, William Robertson, **42**, 99n
Davies-Prowles, Paul, **56**, 5n
Davis E., **12**, 133; **15**, 137
Davis, Alan, **5**, 119
Davis, Arthur G., **20**, 147; **33**, 11
Davis, Ashley M., **42**, 152, 162
Davis, Blevins, **4**, 124, 125
Davis, Buffy, **44**, 198
Davis, Carl, **43**, 215
Davis, Deirdre, **47**, 216
Davis, Geoffrey V., **55**, 272n
Davis, Herbert, **31**, 29n; **34**, 128n; **55**, 266n
Davis, J. M., **14**, 145
Davis, Jo Ann, **29**, 170
Davis, John, **17**, 31n
Davis, Lloyd, **48**, 259; **58**, 314, 331, 333; **60**, 343
Davis, Madison J., **58**, 358
Davis, Mary (Moll), **43**, 96, 98; **53**, 149n
Davis, Michael Justin, **41**, 220
Davis, Natalie Zemon, **42**, 50n; **46**, 18n, 107n, 131; **55**, 40, 193n
Davis, Norman, **24**, 159; **59**, 46
Davis, Philip, **50**, 239, 240, 251; **53**, 110n; **58**, 316
Davis, Richard, **4**, 82
Davis, Stringer, **47**, 95
Davis, Tom, **35**, 184n
Davis, Walter R., **23**, 164n; **32**, 50n, 51n, 60n, 61n; **39**, 131n
Davison, Belinda, **43**, 214; **51**, 207; **52**, 222, 226.
Davison, Frances, **57**, 204
Davison, Francis, **3**, 52; **15**, 102, 109n; **42**, 184
Davison, Jules, **43**, 211
Davison, Peter, **51**, 171, 312–14; **55**, 160n, 164n, 381; **56**, 316
Davison, Peter H., **19**, 147; **22**, 179; **25**, 191; **26**, 35n, 38n, 180; **27**, 181; **31**, 192; **32**, 238–41; **33**, 206; **35**, 237
Davison, Peter J., **46**, 191; **49**, 210n, 239, 331–2, 334
Davison, Secretary, **1**, 125
D'Avray, D. L., **33**, 204
Davril, R., *Le Drame de John Ford*, **14**, 12
Davy, John, **17**, 230
Davy, Sarah, **49**, 303
Davy, Sir Humphrey, **23**, 103, 105
Daw, Carl P., Jr, **23**, 169
Daw, Sir John, **50**, 71
Dawe, George, **49**, 123
Dawes, James, **49**, 794
Dawes, Robert, **37**, 183
Dawison, Bogumil, **24**, 100; **42**, 199; **48**, 10
Dawkins, Peter, **46**, 200
Daws, Nick, **53**, 320
Dawson, Anthony B., **37**, 66n; **43**, 17n; **50**, 262; **52**, 62n; **54**, 132n, 314–15; **56**, 99n; **57**, 342; **58**, 43, 351, 357; **59**, 22n11, 27n33, 31, 35n73, 36; **60**, 355
Dawson, George, **7**, 90, 92–3, 94; **18**, 20
Dawson, Giles E., **1**, 73; **4**, 162; **6**, 171; **7**, 91, 146n; **10**, 88n; **14**, 151; **18**, 15, 16; **25**, 200; **27**, 93, 134n; **31**, 193, 196; **37**, 215n; **38**, 14n; **41**, 20n; **47**, 45, 46n, 49n; **52**, 4n; **55**, 259
'Copyright of Shakespeare's Dramatic Works' reviewed, **1**, 130
'Three Shakespeare Piracies in the Eighteenth Century', **3**, 152
Dawson, J. P., **29**, 96n
Dawson, R. MacG., **41**, 221
Day, Angel, *The English Secretarie*, **1**, 70
Day, Angela, **50**, 76
Day, Barry, **51**, 215n; **52**, 8n, 10n
Day, C. L., **15**, 7
Day, John, printer, **17**, 205, 208
Day, John, **3**, 45; **15**, 169, 180; **18**, 188; **25**, 138, 149; **29**, 23; **34**, 190; **38**, 253; **42**, 212; **43**, 131n; **49**, 101; **55**, 375, 378; **59**, 71, 72, 73, 74, 75, 77
The Blind Beggar of Bednall Green, **14**, 6
Dead Man's Fortune, **3**, 52
An Humourous Day's Mirth, **12**, 20
The Isle of Gulls, **11**, 103
The Parliament of Bees (MS.), **3**, 52
Peregrinatio Scholastica (MS.), **3**, 52
Day, Moira, **50**, 36n
Day, Nicholas, **51**, 237
Day, Richard Digby, **44**, 198
Day, Simon, **57**, 262
Day, William, Keeper of Newgate, **17**, 94

Day-Lewis, Daniel, **43**, 195; **44**, 193
Day-Lewis, Sean, **47**, 9, 10n
Dayolle, Victoria d'Ayola, **38**, 56
Dazai, Osamu, **48**, 106
Dazhong, Lu, **45**, 89n
Dazzi, Gaultiero, **49**, 280; **52**, 259
Deacon, Brian **42**, 157
de Acuna, Hernando, **54**, 92n
Dead Man's Fortune, The, **12**, 48
'Shakespeare in the Opera House', **18**, 75–93
Dead Poets Society, **52**, 290
Dead White Males, **51**, 269
de Almeida, Hermione, **45**, 39a
Dean, Antony, **41**, 188
Dean, Basil, **2**, 11; **35**, 2; **55**, 129
Dean, James, **52**, 94
Dean, Jimmy, **57**, 156
Dean, John, **31**, 183; **33**, 197; **34**, 167; **39**, 126
Dean, Leonard F., **6**, 10; **7**, 133; **21**, 129n, 132, 142; **23**, 148; **31**, 9n; **32**, 68n; **38**, 2
Dean, Paul, **35**, 178; **36**, 66; **38**, 9, 230; **43**, 46n, 47, 48n, 49n, 55, 233; **46**, 219; **57**, 301
Dean, T. A., **37**, 52
Dean, Trevor, **52**, 297
Dean, Winton, **19**, 151; **20**, 179; **45**, 172; **53**, 172n
'Verdi's Otello; A Shakespearian Masterpiece', **21**, 87–96
Dean-Smith, Margaret, **15**, 8; **55**, 86n
Deane, Anthony C., **44**, 105n
Deane, Derek, **53**, 282; **56**, 296
Deane, Felicity, **55**, 305
Deane, Sarah, **46**, 199
Dear Mister Shakespeare, **51**, 270
Dearden, Ian, **48**, 229
Dearden, Julia, **59**, 309
Dearing, Vinton A., **36**, 114n
De Assis, Machado, **20**, 122
Death of a Salesman, **44**, 114
Death of Robert, Earl of Huntingdon, The, **50**, 287
Death of the Actor, The, **46**, 238
Deats, Sarah Munson, **50**, 42n
de Bagno, Roberta Guidi, **53**, 282
Debdale, Robert, **54**, 119
de Beauregard, Raphaëlle Costa, **46**, 213; **56**, 308
de Beauvais, Vincent, **8**, 4
definition of comedy, **8**, 17
Debenham and Hollingsworth, Messrs, **10**, 130
Debord, Guy, **52**, 199
de Borja, Inigo, **33**, 165
Deboucourt, Jean, **5**, 111
de Boys family, **8**, 7
de Boys, Jaques, **54**, 268
Debrett, J., **51**, 93
de Bry, J. T., and J. L., **48**, 44–6
de Bry, Theodor, **50**, 154; **53**, 201n
De Burgh, **32**, 135
Debussy, C., **18**, 75
A declaration of the causes moving the Queenes Maiestie to send a navy to the seas (1696) **17**, 34 and n.
De Calleja, F. Diego, **23**, 82
Decameron, The, **50**, 23
De Casibus, **54**, 309
De Caus, Isaac, **35**, 135n
De Cazalla, Augustín, **23**, 81
de Certeau, Michel, **49**, 301; **52**, 91n; **57**, 20, 21
Dechart, O, **54**, 140n
De Chastes, Monsieur, **49**, 328
Decker, Christopher, **53**, 105n; **58**, 316, 331
Declercq, Aimé, **8**, 118
De Cortesão, Maria da Sauda, **20**, 123
de Courtivron, Isabelle, **46**, 20n
de Critz, John, **38**, 228; **45**, 110
Decroisette, F., **52**, 129n
De Croy, Anne, **33**, 167n
De Croy, Dorothee, **33**, 167n
Dedalus, Stephen, **45**, 40; **58**, 121
Dedinac, M., **4**, 121
Dedinsky, M. M., **4**, 113, 116n
Dee, Janie, **60**, 325
Dee, Dr John, **3**, 18; **4**, 42; **17**, 28, 39 and n., 142, 144nn; **24**, 166; **29**, 158; **32**, 90n; **43**, 4, 238; **44**, 232; **45**, 72; **54**, 228n
Deegen, Annemarie, **33**, 153n
Deelman, Christian, **18**, 179; **46**, 143n
Deer, Evroy, **52**, 239
Deering, Richard, **13**, 107
Deering, Robert, **53**, 282–3
De Escalante, Bernadino, **32**, 90n
de Falla, Manuel, **45**, 173
De Feria, **54**, 126n
Defesch, Wilhelm, **51**, 84–6, 88–9, 91
Defoe, Daniel, **15**, 126; **19**, 23n; **22**, 175; **43**, 102–3; **50**, 21; **51**, 42, 70, 71; **53**, 165
editions of his work in the Huntington Library, **6**, 57
de Fontenay, M., **56**, 218
DeGangi, Marion, **51**, 276
de Gay, Jane, **52**, 279
Degbye, J., **2**, 27
De George, R. and F., **31**, 54n
de Gomara, Françisco López, **51**, 184
Degrada, Francesco, **39**, 233
De Granada, Luis, **32**, 235
de Grazia, Margreta, **33**, 192, 198; **36**, 170n; **43**, 1n; **44**, 223; **45**, 175–6, 179, 190, 192; **46**, 4, 36n, 37n, 39n, 41n, 138, 143; **47**, 246, 255, 258; **48**, 270–1; **49**, 306, 322; **50**, 58n, 141–2, 248, 273–4; **51**, 7, 67n, 125, 274, 289, 295, 321; **53**, 111n, 238n, 302; **54**, 322–5; **55**, 5–6, 250n; **56**, 39n, 204n; **59**, 17n69, 18n76, 20, 21, 31n51, 85n19, 108–9n3, 110n7, 110, 111, 114n27, 120n46, 124n1, 128, 148n4, 154n34, 257–8, 261, 381, 383; **60**, 168n1.7, 228, 233n57, 254–5
De Groot, H, **9**, 6
de Groot, J. H. **54**, 116n; **56**, 184n, 188n, 192n, 193n
De Groote, Beatrijs, **33**, 153n
Deguchi, Norio, **48**, 109–10
de Guevara, Antonio, **54**, 91
Deguileville, Guillaume, **23**, 168
D'Egville, **10**, 74
De Haven, Carter, **57**, 250
Dehler, Franz, **12**, 116
Dehn, Edmund, **41**, 189
Dehn, Paul, **9**, 133; **49**, 154
de Hoghton, Alexander, **53**, 317

Deighton, K, **29**, 110
Deimling, Hermann, **21**, 65n
Deinhardstein, Johann L., **4**, 127
Deistal, Edith, **39**, 76n
Deitchman, Elizabeth A., **56**, 348
de Jersey, Peter, **46**, 178; **53**, 257–8, 269; **54**, 293
de Jongh, Nicholas, **50**, 34; **60**, 205
de Keys, David, **51**, 263
Dekker, Thomas, **1**, 41, 70, 71; **3**, 15, 45, 50; **4**, 13, 29; **6**, 74n; **7**, 85, 142; **8**, 100; **12**, 144; **13**, 33, 103, 107; **14**, 6, 9, 12, 82, 83, 157, 159; **16**, 95–7, 159; **21**, 48, 112; **22**, 52, 72; **23**, 46, 48; **24**, 40, 163; **25**, 144, 147; **26**, 4, 35, 39, 41, 43, 47, 147, 168, 172; **27**, 176, 178; **28**, 134; **29**, 170; **31**, 33, 193; **32**, 93, 95; **33**, 57, 166, 168; **34**, 161; **35**, 185, 190; **36**, 143–3; **37**, 180, 215; **38**, 86n, 229, 253–4; **41**, 10, 39, 41, 60, 216; **42**, 187, 208n; **43**, 242; **44**, 21, 24, 235; **46**, 225; **47**, 24n, 32, 39, 40, 176, 249; **48**, 256, 266, 277; **49**, 40, 97–9, 101, 103, 106, 107n, 108–9, 303; **51**, 147n, 195n; **52**, 82, 123–5, 127–8, 215–16, 225; **53**, 307; **54**, 14, 18n, 27, 66, 67, 133, 301, 351, 357; **55**, 84–5, 350, 360, 369, 377; **56**, 101; **57**, 217, 233, 234, 333; **58**, 126; **59**, 2, 10, 44, 47, 71, 73, 74, 75, 213, 214, 217, 256, 377, 382; **60**, 105, 128–9, 330, 357
  and London prisons, **17**, 88, 91–2, 93n, 94n, 95–6, 98–9; 207, 208n, 212; **20**, 26n
  Bellman of London, The, **17**, 7
  editions in Huntington Library, **6**, 57
  Gull's Hornbook, The, **10**, 81, 84; **11**, 104
  Honest Whore, The, **3**, 29; **13**, 33, 36, 39n; **14**, 23
  Knight's Conjuring, A, **6**, 74n
  Lanthorne and Candle-Light, **1**, 70
  Old Fortunatus, **16**, 170
  Patient Grissil, **9**, 44, 47n, 48n; **17**, 208; **20**, 24
  Roaring Girl, The, **12**, 46
  Satiromastix, **1**, 41; **12**, 43, 45; **17**, 176
  Shoemakers' Holiday, The, **12**, 3, 41, 48; **14**, 165
  Sun's Darling, The (with Ford, John), **13**, 120
  Sir Thomas More (Dekker's hand in), **2**, 47, 51, 52, 59; **9**, 72, 143
  Wonderful Year, The, **4**, 155
Dekker, Thomas, and Webster, John, *Northwood Ho!*, **8**, 150; **17**, 45n, 94n, quoted 94
  Westward Ho!, **17**, 208; **18**, 35
de Kok, Ingrid, **55**, 274n
Delabastita, Dirk, **48**, 1n, 4n, 5n, 115n; **49**, 286; **58**, 313, 331
de la Boétie, Estienne, **56**, 44
de la Coles, Ufranke, **57**, 234
Delacroix, Eugène, **9**, 62, 65, 148; **13**, 78; **16**, 55; **18**, 126; **20**, 164; **21**, 79–86; **23**, 176; **38**, 234; **48**, 215–16; **49**, 125; **57**, 315
Delacroix, Ferdinand V. E., **45**, 2, 5
de la Cruz, Ramón, **54**, 153
De la Fuente, Constantino, **23**, 81n
de la Marche, Olivier, **54**, 92
de la Mare, Walter, **55**, 90
De Lamartine, A., **49**, 100
Delamere, Robert, **49**, 272; **59**, 320; **60**, 327
Delamotte, Guy, **59**, 343
Delane, Martin (Vicar of St Mary's, Warwick), **60**, 11
Delaney, Shelagh, **56**, 246
Delannoy, Marcel, **6**, 120
Delany, Paul, **31**, 178
de La Primaudaye, Pierre, **22**, 122; **27**, 45n; **29**, 82; **36**, 85n; **38**, 52, 56; **43**, 1n; **46**, 127n, 132n; **57**, 207
  The French Academie, **4**, 27
Delaram, F., engraving of James I, **1**, 32–3, 37n
  portrait of James I, **12**, 28; **13**, 101, 102
de la Ramée, Pierre, **43**, 152, 155
De L'Armessin, Nicolas, **23**, 165n
de la Tour, Frances, **43**, 189; **53**, 248; **54**, 283
Delattre, Floris, **16**, 54
  Shakespeare et la guerre, **2**, 120
de Lauretis, Teresa, **54**, 323
Delbrück, B., **23**, 28n
Delcampe, Armand, **50**, 29n
Del Carro, Emilio, **21**, 32, 38n
Delcourt, Marie, **59**, 228n4
Delehaye, Hippolyte, **54**, 103n
de Léon, **52**, 300
Deleuze, Gilles, **59**, 297,
Delgado, Maria, **59**, 203n28
Del Giudice, Filippo, **52**, 193–4
Delia Mirandola, Pico, **32**, 170n, 174
Delightful History of Celestina, **1**, 70
Delille, Maria Manuela, **30**, 189
Delitzsch, Frantz, **54**, 183, 188
Delius, Nicolaud, **44**, 110n; **5**, 39; **36**, 195; **53**, 2n
Delle Colonne, Guido, **36**, 87n
Deller, Richard, **45**, 108
Del Litto, V., **34**, 6n
Delmouzos, Alekos, **58**, 211
de Loier, Pierre, **57**, 25
Delon, Alain, **15**, 133
Deloney, Thomas, **15**, 34, 35, 40n; **17**, 224 and n; **28**, 55n, 56n; **60**, 75, 255–6
  The Gentle Craft, **5**, 80n; **12**, 141
  Thomas of Reading, **10**, 146
de Longueil, Christophe, **42**, 68
de Loo, Andreas, **42**, 81
De Lorraine, Charles, **38**, 50n, 53
  see Mayenne, Duc de
De Lorraine, Philippe Emmanuel, Duc de Mercoeur, **38**, 50n
Delort, Charles Edouard, **49**, 125
De Loutherborg, Philippe Jacques, **13**, 75; **29**, 176; **37**, 45–7; **49**, 118
Del Sarto, Andrea, **26**, 54; **28**, 143
De Luca, D. M., **28**, 154
De Luca, V. A., **30**, 188
De Luna, B. N., **21**, 145; **24**, 155; **27**, 178
Delve, David, **44**, 202; **52**, 266
DelVecchio, Doreen, **52**, 316; **59**, 223n38
Delvig, Baron Anton A., **5**, 99
De Madariaga, Salvador, *see* Madariaga, Salvador de
de Man, Paul, **40**, 126n; **43**, 63; **46**, 84n; **53**, 48; **54**, 139n
Demanez, Raoul, **7**, 108; **8**, 118
de Manian, Freund, **53**, 300
Demaray, John, **52**, 190; **54**, 322
Demarco, Richard, **44**, 196; **51**, 261
Demastes, William, **51**, 197n
Demay, Henry, **13**, 127
Demeger, Robert, **42**, 137–8; **45**, 133; **49**, 11; **50**, 204, 206; **55**, 327

De Mendonça, Barbara Heliodora C., **23**, 152
'*Othello*: a Tragedy Built on a Comic Structure', **21**, 31–8
De Mendoza, Juan González, **32**, 90n, 91–2
De Mere, Justin, **59**, 344
DeMille, Cecil B., **37**, 52
Demirel, Ziya, **9**, 116
Democritus, **40**, 80
DeMolen, Richard L., **28**, 170; **54**, 92n
de Molina, Tirso, **35**, 108; **51**, 164n
Demoor, Marysa, **40**, 215; **46**, 235
de Monstrelet, Enguerand, **42**, 27–30
De Montemayor, George, **22**, 168; **23**, 141; **27**, 131; **29**, 4
De Montespan, Mme, **22**, 19
de Moratín, Fernández, **54**, 153
de Morla, Francisco, **51**, 185
de Mornay, Philippe, **40**, 79; **54**, 95
Demosthenes, **48**, 33
Λόγοι ιέ (1597), **1**, 69
Dempsey, Charles, **50**, 63
Demster, Thomas, **54**, 138n
de Musset, Alfred, **21**, 81, 83–4; **33**, 197; **40**, 202; 45, 43
De Nagy, N. Christoph, **22**, 166
Denby, David, **53**, 89, 90
Dench, Dame Judy, **15**, 148; **16**, 144; **23**, 132, 134; **25**, 164, 167; **27**, 137–42; **29**, 73; **30**, 169, 172, 173, 176, 177, 179; **33**, 174; **34**, 8; **39**, 183; **40**, 223; **41**, 53, 177; **42**, 130, 132, 149; **43**, 183, 196, 212; **44**, 193, 194; **45**, 157; **46**, 185, 187; **47**, 5, 7, 210; **48**, 234; **50**, 149; **51**, 144; **52**, 322; **53**, 286; **55**, 293; **58**, 163, 164, 269–70, 271, 273, 298, 331, 347; **59**, 169–70; **60**, 317–18, 319
Dench, Jeffrey, **27**, 147, 149; **31**, 147–9; **33**, 172, 176
Deneuve, Catherine, **56**, 256
Dengle, Jak, **14**, 117
Denham, Henry, **54**, 92n
Denham, John, **55**, 86n, 265
Denham, Sir John, **42**, 187
Denincz, Jean, **7**, 110; **11**, 120
Deninx, Jean, **7**, 110
Denkinger, E. M., **19**, 107n
Denkinger, M. **1**, 8; **19**, 107n
Denmark, *see also under* Elsinore
Denmark, Christian IV, King of, **38**, 20
Denmark, report on Shakespeare in, **1**, 115; **2**, 128–9; **6**, 119
Denmark, Shakespeare and importance of Brandes, **3**, 107, 109
influence of Shakespeare, **3**
modern studies, **3**, 109–11
most popular plays, **3**, 113
the nineteenth century, **3**, 107–8
stage-productions, **3**, 112–14
translations, **3**, 111–12
Dennehy, Brian, **52**, 96n
Dennett, Dajiel, **51**, 155n
Dennett, Tyler, **60**, 116n60
Dennie, Joseph, **18**, 102, 108
Dennis, C. J., **49**, 60
Dennis, Carl, **25** 176; **28**, 162
Dennis, John, **10**, 28, 30, 38n; **18**, 2, 112; **21**, 67; **31**, 1, 3; **34**, 11; **37**, 147–8; **40**, 72n, 204; **42**, 181; **46**, 141; **49**, 290; **51**, 4, 5; **52**, 291; **55**, 97, 99n; **58**, 141
Dennis, Steve, **51**, 266
Dennison, Peter, **51**, 80n
Dennison, Phil, **51**, 262
Denny, **3**, 23
Denoon, Donald, **55**, 180n
Densher, Merton, **44**, 41
Dent, Alan, **39**, 3, 76n; **49**, 228
Dent, Edward J., **15**, 5, 7; **51**, 81n; **56**, 150n, 151n; **60**, 187n12
Dent, Kathryn, **59**, 382, 383
Dent, R. W., **19**, 136; **24**, 145, 162n; **33**, 204; **37**, 9; **39**, 225; **40**, 78n; **44**, 245; **46**, 61n; **49**, 51n, 102n; **55**, 23n
Dent, William, **38**, 70–3
Dentith, Simon, **49**, 70n
Denvil, **16**, 104
Denys, Christopher, **47**, 101, 104, 106
Denzinger, Henricus, **32**, 132n
de Oliviera Gomes, Aila, **55**, 392
de Ornellas, Kevin, **59**, 372
de Palma, Brian, **60**, 356
Depardieu, Gerard, **56**, 98, 256
de Pennaforte, Onestado, **55**, 331
de Pizan, Christine, **42**, 31n
De Plano Carpini, Johannes, **32**, 89n
Déprats, Jean-Michel, **49**, 280; **54**, 285; **55**, 392; **58**, 339; **59**, 114n56, 324, 328
de Prez, John, **43**, 217; **44**, 202
De Quincey, Thomas, **21**, 9; **30**, 188; **43**, 258–9
Der Bestrafte Brudermord, **11**, 148; **18**, 110, 191
Derby, Earl of, **21**, 153; **54**, 121; **56**, 242n
Derby, Earls of, *see under* Stanley, Edward, Ferdinando, Henry *and* William
Derby, William Stanley, 6th Earl of, **35**, 72, 75
Derby's Men, see Theatre, Elizabethan, Companies
Dereli, Hâmit, **18**, 130
de Réuck, Jenny, **53**, 304
Derin, Haldun, **7**, 116
Dering Manuscript of *Henry IV*, **1**, 61, 65
Dering, Sir Edward, **56**, 33, 351; **58**, 227, 236; **60**, 272n12
DeRitter, Jones, **51**, 75–6
De Ronsard, Pierre, **26**, 115n
de Rougemont, Denis, **25**, 95; **37**, 107n; **44**, 42, 43n; **55**, 355
Derrick, Kate, **44**, 200
Derrick, Patty S., **56**, 134n
Derricke, John, **17**, 201; **52**, 287
Derrida, Jacques, **37**, 164, 180; **39**, 147; **40**, 32, 186–90; **44**, 68, 219, 220; **46**, 82n, 86, 87, 124; **48**, 252; **50**, 126, 246; **52**, 300, 301; **53**, 24n, 40, 41n, 305, 325; **54**, 311, 323–4; **55**, 69, 272, 275, 284n, 341; **56**, 67, 91; **57**, 32, 33; **58**, 169, 176, 177, 181, 195, 197; **59**, 202, 353; **60**, '82–3, 345, 346
Derrington, Michael, **51**, 263
Derrit, Hilary, **45**, 148
Derry, T. K., **24**, 157
De Rueda y Cuebas, Juan, **23**, 82
Derwent, Clarence, **4**, 124
Desai, Anjana, **42**, 181
Desai, R. W., **34**, 172; **54**, 313; **57**, 320
Desailly, Jean, **10**, 118
De Sainte-Maure, Benoît, **36**, 87n
de St Maur, Nicolas, **51**, 138
de Salvo, Brian, **50**, 227
de Sandoval, Fray Prudencio, **52**, 205n
De Sant' Agata, Francesco, **26**, 112n

De Sant' Hierónimo, Fr. Miguel, **23**, 82
Descartes, René, **2**, 108; **4**, 30; **22**, 23; **24**, 97; **40**, 148; **48**, 161; **52**, 301
Discourse on Method, **2**, 107
Deschamps de Pas, L., **29**, 28
Deschamps, Eustache, **15**, 89
Deschamps, Jean, **13**, 128
Desdemona: A Play About a Handkerchief, **54**, 340
De Selincourt, Ernest, **10**, 25n; **27**, 96n; **32**, 73n; **44**, 109; **46**, 115n; **49**, 62n, 171n; **53**, 13n
Desens, Marliss C., **49**, 303, 304; **55**, 382; **56**, 313
Desgarcins, Mlle, **3**, 102
De Silva, Derek, **27**, 176
Desire and Anxiety: Circulation of Sexuality in Shakespearian Drama, **46**, 207
Des Jardins, Gregory, **37**, 189
Desmet, Christy, **46**, 8, 208; **47**, 225; **48**, 245; **49**, 203n, 208n; **51**, 150, 154n; **54**, 152n, 311; **56**, 157n
Desmond, J., **55**, 239n
Desmonde, William H., **15**, 115
Desné, R., **22**, 175n
de Sola Pinto, Vivian, **55**, 92n
de Sömögyi, Nick, **53**, 309–10; **55**, 390; **56**, 101n
de Sousa, Geraldo U., **54**, 228, 301; **60**, 348
de Souza, Edward, **50**, 212; **52**, 293
De Souza, Peter, **54**, 286
Dessen, Alan C., **22**, 172n; **25**, 182; **28**, 159; **30**, 38, 39; **31**, 59n; **33**, 47, 198; **35**, 172; **38**, 161n, 220, 238; **40**, 75n, 198; **41**, 4, 8n, 76n; **42**, 35n, 38n, 116–18; **46**, 21n; **49**, 23, 25, 27n, 171n, 300–1; **50**, 286; **51**, 285; **52**, 32n, 105n; **54**, 16n, 18n, 20n, 23n, 27n, 28, 36n, 306–7, 356; **55**, 24, 25n, 242; **56**, 5n, 19n; **57**, 328, 332; **59**, 55n16, 62, 182n1; **60**, 109n31
Dessoir, Louis, **24**, 100
d'Este, Isabella, **54**, 194, 198
De Stratford, John, **41**, 219
De Strycker, E., **29**, 30n
De Tervarent, Guy, **26**, 112n
Dethick, William, **1**, 61
Detienne, Marcel, **56**, 40–1
De Thou, Jacques-Auguste, **36**, 145
Det Lille Turneteater Company, **58**, 300
Detmer-Goebel, Emily, **52**, 279; **56**, 304; **60**, 84n2, 85
Detmold, George, **4**, 140n
De Tocqueville, A., **24**, 88
De Torres Naharro, Bartholomé, **23**, 79, 80, 81
de Torrijos, General José Maria, **54**, 82
Detre, Simon, **22**, 120–1, 123
Deubel, Volker, **25**, 190
Deutsch, B., **24**, 1n
Deutsch, Ernst, **12**, 113
Deutsch, Stephen, **42**, 160; **43**, 210
Deutschbein, Max, **2**, 126; **4**, 127; **5**, 112, 114; **10**, 9; **28**, 39n, 40n, 42
Deutsche Shakespeare-Gesellschaft, **2**, 126
De Valois, Marguérite, **38**, 52, 55
De Van, Gilles, **57**, 67
De Veer, Gerrit, **32**, 87
De Vega, Lope, **22**, 167; **24**, 169n
De Velasco, Juan, Duke of Frias, **33**, 163–4
De Velasco, Juan López, **23**, 80
Development of Shakespeare's Theatre, **46**, 231
Development of the Sonnet, An Introduction, The (M. Spiller), **48**, 253
de Vere, Edward, Earl of Oxford, **39**, 224; **54**, 90, 92, 94
Devereux, E. J., **23**, 162
Devereux, James A., **23**, 162
Devereux, Robert, First Earl of Essex, **1**, 39, 71, 127; **2**, 52–3, 145–6; **3**, 10, 25, 27, 28, 29, 30; **4**, 10, 156; **5**, 140; **7**, 105, 145
Devereux, Robert, Second Earl of, **6**, 1, 6–7, 160; **8**, 28; **9**, 12, 24, 25, 26, 27, 155; **11**, 72–3, 90, 96, 138, 145; **14**, 91–2, 102; **15**, 25, 173; **17**, 10–11, 34, 113 and n., 118, 127–8, 132; **31**, 99, 100, 104; **32**, 87n, 227; **38**, 19–22, 24, 52–3, 61; **43**, 235, 238, 240–1, 248; **46**, 12, 13n; **48**, 72, 124, 258; **49**, 184, 299; **54**, 98, 133, 355; **55**, 210–11, 213, 217, 257–8, 373
his son, Robin, **31**, 101
Devereux, Robert, Third Earl of Essex, **9**, 33n
Devil is an Ass, The, **48**, 206; **51**, 143; **54**, 13
Devil's Charter, The, **51**, 7, 143
De Vigny, Alfred, **20**, 164; **21**, 80; **30**, 200
De Vinck, Jose, **56**, 92n
Devine, George, **7**, 126, 127; **8**, 124, 125, 126, 1332, 136–8; **9**, 119, 120; **10**, 124; **12**, 86; **13**, 79, 80; **31**, 151
Devitt, Matthew, **44**, 201; **54**, 289
Devlin, C., **14**, 145; **54**, 119n
Devlin, Christopher, **48**, 72n; **57**, 233
Devlin, Diana, **34**, 180
Devlin, E. S., **53**, 252; **54**, 284; **55**, 324; **56**, 289, 290
Devlin, Joe, **55**, 325; **58**, 264, 265
Devlin, Terry, **48**, 234, 236
Devlin, William, **1**, 99, 102; **5**, 127; **6**, 124; **7**, 124; **58**, 42
De Vogüé, M., **52**, 191
Devon, Helen, **56**, 294
Devonshire, Duchess, **51**, 20n
Devonshire, Duke of (1790–1858), **3**, 45
see also under Libraries
Devonshire, Earl of (Henry Courtenay), **60**, 70
Devonshire, William Cavendish, 5th Duke of, **38**, 71
de Voragine, Jacobus, **33**, 99n; **54**, 103n
De Vos, Joseph, **40**, 215
Devrient, Emil, **38**, 193; **49**, 10, 11
Devrient, Ludwig, **35**, 25
de Vries, Jan Vredeman, **47**, 24
Devrim, Sirin, **15**, 139; **18**, 130
D'Ewes, Sir Simonds, **11**, 108
Dewhurst, Coleen, **18**, 132
De Wilde, G. J., **57**, 94
De Wilde, Samuel, **49**, 123
De Witt, Johannes, **1**, 23, 29; **28**, 127, 131; **29**, 129; **30**, 166, 169; **32**, 189, 191; **36**, 179; **41**, 1, 4, 10, 35–6, 41, 87; **42**, 190; **43**, 151–5, 149, 152; **44**, 231; **47**, 23, 29–42; **50**, 169; **51**, 143; **52**, 3–10, 14, 21; **53**, 233; **57**, 322
Swan Theatre drawing, **1**, 2, 5, 9, 23–4; **2**, 22; **3**, 83, 84, 88, 93, 114; **5**, 143; **6**, 160, 161; **7**, 75, 129, 143; **10**, 77; **11**, 146; **12**, 9, 11, 16, 25, 28, 29, 31, 32, 34, 35, 41, 42, 45, 46, 53, 144; **13**, 113, 119, 120; **15**, 172; **20**, 168
Dews, Peter, **12**, 120; **18**, 70; **41**, 185
Dexter, portrait of Shakespeare, *see under* Shakespeare, portraits
Dexter, John, **18**, 154; **33**, 178–80; **36**, 61n; **43**, 183, 207; **59**, 199n8

Dexter, Sally, **42**, 143; **43**, 216; **44**, 173, 182, 198, 202; **45**, 148, 156; **46**, 188, 189; **47**, 215; **52**, 289; **53**, 254; **54**, 287
Dexter, Simon, **44**, 198
Dezorry, Charles and Bachelet Th., *Dictionnaire général*, **7**, 97
D'Haen, Theo, **53**, 165n; **56**, 158n, 314
D'Heere, Lucas, **29**, 26
Dhirendra, **42**, 151; **43**, 214
D'Hulst, Lieven, **48**, 1n, 4n, 5, 115n
Diaghilev, Serge, **4**, 102; **47**, 93; **35**, 1
Diakonova, Nina, **52**, 285
Dialogue of Dives, The, **15**, 66
Diamond, Arlyn, **37**, 34n
Diamond, Gillian, **47**, 218
Diamond, Jeff, **51**, 223
Diamond, William, **37**, 150n
Diana, **11**, 44
Diar, Alice, **49**, 198
Diaz, Bernal, **51**, 185
Conquest of New Spain, **12**, 142
Diaz, Fenandez, José Ramón, **59**, 372
di Babele, La Zattera, **44**, 196
Dibbelt, Ulrike, **37**, 159
Dibdin, Charles, **18**, 96; **51**, 6
Dibdin, James, **57**, 126
Dibdin, Michael, **50**, 39
Dibelius, W., **10**, 2
Di Biase, Carmine, **49**, 293–4
Dibley, Janet, **42**, 159
DiCaprio, Leonardo, **52**, 88–98, 264; **53**, 96
Dick, Andy, **57**, 186
Dick, Jennifer, **59**, 340
Dick, Philip K., **53**, 164n, 171–2
Dick, Susan, **49**, 10n
Dickens, A. G., **43**, 67; **54**, 126n
Dickens, Charles, **1**, 84; **8**, 61; **14**, 112; **16**, 16; **18**, 7, 20; **22**, 2; **24**, 45; **36**, 149; **41**, 209; **47**, 240; **53**, 103–13; **55**, 143, 179; **56**, 99, 100n, 118, 127, 128; **58**, 44; **60**, 235
David Copperfield, **5**, 44
Dickens, Ian, **45**, 150; **46**, 201; **47**, 213; **48**, 227
Dickens, Mamie, **60**, 235n65
Dickenson, John, **15**, 97n
Dickenson, Nigel, **43**, 215
Dickey, Franklin M., **29**, 82, 83
Not Wisely But Too Well: Shakespeare's Love Tragedies, **12**, 135 and n.; 15, 21
Dickey, Stephen, **41**, 213; **52**, 128n; **60**, 102–17, 117n66
Dickins, Christopher, **44**, 200
Dickins, Richard, **20**, 81n
Dickinson, Albert, **48**, 24n
Dickinson, Desmond, **45**, 49
Dickinson, Emily, **24**, 104; **44**, 206, 241; **56**, 303
Dickinson, Hugh, **38**, 15, 150n
Dickinson, J. W., **18**, 162; **25**, 6n; **29**, 95
Dickinson, T. H., **9**, 110n
Dickmann, I., **32**, 190n
Dicksee, Thomas Francis, **49**, 125
Dickson, George B., **25**, 139, 140
Dickson, Mr and Mrs E. Hal, **49**, 125
Dickson, Judy, **47**, 99
Diconson, Thomas, **48**, 30n, 32n, 48n
Diconson, William, **48**, 31n
Dictionary of National Biography, **11**, 100
Diderot, Denis, **9**, 91, 94; **22**, 175; **24**, 85; **40**, 221; **55**, 55; **57**, 212, 213; **59**, 285–6, 287, 288, 289, 290, 292, 293, 295, 297; **60**, 215, 221n25, 222
Didion, Joan, **57**, 153, 154
Dido, Queen of Carthage, **50**, 43; **54**, 62
Dieckmann, Friedrich, **48**, 175
Diego de Estella, **56**, 194
Diehl, Huston, **51**, 293; **52**, 60n, 61n; **53**, 306; **54**, 60; **55**, 220n, 222n
Diels, Joris, **5**, 108
Dieste, Eduardo, **10**, 143
Dieterle, William, **18**, 73; **39**, 1, 2; **49**, 306
Dietrich, Julia C., **31**, 185
Dietrich, Margaret, **53**, 98–9
Dietrich, Marlene, **59**, 300
Dietrichstein, Franz von, Cardinal, **32**, 196; **36**, 145–6
Diffey, Carole T., **44**, 221
DiGangi, Mario, **47**, 229; **52**, 296
Digby, George, **24**, 110, 111, 113
Digby, Sir John, **16**, 119
Digby, Sir Kenelm, **4**, 93; **11**, 107; **17**, 209; **44**, 123n; **49**, 138n
'Diggers', the, **3**, 34, 41n
Digges, Dudley, **14**, 153; **44**, 77n, 232; **60**, 283
Digges, Leonard, **2**, 39, 40; **3**, 12, 140; **10**, 35; **16**, 118–20; **18**, 179; **20**, 95; **33**, 140, 143n; **38**, 250; **44**, 77n, 232; **46**, 238; **52**, 120–1; **57**, 233; **58**, 205; **59**, 277, 378n6; **60**, 283
Digges, Thomas Posthumus, **9**, 25; **14**, 153; **16**, 118; **17**, 141–3; **27**, 45n; **60**, 283
Stratioticos, **11**, 137
Dignam, Mark, **5**, 127; **12**, 128; **26**, 143, 144; **34**, 154; **39**, 202; **42**, 135
Dijke, Ko van, **18**, 127
Dilis, Jan, **5**, 107, 108; **40**, 215
Dilke, C. W., **13**, 66; **14**, 83
Dillane, Richard, **50**, 212; **60**, 292–3
Dillane, Stephen, **49**, 235, 237–8, 271; **60**, 324
Dilley, Glynn, **45**, 150
Dillon, Charles, **9**, 56; **11**, 124; **38**, 188n; **41**, 225
Dillon, George L., **50**, 227; **59**, 28n35
Dillon, Janette, **34**, 171, 183–4; **35**, 170; **48**, 269, 270, 279; **50**, 78n; **51**, 271–88, 291; **52**, 298; **54**, 330, 332–3; **60**, 58–60, 60n5, 67n18
Dillon, Lisa, **58**, 281
Dilnot, Alan, **46**, 248n
Dilthey, Wilhelm, **2**, 110
DiMatteo, Anthony, **51**, 191n
Dimon, Fotini, **42**, 151
Dindsdale, Reece, **59**, 209
Dinely, Henry, **17**, 118 and n.
Dines, Rebecca, **44**, 191
Dinesen, Isak, **43**, 110, 117–19; **60**, 349
Dingelstedt, F., **15**, 132
Dinshawe, Carolyn, **60**, 81n39
Dio Cassius, **6**, 93n, 140
Dio, Chrysostom, **36**, 85, 87, 95
Diodorus Siculus, **33**, 23; **47**, 26
Diogenes, **26**, 94; **32**, 236
Dionis-Bayer, Manuel, **53**, 275
Dionisotti, Paola, **32**, 202; **43**, 254; **46**, 81; **49**, 265; **60**, 78, 204–5
Dionysius of Halicarnassus, **10**, 74; **28**, 71–4; **30**, 193; **38**, 116

INDEX

Dioscorides, **17**, 159
di Pescara, Giulio, **54**, 91n
DiPietro, Cary, **59**, 150n13
Dipple, Elizabeth, **23**, 166
di Rauso, Margherita, **50**, 38
Dircks, P. T., **27**, 172
Direction for the English Traveller, A., **12**, 107
Di Salsa, Francisco Berio, **21**, 81, 84
Disher, M. Willson, **5**, 137, 138
Disney, Walt, **10**, 117; **13**, 142; **50**, 31–2; **54**, 311; **56**, 158
Disraeli, Benjamin, **45**, 99; **56**, 131, 242n
Disraeli, Isaac, **55**, 82, 90
Diss, Eileen, **35**, 151
Distiller, Natasha, **57**, 159; **60**, 332, 352
Dittersdorf, Karl Ditter von, **60**, 184
Diuguid, Nancy, **46**, 201
Diuzhev, Dmitry, **60**, 300Fig.51
Dives and Pauper, **1**, 67
Dixon, Andy, **52**, 262
Dixon, Joe, **43**, 211; **45**, 130; **47**, 209; **48**, 234; **57**, 285; **59**, 300, 304
Dixon, John, **29**, 34, 37
Dixon, Lake, **49**, 272; **50**, 231
Dixon, Luke, **44**, 200; **45**, 156; **51**, 267; **53**, 284
Dixon, P., **19**, 143
Dixon, Priscilla, **29**, 34, 37
Dixon, Rob, **41**, 186
Dixon, Russell, **41**, 185; **44**, 168
Dixon, Thomas, **2**, 24, 25, 26, 27, 32, 34
Dixon, Vivien, **41**, 187
Dixon, W. H., **23**, 101
Dixon, W. Macneile, **4**, 52; **20**, 160
Djivelegov, A., **54**, 148n; **55**, 148n
Djukić, T., **18**, 134
Dmytryk, Edward, **53**, 111
Doane, Mary Ann, **45**, 47; **52**, 88n
Dobb, Clifford, **19**, 148
'London's Prisons', **17**, 87–100
Dobb, Maurice, **35**, 66n
Dobbeck, Wilhelm, **10**, 150
Dobbins, Austin C., **31**, 180
Dobbs, Brian, **51**, 118n, 122n
Dobell, Linda, **42**, 155
Dobell, Percy J., **1**, 65
Dobie, Alan, **49**, 237; **51**, 248
Dobrée, Bonamy, **7**, 137; **8**, 39n; **11**, 136; **15**, 120; **25**, 2; **26**, 5; **34**, 141n, 142
Dobranski, Stephen, **52**, 280
Dobrzycki, Pawel, **51**, 246; **52**, 257
Dobšinský, P., **4**, 115n
Dobson, Anita, **60**, 321
Dobson, E. J., **23**, 11n; **49**, 38n
Dobson, Mark, **54**, 294
Dobson, Michael, **46**, 4, 139n, 143n; **47**, 256–8, **48**, 51n, 52n; **51**, 2, 9, 14, 18n, 19n, 22n, 46, 67n, 68, 77, 125, 128; **53**, 219, 220n, 238; **54**, 73n, 152n; **55**, 97n; **56**, 117–25, 182n, 205n, 256–86, 314; **58**, 72, 90, 138, 144, 145, 160, 268, 330, 331; **59**, 68n19; **60**, 154, 284
Dobson, Teresa, **52**, 279
Docherty, Stephen, **59**, 342
Dockar-Drysdale, Jonathan, **47**, 102
Dockray, Keith, **56**, 326
Doctor Faustus, **48**, 281, **50**, 48, 53n, 55n; **52**, 143, 298, 305; **54**, 13, 14, 228, 356
Dodar, Abd el, **11**, 91
Dodd, James William, **7**, 26; **49**, 118
Dodd, James, **51**, 107
Dodd, Ken, **56**, 95; **60**, 225, 230n41
Dodd, Kenneth M., **25**, 192
Dodd, Wayne, **22**, 161
Dodd, William, **34**, 15; **43**, 220; **44**, 46n; **45**, 105; **51**, 5, 15, 147–58; **53**, 75n, 80, 301, 311; **54**, 322; **55**, 108–9; **59**, 166
Dodds (Nowottny), W. M. T., **2**, 145; **25**, 5, 8; **28**, 48
'The Character of Angelo' reviewed, **1**, 120
Dodds, Madeleine Hope, **10**, 147; **32**, 153n; **48**, 70n, 79n
Dodds, Megan, **53**, 252
Dodds, Ruth, **48**, 70n, 79n
Dodge, Celia, **42**, 153, 156
Dodimead, David, **12**, 125
Dodin, Lev, **56**, 161; **60**, 313Fig.57, 312–13
Dodoens, Rembert, **56**, 41
Dods, Marcus, **48**, 74n
Dodsley, J., **51**, 6n
Dodsley, Robert, **14**, 81, 82, 83; **20**, 73n, 90, 120n; **32**, 94n; **38**, 131n; **46**, 225
Dodsworth, Martin, **40**, 211; **47**, 189
Dodsworth, Mike, **55**, 324
Doe, Paul, **24**, 158
Doebler, Betty Anne, **22**, 167; **28**, 158
Doebler, John, **18**, 173; **27**, 157; **28**, 162, 170; **29**, 159; **32**, 9, 236; **37**, 66, 194; **41**, 61n
'Orlando: Athlete of Virtue', **26**, 111–17
Doering, Tobias, **57**, 313
Doeselaer, Frans Van, **5**, 107
Doggart, Sebastian, **51**, 266
Doggett, Thomas, **52**, 99
Doh, Herman, **29**, 182
Doheny, Mrs E. L., **6**, 61
Doiashvili, David, **51**, 260
Doig, John, **35**, 178
Dolan, Frances E., **50**, 199n; **54**, 307; **55**, 193; **57**, 128, 315; **58**, 174
Dolan, John P., **44**, 61n
Dolan, Leo, **46**, 197; **47**, 215; **48**, 237; **49**, 269
Dolan, Monica, **48**, 208; **54**, 266, 292; **59**, 340; **60**, 323
Dolby, Thomas, **53**, 216, 228–30
Dolega, Ninka, **1**, 99, 102
Dollerup, Cay, **29**, 173; **30**, 202
Dollimore, Jonathan, **38**, 222; **39**, 103n; **40**, 136, 140n, 143, 190, 212; **41**, 70n, 75, 195; **43**, 1n, 6n, 15n, 16, 239, 253n; **44**, 68, 88, 226; **45**, 160; **46**, 3n, 5, 6, 9n, 40, 48n, 79n, 220, 232; **47**, 9n; **48**, 69n, 88n, 239; **49**, 61, 90, 141n, 312; **51**, 295, 326; **52**, 325; **53**, 290–1; **54**, 230n, 323; **55**, 7, 113n, 167, 209–10; **56**, 76, 203n; **59**, 348; **60**, 159, 168n1.7, 173n8, 233, 236
Dollimore, Jonathan and A. Sinfield (eds.), Political Shakespeare, **48**, 239
Dolman, John, **40**, 79n
Dolmetsch, K., **25**, 117
Dolmetsch, M., **15**, 7
Domenichelli, Mario, **55**, 347
Domingo, Anni, **51**, 222–3

Dominik, Mark, **40**, 226–7
Dominique, Ivan, **7**, 108; **8**, 118
Domou, Fontini, **51**, 220
Don John of Austria, **29**, 26
Don, Robin, **37**, 164; **42**, 162; **46**, 198; **50**, 227
Donachie, Ron, **42**, 153
Donaghy, Pip, **45**, 147
Donaldson, E. Talbot, **42**, 61n; **43**, 69, 70; **47**, 139n
Donaldson, George, **53**, 114n
Donaldson, Gordon, **57**, 73
Donaldson, Ian, **23**, 170n; **26**, 173; **31**, 165; **33**, 184; **37**, 175–6; **41**, 114n; **47**, 133n; **51**, 40n, 291–2; **54**, 33n, 331; **55**, 54n, 381; **60**, 343
Donaldson, Peter S., **48**, 93n, 95n, 96n; **52**, 88n, 109, 189n, 193n, 289; **54**, 317, 339; **57**, 240; **59**, 79; **60**, 355, 360
Donat, Robert, **50**, 147
Donatello, **26**, 116
Donatus, **7**, 23, 89n, 129; **30**, 192; **37**, 13, 15; **54**, 309
Donawerth, Jane L., **32**, 234–5; **37**, 193; **39**, 213–14; **40**, 97n
D'Oncieux, Guillaume, **15**, 97n
Donker, Marjorie, **49**, 77n
Donkin, Eric, **40**, 159, 164
Donne, John, **1**, 44, 69, 71, 77; **3**, 31; **4**, 93; **5**, 89; **6**, 60, 143; **7**, 18, 30, 141; **8**, 20, 32; **9**, 144; **11**, 39; **14**, 80; **15**, 12, 26, 27, 30, 99, 101, 102, 103, 104, 105, 106, 107, 109n; **16**, 10, 11, 13, 171; **17**, 127, 128, 130–1, 135, 143; **19**, 37, 41, 42; **20**, 52, 73n; **23**, 98, 167; **24**, 19; **25**, 190; **26**, 79, 168; **27**, 93, 94, 109, 120; **28**, 43, 44; **29**, 27, 175; **30**, 9; **32**, 222; **34**, 185; **36**, 39–41, 162; **37**, 209; **38**, 135n, 173, 215; **39**, 139n, 218; **40**, 26–7, 44, 227–8, 230; **42**, 195, 198; **43**, 55, 61, 228, 243, 260; **44**, 15, 253; **45**, 19n; **46**, 64, 71, 107, 112n, 116n, 124, 125, 225; **47**, 127n, 130, 134–5; **48**, 254; **49**, 7, 59, 76, 176, 282, 301; **50**, 87, 258–9, 271; **51**, 143, 296; **54**, 15, 35n, 44, 67, 206n; **55**, 54, 360; **57**, 212, 217; **58**, 21; **59**, 94, 95, 254, 262, 267–83, 350, 351; **60**, 224n9
Donne, John (son of above), **59**, 270
Donne, William Bodham, **54**, 82
Donnell, Patrick, **9**, 119
Donnellan, Declan, **41**, 187–8, 190; **42**, 136, 153, 159; **43**, 202, 215; **45**, 128, 130, 146; **46**, 191; **48**, 217; **49**, 273; **52**, 233–4, 266; **53**, 280; **54**, 295; **56**, 161–6, 256, 283, 285; **57**, 293; **58**, 285; **59**, 343, 344; **60**, 299–300
Donnelly, Ignatius, **18**, 112
Donnelly, Pat, **55**, 124n
Donner, H. W., **4**, 161; **14**, 145n; **24**, 146
Donner, Jörn, **36**, 69n, 71n
Donner, Leo, **52**, 259
Donner, Paul, **52**, 259
Donno, Elizabeth Story, **10**, 10; **11**, 141; **40**, 228n, 230–1; **44**, 128n; **46**, 10n, 15n, 16n, 52n; **50**, 82; **52**, 120n 121n; **54**, 322; **56**, 30n, 35n; **58**, 350, 357; **59**, 53n10, 198n4
Donoghue, Denis, **53**, 287
Donohue, Joseph W., Jr, **22**, 174; **25**, 192; **34**, 12n; **35**, 6, 7, 9, 49n; **44**, 152n; **47**, 62n
Donohue, Joseph, **51**, 118n; **57**, 60, 85, 87
Donovan, Emma, **52**, 265
Donovan, James, L., **11**, 139
Donovan, Kevin, **54**, 332
Donow, Herbert S., **23**, 144; **25**, 183
Dood, Alice, **49**, 186
Doody, M. A., **51**, 32n
Doolittle, Hilda (H. D.), **44**, 241
Doona, Liam, **52**, 259; **54**, 291
Doran, Charles, **47**, 92
Doran, Gregory, **41**, 163; **48**, 247n; **50**, 235; **51**, 236, 239–41, 260; **52**, 164, 239–40, 260; **53**, 249–51, 263, 285; **54**, 251–2, 271–3, 287, 293; **55**, 271, 274–5, 278–84, 286, 289–92, 308, 322; **56**, 256, 266, 267–8, 273, 279, 282, 287, 291, 299; **57**, 258, 259, 261, 292, 294, 330; **58**, 167, 186, 187, 189, 269, 270, 271, 273, 274, 277, 281, 282, 298, 305, 306, 336; **59**, 183, 187, 191–2, 298, 304–7, 343, 344, 345, 346; **60**, 72, 73, 81, 79–81, 83, 293–4, 296, 299, 317–18, 319, 324
Doran, John, **9**, 58n, 67n; **11**, 124; **51**, 6n
Doran, Madeleine, **1**, 51–2; **4**, 160; **5**, 150; **6**, 5, 11; **8**, 13n; **10**, 157; **14**, 2, 158; **15**, 179; **17**, 224; **18**, 160, 179; **19**, 125, 137; **20**, 68, 151; **22**, 151, 161; **24**, 146; **25**, 7; **26**, 7; **28**, 161; **29**, 83; **30**, 190; **31**, 3, 62n; **32**, 10; **33**, 183, 190; **34**, 62n, 64, 68, 133n; **37**, 13n, 14; **38**, 9, 16; **41**, 14n, 22n; **42**, 118n; **43**, 135n; **46**, 101n; **49**, 181n; **59**, 41
Endeavors of Art: A Study of Form in Elizabethan Drama reviewed, **8**, 149
Doran, Peter, **42**, 160
Dorangeon, Simone, **39**, 235
Dorchester, Marquis of, **17**, 153
Doré, Gustave, **38**, 189
Doren, Mark Van, **3**, 144; **4**, 6; **6**, 11; **10**, 3, 100, 106n; **15**, 80n; **18**, 7, 8; **19**, 8; **41**, 69
Dorey, T. A., **38**, 123n
Dorfman, Eugene, **53**, 6, 16n
Dorian, William, **58**, 154
Döring, Tobias **56**, 155n; **58**, 60
Dorius, R. J., **15**, 166; **38**, 8, 44n
Dorlandus, Petrus, *Den Spieghel der Salichiet van Elckerlyck* (1495), **5**, 107
D'Orléans, Charles, **15**, 97n
D'Orléans, Henri, **38**, 49n
d'Orléans, Philip, **52**, 257
Dormandy, Simon, **45**, 152; **46**, 163; **47**, 201
Dorn, Dieter, **37**, 161, 200; **40**, 58
Dörnemann, Kurt, **10**, 150
Dornford-May, Mark, **49**, 275
Dörenmatt, **55**, 153
Dorrington, Sir John, **60**, 52
Dorsch, T. S., **10**, 3, 9, 153; **11**, 132, 135n; **20**, 49n; **22**, 114, 116n; **26**, 171n, 176n, **29**, 139; **33**, 200–1; **42**, 201–3, 206; **44**, 69n; **46**, 149n; **50**, 114n, 115, 116n; **51**, 179n; **52**, 308; **55**, 190; **58**, 350, 356; **59**, 189n7
New Arden edition of *Julius Caesar* reviewed, **10**, 152
Dorset, 2nd Marquess of (Thomas Grey), **60**, 69–70
Dorset, Thomas Sackville, 1st Earl of, **35**, 131, 133
Dorsten, J. van, **15**, 128
Dorval, Patricia, **58**, 333
dos Santos, João Caetano, **20**, 121
dos Santos, Marlene Soares, **57**, 327
Dostoevsky, Fyodor M., **5**, 61, 103, 114, **16**, 10; **20**, 148; **26**, 22, 26, 30; **28**, 55; **33**, 181; **39**, 81n, 85; **45**, 4; **57**, 113
Double Falsehood, The, **13**, 157; **54**, 314
Douce, Francis, **4**, 87–8, 91, 93; **10**, 74; **11**, 98; **13**, 78, 105n; **15**, 1, 38, 40n; **18**, 17; **28**, 54; **31**, 42n; 35, 87; **47**, 256; **49**, 79n; **59**, 112–13

Doucha, F., **9**, 103, 105, 110n
Dougal, John, **60**, 205
Dougall, John, **44**, 200
Douglas, Lord Alfred, **3**, 10; **53**, 149; **56**, 136n
Douglas, Audrey, **40**, 217; **47**, 57n
Douglas, David, **18**, 104
Douglas, Gavin, **15**, 127; **53**, 20, 21
Douglas, Mary, **29**, 18; **46**, 110; **51**, 318
Douglas, Mildred, **40**, 38
Douglas, Moggie, **46**, 202
Douglas, Wallace W., **15**, 123n
Douglas-Fairhurst, Robert, **53**, 106n; **58**, 331
Douglas-Walker, K., **19**, 106n
Douglass, Miss, **22**, 128, 130–1
Douin, M., **3**, 99; **9**, 91
Douking, Georges, **11**, 120; **12**, 112
Doulton, Valerie, **45**, 145
Douse, Anthony, **45**, 118
Douthwaite, W. R., **53**, 200n
Doux, M. le, **14**, 103
Dove, Alexander, **15**, 145
Dove, Angie, **41**, 184
Dove, John Roland, **23**, 153; **25**, 181
Dove, John, **58**, 277; **59**, 318, 341; **60**, 324, 329
Dove, Jonathan, **46**, 191; **55**, 323, 330, 332
Dove, Rita, **54**, 312
Dover, Earl of, **17**, 12
Dow, Clare, **42**, 149; **43**, 209
Dowden, Edward, **1**, 48; **2**, 108; **3**, 8, 9; **4**, 1–2, 10, 18; **6**, 1, 3; **8**, 1, 7, 10, 14, 145; **15**, 22, 30n; **16**, 32; **18**, 39, 187; **19**, 35, 36, 43n; **24**, 55, 62, 139, 153; **25**, 1; **27**, 176; **29**, 79, 135; **31**, 1–2, 127n; **32**, 16, 17, 155n; **36**, 100; **37**, 11; **45**, 6, 176; **46**, 235–6; **50**, 176n, 181n; **53**, 92; **56**, 130, 203n; **59**, 2, 153; **60**, 185
  Shakespeare's Mind and Art, **3**, 1
Dowell, George B., **12**, 118
Dowland, John, **1**, 68, 71; **5**, 115; **15**, 6; **23**, 165; **40**, 220
  Pilgrimes Solace, **1**, 70
  Second Book of Songs, **1**, 131
Dowland, Robert, **36**, 147n
Dowling, Clare, **57**, 50
Dowling, Gabby, **45**, 152
Dowling, Joe, **43**, 216; **48**, 232
Dowling, Margaret, **28**, 8n
Dowling, Vincent, **43**, 217
Down, Angela, **47**, 99; **51**, 219; **54**, 253; **57**, 273
Downer, Alan S., **9**, 147; **10**, 149; **12**, 144; **14**, 151; **18**, 185; **19**, 153; **20**, 72n; **21**, 155; **26**, 154; **28**, 139n; **35**, 5, 7n, 9
Downes, John, **14**, 81; **17**, 197; **18**, 35; **43**, 81, 89; **49**, 2; **57**, 84; **58**, 243
Downes, Nicholas, **38**, 111
Downie, Bruce, **60**, 321
Downie, Penny, **40**, 177–8; **42**, 160; **43**, 178, 212; **44**, 202; **47**, 199; **48**, 232; **57**, 279; **58**, 301
Downing, Charles, **15**, 25, 30n
Downing, Jim, **60**, 179
Downs, A. C., Jr, **33**, 148n
Downs, Brian, **24**, 85n; **48**, 119n
Downs, Harold F., **56**, 123
Downton, Thomas, **1**, 71; **32**, 233; **33**, 158–9; **47**, 173; **58**, 229
Dowsing, William, **56**, 36
Dowson, Ernest, **55**, 90
Doyle, Brian, **44**, 105n
Doyle, Jamie, **60**, 285
Doyle, John, **44**, 201; **45**, 145; **47**, 215, 216; **48**, 232; **49**, 271, 277; **50**, 230, 235; **51**, 262
Doyle, Kevin, **44**, 202; **47**, 192
Doyle, Patrick, **42**, 160; **43**, 212; **48**, 85
Doyle, Sheila, **49**, 182n
Doyle, Stephen, **60**, 179n15
Drabble, Margaret, **48**, 261
Dracontius, **15**, 98n
Draffen, Robert A., **25**, 173
Draghi, Giovanni Battista, **51**, 80, 81
Drakakis, John, **39**, 7, 8; **40**, 64n, 87n, 190, 212; **42**, 107n; **43**, 1n, 15, 110n; **44**, 42n, 48n, 66n, 68n, 72n; **45**, 38n; **46**, 4n, 6n, 220; **47**, 73n; **50**, 243, 249; **51**, 274; **52**, 14, 15; **53**, 18n, 234n, 236n, 305; **54**, 73n; **55**, 339; **57**, 321; **60**, 196–213
Drake, Alfred, **4**, 123; **12**, 117
Drake, Fabia, **36**, 75
Drake, James, **35**, 164
Drake, Nathan, **18**, 39; **54**, 72
Drake, Simon, **41**, 189
Drake, Sir Francis, **1**, 71, 123; **5**, 149; **6**, 159; **7**, 96; **17**, 22n, 24–5, 28n, 29, 29n, 32–4, 34 nn., 111, 127, 143; **34**, 114; **52**, 187, 189; **54**, 4, 76
Drakich, Janice, **50**, 93n
Draper, C. L., **4**, 151n
Draper, Jennifer, **45**, 145
Draper, John W., **1**, 15, 127; **2**, 139n; **3**, 25, 137; **5**, 142; **6**, 15n, 157, 160, 162; **8**, 6, 148; **9**, 11; **10**, 8; **11**, 137, 146; **12**, 70n; **16**, 165; **18**, 34; **20**, 82n, 149, 159 **21**, 28n, 142; **22**, 154; **25**, 185; **26**, 163; **32**, 86n, 87n, 94n; **34**, 97–8; **45**, 20; **51**, 190; **52**, 122, 124n; **53**, 60
Draper, R. P., **12**, 137; **44**, 217
Draper, Stuart, **59**, 342, 345
Drašković, B., **18**, 134
Draudt, Manfred, **35**, 186; **36**, 194–5; **37**, 215; **38**, 253; **39**, 247; **40**, 147; **42**, 208, 209; **48**, 262
Dray, Michael, **48**, 237
Drayton, Michael, *see also* Mundy, Anthony, **1**, 61, 67; **2**, 38, 42n; **3**, 10; **5**, 139n; **10**, 141; **13**, 106; **14**, 80, 146; **15**, 30, 49n, 100, 101, 106; **17**, 169, 175, **22**, 170; **23**, 167; **24**, 24; **26**, 14, 103, 107; **34**, 87, 89; **38**, 97n, 98; **41**, 140; **42**, 66, 186; **43**, 247, 249; **46**, 226; **48**, 254; **49**, 314; **54**, 76, 115; **55**, 212n; **56**, 30; **58**, 13; **59**, 71, 72, 74, 77, 78, 78n15; **60**, 335
  Amours, **15**, 109n
  Baron's Wars, **2**, 38
  Caesar's Fall, **2**, 42n
  Ideas Mirror, **15**, 109n
  Poems, **1**, 69
Dream, **49**, 275
Dreams, **52**, 290
Drebbel, Cornelis, *see* Cornelis Drebbel
Dreher, Diane Elizabeth, **40**, 191; **42**, 32n; **51**, 21n
Drennan, William R., **48**, 124n
Dresdel, Sonia, **47**, 94
Dresden, S., **23**, 163n
Dresen, Adolf, **20**, 117; **48**, 174, 175, 178, 180, 183
Dresser, Michael, **51**, 259

Dretske, Fred, **60**, 143, 144, 144n11, 145n15
Drew-Bear, Annette, **27**, 176; **36**, 180; **41**, 212; **48**, 258
Painted faces on the Renaissance Stage: The Moral Significance of Face-Painting Conventions, **48**, 258
Drew, Philip, **33**, 190
Drewe, Thomas, **7**, 58, 59, 62, 63, 64, 67n
Drexel collection, *see under* Libraries
Drexler, Peter, **50**, 263
Drexler, R. D., **35**, 177
Dreyfus, James, **52**, 249
Dreyfuss, Richard, **48**, 191–4; **49**, 122, 271
Driessens, Victor, **5**, 107
Drinda, Horst, **20**, 118
Drinkel, Keith, **41**, 186
Drinkwater, John, **20**, 77; **55**, 134, 135; **58**, 141
Driscoll, James P., **39**, 209–11; **40**, 192
Driver, Rolf, **44**, 197
Driver, Tom F., *The Sense of History in Greek and Shakespearean Drama, reviewed*, **15**, 173–4; **19**, 137; **38**, 10
Droeshout portrait of Shakespeare, *see under* Shakespeare, portraits
Droeshout, Daniel (son of Martin the elder), **60**, 240
Droeshout, Dominick (*née* Verricke, wife of Michael), **60**, 247, 250
Droeshout, Hans (John), **60**, 245
Droeshout, Hendrick, **60**, 245
Droeshout, Janneken (*née* Molijns, wife of Martin the elder), **60**, 237–8, 240, 250
Droeshout, Janneken (sister of Martin the elder), **60**, 246, 249, 250
Droeshout, John (father of Martin the elder), **60**, 237, 243–6, 249–50
Droeshout, John (son of Michael), **60**, 237, 246, 251
Droeshout, Maria (sister of Martin the elder), **60**, 245–6, 249, 250
Droeshout, Martin, **57**, 234
Droeshout, Martin and Michael, **40**, 216; **48**, 28, 113
Droeshout, Martin, the elder *and* the younger, **60**, 233, 238, 237–8, 239, 244, 248, 249n53
Droeshout, Mary (*née* de Looze, mother of Martin the elder), **60**, 243–6, 249–50, 251
Droeshout, Michael (brother of Martin the elder, father of Martin the younger), **60**, 237, 243, 245, 246, 247, 249–51
Droeshout, Susanneken (*née* van der Ersbek, wife of Michael), **60**, 247, 250
Droeshout, William (son of Michael), and family, **60**, 246–7
Dromazos, Stathis, **58**, 217
Dromgoole, Dominic, **54**, 253; **60**, 291–2, 306–7
Dronke, Peter, **34**, 186
Drottningholm Theatre Museum, **12**, 32
Druce, Robert, **54**, 132n
Drucker, Trudy, **46**, 139n; **51**, 68, 76
Drue, Thomas, **42**, 187
Druids, **12**, 8
Drum writers of Sophiatown, South Africa, **60**, 332
Drummond, Roscoe, **49**, 233
Drummond, William of Hawthornden, **2**, 39; **7**, 17; **17**, 216; **23**, 106; **35**, 115n; **44**, 175; **54**, 61
Phoebus Arise, **8**, 99n
Drury, Ken, **47**, 209
Dryden, John, **1**, 45, 62, 65, 72; **3**, 17, 44, 56, 62, 131; **4**, 80, 93; **5**, 25, 52, 53; **6**, 141; **7**, 1, 19, 21, 23, 24n; **8**, 28, 57, 66, 139; **10**, 27, 28, 49n, 50; **11**, 60, 74; **13**, 137–40, 145–6; **14**, 10, 77–81, 83–4, 86; **15**, 5; **16**, 33, 75; **18**, 46, 77, 94; **20**, 1, 4, 6, 9, 11, 133, 160, 169; **21**, 67; **22**, 49, 53, 57, 132; **23**, 150, 173; **24**, 53, 127, 166; **25**, 113, 189; **26**, 6, 67, 159, 175; **28**, 36, 160; **29**, 175; **31**, 173; **32**, 38; **34**, 11, 93, 102, 131; **35**, 47; **36**, 114, 173; **37**, 35, 114–9, 193; **41**, 204; **42**, 196; **43**, 88, 91, 93–103, 105–6; **44**, 49n; **46**, 138, 191, 238; **47**, 255, 259; **48**, 79, 241; **49**, 12; **50**, 147; **51**, 19, 80, 82, 83, 85n, 86–7, 89, 93; **53**, 5, 92, 137n, 149, 171, 217, 336; **54**, 101, 109, 114; **55**, 97, 204n, 265, 269, 322, 361; **56**, 107, 149, 209, 314; **57**, 113, 212, 213; **58**, 140, 149; **59**, 366; **60**, 196, 336
All for Love, **9**, 84, 85n; **10**, 9, 38; **20**, 2
adaptations of *Othello, The Tempest* and *Troilus and Cressida*, **9**, 85n
Aureng-Zebe, **20**, 8, 10
The Conquest of Granada, **20**, 10
Essay of Dramatic Poesy, **10**, 13–14, 25n; **14**, 77, 79
Marriage à la Mode, **12**, 94n
Song for St Cecilia's Day, **11**, 60
State of Innocence, **1**, 66
The Spanish Friar, **10**, 48, 49n
The Tempest: or the Enchanted Island (with Davenant, William), **13**, 137, 139, 147
production at Old Vic reviewed, 137–40
Drye, Austin, **45**, 107
D'Silva, Darrell, **53**, 260
Du Bartas, Guillaume de Saluste, Seigneur, **6**, 82, 83, 88n, 89n; **15**, 105; **17**, 141; **19**, 37; **40**, 80
see also under Sylvester, Joshua
Du Bartas, Silvester, **21**, 48; **24**, 145
Du Bellay, **16**, 12
Duberman, Martin, **46**, 4n
Dubey, Neha, **58**, 278
Dubinski, Roman R., **54**, 70n
du Bois, Oliver, **56**, 86
du Bois, Page, **46**, 94; **53**, 85
Dubois, Claude-Gilbert, **57**, 318
DuBois, W. E. B., **51**, 63, 187n
Du Bos, Charles, **16**, 70
Dubrow, Heather, **36**, 167n; **41**, 197, 205–6; **43**, 16n; **51**, 286; **52**, 281; **54**, 298–9, 321; **56**, 301, 308, 311; **58**, 23, 317, 331; **60**, 351
Duby, Georges, **44**, 51, 52
Du Caine, Andrew, **7**, 67n; **50**, 156; **51**, 291; **58**, 244, 246
Duchêne, Kate, **44**, 195; **46**, 162, 163; **47**, 197, 216; **56**, 343
Duchess of Malfi, The, **50**, 244; **52**, 80; **54**, 317
Ducis, Abbé, **16**, 53, 56n; **20**, 121, 164
Ducis, Jean François, **3**, 99; **9**, 59–61, 91; **21**, 79–80; **24**, 79–86; **30**, 200; **47**, 64; **48**, 4; **54**, 153; **57**, 113, 114, 115; **60**, 215, 217–22
adaptations of Shakespeare, **3**, 99
version of *Othello*, **3**, 99–104
Duckies, V. H., **19**, 106n
Ducreux, Louis, **2**, 124
Dudlay, Adeline, **9**, 67n
Dudley, Ambrose, Earl of Warwick, **11**, 90; **12**, 20n, 95–106; **32**, 89; **54**, 116; **60**, 4–6, 8, 13
Dudley, Anne, **55**, 335

Dudley, Robert, Earl of Leicester, **11**, 90; **13**, 95, 104n; **17**, 23, 122–3, 125, 127; **27**, 118n; **47**, 52–3; **57**, 304
Dudley, Robert, First Earl of Leicester (?1532–88), his company of actors, **6**, 65, 73n, 74n
see also under Theatre, Elizabethan
Dudley, Scott, **60**, 228, 232
Dudley, William, **28**, 144; **38**, 207; **39**, 197; **40**, 173, 180; **41**, 187–8; **42**, 154, 156, 157; **47**, 214; **60**, 307–8
Duesing, Dale, **35**, 145
Dufays, Jean-Michel, **59**, 262n21
Duff, Anne-Marie, **51**, 252
Duff, E. Gordon, **6**, 63n
Duff, J. D., **53**, 79n
Duff, J. Wight, **20**, 25n
Duff, William, **58**, 72, 74
Duffet, Thomas, **20**, 169; **57**, 69
Duffin, Ross W., **58**, 328, 331, 342
Duffy, Atlanta, **52**, 254
Duffy, Christopher, **56**, 292
Duffy, Eamon, **52**, 58n, 59, 66n; **54**, 1, 2, 5n, 18, 19n, 25n, 36n, 57n, 122, 123n, 126n, 314; **56**, 28n, 36; **60**, 231
Duffy, Robert A., **45**, 43n
du Fresne, Graeme **45**, 145
Dugdale, Gilbert, **37**, 198
Dugdale, Sir Thomas, *Antiquities of Warwickshire*, **12**, 105, 106n
Dugdale, Sir William, **13**, 103n, 104n; **27**, 115n; **53**, 208n; **59**, 277, 278, 279; **60**, 243n33, 245n38
Duggan, Sean, **58**, 265
Du Guernier, Louis, **13**, 73, 74; **37**, 42
Duguid, Lindsay, **46**, 178
Duguid, Peter, **12**, 120; **14**, 127
Duijvendak, Han, **49**, 277; **50**, 226
Duke of Saxe-Meiningen's Company, **49**, 126
Duke's Mistress, The, **52**, 81, 84
Duke, John, **7**, 60, 66; **33**, 163
Dukes, Ashley, **55**, 237n
Dulac, Edmund, **9**, 82; **37**, 168; **51**, 188n; **56**, 272
Dulandt, Robert, **36**, 144
Du Laurens, André, **43**, 238; 50, 257
Dullin, Charles, **2**, 123; **14**, 119; **16**, 54; **40**, 2
Dulwich College, **1**, 28; **7**, 60, 61, 85
Dumakude, Daisy, **57**, 163
Dumas-Meurice, **20**, 164
Dumas, Alexandre, **3**, 101; **7**, 109; **9**, 59, 61–3, 67; **15**, 136; **21**, 80; **57**, 115; **59**, 263n24
translation of *Hamlet*, **2**, 116, 123
Du Maurier, Sir Gerald, **2**, 11; **12**, 81
Dumb Knight, The, **11**, 48
Dumesnil, Marie Françoise, **9**, 91
Dumezweni, Noma, **56**, 267; **59**, 341
Du Monin, Edouard, **15**, 105, 106, 110n
Dumont, Gabriel, **47**, 27n
Dumur, Guy, **7**, 110
Dunbar, Florence W., **18**, 170
Dunbar, Mary Judith, **39**, 230
Dunbrow, H., **47**, 131n
Duncan, Barry, **48**, 10n
Duncan, Douglas, **50**, 115n; **56**, 225n
Duncan, E. (*fl.* 1847), **1**, 83
Duncan, Edward, **5**, 134
Duncan, Gillies, **57**, 2
Duncan, Joseph E., **23**, 163
Duncan, King of Scotland, **57**, 71
Duncan, Lindsay, **39**, 198; **52**, 261; **56**, 4n
Duncan, Martin, **42**, 159
Duncan, Mr and Mrs James R., **49**, 125
Duncan-Jones, A. E., and E. E., **14**, 110
Duncan-Jones, Caroline, *Miss Mitford and Mr Harness*, **14**, 110
Duncan-Jones, E. E., **20**, 166; **43**, 52
Duncan-Jones, Katherine, **23**, 166n; **26**, 172; **32**, 231, 236; **37**, 218; **39**, 109n; **42**, 53n, 72n; **45**, 11n; **49**, 59n, 326; **50**, 196n; **51**, 286–7; **52**, 302, 304–5; **53**, 28n, 36n, 146n; **55**, 367, 369; **56**, 64, 95n, 184n, 203n, 215n, 310; **57**, 309; **58**, 5–6, 11, 26, 155, 201, 204; **59**, 220, 220n27, 224, 225, 229, 235, 237; **60**, 256n20, 342
Duncker, A., **33**, 160n
Dunderdale, Sue, **44**, 199
Dundes, Alan, **29**, 15n, 17n; **46**, 109n
Dunhill, Rosemary, **56**, 119n
Dunkel, Wilbur, **7**, 145; **18**, 162; **25**, 6n; **27**, 93n, 94n; **29**, 95
Dunlap, Rhodes, **34**, 182
Dunlop, Frank, **9**, 119; **10**, 125; **14**, 126; **37**, 169; **44**, 91, 96
Dunlop, O. Jocelyn, **56**, 56n
Dunlop, Revd John, **54**, 182n, 183, 185n
Dunn Esther, **24**, 87n, 99n, 103
Dunn, Catharine M., **24**, 151
Dunn, Esther Catherine, **7**, 135; **15**, 23; **18**, 105, 117n
Dunn, Jan, **47**, 218
Dunn, Kate, **56**, 177n
Dunn, Kerry, **47**, 210
Dunn, Lionel, **8**, 123, 124, 126
Dunn, T. M., *Philip Massinger*, **14**, 12
Dunne, A. M., **48**, 114n
Dunne, John, **43**, 216
Dunnett, Dorothy, **50**, 101, 104
Dunning, Nick, **58**, 263
Dunning, Ray, **45**, 154
Dunseath, Thomas K., **53**, 120n
Dunstan [Tunstall], James, **60**, 21
Dunstan, A. C., **46**, 226
Dunsworth, Felicity, **51**, 290
Dunsworth, Geoff., **57**, 186
Duplessis-Mornay, Philippe, **32**, 231; **43**, 238
Dupont, Jacques, **15**, 133
Duport, P., **2**, 116
Duppa, Bishop Bryan, **54**, 58
Jonsonus Virbius, **14**, 90
Dupuy, René, **12**, 111
Durand, W. Y., **12**, 20n; **42**, 117n, 118
Durandus, William, **60**, 233
Durbach, Errol, **48**, 115n
Durden, Richard, **30**, 172; **31**, 142; **46**, 200
Dürer, Albrecht **9**, 100n; **13**, 75, 80n; **19**, 61, 70; **24**, 156; **30**, 119, 123; **49**, 81; **54**, 130–1; **56**, 232; **60**, 224
Durer, Christopher, **32**, 226
D'Urfeé, Honoré, **14**, 15; **20**, 3
Durfey, Thomas, **32**, 98n; **51**, 3, 81; **54**, 42; **56**, 314
adaptation of *Cymbeline*, **9**, 85n
Richmond Heiress, **10**, 144n
During, Simon, **56**, 295n
Dürnhofer, Max, **15**, 29
Durnin, John, **46**, 195; **47**, 214; **48**, 236; **50**, 231; **51**, 257; **52**, 265

Durning-Lawrence, Sir Edwin, **4**, 146
Durozier, Maurice, **52**, 285
Durr, Jason, **45**, 138
Durrant, G. H., **12**, 115; **27**, 167
Durrant, Hugh, **45**, 151
Durrell, Lawrence, **5**, 139
Dürrenmatt, Friedrich, **25**, 174; **40**, 159; **54**, 213–15, 217
Durston, C., **54**, 169n
Durtine, John, **42**, 157; **45**, 147
Du Ryer, Pierre, **15**, 91
Du Sautoy, Carmen, **32**, 209
Dusinberre, Juliet, **29**, 159; **32**, 63n, 96n; **33**, 198; **37**, 4, 55; **38**, 240; **42**, 32n, 168; **44**, 217; **46**, 2, 4–8; **48**, 243; **50**, 262; **52**, 274; **53**, 234n, 307–8; **56**, 95n; **58**, 317, 331; **60**, 96–7n35, 165Fig.28, 366–8, 369
Dutaillis, C. Petit, **2**, 120; **6**, 10
Dutch Courtesan, The, **52**, 297
Dutchess of Suffolk, The, **17**, 175
Duteil de la Rochère, Martine Hennard, **56**, 328
Dutescu, Dan, **20**, 127; **29**, 166
Duthie, D. W., **6**, 4
Duthie, G. I., **1**, 12, 129, 130; **3**, 27; **4**, 157; **5**, 37, 147, 150; **6**, 14, 151, 167–8; **7**, 149, 153; **8**, 81, 83, 97n, 98n; **9**, 1, 6, 150; **13**, 18n; **14**, 158 and n; **15**, 138, 182; **18**, 24, 187; **19**, 130n, 162; **20**, 175; **21**, 137; **23**, 121; **25**, 73n, 74, 77n, 79, 80n; **26**, 184; **32**, 9, 242; **33**, 1–3, 9, 188; **34**, 93, 97n; **37**, 30n, 210; **38**, 254; **42**, 99n; **43**, 267; **48**, 271; **50**, 284; **55**, 16, 28n; **59**, 2n5, 7n27, 8n31
  'Bad' Quarto of Hamlet, **3**, 82n
  Elizabethan Shorthand and the First Quarto of King Lear reviewed, **5**, 151
  Shakespeare's 'King Lear' reviewed, **3**, 147–9
  'Antithesis in *Macbeth*', **19**, 25–33
Dutoit, Jacqueline, **48**, 236
Dutt, Clemens, **57**, 173
Dutt, T. K., **10**, 142
Dutt, Utpal, **59**, 370
Dutton, John and Laurence, **6**, 159, 170; **15**, 64, 71n; **27**, 134; **60**, 21–2
Dutton, Mr, **45**, 113n
Dutton, Peter, **17**, 11
Dutton, Richard, **40**, 211; **41**, 197; **43**, 226, 235–54; **46**, 220, 232, 233; **47**, 249; **50**, 110n, 259; **51**, 290; **52**, 73n, 75n, 281, 285n; **53**, 54n, 71n; **54**, 57n, 98n, 99; **56**, 27n, 217n; **57**, 132; **58**, 3, 15, 172, 333; **59**, 26n27, 220, 221; **60**, 6, 269, 342, 355
Dutu, Alexandru, **19**, 145; **22**, 175n; **24**, 150
  'Recent Shakespeare Performances in Romania', **20**, 125–32
Dutz, Ingold, **37**, 159
Du Vair, Guillaume, **33**, 22
Duval, Alexandre, **58**, 139
Duval, Georges, **2**, 116
Duvignaud, Jean, **10**, 118
Duvivier, Charles, **33**, 163n
Duyckinck, E. A., **18**, 103
Duyle, Maxine, **58**, 302
Dvořák, Anton, **9**, 107
'Dwarf Bob', **27**, 178
Dwyer, Kevin A., **56**, 158n
Dyas, Aubrey, **47**, 91
Dyball, **22**, 128, 131
Dyce, Alexander, **2**, 44; **5**, 27; **14**, 82, 85, 87, 113; **16**, 32; **18**, 35; **23**, 102; **27**, 111n, 112, 115n, 116n, 117n; **29**, 105n, 124; **38**, 105n, 112; **43**, 257; **44**, 120, 138; **49**, 29; **54**, 20n, 354; **56**, 101, 121n, 352; **59**, 54, 87, 214, 216, 221
Dyer, Alan, **60**, 2n6, 10, 10n25
Dyer, Chris, **41**, 159, 184–5, 189; **42**, 152, 157, 161; **43**, 173, 186, 208; **44**, 191, 197; **45**, 146, 156; **46**, 200; **48**, 234; **58**, 305; **59**, 176; **60**, 2n6, 15n41
Dyer, Clint, **60**, 323
Dyer, Sir Edward, **9**, 24, 25; **15**, 101, 102, 109n; **32**, 90n
Dyer, F. E., **17**, 23n
Dyer, Gavin, **14**, 116
Dyer, George, **17**, 65n
Dyer, Kevin, **42**, 157
Dyer, Michael, **53**, 282; **56**, 290; **58**, 299; **60**, 325
Dyer, Richard, **52**, 92n, 96n; **55**, 243
Dyer, T. F. Thistleton, **15**, 97n, 111
Dyke, Daniel, **28**, 48n
Dylan, Bob, **39**, 144n
Dymkowski, Christine, **41**, 226; **55**, 380; **59**, 87n29, 89n34, 202n25, 208n48, 211
Dymling, Carl Anders, **11**, 139
Dymock, Sir Edward, **46**, 33
Dymow, Ossip, **55**, 123–4
Dyos, H., **51**, 77n
Dyson, A. E., **44**, 217
Dyson, H. V. D., **7**, 129
Dyson, Peter, **18**, 168; **57**, 58

E. K. (Edward Kirke), **23**, 166; **46**, 46
Eadie, Brude, **48**, 113n
Eagle, Herbert, **57**, 149
Eagle, John, **11**, 99
Eagle, R. L., **12**, 142; **15**, 16
Eagle, The, ship, **11**, 92
Eagleson, Robert D., **29**, 174; **40**, 219, 236n; **41**, 36n; **51**, 316, 335
Eaglestone, Robert, **55**, 71n
Eagleton, Terry, **22**, 148–9; **25**, 12; **31**, 62n; **35**, 81n; **40**, 77, 78n, 188–9, 192, 212; **41**, 70n, 202; **43**, 10; **45**, 76n, 89; **49**, 90, 284; **51**, 36n; **53**, 48n, 101; **54**, 324; **55**, 4; **56**, 144n, 213; **57**, 331; **58**, 155; **59**, 151n17, 215n10; **60**, 128, 186
Eales, J., **54**, 169n
Ealing Shakespeare Players, **58**, 306
Eames (Emms), Geoffrey, **25**, 141, 146, 147
Eames, Roger, **25**, 147
Earl, D. C., **55**, 199n
Earle, John, **58**, 67
Earle, Stephen, **44**, 202
Early Modern English Dictionary, The (projected), **7**, 2
Earne, Lukas, **58**, 309–12
Eason, Myles, **1**, 109, 110
East Africa, report on Shakespeare in, **7**, 109–10; **9**, 112; **10**, 117; **12**, 110–11
East India Company, **17**, 9, 12, 21, 26, 27, 32
East, Gilbert, **33**, 143; **45**, 109
East, Revd John, **54**, 80, 81n
East, Michael, **1**, 68
  Third Set of Books, **1**, 70
Easthope, Anthony, **44**, 67
Eastman, Arthur M., **19**, 142; **23**, 175

Eastman, Richard M., **46**, 90n
Easton, Richard, **38**, 212; **42**, 129, 131
Eastward Ho!, see under Jonson, Ben
Eastwood, Clint, **44**, 65; **52**, 90
Easty, John, **22**, 133n
Eaton, Bob, **44**, 200; **46**, 201; **54**, 294
Eaton, Sarah, **43**, 232
Eaves, T. C. Duncan, **51**, 27n
Ebb, Fred, **45**, 45
Ebel, Julia, G., **24**, 159
Eberle-Sinatra, Michael, **56**, 151n
Ebert, Carl, **7**, 115–16
Ebisch, W. and Schücking, L. L., *Shakespeare Bibliography*, **6**, 3; **7**, 1
Ebner, Caroline, **49**, 278
Ebner, Dean, **20**, 154
Ebreo, Leone, **15**, 104; **32**, 213, 215; **34**, 102, 184; **49**, 136, 138n
Ebsworth, J. W., **15**, 2; **60**, 275n26
Eburne, Andrew, **53**, 144n
Ecatommiti, **52**, 134
Eccles, Audrey, **46**, 71n, 110n, 114n
Eccles, C. M., **19**, 147
Eccles, John, **18**, 94–5
Eccles, Mark, **2**, 153; **4**, 155; **11**, 105n; **14**, 33n; **17**, 88, 126n; **19**, 160; **24**, 159; **25**, 137; **27**, 99, 102n, 129n; **29**, 33; **35**, 183; **37**, 189; **44**, 230; **45**, 182–3; **47**, 167n; **53**, 228n; **54**, 90n, 95n; **55**, 24n; **59**, 41, 188n6
  Marlowe in London, **14**, 9
  'Martin Peerson and the Blackfriars', **11**, 100–6
Eccleston, Christopher, **56**, 280; **57**, 291
Ecclestone, William, **58**, 232
Echard's *Terence*, **1**, 66
Echeruo, Michael J. C., **19**, 120; **25**, 179; **59**, 81n9
Eckerman, Johann P., **14**, 85, 88n
Eckermann, Johann Peter, **49**, 72
Eckert, Charles W., **39**, 1n, 6, 53n; **45**, 63
Eckhardt, Caroline D., **59**, 243n30
Eckhardt, E., **17**, 45n
Eckhoff, Lorentz, **2**, 128; **9**, 132–3; **10**, 120; **11**, 121; **12**, 139
  William Shakespeare reviewed, **3**, 133
Eckleburg, Dr T. J., **55**, 236
Eco, Umberto, **41**, 198; **51**, 68; **53**, 35n–36n; **60**, 154
Economidis, J., **5**, 112; **6**, 120; **7**, 112
Eddington, Toby, **58**, 307
Eddison, Robert, **1**, 100, 102; **5**, 128; **24**, 3n; **31**, 159
Edelman, Charles, **44**, 217; **47**, 237; **53**, 296; **54**, 315; **57**, 303, 319, 328, 329; **58**, 38, 44, 319, 331
Edelman, Nathan, **59**, 262n18, 262n19
Eden, Kathy, **49**, 193n
Eden, Richard (tr.), **17**, 31, 51; **29**, 5; **51**, 179, 184; **52**, 186; **54**, 229; **56**, 42
Eden, Richard, *History of Travel*, **3**, 17
Edens, Walter, **32**, 226
Edes, Richard, **54**, 62n
Edgar, David, **58**, 156
Edgecombe, Rodney, **43**, 230
Edinborough, Arnold, **8**, 119; **9**, 111; **10**, 116, 149; **11**, 118, 148n; **12**, 145; **13**, 161; **23**, 174n; **24**, 167; **25**, 175
Edinburgh International Festival, **11**, 118; **58**, 300, 302, 307
Edis, Steven, **57**, 264
Edman, Irwin, **25**, 103n
Edmiston, Alan, **52**, 28n
Edmond Ironside, **3**, 51, 52
  conjectural Shakespearian autograph, **8**, 159
Edmond, Lauris, **55**, 172n
Edmond, Mary, **30**, 196; **43**, 94n; **44**, 150n, 230; **45**, 102n, 106n, 114n; **47**, 16, 48n; **57**, 56, 57; **58**, 230; **60**, 237, 238, 240, 240n20, 242, 243, 243n28, 245n34, 245n37, 247, 247n45, 249, 249n53
Edmondes, Sir Thomas, **60**, 54
Edmonds, C. K., **6**, 55, 63n
Edmonds, Robert, **52**, 292
Edmondson, Jim, **59**, 188
Edmondson, Joseph, **41**, 113n
Edmondson, Paul, **54**, 295; **58**, 330; **59**, 39, 200n15, 359, 368; **60**, 193n27
Edmonstone, Susan, **44**, 198
Edmund Ironside, **18**, 181; **40**, 169, 225–6; **47**, 277; **48**, 277; **49**, 298; **50**, 287
Edmunds, *alias* Weston, **26**, 72
Edmunds, Candice, **59**, 344
Edmunds, Eleanor, **44**, 200
Edmunds, John, **21**, 152; **24**, 167
Edward I, **52**, 287; **55**, 23
Edward II, **50**, 41–55; **52**, 275, 296; **54**, 155n
Edward III, **3**, 110, 111, 133; **4**, 7; **7**, 140; **9**, 133; **10**, 143; **14**, 10; **20**, 162; **43**, 261–2; **48**, 277; **49**, 280, 324, 329
  attributed to Shakespeare, **6**, 39–48
  imagery of, **6**, 40–4, 47, 48n
Edward IV, **12**, 48, 54
Edward the Confessor, King of England, **54**, 125; **57**, 30, 31; **60**, 127–8
Edward III, King, **28**, 8, 174; **44**, 56; **52**, 176
Edward IV, King **6**, 60
Edward VI, King, **6**, 66; **15**, 64, 71n; **17**, 54, 59, 104, 109, 115, 118; **30**, 61; **38**, 24; **39**, 226; **43**, 51; **47**, 71; **48**, 71; **52**, 170–1; **54**, 1, 5, 7, 75, 126, 134, 349; **57**, 236
Edward VII, King, **56**, 126
Edward VIII, King, **40**, 159
Edward, Charles, **47**, 207; **48**, 207
Edward, Prince of Wales, **56**, 126–36
Edwardes, Michael, **32**, 87n
Edwardes, Richard, **17**, 195; **42**, 117; **49**, 54; **53**, 234
Edwards, Anthony S. G., **31**, 189, 197
Edwards, Calvin R., **50**, 87n
Edwards, Carlton, **51**, 268
Edwards, Charles, **51**, 220–1
Edwards, Christopher, **34**, 180n; **47**, 12
Edwards, E., **13**, 75; **37**, 43–4
Edwards, Edward, **49**, 118
Edwards, Faith, **48**, 233
Edwards, Gale, **49**, 255–7; **50**, 233; **54**, 312; **56**, 344; **57**, 265, 266, 269; **58**, 279, 302; **59**, 341
Edwards, Geoffrey, **15**, 144
Edwards, Hilton, **6**, 119; **39**, 40n, 48n; **51**, 144
Edwards, J. G., **42**, 26n
Edwards, Lee R., **37**, 24n
Edwards, Malcolm, **44**, 191
Edwards, Manon, **47**, 210
Edwards, Matt, **51**, 266
Edwards, Michael, **45**, 27n
Edwards, Miss (Mrs Mozeen), **51**, 85

Edwards, Nettie, **42**, 149; **43**, 208; **47**, 213; **52**, 265; **53**, 284
Edwards, Paul, **46**, 199; **48**, 236; **51**, 6, 61
Edwards, Philip, **8**, 159; **11**, 149; **13**, 149, 162; **14**, 8; **15**, 111; **18**, 188; **19**, 138; **21**, 145; **22**, 62; **23**, 139–40; **24**, 60n; **25**, 5; **26**, 5, 9, 119n, 155, 167; **28**, 105n; **29**, 1, 2, 4, 9, 10; **30**, 203, 205, 206, 207; **31**, 127, 133, 136–7; **32**, 4, 158n; **33**, 172, 191; **34**, 72, 164, 177–8, 184; **36**, 88n, 181; **38**, 1, 88n, 217, 218; **39**, 230, 243–7; **40**, 194, 234; **41**, 37, 39n, 43n, 120n; **42**, 19n, 23n, 211n; **43**, 22n, 26, 69, 81n, 110, 137n; **45**, 54n, 61, 162, 190n; **46**, 62n, 101n, 241n, 256; **48**, 4; **50**, 54n, 95n, 171n, 181n, 273; **51**, 72, 141–6; **52**, 210n, 273, 298–9; **54**, 20n; **55**, 3, 184–7, 252n, 381; **56**, 330; **58**, 253; **60**, 361
'An Approach to the Problem of *Pericles*', **5**, 25–49
'An Approach to the Problem of *Pericles*' reviewed, **6**, 164–5
'Shakespeare's Romances: 1900–1957', **11**, 1–18
Edwards, Rachael, **60**, 178
Edwards, Richard, **32**, 168n; **44**, 50
Damon and Pithias, **14**, 15, 22; **15**, 4, 173; **20**, 18, 24, 25n
Edwards, Richard, apothecary, **11**, 95
Edwards, Rob, **41**, 184; **44**, 197; **45**, 152; **47**, 185, 189, 195
Edwards, Rory, **48**, 230; **49**, 270; **51**, 211, 213
Edwards, Sally, **44**, 168, 199
Edwards, Sian, **48**, 233
Edwards, Stephen, **42**, 158; **46**, 201; **60**, 326
Edwards, Thomas, **24**, 171; **49**, 290; **51**, 5, 8, 129
Cephalus of Procris, **3**, 54
Edwards, W. A., **14**, 11
Edzard, Christine, **47**, 210; **54**, 312; **55**, 384; **56**, 294; **58**, 185, 341
Eedes, Richard, **2**, 70, 73
Caesar Interfectus, **4**, 91
Efron, Arthur, **46**, 216
Efros, Israel, **14**, 121
Eftimiu, Victor, **20**, 127
Egan, Gabriel, **51**, 333; **52**, 14n; **54**, 316; **56**, 317; **60**, 345–6, 347, 352, 358
Egan, Jane, **47**, 102
Egan, Joseph J., **32**, 235, 245
Egan, Rebecca, **59**, 316
Egan, Richard, **27**, 71, 72, 170
Egan, Robert, **22**, 173; **28**, 118; **38**, 9; **40**, 64
Egeman, F., **20**, 130
Eger, Elizabeth, **58**, 76
Egerton, Francis, First Earl of Ellesmere, **6**, 63n
Egerton, John, 2nd Earl of Bridgewater, **13**, 109
Egerton, Sir John, **6**, 55
Egerton, Judy, **49**, 122
Egerton, Sir Thomas, *see under* Ellesmere, Baron
Egerton, Sir Thomas (Lord Ellesmere), **6**, 54; **17**, 57, 81n, 84, 85, 86; **24**, 158; **27**, 94, 95, 99, 100; **29**, 93, 95, 96n, 97; **59**, 276
his library, 59–60
Eggen, Arne, **6**, 123
Eggers, Walter F., Jr, **30**, 185; **32**, 216, 226
Eggert, Katherine, **48**, 249; **52**, 290; **54**, 320; **58**, 252, 254, 256
Eglington, John, **45**, 40
Egri, Peter, **51**, 282
Ehrentraut, Adolf, **50**, 32
Ehrenzweig, Anton, **40**, 111n
Ehrl, Charlotte, *Sprachstil und Charakter bei Shakespeare*, **12**, 70n; 113; **13**, reviewed, 153
Eickhoff, Louise, **6**, 48n
Eidson, Donald, **22**, 156
Eikhenbaum, B., **23**, 174n
Einberg, Elizabeth, **51**, 10
Einenkel, E., **54**, 103n
Einstein, Alfred, **53**, 172n
Eire, report on Shakespeare in, **6**, 119
Eiseley, Mircea, **33**, 189
Eisenstein, Elizabeth, **50**, 240; **55**, 266
Eisenstein, Sergei, **39**, 107; **47**, 108; **58**, 340
Eisler, Colin, **26**, 115
Eisner, Doris, **7**, 146n; **8**, 118
Eisner, Lotte, **45**, 46n
Ejiofor, Chiwetel, **55**, 306, 331
Ek, Anders, **15**, 138; **36**, 65n, 70–2
Ek, Ingrid, **36**, 65n
Ek, Jens, **14**, 122
Ekdahl Family, **56**, 6n
Ekeblad, Inga-Stina, *see under* Ewbank
Ekeroth, Bengt, **10**, 121
Ekman, Gösta, **3**, 113
Eksteins, M., **37**, 156n
Ekwall, Eilert, **7**, 2
Elafowojo, Femi Jr, **55**, 326
Elam, Harry J., **52**, 34n
Elam, Keir, **39**, 215, 235; **40**, 34–5, 105n; **43**, 249; **50**, 245; **52**, 274; **55**, 182, 238n, 347–8, 353–4; **56**, 95; **59**, 285n3, 361–2
Eland, W., **57**, 210
Elandt, E., **57**, 128
Eld, George, printer, **4**, 162; **12**, 147; **26**, 184; **29**, 181–2
Elder, Mark, **58**, 303
Elderton, William, **17**, 219
Eldon, Lord, **38**, 69
Eleanor, Queen, **42**, 42
Elephant, Order of the, **11**, 124
Eley, Chris, **48**, 229
El Fadil, Siddiq, **46**, 194
El-Gabalawy, Saad, **32**, 228
Elgar, Edward, **60**, 185, 186, 187, 194–5
Elgar, Sir Edward, **45**, 172, 174; **56**, 130
El Greco, **19**, 61; **22**, 59; **26**, 49, 50, 53, 55, 63, 64, 65, 66; **53**, 328
Elia, Norbert, **48**, 26n
Eliade, Loren, **33**, 189
Elias, Norbert, **55**, 240–1
Eliaz, Raphael, **8**, 120; **12**, 114; **14**, 121; **49**, 278
Elider, Alun, **43**, 206
Eliot, Charlotte Stearns, **43**, 122
Eliot, George, **6**, 1; **18**, 40; **19**, 13; **21**, 11n; **26**, 8; **30**, 96, 121; **34**, 34; **43**, 3; **44**, 206, 241; **48**, 3, 157, 261; **49**, 133–4, 138n, 140n; **51**, 32; **53**, 110, 114–26; **54**, 88; **55**, 111n; **56**, 134, 135; **59**, 360
Eliot, Henry, **43**, 125n
Eliot, John, **3**, 10; **7**, 140; **32**, 103n; **33**, 19; **38**, 53; **53**, 19
his life, **6**, 79
Orthoepia Gallica, **3**, 25; described, **6**, 79
Shakespeare's knowledge and use of it, **6**, 80–90; **8**, 147
Survey or Topographical Description of France, **6**, 89n
Eliot, Michael, **41**, 228; **42**, 181, 196
Eliot, Stephen, **41**, 178

INDEX

Eliot, T. S., **1**, 105; **2**, 136; **3**, 21n; **4**, 7, 21, 23–4; **5**, 80n, 87; **6**, 105; **7**, 4, 6, 10, 11, 30, 33, 34, 86, 114; **9**, 2, 8, 13, 14; **10**, 98, 103, 106n; **11**, 36, 136; **13**, 30, 148; **14**, 2, 4, 10, 95, 138, 144, 145n, 160; **15**, 150; **16**, 10, 48, 62; **18**, 9, 41, 114, 117; **19**, 87, 93n, 125 143; **20**, 52; **21**, 4, 6–7, 11n, 45, 67, 68, 77, 128; **22**, 5, 66, 67, 162, 166; **23**, 152; **24**, 19, 39, 41, 42, 46, 116; **25**, 10, 64; **26**, 3, 51; **27**, 11; **28**, 30, 31; **29**, 1, 80, 81, 86, 87; **30**, 4, 5–6, 102, 120; **31**, 173; **33**, 182; **34**, 9, 54, 93; **35**, 171; **36**, 6, 18, 21, 175; **38**, 141n, 154, 246; **39**, 221; **40**, 29, 185–6, 192–3, 207–8; **41**, 45, 141, 200; **42**, 181, 196; **43**, 109, 111, 121–9; **45**, 1, 2, 38, 126; **46**, 61, 62, 132, 206; **47**, 114, 193n, 232; **48**, 65, 282; **49**, 209, 211, 226; **50**, 264; **51**, 1, 36; **53**, 287–8; **54**, 31n; **55**, 132, 360; **56**, 107, 108, 139, 327; **57**, 38, 143, 304; **58**, 1, 122, 124; **59**, 147, 347, 366; **60**, 225n13
Family Reunion, **5**, 79
Marina, **8**, 121
Murder in the Cathedral, **4**, 106
The Cocktail Party, **8**, 109
The Waste Land, **8**, 37; **10**, 40
Eliot, Sir Thomas, **57**, 22, 25
Eliot, Valerie, **43**, 125–6; **49**, 209n
Eliott, Mrs M. L., **32**, 16n
Eliza Sive de Laudibus Augustissimae et Serenissimae Principis Elizabethae, **4**, 155
Elizabeth Charlotte of Brandenburg, **36**, 144
Elizabeth I, Queen, **1**, 71, 82, 125; **2**, 25; **3**, 27, 52; **4**, 39, 78, 95, 154–5; **5**, 132, 139, 142, 149; **6**, 60, 64, 68, 106; **7**, 84; **9**, 71; **10**, 28; **11**, 65, 71, 75, 89–97, 100; **12**, 15–18; **13**, 37, 40n, 104n, 155; **14**, 26–7, 30, 33n, 85, 102–3, 106; **15**, 1, 25, 64, 103; **17**, 5, 10–12; **21**, 48; **23**, 79, 81, 87, 120, 147, 154, 166; **24**, 155, 157; **26**, 37, 38n, 41, 46, 99; **27**, 93, 100, 134; **28**, 3, 7, 8, 9, 15, 20, 21, 22, 23–4, 151, 165, 166; **30**, 132; **31**, 56, 58, 143; **32**, 87–8, 106, 131, 134, 198, 231; **33**, 162–3; **34**, 88–9, 132, 142, 158; **35**, 66, 75, 108, 115, 131; **36**, 93, 146, 165; **37**, 148; **38**, 19–22, 24–5, 57, 61, 122, 131, 133, 215; **39**, 216, 228; **41**, 216, 219; **42**, 2, 3, 5, 21, 77, 162; **43**, 3, 4, 6, 55–7, 104, 238, 241, 247; **44**, 59, 61, 62, 151, 158, 159, 227, 234; **45**, 72, 181, 191; **46**, 10–21 passim, 48, 111, 117, 133, 138, 141, 142, 219, 232, 252; **47**, 47, 52, 115; **48**, 40, 43, 71, 76, 246, 251; **49**, 79, 83, 176n, 327; **50**, 160, 256, 269; **51**, 185, 279, 292–3, 294, 322; **52**, 74, 111, 113, 133, 147, 166, 169–72, 182, 280, 295, 310; **53**, 67, 85, 201, 326; **54**, 2, 6, 18, 19, 35, 61, 75, 78, 90–2, 95, 97–8, 116, 119, 121, 125–7, 132–8, 170, 197–8, 229n, 243, 319, 349; **55**, 29, 30, 36n, 45, 46, 53–4, 64, 122, 213, 357, 373; **56**, 36, 118, 215, 220, 227, 242, 354; **57**, 13, 14, 16, 17, 30, 74, 210, 303, 339; **60**, 72, 82, 113, 119, 121, 344
and navy, **22**, 26, 34, 59, 73, 79, 107, 109–10, 113, 118, 122–5, 127, 129, 166
translation of Plutarch's *Moralia*, **10**, 33
Elizabeth II, Queen, **13**, 130; **39**, 197; **45**, 72
Elizabeth R., **54**, 312
Elizabeth, daughter of James I, **1**, 60; **12**, 144; **43**, 55–7, 59
Elizabeth, Duchess of Brunswick, **33**, 161–2; **36**, 139
Elizabeth, Princess, **26**, 36, 40n, 41, 43, 44, 45, 46, 47, 48; **56**, 10
Elizabeth, Princess of Bohemia, **54**, 134
Elizabeth, Princess, later Queen of Bohemia, **36**, 118, 144; **39**, 131
Elizabethan Homily on Matrimony, **60**, 75
Elizabethan Player, The, **46**, 225, 226
Elkington, John, **56**, 238
Elkins, Paul, **43**, 208
Ellacombe, Revd Henry N., **56**, 39n, 40n
Ellegard, Alvar, **23**, 11n
Ellesmere, Baron, (Sir Thomas Egerton), **29**, 95, 97
Ellesmere, First Earl of, *see under* Egerton, Francis
Ellington, Duke, **53**, 249; **56**, 303–4
Elliot, Eleanor, **13**, 124
Elliot, Marianne, **55**, 322
Elliot, Ward E. Y., **51**, 316, 326–8
Elliott, Denholm, **14**, 133
Elliott, G. R., **5**, 78; **6**, 154; **9**, 14; **10**, 98, 102, 104, 106n; **25**, 81, 83; **52**, 276
Dramatic Providence in 'Macbeth' reviewed, **13**, 147–8; **19**, 7, 51
Flaming Minister. A Study of Othello as Tragedy of Love and Hate reviewed, **8**, 142
Hamlet, Scourge and Minister, **18**, 44
Elliott, J. H., **32**, 90, 93n; **35**, 104n; **44**, 62n
Elliott, John R., Jr, **20**, 155; **21**, 152; **23**, 146, 168; **24**, 161; **38**, 8, 11, 13; **39**, 228; **52**, 312
Elliott, Marianne, **54**, 268, 270; **60**, 302–3
Elliott, Martin, **42**, 214; **43**, 228
Elliott, Michael, **9**, 119; **39**, 89, 90n, 181
Elliott, Robert, **15**, 122
Elliott, Ward E. Y., **59**, 69
Elliott, William, **49**, 116
Elliott-Knight, Susannah, **52**, 233; **50**, 206
Ellis, David, **56**, 305, 307
Ellis, F. S., **24**, 113n
Ellis, George, **14**, 89n; **26**, 3; **32**, 21n, 34n
Ellis, H., **48**, 85n
Ellis, Henry, **54**, 193n
Ellis, Sir Henry, **42**, 26n, 28n; **43**, 51n; **44**, 55n
Ellis, Henry Havelock, **14**, 87, 89n; **56**, 213n
Ellis, Herbert A., **32**, 100n; **38**, 51
Ellis, Hilary, **43**, 207
Ellis, J., **27**, 158
Ellis, J. H., **4**, 74n
Ellis, Jack, **42**, 155; **47**, 192
Ellis, James, **45**, 150
Ellis, John, **39**, 104; **49**, 91n
Ellis, Juniper, **55**, 175n, 177n
Ellis, Lisa, **60**, 293
Ellis, R. L., **28**, 16n; **30**, 172
Ellis, Roger, **35**, 97
Ellis, Thomas, **17**, 31; **32**, 88n
Ellis-Fermor, Una, **2**, 126; **4**, 18, 20; **5**, 81, 84, 88–9, 90, 130, 148; **6**, 10, 75, 147; **7**, 8–9; **8**, 12, 36, 145; **9**, 43n, 134; **10**, 11, 59n; **13**, 146; **14**, 2, 8, 9; **23**, 145; **24**, 42; **25**, 8, 11n; **26**, 3, 4, 89; **30**, 55n; **41**, 64n, 73n; **43**, 6; **51**, 142, 144
Shakespeare the Dramatist reviewed, **3**, 142
Ellison, James, **58**, 321, 331
Ellison, Ralph, **60**, 330
Ellison, Zigi, **44**, 202
Elliston, Robert W., **35**, 18; **47**, 62, 68; **58**, 40
Ellmann, Maud, **56**, 137–45
Ellmann, Richard, **48**, 186n; **53**, 138n; **56**, 137n, 139n, 141n, 143n, 144n
Elloway, D. R., **30**, 206n

Ellrodt, Robert, **18**, 173; **29**, 90; **30**, 193; **56**, 329
'An Anatomy of *The Phoenix and the Turtle*', **15**, 99–110
'Self-Consciousness in Montaigne and Shakespeare', **28**, 37–56
Elm, Suzanna, **54**, 38n
Elmer, Peter, **52**, 297
Elmes, John, **45**, 145
Elms, Lily, **55**, 323
Elmy, Mary, **51**, 120
Else, Gerald F., **23**, 148; **37**, 14n
Elsie and Norm's Macbeth, **43**, 208
Elsinore, **1**, 115
an American production of *Hamlet* at, **4**, 124–5
performances at Kronborg Castle, **3**, 113–14
Elsky, Martin, **50**, 241
Elsom, John, **43**, 172n; **44**, 213; **55**, 160n, 161n, 163n, 168
Elson, John, **2**, 139; **6**, 11
Elson, Louis C., **15**, 3
Elstracke, Renold, **43**, 161; **53**, 201n
Elton, G. R., **28**, 64n, 65; **38**, 225; **40**, 135, 136n, 139n, 212; **48**, 72n; **52**, 168n; **54**, 34n, 126n
Elton, Sir Oliver, **5**, 152; **14**, 101n; **27**, 106n
Elton, W. R., **21**, 134, 136; **25**, 18n; **29**, 89, 184; **41**, 146n, 157; **48**, 272n; **54**, 72n, 322; **56**, 171n; **57**, 202
Elton, William R., **3**, 136; **8**, 11; **19**, 120; **33**, 9, 10, 43n, 60, 92n; **34**, 180n; **38**, 162n; **55**, 14n, 183n, 211; **60**, 369
'Ajax in *Troilus and Cressida*' reviewed, **3**, 139
Elvery, John, **44**, 200
Elvetham, **3**, 93
Elwin, H., **18**, 50–1
Ely Palace portrait of Shakespeare, *see under* Shakespeare, portraits
Elyot, Sir Thomas, **1**, 68; **3**, 6; **17**, 53; **18**, 170; **24**, 66; **28**, 80n; **29**, 85, 87; **30**, 61, 189; **31**, 85–6, 88n, 89–91; **32**, 167n; **33**, 19, 22; **34**, 188; **35**, 115n; **36**, 161, **38**, 40, 43; **43**, 238; **44**, 49, 50n; **50**, 43; **52**, 185n; **55**, 245; **56**, 30, 44; **59**, 363
Preservative agaynst Deth, **1**, 70
The Governour, **5**, 79, 141; **10**, 5
Elze, Karl, **9**, 67; **44**, 110n
Emans, Michael, **57**, 295
Embleton, Ian, **44**, 193
Emden, Cecil S., **11**, 106n; **28**, 154
'Shakespeare and the Eye', **26**, 129–37
Emelyanov, V., **39**, 83n
Emerson, Caryl, **46**, 55n; **57**, 196
Emerson, O. F., **15**, 12
Emerson, Ralph Walderson, **58**, 181
Emerson, Ralph Waldo, **1**, 57; **4**, 146; **14**, 153; **18**, 102–5, 107–8, 111–13; **24**, 87; **44**, 205; **45**, 5n, 6; **50**, 171–2; **53**, 131n, 287, 293, 294; **54**, 302; **56**, 204, 206; **59**, 35n71; **60**, 282
Emerson, Tom, **14**, 128
Emery, Douglas, **8**, 123
Emery, J. K., **27**, 104n
Emery, John, **8**, 122
Emery, Winifred, **32**, 31, 35n
Emett, Rowland, **5**, 129
Emmerová, Jarmila, **21**, 129n
Emmerson, Ian, **13**, 134, 136; **14**, 127, 128; **15**, 146; **41**, 185
Emmerson, Richard, **59**, 247n64
Emmet, Dorothy, **16**, 62n
Emmison, F. C., **32**, 103n
Emney, Mark, **45**, 147; **46**, 197
Empedocles, **15**, 96
Empson, Sir William, **4**, 18–19, 23; **6**, 161; **7**, 134, 136; **8**, 131, 141; **9**, 14, 132, 135, 145; **15**, 61; **18**, 7, 53; **19**, 1; **21**, 3, 5, 9, 140, 155n, 162; **23**, 170; **25**, 5, 8; **29**, 91, 177; **30**, 37; **32**, 54; **33**, 4, 7, 11; **34**, 68; **36**, 160; **37**, 209; **38**, 6, 9, 14; **39**, 145; **40**, 22–4, 26–8, 30–2, 114n, 187, 192–3; **41**, 130; **42**, 165; **43**, 226; **46**, 46n, 125; **47**, 150, 242n; **48**, 267; **49**, 209n; **50**, 196n; **52**, 269, 275, 319; **53**, 18, 308
Essays on Renaissance Literature, **48**, 267
The Structure of Complex Words, **13**, 17, 18n, 19n, 39n
The Structure of Complex Words reviewed, **6**, 152–3
Some Versions of Pastoral, **15**, 108n, 114; **20**, 73n
work on Shakespeare's language, **7**, 10–11
Emre, Mollie, **54**, 37n
Emslie, Macdonald, **10**, 150
Emunds, Karl, **23**, 119
Enck, J. J., **16**, 164
Jonson and the Comic Truth, **14**, 10
Endacott, Charlotte, **59**, 338
Ende, Richard von, **21**, 144
Endel, Peggy, **40**, 209
Endelman, Todd, **48**, 51n
Enemy to the People, **47**, 219
Engel, Erich, **7**, 111; **14**, 119; **48**, 8
Engel, Susan, **36**, 154; **39**, 79n; **42**, 50n, 137, 139; **44**, 184; **45**, 148, 153
Engelen, Julia, **1**, 8; **42**, 47n
Engelmüller, K., **9**, 110n
Engels, Friedrich, **35**, 76; **44**, 31, 223; **45**, 90, 91, 100; **48**, 163, 177; **56**, 220n, 341; **57**, 173; **60**, 127
Engels, Johan, **46**, 178, 192; **47**, 209
England, George, **21**, 65n
England, Martha Winburn, **11**, 147
'Garrick's Stratford Jubilee: Reactions in France and Germany', **9**, 90–100
Englands Helicon, **3**, 54
England's Joy, The Plot of the Play called, **3**, 93–4; **12**, 42
Englands Parnassus, **3**, 54; **8**, 99n; **15**, 23
Engle, Frederick, **52**, 195n
Engle, Lars, **40**, 197; **44**, 42n, 223; **46**, 44n; **48**, 242, 246, 253; **50**, 181n; **51**, 147, 148n, 149, 150, 151n, 152, 158
Shakesperian Pragmatism: Market of his Time, **48**, 242
Engle, Ron, **42**, 199
Englefield, Sir Francis, **17**, 127
Engler, Balz, **26**, 166n; **28**, 172; **31**, 175, 193; **37**, 160n; **41**, 211; **47**, 236; **57**, 115, 327
Engler, James, **21**, 100
Engler, Kristina, **44**, 41n
Englische Comedien und Tragedien, **1**, 64
English Comedy (ed. M. Cordner, P. Holland and J. Kerrigan), **48**, 245
English Dancing Master, The, **55**, 86
English National Opera, **58**, 305
English Patient, The, **54**, 254
English Rose, **54**, 292
English Wagner Book, The, **7**, 69, 75
English, Cory, **59**, 338
English, John, **9**, 120; **12**, 119
English, Richard, **52**, 286
Englishby, Paul, **59**, 304; **60**, 184, 317
Englishe, Lindy, **60**, 202
Engstrom, Bonnie, **49**, 246–7

Engstrom, J. Eric, **21**, 142
Ennius, **35**, 123; **37**, 134
Enright, D. J., **7**, 146; **8**, 139; **9**, 139; **10**, 11; **13**, 150; **24**, 138; **36**, 151
Enright, Nick, **58**, 58
Enriquez, Franco, **15**, 136
Ensensberger, Hans Magnus, **48**, 18
Enterline, Lynn, **50**, 243–4; **51**, 286; **54**, 322; **56**, 30n, 34n; **58**, 249; **60**, 358
Enthoven, Gabrielle, **48**, 55
Entrambasaguas, J. de, **20**, 98, 101, 104n
Epicoene, **50**, 71
Epictetus, **33**, 23
Epp, Garrett, **51**, 290
Epp, Leon, **14**, 116
Epstein, Alvin, **10**, 119
Epstein, Helen, **57**, 152
Epstein, Joel J., **24**, 157
Equiano, Olaudah, **51**, 62, 62, 63
Equity, Courts of, **12**, 95
Erasistratus, **38**, 179
Erasmus, Desiderius, **1**, 52, 68; **7**, 23; **10**, 146; **11**, 143, **13**, 88, 89n; **14**, 143; **15**, 97n; **17**, 60–1; **18**, 176; **20**, 22, 176; **22**, 112; **23**, 80, 144, 161, 162; **27**, 56–69; **29**, 91, 104, 159; **30**, 61–3, 64; **31**, 14, 17, 18, 33; **32**, 136, 163, 166, 168n, 169; **33**, 69, 70, 77n, 92, 200; **34**, 162–3; **37**, 138, 140n, 180–1; **39**, 214; **40**, 98; **42**, 67–70, 77, 81; **43**, 238; **44**, 61; **45**, 167; **46**, 45, 112n, 223; **47**, 23n; **49**, 211; **50**, 111, 113n, 116, 117; **51**, 38n, 136, 296; **52**, 274; **54**, 3, 6, 7, 9, 30, 43, 63, 65, 223, 304; **55**, 200n, 219n, 220, 266, 368, 381; **56**, 41, 43, 44n, 48, 233n, 320; **59**, 227, 361, 363; **60**, 76n19
  Apophthegms, **4**, 67n
  Bellum Erasmi, **1**, 70
Erdman, David V., **43**, 59n
Erdman, Nicolai, **56**, 168n
Erforth, Klaus, **48**, 174
Ergang, Robert, **22**, 169
Ergen, Mehmet, **56**, 288; **57**, 293; **59**, 342
Erickson, Amy Louise, **55**, 39
Erickson, Peter, **42**, 10, 12, 13; **46**, 4, 6 **49**, 65n, 104n; **52**, 295, 325; **53**, 291; **54**, 312; **55**, 8n; **56**, 157n, 302, 330; **58**, 173, 252; **60**, 331, 347–9, 352
Ericson, Sture, **36**, 67
Eriksen, Roy T., **36**, 41–2
Erikson, Erik H., **37**, 99; **40**, 191
Erikson, Jon, **43**, 29n
Erlich, Bruce, **31**, 176; **33**, 191
Ermann, Kurt, **43**, 220
Erne, Lukas, **56**, 355; **57**, 300, 318, 336–7; **58**, 318, 331, 352, 355, 356; **59**, 18n77, 18–19, 20n4, 26n27, 38n88, 97, 124n2, 183n2; **60**, 259n25, 269, 366n6
Ernest, Duke of Bavaria, **36**, 146
Ernst, Fritz, **9**, 85n
Errante, Vincenzo, **1**, 116; **2**, 127
Erskine-Hill, Howard, **26**, 159; **38**, 215; **51**, 51n; **56**, 215n
Ertuğrul, Muhsin, **7**, 116; **9**, 116; **14**, 124; **16**, 137
Ervine, St John, **55**, 130
Esche, Edward J., **57**, 46
Eschenburg, Johann Joachim, **6**, 120; **7**, 111; **14**, 119; **15**, 134; **18**, 174; **26**, 166; **40**, 55n, 58, 61; **57**, 62
Escher, M. C., **44**, 17
Escolme, Bridget, **59**, 372, 373, 375; **60**, 170–82, 182n18
Escudier, Marie, **57**, 65
Esdaile, Katherine, **7**, 139
  English Church Monuments 1510–1840, **4**, 156
Esmein, Adhémar, **32**, 132n
  Le Marriage en Droit Canonique, **13**, 89n
Esmoreit (medieval Flemish play), **5**, 107
Espasa-Calpe, **54**, 155n
Esrig, David, **20**, 129
Esser, V. P. S., **18**, 126
Essex Stairs, *see under* London
Essex, Earl of (Henry Bourchier), (1510), **60**, 68, 69–70
Essex, Earl of (Robert Devereux), **57**, 227; **60**, 367
Essex, Earl of, *see under* Devereux
Essex, Earl of, **21**, 100, 103; **23**, 43, 97; **27**, 129n; **28**, 6, 7, 8, 9, 20, 23, 24; **29**, 168
Essex, First, Second and Third Earls of, *see under* Devereux, Robert
Essex, Sir William, **17**, 99
Esslin, Martin, **21**, 38n; **39**, 169, 171; **45**, 9n; **55**, 158n; **57**, 40, 117; **60**, 102, 229
Est, Thomas, *The Whole Booke of Psalmes*, **3**, 56
Este, Isabella d', **60**, 61
Estensen, Elizabeth, **48**, 198; **56**, 250
Estienne, Charles, **54**, 91
Estienne, Henri, **15**, 90, 97n; **17**, 183
Estock, Simon C., **58**, 314, 331
Estrin, Mark W., **56**, 348
Etchells, Tim, **60**, 155n7
Etherton, Michael, **52**, 163
Etienne, Claude, **5**, 111; **6**, 117; **7**, 108; **8**, 118
Etlin, Andrew V., **31**, 12n
Etterle, Fory, **20**, 126
Etti, Florian, **49**, 278
Ettin, Andrew V., **25**, 176
Euclid, **17**, 66
Eugeniou, George, **60**, 323
Euphuism, **7**, 4, 5
Euripides, **3**, 67; **5**, 53; **6**, 25; **10**, 36; **21**, 75; **22**, 3, 5, 109; **31**, 163; **32**, 220; **33**, 34; **34**, 3; **36**, 13, 14, 16–18, 85; **39**, 169; **40**, 75; **41**, 205; **53**, 49, 58
Eusebius, **33**, 99
Evan, Daniel, **48**, 204, 209
Evans, Anna Laura, **54**, 75n, 76
Evans, Sir B. Ifor, **6**, 151; **19**, 149; **23**, 13n, 48; **32**, 128n
Evans, Bertrand, **5**, 135; **21**, 130; **22**, 25, 26n, 41, 166; **23**, 137; **25**, 3, 9, 54, 90, 110, 192; **31**, 31n; **32**, 3, 7, 8, 59n; **33**, 197; **34**, 163–4; **37**, 3, 8, 17n, 95; **39**, 135n; **49**, 5, 6n, 9n; **52**, 121n; **55**, 196n; **56**, 176; **59**, 41
  Shakespeare's Comedies reviewed, **15**, 162–3
Evans, Camille, **45**, 148
Evans, Carol, **39**, 13
Evans, Daniel, **53**, 259, 271; **56**, 273–4; **57**, 264, 269, 275; **58**, 302
Evans, Dee, **56**, 297; **60**, 328
Evans, E. C., **18**, 173
Evans, Dame Edith, **1**, 105; **2**, 4, 12, 13, 16; **4**, 105, 129; **8**, 31, 130; **12**, 86, 122, 124–5; **13**, 140, 142; **16**, 20, 27; **18**, 133; **23**, 131; **25**, 27, 66; **33**, 85; **34**, 8; **37**, 39; **40**, 12; **41**, 67, 69; **49**, 3, 128; **52**, 28n; **58**, 164
Evans, Faith, **43**, 254

Evans, G. Blakemore, **4**, 91, 140n, 162; **6**, 162; **7**, 148; **8**, 147; **11**, 152–3; **14**, 153; **16**, 172–3; **21**, 162; **23**, 176; **25**, 186, 196; **26**, 181; **28**, 173–7; **29**, 184; **30**, 125n, 208; **31**, 4n, 34n; **32**, 129, 142, 177n, 181n; **33**, 1, 208n; **34**, 121n, 194; **35**, 119n; **36**, 32n; **37**, 15n, 70n, 85n; **38**, 63n, 101, 102n, 104, 115n, 155n, 238n, 241–2; **39**, 42n, 81n, 135n, 236n; **40**, 41n, 72n, 108n, 123n, 217, 228n; **42**, 39n, 208n; **43**, in, 134, 268n; **44**, 123n, 256; **45**, 128n; **46**, 51n; **47**, 162n; **48**, 23n, 35n, 86n; **49**, 19n, 23, 42n, 145n, 163n, 164n, 165n, 168, 172, 174n; **50**, 10n, 143n, 269–71, 276; **52**, 99n; **53**, 12n, 104n; **54**, 62n; **55**, 14n, 226n, 258; **56**, 39n, 45n, 80n, 138n; **57**, 339; **59**, 3, 40, 46, 51–2n6, 56n18, 225, 233; **60**, 63n14, 88n9, 102n1, 109n33, 253, 255n16
Evans, Gareth Lloyd, **32**, 2, 6; **33**, 194; **34**, 172; **41**, 127n; **42**, 35; **44**, 191; **47**, 6, 99; **51**, 144, 145
Evans, Graham, **9**, 121
Evans, Mrs H., **11**, 103
Evans, Henry, **1**, 42; **11**, 100, 102–5 and n.; **58**, 222
Evans, Henry, ed., *see* Leyris, Pierre
Evans, Hugh C., **24**, 153, 157; **32**, 7
Evans, James Roose, **10**, 124; **15**, 145
Evans, Joan, **7**, 5
Evans, John X., **45**, 167; **19**, 132
Evans, K. W., **25**, 181
Evans, Katharine, **49**, 303
Evans, L. A. W., **14**, 127
Evans, Lawrence, **48**, 199; **53**, 262; **56**, 254
Evans, Lewis, **17**, 60, 123; **32**, 165n, 174n
Evans, Lis, **46**, 201; **47**, 210, 212
Evans, M., **29**, 162
Evans, Malcolm, **24**, 52; **40**, 186–8; **50**, 103n; **54**, 73n; **55**, 4; **57**, 28, 29, 32
Evans, Marian, **53**, 116
Evans, Maurice, **1**, 113; **2**, 130; **5**, 115, 116; **7**, 5; **18**, 72; **21**, 65n; **23**, 131; **37**, 200; **43**, 252; **44**, 254–5; **46**, 249; **53**, 171; **56**, 28n
Evans, Morgan, **46**, 227
Evans, N. E., **52**, 103n
Evans, Nathan, **51**, 259
Evans, Oliver, **41**, 69, 70n, 74
Evans, R. H., **38**, 69n
Evans, Robert C., **43**, 243–5; **51**, 292; **54**, 333–4
Evans, Robert O., **34**, 103; **49**, 49, 50n, 51n, 52n; **53**, 47
Evans, Ruth, **59**, 244n36
Evans, Samuel, **54**, 58n
Evans, Sandra, **51**, 260
Evans, Sebastian, **52**, 303
Evans, Stuart, **41**, 227
Evans, Tenniel, **47**, 97
Evans, Thomas, **1**, 41; **45**, 113
Evans, Willa McClung, **19**, 106n; **32**, 242
Evason, Anny, **44**, 200; **47**, 210
Eve, Trevor, **46**, 202
Evein, Bernard, **18**, 122
Evelyn, John, **31**, 139; **59**, 291; **60**, 47n59, 224Fig.39, 223–4, 236
Evelyn, Sir Thomas, **21**, 97, 100
Evenchik, Arthur, **52**, 303n; **54**, 348; **56**, 349n
Evennett, Wallace, **5**, 120; **15**, 144
Everall, Naomi, **57**, 47
Everard, Sir Richard, **38**, 32n
Everett, Barbara, **21**, 10n; **24**, 172n, 173; **25**, 4; **29**, 89; **32**, 12, 53n, 55n, 58–9, 220–1; **33**, 8, 43n; **37**, 185; **39**, 136n; **40**, 206–8, 217, 231–2; **41**, 104n; **42**, 131, 176–7, 184; **43**, 219; **44**, 220; **48**, 127n, 245; **51**, 186n, 285; **53**, 186n; **59**, 41, 47
'*Hamlet:* A Time to Die', **30**, 117–23
Everett, Henry, **59**, 338
Everett, Kenny, **49**, 255
Everett, Marshall, **57**, 253
Everett, Rupert, **54**, 289
Everitt, A. M., **38**, 27n
Everitt, E. B., **27**, 129n
The Young Shakespeare, Studies in Documentary Evidence reviewed, **8**, 159
Evers, Bronia, **56**, 6n, 8
Everyman, **3**, 20; **5**, 107; **11**, 20
Evett, David, **36**, 170n, 178
Evett, Marianne Brish, **49**, 98n, 102n
Evintan, Ahmet, **16**, 137
Evreinov, N. N., **40**, 2; **54**, 142
Ewart, Charles, **57**, 89
Ewbank (née Ekeblad), Inga-Stina, **12**, 142; **14**, 54; **19**, 138; **21**, 138, 146; **24**, 164; **26**, 165; **27**, 163, 177; **29**, 6, 7; **30**, 188, 198; **32**, 220; **33**, 124n, 181; **34**, 7, 72, 164; **37**, 6, 19; **39**, 229; **40**, 11n, 87n; **41**, 120n, 202; **43**, 22n, 137n, 138, 139n; **44**, 217; **45**, 162, 190; **46**, 101n; **47**, 110, 248; **48**, 11n, 115n; **50**, 54n, 95n, 241; **51**, 144, 145; **54**, 152n; **59**, 360, 374
'The Fiend-Like Queen: A Note on *Macbeth* and Seneca's *Medea*', **19**, 82–94
'*Hamlet* and the Power of Words', **30**, 85–102
'"More Pregnantly than Words": Some Uses and Limitations of Visual Symbolism', **24**, 13–18
Ewen, C. H. L., **4**, 47n
Ewen, C. L'Estrange, **17**, 36n
Ewig, Wilhelm, **15**, 29
Ewing, Kenneth, **36**, 21
Ewing, Paul, **58**, 280
Ewing, S. B., *Burtonian Melancholy in the Plays of John Ford*, **14**, 12
Excursions, **52**, 117
Exeter, Countess of, **38**, 28
Existentialism, and stage structure, **12**, 4, 7
Exodus, *see under* Bible, The
Exposicio sancti Hieronymi, **4**, 93
Eyre, Peter, **43**, 212
Eyre, Sir Richard, **43**, 194, 202; **44**, 186, 187, 193; **45**, 153; **47**, 187, 189; **48**, 15, 230; **51**, 246, 249–50, 266; **52**, 257, 284; **55**, 283, 327, 382
Eyre, Ronald, **25**, 164, 166; **33**, 174–5; **35**, 147–9
Eyre, Simon, **26**, 98

Faas, Ekbert, **40**, 194–5
Fabbri, Jacques, **18**, 123
Faber, Caroline, **56**, 279
Faber, M. D., **19**, 124; **24**, 156; **25**, 180; **26**, 162
Fabian, Bernhard, **43**, 263n; **50**, 47n
Fabian, Johannes, **58**, 71, 207
Fabian, John, **29**, 175
Fabian, Robert, **38**, 94
Fabiny, Tibor, **43**, 247
Fabo, Paul, **3**, 104

Fabricius of Aquapendente, **17**, 148
Fabricius, Johannes, **44**, 208, 211
Fabricius, Susanne, **48**, 263
Fabrini, **34**, 85
Fabry, Frank, **37**, 219
Fabyan, Robert, **8**, 146; **11**, 46; **20**, 81n; **33**, 16; **38**, 94; **42**, 26
Faccio, Franco, **18**, 83; **21**, 89
Facius, G. S., **49**, 120–1
Facius, J. G., **49**, 120–1
Facsimile Productions, **58**, 307
Fadiman, Anne, **57**, 127
Fagan, J. B., **4**, 105; **9**, 17, 18
Fagus, *Essai sur Shakespeare*, **2**, 119
Fahlén, Margareta, **11**, 122
Fahm, David, **49**, 246
Fahy, Tom, **43**, 178
Fain, John Tyree, **23**, 156
Fair Em, **3**, 48; **4**, 92; **6**, 58; **9**, 84
Fair Maid of Bristol, The, **1**, 46; **11**, 36; **52**, 85, 136–42
Fair Maid of the West, **52**, 209, 211
Fairbanks, Arthur, **31**, 17n
Fairbanks, Douglas, Snr., **18**, 72; **39**, 79; **45**, 8
Fairchild, A. H. R., **15**, 23, 25, 29; **31**, 15, 16; **39**, 130n
Fairclough, H. Rushton, **38**, 40n, 45n; **39**, 161n; **51**, 176n; **53**, 20n; **56**, 40n
Fairer, David, **59**, 110n7
Fairfax, Edward, **24**, 73n; **38**, 93
Fairfax-Lucy, Alice, *Charlecote and the Lucys* reviewed, **13**, 154
Fairfield, Leslie P., **54**, 103n
Fairholt, Frederick, **1**, 83; **14**, 82; **35**, 14; **59**, 245
Fairthorne engraving of Shakespeare, *see under* Shakespeare, portraits
Faith, Adam, **47**, 101
Faithfull, Marianne, **45**, 59; **56**, 269
Faithorne, William, **10**, 72; **53**, 199, 203n
Falbaire, Charles Georges Feneuillot de, **9**, 91
Falck, August, **43**, 113
Falck, Johan, **9**, 116; **16**, 137
Falckenberg, Otto, **13**, 128
Falco, Raphael, **55**, 360–1
Falconer, A. F., **19**, 148–9
Falconer, Colin, **56**, 293, 298
Falconer, Kern, **58**, 301
Falconer, William Armistad, **54**, 40n
Fale, Thomas, **33**, 140
Falk, Doris V., **21**, 134; **32**, 164n
Falk, Johannes, **48**, 8, 9
Falk, Robert, **20**, 159; **24**, 87n, 99n; **57**, 127
  'Shakespeare in America: A survey to 1900', **18**, 102–18
Falk, Rosalie, **48**, 9n
Falk, Rossella, **13**, 129; **14**, 121; **16**, 136
Falk, Sawyer, **6**, 124
Falkland, Lord (Lucius Carey), **14**, 90
Fall of Coriolanus, The (Tate), **48**, 7
Fallicco, A. B., **49**, 136n
Fallow, T. M., **49**, 185n
Falstaff or The True and Valient Death of Sir John Falsof, **43**, 217; **52**, 266
Famous Victories of Henry the Fifth, The, **1**, 126, 128; **3**, 47; **4**, 87, 95; **6**, 4, 36, 37, 71, 157, 170; **7**, 147; **9**, 84; **10**, 145; **14**, 32; **17**, 194, 200–1; **20**, 24; **44**, 247; **50**, 44, 286; **55**, 18, 29
Fane, Mildmay, Duke of Westmorland, **3**, 52
Fanon, Frantz, **48**, 156; **52**, 163
Fansler, H. E., **20**, 24n
Fantham, Elaine, **41**, 209n
Farber, Leslie H., **37**, 121n, 122n
Farber, Yael, **56**, 282; **57**, 292; **60**, 332
Farely, David, **50**, 234
Faria i Sousa, Manuel de, **60**, 242n26
Farjeon, Herbert, **11**, 128, 135n; **20**, 80; **56**, 102n
  The Shakespearean Scene reviewed, **3**, 135
  edition of *Shakespeare, Complete Works* reviewed, **8**, 158
Farleigh, Lynn, **42**, 155; **45**, 156; **47**, 212
Farley, Frederick, **6**, 122
Farley-Hills, David, **33**, 158; **44**, 210; **47**, 240, 241; **50**, 289; **51**, 328; **53**, 60; **54**, 314; **56**, 101n
Farly, Henry, **50**, 188
Farmer, David, **45**, 2n
Farmer, John, *English Madrigals*, **1**, 70
Farmer, John S., **2**, 44; **8**, 101, 104n; **21**, 65n; **30**, 10n; **32**, 95n, 97n, 98n, 103n, 104n, 138n; **49**, 195n; **54**, 27n
  The Writings of John Bale, **11**, 21n
  (ed.) *Tudor Fascimile Texts*, **3**, 3; **14**, 7
Farmer, Norman, Jr., **24**, 158n
Farmer, Richard, **2**, 109; **4**, 57; **10**, 14; **27**, 106; **40**, 72; **46**, 236–7; **51**, 5; **60**, 253n5
  Essay on the Learning of Shakespeare, **3**, 5, 14; **4**, 56
Farnaby, Richard, **11**, 65
Farnham, Willard, **2**, 143; **4**, 13; **6**, 13; **10**, 8; **19**, 134; **25**, 183; **26**, 89; **27**, 111n; **29**, 81, 103n, 109n; **32**, 163n; **38**, 220; **40**, 70; **57**, 238
  The Medieval Heritage of Elizabethan Tragedy reviewed, **11**, 144; **14**, 3; **20**, 19, 24n
  ed. of *Hamlet*, **12**, 151
  Shakespeare's Tragic Frontier, **19**, 5, 130
  Shakespeare's Tragic Frontier reviewed, **5**, 130
Farnsworth, Paul, **42**, 155; **44**, 195; **45**, 150, 154; **46**, 197; **50**, 225; **52**, 255; **54**, 289
Farquhar, George, **22**, 125
Farquhar, H., **13**, 110n
Farr, David, **56**, 290; **57**, 265, 285, 291, 296; **58**, 299, 303; **59**, 185–6, 328, 339, 345; **60**, 322
Farr, Derek, **39**, 106
Farr, Dorothy M., **22**, 172n
Farr, Edward, **52**, 209n
Farrah, **27**, 150; **29**, 156; **34**, 149; **35**, 149; **37**, 172; **42**, 151; **44**, 200
Farrand, Max, **6**, 55, 62
Farrant, Alastair, **46**, 193
Farrant, Richard, **6**, 65; **15**, 173; **17**, 195
Farrar, J. H., **12**, 22
Farrell, B. A., **35**, 161n
Farrell, John, **47**, 68
Farrell, Kirby, **44**, 208, 211
Farrell, Mrs, **51**, 90
Farrell, Nicholas, **41**, 163, 165, 174; **42**, 151; **43**, 207
Farren, Elizabeth, **37**, 45
Farrow, Kenneth D., **48**, 252; **57**, 77
Fashioning Femininity and English Renaissance Drama, **46**, 208
Fasick, Laura, **51**, 36n
Fassett, Kaffe, **54**, 271; **55**, 322; **56**, 287; **57**, 330
Fastolfe, Sir John, **38**, 86

Faternon, **11**, 71
Fatum Vortigerni (MS.), **3**, 52
Faucit, Helena, Lady Martin, **31**, 188; **32**, 16, 20, 26–8, 32–3; **34**, 1, 175; **35**, 9; **37**, 199; **38**, 196–9; **41**, 24–5; **49**, 123, 135–6, 140; **53**, 110, 125, 126n; **56**, 133, 134; **57**, 91; **59**, 211
Faulkner, T. C., **55**, 263n
Faulkner, William, **40**, 201–2; **60**, 330
Faunt, William, **60**, 47n59
Faure, B., **52**, 129n
Faure, Félix, **9**, 66
Fauré, François, **21**, 135; **26**, 157
Faure, Renée, **5**, 111
Fausset, Hugh I'Anson, **57**, 212
Faustus, **52**, 79, 85
Favila, Marina, **57**, 311
Fawcett, J. H., **43**, 106n
Fawcett, Mary L., **38**, 223
Fawcett, Rupert, **55**, 323
Fawkes, Guy, **26**, 40
Fawkner, H. W., **45**, 165; **46**, 213; **54**, 29n
Fay, Jimmy, **58**, 263
Feakins, Mark, **50**, 228
Feales, William, **18**, 22n
Fearon, Ray, **47**, 199, 216; **52**, 247–8, 263; **53**, 185, 256; **54**, 290; **56**, 257, 272; **57**, 264, 295; **60**, 162, 168n1.9
Fearon, Ricky, **57**, 266; **58**, 304; **60**, 159
Fearson, George, **44**, 106n
Feasey, E., **8**, 116n
Feasey, L., **8**, 116n
Feast of Words, A, **46**, 223
Feast, Michael, **48**, 220–2
Feather, John P., **27**, 178, 190; **29**, 175
Featherstone, Mike, **55**, 240n
Fechter, Charles Albert, **9**, 17, 56; **11**, 124; **28**, 171; **30**, 198; **35**, 32; **38**, 192–3, 196; **41**, 23; **56**, 112
Federbush, Shimon, **54**, 184n
Federn, W., **18**, 180
Fedorovitch, Sophie, **1**, 109
Feher, Michel, **55**, 240n, 241n
Fehling, Jurgen, **52**, 284
Fehr, Bernhard, **44**, 110n
Fehrenbach, Robert J., **24**, 167; **34**, 170; **39**, 231; **41**, 217
Fehrman, Carl, **11**, 141
Fehsenfeld, Martha, **55**, 158n
Feil, Doris, **32**, 63n
Feil, J. P., 'Dramatic References from the Scudamore Papers', **11**, 107–16
Feild, John, **17**, 141
Feinstein, Blossom, **23**, 164n
Feinstein, Elaine, **42**, 152; **43**, 207; **53**, 110; **54**, 340; **55**, 132; **58**, 301
Feis, Jacob, **28**, 41
Fekete, Peter, **54**, 295
Feklistov, Alexander, **60**, 300
Feldman, A. Bronson, **4**, 149; **5**, 140; **7**, 143
Felheim, Marvin, **5**, 135; **23**, 144; **25**, 115, 116; **32**, 25n; **35**, 10; **39**, 76n
Felipe, Tata, **54**, 160, 162
Felix and Philiomena, **7**, 98
Felix, J., **4**, 111–12
Fell, Blair, **58**, 154
Fell, Dr, **35**, 129–30
Fellini, Federico, **52**, 90; **56**, 5, 14
I Vitelloni, **11**, 19
Fellowes, E. H., **15**, 6; **19**, 106n
Felperin, Howard, **21**, 153; **22**, 164; **27**, 168–9; **33**, 188; **34**, 144; **36**, 98n; **38**, 16; **40**, 132, 190, 204; **43**, 16n, 44–5, 48, 55, 131; **44**, 224–5; **46**, 82, 83n, 84, 87, 89; **50**, 242–3; **55**, 232n; **57**, 33, 34
Felsenstein, Frank, **51**, 160n
Felton portrait of Shakespeare, *see under* Shakespeare, William, portraits
Felver, Charles S., **10**, 146; **32**, 6
Fen, Elizaveta, **48**, 118n
Fencl, Antonín, **9**, 104, 106, 110n
Fenkohl, Jörg, **37**, 159n
Fenn, Ezekiel, **42**, 107n; **58**, 236
Fenner, Dudley, **26**, 154; **27**, 84; **49**, 190n; **54**, 169
Fennor, William, **17**, 92n, 95, 97; **54**, 69
Fenouillat, Christian, **54**, 289
Fenson, Jonathan, **58**, 278
Fenton, Edward, **17**, 30, 32
Fenton, Geoffrey, **2**, 74, 75; **34**, 103, 185, 196; **36**, 194; **47**, 164
Certain Tragical Discourses, **15**, 165, 170; **20**, 166
Forme of Christian Pollicie, **2**, 70
Fenton, George, **28**, 146; **54**, 290
Fenton, James, **36**, 155; **37**, 168
Fenton, John, **38**, 23n
Fenton, Mr (servant of the Earl of Warwick), **12**, 96–9
Fenton, Richard, engraver, **13**, 75
Fenton, Sarah-Jane, **42**, 157; **44**, 197
Fentress, James, **52**, 55n, 62
Fenwick, Henry, **39**, 86n, 93, 95–8, 105n, 106, 107n, 108n, 109, 110n; **41**, 72; **45**, 188
Fenwick, Kate, **44**, 201
Feore, Colm, **40**, 160–2, 166; **56**, 4n
Ferber, Michael, **45**, 169
Ferdinand II, Emperor, **33**, 166; **36**, 142, 146; **43**, 56
Ferdinand of Styria, King of Bohemia, **33**, 168; **36**, 145
Ferdinand, Earl of Derby, **57**, 232
Ferdinand, Elector of Cologne, **36**, 146
Ferdinando, Lord Strange, **57**, 227, 233
Ferenczi, Zoltán, **59**, 125–6
Ferguson, Arthur B., **55**, 209n
Ferguson, Everett, **54**, 37n
Ferguson, F. S., **31**, 191; **47**, 24; **55**, 32n
Ferguson, J., **19**, 43n
Ferguson, Liane, **35**, 178, 189
Ferguson, Margaret W., **46**, 60n, 71n, 123n, 131n; **48**, 265; **50**, 195n; **51**, 293, 331; **54**, 134n; **55**, 8n, 117n, 240n
Ferguson, Moira, **46**, 123n, 133n; **49**, 302
Ferguson, W. Craig, **14**, 165n; **18**, 33n, 190; **24**, 176; **27**, 186, 187; **43**, 269; **49**, 325n
Fergusson of Kilkerran, Sir James, **24**, 156
Fergusson, Frances, **46**, 122n
Fergusson, Francis, **7**, 130; **8**, 140; **12**, 150; **15**, 114, 116, 119, 121; **18**, 43–4; **19**, 6, 8; **28**, 104n; **29**, 164; **30**, 104n, 107, 109; **31**, 174; **32**, 6, 50n; **34**, 73; **35**, 97; **37**, 187; **41**, 49
Fermor, Henry, **25**, 144
Fernald, John, **1**, 101
Fernandes, Joy, **60**, 301, 302

Fernandes, Millor, **20**, 123
Fernandez, Karina, **56**, 296
Fernández-Armesto, Felipe, **52**, 205n
Fernando, Marcus, **57**, 295
Ferney, **9**, 94
Fernichel, Otto, **33**, 185
Fernie, Ewan, **58**, 169; **60**, 345–7, 352
Ferrabosco, Alphonso, **2**, 29, 31; **15**, 6; **40**, 220; **48**, 135n
Ferrand, Michele-Eugène, **14**, 119
Ferrandine, Duke of, **60**, 62
Ferrara, Patricia, **47**, 8n
Ferrars, Edward, **15**, 64
Ferrell, Lori Anne, **50**, 255; **54**, 50n, 177n
Ferrer, José, **8**, 122
Ferrero, Anna Maria, **11**, 121
Ferrero, Bonnie, **59**, 127
Ferrero, Guiseppe Guido, **49**, 46n
Ferrero, Mario, **13**, 129; **14**, 121
Ferrers, George, **48**, 257
Ferretti, Dante, **46**, 193
Ferrex and Porrex, **17**, 205–6
Ferrier, Carole, **55**, 174n
Ferrier, Kathleen, **41**, 113
Ferris, Rob, **59**, 294
Ferriss, Suzanne, **60**, 76n22
Ferro, Giovanni, **17**, 183
Ferry, Anne, **51**, 256n; **55**, 338
Festival Players Theatre Company, **58**, 299
Fetherstonhaugh, **3**, 51
Fettes, Christopher, **58**, 304
Feuerbach, Ludwig, **48**, 3; **53**, 117
Feuillerat, Albert, **1**, 10, 65; **2**, 118, 120; **6**, 73n; **9**, 154; **28**, 54n; **33**, 13n, 18n, 19n; **34**, 28n; **40**, 79n; **42**, 2n; **47**, 130n; **50**, 154n; **60**, 58n2
Documents Relating to the Office of the Revels in the Time of Queen Elizabeth, **12**, 21n.; **14**, 5; **15**, 71n
Documents Relating to the Revels at Court, **14**, 5
The Composition of Shakespeare's Plays: Authorship, Chronology reviewed, 158
Feuillet, Octave, *Chamillac*, **9**, 62
Fewson, Jonathan, **54**, 290
Feydeau, Georges, **15**, 133; **22**, 52; **57**, 120
Feyerabend, Sigmund, **43**, 161
Fez, King of, **11**, 90
Ffarington, Sir William, **8**, 7
Ffolkes, David, **1**, 112
Ffowler, Richard, **58**, 224
Ffrangçon-Davies, Gwen, **6**, 123; **7**, 124–5
Fibich, Z., **18**, 76, 86
Fichter, Andrew, **35**, 157n
Ficino, Marsilio, **13**, 158; **14**, 154; **15**, 21, 95, 104; **19**, 121; **31**, 46; **34**, 94–6, 102; **36**, 86n, 90, 91, 94; **48**, 141–2; **59**, 225, 362
Fiedler, Klaus, **40**, 55
Fiedler, Leslie A., **4**, 142–3; **15**, 124n; **23**, 62; **27**, 171; **31**, 130, 136; **33**, 202; **42**, 6n, 32; **43**, 176; **46**, 63, 64, 68; **53**, 147n
Fiehler, Rudolf, **10**, 145; **38**, 14, 94n, 98n
Field, Ann, **51**, 91, 92
Field, Arthur, **9**, 141
Field, Henry, **19**, 102, 105n, 106n
Field, Joan, **41**, 183
Field, John, **1**, 68; **17**, 125 and n.; **60**, 7n10
Field, Nathan, **1**, 44; **5**, 142; **11**, 48; **38**, 85; **42**, 106n; **58**, 223; **59**, 73
Field, Nathaniel, **1**, 38; **17**, 196; **45**, 191
Field, Richard, **2**, 70; **3**, 17; **5**, 146; **7**, 36–7, 38, 39, 40, 41, 46–7; **8**, 55, 159; **14**, 163; **28**, 38; **33**, 14; **44**, 126n, 232; **46**, 249; **54**, 18n, 25n; **57**, 233; **60**, 259
Fielder, David, **41**, 187; **48**, 195; **51**, 210; **52**, 115, 223; **57**, 266
Fielding, David, **43**, 215; **44**, 181, 183
Fielding, Emma, **48**, 203, 207; **49**, 280; **56**, 174–5, 345; **57**, 269, 274, 275; **58**, 268, 299, 302; **59**, 332
Fielding, Fenella, **43**, 211
Fielding, France, **44**, 200
Fielding, Helen, **56**, 175n
Fielding, Henry, **16**, 16, 115; **22**, 2, 5; **29**, 152; **30**, 200; **33**, 188; **36**, 3; **41**, 209; **42**, 100; **43**, 228; **51**, 28, 63; **53**, 129; **57**, 79; **58**, 40; **59**, 32n58
Tom Jones, **12**, 81; **19**, 13
Fielding, J., **32**, 190n
Fielding, Rachel, **44**, 200
Fields, Armond, **57**, 249, 250, 252, 253
Fields, Beverly, **41**, 111n
Fieldson, Peter, **43**, 208
Fienberg, Nona, **43**, 235; **46**, 218; **51**, 286
Fiennes, Joseph, **50**, 206, 213, 215; **51**, 267; **53**, 286; **56**, 118; **57**, 262, 263; **58**, 301, 347
Fiennes, Ralph, **41**, 188; **42**, 48n, 132, 139; **43**, 178, 212; **44**, 173; **45**, 148, 155; **49**, 235, 238–40; **50**, 226; **54**, 246, 254–5, 277; **55**, 323, 330; **59**, 328, 329, 330; **60**, 322
Figg, Olly, **51**, 269
Figgis, J. N., **28**, 65n
Figueroa, John, **48**, 157
Figulus, Carolus, **15**, 97n
Fikhman, Ya'akov, **48**, 63n
Filarete, Antonio, **33**, 145n
Filho, Antunes, **20**, 124
Filipović, R., **4**, 122n
Filippsdottir, Nina Dogg, **57**, 286, 287
Filleul, Nicolas, **15**, 91
Fillingham, John Lloyd, **57**, 285
Finch, Arthur, **13**, 105n
Finch, Jon, **41**, 185; **57**, 147, 148, 149
Finch, M. E., **17**, 73n
Finch, Peter, **6**, 145
Finch, Sarah, **41**, 189
Fincham, F. W. X., **11**, 105n
Findlay, Alison, **49**, 304–5; **51**, 289–301; **54**, 300–1; **55**, 379–80; **58**, 53
Findlay, Deborah, **41**, 165–6, 168; **42**, 154; **44**, 192; **48**, 264; **55**, 318, 321
Findlay, Jim, **44**, 202; **45**, 155
Findlay, Julia, **43**, 212
Findlay, Leslie, **48**, 235
Findley, Timothy, **57**, 298; **58**, 153, 157
Finegan, Amy, **57**, 267
Finegold, Stephen, **54**, 290
Fineman, D. A. **26**, 167–8
Fineman, Daniel, **34**, 18n, 19
Fineman, Joel, **40**, 189–90, 204; **46**, 38n, 44, 91n; **49**, 58n, 203n; **50**, 44n, 46n, 135–9, 141, 143; **53**, 19n, 22n, 23n, 73; **55**, 276
Finet, Sir John, **2**, 25; **11**, 113, 116n; **55**, 93

Fineux, Chief Justice, **52**, 173
Fini, Leonor, **9**, 114; **12**, 111; **18**, 126
Fink, Fritz, **48**, 9n
Fink, Z. S., **8**, 5
Finkel, Simon, **5**, 113; **6**, 121; **10**, 119; **13**, 129
Finkelpearl, Philip J., **24**, 159; **27**, 114n, 119, 120n; **32**, 95n, 104n; **40**, 221; **41**, 197, 217; **42**, 190; **57**, 202; **58**, 205; **59**, 219
Finkelstein, Richard, **54**, 311; **56**, 158n
Finkenstaedt, Thomas, **9**, 134; **29**, 183
Finkerath, William, **53**, 283
Finland, report on Shakespeare in, **1**, 115–16; **2**, 128; **8**, 119; **9**, 112; **10**, 117; **11**, 118–19; **12**, 111; **13**, 126; **18**, 121
Finlay, Alistair, **42**, 159
Finlay, Frank, **60**, 160, 168
Finlay, Ian, **18**, 154
Finley, M. I., **56**, 225n
Finn, Christine, **13**, 137
Finn, Paul, **53**, 280
Finn, Ruth, **55**, 333
Finney, Albert, **31**, 157, 161–2; **37**, 184; **39**, 76, 88; **41**, 47, 49–53; **54**, 249; **56**, 247, 271
Finnis, John, **58**, 321, 332
Finsher (ffinsher), Abigall, **29**, 34, 37
Finsher (ffinsher), Robert, **29**, 34, 37
Fiore, Maria, **15**, 136
Fiorentino, G., *Pecorone*, **3**, 54, 55; **55**, 368
Firat, Mulla, **18**, 130
Firbank, Ann, **52**, 234
Firbank, Ronald, **53**, 139–45, 148–9, 150n; **55**, 343
First Book of Homilies, **60**, 73n4
First English Actresses, The, **46**, 237
First Folio, *see* Shakespeare, William, editions
First Part of the Contention betwixt the two famous houses of Yorke and Lancaster, The, see under 'Contention betwixt the two famous houses of Yorke and Lancaster, The First Part of the', **54**, 13
First Quarto of King Lear, The (ed. J. Halio), **48**, 278n, 281
Firth, C. H., **15**, 6; **55**, 91n
Firth, Colin, **56**, 117, 119
Firth, Jonathan, **48**, 212–3; **49**, 271; **50**, 227
Firth, Kenneth, **6**, 122
Firth, R., **16**, 77–8
Firth, Tazeena, **27**, 146, 151
Fisch, Harold, **21**, 142; **23**, 141; **24**, 148; **25**, 175; **26**, 160–1; **27**, 81–92; **29**, 163; **39**, 139n; **54**, 303–4
  '*Antony and Cleopatra:* the Limits of Mythology', **23**, 59–67
  'Shakespeare and the Puritan Dynamic', **27**, 81–92
Fischer, F. J., **9**, 110n
Fischer, Jan O., **14**, 118
Fischer, Olga, **9**, 104; **58**, 319
Fischer, S., Rowohet, and Goldmann, **13**, 128
Fischer, Sandra K., **44**, 219, 240; **45**, 166
Fischer, Susan, **57**, 31
Fischer, Walther, **6**, 157; **10**, 141
Fischer-Lichte, Erika, **47**, 4, 10; **57**, 169
Fischer-Weimann, Waltrad, **27**, 179n
Fischlin, Daniel, **54**, 340–1; **55**, 132n; **57**, 247
Fish, Charles, **19**, 146; **38**, 14
Fish, Linda T., **46**, 4
Fish, Stanley, **37**, 164, 180; **43**, 23n; **46**, 81; **48**, 64; **49**, 216; **50**, 254; **51**, 284; **54**, 334; **60**, 152–3
Fishburne, Laurence, **51**, 265; **54**, 312; **56**, 112
Fisher, **53**, 226n
Fisher, A. Y., **8**, 8
Fisher, Alan, **44**, 240; **45**, 166
Fisher, Chris, **42**, 150; **43**, 213
Fisher, David, **49**, 279
Fisher, Doug, **42**, 156
Fisher, F. J., **17**, 79n, 116n
Fisher, H. A. L., **51**, 166n
Fisher, Jasper, *The True Trojans*, **11**, 44
Fisher, John, **25**, 144; **28**, 171n; **53**, 200n
Fisher, John Abraham, **51**, 90
Fisher, John, Bishop of Rochester, **52**, 179, 180
Fisher, Lizette Andrews, **31**, 11n
Fisher, Mick, **54**, 287
Fisher, Peter F., **12**, 133
Fisher, Sheila, **55**, 244n
Fisher, Sidney T., **15**, 166; **53**, 196–7, 205–7, 208n, 209, 210
Fisher, Thomas, **5**, 52; **9**, 152; **26**, 74; **43**, 248; **50**, 218; **60**, 226n17
Fisher, Will, **57**, 303, 315
Fishkin, Bobby, **59**, 343
Fishman, J. A., **23**, 11n
Fisk, Erik Steven, **52**, 91n
Fiske, Alison, **25**, 166; **55**, 310; **57**, 265, 285
Fiske, John, **52**, 96n, 97n
Fiske, Roger, **18**, 100n; **19**, 151
Fiske, Stephen Ryder, **35**, 7n
Fitch, Ralph, **32**, 86–7
Fitch, Robert E., **22**, 163; **24**, 138–9, 140
Fitter, Chris, **52**, 109; **54**, 321; **55**, 351
Fitton, Anne, **56**, 62
Fitton, Doris, **6**, 117
Fitton, Mary, **3**, 10; **5**, 137, 138; **9**, 12; **26**, 2; **32**, 96n; **58**, 141
Fitz, L. T., **29**, 165; **32**, 222
Fitz-Geffrey, Charles, **17**, 34n; **50**, 196n
Fitzball, Edward, **20**, 107
Fitzgeoffrey, Henry, **41**, 10
Fitzgerald, F. Scott, **33**, 183
Fitzgerald, Geraldine, **49**, 263
Fitzgerald, Mark, **51**, 265
Fitzgerald, Michael, **49**, 248
Fitzgerald, Percy, **35**, 1, 19
Fitzgerald, Scott, **49**, 67
Fitzgerald, Sheridan, **32**, 203
Fitzgerald, Tara, **49**, 240
Fitzgibbon, H. M., **15**, 7
Fitzherbert, Fr. Thomas, **57**, 18
Fitzherbert, Mrs, **38**, 71, 74; **51**, 13; **56**, 131
Fitzmaurice, Francis Dudley, **59**, 122n54
Fitzmaurice, James, **60**, 336, 353
Fitzpatrick, Joan, **58**, 326, 332
Fitzpatrick, Tim, **52**, 13n
Fitzroy, Augustus Henry, Third Duke of Grafton, **9**, 84–5
Fitzroy, Charles, **11**, 107
Fitzsimons, Raymund, **35**, 8
Fitzwilliam Museum, *see under* Libraries
Five Kings, **39**, 39, 41–6 *passim*, 49, 50, 52
Fixer, John, **21**, 99, 100
Fizer, Irene, **53**, 344
Flachmann, Michael, **46**, 213

Flahiff, Frederick T., **33**, 6n, 35; **37**, 72n; **38**, 162n, 163n, 166n; **41**, 145n, 209; **44**, 86n; **45**, 81n; **55**, 59n
Flamm, Erika, **18**, 172
Flanagan, Richard, **32**, 27
Flanders, Julia, **59**, 85
Flanigan, Tom, **50**, 249
Flannery, James W., **52**, 161n, 162n
Flannery, Peter, **44**, 165
Flasket, John, **60**, 260n28
Flatter, Richard, **3**, 137; **4**, 127; **5**, 7; **6**, 120, 161, 163; **7**, 145; **8**, 118, 153; **9**, 8, 113; **10**, 119, 143; **11**, 41n, 117, 120; **12**, 70n, 137; **13**, 124, 157; **14**, 152; **15**, 131–2, 134, 173, 181; **16**, 63, 65–7, 132; **18**, 185; **19**, 2; **21**, 33, 138; **32**, 152, 156–7
  'Dumb-Show in *Hamlet*' reviewed, **3**, 141
  Hamlet's Father and *The Moor of Venice* reviewed, **4**, 140–1
  Shakespeare's Producing Hand, **2**, 146, 150
    reviewed, **3**, 135
  translation of Shakespeare's plays into German, **7**, 107–8, 111, 112
  Triumph der Gnade reviewed, **11**, 139
Flaubert, Gustave, **6**, 142; **34**, 34; **49**, 209; **56**, 303; **57**, 174
Flaxman, John, **37**, 47
Fleay, Frederick Gard, **1**, 50n; **2**, 35n, 146; **3**, 27; **4**, 158; **6**, 39, 75, 78n; **7**, 66n; **8**, 6; **11**, 105n, 106n; **12**, 140; **15**, 171; **20**, 166; **21**, 16, 27n; **25**, 110; **27**, 106n, 107; **31**, 102; **33**, 164n; **36**, 135, 138n; **38**, 53; **42**, 2n; **43**, 84n; **44**, 152; **45**, 175; **47**, 244; **50**, 277; **53**, 308; **59**, 147
Flecker, James Elroy, **55**, 129
Flecknoe, Richard, **7**, 84, 85, 86; **16**, 96; **17**, 196, 198
Fleeshman, David, **44**, 202
Fleetwood, Kate, **53**, 282; **54**, 263; **58**, 301
Fleetwood, Susan, **23**, 133; **28**, 142, 143; **31**, 160; **34**, 150; **37**, 170; **41**, 50; **45**, 152; **47**, 112; **60**, 79
Fleetwood, William, **44**, 24
Fleg, Edmond, **8**, 118
Fleischer, Ernst, **59**, 133
Fleischer, Martha Hester, **29**, 173
Fleiss, Wilhelm, **37**, 150n
Fleissner, Robert F., **18**, 166; **20**, 163; **22**, 168; **23**, 160; **24**, 146; **25**, 182; **27**, 105–10; **29**, 162; **30**, 201; **31**, 195–6; **32**, 236; **33**, 199, 202; **34**, 172; **35**, 178, 187; **36**, 190, 194; **37**, 191; **38**, 253; **39**, 251; **40**, 204, 236; **43**, 268; **48**, 276n; **52**, 294
  ' "Love's Labour's Won" and the Occasion of "Much Ado" ', **27**, 105–10
Fleming, Abraham, **38**, 41, 42n, 45n, 46n, 110; **42**, 28; **53**, 20, 21
Fleming, Chief Baron, **57**, 14
Fleming, Don, **56**, 8, 14n
Fleming, J., **9**, 85n
Fleming, John F., **19**, 144
Fleming, Juliet, **58**, 156
Fleming, N., **19**, 93n
Fleming, Peter, **49**, 228
Fleming, Tom, **16**, 144; **32**, 203; **39**, 79n
Fleming, William H., **8**, 7–8; **25**, 115
Flemish stage, Shakespearian productions on, **5**, 106–10
Flesch, William, **47**, 8; **58**, 318, 324, 332
Fletcher, A., **46**, 131n
Fletcher, Allen, **16**, 138
Fletcher, Angus, **21**, 145n; **54**, 322
Fletcher, Anthony, **48**, 71n, 72n, 230; **54**, 26n, 166n
Fletcher, Bramwell, **39**, 81n
Fletcher, Brett, **43**, 215
Fletcher, George, **7**, 92; **32**, 17; **57**, 91, 93
Fletcher, Giles (the elder), **2**, 54; **3**, 45; **15**, 101; **42**, 71; **57**, 209
  Licia, **15**, 109n
Fletcher, John, **1**, 40, 44–6, 48–9, 65; **3**, 44, 45, 58, 62; **4**, 129, 160; **5**, 141; **6**, 6, 57, 144; **7**, 6, 45–6, 140, 141, 142, 144; **8**, 52, 55, 56, 66; **11**, 50–3, 58, 59n, 82, 111, 151; **13**, 38, 117, 162; **14**, 163; **15**, 26, 127, 179; **16**, 33, 174–5; **17**, 175, 196–7, 202, 209; **18**, 46, 132, 186–7; **20**, 1–14, 95; **21**, 146; **22**, 157 *(see also* Beaumont and); **23**, 121; **24**, 155; **26**, 8, 34, 42, 169, 177, 184, (and Beaumont) 1, 4, 33, 55, 66, 67, 100; **27**, 176; **28**, 178, 180; **29**, 3, 4, 7, 169, 170; **32**, 93, 241; **34**, 52, 178; **35**, 121, 185; **36**, 107, 109, 110, 114, 188; **37**, 42, 145; **38**, 15, 16; **39**, 133, 230, 235, 239; **40**, 219; **41**, 7, 61, 100–1, 233; **42**, 189, 197–8, 208n; **43**, 25, 43–4, 69, 70n, 71–2, 76–7, 81–9, 257, 269; **44**, 116, 123, 125–8, 131; **45**, 179, 184, 195, 202; **46**, 30, 106, 133, 138, 160; **47**, 33, 252; **48**, 185n, 259, 260, 269, 275, 277; **49**, 102, 304, 324–5; **50**, 152, 169n, 282; **51**, 32n, 95–6, 101, 104–5, 135, 206, 215, 289, 291, 309, 317–18, 334; **52**, 26, 43n, 73, 81, 139, 166n, 211–13, 308; **53**, 285, 300, 338; **54**, 15, 17, 18n, 22, 24n, 25n, 63, 214, 238–9, 241–2, 265, 340, 349–50; **55**, 84, 265, 266, 358–9, 378; **56**, 68, 75n, 77, 78, 146–51, 173n, 314, 339; **57**, 91, 258, 259, 261, 335; **58**, 226, 234, 305, 349, 358; **59**, 2, 22, 23–4, 24n20, 71, 72, 75, 76, 77n12, 98, 214, 218, 219, 220, 221, 222, 259, 260; **60**, 67–8, 81–2, 98, 109, 188, 327, 368
  King and No King, A, **48**, 259
  The Night-Walker, **10**, 150
  see also under Beaumont and Fletcher *and* Beaumont, Francis
Fletcher, Paddy, **41**, 184
Fletcher, Phineas, **3**, 45
  The Locusts, **4**, 155
  Sicelidae (MS.), **3**, 52
Fletcher, Ronald, **48**, 113n
Flickenschildt, Elizabeth, **12**, 112
Fliegelman, Jay, **57**, 129, 133, 135
Flimm, Jürgen, **37**, 162
Flint, Kate, **55**, 108
Flintoff, Ian, **50**, 223
Flon, Suzanne, **12**, 111; **15**, 133
Flood, Griffin, *The Life and death of Griffin Flood informer*, **17**, 91n
Flood, Valentine, **36**, 140
Florenne, Yves, **9**, 113; **18**, 122
Florentius, **8**, 116n
Flores Doctorum, **3**, 15
Florian, Călin, **20**, 129
Florio, John, **2**, 151; **3**, 2, 10, 25; **4**, 9; **6**, 88, 160; **7**, 139; **9**, 141; **10**, 119; **12**, 43; **15**, 100, 127; **17**, 202–3, 225, 234; **23**, 45n; **24**, 76n; **27**, 45n, 50n, 52n, 54n; **28**, 38, 39, 41, 42, 98n, 134; **29**, 79; **32**, 164, 186n; **33**, 19; **38**, 49n, 167n; **46**, 58n, 65; **47**, 161–3; **48**, 31n, 151–2, 154; **49**, 63n; **51**, 136, 161n, 178; **52**, 186, 187n; **53**, 22n; **55**, 253n; **57**, 218, 219, 234; **59**, 359; **60**, 232, 343
  First Fruites, **6**, 73n
  Florios Second Frutes, **9**, 34n
  influence on Shakespeare and Ben Jonson, **7**, 104–5
  translation of Montaigne, **3**, 4, 6
Florio, Michelagnolo, **6**, 160; **10**, 120
Florius, **15**, 90

Florus, Lucius Annaeus, **38**, 119n
Flower, A. C., **29**, 165
Flower, Sir Archibald, **36**, 73
Flower, Barbara, **13**, 165n
Flower, Charles, **42**, 47; **54**, 85
Flower, Edmund, **19**, 106n'
Flower, Edward Fordham, **54**, 84–5
Flower, Sir Fordham, **1**, 107
Flower, John, **11**, 109, 115n
Flower, Sarah (née Martineau), **54**, 85, 87
Flower, Sir William, **54**, 84
Floy, Gregory, **44**, 197; **54**, 290; **56**, 297
Floyd, John, **54**, 231–2
Floyd, Simon, **52**, 258; **55**, 327
Floyd-Wilson, Mary, **57**, 188; **59**, 351, 368
Fluchère, Henri, **4**, 25n; **9**, 67n; **15**, 99, 108n; **16**, 54; **18**, 123; **19**, 143; **20**, 127, 131n; **21**, 137; **51**, 144; **57**, 121
Shakespeare reviewed, **7**, 129
Shakespeare, Dramaturge élisabéthan, **2**, 133, 141
reviewed, **3**, 130, 132–3
'Shakespeare in France: 1900–1948', **2**, 115–25
Fludd, Robert, **13**, 159; **20**, 167; **21**, 155; **23**, 172; **24**, 166; **31**, 185; **50**, 152
Fly, R. D., **28**, 155; **29**, 163; **31**, 57n, 169; **38**, 165n; **40**, 209
Flygare, William, **38**, 233
Flynn, Barbara, **51**, 251
Flynn, Errol, **47**, 95
Flynn, Jerome, **43**, 217
Flynn, John T., **25**, 182
Foà, Arnoldo, **13**, 129
Foakes, R. A., **7**, 132; **9**, 134, 139; **10**, 9; **11**, 139, 151; **12**, 149; **13**, 105n; **14**, 12; **15**, 179; **16**, 162, 165; **17**, 207n; **18**, 163, 186n, 188; **19**, 125, 129; **21**, 145, 153; **22**, 107n, 179; **25**, 4, 9, 12n, 50, 51, 82, 185, 187, 191; **26**, 9, 99n, 153, 170, 173; **27**, 134n, 163; **28**, 153; **29**, 3, 8–9, 42, 43, 127, 128, 129; **30**, 95; **32**, 9; **33**, 113, 139n, 156n, 196; **34**, 58n, 68n, 72, 93n, 164–5; **36**, 95n, 172; **37**, 5, 184; **38**, 5, 15, 16, 139n, 145n, 146n, 147n, 149n; **39**, 238n, 240–2, 249; **41**, 5, 204, 238, 243; **42**, 53, 58n, 60, 182, 190, 203; **43**, 44n, 45, 51n, 55, 59n, 67n, 141n, 146n, 167n, 168, 220, 250; **44**, 149n, 251; **45**, 107n, 183n, 197; **46**, 58n, 65; **47**, 15n, 35, 38, 42, 140, 175n, 222, 224, 232, 241; **49**, 285, 324; **50**, 151–70, 180n; **51**, 57n, 145, 179, 306–7, 329; **52**, 1n, 3n, 10n, 14n, 72n, 166n, 273, 325; **53**, 106n, 197, 339; **54**, 21n, 234, 238–44, 311, 344n, 350, 357; **55**, 1, 3, 6n, 10, 12n, 13, 27n, 28n, 29n, 34n, 36n, 43n, 47n, 55n, 69, 72, 73n, 74, 79, 80, 117, 140, 181, 182n, 189, 190, 381, 382; **56**, 39n, 56n, 93n, 235n, 330; **57**, 306, 317–18, 339; **58**, 34, 90, 92, 93; **59**, 15n65, 36, 36n80, 37n87, 38n87, 42, 47, 219, 375; **60**, 36n3, 38n7, 38n8, 39n9, 40, 40n11, 40n17, 41n18, 41n20, 44, 44n30, 45n40, 45n48, 46n50, 49n2, 75n17, 84n1
'The Text of Coleridge's 1811–12 Shakespeare Lectures', **23**, 101–11
'The Art of Cruelty: Hamlet and Vindice', **26**, 21–31
'*Hamlet* and the Court of Elsinore', **9**, 35–43
'Suggestions for a New Approach to Shakespeare's Imagery', **5**, 81–92
(ed. with R. T. Rickert), *Henslowe's Diary* reviewed, **15**, 171–2; **17**, 207n.
(with R. T. Rickert), 'An Elizabethan Stage Drawing?', **13**, 111–12
Foersom, Peter, translations of Shakespeare, **3**, 108
Foerster, Carl, **9**, 107
Foerster, N., **18**, 118n
Fogarty, Elsie, **52**, 28n
Fogel, Ephim G., **13**, 168; **43**, 59n
Fogerty, Elsie, **56**, 245
Fogg, Nicholas, **41**, 220–1; **44**, 198; **56**, 296
Fogle, French R., **6**, 63n; **46**, 115n
Fogle, Richard Harter, **34**, 143
Foister, Susan, **53**, 203n
Foley, Alice, **58**, 116
Foley, Henry, **24**, 72n; **57**, 18
Folgar, Henry Clay, **55**, 386–7
Folger Shakespeare Library, *see under* Libraries
Folger, Abigail, **57**, 155
Folger, Emily Clare, **1**, 57, 59
Folger, Henry Clay, **1**, 57–78; **3**, 57; **10**, 154; **16**, 1; **36**, 190; **47**, 258
Folger, Peter, **1**, 57
Folios, *see* Shakespeare, William
Folk Dance and Song Society, **12**, 9
Folkenflik, Robert, **30**, 200
Folland, H. F., **28**, 159
Folliot, Denise, **49**, 206n
Folorunsho, Charlie, **48**, 235
Fonagy, Ivan, **53**, 15n
Fonda, Henry, **40**, 102
Fontaine, Fine Time, **56**, 291
Fontane, Theodor, **23**, 122; **35**, 12; **52**, 288; **54**, 335–6; **56**, 130
Fontanel, Geneviève, **57**, 119
Fontanne, Lynn, **5**, 115
Fontenrose, Joseph, **54**, 41n
Foor, Sheila Reitzel, **56**, 152n
Foot, Michael, **37**, 172
Foote, John L., **11**, 123
Foote, Maria, **32**, 34; **52**, 292
Foote, Samuel, **9**, 54; **11**, 123; **14**, 113; **51**, 17; **55**, 105n, 135
Forbes, Brenda, **59**, 67
Forbes, Duncan, **43**, 57n
Forbes, Jill, **43**, 251
Forbes, Leslie, **56**, 302
Forbes, Lydia, **18**, 160
Forbes, Peter, **47**, 213
Forbes, Scott, **39**, 81n
Forbes-Robertson, Sir Johnston, **2**, 5, 6, 19; **4**, 105; **7**, 29; **9**, 16, 17, 23, 57; **14**, 151; **18**, 74, 184; **20**, 81n; **29**, 142; **35**, 33; **39**, 75, 77, 79, 82; **42**, 151; **43**, 252; **48**, 192; **49**, 8n, 128; **56**, 245n; **59**, 150
Forbis, F. J., **15**, 16
Ford, Anne, **47**, 97–8
Ford, Boris, **9**, 132, 144n; **31**, 48n; **44**, 72, 235
Ford, Bruce, **55**, 330
Ford, David, **43**, 217
Ford, Emanuel, **60**, 272n13
Ford, George H., **41**, 108n
Ford, Gerald, **28**, 65; **57**, 138
Ford, Guy, **45**, 63n
Ford, H. L., **7**, 91
Ford, Harrison, **53**, 171, 172n; **56**, 256

INDEX

Ford, James, **44**, 193
Ford, Jane, **53**, 297; **58**, 100, 101
Ford, John, **3**, 45; **6**, 154–5, 157; **7**, 129; **14**, 12, 82–3, 86–7; **18**, 181; **21**, 40; **23**, 171; **24**, 5, 6, 11, 165; **26**, 1, 4, 5, 8, 66, 169; **30**, 4; **31**, 184; **32**, 103n; **33**, 25, 91, 197; **34**, 178; **36**, 142, 175; **37**, 117; **41**, 7, 10, 116n; **42**, 17n; **43**, 129; **44**, 211, 237; **45**, 175, 177; **51**, 101, 289, 327; **54**, 301, 357; **55**, 61, 62, 65–6, 84, 350; **56**, 186; **57**, 300, 336; **59**, 5n15, 184, 213, 214, 217, 376
The Lover's Melancholy, **1**, 127
Love's Sacrifice, **13**, 168; **14**, 165
Perkin Warbeck, **12**, 134; **20**, 162
'Tis Pity She's a Whore, **15**, 133
see also Dekker, Thomas
Ford, John R., **60**, 122n7
Ford, Julia, **42**, 132
Ford, Mark, **48**, 196n
Ford, Rodney, **42**, 157; **44**, 201; **45**, 145; **52**, 258, 261
Ford, Ruth, **4**, 124
Ford, Susan, **58**, 83, 90
Ford, Vanessa, **41**, 185
Ford, William, **4**, 82
Ford, Worthington Chauncey, **24**, 89n
Ford-Davies, Oliver, **31**, 148; **37**, 171; **54**, 253; **56**, 283
Forde, Emanuel, *Montelyon*, **1**, 70
Parismus, **1**, 69
Fordun, **57**, 9
Fordyce, James, **51**, 20
Foreign Shakespeare: Contemporary Performance (ed. D. Kennedy), **48**, 262
Foreman, Richard, **47**, 3
Foreman, Walter C., **35**, 165
Fores, S. W., **38**, 72
Forest, Louise C. Turner, **4**, 11; **7**, 10
'A Caveat for Critics' reviewed, **1**, 119, 126
Forest-Hill, Lynn, **59**, 248n68
Forester, John, **49**, 67n
Forey, Madeleine, **52**, 280
Forgacs, David, **57**, 31
Forker, Charles R., **18**, 167; **20**, 155, 163; **23**, 171n; **24**, 165; **33**, 189; **36**, 169–70; **37**, 215n; **38**, 8, 39, 112n, 227; **43**, 262; **44**, 237; **45**, 162; **50**, 41n, 43n, 55; **52**, 275; **56**, 352–3; **59**, 136n1, 379
Forman, H. B., **14**, 88n
Forman, M. Buxton, **24**, 110n, 114n 116n
Forman, Nelly, **46**, 9
Forman, Simon, **1**, 15; **4**, 42; **11**, 71–5; **14**, 151; **15**, 174; **16**, 175; **19**, 43; **23**, 173; **26**, 81–8; **28**, 4, 5, 7; **29**, 2; **32**, 97; **34**, 183; **44**, 22, 23; **46**, 81n; **47**, 241; **52**, 147, 322; **54**, 307; **57**, 5, 6, 69; **58**, 14; **59**, 379; **60**, 269, 354
Bocke of Plaies, **2**, 147, 148; **4**, 88
his account of *Cymbeline*, **4**, 90
Forman, Walter, Jr, **33**, 31n
Formby, George, **36**, 152; **51**, 220; **56**, 251
Fornara, Lisa, **47**, 218
Forrest, Edwin, **9**, 56; **16**, 104; **18**, 104, 106; **30**, 199; **35**, 9; **45**, 32; **53**, 293; **56**, 100; **57**, 90, 91, 127; **59**, 65, 374
Forrest, G. T., **3**, 89
Forrest, H. R., **7**, 92
Forrest, Ian, **44**, 198, 199; **45**, 155; **47**, 214; **50**, 231; **51**, 264; **55**, 331
Forrest, James F., **27**, 160, 179; **31**, 190
Forrest, Rik, **50**, 227
Forse, James H., **46**, 231; **48**, 263; **50**, 242; **58**, 220
Forset, Edward, **28**, 65–6, 67
Forsett, Edward, *Paedantius*, **6**, 60
Forster Virginal Book (1624), **3**, 56
Forster, E. M., **36**, 33; **53**, 2, 6, 7, 139n; **56**, 138, 139n
Forster, John, **53**, 104, 106n; **57**, 94
Forster, Juliet, **52**, 258
Forster, L. W., **11**, 116n; **16**, 70
Förster, Max, **44**, 108n
Forsyth, Neil, **55**, 383; **56**, 328
Fort, J. A., **3**, 10; **15**, 11, 12
Fort, J. B., **15**, 168; **19**, 140
Fortescue, Sir John, **27**, 72; **29**, 85; **32**, 235; **37**, 192; **43**, 238
Fortescue-Brickdale, Eleanor, **37**, 51
Fortier, Mark, **54**, 340–1; **55**, 132n; **57**, 247
Fortin, René E., **23**, 148; **27**, 165; **28**, 152, 154; **34**, 175; **36**, 167n; **50**, 240; **55**, 215n
Fortune playhouse, **52**, 1–2, 5–6, 10, 12, 14, 19–26, 30–2, 69, 215
Fortune Theatre, *see under* Theatres, Elizabethan
Fortune, Jack, **44**, 193
Fortune's Tennis, **2**, 46, 51; **3**, 50, 52
Foss, E., **17**, 80n
Foss, George, **32**, 29n
Foss, Wenche, **11**, 121
Fosse, Bob, **52**, 98n
Fossey, Brigitte, **57**, 119
Foster, Barry, **45**, 135, 136; **46**, 200; **53**, 283
Foster, Ben, **44**, 193
Foster, Beverley, **44**, 197
Foster, Donald W., **41**, 207, 219, 234; **43**, 258–9, 260–1; **47**, 252n, 261; **51**, 326–7; **54**, 306; **55**, 48n; **57**, 32, 37, 309, 336
Foster, Elizabeth Read, **28**, 25n
Foster, Hal, **49**, 209n
Foster, Joanna, **41**, 186
Foster, Mike, **55**, 257n
Foster, Miles, **56**, 292
Foster, Thomas, **11**, 101
Foster, Verna A., **47**, 230; **48**, 115n
Fotez, M., **15**, 141; **18**, 134
Fothergill, G., **6**, 73n
Fothergill-Payne, L. and P., **51**, 69n
Fotheringham, Richard, **39**, 229
Foucart, Jean, **29**, 29
Foucault, Michel, **40**, 190, 224; **44**, 75; **46**, 1, 2, 3, 41n, 42n, 124, 125, 126n, 130, 134, 235; **48**, 40n; **49**, 61n, 304; **50**, 243, 278, 289; **51**, 150, 151n, 272, 204; **52**, 301; **53**, 39n, 73, 79n, 233–4, 236, 243, 311; **54**, 22, 323, 333; **55**, 6, 210, 240, 242, 337, 359; **56**, 42n, 91, 204, 209, 232, 233n; **57**, 31, 325; **59**, 35, 148n4, 290n29, 364, 365; **60**, 233, 254, 365
Fouch, Richard, **58**, 223
Fouère, Olwen, **48**, 229; **58**, 261
Foulis, Robert and Andrew, **18**, 16
Foulkes, Richard, **23**, 173; **31**, 188; **35**, 9n, 10n; **38**, 236; **41**, 224; **47**, 91n; **49**, 128n; **53**, 108n; **54**, 81n; **56**, 134n, 135n; **58**, 113, 115
Foulkes, William, **17**, 48
Fouquet, **16**, 53
Four Plays in One, **13**, 120; **54**, 25

Fourdrinier, P., **49**, 113n
Fourmantchouk, Anatoly, **49**, 277
Fournier, Camille, **5**, 115
Fourquevaux, Raimond de, **58**, 36
Fowler, A. D. S., **23**, 164; **25**, 183; **26**, 14–15, 173; **27**, 109n
Fowler, Alistair, **19**, 138; **42**, 182; **43**, 245–6; **50**, 248
Fowler, Elizabeth, **51**, 297; **55**, 344; **59**, 361
Fowler, Emma, **43**, 211, 214
Fowler, F. G., **29**, 105n
Fowler, H. W., **7**, 22; **29**, 105n, 106, 108, 109, 110, 112
Fowler, J. T., **49**, 198n
Fowler, James, **41**, 224
Fowler, John, **29**, 32
Fowler, Katherine, **25**, 143; **29**, 32, 33
Fowler, Peter J., **52**, 35n
Fowler, W. Warde, **10**, 6; **40**, 73
Fowles, John, **52**, 317; **53**, 164n; **55**, 175; **56**, 160
Fox, Alice, **34**, 175
Fox, Charles A. O., **11**, 143n
Fox, Charles James, **14**, 83; **38**, 69–73; **51**, 12; **56**, 131
Fox, Emilia, **54**, 253
Fox, James, **45**, 157; **47**, 210; **57**, 147
Fox, Jay, **60**, 178
Fox, John, **58**, 250, 253
Fox, Levi, **5**, 57n, 139; **18**, 178; **19**, 145; **24**, 157; **27**, 175; **39**, 226; **51**, 142; **60**, 1, 1n1, 10n25, 19n48
'An Early Copy of Shakespeare's Will', **4**, 69–77
'The Heritage of Shakespeare's Birthplace', **1**, 79–88
'The Soest Portrait of Shakespeare', **15**, 130n
Fox, Luke, navigator, **17**, 24
Fox, Olly, **60**, 302
Fox, Patsi, **57**, 48
Fox, Paul, **54**, 291
Fox, Richard, Bishop, **32**, 133
Fox, W. M, **11**, 30n
Foxe, John, **12**, 142; **16**, 169; **17**, 110–11, 125; **23**, 169; **28**, 22; **36**, 171; **38**, 24n, 93–4, 97, 99; **43**, 53; **45**, 102; **48**, 39n, 40, 71, 72, 74; **50**, 251; **51**, 296; **52**, 172, 205, 207n, 320; **54**, 4, 9, 35, 39n, 61, 100, 102; **55**, 388; **57**, 242; **60**, 120Fig.18, 118–22
Actes and Monuments, **2**, 139; **6**, 73n
Foxe, Oliver, **49**, 185
Foxon, David, **32**, 96n
Foxton, Richard, **50**, 228, 231
Foy, Eddie (Mr Edwin Fitzgerald), **57**, 249–56
Foy, Robert C., **31**, 5n
Fra Angelico, **19**, 70
Fracci, Carla, **18**, 126
Fradenburg, Louise Olga, **52**, 204n, 214
Frain, James, **56**, 4n, 283; **57**, 45, 52
Fraioli, Deborah, **42**, 31n
Fraisse, Jean-Claude, **56**, 308
Frame, Janet, **55**, 171, 177–80
Frampton, John, **17**, 160; **32**, 90n
France, **1**, 114
Shakespeare in academic studies, **2**, 119–21
authorship controversies, **2**, 118
'discovery' by Voltaire, **2**, 115
early translations, **2**, 116
impressionistic criticism, **2**, 118–19
modern criticism, **2**, 117–21
modern productions, **2**, 122–4
modern translations, **2**, 121–2
romantic criticism, **2**, 116–17
reports on Shakespeare in, **7**, 110–11; **9**, 112–13; **10**, 117–18; **11**, 119; **12**, 111–12; **13**, 127; **14**, 118; **15**, 132; **16**, 133; **18**, 121–3
France, Anatole, **9**, 68n
France, Anna Kay, **31**, 175
France, Richard, **39**, 40n, 49n
Frances, Heidi, **57**, 185
Francesca, Piero della, **15**, 132
Francis I, King, **44**, 56, 61
Francis, Clive, **50**, 212–13; **51**, 267; **54**, 285; **59**, 345
Francis, Derek, **12**, 125
Francis, Duke of Anjou, **54**, 91
Francis, F. C., **5**, 53; **24**, 171n
'The Shakespeare Collection in the British Museum', **3**, 43–57
Francis, Geoff, **56**, 273; **57**, 339
Francis, Marie, **47**, 215
Francis, Matthew, **41**, 189; **42**, 159; **55**, 311–13; **56**, 293
Francis, St, **14**, 152
Francke, A., **5**, 114
Franco, Angel, **17**, 40n
Francolini, Anna, **52**, 232
Franconi brothers, **3**, 100
Francovich, Massimo, **15**, 136
Frank, Arthur, **55**, 240
Frank, Philip, **51**, 258
Frank, Robert G., **55**, 64n
Frankel, William, **38**, 209
Frankforter, A. Daniel, **58**, 358
Frankis, P. J., **10**, 146
Frankl, Paul, **33**, 143n, 145n
Frankland, Tom, **58**, 299
Franklin, Colin, **51**, 7; **59**, 129
Franklin, Helen, **46**, 121, 196
Franklyn-Robbins, John, **44**, 194; **51**, 219
Franko, Mark, **54**, 194; **55**, 241n, 243n, 244–5
Franks, Philip, **36**, 150; **42**, 151; **50**, 104n, 229; **60**, 327
Franks, Tanya, **45**, 152
Franssen, Paul, **54**, 74n, 79n; **58**, 138, 142
Frantz, David O., **53**, 27n
Franz Josef I, Emperor of Austria, **35**, 23; **36**, 77; **44**, 197
Franz, Wilhelm, **7**, 3; **23**, 11n, 13
Shakespeare-Grammatik, **7**, 2
Frascatoro, Girolamo, **17**, 164–5
Fraser, Alice, **47**, 101
Fraser, Annette, **43**, 216
Fraser, Lady Antonia, **43**, 57n
Fraser, Donald, **42**, 151, 161; **46**, 193
Fraser, Duncan, **32**, 222
Fraser, John, **23**, 156; **41**, 184
Fraser, John W., **54**, 39n
Fraser, Laura, **56**, 15
Fraser, Lovat, **4**, 102
Fraser, Meg, **57**, 296; **59**, 314, 339
Fraser, Russell A., **18**, 57n, 164–5; **25**, 190; **27**, 177; **30**, 150; **33**, 35n; **38**, 131n; **40**, 228–30, 236; **56**, 31n, 32n, 34n; **58**, 1, 2, 350, 356; **59**, 81n9
Fraser, Sonia, **52**, 256
Fraser, Toa, **55**, 170, 180

Frati, Carlo, **20**, 26n
Frattaroli, Elio J., **45**, 77n
Fraunce, Abraham, **9**, 24; **42**, 54n, 88; **45**, 181–2; **50**, 58, 139
The Arcadian Rhetorike, **4**, 86
Frawley, Monica, **45**, 152; **52**, 266
Frayn, Michael, **48**, 118n
Frazer, Gordon, **47**, 275
Frazer, Harriet, **51**, 96
Frazer, Sir James George, **7**, 2; **15**, 114, 119; **16**, 38; **18**, 117; **23**, 63; **25**, 108; **38**, 77n; **48**, 240; **52**, 185n; **54**, 31n; **55**, 200n, 206n
Frazer, Winifred L., **32**, 236, 244; **45**, 183
Frazier, Harriet C., **22**, 167n; **25**, 187; **43**, 82–4, 89
Freakley, Vernon, **5**, 120
Frech, Andrew, **53**, 269
Fredegar, **59**, 239
Fredén, Gustav, *William Shakespeare*, **12**, 116
Frederick and Basilea (plot of), **3**, 52; **7**, 85
Frederick II, King of Denmark, **22**, 119; **36**, 139
Frederick V, Palatine of Rhein, **32**, 194
Frederick of Jennen, **3**, 16; **31**, 25n
Frederick, Naomi, **58**, 275, 276; **59**, 341; **60**, 285
Frederick, Prince, **43**, 55–6, 69
Frederick Ulric, Duke of Wolfenbüttle, **36**, 139–40
Fredericke, Caesar, **52**, 208
Free, John, **20**, 26n
Free, Mary, **46**, 6
Freeburg, V. O., **32**, 63n
Freed, Amy, **58**, 154, 158
Freedberg, S. J., **26**, 65n
Freedley, G., **7**, 88n
Freedman, Barbara, **35**, 160; **36**, 170–1; **37**, 35; **49**, 58, 208n, 327–9; **52**, 276
Freedman, W. A., **19**, 134
Freehafer, John, **23**, 157, 170n, 171n, 175n; **24**, 155, 168; **26**, 166, 175; **43**, 81, 82n; **51**, 95n, 96–7, 99–101, 104
Freeland, Mark, **42**, 150; **43**, 213
Freeman, A., **18**, 178
Freeman, Arthur, **22**, 167n, 173, 182; **24**, 162, 168n, 171; **27**, 178; **37**, 217n; **54**, 57n, 59n; **60**, 255–6n16
Freeman, Arthur and Janet Ing, **59**, 122n55
Freeman, David, **46**, 199; **51**, 207–9; **52**, 266
Freeman, Douglas S., **6**, 164
Freeman, James A., **29**, 171
Freeman, Jane, **49**, 53n
Freeman, Neil, **56**, 355–6; **59**, 89n34
Freeman, Paul, **51**, 229, 230, 244
Freeman, R. B., **11**, 41n
Freeman, Sir Ralph, **23**, 171
Freeman, Rosemary, **17**, 182n
Freeman, Steve, **54**, 290
Freeman, T. S., **54**, 4n
Freeman, Thomas, **34**, 88
Freer, Coburn, **36**, 180; **56**, 179n
Freese, J. H., **53**, 78n
Freeston, Jeremy, **58**, 186, 193
Freidland, Louis S., **20**, 40n
Freidman, Michael D., **49**, 293
Freiligrath, Ferdinand, **45**, 3, 8, 12
Freindlikh, B., **54**, 149
Freinkel, Lisa, **55**, 339–40
French Theatre, *see* Theatre, French
French, A. L., **21**, 134; **22**, 155; **23**, 145; **24**, 152, 163; **26**, 156; **27**, 31n; **37**, 146n; **38**, 2; **43**, 8n
French, Bruce, **51**, 264
French, Carolyn S., **14**, 143
French, Dawn, **55**, 311; **56**, 293
French, J. Nathan, **36**, 117n
French, James Murphy, **51**, 86n
The Life Records of John Milton, **11**, 106n
French, Leslie, **5**, 120; **8**, 124; **11**, 122; **13**, 131, 135; **18**, 128
French, Marilyn, **37**, 179–80
French, Samuel, **41**, 56
Frenhoff, Rosina, **12**, 114
Frere, Daniel, **43**, 152
Frere, John Hookham, **20**, 93n
Frere, Walter Howard, **25**, 127n; **54**, 123n
Fréron, Elie Catherine, **60**, 221n25
Frescobaldi, G., **15**, 133
Freshwater, Geoffrey, **44**, 158, 164; **53**, 264
Fresneda, Bernardo de, **23**, 81n
Freud, Emma, **41**, 187
Freud, Ralph, **9**, 146n
Freud, Sigmund, **3**, 131; **4**, 11, 140; **7**, 10, 97; **8**, 148–9; **9**, 4, 12–13, 14, 22; **10**, 112; **18**, 40; **19**, 144; **21**, 133; **22**, 15, 16, 65, 145, 146; **23**, 133; **25**, 11; **26**, 59n; **31**, 4; **32**, 117–18; **33**, 189, 192; **35**, 161–2; **36**, 19, 53; **37**, 106, 121n, 122n, 150, 176–7; **39**, 143–4, 146–7; **40**, 35, 94n, 99n, 101–2, 104, 110, 118, 120n, 188, 191, 193, 208; **41**, 129, 196, 212; **42**, 7, 65, 169–72, 178; **43**, 25; **44**, 44n, 47, 53, 75, 211, 213; **45**, 6, 21, 38, 48, 51, 54, 75–7, 100, 135, 137, 167; **46**, 108n, 111n, 112n, 129, 130, 133, 134; **48**, 24, 116, 119, 250, 252, 285; **49**, 7, 58n, 91n, 209n, 211n, 283; **50**, 52, 71n; **52**, 276, 301; **53**, 40n, 48, 82, 85, 297, 306, 320; **54**, 267, 297, 324; **55**, 9, 68n, 69n, 238n; **56**, 113, 138, 163, 311, 327; **57**, 306, 315, 317, 321; **59**, 30, 34n67, 294, 364; **60**, 227, 233, 254
Freund, Elizabeth, **40**, 82; **53**, 296
Freund, Virginia, **11**, 106n, 153
Freund, Walther, **2**, 127
Frey, A. R., **20**, 96
Frey, Charles H., **33**, 188, 202; **34**, 166–7; **35**, 159n; **42**, 175; **43**, 1n, 257; **46**, 88; **59**, 64n5
Frey, David L., **31**, 167; **38**, 5
Freytag, Gustav, **33**, 35
Friar Bacon and Friar Bungay, **50**, 53n; **54**, 227
Fricker, Robert, **5**, 114; **7**, 136; **10**, 106n; **12**, 70n, 138; **14**, 156; **18**, 129; **21**, 129; **28**, 42
Kontrast und Polarität in den Charakterbildern Shakespeares reviewed, **7**, 131
Fridén, Ann, **38**, 234, 237; **41**, 223
Fridner, Elis, **22**, 183
Frieberger, Fred, **53**, 170n
Fried, Erich, **23**, 122; **26**, 166; **37**, 160; **40**, 55; **44**, 213
Frieda, Jordan, **58**, 269; **59**, 339
Friedberg, Emil, **28**, 53n; **32**, 132n
Friedel, Dr, **49**, 131
Friedenreich, Kenneth, **38**, 230n
Friedlander, G., **45**, 89n
Friedlander, Larry, **54**, 339
Friedman, Alan Warren, **30**, 188
Friedman, Alice T., **55**, 374

Friedman, Arthur, **55**, 182, 183
Friedman, Donald M., **23**, 165; **31**, 168
Friedman, Elizebeth, **28**, 15n
Friedman, Jerome, **52**, 205n
Friedman, Martin B., **24**, 183
Friedman, Melvin J., **57**, 119
Friedman, Michael D., **56**, 305
Friedman, W. F., **28**, 15n
Friedman, William F., and Elizebeth S., *The Shakespearean Ciphers Examined*, **12**, 140 and n.
Friedman, Winifred, **49**, 119n, 120–1, 122n
Friedmann, Jane, **16**, 137
Friedrich, Theodor, **9**, 96, 100n
Friedrichsen, G. W. S., **49**, 176n
Friel, Brian, **48**, 2; **60**, 201
Friell, Vincent, **44**, 201
Friend, Gayule, **44**, 201
Friend, Michael, **50**, 228, 229
Friesen, Van, **18**, 40
Friesner, Donald Neil, **23**, 141; **24**, 154, 155
Frigerio, Ezio, **12**, 114
Frings, Cardinal Josef, **4**, 126; **6**, 120; **14**, 156; **18**, 124; **23**, 141
Fripp, Edgar I., **3**, 2, 40n; **4**, 9; **7**, 36, 37; **8**, 7, 11; **10**, 14, 15, 20, 24n, 25n; **26**, 74; **32**, 135n; **39**, 143n; **53**, 64n, 67n; **60**, 1, 1n1, 11n30, 13–14n40
Shakespeare: Man and Artist, **13**, 88n; **15**, 14; **17**, 117n; **18**, 179
Shakespeare Studies, **3**, 2
Frisby, Dominic, **49**, 277
Frisch, Harold, **55**, 242n
Frith, John, **54**, 4, 44, 117
Frith, Mary, **60**, 357
Frith, Roger, **46**, 197
Fritzsche, Hans, **18**, 124
Fritzsche, Max, **24**, 145
Frizell, Andy, **47**, 212
Frobisher, Sir Martin, **17**, 29 and n., 31–2 and nn.; **32**, 88–9
Frodi, Berit, **11**, 122
Frogley, Alain, **60**, 191n23
Frohberg, Egon, **48**, 10n
Froissart, Jean, **3**, 18; **6**, 4, 39; **11**, 143n, 144; **28**, 3; **48**, 89; **52**, 315; **57**, 306
From a Jack to a King, **44**, 196
From Text to Performance in the Elizabethan Theatre, **46**, 228
Fromm, Erich, **60**, 232
Frontain, Raymond-Jean, **46**, 218; **51**, 177n; **53**, 15n
Frost, Christina M., **40**, 203
Frost, David, **19**, 145; **41**, 208, 214
Frost, David L., **22**, 171; **26**, 8; **33**, 190; **34**, 131n; **43**, 243
Frost, Kate G., **38**, 230
Frost, Richard, **49**, 230; **52**, 257
Frost, Robert, **37**, 69; **47**, 272
Frost, William, **12**, 137; **15**, 122
Froude, James Anthony, **10**, 33; **48**, 70n
Froula, Christine, **44**, 206
Frunzetti, Ion, **20**, 127
Fry, Christopher, **7**, 113; **16**, 62; **18**, 119; **49**, 226; **55**, 132
'Letters to an Actor playing Hamlet', **5**, 58–61
Venus Observed, **8**, 109
The Dark is Light Enough, **12**, 125
Fry, Helen, **54**, 294
Fry, Kirsty, **44**, 197
Fry, Mary Isabel, **6**, 57, 63n
Fry, Michael, **45**, 153
Frye, Dean, **20**, 146, 150, 152; **21**, 139; **32**, 6; **55**, 59n
Frye, Northrop, **4**, 142; **8**, 2, 3, 8, 143; **15**, 113, 117, 181; 124n; **18**, 131, 172; **20**, 151–2, 159; **22**, 31, 153, 156–7; **23**, 137; **24**, 148; **25**, 107, 108n; **26**, 167; **27**, 144n; **29**, 3, 4, 7, 8, 9–10; **30**, 147, 149n, 151, 153; **31**, 129, 135–6; **32**, 3–5, 12, 54n; **33**, 188; **34**, 125n; **35**, 116n; **36**, 99, 123; **37**, 2, 3, 5, 9, 10, 36n, 73, 118; **38**, 10, 77; **39**, 123; **40**, 119n, 190; **41**, 193–4; **42**, 196; **43**, 16n, 245; **44**, 89, 205; **46**, 73, 74, 88, 89, 208; **47**, 226; **49**, 69; **51**, 145–6; **52**, 275; **53**, 168n, 288; **54**, 16; **55**, 301; **58**, 57, 314; **59**, 41, 81
'Old and New Comedy', **22**, 1–5
Frye, Roland Mushat, **9**, 139; **10**, 9; **18**, 55, 176–7, 181; **20**, 160, 162; **21**, 148; **22**, 149; **23**, 79, 82, 83, 85, 86–7, 88, 148, 162n, 176n; **25**, 6, 186; **29**, 51n, 64, 89; **33**, 89, 92n, 201; **34**, 142n; **35**, 177; **36**, 175; **37**, 194; **40**, 70; **41**, 222; **42**, 182; **45**, 23–5; **54**, 2, 123n, 298; **60**, 225n11
Frye, Susan, **52**, 114
Fryer, Elizabeth, **25**, 148
Fryer, Peter, **51**, 57n, 59, 61n, 64; **52**, 204n
Fryer, Thomas, **25**, 148
Frykman, Erik, **18**, 128; **23**, 138; **24**, 157
Frykowski, Voityek, **57**, 155
Fuchs, Anne, **55**, 272n, 274, 275n
Fuchs, Barbara, **51**, 279
Fuchs, Georg, **2**, 5
Fuchs, Olivia, **60**, 324, 325
Fudge, Erica, **56**, 228n, 232n; **60**, 129n33
Fueda, Uichiro, **49**, 272
Fuegi, John, **26**, 166, 176; **50**, 41n
Fuerst, W. R., **59**, 210–11
Fugard, Athol, **52**, 156; **55**, 273; **60**, 290
Fujimara, Thomas H., **21**, 131
Fujimura, Misao, **48**, 105
Fujita, Minoru, **26**, 159; **37**, 192
Fukuda, Tsuneari, **11**, 121; **12**, 115; **13**, 130; **15**, 137; **16**, 136; **48**, 108–9; **60**, 131
Fulbecke, William, *An Historicall Collection of the Continuall Factions, Tumults, and Massacres of the Romans*, **10**, 29–30, 34; **17**, 74–5; **18**, 170; **44**, 71
Fulgentius, **26**, 112n
Fulgoni, Andrew, **50**, 167
Fulke, William, **56**, 194n
Fuller, H. De W., **10**, 2
Fuller, Margaret Crane, **53**, 127–36; **55**, 342
Fuller, Mary C., **50**, 260
Fuller, Thomas, **2**, 37; **7**, 84, 89n; **16**, 96; **36**, 173; **38**, 86, 91–2; **54**, 18n, 100, 138; **55**, 264; **59**, 115
Worthies of England, **4**, 88
Fuller, Timothy, Jr., **53**, 127–8, 132, 134
Fuller, William, **52**, 60
Fulwell, Ulpian, *Like Will to Like*, **4**, 92; **51**, 136; **56**, 306
Fumerton, Patricia, **46**, 223; **50**, 78n; **54**, 307, 310; **55**, 374; **60**, 79n33, 184n2
Funeral Elegy, A, **43**, 258
Funeral Elegy on the Death of . . . Richard Burbage, **7**, 84
Funnell, Jenny, **42**, 149
Funnell, Leigh, **41**, 188

Funnyhouse of a Negro, **52**, 34
Funston, J. Louis, **29**, 174
Funtek, A., **4**, 117
Furby, Tim, **47**, 117
Furetière, Antoine, **59**, 264n28
Furman, W. A., **48**, 137n
Furness, Clifton J., **18**, 115, 118n
Furness, Horace Howard, **6**, 2; **8**, 52, 55; **10**, 3, 59n, 151; **11**, 152; **15**, 2, 5; **18**, 102–3, 110–11; **20**, 96; **21**, 22, 52n, 163; **27**, 43n, 107, 108n; **32**, 17, 49n, 85n, 86, 95, 237, 241; **33**, 13n, 16n, 17n, 18n, 19; **35**, 33n, 113; **36**, 61n, 119; **37**, 156; **39**, 139n, 143n, 145n; **40**, 131n; **41**, 56n, 83n, 143n; **45**, 3n, 39; **46**, 10n, 63n, 235; **47**, 165n, 166; **49**, 100n; **53**, 187n; **54**, 129n; **55**, 59n; **59**, 37n87, 53–4, 57n22, 60, 136, 136n1, 140, 199; **60**, 364
  Variorum ed. of *King Lear*, **13**, 10n, 39n
Furniss, W. T., **14**, 11
Furnival, Jason, **56**, 254
Furnivall, Frederick James, **6**, 5; **15**, 2, 34, 181; **16**, 32; **18**, 52; **20**, 166; **21**, 65n; **23**, 168; **24**, 111n, 154; **25**, 1; **27**, 132; **32**, 137n; **33**, 147n; **37**, 152; **39**, 154; **44**, 21n; **46**, 14n, 114n, 115n; **49**, 185n, 186n, 190, 193n, 194n; **51**, 90n; **52**, 19; **53**, 299, 308; **55**, 82n; **56**, 244; **57**, 237; **58**, 171; **59**, 374
Furnivall, Percy, **46**, 114n
Furphy, Joseph, **41**, 209; **43**, 221
Furre, Nicky, **44**, 201
Furse, Robert, **41**, 57n
Furse, Roger, **5**, 121; **6**, 145; **9**, 126; **13**, 79; **39**, 3
Furst, Lilian R., **56**, 206n
Fuseli, Henry (Johann Heinrich Füssli), **5**, 113; **7**, 92; **10**, 71; **13**, 75, 76; **15**, 136; **16**, 171; **18**, 18, 129; **37**, 45, 47–8; **49**, 121–2; **51**, 300; **57**, 157; **58**, 334; **59**, 130–2; **60**, 159, 164, 169n6.9, 354
Fusillo, Robert James, **10**, 147
Fussell, Paul, **44**, 111n; **53**, 150n
Fussner, F. Smith, **20**, 31n; **22**, 147
Futcher, Michael, **44**, 196
Futrall, Elizabeth, **55**, 330
Fuzier, Jean, **34**, 62n; **35**, 177, 189; **38**, 50n, 59n, 223; **39**, 235; **50**, 128
Fynnes-Clinton, Michael, **46**, 240n

Gabain, Ethel, **49**, 128
Gabaleoni, Giovanni Battista, **60**, 357
Gabel, Martin, **39**, 46, 49
Gabiani, Vincenzo, **35**, 110n
Gable, Christopher, **46**, 199; **52**, 263
Gabler, Hans Walter, **23**, 118; **25**, 193; **27**, 190; **32**, 242; **37**, 157n; **43**, 268n
  'Shakespeare Studies in German: 1959–68', **23**, 113–23
Gabold, Anelise, **39**, 79n
Gábor, M., **16**, 135; **18**, 125
Gabriel, Paul, **56**, 238
Gabrieli, Vittorio, **33**, 204; **38**, 101, 110n, 111n, 112; **42**, 83; **54**, 9n; **57**, 225, 227; **59**, 70, 78
Gachechiladze, G., **14**, 148; **48**, 187
Gadamer, Hans-Georg, **37**, 159; **51**, 126–8, 138
Gade, Svend, **45**, 42–4
Gaedertz, K. T., **1**, 2; **12**, 11; **47**, 87
Gager, Jean, **22**, 160
Gager, Valerie L., **53**, 107–9; **56**, 127n, 128n
Gager, William, **4**, 95; **32**, 69, 70; **42**, 55; **46**, 128; **54**, 61, 62
  Dido (MS.), **3**, 52; **4**, 91
  Meleager, **4**, 91
  Oedipus (MS.), **3**, 52
  Rivales, **4**, 95
  Ulysses Redux, **4**, 91
Gaguin, Robert, **42**, 26
Gahagan, Mick, **42**, 155
Gaines, Barbara, **59**, 298; **60**, 305
Gaines, Barry J., **25**, 200; **32**, 225; **35**, 188; **40**, 219; **54**, 152n; **55**, 181n, 391
Gainsborough, Thomas, **9**, 54; **37**, 43; **51**, 4
Gainsford, Thomas, *The Glory of England*, **11**, 96, 97n
Gair, W. Reavley, **24**, 159; **28**, 170; **35**, 174; **36**, 179; **37**, 197; **41**, 61n; **42**, 106n; **46**, 227; **56**, 335
Gairdner, James, **6**, 4; **38**, 187n; **39**, 145n
Gajowski, Evelyn, **46**, 218
Galbraith, V. H., **42**, 26n
Gale, Mariah, **60**, 315, 316
Gale, Thomas, **17**, 154
Galen, Claudius, **6**, 154; **17**, 147–8, 149, 154–5, 156, 159–60; **33**, 204; **38**, 178–9; **46**, 118; **48**, 26; **55**, 63; **59**, 350, 351
Galey, Alan, **59**, 174
Galileo, **17**, 139, 143, 146; **40**, 145, 148; **42**, 208; **55**, 63
Galinsky, H., **15**, 97n
Galinsky, William, **56**, 289
Galitskii, V., **13**, 133
Gallagher, Bernard, **45**, 116
Gallagher, Catherine, **58**, 172
Gallagher, Gus, **60**, 285
Gallagher, Joe, **49**, 274
Gallagher, Lowell, **51**, 296; **54**, 96n, 97n; **60**, 346
Gallagher, Peter, **55**, 328
Galli-Curci, Amelita, **6**, 114
Gallienne, Eva le, **1**, 112–13
Gallop, Jane, **60**, 151
Galloway, David, **23**, 125n, 128n; **24**, 53; **25**, 6n, 191; **26**, 34n, 155n, 166n, 170; **27**, 181n; **28**, 169; **31**, 186; **32**, 161; **35**, 174; **39**, 228; **42**, 105n; **47**, 51n, 54n, 55n, 56n; **55**, 242n; **60**, 2n5
Galloway, Lucinda, **44**, 200
Galloway, Pat, **34**, 159; **39**, 184
Galpin, Francis W., **15**, 6
Galsworthy, John, **4**, 118; **34**, 9; **47**, 108
Galt, John, **35**, 33
Galton, Ray, **56**, 118
Galuzin, Vladimir, **56**, 295
Galvan, Bianca, **12**, 114
Gamaury, Martine Y., **56**, 328
Gambino, Ercole A., **5**, 113
Gamble, John, **19**, 102
Gamble, Peter, **23**, 153; **25**, 181
Gambon, Michael, **35**, 151; **36**, 153; **37**, 172–3; **44**, 186; **45**, 152; **55**, 335; **59**, 299, 324–5, 326; **60**, 322
Game at Chess, A, **52**, 75; **54**, 18, 19, 20n, 21, 22, 25, 27, 29
Gamlin, Yngve, **16**, 137
Ganatra, Nitin Chandra, **52**, 235
Gance, Abel, **39**, 78
Gandhi, Leela, **60**, 84–101
Gandino, Marc'Antonio, **56**, 44n

Gang, T. M., **23**, 165
Ganshof, François L., **44**, 60n
Gants, David, **54**, 332
Ganzel, Dewey, **37**, 217; **47**, 61n; **59**, 88n31
Garabedian, Dirkau, **19**, 140
Garber, Marjorie, **28**, 151; **31**, 166, 174; **34**, 103n; **35**, 156–7; **36**, 177–8; **37**, 178–9; **38**, 231, 240; **39**, 212; **41**, 204; **42**, 170–1; **43**, 8n, 16n, 47n, 94n, 99n; **45**, 100n; **46**, 3, 5, 129n; **50**, 54n; **53**, 146–7; **54**, 130; **55**, 9, 222n, 236n; **56**, 2n; **57**, 33, 337, 339
Garbouz, Oleg, **51**, 261
Garces, Maria Antonia, **56**, 40n, 41n
García, Lorca F., **54**, 340
Garcia, Manuel, **3**, 100
Gardarsson, Gisli Orn, **57**, 287; **58**, 305; **59**, 344; **60**, 326
Garde, Alex, **1**, 115
Gardener, *see* Hathaway, Richard
Gardener, Victor, **59**, 340
Gardette, Raymond, **38**, 223; **54**, 319
Gardiner, Alfonzo, **55**, 107n
Gardiner, Balfour, **11**, 31
Gardiner, Bishop of Winchester, **52**, 172
Gardiner, Caroline, **47**, 213
Gardiner, Janey, **44**, 197; **47**, 210
Gardiner, John Eliot, **51**, 82n
Gardiner, Kenneth, **47**, 214
Gardiner, Michael, **49**, 250
Gardiner, S. R., **28**, 19n; **55**, 94n
Gardiner, S. R. (ed.), **17**, 112n
Gardiner, Stephen, **38**, 24
Gardiner, William, **3**, 3, 28, 29; **8**, 6; **17**, 73; **44**, 249
Gardner, C. O., **40**, 142n
Gardner, Carl, **39**, 104n
Gardner, Edmund, **34**, 95n
Gardner, Gordon, **13**, 138
Gardner, Dame Helen, **4**, 43; **11**, 140; **15**, 99; **18**, 9, 55; **19**, 6, 7, 46–7; **21**, 136, 149; **23**, 87, 137, 151; **24**, 168, 171; **25**, 180; **26**, 79n; **31**, 29n; **32**, 2, 4, 8, 9, 46; **33**, 3, 11, 43n, 181–2; **35**, 156; **36**, 31; **38**, 7n; **44**, 217; **46**, 64; **47**, 275; **49**, 214n; **51**, 145; **57**, 22; **59**, 46, 280, 280n41
'*Othello:* A Retrospect, 1900–67', **21**, 1–11
The Business of Criticism reviewed, **13**, 146
Gardner, J. E., **18**, 131
Gardner, Jimmy, **43**, 201
Gardner, Martin, **56**, 139
Gardner, Melanie, **55**, 138n
Gardner, William, **27**, 94
Gare, Trevor, **49**, 280
Garfield, Andrew, **59**, 327–8
Garfield, Leon, **47**, 219; **53**, 152n
Garganigo, Alex, **57**, 316
Gàrgano, G. S., **7**, 106n
Garland, Patrick, **51**, 267; **53**, 276
Garley, John, **5**, 124
Garmon, Owen, **47**, 214
Garnault, Paul, **41**, 189; **44**, 199; **45**, 155; **48**, 230; **51**, 268; **52**, 255; **54**, 291; **55**, 328
Garnault, Ruth, **45**, 155; **46**, 192; **47**, 210; **48**, 230; **49**, 275; **53**, 276
Garneau, Michael, **48**, 228
Garner, Brian A., **45**, 82n
Garner, Brian R., **38**, 219n
Garner, Chris, **48**, 213
Garner, Nina, **55**, 313
Garner, Shirley N., **43**, 230; **44**, 208; **50**, 247–8
Garner, Stanton B., Jr, **34**, 174; **55**, 239n
Garnet, Father Henry, **10**, 136; **29**, 32; **36**, 174; **57**, 13
Garnet, Father Richard, **19**, 52, 54n
Garnett, Constance, **48**, 118n
Garnett, Richard, **41**, 189; **43**, 112; **58**, 143
Garnier, Ph., **9**, 63
Garnier, Robert, **10**, 4; **19**, 146; **27**, 173; **32**, 231; **37**, 191
Cornélie, **10**, 5
Garran, Gabriel, **18**, 122
Garrard, George, **11**, 111, 113, 116n
Garrard, Hadrian, **51**, 260
Garrett, Almeida, **18**, 127
Garrett, John, **9**, 133; **29**, 41n; **32**, 6; **33**, 47n; **46**, 105n; **49**, 154n
Garrett, Nicholas, **57**, 293
Garrick, David, **1**, 60, 73; **3**, 43–4, 47, 51, 57n; **4**, 81, 94; **5**, 51; **6**, 61; **7**, 26, 28, 30, 52, 121; **8**, 69; **9**, 54, 55, 57–8, 59, 65, 90–100; **10**, 72, 73, 150; **11**, 123, 147; **12**, 8, 9, 81, 140; **13**, 74, 75, 80n, 159; **14**, 81, 113; **15**, 2, 153, 173; **16**, 110, 113; **18**, 16, 63, 67, 68, 72, 77–8, 102, 184; **19**, 24n, 151; **21**, 117; **22**, 129, 133; **23**, 173; **24**, 14, 43, 81, 84n; **25**, 48, 113n, 192; **29**, 143, 146, 177; **30**, 189, 198, 200, 201, 206; **32**, 27, 30, 33n, 38; **33**, 190; **34**, 12n, 186; **35**, 5, 48; **36**, 180; **37**, 34, 45, 147, 199; **38**, 70, 236–7, 242; **39**, 230, 233; **40**, 34; **42**, 37, 137, 199; **43**, 99, 104–5, 232; **44**, 207, 221; **45**, 2, 33n; **46**, 143; **47**, 91, 257; **48**, 51, 60; **49**, 2, 4, 7, 14, 74, 111, 113–16, 118, 119n, 122n, 285; **50**, 262; **51**, 3, 5, 6, 9, 10, 11, 12, 14, 15, 19n, 21–6, 27, 59, 61, 62, 63–4, 66, 67, 86n, 88, 89, 107, 109–23, 129; **52**, 149, 152, 200, 291, 292; **53**, 218n, 301, 319, 327; **54**, 42, 46–53, 56; **55**, 96, 105n, 170, 376, 380; **56**, 97, 111, 283; **57**, 55, 59, 60, 62, 67, 81, 82, 83, 84, 85, 86, 87, 88, 90, 91, 93, 94, 95, 115, 130, 131, 134, 135; **58**, 40, 42, 43, 72, 74, 334; **59**, 263, 286n4, 287–8, 289, 291–2, 297; **60**, 80n34, 188
Florizel and Perdila, **6**, 58
Jubilee, **1**, 81; **18**, 17, 94, 96–7, 179
Garrick, Vakhtang, **48**, 189
Garrity, Freddy, **43**, 214
Garrivier, Raymond, **13**, 127; **18**, 122
Garrod, H. W., **14**, 100n; **15**, 79n
Garson, Barbara, **57**, 138, 144
Gartenberg, Patricia, **33**, 186
Garter, Bernard, **39**, 228
Commody of . . . Susanna, **1**, 64
Garter, Thomas, **32**, 128n; **33**, 193
Gartland, Roger, **44**, 197
Garton, Charles, **51**, 180
Gartside, Julian, **45**, 150
Gartside, Kate, **44**, 197
Gartside, Rachel, **46**, 196
Garven, Jamie, **47**, 214; **49**, 272, 279
Garvin, Paul L., **60**, 228n31
Garway, William, customs farmer, **17**, 9
Gary, Giles, **58**, 232
Gascoigne, Andrea, **47**, 218

Gascoigne, George, **6**, 64; **7**, 7, 14; **17**, 226; **18**, 159; **21**, 52; **26**, 172; **41**, 117; **42**, 54n, 187; **46**, 225; **49**, 79, 80; **50**, 66, 74n, 76n, 115; **51**, 322; **56**, 56; **58**, 28
The Glasse of Governement, **4**, 94
Jocasta (MS.), **3**, 52
Supposes, **12**, 141
Gash, Anthony, **52**, 274
Gaskell, Charles Milnes, **24**, 88
Gaskell, Philip, **49**, 326; **55**, 266
Gaskell, Roger, **59**, 116n36
Gaskill, Howard, **59**, 112n19
Gaskill, M., **54**, 166n
Gaskill, William, **18**, 67; **33**, 173; **55**, 160n
Gasper, Julia, **47**, 249
Gassendi, Pierre, **22**, 23
Gassman, Vittorio, **5**, 113; **7**, 112; **8**, 120; **11**; 121; **12**, 114; **14**, 121
Gastambide, Ariane, **47**, 218
Gaston, Robert, **8**, 125
Gataker, Thomas, **58**, 256
Gatch, Katherine H., **38**, 96n
Gatczyński, Konstanty Ildefons, **9**, 115
Gates, Henry L., **39**, 171n
Gates, Sir Thomas, **17**, 33; **54**, 232–3
Gateway Theatre Company, **58**, 299
Gatti, Hilary, **44**, 216
Gatty, Mr and Mrs, **14**, 114
Gaudet, Paul, **41**, 208; **48**, 246
Gaudry, Joseph, **51**, 91
Gaulis, Louis, **12**, 117
Gaultier, Jean Jacques, **12**, 111
Gaunt, D. M., **23**, 161
Gaunt, William, **46**, 195; **57**, 283
Gaussin, Jeanne-Catherine, **3**, 99; **9**, 91
Gautier, Théophile, **6**, 142; **9**, 62; **45**, 1, 2; **56**, 135
Gauvain, C. J. W., **14**, 127
Gavanelli, Paolo, **55**, 328; **56**, 293
Gaw, Allison, **1**, 8; **3**, 27; **33**, 158
Gawain and the Green Knight, **7**, 19
Gawdy, Francis, **17**, 80
Gawdy, Philip, **33**, 154; **55**, 53
Gawin, Gabriel P., **42**, 149, 155
Gay, E. F., **3**, 34, 35; **6**, 59; **53**, 63n, 66n
Gay, John, **20**, 120n; **51**, 69, 72n; **60**, 136n19
The Beggar's Opera, **4**, 102
The Shepherd's Week, **8**, 47
Gay, Penny, **48**, 243; **53**, 293–4; **54**, 307, 312; **56**, 165; **58**, 48, 91, 350, 351, 357; **59**, 206n40
Gayley, C, *Beaumont the Dramatist*, **14**, 12
Gayley, Charles, **8**, 1; **43**, 85, 87
Gaylord, Christian, **60**, 180
Gaynor, Peter, **58**, 265, 266
Gayton, Edmund, **7**, 70; **16**, 96; **51**, 97n; **54**, 66; **56**, 120n
Gearin-Tosh, Michael, **25**, 177
Geary, Carl, **58**, 190
Geary, Keith, **44**, 42n; **46**, 5
Gebhardt, Peter, **37**, 160n
Geckle, George, **25**, 176; **58**, 58
Geddis, Peter, **25**, 165; **41**, 185
Gedge, Morris, **18**, 116
Geduld, Harry, **39**, 4
Gee, Henry, **54**, 123n
Gee, John, **17**, 192; **56**, 120n, 197n, 200
Gee, N. C., **13**, 105
Gee, Prunella, **49**, 279
Geelan, Christopher, **46**, 199; **47**, 213; **50**, 232; **54**, 284; **55**, 326, 327; **56**, 289, 294, 295; **57**, 295; **58**, 299
Geele, Thomas, **11**, 98
Geertz, Clifford, **35**, 66n; **48**, 13
Gelb, Hal, **25**, 176
Gelber, Norman, **23**, 169
Gelder, Ian, **45**, 154
Gell, Robert, **46**, 31n
Geller, Lisa, **35**, 156–7
Gellert, Bridget, **22**, 168; **24**, 145
Gellibrand, Henry, **17**, 144; **43**, 155
Gellner, Julius, **5**, 112–13; **6**, 121; **10**, 119; **15**, 144
Gelmetti, Gianluigi, **55**, 330
Gémier, Firmin, **2**, 123; **14**, 119; **15**, 133; **16**, 54
Geminus, Thomas, **17**, 148, 157, 157n
Gemma, Frisius, **17**, 64
Gemmel, Ruth, **49**, 276
Gems, Pam, **45**, 137
Genast-Merian, E., **14**, 156
Genée, P., **9**, 110n
Generosa, Sister M., **31**, 33n
Genest, John, **10**, 76n; **32**, 37, 38n, 39n; **51**, 117; **53**, 217n; **55**, 96
Génestal, Robert, **32**, 132n
Genet, Jean, **22**, 27, 28; **32**, 4; **43**, 251; **57**, 119
Genn, Leo, **7**, 125
Genster, Julia, **45**, 167
Gent, C. I., **26**, 155
Gent, Lucy, **41**, 116n; **47**, 24n; **55**, 240n, 242n, 250n
Gent, R. U. G., **40**, 215n
Gentile, Giovanni, **34**, 57n
Gentili, Alberico, **32**, 69; **46**, 252
Gentili, S., **30**, 64, 68, 69
Gentili, Vanna, **24**, 162; **44**, 214
Gentillet, Innocent, **2**, 72, 75; **3**, 141; **21**, 143–4; **56**, 225, 226
Contre-Machiavel, **1**, 125
Gentleman, David, **49**, 129
Gentleman, Francis, **2**, 109; **18**, 37; **20**, 75, 77, 81n, 82n; **34**, 13, 14, 16n; **37**, 85n, 146–7, 148n; **43**, 105–6; **45**, 18, 26; **49**, 2, 115; **51**, 58, 63–5; **53**, 100, 101–2, 214–20, 223, 225–6, 231–2; **57**, 59, 60, 61, 85, 86; **59**, 166
The Gentleman's Magazine, **59**, 126, 127
Gentleman, R. T., **50**, 145n
Gentrup, William F., **57**, 126, 188
Gentry, Curt, **57**, 146
Genzel, H. J., **26**, 157
Geoffrey of Monmouth, **3**, 18; **11**, 44, 45; **13**, 41, 44, 46; **28**, 120; **33**, 16; **59**, 240–1, 243
George a Greene, The Pinner of Wakefield, **4**, 94; **54**, 62
George I, King, **51**, 47–50, 52, 55
George II, Duke of Saxe-Meiningen, **35**, 13, 14
George II, King, **45**, 35
George III, King, **3**, 43, 44, 47, 55, 56, 57n; **13**, 40n; **19**, 143; **38**, 71, 73, 75; **51**, 113n; **55**, 174
George IV, King, **38**, 69, 73, 75; **45**, 97; **51**, 4, 12–13; **56**, 126
George V, King, **3**, 56; **40**, 159; **44**, 106, 108
George, Colin, **46**, 203; **50**, 236; **55**, 335

George, David J., **25**, 188; **32**, 233; **35**, 186; **36**, 173; **37**, 196; **44**, 242; **53**, 71n; **55**, 247n; **58**, 240, 358
George, Janet, **48**, 236
George, Jenni, **44**, 202
George, Kathryn, **44**, 198
George, Louise W., **7**, 146n
George, M. Dorothy, **38**, 69n, 70n
George, Martin, **42**, 149
George, Rose, **56**, 248n
George, Sally, **45**, 154
George, Stefan, **15**, 11; **32**, 224
George, William, Elector of Brandenburg, **36**, 144
Georges, Robert A., **29**, 15n, 17n
Gephard, Erwin, **45**, 43n
Gerard de Narbon, **11**, 72
Gerard, *Entertainment in Norfolk and Suffolk*, **1**, 64
Gerard, Albert, **12**, 132; **15**, 167; **19**, 136; **46**, 62n; **48**, 255
Baroque Tragedies, Comparative Essays on Seventeenth-Century Drama, **48**, 255
'"Egregiously an Ass": The Dark Side of the Moor. A view of Othello's Mind', **10**, 98–106
Gerard, John, **17**, 150, 160; **37**, 217; **50**, 71n; **56**, 42n
Herball, **6**, 169–70
Gerard, Sir Thomas, **11**, 92; **21**, 103; **32**, 107; **54**, 230n
Gerasimov, Mikhail, **47**, 179
Gerber, Douglas E., **54**, 209n
Gerbier, Sir Balthazar, **2**, 25, 26, 35n
Gerchow, Frederick, **19**, 101
Gerevini, Silvano, **12**, 114, 151; **26**, 183
S. Gerevini's *Il Testo del Riccardo III*, **12**, 114, 151; **13**, 41, 156
Gerhard, Per, **16**, 137
Gericke, Robert, **8**, 97n, 98n; **49**, 35
Gerlach, John, **28**, 171n; **39**, 6
German, Sharon, **19**, 120
German Theatre, *see* Theatre, German
Germany, report on Shakespeare in, **3**, 117; **4**, 126–8; **5**, 112; **6**, 119–20; **7**, 111–12; **8**, 119; **9**, 113; **10**, 119; **11**, 120–1; **12**, 112–13; **13**, 128; **14**, 119; **15**, 134; **16**, 133–4; **18**, 123–4; **20**, 117–20
translation into German, **4**, 126–7
Shakespeare productions in, **16**, 18
Germer, Rudolf, **14**, 138; **20**, 158
Gérome, Raymond, **6**, 118; **7**, 108
Gerould, G. H., **17**, 172n
Gerrard, Sir Gilbert, **38**, 31n
Gerrig, Richard J., **58**, 23
Gerritsen, Johan, **42**, 190; **43**, 144; **50**, 169n
Gerschow, Frederic, **36**, 145; **41**, 92n
Gershwin, George, **45**, 126
Gerson, Jean, **42**, 31n
Gerstenberg, Hermann, **9**, 96, 99, 100n; **14**, 156; **18**, 174
Gerstner-Hirzel, Arthur, *The Economy of Action and Word in Shakespeare's Plays*, **12**, 70n, 116; **10**, 147
Gerussi, Bruno, **14**, 117; **16**, 153
Gervais, David, **38**, 234
Gervinus, Georg Gottfried, **3**, 110; **18**, 109; **20**, 97; **27**, 106n; **31**, 3n; **37**, 152; **40**, 72; **43**, 112n; **44**, 110n; **45**, 3
Gerzina, Graham, **51**, 57n
Gerzina, Gretchen, **51**, 60, 61n, 63n
Gesner, Carol, **14**, 148; **25**, 178; **29**, 6; **54**, 212n
Gesner, Conrad, **15**, 97n; **17**, 39, 150
Gesta Grayorum, **1**, 65; **3**, 52; **5**, 39; **10**, 39; **13**, 41, 44, 46; **16**, 38; **17**, 51n, 172
Gethner, Perry, **42**, 198n
Getty, Gordon, **42**, 162
Geulen, Eva, **55**, 78n
Gevers, Jos, **5**, 108–9; **7**, 108
Gevisser, Mark, **55**, 281
Geyer-Ryan, Helga, **44**, 44n
Ghana, Shakespeare in, **16**, 77–82
Ghandi, Leela, **48**, 241
Ghazoul, Ferial, **52**, 278
Gheeraert-Graffeuille, Claire, **58**, 333
Gheeraerts, Marcus, **1**, 71; **13**, 104n; **47**, 175, 176; **53**, 201n
Gheeraerts, Marcus II, **60**, 249n53, 251
Ghent, Stage of 1539, **12**, 5
Gheorghe, Tudor, **46**, 196
Gheorgiu, Mihnea, **19**, 145n; **20**, 127, 131n
Gheyn, Jacob de, **58**, 37
Ghiberti, Lorenzo, **40**, 76
Ghir, Kulvinder, **58**, 278
Ghose, Sisirkumar, **22**, 166, 176
Ghose, Zulfikar, **47**, 232
Ghosh, Prabodh Chandra, **21**, 138
Ghosh-Schellhorn, Martina, **60**, 359
Giamatti, A. Barlett, **40**, 123n
Gianakaris, C. J., **23**, 170; **32**, 225; **41**, 195n, 208n; **46**, 93n
Giancarlo, Matthew, **56**, 310
Giannachi, Gabriella, **53**, 153n; **58**, 358; **60**, 155n6
Gianni, Lapo, **15**, 98n
Giantvalley, S., **39**, 76n
Gibberman, Susan R., **53**, 179n
Gibbins, Thomas, **58**, 246
Gibbon, Edward, **10**, 31, 37
Gibbon, J. M., **15**, 7
Gibbon, Piers, **45**, 150
Gibbons, Brian, **22**, 171; **34**, 102n, 103n, 187–9; **35**, 189; **36**, 174, 176, 178; **37**, 201, 218; **38**, 28n; **42**, 181, 183; **46**, 241, 243–7, 248n, 253; **47**, 224; **48**, 249, 281; **49**, 27, 33, 53, 57n, 70n, 75–7, 105, 145n, 164n, 172; **50**, 113n; **52**, 134, 140; **53**, 174n; **54**, 319; **55**, 196, 197; **56**, 89n; **58**, 308; **60**, 368, 369
Gibbons, Fiachra, **60**, 169n9.3
Gibbons, Orlando, **13**, 107, 110n; **15**, 6; **40**, 220; **49**, 320
Madrigals (1612), **1**, 70
Gibbs, Alderman of Stratford-upon-Avon (*fl.* 1883), **60**, 234
Gibbs, Edward, **1**, 85
Gibbs, James, **39**, 170n, 171n
Gibbs, Nathalie, **54**, 288, 295
Gibbs, Willard, **24**, 97
Gibbyns, **11**, 102, 103
Gibinska, Marta, **49**, 309
Gibran, Khalil, **36**, 1, 10
Gibson, Anthony, **47**, 142
Gibson, C. A., **24**, 165; **30**, 207
Gibson, Clive, **43**, 81n
Gibson, Colin, **52**, 210n; **55**, 252n
Gibson, Edgar C. S., **54**, 122n
Gibson, Elizabeth, **51**, 84n
Gibson, F. D., *Sport in Shakespeare*, **11**, 59n
Gibson, Gail McMurray, **49**, 300; **52**, 66n
Gibson, Geoffrey, **35**, 31n

Gibson, James, **47**, 49n, 54n
Gibson, James M., **52**, 83n
Gibson, Jonathan, **58**, 7, 145; **59**, 116, 120n45
Gibson, Joy Leslie, **55**, 379; **58**, 220
Gibson, Matthew, **11**, 114n
Gibson, Mel, **45**, 12, 53, 61, 62; **46**, 193; **49**, 235; **58**, 193
Gibson, Melissa, **47**, 1n
Gibson, Neil, **9**, 120
Gibson, Paul, **42**, 156
Gibson, Rex, **46**, 240n; **49**, 144n; **51**, 315; **53**, 151n, 151n; **55**, 197; **56**, 173n, 302
Gibson, Richard, **60**, 59n3
Gibson, S., **55**, 264n
Gibson, Strickland, **4**, 82, 83; **6**, 33n
Gibson, Tim, **60**, 178
Gibson, Walter C., **49**, 81n
Gibson, Wilfred Wilson, **55**, 135
Gibson, William, **58**, 143
Gibson-Maxwell, Clara, **44**, 194
Gide, André, **1**, 114; **2**, 121, 123; **7**, 108; **9**, 67; **10**, 50, 59n; **15**, 132; **16**, 70, 74; **18**, 122; **24**, 6, 12; **28**, 43, 107; **43**, 28; **48**, 6; **50**, 126–7, 129, 131
Gidion, H., **26**, 166n
Gielen, Josef, **16**, 132
Gielgud, Eleanor, **35**, 7
Gielgud, Sir John, **2**, 10, 12, 14, 15, 16, 17; **3**, 114; **4**, 99, 137; **5**, 120; **6**, 143, 144, 145, 146; **7**, 30, 146n; **8**, 130; **9**, 19, 20–1, 22–3, 54, 57; **10**, 123, 124, 130; **11**, 128, 135; **12**, 74, 86, 116, 122–6; **13**, 79; **14**, 121; **16**, 20, 22–3, 26–7, 37, 134; **18**, 64, 72, 133, 186; **19**, 116; **20**, 145; **21**, 115–19, 122, 125; **23**, 131, 174; **24**, 3, 43; **25**, 29; **27**, 142, 145; **28**, 148; **32**, 29, 31, 32, 35–6; **35**, 7, 160, 172; **36**, 73n, 81, 84, 165; **38**, 237; **39**, 86, 105; **40**, 12, 13, 16, 36–7, 223; **41**, 47, 55–7, 59, 60, 226; **42**, 199; **43**, 110, 117, 183; **45**, 54–8, 76; **49**, 3, 128, 226, 235; **50**, 149; **51**, 144; **53**, 327; **54**, 254; **55**, 172, 293; **56**, 245, 257, 342; **57**, 159, 177, 258; **58**, 42; **59**, 66
  'Tradition, Style and the Theatre Today', **4**, 101–8
Gielgud, Kate Terry, **35**, 7
Gielgud, Val, **35**, 7; **39**, 7, 8n
Gierow, Karl Ragnar, **10**, 121; **13**, 131; **16**, 137
Gieskes, Edward, **53**, 308; **57**, 202
Giffard, Henry, **46**, 140
Giffard, Humphrey, **17**, 96n
Gifford, George, **43**, 86n
Gifford, H., **13**, 168
Gifford, Helen, **45**, 173
Gifford, Sir Thomas, **12**, 99
Gifford, William, **12**, 37; **14**, 13, 82, 84, 87; **54**, 20n; **56**, 121n
Gift, Roland, **45**, 153
Gigas, Emile, **20**, 98
Gigli, Lorenzo, **5**, 113
Gignoux, Hubert, **9**, 113; **11**, 119; **12**, 112
Gilad, Dan, **9**, 114
Gilbert and Sullivan, **22**, 2
Gilbert, Allan H., **8**, 139; **9**, 137n, 140n; **10**, 49n; **14**, 64, 65n; **16**, 170, 176; **17**, 185n; **19**, 133; **25**, 110; **28**, 104; **32**, 11
  The Symbolic Persons in the Masques of Ben Jonson, **14**, 10
Gilbert, A. J., **27**, 179
Gilbert, Bridget, **22**, 156
Gilbert, Creighton, **23**, 165
Gilbert, Douglas, **57**, 255
Gilbert, Sir Humphrey, **17**, 32 and n., 39, 74n; **32**, 89n
Gilbert, James, **60**, 184
Gilbert, John, **11**, 118; **59**, 374
Gilbert, Sir John, **13**, 77, 80n
Gilbert, Kenneth, **42**, 154; **47**, 99, 100
Gilbert, Miriam, **47**, 239; **50**, 49n
Gilbert, Ruth, **60**, 129n33
Gilbert, Stuart, **24**, 158n; **56**, 143n
Gilbert, Sir W. S., **12**, 85; **16**, 103; **22**, 5; **35**, 16; **40**, 6
Gilbert, W. S. and Sir Arthur Sullivan, **41**, 225; **42**, 91; **45**, 122, 152
Gilbert, William, **17**, 28 and n., 142–3; **50**, 228
  De Magnete, **1**, 68
Gilbert, Yvonne, **60**, 80
Gilbertson, William, **55**, 32
Gilbertus, **24**, 146
Gilbreath, Alexandra, **53**, 263–4; **54**, 257–8, 272–3; **55**, 322, 331; **56**, 287, 296; **57**, 259, 261; **58**, 305, 335; **59**, 344, 345; **60**, 72, 73, 79–81, 83, 293, 318, 319
Gilburne, Samuel, **55**, 387
Gilby, Anthony, **34**, 185; **49**, 190n
Gilda, Leslie, **41**, 190
Gildas, **59**, 249, 252
Gilder, Rosamond, **8**, 122; **9**, 20–1, 117
  'Shakespeare in New York: 1947–1948', **2**, 130–1
Gilder, Sean, **43**, 214
Gildon, Charles, **20**, 76; **21**, 67; **24**, 168; **34**, 11; **38**, 236; **42**, 19, 199; **43**, 103; **46**, 41; **50**, 140; **51**, 5, 8, 69n; **53**, 217, 332; **55**, 97; **58**, 72, 141; **59**, 231
  adaptation of *Measure for Measure*, **9**, 85n
Giles, Caroline, **55**, 328
Giles, David, **9**, 119; **41**, 227; **60**, 105
Giles, Henry, **53**, 94
Giles, Kate, **60**, 1, 15, 15n42, 16
Giles, Launcelot, **19**, 103
Giles, Nathaniel, **58**, 222
Gilhuys, Charles, **5**, 108
Giliov, Ilya M., **52**, 285
Gill, **4**, 125
Gill, Maud, **55**, 135
Gill, Peter, **28**, 144; **35**, 150; **42**, 152; **59**, 344; **60**, 326
Gill, Roma, **33**, 97n; **38**, 230; **39**, 247; **44**, 233; **46**, 234; **50**, 255; **53**, 23n; **56**, 75n; **57**, 215
Gill, Samuel Thomas, **35**, 31
Gill, Stephen, **53**, 106n, 114n
Gill, William Arthur, **49**, 206n
Gillen, Aidan, **55**, 316–17, 332
Gillespie, Kim, **53**, 275
Gillespie, Norman, **37**, 198n
Gillespie, Robert, **48**, 204; **58**, 299
Gillespie, Stuart, **55**, 368; **59**, 361, 366–7
Gillet, Joseph E., **23**, 80; **54**, 193n
Gillet, Louis, **3**, 98, 106
  Shakespeare, **2**, 119
Gillett, Aden, **60**, 325
Gillett, Peter J., **29**, 174; **32**, 219, 234
Gillhouley, James, **13**, 135; **15**, 146
Gilliatt, Penelope, **32**, 209; **49**, 232
Gillibert, Jean, **18**, 122
Gillick, Gordon, **43**, 208, 210

Gillick, Victoria, **57**, 41
Gillie, Christopher, **12**, 137
Gillie, David, **44**, 195
Gillies, Alexander, **9**, 99, 100n
Gillies, Andrew, **39**, 181
Gillies, David, **47**, 218
Gillies, Helena, **43**, 214
Gillies, John, **48**, 241; **50**, 249; **52**, 51–2, 187, 188n, 204n; **54**, 37n; **55**, 344, 385; **57**, 171; **58**, 30, 31
Shakespeare and the Geography of Difference, **48**, 241
Gilligan, Carol, **53**, 91
Gillingham, John, **38**, 205
Gillman, James, **23**, 101
Gillman, Tracie, **43**, 205
Gillray, James, **38**, 69–73; **44**, 207; **51**, 11, 300; **56**, 131
Gilman, Albert, **40**, 91n; **46**, 43n
Gilman, Charlotte Perkins, **51**, 280
Gilman, David, **48**, 231
Gilman, Ernest B., **31**, 181; **33**, 196; **35**, 175; **38**, 6; **52**, 59n
Gilman, Herbert, **36**, 168
Gilman, Sander L., **53**, 15n, 16n
Gilman, Todd S., **50**, 273
Gilmore, David, **43**, 217
Gilmore, David D., **57**, 83
Gilmore, John, **57**, 146, 154, 156
Gilmore, Martin Scott, **55**, 330
Gilmour, Maurice, **53**, 152n; **57**, 162, 163
Gilmour, Soutra, **56**, 296
Gilson, Edmund, **6**, 57
Gimblett, Claire, **53**, 284
Gimblett, Matt, **52**, 263; **53**, 284; **54**, 291; **59**, 341, 342
Ginman, John, **41**, 158
Ginsberg, Ernst, **5**, 114
Giorgi, Elsa De', **5**, 113
Giorgione, **11**, 121
Giotto, **14**, 149
Giovanelli, Craig, **55**, 325
Giovanni (Fiorentino) Ser, **37**, 56; **47**, 161, 166–7; **54**, 89
Giovio, Paolo, **17**, 183
Giovius, Paulus, **29**, 171
Giraldi, G. B., *see under* Cinthio
Girard, René, **29**, 14n; **35**, 154; **36**, 48, 49n; **37**, 70; **38**, 79, 83; **42**, 32–4, 164, 178; **46**, 206; **50**, 44n; **51**, 159n, 170n; **53**, 116, 305; **56**, 72
Giraudoux, Jean, **2**, 120; **22**, 21, 28, 29, 32, 38
Girouard, Mark, **35**, 133; **45**, 110; **47**, 17n, 21n
Giroux, Robert, **36**, 173
Girtin, John, **59**, 115–16
Girtin, Thomas, **59**, 116n31
Griston, Thomas, **17**, 70n
Gisbourne, Karen, **46**, 198
Gischia, Léon, **14**, 118
Giselinus, Victor, **55**, 266
Gissenwehrer, Michael, **57**, 169
Gissing, George, **18**, 20
Gittings, Clare, **60**, 231
Gittings, Robert, **15**, 136
Shakespeare's Rival reviewed, **15**, 168–9
Giucci, Caetano, **37**, 50–1
Giurchescu, Lucian, **20**, 126, 128
Giuseppi, M. S., **33**, 166n; **54**, 133n
Giustinian, Giorgio, **3**, 30
Givan, Christopher, **34**, 175
Givda, Avni, **9**, 116; **18**, 130
Given, Seon, **56**, 141n
Givens, Craig, **48**, 229
Gizhimkreli, Michael, **48**, 187n
Gjersöe, Per, **10**, 120
Gl' Ingannati, **14**, 153; **52**, 120
Gladstone, William E., **14**, 79; **24**, 92; **56**, 242n
Glaister, Gerard, **9**, 119
Glancey, Jonathan, **57**, 51
Glapthorne, Henry, **3**, 51; **47**, 33; **58**, 236
Glare, P. G. W., **50**, 197n; **52**, 185n
Glaser, Milton, **49**, 129
Glaser, Sheila Faria, **52**, 198n
Glasgow Repertory Company, **58**, 298, 301, 302, 303, 304
Glasheen, Adaline, **56**, 144n
Glasier, Phillip, **44**, 131n, 132n, 133n, 134n, 141n
Glasser, Stanley, **41**, 189
Glavin, John, **43**, 265n; **53**, 111n, 113, 142; **56**, 127n
Gleason, John B., **36**, 179; **43**, 144n; **52**, 5
Gleckner, R. F., **14**, 145
Glen, Hamish, **43**, 205; **48**, 230; **54**, 289; **57**, 293
Glen, Iain, **46**, 192; **47**, 189, 210; **48**, 210–11; **49**, 271
Glendinning, Hugo, **59**, 331
Glenham, Edward, **17**, 34 and n.
Glenister, Robert, **48**, 228; **52**, 238, 241–2
Glenn, John, **52**, 192n
Glenn, Susan A., **55**, 119n
Glentoran, John, **43**, 210; **47**, 214
Glenville, Peter, **5**, 116
Gless, Darryl J., **34**, 165, 174
Gli Duoi Fratelli Rivali, **8**, 4
Glick, Claris, **18**, 184; **23**, 173
Glick, Thomas F., **35**, 104n
Gligore, Ana-Maria, **29**, 166
Glinka, Michael I., **45**, 173
Glišić, M., **15**, 140
Glittenberg, Rolf, **54**, 288
Globe Theatre, *see under* Theatres, Elizabethan
Gloewacki, Janusz, **50**, 227
Gloriant (medieval Flemish play), **5**, 107
Glossop, Joseph, **47**, 63, 238
Gloucester, city of, **17**, 13, 167–8
Glover, A. and Waller, A. R. (eds.), *The Works of Francis Beaumont and John Fletcher*, **14**, 8
Glover, Arnold, **15**, 40n; **54**, 66n
Glover, Brian, **27**, 148–9; **47**, 216
Glover, James, **58**, 167; **271**, 272, 273
Glover, Jamie, **51**, 259; **52**, 256
Glover, Julia, **60**, 115–16
Glover, Julian, **18**, 153; **31**, 150; **45**, 117, 139, 141; **46**, 193; **49**, 11, 244–5, 250–1; **51**, 259; **55**, 305, 332; **56**, 281, 291; **59**, 322; **60**, 329
Gluck, **18**, 77
Gluckman, Max, **50**, 69, 70
Glumov, **5**, 117
Gnedich, Nicolai I., **5**, 105n
Gnedich, Pyotr, **56**, 161
Go, Kenji, **57**, 309
Goad, Thomas, **54**, 19n, 23

Godard, Jean-Luc, **43**, 207; **45**, 67; **57**, 330
Godber, John, **44**, 202; **59**, 339
Goddard, Beth, **46**, 199
Goddard, Harold C., **10**, 59n; **15**, 40n; **19**, 7–8; **27**, 72; **30**, 49n, 51n; **36**, 44; **37**, 33n; **45**, 18n; **50**, 177n; **52**, 270; **60**, 96n33
The Meaning of Shakespeare reviewed, **6**, 147–8
Goddard, Michael, **43**, 214
Godelier, Maurice, **35**, 66n
Godfrey, Derek R., **5**, 133–4; **12**, 124; **14**, 132, 133; **16**, 151; **25**, 166; **26**, 162; **34**, 149
Godfrey, Edward, **19**, 106n
Godfrey, Oliver, **49**, 276
Godfrey, Patrick, **33**, 169, 174; **43**, 185; **51**, 208
Godfrey, Paul, **46**, 202; **48**, 237
Godfrey, Walter H., **3**, 89; **7**, 80n; **12**, 10, 11; **45**, 109n; **47**, 24n; **60**, 40n10
Godsalve, William H. L., **49**, 307
Godshalk, William Leigh, **20**, 166; **21**, 153; **23**, 143; **26**, 174n; **27**, 92n, 167; **28**, 152, 162, 167; **31**, 171; **33**, 203; **37**, 20n; **40**, 63n, 64n; **52**, 111n
Godsiashwili, **12**, 118
Godunov, Boris, **11**, 93, 96; **48**, 114–15
Godwin, Christopher, **57**, 275; **58**, 268; **59**, 339
Godwin, Doran, **45**, 150
Godwin, E. W., **10**, 71, 75; **29**, 176; **31**, 188; **32**, 19; **35**, 10; **41**, 224; **56**, 135n
Godwin, J., **50**, 152n
Godwin, Jean, **45**, 151
Godwin, Mary, **10**, 111
Godwin, Richard, **58**, 223
Godwin, Simon, **55**, 322
Godwin, Thomas, **47**, 26
Godwin, William, **13**, 76
Goebbels, Joseph Paul, **37**, 155–6
Goethe, Johann Wolfgang von, **4**, 118; **6**, 107; **7**, 112; **9**, 2, 81, 94, 95–8, 110n; **12**, 79, 80; **13**, 148; **14**, 85; **16**, 10, 63, 70, 134; **18**, 37–9, 44, 79, 104, 114; **21**, 81, 88; **23**, 122; **24**, 145; **26**, 157, 166; **30**, 3, 201; **31**, 2n; **33**, 192; **34**, 14; **35**, 166; **37**, 145, 150, 155; **40**, 58; **41**, 209; **42**, 100; **43**, 112, 220; **44**, 107, 109, 110; **45**, 3, 8, 15, 26, 38–40; **48**, 4n, 9, 10, 105, 183; **50**, 128, 180; **53**, 92, 110; **54**, 141; **56**, 208; **57**, 61, 63, 171
Conversations with Eckermann, **14**, 88n
Faust, **9**, 97
Wilhelm Meister, **9**, 65
Goetsch, Paul, **53**, 2n, 6n; **56**, 305, 329, 330
Goetz, H., **18**, 86
Goevrot, Jehan, **50**, 21, 22, 25
Gofer, Felix, **42**, 158
Goffe, Thomas, **11**, 102; **54**, 62
Goffman, Erving, **29**, 20n; **57**, 308; **58**, 23; **60**, 148
Gogan, Valerie, **45**, 157; **46**, 202
Gogol, Nikolai Vasilevich, **9**, 120; **16**, 10; **19**, 23n; **39**, 81n, 85; **55**, 115
Gohlke, Madelon, **35**, 159n
Gohn, E., **19**, 137
Gokak, V. K., **19**, 138
Gökçer, Cüneyt, **9**, 116; **13**, 132; **14**, 124; **16**, 137; **18**, 130
Gökmen, Muzaffer, **16**, 137
Golata, John, **55**, 145n
Gold, C. H., **15**, 181
Gold, J., **19**, 124
Gold, Jack, **39**, 93–4, 99–102; **41**, 227
Gold, Käthe, **5**, 114; **11**, 117
Gold, Louisa, **48**, 235
Gold, Max, **45**, 151
Goldast, Melchior, **15**, 94, 98n
Goldberg, Andrew, **58**, 299
Goldberg, David Theo, **48**, 60n
Goldberg, Jonathan, **40**, 78n, 212; **41**, 195; **43**, 3n, 57n, 265n, 266; **44**, 219, 226; **46**, 43n, 48n, 93n; **48**, 26n, 28, 75n; **49**, 61n; **50**, 43n, 65, 109, 250; **51**, 130, 317; **52**, 93n, 97, 325; **54**, 134n; **55**, 3–4, 342; **57**, 28, 30, 99; **58**, 27, 315; **59**, 16–17, 61n30, 80, 81, 83n15, 84n17
Goldberg, Lea, **12**, 114
Goldberg, Rita, **51**, 42
Goldberg, S. L., **28**, 155, 156; **33**, 11, 43n, 44, 53n, 202; **38**, 153; **49**, 203n
Golden Legend, The, **20**, 24
Golden, Murray, **53**, 170n
Golder, J. D., **26**, 161; **47**, 157n; **57**, 114; **60**, 218, 221n25
'*Hamlet* in France 200 Years Ago', **24**, 79–86
Goldhammer, Arthur, **50**, 78n
Goldie, Hugh, **8**, 125
Goldie, Terry, **57**, 145
Goldin, Brett, **60**, 285–6
Golding, Arthur, **3**, 14, 19; **11**, 103; **13**, 39n; **15**, 14, 26, 29; **16**, 170; **19**, 57, 81n, 93n; **21**, 150; **23**, 85, 161, 166; **24**, 156, 159, 162; **25**, 125, 137; **26**, 104; **27**, 160, 179; **30**, 153n; **32**, 73–5, 145–8, 150, 174, 230–1; **33**, 19; **34**, 184, 188; **36**, 86, 175; **37**, 207; **39**, 123–5, 127–8, 132; **41**, 133–9, 140n, 141–3; **42**, 53–64, 72, 74, 75, 196; **43**, 41n; **46**, 53n, 117, 221; **47**, 131n, 141, 145–6, 149, 150; **49**, 62; **50**, 83, 198, 251; **51**, 180n; **52**, 280; **53**, 14–16, 17n, 18, 21, 31, 33, 37; **54**, 31; **55**, 25, 200, 202–5, 207, 349; **56**, 27, 28n, 29–30, 38, 41, 57, 64, 84n; **59**, 367; **60**, 273
translation of Ovid's *Metamorphoses*, **3**, 54; **4**, 9, 87; **8**, 94; **10**, 18–24, 25n, 26n, 43, 44, 45
translation of Seneca's *De Beneficiis*, **10**, 34
Golding, Louis T., *An Elizabethan Puritan*, **11**, 105n
Golding, Percival, **11**, 103, 104; **22**, 153
Golding, S. R., **6**, 48n
Goldingham, C. S., **17**, 23n
Goldman, Donald L., **10**, 121
Goldman, Lisa, **43**, 216
Goldman, Lloyd, **23**, 167n
Goldman, Lucien, **36**, 45–6
Goldman, Michael, **27**, 171; **28**, 105n, 111; **29**, 8; **30**, 48n, 139, 147, 190; **43**, 250; **44**, 220; **46**, 239; **55**, 225n, 228n
Goldman, Michael R., **31**, 173; **33**, 181; **35**, 169; **38**, 16, 164; **39**, 136n, 211
Goldmann, Lucien, **53**, 305
Goldoni, Carlo, **20**, 127; **47**, 193n
Goldring, Beth, **37**, 209
Goldsmith, Edward, **48**, 39n, 44
Goldsmith, Oliver, **4**, 104; **22**, 2; **51**, 21; **53**, 105; **59**, 289, 297
Goldsmith, R. G., **32**, 6
Goldsmith, Robert Hillis, **13**, 155, 164; **25**, 50, 51; **27**, 59n, 113n; **29**, 111n, 116; **35**, 87n
Wise Fools in Shakespeare, **13**, 39n
Wise Fools in Shakespeare reviewed, **10**, 135

Goldsmith, Ulrich K., **5**, 136; **15**, 17
Goldstein, Jonathan, **45**, 154; **47**, 217; **49**, 274, 279
Goldstein, Leonard, **20**, 153; **22**, 162; **34**, 31n
Goldstein, N. L., **29**, 162
Goldstein, Philip, **36**, 169
Goldstein, Ruth M., **56**, 5n
Goldwell, Thomas, **56**, 198
Goldwyn, Sam, **29**, 64
Golfing, Francis, **53**, 100n
Goll, August, *Criminal Types in Shakespeare*, **3**, 109
Gollancz, Sir Israel, **8**, 3, 8; **10**, 49n; **15**, 5, 99; **31**, 15n; **44**, 106; **55**, 141n
The Shakespeare Classics, **3**, 6
Golomb, Harai, **48**, 115n; **53**, 296; **54**, 182n, 184n, 187n
Golombek, H., **35**, 115n
Goltz, Hubert, **10**, 34
Golubentsev, **5**, 117
Gomara, Françisco López de, **51**, 185
Gombosi, Otto, **15**, 7
Gombrich, Sir Ernst, **15**, 98n; **31**, 16; **34**, 40; **40**, 75n; **56**, 312
Gomer, Russell, **49**, 272
Gomersall, Robert, **50**, 152; **54**, 62
Gomes, Eugenio, **10**, 115; **15**, 168
Gómez, Lucas, **54**, 152n, 160, 163
Gomez, Nicolas Wey, **52**, 188n
Gomme (*née* Merck), Alice Bertha, Lady Gomme, **17**, 174; **60**, 187
Gomme, Allan, **52**, 17n, 32n
Gomme, Arnold Wycombe, **52**, 17n
Gomme, Laurence, **52**, 17n
Gondomar, Conde de, **23**, 86–7
Gondris, Joanna, **53**, 341; **53**, 344; **55**, 259n; **59**, 124n2, 128
Gonet, Stella, **44**, 193; **48**, 202–3, 220–2; **49**, 273, 275
Góngora, Luis de, **23**, 82; **56**, 40
Gonshaw, Francesca, **45**, 146
González, José Manuel, **47**, 258
Gonzaga, Curzio, **14**, 153; **47**, 169
Gonzaga, Maria Ludvica, Queen of Poland, **32**, 191
Gooch, Bryan, **51**, 4, 6, 81n
Gooch, Bryan N. S., **45**, 171n; **56**, 330
Gooch, Jane L., **55**, 30n
Good, Christopher, **55**, 297, 300
Good, Jack, **9**, 120
Goodal, Thomas, **2**, 48, 49, 60n
Goodall, Howard, **44**, 192; **45**, 150; **46**, 192, 200; **56**, 294
Goodbody, Buzz, **24**, 117, 118, 130; **27**, 148; **29**, 151, 153; **40**, 16; **47**, 3, 5, 11; **55**, 295; **60**, 359
Goodchild, Tim, **45**, 154; **47**, 217; **51**, 235
Goode, Daniel, **52**, 229
Goodere, Sir Henry, **3**, 5
Goodfellow, Donald M., **19**, 135
Goodman, Alice, **40**, 207
Goodman, Benny, **13**, 142
Goodman, Bishop, **54**, 136n
Goodman, Ellen, **52**, 93n
Goodman, Henry, **37**, 168–9; **48**, 225; **53**, 268–70; **54**, 288; **56**, 266; **57**, 277, 278; **58**, 304
Goodman, Jennifer, **45**, 183–4
Goodman, John, **12**, 96–7; **60**, 116
Goodman, Julia, **44**, 196
Goodman, Lizbeth, **50**, 256; **53**, 110n
Goodman, Lynne, **52**, 157
Goodman, O. B., **25**, 200
Goodman, William, **53**, 278
Goodman-Hill, Tom, **52**, 230
Goodnight, Desdemona (Good Morning, Juliet), **49**, 276
Goodrun, John, **42**, 154
Goodspeed, Kelvin, **50**, 230
Goodstein, Peter, **24**, 160
Goodwin, John, **41**, 45n; **56**, 249n; **60**, 229n33
Goodwin, Peter, **42**, 187
Goodwin, Thomas, **58**, 224
Goody, Jack, **24**, 48; **42**, 93n; **55**, 37n; **58**, 315
Goodyere, Sir Henry, **44**, 133
Googe, Barnabe, **15**, 14; **34**, 98
Eglogs, **5**, 53; **8**, 145
Goold, G. P., **53**, 27n; **54**, 31n; **56**, 40n
Goold, Rupert, **53**, 282; **60**, 314–15, 316, 321
Goolden, P., **10**, 145; **29**, 13n; **46**, 109
Gorak, Jan, **51**, 2n
Gorbachev, Raisa, **47**, 194
Gorbelly, **49**, 272
Gorboduc, **3**, 67; **9**, 143; **10**, 138
Gorboduc, see also The Tragedy of Ferrex and Porrex
Gordin, Jacob, **55**, 114–27
Gordon, Andrew, **57**, 207
Gordon, Bruce, **54**, 7n
Gordon, Clare C, **47**, 178
Gordon, David J., **7**, 11n; **8**, 4; **14**, 11; **19**, 29, 130; **23**, 148; **35**, 116n; **40**, 110; **43**, 245; **46**, 96, 116
Gordon, G. S., **4**, 4–5; **7**, 5, 24n; **8**, 1; **22**, 7, 14n; **23**, 11n, 13n; **26**, 73; **59**, 254n2, 262n18
Gordon, Giles, **36**, 22n, 25
Gordon, Kit, **60**, 174, 180
Gordon, Michael, **51**, 226; **52**, 259
Gordon, R. G., **3**, 137
Gordon, Sarah, **54**, 286; **56**, 289
Gordon, Serena, **47**, 218
Gordon, Stuart, **44**, 203
Gordon-Clark, Lucy, **51**, 264; **58**, 307
Gore-Langton, Robert, **60**, 168n3.5
The Gorgeous Gallery of Gallant Inventions, **60**, 254
Gorfain, Phyllis, **31**, 166; **32**, 225; **43**, 138; **46**, 109, 209
'Puzzle and Artifice: The Riddle as Metapoetry in *Pericles*', **29**, 11–20
Gorga, Simona, **56**, 329
Gorge, Sir Arthur, *Olympian Catastrophe*, **6**, 60
Gorges, Arthur, **53**, 79n
Goring, George, **55**, 93n
Goring, Sir Henry, **51**, 57
Goring, Lord, **11**, 108, 114
Goring, Marius, **7**, 126, 127; **16**, 22, 144; **27**, 142; **44**, 243
Gorki, Maxim, **4**, 120; **16**, 10, 11, 15; **19**, 24n; **23**, 176; **40**, 58, 60; **54**, 144–5
Görlach, Manfred, **56**, 310
Görne, Dieter, **22**, 164; **32**, 217
Gorley, Putt, S., **24**, 165
Gorrie, John, **57**, 40
Gorton, Rachael, **45**, 148
Gorvin, Joana Maria, **12**, 113; **13**, 128
Goslicius, L. G., **22**, 168
The Counsellor, **3**, 54

Gosse, Edmund, **7**, 56n; **48**, 116; **54**, 81; **56**, 206n, 214
Gosse, Philip, **54**, 81
Gossett, Susan, **55**, 244n
Gossett, Suzanne, **27**, 178; **39**, 231; **42**, 187n; **44**, 256; **49**, 312; **51**, 32n; **56**, 105n; **57**, 342; **58**, 343–5, 352, 357; **59**, 213, 214, 215, 216–17, 218, 220, 221–2, 223, 369
Gossip, Christopher J., **55**, 247n
Gossman, Lionel, **22**, 23
Gosson, Henry, **3**, 151; **5**, 26; **25**, 145
  his quarto of *Pericles*, **5**, 26–38
Gosson, Stephen, **3**, 16; **8**, 4; **9**, 153; **13**, 159; **15**, 64, 178; **29**, 174; **42**, 115; **43**, 233; **48**, 135; **51**, 281; **54**, 13; **55**, 221, 229, 238; **56**, 32, 33, 44; **58**, 221; **59**, 290; **60**, 280n44
  The Trumpet of Warre. A Sermon, **9**, 34n
Gostelow, Gordon, **25**, 169–70; **41**, 189
Gostelow, Harry, **51**, 225
Gosynhill, Edward, **32**, 97
Got, Edmond François Jules, **9**, 64
Gother, John, **51**, 132, 133n
Gotlieb, Phyllis, **53**, 173n
Gottfried, J. L., *Neuwe Archontologia Cosmica*, **1**, 31
Gottfried, R., **25**, 138n
Gottschalk, Katherine K., **46**, 248n
Gottschalk, P., **27**, 157; **28**, 154
Gottsched, Luise, **53**, 298–9
Gottwald, Klement, **10**, 116; **14**, 118
Gouch, Anthony, **25**, 147; **29**, 34
Gouge, William, **27**, 90; **55**, 357
Gough, Alexander, **58**, 225, 234
Gough, Denise, **59**, 312
Gough, Maria, **43**, 214
Gough, Orlando, **44**, 191; **45**, 153; **46**, 201; **55**, 316
Gough, Rebecca, **58**, 306
Gough, Richard, **4**, 93; **6**, 57
Gough, Robert, **58**, 225
Gough, Toby, **53**, 276; **54**, 288, 293
Gould, Dorothy Ann, **55**, 271; **60**, 290, 291
Gould, Gerald, **6**, 12; **36**, 159; **52**, 112; **58**, 122, 165, 167
Gould, Jay, **24**, 94
Gould, Michael, **51**, 208; **55**, 305
Gould, Rupert, **58**, 304
Gould, William, **57**, 255
Goulding, Daniel J., **57**, 149
Goulish, Matthew, **60**, 155n7
Gounod, Charles F., **3**, 100; **18**, 86; **49**, 4, 14, 285
  opera on *Romeo and Juliet*, **6**, 114
Gourlay, P. S., **26**, 161
Gourmont, Rémy de, **6**, 143
Govil, O. P., **60**, 352
Gow, Gordon, **26**, 140n
Gowan, Pat, **45**, 154
Gowda, H. H. Anniah, **41**, 204
Gower, John, **1**, 55; 10, 145; **14**, 100; **15**, 97n; **17**, 172; **24**, 60, 101, 108, 109, 111, 112, 114, 115; **29**, 30; **31**, 183; **37**, 214; **50**, 138n, 160; **54**, 38; **55**, 204; **56**, 30; **57**, 210, 314, 340; **59**, 258, 259, 265
  Confessio Amantis, **1**, 55, 67, 71; **4**, 87
Gower, Lord Ronald, **56**, 136
Gower, William, **4**, 94
Gowing, Laura, **54**, 173
Gowrie brothers, **44**, 155n
Gowrie, Earl of, **36**, 166, 174; **44**, 155n
Goy-Blanquet, Dominique, **44**, 60n; **46**, 130n; **49**, 207n; **53**, 164n; **56**, 308, 326; **57**, 113; **58**, 327, 332; **59**, 371–2
Goya, Francisco, **60**, 161, 169n5.9
Gözey, Gölistan, **18**, 130
Graatkjer, Axel, **45**, 43n
Grabau, Carl, **44**, 108n
Gräber, Eisig, **54**, 183n
Grabes, Herbert, **37**, 188
Grace, Francis, **40**, 219
Grace, W. G., **5**, 2
Gracian, Geronymo, **56**, 189
Gradwell, Henry, **58**, 224
Grady, Hugh, **45**, 159, 160; **47**, 71n; **49**, 201n, 289; **51**, 272; **54**, 323–4; **55**, 339–41; **56**, 306, 342; **58**, 170, 171, 172, 173, 174, 175, 180; **59**, 148, 151n20
Gräf, Hans Gerhard, **57**, 64
Graff, Gerald, **52**, 109; **59**, 89n34; **60**, 143, 151
Graffman, Göran, **16**, 137
Grafton, Augustus Henry Fitzroy, Third Duke of, *see under* Fitzroy
Grafton, Richard, **8**, 146; **16**, 169; **28**, 4; **33**, 99n; **36**, 171; **38**, 94; **42**, 27; **54**, 9
Graham, Cary B., **8**, 143
Graham, Catherine, **56**, 342
Graham, Cyril, **56**, 136
Graham, Desmond, **52**, 273
Graham, J., **51**, 64–5
Graham, K. L., **18**, 131
Graham, Kenneth, **53**, 57; **58**, 171
Graham, Martha, **48**, 233
Graham, Sam, **51**, 262
Graham, Tony, **49**, 270
Graham, Walter, **43**, 82n, 84; **51**, 95n, 96–102, 104
Graham-White, Anthony, **49**, 325, 326
Grainer, J. Ellen, **55**, 271n
Grammaticus, Saxo, **27**, 172; **29**, 171; **53**, 6
Gramms, Eike, **44**, 195
Gramond, Louis de, **3**, 106n
Gramsci, Antonio, **44**, 213; **53**, 291
Grandage, Michael, **53**, 284; **54**, 268–71; **55**, 322; **56**, 256, 264, 273, 275–7; **57**, 264, 295, 297; **58**, 303, 306; **59**, 301
Grande, Troni, **54**, 306
Grandval, Charles François Racot de, **9**, 91
Grane, Henry, **7**, 108
Grangé, Henri, **15**, 133
Grange, Robert, **44**, 194
Granger, F., **10**, 2
Granger, James, **6**, 61
Granger, Timothy, **50**, 192
Gransden, A., **44**, 58n
Grant, David, **51**, 263
Grant, Duncan, **41**, 57
Grant, Fraser, **51**, 264
Grant, J. E., **14**, 145
Grant, John, **53**, 165n; **55**, 64n
Grant, Kerry S., **51**, 84n
Grant, Maurice Arnold, **47**, 174n
Grant, P., **27**, 158
Grant, Patrick, **31**, 181
Grant, Steve, **45**, 53n, 61n

Grant, Thomas Mark, **27**, 175–6
Grant, Ulysses S., **24**, 91, 92, 93, 94; **54**, 75
Granval, Jean-Pierre, **18**, 122
Granville George, **52**, 99
Granville, George, Baron Lansdowne, **13**, 138; **20**, 169; **46**, 138, 139, 140n; **48**, 54; **51**, 3n, 87
Granville, Revd G., **54**, 85
Granville-Barker, Harley, **1**, 4, 8, 14, 15, 16, 43, 121; **2**, 84, 132; **3**, 40, 41n, 135; **4**, 10, 98, 101–2, 103, 105, 129, 131; **5**, 87; **6**, 12, 148; **7**, 25, 32, 33, 80n, 123, 127, 138; **8**, 5, 8, 52, 75, 80; **9**, 2, 7, 8, 9, 14, 15, 18, 19, 20, 51, 57; **10**, 1, 3, 6, 7, 50, 75, 88n, 148, 149; **11**, 46; **12**, 9, 11, 56, 65, 78, 81, 129n, 144; **13**, 17; **14**, 129, 159; **15**, 5; **18**, 41, 63–4, 67, 69, 184, 186; **20**, 76, 80, 81n, 127, 169; **21**, 1–2, 27n, 153; **23**, 11n; **24**, 1, 167; **25**, 8, 153, 155, 172; **26**, 5; **27**, 48; **28**, 47n, 168; **29**, 48, 55, 56n, 161; **31**, 142, 151, 188; **32**, 23, 155–6, 159n; **33**, 28n, 29n, 45n, 65; **34**, 187; **35**, 1–3, 11, 12, 183; **36**, 79, 80, 97; **37**, 152; **38**, 50n, 51n, 236; **39**, 2, 7, 135n, 215; **40**, 1, 13, 72, 127n, 222–3; **41**, 56–9, 86, 208, 226; **45**, 9; **46**, 184; **47**, 1, 90, 159, 237; **49**, 9, 12, 75, 206n; **51**, 141, 144, 229; **52**, 28n, 290, 311; **53**, 233; **54**, 304; **55**, 4, 56, 129; **59**, 149–50, 204, 208; **60**, 187–8, 189n17
  Companion to Shakespeare Studies, **12**, 11
  contributions to Shakespeare production, **2**, 1, 4, 6, 7–10, 13, 14, 15, 17, 19, 20
  Prefaces to Shakespeare, **7**, 29–30; **12**, 56, 64, 70n.; **13**, 18n; **14**, 55n, 75n
  study of *Coriolanus*, **2**, 113, 138
  views on Elizabethan acting, **2**, 31
  work on Shakespeare discussed, **4**, 17–18
Gras, Henk, **43**, 242–3; **44**, 218; **58**, 200, 203, 204
Grass, Günter, **56**, 288
Grassby, Juliette, **44**, 202
Grassilli, Raoul, **16**, 136
Grasso, Giovanni, **49**, 230
Gravelot (Hubert François Bourguignon), **4**, 86; **13**, 73, 80n; **37**, 43–4; **49**, 113; **59**, 131
Graves, Frank, **8**, 120
Graves, R. B., **36**, 180; **38**, 228; **54**, 336–7; **60**, 37n6
Graves, Robert, **15**, 116, 117; **17**, 171; **25**, 126, 132; **26**, 112n; **31**, 50n; **32**, 214; **33**, 81; **36**, 39–42; **43**, 24; **44**, 66n; **55**, 86n, 89n
Graves, T. S., **12**, 17, 42
  The Court and the London Theatres during the Reign of Elizabeth, **12**, 20n, 21n
Graves, Wallace, **28**, 166
Gravina, Carla, **15**, 136
Gray's Inn, *see under* London
Gray, Austin K., **3**, 5; **8**, 6; **10**, 2; **35**, 87–8, 98
Gray, Cecil G., **5**, 139n; **6**, 159
Gray, Douglas, **57**, 242
Gray, Francine du Plessix, **49**, 209n
Gray, Henry David, **1**, 8, 9; **3**, 28, 31, 75, 78, 83; **5**, 140, 151; **9**, 6, 33n; **27**, 106, 107, 108
  'The Chamberlain's Men and *The Poetaster*', **2**, 144
  'Shakespeare's Rival Poet' reviewed, **3**, 139
Gray, H., **39**, 39n
Gray, Henry, **60**, 227
Gray, J. C., **39**, 215; **43**, 8n, 18n; **55**, 200n
Gray, J. W., **32**, 137n
Gray, James, **30**, 201–2
Gray, John, **56**, 207n
Gray, Lord, **54**, 133
Gray, Madeleine, **55**, 36n
Gray, Oliver, **51**, 162; **53**, 283; **54**, 294; **55**, 331; **56**, 294; **57**, 290
Gray, Robert, *A Good Speed to Virginia*, **1**, 69
Gray, Ronald, **59**, 228n5
Gray, Stephen, **18**, 128
Gray, Stewart, **43**, 205
Gray, Terence, **2**, 15; **12**, 129n; **47**, 93
Gray, Thomas, **2**, 83; **5**, 59; **52**, 254
Gray, Sir Thomas, **49**, 184
Gray, Willoughby, **1**, 99
Gray, Zachary, **3**, 14
Graysonesque, Larry, **58**, 272
Graziani, R. I. C., **14**, 11
Graziani, René, **23**, 166n, 167n; **40**, 217
Graziano, Michael S. A., **60**, 144n11
Graziosi, Franco, **12**, 114; **14**, 121
Great Assizes Holden in Parnassus, The, **14**, 64
Great Pike Garden, **1**, 31
Greaves, Lennox, **44**, 201
Greaves, Ralph, **60**, 189n17
Greaves, Richard L., **49**, 190n
Greaves, Roger, **45**, 46n
Grebanier, Bernard, **18**, 161; **21**, 149–50; **30**, 198–9; **45**, 43; **59**, 108n2
Grebgell, Caroline, **51**, 257
Greci, José, **15**, 136
Greco, A., **27**, 167
Greco, Giacchino, **35**, 113
Greco, John, **42**, 156, 159; **44**, 191, 192, 196; **45**, 148, 155
Grécourt, Jean B. de, **5**, 93
Greece, report on Shakespeare in, **2**, 127; **4**, 128; **5**, 112; **6**, 120; **7**, 112; **10**, 119; **11**, 121; **12**, 113; **15**, 134; **16**, 134; **18**, 124
Green, A. J., **8**, 141; **9**, 8–9
Green, A. Wigfall, **27**, 114n, 115, 116n, 118n; **32**, 103n; **57**, 202
Green, Alistair, **56**, 288
Green, André, **40**, 110; **56**, 138
Green, D. B., **14**, 156
Green, David C., **33**, 197; **34**, 167
Green, Douglas, **57**, 330
Green, F. C., **24**, 80
Green, George Smith, **51**, 138
Green, Hegelian T. H., **56**, 205–6
Green, Henry, **5**, 27; **25**, 99n; **31**, 50n
Green, J. R., **6**, 2
Green, John, **13**, 154; **32**, 192n, 194–7; **33**, 156, 160, 162–4, 166–8; **36**, 137–9, 141–7 *passim*; **38**, 227
Green, Julius, **44**, 203
Green, London, **39**, 233
Green, Lorne, **10**, 116
Green, Mary Anne Everett, **53**, 70n
Green, Paul, **58**, 139
Green, Peter, **53**, 26n
Green, R. H., **15**, 98n
Green, Roger L., **18**, 179
Green, Thomas, **27**, 99
Green, Ti, **53**, 277; **54**, 294; **55**, 326
Green, William, **18**, 188–9; **25**, 109, 110; **37**, 1n

Greenaway, Peter, **48**, 263; **49**, 308; **52**, 197, 290; **53**, 149n, 168n, 328, 330; **57**, 330; **58**, 349; **59**, 293
Greenbaum, Sidney, **53**, 14n
Greenberg, Clement, **52**, 192
Greenberg, David F., **44**, 52n
Greenberg, Martin, **43**, 221
Greenberg, Robert A., **11**, 137
Greenblatt, Stephen J., **36**, 51; **37**, 193; **40**, 139n, 142, 190, 212; **41**, 2, 3n, 194; **42**, 41, 167, 191; **43**, 2, 16, 31n, 224, 239–40; **44**, 47n, 51n, 70, 81n, 205, 219, 224, 232, 237; **45**, 37, 160, 162, 181; **46**, 3, 51, 52, 62n, 135n, 152n, 216, 220; **47**, 30n, 246–7; **48**, 32n, 69–70, 88, 97n, 128n, 148, 150n, 155, 267; **49**, 59, 208n, 212n, 213–14, 312; **50**, 247; **51**, 146, 171n, 178, 184, 285, 302, 303, 305, 333; **52**, 107–13, 118, 130, 201; **53**, 38n, 97, 185, 298; **54**, 21–2, 26n, 29, 59–60, 124n, 127n, 139n, 153n, 307, 319, 323; **55**, 3n, 5–7, 99n, 104n, 219n, 336–8, 346, 355, 359–61, 382; **56**, 111, 159, 173, 312, 313, 320, 351; **57**, 5, 137; **58**, 1, 5, 7, 16, 17–18, 19, 22, 34, 45, 46, 172, 173, 174, 177, 179; **59**, 3, 36, 89n34, 252n97, 348; **60**, 104–5n13, 113n47, 114n52, 145n16, 235
Greene, Douglas E., **44**, 220
Greene, G. S., **25**, 137n
Greene, Gayle, **35**, 159–60; **37**, 3n; **40**, 83n, 92n, 101n; **41**, 65n, 68, 74; **46**, 6n, 9n; **48**, 132n; **49**, 66n; **50**, 247; **60**, 84–5n2
Greene, Graham, **3**, 67; **10**, 136; **27**, 149; **53**, 144
Greene, Jeffrey, **33**, 164
Greene, Jody, **56**, 229, 230
Greene, John, **28**, 172
Greene, John, *Refutation of the Apology for Actors, A*, **20**, 23
Greene, John C., **48**, 8n
Greene, Joseph, **3**, 2; **4**, 72–3; **5**, 57; **19**, 145
Greene, Revd Joseph, **56**, 187, 188, 199
Greene, Nicholas, **56**, 218n, 222n, 224n
Greene, Richard, **51**, 6n
Greene, Richard, of Lichfield, **1**, 81, 87n
Greene, Robert, **1**, 38, 70; **2**, 120; **3**, 2, 23; **4**, 7, 29, 56, 143, 146, 149; **5**, 139; **6**, 5, 15n, 39, 40, 72, 158, 159, 169, 170; **7**, 7, 8, 24n, 51, 137, 140, 141, 147–8, 149; **8**, 3, 56, 103; **9**, 143, 153; **10**, 12, 69, 144, 145, 146; **11**, 142, 151; **14**, 7, 26, 29, 31–3, 82; **15**, 113; **16**, 167, 169–70, 173; **17**, 95, 126, 136, 201, 203; **22**, 51, 52; **23**, 88n, 160, 169; **24**, 176; **25**, 188; **26**, 46, 182; **27**, 16, 130, 132, 134; **28**, 45; **29**, 4, 6, 169; **30**, 14, 79, 196; **31**, 13; **33**, 123–38 *passim*, 197, 203; **34**, 179; **35**, 186, 189; **36**, 116n, 117; **37**, 20; **38**, 131n, 134; **39**, 130, 224; **42**, 63; **43**, 234; **44**, 23, 131; **46**, 12n, 89; **47**, 113, 140; **48**, 266; **49**, 15, 25; **50**, 53n, 268; **52**, 77, 100, 125–7, 323; **53**, 334; **54**, 41, 57, 118, 227, 309; **55**, 18, 21, 23, 24n, 29, 30n, 368; **56**, 61n, 144n, 248; **57**, 208, 212, 216, 217, 218; **58**, 247; **59**, 42, 73, 356; **60**, 274n22
Alphonsus, King of Aragon, **7**, 84; **10**, 86n; **12**, 19, 35, 55n; **13**, 122, 167n
Defence of Coneycatching, **15**, 71n
Euphues his Censure to Philautus, **9**, 142
Farewell to Folly, **15**, 71n
Francesco's Fortunes, **15**, 71n
Friar Bacon and Friar Bungay, **1**, 46; **4**, 95; **8**, 102–3; **13**, 73, 167n; **17**, 200
Greene's Funerals, **4**, 63
Greene's News from Heaven and Hell, **15**, 72n
Greene's Vision, **15**, 72n
Groatsworth of Wit, **1**, 63; **2**, 52; **3**, 54; **4**, 57, 59–66, 88, 153; **5**, 139; **9**, 143; **10**, 144; **15**, 62–72; **54**, 118
James IV, **6**, 159; **11**, 48, 74; **12**, 20
Looking Glass for London and England (with Thomas Lodge), **10**, 87n; **13**, 167n; **15**, 40n
Menaphon, **11**, 151; **15**, 66
Orlando Furioso, **1**, 64; **2**, 152; **4**, 63; **6**, 170; **7**, 83, 85, 147; **9**, 78–9; **13**, 167n
Pandosto, **1**, 62; **3**, 54; **4**, 87; **9**, 142; **10**, 33; **11**, 24, 31
Perimedes the Blacksmith, **6**, 79; Preface to, **8**, 102; **15**, 72n
relation of *Pandosto* to *The Winter's Tale*, **6**, 143–4
Tragical Reign of Selimus, **12**, 20, 142; **20**, 24
Greene, Roland, **51**, 297; **55**, 344
Greene, Susan, *see* Baskervile, Susan
Greene, Thomas, **7**, 61, 62, 63, 64, 65, 67n; **15**, 164
Greene, Thomas M., **21**, 148; **26**, 153; **33**, 161, 163–4; **36**, 144, 172; **38**, 252n; **40**, 75n, 215; **42**, 9, 67n; **46**, 45n; **50**, 87n
Greene's Tu quoque, **17**, 208; **55**, 378
Greeneham, Richard, **25**, 148
Greenfield, Jon, **51**, 205n, 298; **52**, 39n; **60**, 23–34, 34n32, 36, 38Fig.10, 39Fig.11, 40n13, 41, 41n21, 43, 43n26, 44n29
Greenfield, Peter, **40**, 217; **44**, 151; **47**, 57n
Greenfield, Sayre, **49**, 295
Greenfield, Thelma Nelson, **8**, 142; **9**, 138; **20**, 49n; **22**, 164; **29**, 55n–6n; **36**, 103n; **38**, 5n; **43**, 135n; **55**, 59n
Greenhalgh, Susanne, **57**, 40, 46, 47; **58**, 187; **60**, 355
Greenhill, J., **51**, 90n
Greenhow, Anna, **44**, 195
Greenlaw, Edwin A., **6**, 7; **8**, 2; **38**, 122n; **40**, 123n; **46**, 51n; **57**, 197
Greenleaf, W. H., **56**, 206n
Greenslade, F. L., **50**, 142n
Greenstreet, James, **7**, 57
Greenwald, Michael L., **38**, 226; **40**, 223–4; **60**, 132n10
Greenwood, John, **42**, 197; **54**, 96n
Greenwood, Katarzyna, **56**, 328
Greenwood, Paul, **40**, 177–8; **47**, 206; **51**, 235; **59**, 345; **60**, 209, 211
Greenwood, Sarah, **41**, 189
Greer, C. A., **3**, 23; **6**, 11; **7**, 145; **9**, 137, 143n
Greer, David, **19**, 151; **26**, 173; **44**, 238
Greer, Germaine, **40**, 193; **46**, 131n; **55**, 174
Greer, Talt, **60**, 179
Greet, Ben, **2**, 4; **20**, 77, 80; **47**, 238; **52**, 28n; **54**, 265
Greetham, D. C., **39**, 248n; **40**, 227n, 233; **43**, 264n; **55**, 183n, 257n
Greg and Boswell, *Records of the Court of the Stationers' Company*, **11**, 154
Greg, Sir Walter Wilson, **1**, 4, 7, 9, 12, 21, 37n, 63, 78n, 129, 131; **2**, 19, 52, 108, 113, 152; **3**, 3, 23, 24, 25, 26, 27, 28, 29, 30, 31, 32n, 50, 51, 52, 74, 143, 147, 148, 149; **4**, 9, 58, 60, 66, 67n, 90, 91, 157–8, 160; **5**, 3, 20, 24, 25, 46n, 51, 52, 54, 145–6; **6**, 57, 75, 161, 163–4, 168, 169, 171, 172; **7**, 3, 6, 11, 36, 49–50, 51, 52, 56n, 86, 149, 151–2, 153; **8**, 2, 81, 82, 83–4, 89, 90, 97n, 98n, 104n, 105n, 106, 153, 155, 156, 157; **9**, 4, 6, 73, 74, 75, 76, 77, 78, 79, 80n, 145n; **10**, 3, 88n, 152; **11**, 21, 30n, 78–84, 86, 87n, 88n; **12**, 55n, 148, 149, 150; **13**, 165; **14**, 7, 8, 106, 151, 161; **15**, 3, 4, 171, 176–7; **16**, 6, 180, 181; **17**, 205n, 206–9, 213; **18**, 21n, 24–6; **19**, 155n, 157n; **20**, 173; **21**,

159; **23**, 179; **24**, 172, 177; **25**, 7, 73n, 75n, 76n, 110, 197, 199, 200; **26**, 13n, 16n, 35n, 180, 183, 184; **27**, 133, 185; **28**, 175; **29**, 117, 127, 128; **30**, 202, 208, 209; **31**, 95n, 102n, 191, 193; **33**, 1, 2–3, 32n, 143n, 153, 154, 158, 159; **34**, 62n; **35**, 190; **36**, 108, 109, 112, 115n, 140, 144, 147, 189; **37**, 2, 210, 211, 217, 218n; **38**, 89, 101–6, 110, 243, 252, 254; **39**, 248; **40**, 145, 218; **42**, 16n, 77n, 78n, 79, 119, 125, 190, 202, 208; **43**, 6n, 81n, 265; **44**, 114, 146, 151n, 152, 230, 233n; **45**, 109n, 175, 193–5; **46**, 12n, 228, 229, 230; **47**, 15n, 241; **48**, 277, 287; **49**, 27; **50**, 142, 151, 170, 271–2, 283–5, 289; **51**, 129, 290, 309, 314, 330; **52**, 69, 77n, 84–5; **53**, 334; **54**, 353, 357; **55**, 12, 13, 14n, 16, 17, 19, 21, 22n, 26n, 27–8, 29n, 31n, 32, 33n, 34, 264, 389n, 394; **56**, 169, 170, 172; **57**, 202, 225, 227, 228, 231, 232; **58**, 353; **59**, 1, 4, 6, 7–8, 9–10, 11, 12, 13, 14, 17n70, 21, 23–4, 26, 26n28, 28–30, 31, 33–4, 69n1, 86, 154n35, 156, 382; **60**, 49n2, 50n4, 266n40, 266n41
Bibliography of the English Printed Drama to the Restoration, **12**, 146–7; **13**, 163; **14**, 5
(ed.) *Dr Faustus*, **14**, 44n
edition of *Sir Thomas More*, **2**, 44, 47, 50, 51, 56, 57, 60
The Editorial Problem in Shakespeare, **13**, 162; **14**, 157
Elizabethan Dramatic Documents, **11**, 83, 88n; **14**, 5
English Literary Autographs, **2**, 54
Henslowe's Diary, **14**, 5; *Henslowe Papers*, **12**, 21n; **13**, 111–12; **14**, 5
List of English Plays written before 1643 and printed before 1700, **14**, 5
List of Masques, Pageants, &c., **14**, 5
Pastoral Poetry and Pastoral Drama, **14**, 2
Shakespeare First Folio, The, **9**, 148–9; **11**, 30n, 87n, 88n; **13**, 123n, 162
Shakespeare Quarto Facsimiles 9 and 10, **12**, 150
Some Aspects and Problems of London Publishing 1550–1650, **11**, reviewed, 154
Variants in the First Quarto of 'King Lear', **2**, 152
Gregerson, Linda, **49**, 302
Gregg, K. L., *Thomas Dekker*, **14**, 12
Gregg, Pauline, **43**, 56n
Gregg, Tresham D., **54**, 74–6, 78; **58**, 138, 142, 144
Grego, J., **38**, 69n
Gregor, Joseph, **1**, 11, 115; **5**, 110n; **7**, 128; **10**, 76n
Gregor, Keith, **58**, 139
Gregorie, Edward, **6**, 60
Gregorie, Randall, **49**, 186
Gregory of Nyssa, **57**, 244
Gregory the Divine, Saint, **49**, 80
Gregory XIII, Pope, **33**, 154; **54**, 2
Gregory, Dr John, **51**, 21n
Gregory, Michael, **46**, 195
Gregory, Miles, **56**, 287, 289, 293, 298; **57**, 291, 292, 296; **59**, 342–3
Gregory, Saint, **20**, 26n; **54**, 130
Gregory, T. S., **4**, 140n
Gregorye, Richard, **25**, 147
Gregson, Edward, **43**, 212; **46**, 193
Greif, Heinrich, **48**, 172
Greif, Karen, **36**, 169
Greig, Noel, **58**, 358
Greig, Tamsin, **60**, 302, 303, 309, 310
Greimas, A.-J., **41**, 122
Grein, J. T., **14**, 117
Grein, W. T., **5**, 108, 109
Greiner, Norbert, **37**, 158n
Grelon, F., **19**, 126
Grendon, John, **34**, 89n
Grene, Christopher, **56**, 193n
Grene, David, **22**, 163; **43**, 115n; **48**, 115
Grene, Nicholas, **35**, 159, 160; **46**, 216, 217; **56**, 323, 325
Grenender, M. E., **32**, 235
Grenewy, Richard, **28**, 67
Grennan, Eamon, **31**, 184; **33**, 200; **38**, 13; **40**, 67
Grennell, Michael, **52**, 262; **58**, 261
Grenville, Keith, **47**, 101
Grenville, Sir Richard, **17**, 22, 30
Grenville, Sir Thomas, **3**, 44, 47, 55
Gresham College, **17**, 71, 144
Gresham, Sir Thomas, **17**, 9; **53**, 204; **60**, 227
Grétry, A. E. M., music for *Othello*, **3**, 102
Greville, Fulke, **3**, 11; **5**, 141; **11**, 105; **14**, 66–75 *passim*; **15**, 102; **17**, 42n, 118; **21**, 112; **23**, 166; **27**, 117n; **30**, 64, 158; **37**, 189; **38**, 122; **39**, 226; **59**, 71, 229
Alaham, **14**, 66, 75n
Life of Sir Philip Sidney, **14**, 75n
An Inquisition upon Fame and Honour, **14**, 75n
Mustapha, **1**, 65
A Treatise of Monarchy, **14**, 75n
A Treatise of Religion, **14**, 75n
Greville, Sir Fulke, **41**, 220; **44**, 8, 227; **46**, 219; **53**, 72n; **54**, 355; **60**, 13
Grévin, Alfred, **10**, 4
Grew, John, **42**, 153
Grewal, Shiv, **42**, 157; **44**, 199
Grewar, Andrew, **55**, 247n
Grewe, Wilhelm, **48**, 62n
Grex, John, **41**, 186
Grey, Earle, **10**, 111; **14**, 117
'Shakespeare Festival, Toronto, Canada', **10**, 111–14
Grey, Sir, J. F., **15**, 130
Grey, Lady Jane, **52**, 171n
Grey, Lord John, **12**, 99
Grey, Lord, of Wilton, **4**, 154
Grey, Oliver, **52**, 262
Grey, Richard, **48**, 231
Grey, Roger, 10th Earl of Stamford, **15**, 130
Grey, Terence, **53**, 233
Grey, Zane, **53**, 168n
Greyerz, Georg von, **38**, 145n
Gricius, Jonas, **39**, 83n
Grief, Michael, **53**, 309
Grieg, Edvard, **47**, 92
Grierson, Sir Herbert J. C., **9**, 25, 26; **19**, 8; **43**, 55n; **46**, 71n, 142n; **55**, 54n
Letters of Sir Walter Scott, **14**, 89n
Grieve, J. H., **20**, 107–11
Grieve, Thomas, **13**, 80n; **20**, 107–11; **41**, 26–7, 29, 34
Grieve, Walford, **41**, 25–7, 29, 34
Grieve, William, **20**, 107–11
Grieves, **22**, 175
Griffin, Alice, **10**, 149; **12**, 145
Griffin, Bartholomew, **26**, 103, 107, 108–9; **60**, 255–6
Fidessa, **15**, 41, 42

Griffin, Ben, **44**, 181n
Griffin, Benjamin, **51**, 52n; **56**, 324; **57**, 316; **58**, 327
Griffin, Eric, **52**, 206
Griffin, Gerald, **46**, 248
Griffin, Hayden, **33**, 179; **37**, 170; **41**, 185; **42**, 152; **44**, 192; **48**, 232; **54**, 287; **55**, 303, 331; **56**, 287, 291, 327
Griffin, Henry, **19**, 103; **33**, 168
Griffin, John, **25**, 148, 149
Griffin, Julia, **55**, 343
Griffin, Marshall, **55**, 324
Griffin, Miriam T., **33**, 91
Griffin, Robert J., **19**, 139
Griffin, Robert P., **27**, 177
Griffin, W. J., **18**, 192
Griffith, D. W., **39**, 75n
Griffith, Elizabeth, **2**, 109; **51**, 5, 6; **53**, 89, 94
Griffith, Hubert, **52**, 288
Griffith, Hugh, **6**, 132, 135; **18**, 147, 152
Griffith, Kenneth, **42**, 158
Griffith, W., **13**, 110n
Griffiths, A., **17**, 91n
Griffiths, Derek, **48**, 206
Griffiths, G. S., **10**, 10
Griffiths, Gareth, **48**, 157n
Griffiths, J., **48**, 71n, 73n, 83n
Griffiths, Jane, **53**, 20n
Griffiths, John, **60**, 73n4
Griffiths, Paul, **49**, 301
Griffiths, Richard, **31**, 142; **32**, 203, 208; **33**, 178; **37**, 170
Griffiths, Samantha, **43**, 214
Griffiths, Trevor, **31**, 188; **35**, 10
Griffiths, Trevor R., **43**, 1n
Grigg(e)s, John, **60**, 29, 43–4
Griggs, John, **43**, 141, 146; **44**, 230, 231; **45**, 102, 103, 106
Grignion, Charles, **49**, 118
Grigore, Dan, **45**, 146
Grigori, Ferdinand, **35**, 26n
Grigson, Geoffrey, **36**, 30n
Grillo, John, **36**, 155
Grillparzer, Franz, **20**, 4
Grimald, Nicholas, **25**, 99; **26**, 112n; **54**, 62n
Grimaldi, Joseph, **37**, 166
Grimble, Ian, **46**, 12n
The Harington Family, **14**, 109n
Grimes, Jeremy, **47**, 4n
Grimley, Daniel, **60**, 185n5, 194–5
Grimm, Friedrich Melchior, Baron von, **9**, 91
Grimm, Wilhelm and Jakob, **36**, 139; **37**, 53
Fairy Tales, **8**, 136
Grimmwood, Chris, **42**, 155
Grimsdiche, Christian, **49**, 194
Grindal, Edmund, **17**, 125
Grindley, David, **54**, 290
Grinke, Paul, **60**, 255–6n16
Grisolli, Afonso, **57**, 327
Grisoni, Guiseppe, **51**, 11
Gritton, Susan, **55**, 313
Grivelet, Michel, **14**, 65n; **18**, 176; **19**, 125; **21**, 142; **24**, 149; **25**, 173; **27**, 157; **30**, 190; **34**, 85n; **38**, 10, 238n; **52**, 323; **59**, 194n7, 196–7
'The Simplicity of Thomas Heywood', **14**, 56–65
'Shakespeare as "Corrupter of Words"', **16**, 70–6
'Shakespeare, Molière, and the Comedy of Ambiguity', **22**, 15–26
'Shakespeare's "War with Time": the Sonnets and *Richard II*', **23**, 69–78
Thomas Heywood et le drame domestique élizabéthain, **14**, 12
Grix, Jost, **50**, 38
Grob, Alan, **50**, 55n
Grock, **36**, 152; **37**, 168
Groise, Ljuben, **32**, 224
Gronaman, Sibilla (Mrs Sibilla), **51**, 83
Grönbech, Vilhelm, **3**, 109
Groom, Bernard, **23**, 13n, 21n; **47**, 153n
Groot, J. H. de, *The Shakespeares and 'The Old Faith'* reviewed, **1**, 123; **3**, 73n, 139
Gros Louis, Kenneth R. R., **23**, 163
Grosart, Alexander B., **8**, 148; **15**, 25; **21**, 140; **23**, 43n; **26**, 39n; **38**, 86n, 187; **41**, 60n; **54**, 133n; **55**, 84n; **57**, 212
The Complete Poems of Sir John Davies, **12**, 20n
Grose, Carl, **60**, 310–11, 312
Grose, Francis, **32**, 99n
Gross, Alan Gerald, **22**, 156; **23**, 146; **24**, 78
Gross, Harvey, **43**, 24n
Gross, John J., **15**, 123n; **43**, 200; **47**, 238–9, 245n, 252n, 269; **48**, 67n; **51**, 8; **52**, 99, 100; **56**, 303, 304; **57**, 118, 321
Gross, Kenneth, **55**, 338–9; **57**, 25
Gross, Manfred, **23**, 120
Gross, Mary J. H., **31**, 197
Grossberg, Lawrence, **56**, 70n
Grosskurth, Phyllis, **19**, 143
Grossman, Atina, **45**, 45, 46
Grossman, Marshall, **54**, 322
Grote, George, **56**, 207
Grotius, Hugo, **11**, 107; **44**, 62n
Groto, Luigi, **20**, 96, 99; **34**, 103–4
Adriana (1578), **7**, 101–2
Grotowski, Jerzy, **25**, 28; **46**, 171; **47**, 3; **50**, 38
Grove's Dictionary of Music and Musicians, **11**, 100
Grove, Fred, **25**, 119n
Grove, Mr, **22**, 128, 131
Grove, Robin, **43**, 10n
Grover, P. R., **22**, 158
Groves, Beatrice, **60**, 114n53
Groves, John Finlayson, **56**, 247n
Grubb, Shirley Carr, **39**, 251
Grube, Max, **35**, 14
Grüber, Klaus Michael, **37**, 162
Grudin, Robert, **30**, 184; **40**, 125n; **55**, 211, 212n
Gruenspan, Bertha, **32**, 127n
Gruhn, Klaus, **23**, 120
Grund, Manfred, **42**, 159
Gründgens, Gustaf, **3**, 114; **4**, 127; **6**, 117; **37**, 200
Grünewald, Matthias, **56**, 232
Grundlehner, Philip, **32**, 224
Grundy, Joan, **18**, 180; **24**, 16; **32**, 214
'Shakespeare's Sonnets and the Elizabethan Sonneteers', **15**, 41–9
Gruneburg, M. M., **42**, 89n, 93
Gruner, B. R., **35**, 164n
Gruner, E. Hamilton, **58**, 143
Grüttner, Theo, **37**, 158n

Gruyter, Dom De, **6**, 163n; **10**, 115; **12**, 110
Gruyter, Dom de, and Hayward, Wayne, 'Shakespeare on the Flemish Stage of Belgium, 1876–1951', **5**, 106–10
Gruyter, J. O. de, **5**, 108
Grylls, William, **5**, 50–1
Gryndall, W. G., **44**, 135, 139n
Grzegorzewska, Margorzata, **53**, 293
Guadagni, **18**, 77
Guard, Pippa, **31**, 142
Guare, John, **57**, 256
Guarini, Battista, **8**, 55; **30**, 192; **40**, 109, 117
Guarini, J. F., **28**, 104
Guarnieri, Anna Maria, **14**, 121; **16**, 136; **18**, 126
Guarred, Benjamin, **18**, 17
Guazzo, Steven, **20**, 18; **57**, 207
Guazzo, William, **50**, 78
Gucht, Michael van der, **37**, 42
Gudbrandsson, Runar, **52**, 256
Gudgeon, Vernon, **46**, 201
Guernier, Louis du, *see* Du Guernier, Louis
Guerrieri, Gerardo, **7**, 112; **9**, 114; **13**, 129; **14**, 121; **18**, 126
Guevara, A. de, **2**, 73, 75; **32**, 167n
Decada (Edward Hellowes' translation), **10**, 31–2
Dial of Princes (Sir Thomas North's translation), **2**, 70; **10**, 31
Guevara, Luis Velez de, **20**, 18, 26n, 99
Guffey, George Robert, **36**, 114n; **43**, 91n; **51**, 80n
Guggenheim Memorial Foundation, **12**, 46n
Guglia, Eugen, **35**, 27n
Guha, P. K., **19**, 127; **22**, 160
Guibbory, Achsah, **48**, 83n
Guicciardini, Francesco, **17**, 65
Guida, Wandisa, **14**, 121
Guiderius, **11**, 46
Guidi, A., **14**, 146, 148
Guilday, Peter, **29**, 21n
Guildhall, The, London, **3**, 2
Guilds, of the Middle Ages, **12**, 5
Guilford, Sir Henry, **60**, 68
Guilfoyle, Cherrill **41**, 208; **42**, 177, 182; **43**, 234; **44**, 211; **53**, 304
Guilfoyle, Mollie, **50**, 233
Guilhamet, L., **29**, 162
Guillaumot, Bernard, **18**, 122
Guillemeau, James, **46**, 71n, 118n
Guillén, Claudio, **31**, 54
Guillory, John, **59**, 35n71
Guilpin, Edward, **15**, 168; **17**, 130–2, 135
Guilpin, Everard, **28**, 180; **47**, 32, 176; **58**, 205
Guinle, Francis, **50**, 257
Guinn, Alana, **46**, 193
Guinness, Sir Alec, **1**, 98, 102, 103, 106; **4**, 105; **8**, 128, 129; **9**, 19, 22; **10**, 149; **16**, 27, 152; **45**, 192; **49**, 229; **50**, 29; **59**, 199n8
Guinness, Peter, **39**, 196, 197
Guiry, Tom, **57**, 186
Guise and Disguise: Rhetoric and Characterisation in the English Renaissance (L. Davis), **48**, 259
Guiseppi, M. S., **57**, 13
Guizot, François, **2**, 116; **5**, 105n; **20**, 164; **60**, 215
Guj, Luisa, **41**, 207
Gulbenkian Studio (Newcastle-upon-Tyne), **58**, 304
Gulick, C. B., **25**, 100n
Gulick, Sidney L., junior, **9**, 141n
Gulliford, Hermione, **53**, 272; **56**, 266, 293
Gumbrecht, Hans Ulrich, **60**, 122–3, 124, 143, 144
Gumperz, John J., **57**, 205
Gün, Melek, **9**, 116
Gunby, D. C., **22**, 172n; **24**, 165
Gunby, David, **52**, 69n; **59**, 215; **60**, 109n33
Gundolf, Friedrich, **9**, 99, 100n; **15**, 132; **16**, 63; **18**, 174; **20**, 127; **26**, 166; **37**, 155; **44**, 109, 110; **48**, 3
Gunmere, Richard M., **33**, 90n
Gunn, Ben, **55**, 317
Gunn, Giles, **47**, 30n
Gunn, J. A. W., **23**, 162
Gunn, Jacqueline, **44**, 202; **46**, 195, 197
Gunn, James, **53**, 283
Gunn, Margo, **44**, 202
Gunn, Michael, **44**, 199
Gunter, Edmund, **17**, 72, 143, 144; **43**, 152
Gunter, Jean, **48**, 230
Gunter, John, **36**, 149; **43**, 194; **44**, 193; **46**, 165, 200; **47**, 209; **49**, 251, 279; **50**, 211, 228; **51**, 247, 267, 268; **52**, 257; **58**, 298
Gunther portrait of Shakespeare, *see* under Shakespeare, William, portraits
Günther, Alfred, **5**, 114
Der junge Shakespeare reviewed, **3**, 138
Günther, Frank, **37**, 160; **43**, 223; **49**, 278
Günther, Hans F. K., **48**, 63n, 66
Gunther, R. H., **46**, 12n
Günther, Peter, **23**, 154
Gunthio, Ambrose, **6**, 162
Guntner, J. Lawrence, **50**, 263–4; **52**, 283; **55**, 383
Gupta, S. C. Sen, **19**, 131–2, 140; **21**, 153; **28**, 12; **29**, 88
Gurnett, Jane, **45**, 122
Gurnock, Richard, **18**, 154
Gurr, Andrew, **15**, 172; **18**, 182; **20**, 168; **21**, 155; **25**, 188, 189; **26**, 164; **28**, 158; **31**, 7n, 27n; **33**, 146n, 200; **35**, 175; **38**, 15, 92n, 224, 225; **39**, 229, 238–40, 249; **40**, 212; **41**, 7n, 22n, 104n, 214–15, 218; **42**, 101n, 102–5, 186, 188, 194; **43**, 141, 142n, 143n, 145, 146n, 147–9, 168, 250, 253; **44**, 67n, 152n, 231; **45**, 7, 104, 107n; **46**, 12n, 20n, 30n, 43n, 241n, 251–2; **47**, 19n, 25n, 30n, 34n, 47, 59, 176n, 251n; **48**, 33, 243; **49**, 14, 15n, 314, 318; **50**, 113n, 261; **51**, 194n, 195n, 285, 298, 302; **52**, 8, 9n, 10n, 11n, 12, 13n, 14n, 42, 44n, 47n, 74n, 76n, 79n, 81n, 85n, 107n, 135n, 278; **54**, 59n, 308; **55**, 18n, 27n, 34, 189, 235n, 236, 252, 374, 389; **56**, 55n, 61n, 97, 217n, 218n, 225n; **57**, 339; **58**, 3, 358; **59**, 17n70, 18n81, 35n73, 183n2, 255n5, 381, 383; **60**, 1, 1–2n4, 4, 4n7, 7n12, 7n15, 9, 9n20, 9n21, 10, 13n37, 21–2, 24, 25, 25n7, 28n13, 30, 31, 36, 37n6, 41n21, 43, 43n26, 43n27, 44, 44n29, 45n39, 46, 46n52, 103n8, 122n7
'*Coriolanus* and the Body Politic', **28**, 63–9
'*Henry V* and the Bees' Commonwealth', **30**, 61–72
'Who Strutted and Bellowed?', **16**, 95–102
Gury, Jacques, **30**, 200
Gürzap, Alev, **18**, 130
Gusson, Mel, **41**, 47
Gutenberg, Project, **59**, 173, 179
Guthke, Karl S., **14**, 156; **18**, 174

Guthrie, Sir Tyrone, **2**, 13, 15, 17, 19; **4**, 99; **5**, 119; **7**, 107, 114, 124; **8**, 118, 124; **9**, 19–20, 111; **10**, 85, 89n, 116, 130, 134, 149; **11**, 118, 131; **12**, 123, 125, 126; **13**, 129, 140–2, 145, 163; **14**, 117, 126, 136; **15**, 151; **16**, 18, 24–5, 26, 152, 153; **18**, 67, 131; **20**, 113, 133; **22**, 79; **24**, 53; **25**, 45n, 66–7; **30**, 83; **31**, 144, 145, 188; **34**, 8; **35**, 2; **39**, 185, 188; **41**, 67–8; **45**, 54; **47**, 1, 2, 90, 97, 238; **48**, 67, 265; **50**, 31, 32; **53**, 233, 237, 240–3; **56**, 10, 113; **58**, 125; **59**, 371
  production of *Henry VIII*, **3**, 120–9
  'Shakespeare at Stratford, Ontario', **8**, 127–31
Gutierrez, Nancy A., **39**, 251; **44**, 227; **51**, 279; **53**, 291
Gütschow, C. von, **9**, 100n
Guttman, Selma, **8**, 4
  Foreign Sources of Shakespeare's Works, **2**, 139
Güvenc, Nedret, **18**, 130
Guy earl of Warwick, The Tragical History, Admirable Atchievements and various events of, **60**, 342–3
Guy, Henry, **57**, 297
Guy, Jeff, **52**, 160n
Guy, John, **52**, 168n; **54**, 98n, 169n
Guy, John A., **55**, 37n, 210n
Guy, Josephine, **51**, 128n
Guyot, Charly, **18**, 129
Guzmán, Gaspar de (Count-Duke of Olivares), **60**, 240
Gwen, Hayden, **51**, 263
Gwillim, John, **12**, 123; **41**, 106n
Gwilym, Mike, **30**, 175; **35**, 147; **36**, 149, 153; **44**, 177; **56**, 267
Gwinn, Matthew, **19**, 3; **32**, 245
Gwyn, Peter, **44**, 11n
Gwynn, Nell, **37**, 58
Gwynn, Robin D., **54**, 50n
Gwynne, Edward, **1**, 58; **3**, 44, 47; **4**, 93
Gwynne, Hayden, **48**, 202–3, 207
Gwynne, Haydn, **60**, 318, 319
Gwynne, Michael, **3**, 122
Gyller, Harald, **9**, 141n
Gyllome, ffoke, **10**, 144n
Gyseghem, André van, **5**, 119, 120; **15**, 146

Haaker, Ann, **22**, 174; **32**, 94n; **41**, 5, 6n; **55**, 85n
Haas, Rudolf, **29**, 184n; **60**, 369n8
Haas, Virginia Westling, **59**, 158n5
Habenicht, Rudolfe, **32**, 164n
Haberdashers' Company, **11**, 102
Habermann, Ingrid, **58**, 314
Habermas, Jürgen, **51**, 272; **59**, 149n9, 151n16
Habib, Imtiaz, **47**, 225; **54**, 301
Habibullah, Waris, **15**, 145
Habicht, H., **32**, 224
Habicht, Werner, **23**, 112; **24**, 145; **28**, 168; **31**, 175; **37**, 156n, 157n, 158n, 161n; **39**, 219n, 235; **41**, 198n, 245n; **42**, 166; **43**, 266n; **45**, 28n; **47**, 236n; 48, 5, 7, 61n; **49**, 76n; **52**, 103n; **56**, 301, 317; **59**, 195
  'Shakespeare Studies in German, 1959–68', **23**, 113–23
Habima Players, *see under* Theatres
Habington, William, **17**, 199
Hachemi, Liliane el, **40**, 52n
Hack, Keith, **28**, 143, 146, 147
Hackel, Heidi Brayman, **51**, 290; **59**, 18n78; **60**, 268, 268n3
Hackenbroch, Yvonne, **47**, 173n
Hacket, Cicely, **58**, 143
Hacket, John, **54**, 62n
Hackett, Claire, **45**, 156
Hackett, Helen, **52**, 276, 278; **54**, 126n, 314; **56**, 215; **57**, 316
Hackett, James Henry, **18**, 104, 106, 107; **24**, 88, 101; **28**, 139n; **56**, 100n, 129, 132; **60**, 116
Hackforth, R., **24**, 51; **36**, 85n
Hacks, Peter, **48**, 178
Haddington Masque, **52**, 190
Haddington, Ellie, **45**, 156
Haddon-Haines, Richard, **43**, 208, 212
Hadfield, Andrew, **48**, 257; **54**, 229n; **56**, 215–26; **57**, 30, 302; **58**, 326, 332; **59**, 360–1; **60**, 339–41, 352
Hadfield, Mark, **44**, 202; **52**, 230
Hadfield, Paul, **59**, 368
Hadley, Michael, **51**, 224, 226
Hadow, Sir W. H., **15**, 15
Haeckel, Ernst, **24**, 97
Haegeman, Liliane, **53**, 14n
Haehlen, J., **26**, 166
Haell, Michael, **49**, 191
Haeussermann, Ernst, **35**, 21n
Haffenden, John, **47**, 242n; **48**, 267–8
Haffenreffer, Karl, **30**, 195
Hafler, Max, **45**, 147; **46**, 191
Haft, Linal, **47**, 101; **48**, 215
Hagar, Alan, **45**, 160
Hagberg, Carl August, **9**, 116; **14**, 123; **15**, 138; **18**, 128; **36**, 70; **43**, 113; **48**, 3, 4
Hagel, Ursula, **48**, 227
Hageman, Elizabeth H., **39**, 231; **42**, 187
Hagen, E. A., **32**, 195n, 196n
Hagen, Sheri, **60**, 287
Hagen, Uta, **60**, 365
Hagens, Gunter von, **60**, 227n25
Haggard, Frank E., **31**, 195; **38**, 248
Haggard, Miss, **14**, 111
Hagstrum, Jean, **31**, 14
Hague, Richard, **49**, 274
Hahlo, Peter, **53**, 276
Hahn, W., **1**, 113
Hahn, Wiktor, *Shakespeare w Polsce* reviewed, **13**, 154; **14**, 123
Hai, Zafar, **16**, 135
Haie, **11**, 46
Haigh, Christopher, **43**, 67; **54**, 1, 2, 94n, 95, 126n; **56**, 28n
Haigh, Colin, **46**, 195
Haigh, David, **45**, 138–9; **46**, 196
Haight, Gordon S., **53**, 114n, 116n, 121n
Hai-Ming, Wei, **45**, 149
Hainaux, René, **6**, 118
Haines, Charles, **9**, 100n; **33**, 189; **37**, 116n, 124n, 125n; **38**, 248; **41**, 93n; **53**, 8n
Haines, Richard Haddon, **55**, 271n
Hainsworth, J. D., **30**, 200; **54**, 47n
Hair, Paul, **32**, 137n; **49**, 185n
Haislund, N., **23**, 13n
Haitink, Bernard, **55**, 328
Hajdukowicz, B., **1**, 113
Hakari, Markka, **55**, 325
Hake, Edward, **17**, 75n, 85 and n.; **29**, 93; **39**, 231
Hakewill, George, **47**, 26

Hakluyt, R., **21**, 106n
Hakluyt, Richard, *Principal Navigations*, **3**, 25
Hakluyt, Richard, the elder, **32**, 87n, 88, 104n
Hakluyt, Richard, the younger, **32**, 86n, 87, 89n; **39**, 153
Hakluyt, Richard, **16**, 77; **17**, 28, 30n, 31 nn, 32 and n, 34 and n, 36n, 39–41, 51 and n, 52 and n; **48**, 32; **51**, 135; **52**, 101n, 102n, 208n
Hakola, Liisa, **42**, 200
Halász, G., **2**, 127; **3**, 117
Halbwachs, Maurice, **52**, 61–2
Halcrow, Ian, **44**, 196
Haldane, Viscount, **44**, 108
Hale, D. C., **26**, 158
Hale, David George, **23**, 163; **28**, 63n; **32**, 95n
Hale, Edward Everett, Jr, **47**, 87n
Hale, George E., **6**, 62
Hale, J. R., **22**, 159; **48**, 130n; **50**, 154n
Hale, John K., **13**, 136; **14**, 127, 128; **15**, 145; **35**, 157n, 158; **51**, 275
Hale, W. Hale, **49**, 198n
Hales of Eton, **26**, 166, 175
Hales, J. W., **39**, 154
Hales, John W., **10**, 14; **15**, 2, 34; **19**, 74n; **53**, 278
Hales, Jonathan, **48**, 233; **50**, 232
Hales, Nancy K., **35**, 179; **46**, 6
Haley, David, **32**, 246; **33**, 203; **47**, 229
Halfen, Josef, **11**, 122
Halio, Jay L., **18**, 160, 164; **22**, 157, 158, 166; **25**, 94n; **27**, 160; **28**, 171n, 179; **32**, 8–9, 226; **33**, 2n, 28n, 78n, 181n, 208n; **34**, 94n; **36**, 31n; **38**, 155n; **39**, 229n; **40**, 217; **46**, 61n, 155n; **47**, 259–64, 266, 269–71; **48**, 278–81; **49**, 44n, 173n, 219n, 221n, 305–6; **50**, 273n, 283, 286–7; **51**, 284, 328; **52**, 99n, 100, 104; **53**, 295, 338–9; **54**, 234n, 237n, 306, 345; **55**, 2n, 96n, 226n; **57**, 148, 312, 330; **58**, 341; **59**, 170
Halkett, Anne, **17**, 176n
Halkin, Simon, **5**, 113; **13**, 129
Hall, Anmer, **4**, 106
Hall, Arthur, **17**, 78
Hall, Ben, **45**, 153
Hall, Berta, **16**, 137
Hall, Candida, **43**, 208
Hall, Christopher, **17**, 32
Hall, Clayton Morris, **33**, 22n
Hall, E. Vine, *Testamentary Papers*, **3**, 2
Hall, Edward (chronicler), **3**, 4, 18, 23, 26, 66, 138; **5**, 104, 139n; **6**, 3, 9, 10, 26, 33n, 34n; **24**, 63; **25**, 172; **27**, 28n, 72; **28**, 2, 3; **29**, 84; **37**, 27n, 75; **38**, 37, 46, 93–4, 110; **42**, 18, 26–8, 30, 31, 32, 46; 43, 50, 51n; **44**, 3n, 8, 15, 19, 55, 57, 59; **47**, 70n, 72n, 147; **50**, 232; **51**, 135; **52**, 172n, 174n, 179, 180, 230–1, 244, 256; **53**, 275, 285; **54**, 4, 9, 194, 195n, 353; **55**, 286, 306–8, 324, 393–4; **56**, 280–1, 290, 291, 353; **57**, 291, 292, 293; **58**, 301, 303; **59**, 189–90, 316–18, 319; **60**, 59n3, 63, 64, 66–7, 68–71, 328–9
  Chronicle, 4, 148n; **9**, 144n; **14**, 33; **16**, 169; **17**, 107–8, 225; **20**, 41
  as a source for Shakespeare, **6**, 7, 11
Hall, Edward (director and actor), **54**, 274, 280–2
Hall, G. K., **28**, 172n
Hall, Gaston, **47**, 252n
Hall, Henry, **57**, 326–7
Hall, Izzie, **55**, 334
Hall, Jennifer, **37**, 170
Hall, Dr John, **2**, 144; **4**, 70–1, 75–6; **5**, 57; **6**, 59; **14**, 110; **17**, 14, 154; **19**, 36; **40**, 217; **41**, 221; **47**, 175n; **53**, 285
Hall, Jonathan, **49**, 291; **52**, 274
Hall, Joseph, **2**, 54; **16**, 98; **17**, 26, 130–5, 193–4; **20**, 65, 68; **21**, 140; **22**, 38, 39, 182; **23**, 98; **30**, 49n; **32**, 101n; **33**, 93; **46**, 225; **47**, 177
  The King's Prophecie (1603), **5**, 138n, 149
Hall, Kim, **45**, 48; **50**, 260; **51**, 279; **52**, 204n, 213n; **53**, 291
Hall, Lawrence S., **19**, 133–4
Hall, Lucy, **49**, 239, 271
Hall, Marie Boas, 'Scientific Thought', **17**, 138–51
Hall, Pauline, **3**, 118
Hall, Peter J., designer, **15**, 147
Hall, Sir Peter, **8**, 124, 125; **9**, 119; **11**, 134; **12**, 120; **13**, 135, 142–5; **14**, 127, 129–33, 136; **15**, 144–6, 148, 151; **16**, 24, 27; **18**, 67, 133, 149, 151; **19**, 111, 117–18; **20**, 133–5, 140; **21**, 119, 120, 121; **22**, 136, 138; **23**, 132, 133; **24**, 117, 128, 177; **26**, 139, 141; **28**, 121, 171; **31**, 141, 142, 149, 151–2, 155, 158n, 159, 160, 162; **32**, 79, 201; **33**, 179; **34**, 8, 152, 154; **35**, 144–6, 147; **36**, 159; **37**, 184; **38**, 17; **39**, 191, 192; **40**, 19, 180, 205, 210, 223; **41**, 45–53, 67, 165, 176, 178; **42**, 139–45, 148, 149; **43**, 171–2, 183–6, 188, 194, 196, 202, 205, 215–16; **44**, 95, 197; **45**, 9, 10, 12, 57, 58, 63, 121, 189; 46, 165, 168, 184, 201; **47**, 99, 209; **48**, 14, 282; **49**, 199, 226, 232, 235, 237, 250–2, 271, 290; **50**, 31, 114n, 228; **51**, 246–7; **52**, 257, 321–2; **54**, 274; **55**, 171, 231, 293; **56**, 246, 249, 295; **57**, 265, 266, 267, 269; **58**, 206, 298, 337; **59**, 307, 338; **60**, 229, 313–14, 324, 325, 329
  production of *Twelfth Night*, **12**, 126–9
Hall, Radclyffe, **58**, 125
Hall, Rebecca, **57**, 267; **58**, 298; **59**, 338
Hall, Stuart, **52**, 204n
Hall, Susanna, **14**, 110, 113; **17**, 14
Hall, Thomas, **51**, 270
Hall, Vernon, **54**, 90n
'Hall, W.', **36**, 190
Hall, William, **40**, 217; **58**, 224
Hallam, Elaine, **43**, 214
Hallam, Lewis, **18**, 102, 104, 105, 108; **30**, 199; **57**, 128
Hallberg, Edith, **57**, 165, 167
Halle Orchestra, **58**, 303
Halle, Charles, **41**, 24
Halle, Edward, **8**, 146; **48**, 85, 89
  Chronicle, **8**, 148
Halle, M., **23**, 11n
Hallen, A. W. C., **25**, 139n
Hallett, Charles A., **24**, 164; **45**, 19n, 22n, 161
Hallett, Charles and Elaine, **35**, 162
Hallett, Elaine S., **45**, 19n, 22n, 161
Halley, Janet E., **44**, 81, 82n; **55**, 244n
Halliday, A. J., **10**, 75; **49**, 1n; **54**, 87
Halliday, F. E., **9**, 134; **27**, 106n; **36**, 55n; **43**, 18n; **46**, 104n
  The Cult of Shakespeare, **12**, 140 and n.
  Life of Shakespeare reviewed, **15**, 168
  Shakespeare: a pictorial biography reviewed, **11**, 136, 142
  A Shakespeare Companion 1550–1950 reviewed, **6**, 157
  Shakespeare and his Critics, **12**, 139 and n.
  Shakespeare and his Critics reviewed, **4**, 145–6

Halliday, John, **43**, 249; **55**, 196n
Halliday, Michael, **44**, 199
Halligan, Liam, **42**, 136
Hallinan, Tim, **36**, 172; **39**, 10n, 97, 104n, 109n
Halling, A., **3**, 112
Halliwell, Sarah, **49**, 115n; **51**, 10n
Halliwell, Steve, **42**, 155
Halliwell-Phillipps, J. O., **1**, 1, 57, 59, 62, 70, 73, 83, 86, 87 nn., 128; **3**, 5, 11, 45–6; **4**, 72, 73, 161; **5**, 46n, 57n; **6**, 5; **7**, 90; **8**, 153; **9**, 34n, 156; **13**, 163; **14**, 82; **15**, 2; **17**, 172n; **19**, 81n; **23**, 102; **25**, 200; **27**, 97n, 106n; **28**, 179–80; **29**, 168; **32**, 151–2, 241; **38**, 86, 97n, 99; **41**, 217; **44**, 149; **46**, 31n; **49**, 18n, 184n; **53**, 206n, 341; **54**, 115, 134n; **56**, 185n, 187n; **59**, 149; **60**, 1, 13n40, 234
  Autobiography and Correspondence of Sir Simonds D'Ewes, **11**, 115n
  Outline of the life of Shakespeare, **3**, 1; **13**, 88n
Hallma, Henry, **36**, 175
Halloren, Barry, **49**, 273
Hallqvist, Britt, **42**, 150
Hallstead, R. N., **22**, 161
Hallström, Per, **36**, 70
Hallward, Basil, **56**, 137
Halperin, David, **53**, 80; **56**, 105n
Halpern, Baruch, **48**, 89n
Halpern, Richard, **48**, 152n, 240, 247; **52**, 161; **55**, 5–6, 74n, 75, 341; **57**, 2, 303, 304; **59**, 149n9
Halpin, M., **55**, 249n
Halprin, N. J., **49**, 100n
Halpin, Nicholas, **56**, 114
Hals, Frans, **39**, 109
Halsey, Frederick R., his library, **6**, 54
Halstead, Edward, **42**, 154
Halstead, W. L., **31**, 33n
Halstead, William P., **34**, 186; **35**, 5–6; **36**, 74n; **45**, 32n; **53**, 216; **59**, 201
Halter, P., **32**, 224
Halverson, John, **42**, 177; **48**, 251; **49**, 286
Ham, Jennifer, **51**, 176n
Hämäläinen, Ekke, **13**, 126
Hamblen, Abigail Ann, **55**, 145
Hambleton, T. Edward, **8**, 122
Hamblin, Eliza, **32**, 23n
Hamblin, Thomas, **18**, 106–7
Hamburger, Maik, **37**, 160; **40**, 52n, 53n; **48**, 178, 184n; **52**, 284
Hamburger, Michael P., **20**, 117; **23**, 151; **31**, 175; **50**, 130n
Hamer, Douglas, **23**, 161n; **24**, 155; **28**, 49n, 166; **32**, 43n; **39**, 223; **51**, 54n
Hamer, E., **15**, 17
Hamer, Mary, **40**, 222; **50**, 247; **53**, 302–3
Hamill, M. J., **51**, 171n
Hamilton, A. C., **18**, 168; **22**, 151; **26**, 174; **27**, 11n, 17n, 18; **29**, 88; **32**, 226; **38**, 4; **48**, 43n; **50**, 254; **57**, 247
Hamilton, A. H. A., **17**, 83n
Hamilton, Alastair, **44**, 82n
Hamilton, Alice, **47**, 49n
Hamilton, Carolyn, **52**, 159n, 160n, 164n
Hamilton, Charles, **47**, 241; **51**, 96n
Hamilton, D. M., **27**, 167
Hamilton, Donna B., **28**, 157, 167; **37**, 192; **44**, 222; **45**, 171; **47**, 230; **48**, 136n; **54**, 10n, 50n, 58n, 72n, 73, 96n, 322; **55**, 344
Hamilton, Edith, **36**, 85n; **49**, 61n
Hamilton, Emily, **54**, 294
Hamilton, Gary D., **54**, 98n
Hamilton, Henry, **29**, 136
Hamilton, James, 3rd Marquess and 1st Duke of, **11**, 109
Hamilton, James, **56**, 6n
Hamilton, John, **55**, 234n
Hamilton, Lionel, **12**, 119; **13**, 134; **14**, 127; **47**, 96–8, 102, 106
Hamilton, Victoria, **50**, 206, 213–14; **51**, 248, 267; **54**, 268–72; **55**, 322
Hamilton, William, **36**, 94n; **49**, 119; **59**, 132, 379
Hamlet Improvised, **43**, 207
Hamlet, The Tragedy of a Fat Man, **47**, 211
Hamlet (Russian version), **49**, 308
Hamletmachine, **54**, 340
Hamlett, Dilys, **50**, 235
Hamlett, Katherine, **43**, 267
Hamley, Sir Edward Bruce, **54**, 72; **58**, 143
Hamlin, William M., **48**, 248; **51**, 178, 179n
Hamlyn, Paul, **49**, 129
Hamlyn, Robin, **37**, 45n
Hamm, Nick, **42**, 150
Hammel, Robert C., **60**, 182
Hammelmann, Hanns, **37**, 42
Hammer, Ina, **39**, 76n
Hammer, Paul E. J., **54**, 97n–98n
Hammerle, Karl, **8**, 143; **9**, 142; **12**, 137; **14**, 155
Hammerschmidt, H., **37**, 156n, 158n
Hammersmith, James P., **33**, 201; **35**, 188; **36**, 193; **39**, 139n; **40**, 235n; **41**, 230n
Hammerton, Stephen, **58**, 231, 235
Hammond, Antony, **36**, 184–5, 193n; **42**, 181; **50**, 289; **52**, 69n, 316; **55**, 20, 22, 187–8; **57**, 235; **59**, 223n38
Hammond, Brean, S., **51**, 96n
Hammond, Gerald, **35**, 168
Hammond, Jonathan, **52**, 156
Hammond, Kay, **27**, 142
Hammond, Mona, **48**, 196; **49**, 272
Hammond, P. W., **45**, 167; **49**, 334; **51**, 334; **57**, 303; **59**, 15n65, 361, 368; **60**, 112n41
Hammond, William, **44**, 123
Hamo, **11**, 46
Hampden, Walter, **1**, 113
Hampson, Christopher, **59**, 344; **58**, 136
Hampton, William, **11**, 124
Han, Shishan, **57**, 174
Han, Tien, **6**, 115, 116
Hancock, J. L., **20**, 25n
Hancock, Lewis, **47**, 217; **52**, 259
Hancock, Phyllida, **46**, 178, 184
Hancock, Sheila, **35**, 143–4, 148–9
Handel, George Frederick, **3**, 56; **9**, 97; **18**, 77, 78; **21**, 96; **41**, 160; **49**, 12; **50**, 150; **54**, 53, 54; **56**, 280
Handke, Peter, **60**, 104
Handleman, Don, **56**, 25n
Handley, Tommy, **19**, 36
Handlyng Sin, **1**, 71
Handover, P. M., **54**, 133n

Hands, Robert, **53**, 284; **56**, 279; **57**, 265
Hands, Terry, **23**, 132, 133; **24**, 118, 119, 120, 129, 131; **25**, 153, 155, 158, 164; **27**, 144, 150, 151; **29**, 154, 155; **31**, 148–51; **32**, 223; **33**, 169, 170; **34**, 149, 150; **35**, 149–50; **36**, 59, 63, 120n, 129n, 152; **38**, 17, 195n; **39**, 185, 205; **40**, 177–8; **41**, 171, 188, 191; **42**, 151, 160, 200; **43**, 171, 184–5, 192, 196, 203, 250; **44**, 102, 163, 164, 190, 192, 200; **45**, 121, 124, 139, 148, 187; **47**, 121, 124; **49**, 10, 13, 260–3; **50**, 69n, 230; **52**, 286; **53**, 309; **54**, 280, 287, 294; **56**, 113, 240, 279, 291, 343; **57**, 279, 291, 293; **60**, 328
Handwriting, Elizabethan, **2**, 54–8
  see also under Shakespeare, William, handwriting and signatures
Handy, Scott, **52**, 236–8, 240; **55**, 301
Hanford, J. H., **14**, 98, 101n
Hanger, Colonel, **38**, 70–1
Hanger, Eunice, **14**, 116
Hanger, George, Baron Colerain, **56**, 131
Hanham, Alison, **38**, 2
Hanham, Jacquie, **54**, 291
Hanke, Lewis, **32**, 93n
Hankey, Fiona, **56**, 298
Hankey, Julie, **35**, 11; **41**, 225; **42**, 250; **46**, 62; **49**, 292; **51**, 58; **52**, 203n; **53**, 110n; **56**, 132n; **59**, 201, 202n24, 371, 375
Hankin, St John, **56**, 102
Hankins, John Erskine, **11**, 146; **14**, 165, 166; **15**, 14, 17; **33**, 194–5; **34**, 98n; **35**, 119; **36**, 85, 91n; **40**, 70; **45**, 22n
  Shakespeare's Derived Imagery reviewed, **8**, 145
Hankiss, Elemér, **40**, 35
Hanley, Hugh A., **18**, 178
Hanlon, Roy, **53**, 260
Hanmer, Sir Thomas, **3**, 50; **4**, 85, 86, 162; **5**, 51; **8**, 52; **9**, 93; **10**, 28; **13**, 73, 74, 80n; **14**, 78; **18**, 15, 16; **27**, 49n; **31**, 190; **33**, 210; **35**, 183; **42**, 203; **48**, 284; 49, 113–14; **50**, 277; **51**, 4, 7, 8, 10; **53**, 342–3; **54**, 56, 210; **59**, 52, 56–7n20, 59, 60, 88, 131
Hann (stage designer, 1882), **49**, 126
Hann, T., **26**, 142
Hann, Walter, **41**, 26, 31
Hanna, Ralph, **55**, 183n
Hanna, Sara, **54**, 37
Hannaford, Ivan, **52**, 205n
Hannaway, Sean, **55**, 296
Hannay, Margaret P., **44**, 240
Hannay, Patrick, **60**, 283n52
Hannigan, Eithne, **42**, 157
Hannigan, J. E., **3**, 3
Hansen, Carol, *Woman as Individual in English Renaissance Drama: A Defiance of the Masculine Code*, **48**, 258
Hansen, Jørgen Wildt, **30**, 193
Hansen, Miriam, **45**, 45n
Hanson, Alexander, **53**, 268
Hanson, Elizabeth, **53**, 319
Hanson, Ellis, **53**, 139n, 140n
Hanson, L. W., 'The Shakespeare Collection in the Bodleian Library, Oxford', **4**, 78–96
Hanson-Smith, Elizabeth, **41**, 114n
Hansson, Lars, **10**, 121
Häntsch, Thomas, **37**, 157n
Hanuš, Jan, **11**, 118; **13**, 126
Hanway, Mary Ann, **43**, 107
Hapgood, E. R., **27**, 144n
Hapgood, Elizabeth Reynolds, **34**, 9n
Hapgood, Hutchins, **55**, 122, 123n
Hapgood, Isabel, **45**, 4n
Hapgood, Norman, **57**, 255
Hapgood, Robert, **18**, 158, 162, 169; **19**, 132, 133; **20**, 148, 154, 155; **22**, 155; **24**, 154, 161; **25**, 3n; **26**, 159; **27**, 144n; **35**, 7n; **37**, 105n; **38**, 3; **39**, 136n; **40**, 35; **41**, 202, 227; **43**, 236–8; **44**, 111n; **48**, 35n; **53**, 327; **56**, 98n, 100n; **57**, 339
  'Hearing Shakespeare: Sound and Meaning in *Antony and Cleopatra*', **24**, 1–12
  'Shakespeare and the Ritualists', **15**, 111–24
  'Shakespeare's Thematic Modes of Speech: *Richard II to Henry V*', **20**, 41–50
Haponski, W. C., **26**, 176n
Happé, Peter, **48**, 266; **57**, 239; **59**, 250n84
Harada, Tamotsu, **60**, 304
Harambašić, A., **4**, 117
Harari, Josué V., **37**, 70n; **60**, 254n11
Haraszti, Gyula, **59**, 126
Harbage, Alfred B., **1**, 4, 6, 7, 8; **2**, 43n, 134, 153; **4**, 11, 16, 91, 155–6; **5**, 138; **6**, 11; **7**, 5, 7; **8**, 9; **10**, 138, 147, 148, 149; **11**, 153; **12**, 1, 70n; **13**, 165; **14**, 3; **15**, 10, 114, 123n; **16**, 165, 178; **18**, 3, 21, 62–7, 131, 180; **19**, 143–4; **20**, 114, 120n; **21**, 65n, 129, 141; **24**, 163, 172n, 173, 174; **25**, 8, 171; **26**, 7, 55n, 100, 168; **29**, 87, 167, 170, 172; **30**, 14, 109; **31**, 63n, 128n, 132, 191; **34**, 42n, 133n, 136; **35**, 172; **36**, 58n, 97n; **38**, 51, 53, 54n; **41**, 6, 7, 215; **42**, 1; **43**, 16n, 82n; **44**, 243; **45**, 185; **51**, 96n; **53**, 104; **58**, 200, 356; **59**, 40–1, 42, 71n9
  Annals of English Drama 975–1700, **14**, 14n
  As They Liked It reviewed, **1**, 119, 120; **3**, 7
  Shakespeare's Audience, **3**, 7
  Shakespeare and the Rival Traditions, **12**, 140; **14**, 2
  Shakespeare and the Rival Traditions reviewed, **7**, 141–2
  Theatre for Shakespeare, **12**, 70n; **14**, 13
  Theatre for Shakespeare reviewed, **10**, 148
Harben, Henry A., **53**, 212n
Harbord (Harbert), Thomas, **5**, 55
Harbord, Rebecca, **42**, 159
Harbour, Michael, **47**, 101
Harcombe, Sebastian, **50**, 206, 211
Harcourt, John B., **16**, 158–9; **19**, 11, 74n; **28**, 158; **29**, 170; **35**, 87n
Harcourt, L. W. V., **6**, 4
Harcourt, Robert, **17**, 33
  Relation of a Voyage to Guiana, **1**, 68
Hard Day's Bard, A, **44**, 203
Hardie, Martin, **55**, 137–8
Hardie, Philip, **56**, 29n
Hardiman, Terence, **22**, 141
Hardin, Richard F., **43**, 9n; **46**, 224; **55**, 36n
Harding, Allison, **44**, 201
Harding, D. W., **24**, 145
Harding, Davis P., **5**, 141; **8**, 12; **9**, 146; **13**, 86, 88n, 89n; **25**, 6n; **32**, 129n; **43**, 50n
Harding, Edward, **13**, 76
Harding, Peter, **48**, 236
Harding, Samuel, **54**, 62
Harding, Sylvester, **47**, 174
Harding, Thomas, **17**, 121

Hardinge, George, **51**, 5
Hardison, O. B., Jr, **24**, 162; **26**, 174; **30**, 194; **35**, 164; **41**, 144; **49**, 164n; **50**, 147; **55**, 221n
Hardman, Christopher, **48**, 247; **49**, 79n
Hardman, Phillipa, **49**, 79n
Hardouin, Jean, **32**, 132n, 134n
Hardt, Ernst, **44**, 108n
Hardwick, J. M. D., **35**, 8
Hardwick, Paul, **14**, 133; **16**, 150–1; **57**, 340
Hardwick, **12**, 11
Hardy, Barbara, **13**, 151; **32**, 2; **35**, 82; **42**, 185; **43**, 233; **44**, 217–18; **52**, 269; **53**, 2n, 39, 41, 46, 159n, 161; **54**, 132n
Hardy, Dudley, **49**, 128
Hardy, J. P., **34**, 168
Hardy, John, **21**, 149
Hardy, Laurence, **9**, 129
Hardy, Noel, **38**, 237
Hardy, Robert, **3**, 128; **8**, 133; **13**, 140; **52**, 256; **53**, 276
Hardy, Thomas, **5**, 130; **8**, 24; **14**, 156; **16**, 16; **24**, 37, 38, 46; **30**, 3; **36**, 95n, 128; **46**, 32; **49**, 134n, 140; **53**, 115; **54**, 76; **56**, 134, 135
Jude the Obscure, **3**, 67
The Return of the Native, **12**, 137
Hardy, W. J., **25**, 139
Hardyng, John, **8**, 146; **33**, 99n; **48**, 70n
Hare, Arnold, **35**, 8; **41**, 225; **47**, 27n; **51**, 107n, 118n
Hare, Augustus, **7**, 34
Hare, David, **41**, 174, 176, 185; **42**, 151; **43**, 224; **55**, 180
Hare, John, **35**, 16
Hare, Julius Charles, **37**, 152
Hare, Robertson, **56**, 177
Harewell, Anne, **12**, 99
Harewell, John (Lord of the Manor of Lucies), **12**, 99, 102
Harewood, David, **43**, 213; **46**, 198; **48**, 197; **51**, 253–4; **52**, 262; **53**, 185, 192; **57**, 45; **59**, 325–6; **60**, 160, 162, 168n1.9
Harford, Richard, **49**, 272
Harfouch, Corinne, **42**, 159
Hargrave, Francis, **29**, 97n
Hargreaves, David, **55**, 310
Hargreaves, H. A., **25**, 181
Harington family of Burley-on-the-Hill, **14**, 103–7; **16**, 165
Harington, Sir John, **1**, 72; **8**, 6; **17**, 130 and n., 153, 162 and n.; **27**, 136n; **28**, 21; **35**, 112n; **38**, 20–1, 248; **45**, 181; **46**, 10–18, 12n, 19n, 21, 225; **47**, 130n, 165, 274; **52**, 274; **53**, 307; **56**, 218; **58**, 351
Metamorphosis of Ajax, **4**, 65
Orlando Furioso, **3**, 54; **7**, 36, 38
trans. *Orlando Furioso*, **14**, 163; **18**, 191
Hariot, Thomas, **3**, 10; **17**, 28n, 28–9
New Found Land of Virginia, **1**, 69
Harker, J. C., **13**, 79; **26**, 142
Harker, Mrs, **41**, 27
Harlan, Manuel, **59**, 302, 311, 321
Harland, George, **15**, 145
Harle, John, **50**, 235; **55**, 325
Harleian Miscellany, The, **9**, 34n
Harlem Duet, **54**, 340
Harleth, Gwendolen, **56**, 135
Harley, Edward (1689–1741), Second Earl of Oxford, **2**, 44; **5**, 55, 56
Harley, J. P., **58**, 337
Harley, Lady Brilliana, **49**, 300
Harlow, Alvin F., **57**, 249, 252, 253
Harlow, Barbara, **46**, 124n
Harlow, C. G., **20**, 162; **21**, 152; **24**, 159
Harlow, George Henry, **51**, 114, 115
Harman, Mr Justice, **40**, 169
Harman, R. A., **17**, 214n
Harman, Thomas, **38**, 27; **44**, 21, 23n; **52**, 125; **55**, 83, 84
Harman, William, **49**, 164n
Harmanus, Jo, **48**, 32n
Harmer, L. C., **48**, 31n
Harmon, Alice, **28**, 39, 40; **29**, 81
Harmston, Joe, **52**, 266; **55**, 324
Harmsworth, Sir Leicester, **1**, 58, 67–8
Harned, Jon, **60**, 351
Harner, James L., **51**, 334
Harness, William, **14**, 86, 110–15
Harnisch, Hoffman, **20**, 122
Harp, Richard, **56**, 147n
Harper, J. W., **35**, 116n; **37**, 85; **44**, 120; **47**, 245
Harper, Samuel, **3**, 44
Harpsfield, Nicholas, **38**, 94; **42**, 79n, 83; **43**, 50, 52; **50**, 251
Harrier, R. C., **14**, 141; **18**, 170; **50**, 47n
Harrington, James, **56**, 325
Harrington, Lord, **26**, 41
Harrington, William, **13**, 83; **32**, 133
Commendacions of matrymony, **13**, 83, 88n
Harriot, Thomas, **38**, 49n, 53; **52**, 109–11
Harris, Alexander, Warden of the Fleet Prison, **17**, 99
Oeconomy, **17**, 94n, 99n, 253
Harris, Amanda, **44**, 166; **45**, 154; **46**, 175, 177; **47**, 217; **51**, 264; **54**, 251, 253; **55**, 326; **57**, 277; **58**, **281**; **59**, 305–6, 312, 313; **60**, 78, 79
Harris, Anthony, **34**, 182n
Harris, Arthur, **52**, 19n
Harris, Arthur J., **25**, 192; **47**, 83n
Harris, Augustus, **10**, 75; **16**, 116; **35**, 19
Harris, B., **41**, 83n
Harris, Bernard, **13**, 155; **16**, 157n; **17**, 46n; **20**, 49n; **21**, 127n, 140; **25**, 84n; **26**, 9, 24n; **29**, 3; **30**, 148n; **32**, 1; **33**, 8n; **34**, 54n, 58n, 103n, 133n, 189; **35**, 113n; **36**, 50n, 97; **37**, 5, 56n; **38**, 8n, 80n; **39**, 135n, 139n, 145n; **43**, 23n, 26n; **45**, 7; **46**, 21n, 101n
'A Portrait of a Moor', **11**, 89–97
'Dissent and Satire', **17**, 120–37
Harris, Beth, **47**, 99
Harris, Bob, **42**, 157
Harris, Caroline, **54**, 258
Harris, Charles, **54**, 193
Harris, Corrine, **42**, 157
Harris, Dave, **41**, 187
Harris, Duncan J., **31**, 172; **32**, 226
Harris, Frank, **3**, 8; **4**, 6; **12**, 138; **16**, 34; **29**, 133, 135, 139; **54**, 71; **58**, 121, 141, 146
The Man Shakespeare, **3**, 9
Harris, Gil, **60**, 226n16
Harris, Harry, **49**, 273
Harris, J., **43**, 162n
Harris, John, **28**, 170; **30**, 157–8, 161; **33**, 145n; **35**, 133n, 135n; **36**, 115n; **48**, 231
Harris, John W., **19**, 127

Harris, Jonathan Gil, **49**, 289; **57**, 303, 315, 333; **58**, 28, 311, 332
Harris, Julie, **14**, 117
Harris, Kate, **41**, 114n
Harris, Kathryn M., **25**, 173
Harris, Laurie L., **40**, 210n
Harris, Margaret, **50**, 263
Harris, Peter, **52**, 259
Harris, Rennie, **56**, 296; **57**, 296
Harris, Richard, **54**, 253
Harris, Robert, **1**, 107, 108, 109; **11**, 135
Harris, Sophia, **50**, 263
Harris, Thomas, **29**, 34, 35, 36, 37–9
Harris, Valentine, **60**, 50, 51n13
Harrison, C. T., **26**, 167
Harrison, Cathryn, **47**, 209
Harrison, Christopher, **55**, 37n
Harrison, Claire, **44**, 200
Harrison, E. E., **53**, 208n
Harrison, G. B., **2**, 52; **3**, 26, 30; **4**, 10; **6**, 6; **7**, 83–4; **9**, 48n, 152; **10**, 3; **11**, 148n, 153; **13**, 165, 168n; **14**, 157n, 166 and n; **15**, 5, 71n, 72n; **17**, 50n; **18**, 20, 131; **19**, 2, 5, 24n, 142; **21**, 138, 141, 157; **26**, 50; **27**, 16n, 21n; **28**, 118n; **30**, 15; **32**, 100n; **51**, 141, 185; **52**, 303; **53**, 70n; **55**, 82n; **59**, 40, 42, 43, 81n9
Elizabethan Journals, **3**, 6
'A Note on *Coriolanus*', **2**, 150
The Penguin Shakespeare, **2**, 153
Penguin editions of *Richard the Third* and *Love's Labour's Lost* reviewed, **8**, 158
Shakespeare's Tragedies reviewed, **6**, 152
Harrison, James, printer, **18**, 17
Harrison, John, **5**, 120; **8**, 123, 125; **9**, 119, 121; **12**, 119; **15**, 141; **42**, 149; **44**, 202
Harrison, John L., **8**, 140
Harrison, Nigel, **43**, 209
Harrison, R. C., **18**, 118n
Harrison, Robert Pogue, **48**, 159, 160n
Harrison, Sara, **60**, 325
Harrison, Scott Michael, **48**, 70n
Harrison, Stephen, **26**, 39n
Harrison, Thomas P., junior, **3**, 6; **11**, 141; **19**, 120; **23**, 11n, 141n; **26**, 172; **38**, 2n
Harrison, Tony, **41**, 126n; **53**, 105n; **56**, 238, 240, 241, 242, 247
Harrison, W. A., **51**, 81n
Harrison, Wilfred, **40**, 222, 235
Harrison, William, **6**, 162; **29**, 22, 24; **30**, 8; **46**, 233; **50**, 144; **51**, 311; **57**, 43; **59**, 245n45
Description of Britaine, **11**, 44–6; **12**, 20n; **17**, 73n, 91n, 163
Description of England, **1**, 29
Description of Scotland, **4**, 40
Harron, Mary, **58**, 189
Harrop, John, **60**, 147, 147n19
Harryson, William, **60**, 21
Harsnape, Jane, **7**, 139
Harsnett, Samuel, **11**, 143; **12**, 142; **13**, 34, 36, 39; **17**, 52; **24**, 71, 72, 77; **26**, 71–2; **27**, 172, 173; **28**, 119; **29**, 24; **30**, 193; **32**, 229; **33**, 13, 19, 195; **36**, 112n; **38**, 99, 234; **39**, 223; **41**, 143n; **42**, 167; **44**, 22, 234; **47**, 254–5, 259; **50**, 149; **52**, 278; **54**, 21, 23, 26n, 57n; **55**, 6, 17, 368; **58**, 16, 17, 18, 19, 20, 21
A Declaration of Egregious Popish Impostures, **3**, 17, 54; **5**, 134; **10**, 136
Hart family (of Stratford-upon-Avon), **1**, 80, 81, 82, 87n; **4**, 71, 75–6; **5**, 56–7; **14**, 112
Hart, Alexander, **52**, 190n
Hart, Alfred, **1**, 13; **3**, 29; **4**, 7; **6**, 4, 7, 39, 47; **11**, 51; **25**, 74n, 76n; **29**, 84; **30**, 6, 89, 90n; **38**, 246; **42**, 205; **48**, 271; **49**, 28–34, 40; **52**, 81n, 82n, 84, 86; **55**, 16n; **57**, 243; **59**, 7n27
on the authorship of *Edward III*, **6**, 40
Shakespeare and the Homilies, **11**, 59n
Hart, Charles, **56**, 294; **58**, 241
Hart, Clive, **24**, 165; **56**, 138n
Hart, Dee, **42**, 159; **45**, 148; **46**, 199
Hart, E. L., **18**, 162, 172
Hart, H. C., **3**, 69; **5**, 19, 20, 80n; **6**, 2; **7**, 4, 5, 103; **8**, 6; **19**, 94n; **27**, 112, 119, 120, 121, 122; **37**, 92n
Hart, James, **39**, 2n; **51**, 80; **53**, 279
Hart, John A., **24**, 175
Hart, John, grammarian, **7**, 35, 36
Hart, Jonathan, **48**, 240
Hart, Joseph C., **46**, 143
Hart, Kingsley, **18**, 121
Hart, Lorenz, **45**, 146
Hart, Thomas, **56**, 186–7, 189
Hart, Valerie, **58**, 321, 333
Hart, William, **58**, 241
Hart-Davis, Sir Rupert, **29**, 133n, 139n; **35**, 6
Harting, James Edward, **21**, 142; **44**, 131n, 142n
Hartington, Daniel, **49**, 125
Hartlaub, Gustav F., **4**, 127
Hartley, L. P., **56**, 14n, 33n
Hartley, Lodowick, **25**, 182
Hartley, William, **3**, 24; **8**, 7
Hartman, Geoffrey, **40**, 82n, 189–90; **41**, 106n; **43**, 253n; **44**, 33n; **45**, 40n; **46**, 7n, 45n, 82n, 84, 134n; **48**, 26n; **49**, 207n; **50**, 241; **51**, 285; **54**, 132n, 139n; **55**, 5n
Hartman, Herbert, **41**, 138n
Hartmann, G., **47**, 131n
Hartmann, Georg, **1**, 8
Hartmann, Herbert, **32**, 168n; **38**, 83
Hartmann, Jonathan, **60**, 230
Hartmann, Robert, **24**, 97
Hartnoll, Gillian, **39**, 75n
Hartnoll, Phyllis, **1**, 160; **19**, 151; **45**, 171; **49**, 111n; **53**, 172n, 241
Hartop, Job, **16**, 77; **17**, 32
Hartsock, Mildred E., **21**, 132; **22**, 114; **24**, 153
Hartweit, L., **49**, 328n
Hartwell, Peter, **48**, 230
Hartwig, Joan, **25**, 177; **27**, 158; **28**, 162; **29**, 52n; **33**, 136n, 188; **37**, 194; **38**, 220; **43**, 22n; **51**, 177n, 181n; **53**, 15n, 16n, 19n
Hartz, Alisa, **56**, 348
Harvard *see under* Libraries
Harvard '47 Workshop', **1**, 13
Harvey, A. D., **48**, 248
Harvey, David, **50**, 32
Harvey, Elizabeth D., **52**, 145n; **55**, 244n; **60**, 255n15

Harvey, G. H., **13**, 78, 80n
Harvey, Gabriel, **1**, 71; **2**, 54; **3**, 25, 28; **4**, 62; **5**, 138; **6**, 79; **7**, 7; **8**, 6; **10**, 144; **11**, 142, 145; **12**, 31, 135; **13**, 110n; **15**, 128; **17**, 49, 65, 121, 125; **18**, 35; **21**, 48; **23**, 171n; **24**, 77, 159; **26**, 20; **27**, 117n, 130; **28**, 45; **30**, 209; **34**, 85, 90; **38**, 49n, 51, 53, 122; **39**, 224; **40**, 215; **42**, 55; **43**, 269; **46**, 223; **56**, 44; **57**, 197, 214, 216, 217, 218, 309; **60**, 269
Marginalia, **9**, 24–6, 33
Harvey, John W., **15**, 165; **17**, 127; **53**, 107, 109
Harvey, Lawrence, **49**, 156
Harvey, Lois, **45**, 131, 150
Harvey, Marcus, **57**, 51
Harvey, Martin, **2**, 10; **36**, 180n, 181; **44**, 194; **47**, 211
Harvey, Nancy L., **24**, 148
Harvey, Richard, *An Astrological Discourse*, **9**, 34n
Harvey, Richard, **17**, 126
Philadelphus, **11**, 44, 49n
Harvey, Rupert, **47**, 92, 106
Harvey, Tamara, **58**, 280; **59**, 342
Harvey, William, **6**, 66; **34**, 86n; **38**, 179; **55**, 63–4
Harvey, Dr William, **11**, 72; **15**, 174; **17**, 71, 148, 152n, 155
Harvey, Sir William ('Mr WH'), **18**, 178; **20**, 161; **24**, 151; **25**, 4
Harvey/Nashe pamphlets, **44**, 232
Harwood, Frank, **10**, 125; **12**, 119; **13**, 135
Hasegawa, Hirosha, **49**, 272
Haselkorn, Anne M., **45**, 160
Hasell, Captain Robert, **2**, 26, 32, 34, 35
Hasenberg, Peter, **37**, 158n
Hasker, Richard E., **7**, 151; **11**, 152
Haskins, Theresa, **52**, 258
Hasler, Jörg, **23**, 143; **25**, 184; **29**, 161; **32**, 4, 7, 10, 12; **37**, 158n; **39**, 230; **50**, 130n
Hasler, P. W., **54**, 96n
Haslop, Henry, **17**, 34
Hassall, Anthony J., **55**, 174n
Hassall, Christopher, **55**, 128n, 129n, 135n
Hassall, W. O., **11**, 97n
Hassan, **11**, 130
Hassel, R. Chris, Jr, **27**, 164; **31**, 5n; **34**, 162–3, 178–9, 184; **36**, 176; **38**, 49n, 53n, 55n; **40**, 205; **41**, 226–7; **47**, 228; **48**, 251
Hassell, Chris R., **25**, 179
Hasson, Ann, **56**, 4n
Hastings family, **48**, 260
Hastings, Henry, Third Earl of Huntingdon, **6**, 60
Hastings, Ian, **48**, 232
Hastings, W. T., **5**, 91n; **12**, 145; **15**, 111; **19**, 123
Hastrup, Kirsten, **46**, 110n
Hatchard, **18**, 18
Hatcher, O. L., *John Fletcher*, **14**, 12
Hatchman, Richard, Keeper of Newgate, **17**, 93n
Hatchuel, Sarah, **58**, 334, 340, 341, 342; **59**, 371–2; **60**, 355
Hatcliffe, William, **28**, 165; **32**, 227
Hatfield, Hurd, **6**, 124; **7**, 116
'Hathawa, Hanna', **36**, 10
Hathaway, Agnes, **12**, 95
Hathaway, Ann, **56**, 142, 143
Hathaway, Anne, **3**, 9; **12**, 95, 97–8, 102–6; **14**, 111–13; **23**, 159; **26**, 164; **36**, 10; **42**, 185; **46**, 142; **54**, 117, 121
see also under Stratford-upon-Avon
Hathaway, Baxter, **46**, 93n, 217
Hathaway, Michael, **23**, 163n
Hathaway, Richard, of Shottery, **12**, 95–106; **58**, 13
Hathaway, Richard, *see* Mundy, Anthony
Hatherell, William, **49**, 125, 128
Hathway, Richard, **26**, 103; **46**, 226; **59**, 71, 72, 74, 77, 78, 78n15
Hatlen, Burton, **52**, 280
Hatley, Tim, **45**, 154; **46**, 165, 202; **47**, 216; **48**, 237; **52**, 251; **53**, 274; **55**, 323; **56**, 288
Hattaway, Michael, **37**, 183–4; **41**, 9; **43**, 4n; **44**, 20n, 251–2; **45**, 184; **46**, 133n, 241, 249, 250, 251, 254; **47**, 264–6; **49**, 308; **50**, 250; **53**, 167n, 294; **54**, 33n, 58n, 352; **55**, 382, 383, 388–9; **56**, 34n, 147n; **57**, 69; **59**, 71n9, 372; **60**, 105n17
Hatto, A. J., **15**, 21
Hatto, Arthur T., **49**, 6n
Hatton, Denys Finch, **43**, 117
Hatton, Ragnhild, **57**, 74
Hatton, Sir Christopher, **13**, 104n; **17**, 11, 16; **28**, 23, 24; **29**, 94; **48**, 40n
Hatzidakis, M., **7**, 112
Hatziscos, Nicos, **11**, 121; **10**, 119
Häublein, Renata, **56**, 315
Hau'ofa, Epili, **55**, 180n
Haugaard, William P., **54**, 123n, 125n
Hauger, George, **27**, 144
Haughton, David, **44**, 198
Haughton, William, **17**, 43–4; **32**, 198; **47**, 36; **55**, 377; **59**, 71, 72, 73
Haunch, T. O., **51**, 55n
Hauptmann, Gerhart, **16**, 10, 14, 134; **35**, 21; **44**, 108n, 109n; **55**, 115
Hauser, Arnold, **26**, 49, 50, 54, 58, 59n, 60n, 61n, 63, 64, 65; **28**, 152–3
Hauser, Frank, **9**, 22, 121; **13**, 135; **14**, 127; **15**, 145; **20**, 81n; **27**, 140
Hausted, Peter, **11**, 108, 115n; **55**, 93
The Rival Friends, **11**, 108
Havard, Dr William, **18**, 95, 96, 100n
Havas, Adolf, **59**, 126
Havel, Václav, **48**, 165–7
Havelock, E. A., **24**, 50n
Havely, Cicely, **27**, 157; **32**, 155
Havergal, Giles, **48**, 235; **52**, 255; **56**, 294
Haviland, William, **25**, 118
Havilland, Olivia de, **5**, 115, 116
Havrevold, **5**, 113
Haw, Richard, **42**, 157
Hawarde, John, **33**, 147n
Hawes, Craven, **13**, 79
Hawes, Stephen, **59**, 364
Hawke, Ethan, **55**, 324; **58**, 189, 334; **60**, 355
Hawkes, A. J., **13**, 103n
Hawkes, David, **54**, 322; **57**, 303, 304; **59**, 355
Hawkes, Terence, **24**, 6n; **25**, 173; **26**, 165; **28**, 150, 155; **31**, 173; **32**, 179n; **33**, 43n; **34**, 62n; **35**, 66n, 159, 172; **38**, 218; **39**, 136n, 146; **40**, 185–6, 189; **41**, 202; **42**, 165; **43**, 11n, 15n, 110n, 124, 221; **44**, 111n; **45**, 18n; **46**, 206, 219; **47**,

71, 72n, 73, 74n; **48**, 64, 244; **49**, 71n, 208, 288; **50**, 22n, 32; **51**, 14, 146, 147, 274, 275; **52**, 14–16, 101, 202n, 276; **53**, 293; **54**, 72n, 132n, 311; **55**, 4, 71n, 107n, 339; **56**, 39n, 74n, 203n, 205n, 239, 327, 349n; **58**, 130, 170–1, 175, 177–8, 178, 180, 313; **59**, 153n31, 359; **60**, 121n6, 155, 161
'Shakespeare's Talking Animals', **24**, 47–54
Hawkes, Terry, **13**, 153, 158; **14**, 141, 143; **15**, 165, 181–2; **16**, 158; **19**, 11, 121–2, 127, 133
Hawkesworth, James, **17**, 227
Hawkesworth, Walter, **49**, 300
Labyrinthus, **4**, 91
Leander (MS.), **3**, 52
Hawkins, Alexander, **11**, 100, 102–5, 105n
Hawkins, Harriett, **23**, 170; **27**, 162; **28**, 89, 91, 100n; **31**, 107n; **32**, 130, 131, 232; **36**, 169; **39**, 230; **42**, 169n, 180; **43**, 230; **48**, 243; **49**, 282; **53**, 165n; **56**, 148n
Hawkins, Jack, **1**, 115; **3**, 105; **5**, 116; **49**, 229
Hawkins, John, musician, **15**, 1
Hawkins, John E., **18**, 57n
Hawkins, Sir John, **3**, 56; **17**, 21, 25–6, 29, 31, 34, 143; **51**, 27n; **54**, 129n
Hawkins, Leader, **42**, 155; **52**, 222, 227
Hawkins, Michael, **57**, 8, 27
Hawkins, Richard, **17**, 25; **58**, 38, 350
Hawkins, Roger, **55**, 324
Hawkins, Sally, **54**, 291
Hawkins, Sherman, **22**, 153; **32**, 5; **35**, 70n; **37**, 36n; **38**, 13, 79n; **44**, 208; **45**, 163
Hawkins, Thomas, *The Origin of the English Drama*, **14**, 81
Hawkins, Revd Thomas, **4**, 85
Hawkins, William, **51**, 19n
Hawksford, Daniel, **57**, 275, 296
Hawley, Judith, **55**, 107; **52**, 273
Haworth, David, **51**, 264; **54**, 287
Haworth-Booth, Mark, **60**, 230n39
Hawthorne, Denys, **48**, 222–3; **49**, 272
Hawthorne, Nathaniel, **14**, 153; **18**, 115, 116; **24**, 169; **53**, 131n
Hawthorne, Sir Nigel, **47**, 97; **54**, 247–8, 286, **58**, 335, 355; **59**, 370–1
Haxton, Elaine, **11**, 117
Hay, Andrew, **41**, 185; **42**, 155; **47**, 217, 218; **49**, 280; **51**, 264; **59**, 346
Hay, Denys, **17**, 38; **38**, 11; **52**, 174n
Hay, Eloise, **45**, 12n
Hay, Sir James, **29**, 4
Hay, John, **24**, 90, 102, 103; **46**, 199
Hay, Lord, **43**, 248
Hay, Lucy, Countess of Carlisle, **11**, 111, 113
Hay, Malcolm, **55**, 160n, 166n, 167n, 168n
Hay, Will, **4**, 133
Hayashi, Masumi, **60**, 138n25
Hayden, Liza, **57**, 277
Hayden, Oliver, **46**, 199
Haydn, Franz Joseph, **18**, 100; **32**, 79; **36**, 82
Haydn, Hiram, **29**, 85; **33**, 25n; **36**, 45n; **56**, 84n
Haydock, George, **49**, 190
Haydon, Benjamin Robert, **13**, 61, 68n
Hayek, F. A., **56**, 206n
Hayes, Ann L., **5**, 105n; **19**, 127
Hayes, Chris, **41**, 189
Hayes, Dermot, **41**, 190; **44**, 195
Hayes, George, **9**, 57; **11**, 124; **36**, 75, 78
Hayes, Gerald R., **54**, 98n
Hayes, Helen, **5**, 115
Hayes, Hugh, **43**, 206
Hayes, James, **39**, 195; **45**, 156; **54**, 262
Hayes, Malcolm, **9**, 120
Hayes, Nuala, **45**, 217
Hayes, Patricia, **28**, 144, 145
Hayford, Harison, **45**, 1n
Haygarth, Tony, **42**, 145–6; **47**, 212
Hayles, Nancy K., **34**, 173; **36**, 166–7
Hayley, William, **49**, 122n
Hayman, Francis, painter, **4**, 86; **13**, 73, 74, 80n, 159; **31**, 190; **37**, 194; **49**, 113–14; **51**, 10, 107, 120–2; **59**, 131–2
Hayman, Ronald, **17**, 69n, quoted 69; **24**, 131n; **32**, 35; **36**, 22n, 26n; **42**, 87n; **48**, 177n; **50**, 172n, 173n
Hayne, Victoria, **47**, 229
Haynes, Alan, **48**, 135n
Haynes, F. O., **29**, 94, 98, 100
Haynes, John, **57**, 262
Haynes, Jonathan, **42**, 195n; **47**, 248
Haynes, Stephen, **45**, 146
Hays, David, **47**, 211
Hays, Michael L., **29**, 185; **30**, 208; **40**, 210; **58**, 328, 332; **59**, 69n2
Hayter, A., **26**, 161
Hayter, David, **41**, 186
Hayter, James, **47**, 92
Hayter, John, **49**, 123
Hayter, Richard, **14**, 126
Hayton, Alison G., **42**, 178
Hayward, John, **28**, 8, 9; **38**, 22; **43**, 240; **45**, 180; **58**, 17
Hayward, Sir John, **17**, 113n; **51**, 322
Hayward, Sir Ronald, **32**, 90n
Hayward, Susie Lee, **46**, 182
Hayward, Wayne, **6**, 163n
see also under Gruyter, Dom
Haywarde, Richard, **58**, 230
Haywell, F., **41**, 28
Haywood, Charles, **15**, 173; **23**, 175; **24**, 154, 168n, 169
Hazard, Ranulph, **58**, 84
Hazeldine, James, **35**, 150
Hazlett, John, **50**, 231
Hazlitt, W. Carew, **15**, 1, 26; **17**, 169n; **21**, 65n; **22**, 8; **27**, 111n; **28**, 38; **38**, 131n; **40**, 35, 63, 127n
Hazlitt, William, **2**, 19, 109; **4**, 3, 146; **5**, 98, 105n; **6**, 140, 143; **7**, 25, 27, 28, 127; **8**, 1, 28; **10**, 73, 74, 76n; **11**, 132; **14**, 56, 64, 84; **15**, 22; **18**, 3, 34, 38, 50, 72, 104, 108, 113; **20**, 79; **21**, 3, 107; **22**, 8; **24**, 45; **25**, 199; **26**, 90, 140; **29**, 105n, 134, 143; **32**, 17, 18, 21; **34**, 21, 51, 52; **35**, 6, 43–55, 155, 158; **37**, 142, 185, 201; **38**, 194; **39**, 175; **41**, 67, 199, 224; **42**, 38–40; **43**, 112n; **45**, 5, 8, 10, 18, 38, 39; **46**, 220; **47**, 107; **49**, 113n, 123n, 131–40, 214, 216, 229, 231; **51**, 113, 115, 118, 130; **52**, 111n, 131n; **53**, 92, 287; **54**, 66, 138–9, 319; **55**, 9, 10, 107, 109n, 337–8, 344; **56**, 130, 203, 204n, 206; **57**, 29, 88, 171, 211; **58**, 85, 92; **59**, 31, 35n71, 38, 134, 153
Head, Bessie, **40**, 135
Head, Franklin Harvey, **56**, 124
Headley, William, **49**, 193

Heal, Ambrose, **59**, 116, 116n34
Heale, William, **46**, 128
Healey, Chadwyck, **52**, 190n, 315; **59**, 210n56
Healey, Emma, **45**, 153
Healey, Michael, **55**, 380
Healey, Thomas, **51**, 7, 278
Health to the Gentlemanly Profession of Serving-Men, **17**, 11
Healy, Margaret, **58**, 332
Healy, Mark, **56**, 289
Healy, Philip, **53**, 145n, 303
Healy, Thomas, **46**, 134n; **48**, 259; **54**, 315, 321
Heaney, Seamus, **45**, 12; **52**, 286; **60**, 223
Heap, David, **48**, 229
Heap, Richard, **42**, 158
Hearne, Thomas, **4**, 82
Hearnshaw, F. J. C., **6**, 3
Heartbreak Productions, **58**, 302, 303
Heath, Baron, **52**, 214n
Heath, Benjamin, **51**, 134
Heath, Caroline, **8**, 74
Heath, D. D., **28**, 16n
Heath, Robert, **55**, 268n
Heath, Stephen, **53**, 39n
Heath, Tim, **41**, 191
Heath, William, **38**, 73; **51**, 13
Heather, Roy, **50**, 228; **53**, 276; **54**, 276
Heaton, Raymond Henniker, **9**, 115
Heauen of the Mynde, **8**, 100, 101, 104n
Heawelon, **11**, 71
Heawood, Edward, **23**, 127
Hebden, Karen Louise, **58**, 279; **59**, 341; **60**, 323
Hebden, Malcolm, **41**, 187; **43**, 216
Hebel, J. William, **38**, 97n; **55**, 212n
Heber, Richard, **6**, 63n
Hecht, Anthony, **50**, 269
Hecht, Hans, **30**, 164n
Hecht, Werner, **48**, 8n
Heckscher, William S., **31**, 16; **48**, 26n; **60**, 103n5
Hedbäck, Ann Mari, **55**, 258, 263n; **59**, 56n18
Hedgcock, Frank A., **9**, 100n
Hedge, Julia, **58**, 119
Hedgeman, Thomas, **11**, 103
Hedley, Jane, **48**, 254; **57**, 186
Hedrick, Donald K., **33**, 199; **52**, 289; **55**, 346, 348; **57**, 118; **58**, 328, 332
Heeley, Desmond, **39**, 182
Heer and Romeo, **47**, 217
Heffer, Richard, **42**, 156
Hefferman, Carol Falvo, **50**, 257
Heffner, Ray L., Jr, **14**, 4; **28**, 8n; **30**, 186; **32**, 226
Hefford, Wendy, **60**, 247n43, 247n44
Hefner, Hugh, **57**, 145–58
Heftrich, Eckhard, **43**, 223; **44**, 109n
Hegarty, Tony, **44**, 197; **45**, 147; **46**, 191
Hegel, Georg Wilhelm Friedrich, **4**, 3; **20**, 160; **22**, 36, 37; **24**, 97; **40**, 188; **45**, 5, 89, 92; **52**, 300; **53**, 305; **54**, 323–4; **55**, 81; **56**, 322
Hegenbarth, Josef, **14**, 156
Heiberg, Johanne Luise, **29**, 145–9; **31**, 173, 188
Heidegger, Martin, **12**, 110; **49**, 283; **58**, 180; **59**, 357; **60**, 122n9
Heidelberg, **3**, 96
Heidemann, Conrad, **32**, 193
Heighham, John, **56**, 195
Heilbron, Vivien, **44**, 194
Heilbrun, Carolyn G., **12**, 136; **32**, 63n; **46**, 4; **59**, 80n3
Heilman, Robert B., **4**, 20, 25, 141–2; **5**, 85, 87, 88; **7**, 10; **10**, 106n, 139; **11**, 142; **15**, 116, 121; **18**, 9, 54; **19**, 128, 129; **20**, 157; **21**, 8, 62, 63, 131, 137, 150–1; **27**, 27n, 28n; **32**, 226; **33**, 4, 8, 43n; **37**, 6, 33, 35; **38**, 160; **41**, 146n; **44**, 86n, 217; **45**, 80; **51**, 145
  Magic in the Web, **12**, 131 and n., 132–3
  'The Criminal as Tragic Hero: Dramatic Methods', **19**, 12–24
  This Great Stage, **13**, 18n
  This Great Stage reviewed, **3**, 130, 134
Heilpern, John, **24**, 131n
Heim, Michael Henry, **48**, 118n
Heine, Heinrich, **8**, 28; **48**, 65–7; **56**, 303
Heinemann, Margot, **31**, 63n, 175; **34**, 181; **38**, 228; **40**, 140n, 191, 209; **44**, 22n, 34n; **46**, 234; **52**, 273, 325; **54**, 58n; **55**, 92n, 255n; **60**, 173
Heinrich, Theodore A., **6**, 62
Heinwein, Gottfried, **44**, 197
Heinz, Wolfgang, **20**, 117; **48**, 173, 179–80, 182, 183
Heir, Robert, **35**, 35
Heisenberg, Werner, **40**, 148, 196; **42**, 208
Heiskanen, Kari, **55**, 325
Heisler, Ron, **44**, 232
Heitmann, Renate, **57**, 183
Helgerson, Richard, **26**, 165; **30**, 195; **39**, 139n; **40**, 123n; **46**, 105n; **50**, 44, 143; **51**, 19n; **52**, 56–7; **54**, 307; **56**, 324; **57**, 197; **60**, 184n2
Helicopter, Bell, **56**, 287
Heliodorus of Emasa, **20**, 9; **53**, 8, 9
  Æthiopica, Thomas Underdowne's translation of, **8**, 52
Hellenga, Robert R., **30**, 184–5; **36**, 180
Heller, Agnes, **35**, 76n
Hellman, G. S., **9**, 100n
Hellman, Lillian, **55**, 116n
Hellowes, Edward, *see under* Guevara, Antonio de
Helmer, Nora, **55**, 121
Helmes, Henry, **57**, 204
Helmholz, R. H., **49**, 183n, 188n
Helms, Lorraine, **43**, 253–4; **46**, 6, 151n; **49**, 61n, 284; **52**, 279
Helper, Courtney, **53**, 282
Helpmann, Robert, **1**, 104; **6**, 142, 145; **8**, 133; **9**, 22, 119; **10**, 123; **11**, 134; **12**, 119; **13**, 80; **37**, 169
Helps, James, **50**, 230
Helsztyński, Stanisław, **9**, 115; **10**, 120, 142; **11**, 121; **12**, 115; **13**, 154; **14**, 122; **15**, 137; **16**, 136; **19**, 145; **20**, 159, 164
Heltzel, Virgil B., **6**, 60; **31**, 91n
Helyar, Mark, **50**, 228
Hemelryk, Stephi, **43**, 205; **44**, 193
Heminge, Joseph, **2**, 69
Heminge, William, **7**, 1, 24n, 46, 51, 53–4, 57, 59, 138, 144
Heminges, John, **1**, 25, 38, 41, 42, 46, 57; **2**, 31; **3**, 144, 147, 151; **4**, 56, 76, 159; **5**, 140, 145; **8**, 90; **9**, 29, 34n, 76, 155; **10**, 156, 157; **11**, 82, 151; **12**, 148; **13**, 166; **14**, 90, 97; **16**, 8; **18**, 11, 21, 102; **28**, 173, 177; **32**, 108; **33**, 81; **34**, 61; **36**, 174, 191; **37**, 75, 213; **38**, 91–2; **39**, 250; **40**, 231; **41**, 39, 229; **42**, 17, 24, 63; **43**, 43–4; **44**, 113, 114, 149, 232; **45**, 107, 113; **47**, 175; **48**, 28; **49**, 40, 323; **52**, 76, 306, 320, 322; **53**, 342; **54**, 67; **55**, 34, 264; **56**, 60, 61, 354; **57**, 224,

232; **58**, 10, 74, 226, 230, 231, 237; **59**, 9, 25, 25n26, 27, 382; **60**, 56, 266, 268–9, 270, 277–8, 281, 283, 336, 368–9
Heminges, William, **42**, 187; **58**, 226
Hammings William, **17**, 202
Hemingway, Ernest M., **53**, 171
Hemingway, Polly, **45**, 149; **47**, 186, 216; **48**, 198–9; **56**, 247
Hemingway, Samuel B., **3**, 27; **6**, 8; **7**, 133; **13**, 163; **25**, 111n; **38**, 85, 86n, 90n
Hemlow, Joyce, **51**, 5n
Hemming, Sarah, **56**, 236n, 249n
Hemmings, F. W. J., **55**, 143n
Henders, Richard, **53**, 269
Henderson, Andrea, **44**, 237
Henderson, Anthony G., **42**, 96
Henderson, Diana E., **51**, 290; **52**, 290; **54**, 310; **58**, 316, 332; **59**, 263n24; **60**, 354–6, 360
Henderson, Fiona, **41**, 191
Henderson, Hamish, **17**, 173
Henderson, Hanford, **16**, 171
Henderson, Ian, **45**, 152
Henderson, Jeffrey, **32**, 99n
Henderson, John, **9**, 54; **11**, 123
Henderson, Katherine User, **48**, 29n
Henderson, Marina, **49**, 116
Henderson, Mark, **55**, 312, 323, 330, 332
Henderson, Rosalind, **48**, 231
Henderson, Shirley, **42**, 144; **48**, 235
Henderson, T. F., **14**, 88n
Henderson, W. B. Drayton, **28**, 39n
Hendrick, Daniel, **47**, 178
Hendricks, Margo, **48**, 256–7; **49**, 207n; **50**, 244, 249; **52**, 95n, 202n; **53**, 290, 291; **56**, 74; **59**, 372–3
(ed. with P. Parker), *Women, 'Race' and Writing in the Early Modern Period*, **48**, 256; **56**, 74
Hendricks, Marina, **49**, 116
Hendrickson, W., **7**, 4
Hendry, James, **50**, 235
Heneage, Sir Thomas, **21**, 104; **54**, 98n
Hengist, King of Kent; or, The Mayor of Queenborough, **52**, 81; **54**, 23n
Hening, Marc Von, **55**, 159n
Heninger, S. K., Jr, **11**, 140, 146; **15**, 166; **23**, 163; **24**, 158; **28**, 161; **36**, 104n
Henke, James T., **29**, 174; **33**, 197; **49**, 99n, 101n
Henke, Robert, **47**, 230; **51**, 285; **52**, 274
Henkel, Arthur, **26**, 117n
Henley, John, **55**, 93
Henley, W. E., **14**, 88n; **31**, 34n; **32**, 97n; **53**, 56n; **56**, 134
Henn, Hans Georg, **23**, 122; **26**, 166
Henn, T. R., **15**, 119, 120; **16**, 48; **26**, 165; **44**, 131n, 134n
The Harvest of Tragedy reviewed, **11**, 138
Henneberg, Claus, **44**, 195
Hennedy, H. L., **41**, 145n
Hennegan, Nick, **50**, 227
Henneke, Agnes, **6**, 6
Hennel, Charles, **53**, 116
Henneman, J. B., **6**, 5
Hennessy, Robert, **6**, 119
Henning, Hans, **29**, 177
Henning, Standish, **22**, 182; **24**, 156; **49**, 96n
Henri III, King of France, **4**, 148, 155; **6**, 79; **7**, 105
Henri IV, King of France, **3**, 24; **6**, 79
Henries, The, **43**, 171–3, 180
Henrietta Maria, Queen, **2**, 33; **11**, 108–14; **38**, 91
her company of actors, *see under* Theatre, Elizabethan, companies
Henrikson, Anders, **14**, 123
Henriksson, Alf, **15**, 138
Henriques, Alf, **3**, 111; **4**, 152
'Shakespeare and Denmark: 1900–1949', **3**, 107–15
Henriques, Veronica, **19**, 24n
Henry I, King of England, **60**, 75
Henry II, King of England, **54**, 125
Henry II, King of France, **54**, 194n
Henry III, King, **54**, 125
Henry IV, King of England **28**, 8; **38**, 93, 95–6
Henry IV (of Navarre), King of France, **14**, 102; **15**, 105; **17**, 26, 34; **29**, 26, 27, 28; **36**, 176
Henry V, King of England, **6**, 65, 70; **30**, 5; **38**, 93, 95, 97; **43**, 104; **44**, 55–8, 63; **48**, 85–6, 90, 260; **51**, 56n; **54**, 100–1; **60**, 117n66
Henry VI, King, **6**, 66; **30**, 45; **44**, 55, 60; **54**, 124
Henry VII, King, **3**, 53; **6**, 36; **17**, 78; **26**, 44, 45n; **28**, 20; **33**, 16; **42**, 17n; **52**, 171; **54**, 124, 125, 133n, 134, 135, 194n, 195n; **60**, 60
Henry VIII, King, **1**, 71; **3**, 25, 56; **6**, 65; **9**, 71; **11**, 71; **13**, 37, 40n, 76, 105n; **17**, 5, 21, 78, 107, 109, 157, 200, 229, 234–6; **26**, 41; **28**, 18, 20, 21, 63, 165, 166; **30**, 63, 192; **32**, 194; **33**, 145; **34**, 180; **38**, 20, 23–5; **43**, 50; **44**, 234, 237; **46**, 20; **48**, 70, 71; **50**, 160; **52**, 101, 103, 166–9, 172–9, 181–2; **54**, 1, 2, 117, 121, 126, 197n, 242–4; **55**, 64; **60**, 59, 60, 62, 66–71, 118, 121, 188–9
decree concerning education, **17**, 59–60
statute concerning vagrants, **17**, 8
Henry V (film) **49**, 308
Henry Frederick, Prince of Wales (son of James I), **1**, 72; **2**, 26; **3**, 51; **7**, 85; **11**, 114; **12**, 144; **15**, 6, 125; **17**, 162; **26**, 36, 40n, 41, 43, 44, 45, 46, 47, 48; **29**, 4; **31**, 101, 103; **33**, 162; **35**, 133; **36**, 110, 140; **43**, 56, 95; **44**, 154; **54**, 134, 136, 349; **56**, 216, 217, 221
Henry Julius, **33**, *see* Brunswick-Wolfenbüttel, Duke of, **36**, 135, 139
Henry, Akiya, **57**, 264
Henry, Earl of Lincoln, **46**, 33
Henry, Guy, **47**, 184, 206; **51**, 229, 235; **53**, 249; **55**, 290, 310; **56**, 291, 298; **57**, 292, 297; **58**, 167, 272, 298, 335
Henry, John, **48**, 31n
Henry, Julie, **47**, 213
Henry, Lenny, **60**, 162
Henry, Louis, **47**, 232
Henry, Martha, **16**, 154; **31**, 144–5; **34**, 43; **36**, 60
Henry, Niall, **51**, 258; **52**, 260
Henry, Prince, *see* Henry Frederick, Prince of Wales
Henry, William, **21**, 149
Henryson, Robert, **10**, 17; **36**, 87; **44**, 238; **47**, 254; **57**, 216, 306
Hensel, J. D., **18**, 79
Henshall, Douglas, **47**, 213
Henslowe, Francis, **55**, 29

Henslowe, Philip, **1**, 9, 25; **2**, 51, 53; **3**, 17, 23, 29, 30, 52, 127; **4**, 149; **7**, 50, 59, 60, 72, 80n, 147; **8**, 7, 106–7, 108; **12**, 18, 19, 21n, 150; **13**, 111, 112, 160; **14**, 5, 25, 31; **15**, 172; **16**, 168, 173; **17**, 43, 51, 88n, 202, 207; **23**, 173; **26**, 42, 168; **27**, 134, 135, 136, 173; **28**, 3; **29**, 34, 127–32; **30**, 202; **31**, 185; **32**, 103, 194, 197–8, 233; **33**, 140, 143, 149, 156, 157–8, 159, 160, 162–3, 168; **34**, 179; **35**, 190; **36**, 141–2; **37**, 183, 215, 217; **38**, 90, 91n, 97, 247; **39**, 227, 229; **40**, 219; **41**, 5, 6, 39, 91n, 216, 221; **42**, 115n, 190–1; **43**, 141, 146–8, 243, 262; **44**, 146, 148, 149n, 152, 153, 155, 230, 231, 233n; **45**, 102, 107–9, 183; **46**, 231, 233n; **47**, 15, 16, 19, 23n, 31, 35, 42, 172, 174n, 175, 178n, 239, 241; **48**, 277; **49**, 18, 23, 105n, 318; **52**, 4, 10, 71, 73–4, 78, 80, 81, 82; **54**, 21, 337, 357; **55**, 12, 28, 29, 34, 252, 372, 376, 377; **56**, 344; **57**, 333; **58**, 13, 228, 229; **60**, 24, 29n18, 28–9, 30, 31, 35, 36, 37, 44–5, 46, 47, 49–56, 56n37, 74, 75, 356
Diary, **1**, 71; **2**, 52; **8**, 104, 107n; **10**, 69
his companies, **8**, 104
Henson, Basil, **34**, 154
Henson, Nicky, **39**, 191, 198–200; **44**, 198; **59**, 314
Hentsch, Jürgen, **20**, 119; **48**, 179
Hentschel, Evelyn, **37**, 157n
Hentschel, Irene, **41**, 60
Hentz, Louise, **21**, 134
Hentzner, Paul, **17**, 3, 7; **54**, 191; **60**, 44, 45
Henze, Hans Werner, **57**, 310
Henze, Richard, **25**, 176, 179, 180; **27**, 170; **28**, 161; **29**, 162; **32**, 8, 100n
Hepburn, Katharine, **4**, 123; **5**, 115; **7**, 116; **12**, 117; **15**, 139
Hepkowski, James, **57**, 116
Heppenstall, Rayner, **5**, 134; **56**, 102n
Heptinstall, John, **55**, 264
Hepton, Bernard, **7**, 125; **13**, 134; **14**, 126; **15**, 144
Hepworth, Mike, **55**, 240n
Heracleitus, **30**, 119
Herbert of Cherbury, Lord, **5**, 139n; **19**, 37
Herbert, A. G., **57**, 242
Herbert, A. S., **54**, 6
Herbert, George, 1st Baron of Cherbury, **7**, 11; **15**, 92; **19**, 37; **32**, 241; **36**, 11, 19, 45, 162; **39**, 232; **40**, 227; **43**, 54, 244; **44**, 131; **49**, 67, 282; **51**, 296; **53**, 52, 306; **54**, 15; **55**, 346
Herbert, Henry, **52**, 72–6, 81; **55**, 378; **58**, 223, 241
Herbert, Henry, Earl of Pembroke, **32**, 89; **44**, 229, 241
Herbert, Sir Henry, **3**, 51; **4**, 91; **7**, 66; **10**, 88n; **11**, 109–10, 115n; **29**, 51n; **38**, 227n; **40**, 218; **42**, 186, 189; **46**, 232n, 233; **50**, 254, 255, 259; **59**, 22–3n13
see also under Master of the Revels
Herbert, Jeremy, **53**, 254; **54**, 287; **55**, 332; **56**, 297
Herbert, Jocelyn, **43**, 207, 215
Herbert, John, Secretary, **11**, 93
Herbert, Louisa, **32**, 35n
Herbert, Mary (*née* Sidney, Countess of Pembroke), **6**, 93; **11**, 108; **19**, 146, 150; **32**, 88, 89, 231; **37**, 191; **46**, 225; 48, 284; **60**, 344
Antonius, **10**, 5; **11**, 143
Herbert, Philip (4th Earl of Pembroke), **1**, 71; **57**, 333; **60**, 368
Herbert, T. Walter, **5**, 136; **10**, 141; **13**, 167; **14**, 152; **19**, 136, 150; **33**, 189, 195; **48**, 136n
Herbert, William, 3rd Earl of Pembroke (1580–1630), **3**, 31; **4**, 156; **5**, 138; **7**, 68n; **13**, 155; **15**, 12; **20**, 162, 172; **21**, 141; **27**, 134; **28**, 165; **30**, 102, 181, 182; **32**, 89; **35**, 174; **42**, 184, 188–9; **44**, 232; **48**, 131n; **49**, 116; **54**, 295; **57**, 333; **60**, 54, 266, 368
Herbrüggen, Hubertus S., **42**, 82n
Herder, Johann Gottfried von, **9**, 94, 95, 96, 97, 99, 100n; **10**, 150; **37**, 151n; **44**, 109; **46**, 43n; **53**, 287; **54**, 324; **56**, 208
Herendeen, W. H., **45**, 186
Hereniko, Vilsoni, **55**, 180n
Herford, C. H., **1**, 3; **5**, 105n; **6**, 2, 11, 14; **7**, 1; **8**, 9; **10**, 24n, 26n; **11**, 115n; **14**, 8, 44n; **15**, 26, 40n; **25**, 100n; **26**, 39n; **27**, 106n, 112n, 118, 120, 123, 124, 125, 126; **32**, 40n; **34**, 134n; **35**, 79n, 137n, 139n; **36**, 117n, 188n; **38**, 132n; **41**, 95n, 119n, 220; **44**, 106n, 175; **46**, 15n, 56n, 74n, 111n; **47**, 17n, 176n; **49**, 108n; **52**, 68n, 190n; **53**, 18n, 22n, 91n; **54**, 14n, 58n, 331–3; **55**, 20, 21n, 84n, 244n; **57**, 19, 212; **59**, 213n1, 223
Recent Shakespearian Investigation, **3**, 11
Herford, C. H. and Simpson, P., (eds.), *The Works of Ben Jonson*, **7**, 11n; **14**, 8, 44n
Herford, C. H., and E., **32**, 40n
Hergel, Knut, **10**, 120
Hergešić, J., **4**, 122n
Herlie, Eileen, **13**, 125; **45**, 55
Herlihy, David, **59**, 265n29
Herman, Martin, **52**, 222
Herman, Peter C., **49**, 286
Herman, Vimala, **57**, 205
Hermantier, Jean, **10**, 118
Hermantier, Raymond, **11**, 119; **18**, 123
Hermerén, Goran, **40**, 75n
Hermes, **20**, 26n
Hermogenes, **31**, 17
Hermon, David, **53**, 281
Hern, Nick, **48**, 12n
Herndl, George C., **25**, 180
Herod, **12**, 3; in early drama, **17**, 191–2
Herod and Antipater, **7**, 82
Herodotus, **15**, 102; **31**, 183; **33**, 197
Hérold, Ferdinand, **38**, 190
Heron, Jonathan, **56**, 8n
Herrand, Maurice, **7**, 111
Herrera, Andrea O'Reilly, **56**, 152n
Herrey, Hermann, **12**, 144
Herrick, Marvin T., **8**, 2; **10**, 49n; **35**, 110; **37**, 14n; **40**, 109n
Comic Theory in the Sixteenth Century, **14**, 3
Herrick, Robert, **13**, 106; **17**, 169, 175–7, 196; **19**, 60; **32**, 99n; **39**, 232; **40**, 227; **47**, 46
Herringman, Henry, **3**, 48; **4**, 91; **5**, 51, 52; **9**, 84; **55**, 265, 267–9
Herringman, John, **27**, 191
Herrmann, Anne, **43**, 253–4
Herrmann, H. J., **20**, 25n
Herrup, Cynthia, **54**, 166; **55**, 42
Hersey, David, **45**, 149
Hersey, Demetra, **45**, 149
Hersey, George, **47**, 21n, 23n, 24n
Hersov, Gregory, **43**, 211; **47**, 217; **48**, 228; **53**, 276; **54**, 249, 286
Hertford, Earl of, **25**, 188
Hertford, John, **1**, 67
Hertford, Lady, **38**, 73–4
Hertford, Lord (of Ragley), **14**, 115
Hertz, Robert, **48**, 24n

Hertzog, **9**, 100n
Hervey, Elizabeth, **21**, 97, 100
Hervey, Frances, **21**, 97, 100
Hervey, Gawen and Roger, **21**, 97
Hervey, Henry, **21**, 97
Hervey, of Kidbrook, *see* Kidbrook
Hervey, William, 'of Chessington', **21**, 97–105; **23**, 160
Hervey, William, **23**, 160
Hervey, Sir William, **5**, 148; **7**, 139
Herwegh, G., **23**, 174
Herz, Emil, **33**, 164n; **52**, 315n
Herz, Michael, **53**, 283
Herz, S., **32**, 194n, 195
Hescott, Thomas, **59**, 344
Hesiod, **10**, 43; **15**, 102; **25**, 99
Hesker, Andrew, **50**, 209
Hesketh, Bartholomew, **54**, 120n
Hesketh, Richard, **57**, 232, 233
Hesketh, Sir Thomas, **6**, 159; **7**, 139; **54**, 121
Hess, Andre, **52**, 207n, 209n
Hess, Andrew, **55**, 344
Hess, Nigel, **42**, 160; **45**, 146; **46**, 194; **47**, 207; **48**, 230; **49**, 280
Hessels, Joannes Henricus, **53**, 202n; **60**, 240n20
Hestcott, Thomas, **57**, 293
Hetherington, Robert A., **39**, 79n, 83n
Hetherington, William, **45**, 156; **50**, 235
Hethmon, R. H., **20**, 154
Heuer, Hermann, **4**, 127; **5**, 112; **6**, 156; **8**, 139; **9**, 140; **10**, 59n; **12**, 138; **32**, 223; **53**, 74n, 84n
'From Plutarch to Shakespeare: a Study of Coriolanus', **10**, 50–9
Heufeld, **9**, 110n
Heun, H. G., **18**, 174
Heuss, Bundespräsident, **12**, 113
Hewes, Henry, **18**, 132
Hewison, Robert, **49**, 245; **52**, 35n
Hewitt, Bernard, **52**, 7n
Hewitt, Craig, **43**, 209; **45**, 153; **49**, 270
Hewitt, Douglas, **15**, 114
'The Very Pompes of the Divell' reviewed, **3**, 142
'Hewlands', Hathaway family home, **12**, 100, 103
Hewlett, M., **8**, 10
Hewson, Lance, **59**, 195n10
Hexham, H., **23**, 34
Hext, Edward, **44**, 20, 21
Heyd, Michael, **54**, 65n
Heyden, Pieter van der, **37**, 136
Heylar, Mark, **51**, 266
Heylyn, Peter, **19**, 5; **26**, 81n; **54**, 50; **56**, 227, 228; **57**, 72, 73
Heyme, Hansgünter, **37**, 161
Heyningen, Miss C. van, **5**, 112
Heyse, Hans Joachim, **18**, 124
Heywood, Abel, **18**, 19
Heywood, Jasper, **55**, 65, 348
Heywood, John, **9**, 25; **17**, 200; **35**, 175, 190; **42**, 187; **54**, 24; **57**, 239
Play of Love, **14**, 22
Heywood, Thomas, **1**, 38, 70, 75; **2**, 46, 47, 51, 59; **3**, 45, 50, 151; **4**, 29, 58; **6**, 74n; **7**, 6, 58, 59, 60, 64, 66, 67n, 68n, 83, 84, 86, 87, 88, 89n; **8**, 38, 158; **9**, 149; **11**, 20–1, 22, 135n, 149; **13**, 100; **14**, 12, 13, 56–65 *passim*, 153; **15**, 8; **16**, 95–7; **17**, 52, 197, 205–9, 211, 216, 221–2; **18**, 188; **19**, 1, 105n; **20**, 4, 91; **22**, 21, 52; **23**, 76, 171; **24**, 54, 155n; **26**, 9, 41, 103, 168, 169; **27**, 129; **29**, 104, 170, 182; **30**, 198; **31**, 33; **32**, 69, 95, 102n, 166n; **33**, 160, 164–5, 168; **34**, 89; **36**, 117, 142–3, 174; **37**, 215; **41**, 11, 35, 37, 39–43, 91–2, 95–6, 102, 106, 134, 216; **42**, 15n, 100, 116, 118n, 187, 212; **43**, 263; **44**, 19n, 65, 66; **45**, 184; **46**, 228, 235; **47**, 33, 39, 40, 163, 247, 249; **48**, 39, 147, 254, 258; **49**, 40, 105; **50**, 52n, 147, 256; **51**, 297; **52**, 60, 209, 211, 296; **53**, 36n, 326; **54**, 193, 356; **55**, 219n, 225, 229n, 236, 263, 266, 358; **56**, 30, 324, 339; **57**, 233, 278, 309, 316; **58**, 10, 61, 62, 221; **59**, 10, 72, 73, 74, 75, 77, 78, 217, 377; **60**, 252, 253, 253n5, 255, 264–5, 270n5, 282–3, 357
Apology for Actors, **3**, 93; **7**, 87, 88
The Brazen Age, **8**, 109; **11**, 135n
The Captives (MS.), **3**, 51
The Captives, **14**, 56, 64
A Curtaine Lecture, **1**, 70
The English Traveller, **14**, 56–65
The Escapes of Jupiter (MS.), **3**, 51, 52
Fair Maid of the Exchange, **1**, 64; **11**, 51, 52, 54; **13**, 105n
Four Prentices, **1**, 64
1 The Fair Maid of the West, **11**, 20–1, 22
Fortune by Land and Sea (with Rowley, William), **13**, 122
The Golden Age, **12**, 51
his hand in *Sir Thomas More*, **9**, 72
If You Know not Me, **1**, 64
2 If You Know Not Me, You Know Nobody, **12**, 48
The Iron Age, **6**, 157
Maidenhead Well Lost, **13**, 99, 100, 102
Marriage Triumph, **1**, 64
Rape of Lucrece, **13**, 107; **14**, 9; **15**, 40n, 91
The Wise Woman of Hogsdon, **4**, 41
A Woman Killed with Kindness, **10**, 100, 139; **12**, 54; **14**, 56–7, 65
The Silver Age, **12**, 50 51
Heywood, Tim, **54**, 291
Hiatt, Charles W., **43**, 255; **45**, 185n
Hibbard, George R., **19**, 136, 150; **21**, 158; **22**, 171, 178; **23**, 152; **24**, 172n, 173; **25**, 185; **27**, 171; **28**, 178; **29**, 109n; **30**, 9n, 198, 210; **32**, 219; **33**, 191; **34**, 138n, 164; **35**, 166, 174; **37**, 23, 25, 36, 38n; **38**, 6, 13, 82; **39**, 215, 230; **40**, 234; **41**, 37, 145, 241–2, 245n; **42**, 211n; **43**, 6n 70n; **44**, 253–4; **45**, 3n, 53; **46**, 101n, 127n, 254; **48**, 128n; **49**, 329; **50**, 176n, 178n, 180; **52**, 18n; **55**, 1; **56**, 171n; **57**, 203; **59**, 47; **60**, 84n2, 361
Critical Studies, *reviewed:* (1967), **21**, 127–41
(1968), **22**, 145–66
(1969), **23**, 49–58
'George Chapman: Tragedy and the Providential View of History', **20**, 27–32
'*Henry IV* and *Hamlet*', **30**, 1–12
'*Othello* and the Pattern of Shakespearian Tragedy', **21**, 39–46
Thomas Nashe reviewed, **16**, 168
'Words, Action, and Artistic Economy', **23**, 49–58
Hibbert, Christopher, **53**, 209n
Hibbert, Karl, **44**, 193; **45**, 146
Hibbert, Maureen, **43**, 207
Hibernicus, Thomas, **3**, 15; **20**, 26n
Hickey, Brian, **44**, 192
Hickman, Rose, **50**, 255

Hickmott, Alaine, **42**, 154
Hickox, Richard, **53**, 280; **60**, 189n18
Hicks, Alderman Baptist (Viscount Camden), **17**, 12
Hicks, Greg, **44**, 196; **48**, 233; **51**, 247, 249; **55**, 308; **56**, 291; **57**, 258, 265, 285, 291; **58**, 299; **59**, 340; **60**, 323
Hicks, L., S.J., **17**, 127n
Hicks, Penelope, **50**, 289
Hickscorner (1516), **6**, 72
Hickson, S., **4**, 159–60
Hidi, Suzanne, **53**, 5n
Hieatt, A. Kent, **27**, 109n; **38**, 234
Hieron, Samuel, **50**, 196n
Higbee, Helen, **55**, 370
Higden, Ranulf, *Polychronicon*, **1**, 67
Higdon, David Leon, **53**, 117
Higgins, Clare, **43**, 197, 201; **44**, 184, 198; **45**, 148, 153; **46**, 182–4; **47**, 209; **59**, 293, 294, 295–7
Higgins, George, **11**, 97n; **13**, 103n
Higgins, J., **27**, 172
Higgins, John, *Queen Cordila*, **6**, 57; **13**, 41, 44–6; **33**, 17
Higgins, Michael, **14**, 11
Higgins, Paul, **57**, 269, 294; **58**, 302
Higgons, Bevill, **46**, 138, 139, 141, 143; **51**, 3n; **58**, 140, 141
Higgs, Michael, **51**, 226
Higham, Charles, **39**, 69n
Highfill, Philip H. Jr., **53**, 327; **40**, 83n, 84n; **49**, 116n; **51**, 4, 82n
Highley, Christopher, **46**, 216; **52**, 286–7; **53**, 324; **59**, 361
Highway to Heaven, The, **15**, 66
Higlett, Simon, **41**, 183, 187, 189; **42**, 155, 160; **43**, 210–11; **44**, 199, 202; **45**, 146
Hilar, K., **9**, 109, 110n
Hildebrand, John, **55**, 90
Hildebrandt, Herbert W., **53**, 13n
Hildenbrand, Dan, **45**, 155
Hildy, Franklin J., **52**, 11, 12, 13, 30n, 32n; **47**, 19n, 82n, 84n, 179n; **60**, 40
Hill, A. A., **9**, 47n
Hill, Aaron, **51**, 56n, 112, 299
Hill, Adam, **57**, 237, 238
Hill, Annabel, **55**, 330
Hill, Charles Jarvis, **5**, 5; **19**, 12, 23n; **31**, 106n
Hill, Christopher, **17**, 72n; **29**, 90; **31**, 106n, 113n; **32**, 55n; **35**, 66n; **40**, 136n, 137n; **43**, 152; **44**, 79; **55**, 171; **57**, 247
Hill, Dave, **56**, 250
Hill, David, **47**, 186; **49**, 254
Hill, Dominic, **54**, 286; **56**, 298; **57**, 295; **58**, 307; **59**, 340
Hill, Errol, **26**, 176n; **48**, 196n
Hill, G. Birkbeck, **21**, 10n; **24**, 37n
Hill, Geoffrey, **23**, 155; **36**, 103; **56**, 311
Hill, James L., **40**, 208–9, 221; **46**, 7
Hill, John, **51**, 109n, 111n; **59**, 287–9, 297
Hill, Liz, **49**, 276
Hill, Margery, **45**, 105
Hill, Mark, **53**, 284
Hill, Patricia, **12**, 109
Hill, Peter, mariner, **17**, 27 and n.
Hill, R. F., **11**, 155; **12**, 136; **13**, 152; **16**, 162–3; **19**, 130, 135; **21**, 146; **27**, 33; **30**, 183; **38**, 8; **44**, 218; **55**, 84n
'The Composition of *Titus Andronicus*', **10**, 60–70
Critical Studies, *reviewed:* (1976), **30**, 181–90
'*The Merchant of Venice* and the Pattern of Romantic Comedy', **28**, 75–87
Hill, Robert, **45**, 106; **56**, 200
Hill, Roger, **59**, 63–8
Hill, Rosemary, **51**, 259
Hill, T. H., **18**, 191
Hill, Thomas, **24**, 68; **45**, 105; **50**, 153
Hill, Tracy, **56**, 320
Hill, W. Speed, **39**, 248n; **40**, 227n, 233n; **43**, 264n; **51**, 329–31; **54**, 129n; **55**, 3n
Hille, Anastasia, **47**, 191; **48**, 218–19; **49**, 273; **50**, 203; **52**, 223, 226–7; **53**, 274; **56**, 269, 271; **57**, 298
Hillebrand, Harold N., **1**, 7, 10; **7**, 149; **8**, 11; **11**, 103–5, 105n; **25**, 9; **34**, 23n; **35**, 8; **36**, 85n; **52**, 119
Hiller, Wendy, **12**, 83, 84
Hillet, Roger, **6**, 70
Hilliard, Nicholas, **13**, 104n, 143; **32**, 227
Hillman, David, **50**, 242; **52**, 271; **53**, 296
Hillman, Richard, **40**, 209; **46**, 209, 210; **51**, 289–90; **56**, 322, 326, 327
Hills, Mathilda M., **31**, 171
Hillyard, Nicholas, **4**, 130
Hilpert, Heinz, **4**, 126, 127; **5**, 112; **6**, 120; **8**, 119; **9**, 113; **10**, 119; **14**, 123; **18**, 124
Hilprecht, Uwe, **40**, 58n
Hilský, Martin, **48**, 167, 169; **60**, 335
Hilton, Andrew, **47**, 214; **50**, 230; **55**, 325, 328; **56**, 288; **57**, 297; **58**, 298, 306; **59**, 340; **60**, 326
Hilton, John, **58**, 246
Ayres, **1**, 70
Catch that Catch can, **3**, 56
Hilton, Julian, **40**, 216
Hilton, Paul, **52**, 222–3
Hilton, Spencer, **51**, 258
Hilton, Walter, **6**, 59
Hilyer, Louis, **43**, 213; **50**, 214; **54**, 266, **58**, 290
Himmelfarb, Gertrud, **28**, 21n
Hinchcliffe, Edgar, **23**, 165n
Hind, Arthur M., **1**, 37n; **11**, 99n; **17**, 34n; **43**, 161n; **50**, 169; **53**, 196; **54**, 136n; **60**, 237n2, 243n28
Hind, John, **60**, 272n13
Hinde, R. A., **55**, 187n
Hinderer, Walter, **57**, 62
Hindle, Steve, **50**, 70n
Hindley, Charles, **57**, 239
History of the Cries of London, **13**, 110n
Hindley, Myra, **57**, 43, 51
Hindmarsh, Joseph, **55**, 263, 269n
Hinds, Andrew, **54**, 294
Hinds, Andy, **42**, 153; **58**, 265, 266
Hinds, Ciaran, **43**, 213; **44**, 173; **45**, 156
Hinely, Jan Lawson, **35**, 155
Hingley, Ronald, **45**, 4n; **48**, 118
Hinkle, G. K., **15**, 12
Hinks, Brent, **56**, 8n
Hinksey, S., **55**, 30n
Hinman, C. K., **11**, 150, 154–5; **12**, 149; **13**, 161, 164; **14**, 6, 158, 159, 161, 166n; **16**, 6; **17**, 210 nn; **18**, 21n, 131, 186, 190; **19**, 155, 162–3; **20**, 176, 178

Six Variant Readings in the First Folio of Shakespeare reviewed, **15**, 175–7
'Shakespeare's Text—Then, Now and Tomorrow', **18**, 23–33
Hinman, Charles, **52**, 4n; **55**, 54n, 386
Hinman, Charlton, **1**, 77n; **2**, 150, 153; **3**, 149; **5**, 47, 147; **7**, 152; **8**, 153–4; **9**, 151, 156; **10**, 153–5; **23**, 184, 185; **24**, 170, 171, 172, 174; **25**, 129; **26**, 177, 182, 183; **27**, 179, 181, 182, 183, 184, 189, 190; **30**, 206; **31**, 49n, 191–2; **32**, 237; **33**, 2, 208, 210; **34**, 193–4; **36**, 191; **37**, 210–11, 218; **38**, 92n; **44**, 127, 128; **45**, 197n; **46**, 47n; **47**, 163n; **53**, 214n, 341; **59**, 1, 4, 40, 81–3, 159, 160, 379; **60**, 224n8
Hintermann, Carlo, **18**, 126
Hinton, Spencer, **57**, 295
Hippocrates, **17**, 152–5, 161
Hird, Thora, **33**, 174
Hiroshima mon Amour, **55**, 154
Hirota, Joji, **43**, 211
Hiroyuki, Sanada, **54**, 286
Hirsch, E. D. Jr, **51**, 126–8, 130, 138, 139; **53**, 302; **54**, 216, 220
Hirsch, John, **39**, 179–83; **40**, 155; **60**, 174
Hirsch, Richard S. M., **29**, 170; **50**, 46n
Hirschfeld, Heather, **59**, 220
Hirsh, James E., **36**, 160–1; **38**, 10; **40**, 71n; **51**, 291–2; **55**, 351; **56**, 355; **57**, 343; **58**, 31, 322, 332; **59**, 354
Hirst, David L., **45**, 72n
Hirst, Derek, **44**, 77n
Hirst, Paul Q., **48**, 69n
Hirst, Steven, **49**, 278
Hirt, H., **23**, 28n
Hiscock, W. G., **4**, 96n; **10**, 147n; **60**, 223n5
History of King Lear, The, **54**, 340
History of Tom Thumb, The, **3**, 45
History Plays, The, **46**, 215
Histriomastix, **8**, 103, 105n; **9**, 29; **14**, 28, 31, 33n; **15**, 63
Hitchcock, Alfred, **26**, 175; **34**, 41; **39**, 2, 82, 116; **54**, 246; **56**, 10; **57**, 147
Hitchcock, Elsie V., **42**, 79n
Hitchcock, Tricia, **45**, 63n
Hitchens, Mr (or Higgins), **14**, 110
Hitler, Adolf, **8**, 109; **9**, 125; **48**, 175, 176; **52**, 193; **54**, 238; **55**, 165
Hjelm, Keve, **14**, 123
Hjort, Greta, **8**, 83, 96, 97n
Hjort, Hjalmar, **48**, 6n
Ho Chi Minh, President, **57**, 138
Hoadley, Dr, **51**, 107n
Hoadly, John, **54**, 47
Hoak, Dale, **49**, 286
Hoare, Alexandra, **60**, 169n5.9
Hoare, Quintin, **56**, 140n
Hobart, Sir Henry, **17**, 81n
Hobbes, Thomas, **4**, 25; **11**, 107; **20**, 6, 146; **23**, 145; **24**, 20; **25**, 18n; **28**, 65; **33**, 5; **49**, 138n, 304; **50**, 144; **52**, 271; **54**, 127; **57**, 28, 57; **59**, 351
Hobbs, Cecily, **43**, 210
Hobbs, Mary, **33**, 207–8
Hobbs, Paul, **51**, 267
Hobby, Elaine, **49**, 302
Hobday, C. H., **1**, 126; **20**, 158; **23**, 147; **30**, 53n; **60**, 256n17
'Imagery and Irony in *Henry V*', **21**, 107–13
'Shakespeare's Venus and Adonis Sonnets', **26**, 103–9
Hobson, Elizabeth, **49**, 232
Hobson, Sir Harold, **12**, 2; **15**, 147; **16**, 28; **24**, 43; **27**, 34n; **31**, 145; **32**, 32, 35n; **37**, 184; **49**, 225–34
Hoby, Sir Edward, **3**, 26; **13**, 156; **28**, 4, 6; **30**, 199; **35**, 178; **58**, 37
Hoby, Sir Thomas, **25**, 103n; **27**, 56n; **31**, 85, 87n; **38**, 31; **46**, 57, 114n, 133n; **48**, 73n, 78n; **50**, 71n; **54**, 106n; **60**, 62
Hoccleve, Thomas, **6**, 59; **30**, 65n; **38**, 86; **54**, 107
Hockey, Dorothy C., **12**, 133; **14**, 143, 147; **19**, 133; **20**, 148; **25**, 93; **32**, 12; 49n
Hocquard, Bruno, **41**, 186
Hodek, Břetislav, **8**, 119; **9**, 111; **10**, 117; **11**, 118; **12**, 110; **18**, 121; **48**, 163n
Hodgdon, Barbara, **35**, 172; **39**, 53n, 85n; **45**, 168; **46**, 218; **47**, 149n, 235; **48**, 241; **49**, 96n; **50**, 35, 40; **51**, 314–15; **52**, 45, 200, 290; **53**, 296, 304; **54**, 312, 317; **55**, 273n, 280n, 352; **56**, 248n; **57**, 42; **58**, 189, 340, 355, 356; **59**, 210; **60**, 80n36, 72–80, 83n44, 110n36, 117n65, 355, 360
Hodgdon, Tracey, **60**, 182n18
Hodge, Alison, **58**, 358
Hodge, Bob, **55**, 5n
Hodge, Douglas, **41**, 184; **48**, 224; **56**, 257, 271; **57**, 298; **60**, 308–9
Hodge, Harold, (H.H.), **29**, 139
Hodge, Robert Lee, **52**, 40
Hodgen, Margaret T., **7**, 140; **28**, 37; **38**, 167n
Hodges, C. Walter, **4**, 97, 152; **5**, 143; **6**, 71; **7**, 72, 75, 76, 143; **8**, 116n; **10**, 85, 88n; **12**, 24, 55n; **14**, 150; **16**, 152; **18**, 134; **24**, 174; **28**, 132, 135, 167–8; **29**, 130, 131; **30**, 196; **33**, 147–50; **36**, 178–9; **37**, 196; **38**, 238; **40**, 214; **41**, 3, 37, 86; **42**, 115n; **43**, 144, 168n; **44**, 243; **47**, 19n, 78n; **49**, 23; **52**, 3–4, 9n, 11n, 32n, 183n; **53**, 196, 197n
The Globe Restored, **12**, 20n, 21n, 42; **13**, 120, 123n; **14**, 13
The Globe Restored reviewed, **8**, 151–2
'The Lantern of Taste', **12**, 8–14
'Unworthy Scaffolds: A Theory for the Reconstruction of Elizabethan Playhouses', **3**, 83–94
Hodges, M. K., **13**, 104n, 105n
Hodges, R., **50**, 58
Hodges, W. C., **22**, 35, 173
Hodgetts, Michael, **57**, 17
Hodgkin, Katharine, **44**, 228
Hodgkins [Hodgskin], John, **60**, 12n33
Hodgkins, Tom, **56**, 265
Hodgkinson, John, **56**, 266; **57**, 262; **60**, 306
Hodgson, Edward, **19**, 103
Hodgson, Geraldine, **10**, 10
Hodgson, John A., **32**, 222
Hodgson, publisher, 1823, **49**, 113
Hodgson, William, **25**, 146
Hodgson-Wright, Stephanie, **55**, 379–80
Hodnett, Edward, **59**, 130n36, 131n44, 131–2
Hodson, Donal, **8**, 123
Hoeflich, Michael, **55**, 36n
Hoefnagel, Georg, **1**, 26
Hoefnagel, Joris, **26**, 112n
Hoel, Willi, **10**, 120

Hoeniger, F. David, **5**, 136; **10**, 141; **11**, 144; **15**, 124n, 169, 180; **18**, 171, 188; **21**, 149; **23**, 180; **24**, 106, 110, 113n; **25**, 137n; **29**, 11n, 22; **31**, 5n, 166; **37**, 214; **38**, 163n, 252; **43**, 131, 135n; **46**, 223; **52**, 316, 317; **55**, 61, 62; **59**, 259n14
'Shakespare's Romances since 1958: A Retrospect', **29**, 1–10
Hoenselaars, A. J., **47**, 249n; **48**, 257; **52**, 274
Hoenselaars, Ton, **54**, 74n, 78n, 152n; **56**, 215n, 315; **57**, 327; **58**, 208, 312, 333, 334, 339, 342
Hoepfner, Theodore C., **9**, 138; **11**, 140
Höfele, Andreas, **37**, 158n; **56**, 227–35, 312, 320; **58**, 326, 332; **60**, 122n7, 118–22, 129n33
Hoffman, Alice, **55**, 111n
Hoffman, Calvin, **10**, 119, 120; **58**, 151
The Man who was Shakespeare, **14**, 10
The Man who was Shakespeare reviewed, **10**, 143
Hoffman, Dustin, **43**, 183–4, 188; **44**, 95, 197
Hoffman, E. T. A., **9**, 148
Hoffman, Michael, **54**, 289; **58**, 185, 340
Hoffmann, D. S., **20**, 170
'Some Shakespearian Music, 1660–1900', **18**, 94–101
Hoffmann, Friedrich, **13**, 156
Hoffmann, Gerhard, **21**, 143; **26**, 166n
Hoffmannsthal, Hugo von, **14**, 156
Hoffmeier, Dieter, **21**, 149; **22**, 162, 175n
Hofmann, Norbert, **37**, 160n
Hofnagel, Joris, **49**, 262
Hofstadter, Douglas, **40**, 82n
Hogan, Charles Beecher, **7**, 145; **31**, 188; **32**, 37; **43**, 101n; **49**, 111n, 113n; **51**, 59n, 79n; **53**, 217n, 226n; **56**, 351n
Shakespeare in the Theatre, 1701–1800 reviewed, **11**, 147; **13**, 145n; **20**, 72n, 73n
Hogan, Floriana T., **31**, 185
Hogan, J. J., **16**, 178
Hogan, Jerome W., **29**, 175
Hogan, Robert, **54**, 77n
Hogarth, Georgiana, **60**, 235n65
Hogarth, Paul, **49**, 129
Hogarth, William, **10**, 76n; **30**, 164, 165; **45**, 143; **47**, 27; **48**, 57; **51**, 4, 10, 12, 15, 60, 62, 66, 70, 107, 119, 121, 123; **60**, 354
The Analysis of Beauty, **10**, 72
Hogben, Rita, **45**, 155
Hoge, James O., **31**, 191
Hogenberg, Franz, **53**, 198, 203n, 212n
Hogg, Ian, **26**, 143, 148; **39**, 79n; **51**, 239–40; **54**, 271; **55**, 306–7; **56**, 291; **57**, 292; **60**, 310
Hogg, James, **27**, 175; **29**, 166, 173; **34**, 167; **41**, 157n
Hoggart, Ian, **57**, 281
Hoggart, Richard, **56**, 239, 240
Hogge, Ralph, **60**, 53
Hoghton, Alexander, **39**, 223; **54**, 119–21; **56**, 192
Hoghton, Richard, **54**, 119, 120
Hoghton, Thomas, **53**, 317; **54**, 119, 121
Hogrefe, Pearl, **3**, 137
Hogwood, Christopher, **51**, 82n
Hoheisel, Tobias, **45**m, 119; 46m, 194; **49**, 258; **50**, 232
Hohenberg, *see* Braun
Hohenheim, Theophrastus von, *see* Paracelsus
Hohenzollern, Count of, **36**, 146
Hohnshed, Raphael, **54**, 4, 9, 90n, 213n
Hoius, Andreas, **29**, 28, 29, 30
Holaday, Allan, **14**, 9, **23**, 144; **34**, 89n; **36**, 144; **41**, 117n; **42**, 208n; **48**, 39n
Holahan, Michael, **52**, 277
Holbein, Hans the Younger, **13**, 76; **15**, 127; **24**, 158; **42**, 81; **49**, 79, 81, 82; **54**, 304
Holbrook, Peter, **48**, 259; **54**, 197n; **55**, 240n, 241n, 243n, 244n; **56**, 203–14
Holcombe, Thomas, **58**, 233, 237
Holden, Anthony, **53**, 317–18; **56**, 184n, 192n; **58**, 2
Holden, Michael, **52**, 42, 44n
Holden, William, **32**, 104n
Holden, William H., **30**, 164n
Holden, William P., **9**, 152n
Holder, William, **55**, 264
Holderness, Glen, **44**, 195
Holderness, Graham, **35**, 178; **38**, 226; **39**, 103; **40**, 187–8; **41**, 227; **42**, 164, 178; **43**, 225; **44**, 27n, 105n, 217; **45**, 160, 187n; **46**, 160n, 215, 254; **47**, 8n, 9n, 235; **48**, 69–70, 77, 268–71; **49**, 61n, 153, 308, 321; **50**, 243, 272–5, 277; **51**, 129, 274; **52**, 15n, 43n, 313; **53**, 236n; **54**, 73n, 319–20; **56**, 346–7; **57**, 167; **58**, 172, 321; **59**, 16n68; **60**, 228n29, 223–8, 235n66
Holding, Edith M., **34**, 173; **35**, 10; **36**, 181; **38**, 199n; **51**, 45n, 55n
Holding, Peter, **46**, 238–9; **49**, 2n, 10, 14
Holdsworth, R. V., **34**, 140n; **37**, 219; **40**, 226n; **42**, 213; **44**, 234
Holdsworth, W., **17**, 77n, 85n
Holdsworth, Sir William, **51**, 165n; **55**, 39n
Hole, John, **46**, 32
Hole, Richard, **34**, 12, 19n
Hole, Sandra, **23**, 153
Hole, William, **43**, 160–1; **48**, 267
Holiday, B., **17**, 175
Holinshed, Raphael, **1**, 38; **2**, 148; **3**, 4, 6, 18, 23, 25, 26; **4**, 27, 87, 142n; **5**, 66–8, 87, 104, 135; **6**, 3, 9, 11, 19, 26, 33n, 34n, 35n, 73n; **8**, 146; **10**, 140; **11**, 42–6, 49n, 143; **12**, 142; **13**, 30, 41, 44–6; **14**, 33, 40, 153; **16**, 169; **17**, 48n, 85, 91n, 107, 163n; **19**, 2–5, 8, 45, 50, 65, 80, 83, 91–2; **20**, 28, 41, 78, 81n; **21**, 111, 132, 151; **23**, 146, 160; **24**, 63–4, 163; **25**, 172; **26**, 36n, 42, 81, 82, 83, 84, 85n, 86, 87, 113, 157; **27**, 35, 36, 131, 172; **28**, 1, 3, 12, 120; **30**, 8, 49n, 53; **31**, 25n, 34, 41n; **32**, 198, 236, 245; **33**, 14, 16, 17; **36**, 171; **37**, 75n, 76; **38**, 11, 37, 42, 46, 61, 63, 67, 93n, 94, 110–12; **39**, 40, 42, 49, 154; **40**, 10; **41**, 196; **42**, 18, 19, 25–35, 42, 43, 49n, 182, 192; **43**, 49, 63; **44**, 3n, 8, 12, 15; **46**, 233, 252; **47**, 113n, 154n; **48**, 70n, 72n, 75, 85, 89; **49**, 286; **50**, 14n, 42, 44n, 50, 51, 54, 106, 144, 194, 195n; **51**, 135, 311, 322; **52**, 147, 168–9, 172, 174, 176, 178–80, 286, 315, 322; **53**, 6, 60, 176, 179–81, 339; **55**, 19, 22, 23, 47, 291, 368, 371; **56**, 281, 321, 345, 353; **57**, 11, 30, 36, 43, 69, 71, 72, 76, 77, 80, 126; **59**, 220, 245–6, 255; **60**, 58n2, 59, 62n13, 67, 67n17, 106, 111n38
Chronicle of England, **4**, 37
Chronicle of Scotland and *Cymbeline*, **4**, 29–30
Chronicle of Scotland and *Macbeth*, **4**, 31, 35–47
Hollaender, A. E. J., **6**, 73n
Holland, Aaron, **7**, 59, 60, 67n
Holland, Abraham, **11**, 98
Holland, Charles, **57**, 86
Holland, Compton, **11**, 98
Holland, Earl of, *see under* Rich, Henry

INDEX

Holland, Henry, **11**, 98; **28**, 119
Herωologia Anglica, **1**, 33
Holland, Hugh, **48**, 29
Holland, J. F., **26**, 164
Holland, Merlin, **56**, 136n
Holland, Norman N., **11**, 137; **13**, 161; **18**, 156; **19**, 127; **20**, 150, 156; **22**, 145–6, 166; **31**, 10n; **32**, 152, 155; **37**, 164; **43**, 231; **44**, 208; **46**, 74n; **59**, 41
Holland, Peter, **42**, 87n; **43**, 96n; **45**, 161; **47**, 4, 7n, 117; **48**, 16n, 61n, 117n, 245; **49**, 104n, 294, 308, 320–1; **50**, 248; **51**, 2; **52**, 98n, 283, 286, 288–9; **53**, 25n, 55, 149n, 174n, 232n, 331–2, 335; **54**, 152n; **55**, 170n, 220n, 382; **56**, 39n, 105n, 120, 121, 161–6, 168n, 253, 312; **57**, 318, 319; **58**, 349; **59**, 51–2, 89n34, 212n63, 374; **60**, 44n32, 80n36, 342, 357–8, 360
Holland, Philemon, **11**, 98; **23**, 61; **31**, 183; **33**, 55; **34**, 65n; **38**, 115–16, 120, 185; **43**, 160; **44**, 66; **50**, 70n, 138n; **51**, 177, 178n; **53**, 68, 78n; **54**, 40; **56**, 40n, 42n, 44, 63n; **57**, 18
trans. of Pliny, **8**, 147; **13**, 158
trans. of Plutarch's *Moralia*, **12**, 91, 92, 93
Holland, Robert, **57**, 239
Holland, Vyvyan, **53**, 139n
Hollander, John, **40**, 71; **43**, 23n; **45**, 172; **56**, 42n
Hollander, Tom, **45**, 128
Hollands, Guy, **57**, 297
Hollar, Wenceslaus, **1**, 26, 34–5, 37n; **2**, 21–3; **9**, 106; **12**, 22, 29, 30; **28**, 130, 134, 167; **31**, 139; **32**, 189, 191; **33**, 147–50, 151n; **36**, 178; **37**, 196; **41**, 1, 5; **42**, 194; **43**, 144–5; **47**, 31, 41; **50**, 151; **52**, 3, 6, 8, 10, 11, 12, 15, 192; **53**, 197, 198, 200n, 203n, 204, 205, 208n; **60**, 32, 39, 40
'Long View', **1**, 34–5; **6**, 161
sketch of London, **7**, 75
Holleran, James V., **44**, 221
Holles, G., *Memorials of the Holles Family, 1439–1656*, **13**, 104n
Holliday, Barten, **54**, 62n
Holliday, Billie, **56**, 155
Holliday, William, **7**, 90
Hollindale, Peter, **44**, 217
Hollingbery, Vilma, **47**, 102
Hollingdale, R. J., **36**, 46n; **50**, 172n, 173n, 180n; **55**, 73n
Hollingsworth, *see* Debenham
Hollingsworth, Thomas, **53**, 226n
Hollingworth, Simon, **48**, 235; **50**, 226
Hollins, Charlie, **58**, 300
Hollis, Derek, **44**, 197
Hollmann, Reimar, **11**, 148n
Holloway, Baliol, **49**, 230; **2**, 14
Holloway, James, **53**, 275
Holloway, John, **8**, 145; **21**, 4, 5; **23**, 66; **33**, 10, 43n; **37**, 164; **45**, 24n
The Story of the Night reviewed, **16**, 155–7, 161; **18**, 43, 59, 60; **19**, 7
Holloway, Jonathan, **44**, 201; **48**, 231; **50**, 180; **54**, 285
Holloway, Nina, **41**, 186; **42**, 160
Holloway, Stanley, **45**, 56
Holly, M., **28**, 155
Holm, Ian, **13**, 144; **16**, 151; **18**, 150, 151, 166; **20**, 135, 137, 140, 141; **30**, 22; **44**, 194; **46**, 193; **51**, 246, 249–52; **52**, 257; **58**, 206
Holm, Sarah Jane, **48**, 237; **49**, 246
Holman, C. Hugh, **49**, 164n
Holman, Clare, **45**, 117–18, 127; **46**, 198; **52**, 243, 265
Holman, Joseph George, **49**, 119, 121
Holman, Peter, **51**, 80n; **55**, 255n
Holman, Roger, **39**, 75n
Holme, Wilfrid, **48**, 71
Holmedon, Sir Edward, **11**, 92, 94
Holmer, Joan Ozark, **33**, 199; **35**, 187; **36**, 170, 193, 194n, 195; **39**, 226; **47**, 227; **48**, 251; **54**, 89n; **57**, 319
Holmes, Christopher, **56**, 342
Holmes, David W., **23**, 170
Holmes, Denis, **27**, 147
Holmes, Elizabeth, **4**, 18; **5**, 81; **7**, 8; **18**, 53; **33**, 109
Holmes, Jonathan, **58**, 334, 335, 336, 342
Holmes, Martin, **5**, 144n; **14**, 154; **17**, 29n; **19**, 151; **22**, 175n; **23**, 162n; **31**, 63n; **33**, 196; **60**, 115n57
Shakespeare's Public reviewed, **14**, 151
Holmes, Nathaniel, **18**, 112
Holmes, P. J., **54**, 95n, 97n
Holmes, R., **22**, 166
Holmes, Sean, **55**, 311; **56**, 293; **57**, 269, 277, 278; **58**, 302, 304; **59**, 185; **60**, 304–5
Holmes, Sherlock, **45**, 176
Holmes, Thomas, **2**, 148
Holmes, Urban Tigner, Jr, **40**, 80n
Holquist, Michael, **40**, 78n; **44**, 70; **46**, 55n; **49**, 70n; **57**, 196
Holroyd, Michael, **54**, 71n; **56**, 245n
Holsey, Richard, **53**, 197
Holst, Gustav, **18**, 75, 87; **56**, 130; **60**, 185, 186, 187, 189, 195
Holston, Melissa, **55**, 332; **56**, 298
Holt, Charles Lloyd, **23**, 156
Holt, Emily S., **60**, 74n12, 75n16
Holt, Leigh, **31**, 172
Holt, Michael, **45**, 147, 152
Holt, Thelma, **47**, 192, 211; **48**, 233; **54**, 286, 287; **58**, 300, 305
Holtom, William, **1**, 85
Holtz, Jürgen, **48**, 181
Holtzman, Wilhelm, **56**, 44n
Holtzmann, Thomas, **16**, 133; **48**, 229
Holwell, John, **53**, 207
Holy Disorders, **50**, 101n, 106
Holy Sonnets (J. Donne), **48**, 254
Holywell, **8**, 7
Holzberger, William G., **40**, 35n; **54**, 66n
Holzknecht, Karl J., **4**, 151
Studies in the English Renaissance Drama in memory of K.J. Holzknecht reviewed, **14**, 140, 141, 145
Holzworth, Pit, **48**, 232
Homan, Sidney R., **24**, 163; **25**, 175, 181; **26**, 156; **27**, 170; **35**, 171–2; **36**, 162; **41**, 201; **42**, 214; **43**, 231; **44**, 208; **45**, 81; **46**, 74n; **47**, 149n; **53**, 295; **55**, 242n
Homer, Christopher, **42**, 155
Homer, **5**, 53; **6**, 152; **9**, 81, 96, 102, 134, 142; **10**, 15, 35; **13**, 61; **15**, 96; **20**, 22; **22**, 15, 147, 168; **23**, 21, 97; **27**, 119; **30**, 190; **31**, 6, 7, 17; **34**, 89; **36**, 85; **39**, 143, 160, 168; **41**, 133n; **45**, 161; **48**, 13, 148; **50**, 144; **51**, 29; **54**, 32, 86, 229; **55**, 21, 199, 200, 208, 340, 368; **56**, 31
Iliad, **8**, 38; **9**, 136
Odyssey, **4**, 31
Homewood, Bill, **45**, 153
Homilies, Book of, **3**, 66, 67; **6**, 7; **7**, 6; **17**, 106–10
Homilies, First Book of, **60**, 73n4

INDEX

Honan, Park, **47**, 242n; **53**, 152n, 317–18; **54**, 67n, 117n, 239n; **57**, 233; **58**, 5, 155; **60**, 1n2
Hondius, Ludovicus, **1**, 35n, 36n; **8**, 116n; **17**, 144n
'View of London', **1**, 31–2, 33, 37n
Honer, Chris, **47**, 214; **48**, 232; **50**, 235; **51**, 258; **55**, 327
Honest Whore, The, **52**, 215–17, 224–6
Honey, John, **56**, 242n, 243, 244n
Honey, William, **23**, 159
Honeyman, John, **58**, 225, 234
Honeyman, Richard, **58**, 225
Hong, Edna H., **45**, 3n; **57**, 96, 99
Hong, Howard V., **57**, 96, 99
Honig, Edwin, **7**, 136; **10**, 11
Honigmann, Ernst A. J., **8**, 147; **9**, 142, 143, 151, 153; **11**, 145; **14**, 153; **16**, 100, 169; **18**, 41; **19**, 124, 152, 161; **20**, 166, 178; **21**, 145; **22**, 179–80, 181; **24**, 77n; **25**, 145, 194n, 196; **27**, 112n, 113, 116n, 132n; **29**, 25, 104; **30**, 187–8, 206; **31**, 7n, 59n, 195; **33**, 2, 28n, 75n; **34**, 68, 73, 164; **35**, 177; **36**, 173, 177, 189; **37**, 1, 149n; **38**, 12, 100n, 113, 178n, 185n, 218–19, 243; **39**, 145n, 158n, 219, 223, 225, 228, 249n; **40**, 153n, 202, 216, 232; **41**, 39n, 93n, 208, 219; **42**, 39n, 40, 43n, 46n, 49n, 106–7, 181, 193; **43**, 7n, 49n, 219, 241, 243, 256; **44**, 71n, 115n, 210, 218, 251; **45**, 190, 201; **46**, 106n, 249; **47**, 166n, 242, 251; **48**, 84n, 255; **49**, 34, 203n, 219; **50**, 95, 278n, 280–5; **51**, 160n, 296, 307–10; **52**, 103n, 104, 273; **53**, 176n, 180n, 183n, 185, 188n, 190n, 213–14, 232; **54**, 26n, 67, 72n, 100, 120n, 356; **55**, 37n, 187, 381; **57**, 229; **58**, 3–4, 353; **59**, 11–12, 15–16, 21, 22n11, 26, 26n28, 37n85, 47, 70n2, 382, 383; **60**, 162, 165, 166, 168, 249, 366
'The Date of *Hamlet*', **9**, 24–34
'Re-enter the Stage Direction: Shakespeare and some Contemporaries', **29**, 117–25
Studies on Shakespeare's Life, Times and Stage, *reviewed*, **21**, 141–57
Honneyman, David, **44**, 231–3
Honyman, Philip, **11**, 94
Hood, Ella, **45**, 151
Hood, Robin, **34**, 189
Hood, Thomas, **17**, 71, 144; **41**, 108
Regiment of the Sea, **1**, 68
Hook, F. S., **15**, 181
Hook, Frank S., **55**, 24n, 30n
Hook, Lucyle, **18**, 183
Höök, Marianne, **36**, 69n
Hook, Nigel, **52**, 263
Hooke, Henry, **2**, 70, 72
Hooker, Edward Niles, **51**, 45n; **53**, 221n
Hooker, Elizabeth R., **28**, 42n, 64, 65, 66; **29**, 79
Hooker, John, **42**, 28; **60**, 3
Hooker, Richard, **3**, 134; **4**, 25; **8**, 57, 117n; **14**, 143; **16**, 38, 125; **17**, 104, 110–12, 126; **19**, 60, 63, 64, 67n; **20**, 146; **23**, 106; **25**, 76n; **29**, 85, 86, 87, 88, 158; **33**, 5; **37**, 192; **38**, 2, 39; **43**, 237–8; **50**, 239; **54**, 14n, 129, 130; **55**, 230n
Ecclesiastical Polity, **1**, 131
Hooks, David, **18**, 132
Hooper, Ewan, **47**, 218
Hooper, Jim, **45**, 154; **51**, 224; **52**, 259
Hooper, John, Bishop, **13**, 87, 89n; **17**, 106; **32**, 133, 134n, 141
Hooper, Richard, **25**, 99n
Hooper, Warren, **48**, 235
Hoover, Claudette, **51**, 183n
Hope playhouse, **52**, 2, 8, 9, **11**, **52**, 53n, 68
Hope Theatre, *see under* Theatres, Elizabethan
Hope, A. D., **26**, 159
Hope, Anthony, **25**, 166
Hope, Jonathan, **45**, 202; **46**, 214; **48**, 277–8; **51**, 96; **54**, 17n, 241n; **57**, 196; **58**, 319–20, 332; **59**, 6n22, 50n3, 55, 62n31, 259n13, 260; **60**, 368
The Authorship of Shakespeare's Plays, **48**, 277
Hope, Julia, **43**, 212
Hope, Rickhard, **55**, 314
Hope-Wallace, Philip, **39**, 7, 76n; **49**, 228
Hopkins, Anthony, **41**, 53, 175–7, 185; **42**, 149, 152; **45**, 59; **54**, 293; **56**, 4n, 15, 247; **57**, 317
Hopkins, Arthur, **52**, 292
Hopkins, Daniel, **49**, 277
Hopkins, David, **37**, 190; **42**, 196; **59**, 366
Hopkins, Dorothy, **56**, 200
Hopkins, Gerard Manley, **35**, 33; **41**, 108
Hopkins, John, **27**, 141; **54**, 24; **55**, 291, 309; **56**, 40n, 267; **60**, 296Fig.50, 297–8
Hopkins, Laura, **54**, 284
Hopkins, Lisa, **45**, 152; **51**, 291; **52**, 272; **54**, 313; **56**, 347; **57**, 304, 313, 318; **59**, 348, 360; **60**, 334, 352
Hopkins, Mark, **47**, 213
Hopkins, Phil, **60**, 305
Hopkins, Priscilla (Mrs Kemble), **53**, 327
Hopkins, Richard, **56**, 194
Hopkins, Robert Innes, **50**, 216; **51**, 258; **53**, 266; **54**, 292; **55**, 305–6, 331
Hopkins, S. V., **38**, 26n
Hopkins, Vivian C., *Prodigal Puritan: A Life of Delia Bacon* reviewed, **14**, 153
Hopkins, William, **51**, 91n
Hopkinson, Bill, **45**, 151
Hopkinson, Francis, **18**, 108
Hoppe, H. R., **2**, 153; **3**, 26; **4**, 152, 158; **5**, 46n, 47, 150; **7**, 149; **8**, 82; **13**, 163; **22**, 182; **24**, 176; **25**, 73n, 77; **33**, 163n, 167–8; **49**, 27–44; **50**, 284; **59**, 7n27
The Bad Quarto of 'Romeo and Juliet', **3**, 149–50
'John of Bordeaux' reviewed, **1**, 130
Hoppner, John, **51**, 10; **59**, 131n47
Hopwood, C. H., **17**, 79n
Horace, **1**, 51; **4**, 68n; **10**, 15, 146; **11**, 21, 71, 73, 151; **15**, 64; **17**, 61, 64; **19**, 56; **20**, 22; **22**, 47, **27**, 62, 119, 122, **30**, 192; **31**, 19; **34**, 13n; **35**, 121, 123; **37**, 144, 148; **38**, 42, 215; **40**, 34; **42**, 74; **47**, 26; **50**, 1; **51**, 176; **55**, 21, 197, 199, 201, 202, 206, 208; **57**, 210, 220, 221; **59**, 289
Epistles, **4**, 65–6
Odes, **10**, 5
Horalék, Karel, **21**, 153
Horan, Gerard, **46**, 187
Horapollo, **17**, 184
Hordern, Sir Michael, **8**, 133, 134–5, 138; **32**, 203; **39**, 86, 88–90; **41**, 60, 228; **42**, 37; **45**, 72, 192; **49**, 160
Horestes, **17**, 220; **20**, 18, 19, 24
Horio, Yukio, **54**, 247, 286
Horman, William, **33**, 19, 20
Horn, C. F., **18**, 40, 99
Horn, R. L., **36**, 193
Horn, Robert D., **11**, 148n; **16**, 171n

Hornblower, Henry, **52**, 36
Hornbrook, David, **42**, 164
Hornby, James, **47**, 104
Hornby, Mrs, **1**, 81, 87n
Hornby, Richard, **52**, 44n, 115n, 117, 118n; **60**, 147n19
Horne, David H., **7**, 142
Horne, R. C., **37**, 190; **38**, 227
Horne, Richard H., **36**, 175
Horneby family (of Stratford-upon-Avon), **1**, 86
Hörner, Hans, **7**, 116
Horney, Karen, **45**, 165; **46**, 215
Horniman, Annie E. F., **8**, 77; **47**, 91
Hornstein, Gabriel, **59**, 157, 163n20
Hornstein, L. H., **5**, 91n
Hornyold-Strickland, H., **13**, 105n
Horobetz, Lynn K., **23**, 174n; **26**, 176n
Horovitch, David, **45**, 155; **57**, 276
Horowitz, David, **20**, 157; **28**, 110n
Horowitz, M. C., **48**, 137n
Horrox, Alan, **51**, 263
Horrox, Rosemary, **59**, 263n24
Horsefall, Chalkie, **52**, 265
Horsey, Sir Jerome, **17**, 22
Horsfall, Bernard, **38**, 205–6; **54**, 268
Horsfield, Margaret, **39**, 7, 8n
Horsman, E. A., **14**, 14n; **27**, 189; **46**, 31n; **50**, 188n
Horsman, Kim, **40**, 158
Horspool, David, **52**, 94n
Hortmann, Wilhelm, **50**, 30n, 37n, 38, 39n; **52**, 284
Horton, Andrew, **39**, 39n
Horton, Edward, **58**, 234
Horton, Priscilla, **13**, 77; **53**, 104
Horton, Thomas B., **49**, 324–5; **54**, 241n
Horváth, Lázár Petrichevich, **54**, 55
Horwich, Richard, **25**, 188; **31**, 165; **42**, 175, 214; **43**, 226; **56**, 101n; **57**, 28
Horwitz, Tony, **52**, 38n, 40n
Horwood, Arthur, **54**, 292; **58**, 306
Hosier, Kevin, **58**, 299
Hosking, G. L., **6**, 160–1; **47**, 172n
Hoskins, Bob, **46**, 68
Hoskins, Edgar, **56**, 196n
Hoskins, George, yeoman, **17**, 20
Hoskins, John, **49**, 81; **57**, 207; **60**, 223
Hoskins, W. G., **38**, 27n
'Provincial Life', **17**, 13–20
Hoskyns, John, **27**, 120
Hoskyns, Tam, **42**, 129, 131; **43**, 205
Hosley, Richard, **7**, 149; **8**, 97n, 98n, 99n; **9**, 146, 150; **11**, 146, 148n, 155; **12**, 55n, 65, 144; **13**, 160; **14**, 150; **15**, 172, 180; **16**, 175; **18**, 180n, 183; **19**, 146, 153; **20**, 168, 176; **21**, 145, 150, 151; **22**, 35, 173, 183; **23**, 127, 128, 160–1, 185; **24**, 168; **25**, 73n; **26**, 9, 96n; **27**, 77n, 135, 175, 190; **28**, 133; **29**, 171, 172; **30**, 196; **31**, 5n; **33**, 147, 149, 150, 198; **34**, 179–80, 189; **35**, 174; **36**, 178, 185; **38**, 9n, 11; **40**, 70n; **41**, 3–5, 36n, 86–7, 93n; **43**, 144–5, 168n; **44**, 243; **47**, 32n, 34; **48**, 85n; **49**, 21–3; **50**, 272; **52**, 4–7, 10, 11n, 13n; **59**, 41, 47, 159n8
'The Discovery-space in Shakespeare's Globe', **12**, 35–46
'Shakespeare's Use of a Gallery over the Stage', **10**, 77–89
'Was there a Music-room in Shakespeare's Globe?', **13**, 113–23
Hosokawa, Toshio, **57**, 293
Hostos, E. M. de, **19**, 124
Hotine, Margaret, **35**, 177–8; **36**, 176; **37**, 190; **41** 21; **44**, 234
Hotson, Leslie, **1**, 9, 76, 128; **2**, 151; **3**, 10, 11, 12, 27, 28, 29; **4**, 8; **5**, 138, 148–9; **6**, 80, 88n, 159; **7**, 70, 139; **8**, 5, 6, 11, 13n, 149, 150–1; **9**, 145, 146, 148; **10**, 135, 147; **11**, 97n, 148; **12**, 1, 18, 21n, 43; **13**, 73, 97–8; **14**, 13, 33n, 91; **15**, 10, 12, 112; **16**, 30, 118–19, 152; **17**, 73n; **18**, 183, 188; **19**, 3, 143–4; **20**, 158; **21**, 147; **25**, 109, 110; **27**, 94, 119n; **28**, 125, 134; **29**, 179; **30**, 167n; **31**, 18n; **32**, 96n, 110n, 137n, 152, 227–8; **35**, 87, 135; **37**, 196; **40**, 214; **41**, 3n; **47**, 88n; **49**, 327; **53**, 196–7, 205, 206n; **54**, 59n, 120n; **57**, 234; **58**, 199; **60**, 283n53
The Assassination of Christopher Marlowe, **14**, 9
The Commonwealth and Restoration Stage, **13**, 120
The First Night of Twelfth Night, **12**, 20n, 21n; **14**, 13
I, William Shakespeare, **3**, 3
'The Projected Amphitheatre', **2**, 24–35
Shakespeare's Motley, **13**, 80n, 104n, 105n
Shakespeare's Motley reviewed, **7**, 143–4
Shakespeare's Sonnets Dated reviewed, **4**, 148–9, 153–6
Shakespeare versus Shallow, **3**, 3
Shakespeare's Wooden O, **14**, 13; reviewed, **14**, 149–50
Houbart, J., **11**, 119
Houben, Heinrich Hubert, **48**, 10n
Houbraken, Jacobus, **51**, 14
Houghtelling, Ayres, **47**, 258
Houghton, Alexander, **3**, 2; **4**, 148n; **5**, 139n; **6**, 158; **8**, 148; **10**, 144n; **13**, 104n; **24**, 155; **28**, 166
Houghton, Arthur Amory, **1**, 70, 71
Houghton, Martin, **47**, 213–14
Houghton, Norris, **2**, 131; **8**, 122
Houghton, Ralph E. C., ed. of *Lear*, **12**, 151
Houghton, William, **4**, 148n; **23**, 160
Houghton Library, *see under* Libraries
Houghtons of Lancashire, **44**, 231
Houk, Raymond A., 'Shakespeare's *Shrew* and Greene's *Orlando*', **2**, 152
Houlbrooke, Ralph, **38**, 31n, 32n; **49**, 182, 190n, 197; **54**, 123
Houliston, Victor, **55**, 229n
Hourani, Albert, **52**, 207n
House, Madeline, **53**, 103n
Houseman, John, **5**, 116; **8**, 122; **11**, 123; **12**, 117; **31**, 173; **39**, 40; **44**, 243
Houser, David J., **28**, 168
Housman, A. E., **5**, 1, 2, 5, 147; **23**, 176; **51**, 130, 131; **58**, 353; **59**, 29–30
The Shropshire Lad, **12**, 9
Houston, John Porter, **43**, 18n, 19n; **46**, 93n
Houston, P. H., **4**, 147
Houston, William, **53**, 260, 284; **54**, 278–80; **55**, 324; **56**, 248, 289, 290
Houtchens, C. W., **57**, 88
Houtchens, Lawrence and Caroline Washburn, **35**, 6n
Hovenden, R., **25**, 143n
Hovenden, Valery, **14**, 127; **15**, 145
How a Man May Choose a Good Wife from a Bad, **52**, 137n
Howard family, **3**, 29; **8**, 7

Howard, Alan, **22**, 140; **24**, 122, 130; **25**, 70; **28**, 139; **29**, 154–5, 156; **31**, 150; **33**, 177–8; **43**, 250; **44**, 165; **47**, 189–91; **48**, 203, 230; **51**, 246–7, 249; **52**, 257; **54**, 253, 283; **57**, 81; **60**, 329
Howard, Charles, 11th Duke of Norfolk, **11**, 107
Howard, Charles, Earl of Nottingham Lord High Admiral, **11**, 93; **23**, 44, 45; **24**, 157; **25**, 188; **32**, 198; **33**, 153–4, 168; **44**, 232
Howard, Sir Edward, **60**, 68
Howard, Lady Frances, **15**, 168; **26**, 57; **43**, 248; **46**, 212; **49**, 184; **50**, 260; **51**, 291; **56**, 224n
Howard, Frank, **7**, 92; **13**, 75, 76
Howard, George E., **32**, 132; **49**, 183n
Howard, Helen, **44**, 196
Howard, Henry, Earl of Surrey, **3**, 65; **14**, 146; **16**, 12; **20**, 162; **51**, 135; **56**, 30
Howard, Lord Henry, **54**, 133n, 170
Howard, James, **21**, 156; **49**, 2, 111
Howard, Jean E., **34**, 176; **35**, 155; **40**, 213; **41**, 8n, 196, 204; **42**, 163; **43**, 15n; **44**, 41n, 42n, 68n, 105n; **46**, 6, 9n, 20n; **47**, 82n; **48**, 256; **50**, 109n; **51**, 281; **52**, 30n, 279; **53**, 234n, 299; **54**, 310; **55**, 239, 338, 341–2, 352, 355, 373; **56**, 27n, 204n; **57**, 132; **58**, 170, 172; **60**, 109n34, 168, 348, 357
Stage and Social Struggle in Early Modern England, The, **48**, 256
Howard, John, **17**, 90
Howard, L., **26**, 154
Howard, Leslie, **9**, 21, 57; **18**, 73; **27**, 138; **40**, 4; **49**, 153–4
Howard, Lord, of Effingham, engraving of, **17**, 34n
Howard, Lord Thomas, **21**, 103; **60**, 69
Howard, Pamela, **41**, 189; **49**, 273; **50**, 219; **59**, 208–10
Howard, Philip, First Earl of Arundel, **54**, 91, 96
Howard, Richard, **46**, 58n, 92n; **56**, 232n
Howard, Robert, **55**, 267
Howard, Sally, **46**, 198
Howard, Sidney, **8**, 122
Howard, Skiles, **47**, 227; **54**, 195n; **55**, 241, 242, 243n, 244, 245n, 255; **60**, 60n6
Howard, Stephanie, **41**, 159, 184–5, 187; **43**, 173
Howard, T. C., **48**, 201; **56**, 237
Howard, Thomas, 1st Earl of Suffolk, **18**, 192; **32**, 227
Howard, Tony, **52**, 290; **55**, 383; **56**, 5n, 10n
Howard-Hill, Trevor H., **20**, 178; **23**, 176, 177, 178–9, 184; **24**, 172n; **25**, 199n, 200; **26**, 179; **27**, 181, 182, 183, 184, 188; **29**, 181, 184; **30**, 207; **32**, 241, 245–6; **34**, 193, 196; **35**, 186; **36**, 107n, 109, 110, 114n, 120n, 190; **37**, 215n; **39**, 248, 249n; **40**, 151n, 152n, 219, 229; **41**, 232; **42**, 189–90; **43**, 262, 264–5; **44**, 123n, 125n, 236; **45**, 195n; **46**, 247; **47**, 244–5, 260; **48**, 272; **50**, 258, 282; **52**, 324; **54**, 19n; **55**, 258; **59**, 11, 15n64, 69n1, 92n3, 99n11
Howarth, David, **47**, 18n
Howarth, Herbert, **16**, 164; **19**, 150; **20**, 153; **29**, 88; **32**, 10; **38**, 145n
'Shakespeare's Gentleness', **14**, 90–7
Howarth, R. G., **12**, 138 and n.; **23**, 171n; **30**, 164
Howden, Kathryn, **47**, 217
Howe, Elizabeth, **46**, 237–8; **51**, 4; **53**, 149n
Howe, Florence, **53**, 134n
Howe, George, **9**, 19
Howe, Irving, **55**, 115, 124n
Howe, James, **48**, 242
Buddhist's Shakespeare, Affirming Self Deconstruction, **48**, 242
Howe, Jenny, **41**, 187
Howe, John (Baron Chedworth), **53**, 344
Howe, P. P., **14**, 88n; **32**, 17n; **35**, 6, 43, 48–9, 53; **37**, 142n; **40**, 127n; **45**, 39n; **49**, 214n; **54**, 138n; **55**, 9n, 22n, 123n
Howe, Quincy, Jr, **40**, 83n
Howe, Steve, **45**, 151
Howell, Anthony, **54**, 256–7, 267, 272
Howell, Eleanor, **59**, 345
Howell, James, **7**, 40; **57**, 216
Howell, Jane, **39**, 82, 92, 96, 100, 101, 103–6, 108–11; **41**, 227; **43**, 171–2; **44**, 192; **47**, 11; **53**, 328; **56**, 5, 346; **59**, 372
Howell, Robert, **22**, 170; **49**, 272; **53**, 257, 281; **54**, 293
Howell, Stephen, **41**, 186; **42**, 154; **43**, 208
Howell, T. B., **38**, 21n
Howell, Thomas, **46**, 99; **56**, 29n; **57**, 20
Howell, Wilbur S., **32**, 171n; **40**, 97n
Howells, William Dean, **18**, 103; **24**, 104
Howerd, Frankie, **48**, 206; **50**, 212
Howes, Edmund, **43**, 43n; **53**, 63n; **58**, 63
Howes, John, **12**, 100; **17**, 55n
Howey, David, **42**, 134
Howgego, J. L., **6**, 73n
Howland, Gerard, **40**, 178; **41**, 191; **42**, 160
Howlett, D. R., **52**, 186
Howlett, Kathy M., **60**, 348
Howlett, Noel, **47**, 95
Howlett, Robert, **30**, 164
Howling, Alice, **49**, 190
Howse, Hugh, **39**, 234
Howson, Helena Kaut, **48**, 227
Hoy, Cyrus, **14**, 6, 8, 12; **18**, 160, 187; **28**, 2, 3, 152–3; **33**, 188; **34**, 190; **35**, 174; **36**, 107n; **38**, 229; **40**, 226; **41**, 91n; **43**, 18n, 86n, 87–8; **44**, 123n, 126n; **45**, 202; **46**, 92n, 226; **49**, 324; **50**, 241; **51**, 317, 334; **52**, 166n; **54**, 241n; **56**, 169n; **58**, 348; **59**, 214, 220, 260
'Jacobean Tragedy and the Mannerist Style', **26**, 49–67
Hoye, André van, *see* Hoius
Hoyle, James, **26**, 156; **30**, 185; **32**, 231
Hoyle, Richard, **55**, 36n
Hozier, Anthony, **34**, 180
Hrušinský, Rudolf, **14**, 118
Hsia, R. Po-chia, **51**, 165; **54**, 35n
Hsing-Kuo, Wu, **45**, 149; **57**, 177, 180, 181, 182
Hsui-Wei, Lin, **57**, 181, 182
Huang, Fumei, **57**, 180, 181
Huang, Zuolin, **57**, 169, 171, 173, 174, 177, 178, 180
Huarte, Juan, **29**, 81
Hubaux, Jean, **15**, 109n, 110n
Hubball, Tim, **46**, 194
Hubbard, F. G., **9**, 5
Hubbard, William, **20**, 20; **56**, 29n
Huber, Anneliese, **23**, 119n
Huber, C. A., **31**, 193
Huber, E., **30**, 208–9
Huberd, Edward, **27**, 99, 101, 102
Hubert, Judd D., **41**, 223
Hubert, Richard, **60**, 359–60
Hubler, Edward, **4**, 143; **5**, 138; **13**, 148; **15**, 16, 124n; **16**, 171n; **19**, 135; **31**, 127n; **59**, 41
Huckell, John, **43**, 104
Hudd, Roy, **44**, 203; **46**, 197

Hudd, Walter, **1**, 107; **12**, 120; **59**, 198–9
Huddleston, Bridget, **13**, 92, 104n
Huddleston, Sir Ferdinand, **13**, 92, 97, 104n
Huddleston, Sir William, **13**, 92, 104n
Hudson, A. K., **10**, 108
Hudson, Henry, **54**, 101
Hudson, Henry N., **18**, 102, 108–9, 111; **27**, 192; **32**, 16; **59**, 81n9, 86, 87
Hudson, Hoyht H., **49**, 81n; **57**, 207
Hudson, Kenneth, **24**, 40; **25**, 185
'Shakespeare's Use of Colloquial Language', **23**, 39–48
Hudson, Richard, **43**, 188, 215; **44**, 194
Hudson, T., **60**, 252n3
Huebert, Ronald, **49**, 211n
Huei-min, Lee, **45**, 149
Hues, Robert, **17**, 28
Huesmann, Heinrich, **23**, 122; **37**, 159n
Huffman, Clifford Chalmers, **31**, 7n; **38**, 128; **43**, 269; **44**, 2n, 8n
Hug, John, **47**, 216; **48**, 232
Hughes, A., **44**, 76n
Hughes, Alan, **35**, 9, 175; **49**, 4n, 111n, 126, 317–19; **51**, 324; **55**, 199n, 203; **60**, 2n6, 11n30, 13
Hughes, Arthur, **55**, 138n
Hughes, Declan, **54**, 266
Hughes, Geoffrey, **31**, 171; **40**, 142n; **50**, 24
Hughes, Glenda, **48**, 235
Hughes, Gwenda, **42**, 152; **52**, 263; **53**, 281; **54**, 281; **56**, 296
Hughes, Henry, **28**, 38n
Hughes, Ian, **47**, 184, 200; **53**, 265; **54**, 266; **55**, 313
Hughes, Jo, **46**, 192
Hughes, John, **27**, 191; **34**, 11; **37**, 145; **51**, 22n, 87
Hughes, Lee, **37**, 35
Hughes, Mari Rowland, **48**, 227
Hughes, Merritt Y., **46**, 112n; **49**, 168n; **55**, 230n; **57**, 71, 92
Hughes, Michael, **45**, 154
Hughes, Paul L., **30**, 161n, 163n; **33**, 147n; **57**, 237
Hughes, Peter, **15**, 146
Hughes, Robert, **26**, 78n; **55**, 174
Hughes, Sean, **59**, 310–11
Hughes, Ted, **46**, 206, 207; **48**, 194; **52**, 286; **53**, 187n; **54**, 31; **56**, 158, 159, 160, 239; **57**, 331; **58**, 261, 349; **59**, 362
Shakespeare and the Goddess of Complete Being, **46**, 206
Hughes, Thomas, *Gismond of Salerne*, **20**, 17, 24
The Misfortunes of Arthur, **12**, 48; **20**, 17, 24
Hughes, William, as the 'W.H.' of the *Sonnets*, **5**, 139n; **7**, 139; **10**, 141
Hughes, Willie, **56**, 137
Hughes, Zelina, **55**, 326
Hughes, Zerling, **51**, 264
Hughes-Hughes, A., **11**, 106n
Hughey, Ruth, **46**, 13n
Hugo, François Victor, **2**, 116, 121; **7**, 108; **8**, 118; **9**, 65; **12**, 111, 117; **14**, 123; **15**, 168; **16**, 54; **20**, 164; **60**, 217
Hugo, Jean, **49**, 129
Hugo, Joseph, **57**, 115
Hugo, Victor, **2**, 116, 118; **3**, 98; **4**, 1; **16**, 10, 14, 53–4, 70, 75; **21**, 80; **47**, 165n; **48**, 5, 6, 8; **55**, 115; **56**, 205, 206n; **57**, 115, 116; **59**, 263n24; **60**, 217, 218–19
Hernani, **3**, 102–3
Hugo-Daly, Peter, **45**, 139
Hugon, Cecile, **39**, 143n
Huisman, Jacqueline, **6**, 118; **7**, 108
Huisman, Jacques, **6**, 118; **7**, 108
Huizinga, Johan, **14**, 16; **49**, 79n
Huling, Lorraine, **39**, 76n, 78
Hull, Keith, **32**, 226
Hull, Thomas, **35**, 3
Hulley, Karl K., **47**, 147n; **53**, 33n
Hulme, Hilda M., **6**, 158; **9**, 134; **11**, 137, 138; **12**, 143, 151–2; **13**, 154, 168, 169n; **16**, 179; **19**, 141; **20**, 163; **23**, 11n; **25**, 181; **30**, 204; **34**, 62n; **42**, 205, 210n; **50**, 52n; **59**, 49n1
Explorations in Shakespeare's Language reviewed, **16**, 179
Hulme, Peter, **40**, 64n; **43**, 1n, 15; **51**, 274; **54**, 226n, 232n; **55**, 343; **56**, 314; **58**, 349, 357
Hulme, T. E., **16**, 34
Hulme, W. H., **19**, 74n
Huloet, Richard, **23**, 28; **42**, 58; **56**, 57n
Hulse, S. Clark, **31**, 13n; **32**, 213, 232; **33**, 191; **56**, 34
Hulshof, A., **1**, 23
Humbert, Pascal, **44**, 194
Humble, George, **53**, 201n
Hume, Alexander, **57**, 237, 238
Hume, Anthea, **43**, 235, 241; **54**, 4n
Hume, David, **9**, 94; **16**, 35; **24**, 97; **37**, 149–51; **43**, 57; **46**, 153; **51**, 1, 271; **59**, 130
History of Great Britain, **14**, 80, 88n
Hume, Martin A. S., **31**, 179; **54**, 126n
Hume, Robert D., **28**, 157; **49**, 115n; **51**, 48n, 273; **57**, 11, 12, 84
Hume, S. J., **59**, 210–11
Humfrey, Duke of Gloucester, **4**, 93
Humfrey, Pelham, **18**, 94; **51**, 80, 81
Hummelen, W. M. H., **36**, 178
Humorous Lieutenant, The, **54**, 214
Humphrey, Mrs Hannah, **38**, 69, 70, 73
Humphrey, Ozias, **1**, 62
Humphreys, A. H., **41**, 232
Humphreys, Arthur R., **19**, 132, 162–3; **20**, 72n, 73n, 173–4; **22**, 154, 179; **25**, 141n, 173, 199; **26**, 177; **27**, 37n, 131n; **30**, 29n, 35n, 37, 38, 40n, 42n, 43n; **31**, 87n; **34**, 106n, 109; **36**, 186–7; **38**, 1, 10, 15, 44n, 62n, 63n, 77n, 85, 86n, 87, 89, 250–1; **40**, 74n, 84n; **42**, 181, 182, 203, 204n, 206; **44**, 66n, 69n, 71n; **45**, 91n; **49**, 310; **54**, 238n, 239n; **57**, 239, 244; **59**, 47
New Arden edition of *I Henry IV* reviewed, **16**, 172–3
Humphreys, Clare, **44**, 200
Humphries, Barry, **47**, 204
Humphries, Charles, **51**, 89n
Humphries, W. Lee, **48**, 89n
Humpston, Charlotte, **44**, 201
Hün, Agâh, **18**, 130
Hungary, report on Shakespeare in, **2**, 127, 128; **12**, 113–14; **13**, 129; **14**, 120; **15**, 135; **16**, 134–5; **18**, 124–5
see also under Translations
Hunkes (Harry), a bear, **8**, 106, 107n
Hunnis, William, **17**, 195
Hunsdon, First Lord, *see under* Carey, Henry
Hunsdon, Lord (Henry Carey), Lord Chamberlain, **16**, 172; **18**, 188; **49**, 327–8; **54**, 98n, 99
Hunsdon's Men, *see under* Theatre, Elizabethan, companies
Hunt, Albert, **50**, 263
Hunt, Althea, **6**, 124

Hunt, Andrew, **52**, 266
Hunt, Ava, **42**, 157
Hunt, Charles, **10**, 124
Hunt, Christopher, **27**, 106n
Hunt, David, **57**, 296
Hunt, Sir David, **28**, 134n
Hunt, H. O., **1**, 86
Hunt, Holman, **46**, 242–3
Hunt, Hugh, **1**, 100; **4**, 138; **5**, 119, 120, 121, 122, 124; **7**, 123–4; **8**, 123; **9**, 8, 22; **10**, 115; **11**, 117; **12**, 109; **13**, 124; **18**, 61; **24**, 167; **34**, 117n; **38**, 50; **41**, 57n; **47**, 90
  production of *Love's Labour's Lost*, **4**, 129–35
Hunt, John, **27**, 101, 102, 103; **42**, 179
Hunt, John Dixon, **27**, 163; **44**, 236
Hunt, John S., **54**, 226–7
Hunt, Leigh, **7**, 27, 28; **13**, 59, 65, 68n; **14**, 83, 88n; **16**, 78; **29**, 143; **32**, 22n; **35**, 6, 43–8, 54–5; **42**, 37–9; **53**, 113n; **57**, 88
Hunt, Lynn, **47**, 10n
Hunt, Marsha, **37**, 169
Hunt, Martita, **9**, 20; **56**, 113
Hunt, Maurice, **41**, 213; **42**, 182; **43**, 139n, 234; **45**, 170; **48**, 246; **49**, 289; **50**, 245; **51**, 285; **54**, 41n; **55**, 351; **56**, 307–8; **57**, 315; **58**, 321, 325, 332; **60**, 331, 347–9, 352
Hunt, R. A., **48**, 267
Hunt, R. W., **2**, 148; **4**, 88; **26**, 81, 82
Hunt, Simon, **54**, 118, 120, 307; **60**, 184n2
Hunt, Steve, **53**, 278
Hunt, W. H., **25**, 139n, **27**, 129n
Hunt, William, **54**, 47
Hunter, A. E., **19**, 8
Hunter, Chris, **35**, 149
Hunter, Christopher, **57**, 295
Hunter, Edwin R., **23**, 100n
Hunter, George K., **9**, 137; **12**, 136; **13**, 163; **14**, 146; **15**, 181; **16**, 165n, 167; **17**, 37–52, 46n; **18**, 34, 60, 159; **19**, 123, 148, 150, 163; **21**, 127, 137, 158; **22**, 14n, 79, 80, 83, 88, 151, 173; **23**, 152, 167, 169; **24**, 165; **25**, 2, 4, 47n; **26**, 24n, 119, 177–8; **27**, 106n, 190; **29**, 8, 9, 42–3, 163; **30**, 35, 73, 75, 81n, 125, 127, 128, 133n, 135, 192; **32**, 2, 7, 10, 12, 55, 83, 93n, 214; **33**, 1, 83n, 91n, 182, 195–6; **34**, 72, 105n, 164; **35**, 106, 160n; **36**, 50n, 174, 180; **37**, 4, 5, 100n, 107n, 110n, 184, 190; **38**, 13, 54, 249; **39**, 139; **40**, 202, 206; **41**, 93n, 120n, 124, 149n, 202, 204; **42**, 1n, 3n, 104n; **43**, 5, 22n, 137n; **44**, 119; **45**, 7, 189–90, 203n; **46**, 101n, 227; **47**, 71n, 154n; **49**, 88n, 204n; **50**, 54n, 95n, 178n, 184n; **51**, 145, 311, 324, 334; **52**, 204n, 273; **53**, 323; **54**, 196n; **55**, 200, 200n, 236n; **56**, 62n, 205, 206n, 212n, 222n; **57**, 342; **58**, 327, 335; **59**, 47, 54n13, 54n14
  'Elizabethans and Foreigners', **17**, 37–52
  '*Macbeth* in the Twentieth Century', **19**, 1–11
  'Shakespeare's Earliest Tragedies: *Titus Andronicus* and *Romeo and Juliet*', **27**, 1–9
  'Seneca and the Elizabethans: A Case-Study in "Influence" ', **20**, 17–26
Hunter, Glen D., **36**, 182n
Hunter, Graham, **49**, 274; **51**, 263
Hunter, I. M. L., **42**, 87n, 93
Hunter, Ian, **18**, 73
Hunter, John, **22**, 125
Hunter, Joseph, **3**, 50; **36**, 195n; **53**, 87n
Hunter, Kathryn, **46**, 169, 171; **47**, 218; **48**, 225, 230; **51**, 245–7; **52**, 257; **53**, 261; **54**, 283; **57**, 261, 277; **58**, 304, 305; **59**, 318–19; **60**, 326
Hunter, Kelly, **48**, 194; **49**, 270; **55**, 291
Hunter, Lynette, **45**, 167; **55**, 183n, 354; **59**, 372–3, 375
Hunter, Sir Mark, **2**, 39; **10**, 9; **26**, 97; **29**, 80; **32**, 226
Hunter, Meredith, **57**, 156
Hunter, Michael, **52**, 35n, 41n
Hunter, Reginald D., **60**, 167Fig.30
Hunter, Robert Grams, **21**, 127; **25**, 4, 6, 58n, 175; **28**, 161; **29**, 8, 59n; **31**, 170; **32**, 4, 59n; **33**, 10, 92n; **40**, 198; **42**, 6n, 185
Hunter, Robert, **54**, 83n, 87n; **55**, 93
Hunter, Robin, **41**, 188
Hunter, S., **24**, 165
Hunter, Thomas, **19**, 106n
Hunter, William B., Jr, **25**, 180; **38**, 235; **39**, 225
Huntingdon, Third Earl of, *see* Hastings, Henry
Huntington Library, *see under* Libraries
Huntington, Collis P., **6**, 53
Huntington, Henry Edwards, **1**, 58, 66; **49**, 116
  the growth of his library, **6**, 53–5, 61–2, 63n
Huntley, Frank L., **19**, 3, 126
Huntley, Muir (designer), **50**, 235
Huon of Bordeaux, **4**, 158
Huppe, Bernard F., **42**, 3n
Hurd, Richard, **14**, 99; **17**, 181
Hurdis, Mary, **56**, 201
Hurley, Colin, **42**, 151, 161; **44**, 190, 192, 193; **45**, 153; **51**, 242; **53**, 260
Hurley, Robert, **46**, 41n, 126n; **53**, 79n, 233n
Hurok, Sol, **4**, 123
Hurren, Kenneth, **50**, 35n
Hurry, Leslie, **8**, 133; **9**, 22; **13**, 79; **14**, 130
Hurst, Richard, **52**, 264
Hurstfield, Joel, **17**, 127–9 and nn.; **18**, 21n; **19**, 146n, 149; **26**, 171; **29**, 90; **30**, 1; **33**, 181; **35**, 72n; **38**, 11; **49**, 181n; **54**, 170n
  'The Politics of Corruption in Shakespeare's England', **28**, 15–28
Hurston, Zora Neale, **56**, 157
Hurt, John, **39**, 89n
Hurtgen, Charles, **23**, 158, 174n
Hurwitz, Mashe, **55**, 122n
Hurworth, Angela, **54**, 321
Husain, Adrian A., **59**, 365
Husak, Gustav, **36**, 27
Husee, John, **17**, 226–9, 234, 237–9
Huskyn, **54**, 44
Huss, John, **9**, 110n, 118
Hussey, Dyneley, **21**, 96
Hussey, Sir Roger, **56**, 37
Hussey, S. S., **38**, 234
Huston, J. Dennis, **25**, 177; **28**, 161; **31**, 165; **37**, 15n, 37n
Hutchens, Eleanor N., **18**, 165
Hutcheon, Maxwell, **46**, 175–6
Hutcheson, W. J. Fraser, **5**, 139n
Hutchings, Geoffrey, **25**, 164; **33**, 169, 170; **35**, 148
Hutchings, William, **40**, 204; **59**, 157n1
Hutchins, Barbara, **10**, 125

Hutchinson, Christopher, *see* Beeston, Christopher
Hutchinson, Derek, **41**, 178; **45**, 148
Hutchinson, Lloyd, **53**, 261; **55**, 306; **56**, 297
Hutchinson, Robin, **13**, 105n
Hutchinson, Thomas, **53**, 105n; **55**, 106n
Hutchinson, W., **13**, 104n
Hutchison, Neil, **13**, 124
Huth, Alfred, **3**, 44–5
Hutson, Lorna, **48**, 259; **49**, 196n; **51**, 295
Hutson, Martin, **57**, 285; **59**, 301–3
Hutt, Peter, **58**, 158
Hutt, William, **16**, 153, 154; **31**, 146; **34**, 156–60; **37**, 85; **39**, 188
Huttar, Charles A., **23**, 158
Hutten, Leonard, *Bellum Grammaticale*, **4**, 95
Hüttner, Johann, **35**, 23n
Hutton, J., **31**, 136n
Hutton, James, **15**, 9
Hutton, John, **17**, 227
Hutton, Luke, **17**, 95 and n.
Hutton, Richard W., **49**, 119n
Hutton, Ronald, **43**, 93; **54**, 69n
Hutton, Sarah, **48**, 31n, 260
Hutton, Thomas, **19**, 106n
Hutton, V., **25**, 182
Huxley, Aldous L., **19**, 58; **20**, 33; **25**, 185; **34**, 145; **38**, 173; **53**, 164n
  Point Counter Point, **8**, 14–15, 20
Huxley, Julian, **52**, 191
Huxley, T. H., **54**, 80, 83–4
Hviezdoslav (Pavol Országh), **4**, 109
HWS Rembiko Project (Edinburgh), **58**, 304
Hyde, Anne, **43**, 97
Hyde, Sir Edward, Earl of Clarendon, **43**, 97
Hyde, H. Montgomery, **45**, 41n
Hyde, Isabel, **15**, 165
Hyde, John, **13**, 135
Hyde, Jonathan, **34**, 151; **36**, 151; **37**, 173; **41**, 186; **45**, 119, 120; **46**, 194
Hyde, Mary, **20**, 163
Hyde, Mary Crapo, **4**, 147
Hyde, Nicholas, **28**, 68
Hyde, Ralph, **53**, 196n, 201n
Hyde, Thomas, **40**, 221
Hyland, Frances, **9**, 111; **10**, 116; **36**, 58
Hyland, Peter, **32**, 216; **37**, 55, 58n; **40**, 209; **47**, 233; **51**, 273; **57**, 310; **60**, 259n26
Hylton, Jeremy, **52**, 185n
Hyman, Earle, **12**, 117; **18**, 133
Hyman, Lawrence W., **19**, 53, 54n; **25**, 179; **29**, 163
Hyman, Paula, **55**, 119n
Hyman, Stanley Edgar, **15**, 123n; **26**, 162; **34**, 68n; **40**, 127n; **41**, 129, 131
Hyman, William, **21**, 144; **25**, 179
Hymenaei, **52**, 190
Hymer, Nicholas, **42**, 134, 144–5, 148, 153
Hymes, Dell, **57**, 205
Hynd, J., **54**, 163n
Hynes, Samuel, **14**, 145; **31**, 14n
Hyrd, Richard, **56**, 43n
Hysel, F. E., **32**, 190n
Hytner, Nicholas, **40**, 174; **41**, 183; **43**, 202, 215; **44**, 178–86; **46**, 188; **47**, 201, 264; **48**, 196; **49**, 334; **52**, 289, 325; **55**, 55, 286n, 292, 294, 317–21, 334, 380; **56**, 276, 298; **57**, 258, 259, 264, 279, 280, 281, 283, 284; **58**, 59, 301; **59**, 87n29, 177, 184, 186, 187, 321, 322, 323–7; **60**, 322
Hyu, Paul Courtenay, **56**, 296

'I.C.', **34**, 88
Iago, **47**, 216
Iamblichus, **59**, 228
Ibanez, Susana, **44**, 197
Ibbotson, Piers, **41**, 178
Ibsen, Henrik, **4**, 17, 98, 128; **6**, 25, 140, 147; **7**, 11; **8**, 38; **12**, 79; **16**, 14; **19**, 24n, 123; **22**, 3, 35, 163; **24**, 13, 14, 43; **29**, 9, 136, 146; **30**, 85, 86n, 189; **34**, 2, 6; **35**, 21; **36**, 65, 125; **37**, 207; **39**, 94, 170; **43**, 110, 114–17, 119; **47**, 193n; **48**, 10–12, 10, 115–16, 118–19, 191; **55**, 115; **57**, 92, 120; **59**, 374
  Lady from the Sea, **11**, 20
  Peer Gynt, **1**, 103; **4**, 106
I-che, Teng, **6**, 114
Ichikawa, Mariko, **54**, 308; **57**, 332
Ichikawa, Somegorō, **46**, 193; **54**, 111; **60**, 137n21
Ichimura, Masachika, **57**, 270, 271
Iden, Peter, **37**, 161n
If It Be Not Good, the Devil Is In It, **52**, 82
If This be not a Good Play, the Devil is in it, **54**, 14, 66
If We Shadows, a Midsummer Night's Dream for the twentyfirst century, **49**, 275
If You Know Not Me You Know Nobody, **52**, 60
Iffland, August Wilhelm, **35**, 25
Ignatius, St, **55**, 229n
I Hate Horatio, **49**, 271
Ikonen, Ansa, **10**, 117
Il Pecorone, **55**, 368
Ilie, Gheoghe, **49**, 249
Iljovski, V., **4**, 118; **15**, 142
Ilkley, William, **44**, 202
Illich, Ivan, **46**, 42n
Illsley, W. A., *A Shakespeare Manual for Schools*, **12**, 146 and n.
Illyria Theatre Company, **58**, 302
Ilmari, Wilho, **1**, 116; **9**, 112; **10**, 117
Ilsever, Üner, **14**, 123
Imagery in Shakespeare's plays, *see under* Shakespeare, William, imagery
Imani, Heather, **47**, 217
Imhof, Rudiger, **42**, 178
Imlah, Mick, **58**, 331
Immermann, Karl, **1**, 2
Impey, Oliver, **50**, 190n
In Another Country, **46**, 208
Incest, Drama and Nature's Law 1500–1700 (R. McCabe), **48**, 241
Inchbald, Mrs Elizabeth, **13**, 139; **18**, 18; **51**, 21; **58**, 88, 90
Independent Ballet Wales, **58**, 306
India, report on Shakespeare in, **14**, 120; **15**, 135; **16**, 135
Ing, Catherine, **7**, 4; **15**, 8
  Elizabethan Lyrics reviewed, **6**, 155–6
Ingalls, James F., **49**, 274
Ingamells, Rachel, **53**, 173n

Ingelend, Thomas, **17**, 49n
Ingham, Barrie, **23**, 134; **28**, 147; **51**, 260
Ingham, Patricia, **22**, 182
Inglar, William, **21**, 100
Ingleby, C. M., **8**, 55; **23**, 102, 103; **56**, 99n, 101n; **59**, 270–1, 280, 283; **60**, 234, 234n60, 235
Ingledew, John, **25**, 94n
Inglis, Esther, *Les CL Pseaumes de David*, **1**, 72
Octonaries, **1**, 72
Inglis, Fred, **46**, 239
Inglis, Margaret, **9**, 115; **18**, 128
Inglis, Rob, **46**, 195
Ingram, Angela J. C., **38**, 230
Ingram, Anthony, **35**, 176–7
Ingram, Sir Arthur, **17**, 12
Ingram, David, **17**, 31–2
Ingram, E., **50**, 153n
Ingram, Elizabeth Morley, **54**, 92n, 95n
Ingram, J. H., *Christopher Marlowe and his Associates*, **14**, 9
Ingram, Loveday, **49**, 280; **56**, 266, 293; **57**, 294
Ingram, Martin, **38**, 30n; **46**, 32, 33, 69, 131; **49**, 182n, 183n, 188n, 197n, 198; **51**, 42n; **54**, 171
Ingram, R. W., **19**, 128; **27**, 172; **29**, 2; **30**, 198; **39**, 215, 228; **47**, 51n; **57**, 238; **60**, 8n17
Ingram, W. G., **19**, 161; **31**, 164; **34**, 180; **40**, 41n, 218; **56**, 72n, 74n
Ingram, William, **26**, 175–6; **28**, 168; **41**, 221, 242; **44**, 147, 148n, 150n, 153n; **45**, 102n, 105n; **46**, 232; **47**, 51; **50**, 161n; **60**, 45n41, 54n25
Innes, Christopher, **38**, 236; **58**, 159, 358
Innes, Michael, **5**, 134; **9**, 13; **56**, 102n
Innes, Paul, **51**, 294–5
Innocent III, Pope, **20**, 26n; **32**, 132n; **49**, 80
Innocent, Harold, **38**, 207, 211, 213
Innogen, **11**, 43, 44
Inns of Court, *see under* London
Ino, Mikio, **19**, 141
Inoue, Hidenori, **60**, 130, 135–40
Inoue, Yasushi, **60**, 135–6n18
Inshaw, David, **49**, 129
Institor, H., **28**, 119
Institution of a Gentleman (1555), **14**, 90
Intertextuality in Romance and Renaissance Drama: The Staging of Nostalgia, **46**, 210
Ionesco, Eugène, **16**, 19, 34, 70, 150; **18**, 156; **22**, 4; **24**, 19; **43**, 222; **55**, 153, 346; **57**, 112, 114, 116, 119–24
Ionescu, Serban, **46**, 196
Ioppolo, Grace, **43**, 265n; **46**, 149n, 256, 257; **49**, 34; **52**, 325; **55**, 381, 382; **60**, 157n16
Ipatov, V. M., **54**, 148n
Ipi Tombi, **52**, 156
Irace, Kathleen O., **45**, 198–9; **46**, 254; **49**, 27, 30, 35, 313, 330–1; **52**, 311–12; **56**, 95n; **59**, 8, 383
Irby, James E., **34**, 161n
Ireland, David, **59**, 340
Ireland, Kenny, **44**, 195; **48**, 232; **50**, 227; **51**, 263; **52**, 261; **54**, 287; **55**, 331
Ireland, Samuel and William, **41**, 24
Ireland, Samuel, engraver, **1**, 82, 87n; **3**, 53; **5**, 57n; **24**, 168; **51**, 47n; **56**, 188; **59**, 109, 111, 118
Ireland, William Henry, forger, **3**, 53; **6**, 60; **21**, 149; **25**, 187; **29**, 136; **43**, 88; **47**, 256; **51**, 269; **52**, 266; **53**, 318; **54**, 50n; **55**, 90; **56**, 188; **59**, 108–22, 122n57
Ireson, J. C., **57**, 115
Irigaray, Luce, **50**, 247; **56**, 146–7, 158
'Irish Revival', dramatists of, **16**, 62
Irish, Neil, **53**, 283; **54**, 285; **55**, 333
Irons, Jeremy, **40**, 177, 180–1; **41**, 188, 191; **42**, 156, 160
Irons, Nicholas, **53**, 282
Irvin, Eric, **24**, 167n
'Shakespeare in the Early Sydney Theatre', **22**, 125–33
Irvin, Polly, **42**, 152; **44**, 201; **52**, 254
Irving, George, **46**, 202; **48**, 193
Irving, H. B., **9**, 17, 20
Irving, Sir Henry, **1**, 61, 72; **2**, 1, 2, 9, 19; **4**, 102, 105; **5**, 107, 144n; **7**, 29, 121, 122; **8**, 69, 75; **9**, 17, 18, 21, 56; **10**, 76n, 149, 150; **11**, 124; **13**, 79; **14**, 151; **16**, 21; **18**, 59, 60, 63, 67, 72, 104; **23**, 173; **24**, 14, 37; **25**, 118; **28**, 171; **29**, 138, 142, 143, 176; **31**, 188; **32**, 18, 19, 21, 27n, 29, 30, 31, 32, 33n, 35; **34**, 115; **35**, 2, 3, 8, 9, 12, 14, 16, 17, 19, 34, 175; **36**, 74; **38**, 209; **40**, 1, 12, 39; **41**, 23, 56, 224; **44**, 106n; **45**, 32, 35; **48**, 67; **49**, 2, 4, 111, 126, 136, 306; **50**, 262; **52**, 99, 104–5, 292; **53**, 229, 230n, 327; **54**, 249, 315; **56**, 111, 112; **57**, 68, 81, 83, 91, 92, 93, 94; **59**, 65, 150, 202, 286–7, 294, 374
Irving, Lawrence, **35**, 9; **52**, 105n
Irving, Michael, **42**, 153; **47**, 104
Irving, Washington, **1**, 81, 82; **9**, 102, 110n; **14**, 111; **15**, 136; **35**, 104n; **43**, 228; **54**, 302; **58**, 143
Isaac, Megan Lynn, **56**, 301
Isaacs, J., **1**, 10; **10**, 144; **11**, 148; **15**, 8
Isaacson, Hertha, **9**, 100n
Isabella of the Netherlands, Archduchess, **3**, 87–8
Isabella, sister of Philip III, **33**, 162
Isabelle of France, Queen of England, **60**, 75
Isaiah, **36**, 15
Isaksen, Ike, **50**, 229; **57**, 126
Iselin, Pierre, **47**, 230
Isene, Ola, **10**, 120; **11**, 121
Iser, Wolfgang, **37**, 159; **41**, 204; **55**, 155
Isham, Sir Gyles, **9**, 17, 141
İşhan, Fuat, **18**, 130
Ishanturayeva, Sara, **6**, 125
Isherwood, Christopher, **36**, 30; **49**, 227
Isherwood, Millicent, **15**, 144
Ishi, Mitsuru, **56**, 289
Island Princess, The, **52**, 211–13
Isler, Alan D., **22**, 155, 171; **23**, 166; **25**, 174; **52**, 256
Isleworth Actors Comapny, **58**, 306
Islip, Adam, **54**, 94n, 96; **55**, 29n, 30n
Isocrates, **7**, 135
Ad Demonicum, **11**, 139
Isoda, Aki, **42**, 162; **51**, 262
Isozaki, Arata, **46**, 193
Israel, Jonathan I., **60**, 239n13
Israel, report on Shakespeare in, **5**, 113; **6**, 121; **8**, 120; **9**, 114; **10**, 119; **12**, 114; **13**, 129; **14**, 120
The Children of, **8**, 17
Israel, Robert, **50**, 231
Iswolsky, Helene, **44** 69n; **46**, 18n; **55**, 240n
Italy, as setting for Elizabethan literature, **17**, 45–8

INDEX

Italy, report on Shakespeare in, **1**, 116; **2**, 127, 129; **3**, 117–18; **4**, 128; **5**, 113; **6**, 121; **7**, 112–13; **8**, 120; **9**, 114; **10**, 119–20; **11**, 121; **12**, 114–15; **13**, 129; **14**, 121; **15**, 136; **16**, 135–6; **18**, 125–6
  Elizabethan conception of, **7**, 95–6
  Shakespeare's knowledge of, **7**, 96–106
Itzhaki, Yedidia, **53**, 303–5
Iures, Marcel, **48**, 17, 19; **49**, 277
Ivan IV, Tsar, **17**, 22
Ivanov, D. V., **54**, 140n
Ivanov, Vyacheslav, **54**, 140–2, 145
Ivanovich, Dimitry, **48**, 144
Ive, Paul, **58**, 36
Ivernel, Daniel, **18**, 123
Ives, E. W., **15**, 172; **17**, 73–86, 78n; **19**, 148; **38**, 21n; **44**, 17
  'The Law and the Lawyers', **17**, 73–86
  Tom Skelton—A Seventeenth-century Jester, **13**, 90–105
Ivory, Abraham, **58**, 243
Ivory, James, **57**, 262
Iwai, Katsuhito, **45**, 89
Iwasaki, I., **26**, 161
Iwasaki, Soji, **28**, 157; **38**, 10; **46**, 214; **22**, 161; **27**, 179
Iwaszkiewicz, Jarosław, **9**, 115
Iwuji, Chuk, **55**, 296
Iyengar, K. R. S., **19**, 137; **20**, 156
Izdorczyk, Zbigniew, **57**, 242
Izod, Mrs, **1**, 83
Izubuchi, Hiroshi, **50**, 248

Jaarsma, Richard J., **47**, 156n, 157n, 158n, 159
Jack, A. A., **9**, 9
Jack, Hannah, **52**, 263
Jack, Ian, **14**, 11; **41**, 109n
Jack, Jane H., **10**, 140, 145; **19**, 3, 8
Jack Juggler, **1**, 64; **20**, 64
Jackson, Adrian, **47**, 214; **57**, 272; **58**, 304; **60**, 314
Jackson, Andrew, **24**, 88
Jackson, Anthony R., **52**, 37n
Jackson, Sir Barry, **1**, 107; **2**, 10, 12–13, 14, 15; **4**, 106; **7**, 107, 125, 146; **9**, 18, 19, 57–8; **11**, 124; **12**, 80, 82; **16**, 19, 25, 26; **35**, 2; **38**, 17; **40**, 16; **43**, 172; **47**, 90, 91; **48**, 194, 264; **50**, 30; **51**, 141, 144; **52**, 288; **55**, 133; **56**, 123
  'On Producing *Henry VI*', **6**, 49–52
  'Producing the Comedies', **8**, 74–80
Jackson, Berners A. W., **25**, 173n; **26**, 176n; **27**, 163n, 166n, 172; **31**, 6n; **32**, 63n, 223; **34**, 106n
Jackson, G. Maxwell, **12**, 119
Jackson, Gabriele Bernhard, **34**, 131, 135n; **42**, 187n; **43**, 9n; **46**, 117n
Jackson, Glenda, **33**, 178; **41**, 46; **44**, 95; **54**, 312
Jackson, Henry, **10**, 14, 15, 25n; **46**, 62, 64
Jackson, Holbrook, **33**, 86n; **46**, 118n
Jackson, Howard, **35**, 169–70
Jackson, J. R. de J., **19**, 143; **21**, 141; **23**, 175
Jackson, James L., **18**, 57n; **35**, 178, 189
Jackson, John E., **56**, 328
Jackson, MacDonald P., **18**, 181; **20**, 162, 178; **21**, 146; **26**, 172–3; **29**, 171, 181–2; **32**, 237, 243–4; **34**, 190, 193; **35**, 190; **36**, 184n, 192; **40**, 156, 224, 235n; **41**, 231n, 232, 236n; **42**, 43n, 200; **43**, 268n; **44**, 233; **45**, 201–3; **46**, 257n; **49**, 319; **50**, 287–8; **51**, 317, 324, 327–8, 334; **52**, 297n, 317; **54**, 322; **57**, 300, 309, 339; **58**, 343, 357; **59**, 6n21, 6n22, 22n11, 31, 32n59, 70n5, 70n8, 216, 217, 218; **60**, 109n33
Jackson, Nancy, **7**, 125
Jackson, Peter, **14**, 126
Jackson, Philip, **47**, 187
Jackson, R. L. P., **46**, 219
Jackson, Richard, **49**, 232
Jackson, Russell, **29**, 176; **31**, 187; **32**, 19n; **34**, 172; **37**, 198, 199; **39**, 13, 220; **41**, 23n; **42**, 39n, 199; **43**, 185; **44**, 94n; **46**, 7, 256n; **48**, 205, 264; **49**, 116n, 128n; **50**, 262–3; **51**, 3; **52**, 193n; **53**, 236; **54**, 306, 335–6; **55**, 382–3; **56**, 113n, 136n; **59**, 203n28, 203n32; **60**, 168
Jackson, Samuel L., **56**, 305
Jackson, Shannon, **60**, 168
Jackson, Vincent, **15**, 3
Jackson, W. Spencer, **10**, 76n; **49**, 113n
Jackson, William, **36**, 140; **51**, 91, 93
Jackson, William A., **6**, 61; **11**, 98, 154; **15**, 128; **17**, 31n; **31**, 191; **55**, 32n; **60**, 266n40
Jack Straw, **17**, 43; **52**, 85
Jacob and Esau, **17**, 201; **20**, 25n, 64
Jacob, Giles, **17**, 91n
Jacob, Irene, **51**, 265
Jacob, J., **17**, 171n
Jacob, Joseph, **52**, 210n
Jacob, Margaret, **51**, 55n
Jacob, Rik, **13**, 125
Jacobi, Sir Derek, **36**, 152, 154; **39**, 93, 105; **43**, 180, 183–4, 206, 213, 250–1; **44**, 194, 200; **45**, 53, 56, 60–2, 157, 192; **47**, 7n; **48**, 208, 223, 231; **50**, 262; **51**, 259; **54**, 249; **56**, 167–9, 173, 257, 273–5, 277; **57**, 81, 171, 264, 297; **58**, 306
Jacobi, W., **8**, 8
Jacobs, Alfred, **53**, 294
Jacobs, Arthur, **41**, 225
Jacobs, Edward C., **32**, 235
Jacobs, Henry E., **33**, 188n; **46**, 92n; **54**, 41n
Jacobs, Joseph, **48**, 47n, 187n
Jacobs, Kathryn, **57**, 311
Jacobs, Nicholas, **29**, 175
Jacobs, Richard, **34**, 185, 195–6
Jacobs, Rik, **10**, 115
Jacobs, Sally, **24**, 125; **33**, 177; **48**, 202
Jacobson, Claire, **35**, 66n
Jacobson, Howard, **43**, 10n
Jacobson-Gonzalez, Max, **45**, 146
Jacobus, Mary, **52**, 63
Jacquemont, Maurice, **10**, 118; **12**, 112; **14**, 119
Jacquet, Roger, **57**, 119
Jacquot, Jean, **7**, 11n, 142; **9**, 113; **10**, 118; **11**, 120; **12**, 112; **13**, 160; **15**, 9, 138; **16**, 56; **18**, 185; **19**, 105n; **20**, 18, 168; **27**, 170; **43**, 158n; **48**, 137n; **50**, 30n
  George Chapman, **14**, 12
  Les Fêtes de la Renaissance, **12**, 144
Jaeger, Ronald, W., **26**, 173
Jaffa, Harry V., **56**, 222n
Jaffe, Monte, **44**, 195; **46**, 194, 200
Jaffrey, Raza, **58**, 278
Jaffrey, Saeed, **44**, 198
Jagendorf, Zvi, **53**, 299
Jäger, A., **59**, 134n63

Jaggard, Isaac, **13**, 163, 166; **14**, 158 and n., 161, 162; **24**, 170, 178; **60**, 263, 266
Jaggard, Isaac and William, **53**, 78n, 337
Jaggard, John, **60**, 256, 257
Jaggard, William, bibliographer, printer of the First Folio, **1**, 57, 59, 75; **3**, 47, 145; **5**, 21, 22, 23, 24n, 145, 147; **6**, 167, 170, 171; **7**, 52, 54, 151, 153; **8**, 95, 154, 155, 156; **9**, 84, 155; **10**, 152, 156; **11**, 85, 150, 151, 154; **12**, 147–9; **14**, 166; **16**, 177; **18**, 11; **20**, 172; **21**, 160, 162; **22**, 181, 182; **23**, 185; **25**, 197; **26**, 41, 103–4, 109, 181, 182; **27**, 180, 181, 182, 185; **28**, 180; **29**, 178; **32**, 108; **33**, 2, 205; **34**, 186; **36**, 191; **37**, 206, 209; **38**, 91n; **42**, 70, 123–4; **43**, 82n; **44**, 113, 114; **46**, 249; **47**, 260, 270; **48**, 279; **49**, 116n; **59**, 128, 129, 132, 133, 134; **60**, 258, 252–8, 266n42
Shakespeare Bibliography, **3**, 48; **7**, 91
Jagger, Mick, **57**, 145–58
Jago, David M., **32**, 217
Jahali, Faezeh, **60**, 301Fig.52
Jahn, J. D., **27**, 156
Jakobson, Roman, **31**, 54n, 56n; **35**, 117n; **54**, 153n
Jakubec, Jan, **4**, 115n
James I, King (James VI of Scotland), **1**, 21, 32, 71, 82, 125; **2**, 24, 25, 31, 34, 70, 146, 148; **3**, 35, 52, 93; **4**, 10, 35, 36–7, 38 *ff.*, 95, 155–6; **5**, 68, 138n, 140, 149; **6**, 106, 161–2; **7**, 39, 68n, 85, 114; **9**, 11, 12, 89n; **10**, 28; **11**, 63, 71, 76, 100, 103–5, 114n, 115n; **12**, 137n; **13**, 104n; **14**, 27, 80, 85, 155–6, 159; **15**, 1, 125; **17**, 5, 10, 12, 26–7, 29, 29, 35, 49, 56, 80, 109, 112, 118, 128, 164; **19**, 2–3, 8, 45, 52, 59, 62–4; **20**, 163; **21**, 47–9, 52, 130, 135, 140; **23**, 120, 121, 151, 162; **25**, 7, 180; **26**, 34, 35, 36, 37, 40, 41, 42, 43, 44, 45, 46, 47, 72, 98; **27**, 95, 133, 172; **28**, 15, 16, 19, 20, 21, 22, 23, 24, 25, 27, 28, 64, 65, 68, 93, 117–23, 163, 170; **29**, 3, 4; **30**, 161, 162, 165, 195; **31**, 41, 101, 102, 103, 104; **32**, 134, 198, 231, 245; **33**, 147, 162, 168; **34**, 142, 180, 183; **35**, 72, 129, 130, 131, 132, 133, 136, 138, 178; **36**, 139, 165, 174; **37**, 197; **38**, 19, 20, 21, 24, 59, 85, 128, 215; **39**, 219; **40**, 138–9, 199, 218; **41**, 216; **42**, 197; **43**, 3, 4, 7, 55–7, 63–4, 81, 92–3, 95, 97, 146, 225, 238, 240–2; **44**, 75, 77, 78, 82, 83, 128, 154, 155, 158, 159, 226–8, 247; **45**, 109, 110; **46**, 26n, 217, 219, 234, 245; **47**, 24, 47, 50, 53, 59n, 113, 115, 172, 245, 261; **48**, 52, 114, 137, 251, 257, 259; **49**, 16, 20; **50**, 19–21, 142, 242, 245, 260, 268–9; **51**, 276, 284, 293, 317, 334; **52**, 80, 133–5, 143, 145, 147, 182, 214, 293; **53**, 64, 66, 68–9, 201, 326; **54**, 5, 6, 34, 40, 43–4, 5, 61, 62n, 129, 132–6, 138, 168–70, 177–9, 194, 196–8, 349; **55**, 6, 36n, 37n, 40, 43, 45–7, 50–1, 86, 93, 226, 234, 245, 357, 370–1; **56**, 71, 215–22, 225, 226, 354; **57**, 1, 2, 4, 5, 6, 8, 9, 12, 13, 21, 27, 30, 31, 36, 70, 72, 73, 74, 137, 191, 192, 247, 316; **59**, 144, 145, 250, 251n90, 253, 379–80; **60**, 51, 53, 113, 119, 121
Basilikon Doron, **1**, 21; **2**, 70, 72, 73, 75; **4**, 39, 40; **5**, 68; **6**, 157; **10**, 145; **19**, 3, 150; **20**, 153
connection with Amphitheatre plans, **2**, 26, 27, 28
Counterblaste to Tobacco, **19**, 36, 48
Daemonologie, **1**, 71; **4**, 41, 42, 43, 47n; **15**, 112; **19**, 4, 37
Fruitful Meditation, **10**, 140
interest in theories of government, **2**, 70
treatise on government, **4**, 36
True Lawe of Free Monarchies, **2**, 70
James II, King, **17**, 176
James IV, King of Scotland, **26**, 44
James, Adam, **54**, 250
James, Caryn, **45**, 53n
James, Clive, **36**, 23n; **55**, 174
James, D. G., **5**, 83; **9**, 2, 4, 14–15; **10**, 99; **13**, 17, 18, 30; **15**, 121; **18**, 42, 43; **21**, 2; **22**, 165; **29**, 5, 87, 89; **33**, 7, 8; **43**, 16n; **46**, 145n
The Dream of Learning, **13**, 18n, 19n
The Dream of Learning reviewed, **6**, 148–9
'Keats and *King Lear*', **13**, 58–68
The Life of Reason, **13**, 39n
James, Darius, **52**, 261; **53**, 284–5; **54**, 295; **55**, 323; **56**, 294, 296; **57**, 296; **59**, 344; **60**, 321, 325
James, Deborah, **50**, 93n
James, Emrys, **23**, 132; **25**, 167; **28**, 139; **29**, 155; **31**, 147, 149, 150; **32**, 223; **37**, 165, 172; **57**, 279
James, Finlay, **7**, 125; **13**, 139
James, Gerald, **26**, 144, 145
James, Geraldine, **42**, 140; **43**, 188, 206; **44**, 197; **60**, 309
James, H., **55**, 203n
James, Heather, **52**, 271; **59**, 367
James, Henry, **4**, 50; **7**, 29; **17**, 43; **18**, 116; **20**, 33, 35, 36, 40n; **21**, 141; **22**, 5; **24**, 104; **30**, 89, 93, 94; **31**, 62n; **32**, 183; **34**, 65; **35**, 33; **36**, 32, 33n, 36; **43**, 112; **46**, 131n; **49**, 4, 14, 67; **51**, 28; **53**, 7, 117–18, 120, 192, 297; **56**, 86–7, 126; **57**, 92, 127; **59**, 360
James, Revd J. A., **54**, 81
James, Jamie, **54**, 25n
James, Jeremy, **49**, 277
James, Karl, **42**, 151; **47**, 215; **48**, 234; **49**, 277; **51**, 258; **53**, 279
James, Lennie, **48**, 226; **50**, 202–3; **51**, 269
James, Louis, **25**, 117, 118; **35**, 12n
James, Mervyn, **44**, 13n; **55**, 211n
James, Mike, **44**, 200
James, Oscar, **35**, 151; **53**, 259
James, P. D., **55**, 148
James, Paul, **51**, 257; **54**, 284
James, Peter, **44**, 102
James, Polly, **25**, 168
James, Dr Richard, **3**, 53; **38**, 86, 87, 94, 97, 98n, 99; **41**, 217; **54**, 100
James, Rosalind, **59**, 342
James, Sid, **57**, 260
James, Thomas, **4**, 78, 79; **59**, 254n1
James, Trilby, **45**, 156
James, William, **54**, 29–30
Jameson, Mrs A. B., **4**, 3; **20**, 73n
Jameson, Anna, **32**, 15, 16, 17; **38**, 198; **44**, 206, 241; **46**, 142n, 143n; **49**, 131–4; **51**, 280; **53**, 92, 94, 110, 312; **54**, 323; **55**, 109–11; **56**, 132, 304; **58**, 98, 104, 179; **59**, 85–7
Jameson, Anne, **47**, 97
Jameson, Caroline, **42**, 54n, 57n
Jameson, Fredric, **44**, 67; **48**, 15; **49**, 90, 91n; **50**, 243; **53**, 164n; **56**, 10; **57**, 48, 50; **58**, 189, 193; **59**, 151n17; **60**, 333
Jameson, Louise, **52**, 260
Jameson, Stephen, **45**, 145; **48**, 231; **49**, 273; **50**, 230; **58**, 299; **60**, 324
Jameson, Susan, **44**, 196
Jamete, Esteban, **23**, 80, 81
Jamicson, Bruce, **53**, 277; **55**, 323; **59**, 339–40
Jamieson, Eve, **49**, 274

Jamieson, Mark, **45**, 153
Jamieson, Michael, **28**, 89n; **32**, 2, 9; **41**, 63n; **42**, 99n, 100n, 108n
'The Problem Plays, 1920–1970: a Retrospect', **25**, 1–10
Jamieson, Nigel, **44**, 196
Jamieson, Thomas H., **23**, 147; **32**, 165n
Jamois, Marguerite, **16**, 133
Jan, Sara, **59**, 374
Janakiram, Alur, **32**, 213, 215; **34**, 184
Janaro, R. P., **8**, 141–2; **9**, 11–12
Jancsó, Adrienne, **14**, 120
Janelle, P., **17**, 124n
Janicker, Irene, **23**, 170
Janjua, Kaleem, **51**, 222–3
Janko, J., **9**, 106
Jankowski, Theodora A., **44**, 227; **53**, 299
Janowitz, Henry D., **42**, 213
Jansen, Catherine, **44**, 195
Jansohn, Christa, **57**, 310
Janson, H. W., **26**, 116n; **37**, 134n, 136, 137, 139n
Janssen family of stonemasons, Gheerart Janssen's bust of Shakespeare, **3**, 4
the Janssens family, **7**, 139
Janssen, Gheerart (Gerard Johnson), **40**, 216; **57**, 234
Janssen portrait of Shakespeare, *see under* Shakespeare, William, portraits
Janzen, Henry D., **44**, 256
Japan, report on Shakespeare in, **11**, 121; **12**, 114; **13**, 130; **14**, 121; **16**, 136
Jaques, Francis, **44**, 256
Jardine, Alice, **46**, 4
Jardine, Lisa, **38**, 224; **41**, 198; **42**, 107n; **46**, 6, 9n; **47**, 228; **49**, 205n; **50**, 66n, 71n, 237–8, 240, 254; **51**, 38n; **53**, 234n; **56**, 204n, 313; **57**, 207; **58**, 51, 52, 253
Jardine, Luke, **56**, 261
Jardine, Mick, **53**, 322
Jarman, Anthony, **47**, 18n
Jarman, Chris, **60**, 298
Jarman, Derek, **39**, 77; **45**, 63n, 67, 71–3; **50**, 264; **53**, 149n; **56**, 158; **60**, 199
Jarman, Edward, **47**, 18n
Jarrett-Kerr, Martin, **30**, 63n, 65
Jarry, Alfred, **55**, 346; **57**, 112, 114, 116, 117–19, 121, 123, 124, 125
Jarvis, Andrew, **42**, 94, 161; **43**, 173, 181; **44**, 193, 242; **45**, 133, 146; **46**, 178; **49**, 273; **51**, 266; **52**, 265; **60**, 210
Jarvis, Frank, **41**, 183; **58**, 298; **59**, 343
Jarvis, Martin, **45**, 122
Jarvis, Rachel, **51**, 260
Jarvis, Simon, **49**, 322–3; **51**, 7, 125n, 129, 138; **58**, 11; **59**, 124n2, 128
Jarvis, William, **14**, 120; **15**, 136; **16**, 135
Jason, Neville, **52**, 293
Jaspers, Karl, **19**, 23
Jaster, Margaret Rose, **56**, 305
Jastrzębiec-Kozłowski, Czesław, **9**, 114
Jauch, Sharon L. Jansen, **38**, 231
Jauslin, Christian, **37**, 200n
Jauss, Hans Robert, **37**, 159; **51**, 126, 131, 139; **55**, 112, 113n
Javitch, Daniel, **40**, 123n; **50**, 65, 71n
Jay, Anjali, **60**, 285
Jayasundera, Thusitha, **50**, 217–18; **52**, 235
Jayes, Catherine, **50**, 235; **55**, 328
Jayne, Sears Reynolds, **19**, 119; **21**, 131; **34**, 94n; **36**, 90n; **49**, 209n
Jeaffreson, John Cordy, **17**, 10n, 83n, 91n; **25**, 139, 140n; **36**, 137n; **60**, 74n12, 75n14, 75n18, 76n20
Jeanneret, Michel, **46**, 223
Jeans, H. R., **39**, 43n
Jeans, Ursula, **5**, 122
Jeauneau, René, **11**, 120; **12**, 112; **15**, 133
Jeayes, I. H., **55**, 54n
Jebb, Sir Richard, **53**, 54n
Jed, Stephanie, **49**, 312; **53**, 303
Jeffares, A. Norman, **23**, 146
Jefferies, Richard, **58**, 123
Jefferson, D. W., **23**, 141n; **30**, 11n; **36**, 103n; **39**, 171n
Jefferson, Thomas, **18**, 103; **57**, 129
Jeffery, David, **50**, 29n
Jeffes, Agnes, **33**, 157
Jeffes, Anthony, **33**, 157, 158, 159; **38**, 227
Jeffes, Elizabeth, **33**, 157
Jeffes, Humphrey, **4**, 158; **33**, 157, 158, 159
Jeffes, John, **33**, 157
Jeffes, Richard, Jr, **33**, 157
Jeffes, William, **33**, 157
Jefford, Barbara, **4**, 136–7; **6**, 132; **8**, 138; **16**, 22; **25**, 29; **27**, 142; **31**, 160; **44**, 164, 192; **46**, 166, 167; **47**, 209; **54**, 254–5; **56**, 276, 278; **58**, 56, 57
Jeffrey, D. L., **27**, 158
Jeffrey, Francis, **14**, 83
Jeffrey, Francis Lord, **53**, 104
Jeffrey, L. N., **26**, 161
Jeffrey, Peter, **39**, 196, 197, 202, 203; **41**, 71; **42**, 154; **44**, 186; **45**, 148
Jeffreys, M. D. W., **12**, 137
Jeffs, R., **25**, 149
Jegede, Tunde, **42**, 156
Jehne, Martin, **59**, 355
Jekyll, Joseph, **51**, 63
Jellicoe, Ann, **55**, 160
Jemie, Onwuchekwa, **39**, 175
Jenainati, Cathia, **56**, 8n
Jenkin, Bernard, **7**, 72, 74; **10**, 3; **41**, 86
Jenkins, Anthony W., **31**, 189, 197
Jenkins, Gladys, **24**, 71n, 72n
Jenkins, Harold, **4**, 158; **7**, 107; **8**, 143, 157; **9**, 7, 154n, 155; **10**, 136; **11**, 140; **14**, 162, 164; **16**, 168; **18**, 66; **19**, 124; **20**, 72n, 147; **25**, 196; **26**, 117n; **28**, 153; **30**, 201; **31**, 35; **32**, 8, 45n, 64n, 80, 82, 83–4; **33**, 73; **34**, 105n, 188, 196; **35**, 119n, 177, 184; **36**, 23n, 55, 181–2, 186n; **37**, 198; **38**, 1, 11, 13, 81, 101, 104; **39**, 244, 245; **41**, 13, 37, 241; **42**, 181, 211n; **43**, 267; **45**, 10, 17n, 195n; **48**, 269; **49**, 320; **50**, 198n; **52**, 120n; **54**, 127n; **56**, 93n, 330; **58**, 349, 353; **59**, 6n23, 40, 69n1; **60**, 361, 363
'As You Like It', **8**, 40–51
'"Hamlet" Then Till Now', **18**, 34–45
'Shakespeare's History Plays: 1900–1951', **6**, 1–15
Structural Problems in Shakespeare's Henry the Fourth reviewed, **11**, 138
'The Tragedy of Revenge in Shakespeare and Webster', **14**, 45–55

Jenkins, Henry, **52**, 91n, 92n, 96n
Jenkins, Martin, **44**, 102
Jenkins, Raymond, **19**, 120
Jenkins, Tauriq, **60**, 289
Jenkins, Thomas, **8**, 149; **10**, 13
Jenkins, Warren, **5**, 119
Jenkyns, Richard, **54**, 86
Jenn, Stephen, **44**, 197
Jennens, Charles, **4**, 81; **13**, 74; **57**, 341; **58**, 353; **59**, 163
Jenner, Caryl, **8**, 125
Jenner, Michael, **43**, 209
Jenner, Thomas, **12**, 107, 108n
Jennings, Alex, **42**, 135; **45**, 116, 153; **48**, 202–3, 220–2; **49**, 273, 275; **51**, 231, 242–4, 265; **52**, 255, 262, 289; **55**, 291, 313, 318, 320, 321; **56**, 4n, 298
Jennings, Paul, **23**, 39
Jennings, Sue Emmy, **54**, 291
Jensen, Ashley, **54**, 249–50
Jensen, Ejner, J., **24**, 166n; **41**, 35, 42
Jensen, Jan, **53**, 282
Jensen, Johannes V., **3**, 110, 113
Jensen, Mary Ann, **45**, 51n
Jensen, Michael P., **59**, 161n14, 183n4
Jensen, Niels L., **19**, 140, 145
Jensen, Pamela, **51**, 282
Jensen, Phebe, **50**, 279–81
Jensen, Soren Elung, **39**, 79n
Jentsch, Otto, **60**, 227n24
Jephcott, Edmund, **48**, 26n; **51**, 126n; **55**, 240n
Jephson, Emily, **59**, 122n54
Jephson, Revd John M., **54**, 55
Jepson, Laura, **27**, 11n
Jepson, May, **55**, 330
Jepson, Paul, **44**, 191
Jerónimo, Gilberto, **54**, 152n, 160, 163
Jerome, **15**, 90, 97n; **20**, 26n
Jerome, Ben M., **57**, 249, 256
Jerome, Roger, **12**, 120
Jerome, Sophronius E. H., **54**, 43
Jerrold, Blanchard, **38**, 189
Jerrold, Douglas, **2**, 2; **22**, 128
Jerry McGuire, **55**, 341
Jerusalem, **17**, 38, 42, 44, 46
Jesenská, Zora, **4**, 110–11; **16**, 133
Jespersen, Otto, **3**, 109; **23**, 13, 28; **25**, 192
Growth and Structure of the English Language, **7**, 2
Jess-Cooke, Carolyn, **60**, 355
Jesson, Paul, **45**, 117, 156; **46**, 7, 182; **49**, 245; **51**, 239–41, 243, 260; **56**, 261; **59**, 318; **60**, 310, 329
Jeter, Camille L., **47**, 211
Jeter, Derek, **60**, 144–5
Jetter, Kurt, **23**, 118
Jew, The, **14**, 32
Jew of Malta, The, **52**, 78, 105; **50**, 238, 255
Jew of Venice, The, **52**, 99; **20**, 169
Jew of Venice, The (Granville), **48**, 54
Jewel, John, **23**, 84; **54**, 69n; **57**, 200; **59**, 265n30
Jewel, Bishop John, **9**, 25; **17**, 106, 121
Jewell, Sharon L., **56**, 152n
Jewell, Simon, **30**, 196; **44**, 150; **47**, 48, 51
Jewers, Ray, **35**, 148
Jewett, Henry, **53**, 216, 230
Jewkes, Wilfred T., **20**, 15n, 154; **41**, 93n; **53**, 2n; **59**, 11; **55**, 28n, 30n
Act Division in Elizabethan and Jacobean Plays, **13**, 117
Jewkesbury, Edward, **42**, 131
Jewne, Clayton, **53**, 275
Jha, A., **8**, 9
Ji, Junxiang, **57**, 176
Jian, Sheng Chuan, **42**, 152
Jiang, David, **57**, 170
Jiang, Liu, **57**, 173
Jiang, Qing, **57**, 172
Jiao, Juyin, **57**, 171
Jiaxiu, Sun, **45**, 89n
Jiji, Vera M., **30**, 183
Jirásek, A., **9**, 108
Jitianu, Dan, **45**, 146
Jo, Haruhiko, **43**, 215
Joan of Arc, **38**, 223; **42**, 23–35; **44**, 58, 227
Joan of Habsburg, **7**, 105n
'Joan. Patridophilus' (*pseud.*), **60**, 277n36
Joanny (Jean-Baptiste-Bernard Brisebarre), **3**, 103
Jobin, Sybille, **37**, 158n
Jobson, Rebecca, **51**, 258
Jochum, Klaus Peter, **33**, 196–7
Jochums, M. C., **26**, 154
Jodelle, Etienne, **6**, 93n; **24**, 157
Jofen, Jean, **26**, 172
Johan Johan, **13**, 153
Johan the Evangelyst, Enterlude of, **3**, 45
Johansen, Ib, **48**, 263
Johansson, Mats, **18**, 128
Johansson, Mia, **55**, 331
Johansson, Stig, **49**, 328n; **53**, 39n
John de Trevisa, **37**, 86
John of Bordeaux, **52**, 85; **2**, 52
John of Gaunt and Robin Hood and Little John, **55**, 29n
John of Salisbury, **56**, 82n
John Sigismund, Elector of Brandenburg, **36**, 139
John, Anthony, **5**, 119
John, Sir Elton, **45**, 173; **52**, 317
John, Errol, **38**, 213
John, Ivor B., **6**, 35n
John, King, **48**, 71
Johnes, Richard, **60**, 21
Johns, Adrian, **60**, 253, 265–6
Johns, Martin, **45**, 154; **55**, 331
Johnson family of stonemasons, *see* Jannssen
Johnson, Andrew, **44**, 200
Johnson, Anthony L., **40**, 205
Johnson, Barbara A., **42**, 178; **57**, 242
Johnson, Carl, **45**, 152
Johnson, Celia, **39**, 105; **49**, 160
Johnson, Charles, **26**, 114n; **32**, 37–48; **34**, 173; **51**, 45–56; **53**, 301
Johnson, Claudia, **58**, 74, 75, 76, 78, 80, 85
Johnson, Cornelius, **43**, 155; **60**, 223, 249n53
Johnson, Darlene, **49**, 243
Johnson, David, **39**, 189; **50**, 143, 265; **52**, 158n

Johnson, Edward, **2**, 29, 31
Johnson, Ewart, **15**, 145
Johnson, Francis R., **7**, 10; **15**, 176n; **17**, 140n; **19**, 83, 93n
'Printers' "Copy Books"' reviewed, **1**, 131
'Shakespearian Imagery and Senecan Imitation', **2**, 136
Johnson, Geordie, **48**, 236
Johnson, George, **49**, 185
Johnson, Gerald D., **35**, 186; **41**, 14n; **50**, 142, 143n
Johnson, Gloria, **13**, 161
Johnson, Henry Erskine, **11**, 124; **33**, 146n
Johnson, J., **43**, 105n
Johnson, James Turner, **27**, 90n; **48**, 88n
Johnson, Joseph, **55**, 108
Johnson, Judith, **59**, 342
Johnson, Karl, **45**, 63n
Johnson, L. Staley, **46**, 16n, 17n
Johnson, Ladybird, **57**, 136
Johnson, Laurence, **16**, 100
Johnson, Lawrence, **50**, 151, 153
Johnson, Lee, **21**, 81, 84
Johnson, Lesley, **59**, 243n34
Johnson, Linton Kwesi, **48**, 156
Johnson, Lyndon Baines, **18**, 133; **57**, 138, 139, 140, 142, 144, 188
Johnson, Mary, **29**, 34, 37
Johnson, Nora, **52**, 280; **53**, 299
Johnson, Oliver, **43**, 206
Johnson, R. Brimley (ed.), *Letters of Mary Russell Mitford*, **14**, 88n
Johnson, Ralph, **20**, 22
Johnson, Randy, **50**, 199n
Johnson, Rebecca, **53**, 284; **57**, 290; **59**, 301, 302, 303
Johnson, Richard, **11**, 133, 134; **12**, 128; **15**, 147; **16**, 27; **24**, 3n, 8; **26**, 146–7; **38**, 249; **39**, 108; **46**, 182, 183, 184; **47**, 209
Johnson, Richard, *Golden Garland of Princely Delight*, **15**, 40n
Choyce Drollery; Songs and Sonnets, **15**, 40n
Johnson, Richard, Keeper of Newgate, **17**, 93, 220n
Johnson, Robert, **9**, 86, 89n; **11**, 63–6, 69n; **15**, 6; **19**, 105n; **40**, 220; **45**, 172; **48**, 248; **51**, 311
Johnson, Robert Carl, **23**, 168; **24**, 160, 161; **25**, 182
Johnson, S. F., **7**, 130–1; **13**, 168; **14**, 165; **45**, 24n
Johnson, Dr Samuel, **1**, 60; **2**, 109; **3**, 22, 47, 49; **4**, 3, 4, 6, 10, 57–8, 66n, 80, 86, 87, 129; **5**, 1, 51, 105n; **6**, 104–5; **7**, 1, 28, 52, 135; **8**, 52; **9**, 93, 105; **10**, 12, 24, 26n, 28, 85; **12**, 148; **14**, 49, 55n, 78, 80, 142; **15**, 28, 33, 136; **16**, 31–2, 33–4, 51; **18**, 4, 6, 8, 9, 16–19, 108; **19**, 5, 34, 42, 76; **20**, 7, 85–6; **21**, 3, 4, 6, 28n, 149; **22**, 12, 158; **23**, 137, 175; **24**, 18, 48, 107, 153, 177; **25**, 45, 46, 53, 57, 60, 111n; **26**, 71n, 123, 181, 182; **28**, 57, 89, 90–1, 112, 125; **30**, 3n, 58n, 96n, 110, 121, 187, 201, 202; **31**, 1, 5, 9, 10, 105, 111n, 112; **32**, 71, 154n; **33**, 18, 32, 39, 53, 190, 192; **34**, 6, 11, 14, 15, 16, 19, 51, 54, 93n, 104, 144, 168, 170; **35**, 45; **36**, 28, 163, 195; **37**, 45, 100, 142, 147, 149, 150; **38**, 29, 51, 151, 164, 165, 177, 179, 252; **39**, 135, 136, 138, 177, 220; **40**, 72, 137; **41**, 151; **42**, 20, 38–40, 99, 100; **43**, 220, 225; **44**, 131, 138, 139, 207, 246, 251; **45**, 16–18, 91, 130; **46**, 107, 108, 236–7, 242; **47**, 79, 255–6, 266; **49**, 5, 9, 11, 118, 218, 228, 322, 325; **50**, 101–3, 109; **51**, 2, 4, 6, 7, 27, 28, 34, 55–6, 111, 135, 137, 138, 139, 282; **52**, 275, 317–18; **53**, 7, 18, 60n, 72, 92–3, 213, 219, 220, 225–6, 231–2, 337, 342–3; **54**, 10; **55**, 2, 68–70, 77, 97, 102–5, 355, 361, 388; **56**, 99, 209–10; **57**, 28, 85, 112, 115; **58**, 92, 130, 132, 353; **59**, 30n46, 32n58, 43, 57, 59, 93, 115, 125, 127, 128, 130, 133–4, 145, 145n42, 153, 166n30; **60**, 214, 364
Dictionary, **14**, 80
edition of Shakespeare (1765), **4**, 56, 162–3
Proposals for printing the Dramatick Works of William Shakespeare, **11**, 83; **14**, 55n, 81
Proposals for Printing a New Edition of the Plays of William Shakespeare, **4**, 52
The Rambler, **10**, 33; on *Macbeth*, **4**, 53
Johnson, Stan, **44**, 199
Johnson, Stuart, **43**, 206; **46**, 197
Johnson, Thomas, **53**, 279
Johnson, W., **42**, 200
Johnson, Walter, **3**, 3; **43**, 110n; **48**, 3n
Johnson, Wil, **52**, 222, 226; **59**, 343
Johnson, William, **19**, 103; **29**, 34, 37; **30**, 196; **39**, 79n; **49**, 300; **60**, 21–2
Johnson-Haddad, Virginia, **60**, 348–9
Johnston, A., **18**, 167
Johnston, Adrian, **43**, 213; **44**, 197, 201; **49**, 270; **51**, 270
Johnston, Alexandra F., **11**, 99n; **34**, 180n; **43**, 149n, 155n; **47**, 53n; **49**, 16n; **52**, 78n; **53**, 325; **57**, 333
Johnston, Arthur, **46**, 98n
Johnston, Craig, **60**, 310
Johnston, Denis, **1**, 97
Johnston, G. B., **16**, 169
Johnston, Mrs H., **32**, 33
Johnston, H. E., **9**, 55
Johnston, John, **54**, 51; **55**, 134n
Johnston, Margaret, **10**, 131, 132; **14**, 144
Johnston, Susan, **53**, 96
Johnstone, Iain, **45**, 156; **46**, 201; **49**, 270
Jolas, Eugene, **56**, 141n
Joll, Evelyn, **49**, 123n, 125n
Jolles, Frank, **23**, 122
Jolly, Daniel, **60**, 246, 251
Jomes, Richard, **56**, 264
Jonassen, Frederick, **45**, 178
Jones, Andrew, **54**, 288
Jones, Ann Rosalind, **49**, 303; **53**, 15n–16n, 297; **55**, 371–3; **58**, 34, 40, 41, 70; **60**, 73n3
Jones, Bob, Junior, **12**, 118
Jones, C. P., **53**, 77
Jones, Charlotte, **56**, 289; **57**, 291; **58**, 300; **59**, 339
Jones, Dan, **50**, 228
Jones, Daniel, **7**, 3; **32**, 194
Jones, David, **22**, 139–40; **23**, 132; **27**, 146, 148; **31**, 145; **33**, 173, 187; **39**, 94n, 95–7; **41**, 227
Jones, David E., **20**, 154; **43**, 267
Jones, Doris L., **47**, 4n
Jones, Dudley, **1**, 109; **10**, 130
Jones, E. L., **25**, 94n
Jones, Eldred D., **19**, 149–50; **35**, 106; **42**, 101n; **48**, 127n; **50**, 120; **51**, 160n; **52**, 102n, 204n
Jones, Elinor Morgan, **52**, 260

Jones, Emrys, **23**, 162n; **26**, 151; **27**, 159; **29**, 3, 4, 67, 160; **31**, 163, 169; **32**, 239; **33**, 12, 177, 198, 201; **34**, 107, 108; **35**, 109n, 110n, 111n; **36**, 152, 161; **37**, 117; **38**, 5, 9, 10, 99n, 202, 203; **39**, 230; **40**, 70, 71n, 75n, 205; **41**, 131; **44**, 245; **45**, 193n; **46**, 224–5; **48**, 273; **49**, 146; **53**, 177; **55**, 200n, 212n, 244–5; **56**, 312; **57**, 236; **59**, 372
'*Othello, Lepanto*, and the Cyprus Wars', **21**, 47–52
Jones, Eric, **14**, 128
Jones, Ernest, **2**, 138; **4**, 11; **5**, 131; **9**, 2, 12–13, 15; **19**, 132; **20**, 147; **21**, 133; **30**, 112, 113, 114; **32**, 100n; **40**, 1; **43**, 252; **45**, 6, 40, 44, 48, 51, 54, 75; **53**, 242; **57**, 306
Jones, Ernst, **56**, 113
Hamlet and Oedipus reviewed, **4**, 140
Jones, Fanny, **43**, 209
Jones, Freddie, **45**, 123–4
Jones, Gemma, **35**, 148; **36**, 153; **37**, 164, 166, 170; **39**, 233; **46**, 83n, 174, 180, 181
Jones, George, **1**, 83
Jones, Gillian, **59**, 205
Jones, Gordon P., **33**, 191; **37**, 195; **46**, 43n
Jones, Griff Rhys, **46**, 201; **47**, 210
Jones, Griffith, **33**, 173; **41**, 169
Jones, Gwilym P., **32**, 43n; **51**, 54n
Jones, H. S., **56**, 210n
Jones, H. W., **15**, 180; **35**, 183n
Jones, Mrs Harriet, **22**, 128, 130–2
Jones, Harris, **36**, 144, 145, 147
Jones, Henry Arthur, **34**, 9
Jones, Inigo, **1**, 11; **7**, 144; **10**, 71; **12**, 13; **20**, 21; **23**, 125–9; **24**, 13; **26**, 33, 35, 41, 45, 57–8, 169; **28**, 168, 170; **29**, 2; **30**, 157–68, 191; **31**, 102, 186; **32**, 233; **33**, 140, 145, 198; **35**, 129, 132, 133, 134, 135, 136, 137, 138, 139n; **36**, 115n; **37**, 196, 197; **39**, 227, 228; **41**, 1, 2, 5, 49; **42**, 194, 197; **43**, 160, 162, 167n, 236; **45**, 109–11; **47**, 16n, 18, 27, 84; **48**, 140; **49**, 17; **50**, 165; **52**, 47, 79n; **53**, 326; **55**, 249–50, 347; **56**, 217; **60**, 32, 54, 58, 114–15
drawings of Bankside, **1**, 33–4
Jones, J. H., **26**, 162
Jones, J. T., **2**, 151
Jones, Jack, **58**, 229
Jones, James, **34**, 185
Jones, James Earl, **39**, 86
Jones, Jeanne, **60**, 10–11
Jones, Jo L. A., **45**, 147
Jones, John, **9**, 135; **41**, 194, 205; **50**, 278–9, 281; **55**, 55
Jones, John, of Gelli Lyfdy, calligrapher, **17**, 100
Jones, Kirsty, **60**, 321
Jones, M. W., **15**, 169
Jones, Malcolm, **44**, 197; **50**, 257; **60**, 241n24, 241n25
Jones, Margo, **2**, 129; **5**, 116; **6**, 124; **9**, 117
Jones, Marion, **20**, 73n; **41**, 224
Jones, Mark Lewis, **46**, 162; **47**, 206; **51**, 207, 215; **53**, 244, 246; **54**, 286
Jones, Matthew, **46**, 202
Jones, Mike, **46**, 192
Jones, Millard T., **28**, 180; **30**, 206
Jones, Monique, **52**, 255
Jones, Nicholas, **53**, 272; **54**, 289; **60**, 306–7
Jones, Norman L., **52**, 103, 104n; **53**, 67n; **54**, 125n; **56**, 28n
Jones, Osheen, **56**, 4n, 14
Jones, Ozzie, **52**, 262
Jones, Pam, **51**, 263
Jones, Paul, **42**, 157; **44**, 194
Jones, Peter, **32**, 213
Jones, Richard, **32**, 194, 196, 197; **33**, 153, 154, 157, 158–9; **36**, 140–1, 144, 145, 147; **50**, 153–4; **53**, 277; **57**, 294; **58**, 228, 229
Jones, Robert, **15**, 6; **42**, 155; **44**, 238; **48**, 235; **51**, 239, 260, 269; **52**, 260, 263; **53**, 255, 263, 285; **54**, 290
First Booke of Songs & Ayres, **3**, 56
manuscript poem of, **1**, 71
Jones, Robert C., **21**, 100; **30**, 192
Jones, Robert Edmond, **9**, 18; **35**, 2; **41**, 58–60; **58**, 358
Jones, Ron Cephas, **58**, 304; **60**, 162
Jones, Tina, **47**, 214
Jones, Toby, **51**, 220; **58**, 275
Jones, Tom, **45**, 157; **57**, 155
Jones, Trent, **46**, 202
Jones, Ursula, **50**, 217
Jones, W. J., **17**, 75n; **22**, 169; **27**, 94n, 101, 103; **29**, 93n, 94n, 95n, 96n, 99n
Jones, William, **21**, 100; **25**, 148; **33**, 14; **43**, 152, 155, 158, 161; **51**, 199n; **60**, 113n48
Jones, William M., **19**, 147
Jones, Zachary, **23**, 160
Jones-Davies, Marie-Thérèse, **19**, 135; **22**, 172n; **28**, 162; **39**, 230; **44**, 60n; **50**, 257; **56**, 310
Un Peintre de la Vie Londonienne: Thomas Dekker, **14**, 12
Jones-Davies, Margaret, **58**, 312
Jones-Davies, Sue, **44**, 196
Jong, Erica, **44**, 41
Jonic, Bettina, **48**, 231
Jonne, Nicholas, **51**, 262
Jonns, Daniel, **22**, 121
Jonson, Ben, **1**, 29, 54, 61, 71, 82, 103, 126; **2**, 59, 60, 120; **3**, 1, 14, 17, 19, 22, 30, 45, 48, 65, 66, 89, 90, 137, 139; **4**, 4, 29, 93, 95, 129, 149, 157; **5**, 53; **6**, 57, 61, 72; **7**, 1, 3, 4, 6, 7, 11n, 17–18, 23, 24, 84, 86, 87, 88, 89n, 100, 105, 138, 141, 142, 144; **8**, 6, 11, 17, 18, 38, 61, 66, 159; **9**, 11, 70, 144; **10**, 3, 11–14, 21, 23–4, 34–6, 37, 77, 144, 146; **11**, 21, 30n, 64, 65, 69, 71, 72, 73, 74, 85, 99, 102, 105, 107, 109, 115n, 116n, 137; **12**, 17, 86, 134, 140, 143, 144; **13**, 153; **14**, 4, 8, 10, 14n, 27, 29, 31, 44n, 76, 77, 80, 81, 82, 84, 87, 90, 97, 101n, 105, 146, 154; **15**, 3, 8, 27, 62, 99, 102; **16**, 4, 11, 77, 95–7, 126, 164; **17**, 9–12, 46–7, 50n, 51, 63, 73, 136, 171, 177, 183–4, 192, 195–7, 204–5, 207, 212, 216–17, 219; **18**, 46, 187; **19**, 37, 56, 58–9, 86, 145; **20**, 3, 29, 54, 55, 84, 86, 92, 117, 151, 163; **21**, 48, 52n, 67, 140, 145, 161; **22**, 1, 2, 8, 35, 43–6, 47–9, 51–8, 109, 110, 111, 115, 171, 172; **23**, 33, 46, 100, 119, 141, 160, 167n, 169–70; **24**, 13, 40, 47, 48, 52, 62, 68, 107, 127, 146, 150, 164, 165; **25**, 9, 68, 78, 100, 104n, 125, 162, 190, 193; **26**, 1, 3, 4, 15, 33, 34, 35, 39, 40, 41, 45, 48, 56–7, 90, 94, 96, 168, 169, 170; **27**, 83, 112, 119, 120, 121, 122, 123, 124, 126, 127, 135, 176, 178; **28**, 57, 59, 134, 149, 164, 174; **29**, 9, 110, 170, 184; **30**, 3, 4, 89, 191, 195, 196, 201; **31**, 1, 4, 33, 46–7, 100–1, 102, 103, 111n, 158n; **32**, 10, 40n, 79; **33**, 184, 194, 199, 205; **34**, 52, 53, 118n, 131–47, 161, 178; **36**, 53, no, 117, 119, 120, 168, 173, 174, 188; **37**, 58, 87n, 117, 145, 188, 189; **38**, 42n, 86, 92n, 122, 128, 132, 141, 143, 215, 216, 219n, 229,

230, 234, 251; **39**, 224, 226, 230, 231, 235; **40**, 220–1, 227–8; **41**, 10, 22n, 95n, 96, 119, 132, 220; **42**, 54n, 63, 64n, 75, 106, 112, 128, 184, 187, 197, 198, 206, 212; **43**, 4, 93, 161, 226, 242–5, 247–8, 264, 270n; **44**, 6, 7, 8, 10, 13, 14n, 15, 21, 114, 116, 125, 127, 128, 131, 133, 136n, 142n, 153, 175, 218, 231–2, 235–6, 238; **45**, 109, 110, 162, 183, 186–7; **46**, 11, 14, 15n, 29, 30, 31, 56, 58, 74, 111, 116, 117, 125, 133n, 138, 145, 156, 208, 212, 223, 224; **47**, 16, 26, 32, 46–8, 67, 115, 176, 233, 243, 256; **48**, 28, 123, 127, 137n, 259, 266, 273; **49**, 40, 43, 108–9, 282, 291, 293, 299, 301; **50**, 1, 48, 58, 65, 109, 110, 188n, 259; **51**, 18, 31, 53n, 67, 87, 135, 147n, 159, 289, 291, 292, 294, 296, 332, 334; **52**, 23, 68, 80, 84, 120, 134–6, 143, 190, 196, 296; **53**, 18, 20, 22, 32, 71n, 90, 91n, 288, 321–2, 333; **54**, 11, 13, 14n, 21n, 22–4, 28, 56, 57–8, 61–6, 68–9, 73, 76–8, 197, 299, 301, 304, 307, 312, 331–4, 351, 357; **55**, 45n, 54, 84–5, 91, 244, 263, 266, 348, 350, 351, 369, 372, 373, 381; **56**, 2n, 29, 32, 60, 101, 118, 121, 122, 146–7, 148, 151, 159, 217, 218, 225, 312, 354; **57**, 1, 13, 18, 26, 33, 210, 212, 213, 214, 215, 217, 218, 219, 220, 221, 224, 315, 333; **58**, 10, 14, 15, 16, 17, 19, 20, 32, 65, 66, 71, 199–207, 223, 231, 232, 243; **59**, 2, 71, 72, 73, 74, 75, 76, 77n12, 142, 191–2, 206n41, 213, 214, 216, 219–20, 221–3, 225, 228, 253, 267–8, 277, 280, 356, 358; **60**, 58, 66, 77, 188, 237, 270, 341, 343, 357
attitude to *Pericles*, **3**, 151–2
greater popularity than Shakespeare, **1**, 44
Herford-Simpson edition, **4**, 160
his orthography in relation to Shakespeare's, **7**, 35–6, 39–42, 45, 46, 47n
and the King's Men, **1**, 43–4
MSS. of masques, **3**, 51
plays written for Blackfriars, **1**, 44
relations with Shakespeare, **2**, 36–43
and the respectability of the theatre, **1**, 40
satirized by Shakespeare, **3**, 140
and the 'War of the Theatres', **1**, 41
WORKS **11**, 85
Alchemist, **1**, 44, 104; **4**, 95; **9**, 122; **11**, 71, 74, 77n; **13**, 130; **16**, 56n, 138
Bartholomew Fair, **1**, 44; **10**, 69; **13**, 107; **14**, 14n
The Case is Altered, **1**, 44, 64; **8**, 104; **14**, 33n
Catiline, **1**, 44, 64; **2**, 42; **10**, 35, 36; **18**, 36
Chloridia, **1**, 64; **11**, 116n; **14**, 11
Cynthia's Revels, **1**, 44; **2**, 38; **9**, 11, 143; **11**, 100, 104; **13**, 123n; **15**, 173
The Devil is an Ass, **1**, 44; **9**, 86; **10**, 87n; **11**, 71, 72
Discoveries, **2**, 38–9, 41; **8**, 68n; **10**, 26n
Eastward Ho!, **1**, 44, 64; **7**, 57, 106n; **12**, 41; **17**, 88, 203; **50**, 289; **54**, 64, 357
Epicoene, **1**, 44; **13**, 120; **14**, 79; **15**, 40n
Every Man in his Humour, **1**, 43; **2**, 36, 38, 152; **8**, 104; **12**, 54; **18**, 63; **52**, 19, 274
Every Man out of his Humour, **1**, 43; **2**, 36; **7**, 75; **9**, 29, 32; **11**, 30n; **12**, 36, 38, 46; **13**, 102, 116; **43**, 242; **52**, 80
Execration upon Vulcan, **1**, 29
Gypsies Metamorphosed, **6**, 60
Highgate Entertainment, **11**, 100
Hymenaei, **1**, 43
Lord Haddington's Masque, **1**, 43
Love Freed from Ignorance and Folly, **11**, 107
Lovers made Men, **4**, 92
Love's Triumph through Callipolis, **1**, 64; **11**, 116n
The Magnetique Lady, **1**, 44; **11**, 109; **12**, 29
Masque of Augurs, **1**, 55
Masque of Beauty, **1**, 43
Masque of Blackness, **1**, 43; **12**, 143
Masque of Gipsies, **14**, 8
Masque of Queens, **4**, 42; **11**, 71
Neptune's Triumph for the Return of Albion, **11**, 116n
New Inn, **1**, 44
Oberon, the Fairy Prince, **11**, 65, 107, 115n
Pan's Anniversary, **1**, 54
Poetaster, **1**, 41, 44; **3**, 29, 140; **5**, 140; **9**, 11, 41, 143; **11**, 100; **12**, 17, **15**, 65
The Sad Shepherd, **11**, 71
Sejanus, **2**, 40; **4**, 54; **5**, 142; **6**, 54; **7**, 136; **9**, 144; **10**, 35; **12**, 36, 41; **20**, 28; **52**, 134–6; **54**, 21n, 22–4
Staple of News, **1**, 44; **2**, 40
Timber, **14**, 43
Volpone, **1**, 105; **2**, 123; **4**, 95; **7**, 114; **8**, 120; **12**, 44, 48, 138; **16**, 20
Joplin, Janis, **57**, 156
Joplin, Patricia Klindienst, **44**, 35n; **48**, 42n
Joppien, Rüdiger, **29**, 176
Jordan, A. C., **57**, 159
Jordan, Chris, **42**, 155; **50**, 235
Jordan, Constance, **46**, 123n
Jordan, Dora, **56**, 132
Jordan, Emily Clare, *see* Folger, Emily Clare
Jordan, Hoover H., **5**, 135
Jordan, John, **56**, 185–90, 201
Jordan, John E., **4**, 160
Jordan, Mrs, **18**, 98; **32**, 33; **34**, 175
Jordan, R., **24**, 166
Jordan, Thomas, **16**, 166; **52**, 99; **55**, 94–5; **58**, 238, 240, 244
Jordan, W. K., **17**, 55n, 57–8, 62
Jordan, William, **7**, 61
Jordan, William Chester, **37**, 186
Jordanova, Ludmila, **60**, 223n6
Jorden, Edward, **13**, 34
Jorge, Maria do Céu Saraiva, **18**, 127
Jorgens, Elise Bickford, **48**, 136, 137n
Jorgens, Jack J., **28**, 171n; **38**, 18; **39**, 4, 5, 53n, 69n, 81n, 91, 94, 96; **45**, 63; **49**, 159; **53**, 329; **57**, 145, 155; **60**, 354
Jorgens, Jack L., **56**, 3n
Jorgensen, Paul A., **3**, 137; **4**, 147, 151; **5**, 135, 142; **9**, 136; **10**, 8, 142; **14**, 144; **15**, 10; **16**, 161–2; **18**, 176; **19**, 123, 127, 151; **20**, 151; **22**, 161; **24**, 153; **25**, 93; **29**, 160; **30**, 64n, 65n, 68; **31**, 189; **32**, 11–12; **33**, 113, 144; **38**, 11, 15; **49**, 156n; **50**, 102
Shakespeare's Military World reviewed, **11**, 145
Josef II, Emperor of Austria, **35**, 22, 23
Conscience and the King. A Study of Hamlet reviewed, **8**, 140–1
Elizabethan Acting, **12**, 56, 65; **14**, 12
The Tragic Actor reviewed, **14**, 151
Joseph, Bertram L., **5**, 143–4; **7**, 7, 27, 85; **9**, 8, 144, 147; **10**, 147; **12**, 70n; **18**, 182; **20**, 64, 72n, 73n; **32**, 174n; **33**, 92, 93; **35**, 7n, 33n; **42**, 100n, 102n; **45**, 20; **48**, 33; **55**, 242n
Joseph, Joanna, **53**, 286
Joseph, Lois, **21**, 141

Joseph, Sister Miriam, **2**, 133, 134; **4**, 9; **5**, 82; **7**, 7; **16**, 158; **18**, 167; **27**, 84n; **30**, 89; **34**, 62n; **45**, 21, 22; **49**, 47, 49n, 53n; **53**, 154n; **54**, 123n; **55**, 24n
Joseph, of Exeter, **34**, 186
Joseph, Paterson, **44**, 173, 183; **45**, 148; **50**, 223; **57**, 295
Joseph, Paul, **59**, 340
Joseph, Phil, **48**, 232
Joseph, Phillip, **52**, 262
Joseph, Robert, **5**, 116
Joseph, Stephen, **26**, 140; **53**, 236
Josephs, Phili, **46**, 195
Josephson, Lennart, **15**, 138
Josey, Christopher, **54**, 289
Joshi, B. N., **19**, 141
Josten, Walter, **4**, 127; **7**, 111; **16**, 63, 66
Joubin, André, **21**, 86n
Joughin, John, **51**, 277–8; **56**, 306
Joukovsky, Françoise, **44**, 36n
Jourdain, Margery, **43**, 176; **54**, 309
Jourdan, Gabrielle, **53**, 270–1
Jourdan, Sylvester, *Plaine Description of the Bermudas*, **1**, 69; **3**, 54; **17**, 33, 151n, **25**, 127n
Jouve, Pierre-Jean, **9**, 113; **10**, 142; **13**, 154
Jouvet, Louis, **2**, 123; **40**, 2
Jovanović, Lj., **4**, 121; **15**, 141, 142
Jovanovich, Harcourt Brace, **43**, 57n
Jowett, Benjamin, **36**, 86n; **50**, 142n; **54**, 80, 85
Jowett, David, **57**, 277
Jowett, John, **38**, 88n, 92n, 251, 253; **39**, 238–40; **40**, 156n, 207, 226n; **41**, 217, 228n, 230n, 231, 237, 239, 243; **42**, 25n, 46n, 49n, 93n, 202n; **43**, 43n, 255–6, 262, 264; **44**, 69n, 115n, 248, 249, 252–3; **45**, 37n, 82n, 198; **46**, 244, 246; **48**, 272, 275–7, 281; **49**, 28n, 49n, 50, 163n, 165n, 311n; **50**, 280; **51**, 302–36; **52**, 166n, 320; **54**, 322, 344–7; **55**, 194n, 257n, 280n, 390; **56**, 95n, 171; **58**, 345–55, 357; **59**, 5n17, 9, 12n51, 69n1, 76n10, 77n11, 84n17, 93, 124n2, 213, 218, 376, 377–8, 383; **60**, 66n16, 358
Jowitt, J. A., **41**, 65n, 67n; **53**, 41n
Joyce, George H., **32**, 132n, 135n, 137n
Joyce, James, **7**, 4, 97; **15**, 30n; **16**, 34; **18**, 117; **26**, 92; **34**, 54; **36**, 44, 49; **39**, 145n; **41**, 209; **45**, 7, 12, 40n; **49**, 7; **50**, 31; **53**, 3, 110, 294, 297, 343; **54**, 345; **56**, 137–45, 312; **58**, 121, 127
  Ulysses, **5**, 134; **12**, 138
Joyce, Michael, **41**, 186; **45**, 147; **59**, 225n3
Joyce, Nora Barnacle, **56**, 137
Joyce, Rachel, **50**, 205–6; **53**, 256
'J.S.', **23**, 171
Juby, Dick, **58**, 229
Jubye, Edward, **1**, 71; **33**, 158
Judas Iscariot, **36**, 194
Judge, Ian, **44**, 176, 177, 179; **45**, 146; **46**, 194; **47**, 205, 207; **48**, 205, 207, 230; **49**, 279; **50**, 211–16, 228; **51**, 230, 234, 235, 267, 268; **52**, 289; **57**, 263
Judges, A. V., *The Elizabethan Underworld*, **13**, 105n; **17**, 95n, 253; **26**, 71n; **52**, 123n, 125n, 127n
Judith, Madame, **9**, 67n
Juel-Jensen, Bent, **24**, 159
Jugge, Richard, **50**, 142
Jukes, Rick, **50**, 229
Julia, Raôul, **35**, 158; **37**, 39n
Julius Caesar, **31**, 10
Julius Caesar (V. Thomas, Harvester New Critical Introductions), **46**, 217; **48**, 255
Julius, Cotton, **54**, 123n
July and Julian, **20**, 25n
Jump, John D., **25**, 185; **30**, 185; **42**, 80n
Jung, Carl Gustav, **7**, 8, 10; **21**, 133; **22**, 146; **23**, 133; **27**, 171; **39**, 209–11; **40**, 191–2; **44**, 213; **59**, 228n5, 235n14
Jung, J., **36**, 44n
Jungman, Robert E., **32**, 234; **57**, 302
Jupe, Edward, **19**, 103
Jupp, E. B., **45**, 111n
Jürgens, Hanna, **60**, 316–17
Jurkka, Jussi, **13**, 126
Jusserand, Jean Adrien Antoine Jules, **9**, 92
Jusztusz, Pál, **12**, 114
Juvenal, **17**, 61; **27**, 119; **44**, 61
Jylhä, Yrjö, **10**, 117

Kaaya, Brad, **56**, 295
Kabel, Rolf, **48**, 10n
Kable, William S., **21**, 162; **22**, 181; **26**, 182; **27**, 185
Kacer, Jan, **48**, 167–8, 169n
Kachalov, Vladimir, **54**, 144, 151
Kachler, K. G., **11**, 147n; **28**, 172n
Kachur, B. A., **46**, 218; **47**, 231
Kaczynski, Juggen, **45**, 89n
Kadeřávek, Emil, **13**, 126
Kae-Kazim, Hakeem, **41**, 185; **44**, 199; **45**, 148; **48**, 230
Kael, Pauline, **39**, 44n, 79; **57**, 148
Kafka, Franz, **36**, 21, 22, 28, 71; **45**, 10; **48**, 5, 166, 189
Kafno, Paul, **39**, 13n; **59**, 199n8
Kahan, Jeffrey, **50**, 287; **53**, 318
Kahi, Masato, **42**, 153
Kahn, Coppélia H., **29**, 11n, 16; **31**, 11, 20n, 164; **37**, 33n, 34–6, 39n, 40n; **38**, 240; **41**, 106n, 198; **42**, 12; **43**, 1n, 29n, 114; **44**, 33n; **45**, 38n; **46**, 3, 9n, 92n, 95n, 101n, 117n; **49**, 65n, 66n, 88, 104n, 168n; **50**, 44n, 102, 108, 247; **51**, 280–1, 284, 286; **52**, 279, 295, 325; **53**, 34, 83n; **54**, 227n; **55**, 8, 117, 118; **56**, 158n, 218n, 229, 234; **57**, 339; **60**, 96n33
Kahn, Michael, **51**, 299; **59**, 298
Kahn, Paul, **55**, 355–6
Kahn, Sholom J., **12**, 143
Kahn, Victoria, **51**, 184n; **55**, 213n, 220n; **58**, 322, 332
Kahrl, George M., **51**, 5; **54**, 46n, 47n, 56n; **57**, 59
Kahrl, Stanley J., **47**, 49n
Kaibel, Franz, **44**, 109n
Kaige, Chen, **48**, 24
Kainz, Josef, **35**, 28–9; **37**, 199
Kaiser, Gerhard W., **23**, 120; **32**, 220
Kaiser, Walter, **19**, 132; **29**, 91; **46**, 12n; **55**, 232n
Kalb, Jonathan, **55**, 238n
Kalinina, Elena, **60**, 313Fig.57
Kallai, F., **14**, 120; **16**, 135
Kallman, Chester, **52**, 309
Kalmey, Robert P., **33**, 187
Kalson, Albert E., **18**, 184; **29**, 176
Kalthoeber, C., **4**, 80
Kamara, Paddy, **43**, 213

INDEX

Kamaralli, Anna, **58**, 48
Kamarás, Gy., **14**, 120
Kamashev, I. S., **5**, 105n
Kames, Lord (Henry Home), **18**, 47; **34**, 11; **37**, 143, 149, 151n; **60**, 216
Kaminska, Esther Rachel, **55**, 115, 125
Kaminska, Ida, **55**, 115, 124–5
Kaminski, Roman, **40**, 56
Kampen, Claire van, **60**, 229
Kamps, Ivo, **46**, 205; **48**, 88n, 89n; **52**, 109n; **55**, 351; **58**, 173; **54**, 28n, 311
Kamuf, Peggy, **55**, 69n, 272n
Kana, Okko, **55**, 325
Kanagaki, Robun, **46**, 193; **48**, 102–3; **54**, 111
Kancheli, Ghia, **47**, 211
Kander, John, **45**, 45
Kane, George, **49**, 332
Kane, John, **24**, 125n; **42**, 147–8; **51**, 228; **52**, 266
Kane, R. J., **29**, 24n
Kani, John, **43**, 212; **55**, 271, 273–7; **58**, 350; **59**, 371; **60**, 290, 291Fig.47, 291, 359
Kanini, Mary, **23**, 162n
Kannengiesser, P., **10**, 3
Kant, Immanuel, **9**, 94; **24**, 97; **35**, 76; **37**, 143, 151; **45**, 5; **51**, 1; **55**, 355; **56**, 91; **57**, 310; **58**, 182, 183
Kantak, V. Y., **18**, 156; **19**, 141; **24**, 148; **32**, 10
'An Approach to Shakespearian Comedy', **22**, 7–14
'An Approach to Shakespearian Tragedy: The "Actor" Image in *Macbeth*', **16**, 42–52
Kanter, Catherine, **53**, 272
Kantorowicz, Ernst H., **19**, 125; **27**, 44; **28**, 2, 63; **35**, 74; **38**, 11; **43**, 3n; **44**, 209; **46**, 224; **50**, 44n, 250; **54**, 128; **55**, 36n; **57**, 27, 247
Kaplan, Donald, **60**, 146n17
Kaplan, E. Ann, **52**, 96n
Kaplan, Joel H., **24**, 160, 163, 164; **31**, 33n; **34**, 118n; **47**, 3n
Kaplan, Justin, **56**, 203n
Kaplan, M. Lindsay, **46**, 212; **52**, 293n, 299; **53**, 86n; **56**, 75n; **58**, 252, 254, 256
Kaplan, Paul H. D., **42**, 199; **51**, 64n
Kaplangi, Birsen, **18**, 130
Kapner, Mitchell, **55**, 332
Kapoor, Kiran, **15**, 136
Karaali, Oguz, **14**, 124
Karagiorgos, Panos, **58**, 209
Karamzin, Nicolai M., **5**, 95, 98
Karanth, B. V., **59**, 370
Karapetian, O., **13**, 132
Karasholi, Adel, **32**, 217
Karim-Cooper, Farah, **60**, 359, 361
Karl, Joseph, **6**, 121
Karlin, Miriam, **36**, 153
Karm, Kaarel, **12**, 118
Karr, Judith M., **18**, 168–9; **20**, 49n
Karrer, Wolfgang, **53**, 168n
Karson, Nat, **4**, 124
Karthaios, Kleandros, **2**, 127; **4**, 128; **5**, 112; **6**, 120; **10**, 119; **11**, 121; **12**, 113; **18**, 124
Kartheos, K., **58**, 210, 217
Kasamatsu, Yasuhiro, **53**, 275
Kasimov, N., **13**, 132
Kastan, David Scott, **34**, 185; **38**, 10; **43**, 13n, 45n, 46; **48**, 89n; **49**, 310; **50**, 141n, 143n; **51**, 296, 313, 329, 332; **52**, 71n, 81n, 304n; **53**, 331, 333; **54**, 34n, 57n, 122n, 128n, 130, 309–11; **55**, 28n, 354–5; **56**, 28n, 350–2, 354–5; **57**, 196; **58**, 130, 170, 174, 349; **59**, 18n75, 25, 27n30, 38n88, 110n12, 124n2; **60**, 253, 268n1, 362
Katajisto, Martti, **12**, 111
Katayev, Valentin, **27**, 143
Kate and Petruchio, **52**, 193
Katherens, Gilbert, **47**, 15n
Katherine of Aragon, Queen of England, **26**, 41; **43**, 50; **52**, 168–71, 174–82; **60**, 60, 68, 69, 70
character of, **60**, 100–1
Katherine of Sutton, abbess of Barking, **19**, 69
Kathman, David, **58**, 220
Katz, David S., **48**, 51n; **51**, 160n, 161n, 165n
Katz, Leslie S., **49**, 293; **55**, 346
Katz, Richard, **58**, 275
Kau, Joseph, **29**, 171
Kauffmann, Angelica, **51**, 14, 301; **59**, 131n47
Kauffmann, Stanley, **39**, 75
Kaufman, E. K., **13**, 156n
Kaufman, Helen A., **9**, 141, 142; **12**, 142; **14**, 153
Kaufman, Lloyd, **52**, 90n; **53**, 283; **55**, 384
Kaufmann, R. J., **20**, 154; **22**, 160; **25**, 9, 14n, 19n; **26**, 158; **41**, 67
Kaufmann, Walter, **45**, 3n; **50**, 171n, 172n, 174n, 175n; **55**, 73n; **56**, 208n
Kaula, David, **16**, 159; **18**, 173; **21**, 135; **27**, 167; **30**, 184, 192–3; **33**, 18n; **36**, 172; **38**, 231; **40**, 75n; **54**, 36n
'*Hamlet* and the "Sparing Discoverie"', **24**, 71–7
Kaurismaki, Aki, **45**, 147
Kaut-Howson, Helena, **42**, 149; **49**, 273; **51**, 245–6; **52**, 254, 256, 261; **55**, 309; **56**, 297
Kautz, Sebastian, **58**, 299
Kavanagh, Anne, **42**, 149
Kavanagh, John, **43**, 216
Kavanagh, Rachel, **58**, 302, 307
Kavanagh, Robert Mshengu, **52**, 156n, 157, 158n
Kavanaugh, Rachel, **52**, 260; **54**, 265, 294; **55**, 309, 329; **56**, 266, 291; **57**, 262, 265, 269, 290, 294; **59**, 184, 186; **60**, 305–6, 321
Kavanaugh, Rebecca, **53**, 279
Kavli, Karin, **36**, 71
Kavros, H. E., **33**, 203
Kawachi, Yoshiko, **32**, 241, 242; **41**, 214–16; **53**, 293; **54**, 304; **56**, 330
Kawai, Shoichiro, **50**, 248
Kawakami, Otojiro, **48**, 104
Kawamura, Takeshi, **48**, 109
Kawatake, Toshia, **48**, 100
Kay, Barnaby, **59**, 313
Kay, Bernard, **48**, 193–4
Kay, Carol McGinnis, **26**, 157; **33**, 188n; **46**, 92n
Kay, Charles, **55**, 335; **58**, 270, **271**
Kay, David, **59**, 214, 216, 221–2, 223
Kay, Dennis, **58**, 2, 4, 60, 61, 71
Kay, Jonathan, **49**, 274
Kay, Lisa, **57**, 297
Kay, Richard, **40**, 183; **41**, 184

Kay, W. D., **55**, 263n
Kayan, Sabih, **7**, 116
Kayser, Wolfgang, **35**, 175
Kazasoglou, G., **7**, 112
Kazek, John, **56**, 294
Keach, William, **32**, 231–2; **36**, 166; **47**, 129n; **56**, 28n, 30n, 34n, 35n, 38n
Kealey, Patrick, **56**, 297
Kean, Charles, **1**, 72; **2**, 1, 2, 18; **6**, 50; **7**, 34, 145; **8**, 74–5, 78, 80, 152; **9**, 55, 56; **10**, 74; **11**, 124; **13**, 77, 78; **16**, 104, 110–14, 116; **18**, 106; **19**, 153, 154; **20**, 107, 109–11; **22**, 133; **24**, 168; **25**, 113, 114, 115, 116, 119, 120, 121; **29**, 176; **32**, 29, 35n; **35**, 3, 7, 8, 12, 18, 19, 20, 34, 36, 37; **37**, 199; **38**, 188, 189, 191, 194, 195, 199; **39**, 230; **40**, 66; **41**, 23–34, 224; **42**, 38; **43**, 212; **47**, 1; **49**, 126, 229; **52**, 288, 290; **54**, 41, 335; **56**, 120, 126; **57**, 150, 326
Kean, Edmund, **1**, 61; **2**, 19; **3**, 101, 102; **6**, 143; **7**, 25, 27–8, 29; **9**, 55, 61; **10**, 73, 76n; **11**, 124; **13**, 77; **14**, 151; **18**, 67, 72; **21**, 80; **23**, 122; **28**, 139; **29**, 143, 177; **30**, 198; **35**, 5, 8, 33, 34–5, 43–54 *passim*; **37**, 142, 201; **38**, 192; **39**, 233; **44**, 242; **45**, 116, 173; **47**, 66–7; **48**, 7; **51**, 117–19, 130; **52**, 99, 100, 104–5, 288, 291; **53**, 292, 296, 327; **55**, 56, 96; **56**, 111, 113; **57**, 68, 81, 82, 84, 87, 88, 90, 94, 326; **59**, 374
Kean, Mrs Charles (Ellen), **22**, 133; **32**, 29n, 32, 33, 35n; **35**, 8; **38**, 196; **40**, 67; **41**, 26–7; **42**, 38; **57**, 334
Kean, Sidney, **42**, 151
Keane, Doris, **9**, 17
Keane, James, **51**, 266
Keane, Will, **58**, 304
Kearney, Gillian, **47**, 216; **54**, 250
Kearns, Sean, **58**, 263
Keast, W. R., **18**, 54; **33**, 4, 8
Keate, Edith M., **12**, 20n
Keating, Charles, **28**, 142
Keating, James, **56**, 187
Keatman, Martin, **50**, 65n
Keaton, Michael, **48**, 233; **60**, 355
Keats, John, **3**, 80; **4**, 10, 20–1; **5**, 1; **8**, 32, 120, 146; **9**, 138; **10**, 20, 25n; **13**, 58–68; **14**, 83; **15**, 22, 41, 50, 74, 79n, 80n, 108; **16**, 10; **18**, 113; **21**, 129; **22**, 8, 146, 164, 166, 175; **23**, 98; **24**, 35, 44, 108, 110, 114, 115, 127; **31**, 135n; **35**, 45, 46n, 167; **36**, 44; **37**, 207, 212; **40**, 200–1; **41**, 5, 103–18, 223; **42**, 68; **43**, 229; **46**, 158n; **48**, 157; **49**, 139; **52**, 322; **53**, 55; **54**, 127n, 209, 340; **55**, 96; **56**, 243n, 280, 311; **57**, 35; **58**, 92
  Endymion, Hyperion, Ode on a Grecian Urn, **10**, 16
Keats, Thomas, **13**, 59, 66
Keble, John, **54**, 83, 87
Keble, William, **7**, 58, 59, 61, 65–6, 68n
Kederminster Pharmacopolium, 17, 152n
Kedrov, M., **12**, 118
Keeble, N. H., **49**, 303
Keefe, Barrie, **43**, 208
Keefe, Maryellen, **57**, 320
Keegan, Shelagh, **41**, 187; **46**, 202; **48**, 231
Keeling, Captain William, **28**, 6; **60**, 363
Keely, Nula, **43**, 206
Keen, A., **54**, 120n
Keen, Alan, **3**, 4, 138; **4**, 148n; **5**, 139n; **6**, 11, 158–9; **10**, 144n
Keen, Alan, and Lubbock, Roger, *The Annotator. The Pursuit of an Elizabethan Reader of Halle's Chronicle Involving some Surmises about the Early Life of Shakespeare* reviewed, **8**, 148
Keen, Geoffrey, **11**, 132, 134
Keen, Malcolm, **5**, 116
Keen, Maurice H., **38**, 11; **44**, 59n
Keen, Will, **53**, 266; **55**, 334; **57**, 273
Keenan, Rory, **58**, 262
Keenan, Sinéad, **59**, 306
Keenan, Siobhan, **52**, 14n; **60**, 1, 2n4, 2n5, 13n39, 17n45, 22, 23
Keenan, Will, **53**, 282
Keene, Derek, **55**, 373
Keene, Donald, **54**, 109n
Keene, Laura, **22**, 133; **35**, 31
Keenlyside, Simon, **59**, 345
Keep the Widow Waking, **1**, 9
Keepax, Eve, **48**, 233, 237
Keere, Pieter van den, **1**, 27
Kees, Weldon, **40**, 38
Keesee, Donald, **46**, 125n
Keetch, Anthony, **45**, 150
Keeton, George W., **8**, 5; **22**, 169–70; **29**, 96, 98; **43**, 59n
Keevil, J. J., **17**, 25n
Kehler, Dorothea, **45**, 160; **46**, 208; **49**, 96n; **50**, 288; **55**, 351
Keifer, Frederick, **49**, 293
Keightley, Thomas, **19**, 76; **36**, 195n; **45**, 256
Keil, Harry, **12**, 143
Keir, Sir David Lindsay, **52**, 182n
Keith, Sir Arthur, **60**, 234n64
Keith, B. F., **57**, 255
Keith, Ian, **6**, 124
Keith, Linda, **55**, 170n
Keith, Penelope, **39**, 105; **45**, 151
Keith-Johnston, Colin, **9**, 19, 57, 58
Kellan, Ian, **51**, 267
Kellaway, Kate, **60**, 171
Keller, Christa, **16**, 133
Keller, David, **56**, 295
Keller, Gottfried, **18**, 129
Keller, Willy, **10**, 143
Keller, Wolfgang, **6**, 6; **8**, 11; **10**, 2; **44**, 110n, 111n
Kellett, E. E., **4**, 18; **18**, 49, 52–3
Kelley, Donald, **49**, 199n
Kelley, Paul, **46**, 240n
Kellgren, Ian, **43**, 209
Kelliher, W. Hilton, **25**, 192; **28**, 38n; **44**, 231; **46**, 249n
Kellison, Matthew, **29**, 21
Kellner, Leon, **5**, 6; **31**, 196; **32**, 116n; **34**, 196; **35**, 181n
  Restoring Shakespeare, **2**, 57
Kellocke, Thomas, **8**, 107n
Kelly, Cara, **47**, 188
Kelly, Darian, **43**, 212
Kelly, Darragh, **46**, 198; **54**, 253
Kelly, Edward, **11**, 71
Kelly, F. L., **28**, 158
Kelly, George, **55**, 338
Kelly, Gerard, **47**, 192
Kelly, Grace, **56**, 14
Kelly, H. H., **29**, 88
Kelly, Helen M., **59**, 208

INDEX

Kelly, Henry Ansgar, **25**, 172–3; **38**, 2; **43**, 54n; **44**, 2n, 220; **47**, 254; **52**, 177n, 178, 179, 180; **54**, 242n
Kelly, John Alexander, **9**, 98, 100n
Kelly, Jude, **48**, 235; **49**, 273; **50**, 228; **53**, 266; **54**, 287, 292; **59**, 208–10
Kelly, Linda, **35**, 9; **51**, 113n, 115n, 116n, 117n, 118n
Kelly, Matthew, **59**, 314–16; **60**, 328
Kelly, Michael, **18**, 97, 98, 100; **51**, 93
Kelly, Robert L., **23**, 147
Kelly, T., **27**, 165
Kelly, Thomas, **32**, 9
Kelly, Thomas E., **59**, 245n44
Kelly, William, **12**, 21n; **35**, 31
Kelly-Gadol, Joan, **46**, 134n; **59** 265n29
Kelsall, Freda, **48**, 236
Kelsay, John, **48**, 88n
Kelsey, David, **47**, 102, 104, 106, 214
Kelso, Ruth, **31**, 85n, 86n, 88n, 91n
Kelterborn, Rudolf, **46**, 199
Kelway, Anne, **14**, 103
Kemble, Charles, **1**, 61; **2**, 1, 19; **3**, 101, 102; **9**, 55, 61; **10**, 73, 74, 76n; **11**, 124; **16**, 110, 112, 114; **19**, 151, 154; **20**, 108–9, 164; **21**, 80; **30**, 200; **32**, 30, 32, 34, 38; **35**, 8, 13, 18; **37**, 48, 85; **42**, 47; **49**, 123; **51**, 108, 116; **53**, 226n; **55**, 96, 380; **56**, 111; **57**, 84; **58**, 139
Kemble, Elizabeth, **49**, 118
Kemble, Frances Anne (Fanny), **9**, 148; **18**, 104; **22**, 121, 174; **32**, 28, 30; **35**, 8; **38**, 199; **49**, 123; **54**, 82; **56**, 132 and n.; **59**, 87–8, 89
Kemble, John Mitchell, **54**, 82
Kemble, John Philip, **2**, 1; **3**, 53; **4**, 81; **6**, 54; **7**, 28, 123; **9**, 54; **10**, 30, 71, 73; **11**, 123, 124; **13**, 76, 139, 145n; **15**, 172; **18**, 104; **19**, 107; **23**, 173; **24**, 17, 168; **25**, 185; **29**, 176, 177; **32**, 34, 35; **34**, 12, 17–18, 182; **35**, 3, 5, 8, 9, 17, 18, 49, 54, 55; **37**, 198, 199; **38**, 243–4; **42**, 37, 47; **43**, 99, 106; **44**, 207, 221, 242; **45**, 32, 34; **47**, 262; **48**, 7; **49**, 119, 121, 285; **50**, 277; **51**, 11, 59, 66, 82n, 93, 94, 108, 112–18, 300; **52**, 291; **53**, 216–20, 224–5, 226n, 227–31, 262, 296, 327; **57**, 87, 88, 89, 177; **59**, 112n20, 122n54, 199–200, 204
  Laurence portrait of, **11**, 124
Kemble, Mrs John (Priscilla Hopkins), **51**, 4; **53**, 327
Kemble, Roger, **42**, 38n
Kemble, Stephen, **35**, 44; **60**, 115–16
Kembles, the, **31**, 188
Kemenov, V., **2**, 126
Kemp's Nine Daies Wonder, **17**, 175
Kemp, Dominic, **45**, 155
Kemp, Lindsay, **44**, 198; **45**, 69
Kemp, Peter, **43**, 198
Kemp, Robert, **3**, 104
Kemp, Ross, **58**, 305
Kemp, T. C., **7**, 146n; **9**, 147; **12**, 129n; **36**, 79; **38**, 50n
  'Acting Shakespeare: modern tendencies', **7**, 121–7
Kemp, Sir Thomas, **44**, 232
Kemp-Welch, Joan, **47**, 95
Kempe, Margery, **49**, 300; **56**, 313
Kempe, William (Will), **1**, 8, 39, 129, 130; **3**, 27; **5**, 122; **8**, 73; **9**, 147; **14**, 76; **15**, 62; **17**, 194–5, 197; **21**, 113; **22**, 39, 40, 121; **25**, 161, 165, 166, 167; **28**, 177; **32**, 6, 87n, 163n, 194, 238; **34**, 101; **35**, 87, 88, 93, 98; **37**, 198; **38**, 95; **39**, 228; **41**, 127, 217–18, 220; **42**, 63, 199, 204; **43**, 233; **44**, 232; **45**, 107; **46**, 252; **47**, 81, 251; **49**, 19; **50**, 87; **54**, 193; **55**, 373; **56**, 62, 63, 64, 66, 95, 97, 99; **57**, 232; **58**, 31, 62, 348; **60**, 114, 367
Kempe, William, schoolmaster, **17**, 55n
Kempis, Thomas à, **1**, 67
Kempner, Teddy, **44**, 202
Kendal, Felicity, **34**, 154, 155; **43**, 183; **44**, 198
Kendal, Geoffrey, **59**, 370
Kendal, Gillian, **53**, 296–7, 306
Kendal, Madge, **56**, 130, 134
Kendal, Mrs, **4**, 105; **32**, 23, 24, 26n
Kendal, William Hunter and Dame Madge, **35**, 16
Kendall, Anne, **11**, 100–3, 105n
Kendall, Edmund, **11**, 100–2, 105n
Kendall, Gillian Murray, **44**, 220
Kendall, Lisa, **56**, 298
Kendall, Thomas, **11**, 100–5, 105n
Kendals, the, **32**, 19
Kendrick, A. F., **17**, 182n
Kendrick (Kenwrick), Revd Edward, **5**, 55
Kendrick, T. D., **35**, 103n
Kendry, Keith, **44**, 201
Kenilworth, **3**, 93
Kennan, Siobhan, **51**, 298
Kennedy, Adrienne, **52**, 34
Kennedy, Alan, **46**, 199
Kennedy, Andrew, **48**, 115n
Kennedy, C. W., **14**, 11
Kennedy, Dennis, **31**, 187; **40**, 222–3; **41**, 226; **47**, 237; **48**, 15, 188, 262; **49**, 247n; **52**, 41, 44n, 92, 155, 161n, 162n, 163n; **53**, 239n, 309; **57**, 327; **58**, 339; **60**, 138, 169
Kennedy, Jacqueline, **57**, 152
Kennedy, Joe, **57**, 141
Kennedy, John, **39**, 144n
Kennedy, John F., **18**, 133; **28**, 15, 28; **57**, 138, 139, 140, 141, 146, 152
Kennedy, Jonathan, **54**, 295
Kennedy, Judith M., **22**, 168; **54**, 303
Kennedy, Kenneth A. R., **47**, 178n
Kennedy, Laurence, **45**, 131, 150
Kennedy, Michael, **60**, 189n18, 192n24
Kennedy, Milton Boone, **7**, 7; **31**, 8, 9n, 10
Kennedy, Patrick, **17**, 173n
Kennedy, Richard F., **53**, 335, 344; **54**, 303
Kennedy, Robert F., **57**, 139, 140, 144, 146
Kennedy, Tom, **56**, 254
Kennedy, William, **43**, 234
Kenner, Hugh, **55**, 158n
Kenner, Ron, **57**, 146, 154
Kennet, W., **27**, 61, 62, 63, 64, 65, 66, 67, 68
Kenneth I, King of Scotland, **57**, 72
Kenneth III, King of Scotland, **57**, 70, 71
Kenny, Anthony, **43**, 260n
Kenny, Neil, **50**, 199n
Kenny, Dr Paul, **55**, 148n
Kenny, R. W., **24**, 157
Kenny, Shirley Strum, **43**, 103n
Kenny, Thomas, **6**, 5; **27**, 106n
  Life and Genius of Shakespeare, **3**, 23
Kenrick, William, **34**, 15; **51**, 8; **56**, 118

Kent, Diana, **42**, 155
Kent, Faith, **45**, 157
Kent, Jonathan, **46**, 191; **49**, 235, 238, 250; **50**, 226; **54**, 254; **55**, 316–17, 323, 330, 332; **56**, 276, 283, 297; **57**, 259, 287, 288, 292; **58**, 300; **60**, 323
Kent, Nicholas, **50**, 229
Kent, T. van den Berg, **40**, 196
Kenter, Yildiz, **13**, 132; **14**, 123
Kenton, Godfrey, **47**, 96, 97
Kenton, Mary, **47**, 97
Kentrup, Norbert, **52**, 219; **53**, 279
Kenya, report on Shakespeare in, **14**, 121; **15**, 137
Kenyon, J. P., **54**, 34n; **57**, 14
Kenyon, Nicholas, **55**, 198n
Kenyon, Roland, **45**, 63n, 69
Keown, Michelle, **55**, 170n, 177n
Kepler, Johannes, **17**, 65, 139–40, 143; **20**, 3; **40**, 145n; **42**, 208; **48**, 181; **55**, 63
Ker, W. P., **8**, 8; **10**, 25n; **26**, 76n; **31**, 77n; **55**, 204n; **56**, 209n; **59**, 263, 264n26
Kermode, Sir Frank, **9**, 136, 151; **11**, 30n; **16**, 159–61; **17**, 33n; **18**, 8, 9, 172; **20**, 161; **22**, 153; **25**, 8, 125, 126; **28**, 117, 119n, 122, 174; **29**, 5, 44; **30**, 149, 151, 152; **31**, 46; **32**, 1, 179, 181n; **33**, 27n, 34n; **34**, 103n; **35**, 102n, 113n, 114, 116n; **36**, 98n, 115–16, 119n; **37**, 5, 11, 6911, 150n; **38**, 145n, 167n, 170n, 171, 172n, 173; **39**, 6, 80, 123n, 159, 162n, 162, 163, 210; **40**, 187; **43**, 16, 34, 37, 41n, 43–6, 47n, 52; **44**, 77n; **45**, 16n, 24n; **46**, 88; **48**, 155; **51**, 145; **52**, 189n; **53**, 39, 40, 41n, 336; **54**, 242; **55**, 3, 10, 68n, 81n, 152, 155; **56**, 42n; **57**, 2, 3, 29, 150, 196; **58**, 250, 329, 332; **59**, 41, 81
Kern, Edith, **57**, 119
Kernan, Alvin B., **9**, 137; **24**, 151; **28**, 150, 170; **29**, 171, 172; **32**, 224; **33**, 47n, 181; **34**, 135n, 140n, 165, 172; **37**, 87n; **38**, 5, 160n; **40**, 136n; **41**, 5n, 36n, 204; **43**, 8n; **44**, 217; **52**, 133; **53**, 32n; **56**, 219n; **59**, 41, 219n25
Kernan, David, **42**, 162
Kernodle, G. R., **1**, 11; **3**, 93; **4**, 100n; **14**, 150; **15**, 113; **17**, 202; **28**, 170; **36**, 178; **52**, 4, 7n; **55**, 242n
  From Art to Theatre, **3**, 86; **12**, 20n
  'The Open Stage: Elizabethan or Existentialist?', **12**, 1–7
Kernot, Vivienne, **7**, 126
Kerr family, bookplate of, **9**, 84
Kerr, Heather, **48**, 250
Kerr, James, **56**, 298
Kerr, Maddy, **55**, 322; **59**, 338
Kerrigan, John, **35**, 163; **36**, 186–8, 195n; **37**, 18n, 208, 215–17; **38**, 49n, 54n, 253; **39**, 249; **40**, 146n, 147; **41**, 104n, 105n, 242; **42**, 72n, 74, 210, 213n; **43**, 232; **44**, 219, 254; **46**, 35, 41n, 46n, 225, 226, 249n; **48**, 245; **49**, 104n, 320; **50**, 74n, 246, 270–1; **51**, 328; **52**, 275; **54**, 28n; **55**, 2, 198; **56**, 311–12, 330; **58**, 24, 25, 26, 29, 327; **59**, 225, 233; **60**, 193n28
Kerrigan, Patricia, **42**, 159; **44**, 158, 160, 161, 191
Kerrigan, William W., **49**, 301; **54**, 316; **56**, 349n
Kerryson, Paul, **45**, 153; **53**, 281; **60**, 323
Kershaw, David, **42**, 158
Kershaw, Noreen, **42**, 153, 155; **44**, 203
Kersten, Dorelies, **18**, 160
Kerswell, Gillian, **45**, 154
Kéry, Lásló, **14**, 120; **18**, 125; **25**, 179
Kesey, Rory, **51**, 267
Kestelman, Sara, **24**, 124; **33**, 180; **54**, 260–1
Ketch, Jack, **57**, 87
Kethe, William, *Tye thy Mare Tom Boye*, **1**, 70
Kett, Roger, **44**, 18
Kettell, Richard, **45**, 102
Kettle, Arnold, **15**, 140; **19**, 149n; **20**, 116, 143n, 144–5; **21**, 141; **25**, 13n; **30**, 114; **39**, 13n; **44**, 75; **49**, 204n
Kewes, Paulina, **53**, 323
Key, Cecilia, **49**, 185
Keyishian, Harry, **59**, 157n1
Keymis, Lawrence, **17**, 32 and n.
Keyn, Ulf, **48**, 178n
Keyne, Andrew *see* Cane, Andrew
Keynes, Sir Geoffrey, **13**, 76; **55**, 64n, 264n
Keynes, J. M., **40**, 21, 30–1
Keys, Laura, **43**, 231
Keysar, Robert, **11**, 100
Keyser, C. E., **57**, 236
Kezar, Dennis, **52**, 280; **59**, 355
Khan, Nicholas, **54**, 267
Khanna, Urmilla, **32**, 221
Khayyam, Omar, **36**, 7
Khidoyatov, Abrar, **5**, 117
Khodshaev, K., **13**, 132
Khorava, **16**, 15
Khruschev, Nikita, **54**, 149, 150
Kiasashvili, Nico, **14**, 148; **15**, 168; **29**, 167; **48**, 187, 188n
Kidbrook, Lord Hervey of, **21**, 98–9, 100
Kidd, Delena, **43**, 212; **44**, 200; **45**, 148; **46**, 201
Kidd, John, production of *1 Henry IV* reviewed, **6**, 134–7
Kidnie, Margaret Jane, **55**, 183n, 384; **58**, 352, 354, 355, 356; **59**, 20n4, 38n88, 124n2; **60**, 366n6
Kiefer, Frederick, **38**, 220, 221; **41**, 213n; **46**, 213; **51**, 296–7
Kiendl, Teddy, **43**, 213; **47**, 212
Kierkegaard, Søren Aabye, **12**, 110; **29**, 145, 146; **36**, 30, 31, 32, 33, 50, 51; **38**, 218; **45**, 3; **53**, 48n; **56**, 91; **57**, 96–111
Kiernan, Michael, **50**, 72n, 79n
Kiernan, Pauline, **49**, 295; **50**, 238–9, 251; **52**, 44n; **53**, 35, 324–5; **54**, 9, 10; **55**, 349; **58**, 200
Kiernan, Victor G., **20**, 144; **47**, 223; **55**, 5
Kiernander, Adrian, **56**, 105n; **57**, 145
Kiessling, Nicolas K., **31**, 190
Kiknadze, Vassil, **48**, 188n
Kilbey, James A., **25**, 183
Kilfeather, Siobhán, **58**, 191
Kilgour, Maggie, **51**, 181n
Kiliaan, Cornelius, **55**, 266
Kilkenny, **12**, 21n
Kill, Reinhard, **50**, 37n
Killeen, Derek, **49**, 275; **51**, 268
Killeen, J. F., **31**, 189, 197
Killerby, Barry, **44**, 202; **47**, 214
Killick, David, **44**, 177; **45**, 148
Killigrew, Sir Henry, **48**, 266; **54**, 62
Killigrew, Thomas, **14**, 78; **23**, 126; **60**, 367
Killigrew, Thomas, the elder
  Cecilia and Clorinda, **1**, 66
  The Parson's Wedding, **10**, 88n
Killigrew, Sir William, *Siege of Urbin*, **4**, 94
Killim, Andrew, **41**, 185

Killoran, John, **47**, 213
Kilpatrick, Ross, **38**, 233
Kilroy, Thomas, **36**, 1n
Kimak, Bridget, **46**, 200; **50**, 232; **52**, 254, 255, 264; **54**, 284
Kimberley, M., **56**, 136n
Kimborough, Robert, **16**, 181; **19**, 134; **25**, 9, 176; **36**, 178; **60**, 257n22
Kimura, Shinji, **60**, 131n6, 133n12, 130–3, 135, 140
Kinal, Argun, **18**, 130
Kincaid, A. N., **35**, 178
Kincaid, James R., **56**, 9n
Kindermann, Heinz, **28**, 172n; **35**, 4
King is Alive, The, **55**, 74, 75n
King Kong, **52**, 156–7
King Leir, The True Chronicle History of, **3**, 17, 30, 31, 45, 54, 110; **4**, 32–3; **6**, 170; **9**, 84; **11**, 44; **13**, 30, 41, 43–5, 48n, 158; **14**, 32; **17**, 51n, 172; **20**, 24, 28; **55**, 12–35, 368; **60**, 253
King of England, **43**, 208
King Stephen: A Dramatic Fragment, **54**, 340; **55**, 340
King's Men, *see under* Theatre, Elizabethan, companies
see also Chamberlain's Men
King's Player, The, **49**, 280
King's Revels, The, **17**, 208; **43**, 152
King, Alison, **55**, 333
King, Arthur H., **7**, 4; **10**, 11; **23**, 11n
King, Bruce, **46**, 234, 235
King, Captain, **11**, 93
King, Clarence, **24**, 101, 102n
King, Danielle, **58**, 298
King, David, **9**, 124
King, Donald A., **55**, 219n
King, Francis, **57**, 179
King, Henry, **54**, 58n
King, James, **54**, 54n
King, John, **7**, 58, 59, 60, 63, 64, 67n
King, John N., **44**, 227
King, Laura Severt, **47**, 235
King, Lucille, **6**, 7; **29**, 84
King, Mackenzie, **39**, 144n
King, Margaret, **56**, 205n
King, Martin Luther, Jr, **57**, 138, 146
King, Michael, **55**, 178n
King, Nichola, **55**, 73n
King, Paul, **56**, 297
King, Peter, **41**, 185
King, Ros, **54**, 322; **55**, 183n; **58**, 350, 356; **59**, 358, 368
King, Rosalind, **41**, 188; **53**, 178n, 281
King, S. K., **8**, 121
King, Shelley, **48**, 237
King, Sigrid, **57**, 227
King, T. J., Professor, **20**, 168; **25**, 190; **28**, 169; **31**, 179, 187; **32**, 234; **35**, 186; **41**, 4, 5, 21; **46**, 230, 231; **47**, 90n; **52**, 26n; **53**, 196n
King, Thomas, **51**, 11, 121
King, Walter N., **14**, 147; **19**, 137; **23**, 144; **32**, 11, 49n, 52n, 56n, 57n, 60n
Kingdon, Robert, **48**, 76n; **54**, 95n
Kinge, William, **45**, 109n
Kingman, Philip, **33**, 203
Kingsford, Charles Lethbridge, **6**, 4, 7; **23**, 45n; **29**, 79; **38**, 11, 86n; **42**, 26; **44**, 57n, 59n; **53**, 212n; **54**, 34n; **60**, 46n56, 46n57, 46n58
Kingsford, R. J. L., **51**, 142
Kingsley, Ben, **24**, 125n; **29**, 152–3; **33**, 169, 176–7; **39**, 97, 191, 204–6; **40**, 16; **41**, 188; **42**, 200; **45**, 172; **56**, 113; **60**, 161, 164, 168
Kingsley, Charles, **36**, 175; **44**, 135; **54**, 86
Kingsley, Edmund, **59**, 339; **60**, 298
Kingsley-Smith, Jane, **54**, 224n
Kingsman, Robert, **33**, 160
Kingsmill, Andrew, **49**, 190n
Kingsmill, Hugh, **18**, 7; **54**, 71–2
Kingsolver, Barbara, **56**, 315
Kingston, Alex, **45**, 148, 152
Kingston, Felix, **24**, 72n
Kingston, Jeremy, **50**, 34; **51**, 223; **58**, 52
Kingston, John, **54**, 92n
Kingston, Mark, **45**, 157
Kingston, Sir William, **17**, 231; **60**, 69–70
Kinkaid, A. N., **27**, 178
Kinkead-Weekes, Mark, **46**, 123n; **51**, 28, 34n
Kinley, Matthew, **46**, 196
Kinloch, Maggie, **47**, 216; **50**, 233
Kinlock, William, **48**, 135n
Kinnaird, John, **31**, 176, 190
Kinnear, B. G., **31**, 128n, 133n; **32**, 149n
Kinnear, Rory, **57**, 274
Kinnear, Roy, **42**, 92
Kinney, Arthur F., **29**, 174; **43**, 233; **45**, 162; **49**, 45n, 46n, 55; **50**, 116–17, 246; **52**, 276; **54**, 306; **55**, 221n, 351; **56**, 93n, 315, 327, 330; **57**, 126, 188, 227; **59**, 69–70n2; **60**, 280n44
Kinney, Clare, **45**, 168
Kinnock, Neil, **45**, 119
Kinpel, Ben D., **51**, 27n
Kinsman, Robert S., **33**, 92n
Kip, J., **30**, 164n
Kipling, Gordon, **43**, 182; **54**, 194n
Kipling, Rudyard, **25**, 125; **48**, 9n; **53**, 336; **54**, 73, 76; **55**, 90
Kircheva, Olga, **10**, 115
Kirchheim, Astrid, **37**, 158n
Kirchmeyer, Thomas, **17**, 51n
Kirchner, Gustav, **20**, 157
Kirchner, Walter, **22**, 124n
Kireevsky, Ivan V., **5**, 100–1
Kirham, Margaret, **58**, 85
Kirimi, Kananu, **55**, 331; **56**, 271–3; **59**, 314, 344; **60**, 328
Kirjavainen, Kalle, **10**, 117
Kirk(mann) John (Johann), **22**, 119–20
Kirk, G. S., **31**, 50n
Kirk, R. E. G. and Ernest F., **60**, 238n7, 238n8, 245n34, 245n35, 245n36, 245n37, 245n38, 245–6n39, 248
Kirk, Robert, **53**, 54
Kirk, Rudolf, **33**, 22n
Kirkall, Edward, **59**, 131
Kirkall, Elisha, **10**, 72; **49**, 112–13
Kirke, Edward (E. K.), **46**, 46
Kirkham, Edward, **1**, 50; **11**, 100–4, 105n
Kirkland, Kendal, **53**, 274
Kirkman, Francis, **27**, 175; **60**, 115
The Witts, **11**, 146; **12**, 32, 42; **13**, 114, 115

Kirkman, Revd J., **18**, 51–2
Kirkpatrick, John, **42**, 159
Kirkpatrick, R., **31**, 174, 184
Kirkpatrick, Robin, **55**, 344
Kirov, Todor T., **23**, 142
Kirsch, Arthur C., **22**, 164, 175; **24**, 168; **29**, 3, 9; **30**, 184; **31**, 105, 106n, 107n, 109, 111, 112; **35**, 162; **37**, 110, 144n, 176–8; **40**, 125n, 212; **44**, 90; **45**, 165; **48**, 151n, 248; **49**, 204, 206, 212, 214n, 215n
'The Integrity of *Measure for Measure*', **28**, 89–105
Kirsch, James, **21**, 133
Kirschbaum, Leo, **3**, 28; **4**, 147, 152; **5**, 25; **6**, 5; **7**, 140, 148, 153; **9**, 24, 25, 26, 33n; **10**, 9, 10, 103; **11**, 139, 140; **12**, 137n; **15**, 159, 164; **17**, 207n; **19**, 10; **23**, 148, 160; **24**, 77n; **25**, 75n, 76n, 79n; **38**, 12, 154n, 254; **43**, 9n; **60**, 266n40
'Albany', **13**, 20–9
Shakespeare and the Stationers reviewed, **10**, 157–8
Kirshenblatt-Gimblett, Barbara, **52**, 38n, 45
Kirsner, Robert, **51**, 161n, 162n
Kirst, Klaus-Dieter, **40**, 55
Kirstein, Lincoln, **7**, 116
Kishi, Tetsuo, **48**, 11n, 184n; **53**, 293; **55**, 219n, 259n; **59**, 370–1, 375
Kiss Me Kate, **42**, 157; **43**, 214
Kiss, Ferenc, **13**, 129; **16**, 135
Kissoon, Jeffery, **28**, 148; **45**, 152; **46**, 189, 191; **47**, 195–6, 215; **48**, 233; **49**, 279; **50**, 229; **55**, 303; **59**, 341
Kistner, A. L., **28**, 155
Kistner, M. K., **28**, 155
Kitamura, Tokoku, **48**, 105
Kitchen, Michael, **38**, 252; **40**, 179, 181; **42**, 156
Kitchen, Robert, **11**, 92
Kitchin, G. W., **48**, 48n
Kitchin, Laurence, **19**, 154; **20**, 170; **30**, 144; **36**, 72n; **39**, 76, 91, 94
'Shakespeare on the Screen', **18**, 70–4
Kite, Mr, **14**, 111
Kitt, Johann Jakob, **23**, 154
Kitto, H. D. F., **15**, 163; **18**, 44; **23**, 154; **27**, 160
Form and Meaning in Drama, **11**, 138
Kittredge, George Lyman, **1**, 76; **4**, 7, 8; **6**, 13, 14, 48n; **9**, 48n; **10**, 3; **12**, 37; **15**, 5, 15, 181; **17**, 33n; **19**, 2, 4, 12, 125, 161; **24**, 2n, 4; **25**, 51; **27**, 130n; **30**, 91n; **32**, 175n; **33**, 121, 205; **34**, 91n; **38**, 254; **44**, 205; **45**, 23; **48**, 187; **49**, 168, 208; **53**, 232n; **55**, 13; **59**, 3; **60**, 364
Witchcraft in Old and New England, **11**, 77n
Kivimaa, Arvi, **8**, 119; **10**, 117; **11**, 119
Kjellmer, Göran, **23**, 138; **24**, 157
Klaff, Jack, **45**, 149, 152
Klain, Hugo, **4**, 120, 121; **18**, 134, 135
Klassen, Stanislav, **49**, 277
Klášterský, Antonín, **9**, 104
Klatzkin, Raphael, **6**, 121; **13**, 129
Klatzow, Peter, **49**, 271
Klause, John, **42**, 185; **53**, 33; **57**, 300
Klawitter, George, **60**, 256n19
Kleb, William E., **31**, 187–8; **35**, 10
Klebe, G., **18**, 87
Klee, Wanda G., **56**, 315
Klein, Beverly, **55**, 306
Klein, Calvin, **51**, 209
Klein, David, **10**, 9; **14**, 13; **17**, 195; **18**, 62–3, 183; **22**, 173
Klein, Ernest, **40**, 70
Klein, Holger, **47**, 130n, 273n; **50**, 129n
Klein, Joan Larsen, **30**, 194; **34**, 174; **36**, 24; **47**, 242n
Klein, Julius Leopold, **20**, 95–6, 103, 104n; **33**, 18
Klein, Karl, **56**, 224n, 226n, 227n
Klein, Melanie, **33**, 186
Klein, Richard, **29**, 20n
Klein, Theodore M., **42**, 34n
Klein, Ursula, **29**, 177; **30**, 201
Kleinau, Willy A., **48**, 473
Kleinburg, Seymour, **46**, 5
Kleinstück, Johannes, **9**, 137; **11**, 137
Kleist, Heinrich von, **56**, 238; **14**, 156; **37**, 155
Klene, J., **29**, 164
Klene, Sr Jean, **51**, 331
Klethen, Raf, *see* Cletten, Raf
Kleyne, Magda, **7**, 108
Klima, Kevin, **51**, 299
Klima, Slava, **51**, 84n
Kliman, Bernice W., **37**, 200; **38**, 219; **43**, 251; **45**, 27n, 43n; **46**, 254n; **48**, 263; **50**, 262; **52**, 303n, 312, 323–4; **53**, 304, 341–3; **55**, 222n; **56**, 302, 317, 329; **57**, 40, 145, 148, 341, 343; **58**, 340; **59**, 157–61, 173–4; **60**, 218n18
Klinck, Dennis R., **31**, 190
Kline, Kevin, **45**, 43n; **54**, 290; **58**, 47
Klockars, Carl B., **45**, 92n
Kloos, Wolfgang, **56**, 155n, 317
Klopstock, Friedrich, **9**, 95
Klose, Dietrich, **23**, 143
Klosovā, Ljuba, **22**, 175n
Klotz, Günther, **29**, 175; **44**, 72n; **47**, 236n
Klotz, Volka, **18**, 172
Klug, Ernst, **9**, 116
Kluge, F., **23**, 28n
Knack to Know a Knave, A, **52**, 125; **3**, 24; **4**, 149; **10**, 2, 70n, 146n; **17**, 195; **50**, 286
Knack to Know an Honest Man, A, **4**, 149
Knalfa, Louis A., **24**, 158n; **57**, 14
Knapman, David, **41**, 183; **42**, 149, 154; **44**, 197; **52**, 260; **53**, 279; **54**, 294
Knapp, Jeffrey, **47**, 246; **48**, 249; **54**, 67n, 69n, 231n; **56**, 319–20, 322; **59**, 356–7, 362, 368
Knapp, Peggy Ann, **39**, 126n
Knapp, Robert S., **43**, 238–9, 252; **50**, 241
Knapp, Steven, **51**, 130
Knapper, M. M., **48**, 74n
Knave in Graine, The, by J. D., **17**, 98n
Knell, William, **6**, 74n; **44**, 149; **58**, 62
Kneller, Clive, **41**, 184, 188
Kneller, Sir Godfrey, **1**, 62
Knelman, Martin, **39**, 179
Knevet, Sir Edmund, **52**, 173–4
Knevet, Sir Thomas, **60**, 68
Knewstub, John, **44**, 82n
Kniazevsky, B., **23**, 165
Knight of Malta, The, **52**, 212, 213n; **54**, 18n
Knight of the Burning Pestle, The, **52**, 148n
Knight's Tale, The, **54**, 25n
Knight, Anderson, **42**, 160

Knight, Charles, **6**, 61; **7**, 90, 92, 96; **9**, 100n; **10**, 74, 76n; **13**, 77, 78, 80n; **15**, 2, 5; **16**, 32; **18**, 20; **22**, 183; **25**, 110; **27**, 106n; **31**, 2; **32**, 17; **37**, 208; **38**, 187; **56**, 228n; **59**, 87, 125

Knight, Christopher, **52**, 256

Knight, David Vaughan, **59**, 340

Knight, Edward, **11**, 82, 83; **12**, 150; **28**, 180, 181; **36**, 191; **44**, 114n; **52**, 72; **59**, 218

Knight, Floyd, **58**, 301

Knight, George Wilson, **1**, 121; **2**, 136; **3**, 66, 69, 72; **4**, 18, 152–3; **5**, 62, 66, 81, 83, 85, 88, 138, 149; **6**, 6, 8–9, 35n, 150, 151; **7**, 10, 114, 137; **8**, 8, 11, 12, 16, 17, 33, 34, 35, 52, 111–12, 117n, 146; **9**, 14, 115, 132, 135, 140; **10**, 1, 7–8, 98, 106; **11**, 42, 45–7, 49n; **13**, 146–8; **14**, 47, 55n, 138, 156n; **15**, 7, 16, 17, 20, 26, 28, 100, 102–5, 108n, 109n, 113–16, 120–1; **16**, 32–3, 50; **17**, 36; **18**, 40–2, 53–5, 166; **19**, 2, 6–7, 10, 12, 23n, 25, 28, 45, 54n, 62, 83, 92; **20**, 114, 119, 120n, 147, 150, 160; **21**, 2, 3, 7, 11n, 62, 120, 137, 142, 148; **22**, 79, 80, 81, 149, 162; **23**, 151; **25**, 2, 4, 5, 8, 11n, 16n, 29, 39n, 64; **26**, 89, 127n, 151, 162, 167; **27**, 71, 82n; **28**, 89n; **29**, 1, 8, 9, 51, 88, 89, 103n; **30**, 112n; **31**, 9, 27, 29, 59n, 128n, 135, 151, 171, 173; **32**, 56n, 59n, 156n, 214, 226; **33**, 6, 43n, 47, 130; **34**, 9, 164; **35**, 171; **36**, 43, 44, 48, 49, 52; **37**, 99, 100, 107n, 182; **38**, 139n, 226, 254; **39**, 57, 59, 125, 126, 143n, 170–2, 177, 207, 208, 218; **40**, 22, 24, 31, 186; **41**, 63, 68, 193–4, 200; **42**, 165; **43**, 16n, 22n, 44n, 45n, 85n, 127n, 131, 135n; **44**, 86n; **45**, 6, 19, 57, 65, 159, 189; **46**, 93n, 94n, 95, 101n; **50**, 95, 107n, 172n, 176, 182, 183n, 184n; **51**, 144, 146; **52**, 317; **53**, 337; **54**, 127n, 202n; **56**, 205n, 235n; **57**, 38, 337; **58**, 50, 261; **59**, 225; **60**, 101

  critical influence, **4**, 20–4

  The Crown of Life reviewed, **1**, 119

  The Sovereign Flower reviewed, **13**, 147

  The Wheel of Fire, **3**, 132

  work on Shakespeare's imagery, **7**, 8–9

Knight, Grant C., **24**, 98

Knight, Harold, **49**, 128

Knight, John, **12**, 100

Knight, Joseph, **32**, 26; **35**, 7; **55**, 267; **56**, 134, 135n

Knight, Kevin, **49**, 270

Knight, Dame Laura, **49**, 128

Knight, Mark, **49**, 277

Knight, Philip, **19**, 103; **45**, 149

Knight, Stephen, **56**, 205n

Knight, Tom, **42**, 154

Knight, Trevor, **49**, 273

Knight, W. F. Jackson, **31**, 50; **39**, 35

Knight, W. Nicholas, **28**, 164–5; **29**, 95n, 96; **40**, 161n; **43**, 232

  'Equity, *The Merchant of Venice* and William Lambarde', **27**, 93–104

Knight, Wilson, **49**, 201

Knight-Webb, Trish, **48**, 227; **52**, 254; **53**, 279; **54**, 292; **56**, 290

Knightley, Will, **42**, 155

Knights, L. C, **4**, 10, 23, 147; **5**, 71, 81; **6**, 12, 156; **7**, 11, 128–9, 134; **8**, 12, 33; **9**, 132, 136, 144; **10**, 1, 8, 59n, 135, 140; **13**, 81, 84; **15**, 11, 17, 80n; **16**, 34, 43, 47–9, 59, 61; **17**, 129n; **18**, 43, 55, 170; **19**, 6, 7, 12, 20, 22, 25, 33n, 54n, 77, 126, 130; **20**, 36, 40n, 119, 120, 143–4, 146; **21**, 137; **22**, 147, 158, 162; **23**, 42, 66n, 69, 144, 152, 155; **25**, 5, 8, 12n, 185; **26**, 76; **27**, 54n; **28**, 21n, 89, 107; **29**, 87, 165; **30**, 44n, 112n; **31**, 48, 127n, 167; **32**, 139n, 213, 214; **33**, 3–4, 4–5, 43n, 181, 187; **34**, 1, 9, 72, 141n, 164, 168–9; **35**, 171; **36**, 44, 48; **37**, 10; **38**, 3, 10, 13; **39**, 220, 221; **40**, 23–5; **45**, 8n, 18n; **49**, 210–12; **50**, 176n; **53**, 89n, 91, 92; **54**, 299; **56**, 212, 245; **57**, 38, 39, 40

  An Approach to Hamlet reviewed, **15**, 163–4

  Drama and Society in the Age of Jonson, **2**, 143; **14**, 2

  Shakespeare's Politics, **12**, 138 and n.

  Some Shakespearean Themes reviewed, **14**, 138

Knijiga, Narodna, **15**, 142

Knobel, E. B., **8**, 110

Knoepflmacher, U. C., **53**, 119n

Knoespel, Kenneth, **50**, 82n

Knoll, Robert E., **34**, 142n

Knolles, Richard, *Generall Historie of the Turkes*, **5**, 144n; **10**, 29; **16**, 40; **17**, 40n; **21**, 40, 48, 51, 52; **38**, 245; **47**, 252n; **52**, 206n, 210n

Knollys, Sir Francis, **28**, 8

Knollys, Lettice, Countess of Leicester, **11**, 111

Knollys, Sir William, **8**, 7

Knoop, Douglas, **32**, 43n; **51**, 54n

Knoop, Douglas and Jones, G. P., **17**, 67n

Knopf, Alfred A., **48**, 186n

Knoppers, Laura Lunger, **48**, 247; **50**, 199n

Knorr, Friedrich, **11**, 140; **14**, 147

Knortz, Karl, **18**, 110

Knott, Amanda, **46**, 192

Knott, Betty I., **42**, 68n; **56**, 45n

Knott, John, **54**, 34n

Knowland, A. S., **12**, 145; **14**, 141; **25**, 9

Knowler, William, **11**, 116n

Knowles, Conrad, **22**, 127–8, 129–32; **35**, 31

Knowles, James Sheridan, **1**, 84; **35**, 53; **41**, 225; **42**, 186n; **53**, 108; **54**, 81, 314, 333

Knowles, Mrs, *see* Jones, Mrs Harriet

Knowles, Ric, **58**, 339, 342; **60**, 154–5, 156

Knowles, Richard, **21**, 132, 153; **25**, 96n, 97n, 99n, 172; **26**, 112n, 114n, 115n; **27**, 172, 190; **32**, 237–8; **33**, 209; **36**, 63, 191, 192n; **37**, 71n; **40**, 70n; **41**, 245n; **42**, 125; **49**, 217n, 218n, 219n, 220, 333; **51**, 307; **52**, 274–5; **54**, 321–2; **55**, 3; **59**, 15n65, 136–7n4, 159n8

Knowles, Richard Paul, **38**, 219n; **53**, 236n

Knowles, Ronald, **51**, 285; **54**, 352–3; **56**, 323; **57**, 238, 340

Knowlton, E. C., **6**, 15n

Knowlton, Jean, **23**, 172

Knox, Alexander, **7**, 125

Knox, Bernard M. W., **20**, 35, 40n; **22**, 49

Knox, Dilwyn, **48**, 31

Knox, John, **1**, 67; **54**, 75; **57**, 70

Knox, Kathleen, **55**, 113n

Knox, Patrick, **46**, 160; **47**, 211; **49**, 277; **51**, 269

Knox, T. F., **56**, 193n

Knudsen, Hans, **10**, 150n

Knudsen, Kolbjörn, **11**, 122

  of *Hamlet* and *The Taming of the Shrew*, **9**, 103

Knut, Lea, **9**, 114

Knuth, Gustav, **15**, 138

Knutson, Roslyn Lander, **39**, 229; **46**, 231, 232n; **47**, 239–40; **49**, 326; **51**, 294; **52**, 80n, 135n, 137n; **54**, 310; **55**, 34; **57**, 5, 333–4

Knutton, Dominic, **56**, 292

Knyvett, Francis, **48**, 72
Ko, Yu Jin, **52**, 272; **54**, 321; **59**, 351–2, 368
Kobayashi, Ichizō, **60**, 131
Kober, Erich, **35**, 29n
Kobialka, Michal, **49**, 309
Koblar, F., **4**, 118
Koch, Frederick, **56**, 343
Kocher, Paul H., **9**, 139; **19**, 36, 43n; **33**, 55n
Christopher Marlowe, **14**, 10
Kodama, J. Hisao, **19**, 133; **26**, 153
Koefoed, H. A., **6**, 48n
Koenig, Rhoda, **49**, 266
Koeppel, Richard, **4**, 161
Koestenbaum, Wayne, **50**, 49n
Kofman, Sarah, **44**, 44n
Koh, Suk-koo, **59**, 90n37
Kohl, Norbert, **23**, 117
Kohlberg, Lawrence, **53**, 91
Kohler, Estelle, **24**, 124; **25**, 66; **27**, 147, 150, 151; **41**, 178–9, 181, 187; **42**, 159; **44**, 177; **48**, 146, 148; **49**, 274; **53**, 265; **58**, 50
Kohler, Eugene, **20**, 104n
Kohler, Josef, **44**, 109n
Kohler, Richard, **33**, 140n
Kohout, Pavel, **36**, 26
Koht, Halvdan, **43**, 115n
Kohut, Heinz, **49**, 287
Kökeritz, Helge, **2**, 151, 152; **8**, 122; **9**, 47n, 133–4, 152; **12**, 133; **13**, 167; **17**, 224; **23**, 11n; **25**, 93; **26**, 171; **27**, 189; **32**, 100n; **47**, 156n; **50**, 14, 58; **56**, 52, 53; **57**, 224; **59**, 4
Shakespeare's Pronunciation, **7**, 3–4, 24n, 114–15
reviewed, **8**, 158–9
Kökeritz, H., and Prouty, C. T., *Facsimile of the First Folio*, **12**, 70n
Kokkos, Yannis, **52**, 285
Köknar, Ergun, **18**, 130
Kokoschka, Oscar **6**, 120
Kolakowsky, L., **29**, 91
Kolár, F., **9**, 108
Kolar, J. J., **9**, 107
translation, of *Macbeth*, **9**, 102, 103
of *The Merchant of Venice*, **9**, 102, 103
Kolata, Gina, **40**, 228n
Kolb, Robert, **57**, 237
Kolbe, F. C., **4**, 18; **5**, 91n; **7**, 8; **12**, 115; **19**, 25, 36, 43n, 54n
Kolin, Philip C., **26**, 172; **28**, 167; **29**, 174; **31**, 185; **32**, 225; **33**, 30n; **38**, 236; **40**, 201; **46**, 2, 4, 8; **51**, 286; **56**, 34n; **59**, 353
Kollek, Peter, **48**, 10n
Koller, A. M., **35**, 14n
Kollman, Judith, **51**, 177n, 183n, 188
Kolodny, Annette, **53**, 131, 133, 134n
Kolowrat, Count, **9**, 110n
Kolstad, Lasse, **14**, 122
Koltai, Ralph, **32**, 202, 208; **34**, 150; **36**, 152; **39**, 203, 205; **41**, 188, 190
Kolve, V. A., **28**, 91n
Komarova, Valentina P., **40**, 63n
Komine, Lily, **60**, 304
Komisarjevsky, Theodore, **2**, 19; **4**, 103, 132; **25**, 81, 88; **28**, 171; **36**, 73–84; **40**, 13; **46**, 187; **55**, 293; **57**, 328
Komuro, Kutsuzan, **60**, 132n9
Konarska, Joanna, **10**, 120
Kondras, Paul, **43**, 210; **44**, 199; **45**, 155; **50**, 235
Koneski, B., **15**, 142
König, Herbert, **48**, 184
König, Ralf, **56**, 315
Konigson, Elie, **52**, 129n
Könnecke, Gustav, **32**, 189n
Konszul, André, **12**, 139
Koontz, Claudia, **46**, 134n
Koopmann, Helmut, **57**, 62
Kopecký, Jan, **21**, 129
Köpeczi-Bócz, I., **16**, 135
Koppenfels, W. von, **26**, 154
Korat, Asuman, **16**, 137
Korda, Natasha, **50**, 245; **55**, 341; **56**, 339–40; **57**, 333; **58**, 321; **60**, 226n16, 357
Korn, Jeffrey, **43**, 214
Körner, Dietrich, **40**, 57
Korner, Otto, **54**, 285
Kornilova, H., **23**, 175
Korninger, Siegfried, **12**, 110; **21**, 143; **23**, 115; **41**, 213
Die Naturauffassung in der Englischen Dichtung des 17. Jahrhunderts reviewed, **11**, 145
Kornstein, Daniel J., **51**, 159, 160; **59**, 359, 368
Korsunovas, Oskaras, **58**, 303
Kortner, Fritz, **10**, 119; **12**, 112; **13**, 128; **15**, 134; **16**, 134; **18**, 124; **52**, 284
Kortright, Guy, **8**, 78
Korzybski, Alfred, **56**, 87
Kosintsev, Grigori, **43**, 251; **44**, 223; **45**, 4, 63, 65; 47, 112; **60**, 312
Kosintzer, G., **16**, 139
Koskimies, Rafael, **8**, 119; **9**, 112; **10**, 117; **11**, 119; **12**, 111; **25**, 183
Kosok, Heinz, **56**, 314
Koss, Siegfried, **30**, 202
Kossak, Saskia, **60**, 356, 361
Kossmann, E. H., **28**, 24n
Kostetzk, E. G., trans. of *Romeo and Juliet*, **13**, 154
trans. of *Sonnets*, **13**, 154
Kostial, Hermann, **32**, 97n
Kostic, L., **4**, 117
Kostic, Veselin, **40**, 216
Kostressen, Johan, **36**, 144
Kosztolányi, Dezsá, **3**, 117
Koszul, André, **2**, 122; **10**, 142; **16**, 54; **25**, 126
Koteliansky, S. S., **24**, 38n
Kotsur, Troy, **47**, 211
Kott, Jan, **16**, 136; **18**, 121, 174; **19**, 9, 35, 43, 126; **20**, 145; **21**, 74, 129; **22**, 30, 159; **23**, 119; **24**, 154; **25**, 19n, 22, 23n, 28, 171, 186; **27**, 159; **28**, 156; **30**, 195; **31**, 53n, 181; **33**, 3, 47, 187; **35**, 74; **36**, 165; **37**, 140n, 159; **38**, 1, 17, 145n, 232; **39**, 57, 60n, 81, 82, 165, 168, 235; **40**, 1, 4; **41**, 68, 73–4, 145; **42**, 18; **43**, 18, 24, 176; **44**, 213; **45**, 9, 11; **46**, 188; **47**, 111; **50**, 38; **51**, 300; **53**, 51; **54**, 149, 152, 164, 309; **55**, 72, 75, 153–4, 159–60; **56**, 9; **57**, 114, 121, 122, 123, 149, 152, 331
Kotz, Adam, **48**, 218–19; **49**, 273
Kotzebue, August Friedrich Ferdinand von, **38**, 191
Koun, Charles, **7**, 112; **11**, 121
Koun, Karolas, **49**, 13

Kouyaté, Sotigui, **45**, 155; **50**, 39
Kovar, Leo, **40**, 94n
Kovel, Joel, **45**, 89n
Ković, P., **15**, 142
Kowzan, Tadeusc, **40**, 34
Koyro, H. J., **37**, 160n
Koyro, Hans Georg, **23**, 122
Kozicki, Henry, **44**, 145n
Kozikowski, Stanislaus, **53**, 303
Kozikowski, Stanley J., **36**, 166n
Kozintsev, Grigori, **21**, 128; **27**, 179n; **33**, 28, 34; **34**, 39; **36**, 160; **39**, 4, 5, 65, 75, 81, 83–6, 88, 94, 249; **40**, 38; **53**, 111; **54**, 149, 150–1, 309; **55**, 383; **56**, 98n, 99
Kozlenko, William, **57**, 69
Koźmian, Stanisław, **10**, 120; **14**, 122; **15**, 137
Kozuka, Takashi, **60**, 6n9, 341–3, 352–3
Krabbe, Henning, **27**, 192; **29**, 148n; **31**, 173, 188
'A Danish Actress and her Conception of the Part of Lady Macbeth', **29**, 145–9
Krabbe, K., **18**, 134
Kracauer, Siegfried, **45**, 44n
Krafft, John, **22**, 119–20
Kraft, Barry, **59**, 161n14
Kraft-Ebing, Richard von, **45**, 20n
Kramer, Daniel, **56**, 295
Kramer, Heinrich, and Sprenger, James, *Malleus Maleficarum*, **10**, 140
Kramer, Joseph E., **25**, 176; **28**, 181
Kranendonk, A. G. van, **2**, 126, 140, 141
Kranidas, Thomas, **19**, 136
Krantz, Albert, **24**, 156; **29**, 171
Kranz, David L., **58**, 318, 332
Krapp, G. F., **7**, 4
Krapp, G. P., **25**, 3
Krásnohorska, **9**, 107
Kraszewski, Joseph Ignatz, **9**, 110n
Kraus, Jaroslav, **14**, 118; **16**, 133
Kraus, Karl, **14**, 116; **32**, 224
Krause, W., **32**, 195n, 198n
Krauss, Jennifer, **40**, 234
Krauss, Rosalind, **52**, 192n
Krauss, Werner, **5**, 112; **6**, 117; **12**, 112; **13**, 124; **40**, 40; **48**, 173
Kreft, B., **15**, 141–3
Kreider, P. V., **14**, 11
Kreiger, Murray, **19**, 139
Kreilkamp, Ben, **60**, 179–80, 180
Krejca, Otomar, **18**, 120
Kreps, Barbara, **54**, 321; **57**, 340
Kresnik, Johann, **44**, 197
Kress, Gunther, **55**, 5n
Kreuger, Robert, **44**, 69n
Kreyssig, Friedrich, **2**, 108; **44**, 110n
Krieder, Paul, **39**, 138
Krieger, Elliot, **34**, 162, 173; **37**, 4, 10
Krieger, Murray, **31**, 128n
Krige, Uys, **18**, 128
Krikunov, Igor, **45**, 151
Kris, Ernst, **40**, 119n; **57**, 241
Krishnankutty, Sadanam, **45**, 148
Kriśković, V., **4**, 122n
Kristeller, Paul Oskar, **29**, 91; **33**, 22; **36**, 91n
Kristeva, Julia, **47**, 247; **54**, 323; **55**, 239; **56**, 67; **58**, 312; **59**, 294–5, 362
Kristiansen, Henning, **39**, 79n
Kristjansson, Vikingur, **57**, 286
Križák, Bohuslav (Michal Bosý), **4**, 109; **9**, 110n
Krizanovski, Alexander, **45**, 151
Krohg, Guy, **2**, 128
Krohn, Eino, **10**, 117
Król-Kaczorowska, B., **32**, 192n
Kroll, Richard, **57**, 57
Krömer, Bärbel, **56**, 315
Kronenberger, Louis, **24**, 98
Kronenfeld, Judy Z., **31**, 182; **33**, 189; **47**, 233; **52**, 277; **53**, 304; **55**, 92n; **56**, 85n
Krontiris, Tina, **58**, 208
Kross, Jaan, **23**, 159
Krueger, Robert, **40**, 80n; **54**, 196n; **57**, 206
Kruger, Loren, **55**, 271n, 275, 281–2, 283n; **58**, 358
Krull, Marianne, **37**, 150n
Krupinski, Renny, **56**, 292
Kruschelnitzkü, M., **15**, 140
Krutch, Joseph Wood, **32**, 44n; **45**, 7; **55**, 155
Krzyzanowski, Juliusz, **3**, 118
Kubiak, Zygmunt, **14**, 122
Kübler-Ross, Elisabeth, **37**, 186
Kubrick, Stanley, **53**, 193
Küchelbekker, W. K., **23**, 174
Kuckhoff, Adam, **48**, 172
Kuckhoff, Armin-Gerd, **20**, 150; **23**, 142, 174n; **25**, 186; **26**, 166; **32**, 224; **48**, 171, 179
Kücümen, Z., **18**, 130
Kudō, Kankurō, **60**, 130, 135–40
Kugel, Alexandr, **54**, 144
Kuhl, E. P., **3**, 25; **15**, 23; **16**, 170; **32**, 98n
Kuhn, Maura Slattery, **31**, 165, 189
Kuhn, Sherman, **52**, 186n
Kuhn, Thomas S., **35**, 173; **54**, 315; **59**, 28n37
Kuin, R. J. P., **33**, 203
Kujoory, Parvin, **30**, 191
Kukowski, Stephan, **51**, 96, 104, 105
Kulkarni, H. B., **19**, 126
Kuller, Deborah, **55**, 228n
Kullmann, Thomas, **44**, 212
Kulp, B., **55**, 221n
Kumar, Kalamandalam Manoj, **45**, 148
Kumar, Mihir, **22**, 166
Kummer, Friedrich, **48**, 10n
Kumonosujo (The Castle of Cobwebs), **12**, 115
Kunene, Masizi, **52**, 160
Kuner, Mildred C., **23**, 174n; **24**, 167
Kunkel, Kathryn, **47**, 231
Kunstler, Ernst, **10**, 145; **11**, 143n
Kunz, G. F., **49**, 190
Kunz, Harald, **10**, 150n
Kunz, Simon, **42**, 150
Kupke, Peter, **48**, 180
Kupper, Hans Jürg, **32**, 217
Küpper, Reiner, **37**, 160n
Kupperman, Karol Ordahl, **54**, 232n
Kurbas, Les, **56**, 342; **58**, 338
Kurdoğlu, Haluk, **18**, 130

INDEX

Kureishi, Hanif, **57**, 272
Kuriharar, Komaki, **42**, 153
Kurke, Eduard, **23**, 149
Kurland, Stuart M., **43**, 55n, 67n; **48**, 251; **54**, 127n
Kurosawa Akira, **12**, 115; **39**, 4, 6, 13n, 65, 67, 70–4; **40**, 4; **41**, 227; **43**, 251; **45**, 63–5; **48**, 263; **49**, 284; **53**, 111; **55**, 383; **56**, 347; **57**, 172, 182; **58**, 337; **59**, 370, 371; **60**, 135, 138, 355
Kurtzweig, Gisela, **11**, 120
Kuruç, Bozhurt, **14**, 124; **15**, 138
Kuschnia, Michael, **48**, 172n
Kushari, K., **19**, 141
Kussmaul, Ann, **50**, 258
Kussmaul, Paul, **37**, 159n
Kustow, Michael, **50**, 34; **55**, 279
Kutlu, Gülgun, **12**, 117
Kuznets, Lois, **56**, 9n
Kuznetson, V., **13**, 133
Kvapilová, Hana, **9**, 107
Kvapil, Jaroslav, **9**, 108–9, 110n
Kwa Zulu, **52**, 156
'Kyd, Thomas' (pseudonym), **7**, 10
Kyd, Thomas, **1**, 114; **2**, 46; **3**, 52, 62, 109, 110; **5**, 139; **6**, 72, 74n; **7**, 14, 83, 85, 95, 96; **8**, 103, 106; **9**, 26, 153; **14**, 34, 89n; **16**, 37, 98; **17**, 202; **19**, 1, 64, 150; **21**, 25, 150; **22**, 54, 152, 159, 171; **23**, 28n, 49, 117, 160, 169; **24**, 32, 44, 142, 162, 174; **26**, 1, 41; **27**, 173, 178; **30**, 110, 119; **32**, 145, 146, 156, 158, 218; **33**, 25, 33n; **34**, 86–7, 89; **37**, 191; **38**, 122, 220; **39**, 143, 146, 147, 217; **40**, 10; **41**, 7; **42**, 127; **43**, 268; **44**, 131, 148, 149, 153; **45**, 191; **47**, 273; **49**, 57; **53**, 180, 320; **54**, 301, 351; **55**, 21, 23, 24n, 220, 360, 369; **59**, 219, 293
  Cornelia, **9**, 139; **10**, 5; **11**, 137, 143n; **20**, 84
  Spanish Tragedy, **1**, 64, 125; **3**, 26, 112, 138; **6**, 71, 72, 74n; **9**, 41; **10**, 3, 69, 139, 143
  The Spanish Tragedy, **13**, 33; **14**, 8, 10, 50, 82, 105; **15**, 113; **20**, 17, 20, 24
Kyle, Barry, **32**, 201, 205–7; **33**, 176; **37**, 163, 165; **38**, 212; **40**, 175–6, 180; **41**, 190; **42**, 156, 160, 200; **43**, 254, 258; **44**, 158, 168, 191; **49**, 2n; **54**, 265; **55**, 303–5; **56**, 291; **57**, 261, 277; **58**, 48, 304; **59**, 185
Kyle, Chris, **57**, 315
Kymbeline, **11**, 42–6
Kynaston, Edward, **58**, 237, 243, 244
Kynaston, S., **60**, 46n55
Kynaston, Thomas, **58**, 243
Kyncl, Ivan, **57**, 280, 283
Kyndersley, Anne, **32**, 88, 89
Kyrnman, Steve, **53**, 276
Kyte, Sir William, **5**, 56

La amon, **59**, 241–2
Labaña, Juan Bautista, **20**, 101
Labanowski, John, **45**, 154; **59**, 338
Labé, Louis, **15**, 98n
La Belle, Jenijoy, **35**, 178
Laboulle, Louise J., **59**, 41n
Labov, W., **23**, 111n
La Branche, Anthony, **21**, 132; **22**, 163n
La Bruyère, **26**, 89
La Calprenéde, G. de, **20**, 5, 6, 9
Lacan, Jacques, **40**, 110, 190; **44**, 43, 213, 220; **48**, 252; **49**, 58n, 67, 88, 215n, 308; **50**, 244, 247–8, 251; **51**, 284, 289; **53**, 73, 306, 320, 325; **54**, 130, 322, 323, 324; **56**, 145, 311, 330; **57**, 313; **58**, 175; **59**, 350, 353, 364; **60**, 233, 236, 346, 351
LaCapra Dominic, **58**, 170
Lacerda, Carlos, **20**, 123
Lacey, Robert, **56**, 217n
Lacey, Josh, **51**, 269
Lachmann, Karl, **25**, 195
Lacoue-Labarthe, Philippe, **59**, 286, 289–90, 291
Lacquer, Tom, **54**, 166
Lactantius, Lucius, **14**, 143; **15**, 100, 102, 106–7, 109n, 110n; **46**, 122
  De Phoenice, **15**, 29
Lacy, John, **51**, 86
  adaptation of *The Taming of the Shrew*, **9**, 85n
  Sauny the Scott, **9**, 85n
Lacy, Walter, **32**, 30, 31n, 35
Ladkins, Robert, **25**, 149
Ladle, John, **43**, 213
Ladurie, E. Le Roy, **52**, 128
Lady Alimony, **13**, 123
Lady Elizabeth's Men, **44**, 153; **47**, 51, 53, 55–6
Lady Macbeth, **47**, 214
Lady Mother, The, **3**, 51, 52
Lady of Belmont, The, **55**, 130
Lady of Pleasure, The, **52**, 296
Lady Rhetoric, **12**, 5
Lady's Tragedy, The, **54**, 27, 30
Læstadius, Lars-Levi, **9**, 116
Laevius, **15**, 109n
La Farge, John, **24**, 96
Laffay, Albert, **39**, 91, 92
Lafforgue, R., **13**, 127; **14**, 119
La Fontaine, **22**, 16, 20
Lafontaine, H. C. de, **19**, 106
Laforgue, Jules, **9**, 148; **45**, 2
Lagarde, Fernand, **23**, 171n
Lagarde, Jean-Jacques, **18**, 122
Lagénie, Jean, **11**, 120
Lagerwall, Sture, **16**, 137
Lagowski, Joseph J., **55**, 178n
Lagrenée, Jean Jacques, **60**, 221
Laguardia, Eric, **20**, 49n; **22**, 170; **38**, 5
Lahr, John, **60**, 146n17, 146n18, 147n22
Laidlaw, J. C., **23**, 141n
Laine, Edvin, **10**, 117
Laing, R. D., **40**, 145; **42**, 208; **48**, 285; **56**, 265
Laing, Samuel, **41**, 156n
Laing, Stewart, **41**, 183; **42**, 156; **44**, 75, 196; **50**, 207, 236; **51**, 261
Laird, David, **19**, 127
Laird, Trevor, **44**, 198; **45**, 152
Lait, Fiona, **56**, 273
Lajcha, Ladislav, **18**, 121
Lake, David J., **24**, 155; **30**, 207; **31**, 184, 187, 193; **32**, 243; **34**, 190; **38**, 86n; **40**, 226; **59**, 222n34
Lake, James, **50**, 55n
Lake, Peter, **44**, 75; **48**, 257; **54**, 2, 34n, 35n, 89–90, 94, 166n, 167n, 169n, 172n; **56**, 28n, 217n; **58**, 330; **59**, 249n77

INDEX

Lake, Sir Thomas, **1**, 43, 44; **53**, 71
Lal, Ananda, **59**, 369–70
Lallias, Jean-Claude, **52**, 285–6
Lally, Steven, **56**, 57n; **57**, 210
Lalou, René, **2**, 121; **7**, 146n
La Mar, Virginia A., **13**, 165; **14**, 166n
Lamartine, Alphonse de, **2**, 116
Lamb, Charles, **3**, 44; **7**, 26, 127; **9**, 136; **13**, 5, 80; **14**, 57, 82–4, 163; **18**, 108, 113, 114; **23**, 105; **24**, 1n, 168; **25**, 185; **29**, 134, 177; **32**, 20, 63; **36**, 53, 78; **37**, 10, 185; **42**, 214; **45**, 18, 19, 26; **47**, 257; **49**, 128; **50**, 41; **51**, 119, 246; **53**, 10, 151–2, 162, 287, 292, 296; **55**, 68, 96, 106–7, 111; **57**, 115; **58**, 264
  Extracts from the Garrick Plays, **14**, 84
  Letters, **14**, 88n
  Specimens of English Dramatic Poets, **4**, 24
  Specimens of English Dramatic Poets, **14**, 82, 83, 163n
  Tales from Shakespeare, **13**, 76
Lamb, Larry, **55**, 299
Lamb, Margaret, **29**, 175; **35**, 175; **36**, 81; **41**, 85n, 87
Lamb, Mary, **24**, 1n; **32**, 20; **36**, 53; **42**, 214; **44**, 206, 241; **49**, 128; **53**, 10, 151–2, 162; **55**, 107n
Lamb, Mary Ellen, **47**, 150n; **51**, 182; **58**, 248, 252, 257, 258
Lamb, Sidney, **59**, 89n34
'Lambard' Volume of Plays, **1**, 65
Lambarde, William, **17**, 113; **27**, 93–104; **28**, 3, 8, 9, 131n, 164–5; **29**, 95n, 96n, 97; **38**, 19, 61; **47**, 41–3
  Archaionomia, **1**, 61; **3**, 4; **12**, 142
  Perambulation of Kent, The, **12**, 28
Lambert, Christ, **51**, 260
Lambert, D. H., *Cartæ Shakespeareanæ*, **3**, 1
Lambert, David, **43**, 215
Lambert, Edmund, **27**, 97, 98, 102, 103, 104
Lambert, J. W., **39**, 85, 86
Lambert, John, **27**, 98–104
Lambert, José, **48**, 4n
Lambert, Ladina Bezzola, **57**, 115
Lambert, Mark, **58**, 270
Lambert, Peter, **9**, 119
Lambin, G., **7**, 96, 97, 99, 104, 105n, 106n; **19**, 133; **21**, 162; **22**, 160, 164; **25**, 53; **30**, 201
Lamble, Anthony, **45**, 152; **46**, 202; **54**, 254; **56**, 293, 296; **57**, 269
Lambley, Kathleen, **6**, 80; **28**, 38n
Lambrechts, Guy, **19**, 141; **21**, 151; **23**, 74, 160
Lamentable Song of the Death of King Lear and his Three Daughters, A, **13**, 41, 44–7
Lamming, George, **48**, 155–6; **56**, 146n
Lamont, Claire, **53**, 178n; **55**, 107n, 181n
Lamont, Rosette C., **50**, 39n; **57**, 119, 124
Lamos, Mark, **39**, 185, 186, 188; **53**, 285
La Motte, **38**, 57, 58
  see also Pardieu, Valentine
Lamour, Brigid, **53**, 284
Lampe, James, **51**, 19n
Lampe, John Frederick, **18**, 97; **32**, 42; **56**, 122; **59**, 342
La Peña, Francisco de, **60**, 238–9
Lampert, Lisa, **58**, 310, 332
La Place, Pierre-Antoine de, **60**, 217–18, 221
Lamson, Roy, **15**, 40n
Lan, David, **55**, 325; **59**, 186, 311, 310–12; **60**, 320
Lanari, Antonio, **57**, 65
Lancashire, Ann Begor, **30**, 127, 134n
Lancashire, Anne C., **23**, 143; **24**, 148, 162n, 163; **39**, 216; **46**, 22; **52**, 75n
Lancashire, Ian, **38**, 226
Lancaster, David, **44**, 196
Lancaster, James, **17**, 34, 51
Lancelot van Denemarken (medieval Flemish play), **5**, 107
Land, Peter, **35**, 144
Landa, José A. G., **53**, 40n
Landa, Louis, **50**, 21n
Landau, Aaron, **57**, 301
Landau, Jack, **11**, 123; **16**, 138
Landen, Dinsdale, **45**, 122; **47**, 215
Lander, Gina, **42**, 149
Lander, James, **48**, 135n
Lander, Jesse M., **51**, 296; **57**, 319
Landi, Ortensio, **54**, 91n
Landino, Christophe, **15**, 95, 96; **34**, 85
Landis, John Hutton, **40**, 204
Landon, H. C. Robbins, **32**, 81
Landon, Richard, **43**, 268n
Landon-Smith, Kristine, **43**, 210
Landovsky, Pavel, **36**, 26, 27
Landow, George, **60**, 155
Landqvist, John, **43**, 109n, 110n; **48**, 3n
Landry, Donna, **37**, 176n; **51**, 6n
Landry, Francis, **50**, 36n
Landry, Hilton, **18**, 172; **22**, 165; **31**, 127, 163, 164
Landstone, Charles, **51**, 144
  'Four Lears', **1**, 98–102
Landt, D. B., **21**, 152; **37**, 87n; **38**, 14
Lane, Allen, **59**, 42
Lane, Anthony, **52**, 90
Lane, Revd Edmund, **4**, 69
Lane, Emile, **5**, 111; **7**, 108
Lane, John, **34**, 88
Lane, Nancy, **57**, 119
Lane, Ralph, **48**, 138
Lane, Richard, **27**, 99
Lane, Rob, **53**, 276
Lane, Robert, **48**, 250; **50**, 227
Laneham (Lanam), John, **6**, 74n; **60**, 21
Laneham, Robert, **15**, 71n
Lang, A., **11**, 99n
Lang, Alexander, **40**, 55–8, 61; **48**, 183; **52**, 283
Lang, Andrew, **40**, 215; **42**, 25n; **46**, 235
Lang, Cecil Y., **56**, 127n
Lang, Clemens, **48**, 65–6
Lang, Matheson, **7**, 146; **9**, 16; **11**, 124; **18**, 74; **49**, 230
Lang, Peter, **48**, 258; **54**, 306; **56**, 301, 314
Lang, Robert, **49**, 274; **54**, 289
Langaren, Jacobus van, **12**, 107
Langbaum, Robert, **11**, 140; **43**, 117n
Langdale, Alban, **4**, 155; **17**, 122
Langdon, Anthony, **24**, 118
Langdon, Stephen, **38**, 133
Lange, Bob de, **14**, 122
Lange, Hartmut, **48**, 178
Lange, Jessica, **52**, 257; **54**, 293; **56**, 4n
Lange, V., **37**, 152n

Langebank, Alexander Halevi, **54**, 183n
Langenfelt, Gosta, **10**, 146
Langer, Susan, **22**, 9
Langer, Susanne K., **41**, 117
Langer, Suzanne, **10**, 109; **32**, 8; **39**, 1, 2n, 234
Langfield, Angela, **44**, 193
Langford, Larry, **38**, 232; **47**, 141n
Langgaard, Riued, **51**, 259
Langham, Michael, **5**, 111, 119; **6**, 118; **7**, 107, 113, 114; **10**, 115, 116, 129; **12**, 119; **13**, 125; **14**, 117, 135–7; **15**, 145, 146; **16**, 18, 153–4; **38**, 50; **39**, 188; **53**, 235
Langham (Laneham), Robert, **33**, 203; **60**, 337
Langhans, Edward A., **20**, 168; **49**, 111n, 116n; **51**, 4, 82n, 91n
Langhoff, Thomas, **40**, 58–9, 61
Langhoff, Wolfgang, **48**, 173
Langhorne, William, **11**, 102
Langland, William, **57**, 243, 245, 246
Piers Plowman, **6**, 59; **8**, 20, 21; **13**, 106; **17**, 50
Langley, Francis, **1**, 9, 25; **3**, 3; **6**, 160; **7**, 60, 61; **19**, 103; **28**, 168; **40**, 214; **44**, 148, 151; **47**, 42, 241; **49**, 19; **60**, 54
Langner, Lawrence, **7**, 117; **8**, 122
Langridge, Michael, **45**, 154
Langridge, Stephen, **49**, 275; **54**, 285
Langsam, G. G., **6**, 10
Langsford, Rod, **45**, 147
Langton, Stephen, **17**, 106
Langtry, Lillie, **6**, 140; **56**, 134
Langworthy, Charles, **42**, 206
Lanham, John, **27**, 134
Lanham, Richard A., **26**, 174n; **38**, 6; **40**, 93n, 97n, 99n; **49**, 46, 55, 216; **55**, 219n, 221
Lanier, **18**, 103
Lanier, Douglas M., **47**, 225; **50**, 241, 262; **53**, 86n, 330; **56**, 347–8; **57**, 256; **58**, 156, 158, 190; **60**, 130, 133n13, 139n29, 355, 360
Lanier, Emilia Bassano (Lanyer, Aemilia), **38**, 229; **42**, 186–7; **49**, 301; **51**, 161n, 279, 296; **55**, 341
Lanier, Innocent, **2**, 29, 31
Lanier, Nicholas, **40**, 220
Lanman, Henry, **34**, 180; **44**, 147, 148; **60**, 50, 53
Lanquet, Thomas, **42**, 27n
Lansbury, Angela, **41**, 50
Lansbury, David, **43**, 217
Lansdowne, B. L., **30**, 166n; **33**, 141n; **44**, 115–23; **47**, 17n
Lant, Thomas, **44**, 252
Lapides, Fred, **51**, 315
Laplanche, Jean, **44**, 43n; **49**, 58n
Lapotaire, Jane, **28**, 144, 148; **32**, 209; **47**, 183, 211; **51**, 240–1, 260, 270; **53**, 329
Lapsley, Robert, **45**, 49n
la Pucelle, Joan, **43**, 176; **55**, 287; **56**, 248
Laqueur, Richard, *Shakespeares dramatische Konzeption* reviewed, **10**, 138
Laqueur, Thomas, **45**, 37; **46**, 1, 2, 42, 44, 114n, 118n, 124n, 125n, 132n; **47**, 10n; **48**, 26n; **53**, 18, 298; **56**, 230
Lara, Mile, **3**, 103
Larder, Brian, **51**, 260
Larke-Smith, Betty, **47**, 95
Larkin, James F., **30**, 161n, 163n; **33**, 147n; **42**, 129; **45**, 151; **57**, 237
Larkin, Maeve, **50**, 216, 218; **60**, 288
Larminie, Vivienne, **38**, 32n
Larmour, Brigid, **42**, 149; **47**, 214; **52**, 265
Larner, Christina, **57**, 2
Larocca, John J., **54**, 94n
Laroche, Benjamin, **2**, 116
La Rochefoucauld, **28**, 48n; **42**, 96
Laroque, François, **37**, 190; **38**, 232; **41**, 228; **42**, 196; **46**, 30n, 209; **49**, 69, 77n; **50**, 246, 257; **51**, 283; **52**, 274, 285; **53**, 15n; **54**, 319; **56**, 39n, 328; **57**, 221, 238; **58**, 321, 327, 333; **59**, 257, 361
Larpent, John, **6**, 59–60
Larra, Mrs, **22**, 131
Larsen, Gunnar, **11**, 121
Larsen, Kenneth J., **57**, 243
Larson, Kenneth E., **45**, 159
la Rue, Danny, **43**, 249
Larum for London, A, **6**, 48n; **52**, 6, 7
Las Casas, Bartolome de, **17**, 42; **52**, 188
Lascelles, G., **44**, 131n
Lascelles, Mary, **8**, 13, 26n; **15**, 171; **18**, 158; **25**, 7; **26**, 120; **28**, 89, 100n, 155; **31**, 147; **32**, 9, 10; **37**, 90
'*King Lear* and Doomsday', **26**, 69–79
Shakespeare's Measure for Measure reviewed, **8**, 140
Lascombes, André, **51**, 283
Laseur, Cees, **13**, 130; **14**, 122
Laski, Harold, **27**, 83n
Laski, Marghanita, **56**, 246
Laslett, Peter, **38**, 27n, 29; **46**, 79n
Lass, Roger, **55**, 354
Lasserson, Rachel, **48**, 236
Lasso, Orlando di, *Receuil du Mellange*, **1**, 70; **13**, 161; **26**, 173
Last Things and Last Plays: Shakespearian Eschatology, **46**, 213
Last, B. W., **51**, 69n
Laszlo, Carl, **49**, 122
Lateiner, Joseph, **55**, 122n
Latham, Agnes, **29**, 177; **32**, 2, 6, 9, 37, 64n; **33**, 69n, 70n; **35**, 81n; **41**, 160–1; **43**, 32; **46**, 11n, 12n, 15n; **53**, 53; **54**, 115; **60**, 58n1
Latham, Grace, **18**, 52
Latham, Jacqueline E. M., **30**, 195; **31**, 171–2; **32**, 101n, 231, 236; **34**, 176
'*The Tempest* and King James's *Daemonologie*', **28**, 117–23
Latham, M. W., **8**, 5, 6
Latham, R. E., **20**, 59n; **21**, 100
Latham, Robert, **43**, 98n; **51**, 80n
Latham, Stuart, **8**, 123, 126
Latham, Symon, **44**, 139, 140n, 141
Lathom, Lord, **4**, 106
Latimer, Hugh, Bishop of Worcester, **12**, 99, 105n; **17**, 18, 54, 104–5, 109; **31**, 120; **33**, 93; **48**, 72; **54**, 4, 5, 35
Latimer, Lucia, **57**, 296
Latimer, Sally, **8**, 125
Latimer-Gregory, Miles, **57**, 297
Latour, Bruno, **59**, 32n60
Latter, D. A., **30**, 196
'Sight-Lines in a Conjectural Reconstruction of an Elizabethan Playhouse', **28**, 125–35
Laube, Heinrich, **15**, 132; **35**, 22, 23, 24, 25, 26
Laud, Archbishop William, **4**, 79, 83; **11**, 107; **17**, 66, 100; **54**, 18, 58–9
Laugh and Lie Downe, **13**, 103

Laughlin, Charles D. Jr., **55**, 248–9
Laughton, Charles, **12**, 129n; **13**, 144; **25**, 64; **42**, 103
Laughton, J. K. (ed.), **17**, 21n, 22n
Launching of the Mary, **11**, 80, 81
Laurence, Dan H., **35**, 8n
Laurence, Jordan, **13**, 135
Laurence, Margaret, **44**, 241; **53**, 164; **56**, 302
Laurence, Michael, **6**, 119
Laurenson, James, **31**, 148, 149, 150; **33**, 176; **46**, 191; **47**, 191
Laurentius, **17**, 200
Laurie, John, **14**, 116
Laurie, Margaret, **51**, 80, 81
Laurier, Angela, **46**, 187–8; **47**, 215; **50**, 35
Laurier, Jay, **36**, 82, 83
Lauten, Flora, **53**, 283
Lavagnino, John, **54**, 14n; **58**, 354, 356
Lavasher, John, **19**, 106n
Lavater, Johan Caspar, **51**, 114
Lavater, Lewis, **58**, 46
Lavater, Ludwig, **19**, 58; **27**, 173; **32**, 231
Of Ghosts, **3**, 21n; **50**, 196n
Three Christian Sermons, translated by W. Barlow (1596), **4**, 159
Lavelle, J., **1**, 114
Lavender, Andrew, **56**, 345–6; **59**, 208n48; **60**, 141–2, 151, 152
Laver, James, **10**, 72, 76n; **21**, 155
Laverdin, Marshal de, **11**, 108
Lavers, Annette, **44**, 66n
Lavery, Bryony, **51**, 259; **52**, 279
La Vey, Anton, **57**, 154
Lavin, J. A., **23**, 162; **24**, 176; **25**, 191; **26**, 184; **27**, 166; **28**, 169; **42**, 105n; **55**, 29n, 30n
Lavington, Sir James, **43**, 107
Lavrovsky, Leonid, **60**, 327
Law, Alma H., **48**, 115n
Law, E., **15**, 7
Law, Ernest, **36**, 115n; **60**, 54–5, 56
Law, Maggi, **43**, 205
Law, Phyllida, **45**, 151
Law, Robert Adger, **1**, 122; **3**, 23, 28; **4**, 142n; **5**, 135; **6**, 11, 13, 17, 21; **8**, 143; **9**, 143, 144n; **10**, 2; **11**, 138, 142; **12**, 142; **14**, 163 and n; **27**, 133n; **31**, 12n, 94, 98n; **38**, 1, 14, 15; **55**, 19, 20, 21, 22n, 200n
'Belleforest, Shakespeare and Kyd', **2**, 140
Law, T. G., **24**, 71n
Lawes, Henry, **6**, 55; **33**, 208
Lawes, William, **19**, 105n; **26**, 33; **32**, 242
Lawford, Thomas, **60**, 112
Lawler, Dennis, **47**, 68n
Lawless, Donald S., **23**, 171n; **32**, 235; **33**, 203; **34**, 186; **35**, 177
Lawlor, John, **5**, 132–3; **10**, 135; **12**, 138; **15**, 158; **16**, 59, 157–8, 169–70; **19**, 6, 141; **25**, 189; **28**, 170; **29**, 4
The Tragic Sense in Shakespeare reviewed, **15**, 157–8
Lawner, Lynne, **53**, 32n
Lawrance, Will, **46**, 161
Lawrence, Arthur, **47**, 96
Lawrence, Charles E., **58**, 145
Lawrence, D. H., **16**, 34; **20**, 144; **21**, 44; **24**, 31, 35; **26**, 8; **40**, 204; **42**, 3n; **45**, 109n; **46**, 123; **56**, 303
Lawrence, Errol, **52**, 208n
Lawrence, French, **51**, 6
Lawrence, Gary, **46**, 68; **47**, 216
Lawrence, Jason, **55**, 347; **59**, 362; **60**, 343, 353; **54**, 178n; **60**, 229n36
Lawrence, Josie, **49**, 255–6; **50**, 234; **52**, 261; **58**, 280; **59**, 342; **60**, 78
Lawrence, Judiana, **39**, 218
Lawrence, L. A., **13**, 110n
Lawrence, Robert, **60**, 229n36
Lawrence, T. J., **47**, 83n
Lawrence, Sir Thomas, **10**, 73; **49**, 119; **51**, 11, 112–15, 119
Lawrence, W. J., **1**, 4, 8, 10; **4**, 11, 98; **6**, 74n; **7**, 72, 74, 80n; **9**, 26, 29, 33n; **10**, 88n, 152; **11**, 64, 69n; **12**, 9, 11; **15**, 7, 9, 10n; **47**, 24n, 83, 90n; **52**, 18n; **60**, 40n10
Pre-Restoration Stage Studies, **13**, 123n
The Physical Conditions of the Elizabethan Public Playhouse, **12**, 33
The Elizabethan Playhouse, **13**, 113, 123n
Lawrence, W. N., **49**, 181n
Lawrence, W. W., **2**, 138; **3**, 69; **4**, 13; **8**, 10, 12; **11**, 45; **13**, 88n, 153; **25**, 2, 3, 5, 6, 7, 8; **26**, 119; **29**, 51, 53; **32**, 135n, 156; **49**, 181n
Shakespeare's Problem Comedies, **2**, 143; **3**, 7; **11**, 49n
Lawrenson, T. E., **19**, 143; **43**, 158n
Lawry, Jon S., **19**, 123; **27**, 165; **32**, 87n, 100n; **34**, 176
Lawson, Adrian, **44**, 198
Lawson, Aletta, **42**, 155
Lawson, Kyle, **60**, 168n4.1
Lawson, Leigh, **43**, 188; **44**, 197
Lawson, Maria, **59**, 344
Lawson, Nigel, **40**, 208
Lawton, Richard, **52**, 158n
Lax, Annecy, **54**, 293
Layamon, **33**, 16
Layden, Penny, **52**, 238–9; **54**, 262
Layer, Christopher, **51**, 57
Layton, Elizabeth, **57**, 127, 136
Layton, John, Keeper of Newgate, **17**, 93n
Lazar, Andrew, **54**, 292
Lazare, Katherine, **59**, 338
Lazaridis, Stefanos, **41**, 168; **42**, 158
Lazarowicz, Klaus, **60**, 128n31
Lazarus, **11**, 40
L., E., contribution to *Sorrowes Joy* (1603), **4**, 155
Lea, Henry Charles, **35**, 104n
Lea, James, **5**, 149
Lea, Kathleen M., **1**, 8; **8**, 3; **25**, 125n; **34**, 169; **52**, 122n; **54**, 193n, 196; **55**, 247n
Italian Popular Comedy, **14**, 3
Lea, Philip, **30**, 164n
Leach, A. F., **17**, 58, 59n
Leach, Edmund, **29**, 18n; **35**, 66n, 70n
Leach, Francis, **13**, 110n
Leach, Robert, **50**, 225; **57**, 302
Leach, Susan, **49**, 142n
Leacroft, Helen, **47**, 2n
Leacroft, Richard, **43**, 158n; **47**, 2n
Leadbitter, Bill, **44**, 199
Leaf, Claudia, **58**, 154
Leahy, William, **57**, 319
Leake, John, **53**, 200n
Leake, W., **5**, 52
Leake, William, **55**, 33

Leaming, Barbara, **57**, 155; **59**, 68
Lear, Edward, **55**, 139n
Learning to Curse, **46**, 220
Learning, Barbara, **39**, 71n
Learning, Thomas, **55**, 367
Lear's Daughters, **43**, 207; **54**, 340
Leason, John of Hersley, **14**, 166; **27**, 182
Leatherbarrow, Tom, **43**, 214; **44**, 202; **45**, 149, 150; **46**, 194, 203
Leavenworth, Russell E., **29**, 174; **45**, 26n
Leavis, F. R., **4**, 10, 23, 24; **6**, 153; **7**, 11; **8**, 12, 22; **9**, 132; **10**, 9, 103, 106n; **11**, 44; **12**, 132n; **14**, 144; **18**, 9; **19**, 5, 143; **21**, 4, 5, 9 10n 11n, 28n, 62; **23**, 152; **25**, 5, 7, 29; **26**, 123n; **27**, 82n; **32**, 139; **34**, 1, 9, 54, 57, 66, 68; **36**, 103; **37**, 6, 131; **38**, 246; **40**, 24–31, 192; **41**, 45, 211; **42**, 165, 181; **44**, 217; **45**, 57; **47**, 73; **49**, 212; **51**, 146; **53**, 288; **56**, 208n, 209n; **57**, 38; **60**, 186
(ed.) *Determinations*, **14**, 11
The Common Pursuit, **11**, 49n
Leavis, Queenie, **47**, 109
Lebedev, Georgia Pavel, **48**, 186
Lebègue, **20**, 25n
Lebesque, Morvan, **18**, 123
Le Blanc, Abbé Jean-Bernard, **3**, 136; **24**, 79; **60**, 215, 217
Le Bossu, René, **8**, 58–9; **37**, 148
Le Brun, Charles, **51**, 111–12, 114, 119
Lecarte, Irène, **7**, 108
Lecca, Marie-Jeanne, **52**, 254
LeClaire, Guy, **13**, 124
Le Clercq, Jacques, **46**, 117n
Leconfield, Lord, **17**, 28
Lecoq, Anne-Marie, **31**, 15n
Lecoq, Jacques, **46**, 169; **60**, 166, 169n4.1
Le Comte, Edward S., **5**, 140; **9**, 12; **15**, 173; **23**, 167n
Lecotteley, Charles, **15**, 133
Lecoux, Paul, **55**, 330
Le Coz, Anne, **44**, 195
Leday, Sadanam Annette, **45**, 148
Ledbetter, Robert, **32**, 196, 197; **33**, 160, 162, 164
Ledebur, Ruth F. von, **37**, 156; **42**, 175
Ledger, Heth, **54**, 292
Ledwell, Jane, **55**, 170n
Lee, Adrian, **47**, 215; **50**, 216; **53**, 284; **54**, 288
Lee, Brian, **41**, 186
Lee, Bruce, **57**, 146
Lee, Francis, **56**, 237
Lee, Guy, **46**, 111n
Lee, Henry, **53**, 323–4
Lee, Sir Henry, **46**, 115n, 225n; **60**, 351
Lee, Jenny, **51**, 267; **55**, 328; **58**, 117
Lee, John, **55**, 337–8; **56**, 147n
Lee, Jongsook, **46**, 61n
Lee, Maurice, Jr, **44**, 226–7
Lee, Nathaniel, **55**, 97
Lee, Paul, **8**, 123
Lee, Robert, **33**, 163, 167n; **36**, 135, 138n
Lee, Sir Sidney, **1**, 37n; **2**, 14, 16, 41; **3**, 6, 9; **4**, 1–2, 7, 10; **5**, 147; **7**, 50, 52, 53, 82; **8**, 153; **11**, 79–82; **12**, 138; **15**, 6, 11, 12, 14, 15, 18, 29, 30, 100, 109n; **17**, 37n; **23**, 91; **26**, 107; **28**, 39n; **29**, 140–1; **35**, 1; **38**, 52; **42**, 67n, 70n; **43**, 112n; **44**, 110n; **46**, 35n; **47**, 134n; **48**, 276, 277; **53**, 69n; **55**, 14n, 32, 386–8; **58**, 1, 119, 121; **59**, 4, 25, 152, 153
Facsimile of the First Folio, **11**, 80, 87n
Life of Shakespeare, **3**, 8
Stratford-upon-Avon, **3**, 2
Lee, Spike, **60**, 330
Lee, Vernon, **7**, 95
Lee, Virgil, **29**, 174
Lee, William, **33**, 167
Leech, Clifford, **5**, 136; **7**, 107, 146; **8**, 12, 14, 15, 16, 17; **11**, 139; **13**, 149, 152, 156, 166; **14**, 8, 163–4; **15**, 24, 113, 118, 121, 138, 160, 179; **18**, 34, 62, 65, 170; **19**, 142, 153; **20**, 158; **21**, 129, 131, 135; **23**, 132, 149–50, 180, 181; **24**, 11, 143, 150, 176; **25**, 3, 6, 47, 48, 60n; **26**, 166; **27**, 157n, 158n, 164n, 165n, 170n, 179n, 188; **28**, 77n, 153, 169; **29**, 1, 6, 89, 171; **30**, 9n, 11n, 37, 39; **31**, 5; **32**, 7, 8, 53n; **33**, 7, 147n, 188; **36**, 57n; **37**, 5, 20n, 55n, 106n; **38**, 12, 13, 134, 135, 142; **40**, 153n; **43**, 38, 70, 74n; **46**, 227; **49**, 96n, 105n; **51**, 96n; **52**, 6n; **54**, 350; **56**, 78n; **58**, 348
John Ford and the Drama of his Time, **14**, 12
John Webster, **14**, 11, 55n
'The "Meaning" of *Measure for Measure*', **3**, 66–73
Shakespeare's Tragedies reviewed, **5**, 130–1
'The Structure of the Last Plays', **11**, 19–30
'Studies in Shakespearian and Other Jacobean Tragedy, 1918–1972: A Retrospect', **26**, 1–9
'Studies in *Hamlet*, 1901–1955', **9**, 1–15
'The Unity of *2 Henry VI*', **6**, 16–24
Leech, Geoffrey, **53**, 14n
Leech, Susan, **55**, 329
Leedam, Thomas, **11**, 100
Leedham-Green, E. S., **56**, 197n
Leeds University Library *see under* Libraries
Leefe, Reginald, **2**, 19
Lees, F. N., **10**, 11, 59n; **19**, 147; **21**, 52n; **30**, 195; **54**, 223n
Lees, R. B., **23**, 14n
Leeves, Luke, **59**, 345
Le Fanu, Sheridan, **58**, 193
Lefebvre, Henri, **54**, 330; **55**, 248n; **60**, 346
Lefebvre, Léon, **33**, 162, 163n
Lefevere, André, **48**, 4n
Le Fevre, Raoul, **35**, 179; **36**, 87n; **41**, 70n
Lefkowitz, M., **19**, 106n
Lefranc, Abel, **2**, 118; **3**, 11; **7**, 97, 139; **9**, 12, 141; **38**, 52; **57**, 211
A la Découverte de Shakespeare, **2**, 120
reviewed, **1**, 124–5
Lefton, Sue, **52**, 226
Legat, Francis, **53**, 109n
Legate, John, **27**, 190
Legend of Good Women, **54**, 303
Legg, Leopold G. Wickham, **54**, 125n; **60**, 113n44
Leggatt, Alexander, **24**, 164; **26**, 155; **28**, 82, 159–60; **29**, 171, 172; **31**, 173; **32**, 4, 5, 7, 12; **35**, 91; **37**, 4, 7, 11, 67, 103n; **39**, 216; **41**, 5n, 36n; **42**, 10n, 165, 168–9; **43**, 46, 53n, 54, 229; **44**, 71n, 256; **45**, 187–8; **47**, 249–50; **51**, 69n, 292; **52**, 276; **53**, 288–9, 292–3, 306, 307; **54**, 307, 340; **55**, 381; **57**, 200, 333; **58**, 350, 356; **59**, 347–8, 367, 368; **60**, 349, 353
Legge, Thomas, Dr, **42**, 20, 21; **45**, 185; **49**, 300
Richardus Tertius (MS.), **3**, 52; **4**, 91; **6**, 60; **20**, 17, 24
Legh, Gerard, **27**, 14n, 118n; **41**, 106n
Legman, Gershon, **32**, 99n

INDEX

Legouis, Emile, **1**, 118; **2**, 119, 122; **10**, 142; **16**, 54; **55**, 145, 146n
Legouis, Pierre, **19**, 141; **30**, 193; **55**, 145n, 204n
'*Titus Andronicus*, 111, i, 298–9', **28**, 71–4
Legrand, Julie, **42**, 140
LeGros, James, **57**, 186
Leguizomo, John, **52**, 90
Le Hardy, William, **25**, 139, 140n
Lehman, Courtney, **52**, 279; **60**, 169n6.2
Lehmann, Beatrix, **1**, 108, 110; **27**, 153
Lehmann, Courtney, **56**, 347; **57**, 145, 330; **58**, 161, 194
Lehmann, Elmar, **47**, 236n; **56**, 235n
Lehmann, H. T., **28**, 53n
Lehmann, Paul, **59**, 262n18
Lehmann, Wilhelm, **49**, 123
Lehmberg, Stanford E., **32**, 167n; **54**, 20n
Lehnert, Martin, **19**, 145; **20**, 169; **22**, 166; **32**, 223
Lehto, Leo, **9**, 112; **10**, 117; **13**, 126
Le Huray, Peter, **54**, 20n
Leibnitz, Gottfried Wilhelm, **35**, 76n; **45**, 5
Leibovici, Leo, **38**, 207
Leicester, countess of, *see under* Knollys, Lettice
Leicester, Earl of (Robert Dudley), **60**, 4–7, 8, 11, 54
Leicester, Earls of, *see under* Coke, Robert, Dudley, Robert, *and* Sidney, Robert
Leicester, Robert Dudley, Earl of, **27**, 129; **28**, 20, 23, 24, 151; **35**, 115; **38**, 21, 22; **43**, 247; **44**, 234, 236, 240; **48**, 266; **54**, 74, 116, 118, 192; **59**, 229
Leicester's Men, *see under* Theatre, Elizabethan, companies
Leider, Emily W., **24**, 146
Leigh, Alan, **41**, 189; **43**, 210
Leigh, Andrew, **52**, 28n
Leigh, J. H., **25**, 118
Leigh, John, **59**, 76
Leigh, Mike, **28**, 137
Leigh, Richard, **17**, 34n
Leigh, Sir Robert, **7**, 58, 59, 63, 64, 65, 67n; **25**, 144
Leigh, Valentine, **33**, 141, 143n
Leigh, Vince, **59**, 318
Leigh, Vivien, **3**, 114; **6**, 123, 140, 141–2, 145; **7**, 146n; **9**, 126, 129; **13**, 70; **15**, 141; **16**, 24, 132; **48**, 227
Leigh, William, **50**, 194; **58**, 144
Leigh-Hunt, Barbara, **30**, 173
Leigh-Noel, M., **51**, 180
Leighton, Frederick, **49**, 125–6
Leighton, Margaret, **1**, 98, 102; **18**, 133; **24**, 3n; **36**, 81
Leighton, Margaret (*ob.* 1908), **7**, 92
Leimberg, Inge, **22**, 151–2; **23**, 117, 119; **24**, 153; **26**, 163; **34**, 95, 96, 101, 104n; **50**, 111n
Leinwand, Theodore B., **44**, 226; **54**, 299; **55**, 359
Leiser, Moshe, **54**, 289; **58**, 300
Leishman, James Blair, **6**, 158; **7**, 106n; **14**, 145; **15**, 18n 71n, 72n, 168; **17**, 130n; **22**, 82, 90; **23**, 41n, 69–70; **29**, 47; **31**, 128n; **32**, 101n, 103n; **42**, 74n; **46**, 16n; **49**, 98n; **56**, 65n
Themes and Variations in Shakespeare Sonnets reviewed, **16**, 170–1
Leisi, Ernst, **18**, 129; **20**, 174; **21**, 162; **23**, 118, 185; **24**, 149; **25**, 5; **27**, 189; **31**, 175; **32**, 224; **37**, 161n; **41**, 245n; **59**, 193–4, 195, 196n14, 196n15
Leiter, Samuel L., **50**, 30n
Leith, Alastair, **45**, 148
Leitzmann, Albert, **9**, 100n; **57**, 64
Leja, Matthias, **49**, 278
Lejeune, Oscar, **7**, 108; **8**, 118
Lekain, Henri Louis, **9**, 91
Lekes, Edmund, **54**, 97n
Le Laboureur, J., **32**, 191
Leland, John, **49**, 79; **52**, 59n; **59**, 261n17
Leland's Collecteana, **1**, 36n
Lelyveld, Toby, **35**, 1; **48**, 54n
Lemaître, Frederick, **3**, 100; **28**, 148
Lemaître, Jules, **9**, 65, 68n
Lemarchand, Jacques, **10**, 118
Lembcke, Edvard, **48**, 4n
translations of Shakespeare, **3**, 108, 111
Lemêtre, Jean-Jacques, **52**, 286
Lemmon, J., **19**, 31, 33n; **28**, 150
Lemon, Mark, **56**, 127
Lemon, R., **23**, 41n
Lemon, Rebecca, **57**, 36
Lemonnier, Léon, **2**, 120
Le Motteux, Peter, **46**, 14n
Lemouton, Emilia, **53**, 319
Lemprière, John, **10**, 20
Lendon, Jon E., **52**, 186n
Leney, William, **51**, 64–5
Lengeler, Rainer, **37**, 158n
L'Engle, Madeleine, **53**, 136
Lengler, **23**, 119; **26**, 161
Lengyel, Gy., **16**, 135; **18**, 125
Lenin, Vladimir Ilitch, **48**, 189; **49**, 91n; **54**, 145n, 146
Lenkiewicz, Rebecca, **58**, 302
Lennam, T. N. S., **23**, 169; **25**, 191; **27**, 163
Lennartz, Monika, **40**, 60
Lennix, Harry, **56**, 4n
Lennon, John, **54**, 246; **57**, 155, 156
Lennox, (Mrs) Charlotte, **33**, 18; **34**, 13, 15; **37**, 142; **51**, 5, 6; **53**, 213, 214n, 219, 220, 231–2; **55**, 106
Lennox, Duke of, *see* under Stuart, Ludowick,
Lennox, James Stuart, 4th Duke of, **38**, 122
Lennox, Patricia, **54**, 312
Lennox-Boyd, Hon. Christopher, **49**, 115; **51**, 10
Leno, Dan, **7**, 123; **29**, 143; **36**, 152
Lenska, Ruala, **51**, 261
Lent, Johan A., **60**, 133n13
Lents, Cheryl Blair, **32**, 101n
Lenz, Bernard, **37**, 158n; **47**, 236n; **56**, 235n
Lenz, Carolyn Ruth Swift, **35**, 159; **37**, 3n, 33n; **40**, 92n, 101n; **41**, 65n, 74n; **46**, 6n; **48**, 132n; **49**, 66n; **60**, 84–5n2
Lenz, J. M. R., **9**, 96, 99, 100n
Lenz, John W., **37**, 151n
Lenz, Joseph M., **36**, 166; **48**, 243
Leo the Great, Pope, **57**, 245
Leo X, Pope, **60**, 62n10
Leo, F. A., **10**, 59n
Leo, Johannes, **11**, 95, 97n
A Geographical Historie of Africa, **11**, 97n
Leon, H. J., **38**, 39
Leon, Rigoberto Cordero y, **7**, 133
Leonard, David, **49**, 271, 277
Leonard, E. M., **53**, 62n
Leonard, Janet S., **38**, 227

Leonard, Nancy S., **34**, 170–1; **35**, 159
Leonardo da Vinci, **15**, 136, 165; **23**, 163; **32**, 203; **45**, 5
Leoncavallo, Ruggiero, **45**, 173
Pagliacci, **8**, 71
Leone, Leonard, **36**, 178n; **43**, 144n; **52**, 9n, 11n
Leone, Sergio, **52**, 90
Leonhardt, R. W., **48**, 9n
Leontiev, A. N., **54**, 145n
Leontovich, Eugenie, **36**, 81; **46**, 187
Leopold I, Emperor, **18**, 78
Lepage, Robert, **46**, 187–9; **47**, 215; **48**, 228; **49**, 306; **50**, 35, 36, 39; **51**, 193, 259, 284; **52**, 255; **54**, 312, 313; **56**, 345, 346
L'Epine-Smith, Jane, **45**, 149
Le Poulain, Jean, **15**, 133
Leppänen, Glory, **10**, 117; **11**, 119
Le Prevost, Nicholas, **44**, 195; **51**, 215; **54**, 270–1; **56**, 267–8; **57**, 294
Leret, Xavier, **50**, 234; **57**, 297; **60**, 326
Lerma, Duke of, **23**, 87n
Lerner, Laurence, **14**, 154; **21**, 142; **25**, 81n; **31**, 184; **32**, 2, 223; **42**, 196; **52**, 101
Le Roux, Hugues, **9**, 63, 68n
Leroy, Maxime, **15**, 109n, 110n
Lerse, Franz Christian, **9**, 95, 96, 97
Les Atrides, **30**, 33
Lesay, Franck, **54**, 319
Lescure, Jean, **11**, 120; **12**, 112
Leskov, Nikolai, **52**, 285; **57**, 113
Leslie, Bishop John, *De Origine, Moribus et Rebus Gestis Scotorum*, **4**, 47
Leslie, Charles Robert, **51**, 116, 117
Leslie, John, **17**, 122; **19**, 3, 147; **27**, 172
Leslie, Michael, **53**, 326
Leslie, Nancy T., **28**, 169n
Leslie, R. F., **41**, 156n
Lesnick, Henry G., **23**, 169
Lessay, Franck, **56**, 39n; **57**, 221
Lesser, Anton, **34**, 151; **36**, 155; **39**, 191; **41**, 72, 190; **43**, 177–8, 212; **45**, 116, 139, 153, 157; **46**, 175–7, 180; **47**, 217; **52**, 267, 293; **57**, 274; **58**, 299; **59**, 328, 329; **60**, 322
Lesser, Simon O., **25**, 181
Lesser, Zachary, **60**, 368–9
Lessing, Doris May, **55**, 115
Lessing, Gotthold Ephraim, **9**, 94, 96, 97, 99, 100n; **16**, 14, 134; **18**, 114; **22**, 35, 166; **26**, 167; **37**, 152, 155; **40**, 58; **43**, 249; **45**, 159
Lessingham, Jane, **53**, 327
Lester, Adrian, **45**, 128–9; **46**, 9, 191; **54**, 269–70; **55**, 301–2; **56**, 97, 100, 164, 289; **57**, 258, 280, 282, 283; **58**, 301; **59**, 177
L'Estrange, Sir Nicholas, **56**, 60n
Letchford, Mabel, **10**, 113
Le Tourneur, Etienne-François-Louis-Honoré, **57**, 114, 115
Le Tourneur, Pierre, **2**, 115, 116; **5**, 105n; **9**, 92–4, 110n; **16**, 53; **24**, 86; **45**, 159; **48**, 8; **60**, 215, 216
translation of Shakespeare, **3**, 98
Le Touzel, Sylvestra, **46**, 201; **51**, 219
Lett, Ray, **42**, 153; **43**, 216; **45**, 150; **47**, 104, 106; **50**, 235
Letters of Horace Howard Furness, The, **46**, 235
Letts, Crispin, **51**, 255
Letts, Dominic, **49**, 247
Letts, M., **17**, 39n
Letts, Pauline, **47**, 99
Leukhardt, Josh, **56**, 295
Levack, Brian P., **57**, 9
Levant Company, **11**, 90, 92, 93, 96; **17**, 9, 21, 37n
Leveaux, David, **45**, 116–19; **46**, 198; **49**, 9n; **60**, 137n21
Levenson, Jill L., **27**, 158; **31**, 181; **38**, 233; **39**, 139n; **41**, 209; **42**, 199; **49**, 7, 8, 14n, 74n, 99n, 159n, 163n; **52**, 18n, 91n; **53**, 293; **54**, 22n, 307, 347–8; **55**, 3n, 271n, 391; **58**, 138, 145, 148; **59**, 359–60
Lever, J. W., **6**, 169; **7**, 133, 140; **9**, 145n; **12**, 142; **14**, 155–6; **15**, 13, 15, 16, 44, 45, 52, 61n; **18**, 173; **20**, 174; **22**, 82; **23**, 69; **25**, 7; **26**, 9, 122, 126, 127n, 177; **27**, 92n; **28**, 79n, 90n; **30**, 191; **31**, 100, 106n, 127n, 128n, 129, 130, 133, 136, 180; **32**, 107; **33**, 19n; **35**, 179; **37**, 90, 92, 93n; **40**, 107n, 109, 111, 113n, 115, 117, 139n, 140n; **41**, 70n; **42**, 67n, 75n; **44**, 254–5; **46**, 112n, 244; **53**, 30n, 37n, 228n; **55**, 196; **58**, 51
The Elizabethan Love Sonnet reviewed, **10**, 141
'Shakespeare and the Ideas of his Time', **29**, 79–91
'Shakespeare's French Fruits', **6**, 79–90
'Twentieth-century Studies in Shakespeare's Songs, Sonnets, and Poems. 3. The Poems', **15**, 18–30
'Venus and the Second Chance', **15**, 81–8
Lever, K., **14**, 10
Lever, Katherine, **59**, 188
Lever, Thomas, **17**, 115
Leverenz, David, **45**, 38n
Leveridge, Richard, **18**, 98, 100; **19**, 151; **51**, 48n; **56**, 122
Leverson, Ada, **53**, 138
Levey, Barnett, **22**, 126–8
Levi, A. H. T., **42**, 68n
Levi, Peter, **48**, 60
Lévi-Strauss, Claude, **22**, 16; **29**, 11n, 12n; **31**, 56; **35**, 65, 66, 67, 70, 73, 74, 76; **37**, 188; **40**, 186; **50**, 109, 243
Levin, Bernard, **31**, 151n; **33**, 171n; **55**, 277; **56**, 248
Levin, Carole, **46**, 111n; **52**, 114n; **54**, 93n
Levin, D., **22**, 175n
Levin, Harry, **11**, 153; **15**, 123, 165; **18**, 43, 44, 158; **19**, 126; **20**, 158; **24**, 150; **25**, 111; **27**, 61n, 63n, 65n, 67n; **28**, 40, 41, 47n, 108, 157, 174, 178; **29**, 167; **31**, 46, 174; **33**, 3, 35n, 38, 39, 47n; **34**, 96n; **35**, 97; **36**, 164; **38**, 13, 160, 161; **39**, 140, 143n; **40**, 137–8; **41**, 202; **43**, 16n; **45**, 8, 62, 76n; **48**, 9n; **49**, 51, 63n, 94n, 100; **51**, 145; **53**, 43; **59**, 41
The Overreacher, **14**, 10
The Question of Hamlet reviewed, **14**, 140
'Shakespeare's Misanthrope', **26**, 89–94
'Two Magian Comedies: *The Tempest* and *The Alchemist*', **22**, 47–58
Levin, J. D., **20**, 159
Levin, Joanna, **57**, 32, 312
Levin, Kate, **51**, 292
Levin, Richard A., **19**, 140, 147; **20**, 158; **22**, 172n; **24**, 162; **25**, 182, 192; **26**, 4, 173, 184; **27**, 191; **28**, 7, 151, 163; **29**, 167; **32**, 6, 227; **33**, 183–5, 186, 204, 206n; **34**, 70, 170, 186; **36**, 169, 170, 177, 190, 194; **37**, 158, 164, 218; **38**, 9; **39**, 225, 240; **40**, 197, 213, 225n; **41**, 128, 141; **42**, 168; **43**, 253–4; **44**, 122n, 205, 225–6, 244; **45**, 179n; **46**, 20n; **47**, 176n; **50**, 242; **52**, 325; **53**, 322; **54**, 189n, 315, 323; **55**, 19; **56**, 330; **57**, 316, 318; **58**, 325, 332; **59**, 376n2
Levin, Yuri D., **23**, 159, 174n; **48**, 4n; **52**, 285
Levinas, Emmanuel, **58**, 176; **60**, 346

Levine, Joseph, **51**, 138
Levine, Laura, **44**, 44n; **46**, 6, 20n; **49**, 304; **52**, 279, 293n; **56**, 75, 233n
Levine, Lawrence, **57**, 250, 253, 255; **58**, 116
Levine, Michael, **46**, 188; **47**, 215
Levine, Mortimer, **52**, 171n
Levine, Nina, **53**, 308
Levine, Robert T., **34**, 185, 195
Levins, Peter, **42**, 58n; **56**, 58n
Levinson, Judith, C., **28**, 173
Levinson, Stephen C., **50**, 98n
Levinta, Doina, **50**, 234
Levitan, Isaak, **48**, 117
Levitch, Timothy Speed, **57**, 186
Leviţchi, L., **20**, 127; **29**, 166
Levith, Murray J., **43**, 227; **57**, 319; **58**, 312, 332
Levitsky, Ruth M., **20**, 148; **27**, 158, 159; **31**, 180; **32**, 235; **33**, 201
Leviush, Zalman, **9**, 114; **14**, 121
Levon, Katrina, **45**, 125, 148
Levring, Kristian, **55**, 74; **56**, 291; **58**, 185
Levy, Adam, **54**, 276, 278; **57**, 281; **59**, 318; **60**, 310
Levy, Charles S., **24**, 159
Levy, Deborah, **56**, 343
Levy, Eric P., **56**, 329
Levy, F. J., **26**, 174n; **38**, 11; **42**, 29; **55**, 209n, 213n
Levy, M. J., **51**, 4
Levy, Milton A., **15**, 171
Lewalski, Barbara Kiefer, **18**, 161–2; **20**, 153; **23**, 144; **24**, 156; **25**, 103n, 104n; **32**, 49n; **33**, 67n; **34**, 117; **43**, 97n; **49**, 303; **51**, 164n; **55**, 244n
Lewes, George Henry, **29**, 134; **35**, 32, 34; **48**, 4; **49**, 133
Lewi, Angela, **42**, 81n, 82n, 83n
Lewik, Wlodzimierz, **16**, 136
Lewin, John, **43**, 211
Lewin, Roger, **45**, 191n
Lewinsky, Josef, **33**, 26n
Le Winter, Oswald, **49**, 72n
Lewis Frederick of Würtemberg, **36**, 140
Lewis, Anthony J., **25**, 184; **26**, 175; **32**, 234; **46**, 211; **51**, 69n
Lewis, B. Roland, **4**, 74n; **59**, 276n24
The Shakespeare Documents, **3**, 4
Lewis, Barbara, **53**, 286
Lewis, C. M., **9**, 9, 11
Lewis, C. S., **1**, 121; **4**, 24, 52, 162; **6**, 101; **9**, 14, 135–6; **15**, 21, 24, 27, 30n, 104, 108n; **17**, 40n, 41, 224–5; **18**, 41–2, 44; **23**, 158; **24**, 40; **28**, 43; **30**, 82; **31**, 137; **36**, 44, 45; **37**, 14n; **41**, 148; **43**, 264; **45**, 76n; **53**, 30; **54**, 206; **55**, 349; **56**, 28; **57**, 200; **59**, 265
Lewis, Cecil Day, **5**, 88
Lewis, Charlton T., **52**, 185n
Lewis, Cynthia, **48**, 170; **52**, 272; **60**, 348
Lewis, D. B. Wyndham, **4**, 6–7
Lewis, Damian, **48**, 235; **49**, 271; **51**, 228, 230, 231; **52**, 255
Lewis, David, **43**, 217; **53**, 90
Lewis, Elle, **49**, 273
Lewis, Kevin, **45**, 155
Lewis, Margaret, **55**, 171n
Lewis, Maria, **53**, 116
Lewis, Michael, **5**, 149; **17**, 22n
Lewis, P. E., **51**, 72n
Lewis, P. S., **44**, 58n
Lewis, Peter, **39**, 169, 170n, 172
Lewis, Richard, **43**, 210
Lewis, Robert E., **49**, 79n
Lewis, Roger, **32**, 24
Lewis, Samantha, **48**, 234
Lewis, Stephen Brimson, **53**, 249; **54**, 252, 288, 293; **55**, 325; **56**, 291; **57**, 259, 292; **59**, 304; **60**, 317
Lewis, W. W., **51**, 5
Lewis, William, **49**, 123
Lewis, Wyndham, **16**, 34; **21**, 5; **22**, 8
Lewkenor, Sir Lewis, **2**, 25; **11**, 92–3, 116n, 143; **19**, 146; **26**, 172; **48**, 123–5; **54**, 92n
Lewkowicz, Karl, **59**, 342
Ley, Charles David, **6**, 154
Ley, Stephen, **45**, 155
Leyland, Peter, **4**, 155
Leyris, Pierre, **26**, 164; **50**, 130
Leyris, Pierre and Evans, Henry, *œuvres Complètes de Shakespeare* reviewed, **13**, 153–4
Leyshon, Andrew, **60**, 187n13
Lezra, Jacques, **52**, 300
Li, Jianwu, **57**, 170, 174, 175, 176
Li, R., **57**, 171
Li, Zhen, **57**, 176
Liber Regalis, **60**, 113
Liberles, Robert, **48**, 52n
Liberty, Kate, **42**, 157
Libes, I., **8**, 120
Libo, Kenneth, **55**, 115n
LIBRARIES
Ashmolean Museum, **4**, 93
Balliol College, **16**, 118, 120
Birmingham Public, **13**, 77, 80n
Birmingham Shakespeare Memorial Collection, **7**, 90–4; **12**, 119
Birmingham Reference Library, **1**, 73
Bodleian Library, **3**, 47; **4**, 78–96; **6**, 62; **7**, 56, 114; **10**, 154n; **11**, 64, 98; **13**, 109, 165
background literature, **4**, 92–3
collections relating to Shakespeare: growth of Shakespeare collection, **4**, 78–84
copies of Quartos and Folios, **4**, 84–6
Douce collection, **4**, 87–8
Malone collection, **4**, 80–1, 86, 87, 91–2, 93, 95
plays earlier than 1700, **4**, 91–2, 93–4
Rawlinson collection, **4**, 91, 94
source and allusion books, **4**, 86–91
Turbutt First Folio, **4**, 82–4
Bridgewater, **12**, 107; **13**, 108–9, 110n
British Museum, **3**, 43–57; **4**, 72, 74n, 79, 84, 85, 87, 93; **5**, 50; **6**, 62, 160, 172; **7**, 49, 51, 52; **10**, 154n; **11**, 64–6, 78, 80, 98; **12**, 107, 125; **13**, 80n, 105n, 107–10, 165; **14**, 81
Ashley library in, **3**, 45
collections relating to Shakespeare: Garrick's library, **3**, 43–4
copies of Quartos and Folios, **3**, 47–8
Elizabethan MSS., **3**, 50–3
George III, **3**, 44–5
J. O. Halliwell-Phillipps, **3**, 45–6
music, **3**, 55–6

LIBRARIES (*cont.*)
Portland Papers in, **5**, 55, 57n
'Shakespeariana', **3**, 49–50
Shakespeare exhibition (1923), **3**, 49
sources and allusions, **3**, 54–5
Cambrai, **12**, 32
Charlemont Library, **4**, 81
Columbia, Theatre Museum at, **1**, 13
Congress, Library of, **1**, 58, 76
Corpus Christi College Library, Oxford, **4**, 94
Devonshire, Duke of (1790–1858), his library, **6**, 54
Drexel collection, **9**, 89n
Emmanuel College Library, Cambridge, edition of *Othello* in, **5**, 54
Fitzwilliam Museum, **12**, 32
Fitzwilliam Museum, Cambridge, editions of Shakespeare in, **5**, 54
Folger Shakespeare Library, **1**, 17, 19, 21, 57–78; **2**, 150; **3**, 47, 49, 57; **4**, 72, 74n, 82, 84–5, 93; **5**, 51, 147; **6**, 162, 163, 171, 172; **7**, 91; **8**, 153–4; **10**, 2, 87n, 150, 153, 154; **13**, 74, 80n, 105n, 159, 163; **16**, 1–3, 6; **22**, 151; **27**, 104
activities, **1**, 74–7
biography and iconography, **1**, 61–2
collections: Americana, **1**, 69
early printed books (non-dramatic), **1**, 67–70
English drama, **1**, 63–6
Incunabula, **1**, 73
influence and reputation, **1**, 63
MSS. (non-dramatic), **1**, 70–2
modern books and MSS., **1**, 73
origins, **1**, 57–60
Shakespeare's text, **1**, 59–61
Song-Books, Elizabethan and Jacobean, **1**, 68–9, 70
Sothern-Marlowe material in, **1**, 72
sources, **1**, 62–3
stage-history, **1**, 72
Harvard, **12**, 107
Houghton Library, **10**, 154n
Huntington Library, **3**, 57; **4**, 84–5, 93; **6**, 170; **8**, 104n, 105n; **11**, 98; **12**, 107; **13**, 108–9, 110n
documents relating to Warwickshire, **6**, 59
family papers, **6**, 60
its growth and collections of Shakespeariana and early books described, **6**, 53–63
John Rylands, **13**, 104n, 105n
King's College Library, Cambridge, editions of Shakespeare in, **5**, 54
Martin Bodmer Library (Bibliotheca Bodmeriana), **8**, 98n
Bibliotheca Bodmeriana described, **8**, 81–5
Rosenbach collection, **7**, 115; **8**, 82, 84, 85n
New York Public Library, **3**, 48; **6**, 171
Pembroke College Library, Cambridge, editions of Shakespeare in, **5**, 54
Pepys, **13**, 106, 108, 109
Shakespeare's Birthplace Library, **10**, 152
Stadtbibliothek, Zürich, **5**, 46n
Stockholm, Royal Library of, **1**, 28
Trinity College Library, Cambridge, Shakespeare collection described, **5**, 50–4
University College, Cardiff, **13**, 80n
University of Leeds, **11**, 59n
University of Minnesota Library, **10**, 154n
University of Pennsylvania Library, **5**, 144n
University of Virginia Library, **10**, 154n
Victoria and Albert Museum, **13**, 80n
Worcester College Library, Oxford, **4**, 94–5
Wigan Public, **13**, 105n
Libro de Apolonio, **9**, 140
Licata, Salvatore J., **56**, 73n
Lichfield, Richard, **60**, 337
Lichtenberg, Georg Christoph, **9**, 98, 100n; **21**, 125n; **29**, 143; **51**, 115–16; **58**, 40, 43
report of Garrick's acting, **7**, 121–2
Lichtenfels, Peter, **59**, 372–3, 375
Lichtenhahn, Fritz, **24**, 145
Lickendorf, Elizabeth, **55**, 276n
Liddell, J. R., **4**, 96n
Liddell, Mark Harvey, **26**, 82n, 85
Lide, Sven, **48**, 6n
Lidgard, Carolyn, **55**, 172n
Lidstone, Gerald, **47**, 213
Lie, Nadia, **53**, 165n; **56**, 158n, 314
Liebermann, F., **6**, 4
Liebknecht, Wilhelm, **45**, 90
Liebler, Naomi Conn, **36**, 171–2; **48**, 250–1; **50**, 104n, 246; **53**, 305; **56**, 102; **58**, 327; **59**, 355; **60**, 114n49
Liechtenstein Gallery, **12**, 32, 33
Life of Alexander (Plutarch), **48**, 250
Light, John, **60**, 304, 316
Lightbody, David, **51**, 261
Lightbown, R., **43**, 155n, 160n
Ligier, Pierre-Matthieu, **3**, 101
Lilburne, John, **17**, 85; **23**, 167
Liliev, Nikolai, **10**, 115; **13**, 125
Lillich, Meredith, **49**, 157
Lillo, George, **9**, 94; **43**, 103n; **46**, 139; **51**, 18–19, 24, 67–77; **53**, 301
Lilly, Joseph, **32**, 98n
Lilly, William, **34**, 183; **44**, 250
Lillywhite, Lisa, **51**, 264
Lily, William, **17**, 58–9; **35**, 123, 124
A Shorte Introduction of Grammar, **4**, 86
Lim, C. S., **37**, 189n
Lim, Walter S. H., **56**, 318
Lima, Carlo, **15**, 136
Limbird, John, **18**, 19
Limon, Jerzy, **36**, 140, 143n, 144; **39**, 227; **40**, 220–1; **47**, 259; **52**, 82n; **54**, 192n, 196, 317
Limouze, Henry S., **37**, 193n
Lin Shu, **36**, 53
Lin, Hsiu-Wei, **57**, 177, 181, 182
Lin, Tung-Chi, **34**, 195
Linacre, Thomas, **17**, 64, 155
Linares, Gabriel, **54**, 154n
Linche, Richard, **50**, 63
Lincoln, Abraham, **18**, 105; **24**, 99; **50**, 3; **60**, 116, 176
Lincoln, Mary, **42**, 149
Lind, Jenny, **29**, 146
Lind, Millard, **48**, 86n, 87
Linda, J., **9**, 102
Lindabury, R. V., **6**, 6
Lindeheim, Nancy R., **26**, 174

Linden, Stanton J., **33**, 204
Lindenbaum, P., **29**, 161–2
Lindenberger, Herbert, **38**, 9
Linder, Hans R., **12**, 144
Lindford, Peter, **56**, 292
Lindheim, Bogislav von, **9**, 134; **23**, 13n
Lindheim, Nancy R., **37**, 72n; **44**; 86n
Lindley, Arthur, **57**, 51
Lindley, David, **44**, 217, 238; **46**, 205; **48**, 142n; **50**, 241, 260; **56**, 219n, 224n; **57**, 337–8; **59**, 89n34, 89, 90; **60**, 188, 356, 361
Lindley, K. J., **50**, 261
Lindroth, Colette, **24**, 99n
Lindroth, James, **24**, 99n
Lindsay, Alexander, 25th Earl of Crawford, **13**, 92, 104n
Lindsay, Barbara N., **23**, 179
Lindsay, David, 28th Earl of Crawford, **13**, 90, 105n
Lindsay, Sir David, **53**, 326
A Satire of the Three Estates, **4**, 99–100
Lindsay, Jack, **6**, 79, 80, 85
Lindsay, James, 24th Earl of Crawford, **13**, 92, 96
Lindsay, Katrina, **59**, 300
Lindsay, Marshall, **31**, 164
Lindsay, Robert, **39**, 108; **47**, 10; **52**, 245–6; **53**, 281
Lindsay, Wallace M., **46**, 116n
Lindsey, E. S., **15**, 7
Lindström, Åoke, **18**, 128
Lindström, Erik, **3**, 114; **18**, 121
Lindström, Hans, **43**, 112n, 113n
Lindtberg, Leopold, **9**, 116; **13**, 124, 125; **15**, 132; **16**, 132; **24**, 145; **28**, 172n; **37**, 162n
Line, Jill, **59**, 362
Line, Kit, **45**, 156; **46**, 197
Lineham, Rosaleen, **43**, 216
Linehan, Conor, **55**, 332; **59**, 299
Linehan, Niamh, **58**, 263
Linford, Anthony, **47**, 102n
Linford, Peter, **45**, 157
Ling, Nicholas, **3**, 19; **20**, 26n; **26**, 184; **28**, 41n; **35**, 79n; **38**, 245–6; **60**, 255, 260–4, 267
Ling, Peter, **43**, 205
Lingard-Lane, Jon, **46**, 194
Lings, Martin, **21**, 128
Link, Franz H., **37**, 158n
Linker, Robert White, **40**, 80n
Linklater, Kristin, **51**, 276–7
Linley, Thomas, Sr, **51**, 6, 90n, 93
Linley, Thomas, Jr, **18**, 96, 98; **51**, 91
Linley, William, **15**, 3; **18**, 98
Linnell, Rosemary, **34**, 180; **53**, 196, 197n, 206n
Lintern, Richard, **53**, 252
Linthicum, M. Channing, **1**, 8; **6**, 93n; **60**, 74n8, 74n9, 75n13, 76n23
Linton, Joan Pong, **53**, 324
Linton, W. J., **1**, 83
Lintott, Bernard, **46**, 41n
Linz-Roberts, Jane, **42**, 152
Lion, The, ship, **11**, 90
Lipka, L., **23**, 23n
Lipman, Maureen, **27**, 149; **56**, 247
Lippincott, H. F., **29**, 174; **30**, 194
Lippincott, Joshua Ballinger, **45**, 39
Lipscomb, Edward, **55**, 328, 329, 333
Lipscombe, John, **45**, 112
Lipsius, Justus, **15**, 97n; **33**, 14–16, 17, 19, 20–5; **36**, 179; **46**, 99; **54**, 40
de Amphiteatris, **2**, 30
Liptzen, Keni, **55**, 115, 124–5
LiPuma, Edward, **57**, 26
Lirondelle, A., **5**, 105n
Lisle family, letters, **17**, 226–39; **59**, 359
Viscount (Arthur Plantagenet), **17**, 226–7, 231, 233–5, 237–9
Honor (*née* Grenville), **17**, 226, 230, 234, 237
Lisle, Rouget de, **18**, 81
Lister, David, **60**, 230n40
Liszt, Franz, **37**, 201; **60**, 195
Litde, David M., **54**, 47n
Literature And Degree in Renaissance England: Nashe, Bourgeois Tragedy, Shakespeare (P. Holbrook), **48**, 259
Literature, Politics and National Identity: Reformation to Renaissance (A. Hadfield), **48**, 257
Lithgow, Arthur, **11**, 123; **15**, 139; **18**, 132
Lithgow, William, **17**, 33
Litson, Jo, **52**, 91n
Little Bit of Fluff, A, **9**, 17
Little Device for Henry VII, **60**, 112n42, 113n44
Little, Arthur L., Jr, **47**, 233; **49**, 207n
Little, David M., **9**, 100n; **48**, 88n; **51**, 5
Little, Steve, **59**, 342
Littledale, Harold, **11**, 50, 55, 59n
Littleton, Betty J., **24**, 160n
Littlewood, J. C. F., **22**, 163
Littlewood, Joan, **8**, 123; **10**, 123; **12**, 120; **16**, 143; **18**, 65, 147, 153–4; **53**, 328; **59**, 203
Livermore, Ann, **21**, 152
Livesey, Gerry, **50**, 228
Livesey, Julie, **53**, 262
Livesey, Peggy, **36**, 81
Livesey, Roger, **5**, 122, 125; **6**, 138, 139
Livingston, Meg Powers, **55**, 378
Livingston, Paisley, **53**, 90n
Livingstone, Sid, **29**, 152
Livy, **4**, 28; **10**, 25n, 29, 31, 34, 38n; **15**, 23, 29, 89; **17**, 61; **28**, 67, 71–4; **30**, 193; **31**, 15; **38**, 39, 115, 116, 119–25, 128, 129, 185; **40**, 75; **41**, 105, 117; **42**, 118; **44**, 8, 34; **47**, 131n; **48**, 8, 39n; **50**, 138; **53**, 61, 69; **55**, 199, 204, 208, 209; **56**, 14
L., J., *see under* Lea, James
Llewellyn, Nigel, **55**, 240n, 242n, 250n; **60**, 223n4, 231n47, 232
Llewellyn, Roger, **47**, 212
Llewellyn-Jones, Lloyd, **49**, 278; **51**, 262; **52**, 256
Lloyd, Bernard, **27**, 151; **35**, 143, 144; **44**, 191, 194; **45**, 132
Lloyd, Emily, **58**, 300
Lloyd, Revd Evan, **54**, 52n
Lloyd, Janet, **40**, 198n; **46**, 209
Lloyd, Matthew, **51**, 257, 263
Lloyd, Michael, **14**, 142, 154; **15**, 174; **18**, 171; **23**, 61n; **30**, 195; **31**, 33
'Cleopatra as Isis', **12**, 88–94
Lloyd, Norman, **11**, 123; **59**, 67
Lloyd, Peter, **44**, 232

INDEX

Lloyd, Phyllida, **41**, 188; **42**, 156; **44**, 192; **45**, 156; **46**, 256; **48**, 223–4; **52**, 289; **57**, 258, 261, 293; **58**, 305
Lloyd, Robert, **39**, 79n
Lloyd, W. F., **53**, 64n, 66
Lloyd, William, **59**, 382, 383
Lloyd, William Watkiss, **10**, 38n
Lloyd Evans, Gareth, **16**, 161; **20**, 165; **22**, 175; **23**, 174n; **24**, 117, 137, 167; **26**, 175; **27**, 137–42, 163, 169–70; **28**, 103n; **29**, 48, 91
Conversation with Judi Dench, **27**, 137–42
'Directing Problem Plays': interview with John Barton, **25**, 63–71
'Interpretation or Experience? Shakespeare at Stratford', **23**, 131–7
'The Reason Why: The Royal Shakespeare Season 1968' *reviewed*, **22**, 135–44
'Shakespeare and the Actors: Notes towards Interpretations', **21**, 115–25
'Shakespeare, the Twentieth Century and "Behaviourism" ', **20**, 133–42
Lloyd-Jones, Hugh, **35**, 162
Lloyd-Pack, Roger, **42**, 158
Lloyds, Frederick, **41**, 26
Lluellyn, Martin, **17**, 177
Loach, Kenneth, **15**, 144
Loades, David M., **52**, 168n, 171n; **54**, 125n
Loarte, Gaspar, **56**, 195–6
Löb, Ladislaus, **31**, 184; **32**, 223
Lobban, Michael, **55**, 37n
Locatellus, Bonetus, **10**, 49n
Lock, Kate, **42**, 160
Locke, John, **8**, 57, 58; **9**, 94; **18**, 47; **20**, 83, 87; **22**, 145; **38**, 179; **46**, 79; **49**, 304; **51**, 73, 136; **56**, 91; **59**, 130
Locke, Matthew, **18**, 94, 98; **19**, 151; **35**, 36; **38**, 197; **51**, 80, 81
Locke, Philip, **24**, 118
Lockett, Carol, **51**, 292
Lockey, Rowland, **42**, 80, 81, 83
Lockhart, Adrienne, **30**, 202
Lockhart, Calvin, **26**, 148–9
Lockhart, John Gibson, **18**, 19; **56**, 128
Lockhart, Robert, **44**, 197
Lockie, D. McN., **33**, 166n
Lockie, David, **11**, 97n
Lockyer, Mark, **47**, 199, 204–5; **49**, 242–3, 255; **54**, 262–3; **59**, 345
Lockyer, Paul, **58**, 301
Lockyer, Roger, **38**, 23n; **43**, 238; **56**, 216n, 218n, 219n, 221n
Locrine, **4**, 92; **6**, 34n; **9**, 84; **10**, 143; **11**, 44; **12**, 20; **13**, 156; **14**, 10, **17**, 212; **20**, 24; **48**, 277; **55**, 30n
Lodge, David, **35**, 117n; **45**, 126; **58**, 130
Lodge, John, **7**, 117
Lodge, Thomas (*see also* Greene, Robert), **10**, 35, 70n; **11**, 143n; **14**, 7, 23, 29; **15**, 101, 127; **17**, 41, 51, 130; **18**, 34; **23**, 88n, 98; **26**, 113, 115; **27**, 130, 173; **28**, 167 29; **29**, **31**, 2, 183; **32**, 232; **33**, 72; **34**, 184; **38**, 131n, 220; **40**, 135n, 225; **42**, 71n; **44**, 20, 21; **45**, 15, 19; **46**, 10, 16, 17, 20, 41n, 224; **47**, 273; **50**, 20, 22n, 23, 25, 255; **51**, 135; **54**, 57, 115, 118; **55**, 21, 22, 23, 24n, 25; **56**, 44, 87, 89, 101, 328; **58**, 25, 183; **60**, 52
A Looking Glass for London and England, **1**, 64; **10**, 87n
Phillis, **15**, 46, 109n
Poore Man's Talent, **1**, 71
Rosalynde, **1**, 62; **3**, 18; **4**, 87; **8**, 1, 41, 42, 46, 47–8; **10**, 33; **15**, 170
translation of Seneca's *De Beneficiis*, **10**, 34, 38n
Wounds of Civil War, **11**, 48; **13**, 167n
Lodovici, Cesare Vico, **11**, 121; **12**, 114; **13**, 129; **15**, 136
Loeb, James, **47**, 128; **56**, 41n; **59**, 194
Loeben, Maria-Beate von, **23**, 118
Loeffler, Peter, **29**, 176
Loehlin, James N., **51**, 299; **52**, 289; **56**, 4; **57**, 328; **58**, 339; **60**, 360
Loengard, Janet S., **41**, 5; **44**, 147; **60**, 41n18, 42n23, 43n28
Loewenstein, Joseph F., **43**, 239–40, 265n, 266; **54**, 333; **59**, 33n65; **60**, 253–4
Lofaro, Michael, **32**, 225
Loftis, John, **32**, 42n, 46n; **51**, 46n, 52n, 76, 185
Loftus, Suzanne, **56**, 292
Logan, George M., **23**, 169; **31**, 183
Logan, Gerard, **49**, 261
Logan, Phyllis, **55**, 327
Logan, Terence P., **33**, 198
Logan, W. H., **53**, 217n
Logeman, Henri, **5**, 110n
Loggan, D., **30**, 163n
Loggins, Vernon, **51**, 282
Löhken, Silvia, **40**, 54
Loiseau, J., **10**, 142
Lok, Anne, **60**, 333
Lok, John, **52**, 208
Lökkeberg, Georg, **7**, 114; **8**, 120
Lomax, Harry, **10**, 123; **12**, 119; **13**, 135; **14**, 127
Lomazzo, **31**, 19
Lombard, Bernard, **39**, 139n
Lombard, Peter, **39**, 139n
Lombardo, Agostino, **15**, 136; **23**, 153–4; **44**, 217; **48**, 257; **59**, 194n7
Il Dramma Pre-Shakespeariano reviewed, **11**, 144
Lombardo, Greg, **58**, 189
Loncq, Caroline, **44**, 177; **45**, 125; **47**, 213
Loncraine, Richard, **51**, 266; **52**, 289; **55**, 382; **56**, 3; **58**, 185; **59**, 371, 372
LONDON, **3**, 1, 2, 3, 16; **4**, 70, 73, 79, 81, 83; **5**, 55; **6**, 159, 168; **11**, 117, 124, 128; **12**, 2, 3, 5–6, 16, 17, 19, 22; **17**, 3–12
apprenticeship, **17**, 67–8
Bermondsey Church, **3**, 28
Blackfriars, **3**, 26, 50; **4**, 70, 76; **52**, 69, 79, 81–3, 143
boundaries, **17**, 3–4
Bridewell Dock, **1**, 30
Carpenters' Hall, **6**, 65
the City, **17**, 4–5, 8–11
city and City (definition of), **17**, 4n 4
College of Physicians, **11**, 73
Cripplegate, **3**, 3; **11**, 100
companies, **17**, 6, 68, 70, 150, 157–9
Denmark House, **11**, 109, 110
Dulwich College, **7**, 60, 61, 85
Essex Stairs, **1**, 30
Finsbury Fields, **3**, 24
Gray's Inn, **3**, 24, 25; **4**, 69; **8**, 7; **11**, 103, 146; **12**, 21n
Guildhall, **12**, 19
Inns of Court, **12**, 18; **8**, 11, 32, 107n; **17**, 71–2, 78–9

hospitals, **17**, 7, 153, 158, 164
hours of work in, **17**, 17
official pest-house, **17**, 8, 166
opportunities for self-education in, **17**, 70–2
overcrowding, **17**, 162
prisons, **17**, 4, 87–100
sewage, **17**, 161–2
and Venice, **17**, 46–7
water and food supply, **17**, 5–6
Bishopsgate, **12**, 20n
Gravesend, **11**, 92
inns as theatres, **6**, 64–5
Hampton Court, **11**, 92, 97, 110, 114, 115n; **12**, 16; size of the hall, 15
Islington, **11**, 71
London Bridge, **1**, 30, 33, **17**, 5, 162
Lumbard Street, **11**, 98
Maid Lane, **1**, 29, 30
Maiden Lane, **12**, 143
Mermaid Inn, **3**, 3
Middle Temple, the, **3**, 53; **4**, 149
Montagu House, **3**, 44
Moorfields, **7**, 71
National Maritime Museum, Greenwich, **8**, 116n
Newgate, **11**, 103
Newington, **11**, 100
Nonsuch, **11**, 92
Oatlands, **11**, 93
Paris Garden, **3**, 3; **7**, 71
Paris Garden Manor, **1**, 29
Parish of St Olave, **11**, 100
Public Record Office, the, **3**, 2, 3; **4**, 88; **11**, 100
Requests, Court of, **7**, 64, 67n
Royal Exchange, **1**, 26; **11**, 92
St Andrew's, Holborn, **11**, 100
St Clement Dane's, **11**, 102, 103
St George's, Southwark, **1**, 33
St Mary Overie's, **1**, 25, 26, 30, 31, 32, 33, 34, 36n; **2**, 23
St Olave's, Southwark, **1**, 32; **2**, 21
St Paul's, **1**, 26, 33; **11**, 105
Silver Street, **11**, 100
Scriveners Company, **4**, 70
Somerset House, **1**, 30; **4**, 71, 73; **11**, 109, 110, 114
Southwark, **1**, 25–6, 27, 30, 31; **3**, 3, 142; **11**, 34
Southwark Cathedral, *see* St Mary Overie's
Strand, **11**, 92, 100
Suffolk Place, **1**, 26
Temple, the, **5**, 50
Thames Street, **11**, 72
Trinity Hall, used as a theatre, **6**, 64–74
Westminster, **17**, 4
Westminster Abbey, **6**, 70, 73n
Westminster Hall, **17**, 75–7, 81, 85–6
Wesminster School, **11**, 103
Whitehall, **1**, 33
Whitehall, Banqueting House, **11**, 107, 110–11, 114
Whitehall Masquing House, **11**, 111–13, 114
Winchester House, **1**, 25, 26, 27, 30, 31, 36n; **2**, 23
York House, **1**, 26
London Bibliographical Society, **4**, 83; **7**, 49, 50
London Lickpenny, **13**, 106
London Prodigal, The, **1**, 46; **4**, 92; **9**, 84; **12**, 36; **15**, 134; **16**, 134; **48**, 277
Londré, Felicia Hardison, **36**, 21n
Loney, Glenn, **44**, 243; **49**, 172n
Long, A. A., **46**, 145n
Long, E. T., **26**, 74n
Long, Jane, **43**, 96, 98
Long, John, **20**, 151
Long, John H., **4**, 149, 162; **5**, 140; **6**, 171; **8**, 153; **10**, 141; **15**, 9; **32**, 6; **33**, 76n; **36**, 115n; **51**, 311; **55**, 86
Shakespeare's Use of Music reviewed, **10**, 150
Long, Kenneth R., **54**, 20n
Long, Michael, **30**, 186, 187; **36**, 48, 49; **44**, 215; **46**, 220
Long, William B., **35**, 186; **40**, 218; **42**, 202; **43**, 262; **48**, 271, 272; **50**, 276n; **51**, 332; **52**, 70, 71; **59**, 11, 12
Longenbaugh, John, **48**, 236; **49**, 279
Longer Thou Livest, The, **55**, 86n
Longford, Lord, **57**, 51
Longhi, Kym, **60**, 181–2
Longhurst, Derek, **39**, 103; **42**, 164; **60**, 228n29
Longhurst, Tony, **49**, 273
Longinotto, Kim, **60**, 131n3
Longinus, Dionysius Cassius, **50**, 245; **54**, 29; **59**, 165–6
Longmate, Barak, **59**, 119, 121
Longmore, Wyllie, **42**, 149; **44**, 199
Longrigg, James, **38**, 186n
Longueville, Duc de, **38**, 49n
Longus, **14**, 148
Longworth, Toby, **51**, 233
Lonicerus, **23**, 169
Lonsdale, Roger, **53**, 105n
Lontay, Mrs Margit, **18**, 125
Looby, Christopher, **57**, 130, 133
Loofbourow, J. W., **43**, 102
Looke about you (1600), **17**, 99n; **55**, 23; **60**, 105
Loomba, Ania, **43**, 99, 105n, 221–2; **49**, 202, 206, 213; **50**, 242; **51**, 274, 278; **52**, 202n, 213n; **53**, 290, 291, 293, 312; **54**, 233n, 302; **55**, 352; **56**, 204n; **60**, 162, 168n4.4
Loomes, Brian, **60**, 246n42
Loomie, Albert J., **29**, 21n, 30n; **55**, 93n
Loomis, Catherine, **46**, 95n
Loomis, Edward Alleyn, **11**, 148
Looney, J. Thomas, **59**, 358
Lootens, Tricia, **56**, 132n
López, Francisco, **54**, 154
Lopez, Dr Roderigo, **5**, 140; **17**, 49–50, 128
Lopokova, Lydia, **58**, 125
Lora, José García, **9**, 140
Loraine, Robert, **2**, 4
Loraux, Nicole, **53**, 305
Lorca, Frederico García *see* García Lorca F.
Lord Chamberlain – King's Men, *see under* Theatre, Elizabethan, companies
Lord, Arthur, **12**, 120
Lord, George de Forest, **37**, 185n; **38**, 252n
Lord, Gisela, **24**, 153
Lord, Suzanne, **58**, 358
Lordi, Robert J., **14**, 153
Lords and Ladies of London, The, **52**, 298
Lorenz, K. Z., **53**, 156n

Lorimer, R. L. C., **50**, 229; **57**, 126
Lorkin, Thomas, **3**, 53; **43**, 43n
Loshak, David, **59**, 116n31
Lotan, Yael, **55**, 37n
Lothar, Rudolf, **35**, 22n, 29
Lothian, John M., **21**, 140; **29**, 177, 178; **32**, 64n, 74n; **35**, 80n; **50**, 65n; **52**, 130n; **56**, 174n; **59**, 52n9, 53–4, 57n22
King Lear: A Tragic Reading of Life reviewed, **4**, 141
Lotman, Yuri, **53**, 9–10; **60**, 120, 121
Lott, Felicity, **35**, 145
Lotto, Lorenzo, **37**, 176
Loughnan, Michael, **45**, 154
Loughrey, Bryan, **38**, 234; **46**, 160n, 254; **48**, 268–71; **49**, 321; **50**, 273; **51**, 128, 274; **52**, 313; **59**, 16n68; **60**, 225n14
Louis XIV, King, **16**, 53; **22**, 19
Louis-Philippe, King of France, **3**, 101
Lounsbury, T. R., **4**, 2; **9**, 100n
Lövberg, Aase Nordmo, **6**, 123
Love, **47**, 219
Love in a Forest, **52**, 275
Love is All There Is, **52**, 90
'*Love lyes a bleedinge*', **4**, 88
Love Story in Shakespearian Comedy, The, **46**, 211
Love Suicides at Amijima, The, **54**, 109
Love Suicides at Sonezaki, The, **54**, 109
Love's Changelings Change, **13**, 120
Love's Labour's Won, **12**, 141
Love's Victory, **55**, 380
Love, **6**, 59
Love, Alison, **39**, 169, 170n, 175n
Love, Harold, **27**, 188; **35**, 33n; **59**, 26n27, 113n23, 118
Love, John M., **31**, 165–6
Love, K. J. P., **52**, 297
Love, Patti, **44**, 194
Loveday, Thomas, **58**, 239
Lovejoy, Arthur O., **6**, 8; **7**, 4; **27**, 44; **29**, 85; **37**, 69n; **44**, 205
Lovell, Sir Robert, **21**, 100
Lovell, Thomas, **58**, 239
Lover's Complaint, **1**, 124
Loves Martyr, *see under* Chester, Sir Robert
Lovesick King, **54**, 18n
Lovett, David, **34**, 12n
Low Countries, prisoners from, in Barbary, **11**, 90–2
Low Countries, the stage of, **12**, 4
Low, Anthony, **23**, 171n; **25**, 181; **54**, 314–15; **60**, 231
Low, Donald A., **24**, 178
Low, Jennifer A., **58**, 323, 332
Lowe, Kate, **52**, 297
Lowe, Ken, **58**, 306
Lowe, Lisa, **46**, 93n
Lowe, Nicholas, **58**, 239
Lowe, R. W., **27**, 106n; **35**, 6, 43; **57**, 94
Lowe, Sir Thomas, **8**, 109–10; **11**, 102
Lowell, James Russell, **18**, 39, 103, 105, 109, 110, 111, 113–14; **24**, 87, 89, 99, 102, 103, 104; **45**, 6
Lowen, John, **11**, 109; **17**, 197; **18**, 63
Löwenadler, Holger, **11**, 122
Lowenthal, David, **52**, 270, 278
Lower, Charles B., **25**, 184; **38**, 236; **49**, 161n; **53**, 333
Lowers, James K., **48**, 71n
Lowes, J. L., **6**, 87; **8**, 116n; **14**, 153
Lowes, John Livingston, **25**, 127, 128; **26**, 99n; **32**, 229
Lowin, John, **38**, 91; **47**, 240; **52**, 82
Lownes, Victor, **57**, 146
Lowrie, W., **36**, 50n
Lowry, Betty, **39**, 42n, 43n
Lowry, J. S., **37**, 194
Lowry, Malcolm, **42**, 207
Loyd, Ludowicke, **42**, 54n
Loyola, **54**, 62n
Lubbock, R., **54**, 120n
Lubbock, Roger, *see* Keen, Alan
Luborsky, Ruth Samson, **50**, 153; **54**, 92n, 95n
Lucan, **10**, 48; **11**, 71; **15**, 24; **19**, 56; **23**, 169; **31**, 183; **38**, 181; **42**, 66; **53**, 78, 79, 83
Lucara, Lucia, **53**, 282
Lucas, E. V., **14**, 88n; **37**, 52n
Lucas, F. L., **3**, 21n; **26**, 4; **40**, 25; **50**, 289
ed, *The Complete Works of John Webster*, **14**, 8, 65n; **19**, 93n
Lucas, J., **55**, 143n
Lucas, Sir John Seymour, **52**, 30
Luccock, Halford, **24**, 88n
Luce, Morton, **26**, 72n; **56**, 174n; **59**, 81
Luce, Richard, **44**, 72
Luce, T. J., **38**, 116, 117n
Luchinger, Peter, **59**, 342
Lucian, **9**, 143; **20**, 22; **22**, 5; **27**, 111, 116n, 117, 119, 121n, 127; **29**, 103, 104, 108, 109, 110, 111, 112, 116; **30**, 195; **31**, 182; **54**, 304; **56**, 225, 230n; **58**, 247
Luckay, Róbert, **60**, 312
Luckham, Claire, **47**, 210
Luckham, Cyril, **1**, 101, 102; **11**, 132; **12**, 127–8
Luckhurst, Mary, **53**, 153n
Luckhurst, Roger, **55**, 73n, 74n, 80n
Lucking, David, **44**, 218
Luckyj, Christina, **44**, 237
Lucretius, **5**, 2; **10**, 42; **15**, 81; **20**, 22; **23**, 36; **25**, 128; **39**, 127n; **52**, 300
De Rerum Natura, **15**, 83
Lucskay, Robert, **59**, 318–19
Lucy, C. Hartwell, **4**, 69
Lucy, Frances, **3**, 28
Lucy, Sir Thomas, of Charlecote, **3**, 10; **4**, 151; **12**, 95–106; **13**, 154; **14**, 112, 113; **46**, 142; **54**, 116; **58**, 143; **60**, 13
Lüdecke, H., **5**, 114; **6**, 124, 161; **7**, 115; **12**, 116
Luders, Alexander, **38**, 75; **53**, 71n
Ludlan, Dave, **45**, 157
Ludlow Festival, **58**, 302, 307
Ludovici, Cesare Vico, **3**, 118; **4**, 128; **6**, 121; **7**, 112–13; **8**, 120; **9**, 114; **10**, 120
Ludus Coventriae: Woman Taken in Adultery, The, **20**, 66
Ludwig, Otto, **16**, 67; **44**, 110n
Luft, Friedrich, **48**, 172
Luft, Herbert G., **45**, 44n
Lugné-Poe, Aurélien-Marie, **9**, 67, 68n; **57**, 117
Luguet, H., **9**, 63
Luhrmann, Baz, **52**, 88–98, 197–200, 264; **53**, 96, 163; **54**, 317, 347; **55**, 341, 352, 354, 382; **56**, 3, 5n, 114, 347; **58**, 185
Luigini, Alexandre Clément Léon Joseph, *Egyptian Ballet*, **8**, 75; **48**, 227
Luis de Granada, **23**, 82, 87; **56**, 194

Lukacher, Ned, **49**, 283; **53**, 80
Lukács, Georg, **36**, 45; **51**, 272
Lukács, M., **14**, 120; **18**, 125
Lukavský, Radovan, **14**, 118; **48**, 165n
Lukes, Milan, **41**, 245n
Lukis, Adrian, **56**, 292
Lullo, Giorgio De, **6**, 121; **13**, 129; **15**, 135–6
Lully, Jean Baptiste, **51**, 81
Lumby, J. R., **28**, 27n
Lumbye, H. C., **29**, 145
Lumiansky, R. M., **41**, 145n; **57**, 242
Lumley portrait of Shakespeare, *see under* Shakespeare, William, portraits
Lumley, Lady Jane, *Iphigenia in Aulis* (MS.), **3**, 52
Lumley, Lord, **17**, 71, 153
Lumsden, David, **15**, 8, 10
Lumsden, Richard, **43**, 206
Lunacharsky, **21**, 128
Lunghi, Cherie, **30**, 172, 174; **33**, 171
Lunn, Jonathan, **43**, 210
Lunt, Alfred, **5**, 115
Lupton, Donald, **55**, 85n; **58**, 38
London and the Country Carbonadoed, **13**, 106
Lupton, Julia Reinhard, **41**, 198; **49**, 67n; **52**, 202–3, 206, 278; **54**, 185n; **55**, 9, 342, 346; **59**, 352, 368
Lupton, Thomas, **37**, 92n; **55**, 85
Lusardi, James P., **45**, 188; **47**, 42; **53**, 17, 208n; **56**, 337
Luscombe, Christopher, **47**, 199, 205–6; **49**, 280; **51**, 231, 235; **53**, 328; **60**, 305
Luscombe, Tim, **45**, 57, 130, 131, 150
Lust's Dominion, **6**, 155; **17**, 51n
Lutas, Muazzez, **9**, 116
Lute, Karen, **54**, 292
Luterkort, Ingrid, **36**, 67
Luther, Martin, **1**, 67; **23**, 80, 86; **26**, 49; **28**, 53, 56n; **33**, 92–3; **36**, 50; **42**, 176; **43**, 65, 237; **44**, 23; **45**, 25; **51**, 296; **53**, 320; **54**, 7, 10, 35, 139, 298; **55**, 220; **57**, 115, 237, 242; **58**, 208
Lüthi, Max, **7**, 135; **14**, 156n; **15**, 138; **18**, 129; **20**, 159; **21**, 153; **23**, 114; **43**, 5, 6, 239
Shakespeares Dramen reviewed, **11**, 136; **12**, 113
Luthuli, Albert, **55**, 275
Lutkehaus, Ludger, **45**, 100n
Lutyens, Edwin, **47**, 82, 88; **52**, 30
Lutz, Bruno von, **37**, 159n
Lutz, Ton, **14**, 122
Luzán, Ignacio de, **20**, 102
Lyas, Michael, **48**, 237
Lyddiard, Alan, **44**, 201; **45**, 156; **52**, 265
Lydgate John, **4**, 78; **6**, 59; **8**, 17, 31; **9**, 142; **10**, 36; **13**, 160; **21**, 150; **22**, 118n; **24**, 60; **35**, 114; **36**, 87n; **37**, 207; **47**, 254; **49**, 79, 85n; **55**, 368; **57**, 218
Lydon, Daniele, **48**, 193–4
Lyell, James P., **11**, 154
Lyle, E. B., **24**, 179; **26**, 172; **27**, 159, 179; **32**, 235, 245
Lyle, Emily, **44**, 68n
Lyle, J. V., **36**, 140n
Lyly, John, **1**, 11; **2**, 54, 120, 149; **3**, 16; **4**, 29, 49, 143; **7**, 5, 8, 141; **8**, 2, 3, 58, 64, 65, 67, 103, 147; **10**, 12, 69; **12**, 55n, 133; **14**, 7, 15–24 *passim*, 82; **15**, 5, 14, 65, 69, 70, 100, 113; **16**, 165, 167; **17**, 126, 129, 169, 171, 198, 206, 208, 236–7; **21**, 131; **22**, 36, 69; **23**, 169; **24**, 44, 71, 162; **26**, 153; **28**, 41n, 76, 80n; **29**, 174; **30**, 125–34, 198; **31**, 18, 85n, 117; **32**, 166; **33**, 200; **34**, 30n, 31; **35**, 80; **36**, 172; **37**, 19, 20, 191; **38**, 40, 43, 44n, 231, 232; **41**, 222; **42**, 1–13, 106–7; **44**, 50, 250; **46**, 56, 57, 105, 227; **48**, 259; **49**, 81; **50**, 58; **51**, 136, 292–3; **52**, 79, 82; **54**, 91, 196, 309; **55**, 25, 207n; **56**, 44, 45, 222, 249; **57**, 336; **59**, 71
Campaspe, **1**, 64; **5**, 139; **6**, 82; **8**, 147; **14**, 17, 20, 21; **15**, 69
Endimion, **14**, 16, 20, 23, 24n
Euphues, **3**, 54; **4**, 50
Euphues and his England, **7**, 15, 84
Gallathea, **14**, 17, 18, 24 and n; **15**, 70
Harefield Entertainment, **1**, 65
Love's Metamorphosis, **14**, 18
Midas, **15**, 69
Mother Bombie, **4**, 41
Pappe with an Hatchet, **15**, 71n
Sapho and Phao, **4**, 95; **14**, 16, 18, 20, 21, 24n; **15**, 70, 72n
The Woman in the Moon, **8**, 109; **14**, 18; **15**, 70
Lyly, William, **46**, 42
Lyn, Carmen, **43**, 209
Lyn, Timothy, **41**, 189
Lynch, Alfred, **56**, 248
Lynch, Barry (Finbar), **45**, 127, 128; **46**, 202; **47**, 195; **48**, 203, 216, 221; **49**, 270, 275; **51**, 251; **52**, 253; **58**, 301, 304; **56**, 4n, 7n
Lynch, David, **54**, 303
Lynch, John Patrick, **43**, 219, 238; **48**, 228
Lynch, Kathryn L., **42**, 183; **54**, 303
Lynch, Stephen J., **56**, 67; **58**, 330, 332
Lynch, Susan, **48**, 224
Lynche, Richard, *Diella*, **1**, 69; **26**, 112n
Lynd, J. J., **31**, 57n
Lyndhurst, Nicholas, **60**, 329
Lyne, Raphael, **56**, 28n, 29n
Lynn, Jack, **42**, 149
Lyon, A., **56**, 46n
Lyon, David, **43**, 178; **51**, 251
Lyons, Bridget Gellert, **25**, 189; **32**, 218; **41**, 145
Lyons, Charles, **22**, 160
Lyons, Clifford P., **13**, 153; **18**, 175; **19**, 135, 153
Lyons, John Coriden, **40**, 80n
Lyons, Lisa, **57**, 138, 143
Lyons, Paddy, **53**, 27n
Lyons, Robert, **53**, 327–8
Lyons, Susan, **58**, 58
Lyotard, Jean-François, **55**, 73n
Lyte, Henry, **56**, 41
Lyth, Claire, **41**, 186; **43**, 206; **44**, 203; **45**, 156; **46**, 195, 201; **47**, 209, 212; **50**, 233; **51**, 258; **52**, 254
Lythe, S. G. E., **9**, 144
Lyttle, David, **7**, 113
Lytton, Bulwer, **55**, 143
Lytton, Edward, **53**, 105
Lytton, Emily, **52**, 30n
Lyubimov, Yuri, **44**, 193

Maas, H., **1**, 10
Maas, Paul, *Textual Criticism* reviewed, **13**, 165

Mabbe, James, **3**, 12; **16**, 118–20; **20**, 95, 79
as 'I. M.' of First Folio, **3**, 140
Mabley-Allen, Don, **60**, 180
McAdam, Ian, **51**, 293; **53**, 322–3
McAfee, Helen, **37**, 58n
McAleer, Des, **42**, 136; **51**, 261; **58**, 278; **59**, 345
McAlindon, Thomas, **23**, 150; **25**, 13n, 14n, 24n, 182; **26**, 155; **28**, 149–50, 155; **31**, 10; **38**, 6, 231; **45**, 164–5; **48**, 253; **50**, 251; **51**, 158n; **55**, 210n, 218n, 220n; **56**, 319, 320, 325–7; **57**, 239; **58**, 325
Shakespeare's Tragic Cosmos, **48**, 253
McAllister, Peter, **50**, 227; **53**, 284
Macallum, Sir Mungo, **22**, 170
McAndrew, Deborah, **49**, 254; **56**, 254
McAndrew, John, **45**, 152; **51**, 221
MacAnmich, Cal, **51**, 258
McArdell, James, **13**, 74; 49, 115
McArdle, Aidan, **53**, 255, 272–3; **55**, 288; **56**, 295
MacArthur, David, **42**, 155
McArthur, H., **14**, 145n
McArthur, Molly, **2**, 16
McAtackney, L., **60**, 37n5
Macaulay, Alastair, **52**, 43n
Macauley, Alistair, **60**, 80
Macaulay, G. C., **14**, 163n; **24**, 109n; **57**, 210
Macaulay, Peter Stuart, **57**, 246
Macaulay, Rose, **17**, 223–5, 228
Macaulay, Thomas Babington, Lord, **7**, 31; **21**, 68; **38**, 180; **47**, 255–6
McAuliffe, Nichola, **42**, 157; **48**, 235; **49**, 274; **58**, 305
McAvoy, William Charles, **10**, 146n; **27**, 59n
McBean, Angus, **60**, 78
Macbeth, King of Scotland, **57**, 70, 71, 73, 74
Macbeth, the Musical, **49**, 273
McBride, Charles, A., **55**, 272n
McBride, Maria-Odilia Leal, **55**, 272n
McBride, Phyllis, **55**, 342
McBride, Tom, **33**, 200; **38**, 145n
McBurney, Simon, **46**, 169, 170, 171; **53**, 153n; **58**, 269, 274–7, 275; **59**, 188, 341; **60**, 284–5
MacCabe, Colin, **43**, 233; **55**, 8n
McCabe, Richard A., **40**, 174; **41**, 178, 181; **43**, 200; **44**, 198; **46**, 172, 173, 176; **48**, 241; **49**, 262–3; **50**, 212; **52**, 249–50; **53**, 250–1, 255; **54**, 290, 293; **55**, 292; **56**, 34n, 217n; **60**, 162,168n1.9, 309–10
McCabe, William H., **29**, 23n
MacCaffrey, Wallace T., **17**, 11n; **55**, 210n
McCall, Gordon, **50**, 36
McCall, Marsh H., **31**, 13n
McCallin, Clement, **13**, 124; **24**, 118; **31**, 148
McCallin, Tanya, **49**, 271; **50**, 232
McCallum, Eileen, **54**, 258
McCallum, Joanna, **48**, 206; **51**, 230, 235; **55**, 323
MacCallum, M. W., **4**, 9; **6**, 2; **10**, 1, 4, 6, 50–1, 52, 57; **11**, 132; **31**, 2–3, 7; **40**, 72, 74; **53**, 80n, 81n
Shakespeare's Roman Plays, **11**, 135n
McCandless, David, **49**, 293 **58**, 50
McCandless, Michael, **22**, 163
McCann, Gary, **52**, 264; **54**, 294
MacCannell, Dean, **52**, 39, 40n
McCarey, Jo, **47**, 213
McCarron, William E., **20**, 166
McCarthy, Barry, **54**, 273
McCarthy, Desmond, **34**, 8; **59**, 149n11
McCarthy, Henry, **9**, 120
McCarthy, Lillah, **2**, 4; **52**, 28n
McCarthy, Maggie, **59**, 328
McCarthy, Marie, **55**, 292
McCarthy, Mary, **36**, 151
McCarthy, Penny, **60**, 336–7, 353
McCartney, Eugene Stock, **56**, 40n
McCartney, Sir Paul, **42**, 160
MacCary, W. Thomas, **44**, 49n
McClary, Susan, **54**, 199n; **55**, 241n
McClellan, Kenneth, **5**, 120; **42**, 155; **46**, 194
McClintic, Guthrie, **2**, 130, 131
McCloskey, J., **18**, 166
McCloud, Randall, **59**, 161
McCluhan, Marshall, **43**, 252
McClumpha, C. F., **15**, 12
McClure, Donald S., **60**, 109n33
McClure, Leonard, **43**, 211
McClure, Norman Egbert, **11**, 115n; **13**, 110n; **15**, 125; **31**, 99n; **46**, 14n; **55**, 93n
The Letters and Epigrams of Sir John Harington, **14**, 109n
McClure, Peter, **44**, 227
McClure, Rob, **39**, 189
McCluskey, Mary, **55**, 326
McCluskie, Kathleen, **39**, 230
Maccoby, Hyam, **25**, 179
Maccoll, Alan, **23**, 167n
MacColl, E., **55**, 108n
McCollom, William G., **22**, 154; **32**, 6, 56n; **15**, 113, 121
McCombie, Frank, **29**, 164; **32**, 235; **35**, 167, 177
'Hamlet and the *Moriae Encomium'*, **27**, 59–69
McCoog, Thomas, **54**, 94n; **56**, 193n
McConachie, Bruce A., **47**, 10n; **52**, 37n; **59**, 212n63
McCorkindale, Don, **45**, 155
McCormack, Colin, **45**, 149; **52**, 231
McCormack, David, **41**, 191
McCowan, George, **38**, 139n, 140
McCowen, Alec, **39**, 105; **43**, 217; **47**, 203; **48**, 236
McCown, Gary M., **30**, 194; **49**, 100n
McCoy, Richard C., **34**, 28n; **51**, 296; **54**, 136n; **57**, 316; **58**, 317, 332
McCoy, Sylvester, **40**, 183
MacCracken, Eleanor, **6**, 63n
McCracken, George E., **30**, 62n; **54**, 33n
MacCraig, Norman, **45**, 61
McCrea, Scott, **59**, 358–9, 368
McCredie, Andrew D., **51**, 87n
McCreery, Kathleen, **42**, 157
McCrindle, Joseph F., **36**, 22n
McCrink, Paul, **56**, 237
McCrory, Helen, **56**, 262, 263; **59**, 311, 312; **60**, 320
McCrystal, Cal, **56**, 297
McCrystal, Kiernan, **43**, 213
McCullen, J. T., **14**, 10; **19**, 127
MacCulloch, Diarmaid, **54**, 7n, 123; **59**, 250n79
McCulloch, Ian, **42**, 161

McCullough, Andrew, **39**, 76n
McCullough, Christopher, **41**, 227; **42**, 164; **49**, 153–4, 308
McCullough, Peter, **56**, 217n
McCunn, Hamish, **45**, 173
McCurdy, Harold Grier, *The Personality of Shakespeare. A Venture in Psychological Method* reviewed, **8**, 148–9
McCurdy, Peter, **51**, 205; **52**, 11n, 12
McCusher, Mary, **43**, 208
McCusker, Frank, **47**, 210
McCusker, Stella, **58**, 266, 267
McCutchan, J. W., **4**, 146n
McCutcheon, Elizabeth, **23**, 167n
McDermott, Phelim, **42**, 150; **52**, 260; **60**, 329
McDiarmid, Ian, **38**, 204, 209; **47**, 7; **55**, 317, 332; **56**, 297; **60**, 323
McDiarmid, Matthew, **11**, 137, 143n; **12**, 142
McDonagh, Philomena, **43**, 208
McDonald, Alasdair, **50**, 229
McDonald, Andrew, **46**, 191; **48**, 231
MacDonald, Ann-Marie, **54**, 312
McDonald, Antony, **43**, 206; **44**, 191; **45**, 117, 153
McDonald, Camden, **45**, 151; **46**, 200; **51**, 262
McDonald, Charles O., **18**, 166
Macdonald, David, **53**, 277
Macdonald, Dwight, **57**, 139
MacDonald, George, **56**, 101
Macdonald, Heather, **39**, 186
Mcdonald, Hettie, **45**, 151
Macdonald, Hugh, **53**, 33n
MacDonald, James, **43**, 214; **55**, 316, 332
McDonald, James, **47**, 212; **48**, 234; **56**, 297
McDonald, Jan, **35**, 3n; **36**, 180
MacDonald, Joyce Green, **48**, 255; **51**, 63, 278–9; **60**, 169n5.2, 349
MacDonald, Mairi, **56**, 184n
MacDonald, Michael, **41**, 222; **43**, 2n; **45**, 177–8; **57**, 312; **58**, 324
McDonald, N., **39**, 76n
McDonald, P. Jackson, **54**, 16n, 24n
Mcdonald, Peter, **53**, 114n
Macdonald, R. D., **15**, 144
MacDonald, Ramsay, **40**, 21
Mcdonald, Rod, **45**, 63n
McDonald, Ronald R., **50**, 250
McDonald, Russ, **34**, 176; **36**, 168; **43**, 230, 243–4; **44**, 219; **46**, 7; **48**, 241; **54**, 58n, 309, 310; **56**, 302–3, 310; **57**, 28, 196; **58**, 207, 330; **59**, 94n6, 360
Shakespeare Reread: The Texts in New Contexts, **48**, 241, 252
Macdonald, Sheila, **53**, 274
MacDonald, Trevor, **57**, 45
MacDonnell, Chris, **42**, 158
McDonnell, Robert F., **30**, 150
McDougall, Irene, **41**, 184; **59**, 340
McDougall, Roger, **13**, 124
McDowell, John H., **52**, 7n
'Medieval Art in Shakespearian Staging' reviewed, **3**, 140
Mace, Nancy A., **44**, 242
McEachern, Claire, **43**, 225; **48**, 249; **51**, 296; **54**, 124n, 304; **56**, 307; **59**, 378–9, 383
McElderry, B. R., Jr, **43**, 124n
McElroy, Bernard, **28**, 152, 155; **34**, 135, 137; **55**, 211, 212n
McElroy, John F., **27**, 176
McElwee, W. L., **14**, 127; **15**, 145
McEnery, John, **33**, 176; **51**, 209, 210–11, 213; **52**, 223, 227; **53**, 246; **59**, 318
McEnery, Peter, **19**, 114; **20**, 134; **31**, 147, 149; **33**, 172; **37**, 173; **54**, 259; **55**, 185n, 305, 323
McEvoy, Sean, **60**, 349–50, 353
MacEwan, E. J., **33**, 35n
McEwan, Geraldine, **12**, 127–8; **42**, 129; **43**, 183, 205; **44**, 194; **47**, 211
McEwan, Ian, **55**, 186n
MacEwen, Molly, **1**, 95, 96
McEwan, Neil, **30**, 188
McEwan, Paul, **56**, 264, 265
Macey, Samuel L., **32**, 236
McFadden, Claron, **54**, 289
McFadden, Fred R., Jr, **29**, 183
MacFadyen, Angus, **56**, 4n
MacFadyen, Matthew, **52**, 234; **53**, 280; **59**, 324–5, 326–7; **60**, 322
McFadyen, Myra, **45**, 156
McFarland, Angus, **54**, 26
McFarland, T., **27**, 168
McFarlane, Brian, **52**, 193n
McFarlane, Colin, **48**, 233
MacFarlane, Fenella, **55**, 377
MacFarlane, I. D., **57**, 115
McFarlane, J. W., **43**, 115n, 116n
McFarlane, K. B., **38**, 11
McFarlane, Robert, **59**, 205
McFetridge, Paula, **49**, 278
Macfie, Pamela Royston, **57**, 302
McGann, Jerome J., **40**, 232n; 50, 280; **51**, 321, 323–4, 329; **53**, 213n; **57**, 136; **59**, 15, 20, 37–8n87, 88n32
McGarricle, Perse, **58**, 130
McGee, Arthur R., **18**, 168; **21**, 137; **42**, 176–7; **45**, 22, 24, 25; **54**, 123n
'*Macbeth* and the Furies', **19**, 55–67
McGee, C. E., **39**, 216; **43**, 266; **44**, 149n; **46**, 227
McGiffert, M., **54**, 169n
McGill, Donald, **46**, 122
McGill, Stewart, **58**, 303, 306; **59**, 343; **60**, 322, 326
McGill, Stuart, **57**, 292
McGinn, Bernard, **59**, 242n24, 249n72
McGinn, D. G., **18**, 35
McGinn, D. J., **2**, 135, 151; **25**, 5
McGinn, Donald, **49**, 190n
McGinness, Frederick J., **54**, 93n
McGinty, Terry, **45**, 150
McGlinchee, Claire, **10**, 146n; **16**, 172n; **35**, 32n
McGlone, Jackie, **56**, 240n
McGlynn, John, **46**, 195
McGovern, Barry, **58**, 262
McGovern, Tom, **51**, 263; **54**, 287
MacGowan, Kenneth, **41**, 58–60
McGowan, Alistair, **60**, 317
McGowan, Julian, **45**, 152; **49**, 277; **51**, 258
McGowan, Kenneth, **9**, 146
McGowan, Kevin, **42**, 151
MacGowran, Jack, **39**, 79n
McGrade, Arthur Stephen, **54**, 14n

INDEX

McGrane, Laura, **57**, 186
McGrath, Anne, **1**, 101, 102
McGrath, Elizabeth, **42**, 157
McGrath, John E., **58**, 358
McGrath, John, **44**, 73n
McGrath, Patrick, **22**, 169; **24**, 71n
MacGregor, Arthur, **50**, 190n
MacGregor, Barry, **34**, 159
MacGregor, George, **48**, 227
McGregor, Graham, **41**, 200n
MacGregor, Joanna, **42**, 159; **51**, 264
MacGregor, John, **9**, 130
McGugan, Ruth, **27**, 190; **40**, 70n; **59**, 159n8
McGuinness, B. F., **48**, 120n
McGuinness, Clodagh, **47**, 216
McGuinness, Frank, **48**, 23, 50; **52**, 266; **58**, 152, 157, 260
McGuire, Joshua, **55**, 291
McGuire, Philip C., **28**, 154; **38**, 153n, 165n, 235n; **40**, 196; **43**, 200; **45**, 80n, 81; **46**, 255; **47**, 149n; **48**, 244; **50**, 49n; **53**, 214–15, 232n, 304; **55**, 58n; **56**, 69n
  Shakespeare: The Jacobean Plays, **48**, 244
McGuire, Richard L., **22**, 156
Mach, Ernst, **24**, 97
Mácha, **9**, 102
Machabeli, Avané, **48**, 185–7
Machabeus, Judas, **29**, 26, 27, 28–9
McHale, Dominic, **49**, 271; **51**, 259
Macherey, Pierre, **31**, 62n; **44**, 67
Machiavelli, Niccolò, **1**, 68; **3**, 7; **4**, 7, 14; **5**, 72, 73; **7**, 103, 129; **10**, 11; **17**, 65, 216; **20**, 28, 52, 54–6; **21**, 143–4; **22**, 115, 148; **23**, 145, 162; **24**, 158; **26**, 49; **27**, 45, 46, 53, 72, 74–5; **28**, 10; **29**, 79, 80, 85, 88, 90, 164; **31**, 180; **33**, 5, 21, 200; **37**, 96, 38, 115, 122–4, 128, 215, 216, 220; **39**, 57, 58, 62; **41**, 198; **43**, 238, 249; **44**, 6, 11, 35, 36, 57, 61, 62; **48**, 85, 88–93, 127; **49**, 195, 196n; **51**, 177, 184; **52**, 274; **55**, 209, 212, 213–14, 296, 355; **56**, 225, 226, 318, 322; **57**, 34, 240; **59**, 361, 365
  The Prince, **3**, 141; **20**, 55, 59
Machin, Lewis, **1**, 64; **32**, 192n
Machin, Richard, **32**, 195; **33**, 162
Machlin, Gareth, **57**, 291
Machon, Louis, **48**, 93n, 95n, 96
  Diary, **6**, 73n
Machyn, Henry, **60**, 46
McIlwain, Charles Howard, **28**, 64n, 68; **43**, 63n; **54**, 129n; **55**, 44n; **57**, 70
McIlwaine, Mandy, **44**, 202
McIlwraith, A. K., **2**, 14; **4**, 92; **5**, 47; **11**, 52
McLeary, Paul, **55**, 316
McInally, Jane, **54**, 288
McInnery, Lizzie, **42**, 162
McInnery, Tim, **41**, 184; **45**, 122
Macintosh, Angus, **32**, 6
McIntosh, Angus, **18**, 160, 166; **23**, 11n; **26**, 164n
McIntosh, Genista, **47**, 121
McIntosh, Gina, **53**, 322
McIntosh, Shona, **56**, 292
McIntyre, Alasdair, **51**, 271; **53**, 91; **47**, 95
MacIntyre, Jean, **41**, 210; **42**, 112; **51**, 290
MacIsaac, W. J., **25**, 17
McIver, Bruce, **49**, 143n, 284
McJannet, Linda, **53**, 340–1, 344
Mack, Loulou, **55**, 272n
Mack, Maynard, **15**, 161; **18**, 42–4, 175; **19**, 10, 120; **20**, 49n, 145; **26**, 9, 96; **27**, 161; **28**, 111; **32**, 164n, 174; **33**, 5, 8, 11, 46, 68n, 183, 185; **34**, 133, 134, 170, 176–7; **35**, 12, 99, 155–6; **36**, 44, 80, 188n; **37**, 72n, 185n; **38**, 80, 153, 154, 155n, 159, 163, 164n, 166n, 252n; **40**, 5, 139n; **41**, 78n; **44**, 205; **45**, 7, 8, 10, 196; **51**, 139n; **55**, 231; **59**, 41
Mackail, J. W., **1**, 14; **4**, 5; **5**, 152
Mackay, Eileen, **18**, 163
Mackay, John, **56**, 292; **57**, 297
McKay, Malcolm, **51**, 213–15
McKay, Maxine, **19**, 136; **29**, 94, 95–6, 98
McKay, Tom, **57**, 283
Mackay, Mr, **22**, 130–1
McKee, Malcolm, **49**, 280
McKeen, David B., **19**, 147; **38**, 86n, 90n, 98; **54**, 97n, 98n
McKeithan, D. M., **4**, 9, 34n
  The Debt to Shakespeare in Beaumont and Fletcher's Plays, **14**, 12
McKellan, Martin, **43**, 206–7; **46**, 193; **52**, 261; **53**, 275
McKellen, Sir Ian, **23**, 131; **26**, 140; **30**, 169, 173, 174, 177, 178; **39**, 191–3; **40**, 36, 39; **41**, 53, 1911, **42**, 162; **43**, 194–5, 217; **44**, 184–9, 199; **45**, 148, 153; **47**, 5, 7, 9, 11–13; **48**, 7, 16, 19; **49**, 13; **51**, 266; **52**, 284, 289; **53**, 193, 266; **54**, 292; **55**, 282, 345, 382; **56**, 247, 347; **57**, 269; **59**, 169–70, 371; **60**, 351, 365–6
McKelvey, John, **12**, 121; **13**, 134
McKenna, Ged, **47**, 213
McKenna, Jayne, **51**, 226; **55**, 309–10
MacKenna, Stephen, **36**, 91n
McKenna, Virginia, **6**, 143
Mackenzie, Agnes More, **4**, 4
Mackenzie, B. A., *Shakespeare's Sonnets*, **3**, 10
  reviewed, **1**, 123–4
MacKenzie, Clayton, **44**, 27n; **55**, 360
Mackenzie, Sir Compton, **18**, 74
McKenzie, D. F., **13**, 166; **14**, 161 and n., 166n; **17**, 68n; **20**, 177; **23**, 184–5; **25**, 191; **26**, 180; **27**, 180, 190; **28**, 174; **37**, 211; **38**, 251; **40**, 235; **59**, 20, 27, 34, 112
McKenzie, Donald, **52**, 143
Mackenzie, Ellie, **47**, 213; **50**, 226
McKenzie, Sir George, **57**, 70, 73
Mackenzie, Henry, **14**, 83; **18**, 37; **34**, 12, 13, 14, 16, 18n, 19, 20, 21; **45**, 15
McKenzie, Henry, **2**, 109
Mackenzie, James J., **11**, 139; **24**, 178
Mackenzie, W. Roy, **32**, 101n
McKeon, Kevin, **47**, 218
McKern, Abigail, **58**, 336
McKern, Leo, **5**, 122, 128; **8**, 137; **27**, 140; **39**, 89n, 90
Mckern, Robert, **45**, 151
McKernan, Luke, **52**, 185n
Mackerras, Charles, **58**, 302
McKerrow, Ronald B., **1**, 12; **2**, 19, 113; **3**, 31; **4**, 58, 67n; **5**, 10, 11, 12, 47, 54; **7**, 3, 11, 49–50, 51, 52, 55n, 153; **8**, 82, 91; **10**, 2, 70n; **11**, 78, 81, 83–7, 87n, 88n; **13**, 163; **14**, 7; **15**, 40n, 72n, 128; **16**, 6; **17**, 210n, 212n; **18**, 12–13, 14, 16, 17, 24–5, 27; **19**, 155n, 156, 160–1; **23**, 162n; **24**, 170; **26**, 45n; **28**, 175; **32**, 149n; **36**, 57, 140n; **37**, 2, 218n; **38**, 242; **40**, 145; **41**, 235; **42**, 15n, 88n; **43**, 265; **46**, 222; **47**, 24, 37n, 127n, 133n; **48**, 277, 287; **49**, 18n, 81n, 324; **50**,

78n, 142, 272; **51**, 331; **52**, 69; **54**, 63n; **55**, 367, 390; **56**, 31n, 35n, 63n; **57**, 216, 233, 239; **58**, 355; **59**, 1, 2, 10, 12, 13–14, 14n58, 15, 17n70, 30, 45n6, 154, 156, 382
Dictionary of Printers and Booksellers 1557–1640, **14**, 5
Introduction to Bibliography, **14**, 5, 161
Printers and Publishers' Devices 1485–1640, **14**, 5
Prolegomena for the Oxford Shakespeare, **11**, 87n; **14**, 157
(ed.) *Works of Thomas Nashe*, **14**, 5, 33n
McKewin, Carole, **31**, 176; **40**, 101n; **48**, 132n
Mackie, W. S., **23**, 14
Mackiewicz, Lech, **59**, 205
McKillop, Alan D., **42**, 99n
Mackinder, Anthony, **60**, 44n36
McKinder, H. J., **44**, 107
McKinley, Everett, **57**, 138
McKinley, Meier, **54**, 287
McKinnon, Andrew, **59**, 340
MacKinnon, Lachlan, **42**, 173; **45**, 134
Mackintosh, Iain, **30**, 157, 167n, 168; **49**, 114n, 115n, 116n, 118n; **51**, 11n
Mackintosh, M., **54**, 149n
Mackintosh, Mary, **39**, 75n
McKintosh, Peter, **56**, 272, 287
Mackintosh, Steven, **42**, 145
McKisack, Mary, **38**, 11
McKitterick, David, **59**, 122n56
Macklin, Charles, **38**, 209; **42**, 85; **48**, 54–5; **51**, 4, 109, 112, 115; **52**, 99; **53**, 327; **57**, 81, 85, 86, 87, 90; **58**, 262; **59**, 65, 292
Macklin, Thomas, **49**, 119
Mackmin, Anna, **44**, 191; **47**, 213
MacLachlan, Kyle, **58**, 191
McLaren, Graham, **52**, 257; **54**, 286; **59**, 340
McLaren, Moray, '*By Me . . .*' reviewed, **3**, 138
McLarg, Tamara, **44**, 201
McLauchlan, Juliet, **29**, 164
'The Prince of Denmark and Claudius's Court', **27**, 43–57
McLaughlin, Annette, **57**, 263
McLaughlin, John J., **32**, 222
McLaverty, James, **36**, 164–5; **38**, 244n
McLay, Catherine M., **22**, 193; **42**, 7n
McLean, Andrew M., **52**, 283
Maclean, Catherine MacDonald, **34**, 51n
Maclean, Don, **57**, 156
Maclean, Gerald, **49**, 302
Maclean, Hilary, **56**, 264–6
Maclean, Hugh, **15**, 172; **21**, 132; **38**, 154n
MacLean, Ian, **45**, 37; **49**, 194n
McLean, Ruari, **49**, 79n
MacLean, Sally-Beth, **44**, 150n; **47**, 45n, 50n, 51n, 52n, 53n, 251n; **50**, 257; **52**, 293–4; **55**, 12, 18, 19, 29, 30n, 34; **60**, 1, 4, 6–7, 7n10, 7n12, 13n37, 21–2, 54n27
McLeary, Paul, **55**, 316
Maclehose, James, **51**, 4; **60**, 194n31
McLellan, Eric, **31**, 17
McLeod, Marjorie, **6**, 117
Mcleod, Mary, **50**, 223
McLeod, Randall (Cloud, Random), **33**, 208; **34**, 194; **35**, 186, 188; **37**, 208, 210, 212, 213; **39**, 247, 249n; **41**, 245; **50**, 140–1; **51**, 332–3; **52**, 143; **53**, 341, 343; **55**, 3n; **59**, 17, 20, 36–7, 149n8, 162
Maclès, Denis, **18**, 123
MacLiammóir, Micheál, **6**, 119; **18**, 71; **39**, 3, 4, 53n, 54n; **51**, 144; **58**, 263
'Three Shakespearian Productions: A Conversation', **1**, 89–97
Maclise, Daniel, **37**, 48
McLoughlin, Cathleen, **54**, 304
McLuhan, H. M., **6**, 12
McLuhan, Marshall, **33**, 67, 68, 79; **37**, 9; **52**, 191–2, 194; **59**, 377
MacLure, Millar, **9**, 139; **10**, 9; **27**, 175; **28**, 19n
McLuskie, Kathleen E., **26**, 163; **41**, 222; **43**, 253; **45**, 184; **46**, 3, 6, 9n; **47**, 247–8, 250; **48**, 258; **50**, 254; **51**, 290; **53**, 234n; **54**, 303, 317; **55**, 7, 113, 352, 359; **56**, 101, 342; **57**, 167; **58**, 56; **60**, 62n13, 84n2, 140, 355
Dekker and Heywood; Professional Dramatists, **48**, 258
'Shakespeare's "Earth-treading Stars": the Image of the Masque in *Romeo and Juliet*', **24**, 63–9
McLynn, Dr Neil, **53**, 149n
McKnight, G. H., **7**, 4
MacMahon, Aline, **4**, 124
McMahon, Morgan, **22**, 133n
McManaway, J. Q., **30**, 110n
McManaway, James G., **4**, 149, 152; **6**, 163; **8**, 2; **9**, 155n; **10**, 88n, 151n; **12**, 145; **13**, 156, 163; **16**, 6, 166, 171; **18**, 100n, 171; **19**, 119n, 145, 153; **21**, 162; **22**, 167n, 183; **24**, 152n, 169, 171, 172; **25**, 110, 183; **28**, 3n; **29**, 180; **31**, 193; **32**, 10, 237; **36**, 189n; **38**, 14n, 90n, 91; **41**, 20n; **51**, 80n; **52**, 4n, 6n; **56**, 184n, 188n, 189n, 193n
'The Folger Shakespeare Library', **1**, 57–78
'Recent Studies in Shakespeare's Chronology', **3**, 22–33
Woodward and McManaway's *Check List*, **4**, 93
McManaway, Mary R., **25**, 138n
McManus, Barbara F., **48**, 29n
McManus, John, **55**, 248
McMaster, A., **6**, 119
McMaster, Juliet, **24**, 165
McMillan, Dougald, **6**, 54, 60; **16**, 103; **55**, 157n, 158n
Macmillan, Douglas, **51**, 87n
Macmillan, Harold, **55**, 150; **56**, 246
MacMillan, Kenneth, **54**, 258; **56**, 296; **57**, 296; **58**, 305; **59**, 344; **60**, 327
Macmillan, Michael, **10**, 3
McMillin, Scott, **30**, 196; **36**, 189; **38**, 112, 230, 235; **39**, 217, 218, 221, 222; **41**, 14n, 18–21, 215–16, 218, 233n; **42**, 77; **43**, 168n, 262–3; **44**, 149, 150n, 230; **45**, 187–8; **46**, 254–5; **52**, 293–4; **54**, 89; **55**, 12, 18, 19, 29, 30n, 34; **57**, 227; **58**, 350, 356, 357; **59**, 21–3, 24, 25, 26–8, 33, 383; **60**, 1, 4, 6–7, 7n10, 7n12, 13n37, 21–2, 54n27
MacMonnies bust of Shakespeare, **1**, 62
MacMullen, Katherine V., **18**, 170
McMullan, Frank, **8**, 122; **9**, 117, 148; **10**, 88n
McMullan, Gordon, **46**, 214; **48**, 260; **50**, 251; **52**, 212n, 274; **53**, 299–300; **54**, 238n, 314, 348–50; **56**, 69n, 95n, 148n, 149, 150n, 352; **57**, 341; **58**, 145, 349, 356; **59**, 21, 38n88, 213, 213n5, 219, 220, 220n29, 259n12; **60**, 67n17, 67n18, 358
Politics of Unease in the Plays of John Fletcher, **48**, 260
(ed. with Jonathan Hope), *The Politics of Tragicomedy*, **46**, 214
McMullen, Joseph T., **7**, 142–3
McMurray, John, **44**, 194
McNair, Lord, **24**, 156
McNamara, Anne M., **14**, 146

MacNamara, Jo Ann Kay, **54**, 38n
McNamara, Kevin R., **48**, 140n; **55**, 243n
McNamara, P. L., **27**, 157
McNamee, L. F., **14**, 151
MacNaughton, Alan, **1**, 111; **36**, 154; **45**, 117, 153
McNeal, Thomas H., **13**, 158; **38**, 9; **55**, 20, 22n, 23, 25
McNeice, Ian, **36**, 154
MacNeice, Louis, **24**, 44
MacNeil, Colin, **41**, 186; **42**, 154
McNeil, F. Marion, **19**, 57
MacNeil, Ian, **42**, 151; **43**, 206; **48**, 231
McNeill, Hector, **51**, 64
McNeill, John T., **54**, 139n; **55**, 229n; **57**, 237
McNeir, Waldo F., **1**, 8; **14**, 65n; **18**, 183; **20**, 49n, 155; **22**, 183; **23**, 153; **25**, 174; **26**, 158, 163; **29**, 55n; **33**, 47n; **36**, 103n; **38**, 5n; **59**, 81n9
MacNichol, Katie, **51**, 213
McNichol, Stella, **60**, 186n11
MacNulty, Sir Arthur Salusbury, **14**, 154
McNulty, Robert, **35**, 112n
MacOwan, Michael, **2**, 16; **5**, 119; **8**, 124
McPeek, James A. S., **26**, 154; **31**, 33n, 38n; **32**, 11
MacPhee, Wendy, **41**, 183; **42**, 160; **43**, 217; **44**, 193; **45**, 145; **46**, 196; **47**, 214; **48**, 228; **49**, 278; **50**, 231; **56**, 297; **57**, 290
McPhee, Wendy, **51**, 266; **52**, 265; **53**, 274; **54**, 290; **55**, 328; **58**, 307
McPherson, David C., **27**, 165, 179; **37**, 197; **40**, 219; **46**, 224; **48**, 124n; **49**, 301
Macpherson, James, **9**, 102; **59**, 109–10, 112
McQuarrie, Stuart, **43**, 211; **54**, 266, 292
McQueen, Jim, **34**, 159
MacQuoid, Percy, **2**, 6
McRae, Hilton, **39**, 201; **44**, 196; **59**, 301–2, 314, 316; **60**, 321, 327, 328
McRae, K. D., **17**, 214n
Macray, W. D., **4**, 91, 96n
Macready, Carol, **59**, 303
Macready, Charles, **11**, 124; **13**, 77, 80n; **18**, 104, 106, 113, 184; **19**, 154; **30**, 199; **59**, 65, 374
Macready, William, **21**, 62, 80; **22**, 132; **58**, 40, 41
Macready, William Charles, **2**, 1, 2, 19; **3**, 101, 102; **7**, 25, 28–9; **8**, 69; **9**, 55, 61, 140; **10**, 74, 76n; **32**, 21, 30n, 32, 34–5; **33**, 27; **35**, 3, 5, 7, 9, 17, 18, 20, 54, 188; **37**, 199; **39**, 233; **40**, 39; **41**, 26, 28, 224; **42**, 39n; **43**, 223; **44**, 242; **45**, 1, 33, 57; **46**, 170; **48**, 7, 8; **49**, 123; **53**, 104, 108, 109, 110n, 327; **54**, 82; **55**, 96, 145; **56**, 100, 111, 133; **57**, 68, 88, 90, 91, 92, 94, 115, 126, 127, 177, 326; **60**, 288
Macrobius, **4**, 64–5; **15**, 109n; **36**, 91n; **50**, 63
Macropedius, Georgius, **56**, 56n
McRuvie, David, **45**, 148
McShane, Mike, **46**, 198
McSorley, Gerard, **43**, 217
McTeer, Janet, **40**, 172–5; **41**, 183, 188; **42**, 154; **47**, 192–3; **48**, 233; **55**, 74; **57**, 261; **58**, 305
Macus, Leah S., **53**, 40
McVicar, David, **56**, 292
McVicker, **25**, 113–14, 115, 116, 117, 118
Mad Dogs and Englishmen, **43**, 213; **58**, 301
Mad World My Masters, A, **54**, 21, 57, 62
Mad World, My Masters, A, **52**, 215–17, 224, 226–7
Madan, Falconer, **4**, 82, 83, 84, 85, 86
Madariaga, Salvador de, **2**, 137; **3**, 137; **4**, 10, 24; **9**, 11
'Don Juan as a European Figure' reviewed, **1**, 120
'On Translating *Hamlet*', **6**, 106–11
Madariaga, Salvador de, **13**, 148; **19**, 140; **20**, 146
Madden, D. H., *Diary of Master William Silence*, **3**, 6
Madden, D. H., **44**, 131n, 134n, 135n, 138, 142n
Madden, Edward, **57**, 249, 256
Madden, Sir Frederick, **28**, 38n
Madden, John, **56**, 4; **58**, 185
Mäde, Hans Dieter, **20**, 118; **48**, 178, 179n
Madelaine, R. E. R., **37**, 190, 197, 219
Madelaine, Richard, **53**, 304, 327
Madin, Christopher, **55**, 333
Madoc, Philip, **45**, 135, 138; **57**, 294; **58**, 302; **60**, 211–12
Madubuike, Ihechukwu, **39**, 175
Maecenas, **38**, 40
Maede, Hans Dieter, **21**, 133
Maes, Gust, **7**, 108
Maes-Jelinkek, H., **44**, 219
Maeterlinck, Maurice, **2**, 121; **8**, 150; **13**, 30, 31; **15**, 133; **34**, 7; **57**, 121
Life and Flowers, **13**, 39n
Magarshack, David, **26**, 22n; **28**, 55n; **48**, 118
Magee, David, **58**, 140
Magee, Jeff, **57**, 250
Magee, Patrick, **39**, 79n
Magee, W. H., **26**, 155
Magellan, Ferdinand, **52**, 187–8
Magett, Steven, **52**, 72n
Maggiora, Rosa, **44**, 191
Magill, Ronald, **14**, 126
Maginley, Ben, **39**, 75n
Maginn, William, **56**, 128, 129, 131
Magnani, Anna, **36**, 3
Magnetic Lady, The, **54**, 65
Magni, Eva, **6**, 121; **10**, 120
Magni, Marcello, **46**, 171; **52**, 217–18, 225; **53**, 261; **54**, 283
Magnin, Charles, **3**, 102
Magno, Paschoal Carlos, **20**, 122
Magnocavalli, Anniball, **50**, 78
Magnusson, Lynne, **40**, 206; **53**, 288–9, 310; **55**, 182–3, 354; **57**, 196, 200
Magretta, Joan, **39**, 39n
Magritte, René, **44**, 177
Maguin, Jean-Marie, **27**, 173; **31**, 196; **40**, 74; **50**, 129n, 257
Maguire, Laurie E., **39**, 229; **41**, 227; **50**, 141n, 284–6; **52**, 85, 313; **53**, 331n, 332, 335; **54**, 307; **55**, 183n, 194n; **56**, 166; **57**, 305, 313, 317, 337; **59**, 8–9, 17n72, 20n4, 29n38, 33n64, 148, 212, 382, 383; **60**, 100
Maguire, Nancy Klein, **42**, 197; **49**, 302; **51**, 23n; **55**, 97n; **58**, 90, 330
Maguire, Sean, **52**, 263
Mahabharata, **50**, 33
Mahaney, William E., **27**, 177; **29**, 174
Maher, Mary, **57**, 331
Mahl, Mary R., **53**, 24n
Mahler, Margaret, **44**, 208; **49**, 287
Mahn, K. A. F., **15**, 98n

Mahomet III, **11**, 90
Mahon, John W., **42**, 181, 212n; **56**, 89n; **59**, 161n17
Mahood, Molly M., **7**, 5; **15**, 122; **16**, 74; **18**, 53, 173; **22**, 107n, 152, 166, 178; **23**, 67n, 69, 132; **24**, 28; **26**, 165; **28**, 114; **29**, 7; **32**, 214; **34**, 62n, 172; **35**, 80n, 82, 84n; **37**, 1, 124n; **38**, 6; **41**, 84n, 244; **42**, 181; **43**, 230; **46**, 108n; **47**, 226, 269, 271; **48**, 164; **49**, 8, 50, 51, 53n, 99n; **50**, 51, 113n, 270; **51**, 145; **52**, 99n, 106n; **53**, 42, 46; **54**, 89n; **55**, 381; **56**, 97; **57**, 328; **59**, 230
'Love's Confined Doom', **15**, 50–61
Shakespeare's Wordplay, **11**, 41n, reviewed, **11**, 136
Maid Lane, *see under* London
Maid's Metamorphosis, The, **54**, 229
Maid's Tragedy, The, **52**, 43n, 85; **54**, 15
Maidment, James, **53**, 217n
Mailer, Norman, **49**, 212n
Mailer, Sándor, **39**, 236n
Main, Laura, **57**, 295
Main, Richard, **53**, 279; **54**, 294; **56**, 294; **58**, 305
Maintigneux, Sophie, **43**, 207
Mainusch, Herbert, **55**, 181n
Mair, John Dunbar, **59**, 108n2
Mair-Thomas, Sara, **45**, 149
Mais, S. P. B., **55**, 111n, 113n, 130–1
Mais, Sally, **48**, 235
Maisonneuve, E. de, **44**, 23n
Maitland, F. W., *see* Pollock, F.
Maitland, Frederic W., **29**, 94; **32**, 132n, 134n; **43**, 32; **51**, 160n, 165n, 166; **52**, 182n
Maitland, William, **33**, 198
Maitra, Sitansu, **22**, 146
Shakespeare's Comic Idea reviewed, **15**, 163
Major, John, **47**, 221
Major, John M., **14**, 154
Major, T., **13**, 129; **14**, 120
Majumdar, Sarottama, **59**, 370
Makařovský, Jan, **21**, 140
Makarewicz, Andrzej, **11**, 121
Makaryk, Irena R., **56**, 342; **58**, 338, 342; **60**, 334–5, 353
Makeba, Miriam, **52**, 156
Makeham, Mr, **14**, 111, 112
Makhaya, Elliot, **52**, 158n, 164n
Makowska, Helena, **45**, 43n
Makowski, Elizabeth, **54**, 38n
Makris, Solon, **58**, 217
Malá, Otilie, **9**, 108
Malahide, Patrick, **52**, 267
Malakov, Vital, **45**, 151
Malala, Justice, **57**, 165
Malaya, report on Shakespeare in, **7**, 113
Malcolm II, King of Scotland, **57**, 70, 71
Malcolm, J. P., **30**, 164n
Malcolm, Noel, **56**, 120
Malcolm, Roy, **1**, 111
Malcolmson, Cristina, **45**, 160; **51**, 285
Malcontent, The, **52**, 82–3, 134, 297; **54**, 357
Male, David A., **39**, 234
Mâle, Emile, **53**, 15
Maleczech, Ruth, **45**, 51n
Maley, Willy, **51**, 277; **52**, 286; **54**, 315; **58**, 327, 332; **59**, 360–1, 368
Malhar-Shivalingappa, Shantala, **45**, 155
Malherbe, Fontaine, **3**, 98
Malherbe, François de, **9**, 92
Malherbe, M. de, **48**, 144
Malibran, Mme, **21**, 81
Malik, Charlotte, **47**, 218
Malin, Sarah, **57**, 273
Malinoff, Anastasia, **43**, 213
Malinowski, Bronislaw, **48**, 240; **50**, 243
Malipiero, G. F., **18**, 87
Malkiewicz, A. J. A., **38**, 23n
Mallaburn, Tom, **56**, 289, 293; **57**, 291, 292
Mallarmé, Etienne, **9**, 68n, 148; **15**, 109n
Mallarmé, Stéphane, **9**, 68n, 148; **36**, 44; **57**, 114, 115
Mallen, Eric, **55**, 339
Maller, Sandor, **44**, 241
Malleson, Miles, **13**, 139; **27**, 142
Mallet, Andrew, **48**, 236
Mallett, David, **51**, 7
Mallett, Eric, **50**, 217–19
Mallin, Eric, **50**, 22, 238; **54**, 314
Malmö (Sweden), **1**, 58
Malmquist, Sandro, **1**, 115; **3**, 118; **9**, 114; **14**, 123
Malmstróm, Ulla, **36**, 65n, 70
Malone Society, The, **2**, 44; **4**, 81, 95; **7**, 51; **11**, 81, 82, 87n, 88n
Malone, Edmond, **1**, 1, 3, 62, 73; **2**, 108; **3**, 3, 11, 17, 22, 49, 50; **4**, 82, 85–6, 88, 91–2, 93, 95; **5**, 19, 20, 25, 57n; **6**, 3, 4–5, 82, 158; **7**, 5, 76, 140; **8**, 91; **9**, 153, 154; **10**, 20, 22, 26n; **11**, 137; **12**, 8, 9, 148; **13**, 113; **14**, 82; **15**, 1, 2, 11, 12, 24, 30, 38, 40n, 71n; **18**, 17–19, 23, 30; **19**, 2, 104, 105n, 161; **20**, 36, 83, 84, 90, 93n, 171–2; **21**, 101–2, 149; **22**, 145; **24**, 107, 168, 171n, 175, 178; **25**, 111, 125, 187; **26**, 71, 91, 172; **27**, 107, 111n, 129; **29**, 168, 170, 179; **30**, 191, 205; **31**, 194; **32**, 242; **33**, 210; **34**, 14, 18n, 19n; **38**, 253; **39**, 145n, 153n; **40**, 131; **41**, 35, 42, 240; **44**, 115–24, 152; **45**, 175–9, 181, 185–7, 190–2; **46**, 37–43, 46, 138, 236; **47**, 88, 107, 246, 255–7; **49**, 22n, 24, 91n, 322; **50**, 102, 140, 254; **51**, 4, 5, 7, 67n, 136, 286, 321; **52**, 303, 318; **53**, 302, 337, 343, 344; **54**, 115; **55**, 12, 13, 27, 388; **56**, 185–90, 199, 201; **58**, 10, 223; **59**, 30–1, 32n58, 49, 56–7n20, 57n21, 60, 88, 108, 110, 111n14, 112n20, 114n28, 114, 115, 119, 120, 123, 127, 128, 129, 130, 132–3, 134, 199–200, 214, 270, 356, 380; **60**, 253n5, 265n38
Attempt to ascertain the Order of Shakespear's Plays, **4**, 57
A Dissertation on the Three Parts of Henry VI, **4**, 56, 57–8
editions of Shakespeare, **4**, 80–1
History of the Stage, **3**, 1; **12**, 8
interpretation of Greene's 'upstart Crow', **4**, 56–68
on the life of Shakespeare, **3**, 1
Rise and Progress of the English Stage, **14**, 81
Maloney, Michael, **44**, 194; **45**, 117, 118, 140, 141; **46**, 193, 198; **51**, 258; **54**, 248; **59**, 339
Malory, Sir Thomas, **15**, 34, 171; **29**, 123; **57**, 150; **59**, 265
Malpezzi, Frances M., **51**, 177n; **53**, 15n
Maltby, Judith, **59**, 258n10, 265–6n30
Malý, J., **9**, 103, 105, 110n
Mamontovas, Andrus, **54**, 285
Manaka, Hitomi, **60**, 303Fig.53
Mandel, J., **27**, 164

Mandela, Nelson, **52**, 155, 157; **55**, 272, 275, 279; **57**, 165; **60**, 290–1
Mandelbrote, Giles, **55**, 257n
Mandelson, Peter, **56**, 103
Mander, Carel Van, **31**, 16
Mander, Raymond, **7**, 145; **9**, 18, 53; **35**, 11
Mander, Raymond and Mitchenson, Joe, 'Hamlet Costumes: A correction', **11**, 123–4
Mander, Sheila, **48**, 235
Mandeville, Bernard de, *The Fable of the Bees*, **9**, 97
Mandeville, Sir John, **6**, 59; **17**, 39; **30**, 72; **32**, 89n; **50**, 260
Mankind, **1**, 64
Mandolidou, Vasso, **15**, 135
Manet, Edouard, **45**, 125
Manez, Raoul de, **12**, 110
Mangan, Michael, **46**, 217; **50**, 242
Mangan, Teresa, **45**, 151
Manheim, Michael, **28**, 157; **38**, 4; **49**, 308; **50**, 41n
Manheim, Ralph, **50**, 41n
Mani, Marcello, **51**, 245, 247
Manifold, J. S., **15**, 9
Manilius, **51**, 130n
Manim, Mannie, **55**, 274
Manitto, Gary V., **39**, 225
Maniutiu, Mihai, **49**, 277; **50**, 234
Mankiewicz, Joseph, **18**, 71; **45**, 63
Mankind, **52**, 298
Manley, Andrew, **45**, 146; **46**, 199; **47**, 213; **48**, 232; **49**, 274; **50**, 232; **52**, 263
Manley, Frank, **21**, 153; **26**, 157; **39**, 139n
Manley, John Matthews, **55**, 65n
Manley, Lawrence, **49**, 301–2
Manley, Skip, **53**, 243
Manlove, Colin N., **36**, 163–4
Mann, David, **46**, 225, 226
Mann, Dieter, **40**, 56
Mann, F. O., **28**, 56n
Mann, Isabel R., **4**, 152; **18**, 179
Mann, Jill, **44**, 217
Mann, Karen, **41**, 186
Mann, Phyllis, **51**, 142
Mann, Thomas, **10**, 109; **15**, 120; **26**, 163; **29**, 9; **43**, 28; **44**, 41, 44n; **45**, 2; **55**, 343
Mannell, Robin, **46**, 199
Mannering, William, **51**, 221
Manners, Lady Diana, **55**, 135
Manners, Francis, Sixth Earl of Rutland, **3**, 4, 11
Manners, Sir John, **3**, 40; **53**, 67n
Manners, Roger, Fifth Earl of Rutland, **7**, 139
Mannery, Samuell, **58**, 224
Manning, Barbara, **13**, 124
Manning, John, **43**, 246–7; **44**, 236; **45**, 182; **49**, 33n; **56**, 45n, 97n
Manning, Roger B., **24**, 157; **44**, 18n, 19n; **50**, 261
Manning, S., **55**, 239n
Manning, T. D., **17**, 22n
Manningham, John, **3**, 53; **29**, 173; **31**, 177–8; **32**, 102n, 104n; **41**, 221; **42**, 115; **46**, 23; **47**, 240; **52**, 25, 120n; **56**, 64, 256; **57**, 205, 208; **58**, 137, 204; **60**, 360
Mannion, Tom, **42**, 160; **54**, 265; **55**, 307, 329; **56**, 291; **59**, 330, 339; **60**, 320
Mannoni, Octave, **46**, 220; **48**, 155
Manocchio, T., **30**, 188
Mansai, Nomura, **58**, 300
Mansell, Darrell, Jr, **21**, 135
Mansell, Richard, **17**, 34
Mansfield, C., Jr, **48**, 88n
Mansfield, Katherine, **53**, 97–8
Mansfield, Richard, **23**, 131; **52**, 292
Mansi, J. D., **32**, 132n
Manson, Charles, **57**, 145, 146, 154, 155, 156, 157
Mantegna, Andrea, **10**, 71
Mantell, Robert, **57**, 256
Mantua, Duke and Duchess of, **60**, 62
Mantuanus, Baptista, **15**, 97n; **35**, 123
Mantzius, Karl, **1**, 11; **3**, 109–10, 112; **7**, 82
Manuel, Paul, **45**, 154
Manus, Torsten, **36**, 68n
Manutius, Paulus, **38**, 41n
Manvell, Roger, **35**, 9; **38**, 18; **39**, 4, 5, 39, 53n, 75n, 76n, 81, 91, 92, 94; **45**, 59n, 63; **49**, 156–7; **57**, 93
Manwaring, G. E., **17**, 29n
Manwood, Sir Roger, **17**, 85
Manwood, Thomas, **60**, 283
Mányai, Lajos, **16**, 135
Mapes, Stephen, **51**, 258
Maplethorpe, Bernard G., **42**, 158
Mappa Mundi, in Hereford Cathedral, **17**, 39n
Mapstone, Sally, **57**, 126
Maquerlot, Jean-Pierre, **41**, 228; **50**, 241; **53**, 167n
Mar, Earl of, **54**, 134n
Maranda, Elli Köngäs, **29**, 17n
Maranda, Pierre, **29**, 17n
Marathe, Sudhaker, **42**, 181
Marc, Nina, **50**, 227
Marcel, Gabriel, **12**, 111; **28**, 45
Marcell, Joseph, **38**, 213; **42**, 156, 162; **43**, 207; **44**, 202
Marcelline, George, **48**, 140
March, Henry, **45**, 149
March, Olave, **8**, 124
Marc'hadour, G., **21**, 152
Marcham, Frank, **4**, 70
Marchand, H., **23**, 14n, 18, 20, 23n, 28n
Marchant, E. C., **25**, 100
Marchat, Jean, **11**, 120; **12**, 112
Marchena, Juan de, **11**, 91
Marchesi, Concetto, **8**, 120
Marchetti, Leo, **40**, 205
Marchetti, Ludovic, **49**, 126
Marchionne, Claire, **46**, 201; **51**, 239
Marchison, Ruari, **41**, 185
Marchitello, Howard, **52**, 300; **59**, 61n30
Marcos, Comandante, **54**, 157–8
Marcos, Ferdinand, **46**, 238
Marcos, Imelda, **56**, 166
Marcus, G. J., **17**, 22n
Marcus, Jane, **58**, 120
Marcus, Leah S., **43**, 244–5; **45**, 159n; **46**, 16n, 255; **48**, 257; **50**, 254; **51**, 318–20; **52**, 16, 325; **54**, 58, 139; **55**, 6, 44n; **56**, 182n; **58**, 352; **59**, 9n37, 17n72, 21; **60**, 84n2, 366
Marcus, Paul, **42**, 156
Marcuse, Herbert, **37**, 9

Marder, Louis, **5**, 140; **10**, 122; **11**, 123; **12**, 118; **18**, 131, 179; **19**, 143; **21**, 148; **32**, 225; **35**, 191; **40**, 37; **41**, 66
Mardin, Yusuf, **7**, 116; **18**, 130
Mare, Margaret L., **7**, 121; **30**, 165n
Marek, A., **9**, 101–2
Marenco, Franco, **23**, 166
Marendaz, D. M. K., **7**, 114; **9**, 115
Mares, F. H., **22**, 172n; **25**, 180; **32**, 63n; **42**, 203–6; **56**, 169n
Mareuil, Arnaut de, **15**, 98n
Marfleet, Christine, **50**, 229
Margaret of Navarre, **60**, 344
Margaret, Princess, **56**, 10
Margaret, Queen of Scotland, **26**, 44
Margeson, John M. R., **22**, 172; **27**, 157n, 158n, 164n, 165n, 170n, 179n; **30**, 9n; **36**, 57n; **37**, 55n; **40**, 153n; **43**, 70n, 270n; **44**, 250–1
Margolies, David, **42**, 164; **46**, 216, 217; **55**, 5
Margolyes, Miriam, **47**, 210; **52**, 90, 95
Marguerite of Navarre, **46**, 17
Maria Eleonora, Duchess of Königsberg, **32**, 195
Maria Magdalena, Archduchess of Austria, **33**, 166, 168; **36**, 142, 143, 145, 146
Maria of Bavaria, **36**, 145
Maria Theresa, Empress of Austria, **35**, 22n
Mariam, see *Tragedy of*
Mariana, Juan de, **59**, 250
Marienstras, Richard, **19**, 126; **40**, 198; **46**, 130n; **49**, 207n; **50**, 257; **56**, 308, 329, 348; **57**, 125; **59**, 65n6
Marín, Francisco Rodriguez, **20**, 104n
Marín, Luis Astrana, **3**, 118; **9**, 115–16
Marion, Jean-Luc, **60**, 346
Maritain, Jacques, **20**, 116
Marivaux, P. C. de Chamblain de, **3**, 103; **41**, 204
Marjanishvili, Koté, **48**, 187–9
Mark, Thomas Raymond, **19**, 145; **59**, 126n9
Markels, Julian, **19**, 136; **22**, 175n; **24**, 147; **31**, 9n, 11n; **35**, 100
Marker, Frederick J., **35**, 12n; **36**, 65n
Marker, Lise-Lone, **24**, 167; **25**, 191; **36**, 65n
Markham, Clements R., **46**, 17n
Markham, Gervase, **15**, 168; **17**, 152n, 178n; **19**, 76–7; **53**, 323; **55**, 83n, 211; **57**, 321
Markham, Isabella, **46**, 13
Markham, Kika, **40**, 183
Markham, Robert, **46**, 11
Markland, Murray F., **24**, 166n
Marklew, Trudy, **42**, 149
Marks and Gram, **45**, 149
Marks, Carol, **41**, 147n
Marks, Elaine, **46**, 20n
Marks, Lisa, **46**, 201
Marks, Matt, **47**, 213
Marks, Peter, **55**, 73n, 74n, 80n
Marks, Shula, **52**, 154n, 160n
Marks, Stephen Powys, **56**, 337
Markus, Tom, **36**, 58
Márkus, Zoltán, **60**, 334
Marland, Lara, **45**, 150
Marley, Patrick, **43**, 205
Marlorate, Augustine, **28**, 101n
Marlow, Conrad, **41**, 50
Marlow, Metin, **48**, 229; **51**, 264
Marlow, Sam, **60**, 202
Marlowe, Christopher, **1**, 126; **2**, 59, 60; **3**, 10, 52, 62, 138; **4**, 7, 29, 50, 59, 60–1, 63, 150; **5**, 133, 139, 149; **6**, 5, 9, 39, 40, 43, 48n, 72, 159; **7**, 6, 8, 17, 82, 84, 85, 86, 113, 132, 142; **8**, 103, 106, 109, 145, 150; **9**, 137, 144; **10**, 3, 12, 48, 69, 119, 143, 144; **11**, 23, 54, 141; **12**, 112; **14**, 7, 26, 34–44, 68, 142; **16**, 11, 77, 97–100, 167; **17**, 13, 41, 49–51, 88 and n., 135, 194, 196–7, 149; **20**, 1, 17, 24, 52; **21**, 155, 162; **22**, 32, 51, 138, 139, 140–1, 147, 148, 173, 183; **23**, 49, 51, 97n, 117, 121, 141, 148, 149, 154, 155, 159, 166, 169; **24**, 20–1, 22, 23, 40n, 42, 44, 117, 143, 161, 162, 165; **25**, 190; **26**, 3, 6, 8, 9, 54, 103, 108; **27**, 18, 31, 71–9, 130, 132, 135, 176, 178; **28**, 45, 46, 169; **29**, 170; **30**, 4, 5, 11, 14, 198; **31**, 33, 109, 155–62, 170; **32**, 112, 218, 232, 235; **33**, 97, 154, 156, 166, 168, 195, 200; **34**, 52, 53, 172, 188; **35**, 154–5, 185; **36**, 10, 40, 93, 121, 122, 123, 129, 142, 173; **37**, 60, 129, 189, 204; **38**, 3, 4, 53, 178, 181–5, 189, 209, 220, 229; **39**, 143, 217, 225, 235; **40**, 45, 75, 227–8; **41**, 7, 9, 63, 64n, 210; **42**, 33, 55, 56, 65, 66, 80n, 127–8, 196, 208n; **43**, 6–8, 10; **44**, 13, 70, 131, 148, 149, 153, 211, 216, 220, 224, 233, 238; **45**, 179, 183, 184, 186, 192, 200; **46**, 5, 15, 63n, 111, 113, 160, 223, 225, 234, 235; **47**, 113, 127–37, 167, 171, 177–9, 224, 236, 242, 245n, 273; **48**, 8n, 27n, 39n, 40, 266, 277, 281; **49**, 29, 36, 100, 281, 314; **50**, 41–55, 65, 147, 150, 153, 255; **51**, 37, 166, 194, 212, 291, 29; **52**, 77, 99n, 100n, 275; **53**, 23, 24, 33, 78n, 149, 180, 322–3; **54**, 22, 73, 76, 96, 155n, 208, 271, 306, 333; **55**, 19, 20, 21, 23, 25, 65, 213–14, 220, 230n, 347, 349, 350, 360, 361, 369; **56**, 28, 32, 34, 35, 73, 211n, 220, 307, 308, 323, 324, 327, 334, 337, 353; **57**, 15, 31, 215, 222, 223, 224, 231, 232, 233, 277, 302, 319; **58**, 63; **59**, 2, 71, 75, 94, 97, 98, 184–5, 219, 352, 355; **60**, 255–6, 260–1, 262–3, 340, 343, 369
Dido and Aeneas, **11**, 141
Dr Faustus, **1**, 46, 64; **2**, 152; **4**, 27, 30, 41, 42, 43–4, 92; **5**, 141; **6**, 161; **7**, 83, 85, 142; **12**, 37; **13**, 167n; **14**, 8, 10, 34, 36, 40–1, 44n; **15**, 5; **16**, 47, 125, 147; **20**, 59
dating of, **8**, 102–3; **9**, 148
Edward II, **1**, 46, 64; **3**, 25; **6**, 2, 7, 36; **10**, 64, 138; **12**, 134; **14**, 8, 34, 40–2, 44n
handwriting, **2**, 54
Hero and Leander, **1**, 62; **3**, 54; **14**, 44n; **15**, 19, 62
Jew of Malta, **3**, 24; **7**, 83, 86, 87, 96, 142; **10**, 80; **13**, 167n; **14**, 8, 34, 36–8, 41–2, 44n; **20**, 52, 54, 140
Massacre at Paris, **1**, 65; **14**, 8
Shakespeare's debt to, **6**, 7
Tamburlaine, **1**, 64; **2**, 113; **3**, 60, 66; **5**, 139, 144n; **6**, 18, 151, 156; **7**, 83, 85, 86; **10**, 139, 145; **11**, 23; **12**, 2, 3; **13**, 156, 166, 167n; **14**, 8, 10, 34, 36, 38, 40–2, 44; **20**, 99
Tragedy of Dido, **10**, 23
production of, 119; **15**, 133, 167, 179; **16**, 56n, 133; **19**, 147
trans. of Ovid, **14**, 34
Marlowe, Julia, **32**, 22, 23, 24; **56**, 134; **57**, 256
Marlowe, Linda, **45**, 122
Marmion, Shackerley, **2**, 35n; **11**, 110; **28**, 170; **58**, 223
Holland's Leaguer, **2**, 32
Marmion, Simon, **6**, 59
Marmontel, Jean François, **9**, 91, 93; **16**, 53
Marosin, Mircea, **20**, 128
Marotti, Arthur F., **23**, 167n; **46**, 43n; **54**, 95n; **57**, 202, 205; **59**, 118; **60**, 253n5, 255n15

Marowitz, Charles, **25**, 28; **27**, 148; **28**, 138; **29**, 176; **37**, 162; **38**, 237; **39**, 47; **43**, 222–3; **45**, 9, 11, 66, 71; **47**, 3, 112; **52**, 24, 164, 287; **54**, 340; **55**, 166, 345; **56**, 314; **59**, 339, 371
Measure for Measure (adaptation), **47**, 214
Marprelate controversy, **1**, 68; **7**, 49
Marprelate Tracts, William Pierce, edition of, **8**, 105n
The Protestation, **8**, 101
The Reproof of Martin Junior, **8**, 101
Marprelate, Martin, **15**, 65; **17**, 124–6; **37**, 197; **49**, 287; **51**, 322; **54**, 102, 118; **56**, 63; **57**, 237, 239; **60**, 341
Marquard, N. J., **12**, 115
Marquez, John, **59**, 303
Marrapodi, Michele, **41**, 208; **48**, 257; **50**, 241; **52**, 273, 274, 279; **55**, 347; **59**, 361, 362, 368
Marrapodi, Michele, J. Hoenselaars, M. Cappuzzo and L. Santucei (eds.), *Shakespeare's Italy: Functions of Italian Locations in Renaissance Drama*, **48**, 257
Marre, Albert, **6**, 124; **7**, 116, 117
Marriage of Wit and Science, The, **3**, 41n, 52; **4**, 92; **20**, 25
Marrian, F. J. M., **21**, 147n
Marriette, Amelia, **55**, 384
Marriott, Alan, **43**, 207
Marriott, Sir J. A. R., **6**, 6; **29**, 80
English History in Shakespeare, **6**, 3
Marriott, Kate, **49**, 278
Marriott, W. K., **27**, 46n
Marroni, Francesco, **40**, 205
Mars, Mlle (A.-F.-H. Boutet), **3**, 103
Marschall, Wilhelm, **15**, 29
Marsden, Jean I, **43**, 99n; **46**, 143n; **47**, 225; **53**, 220, 221, 223, 301; **51**, 17–26, 67n, 125, 128–9, 131–4, 139; **54**, 42n; **55**, 97n; **57**, 129
Marsden, Robert, **12**, 121
Marsden, Roy, **45**, 149; **47**, 218; **55**, 327; **56**, 298
Marsh, Bower (ed.), **6**, 73n; **17**, 67n; **45**, 102n
Marsh, Derick R. C., **15**, 137; **18**, 162, 171; **20**, 154; **30**, 154; **34**, 96n; **37**, 218; **40**, 203; **43**, 225
Marsh, Dominic, **60**, 306
Marsh, Edward, **55**, 128, 135
Marsh, Jean, **49**, 125n
Marsh, Ngaio, **6**, 122–3; **10**, 149; **12**, 129n; **55**, 170–2, 178, 179, 180
'A Note on a Production of *Twelfth Night*', **8**, 69–73
Marsh, Nicholas, **52**, 272–3; **58**, 330, 332
Marshak, Samuel, **2**, 127; **4**, 125; **5**, 117; **6**, 125
Marshall, Cynthia, **46**, 213; **47**, 228, 234; **49**, 289; **52**, 279; **53**, 82n, 86n, 306–7; **55**, 352; **58**, 324–5, 332, 334, 337, 342
Marshall, David, **37**, 187
Marshall, Dorothy, **49**, 123
Marshall, Frank A., **16**, 32; **53**, 229, 230n
A Study of 'Hamlet', **14**, 164
Marshall, F. M., **32**, 23n
Marshall, Gail, **56**, 134n; **58**, 315; **59**, 374, 375
Marshall, Herbert, **59**, 211
Marshall, Mr, **54**, 84
Marshall, Norman, **9**, 133; **18**, 128; **32**, 36n; **36**, 84n; **47**, 88n
The Other Theatre, **12**, 129n
The Producer and the Play, **12**, 129n
Marshall, Stuart, **51**, 263
Marshall, Tristan, **55**, 370–1
Marshall, William, **6**, 61; **43**, 158, 160, 162–4; **50**, 152; **58**, 257
Marshall's engraving of Shakespeare, *see under* Shakespeare, William, portraits
Marshe, T., **47**, 24–5
Marsland, Andrew, **49**, 273
Marsterson, Thomas, **17**, 68
Marston, Cathy, **59**, 345
Marston, John, **1**, 41, 52, 64; **2**, 148; **3**, 19, 29, 45, 52, 140; **4**, 150, 151; **6**, 72; **7**, 6, 96, 131, 133, 141, 142; **8**, 11, 38, 41; **9**, 10, 11, 34n, 137, 149; **10**, 35, 146; **11**, 100, 103; **12**, 140; **14**, 9, 11, 82; **15**, 8, 99, 105, 108n; **16**, 98; **17**, 43, 45–6, 130–1, 134–5, 183–4, 199, 202, 206, 219n; **19**, 150; **20**, 20; **22**, 52, 164, 171; **23**, 46, 98, 100; **25**, 9, 68, 189, 191; **26**, 9, 55, 57, 99, 153, 169, 173; **27**, 99; **28**, 38, 41; **29**, 2, 3, 7, 9, 10, 170, 184; **30**, 110, 191, 192; **32**, 10, 93, 95, 104, 159n, 192n, 232; **33**, 91, 196; **35**, 33, 81n; **36**, 174; **37**, 180, 197; **38**, 122, 233; **39**, 127; **40**, 215; **41**, 35, 61, 93n; **42**, 104, 107, 187, 194, 197; **44**, 211; **45**, 19n, 20, 185–6, 191; **46**, 20n, 21n, 223, 224, 225; **47**, 47–8, 130, 176–7, 242–3; **48**, 123, 259, 264; **49**, 40, 97n, 98n, 99n, 210n, 212n, 325; **50**, 198n, 246; **51**, 291; **52**, 82, 134, 143, 295, 296–7; **53**, 320; **54**, 15, 16, 17, 20, 21, 62, 64n, 224, 357; **55**, 220, 369; **56**, 38, 101, 121, 217, 335–6, 337; **57**, 209, 219, 234, 333; **58**, 205; **59**, 71, 72, 73, 75, 77, 213, 214, 216, 219–20, 221–3; **60**, 369
Antonio and Mellida, **9**, 11; **13**, 156; **15**, 40n; **20**, 20, 22
Antonio's Revenge, **3**, 139; **9**, 11, 30, 32, 41; **13**, 156; **20**, 28
Dutch Courtesan, The, **14**, 23; **15**, 173
Entertainment, **6**, 60
First Anti-mask of Mountebanks, **6**, 60
Insatiate Countess, **1**, 64
Malcontent, The, **1**, 41–2, 43; **4**, 24; **9**, 30–1, 34n; **13**, 116, 119; **14**, 23 **15**, 40n; **48**, 259
Sophonisba, **4**, 42; **5**, 139; **13**, 113
see also under Jonson, Ben, *Eastward Ho!*
Marston, Westland, **51**, 108n
Marsus, **15**, 94, 97n
Marsus, Paul, **56**, 60
Martelli, Mario, **48**, 93n
Marten, Anthony, **17**, 34 and n.
Marten, Barbara, **45**, 156
Marten, Henry, **36**, 136n
Marti, Mario, **24**, 162n; **50**, 23n
Martial, Marcus Valerius, **17**, 61; **22**, 47; **38**, 42; **56**, 31
Martin Bodmer Library, *see under* Libraries
Martin Marprelate, **60**, 341
Martin, Anthony, **56**, 320–1
Martin, Benjamin, **55**, 94
Martin, Catherine, **52**, 91n
Martin, Christopher, **44**, 195; **47**, 210; **49**, 295
Martin, Denis, **7**, 108; **10**, 115
Martin, Frank, **11**, 117; **18**, 87; **45**, 172
Martin, Graham, **10**, 140
Martin, Gregory, **54**, 43, 91, 93n; **56**, 193
Martin, James, **38**, 71
Martin, John, **47**, 212; **58**, 358
Martin, John E., **53**, 62n, 63n, 64n
Martin, John Rupert, **57**, 215
Martin, L. C., **14**, 8; **31**, 33n
Martin, Lesley, **45**, 151
Martin, Patrick H., **58**, 321, 332

Martin, Peter, **50**, 254; **51**, 7; **54**, 51n; **59**, 30, 30n46, 124n1
Martin, Philip, **31**, 127n, 128, 129, 130, 135n
Martin, Priscilla, **31**, 176; **41**, 64n
Martin, R. W. F., **38**, 240
Martin, Randall, **45**, 163; **55**, 393–6
Martin, Richard, **1**, 71; **27**, 120; **43**, 242; **57**, 208
Martin, Robert, **18**, 17
Martin, Robert Bernard, **56**, 129n
Martin, Ruth, **41**, 189
Martin, St, of Braga, **20**, 22
Martin, Sir Theodore, **35**, 17
Martin, Susanna, **45**, 150
Martin, T., **5**, 53
Martin, Trevor, **39**, 196
Martin, Walter, **20**, 150; **21**, 135; **22**, 166
Martin, William F., **42**, 179
Martin-Davies, Ashley, **48**, 220; **49**, 273; **50**, 203; **51**, 236, 257, 263; **52**, 256, 257; **54**, 292; **55**, 310, 318; **56**, 298
Martin-Harvey, Sir John, **9**, 17, 57; **35**, 2, 20
Martindale, Charles, **42**, 196n; **45**, 161; **46**, 221; **55**, 349, 350; **56**, 28n, 65n; **59**, 225n1, 366–7, 368
Martindale, Joanna, **56**, 30n
Martindale, Michelle, **45**, 161; **46**, 221; **59**, 225n1
Martineau, Jane, **57**, 315
Martineau, Shereen, **58**, 278; **59**, 345
Martines, Lauro, **48**, 126n
Martinet, Marie-Madeleine, **30**, 202, **38**, 231
Martinez-Luciano, Juan V., **38**, 234
Martino, Alberto, **33**, 188n
Martino, Giovanni, **54**, 91n
Martins Penna, Luis Carlos, **20**, 121
Martire, Pietro, **51**, 179
Martyn, Christopher, **60**, 224n7
Martyn, William, **17**, 66; **35**, 79
Martyr, Peter, **54**, 229–30, 232–3
Martz, Leo, **29**, 5
Martz, Louis L., **23**, 87; **34**, 171
Marvell, Andrew, **15**, 99; **33**, 64n; **36**, 7; **38**, 16; **40**, 227; **43**, 238; **44**, 1; **46**, 52; **49**, 301; **50**, 243–4, 258–9; **53**, 33, 58; **56**, 80, 84, 87, 92, 120; **60**, 337
  Horatian Ode, **20**, 30
Marwa, Emil, **51**, 223
Marwick, Arthur, **45**, 180n
Marwick, Kate, **43**, 216
Marx, C. W., **57**, 242
Marx, Eleanor, **45**, 90
Marx, Groucho, **4**, 133; **37**, 167
Marx, Jenny, **23**, 173
Marx, Karl, **23**, 176; **26**, 92; **31**, 56n, 61n, 175; **35**, 65, 66n, 76; **40**, 35, 187–8, 193, 203; **44**, 31, 223; **45**, 89–100; **48**, 163, 166, 177n; **49**, 301; **50**, 274; **52**, 15; **54**, 324; **55**, 341; **56**, 143, 206, 220–1, 341; **57**, 173, 193; **59**, 150n15, 364; **60**, 254, 335
Marx, Steven, **46**, 210; **48**, 89n; **50**, 251; **54**, 308; **58**, 57
Mary Magdalene (Digby), **60**, 81n39
Mary, Princess, **26**, 44n
Mary I, Queen, **13**, 104n; **14**, 30; **35**, 108; **43**, 5; **44**, 106; **48**, 83; **50**, 255, 269; **52**, 170, 171n, 172, 176; **54**, 6, 74–5, 91, 125, 126, 134; **60**, 75
Mary Stuart, Queen of Scots, **1**, 125; **4**, 39; **6**, 1, 60; **12**, 102; **17**, 110, 122, 123; **26**, 36n, 41, 46, 48; **28**, 8, 151, 166; **36**, 174; **42**, 33, 34; **43**, 56–7; **44**, 227; **52**, 171n; **54**, 75, 96, 134, 138; **56**, 217; **57**, 70, 71
Masala, Nomakhosi, **56**, 282
Mascagni, Pietro, **45**, 173
Masefield, John, **4**, 2, 5; **6**, 12; **8**, 4, 8; **9**, 133; **15**, 26; **19**, 9, 49; **25**, 45n, 46; **26**, 103; **27**, 106n; **30**, 43; **36**, 50n; **50**, 2; **55**, 130–1
Masenga, K. E., **9**, 115
Masham, Lady Elizabeth, **38**, 33n
Masham, Sir William, **38**, 32n, 33n
Masina, Giulietta, **56**, 18
Mask of Proteus, **60**, 64
Maskall, Robert, **45**, 102–4
Maskell, William, **56**, 196n
Maslen, R. W., **55**, 349; **60**, 339, 353
Maslin, Janet, **52**, 90n
Mason, Bob, **54**, 268
Mason, Brewster, **19**, 114; **22**, 139, 140; **23**, 132; **29**, 154, 155; **41**, 46; **52**, 309; **57**, 339
Mason, D. J., **15**, 17
Mason, E. C., **4**, 147, 151; **18**, 174
Mason, Edward Tuckerman, **45**, 34n
Mason, Ellsworth, **56**, 141n
Mason, H. A., **21**, 138; **22**, 162; **33**, 11; **34**, 93; **39**, 207
Mason, James, **8**, 118; **9**, 111
Mason, John, **59**, 74
Mason, John, *The Turk*, **12**, 48
Mason, Mr, **14**, 110
Mason, Pamela, **46**, 238–9; **55**, 383; **57**, 343
Mason, Patrick, **51**, 261; **57**, 297; **58**, 263; **59**, 314–16; **60**, 328
Mason, Revd Robert, **4**, 94; **59**, 122n54
Mason, W., *Caractacus*, **13**, 49
Mason, William, **24**, 178
Masque of Oberon, **54**, 197
Masque of Queens, The, **50**, 109–10; **52**, 143
Masque of the Inner Temple and Gray's Inn, **54**, 20
Massa, Daniel, **41**, 64
Massacre at Paris, The, **50**, 286; **52**, 297
Massai, Sonia, **51**, 67–77; **53**, 301; **55**, 257n, 258n; **57**, 342; **58**, 354, 356; **59**, 369, 375
Massarella, David, **42**, 151
Massehian, Houhannes, **24**, 169
Massey, Anna, **41**, 174–5
Massey, Daniel, **37**, 164, 166; **38**, 203, 204; **47**, 205–6; **49**, 100n, 280; **58**, 58; **60**, 204
Massey, Gerald, **15**, 13
  The Secret Drama of Shakespeare's Sonnets, **3**, 10
Massey, M. Kathleen, **53**, 213n
Massey, Raymond, **10**, 122
Massie, Antony, **8**, 125
Massin, Jean, **48**, 5n
Massinger, Philip, **1**, 64; **2**, 120; **3**, 45; **4**, 160; **6**, 57; **7**, 6; **10**, 35; **11**, 51–2, 59n, 80–2, 151; **14**, 12, 13, 81–4, 86–7; **17**, 175, 195, 203; **18**, 46; **20**, 103n; **23**, 88, 171; **24**, 165; **25**, 68–9; **26**, 5, 9, 169; **28**, 180, 181; **30**, 207; **32**, 93; **34**, 178; **36**, 109; **38**, 189; **40**, 220; **41**, 7, 61; **42**, 189; **43**, 86n, 126; **44**, 125–7, 128n, 229; **45**, 184; **47**, 67, 249; **48**, 277; **52**, 206n, 210, 213; **54**, 18n, 357; **55**, 252, 359; **58**, 62, 225, 234, 349; **60**, 278n39
  The Bashful Lover, **13**, 115
  Believe as you List (MS.), **3**, 51; **11**, 80–2; **14**, 13

Massinger, Philip (*cont.*)
The Bondman, **13**, 120
The City Madam, **13**, 115, 120
The Duke of Milan, **6**, 36; **11**, 51; **13**, 115
The Emperor of the East, **4**, 92; **13**, 115
The Fatal Dowry, **13**, 115, 120
The Great Duke of Florence, **15**, 40n
The Guardian, **12**, 42; **13**, 115
The Parliament of Love, **11**, 51
The Renegadeo, **12**, 42
The Roman Actor, **13**, 115, 120
The Spanish Curate, **11**, 51
Unnatural Combat, **7**, 96
A Very Woman, **13**, 115
Virgin Martyr, **1**, 64; **4**, 92
Massingham, Dorothy, **9**, 19
Masson, David I., **9**, 135
Masson, Forbes, **52**, 261; **59**, 300, 314; **60**, 328
Mast, Gerald, **39**, 1n; **57**, 150
Masten, Jeffrey, **51**, 290, 317–18; **55**, 264n; **56**, 78, 312, 324; **59**, 5n16, 213n5, 214n6, 218, 219n24
Master, A. J. R., **9**, 112; **10**, 117; **12**, 111; **18**, 132
Master of the Ceremonies, Office of, **2**, 25
Master of the Revels (*see also* Herbert, Sir Henry), **7**, 61, 151; **52**, 72–6, 81; **55**, 28, 34, 44
Mastering the Revels, **46**, 232
Masterman, Neville, **39**, 236
Masters, Helen, **42**, 153
Masuccio di Salerno, **14**, 64; **20**, 98; **37**, 61
Matadze, M., **14**, 148
Matamoros, Diego, **39**, 182
Matar, Nabil, **59**, 361
Match Me in London, **54**, 18n, 27
Matcham, Frank, **49**, 235
Matchett, William H., **18**, 169; **21**, 140, 151; **24**, 151; **29**, 7, 67; **31**, 184; **36**, 40, 41–2; **38**, 12, 165n; **45**, 80n, 88n
'Some Dramatic Techniques in *The Winter's Tale*', **22**, 93–107
Matchinske, Megan, **53**, 319–20
Matchit, Ambrose, **58**, 239
Matei-Chesnoiu, Monica, **60**, 359, 361
Matejka, Ladislav, **31**, 54n, 55n; **60**, 228n30
Mathesius, V., **9**, 106
Matheson, Anthony, **51**, 269
Matheson, Eve, **45**, 148, 153; **51**, 213
Matheson, Mark, **50**, 249
Matheson, P. E., **46**, 149n
Matheson, T. P., **39**, 103n
Mathew, Frank, **15**, 26
Mathews, Anne, **51**, 107
Mathews, Charles, the elder, **37**, 85
Mathews, Charles, **48**, 262
Othello, the Moor of Fleet Street, **48**, 262
Mathews, Richard, **8**, 124; **9**, 120
Mathias, Sean, **52**, 251–2; **53**, 274
Mathie, Alexandra, **44**, 202; **47**, 210
Mathies, Eberhard, **46**, 194
Mathiesen, Thomas, **57**, 250
Mathieson, Barbara, **54**, 312
Matkowsky, Adalbert, **57**, 68
Matless, David, **60**, 187n13
Matsu, Takako, **60**, 137, 138
Matsuba, Stephen N., **52**, 185n
Matsui, Sumako, **48**, 107
Matsumoto, Kōshirō, **15**, 137; **60**, 137n21
Matsumoto, Toshio, **31**, 30n
Matsuoka, Kazuko, **50**, 248; **53**, 275; **58**, 304; **60**, 137, 304
Mattauch, Hans, **23**, 150, 174n
Matteo, G. J., **29**, 166
Matteo, Gino M., **51**, 58
Mattes, Eva, **49**, 269; **50**, 230
Matthäi, Hans Rudolf, **23**, 120
Matthew, Sir Toby, **11**, 71, 116n
Matthews, Brander, **25**, 3n; **26**, 119; **35**, 15n; **53**, 60
Matthews, Dakin, **60**, 116n63
Matthews, G. M., **20**, 145; **49**, 204n
Matthews, H. M. V., **18**, 157
Matthews, J. Brander, **1**, 13; **4**, 11–12; **8**, 5
Matthews, Jackson, **49**, 206n
Matthews, Peter, **52**, 90
Matthews, R., **29**, 165
Matthews, Robert, **49**, 27, 31
Matthews, Robert A. J., **51**, 105n
Matthews, William, **19**, 135, 150; **43**, 98n; **51**, 80n
Matthey, Pierre-Louis, **1**, 114, 116; **2**, 129
Matthias, Archduke, **33**, 162; **36**, 146
Matthies, Eberhard, **44**, 195
Matthiessen, F. O., **10**, 59n; **18**, 116–17
Matthieu, Pierre, **20**, 18; **43**, 164, 167n
Mattingly, Garrett, **4**, 155; **17**, 22n; **44**, 61n
Matus, Irvin Leigh, **45**, 191; **58**, 2
Matus, Michael, **59**, 303
Matz, Robert, **54**, 321
Maubant, Henri Polydore, **9**, 64
Mauclair, Jacques, **57**, 119
Maud, Jane, **47**, 215
Maude, Aylmer, **54**, 141n
Maudsley, Dr Henry, **45**, 40, 41
Maugham, Somerset, **20**, 81; **21**, 77; **48**, 185
Maule, Jeremy, **41**, 103n; **54**, 197n
Maulnier, Thierry, **7**, 110; **18**, 122
Maunder, Raymond, **59**, 211n58
Mauntz, Alfred von, **15**, 25, 27, 29
Maurer, Desmond, **44**, 192; **53**, 276
Maurer, Margaret, **44**, 218; **52**, 275; **53**, 344; **55**, 244n; **56**, 314
Mauretania, **11**, 89
Mauri, Glauco, **13**, 130; **14**, 121; **18**, 126
Mauriac, Claude, **48**, 6
Maurice the Learned, Landgrave of Hesse-Cassel, **33**, 157, 165
Maurice, Clement, **39**, 77n; **49**, 153
Maurice, Revd F. D., **54**, 82, 86
Maurice, François, **3**, 67
Maurice, of Orange, **33**, 155
Maurois, André, **18**, 123; **19**, 140
Mauron, Charles, **22**, 16
Maurstad, Toralv, **13**, 130
Maus, Katharine Eisaman, **37**, 193; **40**, 206; **43**, 92, 95n, 100n; **46**, 70n, 72, 122n; **49**, 207n, 281; **50**, 254; **51**, 304; **52**, 145n; **53**, 86n; **55**, 218n, 222n, 228n, 244n, 338; **57**, 18, 20, 21; **58**, 249, 317; **59**, 296, 381, 383; **60**, 255n15
Mauss, Marcel, **50**, 243; **55**, 40n, 248n; **60**, 346
Maverick, Ryk, **42**, 152
Maverty, S. C., **28**, 158

Mavor, John, **56**, 227n
Maximilian I, Duke of Bavaria, **36**, 146
Maxwell, Baldwin, **6**, 6; **11**, 153; **17**, 212; **18**, 8; **19**, 124; **26**, 9; **29**, 83n, 180
Studies in Beaumont, Fletcher and Massinger, **14**, 12
Studies in the Shakespeare Apocrypha, **14**, 4
Maxwell, J. C., **2**, 136, 139; **4**, 22, 24, 145n; **5**, 91n, 134, 140, 141, 150–1; **9**, 133, 136, 144; **10**, 49n, 69, 70n, 139, 146n; **11**, 143n, 148n, 149; **12**, 138, 147–8; **14**, 154, 154 and n.; **16**, 83–4, 88, 155–6; **18**, 186–7; **20**, 172, 178; **21**, 146, 147, 153, 155n, 159, 162; **22**, 62, 154, 156, 168; **23**, 151, 161, 180; **24**, 164, 166; **25**, 5, 7, 181; **26**, 105, 184; **27**, 106n, 111n, 112n, 136n, 191; **28**, 181; **29**, 41, 103n, 108, 111n; **30**, 195, 203; **31**, 25n, 112; **32**, 130, 141n, 149n, 234, 245; **33**, 7, 32n, 191; **34**, 85n, 156, 163; **38**, 15, 247, 248; **39**, 250n; **44**, 251, 253; **48**, 39n; **51**, 145; **55**, 207; **57**, 227; **59**, 2n5
'New Arden' edition of *Titus Andronicus* reviewed, **8**, 157
New Cambridge *Pericles* reviewed, **11**, 149
'Shakespeare's Roman Plays: 1900–1956', **10**, 1–11
Maxwell, Mrs L. C., **1**, 73
Maxwell, Mark, **44**, 192
Maxwell, Richard, **58**, 301
Maxwell, Roberta, **39**, 181
Maxwell, Ruth Anderson, **4**, 34n
Maxwell, W. C., **23**, 21n
May, Brian, **45**, 149
May, Jack, **7**, 125
May, Marcel, **28**, 39n
May, Olwen, **56**, 273
May, Stephen W., **27**, 178; **28**, 174
May, Steven, **60**, 366
May, Thomas, **4**, 154; **11**, 64; **14**, 13; **16**, 97; **22**, 4; **55**, 361; **60**, 108–9
The Old Couple, **9**, 86
May, Tim, **45**, 155
May, Val, **9**, 119; **10**, 123; **13**, 134; **14**, 126–8; **15**, 144; **49**, 279; **50**, 232; **51**, 260
Mayall, Hannah, **47**, 214
Maycock, Hazel, **42**, 152
Maycock, Lucy, **44**, 203
Mayde's Metamorphosis, **17**, 169
Mayenne, Charles de Lorraine, Due de, **38**, 50n, 53
Mayer, Claudia, **44**, 192
Mayer, Dorothea, **5**, 115
Mayer, H., **49**, 126
Mayer, Jean-Christophe, **54**, 319
Mayerne, T. T. de, **19**, 43n
Mayes, Ian, **49**, 123n
Mayhall, Jane, **4**, 147
Mayhew, A. L., **42**, 58n; **52**, 186
Maynard, Bill, **45**, 151
Maynard, Charles, **47**, 92, 106
Maynard, Katherine, **47**, 223
Maynard, Terence, **56**, 259
Maynard, Winifred, **40**, 220; **41**, 202
Mayne, Jasper, **3**, 140; **54**, 58n, 62, 64, 65, 68
Mayor, A., **4**, 74n
Mayoux, J. J., **16**, 74
Mays, Joanna, **44**, 162
Mazer, Cary M., **35**, 2n; **38**, 236; **41**, 224; **45**, 27n; **52**, 18n, 24n
Mazibuko, Doreen, **55**, 272
Mazynsky, Valery, **50**, 232
Mazzini, G., **2**, 134
Mazzio, Carla, **53**, 292
Mbatha-Raw, Gugu, **59**, 327–8
Meacham, Standish, **54**, 83n
Meacher, Harry, **51**, 260; **54**, 287, 288
Mead, George Herbert, **60**, 148
Mead, H. R., **6**, 53, 55
Mead, Joseph, **11**, 115n; **54**, 136n
Mead, Margaret, **46**, 122; **48**, 13
Mead, Philip, **48**, 234; **55**, 174n; **56**, 205n
Mead, Philip and M. Campbell (eds), *Shakespeare's Books: Contemporary Cultural Politics and the Persistence of Empire*, **48**, 240
Mead, Spencer, **41**, 186
Meade, Dorothy M., **42**, 195
Meade, Jacob, **47**, 15n
Meade, Joseph, **2**, 35n
Meade, Paul, **48**, 234
Meaden, Dan, **28**, 147
Meader, William G., **32**, 139n
Courtship in Shakespeare reviewed, **11**, 144
Meadowcroft, J. W. R., **23**, 185
Meadows, Alan, **42**, 158
Meadows, Kenny, **7**, 92; **10**, 73
Meads, Chris, **56**, 339
Meagher, John C., **19**, 163; **25**, 200; **27**, 179, 191; **38**, 235; **55**, 241n, 244n, 245
Meaker, Timothy, **56**, 297
Meaning by Shakespeare, **46**, 206
Mearns, Hughes, **47**, 139n
Mears, Catherine, **46**, 180
Mears, Michael, **59**, 345
Mebane, John S., **37**, 191; **47**, 139n; **48**, 141n; **59**, 252n96
Meckier, Jerome, **25**, 185; **53**, 107
Meckler, Nancy, **41**, 190; **46**, 202; **48**, 237; **51**, 267; **58**, 135; **59**, 300–1; **60**, 286, 321
Medcalf, Stephen, **48**, 260
Meddus, Dr., **60**, 54
Medical Journal of Malaya, **11**, 149
Medici, Antonio de', **7**, 97
Medici, Catherine de', **17**, 216; **27**, 172; **36**, 176; **38**, 52, 55; **54**, 194n
Medici, Ferdinando de', **7**, 106n
Medici, Francesco de', Grand Duke of Tuscany, **7**, 97, 105–6n
Medici, Giulio de', **25**, 166
Medici, Lorenzo de', **31**, 46; **60**, 61
Medici, Maria de', **7**, 97
Medicine and Shakespeare in the English Renaissance, **46**, 223
Medieval and Renaissance Drama in England, **46**, 231
Medina, Duke of, **17**, 34n
Medvedev, P. N., **44**, 85n
Medwall, Henry, **14**, 22; **20**, 167; **30**, 36
Fulgens and Lucrece, **14**, 15, 18
Medwin, Thomas, *Life of Percy Bysshe Shelley*, **14**, 88n
Meer, Michael van, **60**, 248–9
Meester, Johan De, **10**, 115; **14**, 122
Megiddo, Adam, **57**, 290

Mehl, Dieter, **16**, 166; **21**, 143; **23**, 115, 116, 172; **25**, 184; **26**, 155, 161, 166, 176; **31**, 181; **32**, 154n; **34**, 101; **37**, 156n; **39**, 219; **41**, 202, 206; **48**, 253; **53**, 293; **54**, 22n; **55**, 3n, 242n, 271n; **59**, 41
Mehl, Dieter and W. Weiss (eds), *Shakespeares Sonette in europaischen Perspäctiven*, **48**, 253
Mehlin, Urs H., **25**, 182
Mehlman, Jeffrey, **49**, 58n; **53**, 40n
Meiklejohn, J. M. D., **55**, 112n
Meillet, A., **23**, 28n
Mein-Smith, Philippa, **55**, 180n
Meinck, Carl, **31**, 11n
Meincke, Günther, **11**, 120
Meinecke, **18**, 130
Meininger Company, **35**, 12, 13–20
Meisel, Kurt, **16**, 133
Meisel, Martin, **41**, 28
Meiss, Millard, **26**, 115n; **33**, 99n
Meissner, J., **33**, 164n, 168n; **36**, 138n, 145n
Meissner, Paul, **2**, 126; **44**, 111n
Mela, José Manuel, **49**, 249
Melanchthon, Philip, **4**, 65; **25**, 188; **32**, 194n; **56**, 44n
Melcher, Terry, **57**, 155
Melchinger, Siegfried, **12**, 145; **18**, 124
Melchiori, Barbara, **44**, 214
Melchiori, Giorgio, **30**, 181; **31**, 164; **36**, 169, 193; **37**, 149n; **38**, 101, 235, 243, 253; **41**, 122, 216, 233n; **43**, 262; **44**, 214, 247–8, 256; **45**, 198; **46**, 255, 257n; **48**, 75n; **49**, 99n, 328–9; **52**, 314–15, 318; **54**, 96n, 353–4; **55**, 184, 185; **57**, 225, 227, 243; **59**, 36, 70, 78, 194n7, 383; **60**, 107n25, 184, 184n3
Melia, Joe, **34**, 149; **35**, 149, 150
Melies, Gaston, **45**, 68n
Méliès, Georges, **45**, 67, 68, 72; **52**, 185n; **55**, 383
Melito of Sardis, Bishop, **33**, 99n
Mellamphy, Ninian, **43**, 230; **55**, 247n
Meller, V., **15**, 140
Mellers, Wilfrid, **9**, 144; **21**, 144
Melling, Richard, **45**, 63n
Mellinger, Leonie, **35**, 148; **44**, 196
Mellor, Anne K., **56**, 153n
Mellor, Aubrey, **49**, 60n
Mellors, Wilfred, **60**, 189n17
Melnitz, William, **9**, 146n
Melo, Jose Manuel, **50**, 234
Melrose, Susan, **55**, 237n
Meltke, Martin, **48**, 183
Melton, Sir John, **8**, 110
Melville, Herman, **10**, 98; **18**, 103–5, 111, 116–17, **20**, 159; **21**, 141; **22**, 175; **26**, 89, 91, 94; **45**, 1; **54**, 302
Moby Dick, **18**, 104, 116; (film version), **18**, 71
Melvin, Jules, **53**, 261–2
Melvin, Murray, **18**, 153
Melzer, Annabelle Henkin, **49**, 153n, 156n, 157n; **52**, 185n
Melzer, Sara E., **54**, 199n; **55**, 241n
Melzi, Robert C., **21**, 152; **25**, 188; **32**, 2; **55**, 247n
Memmo, Paul E., Jr, **21**, 131; **56**, 82n
Menaechmi, **50**, 111n, 115; **54**, 194, 202
Menander, **22**, 4, 35
Ménard, Louis, **3**, 106; **9**, 66
Menart, J., **18**, 134
Mendel, Sydney, **19**, 123
Mendell, C., **19**, 93n
Mendelson, Edward, **36**, 29n, 31n
Mendelssohn-Bartholdy, Felix, **7**, 116; **9**, 111, 116; **11**, 120, 123; **15**, 134; **18**, 75, 81; **35**, 74; **37**, 50; **39**, 241; **40**, 51, 53n; **45**, 173; **47**, 92; **48**, 10, 233; **54**, 289; **55**, 312–13; **56**, 294; **59**, 304; **60**, 185, 187, 325
Mendelssohn-Bartholdy, Jacob Ludwig, **53**, 280, 285
Mendenhall, G. E., **48**, 86n
Mendès, Catulle, **9**, 67, 68n
Mendes, Sam, **44**, 172, 183, 195; **45**, 155; **46**, 162; **47**, 11, 121, 181, 202–5, 216; **48**, 236; **49**, 235, 260; **51**, 252, 255, 283; **52**, 262; **54**, 254, 258, 333; **56**, 256, 259–64; **57**, 297; **59**, 186
Mendham, William, **25**, 144
Mendilow, A. A., **13**, 168; **23**, 138, 186
Mendl, R. W. S., **20**, 160
Mendonça, Barbara H. C. de, **15**, 170
'The Influence of *Gorboduc* on *King Lear*', **13**, 41–8
Mendonça, Carla, **43**, 216; **44**, 194; **45**, 150
Mendoza, Bernardino de, **58**, 37
Menegatto, Beppe, **15**, 136; **18**, 126
Ménendez y Pelayo, M., **20**, 104n
Menenius, **23**, 99n
Menetto, Carlo A., **5**, 113
Mennell, Stephen, **55**, 240n
Mennes, John, **53**, 26n
Menon, Madhavi, **58**, 322, 332
Menotti, Carlo, **45**, 173
Mensaros, Laszlo, **12**, 113
Mentz, Steven R., **58**, 310
Mentzel, E., **33**, 160n, 163; **36**, 138n
Menzies-Kitchin, James, **50**, 231
Merbury, Francis, **3**, 52; **23**, 169; **28**, 177
Mercadente, S., **18**, 80; **19**, 151
Mercator, Gerardus, **8**, 116n
Mercator-Wright projection, **17**, 28, 144
Mercer, Eric, **17**, 182n; **33**, 140
Mercer, Peter, **23**, 152; **42**, 177; **45**, 24
Merchant of Venice, The, **46**, 220
Merchant, Christina, 'Delacroix's Tragedy of Desdemona', **21**, 79–86
Merchant, Ismail, **57**, 262
Merchant, Paul, **21**, 162; **50**, 256
Merchant, W. Moelwyn, **9**, 137; **10**, 141; **11**, 148; **12**, 144, **13**, 80n, 160; **15**, 172; **16**, 171, **19**, 81n, 142; **20**, 169; **21**, 138, 157; **24**, 15n; **31**, 4n, 16n; **35**, 10n, 11; **37**, 10, 41, 45n; **39**, 229; **40**, 212; **41**, 56n, 224; **49**, 113n, 114n, 122n; **51**, 9; **57**, 133; **59**, 130, 131
'Classical Costume in Shakespearian Productions', **10**, 71–6
'Costume in *King Lear*', **13**, 72–80
'His Fiend-like Queen', **19**, 75–81
Shakespeare and the Artist, **13**, 80n, reviewed, **13**, 158–9
Merchant-Ivory, **56**, 8, 267
Mercier, Louis Sébastien, **9**, 91
Mercier, Vivian, **55**, 157n
Merck, Alice Bertha, **52**, 17n
Meredith, Burgess, **11**, 123; **43**, 207
Meredith, Geoffrey, **10**, 124
Meredith, George, **8**, 1; **19**, 13; **22**, 36; **55**, 143; **56**, 134
The Egoist, **4**, 30

Meredith, Ifan, **59**, 344
Meredith, John, **22**, 128–30
Meredith, Mrs, **22**, 128–30
Meres, Francis, **2**, 149; **3**, 24, 28, 29, 144; **4**, 149; **7**, 24n; **12**, 141; **14**, 25, 26, 30, 31; **17**, 130, 182; **21**, 48; **25**, 110; **26**, 108; **27**, 105, 107, 108, 132; **30**, 201; **31**, 127, 138; **35**, 79; **37**, 26; **38**, 52; **39**, 123; **41**, 142; **42**, 63, 65, 66, 70, 73; **46**, 15n, 45; **52**, 99; **55**, 349; **56**, 30, 34, 350; **57**, 218, 223, 224, 302; **60**, 258
Palladis Tamia, **3**, 54; **8**, 100, 104; **9**, 24, 32; **10**, 69; **14**, 29, 76, 88n
Meri, George, **13**, 133; **15**, 167; **16**, 139; **23**, 152, 159; **29**, 166, 167
Meriam, M., **32**, 190n
Merian, Matthew, **50**, 152
Merian, Matthias, **33**, 148
Merian's view of London, **1**, 27, 30, 31, 33, 36n
Merifield, James, **48**, 232; **49**, 271, 277; **50**, 230, 235
Mérimée, Henri, *Spectacles et comédiens à Valencia 1580–1630*, **14**, 109n
Merkouri, Melina, **58**, 217
Merle, Robert, **20**, 131n
Merlin, John Joseph, **51**, 92
Mermaid Inn, *see under* London
Meron, Hanna, **9**, 114; **14**, 121
Meron, Theodor, **48**, 260
Henry's Wars and Shakespeare's Laws: Perspectives on the Law of War in the Later Middle Ages, **48**, 260
Merrells, Simon, **57**, 292
Merriam, Thomas, **34**, 191; **35**, 191; **37**, 215; **39**. 250; **41**, 233n; **43**, 263; **45**, 200, 202n; **49**, 27, 29; **50**, 287; **51**, 105n, 334; **52**, 314, 316
Merridew, John, **56**, 187n
Merrifield, James, **51**, 263
Merrill, Lisa, **57**, 127; **59**, 374
Merrill, Robert, **32**, 214; **33**, 199
Merrill, Thomas F., **23**, 167
Merriman, R. W., **23**, 42n
Merrison, Clive, **39**, 203, 204; **42**, 133; **43**, 212
Merritt, Anna Lee, **49**, 128
Merrix, Robert P., **30**, 56n; **33**, 187; **42**, 182; **49**, 142n
Merry Devil of Edmonton, The, **3**, 48, 112; **7**, 78, 81n; **12**, 44; **52**, 140n
Mertens-Fouck, Paule, **19**, 147n
Merzin, L., **39**, 83n
Mesguich, Daniel, **53**, 168n
Meskhishvili, Giorgi, **47**, 211
Meskhishvili, Lado, **48**, 186
Meskin, Aaron, **5**, 113; **6**, 121; **9**, 114; **10**, 119; **13**, 129
Mesnard, Pierre, **44**, 62n; **53**, 165
Messa, al Hage, **11**, 91, 94
Messalaar, Gerard, **13**, 130
Messalina, **3**, 84
title-page engraving (1640), **4**, 97, 98; **7**, 73, 75; **12**, 42; **13**, 114, 115, 120
Messel, Oliver, **2**, 19; **5**, 116; **12**, 12
Messer, Graeme, **49**, 271
Messiaen, Pierre de, translation of Shakespeare, **1**, 114; **2**, 121
Messimeris, Tassia, **47**, 217
Messina, Cedric, **39**, 94, 95, 105; **45**, 59, 60, 188; **47**, 10, 215; **56**, 346
Messina, Maria Grazia, **59**, 130n41, 131
Messink, James, **9**, 98, 100n
Mestel, Jacob, **55**, 116n
Meszaros, Patricia K., **30**, 186; **37**, 193
Mészéros, Ági, **14**, 120
Mézières, A., **2**, 116, 125n
Metamorphoses, **50**, 82, 83n, 87; **54**, 207, 228, 317
Metastasio, Pietro, **20**, 34, 35
Metcalf, Edgar, **15**, 146
Metcalfe, Carol, **50**, 230; **52**, 254
Meth, Jonathan, **42**, 158
Methodius, Pseudo-, **59**, 241
Methua-Scheller, Maria, **42**, 199
Metro Gilded Balloon Treviot Edinburgh, **58**, 307
Metscher, Thomas, **31**, 175; **32**, 224
Metz, Christian, **39**, 91
Metz, G. Harold, **29**, 170; **31**, 173, 187; **32**, 234; **35**, 191; **36**, 171, 190; **37**, 215n; **38**, 112; **40**, 227n; **43**, 262, 268; **45**, 203n; **51**, 324–5
Metzger, Mary Janell, **52**, 205n, 211, 280
Meulen, A. F. van der, **3**, 88; **12**, 32, 33
Meurice, Paul, **9**, 59, 61–3, 64, 66, 67
Meurling, Per, **7**, 114
Mexía, Pero, **20**, 104n
Mexico, report on Shakespeare in, **3**, 118
Meyer-Baer, Kathi, **54**, 25n, 27n
Meyer, Ann R., **48**, 281; **49**, 334–5; **55**, 3n; **59**, 15n65
Meyer, Anthony, **45**, 63n, 68
Meyer, C. F., **18**, 129; **32**, 197n; **36**, 144n, 147n
Meyer, David, **45**, 63n, 68
Meyer, Edward, **29**, 79
Meyer, Jean, **11**, 119
Meyer, K. F., **17**, 165
Meyer, Marcel, **60**, 290
Meyer, Melinda, **59**, 295
Meyer, Michael, **43**, 115n; **48**, 116n
Meyer, Russell J., **37**, 67n
Meyerbeer, Giacomo, **57**, 65
Meyerhold, Vsevolod, **24**, 125; **27**, 143, 144; **39**, 5, 81n, 85; **40**, 2; **47**, 3; **54**, 142; **55**, 323; **56**, 346
Meyers, Jonathan Rhys, **56**, 4n
Meyersohn, Marylea, **58**, 85, 86
Meyjes, Ben, **55**, 300
Meymott, W. J., **1**, 29
Meyrick, Sir Gelly, **28**, 6–7; **38**, 22, 61; **42**, 193
Meyricke, Samuel, **10**, 74; **20**, 108
M. F., *see under* Mundy, Francis
Mhlongo, Ntombi Nkosi, **57**, 161, 163
Michael, Kathleen, **3**, 123, 127
Michael, Nancy C., **42**, 213
Michaël, Pierre, **6**, 118; **7**, 108
Michaelidis, Costis, **10**, 119
Michaels, Kenneth, **42**, 154
Michaels, Walter Benn, **51**, 130
Michaels, Yomi, **47**, 216
Michaud, M. M., **54**, 97n
Michault, Pierre, **49**, 83
Michel-Michot, Paulette, **23**, 161; **44**, 219
Michel, Andreas, **55**, 73n
Michel, Francisque, **2**, 116
Michel, Keith, **12**, 84

Michel, Laurence, **10**, 145
Michel, Pierre, **44**, 219
Michelangelo, Buonarroti, **15**, 28, 100–1; **19**, 61; **20**, 31; **21**, 3; **22**, 60; **26**, 60, 116; **28**, 55; **36**, 167, 175, 176; **57**, 42
Michelet, Jules, **59**, 263n24
Micheli, Lind McJ., **43**, 52n, 268
Michell, Keith, **5**, 124; **9**, 126; **39**, 105; **46**, 194
Michell, Roger, **42**, 151, 154; **45**, 157
Michelsen, Peter, **35**, 12n
Michelson, H., **17**, 49
Michie, Donald M., **55**, 14n, 32, 33n
Michie, John, **45**, 150
Micklewright, Sara, **58**, 243
Micyllus, **56**, 56n
Middle Temple, *see under* London
Middlemass, Frank, **38**, 212, 213; **39**, 86n, 88
Middlemore, S. C. G., **50**, 174n
Middleton, Alasdair, **42**, 150; **51**, 257
Middleton, Anne, **55**, 183, 192n
Middleton, Christopher, **58**, 62, 66, 304
Middleton, Gren, **53**, 280; **55**, 326
Middleton, Hugh, **2**, 150; **3**, 30
Middleton, Juliet and Grenville, **42**, 158
Middleton, Juliette, **53**, 280
Middleton, Noelle, **6**, 119
Middleton, Richard, **30**, 197
Middleton, Thomas (*see also* Rowley, William), **2**, 152; **4**, 25, 29, 62, 129; **5**, 148; **6**, 57, 157; **7**, 96, 143; **8**, 56, 66; **11**, 63, 116n; **13**, 117; **14**, 11, 13, 82; **16**, 99; **17**, 135, 175, 206; **19**, 1, 2, 58–60; **20**, 2, 54; **21**, 24, 146; **22**, 171; **23**, 46, 132, 133, 170–1; **24**, 40, 179; **25**, 141n; **26**, 4, 5, 7, 8, 9, 39, 54, 56, 57, 66; **27**, 176; **29**, 123, 173; **30**, 161n, 192, 198, 207; **32**, 99n; **34**, 53, 89, 161, 181–2, 190; **35**, 113, 114, 116, 176; **36**, 110, 112, 114n, 117, 124, 126, 133, 174; **37**, 115, 124n, 219; **38**, 85, 86n, 99, 228, 230; **39**, 224; **40**, 216, 219–20; **41**, 7, 116, 231, 233, 239; **42**, 187, 189, 212; **43**, 128, 242, 263; **44**, 24, 79, 114–24, 125n, 127, 128, 153, 234, 247; **45**, 173, 195, 196; **46**, 116n, 124n, 227, 233, 244, 247, 257n; **47**, 48, 176, 243–4, 248–9; **48**, 28, 258, 273n, 275, 276, 277; **49**, 81, 288, 303; **50**, 278, 282, 284; **51**, 101, 212–14, 291, 305, 311, 325, 327; **52**, 43n, 75, 81, 134, 143–4, 147–8, 215, 226–7, 274, 296; **53**, 300, 340; **54**, 13, 14, 18, 19n, 21–2, 23n, 27, 30, 57, 62, 299, 301, 312, 334, 357; **55**, 84n, 257, 350, 358–9, 360, 372; **56**, 31, 32, 101, 224, 337, 339; **57**, 1, 69, 76, 95, 122, 228, 335, 336; **59**, 5, 27, 71, 72, 73, 75, 76, 77, 77n12, 184, 204–6, 208–10, 213, 214, 217, 220, 222; **60**, 66–7, 102n2, 109n33, 113n45, 188, 225–6, 232–3, 266, 266n42, 273, 357, 368
  Black Book, **7**, 69
  The Changeling, **14**, 8, 9
  A Chaste Maid in Cheapside, **13**, 113, 119
  A Game at Chess, **1**, 64, 65; **3**, 52; **4**, 91; **6**, 60; **11**, 116n; **14**, 9
  The Ghost of Lucrece, **1**, 75; **15**, 91
  Hengist King of Kent, **1**, 65, 75; **14**, 9
  The Revenger's Tragedy, **47**, 121; **48**, 251; **54**, 13, 29
  The Roaring Girl, **11**, 104; **12**, 46
  The Spanish Gipsy, **13**, 120
  share in *Macbeth*, **2**, 146, 147–8
  Triumph of Honour, **1**, 64
  The Witch, **4**, 42, 91; **5**, 148; **9**, 86, 89n; **11**, 63, 146; **12**, 137; **13**, 157
  World Tost at Tennis, **1**, 64
  (*and* Rowley, W.), *A Fair Quarrel*, **4**, 91; **9**, 48n
Midgley, Graham, **28**, 85, 86
Midgley, Robert, **49**, 278
Midgley, Robin, **43**, 211; **45**, 154; **52**, 260
Midsommer Actors, The, **50**, 225
Miedzyrzecka, Daniela, **43**, 18n
Mielziner, Jo., settings of, **12**, 7
Mifflin, Houghton, **25**, 186
Mignault, Claude, **56**, 46, 49
Mihailović, D., **18**, 135
Mikalachki, Jodi, **49**, 293; **52**, 271; **56**, 228n
Mikami, Isao, **14**, 121
Mikesell, Margaret Lael, **45**, 169; **49**, 202; **60**, 84n2, 97n36, 98, 99
Mikhailov, A., **12**, 118
Mikheols, Solomon, **13**, 133; **40**, 40
Mikovec, F. B., **9**, 102–3
Mikulicz, Hilde, **6**, 117
Milander, Olof, **41**, 223
Milani, Luciana, **5**, 113
Milano, Alberto, **7**, 116
Milčin, I., **4**, 118; **15**, 142
Mildmay, Sir Humphrey, **47**, 41
Mildmay, Sir Walter, **17**, 127
Miles Gloriosus, **12**, 85
Miles, Ben, **48**, 237; **59**, 321, 322–3; **60**, 326
Miles, Bernard, **8**, 124; **9**, 49, 147; **10**, 85, 89n
Miles, Gareth, **60**, 213, 321
Miles, Geoffrey, **50**, 247
Miles, Kate, **59**, 340
Miles, Maria, **43**, 213; **45**, 122; **46**, 201
Miles, Patrick, **48**, 115n
Miles, Robert, **52**, 201n
Miles, Rosalind, **37**, 90; **41**, 220; **44**, 235
Miles, Vernon Garth, **41**, 208
Miletić, S., **4**, 122n
Milgate, W., **59**, 277n31, 278n33
Milhous, Judith, **30**, 200; **57**, 84
Milićevic, J., **15**, 140
Milićevic, O., **18**, 135
Mill, Anna J., **24**, 160, 161
Mill, Callum, **15**, 146
Mill, John Stuart, **24**, 88; **56**, 206–13
Millais, John Everett, **49**, 125; **60**, 362
Millar, Oliver, **60**, 223n5
Millar, Sheila, **47**, 95
Millar, Sylvia, **39**, 79n
Millard, Barbara C., **44**, 222
Millard, Christopher, **53**, 138n
Millbank, Elizabeth, **42**, 154
Milledge, Katie, **50**, 234
Miller, Anthony, **40**, 204; **45**, 164; **46**, 219; **57**, 145
Miller, Arthur, **12**, 7; **16**, 19; **18**, 155; **20**, 35, 40n; **27**, 81; **47**, 91; **48**, 11, 12; **57**, 119
  Enemy of the People, An, **48**, 11–12
Miller, Dave, **42**, 158
Miller, David, **57**, 31
Miller, David A., **40**, 123n

Miller, David Lee, **48**, 152n, 248; **51**, 167n
Miller, Donald C., **9**, 138
Miller, E. H., **17**, 130n
Miller, F. J., **56**, 59n
Miller, Flora Whitney, **49**, 123
Miller, Frank Justus, **10**, 49n; **32**, 75n; **53**, 15n; **54**, 31n, 207n; **55**, 65n
Miller, Henry, **50**, 188n
Miller, J. Hillis, **53**, 39, 48; **58**, 180, 181
Miller, James, **45**, 151; **47**, 27n
Miller, Joan, **11**, 134; **12**, 84
Miller, Jonathan, **24**, 129, 131; **25**, 154; **27**, 174; **36**, 61, 154, 172; **37**, 59; **38**, 209, 240; **39**, 10, 86, 88, 95, 97–100, 102, 104, 109; **40**, 212; **41**, 67, 72, 168, 228; **42**, 158; **43**, 183, 188–9, 215; **44**, 95, 194, 213: **45**, 188; **48**, 116, 155; **49**, 141, 143n, 145n, 151; **51**, 219–20, 264; **52**, 287, 292; **55**, 186–7, 322, 380; **56**, 346; **59**, 198, 371
Miller, Kenny, **45**, 150; **48**, 235; **53**, 277
Miller, Les, **41**, 186
Miller, Lisa, **54**, 289
Miller, Max, **46**, 173; **51**, 213
Miller, Patrick, **43**, 208; **44**, 195; **48**, 86; **60**, 25n8, 36n2, 37n5
Miller, Paul J. W., **32**, 170
Miller, Perry, **27**, 83n
Miller, Pip, **41**, 186
Miller, Poppy, **52**, 230–1
Miller, R. H., **46**, 13n
Miller, R. P., **14**, 154; **15**, 21
Miller, Richard, **53**, 117n; **56**, 140n
Miller, Rick, **55**, 327
Miller, Robert P., **7**, 137; **53**, 15, 17m, 19n
Miller, Ronald F., **30**, 183
Miller, Shannon, **46**, 219
Miller, Sienna, **59**, 311; **60**, 320
Miller, Stephen, **59**, 383
Miller, Stephen Roy, **53**, 338
Miller, Tice L., **75**, 7n
Miller, Walter, **25**, 99n
Miller, William, **17**, 213n; **42**, 28n; **48**, 7; **49**, 120
Miller, William E., **18**, 180, 183; **31**, 190, 197
Miller, William Ian, **57**, 84
Miller-Schütz, Chantal, **52**, 44n
Milles, Thomas, **21**, 163; **22**, 161, 168
Millfield Theatre (London), **58**, 306
Millington, Sarah, **47**, 213
Millington, Thomas, **46**, 16n
Mills, A. D., **31**, 186
Mills, Alison, **42**, 157
Mills, David, **50**, 257; **57**, 242; **59**, 247n66
Mills, Howard, *Working with Shakespeare*, **48**, 244
Mills, John A., **28**, 171; **45**, 32n, 35
Mills, L. J., **15**, 166; **19**, 129
Mills, Laurens, **56**, 208
Mills, Perry, **46**, 240n
Mills, Tobias, **58**, 62
Millson, Joseph, **57**, 267; **60**, 302, 310
Milmoe, Caroline, **48**, 235
Milne, A. A., **55**, 291
Milne, A. T., **24**, 177n
Milne, Dan, **50**, 217, 219; **52**, 235
Milne, Drew, **56**, 144n
Milne, Evander, **2**, 139
Milne, Lennox, **10**, 125
Milner, Henry, **47**, 63–5, 69
Milner, Ian, **21**, 139
Milner, Peter, **45**, 153
Milnes, Richard Monkton (Lord Houghton), **54**, 82
Milns, William, **59**, 116
Milo, Joseph, **9**, 114; **12**, 114; **18**, 125
Milośević, M., **4**, 121; **15**, 140
Mils, Tobias, **6**, 74n
Milsom, S. F. C., **49**, 188n
Miltitz, Carl Borromacus von, **37**, 46
Milton, Andrew, **56**, 292
Milton, Ernest, **9**, 18, 19, 57; **11**, 124; **23**, 131; **45**, 76
Milton, John, **3**, 14; **5**, 50, 51; **6**, 54, 154, 158; **7**, 1, 24n, 30, 152; **8**, 57; **9**, 82, 84, 97; **10**, 14, 17; **11**, 60, 107, 116n, 145; **13**, 58, 65, 105n; **15**, 21, 26–7, 81, 91; **16**, 168; **17**, 91; **18**, 12, 20, 95; **19**, 55, 57, 59, 60, 65, 81n; **20**, 85; **22**, 1, 56, 170; **23**, 167; **24**, 42, 159; **26**, 114; **32**, 228; **33**, 204; **34**, 185; **35**, 178; **36**, 104, 117, 152, 162; **38**, 69, 218n; **40**, 71, 202; **41**, 109n; **42**, 68; **43**, 121, 228, 238; **44**, 1, 6, 212, 216, 238; **45**, 167; **46**, 112n, 115, 116n, 145; **47**, 245; **48**, 254; **49**, 168, 169, 302, 303; **50**, 1; **51**, 18, 28, 31, 125, 133, 136, 138, 296, 318, 320–1, 326; **53**, 38, 57, 143; **54**, 32, 40, 56, 61, 183, 206, 320, 333; **55**, 230n, 263, 267, 361; **57**, 70, 71, 217, 338; **58**, 73, 249, 255; **59**, 94, 281, 350, 351, 352, 365–6; **60**, 234, 269, 282, 332–3
  Comus, **12**, 107
  Eikonoklastes, **14**, 98, 100
  Hermes, or, a guide to the elements, & c, **5**, 53
  The History of Britain, **14**, 100
  Paradise Lost, **5**, 53, 75; **8**, 24; **13**, 62, 65
  The Reason of Church Government, **14**, 98–101
  Of Reformation, **14**, 101n
Milton, John (father of the poet), **11**, 105
Milton, Jonathan, **46**, 202
Milward, Peter, **18**, 168; **19**, 140; **21**, 148; **22**, 167; **23**, 160; **26**, 162; **28**, 151, 165–6; **41**, 218; **45**, 203; **54**, 25n, 40, 61n, 68n, 120n, 121n, 244n; **55**, 230n, 231n, 234n; **56**, 192n
Mimmack, Peter, **48**, 253; **54**, 294; **56**, 297; **57**, 295; **58**, 302, 303; **59**, 340, 342
Minami, R., **57**, 171
Minazzoti, Christine, **18**, 123
Mincoff, Marco, **2**, 127; **5**, 133; **7**, 140; **10**, 116; **11**, 53, 54; **15**, 170; **16**, 167, 169, 174–5; **19**, 144; **20**, 178; **21**, 135; **22**, 157, 174; **25**, 6, 188; **26**, 13–14, 113n, 117n; **29**, 170; **30**, 125; **32**, 10; **37**, 190; **38**, 12, 247, 249, 250; **42**, 3n; **45**, 203n; **47**, 229; **51**, 324; **54**, 147; **56**, 341
  Christopher Marlowe, **14**, 9
  'Shakespeare and Lyly', **14**, 15–24
  'Shakespeare, Fletcher and Baroque Tragedy', **20**, 1–16
  'The Structural Pattern of Shakespeare's Tragedies', **3**, 58–65
Mind, Will and Understanding, **1**, 64
Minelli, Liza, **57**, 190
Miner, Earl, **36**, 114n; **53**, 40
Minetti, Bernhard, **13**, 128
Mink, Louis O., **44**, 145n
Minks, Wilfried, **37**, 161; **49**, 269; **50**, 230; **55**, 323
Minnequerode, Meade, **18**, 117n
Minnesota University Library, *see under* Libraries
Minoes, Claudius, **40**, 79n; **56**, 49

Minogue, Dannii, **54**, 288, 293
Minogue, Kylie, **54**, 293
Minotis, Alexis, **10**, 119; **12**, 113; **15**, 134, 135
Minsheu, John, **56**, 39; **57**, 204
Minter, Tinch, **43**, 210
Minto, William, **26**, 184
Minturno, A. S., **10**, 48
Mintz, Michael, **55**, 125
Miola, Robert S., **34**, 184; **36**, 171, 175; **38**, 37n, 41n, 215–17; **40**, 75n; **42**, 165; **44**, 9n, 71n; **46**, 221, 222, 223; **47**, 227; **49**, 290; **50**, 111n; **51**, 190n; **52**, 274, 275, 279; **54**, 32n, 33n; **55**, 207n, 211n, 214n, 347, 367, 368; **56**, 218n, 220n, 222n, 225n, 303; **58**, 349, 356; **59**, 250n81, 361; **60**, 84n2
Miracle plays, **7**, 69–70, 73, 76, 82, 99; **17**, 191–2
in Belgium, **5**, 106–7
stages for, **3**, 94
Miranda, Carlos, **44**, 198
Mirandola, Pico della, **15**, 95; **25**, 103; **30**, 190; **44**, 36; **53**, 29; **54**, 227
Mirbeau, Octave, **9**, 67, 68n
Mirren, Helen, **31**, 149; **37**, 172, 173; **40**, 183; **43**, 171; **45**, 63n, 69; **47**, 122; **52**, 251–2; **53**, 274
Mirror for Magistrates, A, **1**, 67; **3**, 18; **4**, 4, 14, 27; **6**, 57, 157; **10**, 3, 20, 29, 31; **11**, 144; **13**, 30; **14**, 26; **15**, 24, 169; **55**, 15, 17, 21
Mish, Charles C., **43**, 102n
Misik, Stefan, **4**, 115n
Miskimin, Alice, **59**, 259n11
Misrule, Lord of, **17**, 19–20, 178–9
Misselden, Edward, *Free Trade*, **1**, 68
Mitchel, **10**, 73
Mitchell, Allan, **45**, 139; **46**, 187
Mitchell, C. Martin, *The Shakespeare Circle*, **2**, 144
Mitchell, Charles, **19**, 132, 136; **20**, 150; **22**, 156
Mitchell, Clare, **51**, 219
Mitchell, Donald, **32**, 81n
Mitchell, E. B., **44**, 142n
Mitchell, Graham, **43**, 205; **44**, 202
Mitchell, J. L., **29**, 183n
Mitchell, John, **42**, 157
Mitchell, Joseph, **51**, 10
Mitchell, Katie, **45**, 157; **48**, 211–14; **49**, 271; **54**, 312; **56**, 343
Mitchell, Laurence, **59**, 346
Mitchell, Lee, **36**, 62
Mitchell, Margaret, **60**, 330
Mitchell, Reg, **52**, 266; **53**, 285; **58**, 154
Mitchell, Roger, **41**, 187
Mitchell, Ruth, **47**, 210; **48**, 213; **49**, 271
Mitchell, Sally, **55**, 112
Mitchell, Sebastian, **43**, 212
Mitchell, Tim, **52**, 249; **54**, 277; **55**, 309
Mitchell, US Senator, **54**, 215
Mitchell, W. J. T., **51**, 130n; **53**, 40n
Mitchell, Warren, **50**, 228
Mitchell, William J., **52**, 196n
Mitchell, Yvonne, **7**, 126–7; **16**, 22; **27**, 142
Mitchenson, Joe, **7**, 145; **9**, 18, 53; **35**, 11; **59**, 211n58
Mitford, Mary Russell, **14**, 88n, 110; **40**, 171
Mittenzwei, Werner, **48**, 174n
Mitterwurzer, Anton Friedrich, **35**, 26–8, 29; **37**, 199; **57**, 68
Mitton, G. E., **1**, 35n
Miu, Maria, **47**, 215
Miyauchi, B., **26**, 159; **33**, 189–90
Mizinova, Lydia, **48**, 117
Mnouchkine, Ariane, **39**, 100; **48**, 15; **50**, 33, 37; **51**, 193; **52**, 162–3, 285–6; **55**, 314
Moberly, Charles, **55**, 107n, 110n
Mocca, Andrea, **48**, 236
Mochalov, M., **2**, 126
Mochalov, P. S., **5**, 118
Mochalov, Rudolf, **9**, 118; **16**, 14
Modenessi, Alfredo Michel, **54**, 152n, 154n, 155n, 156n, 157n; **56**, 347
Modjeska, Helena, **32**, 24; **56**, 134
Modzalevsky, B. L. *and* L. B., **5**, 104
Moens, W. J. C., **53**, 202n
Moffatt, John, **39**, 189
Moffet, Thomas, **43**, 269; **56**, 64n
Moffett, Robin, **18**, 171; **29**, 3
Moffitt, John F., **51**, 176n
Mogann, Maurice, **60**, 194
Mohr, Bruce, **52**, 192n
Mohun, Michael, **58**, 242
Moi, Toril, **46**, 79
Moisan, Thomas, **44**, 41n; **46**, 208; **49**, 50n, 54, 66n, 96n; **50**, 245; **57**, 339; **60**, 92n29
Moiseiwitsch, Tanya, **3**, 120; **6**, 129–31; **7**, 109, 123; **8**, 128, 129, 132; **10**, 85, 116; **11**, 118; **12**, 123; **13**, 129; **14**, 117; **16**, 26, 152; **31**, 145
Moissi, Alexander, **3**, 113; **20**, 121; **49**, 226
Molé, François René, **9**, 91; **60**, 219, 221–2
Molière, Jean-Baptiste Poquelin, **1**, 66; **3**, 103; **4**, 4, 120; **5**, 101, 102, 131; **7**, 110, 111; **10**, 76n; **12**, 1, 2,; **14**, 119, 154; **16**, 14; **20**, 127; **21**, 35, 141; **22**, 1, 2, 8, 15, 16, 17–26, 35; **24**, 38, 149; **26**, 90, 94; **29**, 123; **30**, 117–18; **34**, 2; **35**, 159; **36**, 65; **41**, 204; **47**, 252; **53**, 129; **56**, 260
Amphitryon, **10**, 136
Tartuffe, production in contemporary dress, **8**, 79
Molin, Jean, **11**, 122
Molin, Nils, **8**, 121; **9**, 116, 132; **10**, 121; **12**, 116; **14**, 123; **48**, 4n
Molina, Alfred, **40**, 170–1
Molinet, Jean, **15**, 93
Molineux, Emeric, **32**, 86n
Möller, Niels, **3**, 109, 111
Molloy, Dearbhla, **42**, 130, 131, 153
Molloy, J. Fitzgerald, **57**, 88
Molloy, Kevin, **49**, 279
Moloney, Conor, **59**, 341
Molyneux, Edward, **53**, 310
Molyneux, Emery, **17**, 28 and n.
Momigliano, A., **10**, 38n
Mommsen, Theodor, **5**, 25; **10**, 33, 37; **33**, 99n; **59**, 262n20
Mommsen, Tycho, **59**, 6
Momose, Izumi, **19**, 133
Momoyama, Harue, **45**, 155
Mompesson, Sir Giles, **2**, 26
Mömplegard, Frederick, Count of, **49**, 327–8
Monaghan, J., **6**, 15n
Monardes, Nicholas, **17**, 160
Monastyrsky, P., **16**, 138
Monck, N. J., **8**, 123

Monck, W. Nugent, **1**, 108; **2**, 4, 18; **8**, 123, 125; **14**, 151–2; **47**, 81–9; **52**, 161, 291
'The Maddermarket Theatre and the Playing of Shakespeare', **12**, 71–5
Moncrieff, William, **47**, 63, 69
Mond, Frieda Loewenthal, **52**, 30
Mondadori, Arnoldo, **44**, 256; **46**, 257n
Monette, Richard, **35** 59
Money, John, **8**, 142
'Othello's "It is the cause . . .": an analysis', **6**, 94–105
Monitto, G. V., **37**, 218
Monk, S. H., **20**, 159–60
Monks, Chris, **42**, 154; **43**, 216; **45**, 155; **52**, 263; **54**, 289
Monmouth, Duke of, **43**, 95–7
Monmouth, Geoffrey of, **26**, 35, 36n, 41, 42, 43; **29**, 171
Monnet, Gabriel, **11**, 120; **13**, 160; **16**, 133
Monod, Paul, **51**, 48n, 51n, 54, 55n
Monro, C., **29**, 97n
Monroe, Marilyn, **40**, 56
Monroe, R. D., **16**, 171
Monsarrat, Gilles D., **15**, 175; **38**, 233; **52**, 323; **57**, 300
Monson, Sir William, **17**, 21n
Monsters of the Deep: Social Dissolution in Shakespeare's Tragedies, **46**, 216
Monstrelet, Enguerrand de, **60**, 106
Mont, Pol de, **5**, 107
Montacute, **12**, 11
Montag, Andrea, **43**, 213; **56**, 292
Montagu House, *see under* London
Montagu, Bishop, **56**, 217
Montagu, Duke of, **51**, 55, 62
Montagu, Elizabeth, **51**, 5, 6n; **54**, 56; **57**, 55; **58**, 72–82
Montagu, Jennifer, **51**, 111n
Montagu, Mrs, **25**, 185
Montague Elizabeth, **53**, 92–4
Montague, Helene, **58**, 262
Montague, Lord, **53**, 326
Montague, Michel, **1**, 38, 68
Montague, Sir Edward, **3**, 34
Montague, Walter, **31**, 186
Shepherd's Paradise, **1**, 65; **11**, 109–10, 116n
Montague-Douglas-Scott, Walter, 8th Duke of Buccleuch, **13**, 104n
Montaigne, Michel Eyquem de, **3**, 6, 19, 54, 55; **4**, 7, 9, 14; **7**, 105, 131, 140; **10**, 31, 33, 34, 136; **14**, 60, 103, 148; **16**, 70; **17**, 42, 141, 174; **18**, 41, 112; **20**, 17, 154, 166; **22**, 48; **23**, 45, 161; **25**, 125; **26**, 49; **27**, 44–5, 50, 52n, 56, 173; **28**, 37–50, 98, 167; **29**, 5, 79, 80, 81, 85, 88, 89, 90, 164; **30**, 119, 193; **32**, 186, 231, 235; **33**, 19, 22, 25; **34**, 23; **36**, 176; **37**, 176, 177; **38**, 167, 173, 233, 234; **39**, 159; **40**, 195; **43**, 237–8, 249; **44**, 219, 232; **45**, 167; **46**, 58, 59, 65, 145, 147, 158, 223; **47**, 259; **48**, 31, 151–4, 248; **49**, 63, 211; **50**, 43, 127, 190, 196n, 239, 247; **51**, 178–9, 310; **53**, 14, 22n, 86, 87n, 320; **55**, 220, 232, 253, 368, 381; **56**, 44, 92, 336; **57**, 218; **59**, 257, 361
see also Florio, John
Montale, Eugenio, **1**, 116; **3**, 117; **4**, 128; **8**, 120; **9**, 114
Montalván, Juan Pérez de, **20**, 102, 105n
Monteagle, Lord, **1**, 45; **28**, 6
Montégut, Emile, **2**, 116; **57**, 115
Montemayor, Jorge de, **7**, 98; **14**, 153; **20**, 95
Diana, **3**, 54
Montemore, Sally, **47**, 213
Montesquieu, Charles Louis de Secondat, baron de, **33**, 22
Monteverdi, Giuseppe, **56**, 18
Monteyne, Lode, **5**, 110n
Montfleury, **16**, 53
Montgomerie, William, **11**, 139, 143n; **15**, 112
Montgomery, Earl of (Philip Herbert), **21**, 141; **60**, 54
Montgomery, Elizabeth, **50**, 263
Montgomery, Flora, **60**, 292, 293
Montgomery, Louise, **48**, 235
Montgomery, Mrs, **23**, 44
Montgomery, Robert, **38**, 180, 195
Montgomery, Robert L., **23**, 146, 157
Montgomery, Roy F., **9**, 144
Montgomery, Walter, **35**, 37
Montgomery, William, **40**, 156n, 226n; **41**, 14n, 228n, 230, 244; **42**, 25n, 93n, 202n; **43**, 43n, 264n; **44**, 69n; **45**, 37n, 82n; **49**, 28n, 163n, 165n, 311n; **50**, 280n; **52**, 166n; **55**, 194n, 257n, 280n, 390; **59**, 69n1, 376–7, 378, 383
Montmorency, J. E. G., **15**, 16
Montrose, Louis Adrian, **31**, 165; **36**, 167n; **37**, 19n; **38**, 49n, 54n; **40**, 123n, 212–13; **41**, 196; **42**, 1n, 6, 191; **44**, 239; **46**, 16n, 20n, 111n, 212; **47**, 30n; **48**, 89n; **49**, 197n; **50**, 237–8; **51**, 182–3; **52**, 61n, 275; **54**, 59–60; **56**, 1, 67, 68, 74n, 75, 76; **57**, 339; **58**, 172
Monu, Nicholas, **52**, 217–18; **57**, 295
Monu, Nick, **49**, 276
Moodie, Tanya, **59**, 343
Moody, A. D., **37**, 10
Moody, Jane, **59**, 374
Moody, John, **9**, 121; **10**, 123; **12**, 120; **13**, 134, 135; **51**, 92
Moody, Richard, **35**, 9
Moon, Frank, **55**, 333
Moon, Joan, **43**, 208
Mooney, Michael E., **41**, 121n; **45**, 190n
Mooney, Paul, **42**, 153
Mooney, Thomas, **48**, 233
Moor in English Renaissance Drama, The, **46**, 209
Moore Smith, G. C., **27**, 112, 118
Moore, A. P., **32**, 136n, 137n
Moore, Don D., **36**, 174n
Moore, Donald, **7**, 113
Moore, Dudley, **45**, 172
Moore, Edward M., **31**, 188
Moore, Edward, N., **26**, 175
Moore, Geoff, **41**, 189; **45**, 151
Moore, George, **49**, 10; **58**, 140
Moore, Gerald, **39**, 169, 170n, 172
Moore, Guy, **52**, 222
Moore, Harry Thornton, **59**, 67–8
Moore, Helen, **58**, 170
Moore, Henry, **7**, 127; **42**, 145
Moore, Ian Karl, **52**, 257; **54**, 284
Moore, J. K., **55**, 260–1, 263n
Moore, J. R., **5**, 134, 140; **7**, 135; **8**, 5; **15**, 5; **22**, 175n
'The Character of Iago' reviewed, **1**, 120
Moore, Jeanie Grant, **46**, 208
Moore, John C., **59**, 262–3n22
Moore, John Robert, **35**, 113n; **55**, 247n

Moore, Josephe, **58**, 224
Moore, K. V., **14**, 128; **15**, 146
Moore, Karen, **50**, 226
Moore, Lesley, **43**, 211
Moore, Marianne, **60**, 143–4, 147
Moore, Mavor, **44**, 100n
Moore, Meriel, **1**, 91
Moore, Michael, **51**, 184n
Moore, Nicholas, **53**, 286
Moore, Rachel O., **56**, 10n
Moore, Richard, **47**, 185
Moore, Samuel, **35**, 66n
Moore, Stephen, **36**, 151
Moore, Susan, **58**, 84
Moore, Thomas, **11**, 71
Moore, Tom, **54**, 284
Moore, Wanda, **47**, 101
Moore, William H., **18**, 178; **23**, 167
Moore, Wyke, **41**, 33
Moorey, Frank, **44**, 195
Moorhouse, Jocelyn, **52**, 257
Moorman, F. W., **6**, 4, 39; **20**, 103n
Moorthy, P. R., **27**, 159
Morahan, Hattie, **55**, 297, 309
Moral Universe of Shakespeare's Problem Plays, The, **46**, 220
Morality plays, **5**, 107, 141; **6**, 160; **30**, 36–9, 104, 192
Moran, Chris, **59**, 346
Moran, Janet, **58**, **265**, 267
Morand, P., **9**, 67
Morant, Philip, **1**, 99, 102
Morante, Luis, **54**, 154
Moravec, D., **18**, 134
Moravek, Vladimir, **56**, 292
Moray, Thomas, **21**, 48
Mordaunt, Jane, **20**, 111
Morden, Robert, **30**, 164n
Mordvinor, N., **2**, 106n; **13**, 133; **16**, 15
More Light, **42**, 162; **54**, 73
More, Ann, **23**, 167
More, Anne, **1**, 71
More, Hannah, **51**, 4
More, Henry, **54**, 65n
More, Sir Thomas, **1**, 68; **4**, 27; **7**, 144; **9**, 25, 71–2, 81; **17**, 42, 53, 55, 109, 223; **20**, 22; **23**, 144; **28**, 27, 177, 178; **29**, 86, 121, 159; **30**, 203–4; **32**, 173, 228; **33**, 204; **38**, 2; **39**, 226; **42**, 21; **43**, 50, 54, 238; **44**, 1, 20, 62; **47**, 254; **49**, 79; **50**, 111, 113n, 116, 117; **51**, 294; **52**, 171, 182; **53**, 239; **54**, 3, 9, 43–4, 96; **55**, 83n; **56**, 120, 309
  History of King Richard the thirde, **6**, 34n
More, Sir Thomas, see *Booke of Sir Thomas More*
More, Sir Thomas, **17**, 43, 45–6, 211
More, Sir William, **41**, 217
Morecambe, Eric (John Eric Bartholomew), **60**, 228
Morell, André, **11**, 131
Morell, Janice, **47**, 213
Morellet, André, **9**, 91
Morelli, Cesare, **18**, 95; **21**, 48
Moreschi, Jojo, **46**, 196, 199
Moretti, Franco, **55**, 5; **56**, 140, 141n; **57**, 31
Morgan, Appleton, **7**, 3; **18**, 112; **59**, 157n3
Morgan, Charles, **36**, 81
Morgan, Edwin, **56**, 158
Morgan, Emily, **44**, 199
Morgan, F. C., **33**, 203
Morgan, Francine, **45**, 151
Morgan, Gareth, **16**, 145
Morgan, John, **47**, 174n
Morgan, MacNamara, **51**, 19n
Morgan, Maurice, **57**, 26, 89, 317
Morgan, Morris Hickey, **30**, 159; **35**, 137n; **47**, 23n
Morgan, Norman Louis, **31**, 180
Morgan, Pam, **49**, 279
Morgan, Paul, **18**, 179; **20**, 103n; **30**, 202; **50**, 278
  '"Our Will Shakespeare" and Lope de Vega: An Unrecorded Contemporary Document', **16**, 118–20
Morgan, Priscilla, **13**, 141
Morgan, Shane, **48**, 230
Morgan, Susan, **59**, 85
Morgan, W. W., **26**, 154
Morgan, William, **53**, 200, 205, 207
Morgann, A. E., **38**, 88
Morgann, Maurice, **2**, 19; **4**, 3, 10, 146; **6**, 12, 13; **7**, 133; **8**, 140; **9**, 93, 100n; **15**, 33; **24**, 178; **26**, 167–8; **30**, 3, 35; **34**, 3, 4, 5, 12, 18–19, 169; **35**, 165–6; **37**, 143–5, 147, 150; **41**, 120; **47**, 257; **49**, 206–7; **51**, 1, 5; **52**, 319; **60**, 116, 185
Morgenstern, Joe, **52**, 94n
Mori, Masayuki, **15**, 137
Moriarty, Paul, **32**, 203; **47**, 191
Moricone, Massimo, **46**, 199; **52**, 263
Moringo, M. A., **17**, 40n
Morison, Mary, **43**, 112n
Morison, Patricia, **4**, 123
Morison, Richard, **44**, 20
Morison, Samuel Eliot, **52**, 188n
Morison, Stanley, **42**, 82; **52**, 143
Moriyama, Mirai, **60**, 140
Mork, Erik, **11**, 121
Mörk, Lennart, **13**, 131; **14**, 123; **16**, 137
Morle, Phil, **46**, 193; **48**, 228; **49**, 270
Morley, Christopher, **24**, 122; **26**, 140, 142; **27**, 149; **32**, 204, 206; **33**, 173, 176; **41**, 191; **44**, 166, 192; **47**, 117; **52**, 288
Morley, Henry, **2**, 2; **4**, 22; **8**, 72; **16**, 104; **35**, 6; **38**, 187–200 *passim*; **40**, 210; **48**, 10n, 11; **52**, 180n; **55**, 107, 111n; **58**, 115
Morley, Lord, **54**, 88
Morley, Royston, **10**, 123, 125; **14**, 116
Morley, Sheridan, **45**, 10, 59n; **50**, 34
Morley, Steve, **41**, 185
Morley, Thomas, **1**, 68–9; **5**, 115; **15**, 6, 9, 10n; **17**, 214; **33**, 78n; **40**, 220
  First Book of Ayres, **1**, 68
  First Booke of Consort Lessons, **3**, 56
  Madrigales, **1**, 69
  A Plaine and Easie Introduction to Practicall Musicke, **4**, 149, 162; **5**, 140
  Triumphes of Oriana, **1**, 69
Mörner, Stellan, **1**, 115
Morns, Tom, **54**, 251, 253
Morocco, **11**, 89–97
Morosini, Adèle Rossetti, **59**, 103

Morozov, Mikhail M., **1**, 116, 122; **2**, 126, 127; **3**, 106, 136; **4**, 25n, 122n; **5**, 88; **9**, 117, 118; **16**, 46, 139; **18**, 52; **21**, 129; **34**, 6
'Individualization of Shakespeare's Characters through Imagery', **2**, 83–106
Shakespeare's Language and Style, **2**, 83
Morrell, Geoff, **59**, 205
Morricone, Ennio, **46**, 193
Morris (secretary to Thomas Cranmer), **60**, 121
Morris, B. R., **13**, 156; **14**, 141
Morris, Brian, **24**, 164; **25**, 9, 23n, 24n; **33**, 92n; **34**, 187; **35**, 119n; **36**, 184–6; **37**, 2, 23, 25, 29, 33n, 37n, 38n, 39n, 40n, 184, 204; **38**, 239; **50**, 45n; **55**, 191, 193; **60**, 73n5, 84n1, 84n2, 96, 99n39
Morris, C., **29**, 90
Morris, Cherry, **46**, 162; **49**, 260; **51**, 235
Morris, Christopher, **17**, 113n, 114; **38**, 2
Morris, Griffith, **45**, 109
Morris, Harry, **13**, 156; **22**, 162; **25**, 182; **30**, 183; **38**, 231; **40**, 200; **56**, 81n
Morris, Helen, **23**, 154; **24**, 156
Morris, I., **36**, 142n
Morris, Irene, **28**, 172; **33**, 166, 168; **36**, 142
Morris, Ivor, **12**, 137; **26**, 23, 24; **27**, 155; **33**, 89n
'The Tragic Vision of Fulke Greville', **14**, 66–75
Morris, Jan, **58**, 312
Morris, John, **22**, 169
Morris, Johnny, **23**, 47
Morris, Jonathan, **46**, 240n
Morris, Matthias, **58**, 240
Morris, Max, **9**, 95, 100n
Morris, Mowbray, **35**, 17; **56**, 128n
Morris, P. E., **42**, 89n, 93n
Morris, Peter (German engineer), **17**, 5, 162
Morris, R., **42**, 56n; **46**, 16n
Morris, Siwan, **59**, 345
Morris, Terry P., **46**, 212
Morris, Thomas, **25**, 146; **45**, 109
Morris, Tom, **53**, 285; **55**, 326
Morris, William, **10**, 75; **45**, 123; **53**, 238–9
Morris, William C., **20**, 154
Morrisette, Billy, **57**, 186; **58**, 194
Morrison, Blake, **56**, 238; **57**, 41, 42
Morrison, Campbell, **51**, 237
Morrison, Clive, **42**, 148
Morrison, Conall, **48**, 231; **55**, 332
Morrison, John, **52**, 259
Morrison, Michael A., **52**, 292; **53**, 327
Morrison, Peter, **38**, 230
Morrissey, David, **42**, 138–9; **43**, 207
Morsbach, L., **10**, 9
Morsberger, Robert E., **29**, 174
Morse, Hayward, **42**, 153; **49**, 269
Morse, Ruth, **54**, 182n; **55**, 343; **56**, 300–30; **58**, 308–33
Morse, William R., **45**, 170
Morstin, L., **1**, 113
Morte d' Arthur, **11**, 75
Mortensen, Peter, **20**, 146; **29**, 170
Mortimer, Anthony, **54**, 319
Mortimer, John, **39**, 229; **47**, 251
Mortimer, Maya, **53**, 13n
Mortimer, Raymond, **58**, 123
Mortimer, Terry, **42**, 161; **45**, 146, 156; **46**, 201
Mortimer, Vicky, **45**, 157
Morton, A. L., **19**, 149; **20**, 155; **31**, 61n, 106n
Morton, Alexander, **47**, 213
Morton, Andrew, **38**, 253; **40**, 227n
Morton, Anna, **54**, 289
Morton, John, of Ashby Folville Manor, Leicestershire, **12**, 99
Morton, Luce, **43**, 110
Morton, Mary, **12**, 99
Morton, Dr Nicholas, **48**, 76
Morton, Thomas, Bishop, **35**, 178; **47**, 61, 69; **59**, 374
Moryson, Fynes, **17**, 11, 33, 43; **33**, 156; **43**, 227; **48**, 34, 35n; **54**, 191–2, 193, 195n, 196
Moseley, C. W. R. D., **24**, 163n
Moseley, Humphrey, **11**, 105; **43**, 81; **44**, 126; **45**, 195; **48**, 269; **51**, 95; **52**, 308; **55**, 265, 266, 268n; **59**, 23–6, 27; **60**, 368
Moseley, Sir Nicholas, **1**, 28, 30; **11**, 92, 94
Mosely, Joseph, **56**, 185, 187, 189, 201
Mosenthal, S. H., **18**, 81
Moser, Thomas C., **45**, 12n
Moshinsky, Elijah, **39**, 95, 99, 100, 103, 108–1; **41**, 227–8; **44**, 198, 213; **52**, 244–5; **53**, 281; **56**, 295; **60**, 325
Moss, Arnold, **10**, 122; **39**, 81n
Moss, Peter, **34**, 157; **36**, 59
Moss, Rebecca, **56**, 217n
Mosse, George L., **46**, 137, 138n
Mosse, Miles, **39**, 226; **47**, 227; **52**, 103
Mossman, Judith, **48**, 250; **56**, 223n
Mossman-Ellis, Jo, **42**, 158
Mosteller, Frederick, **40**, 225n
Moston, Doug, **53**, 341
Mote, Humphrey, **17**, 33
Mother Bombie, **50**, 58n
Motives of Woe: Shakespeare and 'Female Complaint', **46**, 225, 226, 249n
Motley, **15**, 147
Motley, John Lothrop, **38**, 58n
Motohashi, Tetsuya (Ted), **48**, 253; **50**, 248; **54**, 305
Motschach, Hermann, **37**, 160
Mott, L. F., **3**, 23
Motteaux, Peter, **51**, 97n
Motten, J. P. Vander, **57**, 234; **60**, 249n53
Motteram, John, **58**, 223
Mottet, Alain, **57**, 119
Motteux, Peter, **49**, 77n
Mottley, John, **55**, 89
Mottley, Peter, **50**, 228; **53**, 276; **60**, 322
Mottram, Caitlin, **59**, 307
Moudouès, Mlle R. M., **11**, 120; **12**, 112; **13**, 128; **14**, 119; **15**, 133
Mouffet, Thomas, **42**, 53, 61n
Of the Silkworms, and their Flies, **12**, 141
Moulay Ahmed el-Mansour, *see under* Muley Hamet
Moule, H. F., **54**, 6
Moulton, Ian Frederick, **51**, 281; **56**, 34n
Moulton, Richard G., **4**, 1, 2, 16; **6**, 26, 33n; **12**, 123, 129n; **19**, 10; **21**, 28n; **37**, 13, 20; **53**, 94; **59**, 140
Mounet, Paul, **3**, 104
Mounet-Sully, Jean, **3**, 103, 104; **9**, 57, 62, 63, 64, 65, 66, 68n; **20**, 164

Mount, Peggy, **38**, 204
Mounteagle, Sir Edward, **12**, 98–9
Mountford, Walter, *The Launching of the Mary* (MS.), **3**, 51, 52
Mountjoy family, **3**, 3, 11; **28**, 38; **40**, 216
see also Belott-Mountjoy suit
Mountjoy, Charles, Eighth Baron, *see under* Blount, Charles
Mountjoy, Christopher, **11**, 100; **25**, 138; **57**, 234
Mountjoy, Mary, **3**, 11, 13
Mourek, V., **9**, 106
Mourt, G., **1**, 69
Mousley, Andrew, **49**, 287; **55**, 350–1
Moussorgsky, M. P., **5**, 100
Mowat, Barbara Adams, **23**, 156; **25**, 184; **31**, 166; **36**, 167; **42**, 197; **43**, 1n, 265n, 266; **44**, 218; **46**, 3; **48**, 247; **50**, 3, 143, 188n, 271–3, 276n, 289; **51**, 290; **52**, 78n; **53**, 331n, 332–3, 344; **55**, 259n, 343; **56**, 27n; **57**, 19, 315; **58**, 322; **59**, 18, 20, 30n46, 31n53, 37n87, 51, 89n34, 124n1
Mowat, John, **41**, 191; **43**, 213; **44**, 203
Mowat, Nick, **49**, 271; **54**, 290
Mowbray, Thomas, **38**, 97n
Mowl, Timothy, **51**, 5n
Moxon, Joseph, **27**, 180, 190; **33**, 140n, 150; **37**, 211; **54**, 343; **55**, 266; **56**, 170; **59**, 13
Mechanick Exercises, **4**, 163; **17**, 211; **18**, 32, 33n; **20**, 177
Moyer, Stephen, **49**, 277
Mozart, Wolfgang Amadeus, **17**, 218; **18**, 75–9, 81, 97; **42**, 113; **44**, 215; **49**, 249, 250
Don Giovanni, **9**, 110n; **32**, 79–84; **34**, 173; **36**, 82; **53**, 172; **56**, 151n, 249
Mozeen, Mrs (Miss Edwards), **51**, 84, 86
Mozley, J. H., **41**, 40
Mráz, A., **4**, 115n
Mrs Piozzi's Tall Young Beau, **46**, 237
Msomi, Welcome, **52**, 154, 157–61, 163–4, 258; **54**, 340; **56**, 292; **57**, 159–67; **58**, 349
Mtwa, Percy, **55**, 274, 275
Muñoz, Luis, **60**, 240
Mucciolo, John M., **54**, 72n, 322, 323; **55**, 183n; **56**, 171n
Mucedorus, **1**, 43; **3**, 48; **4**, 92; **11**, 34, 48; **14**, 20
Mucsi, Zoltàn, **50**, 38
Mudford, Peter G., **25**, 181
Mueller, Dennis M., **25**, 145
Mueller, Janel M., **23**, 167; **51**, 296
Mueller, Martin, **55**, 12n, 19, 21, 25–7
Mueller, Michael, **42**, 150; **52**, 261
Muellner, Leonard, **56**, 41n
Muellner, Mireille, **56**, 41n
Mueschke, Miriam, **22**, 154
Mueschke, Paul, **22**, 154
Mugur, Vlad, **20**, 128
Mühe, Ullrich, **48**, 184
Mühlfeld, W., **10**, 4
Muir, Christopher, **14**, 116
Muir, Edwin, **26**, 76; **29**, 86; **33**, 5; **48**, 6n
The Politics of 'King Lear' reviewed, **3**, 142
Muir, Kenneth, **1**, 14, 121, 126; **3**, 137; **4**, 142n, 147; **5**, 46n, 92n, 134, 146–7; **6**, 148; **7**, 5, 8, 107, 128, 140; **8**, 13n, 117n, 147; **9**, 12, 132, 134, 139, 141, 142, 144; **10**, 6, 25n, 50, 136, 146n; **11**, 59n, 143, 148; **12**, 141–2, 149; **13**, 39n, 40n, 132, 157–8, 162; **14**, 98, 138–9, 153; **15**, 20, 23–4, 26–30, 140, 165, 174, 179–80, 182; **16**, 45–6, 50, 165–6; **18**, 5, 44; **19**, 2, 3, 11, 13, 23n, 24n, 25, 54n, 76, 93n, 122, 138, 139, 140–1, 149; **20**, 82n, 104n, 114, 120n, 131n, 144, 158, 175, 178; **21**, 130, 137, 141, 146; **22**, 62, 152, 155, 163, 180; **23**, 54n, 73n, 156; **24**, 71n, 76n, 106n, 157; **25**, 4, 7, 12n, 39n, 126n, 142n, 185, 196n; **26**, 5, 71, 72, 82, 166, 172; **27**, 18n, 24n, 34, 59n, 133, 145, 146, 154, 156, 170; **28**, 4n, 39, 48, 74, 123n; **29**, 4, 6, 9, 31, 90, 106n, 165; **30**, 15n, 99n; **31**, 10n, 177, 184; **32**, 2, 80n, 228–9, 234, 245; **33**, 1, 3, 7, 8, 1311, 16n, 17n, 19, 29n, 35n, 44n, 75, 79n, 108n, 130n, 182, 194, 204, 207; **34**, 62n, 99n, 161–2, 168, 191; **36**, 55n, 112n, 168; **37**, 2, 4, 116n, 120, 141n, 146n, 205–7, 211–13; **38**, 5, 18, 41n, 49n, 56n, 156, 157n, 158n, 185n, 25m, 254; **39**, 67n, 159, 160, 229n; **40**, 74n, 137n, 141n, 209, 216; **41**, 64n, 67n, 69n, 75, 77n, 120, 143n, 153, 202, 204; **42**, 39, 53, 58, 59, 181, 195n; **43**, 82–3, 86n, 115n, 133; **44**, 46n, 75, 136n; **45**, 99, 100; **46**, 62n, 64n; **47**, 163n, 166n, 167n, 255, 262; **48**, 124n, 279; **49**, 21n, 29n, 47n, 55, 131, 142n; **50**, 3, 235; **51**, 144–5, 175n, 177n, 179n, 315, 328; **52**, 273, 317; **53**, 78n, 338; **54**, 89n; **55**, 12, 13, 14n, 17, 18, 27, 54n, 392; **56**, 64n; **57**, 22, 36, 335; **59**, 41, 42, 44, 47; **60**, 163, 169n5.1
New Arden edition of *King Lear* reviewed, **7**, 149–50
New Arden edition of *Macbeth* reviewed, **5**, 148
edition of *The Painful Adventures of Pericles Prince of Tyre by George Wilkins* reviewed, **8**, 158
'Fifty Years of Shakespearian Criticism: 1900–1950', **4**, 1–25
'Image and Symbol in *Macbeth*', **19**, 45–54
'Madness in *King Lear*', **13**, 30–40
'A Reconsideration of *Edward III*', **6**, 39–48
Shakespeare as Collaborator reviewed, **15**, 169
Shakespeare's Sources reviewed, **11**, 143; **12**, 65, 141; **13**, 157
'Shakespeare's Hand in *The Two Noble Kinsmen*', **11**, 50–9
'Shakespeare's Imagery—Then and Now', **18**, 46–57
'Shakespeare's Poets', **23**, 91–100
'Shakespeare the Professional', **24**, 37–46
'*Timon of Athens* and the Cash-Nexus' reviewed, **1**, 123
'*Troilus and Cressida*', **8**, 28–39
The Voyage to Illyria, **3**, 9
Muir, Willa, **48**, 5, 6n
Muirhead, Jill, **47**, 218
Mukerji, E., **19**, 142
Mukherjee, Debabrata, **41**, 208n
Mukherji, A. D., **21**, 143; **22**, 157
Mulcaster, Richard, **7**, 19, 27; **17**, 56, 57, 60, 64, 129; **26**, 38n, 45n; **28**, 170; **32**, 169n; **39**, 214; **57**, 197, 198, 208
Muldowney, Dominic, **42**, 149; **43**, 212; **44**, 193; **45**, 148, 153; **48**, 230; **52**, 257; **55**, 355
Muldrew, Craig, **55**, 40
Muley Hamet, King of Barbary, **11**, 90–3, 95–6
Mulhall, Stephen, **55**, 71n; **57**, 105
Mulhern, Francis, **40**, 25n
Mulholland, P. A., **41**, 91n
Mulikita, F. M., **52**, 160
Mullaly, Robert, **31**, 187
Mullaney, Steven, **36**, 165–6, 174; **42**, 191–2; **44**, 47, 66, 148; **46**, 19; **47**, 248; **48**, 155, 241; **51**, 333; **52**, 199; **53**, 243; **54**, 127n; **57**, 28
Mullany, Peter, **24**, 165
Mullen, Aaron, **43**, 206
Mullenbrock, Heinz-Joachim, **29**, 184n; **60**, 369n8

Müller, Anja, **56**, 314, 315
Muller, Arthur E., **1**, 72
Müller, F. Max., **54**, 85
Müller, Gerda, **48**, 172
Müller, Heiner, **25**, 173; **42**, 150; **46**, 193, 200; **48**, 178, 182, 183–4; **52**, 284; **54**, 340; **55**, 166, 167
Muller, Herbert, **15**, 113
Müller, Johannes, **29**, 29n
Müller, Wolfgang G., **37**, 157n
Müller, Wenzel, **18**, 79
Müller-Bellinghausen, Anton, **10**, 147; **12**, 70n
Müller-Schwete, Gerhard, **23**, 115n; **37**, 156n, 199n
Mullett, Charles F., **17**, 25n; **50**, 19n
Mullin, Diane, **60**, 179n17
Mullin, Donald, **56**, 132n, 134n
Mullin, Michael, **28**, 171; **31**, 188; **32**, 223; **34**, 186; **35**, 10; **36**, 76; **47**, 6n; **50**, 263; **57**, 147
Mulliner, Thomas, **3**, 56
Mullini, Roberta, **39**, 235
Mullins, Ian, **15**, 144; **41**, 186; **42**, 150, 154
Mulmucius, Dunwalló, **11**, 44
Mulready, William, **13**, 76
Mulryne, J. Ronnie, **20**, 153; **26**, 9; **32**, 2, 11; **42**, 199; **44**, 126; **46**, 116n; **47**, 19n, 118n, 237n, 249; **51**, 205n, 283; **52**, 12n, 13n, 14n, 39n, 107n, 274; **53**, 324, 329; **54**, 194n; **55**, 247n, 347; **60**, 6n9, 1–19, 26n9, 29n19, 29n20, 30n25, 32n29, 34n32, 341–3, 352–3
Mulvey, Laura, **45**, 49; **49**, 208n
Mumford, Lewis, **24**, 87; **51**, 177
Mumford, Peter, **41**, 191; **42**, 156
Mums, Robert, **54**, 290
Munakata, Kuniyoshi, **46**, 257n
Munby, Jonathan, **59**, 299, 301–4; **60**, 321
Munch, Edvard, **44**, 215
Münch, W., **10**, 6
Munda, Constantia, **48**, 29n
Munday, Anthony, **2**, 52; **3**, 50; **12**, 51; **14**, 25–33; **16**, 168; **23**, 161, 171, 181; **26**, 35, 39, 43, 45, 47, 103, 183; **34**, 62n; **35**, 190, 191; **37**, 215; **38**, 97, 101, 106, 109, 110, 113; **41**, 197; **42**, 77, 79, 83; **43**, 262–3; **45**, 157, 202n; **46**, 226; **47**, 47, 167; **50**, 287; **54**, 35–6, 89–99; **57**, 15, 16, 17, 233; **58**, 13, 227; **59**, 5, 71, 72, 74, 77, 78, 78n15, 377
  Brief Chronicle of the Success of Times, **14**, 29
  The Death of Robert, Earl of Huntington (with Chettle, Henry), **14**, 25
  The Downfall of Robert, Earl of Huntington (with Chettle, Henry), **14**, 25, 29
  duration and influence of his work, **8**, 103–4
  The English Romayne Life, **14**, 26
  extemporizer, **8**, 103
  anti-Martinist activities, **8**, 101–2
  Fedele and Fortunio, **13**, 116; **14**, 25, 27–8
  handwriting, **8**, 100–1, 104n, 105n
  John a Kent and John a Cumber, **2**, 51; **6**, 60; **12**, 19, 50, 51; **14**, 25, 28, 29, 32, 33n; **15**, 170
    the dating of, **8**, 100–2
    its relationship to *De Faustus, Friar Bacon and Friar Bungay*, and *A Midsummer Night's Dream*, **8**, 102–3; **10**, 144
  Sir John Oldcastle (with Drayton, Michael, Hathaway, Richard, and Wilson, Robert), **14**, 25
  Palmerin d'Oliva, **1**, 69
  Sir Thomas More, **2**, 45, 47, 49, 51, 53; **8**, 104; **9**, 72–3, 143
  The Set at Tennis, **14**, 31
  Zelauto, **8**, 4
Munday, Sir John, **38**, 110
Munden, R. C., **54**, 170n
Mundorf, Paul, **14**, 119
Mundy, Francis, **6**, 54
Mundy, Peter, **32**, 196n
Munk, Kaj, **3**, 114–15; **36**, 66
Munkelt, Marga, **42**, 207–8; **46**, 255
Munro, Hector Hugh (Saki), **53**, 138–9, 150n
Munro, James, **51**, 264
Munro, John, **3**, 146–7; **10**, 21; **14**, 157; **20**, 97–100, 103, 104n; **26**, 44n; **34**, 11n, 85n; **38**, 176n; **49**, 41n; **57**, 69; **60**, 272n12
  The London Shakespeare reviewed, **13**, 162–3
Munrow, Julia, **41**, 188
Munsche, P. B., **51**, 49n
Munson, William F., **24**, 161
Münsterberg, Hugo, **39**, 1
Munster, Sebastian, **50**, 188n
Müntz, Ludwig, **53**, 15n
Munzer, Bettina, **46**, 201
Murad III, Sultan, **11**, 96; **17**, 214
Murad, Orlene, **36**, 142
Murakami, Takeshi, **50**, 248
Murcell, George, **41**, 188; **42**, 154; **43**, 209, 213
Murchie, Nicholas, **48**, 235
Murchison, Ruari, **42**, 153; **49**, 279; **50**, 229; **51**, 220, 263; **52**, 259; **53**, 282; **55**, 309–10, 333
Murder of Gonzago, The, **50**, 59, 61
Murdoch, Alex, **58**, 307
Murdoch, Dame Iris, **51**, 1; **56**, 302
Murdoch, James, **52**, 288
Murdoch, Rupert, **52**, 198
Murdock, D., **26**, 161
Murdock, George P., **15**, 123n
Muret, Marc Antoine, **10**, 4
Murgatroyd, Olga, **47**, 95
Muriello, Karen Morris, **34**, 186
Murphy, Andrew, **50**, 273, 275, 277; **51**, 274; **58**, 107, 355, 356; **59**, 2n4, 51n5, 124n1, 124, 125, 128, 134, 148n4, 149n6, 149n7, 151n20, 154n34, 360–1, 368
Murphy, Arthur, **20**, 169; **26**, 175; **40**, 204; **48**, 52; **57**, 84
Murphy, Brian, **18**, 153
Murphy, Conor, **51**, 226; **52**, 259
Murphy, G. N., **19**, 125; **20**, 164; **21**, 146–7
Murphy, Gerard, **35** 148; **36**, 153; **40**, 172, 176; **41**, 188, 190; **42**, 154, 160; **45**, 154; **52**, 249; **53**, 277; **55**, 310; **57**, 291, 292
Murphy, James J., **49**, 45n
Murphy, Joe, **50**, 199n
Murphy, John, **58**, 265
Murphy, John L., **23**, 168; **38**, 99n; **42**, 210n; **54**, 25n; **55**, 14n, 104n
Murphy, Julian, **43**, 216
Murphy, Shaney, **46**, 199
Murphy, Terence, **45**, 177–8
Murphy, Tom, **58**, 263
Murray, Barbara A., **56**, 314, 326, 340–1
Murray, Barbara E., **57**, 58

Murray, Braham, **42**, 154; **43**, 209, 216; **45**, 155; **56**, 280; **57**, 295; **59**, 330; **60**, 320
Murray, Brian, **16**, 145; **20**, 134
Murray, Christopher, **35**, 9; **41**, 225; **54**, 81n
Murray, Gilbert, **9**, 13; **10**, 149; **15**, 111, 115; **30**, 103–4, 106, 107; **56**, 206
Murray, H. J. R., **35**, 114n, 115n
Murray, Henry, **13**, 92
Murray, Isobel, **32**, 26n
Murray, Jacob, **59**, 327–8; **60**, 326
Murray, James, **7**, 1
Murray, Janet H., **52**, 93n
Murray, John, **2**, 44; **14**, 86
Murray, John J., **55**, 24n
Murray, John Tucker, **1**, 4, 9; **6**, 74; **17**, 168n; **44**, 149; **47**, 52; **52**, 75n; **60**, 1, 4, 9n21, 21
English Dramatic Companies, **11**, 105n; **12**, 21n
Murray, Joseph, **56**, 296
Murray, Kevin, **44**, 196
Murray, Leigh, **38**, 236
Murray, Lindley, **48**, 99n
Murray, Margaret, **19**, 56–7
Murray, Mein, **45**, 156
Murray, Neil, **44**, 196, 201; **52**, 265
Murray, Patrick, **23**, 137; **26**, 166–7
Murray, Paul, **32**, 6
Murray, Peter, **47**, 174n, 176n
Murray, Sean, **44**, 192; **45**, 152
Murray, W. A., **21**, 137
'Why was Duncan's Blood Golden?', **19**, 34–44
Murrey, Henry, **2**, 34
Murrie, E. B., **15**, 7
Murry, John Middleton, **1**, 121; **2**, 119; **3**, 106; **4**, 9, 13, 19, 20–1, 22, 24; **5**, 91n; **6**, 8, 11, 13; **8**, 3; **10**, 4, 7, 50; **11**, 59; **15**, 26, 79n; **18**, 53; **19**, 6, 50; **21**, 4, 9, 137; **22**, 10, 14n; **23**, 98n; **25**, 107, 111, 155, 158n; **26**, 103; **33**, 105, 106; **36**, 45; **39**, 143n; **41**, 103n, 224; **43**, 229; **44**, 217; **50**, 127; **53**, 97n
Murtagh, Ray, **43**, 208
Musa, Mark, **39**, 57n
Muschg, Walter, **18**, 124; **20**, 147
Muscovy Company, **17**, 27, 30, 32
Musgrave, Sir Richard, **60**, 278n38
Musgrave, Sir William, **4**, 88
Musgrove, S., **10**, 9; **11**, 144; **12**, 138 and n.; **14**, 146; **18**, 163; **23**, 172; **24**, 172; **25**, 179; **32**, 243; **43**, 243
Musiol, M., **19**, 140, 145
Musk, John, **27**, 167n
Mussato, Albertino, **42**, 21
Mussolini, Benito, **37**, 172; **42**, 157
Mustaph, Nirmal, **22**, 157
Musumeci, Irene, **56**, 8n
Mutabilitie, **52**, 266
Mutran, Khali, **36**, 10
Mutschmann, Heinrich, **14**, 100n; **54**, 41n, 116n
Mutu, Tam, **57**, 262
Mwangi, Franky, **56**, 265–6
My Fair Lady, **55**, 309
My Own Private Idaho, **52**, 290; **50**, 264
My Sweet Rose, **49**, 270
Myddleton, Sir Hugh, **17**, 5
Mydell, Joseph, **54**, 268
Myer, Valerie Grosvenor, **51**, 30n
Myers, Bruce, **55**, 301; **56**, 97
Myers, Frederic W. H., **54**, 86
Myers, James Phares, **23**, 170n
Myers, Jeffrey R., **40**, 234
Myers, Keith, **42**, 153; **44**, 191
Myers, Scott, **54**, 250
Myerscough, Damian, **49**, 274
Myerscough-Jones, David, **39**, 109n; **50**, 228
Myerson, Dr George, **55**, 143n
Myerson, Joel, **53**, 130, 131n, 166n
Myhill, Nova, **54**, 321
Mynhardt, Siegfried, **9**, 115
Mynors, R. A. B., **41**, 156n; **53**, 20, 21
Mynshul, Geoffrey, **17**, 95–6, 99
Myrat, Demetrios, **10**, 119; **11**, 121
Myres, Sir John, **20**, 33, 40n
Myrick, Kenneth O., **19**, 119, 125; **29**, 88; **41**, 148–9
Myriel, Thomas, **13**, 107
Mystery plays, (*see also* Miracle plays), **30**, 192

Nabbes, Thomas, **17**, 199; **58**, 235
Nabeshima, Norihiro, **19**, 125
Nabokov, Vladimir, **26**, 89
Nádasdy, K., **14**, 120
Naef, Irene, **30**, 185
Naef, W., **32**, 224
Nagarajan, S., **8**, 140; **11**, 140; **14**, 147, 154; **18**, 162, 163, **19**, 10; **28**, 51n; **32**, 130; **36**, 172; **41**, 208; **42**, 181; **59**, 41
Nagler, A. M., **9**, 146; **10**, 147; **21**, 125n; **41**, 3, 99; **42**, 100n, 104n; **47**, 78n; **52**, 4
Shakespeare's Stage reviewed, **13**, 160
Naiambana, Patrice, **51**, 228
Naik, M. K., **22**, 167
Nair, Kalamandalam Padmanabham, **45**, 148
Nair, Kalamandalam, Unnikrishnan, **45**, 148
Nair, Keezhapadam Kumaran, **45**, 148
Naish, Jenny, **34**, 180
Naito, Kenji, **41**, 103n
Nakagoshi, Tsukasa, **51**, 264; **53**, 275; **57**, 270; **60**, 304
Nakamura, Masanao, **48**, 99n
Nakamura, Shinobu, **57**, 289
Nakamura, Shunichi, **14**, 121
Nakanori, Koshi, **35**, 160n
Nakogoshi, Tsukasa, **50**, 231
Namath, Joe, **57**, 190
Namboodiri, Nelliyode Vasudevan, **45**, 148
Nameri, Dorothy E., **30**, 194; **33**, 197; **55**, 13, 14n
Nancy, Jean-Luc, **58**, 169, 176, 181, 183
Nandy, Dipak, **20**, 145; **30**, 42n
Nangle, Benjamin, **2**, 153
Nannini, Remigo, **39**, 225
Nannus Mirabellius, **36**, 92n
Napier, John, **17**, 71; **28**, 142; **30**, 172, 176; **31**, 141; **33**, 169, 170; **47**, 5, 117, 124
Napoleon I, **3**, 99, 100; **8**, 109; **18**, 78; **28**, 22
Napoleon III, **10**, 33, 37
Naps, John, **44**, 210
Napton, John, **60**, 46
Narasimhaiah, C. D., **19**, 128

Nardi, **21**, 96n
Naremore, James, **28**, 171n; **39**, 43, 69n
Nares, Robert, **19**, 76; **32**, 85
Narita, Tatsuo, **19**, 132n
Narti, Ana Maria, **20**, 131n
Nascimento, Susan Z., **44**, 115n, 124n
Nash, Anthony, **48**, 267
Nash, Damien, **35**, 145
Nash, Eliza (later Bernard, Eliza), **14**, 114
Nash, John, Thomas and Elizabeth, *see* Hall, Dr John, and family
Nash, John, **14**, 110
Nash, Paul, **55**, 128–9, 133–8
Nash, Pip, **41**, 190; **42**, 155; **43**, 208, 214; **46**, 201
Nash, Thomas, **58**, 67, 183
Nash, Walter, **12**, 132; **55**, 354–5
Nashe, Thomas, of Stratford Manor Court, **12**, 97
Nashe, Thomas, **1**, 128; **3**, 25, 45; **4**, 59–60, 62, 64–5; **5**, 133; **6**, 79; **7**, 4, 7, 83, 84, 87, 140, 147, 148; **8**, 6, 110; **9**, 143, 153; **10**, 70n; **11**, 142; **14**, 28, 31, 146, 153; **15**, 63, 72n, 126, 128; **16**, 95–7, 168, 173; **17**, 50, 91, 93, 126, 129–30, 133, 212, 222; **21**, 138; **23**, 160, 169; **24**, 52, 71, 159; **25**, 188; **26**, 170, 184; **27**, 130, 135; **28**, 45n; **32**, 231, 234, 235; **33**, 202, 211; **34**, 185, 194–5; **35**, 175, 179, 184; **36**, 143n, 176; **37**, 190, 191, 215; **38**, 51, 122, 229, 242; **39**, 143; **42**, 15n, 27, 87, 88n, 92, 182, 187; **44**, 233, 250; **45**, 19n; **46**, 133n, 134, 135, 222, 223; **47**, 33, 38, 127n, 130, 132n, 133, 135–6, 273; **48**, 266; **49**, 18, 81, 195n, 323–4; **50**, 78; **51**, 324; **52**, 100, 101, 121n; **53**, 25–8, 31, 36; **54**, 63–5, 69, 224, 351; **55**, 249; **56**, 31, 35, 63, 101; **57**, 216, 217, 218, 222, 224, 239; **59**, 1, 2, 42, 356
  Have with You to Saffron Walden, **14**, 33n
  Pierce Pennilesse, **3**, 54; **8**, 147
  Summer's Last Will and Testament, **15**, 40n
  Terrors of the Night, **20**, 162
  Unfortunate Traveller, **1**, 70; **7**, 95
Nass, Barry, **36**, 175; **41**, 133n
Nassau, Prince Maurice of, **35**, 133
Nasta, Dan, **20**, 126
Natchinski, Thomas, **40**, 92n, 101n
Nath, Prem, **40**, 204
Nathan, Norman, **4**, 149; **7**, 133; **9**, 139; **10**, 136; **14**, 143; **19**, 136; **22**, 164; **24**, 178; **32**, 234, 246; **51**, 186n
Nathoo, Azeem, **59**, 345
National Maritime Museum, Greenwich, *see under* London
Natsume, Soseki, **48**, 106–7
Natural Perspectives Theatre Company, **58**, 300
Natwick, Mildred, **8**, 122
Naughton, John, **59**, 363–4, 368
Nauman, Anna, **52**, 283
Naumann, Walter, **37**, 156n
Navarre, Henry, King of, **38**, 49n, 52, 53, 55–7
Navarre, Margaret of, **33**, 199
Navarro, John, **11**, 110, 116n
  his Company of Spanish Players, **11**, 110
Navon, Arie, **14**, 121
Navratilova, Martina, **60**, 149–50
Nayar, Dahhe, **45**, 153
Nayfack, Nicholas, **53**, 168
Naylor, Andy, **43**, 208, 210
Naylor, Anthony, **55**, 335
Naylor, Ben, **57**, 293; **59**, 339
Naylor, Edward Woodall, **15**, 1, 3, 4, 5, 7–9
Naylor, Gloria, **53**, 136, 166n; **54**, 311; **56**, 146, 156–7, 302
Nazarjan, S., **25**, 6n
Nazianzen, Gregorius, **49**, 80
Nazor, V., **4**, 117
Ncube, Sello-Maake ka, **58**, 281, 282; **59**, 343, 371; **60**, 161
Neal, David, **47**, 211; **52**, 256
Neal, Simon, **57**, 297
Neale, J. E., *Queen Elizabeth*, **3**, 7; **28**, 17n; **38**, 20; **52**, 113n
Neale, Sir John, **17**, 12, n., 120, 127
Neale, Marjery, **45**, 106
Neale, Simon, **45**, 105–6
Neale, Thomas, *The Ward*, **4**, 94
Nearing, Barbara, **39**, 41n
Neat, David, **44**, 192
Nebeský, V. B., **9**, 105
Necker, Suzanne, **53**, 134
Neckham, Alexander, **56**, 83n
Neddaff, Ramona, **55**, 240n, 241n
Nedeva, Madlena, **51**, 223
Nedić, B., **4**, 118, 119; **15**, 142; **18**, 135
Needham, Claudia, **48**, 24n
Needham, Paul, **59**, 114n27
Needham, Peter, **45**, 146
Needham, Rodney, **35**, 73n; **48**, 24n
Needles, William, **16**, 154; **39**, 183; **40**, 157
Neely, Carol Thomas, **29**, 165; **31**, 54n, 164; **35**, 159; **37**, 3n; **40**, 92n, 101n; **41**, 65n, 74n; **42**, 168, 192; **44**, 208, 226, 241; **46**, 3, 6n; **48**, 132n; **49**, 66n; **50**, 247; **51**, 42n; **58**, 22, 249, 324, 332; **60**, 84–5n2
Negri de Bassano, Francesco, *Freewyl*, **1**, 64
Nehamas, Alexander, **50**, 175, 178; **56**, 209, 210n
Neher, Caspar, **29**, 176
Nehru, P., **16**, 135
Neidig, William, **7**, 53; **14**, 161; **27**, 185; **60**, 266n40
Neiiendam, Robert, **29**, 145
Neil, James, **34**, 185
Neild, James, **35**, 34, 37
Neill, Adam, **60**, 289
Neill, Kerby, **7**, 133; **8**, 5; **32**, 56n
Neill, Michael, **23**, 171n; **44**, 221; **47**, 79, 80; **48**, 130, 250, 282–4; **49**, 25, 207n, 209n, 213, 315; **51**, 64, 283; **52**, 297n; **53**, 86n, 290, 291–2, 294; **54**, 16n, 122n, 130; **55**, 54, 359–60; **57**, 19; **58**, 349, 351; **59**, 23n15, 37n87, 48; **60**, 169n5.2, 225, 228, 231, 348, 365–6, 369
Neilson, Adelaide, **32**, 23
Neilson, Francis, **30**, 154n
Neilson, H. V., **11**, 124
Neilson, Julia, **32**, 30, 33; **35**, 7; **56**, 134
Neilson, Tony, **46**, 195
Neilson, William Allan, **1**, 76; **3**, 31; **5**, 5; **19**, 12, 23n; **31**, 106n
Nejgebauer, Aleksander, **15**, 164; **18**, 172
  'Twentieth-century Studies in Shakespeare's Songs, Sonnets, and Poems: 2, The Sonnets', **15**, 10–18
Nekrosius, Eimuntas, **54**, 285
Nelke, Laura, **49**, 119n
Nelligan, Kate, **31**, 147; **39**, 105
Nellist, Brian, **17**, 52n; **50**, 255
Nels, B., **15**, 140

INDEX

Nels, Sofya, **23**, 174n; **54**, 147n, 148n, 149n
Nelsen, Paul, **52**, 13n
Nelson, Alan H., **43**, 167n; **44**, 151n, 225; **47**, 51n; **49**, 300; **50**, 165, 168; **54**, 62n; **57**, 245; **58**, 2, 13, 222; **60**, 342
Nelson, Alfred, **35**, 8
Nelson, Cary, **56**, 70n
Nelson, Cathryn A., **29**, 175
Nelson, Conrad, **48**, 199; **54**, 294; **56**, 251n, 253, 291; **57**, 279; **58**, 301; **60**, 288, 289
Nelson, Gerald **36**, 32n
Nelson, Norman E., **27**, 84
Nelson, Paul, **53**, 213n, 344
Nelson, Ralph, **14**, 125
Nelson, Richard, **45**, 157; **57**, 91
Nelson, Sarah, **47**, 213
Nelson, T. G. A., **37**, 116n, 124n, 125n; **38**, 223; **53**, 8n; **56**, 313
Nelson, Thomas, **27**, 179
Nelson, Tim Blake, **56**, 295
Nelson, Timothy G. A., **24**, 162
Nelson, William, **23**, 163n; **56**, 59n, 60n
Nemerov, Howard, **11**, 137
Németh, Antal, **12**, 113; **14**, 120
Németh, Lajos C., **16**, 135
Nemirovich-Danchenko, Vladimir, **23**, 174n; **41**, 123; **49**, 252; **54**, 142–3
Nemmo, Paul E., **34**, 95n
Nenner, Howard, **54**, 133n; **57**, 70, 74
Nennius, **59**, 241
Neoplatonism, **5**, 72, 73, 80n
Neri, Ferdinando, **1**, 9; **7**, 104
Neri, Nicoletta, **5**, 113; **9**, 114
Nerini, Frances, **53**, 278
Nero, the Emperor, **44**, 66
Nero, **12**, 48
Nesbitt, Francis, **22**, 132; **35**, 31
Nestingen, James A., **57**, 237
Nestroy, Johann, **13**, 125
Nešvera, Josef, **9**, 110n
Nethercot, A. H., *Sir William D'avenant*, **11**, 115n
Netherlands, report on Shakespeare in, **1**, 114; **6**, 121–2; **7**, 113; **12**, 115; **13**, 130; **14**, 121; **18**, 126–7
Nethersole, Reingard, **43**, 230
Netter, Thomas, **54**, 102n
Nettles, John, **32**, 205, 206; **46**, 174, 180, 184; **47**, 219; **49**, 251–2, 260; **50**, 228; **53**, 322
Netto, Jeffrey, **55**, 348
Netzloff, Mark, **58**, 310
Neuhaus, H. J., **29**, 183
Neumeier, John, **37**, 162
Neuner, Gerhard, **37**, 157n
Neveux, Georges, **5**, 111
  translation of *Othello*, **3**, 104–5
Nevill, William, **37**, 190
Neville, Catherine, **49**, 184
Neville, Jenny, **42**, 157, 158; **43**, 206; **45**, 150
Neville, John, **8**, 136; **9**, 124; **10**, 130, 133, 134; **14**, 134; **15**, 141, 145; **27**, 34n, 141; **39**, 186–8; **40**, 155; **56**, 111
Neville, Sir Thomas, **59**, 24n20
Nevinson, Charles, **32**, 134n
Nevinson, J. L., **18**, 180; **22**, 167n
Nevo, Ruth, **22**, 163; **23**, 143; **27**, 155–6; **37**, 3, 13n; **38**, 10, 240; **42**, 6n, 170, 181, 201; **43**, 23n, 24n; **45**, 162; **46**, 109n; **50**, 42; **51**, 168n
Nevrla, František, **16**, 133
New Custome, **4**, 94
New English Dictionary, The, see Oxford English Dictionary
New Historicism and Renaissance Drama, **46**, 220
New Oxford Book of Sixteenth Century Verse, **46**, 224
New Place, *see* Stratford-upon-Avon
'New Place: The Only Representation of Shakespeare's House, from an Unpublished Manuscript', **5**, 55–7
New Shakespeare Company, **58**, 303, 307
New Shakespeare Society, **18**, 51–2
New York City Players, **58**, 301
New York Herald Tribune, **59**, 67
New York Public Library, *see under* Libraries
New Zealand, report on Shakespeare in, **1**, 112; **6**, 122–3; **7**, 113–14
New, John F. H., **24**, 157
Newall, Alex, **20**, 148
Newbolt, Sir Henry, **10**, 4; **56**, 243
Newborough, Mary, **32**, 96n
Newburgh, William of, **55**, 53
Newcastle cycle, **21**, 56, 57
Newcastle, Duchess of (Margaret Cavendish), **60**, 336
Newcastle, Duke of, **48**, 53
Newcastle, William, Duke of, *see under* Cavendish, William
Newce, Captain William, **57**, 13
Newcomb, Lori Humphrey, **57**, 313, 316
Newcomb, Thomas, **44**, 126
Newcourt, Richard, **53**, 199, 203n
Newdigate, Bernard H., **15**, 27; **38**, 97n; **46**, 12n, 14n
Newell, Alex, **42**, 230
Newell, James, **4**, 70
Newes from Scotland, **4**, 41, 42; **17**, 171
Newey, Katharine, **59**, 374
Newey, Vincent, **45**, 162; **57**, 188
Newlin, Jeanne T., **34**, 8n; **35**, 9n
Newlyn, Lucy, **41**, 103n
Newman, Cardinal J. H., **6**, 1
Newman, Dorman, **55**, 263
Newman, Ernst, **60**, 186n9
Newman, Franklin B., **21**, 132; **38**, 15
Newman, Gerald, **51**, 17, 26n
Newman, Henry, **47**, 260
Newman, Jane O., **48**, 255
Newman, John Henry, **54**, 83, 238n
Newman, Karen, **37**, 194; **40**, 222; **41**, 196, 198; **42**, 163; **44**, 42n; **46**, 5, 208; **50**, 243; **51**, 189n; **60**, 92n29, 99n38, 161, 168n3.2
Newport, Christopher, sailor, **17**, 27 and n.
Newport, Rychard, possible identification with Sir Richard Newport of Ercall, **8**, 148
Newport, Sir Richard, **4**, 148n
Newsome, Chloe, **55**, 333
Newth, Jonathan, **59**, 312
Newton, Sir Isaac, **5**, 53; **40**, 145; **42**, 208; **59**, 228
  Principia, **20**, 177
Newton, J. M., **25**, 5n; **34**, 58n, 172
Newton, John, **54**, 54
Newton, Joy, **7**, 116

Newton, Mrs Eric, **13**, 80n
Newton, Steve, **52**, 259
Newton, Thomas, **33**, 90n; **47**, 140; **55**, 65n
Newton-De Molina, David, **42**, 89n
Ney, Marie, **32**, 32
Neylan, John Francis, **9**, 155
Ngbane, Menzi 'Ngubs', **56**, 282
Ngema, Mbongeni, **55**, 274
Ngubane, Ben, **57**, 165
Ngubane, Jordan Kush, **52**, 106n
Nice, Richard, **46**, 45n; **55**, 40n, 248n; **57**, 200
Nichol, John, **18**, 17
Nicholas I, Czar of Russia, **5**, 99–100
Nicholas II, Czar of Russia, **9**, 66
Nicholas of Cusa, **59**, 228, 229
Nicholas, Anna, **52**, 249
Nicholas, John, **60**, 113
Nicholas, Peter, **54**, 271
Nicholas, Thomas, **51**, 184, 185n
Nicholl, Charles, **35**, 176; **38**, 229; **50**, 63n, 65n; **57**, 239; **60**, 343
Nicholl, John, **17**, 33
Nicholls, Anthony, **13**, 142, 144
Nicholls, Derek, **42**, 151
Nicholls, John Gough, **26**, 39n, 74
Nicholls, Kate, **45**, 154
Nicholls, Sutton, **30**, 164n
Nichols, Ann E., **52**, 59n
Nichols, Bill, **52**, 96n
Nichols, John, **47**, 18n; **55**, 226n; **56**, 192, 193, 195; **57**, 210, 214
Progresses and Public Processions of Queen Elizabeth, **11**, 97n; **12**, 20n, 21n; **15**, 1, 2
Nichols, John Bowyer, **59**, 126, 127, 129
Nichols, John G., **35**, 130; **38**, 49n
Nichols, Peter, **51**, 197; **53**, 1
Nichols, Robert, **45**, 4n
Nicholson, Brinsley M., **40**, 228; **41**, 26; **56**, 101
Nicholson, Colin, **56**, 345
Nicholson, E. W. B., **4**, 83–4
Nicholson, Margaret, **38**, 71
Nicholson, Watson, **47**, 61n
Nicholson-Smith, Donald, **44**, 43n; **52**, 199n; **55**, 248n
Nickleby, Nicholas, **11**, 19
Niclaes, Henry, **44**, 82
Nicolai, Carl Otto, **18**, 75, 81–2; **45**, 174; **56**, 130n; **60**, 184, 192n24, 317
Nicolaievsky, Boris, **45**, 90
Nicolau, Florian, **20**, 128
Nicoli, Vincenzo, **45**, 156; **53**, 261; **54**, 283
Nicoll, Allardyce, **1**, 76; **4**, 9–10; **5**, 92n; **6**, 63n, 74n; **7**, 132; **8**, 105n, 116n; **9**, 50, 132; **10**, 59n, 101, 106n; **12**, 129n; **13**, 128, 159; **14**, 150; **15**, 7, 9, 11, 168, 170–1; **16**, 2–3, 7, 103; **17**, 79n 199n; **18**, 181; **19**, 148; **21**, 35, 145, 146; **25**, 45n; **26**, 3, 4, 9; **32**, 38, 43n, 44; **35**, 4; **36**, 121; **39**, 2, 39; **41**, 1, 2, 6, 219; **45**, 8n; **47**, 38; **51**, 141–6; **52**, 7n; **55**, 14n, 259; **57**, 210, 214; **59**, 44
The Elizabethans reviewed, **11**, 145
The English Theatre, **13**, 114
'"Passing over the Stage"', **12**, 47–55
'Studies in the Elizabethan Stage since 1900', **1**, 1–16
(ed.) *Shakespeare Survey* I, **14**, 1, 12, 13
(ed.) *Works of Cyril Tourneur*, **14**, 8
Nicolls, T., **56**, 223n
Nicolson, George, **52**, 315
Nicolson, Marjorie H., **42**, 43n
Niculescu, Miron, **20**, 128
Niebuhr, Reinhold, **36**, 30
Niedecken-Gebhart, H., **33**, 155n, 156; **36**, 139n
Niederstenbruch, Alex, **48**, 61n
Nielsen, Asta, **45**, 42–51
Nielsen, Carl, **3**, 114
Nielsen, Elizabeth, **20**, 150; **36**, 190n
Niessen, Carl, **3**, 117; **33**, 162n; **36**, 138n, 145n, 146n
Nietzsche, Friedrich Wilhelm, **9**, 135; **16**, 34; **22**, 156; **28**, 109; **30**, 186; **35**, 28; **36**, 19; **39**, 171; **40**, 82n, 188; **41**, 207, 212; **42**, 173; **44**, 213; **45**, 3; **46**, 124; **48**, 119; **50**, 171–86; **52**, 301; **53**, 100, 101; **54**, 141, 238, 297; **55**, 73n, 155; **56**, 206–9, 210n, 211; **57**, 107; **59**, 35
Nightingale, Benedict, **41**, 47; **50**, 34; **52**, 117–18, 325; **57**, 177; **60**, 171n4
Nightingale, Jack, **43**, 216
Nijhoff, Martinus, **7**, 108; **13**, 130
Niklaus, Thelma, **21**, 33, 38n
Nikolynkin, Alexandre, **21**, 128n
Nilan, Mary Margaret, **29**, 176; **33**, 10n; **43**, 102n, 103n
'*The Tempest* at the Turn of the Century: Cross-currents in Production', **25**, 113–23
Nilsen, Hans Jacob, **1**, 115; **3**, 114; **7**, 114; **10**, 120
Nilsson, Maj Britt, **16**, 137
Nims, John Frederick, **36**, 86n; **42**, 53n, 54n; **57**, 215
Ninagawa Theatre Company, **58**, 304
Ninagawa, Yukio, **42**, 153; **43**, 215; **47**, 3; **48**, 15, 109–10; **50**, 231; **51**, 264; **53**, 275; **54**, 246–8, 250, 286; **57**, 259, 269, 270, 271, 287; **58**, 268, 304; **59**, 298, 339, 370–1; **60**, 136, 136n19, 137n21, 137, 137n21, 138, 138n24, 303–4
Ninchi, Annibale, **5**, 113
Nirenberg, David, **52**, 207n, 210n
Nisbet, Monika, **46**, 201
Nisbet-Robinson, Neil, **54**, 294
Nisbett, Louisa, **56**, 132, 133, 134
Nisbett, Mrs, **20**, 111; **32**, 30; **34**, 175
Nivelon, Francois, **51**, 108, 109
Nixon, Anthony, **35**, 130n
Nixon, David, **58**, 303, 305; **59**, 342
Nixon, Richard, **37**, 173; **52**, 192; **57**, 188, 190
No Holds Bard, **44**, 203
Noack, Claus, **42**, 159
Noah, **12**, 3
Noakes, Carol, **42**, 156
Nobili, Lila de, **11**, 134; **12**, 127; **13**, 143
Noble, Adrian, **36**, 152, 159; **37**, 163, 164, 168, 173, 185; **38**, 201, 202, 204, 205; **39**, 199, 200; **40**, 174; **41**, 170–1, 175, 179, 183, 186; **42**, 137, 152, 157; **43**, 171, 173, 177, 212, 254; **45**, 119, 124, 139, 140–4; **46**, 11n, 173, 174, 175, 193; **47**, 122–5, 181–3, 185, 193, 199–203, 211, 219; **48**, 202–4, 222–3, 230–1; **49**, 2n, 3, 10–12, 240, 242–5, 275; **50**, 233; **51**, 228, 242; **52**, 236–7, 255, 262, 265, 290; **53**, 283; **54**, 274; **55**, 286, 313; **56**, 4, 6n, 7–10, 14, 253, 256–7, 271–3; **57**, 40, 42, 43, 44, 45, 258, 261, 279, 295, 331; **58**, 58, 336, 337

Noble, Peter, **39**, 54n
Noble, Richmond, **3**, 28; **4**, 9; **8**, 5; **10**, 150; **15**, 5, 6, 7; **25**, 37n, 125, 126, 127n, 130n; **28**, 98n; **29**, 88; **32**, 59n; **41**, 218
'*Nobleman, The*', **4**, 88
Nobody and Somebody, **11**, 44; **55**, 371
Nobre, António, **30**, 189
Nochimson, Richard L., **32**, 222
Nock, Francis J., **9**, 148
Noda, Hideki, **48**, 109, 110; **53**, 329
Noda, Manabu, **54**, 305
Nodelman, Perry, **55**, 161n, 168n
Noël, Jacques, **12**, 111; **57**, 119
Noelte, Rudolf, **37**, 162
Noel-Tod, Jeremy, **54**, 201n
Nogent, Gilbert de, **17**, 38
Nógrádi, R., **14**, 120
Noguchi, Isamo, **13**, 79; **20**, 145
Nohrnberg, James, **46**, 117n
Nöjd, Ruben, **48**, 4n
Nokes, David, **36**, 154
Nolan, John, **53**, 269
Noli, F. S., **15**, 142
Noling, Kim H., **43**, 52n, 56, 57n, 225
Nollen, Elizabeth Mahn, **56**, 152n
Nomura, Mansai, **57**, 288
Nomvete, Pamela, **46**, 201
Nonnos, **47**, 26; **56**, 84
Noonan, J. T., **49**, 184
Noonan, Stephen, **51**, 248; **54**, 252; **58**, 300; **59**, 333
Norberg, Kathryn, **54**, 199n; **55**, 241n
Norbrook, David, **39**, 219n, 226; **41**, 195–6; **44**, 239; **46**, 214; **48**, 257; **50**, 250–1; **53**, 25n; **54**, 9; **55**, 231n; **57**, 71, 126
Norburie, George, **29**, 97n
Norden, John, **1**, 27–31; **2**, 22–3; **17**, 128 and n; **32**, 190; **43**, 141, 144; **47**, 31, 37; **52**, 3; **53**, 203; **60**, 31–2, 38–9, 44, 45
  Speculum Britanniae, **1**, 27, 28, 30
Nordon, Tom, **44**, 203; **46**, 197; **47**, 218; **48**, 237
Nordrum, Lars, **7**, 114
Noreen, Rudolf, **60**, 327
Norem, Lois, **44**, 256
Norfolk, Duke of, **52**, 167–8
Norfolk, Dukes of, **28**, 17–18, 19
Norford, Don Parry, **34**, 170
Nørgaard, Holger, **10**, 145; **19**, 1, 130n, 147; **55**, 207n
Norlund, Johan, **2**, 128
Norman, Arthur M. Z., **10**, 146; **13**, 158
Norman, Philip, **1**, 29
Norman, Robert, **17**, 28
Normand, Lawrence, **45**, 169
Normington, John, **47**, 202, 205; **55**, 319; **58**, **290**; **59**, 340
Norreys, Sir John, **38**, 50n
Norris, Christopher, **47**, 73; **53**, 18n
Norris, J. Parker, **60**, 233–4
Norris, Sir John, **4**, 154
Norris, Stan, **54**, 285
North, Colonel, **45**, 10, 12
North, Marcy L., **60**, 261n31, 265
North, Robert, **55**, 331
North, Roy, **48**, 201; **56**, 237
North, Sir Thomas, **12**, 138; **15**, 177; **19**, 146; **20**, 151; **21**, 14; **22**, 112; **23**, 184; **28**, 66; **29**, 103, 110, 115; **30**, 97, 135, 204, 205; **32**, 167n; **33**, 105, 116n; **34**, 81, 188; **38**, 115, 116, 185, 186, 250; **40**, 69, 72–5, 86n; **41**, 77n, 85; **42**, 196, 206; **44**, 8, 15, 66; **46**, 96, 106; **47**, 23n, 142, 145–6, 149, 151; **48**, 36n, 38n, 40; **53**, 50, 51, 69, 74, 76, 84, 85; **54**, 91, 92n; **55**, 201, 205, 211n; **56**, 42n, 223
  Life of Pelopidas, **8**, 148
  translation of Antonio de Guevara's *Dial of Princes*, **2**, 70; **10**, 31
  translation of Plutarch's *Lives*, **1**, 39; **3**, 6, 18, 54; **4**, 9, 21, 87; **6**, 75, 91–3, 155; **7**, 36, 77, 126; **8**, 54, 147; **10**, 4, 12, 29, 50, 52–8, 59n; **12**, 65, 69, 92–4, 94n
Northam, Jeremy, **44**, 193; **47**, 206
Northampton, Earl of, **42**, 198
Northampton, Henry Howard, Earl of, **35**, 131
Northampton, William Compton, 1st Earl of, **33**, 164
Northamptonshire, **3**, 34
Northbrook, John, **54**, 59
Northcote, **10**, 73
Northcote, James, **49**, 121, 126; **51**, 300; **59**, 131n47, 132
Northcote, Julia Stafford, **51**, 261; **52**, 263; **54**, 290; **55**, 333
Northcott Theatre Company, **58**, 307
Northern Broadsides, **58**, 269, 279, 301
Northern, Michael, **10**, 130
Northey, Christopher, **42**, 160
Northrop, Douglas A., **23**, 166
Northumberland, Countess of, *see under* Cecil, Lady Anne
Northumberland, Earl of, *see under* Percy, Algernon, *and* Percy, Henry
Northumberland, Henry Percy, 9th Earl of, **38**, 29; **44**, 37, 240
Northward Ho!, see under Dekker, Thomas, *and* Webster, John
Nortimo, Jorma, **10**, 117
Norton, Bonham, **55**, 37n
Norton, Caroline, **58**, 102
Norton, F. J., **29**, 16n
Norton, M., **43**, 149n, 158n, 160n, 162n; **50**, 152n
Norton, M. D. Herter, **23**, 164n
Norton, Richard, **48**, 71–2
Norton, Thomas, **30**, 206; **32**, 102n; **33**, 17, 92; **46**, 127n; **48**, 71n, 74n, 82n; **53**, 326; **54**, 27n
Norton, Thomas and Sackville, Thomas, **1**, 126; **6**, 156; **7**, 141; **11**, 144; **14**, 80
  Gorboduc, **11**, 44, 144; **13**, 42–8, 48n; **14**, 80; **15**, 142, 170; **20**, 25n
  see also under Sackville, Thomas
Norway, report on Shakespeare in, **1**, 115; **2**, 128; **3**, 118; **4**, 128; **5**, 113–14; **6**, 123; **7**, 114; **8**, 120; **11**, 121; **13**, 130; **14**, 122
Norwich, **1**, 57; **12**, 71
  Bishop's Palace, **12**, 73
Norwich mystery cycle, **21**, 57
Norwich Players, The, *see* Maddermarket Theatre
Norwood, Richard, **43**, 152
Nosak, Bohuslav, **4**, 115n
Noske, Frits, **57**, 65
Nössig, Manfred, **48**, 175n
Nossiter, Maria, **49**, 116

Nostbakken, Faith, **58**, 330, 332
Nosworthy, James M., **2**, 146, 147; **5**, 151–2; **7**, 139; **9**, 143, 151–2; **10**, 141; **11**, 20, 23, 44, 47, 49n; **13**, 161; **15**, 9, 12; **19**, 1, 2, 93n; **20**, 161, 174–5; **23**, 173, 182, 183; **24**, 172; **25**, 110; **26**, 20n, 81, 82–4, 85n; **27**, 111, 116, 118n, 122n, 127n, 133n; **29**, 1, 45, 52, 53n; **31**, 31n; **32**, 152, 157, 158n, 159n, 227; **34**, 173; **36**, 98n, 100, 102, 105; **39**, 127n, 160; **43**, 18n; **46**, 104n; **49**, 102n; **54**, 208n; **55**, 196, 392; **57**, 209; **59**, 44
'*Hamlet* and the Player who could not Keep Counsel', **3**, 74–82
'The Integrity of Shakespeare: Illustrated from *Cymbeline*', **8**, 52–6
'Music and its Function in the Romances of Shakespeare', **11**, 60–9
'Structural Experiment in *Hamlet*' reviewed, **1**, 119
Notary, Julian, **59**, 244n38, 246n58
'Note on the Swan Theatre Drawing', **1**, 23–4
Notestein, Wallace, **56**, 218n
Noth, Martin, **48**, 86n
Nott-Bower, Jill, **45**, 157
Nottingham Playhouse Theatre Company, **58**, 269, 304
Nottingham, Earl of, *see under* Howard, Charles
Novak, E., **23**, 173
Novak, Maximillian E., **36**, 114n; **43**, 91n; **44**, 49n
Novell, Andrew, **53**, 281
Novelli, **20**, 121
Novello, Ivor, **55**, 135
Novello, Sabilla, **58**, 96
Noverre, Jean Georges, **57**, 61
Novy, Marianne L., **32**, 216; **34**, 171; **37**, 33n. 37n; **38**, 240; **39**, 213; **40**, 126n; **44**, 206, 208, 241; **48**, 261; **49**, 64n, 65n, 134n, 168n, 169n; **53**, 4n, 110n, 117, 118, 119n; **54**, 312; **55**, 147n, 148n; **56**, 156n, 204n, 302, 315; **58**, 84; **60**, 85, 92n29
Engaging with Shakespeare; Responses of George Eliot and other Women Novelists, **48**, 261
Nowell (Blackfriars law-suit), **11**, 102
Nowell, Alexander, **57**, 237
Nowell, Dean, **20**, 25n
Nowosielski, Charles, **43**, 214; **46**, 192; **47**, 210; **48**, 236
Nowottny, Winifred M. T. (W. M. T. Dodds), **7**, 130; **9**, 136; **11**, 139–40; **12**, 137; **14**, 142; **15**, 17, 159; **19**, 127; **20**, 49n, 165; **24**, 25; **25**, 5, 8; **31**, 163; **32**, 214; **33**, 40; **41**, 73n; **52**, 302; **55**, 10; **56**, 230n
'Lear's Questions', **10**, 90–7
'Some aspects of the style of *King Lear*', **13**, 49–57
Noy, Dov, **48**, 56n
Noyes, G. E., **31**, 91n
Noyes, George R., **38**, 170n
Noyes, Robert, **51**, 14
Noyes, Robert Gale, **7**, 137
Nozick, Robert, **55**, 221
Nuffield Theatre Company, **58**, 300
Numan, **54**, 40
Nunes, Carlos Alberto, **10**, 115
Nuñez, Pedro, **17**, 144
Nungezer, Edwin, **1**, 8; **7**, 86, 89n; **22**, 119; **33**, 154, 155n, 157, 167n; **36**, 137, 138n, 141n; **58**, 67
Nunn, Hilary M., **60**, 358–9, 361
Nunn, Trevor, **22**, 141; **23**, 132, 133; **24**, 117, 122, 128n, 130, 131; **25**, 27; **26**, 139, 140, 141, 148; **27**, 137, 138–9; **28**, 137; **29**, 73; **30**, 169–71, 173, 176–8; **31**, 146–7; **33**, 75n, 82, 83, 84, 85, 87, 169; **34**, 156; **35**, 142n, 148; **36**, 149–51, 159; **37**, 184, 199; **40**, 13, 223; **41**, 45, 170; **42**, 136; **43**, 184, 198, 190–2, 203; **44**, 95, 177, 186, 199; **45**, 134, 136, 137, 139, 192; **46**, 68, 196, 200; **47**, 4, 5, 6n, 7, 9, 11–13, 117–18, 124, 126; **48**, 109, 265, 282; **49**, 2n, 289; **50**, 262; **51**, 253, 268; **52**, 266, 286, 290, 308; **53**, 255, 257–8, 260, 267–72; **54**, 267, 288, 293; **55**, 286, 294, 309, 331; **56**, 177, 246n, 247, 266, 281, 347; **57**, 262, 264, 269, 332; **58**, 268, 293, 301, 337, 345; **59**, 190–1, 300, 320–3, 338–9, 373; **60**, 110n36, 211, 295, 307, 326, 360, 365–6
Nussbaum, Martha, **53**, 91
Nüssel, Heide, **23**, 122
Nutt, Joe, **56**, 302
Nuttall, A. D., **20**, 157; **22**, 164; **23**, 151; **25**, 6, 37, 42, 90n; **27**, 170; **29**, 90; **30**, 184; **31**, 106n; **32**, 9; **35**, 114n; **36**, 168–9; **38**, 221n; **40**, 84, 115n; **42**, 196; **43**, 25; **44**, 51n; **49**, 183n, 202, 203n, 214n; **50**, 186n; **51**, 145; **53**, 108n; **54**, 179n, 201n, 207; **55**, 349; **56**, 223n, 224n, 228n; **59**, 366
'*Measure for Measure:* the Bed-trick', **28**, 51–6
Nyberg, Lennart, **43**, 250–1
Nye, Robert, **52**, 266; **56**, 130n, 315
Nyerere, Julius, **36**, 2
Nyman, Heikki, **40**, 29n
Nyrén, William, **10**, 120
Nyusztay, Ivân, **58**, 332

Oakeshott, Walter, **9**, 133; **15**, 72n; **32**, 90n, 91n
Oakley, Francis, **23**, 162
Oakley, Lucy, **49**, 126n, 306; **59**, 130, 130n36, 130n39, 130n40, 131n42, 131n45
Oakley-Smith, John, **52**, 261
Oates, Joyce Carol, **21**, 134; **41**, 64, 67, 73
Obano, Rex, **51**, 241; **52**, 264
Obee, Lois, **47**, 94
Oberer, Walter, **18**, 129
Oberkogler, Friedrich, **37**, 158n
Oberli, Maurice, **2**, 127
Oberndorff, John, **32**, 94n
Oberon, **52**, 190
Obertello, Alfredo, **8**, 120; **11**, 141; **13**, 130; **14**, 148n
Obey, André, **5**, 111; **6**, 118; **11**, 120; **15**, 133
Obolensky, Chloe, **45**, 155
O'Briain, Donnacadh, **58**, 264
O'Brian, Martin, **56**, 293
O'Brian, Patrick, **49**, 114n
O'Brien, Bernadette, **45**, 155
O'Brien, Dermot, **46**, 194; **49**, 274
O'Brien, Ellen, **53**, 294, 295
O'Brien, Ellen J., **37**, 193
O'Brien, Gordon Worth, **14**, 141
Renaissance Poetics and the Problem of Power reviewed, **11**, 144
O'Brien, Jack, **60**, 116n63
O'Brien, Maureen, **45**, 152
O'Brien, Peggy, **49**, 142n
O'Brien, R. V., **54**, 204n
O'Brien, Richard, **56**, 348

O'Brien, Timothy, **24**, 124; **27**, 146, 151; **29**, 176; **33**, 169; **43**, 190; **44**, 193; **45**, 125, 148; **46**, 201; **49**, 261–2; **50**, 230; **54**, 287, 294
O'Byrne, Darren, **58**, 193
O'Callaghan, Michelle, **60**, 283n54
O'Callaghan, Patrick, **54**, 294
O'Callaghan, Richard, **37**, 168, 169; **42**, 150; **59**, 207
O'Callaghan, Sean, **48**, 209
O'Casey, Sean, **1**, 97; **36**, 1, 3, 10
Occhini, Maria, **15**, 136
Occhiogrosso, Frank, **39**, 90n; **57**, 330
O'Chaine, Donatus, **36**, 140
Ochester, Edwin F., **24**, 166
Ockham, William of, **24**, 91
O'Cleary, Joan, **55**, 332
O'Connell, Daniel, **54**, 75
O'Connell, Kate, **42**, 149
O'Connell, Michael, **39**, 229; **57**, 236
O'Connell, Patrick, **41**, 160, 185; **42**, 161
O'Connor, D., **55**, 83n
O'Connor, F., **37**, 213n
O'Connor, Francis, **46**, 197; **53**, 275
O'Connor, Frank, **5**, 92n, **7**; 10
The Road to Stratford reviewed, **3**, 133–4
O'Connor, Garry, **56**, 167n; **58**, 1; **60**, 116n62
O'Connor, John, **49**, 128; **60**, 78n29, 80n34
O'Connor, John J., **24**, 157; **29**, 181; **39**, 89
O'Connor, John S., **31**, 194; **40**, 229
O'Connor, Joseph, **49**, 160
O'Connor, Marion F., **42**, 163; **43**, 15n; **44**, 41n, 68n, 105n; **47**, 82n, 83n; **50**, 109n; **52**, 24n, 30n; **53**, 238n; **54**, 316; **60**, 168
O'Connor, Patrick, **49**, 129n
O'Connor, Robert, **53**, 304
O'Connor, William D., **18**, 107, 112, 114, 115
O'Conor, Joseph, **37**, 168; **39**, 199, 202, 203; **41**, 173; **50**, 223
O'Conor, N. J., **46**, 33n
October, D. C., **57**, 160, 161
O'Dair, Sharon, **48**, 152n, 248; **51**, 167n; **55**, 353; **60**, 141–53, 335
Odajima, Youshi, **42**, 162; **48**, 109–10
O'Day, Trish, **55**, 332
Odell, G. C. D., **10**, 76n; **18**, 117n, **20**, 110, 111n; **29**, 141n; **32**, 37–8, 41–2; **33**, 3, 4, 5, 10, 11, 12, 13, 14, 48n; **34**, 187; **38**, 191n; **41**, 23n; **42**, 47; **43**, 102n; **49**, 2n; **51**, 67n, 69n; **53**, 230
Odland, Bruce, **49**, 274
Odo, Geraldus, **29**, 99
O'Donnell, **56**, 260–1
O'Donnell, Anthony, **46**, 166, 167, 177
O'Donnell, Brennan, **52**, 276
O'Donnell, Fergus, **51**, 227; **53**, 272; **55**, 314
O'Donnell, Peadar, **52**, 286
O'Donoghue, Bryan, **50**, 227
Oedipus, **11**, 20
Oehlenschläger, Adam Gottlob, **5**, 52; **43**, 112
Oenone and Paris, **1**, 75
Oenslager, Donald, **8**, 122
O'Farrell, Nellie, **2**, 35n
Offenbach, **18**, 76
Office of the Revels, documents relating to, **8**, 158
Office of Works, Elizabethan, accounts, **8**, 150–1
O'Flaherty, Mrs, *see* Winstanley, Eliza
Ofluoğlu, Mucip, **16**, 137; **18**, 130
Ogden, David, **45**, 153
Ogden, Dunbar H., **39**, 234
Ogden, James, **42**, 198; **52**, 324; **55**, 3n
Ogden, Paul W., **39**, 234
Oggel, L. Terry, **35**, 5n
Ogilby, John, **53**, 200, 205, 207
Ogilvie, John, **43**, 104
Ogilvy, J. D. A., **27**, 162
Ogilvy, Rachel, **42**, 156
'Ogle the wig-maker', **2**, 52
Ogle, Sir John, **33**, 168
Ogle, M. B., **15**, 15
Oglethorpe, Owen, Bishop of Carlisle, **54**, 125n
Ognell, Andrew, **12**, 98, 101
Ognyanov, Lyubomir, **1**, 114; **3**, 116; **10**, 116; **13**, 125
O'Gorman, Simon, **49**, 273
Oguzalp, Tomris, **12**, 117
O'Hanlon, Jacqui, **46**, 196
O'Hara, David, **43**, 185, 190; **44**, 193, 200
O'Hara, John, **48**, 232; **49**, 280; **52**, 254; **53**, 280
O'Haver, Tommy, **56**, 294
O'Herlihy, Micheal, **6**, 119
Ohlmarks, Åoke, **16**, 137; **18**, 128
Ohm, Karl, **37**, 158n
Ohtomo, Katsuhiro, **60**, 135, 139
Ojetti, Paola, **3**, 118; **12**, 114
O'Kane, Patrick, **54**, 287
O'Kane, Sheelagh, **48**, 236
Okerlund, G., **31**, 95n
Okes, John, **55**, 266
Okes, Nicholas, **2**, 152, 153; **5**, 22; **13**, 99; **14**, 165; **18**, 23; **25**, 197; **28**, 180; **37**, 210, 211; **40**, 150, 152n; **47**, 259, 271; **48**, 287; **50**, 282; **55**, 266; **58**, 350; **60**, 252
Okey, Thomas, **58**, 110
Okhlopkov, Nikolay Pavlovich, **9**, 117, 118; **12**, 118; **15**, 140; **60**, 335
Okonedo, Sophie, **53**, 257; **54**, 293
Olaniyan, T., **51**, 73n
Olaus Magnus, **20**, 26n
Old Law, The, **54**, 357
Old Testament Women in Western Literature, **46**, 218
Old Vic Theatre and Company, London, *see under* Theatres
Old Wives' Tale, The, **52**, 84–5
Oldcastle, *alternative title for 1 Henry IV*, **8**, 158
Oldcastle (Cobham family name), **41**, 217
Oldcastle Controversy, The, **46**, 225, 226
Oldcastle, Sir John (Lord Cobham), **38**, 89, 93–8, 222; **39**, 246; **54**, 100–7, 133; **60**, 341
Oldfield, Ben, **55**, 333
Oldham, John, **49**, 37
Oldknow, Mark, **55**, 332
Oldknow, Sarah, **49**, 277
Oldman, David, **49**, 270
Oldroyd, William, **59**, 340; **60**, 293
Oldys, W., *and* Birch, T., **27**, 56
Oldys, William, **41**, 35; **46**, 41; **54**, 121; **56**, 61
Olgeirsson, Karl, **57**, 286
Oliphant, Dave, **55**, 183n

Oliphant, E. H. C, **2**, 47; **20**, 166; **34**, 190; **43**, 82n, 86; **51**, 96n
The Plays of Beaumont and Fletcher, **14**, 12
Oliphant, Thomas, **9**, 89n
Olivares, Count-Duke of (Gaspar de Guzmán), **60**, 240
Olive, W. J., **5**, 142
Oliver, Alban, **47**, 217
Oliver, Edna May, **18**, 73
Oliver, Gary, **50**, 218; **59**, 339
Oliver, H. J., **12**, 109, 148; **13**, 164; **14**, 142; **21**, 162; **22**, 178; **23**, 180; **24**, 162n; **25**, 198; **27**, 111n, 112n, 113; **28**, 178n; **29**, 103n, 104, 115; **30**, 207, 208; **31**, 185; **33**, 203; **37**, 2, 23, 28, 29n, 34, 39, 203–5, 219; **38** 239; **50**, 20n; **54**, 208n, **55**, 191, 193, 194; **56**, 218n; **60**, 74
The Problem of John Ford, **14**, 12
Oliver, Harold, **59**, 47
Oliver, Jonathan, **45**, 153
Oliver, L. M., **2**, 143; **38**, 94n
Oliver, Peter, **60**, 223
Oliver, Rachel, **52**, 259
Oliver, Roland, **41**, 187; **55**, 325
Oliver, Stephen, **36**, 154; **41**, 169; **42**, 158; **44**, 198; **46**, 200
Oliver, Vic, **47**, 96
Olivier, Laurence (Lord Olivier), **1**, 98, 99, 102, 103, 104, 105; **2**, 18; **3**, 113, 114; **4**, 105, 130; **6**, 121, 123, 136, 141, 142, 143, 145, 146; **7**, 28, 113, 121, 146n; **8**, 130; **9**, 21, 112, 124–30; **10**, 127; **11**, 128; **13**, 70, 79, 128, 161; **15**, 141, 147, 150; **16**, 20, 24, 27; **18**, 68, 71–4, 147, 154–5, 185; **20**, 139, 170; **21**, 115–19, 122, 125, 141; **22**, 94; **23**, 131, 173, 174; **24**, 129; **25**, 28; **26**, 150, 176; **27**, 145; **30**, 144; **31**, 152; **34**, 156; **35**, 32, 189; **36**, 61, 159–60, 165; **37**, 59; **38**, 18, 226; **39**, 2–6, 39, 65, 75, 86, 89, 90, 95, 96n, 136, 175; **40**, 1, 4, 13, 36–7, 64; **41**, 2, 46–7, 51, 53, 57, 60, 177, 226, 228; **42**, 86; **43**, 183, 194, 201, 251–2; **44**, 243; **45**, 8, 35, 40, 47–65, 76, 147, 172; **47**, 48, 97; **48**, 7, 61, 187, 263, 264; **49**, 3, 128, 153–4, 156, 227–34; **50**, 256; **51**, 299; **52**, 71, 99, 104–5, 112, 192–5, 197–8, 200, 291; **53**, 235, 240–2, 327; **54**, 254–5, 312, 313, 321; **55**, 42, 172, 293, 321, 382, 383; **56**, 111, 113, 114, 245–6, 276, 342, 347; **57**, 81, 147, 331; **59**, 372; **60**, 105, 160, 162, 165, 167, 168, 169, 206, 351, 354, 356, 362
film of *Hamlet*, **3**, 119
Olivier, Richard, **51**, 209, 212, 217; **52**, 117, 217, 256; **53**, 279
Ollerenshaw, Maggie, **56**, 252
Olleson, Edward, **44**, 238; **45**, 162
Olley, Francis R., **20**, 148
O'Loughlin, Sean, **5**, 92n; **15**, 20, 23–4, 26–30; **25**, 126n
The Voyage to Illyria, **3**, 9
Olson, Charles, **18**, 116
Olson, Elder, **19**, 122
Olson, Paul A., **12**, 133; **15**, 112; **35**, 72n
Olsson, Yngve B., **24**, 156; **29**, 171; **40**, 209
'Olympiads', **2**, 28, 33
Olympic Games, 1936, **3**, 96
O'Mahoney, Robert, **35**, 154; **48**, 236
O'Malley, C. D., **23**, 163
O'Malley, John W., **59**, 250n81
Omambala, Chu, **53**, 268
Oman, C., **47**, 173n
Omans, Stuart, **24**, 161n
O'Mara, Kate, **42**, 152, 157; **43**, 205; **44**, 191, 196; **45**, 157; **52**, 265
O'Meara, Jean M., **42**, 19n
O'Meara, John, **46**, 218; **51**, 283–4
Omere, Ivy, **52**, 232–3; **53**, 274
Omerod, David, **51**, 182n
Omesco, Ion, **42**, 176
Omotoso, Kole, **36**, 2
Ondaatje, Michael, **50**, 135n
Onderiz, Ambrosio, **20**, 101
Onega, Susana, **53**, 40n
O'Neil, Catherine, **58**, 312, 332
O'Neill, Eliza, **16**, 109; **35**, 51, 54; **42**, 39; **49**, 122–3
O'Neill, Eugene, **18**, 115; **19**, 24n; **34**, 3; **40**, 38; **53**, 188
O'Neill, Maria, **56**, 309
O'Neill, Vincent, **43**, 217
O'Neilly J. G., **54**, 125n
Ong, Walter J., **7**, 3; **9**, 135; **15**, 27; **24**, 47, 48n, 49n; **35**, 66n, 79n; **53**, 91; **59**, 32n57, 91; **60**, 80n38
Onians, Richard Broxton, **54**, 31n
Onions, C. T., **3**, 6; **5**, 20; **7**, 2; **11**, 89; **12**, 6; **16**, 71; **19**, 77; **23**, 36; **34**, 116; **40**, 219, 236n; **41**, 36n; **49**, 176n; **51**, 316, 335; **55**, 190; **56**, 70n
Onymere, Clara, **51**, 222–3
Oparei, Dhobi, **43**, 201; **53**, 258–9; **57**, 295
Ophelia, **47**, 211
Operation Shakespeare, **52**, 266
Opie, Iona, **56**, 2n5
Opie, John, **49**, 121; **59**, 131n47, 132
Opie, Mrs., **53**, 108
Opie, Peter, **56**, 2n5
Oppé, Adolf Paul, **10**, 76n
Oppel, Horst, **4**, 147; **9**, 140; **11**, 142, 144; **12**, 139, 146; **16**, 163; **19**, 128; **23**, 114, 121, 123; **24**, 145; **26**, 163; **34**, 185; **37**, 156II, 159
Oppen, Alice Arnott, **58**, 53
Oppenheimer, J. Robert, **22**, 147
Oram, Christopher, **52**, 254; **53**, 284; **54**, 268; **55**, 322; **56**, 273; **57**, 264
Orange, Linwood E., **32**, 225
Orange, Michael, **40**, 203–4
Orange, Prince of, *see* William, Prince of Orange
Oras, Ants, **8**, 150; **18**, 186; **42**, 206
Orator, The, **54**, 96
Orbay, Ergin, **14**, 124
Orbison, Roy, **44**, 199
Orbison, Tucker, **23**, 171; **39**, 90
Orchard, Andy, **59**, 240n7
Ord, H., **15**, 15
Ordinary, The, **54**, 62, 69n
Ordish, T. F., **1**, 35n, 36n; **42**, 114
Ordýnski, Richard, **4**, 126
O'Reilly, Genevieve, **59**, 321
Orff, Carl, **7**, 111; **18**, 87; **45**, 172
Orgel, Stephen, **24**, 164; **28**, 169, 170; **31**, 98n, 102n; **33**, 145n; **34**, 146; **35**, 66n, 129n, 138n; **36**, 115n; **37**, 193; **39**, 229; **41**, 6, 243–4; **42**, 58n, 175; **43**, 11n, 12, 15n, 27, 92, 94, 95n, 162n, 245; **44**, 44n, 48, 52; **45**, 37; **46**, 5, 6, 9n, 17n, 46n, 47n, 96n, 111n, 117n, 123n; **47**, 17n, 29n, 127n; **48**, 155; **49**, 73n, 312; **50**, 80n, 143, 144, 188n, 195, 267–9, 289; **51**, 275–6, 329; **53**, 148n, 149n, 234n, 305, 337; **54**, 197n, 322; **55**, 186n, 220n, 232n, 237n, 242n, 243n, 244n, 245n; **56**, 73, 105–16, 146–7, 154n, 159, 170n; **57**,

1, 2, 3, 84, 145, 210, 334; **58**, 314, 329, 332, 349; **59**, 36, 38n87, 81, 85, 89, 104n18, 108, 212n63, 362, 381–2, 383; **60**, 44n32, 58n2, 59n3, 60n7, 115n58, 123n16, 357–8, 360
Origen, **57**, 245
O'Riordan, Adam, **13**, 135
O'Riordan, Conal, **8**, 78; **54**, 76–8; **55**, 76–8
Orisayomi, Rufus, **48**, 231; **52**, 258
Orita, Kohji, **46**, 193
Orkin, Martin R., **37**, 190; **41**, 210; **42**, 165–6; **46**, 214; **49**, 285; **51**, 277; **52**, 158n, 202n; **53**, 290, 293, 303; **54**, 233n; **55**, 273; **56**, 204n; **58**, 350; **60**, 331–2, 353
Orlando, **54**, 312
Orlando Furioso, **52**, 77
Orlin, Lena Cowen, **40**, 220; **51**, 186n, 187n; **53**, 299; **54**, 307, 322; **55**, 372–3, 375; **57**, 333; **60**, 259n26
Ormerod, David E., **10**, 123; **27**, 164; **32**, 221, 236; **40**, 215, 219; **47**, 150n
'Faith and Fashion in *Much Ado About Nothing*', **25**, 93–105
Ormerod, Nick, **41**, 187–8, 190; **42**, 153, 159; **43**, 215; **44**, 130, 146; **46**, 191; **48**, 217; **52**, 266; **53**, 28; **54**, 295; **56**, 161, 165
Ornest, Ota, **14**, 118
Ornstein, Robert, **12**, 142; **14**, 141; **19**, 127; **21**, 138–9; **23**, 174n; **24**, 150, 168; **25**, 5n; **26**, 4, 6, 8; **27**, 161; **28**, 2, 3, 5n, 6, 10, 48n; **29**, 87; **30**, 58n, 65, 68; **31**, 95; **33**, 5, 8; **34**, 140; **37**, 102n; **38**, 3, 4, 46n; **40**, 75n; **41**, 64n, 83n, 88n, 203; **46**, 101n, 229n; **48**, 255; **54**, 219n; **55**, 223n
'Shakespearian and Jonsonian Comedy', **22**, 43–6
Shakespeare's Comedies, **48**, 255
Orosius, **59**, 240, 263
O'Rourke, James L., **47**, 234; **55**, 226n; **58**, 311, 332
O'Rourke, Josie, **59**, 307–10
O'Rowe, Mark, **58**, 263
Orpheus, **11**, 60
Orr, Marcus W., **47**, 161n
Orr, Peter, **24**, 3n
Orrell, John, **20**, 166; **31**, 186; **33**, 198; **35**, 135n, 175; **36**, 178, 179; **37**, 195–7; **38**, 228; **39**, 226; **41**, 3, 5, 10n, 37; **42**, 194; **43**, 141, 144–8, 149n, 235–6; **45**, 108n, 109n, 110, 111; **47**, 16n, 19n, 27n, 127n; **49**, 17n; **50**, 165; **51**, 205; **52**, 8–12, 13n, 14n, 39n, 47n; **53**, 197, 208n; **60**, 32, 32n29, 37n6, 45n45, 103n8
'Inigo Jones at The Cockpit', **30**, 157–68
Orrery, Earl of, *see under* Boyle, Roger
Orrock, Sally, **56**, 288
Orsini, Napoleone, **1**, 14, 116
edition of Croce's *Shakespeare* reviewed, **3**, 130, 132
'La critica Shakespeariana' reviewed, **1**, 118–19
Orsino, Don Virginio, **10**, 147
Orszagh, Ladislas, **12**, 114
Ortego, P. D., **26**, 158
Ortelius, Abraham, **15**, 128; **17**, 39; **31**, 18
Theatrum Orbis Terrarum, **17**, 41
Ortiz, Antonio, **29**, 30
Orton, Joe, **53**, 194, 328; **56**, 246
Orwell, George, **13**, 31; **23**, 97; **33**, 7, 8; **37**, 209; **46**, 122; **49**, 95; **56**, 203
Selected Essays, **13**, 39n
Ory, Pascal, **48**, 253
Osanai, Kaoru, **23**, 174n; **48**, 108–9
Osbaldiston, David, **47**, 68
Osborn, James M., **50**, 67n; **54**, 126n; **55**, 267n
Osborne, Francis, **56**, 219, 220, 222
Osborne, Heather, **44**, 195
Osborne, John, **16**, 19; **19**, 24n; **42**, 181; **45**, 59; **48**, 286n; **49**, 230; **55**, 150, 160; **56**, 246
Osborne, Laurie E., **45**, 169, 194n; **50**, 276–8; **51**, 323–4; **52**, 289–90; **53**, 344; **54**, 3n; **55**, 346; **56**, 347; **57**, 83; **58**, 340; **59**, 62, 199, 204; **60**, 360
Osborne, Melanie, **51**, 293
Oscarsson, Per, **8**, 121; **12**, 116
Oseeler, Oliver, **52**, 187n
Osgood, Charles G., **1**, 76; **4**, 162; **40**, 36n; **46**, 51n
O'Shaughnessy, Arthur, **10**, 109
O'Shea, José Robert, **60**, 218n18
O'Shea, Milo, **49**, 161, 172
O'Shea, Steven, **43**, 207
Osler, Sir William, **4**, 84
Osment, Philip, **47**, 218; **54**, 340
Osmond, Rosalie, **32**, 234
Osmond, T. S., **7**, 4
Osmonton, A., **55**, 94
Osmonton, Martha, **55**, 94
Osorio, Elena, **20**, 98, 101
Osselton, N. E., **52**, 273
Ossian, **43**, 104; **59**, 109–10, 112
Ossian (James MacPherson), **5**, 93; **9**, 94, 95, 96, 102
Ost, Geoffrey, **5**, 119; **13**, 134; **14**, 126; **15**, 144
Østerberg, Valdemar, **3**, 110; **4**, 64; **6**, 48n
see also under Translations
Österreichische Shakespeare-Gesellschaft, **2**, 126
Ostler, William, **58**, 233
Ostovich, Helen, **54**, 332–3; **56**, 148n; **58**, 358
Ostrom, Toby, **41**, 191
Ostrovski, A. N., **4**, 120, 125; **22**, 35
Ostrower, Jessica, **60**, 178n14
O'Sullivan, James P., **32**, 63n
O'Sullivan, John, **57**, 136
O'Sullivan, Mary I., **29**, 82
O'Sullivan, Maurice J., **41**, 219; **54**, 75; **56**, 124n; **58**, 138, 140
Otherworldly Hamlet, **46**, 218
Otho, Emperor, **32**, 236
Otis, Brooks, **39**, 168n
O'Toole, Fintan, **58**, 262
O'Toole, Peter, **14**, 135, 136; **16**, 22; **54**, 253; **56**, 247; **57**, 81; **60**, 78, 79
Otskheli, Petré, **48**, 189
Otten, Charlotte F., **34**, 196
Otto, Brian, **41**, 191; **48**, 231
Otto, of Friesing, **33**, 99n
Otto, Teo, **9**, 114; **12**, 144–5
Ottosen, Ingeman, *Shakespeare under Elizabeth*, **3**, 111
Otway, Thomas, **7**, 1–2; **15**, 153; **19**, 153; **25**, 189; **37**, 117; **38**, 73, 190; **42**, 85; **47**, 257; **49**, 2, 111, 113; **53**, 323; **55**, 97
adaptation of *Romeo and Juliet*, **9**, 85n
Venice Preserved, **13**, 38
Ouditt, Sharon, **50**, 247–8
Oulton, Richard, **55**, 29
Our American Cousin, **52**, 34
Out of Joint, **58**, 268

Outhwaite, R. B., **23**, 162n; **49**, 183n
Outlawe, Henry, **11**, 104
Ouzounian, Richard, **40**, 156
Ove, Indro, **46**, 199
Over the Edge, **58**, 305
Over, Alan, **22**, 145; **23**, 50n
Over, G. A., **18**, 56n
Over, William, **55**, 346
Overall, W. H., **1**, 35n
Overbury, Nicholas, **27**, 100
Overbury, Sir Thomas, **11**, 72, 99; **15**, 168; **21**, 140; **24**, 165; **27**, 100; **57**, 213; **58**, 68, 69
Overholzer, Winifred, **14**, 156
Overmyer, J., **26**, 162
Overton, Bill, **44**, 217
Overton, Henry, **13**, 110n
Overton, John, **13**, 109, 110n
Ovid, **1**, 38, 51; **3**, 14, 19; **4**, 9, 28, 87; **5**, 137, 139; **7**, 36; **10**, 2, 17, 18, 64, 69; **11**, 76, 104, 135n; **12**, 136; **13**, 36; **14**, 92, 154; **15**, 20, 23–4, 26, 29, 62, 81–2, 84, 88n, 90, 93, 99, 115, 169; **17**, 61; **19**, 56–7, 59, 81n, 86, 88, 93n, 130; **20**, 20–2, 25n, 164, 166; **22**, 56, 110, 151; **23**, 51, 73, 74, 85, 92, 143, 161, 166; **24**, 166; **25**, 125; **26**, 104, 107, 108; **27**, 2, 16–17, 19, 160, 192; **29**, 5, 175; **30**, 104, 134; **31**, 7, 15, 24, 25, 29, 31, 79, 83; **32**, 73, 74, 75, 145, 146, 147, 230, 232; **33**, 77n, 200; **34**, 103n, 156, 184, 188; **35**, 122, 123; **36**, 86, 104, 167, 171, 175, 180; **38**, 39, 169, 181, 232, 250; **39**, 123–6, 143, 221; **41**, 105, 112, 133–44; **42**, 4, 54–6, 59, 60, 62, 63, 65–76, 182, 196–7; **43**, 5; **44**, 34; **45**, 161; **46**, 15, 54, 56, 219, 221, 225; **47**, 127–37, 141, 145, 147–8, 149n, 253; **48**, 43; **49**, 6, 59, 62–3, 67, 100, 294, 295; **50**, 81–9, 138, 198, 251; **51**, 40, 180, 183, 190; **52**, 185; **53**, 13, 14, 15, 16n, 18, 19, 20, 21, 26, 33, 49–50, 52, 58; **54**, 6, 7, 15, 31–3, 37, 207, 224, 228, 318–19, 333; **55**, 21, 23, 25, 196–208, 346, 348–50, 367–8; **56**, 2, 27–38, 45n, 53, 56–8, 61, 82, 83, 84n, 86; **57**, 302, 306; **59**, 249, 355, 356, 367
  Amores, **15**, 29, 93, 98n, 108n
  Ars Amatoria, **13**, 159; **15**, 98n
  Fasti, **10**, 16; **12**, 141; **15**, 29, 92, 94, 97n
  Heroides, **10**, 22, 23, 26n
  Metamorphoses, **3**, 4, 6; **11**, 76, 77n, 135n; **13**, 39n; **14**, 36, 91, 92; **15**, 14, 28
    (Aldine edition in the Bodleian), **4**, 86; **10**, 14, 15, 18–20, 22–4, 25n, 26n, 40–8, 49n
  see also under Golding, Arthur
Owen, A. E. B., **41**, 114n
Owen, Cathy, **56**, 292
Owen, Clive, **43**, 213
Owen, Geoff, **42**, 155
Owen, Gwenith, **41**, 189
Owen, L., **28**, 162
Owen, Orville Ward, **46**, 235n
Owen, Peter, **51**, 4
Owen, Richard, **54**, 84
Owen, Stephen, **57**, 177
Owen, Susan J., **55**, 97n
Owen, Tom, **60**, 179
Owen, Wilfred, **39**, 169; **46**, 210
Owen, William Otway, **46**, 235n
Owens, Evan, **51**, 84n
Owens, Margaret E., **50**, 257
Owens, Roger, **35**, 160
Owens, Steve, **42**, 151
Owens, W. R., **50**, 256
Owour, Erastus, **53**, 276
Owst, G. R., **20**, 73n; **26**, 76n
Oxberry, William, **24**, 162n; **43**, 106n; **53**, 220n
Oxenford, John, **35**, 7
Oxford Book of Sixteenth-Century Verse, **46**, 224
Oxford, Earl of, his Men, *see under* Theatre, Elizabethan, companies
Oxford, Earl of, **32**, 238; **35**, 72, 75; **46**, 225; **54**, 90, 92, 94
Oxford, Edward de Vere, Seventeenth Earl of, *see under* Vere, Edward de
Oxford, Edward Harley, Second Earl of, *see under* Harley, Edward
Oxford English Dictionary, The, **5**, 20, 24n; **7**, 1, 35; **12**, 25, 37, 107, 151–2
Oxford Shakespeare Company, **58**, 307
Oxford Stage Company, **58**, 299
Oxford University, **3**, 74; **4**, 78, 81, 86, 90, 95
  Christ Church, **12**, 21n
  Oxford Movement, **4**, 81
  1605 pageant at St John's College, **4**, 39
  Trinity Hall, **12**, 16, 19
  see also under Libraries
Oxley, Philip, **44**, 123n
Oyama, Toshikazu, **18**, 167; **19**, 126, 134; **22**, 158; **23**, 154; **48**, 5
Oyama, Toshiko, **19**, 134; **48**, 5
Oyelowo, David, **55**, 288; **56**, 248, 290
Oz, Avraham, **35**, 159; **38**, 226; **43**, 230; **48**, 63n, 262; **49**, 292; **50**, 36n; **53**, 296; **54**, 182n
Ozark, Joan, **45**, 166
Ozawa, Bitaro, **14**, 121
Ozell, John, **51**, 97n
Ozu, Jiro, **11**, 121; **12**, 115; **14**, 121
Özdoğru, Nüvit, **18**, 130

Paavola, Jouko, **10**, 117, **11**, 119; **13**, 126
Pabst, G. W., **45**, 44n
Pacino, Al, **44**, 95; **51**, 265; **55**, 345, 384; **59**, 371, 372; **60**, 354–5, 356
Pack of Patentees, A., **12**, 107
Pack of Puritans, A., **12**, 107
Pack, R. A., **53**, 80n
Pack, Roger Lloyd, **54**, 293
Packard, Frederick C., Jr, **24**, 2n
Packe of Spanish lyes, A (1588), **17**, 34
Packham, Neil, **57**, 297
Packman, Simon, **45**, 155
Pacuvius, **10**, 36
Padamsee, Alyque, **51**, 278
Padel, J. H., **30**, 181; **35**, 174
Padelford, F. M., **23**, 21n; **46**, 51n
Padhi, Shanti, **30**, 184; **40**, 204
Padiila, María Enriqueta González, **54**, 154
Padrin, L., **42**, 21n
Paeper, Veronica, **49**, 271
Paéz Rios, Elena, **60**, 239n13

Pafford, J. H. P., **12**, 143; **13**, 152; **14**, 151, 152; **15**, 9; **18**, 188; **20**, 179; **21**, 148; **24**, 177; **28**, 121n; **29**, 4, 76, 183; **31**, 65n; **35**, 190; **45**, 204; **46**, 84n, 89n; **50**, 268; **54**, 244n
Pagden, A. R., **48**, 39n
Page portrait of Shakespeare, *see under* Shakespeare, William, portraits
Page, Anthony, **14**, 126
Page, John, **58**, 237
Page, Nadine, **32**, 56n
Page, R. B. le, **6**, 162
Page, R. I., **19**, 147
Page, T., **57**, 70
Page, William, **48**, 40
Paglia, Camille, **50**, 38
Pagnani, **5**, 113
Pagnini, M., **34**, 62n
Pagnol, Marcel, **9**, 112
Paige, Deborah, **46**, 202; **47**, 215; **48**, 236; **49**, 274, 280; **51**, 263; **52**, 257
Paillot, Jean Le, **10**, 115
Paine, A. B., **18**, 118n,
Paine, Robert, **50**, 70n
Paine, Thomas, **38**, 72; **57**, 128, 129, 130
Painfull Adventures, The, **52**, 317
Painter, Sidney, **48**, 78
Painter, William, **10**, 16; **20**, 18, 96, 99, 100, 101; **25**, 45, 46, 48, 52, 54, 57; **37**, 99n; **48**, 184; **49**, 1, 45–7, 87, 195n, 197, 198n; **50**, 138; **52**, 210n; **56**, 232
The Palace of Pleasure, **3**, 54; **6**, 39; **10**, 25n, 34; **14**, 53; **15**, 29
Pairy, Natasha, **39**, 81n
Pake of Knaves, A, **12**, 107
Pakledinaz, Martin, **53**, 280; **54**, 289
Paladino, Santi, **10**, 119–20
Palárik, J., **4**, 115n
Palay, Abdurrahmann, **16**, 137
Palfrey, John Graham, **24**, 101n
Palfrey, Simon, **59**, 349–50; **60**, 360
Palgrave, Sir Francis, **56**, 49
Palingenius (Marcellus Palingenius Stellatus), **9**, 25; **34**, 98, 99
Zodiacus Vitae, **8**, 145; **15**, 14, 17
Palitzsch, Peter, **23**, 174n; **37**, 161; **58**, 339
Palladio, Andrea, **30**, 160; **35**, 137; **47**, 24
Palladis Tamia, **52**, 99n
Pallant, Robert, **19**, 104; **33**, 163–4; **46**, 231; **58**, 233
Pallin, Ingemar, **5**, 114; **6**, 123
Pallis, Alex., **10**, 119
Palliser, D. M., **38**, 26n, 28n, 29n
Pallister, Janis L., **50**, 190n
Palme, Olof, **41**, 223; **51**, 199
Palme, Ulf, **14**, 123
Palmer, Alan and Veronica, **36**, 174
Palmer, Alastair, **45**, 151; **46**, 198; **47**, 218
Palmer, Christopher, **32**, 218; **45**, 147
Palmer, D. J., **21**, 134; **24**, 149; **25**, 174, 175; **26**, 154; **27**, 149, 159, 163n, 164, 165n, 167n, 170n; **28**, 104n; **29**, 3; **52**, 103n; **56**, 147n
Critical Studies, *reviewed:* (1973), **27**, 155–72
(1974), **28**, 149–64
(1975), **29**, 157–67
Palmer, Daryl W., **49**, 294; **51**, 278–9; **58**, 312, 332
Palmer, David J., **32**, 5, 7, 9, 48n, 94n, 100n; **34**, 35n, 125n, 173; **35**, 91, 92n, 97n; **37**, 6, 20n, 59, 66n, 184; **38**, 15, 54n, 187n; **39**, 96n, 217, 229n; **40**, 73, 81n, 82n, 83n, 87n; **41**, 127n; **42**, 11n; **43**, 234, 266n; **45**, 28n; **47**, 139n; **49**, 76n; **50**, 82n, 85, 88n; **53**, 2n
Palmer, J., *Ben Jonson*, **14**, 10
Palmer, John, **1**, 120; **2**, 41; **4**, 4, 5; **6**, 10–11; **8**, 1, 7, 28; **10**, 8; **27**, 31n, 32n; **44**, 1; **60**, 51n13
Comic Characters of Shakespeare, **2**, 135
Palmer, Kenneth, **37**, 205–7; **41**, 69n, 70n, 74–5; **42**, 181; **50**, 22n
Palmer, Melvin D., **57**, 74
Palmer, Michael, **52**, 265
Palmer, Mr, **22**, 128–9
Palmer, Paulina, **21**, 149
Palmer, Ralph Graham, edition of Seneca's *De Remediis Fortuitorum* noted, **10**, 146
Palmer, Richard, **41**, 190; **42**, 155; **43**, 214; **44**, 192; **45**, 155; **46**, 196
Palmer, Robert C., **57**, 312
Palmer, Rupert E., **24**, 158n
Palmer, Scott, **57**, 293; **58**, 298, 301; **59**, 343
Palmer, Thomas, **43**, 246
Palmer, W. T., **13**, 104n
Palmerston, Lord, **24**, 92; **54**, 82
Palsson, H., **26**, 164n
Paltrow, Gwyneth, **53**, 286; **58**, 347
Palumbo, Ronald J., **31**, 187
Palus, M., **60**, 37n5
Pandosto, **54**, 41
Pandurović, S., **15**, 140; **18**, 134
Panet, Bridget, **47**, 215
Panja, Shormishtha, **59**, 369
Panofsky, Erwin, **9**, 100n; **20**, 20, 21, 31; **23**, 49n; **25**, 102n, 103, 189; **26**, 57; **29**, 91; **31**, 45, 46, 47; **33**, 99n; **36**, 86n, 91n; **44**, 215; **50**, 65; **56**, 45; **60**, 103n6
Pánstwowy Instytut Wydawniczy, **11**, 121
Pantzer, Katharine F., **23**, 162n; **31**, 191; **54**, 90n; **55**, 32n
Paolucci, Anne, **15**, 166; **20**, 160; **24**, 6n; **31**, 175; **32**, 217; **45**, 89n; **49**, 46n
Papaconstantinou, Nico, **16**, 134
Papamichail, Dimitri, **16**, 134
Papavoine, Louis August, **60**, 184
Pape, Walter, **51**, 9n; **53**, 109n
Papetti, Viola, **44**, 214
Papolos, Demitri F., **45**, 20n
Papolos, Janice, **45**, 20n
Papp, Joseph, **15**, 139; **16**, 138; **31**, 173; **39**, 86n; **45**, 11, 43n; **49**, 271; **57**, 152; **58**, 355
Parabosco, *Il Pellegrino*, **3**, 90
Paracelsus (von Hohenheim), **17**, 149, 160; **19**, 36–7, 39, 40–1, 43n, 44n, 58
Paradin, Claudius, **17**, 182, 187
Paradin, George, **25**, 188
Paradise, Nathaniel Burton, **38**, 132n
Paradyse of daynty devises, The, **4**, 87; **60**, 254
Paramour, Thomas, **42**, 114
Parandowski, Jan, **10**, 120
Parasitaster, or the Fawn, **54**, 14n, 15
Pardieu, Valentine, **38**, 57, 58
see also La Motte

Paré, Ambroise, **17**, 158; **28**, 121; **38**, 180n; **50**, 187, 190n, 193, 194n, 195n; **51**, 176n
Parel, Anthony J., **48**, 93n
Parenti, Franco, **12**, 114; **13**, 129
Parey, Ambrose, **46**, 114n, 119
Parfenov, Alexandr, **52**, 284
Parfitt, David, **42**, 129
Parfitt, G. A. E., **23**, 170; **34**, 131n; **51**, 292
Parfitt, Judy, **45**, 58, 61
Paridon, Egbert van, **14**, 122
Parigi, G., **10**, 72, 76n
Parigot, Guy, **15**, 133; **18**, 123
Paris Garden, *see under* London *and* Theatres, Elizabethan
Paris, Bernard J., **44**, 208; **45**, 165; **46**, 74n, 215
Paris, Dave, **52**, 89
Paris, Jean, **9**, 14, 141
Hamlet ou Les Personnages du Fils reviewed, **8**, 140–1
Paris, Matthew, **12**, 142
Parish, Diane, **46**, 200
Parish, William A., **6**, 63n; **12**, 107
Park, Clara Claiborne, **40**, 92n
Park, Clare, **59**, 334
Park, Katharine, **50**, 187n, 194n
Park, Roy, **37**, 185
Park, The, **43**, 210
Park, Thomas, **38**, 20; **49**, 119
Parke, Francis, **19**, 101–2, 105n, 107n
Parker, A. A., **23**, 84n, 88n; **35**, 108n
Parker, Andrew, **46**, 114n; **50**, 20n; **51**, 19n
Parker, Anthony, **60**, 186n11
Parker, Barbara L., **25**, 181; **49**, 64n, 289; **58**, 332; **59**, 362–3, 368
Parker, Brian, **55**, 43n
Parker, David, **24**, 153
Parker, Dorothy, **28**, 91
Parker, Douglas H., **36**, 194
Parker, Francis, **19**, 106n
Parker, Fred, **49**, 293
Parker, G. F., **43**, 220–1; **44**, 207; **51**, 7; **55**, 103n; **59**, 124n1
Parker, Geoffrey, **38**, 57n
Parker, Hershel, **43**, 1n
Parker, J., **37**, 47
Parker, James, **49**, 120
Parker, John, **25**, 148; **57**, 145, 154; **58**, 172
Parker, Kenneth, **52**, 154n; **54**, 307
Parker, Kirsten, **56**, 267
Parker, Louis N., **60**, 186–7
Parker, Lynne, **54**, 266–7; **55**, 323; **56**, 287
Parker, Marion D. H., **28**, 19n; **37**, 92
The Slave of Life reviewed, **10**, 135–6
Parker, Matthew (Archbishop), **57**, 200
Parker, Mr, **14**, 113
Parker, Nathaniel, **43**, 188
Parker, Oliver, **44**, 199; **51**, 265; **55**, 384; **58**, 185; **60**, 169, 354
Parker, Patricia, **40**, 82n, 189; **41**, 106n; **42**, 164n; **43**, 26n, 224, 253n; **44**, 33n; **45**, 40n; **46**, 7, 45n, 75, 82n, 91, 99, 100, 105n, 134n, 210; **47**, 131n; **48**, 26n, 256–7, 262; **49**, 59n, 205n, 207n, 208, 285; **50**, 237–8, 242; **51**, 295; **52**, 202n, 270; **53**, 12n, 14, 15n, 16, 18, 41n, 298; **54**, 132n, 239n, 244n, 306; **55**, 5n, 342; **56**, 39–54, 71, 75, 313; **57**, 196, 198, 221; **58**, 351
Parker, R. B., **18**, 175; **34**, 182n; **39**, 216; **48**, 282, 285–7; **51**, 213n; **56**, 171n
Parker, Robert W., **26**, 174n
Parker, Roger, **57**, 65
Parker, Roscoe E., **17**, 191
Parker, T. H. L., **46**, 25n
Parker, Theodore, **53**, 131n
Parkes, H. B., **5**, 141
Parkes, Shaun, **49**, 278; **60**, 308–9
Parkes-Davies, Nigel, **44**, 195
Parkhurst, Bishop John (of Norwich), **52**, 60
Parkinson, John, **51**, 84n, 85n, 89; **56**, 41n
Parkinson, Sydney, **55**, 170
Parkinson, Thomas, **49**, 118
Parks, George Bruner, **17**, 40n, 44n; **23**, 164; **32**, 86n, 87n, 88n
Parks, Stephen, **46**, 19n
Parks, Suzan-Lori, **52**, 33–4
Parmigianino, **26**, 50, 54
Parnassus plays, the, see under *Pilgrimage to Parnassus*, and *Return from Parnassus*
Parnell, Charles Stuart, **56**, 144
Parny, Viscount de (1753–1814), **5**, 93
Paroissien, H. F., **59**, 42
Parolin, Peter A., **57**, 313; **59**, 354; **60**, 357, 360
Parr, Anthony, **43**, 270n; **50**, 255; **56**, 149n
Parr, Brian, **43**, 154
Parr, Katherine, **43**, 51; **46**, 17
Parr, Wolstenholme, **34**, 12
Parrish, S. M., **16**, 179
Parrish, Sue, **47**, 210, **58**, 298
Parrot, Henry, **23**, 237
Parrott, Kenneth, **15**, 144
Parrott, Thomas Marc, **3**, 24, 136, 145, 146; **4**, 5; **8**, 1, 2, 4, 7; **9**, 6, 45, 48n; **10**, 2, 4, 70n; **26**, 4, 173; **37**, 11; **55**, 17n
(ed.) *The Comedies of George Chapman*, **14**, 8
(ed.) *The Tragedies of George Chapman*, **14**, 8
The Parrott Presentation Volume, **14**, 11
The Plays and Poems of George Chapman, **15**, 40n
'*Pericles*: The Play and the Novel' reviewed, **3**, 150–1
Shakespearean Comedy reviewed, **4**, 143
Parry, Christopher, **43**, 212; **45**, 145; **46**, 196; **49**, 142n
Parry, Graham, **47**, 237
Parry, Natasha, **13**, 138; **45**, 146; **55**, 301
Parry, P. H., **46**, 7
Parry, R. St J., **10**, 14, 25n
Parry, Simon, **51**, 266
Parry, Vivien, **54**, 287
Parry, William, **54**, 95
Parslow, Nicci, **41**, 187
Parsons, Howard, **5**, 140
Parsons, Philip, **18**, 160
'Shakespeare and the Mask', **16**, 121–31
Parsons, Robert D., **1**, 68; **23**, 161n; **35**, 177; **38**, 97; **52**, 281; **54**, 91, 93n, 94, 95n; **56**, 32, 184, 192–5, 199; **57**, 70
Conference about the Next Succession, **1**, 124
Parsons, Thomas, **58**, 229
Parsons, William Barclay, **23**, 163
Partee, Morris H., **25**, 182
Partridge, A. C., **6**, 6; **7**, 4, 6; **8**, 121, 159, 160; **9**, 115; **10**, 121; **11**, 122; **12**, 116; **15**, 30, 160n; **18**, 128, 186; **31**, 191–2

The Problem of Henry VIII Reopened reviewed, **4**, 159–60
'Shakespeare's Orthography in *Venus and Adonis* and some early quartos', **7**, 35–47
Partridge, Bernard, **13**, 79
Partridge, David, **57**, 296
Partridge, E. B., **33**, 184
The Broken Compass, **14**, 11
Partridge, Eric, **15**, 40n; **27**, 18, 189; **32**, 100n, 103n, 104n; **37**, 124n, 128n; **40**, 117; **46**, 131n, 132n; **51**, 325, 335; **56**, 229n
Shakespeare's Bawdy, **2**, 144
Partridge, Phil, **42**, 158
Paryla, Katja, **52**, 284
Pascal, Blaise, **22**, 16; **29**, 89; **36**, 45
Pascal, Julia, **54**, 286; **56**, 291
Paschall, William, **60**, 51
Pasco, Richard, **7**, 125; **25**, 166, 169, 170; **27**, 149, 150, 152; **28**, 140; **31**, 153, 154; **39**, 240; **40**, 223; **50**, 49
Pascoe, David, **51**, 291; **53**, 103n; **56**, 336
Pasinetti, P. M., **8**, 120
Pasqualigo, Luigi, **14**, 25, 28
Il Fidele, **14**, 27
Pasquier, Paul, **5**, 115
Passe, Magdalen and William, **1**, 33
Passe, Simon van de, **1**, 32
Passionate Pilgrim, **1**, 60, 75, 131; **4**, 85; **5**, 50, 53; **6**, 58; **7**, 53; **9**, 85; **60**, 252–66
Pasta, Mme G., **3**, 100; **21**, 81
Paster, Gail Kern, **30**, 192; **33**, 201; **38**, 128n; **46**, 7, 125n; **48**, 26n; **49**, 212n; **51**, 178n; **53**, 94–5, 96, 298; **54**, 323; **55**, 240, 249n, 340, 374; **58**, 249, 250, 251, 255, 257, 258; **59**, 350, 351, 368
Pasternak, Boris, **1**, 114, 116; **4**, 125; **5**, 117; **6**, 125; **15**, 136; **21**, 11n; **24**, 41; **31**, 175; **39**, 83; **40**, 200–1; **42**, 150; **54**, 150; **56**, 303
Paston, Sir John, **32**, 137
Paston, Lady Katherine, **17**, 227
Paston, Margery, **32**, 137
Pastore, Annibale, **5**, 113
Paszkowski, Józef, **10**, 120; **14**, 122
Patan, Federico, **54**, 154n
Patch, Cardinal Wolsey's Fool, **13**, 100, 104n
Patch, Howard R., **44**, 35n; **49**, 73
Patel, Jyoti, **43**, 213
Pater, Walter Horatio, **4**, 2, 22; **6**, 12; **15**, 19; **22**, 8, 155; **25**, 1; **27**, 146; **28**, 104, 105; **37**, 147, 148n; **38**, 196; **39**, 240; **45**, 44; **56**, 142; **59**, 264
Patericke, Simon, **56**, 225
Paterson, Alan, **51**, 264
Paterson, Caroline, **45**, 156; **47**, 213
Paterson, John, **5**, 133; **30**, 85n
Paterson, Joseph, **56**, 280n
Pateson, William, **60**, 21
Pätges, Christian, **29**, 145
Patmore, Coventry, **7**, 33
Paton, Sir Joseph Noel, **37**, 48–51
Paton, Ruth, **54**, 291
Patrichi, Gina, **45**, 146
Patrick, Anna, **44**, 199
Patrick, David L., **3**, 23; **6**, 4; **7**, 153; **8**, 157; **19**, 163; **23**, 179; **25**, 193; **30**, 209; **49**, 332; **51**, 313
Patrick, F. J., 'The Birmingham Shakespeare Memorial Library', **7**, 90–4
Patrick, J. Max, **8**, 141
Patrick, Julian, **34**, 138n
Patrick, Nathaniel, **15**, 173
Patrides, C. A., **20**, 159
'Patridophilus, Joan.' (*pseud.*), **60**, 277n36
Patrizi, Francesco, **54**, 29n
Patston, Peter, **60**, 169
Patten, William, **42**, 28n
Patterson, Alex, **52**, 266
Patterson, Annabel, **42**, 190; **43**, 56, 240–1, 265n, 266; **44**, 18n, 20n, 209; **47**, 62n; **49**, 285–7; **50**, 254, 276; **51**, 322, 333; **52**, 114, 325; **53**, 65n, 70n, 72n; **54**, 11n; **55**, 6; **56**, 335
Patterson, Frank Allen, **14**, 100n; **54**, 61n
Patterson, Lee, **44**, 151n
Patterson, Michael, **37**, 161n
Patterson, Ronan, **41**, 189; **42**, 151
Patterson, Steve, **54**, 299
Patterson, T., **8**, 127
Patterson, W. B., **59**, 250n81, 252n94
Patterson-Hannay, Margaret, **43**, 57n
Pattinson, Maria, **45**, 149; **52**, 264
Pattison, B., **15**, 7, 8
Pattison, John, **45**, 152
Pattison, Mark, **14**, 98; **17**, 42n; **54**, 80
Patton, Cindy, **50**, 19n
Paturel, Domenique, **18**, 122
Paul III, Pope, **32**, 93n
Paul IV, Pope, **35**, 105
Paul's Boys, The, **47**, 243; **52**, 82, 134
Paul, Anthony, **47**, 234
Paul, David, **15**, 146
Paul, Henry N., **1**, 73, 128; **3**, 27, 29, 30; **4**, 38, 47n; **6**, 33n; **15**, 111; **19**, 2–4, 45, 52, 58, 82, 93n; **21**, 52n; **25**, 111; **26**, 85n; **28**, 123n; **55**, 265; **56**, 215n; **57**, 2, 27, 30, 55, 68
'The First Performance of *Macbeth*', **2**, 148
The Royal Play of 'Macbeth', **13**, 40n, 163
Paul, Kate, **45**, 155; **47**, 214
Paul, St, *see* St Paul
Paulding, J. K., **18**, 103
Paulfreyman, Thomas, **32**, 163n
Paulhan, Jean, **57**, 119
Paulin, Bernard, **19**, 130
Paulin, Roger, **53**, 298–9; **57**, 112; **58**, 312, 332
Pauling, Nicholas, **60**, 290
Pauls, Peter, **55**, 14n
Paulsen, Carl, **15**, 146
Paulson, Ronald, **48**, 57n
Pausanias, **22**, 17; **25**, 103
Pauvert, J.-J., **21**, 86n
Pauwels, Henric, **60**, 240, 251
Pavelka, Michael, **48**, 232; **50**, 235; **53**, 285; **54**, 294; **55**, 324, 327; **56**, 290, 291
Pavier, Thomas, **22**, 181–2; **27**, 181, 182, 185; **32**, 238; **36**, 191, 192n; **38**, 91n; **40**, 219; **44**, 114; **46**, 252; **52**, 136; **55**, 390; **60**, 266
Pavier-Jaggard Quartos, 1619, *see under* Shakespeare, editions
Pavis, Patrice, **52**, 162–3
Pavy, Salathiel (Salomon), **1**, 44; **58**, 223
Pawar, Ram, **60**, 301

Pawlo, Toivo, **15**, 138
Payne, B. Iden, **6**, 124; **9**, 117; **10**, 122; **12**, 118; **16**, 138, **32**, 35n; **36**, 73; **41**, 57; **47**, 95
Payne, John, **43**, 105n, 150, 155–69
Payne, Laurence, **1**, 109, 110; **8**, 124
Payne, M., **28**, 155
Payne, R. J. G., **8**, 123; **9**, 119; **13**, 134; **15**, 144
Payne, Robert, **11**, 102
Payne, Waveney, R. N., **24**, 169; **51**, 3
Payne, William, **60**, 44
Payton, John, **56**, 186, 187
Paz, Octavio, **54**, 164
Peabody, O. W. B., **18**, 108
Peacham, Henry, **1**, 17, 19, 21–2; **7**, 135; **10**, 71; **14**, 107; **17**, 183; **25**, 188; **26**, 98; **32**, 234; **38**, 248; **40**, 97; **41**, 107; **47**, 23n, 29; **50**, 60n, 75; **51**, 143; **53**, 13, 15n, 17, 19n, 21; **55**, 24n; **56**, 42n, 43
The Compleat Gentleman, **1**, 19, 21, 22
Emblemata Varia (MS.), **1**, 21, 71
illustration of *Titus Andronicus*, **3**, 146–7
Sketch of Aaron, **11**, 89
Peacock, John, **55**, 250
Peacock, Philip, **44**, 196
Peacock, Trevor, **51**, 255; **56**, 120
Peak, Phillipa, **57**, 296
Peake, Bladon, **47**, 95, 106
Peake, Joseph J. S., **36**, 86n
Peake, Richard, **48**, 262
Peake, Robert, **56**, 218
Pearce, F. M., **26**, 154; **28**, 162
Pearce, Joanne, **45**, 141; **47**, 183–4; **51**, 228–9
Pearce, Josephine A., **8**, 143
Pearce, Mike, **44**, 192
Pearce, Oscar, **51**, 225
Pearce, Simon, **49**, 276
Pearce, Susan M, **50**, 190n
Pearce, T. M., **14**, 142
Pearce, Zachary, **51**, 137
Pearl, Daniel, **57**, 126
Pearl, Valerie, **54**, 331
Pearlman, Edward, **24**, 167; **41**, 227; **46**, 215; **48**, 243; **49**, 12, 39; **53**, 47; **54**, 55n; **56**, 330; **57**, 145, 155; **58**, 45
Pearmain, Vincent, **5**, 119
Pearn, B. R., **32**, 154n
Pears, D. F., **48**, 120n
Pears, Peter, **49**, 307
Pearsall, Leslie E. F., **20**, 163
Pearson, A. H., **49**, 190n
Pearson, D'Orsay W., **28**, 163, 173; **31**, 4n, 6n; **34**, 176; **43**, 1n, 268
Pearson, Hesketh, **4**, 6; **35**, 9; **46**, 184n; **56**, 130n
Pearson, Jacquelyn, **35**, 178, 179; **36**, 176; **51**, 68, 70, 71, 293; **55**, 23–4
Pearson, John, **14**, 13
Pearson, Karl, **24**, 97
Pearson, Lu Emily, **15**, 20, 21
Pearson, M. N., **52**, 211n
Pearson, Mike, **60**, 154, 155
Pearson, Norman Holmes, **9**, 134
Pearson, Richard, **60**, 322
Pearson, Roberta, **60**, 355
Peasgood, Julie, **33**, 172, 173
Peaslee, Richard, **24**, 126
Peat, Derek, **35**, 166–7; **36**, 172; **38**, 161n
Pebworth, Ted-Larry, **48**, 254
Pecci-Blunt, Anna Laetitia, **14**, 121
Pecheux, M. Christopher, Mother, **29**, 175
Pechter, Edward, **32**, 221; **33**, 202; **40**, 202; **41**, 195n, 222; **43**, 17n; **44**, 85n; **49**, 281; **51**, 273–4; **54**, 334; **56**, 303; **57**, 83; **58**, 326, 332, 349, 356; **59**, 32n58, 32n61, 383
Peck, Bob, **29**, 152; **33**, 169, 174, 176; **36**, 151, 154; **37**, 173; **51**, 263
Peck, Francis, **17**, 11n
Peck, John, **55**, 352
Peck, Linda Levy, **55**, 374
Peck, Russell A., **22**, 162; **38**, 154n
Peckham, Sir George, **54**, 230n
Peckham, Morse, **56**, 169, 170n; **59**, 27n32
Pécsi, Sándor, **16**, 135
Pederson, Lauritz, **22**, 124n
Pedicord, Harry William, **36**, 180; **43**, 105n; **48**, 51n; **51**, 23n, 54; **54**, 49n; **55**, 96n; **57**, 59
Pedley, Anthony, **27**, 153
Peel, Albert, **6**, 60
Peel, Bill, **41**, 58n
Peel, Edward, **48**, 199
Peel, Sir Robert, **45**, 93
Peel, William, **31**, 188
Peele, George, **2**, 120; **3**, 24, 45, 145; **4**, 7, 56, 59, 60, 62, 91, 95, 149; **5**, 139, 150–1; **6**, 39, 40, 72, 169; **7**, 82, 138, 140, 142, 147; **8**, 56, 103, 157; **10**, 2, 12, 60, 69, 70n, 144; **14**, 7, 44n, 82; **15**, 63, 113, 114; **16**, 167; **17**, 172, 201–2; **21**, 131; **23**, 117, 169; **24**, 162; **27**, 130, 132, 135; **28**, 4, 119n; **30**, 79, 121, 198; **33**, 158; **38**, 132, 134, 143, 247; **39**, 217; **42**, 55; **43**, 268; **45**, 91, 184; **47**, 113, **50**, 287–8; **52**, 287; **53**, 180; **54**, 57n; **55**, 23, 24n, 29n, 30n, 199n, 280; **56**, 280, 312; **57**, 335, 336; **58**, 253; **59**, 5, 73
Anglorum Feriae, Englandes Hollydayes, **3**, 52
Battle of Alcazar, **7**, 85, 151
Edward I, **1**, 64; **6**, 36
Honour of the Garter, **3**, 24, 145
King David and Fair Bethsabe, **1**, 64; **5**, 150
Old Wives' Tale, The, **2**, 124; **4**, 42–3; **5**, 141; **15**, 113; **55**, 24n
Pageant before Woolstone Dixie, The, **4**, 92
Soliman and Perseda, **13**, 110n
Peele, James, **17**, 68–9
Peend, Thomas, **23**, 166; **56**, 29n; **60**, 272n13
Peers, E. Allison, **56**, 83n
Peerson, Martin, **11**, 100–6
Mottects or Grave Chamber Musicke, **11**, 105
Private Musicke, **11**, 105
Peery, William, **5**, 142
Pegg, Barry, **53**, 28
Pegg, Nicholas, **50**, 227
Pegge, Samuel, **18**, 17; **35**, 178, 188n
Peguilhan, Aimeric de, **15**, 98n
peine forte et dure, la, **17**, 91 and n, 92n
Peisley, Frederick, **12**, 121
Peleg, Frank, **9**, 114
Pelham, Henry, **48**, 58
Pelham-Holles, Thomas, Earl of Clare, **51**, 52n
Pelikan, Jaroslav, **28**, 53n; **54**, 43n, 139n

Pelka, Valentine, **48**, 288
Pellegrini, Giuliano, **17**, 184n
Pelling, G. B. R., **42**, 196
Pelling, Margaret, **55**, 37n
Peltrault, Claude, **48**, 248; **50**, 196n; **54**, 225n
Shakespeare, La Tempête: Etudes Critiques, **48**, 248
Pember, John, **42**, 159
Pember, Ron, **28**, 144, 145, 146; **45**, 149
Pemberton, Caroline, **49**, 176n
Pemberton, Cathy, **46**, 195
Pembroke Players, **50**, 226
Pembroke's Men, *see under* Theatre, Elizabethan, companies
Pembroke, 5th Earl of, **44**, 240
Pembroke, Countess of, *see* Herbert, Mary
Pembroke, Earl and Countess of, *see under* Herbert, William *and* Mary
Pembroke, Earls of, *see* Herbert, Philip; Herbert, William
Pempelfort, Dr Karl, **48**, 62n
Penasco, S. A., **10**, 139
Pendleton, Thomas A., **42**, 181, 212n; **43**, 263; **44**, 222; **56**, 89n; **59**, 161n17
Pendry, E. D., **27**, 178; **52**, 123n, 125n, 127n; **55**, 84n
Penelope, a Dramatic Opera, **55**, 89
Peniall, Richard, **45**, 113, 114n
Penkethman, William, **51**, 47
Penley, S., and family, **3**, 100
Pennafort, Onestaldo de, **20**, 122, 123
Pennell, Nicholas, **31**, 145; **39**, 180–3, 185, 188; **40**, 156, 158, 168
Penniman, J. H., **1**, 50
Pennington family,
Heloise, **13**, 97
John (Lord Muncaster), **13**, 92
Joseph, **13**, 92, 93
Maria Margaret Frances, **13**, 92
Nicholas, **13**, 93, 94
William (d. 1652), **13**, 92
Sir William, (1655–1730), **13**, 92–3, 96, 104n
Pennington, Mary, **49**, 303
Pennington, Michael, **28**, 147, 148; **30**, 175; **32**, 206, 207, 208; **34**, 153; **38**, 234; **39**, 108; **41**, 121, 160–1, 185; **42**, 129, 161; **43**, 172, 178–81, 183–4; **45**, 130, 132, 146, 156; **46**, 202; **47**, 212, 219; **48**, 21; **49**, 236, 238, 271; **53**, 249–52; **54**, 274, 293; **56**, 96, 175, 257; **57**, 264; **60**, 205
Pennington-Ramsden, Sir William, **13**, 90, 104n, 105n
Pennsylvania University Library, *see under* Libraries
Pennycuicke, Andrew, **58**, 238
Penrose, B., **17**, 38 and n., 40
Penry, John, **17**, 126; **54**, 96
Journal, **6**, 60
Penry-Jones, Rupert, **53**, 250
Pensky, Max, **55**, 76n, 78
Pentelow, Arthur, **47**, 97–8
Penzance, Lord, **18**, 112
Peover, Matt, **58**, 300
Pepperall, Ian, **51**, 258; **53**, 281
Pepys, Elizabeth, **46**, 9
Pepys, *see under* Libraries
Pepys, Mrs Samuel, **10**, 15
Pepys, Samuel, **1**, 28; **10**, 15, 150; **13**, 108, 113, 119; **18**, 35, 38; **22**, 57; **29**, 135; **37**, 58; **43**, 96–8; **49**, 302; **51**, 80; **52**, 148–9; **53**, 200n; **55**, 267; **56**, 118, 119; **57**, 69; **58**, 243; **60**, 47n59
Pequigney, Joseph, **46**, 5, 208; **48**, 254
Peraldus, Guillaume, **14**, 142
Perceval, Luk, **59**, 298; **60**, 286–7
Percival, Richard, **57**, 204
Percy, Algernon, 10th Earl of Northumberland, **11**, 111
Percy, Bishop Thomas, **4**, 85, 86; **15**, 1, 7; **20**, 86; **39**, 154
Reliques of Ancient English Poetry, **13**, 47n; **14**, 81
Percy, C. H. Herford, **52**, 190n
Percy, Sir Charles, **1**, 45; **28**, 6
Percy, Esmé, **2**, 4; **52**, 28n
Percy, Henry, 8th Earl of Northumberland, **3**, 10, 25; **11**, 75
Percy, Sir Jocelyn, **28**, 6
Percy, Robert, **32**, 194
Percy, Sir Thomas, **26**, 40; **33**, 16, 18; **48**, 71; **55**, 86n; **58**, 78
Percy, William, **17**, 202; **32**, 101; **52**, 82; **59**, 72, 75, 76, 77n12
Comedies and Pastorals, **6**, 60
The Faerie Pastoral, **13**, 120
Perera, Suvendrini, **55**, 180n
Pereson, Edward, **6**, 67, 68, 69, 74n
Pereson, John, **6**, 69
Pérez, Antonio, **12**, 141; **14**, 102, 108 n; **31**, 179
Pérez, Manuel, **54**, 154
Perez de Moya, Juan, **23**, 84, 85
Perinet, Joachim, **56**, 151n
Perkin, John, **60**, 21
Perkin, R. L., **16**, 172n
Perkins, Benjamin, **48**, 234
Perkins, Clare, **43**, 207; **46**, 201
Perkins, Jocelyn, **54**, 124n, 125n; **60**, 112n42
Perkins, Matthew, **54**, 284
Perkins, Maxwell, **44**, 118
Perkins, Richard, **7**, 57, 58, 59, 60, 62–3, 64, 65, 67n, 86–7; **9**, 147; **16**, 96; **33**, 164; **47**, 110
Perkins, V. F., **39**, 85
Perkins, William, **2**, 76; **13**, 85; **27**, 83n, 84, 85–8, 90, 91; **28**, 92, 102; **33**, 93; **36**, 162; **38**, 30, 31n; **43**, 7, 61, 237; **54**, 10; **55**, 228, 229; **57**, 244
Christian Equity, **2**, 68, 70, 74–5
Christian Oeconomie, **13**, 88n
Exposition, **2**, 69
Perkinson, R. H., **14**, 11
Pern, Beadle, **11**, 108–9
Perondinus, Petrus, **47**, 177n, 179
Perowne Petersen, Richard F., **54**, 76, 77n
Perowne, J. J. Stewart (Dean of Peterborough), **54**, 134n, 185
Perowne, S. J., **54**, 169n
Perrello, Tony, **52**, 278
Perret, Marion D., **38**, 224n; **59**, 157n1; **60**, 88–9n10
Perrett, A. J., **3**, 147; **5**, 138
Perrett, Wilfrid, **3**, 18; **4**, 9; **26**, 36n, 41n; **27**, 173; **33**, 16n; **55**, 13, 14n, 20–1, 22n, 25
Perrière, Guillaume de la, **17**, 182
Perrin, Alan, **45**, 153
Perrin, Noel, **20**, 163
Perrineau, Harold, **52**, 95
Perring, Philip, **32**, 245
Perry, Clive, **41**, 191
Perry, Curtis, **52**, 295; **55**, 346; **57**, 118
Perry, J. Marsden, **9**, 82

Perry, Thomas A., **8**, 142
Perry, Thomas W., **48**, 51n, 53, 56n
Perry, William, **58**, 235
Perryman, Judith C., **38**, 233
Person, James E., Jr, **43**, 237
Person, Robert, **55**, 229
Personn (Persen), Johann, **22**, 119–21, 123
Persons, George, **29**, 29
Persons, Robert, **17**, 121–4, 127–8; **24**, 71, 72, 74; **28**, 166; **29**, 22, 29, 30; **54**, 116
Pertwee, Sean, **41**, 178; **53**, 278
Perucci, **55**, 248n
Perugino, **26**, 54
Pescetti, Orlando, *Cesare*, **10**, 4–5
Pessanda, Jillia, **60**, 175–6
Pessoni, Michele, **46**, 218
Petöfi, Sándor, **3**, 117; **39**, 236; **53**, 319; **59**, 124, 125–6, 135
Petcher, Edward, **56**, 301
Petcher, Stephen, **42**, 162
Petelius, Pirkka Pekka, **43**, 147
Peter Hall Company, **58**, 298
Peter Martyr, *see* Anglerius
Péter, András, **3**, 117
Peter, John, **41**, 53; **43**, 188–9, 200; **47**, 186; **48**, 223; **52**, 42–3, 115–16, 230; **56**, 236, 238n, 239
Peter, William, **43**, 258–9
Peters, Antony, **46**, 193
Peters, Arthur King, **49**, 129n
Peters, Catherine, **58**, 155
Peters, Clarke, **44**, 199
Peters, Colin, **57**, 258, 266
Peters, Helen, **42**, 195; **46**, 112n
Peters, John, **42**, 155
Peters, Revd Matthew, **49**, 122
Petersen, Per Serritslev, **57**, 149
Petersen, Robert P., **56**, 73n
Peterson, D'Orsay W., **53**, 54n
Peterson, Douglas L., **9**, 143n; **19**, 130, 134; **27**, 169; **29**, 11n, 16n, 53n; **33**, 125; **43**, 131, 133
Peterson, Wolfgang, **59**, 371
Petherbridge, Edward, **38**, 213; **42**, 200; **44**, 94n; **51**, 228–9, 234, 235–6, 244, 268; **54**, 295; **56**, 247
Petherbridge, Jonathan, **41**, 190; **42**, 155; **43**, 205, 208, 214; **46**, 201; **47**, 214; **53**, 279; **56**, 267; **57**, 294, 295
Petit, J.-P., **41**, 228
Petit, Jacques, **14**, 102–4, 107–9; **16**, 165
Petit-Dutaillis, C., *see under* Dutaillis
Petitt, W., **30**, 188
Petowe, Henry, **57**, 222, 223, 224
Petrarch (Francesco Pertarca), **1**, 68; **3**, 15; **4**, 49, 93; **7**, 101; **15**, 34, 95, 98n, 101, 106, 109n; **16**, 12, 125, 127, 131; **23**, 69; **28**, 49; **34**, 85, 95; **37**, 70; **40**, 75; **42**, 4; **43**, 228, 234; **46**, 14, 16; **48**, 286n; **49**, 6, 48, 51–2, 57, 59, 61, 63, 67, 70, 74, 76, 77, 85, 92, 99, 100, 101, 105, 107, 109, 168, 295; **53**, 224; **54**, 318; **56**, 36, 84, 85, 305; **59**, 262, 265; **60**, 234
Petrenko, A., **39**, 83n
Petrić, A., **18**, 134
Petro, Patrice, **45**, 45
Petronella, Vincent F., **28**, 153, 154, 159, 160; **33**, 201; **40**, 204
Petrović, V., **18**, 134
Petrus Lavinius, **56**, 56n
Petry, Michael John, **27**, 177
Pett, John, **19**, 103
Pett, Peter and Phineas, ship designers, **17**, 22
Pettegree, Andrew, **54**, 1n
Pettet, E. C, **2**, 139n, 144; **4**, 150; **5**, 135; **7**, 5, 8; **8**, 3, 11, 113; **9**, 137; **10**, 11; **26**, 98; **28**, 63n, 86n; **29**, 106n; **38**, 129n; **53**, 69, 70
'*Coriolanus* and the Midlands Insurrection of 1607', **3**, 34–42
Shakespeare and the Romance Tradition reviewed, **4**, 143–4
Petti, Anthony G., **31**, 191, 193; **48**, 72n; **54**, 92n
Pettie, George, **31**, 168n, 169n; **41**, 138; **49**, 64; **50**, 69; **60**, 272n13
A Petite Pallace of Pettie his Pleasure, **10**, 41, 43, 45, 49n, 69
Pettie, John, **49**, 123, 294
Pettigrew, H. P., **8**, 5
Pettigrew, Henry, **60**, 310
Pettigrew, John, **25**, 174; **30**, 45n
Pettingell, Frank, **18**, 70
Pettitt, Henry, **29**, 136
Pettitt, Thomas, **37**, 190
Petursson, Sigfus Mar, **57**, 287
Petworth House, **11**, 152
Pevsner, Nikolaus, **35**, 129n
Peymann, Claus, **58**, 340; **60**, 316–17
Peyre, Henri, **20**, 159
Peyré, Yves, **48**, 145n; **50**, 257; **55**, 350; **56**, 329
Peyret, Jean-François, **50**, 128
Pezold, Dieter, **53**, 168n
Pezzana, Giacinta, **54**, 154
Pfeiffer, Michelle, **52**, 257; **54**, 290; **58**, 185
Pfeiffer, Rolf, **37**, 159n
Pfister, Eva, **50**, 37n
Pfister, Manfred, **28**, 159; **37**, 17n, 158; **42**, 166; **43**, 223, 249; **45**, 162; **55**, 196n; **56**, 235n, 315; **58**, 312
Phaedrus, **4**, 65
see also Aesop's *Fables*
Phaer, Thomas, **42**, 54n; **56**, 57, 65; **57**, 217
translation of *Aeneid*, **10**, 25n
Phares-Matthews, Dee Ann, **59**, 161
Pharmacopoeia Londinensis, **17**, 160–1
Phayre, Thomas, **50**, 21n
Phelan, Gerald B., **55**, 213n
Phelan, James, **59**, 89n34
Phelan, Peggy, **60**, 360
Pheloung, Barrington, **48**, 233
Phelps, Charles E., **29**, 94, 95, 96
Phelps, Henry P., **56**, 100n
Phelps, Samuel, **2**, 1, 2–3, 19; **9**, 56; **10**, 74; **11**, 124; **13**, 77; **16**, 33, 104, 112, 113; **19**, 153n, 154; **23**, 173n; **25**, 113, 115; **35**, 3, 9, 12, 20; **37**, 199; **38**, 188, 189, 191, 192, 194–9; **41**, 23–4, 28; **52**, 288; **53**, 229, 239; **54**, 335; **56**, 111, 130; **57**, 326
Phelps, Wayne H., **33**, 203
Phialas, Peter G., **13**, 156; **18**, 169; **19**, 123, 135; **20**, 155; **21**, 130; **24**, 57n, 60n; **32**, 9; **34**, 131n; **37**, 13; **38**, 8, 10, 11n
Philaster (Beaumont and Fletcher), **48**, 259
Philidor, P. A. D., **60**, 184
Philip II, King of Spain, **4**, 155; **12**, 5; **13**, 104n; **14**, 102; **24**, 155; **29**, 22, 27; **35**, 108; **38**, 57; **59**, 246
Philip III, King of Spain, **17**, 26; **23**, 86; **29**, 30, 32n; **33**, 162

Philip, David, **52**, 159n
Philip, I. G., **4**, 96n
Philip, Jules, **48**, 228
Philip Julius, Duke of Wolgast, **32**, 197; **36**, 144–5
Philip, Prince, Duke of Edinburgh, **13**, 130
Philip, Ranjini, **46**, 218
Philipe, Gerard, **16**, 133
Philippide, Alexandru, **20**, 127
Philippou, Nick, **50**, 236; **54**, 292
Philips, Augustine, **11**, 62
Philips, Edward, **14**, 101n
Philips, Julian, **55**, 322; **56**, 273
Philips, Katherine, *Horace*, **1**, 66
Pompey the Great, **1**, 66
Phillip, John, *Patient Grissell* (1568–9), **7**, 144
Phillipou, Nick, **55**, 326
Phillips, A., **57**, 232
Phillips, Ambrose, *Distressed Mother*, **10**, 76n
Phillips, Angela, **45**, 149
Phillips, Augustine, **28**, 6, 7; **40**, 231; **45**, 107; **58**, 69; **60**, 56
Phillips, Edward, **6**, 57
Phillips, G. W., **15**, 14
Phillips, Gary, **54**, 76n, 77n
Phillips, Graham, **50**, 65n
Phillips, Hugh, **30**, 164n
Phillips, James, **58**, 301
Phillips, James Emerson, **10**, 8; **19**, 137; **29**, 83, 84; **31**, 6; **54**, 138n
Phillips, Johnny, **1**, 111; **51**, 97n; **52**, 209n; **54**, 126n; **58**, 285; **59**, 343
Phillips, Leslie, **51**, 235
Phillips, Margaret, **31**, 81n
Phillips, Neil, **45**, 151
Phillips, O. Hood, **19**, 149; **26**, 171
Phillips, Robin, **24**, 121, 129; **31**, 141, 143, 144; **34**, 158, 159, 160; **36**, 60, 63; **39**, 179, 183, 185; **40**, 159, 162, 165
Phillips, Ronald Selwyn, **47**, 216, 217
Phillips, Thomas, **47**, 55n; **51**, 117, 118
Phillips, Tom, **52**, 266
Philomusus, **35**, 81
Philosophers Banquet, The, **20**, 162
Philostratus, **25**, 100n; **31**, 16, 17, 19
Phipps, C. J., **47**, 92
Phipson, Emma, **6**, 48n; **18**, 52
Phocas, Andonis, **16**, 134
Phoenix, The, **52**, 134
Physicians, Royal College of, **17**, 69, 71, 148, 152–7, 160–1, 166
Physiologus, **17**, 151
Piachaud, René-Louis, **10**, 118; **11**, 119; **14**, 123; **42**, 181
translation of *Othello*, **3**, 105; **8**, 121
Piave, Francesco, **57**, 64, 116
Picasso, Pablo, **12**, 12; **29**, 177
Piccini, A., **60**, 37n5
Piccoli, Fantasio, **16**, 136
Pichois, C., **18**, 174
Pichot, Amadée, **57**, 115
Picinelli, Filippo, **29**, 29
Pickard, David, **42**, 156
Pickard, John, **52**, 263
Pickavance, Robert, **53**, 261
Pickering, Anne, **46**, 229n
Pickering, Danby, **52**, 208n
Pickering, Roger, **51**, 112
Pickering, William, **18**, 19; **49**, 79n
Pickeryng, John, **30**, 13, 16
Pickford, Mary, **18**, 72; **39**, 79
Pickles, Chris, **58**, 307; **59**, 338; **60**, 323
Pickup, Rachel, **51**, 222–4; **57**, 287; **59**, 328
Pickup, Ronald, **25**, 27; **50**, 227
Pico della Mirandola, Giovanni, **33**, 22; **34**, 95, 96, 98–9, 100; **43**, 237–8; **53**, 30, 37n; **59**, 365; **60**, 125–6
Oratio de Hominis Dignitate, **1**, 131
Pieraccini, Gaetano, **7**, 105–6n
Pierce, Robert B., **25**, 180; **26**, 156; **30**, 58n; **38**, 4; **54**, 321
Pierce, William, **57**, 238
Pierfederico, Tonino, **13**, 129
Piero, **49**, 157
Pierret, **21**, 80
Pierson, Anne, **51**, 261
Pierson, Peter, **59**, 246n59
Pierson, Thomas, **6**, 74
Pies, Eike, **28**, 172n
Pieters, Jurgen, **60**, 232
Pietsch, Ilse, **37**, 155
Pietschmann, Herbert, **40**, 145; **42**, 208
Pig, John, **58**, 229
Pigafetta, Antonio, **52**, 188n
Pigalle, Jean-Baptiste, **9**, 92
Piggot, Sir Christopher, **57**, 9
Piggott, J. R., **47**, 172n
Piggott, Lester, **56**, 144
Piggott-Smith, Tim, **28**, 142; **41**, 176; **42**, 143–5, 149; **43**, 206, 216; **45**, 147; **49**, 271; **52**, 255; **55**, 308
Pigman, G. W., **40**, 75n
Pile, Bob, **50**, 186n
Pile, Steve, **55**, 248n
Pilford, Jackie, **41**, 184
Pilger, John, **50**, 199n
Pilgrim Trust, **5**, 53
Pilgrim, Geraldine, **49**, 274
Pilgrim, The, **54**, 18n, 24n
Pilgrimage to Parnassus, The, **4**, 91; **20**, 65
Pilikian, Hovhanness, **32**, 222; **47**, 211
Pilkington, Ace, **49**, 159
Pilkington, Francis, *First Book of Songs*, **1**, 70
Pilkington, Revd James, **54**, 36
Pilkinton, Mark C., **47**, 56n; **49**, 16n; **52**, 75n, 78n
Pillchorne, Henry, **51**, 291
Pilon, Frederick, **34**, 12, 14–15
Pilotto, Camillo, **6**, 121
Pimlott, Steven, **42**, 159; **43**, 210; **45**, 116, 119; **46**, 194; **48**, 217, 219, 221–2; **49**, 252, 255, 258–60, 273; **50**, 203–7, 232; **51**, 257; **53**, 247; **54**, 268, 274–80, 283; **55**, 286, 292, 294–301, 307–9, 319, 330; **56**, 97, 288, 295; **57**, 266, 278, 291; **58**, 31, 44; **59**, 188, 321, 327, 333–7; **60**, 322
Pimpernell, Henry, **44**, 210
Pinchard, Betty, **55**, 135
Pinciss, Dr Gerald M., **30**, 196; **33**, 191; **38**, 15; **43**, 237–8; **55**, 18, 123
'Shakespeare, Her Majesty's Players, and Pembroke's Men', **27**, 129–36

Pincombe, Michael, **51**, 292–3
Pindar, **14**, 145; **22**, 15; **54**, 86
Pine, John, **49**, 118
Pine, Robert, **51**, 13
Pinero, Sir Arthur Wing, **4**, 98, 102; **8**, 131; **20**, 81; **29**, 134, 137; **34**, 9; **47**, 108
Piney, Duncan, **45**, 150
Pinfold, Jackie, **43**, 208
Pinhorn, Malcolm, **21**, 148
Pinney, Thomas, **47**, 255n; **48**, 3n; **53**, 114n
Pinnington, Adrian, **50**, 248
Pinnock, Andrew, **39**, 155n
Pinnock, Steve, **44**, 202
Pinski, David, **55**, 124
Pinsky, Leonid, **52**, 285
Pinter, Harold, **16**, 19, 150; **18**, 156; **19**, 24n; **21**, 37; **22**, 28, 32; **23**, 39; **24**, 19, 43; **34**, 37; **36**, 21; **39**, 85; **40**, 149; **43**, 1, 222; **50**, 19; **51**, 194; **56**, 246
The Homecoming, **20**, 137
Pinter, Jack, **55**, 333
Pinto, Ricardo, **44**, 199; **49**, 276; **51**, 259; **52**, 255; **55**, 326
Pinto, V. de Sola, **15**, 7
Piozzi, Hester, **51**, 5, 61
Piper, The, **54**, 77n
Piper, David, **13**, 105n; **15**, 130 and n; **43**, 103n
Piper, Tom, **48**, 230; **51**, 265; **53**, 259, 271, 284; **54**, 256, 258, 289; **55**, 286–7, 331; **56**, 290, 295, 296; **59**, 314
Pirandello, Luigi, **16**, 35, 38; **22**, 28; **36**, 21, 22, 28; **40**, 6; **42**, 103n; **49**, 225; **57**, 119; **60**, 103n4
Pirate Utopia Company, **58**, 302
Pirie, David, **27**, 157; **35**, 97n
Piriz, Roberto Bula, **10**, 142
Pirkhofer, Anton M., **18**, 173; **31**, 164
Pisanello, Vittorio, **9**, 114
Pisarev, Evgeny, **60**, 299–300
Piscator, Erwin, **58**, 130, 133
Piscopo, Vittorio, **12**, 114
Pistoia, Cino da, **15**, 98n
Pitcairn, A. A., **4**, 74n
Pitcher, John, **38**, 232n; **39**, 221; **44**, 63n, 256; **45**, 195, 198n; **49**, 299; **51**, 69n, 291, 230–1; **53**, 326
Pitcher, Seymour M., **27**, 131n
The Case for Shakespeare's Authorship of 'The Famous Victories' reviewed, **16**, 181
Pitman, J. R., **55**, 106n, 108n
Pitman-Wallace, Lucy, **56**, 294; **60**, 323
Pitoëff family, **16**, 54
Pitoëff, Georges, **2**, 123; **7**, 110; **9**, 113; **14**, 119
Pitt, Angela, **42**, 32n
Pitt, William, **51**, 109
Pitt-Rivers, Julian, **47**, 265
Pittock, Malcolm, **38**, 251, 252n
Pittock, Murray G. H., **57**, 73
Pitts, Rebecca, E., **24**, 145
Pivec, Jan, **6**, 118
Pix, Mary Griffith, **43**, 254; **51**, 3n
Pizer, Lois D., **13**, 156n
Pizzi, Pier Luigi, **55**, 330
Pizzoferno, Giovana, **43**, 212
Plaatje, Solomon T., **40**, 135, 143; **52**, 161; **57**, 159–67; **58**, 208; **60**, 332
Place, P. A. de la, **3**, 98; **16**, 53
plague, **17**, 7–8, 165–6, 208
Plaksin, V., **5**, 105n
Planché, James Robinson, **2**, 19; **9**, 55; **10**, 74; **15**, 172; **16**, 103–117; **18**, 184; **20**, 108, 111; **21**, 155; **35**, 13–14, 18; **51**, 116; **53**, 279
Planchon, René, **13**, 127; **15**, 138
Planchon, Roger, **12**, 112; **15**, 133; **16**, 54, 56n; **18**, 122
Plantagenet, Henry, **28**, 120
Plantagenets, The, **43**, 171–81, 184, 212–3, 250, 255; **44**, 199; **54**, 274
Plantin, Christophe, **55**, 265–6; **57**, 221
Plaović, Rasá, **4**, 120–1, 122; **15**, 141
Plash, John, **53**, 282
Plash, Sylvia, **53**, 187
Plashenko, Tamora, **45**, 151
Plastow, Jane, **58**, 358
Plat, Sir Hugh, **17**, 25
Plater, Alan, **60**, 329
Plath, Sylvia, **56**, 159
Plato, **3**, 6; **8**, 145; **10**, 43, 49n, 136; **15**, 21, 96, 143; **16**, 125; **20**, 22; **23**, 93; **24**, 50–1, 52, 148n; **25**, 103; **28**, 29, 43, 63; **29**, 85; **30**, 189; **31**, 7, 17, 197; **32**, 169, 236; **33**, 24; **34**, 23, 95; **35**, 79, 82n, 157, 172, 177; **36**, 85, 86, 90, 91, 92, 93n, 94, 177; **38**, 43, 230n; **39**, 146, 149, 155, 234; **40**, 195; **42**, 16; **44**, 210; **47**, 26; **48**, 141n, 152, 260; **49**, 59, 61–3, 67, 216, 283; **50**, 245; **51**, 177; **52**, 274; **53**, 15, 25n, 320; **55**, 352, 356; **56**, 32, 228, 321, 322; **59**, 225–6, 227, 229, 232, 233, 235–6, 237, 289–90, 293, 295, 362, 363, 365
Phaedrus, **15**, 81, 83
Republic, **4**, 66
Platonism and the English Imagination (A. Baldwin and S. Hutton), **48**, 260
Platt, A., **6**, 39
Platt, Hugh, **30**, 201
Platt, Martin, **44**, 93
Platt, Michael, **30**, 185; **31**, 11n
Platt, Peter G., **54**, 29; **57**, 313
Platter, Thomas, **8**, 150; **11**, 147; **30**, 164; **42**, 115n, 206n; **43**, 147; **44**, 66, 153; **45**, 107; **47**, 265; **52**, 4; **54**, 191, 195–9; **56**, 99; **57**, 327; **58**, 12; **60**, 43, 45, 103
Plautus, Titus Maccius, **3**, 15; **5**, 53; **7**, 111; **15**, 98n; **17**, 61; **18**, 159; **22**, 1, 3, 8, 15, 16, 17, 19, 21, 23, 52; **23**, 161; **25**, 82; **27**, 2, 18, 119; **30**, 192; **42**, 201; **44**, 236; **46**, 221; **47**, 240, 254; **50**, 115–16, 144; **51**, 179, 180n; **52**, 276; **54**, 194; **55**, 194, 368; **56**, 38n; **59**, 367
Aulularia, **12**, 15
Gunaikeion, **14**, 59, 64
Menaechmi, **3**, 53; **10**, 146; **11**, 146
Mostellaria, **14**, 57–9, 61, 64
Play of the Sacrament, The, **17**, 49; **50**, 255
Play of the Weather, The, **4**, 95; **54**, 24, 26
Players of Shakespeare 3: Further Essays in Shakespearian Performance by Players with the Royal Shakespeare Company, The (R. Jackson and R. Smallwood), **48**, 264
Playfair, Nigel, **4**, 102, 105; **47**, 90
Playford, Edgar, **53**, 240
Playford, John, **15**, 3; **55**, 86–8; **60**, 191
Dancing Master, **3**, 56; **11**, 65
Select Ayres, **3**, 56
Plazy, Gilles, **57**, 119

Pleasant History of the Life and Death of Will Summers, A, **13**, 99, 101, 102, 105n
Pleasure Reconciled to Virtue, **54**, 398
Pledger, Christopher, **43**, 209
Pléiade, The, **4**, 49, 50
Plesington (Pleasington), Anne, **25**, 144
Pleskot, Jaromir, **7**, 109; **14**, 118
Plessen, Elizabeth, **49**, 269; **50**, 230
Plimpton, G. A., **1**, 76
The Education of Shakespeare, **3**, 5
Pliny, **17**, 150–1; **31**, 16, 18, 19, 183; **32**, 244; **34**, 65n; **38**, 40, 43, 231; **41**, 139; **50**, 62; **51**, 177; **56**, 40, 41, 46
(*see also* Holland, Philemon)
Plomer, H. R., **55**, 263n, 267n
Plotinus, **15**, 105; **31**, 49; **36**, 86n, 91, 92, 93; **40**, 79; **59**, 228, 236
Plotz, John, **51**, 284
Plowden, Edmund, **29**, 99, 100; **54**, 129, 130; **55**, 40n
Plowman, Max, **4**, 24; **8**, 9; **45**, 9
Plowright, David, **39**, 89n
Plowright, Joan, **44**, 176
Plumfield, Thomas, **58**, 224
Plummer, Christopher, **11**, 118; **13**, 125; **14**, 117; **16**, 18, 153; **18**, 70; **24**, 3n; **36**, 84; **44**, 95, 243; **45**, 147; **53**, 170n
Plummer, Sue, **48**, 228
Plutarch, **1**, 38; **2**, 42, 133; **3**, 6, 17, 36–9, 54; **4**, 27, 28, 87; **9**, 133, 139, 143; **12**, 65–70, 138, 142; **13**, 61, 151; **14**, 33, 153, 154; **15**, 170, 177; **17**, 215–16; **19**, 130, 146; **20**, 14, 22; **21**, 14, 132; **22**, 112, 113, 140, 157; **23**, 60, 61, 62, 63, 95, 96, 161, 184; **24**, 8, 12, 16, 140; **25**, 127, 128, 129; **27**, 111, 112n; **28**, 10, 67; **29**, 103, 104, 105, 111, 116, 170, 171; **30**, 4, 135, 140, 143, 195, 204, 205; **31**, 3, 7, 9, 10, 18, 34, 46, 48, 57n, 183, 197, 198; **33**, 19, 20n, 55, 100, 102, 105, 106, 107, 116, 197; **34**, 81, 83–4, 171, 187; **36**, 18; **37**, 148; **38**, 46n, 115, 116, 120, 121, 124, 125, 129, 176, 185, 217, 233; **40**, 69, 71–6, 81, 86; **41**, 77–8, 85–90, 211; **42**, 196; **44**, 61, 207–8; **45**, 197; **46**, 94, 96, 103, 106, 128; **47**, 142, 145–6, 148; **48**, 8, 33, 36n, 38–40, 250, 285, 286n; **50**, 69, 70, 75n; **51**, 135; **52**, 307; **53**, 50, 51, 54, 58, 60–87, 128, 344; **54**, 6, 7, 10, 12, 28, 40, 224; **55**, 19, 199, 201, 205, 208, 209, 211n, 212, 213, 368; **56**, 14, 42–6, 53, 70, 221, 223; **59**, 363; **60**, 177
Life of Marius, **9**, 85n
Lives, **10**, 2, 3, 4, 5, 7, 12, 29, 31, 32, 33, 34, 35, 50–8, 146
Lives, trans, by Sir Thomas North, **12**, 92–4
Moralia, **10**, 33
Moralia, trans. by Philemon Holland, **12**, 91, 92
see also under North, Sir Thomas, *and* Amyot, Jacques
Pocket Mirror, The, **55**, 179
Pocock, J. G. A., **48**, 125n; **57**, 8; **59**, 255
Pocock, Nicholas, **43**, 50n
Poe, Edgar Allan, **4**, 28; **7**, 97; **9**, 114; **15**, 109n; **21**, 17; **53**, 166n; **55**, 89–90; **60**, 330
Poel, Ella, **52**, 32
Poel, William, **1**, 15, 16, 89; **2**, 1, 2, 4–5, 8, 9, 12, 14, 15, 17, 19, 20; **3**, 74; **4**, 105; **8**, 152; **9**, 18, 19, 57, 147–8; **10**, 75, 149; **11**, 148; **12**, 9, 22, 71, 73, 82, 144; **15**, 5; **16**, 114; **18**, 184, 185; **23**, 123; **25**, 1, 116, 117, 122, 123, 172; **26**, 147, 175; **29**, 140; **32**, 35n, 224; **35**, 1, 2, 3; **36**, 180; **39**, 143n; **40**, 12, 223; **41**, 63n, 67, 73; **43**, 186; **45**, 34n; **47**, 1, 2, 5, 81–8, 90; **50**, 31; **51**, 144; **52**, 17–32, 161; **53**, 233–4, 236–40; **54**, 316; **60**, 187
pioneer work for modern Shakespearian production, **8**, 77–8
Poetaster, **52**, 28n
Poggioli, Renato, **36**, 104; **37**, 69
Pogodin, M. P., **5**, 100
Pogson, Beryl, **5**, 132; **22**, 154
Pogson, Kathryn, **45**, 147; **52**, 217–18, 220, 225
Pogue, J. C., **18**, 180
Pogue, Kate Emery, **60**, 335–6, 353
Pohl, F. J., **16**, 164
Poincaré, Henri, **24**, 97
Pointer, Amanda, **44**, 199
Pointner, Frank Eric, **58**, 317, 332
Pointon, James, **52**, 263
Pointon, Marcia, **51**, 9, 300
Poirer, Michel, **28**, 45n
Poirier, Michel, **2**, 140; **7**, 135
Poirier, Richard, **33**, 4n; **50**, 171n; **59**, 35n71
Poisson, Rodney, **19**, 130; **21**, 163; **22**, 161; **30**, 194; **31**, 164, 190
Poitier, lan, **45**, 155
Poitier, Sidney, **55**, 243
Poklitaru, Radu, **59**, 344
Pokorný, Jaroslav, **10**, 116; **18**, 121
Shakespeares Zeit und das Theater reviewed, **14**, 155
Poland, report on Shakespeare in, **1**, 113; **2**, 128; **3**, 118; **9**, 114–15; **10**, 120; **11**, 121; **12**, 115; **14**, 122; **15**, 137; **16**, 18, 136
Polanski, Roman, **28**, 174; **39**, 4, 65, 67, 69–71, 75; **41**, 227; **45**, 63, 64; **48**, 262; **50**, 262; **53**, 158, 304; **55**, 383; **57**, 145–58
Polevoy, N. A., **5**, 100
Policardi, Silvio, **5**, 113
Polišenský, Josef, **21**, 153; **36**, 146n
Politeuphuia, Wit's Commonwealth, **3**, 19
Poliziano, Angelo, **56**, 44n
Pollack, Ellen, **15**, 145
Pollack, Rhoda-Gail, **32**, 233
Pollard, A. F., **6**, 3
Pollard, Alfred W., **1**, 12; **2**, 19, 44–5; **3**, 3, 28, 29, 31, 44, 45, 47, 50, 57, 143; **4**, 58, 64, 67n, 84, 160; **5**, 3, 25, 50, 51, 52; **6**, 5, 58; **7**, 3, 11, 49, 51, 52–3, 54, 151; **8**, 3, 81, 82, 98n, 100–1, 104n, 105n; **9**, 4, 69, 70, 71, 73, 74, 77, 79n; **11**, 78–81, 83–7, 87n, 88n; **14**, 7, 161; **17**, 208n; **18**, 24; **20**, 175; **21**, 65n; **22**, 180; **23**, 92; **25**, 75n, 79; **26**, 181; **27**, 129; **40**, 145; **42**, 77, 79, 119; **43**, 262; **48**, 277, 287; **49**, 326; **50**, 151, 284; **53**, 334; **54**, 90n, 94n, 95n; **55**, 18, 258–9; **57**, 226, 227, 232, 234; **58**, 141, 227; **59**, 1, 6–7, 9, 10, 11, 33, 69n1, 147, 151, 154–5, 156
King Richard II: a new quarto, **11**, 87n, 88n
Shakespeare's Fight with the Pirates, **11**, 79, 87n; **14**, 5
Shakespeare's Folios and Quartos, **14**, 5
Pollard, A. W., and Redgrave, G. R., *A Short-Title Catalogue, 1475–1640*, **4**, 93, **13**, 109
books in Huntington Library, **6**, 56, 57, 61
reference numbers to books in Trinity College Library, Cambridge, **5**, 51–4
Pollard, Carol W., **38**, 233
Pollard, David L., **44**, 153n
Pollard, William, **44**, 221
Pollen, John Hungerford, **24**, 71n, 77; **54**, 95n
Pollen, J. J., **56**, 193n, 194n, 195n
Pollin, Burton R., **20**, 148
Pollitt, Clyde, **37**, 171

Pollitt, Katha, **52**, 93n
Pollock, F., and Maitland, F. W., *The History of English Law*, **13**, 88n
Pollock, Sir Frederick, **10**, 76n; **32**, 132n, 134n; **35**, 8; **43**, 32; **48**, 7n; **51**, 160n, 165n, 166; **57**, 42, 90
Pollock, Linda, **56**, 2n
Pollock, Walter Herries, **32**, 35n; **35**, 17n; **59**, 286
Polo, Gil, **22**, 168; **29**, 180
Polo, Marco, **32**, 89n
Polonsky, Norma, **13**, 124
Polwhele, Richard, **41**, 109–10
Polyander, John, **60**, 232
Polycarpou, Peter, **41**, 178
Pomeroy, Sue, **59**, 343
Pomfret, John E., **6**, 63n
Pomorska, K., **31**, 54n
Pompeius Trogus, **29**, 25
Pompignan, Le Franc de, **16**, 53
Pompilius, Numa, **38**, 120
Ponce de la Fuente, Constantino, **23**, 81
Ponelle, Jean Pierre, **16**, 134
Ponet, John, Bp of Worcester, **17**, 109 and n.
Pongetti, Henrique, **10**, 143
Poniedzialek, Jacek, **50**, 38
Ponsonby, William, **28**, 54n; **33**, 14
Pontac, Perry, **56**, 296
Pontalis, J.-B., **44**, 43n
Pontanus, Jacobus, **15**, 98n, 101, 106; **29**, 29, 30; **39**, 127n
Ponte, Lorenzo da, **18**, 78
Pontormo, **26**, 50, 51, 54, 55
Ponz de Capduelh, **15**, 93
Poole, Adrian, **41**, 205, 209; **43**, 229; **53**, 119n; **55**, 179n; **56**, 118, 126–36, 308–9, 310; **57**, 117; **58**, 314, 315, 332; **59**, 374, 375
Poole, Eric, **35**, 176; **38**, 227; **55**, 37n
Poole, H. E., **55**, 264n
Poole, John, **42**, 162
Poole, Kristen, **49**, 287; **52**, 274–5; **54**, 100n, 169n; **57**, 239; **60**, 341, 353
A Poore Knight his Pallace of Priuate Pleasures, **60**, 272n13
Poole, R., **27**, 129n
Poole, William, **58**, 318, 332, 333
Pooler, C. Knox, **15**, 11, 12, 18, 19, 22; **31**, 136n; **52**, 302, 303
Poos, L. R., **55**, 37n
Pope, Alan, **47**, 219
Pope, Alexander, **1**, 12; **2**, 83, 109; **3**, 1, 26, 49; **4**, 81, 161; **5**, 15n, 19, 20, 50, 51; **7**, 2, 23, 30; **8**, 52; **9**, 93; **10**, 27, 28; **13**, 61; **14**, 78, 80–1; **15**, 177; **16**, 84; **18**, 12–14, 16, 18, 47; **19**, 143; **21**, 6; **22**, 16; **24**, 175, 176; **25**, 73, 85; **26**, 181, 182; **31**, 1; **32**, 42; **33**, 192, 209; **34**, 51, 54; **35**, 46; **39**, 239, 241; **42**, 205, 207; **43**, 83, 86n, 102–3; **44**, 113, 136n; **46**, 137, 141, 225, 236–7, 250n; **48**, 279; **49**, 113, 314, 322; **51**, 4, 7, 8, 15, 27, 30, 45, 62, 76n, 129, 131, 133, 134, 137, 138, 139, 321; **52**, 99, 275, 303; **53**, 53, 187, 302, 336–7, 342; **54**, 42n; **55**, 2, 389; **57**, 216; **59**, 32n58, 56, 58, 93, 94, 98, 102n15, 104n18, 128, 130, 133, 166, 198n1, 366
  The Dunciad, **5**, 1
  Dunciad Variorum, **20**, 33
  edition of Shakespeare, **4**, 85–6
  Imitations of Horace, **14**, 88n
  Preface to Shakespeare, **9**, 97
Pope, Angus, **43**, 213
Pope, Elizabeth Marie, **4**, 22; **7**, 7; **8**, 12, 16; **10**, 136; **25**, 6; **28**, 94; **32**, 129n
  'The Renaissance Background of *Measure for Measure*', **2**, 66–82
  see also, **3**, 66–73, 137, 141n
Pope, John, **43**, 213; **44**, 196; **46**, 201; **47**, 217; **48**, 237
Pope, Morgan, **60**, 46
Pope, Natasha, **49**, 271
Pope, Thomas, **22**, 121; **32**, 194; **37**, 198; **45**, 107; **54**, 193; **57**, 232; **58**, 10, 230
Pope-Hennessy, John, **26**, 112n, 116n
Popham, John, **57**, 13
Popkes, Stephen, **53**, 173n
Popkin, Richard H., **46**, 145n; **55**, 220
Popović, Vladeta, **5**, 144n; **15**, 140
  'Shakespeare in Post-War Yugoslavia', **4**, 117–22
Popovici, Ileana, **20**, 131n
Popper, Sir Karl, **35**, 165n; **40**, 153
Popple, William, **56**, 98
Poppy, Andrew, **47**, 210
Porath, Orna, **12**, 114; **14**, 121
Porkomy, Jaroslav, **48**, 163n
Porphyry, **17**, 64
Porsinna, Lars, **38**, 117
Porson, Richard, **4**, 56; **5**, 2
Portacio, Tony, **42**, 160; **44**, 193; **48**, 228
Portal, Robert, **47**, 206; **54**, 278
Porter, Andrew, **32**, 84; **39**, 232, 233; **57**, 64, 115
Porter, Carolyn, **43**, 17n
Porter, Charlotte Endymion, **8**, 8; **10**, 14; **17**, 176; **55**, 391n; **59**, 57n22, 137, 138, 139, 136–45, 145n42
Porter, Cole, **4**, 123; **42**, 157; **435**, 126; **56**, 297; **57**, 155
Porter, David, **48**, 248
Porter, Eric, **9**, 124; **14**, 132; **16**, 144, 147, 150; **19**, 114; **22**, 141; **43**, 189; **44**, 194; **45**, 122; **46**, 201; **57**, 40
Porter, Hal, **35**, 32n
Porter, Henry, **2**, 54; **14**, 23; **20**, 175; **40**, 225; **46**, 65; **49**, 97–8, 101–9
  Two Angry Women of Abington, **6**, 88n; **14**, 88n
Porter, Joseph A., **35**, 168–9; **38**, 7; **44**, 215; **46**, 5, 216; **49**, 61n, 63n; **50**, 63; **51**, 8; **55**, 352; **57**, 209, 210
Porter, Katherine Anne, **53**, 136
Porter, Peter, **45**, 57, 122
Porter, R. K., **59**, 132
Porter, Robert, **45**, 115n
Porter, Roy, **51**, 73, 74
Porter, Walter, *Madrigals and Ayres*, **1**, 70
Porter, William, **19**, 103
Porterfield, Robert, **4**, 124; **9**, 117
Portington, William, **45**, 111; **47**, 16–18, 24n
Portland Papers in the British Museum, *see under* Libraries
Porto, Luigi da, **1**, 62; **3**, 54, 55; **20**, 98
Portraits of Shakespeare, *see* Shakespeare, William
Portugal, José Blanco de, **18**, 127
Portugal, report on Shakespeare in, **1**, 116; **3**, 118–19; **18**, 127
Portugal, **11**, 90
Portway, Saskia, **58**, 298

Pory, John, **11**, 95, 97n, 108–10, 115n; **52**, 206n
A Geographical Historie of Africa, **11**, 95, 97n
Poskitt, Kjartan, **43**, 213
Posner, Anna, **57**, 121
Posner, Lindsay, **45**, 152; **54**, 266, 292; **55**, 309–10, 332; **56**, 298; **57**, 297
Postan, Cynthia, **44**, 52n
Postel, Guillaume, **44**, 62n
Postlethwaite, Pete, **40**, 172, 174; **52**, 90, 257
Postlewait, Thomas, **47**, 10n; **48**, 191; **59**, 31n51, 212n63
Postone, Moishe, **57**, 26
Potapenko, Ignaty, **48**, 117
Pott, Mrs Henry, **18**, 112
Potter, Andrew, **53**, 279, 282; **56**, 296
Potter, Dennis, **45**, 126; **53**, 328; **55**, 312
Potter, Frank H., **15**, 3
Potter, G. R., **54**, 139n
Potter, Lois, **28**, 11n; **29**, 160–1; **42**, 197–8; **43**, 270n; **44**, 217, 256; **46**, 214, 241n; **50**, 65; **51**, 309–10; **53**, 295–6, 325; **54**, 306, 322, 333, 338; **56**, 41n, 105n, 113, 114, 181n, 329; **58**, 1; **59**, 213, 215, 216, 218, 221, 222, 259n12; **60**, 167, 169, 259n26
'The Antic Disposition of Richard II', **27**, 33–41
Potter, Nick, **43**, 225; **45**, 160
Potter, Peter, **5**, 120; **8**, 125
Potter, Robert, **29**, 171
Potter, Sally, **54**, 312
Pottle, Frederick A., **34**, 13n; **54**, 50n, 51n, 52n
Potts, Abbie Findlay, **9**, 138, 142, **143**
Shakespeare and 'The Faerie Queene' reviewed, **13**, 157–8
Potts, Andrew, **47**, 216
Pouch, Captain, **3**, 35, 41n
Poulenc, Francis, **57**, 123
Poulsen, Johannes, **3**, 113, 114
Poulsen, Olaf, **3**, 112
Poulton, Diana, **36**, 147n
Poulton, Mike, **49**, 253; **60**, 293
Pound, Ezra, **10**, 18; **14**, 156; **16**, 34; **40**, 193; **42**, 54
Pountney, David, **50**, 235; **52**, 254; **56**, 292; **57**, 294
Pountney, Graham, **55**, 328, 331
Pourtalès, Guy de, **2**, 118, 121; **9**, 67
Poussin, Nicolas, **10**, 37, 72; **13**, 158; **56**, 81n
Povey, Kenneth, **14**, 164; **19**, 163
Powell, Chilton L., **32**, 132n
Powell, Colin, **58**, 25
Powell, Enoch, **44**, 1
Powell, James, **43**, 211; **44**, 202; **56**, 122
Powell, Jocelyn, **27**, 167; **43**, 96
Powell, John, **9**, 119
Powell, L. F., **21**, 10n
Powell, Michael, **46**, 196
Powell, Peter, **8**, 124
Powell, Robert, **53**, 67
Powell, Sandy, **44**, 198
Powell, Stephen, **47**, 218
Powell, William, **51**, 4; **57**, 86
Power of Eloquence and English Renaissance Literature, The, **46**, 223
Power, Dominic, **47**, 214
Power, Jack, **43**, 209; **45**, 151
Power, Patrick, **35**, 146
Powers, Eileen, **44**, 20n
Powers, Sharon B., **48**, 160n; **55**, 1n
Powesland, Pamela, **46**, 220
Powle, Stephen, **27**, 100
Powle, Thomas, **27**, 100, 101, 102, 103
Powlton, Thomas, **60**, 21
Pownell, David, **42**, 162
Powrie, Greg, **56**, 294
Powys, John Cowper, **39**, 169
Poyatos, Fernando, **53**, 4n
Poynet, John, *Politic Power*, **3**, 20
Poynter, F. N. L., **19**, 148
'Medicine and Public Health', **17**, 152–66
Poyntz, Francis, **60**, 247
Praag, Jonas van, **20**, 99, 104n
Praetorius, C., **27**, 132n
Prager, Leonard, **15**, 165; **22**, 175n; **54**, 182n
Praise of Folly, The, **50**, 117
Prakash, Nigram, **15**, 136
Prange, Gerda, **8**, 153; **15**, 9
Prannell, Henry, **11**, 95–6
Pratchett, Terry, **60**, 324
Prats, Philippe, **33**, 165n
Pratt, Josiah, **48**, 40n
Pratt, Samuel M., **20**, 154
Prawer, S. S., **45**, 89, 90, 97
Prayer Book (1549), **17**, 225, 238
Praz, Mario, **1**, 116; **2**, 127; **8**, 120; **9**, 114, 141; **10**, 120; **11**, 121; **12**, 114; **15**, 9; **17**, 181n; **25**, 53n; **34**, 171; **47**, 163n; **50**, 30n
'Shakespeare's Italy', **7**, 95–106
Preface to Shakespeare's Tragedies, A, **46**, 217
Preiss, Richard, **60**, 358
Preljocaj, Angelia, **55**, 331
Prem, **43**, 213–14
Preminger, Alex, **37**, 35n; **49**, 164; **57**, 251
Prendergast, Catherine, **47**, 213
Prendergast, Jane, **52**, 279
Prendergast, Shaun, **42**, 129, 131
Prentice, Herbert, **47**, 92–3, 106
Prentki, Tim, **52**, 163n
Prerogative Court of Canterbury, **4**, 69, 71
Prescott, Anne Lake, **43**, 57n; **45**, 185n; **50**, 254; **51**, 292; **54**, 92n
Prescott, F. C., **33**, 121
Prescott, Paul, **60**, 360
Prescott, W. C., **6**, 61
Presgurvic, Gerard, **57**, 296
Press, Karen, **55**, 274n
Pressler, Charlotte, **55**, 347; **59**, 362
Pressler, Mirjam, **56**, 315
Pressly, William L., **47**, 258; **49**, 116n, 118n, 119n, 122n, 123n
Presson, Robert K., **7**, 134; **8**, 11; **9**, 142; **14**, 154; **21**, 154; **22**, 165; **23**, 170; **25**, 9
Prest, Wilfrid R., **49**, 196n; **57**, 202
Preston, Amyas, **21**, 103
Preston, Claire, **46**, 213
Preston, D. R., **25**, 179
Preston, Elizabeth, **13**, 92
Preston, Mary, **54**, 300

Preston, Thomas, **13**, 92; **17**, 192–3; **55**, 65
Cambyses, **20**, 18, 19, 24, 25n
Preston, Travis, **60**, 324
Pretty, Francis, **17**, 32
Pretty, Stan, **46**, 202
Pretye Complaynte of Peace, A, **1**, 70
Preuschen, Karl Adalbert, **30**, 202
Préville (Pierre Louis Dubus), **9**, 91
Prévost, Abbé (Antoine François Prévost d'Exiles), **16**, 53; **24**, 79; **60**, 218
Price, Andrew, **46**, 192; **47**, 210
Price, Cecil, **13**, 68n; **32**, 42n; **42**, 37n, 85n; **51**, 111n, 115n
Price, Claire, **54**, 270; **59**, 308, 309–10
Price, Curtis A., **38**, 235, 236
Price, Diana, **59**, 277
Price, F. D., **17**, 77n
Price, F. W., **30**, 200
Price, George R., **24**, 163; **33**, 206–7; **34**, 193n; **35**, 186; **39**, 247; **40**, 146, 149, 150, 152; **42**, 209
Price, Henry, **49**, 186, 189
Price, Hereward T., **1**, 129; **6**, 4, 5, 34n; **7**, 10, 147; **8**, 8, 157; **10**, 2; **12**, 142, 151; **14**, 163; **15**, 20, 24, 29; **16**, 167, 174; **24**, 152; **27**, 11n; **31**, 95n, 102n; **38**, 9; **42**, 12
'The First Quarto of *Titus Andronicus*' reviewed, **3**, 143–4
'Function of Imagery in *Venus and Adonis*', **2**, 136
'Mirror-Scenes in Shakespeare', **2**, 134
reviewed, **3**, 144–5
Price, J. G., **18**, 184
Price, J. R., **24**, 152
Price, John Edmund, **32**, 231; **34**, 175; **45**, 109n; **60**, 207
Price, John Edward, **43**, 232
Price, Jonathan R., **28**, 89n; **38**, 13; **42**, 152; **55**, 325
Price, Joseph G., **23**, 151; **25**, 4, 45n, 48n, 50, 51, 56, 57, 60; **27**, 106n; **30**, 80; **35**, 9n, 10, 178; **38**, 8n; **41**, 209; **52**, 284; **53**, 218n, 232n; **54**, 22n; **60**, 334–5, 353
Price, Leontyne, **52**, 95, 97
Price, Matilde, **49**, 189
Price, Maude (Gregorie), **49**, 186, 189
Price, Peter, **24**, 158n
Price, R. T., **15**, 17, 109n
Price, Roger Carson, **31**, 5n
Price, Russell, **49**, 195n; **55**, 209n
Price, S. R. F., **53**, 79n
Price, Sampson, **54**, 178n
Price, Tim, **41**, 189; **43**, 213
Price, Vincent, **57**, 154
Prick of Conscience, The, **6**, 59
Pricke, R., **13**, 109
Pride of Life, The, **3**, 20
Priessnitz, Horst, **37**, 159n
Priest, Dale G., **34**, 185
Priest, Josias, **37**, 41
Priestley, Clive, **44**, 101
Priestley, F. E. L., **44**, 217
Priestley, J. B., **4**, 120; **6**, 13; **19**, 132; **40**, 210; **47**, 91, 105; **48**, 205
Priestley, Tony, **41**, 191
Priestman, Brian, **19**, 151
Prince, F. T., **15**, 18, 22, 24–5, 99, 107, 108n, 167, 178; **23**, 76n, 180; **31**, 13n; **36**, 40n; **41**, 241n
Prince's Men, *see under* Theatre, Elizabethan, companies
Pringle, Bryan, **43**, 216
Pringle, Roger, **43**, 266n; **45**, 28n; **48**, 11n, 184n; **49**, 76n; **52**, 103n; **55**, 219n, 259n
Printing, Elizabethan, *see under* Shakespeare, textual problems
printing, **17**, 205–13
Prior, Camille, **14**, 127
Prior, John, **44**, 155
Prior, Mary, **49**, 303
Prior, Moody E., **3**, 137; **5**, 88, 92n; **6**, 162; **10**, 70, 139; **28**, 10n–11n; **31**, 168; **38**, 4; **40**, 63
'Character in Relation to Action in *Othello*', **2**, 135
The Language of Tragedy, **2**, 136
Prior, Roger, **15**, 144; **29**, 25, 26, 31–2; **42**, 186; **43**, 269
'George Wilkins and the Young Heir', **29**, 33–9
'The Life of George Wilkins', **25**, 137–52
Prioress' Tale, **52**, 101
Priscian, **7**, 22, 23
Priscilla, Queen of the Desert, **52**, 90
Pritchard, Allan, **32**, 228
Pritchard, F. H., **59**, 81n9, 86
Pritchard, Hannah, **51**, 4, 11, 110, 113, 115; **58**, 334
Private Life of Henry VIII, **12**, 129n
privateering, **17**, 24–6, 29, 34–5
Privy Council, **11**, 92–7; **17**, 4, 6, 7, 9, 10, 33, 76, 79, 89, 90, 94, 96, 97, 100
Probus, **15**, 97n
Procházka, Martin, **58**, 314
Proclamation . . . touching the opening of the traffique of Spaine (1603/4), **17**, 35
Proclemer, Anna, **5**, 113; **7**, 112; **10**, 120; **18**, 126
Proclus, **59**, 228
Procopius, **20**, 3
Procter, Francis, **54**, 123n
Procter, Mudita, **52**, 260
Proctor, Bryan Waller, **57**, 88
Proctor, F., **25**, 127n
Proctor, John Ray, **60**, 162, 163, 164
Proctor, Robert, **7**, 56n
'Producing the Comedies', Sir Barry Jackson, **8**, 74–80
Production of English Renaissance Culture, The (D. Miller, S. O'Dair and H. Weber), **48**, 248
Productions of Shakespeare's Plays in the United Kingdom, **1**, 89, 111
Birmingham and Stratford productions of history plays, **6**, 49–52, 129–39; **7**, 118–20, 123–7, 146; **8**, 123–6, 128–9, 132–8
Festival of Britain productions, **6**, 140–6
Henry VIII at Stratford (1949), **3**, 120–9; **4**, 99–100, 130–8; **5**, 119–20, 121–8; **6**, 126–8
productions from 1900 to 1950, **2**, 1–19
productions of comedies from 1856 discussed, **8**, 74–80; **9**, 16–23, 54–8, 119–21, 122–31, 147; **10**, 3, 72–6, 85, 123–5, 126–34, 149
in foreign countries, **2**, 122–4, 128–9, 130–1
open-air productions in Germany, **3**, 95–7
productions in Denmark, **3**, 112–14; **4**, 110–14, 120–2, 123–8; **5**, 108–9, 111–18; **6**, 117–25; **7**, 107–17; **8**, 69–73, 118–22; **9**, 59–67, 102, 107–9, 110n, 111–18, 147; **10**, 87n, 111, 115–22, 149, 150
see also under titles of individual plays and names of countries
Proeschold, Ludwig, **44**, 83n
Progress to Parnassus, **1**, 65

Pröhl, Gerhard, **11**, 120
Prokofiev, Sergei Sergeyevich, **6**, 125; **16**, 15; **30**, 5; **45**, 172–3; **49**, 4, 153, 240, 285; **52**, 263; **53**, 282; **54**, 258, 291; **55**, 331; **56**, 296; **57**, 296; **58**, 305; **59**, 344; **60**, 327
Prokovsky, Andre, **58**, 305
Prölss, Robert, **48**, 10n
Promos and Cassandra, **8**, 16, 25, 27n; **52**, 134
prompt-books, **17**, 209–10
Pronko, Leonard C., **42**, 103n
Propeller Theatre Company, **58**, 303
Propertius, **15**, 97n
Propp, Vladimir, **41**, 122; **53**, 4n, 11, 153n
Proser, Matthew N., **20**, 148, 149; **23**, 148; **26**, 164
Prosetler, Mary, **22**, 109
Proske, Max, **14**, 156n
Prospero and Caliban: The Psychology of Colonization, **46**, 220
Prospero's Books, **52**, 197–8, 289
Prospero's Books. Screen Shakespeare (C. Schatz-Jacobsen), **48**, 263; **49**, 308
Prosser, Eleanor, **18**, 185; **20**, 73n, 166; **22**, 157–8; **26**, 23, 25n, 161; **28**, 37n; **30**, 208; **32**, 174n; **33**, 186; **34**, 9, 172; **35**, 181; **36**, 44; **39**, 221; **44**, 248; **45**, 17n, 18–24; **48**, 151; **50**, 176n, 181n; **54**, 123n; **55**, 258n
Prothero, G. W. (ed.), **17**, 91n
Protheroe, Brian, **48**, 235; **56**, 273; **60**, 323
Protter, Sylvia Alter, **55**, 116n, 119n
Proudfoot, Richard (G. R.), **21**, 146; **22**, 167n; **28**, 181; **29**, 1; **31**, 167; **32**, 106; **34**, 189; **36**, 108n; **37**, 201; **38**, 88n, 233; **41**, 233n; **42**, 161, 181; **43**, 270n; **44**, 83n; **45**, 198n; **46**, 227–8; **47**, 240n; **49**, 310, 324; **50**, 113n; **51**, 331; **52**, 303, 314; **53**, 335, 338; **54**, 350–1; **55**, 390–1; **56**, 94, 169; **57**, 342; **58**, 83; **59**, 6n22, 83, 382–3
Proudhon, P. J., **28**, 65
Proust, Marcel, **28**, 30; **36**, 149
Prouty, Charles Tyler, (*see also under* Kökeritz, Helge), **2**, 153; **4**, 161; **6**, 5, 153; **7**, 143; **8**, 4–5, 8; **9**, 133, 146n, 152, 153–4; **10**, 88n, 89n; **12**, 16, 20n; **13**, 165, 168n; **15**, 170; **19**, 146; **25**, 179; **55**, 24n; **59**, 4, 40
  'An Early Elizabethan Playhouse', **6**, 64–74
  proverbs and puns, **17**, 236–8
  provincial life in Elizabethan England, **17**, 13–20
Prowse, Philip, **51**, 258
Prucha, Jaroslav, **13**, 126
Pruvost, René, **2**, 120; **12**, 139; **14**, 153, 155; **60**, 272n13
Pryce, John, **45**, 109
Pryce, Jonathan, **32**, 202, 206; **41**, 170, 172, 186; **42**, 134, 137; **43**, 254; **46**, 81; **48**, 222; **49**, 257; **50**, 262; **57**, 42, 43; **60**, 205
Prynne, Captain Edward, **11**, 93–4
Prynne, Henry, *Histriomastix*, **14**, 98
Prynne, William, **17**, 217; **32**, 69; **38**, 92n; **46**, 103, 106; **50**, 22; **54**, 58n; **55**, 255n; **58**, 221
Pryor, Felix, **47**, 242–3
Pryse, Marjorie, **31**, 172
Przybos, A., **36**, 147n
Psiharis, Yiannis, **58**, 211
Ptolemy, **3**, 7; **17**, 39 and n., 66, 140–1, 144
Public Record Office, *see under* London
Public, The (El público), **54**, 340
Publius Sicilius, **29**, 170
Puccini, G., **18**, 75
Puckering, Sir Thomas, **11**, 115n
Puddephat, Wilfrid, **43**, 248; **60**, 226n17
Pudovkin, Vsevolod, **47**, 108
Pudsey, Edward, **4**, 90; **36**, 138
Puget, Claude-André, **16**, 133
Pughe, Thomas, **41**, 245n; **43**, 233
Pugin, Augustus, **20**, 109
Pugliatti, Paola Gulli, **34**, 62n; **40**, 205; **47**, 231; **50**, 250; **53**, 308
Puhvel, Martin, **32**, 235
Pujante, Ángel-Luis, **41**, 245n; **51**, 95–105; **53**, 301; **54**, 155n, 156n; **57**, 327; **58**, 312; **59**, 194n7
Pullen, Melanie Clark, **55**, 320
Pulver, Jeffrey, *A Biographical Dictionary of Old English Music*, **11**, 106n; **15**, 4
Punchdrunk Theatrical Experience, **58**, 302
Punk and the Princess, The, **49**, 278
Purcarete, Silviu, **46**, 196; **49**, 245, 247–50, 257; **50**, 234; **52**, 265; **53**, 149n
Purcell, Alice, **42**, 155; **48**, 192; **49**, 271
Purcell, Henry, **7**, 112; **9**, 116; **11**, 65; **12**, 109; **13**, 137; **15**, 5, 9; **18**, 75–7, 94, 98, 100; **37**, 41, 45; **38**, 235; **45**, 172; **49**, 302; **51**, 80–2, 85, 87–93; **52**, 290; **53**, 217; **56**, 142; **57**, 294; **60**, 191
  Golden Sonata, **8**, 71
Purcell, John, **42**, 151
Purchas, Samuel, **17**, 33, 44; **48**, 32; **52**, 206n, 208n; **54**, 136–7
Purchase, Bruce, **35**, 149; **37**, 128n
Purdom, C. B., **6**, 161, 163; **7**, 146n; **20**, 81n
  Harley Granville-Barker reviewed, **10**, 148–9
  Puritan, The, **4**, 91; **9**, 84
Purdon, Noel, **29**, 173
Purdum, Richard, **19**, 140
Purell, Sally, **55**, 30n
Puritan Discipline Tracts, **17**, 124n
Puritan, The, **17**, 212; **48**, 277; **52**, 148n
Purkayastha, Jagodish, **31**, 171
Purkis, E., **43**, 158n
Purkiss, Diane, **57**, 2, 3, 32
Purkyně, Karel, **9**, 107
Purland, T., **1**, 83
Pursley, David, **18**, 130
Purslowe, George, **50**, 156
Purtseladze, Anton, **48**, 186
Purves, David, **57**, 126
Purvis, J. S., **23**, 42n
Püschel, Ursula, **23**, 174n; **26**, 162; **32**, 220
Pusey E. B., **54**, 83
Pusey, Hugh, **58**, 246
Pushkin, Alexander Sergeevich, **5**, 117; **6**, 125; **15**, 143; **16**, 10, 14, 17; **23**, 176; **26**, 167; **56**, 161, 162
  Boris Godunov, **5**, 93, 94–8, 99–100, 101, 102–3, 104, 105n
  The Captain's Daughter, **5**, 104
  Evgeny Onegin, **5**, 93–4
  The Gypsies, **5**, 94
  Little Tragedies, **5**, 101–2, 103, 105n
  Poltava, **5**, 93
  Shakespeare's influence on, **5**, 93–104
  The Stone Guest, **5**, 105n
Putney, Rufus, **8**, 144; **15**, 20, 21, 27

Puttenham, George, **14**, 80; **37**, 180; **40**, 86, 87n, 221; **42**, 53, 66, 67, 70, 73, 92, 93; **43**, 238; **44**, 46–8, 120; **46**, 93, 103, 104; **48**, 257; **50**, 60n, 65, 74, 76, 113, 135–6, 139, 145, 242; **53**, 13, 14, 21, 22; **55**, 24n; **56**, 242; **57**, 12, 28; **58**, 60, 71; **59**, 230
Arte of English Poesie, **4**, 78; **7**, 5, 6, 14, 19–20, 22; **10**, 64
Puttenham, Richard, **22**, 3; **36**, 166; **40**, 98, 103; **41**, 115, 196; **51**, 297
Putzel, Max, **53**, 24n
Puzo, Mario, **53**, 99
Pyant, Paul, **47**, 123; **55**, 323
Pye, Christopher, **44**, 209; **50**, 103, 109; **56**, 139, 316
Pye, Henry James, **20**, 39
Alfred, **20**, 33
Commentary illustrating the Poetic of Aristotle, **20**, 34, 40n
Comments on the Commentators of Shakespeare, **20**, 33, 36, 40n
Pye, Tom, **60**, 172
Pyke, Elaine, **53**, 260
Pyle, Fitzroy, **4**, 9, 142n; **23**, 155–6; **26**, 167; **29**, 1, 2, 4, 6, 67
Pyle, Robert, **49**, 116
Pyle, Thomas, **9**, 48n
Pyman, Avril, **21**, 128
Pynson, Richard, **1**, 67
Pyot, Lazarus, **54**, 96
Pyramus and Thisbe, **49**, 275
Pyrrho, **40**, 80; **46**, 145
Pyrrhus, King of Epirus, **60**, 124n17
Pythagoras, **13**, 36; **15**, 96; **17**, 216; **39**, 123, 149; **42**, 67, 72–4; **46**, 18; **53**, 320
'Symbols and Significances', **17**, 180–7
Textual Studies, *reviewed:* (1968), **22**, 176–83
(1969), **23**, 176–86
(1970), **24**, 170–9
(1971), **25**, 193–200
(1972), **26**, 177–84
(1973), **27**, 179–92
(1974), **28**, 173–81
(1975), **29**, 177–85
(1976), **30**, 203–10
'Verbal Reminiscence and the Two-Part Structure of *The Winter's Tale*, **29**, 67–78

Qarshie, Hugh, **60**, 162, 164, 165, 166, 169
Qipiani, Dimitri, **48**, 185–6
Quadflieg, Will, **5**, 115; **10**, 119
Quaife, G. R., **49**, 198n
Quaritch catalogue (1877), **11**, 105
Quarles, Francis, **17**, 176
Quarles, John, **10**, 72; **34**, 88n
The Banishment of Tarquin, **9**, 85
Quarrell, W. H., **7**, 121; **30**, 165n
Quarshie, Hugh, **40**, 176, 179; **41**, 190; **42**, 160; **44**, 199; **49**, 251–2; **50**, 228; **53**, 185; **59**, 371
Quartermaine, Leon, **1**, 102; **3**, 122; **18**, 73
Quartucci, Carlo, **43**, 209
Quasha, George, **55**, 76n
Quasimodo, Salvatore, **3**, 117; **4**, 128; **6**, 121; **11**, 121; **15**, 136
Quast, Philip, **50**, 212, 214; **57**, 266
Quay Brothers, **51**, 219, 264
Quayle, Sir Anthony, **3**, 122, 123, 125–9; **5**, 119; **6**, 136; **7**, 113; **8**, 137; **9**, 119; **10**, 127; **13**, 70; **16**, 19–20, 25–6; **24**, 3n, 8, 10; **25**, 3, 94n; **26**, 119; **27**, 106n; **39**, 94, 98, 105; **42**, 152; **43**, 183; **45**, 188–9; **48**, 17; **50**, 31; **52**, 319; **54**, 276; **56**, 113
Production of *Henry V* reviewed, **6**, 138–9
Production of *Richard II* reviewed, **6**, 129, 132–4
Quayle, Jenny, **46**, 201; **47**, 207, 212; **51**, 248
Quayle, John, **52**, 237
Queen Elizabeth: or the Origin of Shakespeare, **54**, 74
Queen Elizabeth's Prayer-Book (A Booke of Christian Prayers), **60**, 226n18
Queen's Men, *see under* Theatre, Elizabethan, companies
Queenes Arcadia, The, **11**, 114n
Queenes Maiesties Passage, through the Citie of London the Day before her Coronacion, **17**, 180n
Queensberry, Duchess of, **51**, 61
Quennell, Peter, **18**, 128, 178
Quesnel, Pooky, **59**, 327
Questier, Michael, **54**, 35n, 89–90, 91n, 94n, 167n, 181n
Qui est là?, **55**, 301
Quijano, Margarita, **18**, 167–8
Quiller-Couch, Sir Arthur, **1**, 13; **4**, 11–12, 21, 22, 53; **5**, 131; **6**, 13; **7**, 125; **8**, 12, 41, 42, 44; **9**, 79; **11**, 31, 34, 35, 39, 41n; **12**, 127; **18**, 3, 8, 9, 20; **19**, 8; **24**, 52; **25**, 3, 94n; **32**, 1; **36**, 107n, 115n; **37**, 90n; **40**, 39; **41**, 94n; **44**, 108n, 109, 110, 111, 139, **47**, 275; **54**, 311; **58**, 356; **59**, 2, 40, 147, 152, 153, 153n30, 156
Shakespeare's Workmanship, **3**, 6
Quilley, Denis, **31**, 159; **41**, 50; **49**, 262; **50**, 230; **51**, 248, 267; **53**, 259; **54**, 260; **55**, 323; **56**, 97
Quilligan, Maureen, **46**, 60n, 71n, 123n; **50**, 195n; **51**, 295; **53**, 324; **54**, 134n; **55**, 6n, 8n, 117n, 240n, 250n; **60**, 168, 228, 233n57, 343–4, 353
Quilter, Harry, **32**, 23n
Quin, James, **7**, 28; **10**, 72, 76n; **21**, 117; **37**, 85, 147; **44**, 242; **51**, 60, 109, 113; **53**, 217, 218n; **57**, 60, 86
Quinault-Defresne, A.-A., **3**, 99
Quine, Willard Van Orman, **57**, 313
Quiney Affair, The, **52**, 266
Quiney family, **32**, 228
Quiney, Adrian, **14**, 114
Quiney, Judith, **14**, 113–14; **17**, 14
Quiney, Richard, **10**, 12–13
Quiney, Thomas, **17**, 14; **18**, 178; **28**, 38
Quiney, Thomas and Judith, **4**, 74n, 75–6; **8**, 6
Quinlan, Maurice J., **9**, 143
Quinn, Arthur, **59**, 274n19
Quinn, David Beers, **17**, 26n, 27n, 32n; **19**, 148; **21**, 142; **54**, 230n
'Sailors and the Sea', **17**, 21–36
Quinn, Edward G., **21**, 141; **45**, 172
Quinn, Kenneth, **39**, 168n
Quinn, Michael, **14**, 146; **38**, 2, 8
Quinn, Tammy, **60**, 178
Quinn, Vincent, **56**, 68n
Quinones, Ricardo J., **19**, 131; **29**, 16n; **34**, 26n; **38**, 10
Quint, David, **42**, 68n, 164n; **49**, 59n
Quintela, Paula, **18**, 127
Quintilian, **7**, 85; **30**, 14; **31**, 14n, 17, 18; **42**, 70, 89; **48**, 31n, 136; **55**, 219n; **59**, 230
Quirk, Sir Randolph, **42**, 195; **53**, 14n
Quo Vadis, **10**, 38

Raab, Felix, **21**, 143–4; **29**, 90; **38**, 122n; **55**, 213n; **56**, 225n
Raab, Rudolf, **44**, 111n
Raach, John H., **17**, 155n
Rabanus, Gert, **37**, 160n, 200
Rabb, Ellis, **11**, 123
Rabb, Theodore K., **43**, 63n
Rabelais, François, **1**, 52; **6**, 79; **8**, 59;**22**, 5; **29**, 91; **35**, 175; **40**, 78n; **46**, 10–18, 19n, 117, 130n, 23; **49**, 70, 72, 77; **50**, 127; **51**, 292; **52**, 192; **54**, 304; **55**, 266; **56**, 52; **57**, 212, 213;
Rabinow, Paul, **46**, 124n
Rabkin, Norman, **19**, 130; **20**, 154; **22**, 146–7, 158; **24**, 12, 145n, 161; **25**, 11–12, 16n; **26**, 163; **27**, 164; **29**, 9, 89–90; **32**, 4, 219, 226; **34**, 39n, 145; **35**, 172–3; **37**, 8, 55, 56, 164, 203; **38**, 3, 15, 18n, 131n, 145n; **39**, 51m, 136n, 211; **40**, 36, 148n, 153, 187, 196; **41**, 212; **42**, 173; **43**, 46n, 135n, 226; **44**, 55n, 222; **46**, 93n; **52**, 108n; **53**, 339; **54**, 127n; **55**, 211, 212n, 340; **57**, 236
Raby, Peter, **37**, 200, 201; **57**, 115
Race, Sydney, **6**, 162; **7**, 145; **9**, 145
Rachmaninov, Sergei, **48**, 227
Racine, Jean, **5**, 10, 93, 111; **7**, 110; **10**, 37, 72, 128; **13**, 151; **16**, 74; **20**, 9, 11; **22**, 22, 163; **24**, 38, 79, 81, 83; **27**, 157; **29**, 9, 165; **34**, 2, 6; **35**, 24; **36**, 45; **48**, 7; **50**, 132; **53**, 49–51, 54, 58; **54**, 109; **60**, 215–16, 220n22
Phèdre, **9**, 60
Bajazet, **20**, 11–13
Bérénice, **20**, 2
Racine, Louis, **16**, 53
Rackham, Arthur, **37**, 52, 53; **40**, 173; **49**, 128; **56**, 6, 9, 10
Rackham, H., **39**, 149n; **42**, 88n; **49**, 169n; **50**, 62n
Rackin, Phyllis, **24**, 146; **26**, 159; **33**, 190; **41**, 222; **42**, 32n, 33n, 40n; **44**, 163; **46**, 6, 20n; **48**, 86n, 242; **51**, 281; **52**, 56n, 57n, 178n, 279; **53**, 234n, 299; **56**, 204n; **57**, 318, 319; **58**, 131; **60**, 109n34, 184n2, 190n21, 193
Rackoff, Louis, **36**, 59
Radcliff, Sir Anthony, **11**, 92, 94
Radcliff-Umstead, Douglas, **46**, 5n
Radcliffe, Debbie, **42**, 154; **45**, 149; **46**, 199; **47**, 216
Radcliffe, Margaret, **55**, 53–4
Radcliffe, Mrs, **30**, 200
Radday, Yehuda T., **32**, 115
Radebrecht, F., **9**, 34n
Radel, Nicholas F., **50**, 243; **51**, 291; **60**, 348
Rademacher, Nelly, **12**, 116
Radford, Matthew, **47**, 219
Radford, Michael, **60**, 213, 355
Radford, Richard, **45**, 107
Radford, Thomas, **60**, 52
Radice, Betty, **33**, 77n
Radim, Paul, **35**, 70n
Radin, Victoria, **36**, 151
Radovic, Dj., **18**, 134
Radzinowicz, L., **17**, 83n
Radzins, E., **39**, 83n
Rae, Alexander, **35**, 44
Rae, Nola, **41**, 191; **42**, 155; **43**, 210
Rae, T. I., **21**, 142
Raeck, Kurt, **4**, 152
'Shakespeare in the German Open-Air Theatre', **3**, 95–7
Raevensbusch, R. M. S. van den, **1**, 114
Raevsky, N. N., **5**, 94, 105n
Rafael, **57**, 42
Raffat, Shanaya, **60**, 302
Raglan, Lord, **15**, 124n
Ragon, Michel, **48**, 40n
Ragussis, Michael, **54**, 183n, 184n, 185n
Rähesoo, Jaak, **31**, 175
Raikes, Elizabeth, **55**, 108n
Raimon de Toulouse, **15**, 93
Raimondi, Ezio, **51**, 184n
Raimund, Ferdinand, **13**, 125
Rain, Douglas, **14**, 117; **34**, 157; **38**, 139n
Raine, James, **49**, 184n, 185n, 193n
Raines, James, **32** 137n
Rainoldes, John, **54**, 61; **58**, 221
Rainolds, John, **32**, 69, 70, 71; **39**, 228
Th'overthrow of Stage-Playes, **4**, 94
Rainolds, William, **55**, 234; **56**, 194n
Rains, Claude, **58**, 139
Rainsford family, **8**, 7
Rainsford, Nickie, **44**, 199; **46**, 192
Raison, Jeremy, **51**, 262
Raistrick, George, **38**, 212; **45**, 152
Raith, J., **3**, 21n
Raitt, Jill, **54**, 129n, 139n
Raitt, R. S., **55**, 91n
Raitt, Suzanne, **54**, 312
Rajz, János, **16**, 135
Raknem, Ingvald, **42**, 32n
Rakoff, Alvin, **49**, 153, 160–1
Raksányi, G., **14**, 120
Raleigh (Ralegh), Sir Walter (*ob.* 1618), **1**, 71, 81; **3**, 10, 25; **4**, 149; **6**, 9; **7**, 20; **8**, 6; **9**, 24, 25, 81, 144; **17**, 12, 24, 28–9, 32, 39, 118, 127; **18**, 112; **19**, 65, 150; **20**, 3, 29, 79; **21**, 103; **22**, 147; **23**, 43–4, 161; **26**, 103, 114n; **27**, 56; **28**, 7, 21, 24, 28; **29**, 178; **31**, 48; **32**, 90n, 91n; **34**, 102; **36**, 40, 183; **38**, 49, 53, 122; **40**, 185; **41**, 197; **42**, 71n, 123; **43**, 161; **44**, 11, 37, 232, 237; **45**, 181; **46**, 16, 99n, 225; **48**, 4n; **49**, 131; **50**, 71n, 261; **53**, 33; **54**, 133, 355; **56**, 79, 217; **57**, 12, 20, 22, 85; **60**, 50, 255–6, 260–1
History of the World, **1**, 67; **10**, 29, 31, 38n; **14**, 80; **20**, 27, 28
Raleigh, Sir Walter (1861–1922), **3**, 6, 69, 70, 146; **4**, 4, 5; **5**, 129; **6**, 2; **8**, 4, 7; **9**, 106; **10**, 26n; **15**, 6, 19; **17**, 120; **18**, 4; **20**, 75; **21**, 8, 28n; **25**, 1; **26**, 73; **27**, 112; **56**, 210n; **58**, 123; **59**, 153, 153n30
Johnson on Shakespeare, **11**, 88n; **14**, 88n
Raley, Marjorie, **51**, 279
Ralli, Augustus, **6**, 152; **18**, 118n
Rally, Andrew, **49**, 271
Ralph, Brian, **44**, 197
Ram, Alur Janaki, **23**, 149
Raman, Shankar, **52**, 188n
Ramaswamy, Archana, **60**, 301
Ramberg, J. H., **37**, 44, 45; **49**, 118
Rambuss, Richard, **50**, 65, 76n
Ramel, Henrik, **22**, 121
Ramel, Jacques, **22**, 172n
Ramicora, Dunya, **49**, 274; **50**, 231
Ramm, Dieter, **37**, 158n
Ramm, John, **43**, 210; **59**, 207–8, 211, 334, 335
Ramos, Pericles Eugenio da Silva, **10**, 115; **20**, 123

Rampolokeng, Lesego, **57**, 163
Ramsay, Allan, **39**, 154n
Ramsay, G. D., **17**, 26n
Ramsden, John, **47**, 215
Ramsey, Alasdair, **43**, 206; **46**, 197; **56**, 296
Ramsey, Herbert, **50**, 289
Ramsey, Jarold W., **21**, 138; **25**, 176; **28**, 155; **29**, 173; **56**, 230n
Ramsey, Paul, **31**, 163, 193; **38**, 26n; **46**, 47n; **59**, 69n2, 77n13
Ramsey, Peter, **35**, 66n
Ramsey, Warren, **45**, 4n
Ramster, John, **57**, 294
Ramus, Petrus (*see also* Pierre de la Ramée), **7**, 6, 35; **17**, 65; **18**, 176; **27**, 83, 84; **35**, 79; **42**, 89
Ran (Kurosawa), **48**, 263
Ranald, Margaret Loftus, **18**, 164, 168; **31**, 179; **34**, 174; **42**, 167; **49**, 181n
Rand, Frank P., **5**, 135
Randall, Dale B. J., **39**, 223n, 231; **49**, 27n, 28n
Randall, David A., **1**, 72
Randle, Charlotte, **54**, 266; **55**, 306
Randle, Mary Jo, **42**, 162
Randolph, John, **24**, 93
Randolph, Thomas, **11**, 108, 109; **14**, 13; **17**, 49; **34**, 183; **38**, 86; **60**, 274n23
The Drinking Academy, **15**, 40n
The Jealous Lovers, **11**, 108
Randone, Salvo, **5**, 113; **11**, 121; **14**, 121
Rang, F. C., **15**, 16
Ranin, Matti, **13**, 126
Rank, Otto, **22**, 15
Rankins, William, **17**, 135
Ránky, Gy., **16**, 135
Rann, Joseph, **59**, 56–7n20, 57n21, 60, 62
Ranney, Omar, **10**, 149
Ransom, John Crow, **15**, 16, 17; **31**, 164; **32**, 214; **40**, 201
Ranson, Malcolm, **45**, 149
Ranson, Nichola, **49**, 142n
Ranum, Orest, **50**, 78n
Ranzau, Gert, **22**, 121, 123
Ranzau, Henrik, **22**, 121
Raphael (*see* Sanzio), **26**, 54, 65; **27**, 55; **49**, 157
Rapin, René, **18**, 129
Rapley, Dale, **57**, 264
Rappaport, Gideon, **32**, 234
Rappoport, R., **15**, 137
Rare Triumphs of Love and Fortune, The, **11**, 20–1, 44, 48; **31**, 25n; **54**, 229
Rashleigh, Alasdair, **43**, 206
Rashleigh, Andy, **43**, 206; **49**, 280; **51**, 268
Rasmussen, Börseth, **10**, 120
Rasmussen, Eric, **40**, 235; **43**, 242, 263–4; **44**, 233; 234n; **48**, 281; **53**, 342; **55**, 65n, 259n, 392–6; **56**, 182; **58**, 343; **59**, 157n1, 161, 163n20, 174, 299, 380; **60**, 361–9, 369n8
Textual Companion to 'Dr Faustus' A, **48**, 281n
Rasmussen, Mark David, **58**, 334
Raspa, Anthony, **54**, 35n
Rastall, Richard, **58**, 221, 222
Rastell, John, **17**, 193; **29**, 98, 99n; **52**, 272; **59**, 243, 245
Rastell, William, **11**, 100, 102, 103, 105n
Ratcliff, Derek, **44**, 131n, 132n, 133n
Ratcliffe, Michael, **38**, 209; **40**, 174; **50**, 34
Rathbone, Basil, **49**, 153–4
Rathbone, Niky, **47**, 181; **51**, 257–70
Ratib, Gamil, **11**, 120
Ratnam, Roshina, **60**, 290
Ratsey's Ghost, **18**, 35
Rattigan, Paul, **44**, 200
Rattigan, Terence, **56**, 246
Ratto, Giovanni, **2**, 129
Rattray, R. F., **25**, 1n
Rauber, D. F., **24**, 145
Rauchbauer, Otto, **41**, 211n, 213
Rauschenberger, Maria, **37**, 160n
Rauso, **50**, 39n
Ravelhofer, Barbara, **54**, 197n; **55**, 241, 242, 243n, 249, 255n; **60**, 119n3, 123n16, 356–7, 361
Raven, A. A., **9**, 1; **18**, 34
Raven, C. E., **23**, 45n
Raven, James, **55**, 198
Ravenet, François-Simon, **49**, 115–16
Ravens, Jan, **44**, 202
Ravenscroft, Christopher, **41**, 190; **48**, 236; **60**, 327
Ravenscroft, Edward, **3**, 144; **10**, 39, 49n, 61, 70n; **51**, 19, 324; **55**, 257
adaptation of *Titus Andronicus*, **9**, 85n
Ravenscroft, Thomas, **1**, 68; **15**, 1, 6
Brief discourse . . . on measurable music, **6**, 55
Deuteromelia, **3**, 56; **13**, 107, 110n
Melismata, **13**, 107
Pammelia, **13**, 107
Ravid, Shoshana, 5, 113; **10**, 119; **13**, 129
Ravn, V. C., **22**, 119, 124n
Raw, Laurence J., **52**, 22n
Rawi, Raad, **40**, 174; **43**, 211; **44**, 197; **51**, 227
Rawling, Henry, **13**, 94
Rawlings, Peter, **54**, 302, 303
Rawlins, Thomas, **43**, 149, 151–2, 167–8; **50**, 165
Rawlinson, Thomas, *see under* Libraries, Bodleian
Rawnsley, Andrew, **56**, 93n, 103n
Rawnsley, H. D., **44**, 106n
Ray, George W., **24**, 161
Ray, Isaac, **18**, 39
Ray, Robert H., **31**, 190, 197; **41**, 209
Ray, S. N., **19**, 120
Ray, Satyajit, **48**, 12; **59**, 370
Ray, Sid, **52**, 279
Raymond, Emily, **45**, 155; **48**, 235
Raymond, Gary, **43**, 212; **45**, 150
Raymond, George, **58**, **39**
Raymond, Henry, **24**, 92
Raymond, Maude, **15**, 109n; **57**, 256
Rayne, Stephen, **44**, 202; **47**, 213; **48**, 230
Rayner, Alice, **52**, 34n
Rayner, Lord, **44**, 101
Raynoldes, William, *see* Renolds, William
Raynor, Howard, **55**, 287
Raynsford, Edward, **4**, 70
Raysor, Thomas Middleton, **8**, 26n; **10**, 49n; **14**, 88n; **18**, 38; **23**, 102, 103, 104n, 106, 107, 109, 110; **24**, 44; **25**, 45n; **34**, 12n, 52n, 54n, 104n; **38**, 168n; **43**, 221; **50**, 101n; **54**, 66n
Razum, Hannes, **10**, 148

Razuvgen, Maxim, **49**, 277
Ré, Michel de, **14**, 119
Rea, J., **19**, 137
Rea, J. D., **8**, 4
Rea, John A., **51**, 185–6
Rea, John D., **27**, 59n; **33**, 70n
Rea, Kenneth, **54**, 295
Rea, Leisa, **45**, 148
Read, Conyers, **17**, 109n; **35**, 72n
Read, Joanna, **56**, 292
Read, Simon, **11**, 71
Read, Thomas G., **9**, 120; **10**, 123; **12**, 120
Reade, Charles, **7**, 33; **41**, 24
Reade, John, **58**, 237
Reade, Simon, **49**
Reade, Timothy, **47**, 39; **58**, 237
Readle, Charlotte, **55**, 331
Reagan, Nancy, **57**, 136
Reagan, Ronald, **57**, 143
Realdus Columbus, **17**, 148
Reaney, P. H., **22**, 124n
Reardon, Bernard M. G., **55**, 221n
Reardon, Michael, **47**, 117
Reaske, C. R., **26**, 153; **29**, 175
Reaves, Judy, **46**, 198
Reay, B., **46**, 32n
Rebel Without a Cause, **52**, 90
Rebello, L. F., **18**, 127
Rebelo, L. S., **18**, 127
Rebhorn, James, **57**, 186
Rebhorn, Wayne A., **33**, 199; **44**, 226; **45**, 167; **49**, 45n, 55, 292; **50**, 259
Rebush, Roman, **55**, 123
Recorde, Robert, **17**, 141
Red Bull Theatre, *see under* Theatres, Elizabethan
Red Lion Inn, *see under* Theatres, Elizabethan
Reddaway, T. F., 'London and the Court', **17**, 3–12
Reddington, John, **28**, 171n
Reddington, Ian, **45**, 157; **47**, 213; **54**, 290
Reddish, Samuel, **53**, 327
Rederyker stage, Antwerp, **3**, 86; **17**, 202
Redfern, Walter D., **49**, 98
Redford, Bruce, **51**, 5
Redgewell, Jacqueline, **60**, 288
Redgrave, Corin, **26**, 147; **41**, 185; **42**, 153; **44**, 192; **54**, 251–3; **55**, 326; **56**, 345; **58**, 290; **59**, 318, 340; **60**, 322
Redgrave, G. R., **54**, 90n, 94n, 95n; **59**, 1
Redgrave, G. R., *see* Pollard, A. W.
Redgrave, Jemma, **44**, 195; **47**, 209; **55**, 312; **56**, 293
Redgrave, Lynn, **51**, 270
Redgrave, Sir Michael, **2**, 130, 131; **4**, 133, 157; **6**, 132, 134, 135–6, 138–9; **7**, 126, 127; **9**, 22, 133; **12**, 80; **26**, 147; **40**, 40; **50**, 149; **51**, 270
  production of 2 *Henry IV* reviewed, **6**, 137–8
Redgrave, Vanessa, **16**, 144–6, 150–1; **23**, 132; **28**, 142; **34**, 173; **39**, 181; **40**, 169, 173, 181–3; **41**, 183; 189; **44**, 195; **45**, 59; **50**, 225; **54**, 246, 263–4; **55**, 332; **56**, 345; **60**, 79
Redman, Amanda, **51**, 251
Redman, Crispin, **45**, 146
Redman, Joyce, **1**, 98
Redmayne, Eddie, **56**, 258–9
Redmond, James, **42**, 103n, 195n, 214; **43**, 70n; **45**, 162; **56**, 72n
Redmond, Michael J., **59**, 362
Redmond, Nicola, **44**, 197; **54**, 265; **55**, 329
Redmond, Siobhan, **43**, 205; **45**, 151; **51**, 231–2, 265
Redpath, Theodore, **19**, 161; **31**, 164; **40**, 41n; **41**, 242; **56**, 72n, 74n
Reed, A. W., *Early Tudor Drama*, **14**, 2
Reed, Arthur, **59**, 152–3, 154
Reed, E. B., **15**, 8, 13
Reed, G., **28**, 154
Reed, Henry, **21**, 52n
Reed, Isaac, **3**, 49; **5**, 105n; **18**, 108; **21**, 49–50, 52n; **32**, 242; **33**, 210; **34**, 14; **38**, 97n; **40**, 236; **46**, 236; **59**, 122n54, 125, 127–8
Reed, J. C., **55**, 268n
Reed, Joanna, **50**, 231
Reed, Nancy, **60**, 178
Reed, Robert Rentoul, Jr, **14**, 155; **15**, 170; **23**, 146; **39**, 209
Reed, Sarah, **44**, 200
Reed, Tim, **43**, 210; **45**, 152
Reed, Timothy, **50**, 156
Reed, Victor, **23**, 165n
Reeder, Robert, **57**, 305
Rees, Abraham, **51**, 84n
Rees, B., **13**, 134
Rees, D. G., **21**, 147
Rees, Daniel Evans, **45**, 150
Rees, David Evans, **45**, 155; **47**, 217; **50**, 226
Rees, Elizabeth, **49**, 274
Rees, Ennis, *The Tragedies of George Chapman*, **14**, 12
Rees, Garnet, **57**, 115
Rees, James, **20**, 163
Rees, Joan, **7**, 145; **8**, 152; **9**, 139, 143n; **10**, 4, 5; **14**, 154; **20**, 163; **21**, 145; **23**, 166n; **26**, 34, 36, 165; **32**, 211; **35**, 98; **37**, 13n, 191; **41**, 87n, 212; **45**, 162; **53**, 2n
  'An Elizabethan Eyewitness of *Antony and Cleopatra*?', **6**, 91–3
  'Revenge, Retribution, and Reconciliation', **24**, 31–5
Rees, Roger, **25**, 166; **30**, 176, 178; **33**, 174; **38**, 209–12; **42**, 151
Rees-Jones, S., **13**, 105n
Reese, Gertrude C., **6**, 9
Reese, J. E., **24**, 148
Reese, M. M., **27**, 32n, 41; **29**, 85; **30**, 49n, 56n, 58n; **31**, 93; **38**, 4, 66; **39**, 226; **54**, 215n
  Shakespeare: his World and his Work reviewed, **7**, 138
  The Cease of Majesty reviewed, **16**, 161, 169
Reeve, Alex, **10**, 123; **14**, 124; **47**, 96–7, 106
Reeve, Henry, **24**, 88
Reeve, M. D., **51**, 163n
Reeve, Ralph, **32**, 195; **33**, 162
Reeves, Francis, **56**, 200
Reeves, G. A., **7**, 88n
Reeves, Geoffrey, **39**, 6n; **50**, 263
Reeves, Keanu, **48**, 233
Reeves, Saskia, **42**, 153; **43**, 216; **45**, 127; **47**, 189; **52**, 234; **53**, 280
Refn, Helge, **1**, 115; **18**, 128
Reformation, **17**, 42–3, 105–9, 111
Regan, Linda, **49**, 273
Regan, Vincent, **43**, 206; **45**, 152
Reggiani, Serge, **9**, 112

Reggio, Pietro, **18**, 94; **51**, 80
Regio, R., **10**, 43, 49n
Regiomontanus' prophecies, **17**, 127
Regius, Raphael, **50**, 85n; **56**, 56n, 59
Rehan, Ada, **7**, 29; **32**, 21, 23, 24; **52**, 288; **56**, 134, 135; **60**, 77–8
Reibetanz, John, **32**, 221; **33**, 43, 46, 49–50, 51, 52–3, 60n; **47**, 262
Reichenberg, Suzanne Angélique Charlotte, **9**, 62, 63, 64
Reichert, Günter, **23**, 116
Reichert, John F., **20**, 166
Reichert, Klaus, **53**, 294; **56**, 315
Reid, Alexander, **40**, 178
Reid, Alison, **48**, 237
Reid, B. L., **19**, 124; **20**, 148, 150
Reid, Douglas A., **35**, 12n
Reid, J. D., **55**, 206n
Reid, J. K. S., **54**, 129n
Reid, Kate, **16**, 153
Reid, R. R., **48**, 71n
Reid, Richard Lamer, **55**, 360
Reid, S. W., **26**, 155; **28**, 180; **29**, 181; **30**, 206, 207; **31**, 194; **33**, 208n; **35**, 186; **36**, 191; **37**, 218; **38**, 241n; **39**, 250; **50**, 272n
Reid, Stephen A., **25**, 176
Reidy, Gabrielle, **46**, 171; **51**, 246
Reidy, John, **52**, 186n
Reif, Patricia, **23**, 163
Reilly, J. J., **18**, 118n
Reilly, Jim, **53**, 119, 125n
Reilly, William, **53**, 98
Reiman, Donald H., **19**, 133; **49**, 160n
Reimann, Aribert, **44**, 195; **46**, 194
Reimer, A. P., **40**, 203–4
Reimer, C. J., **4**, 22; **10**, 136
Reimolds, Robert, **32**, 196
Reinell, Sir George, Marshal of King's Bench prison, **17**, 96
Reinelt, Janelle G., **55**, 239n
Reinfandt, Christoph, **56**, 322–3
Reinhard, Kenneth, **49**, 67n; **55**, 9
Reinhardt, Max, **1**, 106; **2**, 1, 3, 128; **3**, 113; **4**, 101, 126; **5**, 116; **8**, 79, 80; **9**, 57; **12**, 79; **13**, 142, 145n; **18**, 67, 73; **44**, 107, 10; **45**, 63; **47**, 3, 237; **48**, 222; **49**, 306; **52**, 284, 290; **56**, 7; **58**, 42
Reinhardt-Thimig, Frau, **6**, 117
Reis, Ilse H., **37**, 159n
Reisz, Karel, **45**, 59
Reitani, Luigi, **59**, 194–5, 196, 197
Reitel, Enn, **39**, 93
Reiter, Rayna, **56**, 74n
Religion
dissent, **17**, 120–9
satire, **17**, 130–1
and travel, **17**, 42–3
and education, **17**, 54
prison, **17**, 88–9, 97
Protestant, **17**, 105–6, 115, 121, 123–6, 130
Roman Catholic, **17**, 106–7, 110, 121–4, 130–1
Relph, George, **1**, 102
Rembrandt van Rijn, **7**, 121; **13**, 75; **24**, 99; **34**, 158; **35**, 36; **39**, 95, 99, 100, 109; **48**, 26; **57**, 157
Remhardt, Max, **35**, 1; **39**, 1, 2, 65, 109; **40**, 2, 51–2, 55, 58
Remick, Lee, **53**, 171
Remy, N., **28**, 121
Renan, Ernest, **3**, 110; **22**, 48, 119, 121, 123
Renard, Christopher, **13**, 135
Renaud, Madeleine, **10**, 118
Rendall, David, **56**, 295
Rendle, Adrian, **56**, 123n
Rendle, William, **1**, 29, 35n; **33**, 147; **47**, 172n
Renegado, The, **52**, 210–13
Renger, Konrad, **60**, 248n50
Reni, Guido, **45**, 117
Rennert, Hugo Albert, *The Life of Lope de Vega*, **20**, 98, 104n, 105n
The Spanish Stage in the Time of Lope de Vega, **14**, 109n
Rennie, Malcolm, **42**, 154
Reno, Raymond H., **19**, 132
Renoir, Jean, **9**, 112; **50**, 30
Renolds, William, **4**, 71, 75
Rentz, Bernhard, **57**, 165
Renwick, W. L., **1**, 130; **10**, 17, 25n
Replogle, Clare, **24**, 143
Reppen, Joseph, **49**, 207n
Requests, Court of, *see under* London
Resch, J., **10**, 3
Resenda, Aimara da Cunha, **57**, 327
Resistable Rise of Arturo Ui, The, **54**, 340
Resnais, Alain, **40**, 118
Respublica, **50**, 255
Restoration Drama, **1**, 65–6
Restoration plays, the printing of, **4**, 163
Retallack, Guy, **56**, 296
Retallack, John, **42**, 155; **43**, 216; **44**, 192, 194; **45**, 150; **46**, 200; **48**, 228, 234; **49**, 277; **50**, 235; **51**, 258; **52**, 231; **53**, 279
Retamar, Roberto Fernández, **48**, 155, 157
Rétoré, Guy, **13**, 127; **18**, 122
Return from Parnassus, The, **2**, 41; **3**, 140; **4**, 91; **14**, 76; **15**, 62, 71n, 72n
Return to the Forbidden Planet, **44**, 201
Retzsch, F. A. Moritz, **7**, 92; **37**, 46, 47, 50, 53
Reusner, Nicholas, **15**, 97n
Revard, Carter, **34**, 196
Revelation, **11**, 60
Revels Accounts, The, **4**, 88–9
Revels Office, **11**, 151; **12**, 16–18
Revels' Players
see under Theatre, Elizabethan, *and* Master of the Revels
Revenge of Bussy D'Ambois, The, **52**, 296
Revill, Clive, **11**, 135
Revill, George, **60**, 187n13
Revill, Melanie, **45**, 63n
Revzin, Philip, **52**, 158n
Rewt, Polly, **51**, 6
Rex, Richard, **54**, 8
Rey, Jean-Pierre, **7**, 108; **8**, 118
Rey-Flaud, Bernadette, **52**, 122n, 129
Reybas, André, **16**, 54, 133; **18**, 123
Reyher, Paul, **1**, 11; **6**, 4, 10, 26, 33n, 34n; **18**, 123; **28**, 42
Essai sur les idées dans l'œuvre de Shakespeare, **2**, 121, 126, 133–4, 141
Reynard, James, **44**, 202; **45**, 149; **46**, 194; **51**, 268; **52**, 264; **53**, 282, 285

Reynold, Gonzague de, *Caliban délivré*, **2**, 127–8
Reynoldes, Edward, **25**, 148
Reynoldes, Richard, *Chronicle of all the Noble Emperours of the Romaines*, **10**, 29, 30
Reynolds (Renaldes), Jane, **36**, 136–7, 142
Reynolds (Stratford Manor Court), **12**, 100
Reynolds, Billie, **49**, 270
Reynolds, Bryan, **55**, 346, 348; **57**, 118, 145, 149; **58**, 333
Reynolds, Carol, **47**, 213
Reynolds, Celia, **42**, 156
Reynolds, Ernest, **55**, 130
Reynolds, Frederick, **20**, 107; **47**, 148; **60**, 190
Reynolds, George Fulmer, **1**, 3–4, 5, 6; **3**, 140; **4**, 11, 151–2; **5**, 143; **7**, 80n; **8**, 11; **10**, 85, 87n, 88n, 89n; **11**, 146; **12**, 65; **14**, 149; **15**, 139; **16**, 166; **22**, 35; **25**, 9; **41**, 4, 5; **47**, 37n, 78n, 89; **52**, 4–5
'*Hamlet* at the Globe', **9**, 49–53.
'*Troilus and Cressida* on the Elizabethan Stage', **2**, 141
The Staging of Elizabethan Plays at the Red Bull Theater, **12**, 42; **13**, 122–3
'Was there a "Tarras" in Shakespeare's Globe?', **4**, 97–100
Reynolds, Gillian, **56**, 249
Reynolds, Henry, **20**, 27
Reynolds, Hilary, **46**, 198
Reynolds, James A., **36**, 177
Reynolds, Jane, **13**, 68n
Reynolds, John, *see* Rainolds, John
Reynolds, John Hamilton, **13**, 58, 61, 68n; **41**, 103–5; **44**, 147; **53**, 64
Reynolds, Sir Joshua, **4**, 80; **6**, 61; **13**, 80n; **37**, 45, 46; **51**, 4, 10, 122; **59**, 132; **60**, 354
Reynolds, Larry, **58**, 172
Reynolds, Miss, **32**, 2911
Reynolds, Peter, **48**, 224
Reynolds, Robert, **36**, 135, 137–8, 139, 142, 144
Reynolds, S. W., **10**, 73
Reynolds, Susan, **59**, 239n2, 240
Reynolds, William, **21**, 148; **48**, 254
Rezepter, V., **16**, 138
Rheam, Sue, **51**, 261
Rhenanus, Johannes, **17**, 196
Rhetoric, Shakespeare's knowledge of theories of, **7**, 6–8, 14–15, 22–3
Rhoads, Diana A., **40**, 194–5
Rhodes, Ernest L., **31**, 185; **33**, 140n
Rhodes, John, **19**, 104; **58**, 243
Rhodes, Justin, **51**, 263
Rhodes, Neil, **35**, 175; **46**, 223; **52**, 286; **58**, 333
Rhodes, R. Crompton, **10**, 89n
Rhys, E., **55**, 139n
Rhys, Matthew, **56**, 4n; **59**, 344
Rhys, Paul, **51**, 250–1; **53**, 253–4; **54**, 284; **58**, 275, 276; **59**, 341; **60**, 285
Rhys, Will, **47**, 211
Rhys Jones, Griff, **45**, 122, 124, 126
Rhys-Davies, John, **31**, 147
Riabov, R., **45**, 89n
Ribeiro, Alvaro, **27**, 178; **33**, 187n; **51**, 5
Ribner, Irving, **3**, 141; **7**, 136, 140; **8**, 144; **10**, 11; **11**, 138–9; **14**, 10, 145 and n; **16**, 44; **19**, 6, 119, 120, 146; **20**, 127; **21**, 151; **22**, 155; **24**, 164; **26**, 7; **27**, 71; **28**, 4n, 7, 9; **29**, 83, 84, 89, 90; **33**, 9; **34**, 91n, 97n; **36**, 93n; **38**, 7; **42**, 15, 117; **44**, 2n, 71n; **45**, 18n, 22n, 23n; **47**, 71n; **48**, 71n; **50**, 181n
The English History Play in the Age of Shakespeare, **12**, 133 and n, 134; **14**, 4
Ricci, Corrado, **1**, 11
Ricci, Digbi, **55**, 279
Ricci, Luigi, **27**, 46n
Ricci, Renzo, **4**, 128; **6**, 121; **10**, 120; **12**, 114
Ricci, Seymour de, **1**, 61, 70
Rice, Charles, **35**, 7n
Rice, Emma, **60**, 310–11, 312
Rice, Eugene F., Jr, **33**, 99n; **54**, 43n
Rice, G. P., **44**, 62n
Rice, J. R., **28**, 156
Rice, John, **26**, 45; **58**, 231–2, 232
Rice, Joseph, **35**, 7
Rice, Julian C., **28**, 155; **40**, 75n
Rice, Peter, **10**, 130
Rich, Adrienne, **44**, 206, 241; **56**, 150
Rich, Barnaby, **17**, 41
Rich, Christopher, **47**, 27
Rich, Frank, **45**, 43n
Rich, Georgina, **59**, 309, 345
Rich, Geraldine, **58**, 278
Rich, Henry, 1st Earl of Holland, **11**, 109, 115n; **14**, 109n
Rich, John, **15**, 173; **47**, 15n, 27; **56**, 351
Rich, Mr, **32**, 103n
Rich, Penelope (*née* Devereux), Lady Rich, **27**, 178; **32**, 235; **54**, 171; **60**, 344
Rich, Sir Richard, **54**, 171
Rich, Townsend, **46**, 10n, 15n
Richard I, King, **14**, 30; **42**, 42
Richard II, King of England, **25**, 188; **48**, 71; **55**, 45; **57**, 236; **60**, 113
Richard III, King of England, **42**, 21; **51**, 116; **54**, 124; **55**, 276; **60**, 112–13
Richard III, fictitious mystery play on, **3**, 53; **11**, 151; **14**, 44n, 166; **16**, 173–4; **20**, 81n, 162, 175
Richard, Duke of York, The True Tragedie of, **3**, 23, 47, 110; **4**, 7, 57, 84; **6**, 4–5, 169; **7**, 147, 148, 151; **9**, 83; **10**, 145; **11**, 151; **14**, 44n, 166; **16**, 173–4; **20**, 81n, 162, 175
Shakespeare Quarto facsimile reviewed, **13**, 164
Richard, Emily, **38**, 211, 212
Richard, J. L., **11**, 119
Richardot, Jean, **33**, 165n
Richards, Bernard, **34**, 185
Richards, Dai, **60**, 198
Richards, I. A., **5**, 83, 91n, 130; **7**, 10, 11; **9**, 132; **10**, 136; **26**, 9; **28**, 29; **36**, 85n; **40**, 32; **45**, 57; **53**, 92
Richards, Inigo, **47**, 27
Richards, Jane, **46**, 196
Richards, Jeffrey, **49**, 307
Richards, Jennifer, **54**, 314
Richards, Joshua, **53**, 263
Richards, Keith, **57**, 152
Richards, Kenneth, **23**, 171n, 172; **35**, 3n, 9n; **39**, 13; **41**, 225; **55**, 247–8
Richards, Laura, **55**, 247–8
Richards, Martin, **52**, 258
Richards, Nathaniel, **43**, 149n, 152, 167n; **50**, 165; **58**, 239
Messalina, **15**, 202

Richards, Peter, **55**, 326
Richards, Sam, **54**, 290
Richards, Sandra, **51**, 3
Richards, Val, **55**, 9
Richardson, Alex, **43**, 217
Richardson, Anthony, **15**, 145
Richardson, Arleigh D., **9**, 134; **15**, 178–9
Richardson, Brian, **44**, 221; **53**, 2, 7
Richardson, David, **37**, 138
Richardson, Guy, **52**, 264
Richardson, Ian, **20**, 139, 140; **21**, 115, 116, 122–5; **22**, 139, 140; **23**, 131; **24**, 117, 119, 121, 124, 130; **25**, 65; **28**, 142, 143, 144, 147; **29**, 146–7, 152, 153, 154; **31**, 153; **39**, 185, 240; **40**, 223; **41**, 47; **50**, 49; **52**, 309
Richardson, J. M., **44**, 239
Richardson, Joy, **48**, 225; **51**, 208
Richardson, Maurice Wigham, **9**, 58n
Richardson, Miles, **59**, 304
Richardson, Miranda, **56**, 117
Richardson, Neil, **45**, 149, 153
Richardson, Nicholas, **4**, 90
Richardson, Sir Ralph, **1**, 103, 105; **2**, 18; **4**, 105; **11**, 128, 130, 131; **16**, 20; **39**, 42, 95n; **48**, 264; **49**, 231; **50**, 29; **55**, 172; **56**, 113; **57**, 81; **60**, 116
Richardson, Robert D. Jr., **53**, 133n
Richardson, Ruth, **60**, 227
Richardson, Samuel, **42**, 99; **51**, 27–43; **53**, 301
Richardson, Steven, **50**, 232
Richardson, Tony, **13**, 135, 140; **14**, 126; **15**, 151; **18**, 67; **45**, 53, 58, 59, 63; **60**, 354
Richardson, W. C., **57**, 202, 204
Richardson, William, **2**, 109; **18**, 37; **34**, 12, 13, 14, 15, 16, 20–1; **37**, 149–51; **43**, 106; **53**, 92, 94
Riche, Barnabe, *Farewell to Militarie Profession*, **4**, 87; **8**, 4; **9**, 142; **29**, 180; **32**, 74; **42**, 54n; **47**, 169; **50**, 68; **58**, 205
Richelieu, Armand Jean du Plessis, due de, Cardinal, **33**, 22
Riches, Anne, **51**, 176n
Riches, Mary Ellen, **57**, 237
Richeson, A. W., **33**, 143n
Richey, M. W., **17**, 27n
Richfield, Edwin, **31**, 148; **34**, 151
Richie, Donald, **39**, 74n
Richle, Wolfgang, **34**, 194; **39**, 219; **40**, 205
Richman, David, **45** 168
Richmond, Duke of, **47**, 18
Richmond, Evelyn B., **15**, 172
Richmond, Hugh Macrae, **23**, 144, 157; **26**, 152, 164; **30**, 47, 52n, 53n; **31**, 5n; **32**, 5; **33**, 199; **36**, 176; **38**, 4, 16, 50n, 4, 55n, 56n, 57n; **42**, 6n; **43**, 44n; **44**, 242; **45**, 187n; **47**, 140n, 231, 238n; **48**, 265; **55**, 344–5; **57**, 148; **58**, 319, 333
King Henry VIII, **48**, 265
Richmond, Velma Bourgeois, **55**, 345–6; **59**, 253n101
Richter, Bodo I. O., **21**, 154
Richter, Helene, **35**, 25n
Richter, Walter, **5**, 114
Rick, L., **32**, 73n
Rickards, Susannah, **46**, 160, 161
Rickert, R. T., **33**, 139n; **41**, 5n; **42**, 190; **43**, 141n; **44**, 149n; **45**, 107n, 183n; **47**, 15n, 175n, 241; **52**, 10n, 14n, 72n; **54**, 21n, 356; **55**, 12n, 27n, 28n, 29n, 34n
and see Foakes, R. A.
Ricketts, Charles, **29**, 141; **55**, 138n
Rickey, Fred, **39**, 81n
Rickey, Mary Ellen, **14**, 10; **18**, 164; **20**, 154; **25**, 12n; **41**, 73n; **54**, 14n
Rickman, Alan, **39**, 202; **42**, 200; **47**, 211; **52**, 251–3; **53**, 274
Rickman, Kate, **45**, 27n
Rickner, George, **19**, 103, 104, 106n
Ricks, Christopher, **27**, 44; **31**, 130; **42**, 210n; **43**, 127n; **46**, 125n
Ricks, Don M., **24**, 152; **38**, 5
Ricktre, R. T., **27**, 134n; **29**, 127, 128, 129
Ricoeur, Paul, **51**, 126
Ricordi, Giulio, **21**, 89
Ricotta, Vincenzo, **41**, 188
Riddell, Derek, **45**, 150
Riddell, James A., **29**, 174; **31**, 168; **51**, 291; **58**, 233
Riddington, Jason, **49**, 271
Riddock, Billy, **42**, 154
Rideout, Esmond, **45**, 153
Rider, Paul, **44**, 202; **45**, 153; **47**, 211; **55**, 312
Rider, Philip R., **34**, 196
Ridgley, Wayne, **60**, 178Fig.32
Ridgway, Lady, **39**, 231
Ridgway, Sir Thomas, **44**, 77
Riding, Alan, **50**, 50n
Riding, Laura, **32**, 214
Ridings, Richard, **44**, 173, 182, 195; **45**, 125, 156
Ridler, Anne, **13**, 148n; **24**, 168; **26**, 119n
Ridley, M. R., **4**, 5; **7**, 55; **10**, 3, 10; **12**, 148, 149; **15**, 26; **21**, 27n; **22**, 180; **23**, 61n; **24**, 3n; **33**, 99n, 116n; **37**, 120n; **38**, 244, 245; **42**, 101n; **50**, 3; **60**, 365
New Arden edition of *Antony and Cleopatra* reviewed, **8**, 157
(ed.) *Marlowe's Plays and Poems*, **14**, 8
Ridley, Nicholas, **52**, 171n; **54**, 4, 35
Ridolfi plot, **17**, 122
Ridoni, Relda, **12**, 114
Ridout, Matthew, **41**, 191; **42**, 210
Ridpath, George, **54**, 58–9, 61
Riebling, Barbara, **60**, 128n30
Riefer, Marcia, **58**, 49
Rieff, Philip, **46**, 111n
Riehle, Wolfgang, **23**, 116; **26**, 158; **47**, 254; **59**, 367
Riemer, A. P., **22**, 162; **24**, 1n; **35**, 157; **42** 183
Riesenberg, Peter N., **55**, 36n
Riewald, J. G., **29**, 134n, 135n; **33**, 154, 155n, 162; **36**, 137, 140
Riffaterre, Michael, **56**, 67
Rigaud, John Francis, **49**, 120
Rigaud, Nadia, **39**, 235
Rigby, Annie, **58**, 304
Rigby, Terence, **49**, 239
Rigg, Dame Diana, **20**, 134; **23**, 132; **39**, 89, 90; **46**, 191
Riggio, Milla Cozart, **49**, 284; **54**, 338
Riggs, David, **26**, 157; **27**, 78–9; **30**, 192; **38**, 4; **42**, 23, 30n, 117; **44**, 235–6; **54**, 23, 66n; **56**, 217n
Riggs, Otis, **1**, 107
Righter, *see* Barton, Anne
Righter, Anne, **18**, 60, 157–8
Righter, William, **25**, 189
Righton, Edward, **35**, 18
Rigney, James, **60**, 233, 234
Rignold, George, **41**, 34; **57**, 326
Rigold, Stuart, **36**, 178

Riley, Josephine, **57**, 169
Rilke, R. M., **16**, 170–1; **32**, 105n
Rilla, Paul, **48**, 172n
Rimbaud, Arthur, **48**, 105
Rimbault, Edward Francis, **9**, 86, 89n; **15**, 2
Rimmell, Nathan, **60**, 326
Rimmington, Noelle, **57**, 155
Rimmon-Kenan, Shlomith, **49**, 57n
Rindisbacher, Hans J., **49**, 209–10, 211n
Rinehart, Keith, **26**, 172
Ring, Maria, **55**, 326
Ringler, Richard N., **23**, 146n
Ringler, William A., Jr, **15**, 8; **16**, 164; **18**, 167, 180; **23**, 172; **27**, 178; **28**, 174; **42**, 47n; **52**, 324; **57**, 212, **60**, 366
Ringrose, John, **47**, 99, 100
Ringwald, Molly, **43**, 207
Rintoul, David, **43**, 213; **46**, 195; **52**, 222, 226–7; **56**, 279; **58**, 299; **59**, 343
Rintoul, Douglas, **57**, 296
Ripa, Cesare, **17**, 183; **36**, 175; **48**, 143–4; **49**, 81; **53**, 15n; **56**, 48, 52; **57**, 14
Ripin, Edwin M., **51**, 92n
Ripley, George, **58**, 132
Ripley, John, **20**, 81n; **34**, 182; **35**, 10, 14; **52**, 291; **53**, 72n
Rippy, Marguerite Hailey, **56**, 347; **60**, 169n6.2
Riss, Arthur, **46**, 219
Rissanen, Matti, **25**, 180; **58**, 319
Rist, Thomas, **54**, 24n, 314–15
Ristine, F. H., *English Tragi-Comedy*, **14**, 3
Ristori, Adelaide, **38**, 196, 197; **41**, 225; **55**, 224n
Ritchie, C. I. A., **17**, 77n
Ritson, Joseph, **14**, 87; **15**, 1; **24**, 171n; **34**, 13n, 14; **46**, 236; **47**, 256
Ritter, P., **18**, 79
Ritter, Peter, **60**, 184
Ritter, Sonia, **41**, 180–1; **50**, 225; **52**, 217, 223, 225; **55**, 330
Ritzer, George, **58**, 194
Riuttu, Leo, **13**, 126
Rivals, The, **54**, 255
Rivers, Anthony, **24**, 72
Rivers, L. Mendell, **57**, 138
Rivett, Alan, **56**, 247n
Rivington (London publisher), **59**, 129, 130
Rivington, F. and C., *Shakespeare*, **13**, 75
Rix, H. David, **55**, 219n
Rizner, L., **4**, 115n
Rizzio, David, **9**, 12
R J Williamson Company, **58**, 298, 300
R., J., remarks on Sonnet 107, **4**, 155
RL (unidentified author), **60**, 337
Roach, John, **13**, 76
Roach, Joseph R., **40**, 221; **47**, 10; **52**, 38, 39n, 43; **54**, 305; **55**, 239n, 242n, 254n, 344; **57**, 82, 86, 135; **59**, 287, 288n21
Roach, Tanya, **49**, 277
Roache, Linus, **41**, 178; **43**, 207; **44**, 180, 183; **45**, 117, 121, 148, 153; **47**, 212; **48**, 234; **54**, 253; **55**, 323, 330
Roaring Girl, The, **54**, 300
Roaring Girl's Hamlet, The, **47**, 210
Roark, Christopher, **42**, 182
Robards, Jason, Jr., **13**, 125
Robarts and Bellamy, **13**, 76
Robbe-Grillet, Alain, **41**, 108
Robbins, R. H. A., **21**, 149; **22**, 182
Robbins, Robin, **40**, 148n, 227n
Robbins, Rossell Hope, **41**, 114n
Robbins, William, **7**, 134
Robert of Gloucester, **33**, 16
Robert, Guy, **55**, 143n, 146n
Roberts, Adam, **44**, 202; **47**, 216
Roberts, Caroline, **53**, 342; **60**, 42n22
Roberts, Chrissy, **44**, 203
Roberts, Christian, **44**, 201
Roberts, Daniel, **55**, 320
Roberts, Eunice, **42**, 153
Roberts, Sir Frank, **18**, 124
Roberts, Gareth, **52**, 297; **54**, 315
Roberts, Gilda, **57**, 67
Roberts, Henry (marine journalist), **17**, 34, 34n, 41
Roberts, Jack, **17**, 244n
Roberts, James, **5**, 52; **6**, 171; 7, 39; **8**, 95; **9**, 7, 152, 153; **10**, 73, 155; **11**, 154; **15**, 179; **24**, 72, 77; **26**, 181; **27**, 136n, 181; **28**, 176, 180; **38**, 246, 253; **48**, 115; **50**, 286n; **60**, 266n41
Roberts, Jane Linz, **47**, 214
Roberts, Jeanne Addison, **25**, 200; **27**, 164; **29**, 162, 180; **30**, 210; **31**, 176, 177; **32**, 246–7; **34**, 165, 166; **35**, 185; **36**, 107n, 110; **39**, 230; **44**, 115n; **45**, 160; **51**, 181, 183n, 186n; **53**, 337; **55**, 181n; **56**, 130n, 227n; **57**, 128, 313; **58**, 349; **59**, 80, 81–2, 83, 84, 90, 105n19
'*The Merry Wives of Windsor* as a Hallowe'en Play', **25**, 107–12
Roberts, John, **60**, 260n28
Roberts, Josephine A, **39**, 231; **42**, 213; **45**, 81, 82; **51**, 331
Roberts, Mark, **55**, 73n
Roberts, Michael, **50**, 188n
Roberts, Neil, **53**, 120
Roberts, Nia, **59**, 338
Roberts, Oswald Dale, **47**, 94, 95
Roberts, Philip, **54**, 166n; **55**, 160n, 166n, 167n, 168n
Roberts, Revd R. E., **54**, 80
Roberts, R. J., **27**, 190
Roberts, R. S., **17**, 155n
Roberts, Robert, **6**, 171
Roberts, Sarah, **42** 159
Roberts, Sasha, **50**, 278; **51**, 6, 279–80; **53**, 299, 302, 303, 305; **57**, 309; **58**, 96; **59**, 18n78, 87n25, 87n26, 87n27
Roberts, Selena, **60**, 145
Roberts, Simon, **45**, 151; **51**, 246
Roberts, Sydney, **26**, 123n
Roberts, W. Rhys, **49**, 193n
Roberts, William, **7**, 58, 61, 68n
Roberts-Baytop, Adrianne, **29**, 173
Robertson, Ben, **43**, 208
Robertson, D. A., **46**, 73n
Robertson, Forbes, **11**, 124; **16**, 23
Robertson, Iain Stuart, **43**, 211
Robertson, John M., **3**, 30, 144; **4**, 7, 23; **6**, 78n; **7**, 6; **9**, 9; **10**, 2, 3; **15**, 12; **16**, 64; **18**, 41; **19**, 1; **20**, 166; **26**, 3; **28**, 37n, 39n 40n, 41, 42; **29**, 115n; **38**, 167n; **47**, 108, 243; **58**, 122; **59**, 147
The Baconian Heresy, **3**, 11
Literary Detection, **2**, 146
Robertson, Jennifer, **60**, 131, 131n3, 131n4
Robertson, Sir Johnston Forbes, *see under* Forbes-Robertson

Robertson, Kate, **42**, 156
Robertson, Roderick, **23**, 168
Robertson, T. W., **56**, 123
Robertson, Thomas, **34**, 9, 12, 13–14, 15
Robertson, Toby, **14**, 127; **40**, 169, 173, 181; **41**, 183, 187, 189, 233n; **42**, 161; **44**, 199; **46**, 193
Robertson, Tom, **2**, 3; **41**, 28
Robeson, Paul, **5**, 115; **38**, 213; **40**, 38; **49**, 226, 230, 288; **51**, 57, 63; **55**, 273; **60**, 365
Robin Goodfellow, **17**, 169 and n
Robin, Armand, **13**, 154
Robins, Cicely, **36**, 136, 142
Robins, George, **1**, 82, 83
Robins, William, **36**, 136; **58**, 237
Robinson, A. H. W., **17**, 27n
Robinson, Clement, **42**, 59n
Robinson, F. N., **32**, 133n, 166n; **36**, 89n; **39**, 150n; **44**, 42n; **47**, 145n; **49**, 73n, 176n; **56**, 57n; **57**, 215
Robinson, F. W., **55**, 113n
Robinson, Forrest G., **24**, 159
Robinson, Fred C., **59**, 262n18, 262n21
Robinson, G., **14**, 82
Robinson, Heath, **5**, 129
Robinson, Henry Crabb, **14**, 86, 89n; **23**, 154; **35**, 7
Robinson, Horace W., **10**, 149
Robinson, Ian, **23**, 154
Robinson, J. W., **19**, 136, 150; **28**, 171; **44**, 244
Robinson, James E., **19**, 137; **22**, 173
Robinson, James F., **28**, 61
Robinson, John, **40**, 219
Robinson, John, of Leyden, **1**, 68
Robinson, Julie-Anne, **45**, 147; **46**, 196; **54**, 295
Robinson, Kate, **51**, 267
Robinson, Lucy, **42**, 159
Robinson, Mrs Mary, **38**, 70; **51**, 4
Robinson, Naomi, **59**, 340
Robinson, Patrick, **57**, 266
Robinson, Peter, **53**, 312; **56**, 310–11
Robinson, Richard, **17**, 75 and n, 77, 79n, 219n; **19**, 86, 94n; **47**, 167; **58**, 232, 241
Robinson, Robert, **23**, 40–1
Robinson, Roger, **55**, 175n
Robinson, Stuart, **59**, 205
Robinson, Thomas, **23**, 102; **36**, 138
The Schoole of Musicke, **3**, 56
Robinson, Tom Osborne, **47**, 93, 95–100, 104–6
Robinson, Tony, **48**, 236
Robsart, Amy, **57**, 304
Robson, Christopher, **44**, 195
Robson, Flora, **2**, 130, 131; **6**, 143; **25**, 64
Robson, Frederick, **16**, 108, 115; **21**, 134
Robson, J. M., **56**, 208n
Robson, Simon, **31**, 190
Robson, W. W., **30**, 188; **32**, 157
Robynson, Ralph (trs.), **17**, 109n
Roche, S. Wallace, **38**, 236
Roche, Thomas P., Jr, **36**, 93n; **43**, 245–6; **46**, 16n; **49**, 168; **52**, 291
Rochefort, H., **9**, 66
Rochester, John Wilmot, 2nd Earl of, *see* John Wilmot, **35**, 154; **44**, 238; **49**, 304
Rochett, W., **27**, 170
Rockas, Leo, **28**, 161; **29**, 165; **31**, 168
Rockefeller Foundation, **4**, 93
Rocket, Gilbert, **60**, 50n5
Rockwell, K. A., **11**, 139
Rocque, John, **30**, 164n
Rodd, Thomas, **4**, 86
Roddman, Philip, **24**, 6n
Roddy, Marsha, **55**, 331
Rode, Helge, *Shakespeare*, **3**, 114
Rodenberry, Gene, **53**, 170
Rodenburg, Patsy, **51**, 276; **56**, 175, 179, 302, 309, 343
Röderer, Johann Gottfried, **9**, 95, 100n
Roderick, Anne, **44**, 191
Rodes, David S., **59**, 169
Rodger, David, **46**, 199
Rodger, Struan, **49**, 265
Rodgers, Richard, **45**, 146
Rodin, Auguste, **22**, 99
Rodinson, François, **48**, 228
Rodriguez, Alex, **60**, 144–5
Rodway, Allen E., **55**, 92n
Rodway, Norman, **24**, 118, 119; **44**, 172, 172, 179, 180; **45**, 148, 156; **51**, 219, 236, 264
Roe, F. Gordon, **22**, 167n
Roe, John, **46**, 241, 247–9; **48**, 255, 260; **53**, 12n; **55**, 349; **58**, 322, 333; **60**, 256, 256n17, 351
Roe, Sir John, **1**, 44; **27**, 178
Roeg, Nicholas, **57**, 147, 148
Roehl, Bernie, **52**, 185n
Roerecke, Edith M., **20**, 151
Roesen, (*see* Righter, Barton), Bobbyann, **8**, 139–40; **22**, 71; **24**, 57n, 58n
Roesslin, Eucharius, **46**, 118n
Roessner, Jane, **34**, 171
Roffe, Alfred, **51**, 89
Rogan, John, **38**, 212, 213
Rogde, Ingolf, **7**, 114
Roger, David, **47**, 218
Rogers, Abraham, **19**, 103
Rogers, Carmen, **8**, 144
Rogers, D. M., **24**, 72n; **29**, 21n; **54**, 95n; **56**, 189
Rogers, David, **59**, 307
Rogers, Edward, **58**, 237
Rogers, G. H., **35**, 32
Rogers, H. L., **19**, 3, 54n
Rogers, Henry, **49**, 198
Rogers, J., **54**, 5n
Rogers, J. K., **38**, 251
Rogers, James E. Thorold, **53**, 62n, 64n, 65, 72n
Rogers, John, **44**, 81n
Rogers, Katherine, **47**, 214
Rogers, Laura, **57**, 277
Rogers, Mike, **57**, 296
Rogers, Nicholas, **48**, 53n
Rogers, Pat, **51**, 51n
Rogers, Paul, **5**, 122, 127; **7**, 124; **9**, 123–30; **10**, 130, 131; **12**, 80, 109; **13**, 124; **20**, 138
Rogers, Rebecca, **57**, 3
Rogers, Robert, **23**, 153; **40**, 11n
Rogers, S., **28**, 154

Rogers, Samuel, **14**, 88n
Rogers, Thomas, **11**, 71; **54**, 169n
Celestiall Elegies, **9**, 34n
Rogers, Thorold, **44**, 63n
Rogers, Timothy, **55**, 129n
Rogerson, Margaret, **34**, 180n; **49**, 16n; **52**, 78n
Rogoff, Gordon, **19**, 154
Rohmer, Rolf, **21**, 149; **22**, 166; **25**, 186; **26**, 166
Röhrmann, H., **7**, 113, 132
Rohrmoser, Günter, **37**, 158n
Rohrsen, Peter, **37**, 157n
Roland, Alan, **40**, 110n
Rolfe, Frederick W. (Baron Corvo), **53**, 144–50; **55**, 343
Rolfe, John C., **30**, 69n
Rolfe, William J., **18**, 102; **59**, 87, 139n8, 140
Rolland, **16**, 10
Rolle, Dietrich, **37**, 159n; **55**, 181n
Rollé, Jacques Hippolyte, **9**, 62, 65
Rolle, John Jeffrey, **58**, 267
Rolle, Richard, **6**, 59
Rolliffe, John, **11**, 95
Rolling Stones, The, **57**, 156
Rollins, Hyder Edward, **1**, 75, 77n; **3**, 31; **4**, 155; **8**, 10; **15**, 6, 11, 13, 17, 19, 20, 26, 30n, 34, 40n, 61n, 98n, 109n; **17**, 220n; **23**, 69n; **25**, 9; **31**, 127n, 136n; **37**, 189; **41**, 103n, 105n, 112n, 116n, 240n; **46**, 35, 37n, 41n, 45n; **55**, 92n, 93; **60**, 258n23, 260n28, 262n33
Romack, Katherine, **60**, 336, 353
Roman de la Rose, **6**, 101
Roman Voices, **47**, 212
Roman, George, **41**, 186; **42**, 160
Roman, Laurence, **44**, 194
Romance, **9**, 17
Romance tradition in Shakespeare, *see under* Shakespeare
Romani, Felice, **18**, 80; **56**, 296; **58**, 305
Romania, Shakespeare performances in, **20**, 125–31
Romano, Giulio, **11**, 40; **15**, 94; **26**, 65; **30**, 202; **31**, 10; **36**, 167; **40**, 76; **42**, 197; **53**, 32n; **54**, 24; **57**, 334; **59**, 257
Romany, Frank, **44**, 219
Romaunt of the Rose, **9**, 25
Romei, Annibale, **16**, 84; **27**, 45n
The Courtiers Academie, **9**, 34n
Romeo, Rosario, **17**, 40n, 246n
Romer, Georg Christian, **60**, 184
Romer, Patrick, **47**, 214
Romeus et Julietta (MS.), **3**, 52
Romney, George, **10**, 73; **13**, 80n; **47**, 174n; **51**, 4, 11, 300; **59**, 131n47, 362; **60**, 354
Ronan, C. J., **26**, 158
Ronan, Clifford, **50**, 258; **59**, 354–5
Ronayne, John, **36**, 178; **51**, 298; **52**, 10, 13, 14
Ronconi, Luca, **15**, 136
Ronde, Th. de, **5**, 110n
Ronder, Tanya, **51**, 257; **56**, 297
Rondiris, Dimitris, **4**, 128; **5**, 112; **12**, 113
Ronel, Avital, **52**, 183n–184n
Ronk, Martha C., **47**, 228; **48**, 251
Ronsard, Pierre de, **15**, 29, 81–2, 84–6, 98n 105–6, 109n; **16**, 12; **17**, 42; **34**, 104; **42**, 71n
Roodenburg, Herman, **48**, 37n; **55**, 241n
Rooney, M., **18**, 73
Roose-Evans, James, **55**, 330; **56**, 292
Root, Amanda, **43**, 208–9; **44**, 172, 195; **45**, 125, 148, 156
Root, Robert Kilbum, **10**, 14, 15, 22, 25n, 26n; **31**, 49n; **54**, 37n; **55**, 349
Roper, Derek, **49**, 308–9
Roper, Lyndal, **52**, 297
Roper, Nigel, **52**, 262; **54**, 287, 290
Roper, William, *Life of More*, **14**, 33
Roppolo, Joseph Patrick, **11**, 147
Roques, Mario, **52**, 129n
Roriczer, Mathes, **33**, 145n
Rorty, A. O., **51**, 155n
Rorty, Richard, **39**, 146n; **40**, 31; **49**, 201; **56**, 204, 205n; **58**, 349; **59**, 28, 28n37, 35n74, 352
Rosalynde, **50**, 255; **54**, 115, 118
Rosand, David, **31**, 18n
Rosanov, M. N., **9**, 96, 100n
Rosati, Salvatore, *Il Giro Della Ruota*, **10**, 11; **13**, 147
Roscius, **7**, 86, 89n; **58**, 61
Roscius, the infant, *see* Betty, Master William Henry West
Roscoe, Ingrid, **51**, 9n
Roscoe, William, **49**, 122n; **59**, 264n27
Rose, The, *see under* Theatres, Elizabethan
Rose, Adam, **19**, 103
Rose, Alison, **38**, 211
Rose, Billy, **39**, 40n
Rose, Clifford, **44**, 194; **47**, 198; **51**, 253, 255
Rose, Ellen Cronan, **32**, 65n
Rose, George Arthur, **3**, 127–8; **6**, 143, 145; **16**, 22; **53**, 144n
Rose, Gillian, **55**, 54n, 80, 81
Rose, Harry, **6**, 59
Rose, Jacqueline, **40**, 207, 211; **45**, 38, 48; **46**, 4; **56**, 204n
Rose, Jonathan, **56**, 245n; **58**, 113, 117
Rose, Lloyd, **39**, 90n
Rose, Mark, **38**, 10; **39**, 135n; **40**, 123n, 209; **44**, 69n, 220; **49**, 214n; **58**, 349
Rose, Marvin, **24**, 160; **26**, 161n
Rose, Mary Beth, **39**, 231; **42**, 2, 12; **43**, 265n; **44**, 52n; **46**, 6, 16n, 107n, 128n; **55**, 250n
Rose, Mr & Mrs Frank W., **49**, 125
Rose, Paul L., **4**, 127; **24**, 147
Rose, Phil, **45**, 150
Rose, Steven, **24**, 149
Rose-Troup, Francis, **48**, 71n
Roselli, *Tractatus*, **1**, 73
Rosen, Alan, **53**, 292, 296
Rosen, Barbara, **28**, 118, 121; **59**, 41
Rosen, Carol, **38**, 50n
Rosen, Charles, **51**, 123
Rosen, David, **39**, 232; **57**, 64, 115
Rosen, Philip, **45**, 49n
Rosen, William, **19**, 8, 9; **21**, 139; **59**, 41
Shakespeare and the Craft of Tragedy reviewed, **15**, 161–2
Rosenbach, A. S. W., **1**, 70, 76; **55**, 386–7
Rosenbach Collection, *see under* Libraries, Bibliotheca Bodmeriana
Rosenbaum, Ron, **59**, 161n14
Rosenberg, Edgar, **24**, 162
Rosenberg, Eleanor, **60**, 6, 7n10
Rosenberg, John D., **21**, 136; **33**, 44, 49
Rosenberg, Mark, **56**, 97n, 98

Rosenberg, Marvin, **8**, 142; **9**, 147; **10**, 139; **12**, 143; **14**, 13; **18**, 184; **21**, 62, 65n; **23**, 173; **26**, 155, 163; **27**, 158; **28**, 171; **29**, 176; **33**, 11, 43n, 45, 46, 46n, 47n, 48n, 52; **34**, 9, 11, 65n, 169; **39**, 9, 82; **40**, 34n; **43**, 231, 250; **45**, 167; **47**, 153n, 154n, 156n, 159, 236, 263; **49**, 147n, 148; **51**, 58, 64, 298–9; **53**, 237n, 294; **55**, 56, 58n, 59, 60n, 223n, 224n, 225, 242n; **57**, 40, 83, 92, 93, 94, 330; **58**, 220, 221; **59**, 200; **60**, 160, 168n2.2
Rosenberg, Mary, **40**, 33
Rosenberg, Ray, **50**, 227
Rosenberry, E. H., **18**, 118n
Rosenblatt, Jason P., **33**, 201; **39**, 145n
Rosenblatt, Mark, **58**, 305, 306
Rosenblum, Joseph, **36**, 175
Rosencrantz and Gildenstern are Dead, **43**, 222
Rosenfeld, Lulla, **55**, 115, 124n, 125n
Rosenfeld, Sybil M., **21**, 146; **22**, 175; **29**, 176; **30**, 197; **49**, 115n, 119n; **56**, 122n
'The Grieves Shakespearian Scene Designs', **20**, 107–12
Rosenheim, Judith, **38**, 219, 253; **54**, 166n
Rosenthal, Laura, **46**, 139n; **53**, 323
Rosenthal, Suzanna, **57**, 292
Rosenwald, Lessing J., **1**, 62, 70, 71
Rosier, James L., **9**, 138; **17**, 32–3
Rosignoli, Maria P., **23**, 162n
Rosinger, Lawrence, **23**, 153, 166n; **30**, 194
Rosmer, Milton, **59**, 203
Ross, Alan S. C., **21**, 147
Ross, Mr and Mrs Alan, **19**, 81n
Ross, Alexander, **56**, 83n
Ross, Charles, **51**, 297
Ross, Cheryl Lynn, **50**, 23n
Ross, D. J. A., **42**, 159; **51**, 108, 109, 115; **54**, 250; **59**, 241n16
Ross, Gary, **56**, 298
Ross, Gordon N., **32**, 236
Ross, Harry, **57**, 293
Ross, Hugh, **41**, 190; **42**, 159; **44**, 160, 162; **47**, 187
Ross, J. J., **41**, 200
Ross, J. M., **48**, 52n
Ross, John C., **59**, 42
Ross, Lawrence J., **13**, 156; **16**, 166; **21**, 136; **23**, 146; **38**, 245n; **39**, 149n, 155n; **41**, 127n; **47**, 78; **52**, 278
Ross, Lesley, **58**, 306
Ross, Ricky, **52**, 261
Ross, Robert H., **55**, 129n, 135n
Ross, William, **15**, 12
Rosser, George C., **19**, 23n
Rosser, Peter, **47**, 95
Rosseter, Philip, **11**, 100; **15**, 6
Rossetti, Christina, **8**, 138
Rossetti, Dante Gabriel, **55**, 138n; **60**, 333
Rossi, Alberto, **7**, 113; **9**, 135
Rossi, Alfred, **53**, 241n
Rossi, Ernesto, **5**, 107; **9**, 57; **20**, 121; **34**, 65; **40**, 222; **41**, 225; **48**, 187; **50**, 35
Rossi, Joan Warchol, **33**, 188
Rossingham, Edmund, **11**, 116n; **54**, 19n
Rossini, Gioacchino, **3**, 100; **18**, 75, 81, 85; **21**, 81, 82, 83–4, 85; **49**, 12; **55**, 329; **57**, 64, 66
Otello, **18**, 80, 82
Rossiter, A. P., **2**, 151; **3**, 26; **4**, 161; **6**, 10, 11, 29, 33n, 34n, 35n; **8**, 34: **9**, 133; **14**, 34; **15**, 118–19, 159–60, 164–5, 167; **19**, 5, 6, 9; **20**, 66, 73n; **22**, 31; **25**, 2, 63; **26**, 120; **27**, 24n, 31n; **28**, 1n, 12, 91n, 100n; **29**, 87, 89; **30**, 140; **31**, 62n 93; **32**, 1, 6–7, 11, 12, 50n, 54, 55n, 58, 60n, 129n; **33**, 200; **37**, 8; **38**, 3, 61; **41**, 68; **42**, 173; **43**, 226; **44**, 15n; **47**, 251; **55**, 21n, 211; **58**, 52, 54, 56; **59**, 188
English Drama from Early Times to the Elizabethans reviewed, **4**, 150
Woodstock reviewed, **1**, 119, 126
Rossiter, Leonard, **49**, 305
Rossiter, Pat, **43**, 209
Rossiter-Smith, H., **19**, 147
Rossky, William, **37**, 187
Rosso, **26**, 50, 51, 54
Rosso, Laurence, **39**, 189
Rosso, Mariselena, **43**, 212; **44**, 200
Rostand, Edmond, **45**, 43
Roston, Murray, **21**, 142n; **22**, 172
Rostova, I., **13**, 133
Rostron, David, **23**, 173; **25**, 192; **35**, 9, 10n
Rota, Giovanni, *see* Vittorini, Elio
Rota, Nino, **57**, 152
Rotas, Basil, **10**, 119; **11**, 121; **12**, 113
Technologika II reviewed, **7**, 112
Rotas, Vassilis, **1**, 116; **5**, 112; **18**, 124; **58**, 208–19
Roth, Cecil, **8**, 149; **19**, 136
Roth, Joanna, **48**, 234
Roth, Michael S., **52**, 64
Roth, R., **10**, 8
Roth, Stephani, **50**, 203
Rothe, Hans, **3**, 119; **4**, 127; **6**, 124; **7**, 111; **9**, 113; **11**, 120; **12**, 112; **13**, 128, 131, 140; **14**, 156; **15**, 134; **16**, 63–5, 66–7; **18**, 185; **23**, 121; **37**, 156n; **59**, 195
Rothenberg, A., **26**, 164
Rothman, J., **27**, 166
Rothmann, Johan, **48**, 27n, 28n
Rothschild, Herbert B., Jr, **27**, 161; **31**, 183; **38**, 14
Rothstein, Eric, **23**, 146n; **53**, 120n
Rothwell family, **4**, 69–70
Rothwell, Kenneth S., **28**, 171n; **39**, 13; **41**, 227; **49**, 153, 156, 157n; **52**, 185n; **54**, 337–8; **57**, 145, 156; **58**, 341
Rothwell, Talbot, **39**, 79n
Rothwell, W. F., **10**, 88n; **13**, 116; **14**, 150; **52**, 6
'Was there a Typical Elizabethan Stage?', **12**, 15–21
Rothwell, William (*or* ? Gilbert), **4**, 69, 73
Rothwell, William, Mayor of Warwick, **4**, 74n
Rotrou, Jean, **22**, 21
Rötscher, H. T., **3**, 110
Rott, Adolf, **13**, 124
Rouault, **12**, 127
Roubillac, Louis François, **54**, 48
Roubillac statue of Shakespeare, **1**, 62; **3**, 44
Roud, Steve, **55**, 53
Rouda, F. H., **16**, 159
Rougemont, Denis de, **15**, 122
Roukin, Samuel, **60**, 293
Roupe, Chris, **45**, 155
Rouquier, Georges, *Farrébique, ou les quatre saisons*, **11**, 19
Rourke, Josie, **57**, 295; **60**, 309Fig.55, 309–10, 325
Rous, John, **4**, 79, 96n

Rouse, John, **48**, 8n; **55**, 281n, 282
Rouse, W. H. D., **10**, 25n, 49n; **16**, 170; **30**, 153n; **32**, 73n, 145n; **39**, 123n; **41**, 134n; **42**, 72n; **46**, 57n; **47**, 26n; **49**, 62n, 126n; **50**, 83n, 198n; **56**, 57n
Rousseau, A.-M., **57**, 113
Rousset, Jean, **28**, 46n
Rousseau, Jean-Jacques, **9**, 91, 94; **26**, 94; **28**, 65; **36**, 124; **43**, 106; **45**, 173; **50**, 173; **54**, 51; **57**, 33
Roussillon, Jean-Pierre, **8**, 118
Routledge, Patricia, **38**, 206
Routledge, R. A., **51**, 165n, 171n
Rouve, Pierre, **5**, 119
Rouvière, Philibert, **9**, 62, 65
Rover, The, **50**, 256
Rovina, Hannah, **5**, 113; **9**, 114
Rowan, D. F., **25**, 191; **28**, 168; **30**, 157, 198; **35**, 174; **43**, 270n; **50**, 165, 168
'A Neglected Jones/Webb Theatre Project: "Barber Surgeons' Hall Writ Large" ', **23**, 125–9
Rowan, David, **53**, 280
Rowan, Dominic, **52**, 230
Rowan, Lorraine, **44**, 195
Rowan, Nicole, **40**, 216
Rowbothum, James, **35**, 115n
Rowe, Clive, **59**, 312
Rowe, Eleanor, **45**, 8n; **48**, 115n
Rowe, George E. Jr, **35**, 176; **42**, 198
Rowe, Katherine A., **48**, 39n, 250; **54**, 317–18; **57**, 132, 186, 188, 194; **58**, 4, 146, 189, 340; **59**, 351, 368
Rowe, Nicholas, **2**, 36, 42n, 83; **3**, 22, 49; **5**, 2, 25, 50, 51, 144; **6**, 58, 77, 81; **7**, 1, 55, 91, 145; **9**, 93, 97; **10**, 13, 14; **12**, 4; **13**, 73; **18**, 13, 14, 23, 189; **24**, 107, 176; **27**, 187, 191; **28**, 75; **29**, 179; **31**, 77, 83; **32**, 234, 246; **33**, 41, 49; **34**, 11, 188; **38**, 87, 98n; **43**, 88, 103, 249; **44**, 113, 129, 236; **46**, 138; **47**, 65, 269; **48**, 284; **49**, 75, 113, 322; **51**, 2, 4, 6, 8, 135; **52**, 291; **53**, 218, 331–2, 335–7, 339–40, 342–4; **55**, 257–8, 260, 270; **56**, 60; **57**, 321; **59**, 32n58, 51, 56, 57, 58, 80, 83, 105–6, 128, 131, 134, 159, 379; **60**, 364
Life of Shakespeare, **3**, 1
Rowe, Peter, **43**, 210; **50**, 229
Rowell, George, **16**, 103; **30**, 200; **32**, 19n; **35**, 2n, 6, 7, 9n; **41**, 224; **47**, 238–9; **49**, 128n, 307
Rowell, Rosie, **42**, 156; **44**, 192
Rowland, Benjamin, Jr, **40**, 76n
Rowland, Beryl, **25**, 176; **51**, 176n, 177n
Rowland, Christine, **41**, 188
Rowland, Richard, **46**, 226
Rowland, Roger, **42**, 155
Rowlands, Samuel, **13**, 110n; **16**, 98; **17**, 174; **18**, 188; **28**, 159; **44**, 19n; **46**, 129n, 225; **50**, 156n; **55**, 82n; **60**, 76, 80n37
Greene's Ghost, **13**, 110n
Rowlandson, Thomas, **13**, 108; **30**, 164, 165; **42**, 38n
'Rowley' poems, **18**, 48, 52
Rowley, Bill, **44**, 203
Rowley, Samuel, **1**, 38; **2**, 152; **3**, 24; **27**, 129; **32**, 233; **38**, 25; **42**, 212; **43**, 48, 51; **44**, 81, 82n, 126, 127; **52**, 24; **54**, 244n, 349; **59**, 71
When You See Me You Know Me, **11**, 61
Rowley, William, **22**, 171; **25**, 138; **26**, 54; **29**, 23, 182; **40**, 216, 226; **44**, 203; **46**, 233; **47**, 33; **48**, 28; **54**, 357; **55**, 84n; **57**, 122; **59**, 72, 73, 74, 213, 214, 217, 220, 222; **60**, 109n33
The Search for Money (1609), **7**, 89n
Rowley, William (*see under* Fletcher, John, Heywood, Thomas, *and* Webster, John),
A Shoemaker a Gentleman, **13**, 113, 119
Rowley, William (and Middleton, T.), *A Fair Quarrel*, **4**, 91
Rowse, A. L., **17**, 77n; **18**, 121, 131, 177–8; **20**, 160, 161; **21**, 97; **28**, 5; **32**, 88n, 97n, 214, 228; **34**, 167; **35**, 66n; **39**, 224, 237, 246, 247; **42**, 186–7; **44**, 62n, 254; **51**, 161n; **56**, 319; **59**, 40
Roxana, title-page engraving (1632), **3**, 84; **4**, 97; **7**, 73; **11**, 146; **12**, 36, 42, 46; **13**, 113
Roxburghe, Duke of, **3**, 44
Roxburghe, Lady, **49**, 299
Roy, Bruno, **49**, 83n
Roy, Mylise, **12**, 117
Roy, S. N., **22**, 175n
Roy, Vladimir, **4**, 110
Royaards, Ben, **7**, 108; **12**, 110
Royal Ballet of Flanders, **58**, 305
Royal Exchange, The, *see under* London
Royal Grammar, The, **7**, 23
Royal National Theatre Education, **58**, 306
Royal Opera Company, **58**, 300, 303
Royal Shakespeare Company, **58**, 268, 298, 299, 302, 304, 305, 306
Royden, Matthew, **15**, 26, 29, 30, 100, 101
Elegy for Astrophil, **15**, 100, 109n
Royle, Carol, **35**, 149, 150; **43**, 210; **45**, 148
Royle, Danny, **54**, 333
Royle, Edwin Milton, **57**, 252, 255
Royle, Nicholas, **55**, 69n
Royster, Francesca T., **54**, 312; **60**, 348
Royston, Richard, **55**, 266
Rozett, Martha Tuck, **44**, 243; **49**, 284–5; **57**, 238; **60**, 348
Rozmovits, Linda, **54**, 315
Rubalcava, Magdalen, **47**, 217
Rubasingham, Indhu, **57**, 296
Rubel, V. L., **23**, 21n
Rubens, Sir Peter Paul, **15**, 19; **29**, 29; **30**, 83; **31**, 45; **52**, 47; **53**, 186
Rubens, Sir Peter Paul, Triumphal Arch at Antwerp, **4**, 100n
Rubenstein, Frankie, **57**, 302
Rubin, Deborah, **56**, 38n
Rubin, Gayle, **56**, 74
Rubin, Ida E., **40**, 75n
Rubin, Leon, **39**, 189, 190; **59**, 183, 184, 185, 188
Rubinstein, Annette, **31**, 175
Rubinstein, E., **25**, 174
Rubinstein, Frankie, **49**, 100n; **50**, 52n; **51**, 325
Rubinstein, H. F., **20**, 162; **58**, 139, 141–2, 146, 324
Rubio, Miguel, **39**, 43n, 44n, 50n
Ruboshkin, Alexander, **45**, 151
Rubow, Paul V., **1**, 115; **2**, 126, 141; **3**, 110–11; **6**, 119; **48**, 4n
Shakespeare og hans Samtidige, **2**, 140
Ruby, Thelma, **39**, 43
Rudanko, Juhani, **47**, 232
Rudd, Niall, **56**, 55n
Ruddock, John, **1**, 109, 110
Rudenstine, Neil L., **22**, 170
Rudhart, Bianca-Maria, **37**, 157n
Rudkin, David, **58**, 154

Rudlin, John, **55**, 247n
Rudman, Michael, **35**, 151; **45**, 151; **47**, 215; **48**, 228; **49**, 278
Rudnytsky, Peter L., **38**, 232; **49**, 207n, 308; **55**, 8
Rudolf II, Emperor, **11**, 90; **29**, 24n; **33**, 162; **36**, 145
Rudolf, Georg, **37**, 158n
Rudolph, J., **26**, 164; **29**, 177
Rudolph, Johanna, **45**, 89n
Rudwick, Paul, **49**, 271
Rudyerd, Sir Benjamin, **27**, 114n; **32**, 102n
Rueff, Jacob, **46**, 115n
Rüegg, August, **23**, 150, 161
Ruelens, Charles, **33**, 163
Ruesch, Jurgen, **40**, 38
Rufini, Sergio, **44**, 217
Ruge, Enno, **56**, 315
Ruggieri, Osvaldo, **12**, 114; **15**, 136
Ruggieri, Ruggiero, **18**, 74
Ruggiero, Guido de, **56**, 208n
Ruggle, George, *Ignoramus*, **4**, 91
Ruggles of Red Gap, **18**, 71
Ruggles, Eleanor, **24**, 100n
Ruggles, Henry, **53**, 94
Ruhl, Ludwig Sigismund, **7**, 92; **37**, 46–8, 50, 53
Ruiter, David, **58**, 327, 333
Rülicke-Weiler, Käthe, **48**, 175n
Rulikowski, M., **1**, 113
Rulton, Robert C., **31**, 181
Rumantseva, Daria, **60**, 313
Rümelin, Gustav, **2**, 108
Runciman, Alexander, **13**, 74, 75; **51**, 13–14
Runciman, John, **13**, 74–6; **41**, 224
Rundle, James U., **24**, 157
Runner, Joshua, **52**, 93
Rupp, E. Gordon, **33**, 92n
Rupp, Stephen, **45**, 171
Ruppel, K. H., **11**, 148; **14**, 152
Ruru, Li, **58**, 334, 338, 342
Ruscelli, Girolamo, **17**, 184; **45**, 182
Rusche, Harry, **23**, 153
Rush, David, **13**, 134
Rush, Geoffrey, **52**, 261; **60**, 49
Rushdie, Salman, **49**, 205, 212
Rushton, Julian, **49**, 285
Rushton, Peter, **49**, 190n
Rushton, Sara, **55**, 309
Ruskin Galleries, Stratford-upon-Avon, **11**, 97n
Ruskin, John, **32**, 15; **52**, 273; **53**, 125, 238; **59**, 264
Russ, J. R., **26**, 165; **29**, 175
Russel, Thomas, **3**, 3, 11, 12
Russell of Liverpool, Lord, **38**, 56n
Russell, Barry, **41**, 190
Russell, Bertrand, *Principles of Social Reconstruction*, **2**, 112
Russell, D. A., **11**, 123, 147
'Hamlet Costumes from Garrick to Gielgud', **9**, 54–8
Russell, Edward, **9**, 17
Russell, Edward, Earl of Bedford, **14**, 103; **32**, 28
Russell, Edward R., **32**, 18
Russell, Hastings, 12th Duke of Bedford, **13**, 104n
Russell, John L., **49**, 138n, 287
Russell, Ken, **52**, 90
Russell, Lord John, **24**, 92, 93
Russell, Lucy Harrington, Countess of Bedford, **14**, 104; **15**, 27
Russell, Pancho, **44**, 200
Russell, Stephen, **31**, 144; **34**, 156, 158; **40**, 165, 168
Russell, Thomas, **16**, 118; **21**, 148; **32**, 137, 142; **44**, 77n
Russell, William, **37**, 187; **51**, 210
Russian theatre, **12**, 8, 13
Russo, Mary, **46**, 144
Ruth, Leon, **12**, 111
Rutherford, Anna, **56**, 156n
Rutherford, Malcolm, **50**, 35
Rutherford, Mary, **28**, 145; **42**, 161
Rutherston, Albert, **8**, 80
Ruthven, Lord, **4**, 36–7
Rutland, Earl of, **21**, 103; **44**, 236
Rutland, Earls of, *see under* Manners, Francis, *and* Manners, Roger
Rutland, Lord, **17**, 185; **18**, 112
Rutledge, Douglas F., **43**, 232
Rutson, Robert, **11**, 102
Rutter, Barrie, **41**, 169; **46**, 202; **47**, 185–7, 216; **48**, 199, 200–4, 232; **49**, 252–4, 275, 276; **50**, 225; **51**, 266; **53**, 262–3, 281; **54**, 286, 294; **55**, 69, 71, 77; **56**, 5, 236, 237n, 238–41, 247, 249, 250, 252, 254, 291, 293; **57**, 278, 279, 293; **58**, 279, 301; **59**, 299–300, 301, 341; **60**, 287–8, 289Fig.46, 320
Rutter, Carol Chillington, **35**, 190–1; **41**, 216; **42**, 115n; **43**, 147n, 254, 262; **44**, 152; **46**, 9n, 11n; **48**, 243; **51**, 285; **52**, 74n; **54**, 151n, 337; **55**, 379, 382, 383; **56**, 1–26, 166, 173n, 236–55; **58**, 220; **59**, 69n2; **60**, 28, 29n17, 29n21, 30n22, 30n23, 31, 45n46, 74, 78n30, 79n31, 82n43, 172, 173, 226n19, 285, 360
Rutter, Joseph, *The Shepheards Holy-Day*, **4**, 154
Ruttkay, Kálmán, **2**, 127; **39**, 236n
Ryall, David, **39**, 195; **51**, 244
Ryan, Anna Livia, **51**, 208, 215; **55**, 317
Ryan, Cathy, **54**, 294
Ryan, Daniel, **53**, 272–3; **54**, 289
Ryan, Francesca, **47**, 195
Ryan, Kiernan, **44**, 41n, 206; **47**, 235; **49**, 94n; **53**, 302; **54**, 155n; **55**, 341; **56**, 317, 336; **58**, 180; **59**, 178
Ryan, Lacy, **51**, 120
Ryan, Lawrence V., **22**, 169
Ryan, Richard, **28**, 7
Ryan, Robert, **8**, 122; **26**, 143
Ryan, Sean, **50**, 199n
Rycenga, John A., **35**, 79n
Rydén, Mats, **31**, 189; **32**, 244
Ryder, Albert Pinkham, **47**, 258
Ryder, Alfred, **18**, 132
Rye, W. B., **36**, 140n
Ryecart, Patrick, **49**, 161
Ryken, Leland, **24**, 159
Rykiel, Sonia, **60**, 76, 82
Rylance, Mark, **36**, 154; **43**, 186–7, 197, 199, 206; **44**, 200; **46**, 200, 238; **47**, 192–3; **48**, 233; **50**, 201–3, 229, 236; **51**, 209–13, 215, 217, 269, 298; **52**, 107, 116–18, 217, 225, 256; **53**, 244, 246–7, 248, 253, 279; **54**, 246, 258, 262–3, 283, 386, 321; **55**, 56n, 292, 315, 323; **56**, 99, 100, 168–9, 256, 258–9, 288; **57**, 81, 276, 297; **58**, 277, 304, 307; **59**, 292, 295, 296, 318, 319–20, 341, 373; **60**, 229, 327

Rylands, George, **2**, 18; **4**, 18, 49; **5**, 87; **7**, 8, 11n, 146n; **8**, 8; **9**, 22, 134; **12**, 82; **13**, 163; **15**, 23; **18**, 53; **19**, 116; **24**, 3n; **40**, 16; **51**, 141–2, 144
'Festival Shakespeare in the West End', **6**, 140–6
'The Poet and the Player', **7**, 25–34
Shakespeare's Poetic Energy reviewed, **8**, 145
Rylands, George *and* Ellis-Fermor, Una, 'London Productions', **1**, 103–6
Rylands, John, **13**, 138; **39**, 250n
Rylands, John, *see under* Libraries
Rylands, W. Henry, **47**, 172n
Rylskii, M., **15**, 140
Rymer, Thomas, **7**, 135; **10**, 27, 28, 98, 99, 106n; **14**, 77; **18**, 2, 7, 9, 35–6, 112; **20**, 7, 8, 9; **21**, 16, 27n, 41, 67–77; **23**, 152; **31**, 3; **33**, 192; **34**, 5, 11, 13; **35**, 109, 111; **37**, 124, 145–8; **43**, 49; **44**, 58n; **46**, 62, 65; **48**, 128; **49**, 210, 309; **51**, 5; **53**, 92, 188; **54**, 302; **56**, 107–9, 110, 114
Ryndin, **9**, 118
Rynell, Alarik, **32**, 109n
Ryner, Bradley, **59**, 62n31
Ryott, Emma, **44**, 202; **47**, 211
Ryskamp, Charles, **54**, 46n, 54n
'Ryther' Maps, **1**, 26
Rytter, Henrik, **12**, 139
Ryuta, Minami, **55**, 385
Ryuzanji, Sho, **48**, 110
Rzepka, Charles J., **48**, 115n

1 Sir John Oldcastle, **60**, 266, 266n42
Saalman, Howard, **33**, 145n
Saatkamp, Herman, J., **54**, 66n
Saba, Sirine, **53**, 272; **56**, 271, 273; **60**, 306
Sabadini, Ada, **8**, 120
Sabbatini, **35**, 138
Sabbattini, Nicola, **52**, 7
Sabbe, Maurits, **5**, 110n
Sabberton, Ken, **48**, 204
Sabinus, Georgius, **39**, 127; **41**, 135–6, 144
Sabol, Andrew J., **15**, 173; **36**, 187n
Songs and Dances for the Stuart Masque reviewed, **13**, 161; **15**, 9
Sabor, P., **51**, 32n
Sabuncuoğlu, Nur, **9**, 116; **15**, 139; **18**, 130
Saccio, Peter, **24**, 162n; **30**, 198; **31**, 167; **38**, 11; **43**, 6n, 45n, 49; **54**, 321; **60**, 96n33
Sacharoff, M., **26**, 155; **27**, 166
Sachs, Albie, **55**, 274
Sachs, Arieh, **23**, 186n
Sachs, Hans, **9**, 94
Sachs, Naomi, **45**, 150, 155
Sachs, Robin, **42**, 155
Sachs, Wulf, **9**, 13
Sackfull of Newes, A, **6**, 64
Sackler, Howard, **24**, 3n
Sacks, David Harris, **55**, 373
Sacks, Elizabeth, **35**, 167
Sacks, Peter, **58**, 61, 70
Sacks, Quinney, **57**, 294
Sackton, A. H., **4**, 147; **5**, 81; **7**, 7
Rhetoric as a Dramatic Language in Ben Jonson, **14**, 10
Sackville, Charles, Earl of Middlesex, **14**, 80
Sackville, Thomas, Lord Buckhurst (*see also* Norton, Thomas), **11**, 93; **17**, 7; **19**, 64
Sackville, Thomas, Lord Buckhurst, **10**, 1, 29; **24**, 157; **30**, 61; **32**, 145, 146; **33**, 17, 153, 154, 157, 160, 161; **35**, 131, **36**, 135, 138n, 139, 141; **44**, 232; **53**, 326; **54**, 27n; **55**, 23
see also under Norton, Thomas, for *Gorboduc*
Induction to A Mirror for Magistrates, **10**, 20
Sackville-Knole MSS., **8**, 107n
Sacrobosco, G., **23**, 167
Sad Shepherd, The, **54**, 66
Sadayacco, Madame, **48**, 104
Sadie, Stanley, **54**, 20n; **57**, 65
Sadler family, **32**, 228
Sadler, D. H., **17**, 28n
Sadler, Hamnet, **43**, 267; **54**, 121
Sadler, John Fippes, **17**, 7; **46**, 118n
Sadler, Judith, **54**, 121
Sadler, Margaret, of Stratford-upon-Avon, **12**, 105n
Sadler, Michael, **41**, 188
Sadler, T., **14**, 89n
Sadler, William, **38**, 33
Saffrey, Michael, **43**, 208
Sagasar, Elizabeth Harris, **48**, 254; **58**, 25
Saha, Narayan Chandra, **21**, 141
Sahel, Pierre, **26**, 158; **38**, 223; **43**, 47n, 48; **44**, 27n; **52**, 167n
Sahinbas, Irfan, **13**, 132; **15**, 139
Sahlins, Marshall, **55**, 40n
Said, Edward, **42**, 34n
Sailors, Elizabethan, **17**, 23–34
St Augustine, **21**, 152; **24**, 140; **27**, 157; **28**, 43; **30**, 61, 63, 64; **33**, 9; **34**, 85, 95; **46**, 98
St Francis Borja, **23**, 82, 83
St James, **35**, 103
St Jerome, **32**, 133n; **34**, 86n
St John of Bletso, **54**, 96
St John of the Cross, **56**, 91
St John Chrysostons, **46**, 98
St John the Divine, **33**, 16n, 101–2, 107–8, 109; **35**, 8n; **46**, 20n
Saint Katherine of Alexandria, **54**, 103
Saint Patrick for Ireland, **54**, 20
St Paul, **13**, 84; **14**, 143; **15**, 96; **17**, 103–4, 108, 114; **27**, 83, 86; **28**, 68; **29**, 5, 170; **30**, 104; **31**, 4–5; **33**, 134, 137; **34**, 162, 163; **59**, 237, 246n, 53, 352
St Sebastian, **34**, 163
St Thomas Aquinas, **37**, 100
Saint-Denis, Michel, **4**, 103; **9**, 113; **10**, 118; **12**, 112; **15**, 133, 147; **19**, 111; **27**, 142; **47**, 3n
Saint-Denis, S. M., **41**, 58n
Saint-Denys, Le Religieux de, **44**, 57n
Saint-Didier, Henri de, **14**, 151
Saint-Etienne, Pasqual de, **35**, 104
Saint-Hilaire, De Queux de, **15**, 97n
Sainte-Albine, Remond, **59**, 288, 289
Sainte-Maure, Benoît de, **10**, 17; **31**, 181
Sainthill, Loudon, **12**, 122
Saintsbury, George, **4**, 5; **6**, 39, 152; **15**, 19, 22, 26; **18**, 12, 20; **38**, 187
Saintsbury, H. A., **55**, 135
Saire, Rebecca, **46**, 167, 177; **49**, 161
Saire, Warren, **47**, 212

Saito, Takeshi, **10**, 142–3
Saitō, Yoshimasa, **60**, 133n12
Saker, Edward, **8**, 75; **31**, 27; **41**, 23n
Saki, *see* Munro, H. H.
Sala, G. A., **35**, 7
Salaman, R. A., **45**, 111n
Šalda, F. X., **9**, 106
Sale, Roger, **22**, 160
Salem, Pamela, **47**, 213
Salem, Peter, **42**, 151; **46**, 194, 202; **47**, 215; **48**, 237
Salerno, **17**, 153
Salerno, Enrico M., **12**, 114
Salerno, Masuccio di, **47**, 167n
Sales, F., **20**, 102
Sales, Roger, **46**, 234–5; **58**, 89
Salesa, Damen, **55**, 176
Salgādo, Gāmini, **27**, 163; **29**, 176; **32**, 2, 22n, 37; **35**, 6; **36**, 81n, 178; **37**, 14, 17n; **42**, 38n, 39n; **46**, 9n, 239n; **52**, 121, 124n, 149n; **55**, 82n; **60**, 168
'"Time's Deformed Hand": Sequence, Consequence, and Inconsequence in *The Comedy of Errors*', **25**, 81–91
Saliceto, Bartolomi di, **15**, 97n
Salieri, Antonio, **58**, 303; **60**, 184, 190
Salih, Tayeb, **53**, 293
Salingar, Leo G., **9**, 144; **12**, 129n; **13**, 153; **21**, 144; **23**, 132; **29**, 157; **31**, 62n, 116; **32**, 5, 100n; **34**, 144, 147; **36**, 169; **37**, 2, 14; **38**, 231, 234; **40**, 69, 198n, 199, 213; **45**, 162; **47**, 147; **52**, 123n, 274; **54**, 303; **57**, 305
Salisbury Court Theatre, *see under* Theatres, Elizabethan
Salisbury, Countess of, **34**, 89
Salisbury, Frank, **1**, 59
Salisbury, John, **6**, 159; **8**, 148
Salisbury, Joyce E., **51**, 176n
Salisbury, Lord, **26**, 46; **29**, 23
Salisbury, Robert Cecil, First Earl of, *see under* Cecil, Robert
Salkeld, Duncan, **47**, 245–6; **59**, 49n1
Salkinson, Isaac Edward, **54**, 182–9
Sallinen, Matti, **55**, 325
Sallust, **10**, 36; **17**, 61; **37**, 148; **38**, 116
Salmi, Mario, **26**, 114n
Salmon, Eric, **14**, 126
Salmon, Vivian, **23**, 11n; **25**, 184; **41**, 241; **42**, 195
'Some Functions of Shakespearian Word-Formation', **23**, 13–26
Salomon, Brownell, **30**, 191, 197; **33**, 197; **35**, 155; **38**, 10; **41**, 91n; **45**, 204n
Salomons, Israel, **48**, 56n
Salter, David, **52**, 259; **53**, 25n
Salter, Dennis, **50**, 35n, 36n; **52**, 155; **53**, 236n; **55**, 172n
Salter, F. M., **20**, 73n
Medieval Drama in Chester reviewed, **11**, 144
Salter, H. E., **30**, 163n
Salter, K. W., **9**, 138n
Salter, Thomas, **56**, 31
Saltman, Andrew, **50**, 233
Salusbury family, **44**, 232
Salusbury, Sir John, **15**, 25, 27, 99; **21**, 140; **43**, 241
Salusbury, Sir Thomas, **1**, 44; **24**, 159
Salutati, Collucio, **15**, 95; **44**, 34
Salvador, Joseph, **48**, 51
Salvayre, Gaston, **18**, 86; **19**, 151
Salvian of Marseille, **29**, 21
Salvini, Guido, **4**, 128; **6**, 121; **20**, 121
Salvini, Tommaso, **30**, 198; **34**, 65n; **35**, 33; **36**, 61; **40**, 38–9, 222; **41**, 225; **50**, 35; **56**, 113
Salzburg Cathedral, **3**, 96
Salzburg Festival, **8**, 118
Salzman, L. F., **33**, 141n; **46**, 133n
Salzman, Paul, **50**, 74n
Salzmann, Friedrich Rudolph, **9**, 95.
Samarin, R. M., **9**, 118; **15**, 140; **21**, 128n
'Our Closeness to Shakespeare', **16**, 10–17
Sambin, Hughes, **47**, 24
Sames, Mawline, **25**, 146–7, 149
Sames, William, **36**, 136n1
Sammelles, Neil, **36**, 21n
Samoilov, Yevgeni, **9**, 117, 118; **16**, 15
Sampley, Arthur M., **10**, 2, 70n; **16**, 170; **55**, 30n
Sampson, Agnes, **4**, 42
see also Witchcraft
Sampson, George, **23**, 87n; **24**, 155; **41**, 157
'Shakespeare and Bach', **1**, 119
Sampson, John, **44**, 199
Sampson, William, **53**, 323; **56**, 120n
Sampson, lost play of, *c.* 1567, **7**, 57
Sams, Eric, **36**, 172; **37**, 215; **39**, 225, 250; **40**, 224–6, 230; **42**, 117, 193–4, 213; **43**, 267; **45**, 195n, 202; **46**, 254n, 255; **49**, 298–9; **50**, 151; **51**, 315–17; **52**, 314; **54**, 67; **56**, 280; **58**, 4
Sams, Jeremy, **42**, 151, 153, 154, 156, 159; **43**, 215; **44**, 191; **45**, 157; **57**, 66
Samson, Charles, **9**, 63, 67n
Samuel Johnson on Shakespeare, **46**, 236
Samuel, Irene, **32**, 183n
Samuel, Norma, **45**, 150
Samuel, Raphael, **44**, 105n; **52**, 35n, 38n, 40n, 44n; **55**, 108n
Samuels, Ernest, **24**, 92n, 93n, 98
Samuelson, David A., **38**, 153n, 165n, 235n; **45**, 80n; **50**, 49n
Samwaise, Magdalen, **29**, 33–4, 35
Sanada, Hiroyuki, **53**, 275; **54**, 247–8; **60**, 137n21
Sancho, Ignatius, **51**, 6, 62–3
Sancroft, Archbishop, **16**, 170; **55**, 87n
Sand, George, **58**, 150
translation of *As You Like It*, **2**, 116
Sandby, Paul, **13**, 108
Sandells, Foulke, **12**, 97–106
Sander, Nicholas, **17**, 121
Sanders, Gerald, **27**, 106n
Sanders, Julie, **53**, 321; **56**, 155n, 302; **60**, 184–95, 195n33, 343
Sanders, Norman, **12**, 55n; **16**, 168; **18**, 185–6; **19**, 120n, 130, 136, 154; **21**, 145; **31**, 176, 177; **32**, 219; **33**, 188; **35**, 182n; **36**, 182–4; **37**, 36n, 75n; **38**, 15, 243–5; **41**, 136n, 139n; **46**, 63, 242, 251n; **47**, 269n; **49**, 211n; **53**, 185, 190n; **58**, 350, 357; **59**, 42; **60**, 84n2
Critical Studies, *reviewed:* (1970), **24**, 137–54
(1971), **25**, 171–86
(1972), **26**, 151–68
'The Popularity of Shakespeare: An Examination of the Royal Shakespeare Theatre's Repertory', **16**, 18–29
'The True Prince and the False Thief: Prince Hal and the Shift of Identity', **30**, 29–34

Sanders, Wilbur, **22**, 147–8; **26**, 8; **29**, 89; **35**, 169–70; **38**, 3; **42**, 180; **43**, 10n, 11n; **50**, 280n; **55**, 231n
Sanderson, Cobden, **5**, 51
Sanderson, James L., **31**, 5n; **58**, 349
Sanderson, Rachel, **57**, 337
Sanderson, Robert, **43**, 61n
Sandes, James, **36**, 136
Sandes, Thomas, **58**, 239
Sandford, Patrick, **41**, 183; **46**, 198; **48**, 235; **50**, 225; **52**, 255; **55**, 332; **58**, 300
Sandler, Hannes, **18**, 119
Sandron, Nahma, **55**, 116n, 122n, 123, 125n
Sands, Cicely (later Browne), **33**, 157; **35**, 136n
Sands, Leslie, **35**, 151
Sandved, A. O., **49**, 328n
Sandys, Sir Edwin, **44**, 77
Sandys, George, **17**, 33; **23**, 161; **39**, 132; **41**, 137, 139, 144n; **42**, 59, 62n; **47**, 147; **50**, 85n; **52**, 203n; **53**, 33; **56**, 29, 57, 83, 88n
Sandys, Sir J. E., **4**, 68n; **59**, 264
Saner, Reginald, **23**, 154; **24**, 168n
Sanford, Hugh, **57**, 222
Sangré, Bakary, **45**, 155; **50**, 39
Sanipoli, Vittorio, **18**, 126
Sankey, Fr William, **18**, 177; **23**, 79, 80–1, 82, 83; **25**, 6n
Sano, Seki, **3**, 118
Santaniello, A. E., **51**, 9
Santayana, George, **2**, 134; **4**, 24; **16**, 45; **39**, 141; **54**, 66
Santhiri, Richard, **45**, 155
Santini, Bruno, **42**, 157; **43**, 208; **46**, 195; **47**, 209; **55**, 330
Santlow, Hester, **32**, 42
Santos, R. J., **60**, 218n18
Santucci, L. Falzon, **48**, 257
Santuccio, Gianni, **6**, 121; **11**, 121; **15**, 136
Sanvic Romain (Robert de Smet), **4**, 152; **5**, 111, **6**, 117; **7**, 108; **8**, 118; **10**, 115
Le Théâtre Élisabéthain reviewed, **10**, 146–7
Sanvoisin, Michel, **56**, 294
Sanzio Raphael, **9**, 99
Sapani, Danny, **47**, 216; **48**, 219; **49**, 272; **51**, 225; **53**, 244; **54**, 286; **59**, 340; **60**, 323
Sapara, Ade, **51**, 207; **54**, 293
Sapientia Solomonis, **3**, 52
Sara, Cathy, **49**, 278
Saravia, Hadrian, **57**, 247
Sarbiewski, Casimir, **32**, 192
Sarbin, Theodore, **51**, 153
Sarcerius, Erasmus, **2**, 75
Sarcey, Francisque, **9**, 63, 65, 68n
Sardou, Victoriën, **22**, 2
Sargeaunt, M. J., *John Ford*, **14**, 12
Sargent, John Singer, **19**, 75; **57**, 93
Sargent, Michael, **59**, 338
Sargent, Nick, **42**, 157; **46**, 192
Sargent, R. M., **5**, 141; **10**, 2; **25**, 188; **27**, 16n
Sarment, Jean, **3**, 103–4; 7, 110
Sarne, Mike, **49**, 278
Sarossy, Gyuri, **56**, 288; **59**, 340
Saroyan, William, **12**, 1
Sarrazin, Gregor, **6**, 11; **7**, 2; **10**, 5; **23**, 22n, 34n; **55**, 192n
Sarrazin, Maurice, **7**, 111; **10**, 118; **18**, 123
Sartain, Donald, **15**, 144
Sarti, Andrea, **55**, 180
Sarton, G., **17**, 28n
Sartre, Jean-Paul, **1**, 97, 98; **12**, 110; **16**, 19; **22**, 5; **28**, 43, 44; **34**, 3, 34; **48**, 156–7; **56**, 303; **57**, 119
Le Sursis, **8**, 34
Sasai, Eisuke, **57**, 288, 289
Sasayama, Takashi, **53**, 329
Saslow, James M., **46**, 4, 17n
Sassen, Saskia, **58**, 197
Satchell, T., **7**, 152
Satin, Joseph, **26**, 161; **33**, 13n, 16, 19
Satire, Elizabethan, **17**, 129–37
Sato, Horishi, **42**, 157
Satz, Stanley, **54**, 68
Saudek, Erik A., **4**, 109, 114; **6**, 118–19; **9**, 104–5, 110n; **10**, 116; **12**, 110; **13**, 126; **14**, 118; **16**, 133; **18**, 121; **48**, 164, 165n
Sauer, Elizabeth, **58**, 358; **60**, 269n4
Sauget, Henri, **15**, 133
Saul, Christopher, **50**, 216; **52**, 236; **59**, 328, 339
Sauli, Alexander, **56**, 188, 192
Saunders, Ann, **33**, 145n; **56**, 337
Saunders, Christopher, **52**, 159n
Saunders, Edward, **29**, 110n
Saunders, F. R., **7**, 143
Saunders, Florence, **32**, 32
Saunders, Francis, **55**, 267
Saunders, George, **23**, 173
Saunders, Henry, **38**, 231
Saunders, J. G., **50**, 249
Saunders, J. W., **9**, 146; **10**, 147; **12**, 55n; **22**, 169
'Vaulting the Rails', **7**, 69–81
Saunders, James, **36**, 21n; **56**, 185n, 187n
Saunders, Jason Lewis, **33**, 22, 23
Saunders, Jennifer, **51**, 213
Saunders, Julie, **43**, 213
Saunders, Norman, **23**, 180n, 181, 183
Saunders, Penny, **59**, 346
Saunders, William, musician, **19**, 101–5, 107n
Saunders, William, Vicar of Wootton Wawen, **12**, 103
Saurin, Bernard Joseph, **9**, 91
Sauss, Everhart, **33**, 155, 157n
Saussure, Ferdinand de, **31**, 54; **47**, 221; **49**, 91n
Sauvage, Catherine, **14**, 119
Sauvage, F., **10**, 142
Savadski, Y., **12**, 118
Savage, D. S., **9**, 14
Hamlet and the Pirates reviewed, **5**, 129
Savage, James E., **27**, 178
Savage, Jerome, **44**, 147, 148
Savage, Paul, **58**, 304
Savage, Richard, **1**, 86; **26**, 74n; **60**, 1, 1n1
Minutes and Accounts of the Corporation, **3**, 2
Parish Registers of Stratford, **3**, 2
Savile, George, Marquis of Halifax, **51**, 21n
Savile, Henry, **17**, 34, 66
Savile, Thomas, **17**, 93
Savill, Arthur, **58**, 223, 224
Savill, Cordaile, **58**, 224
Saviolo, Vincentio, **24**, 144; **32**, 236; **47**, 273; **49**, 164n
Savits, Jocza, **1**, 2; **43**, 113; **47**, 1, 2

Savo, Jimmy, **18**, 126
Savonarola, Fra Girolamo, **56**, 32, 34n
Savory, Abraham, **11**, 71–5, 77n
Savoy, Charles Emmanuel, Duke of, **7**, 105n; **8**, 107; **26**, 46
Saward, William, **58**, 143
Sawday, Jonathan, **50**, 258; **51**, 283; **55**, 54n
Sawyer, E., **44**, 155n
Sawyer, Paul, **25**, 192; **51**, 56n
Sawyer, Robert, **54**, 311, 312; **56**, 136n, 157n; **58**, 314, 333
Saxe-Meiningen, Duke of, **5**, 107; **35**, 18; **40**, 1
Saxl, Fritz, **25**, 189; **58**, 247
Saxo Grammaticus, **3**, 55; **4**, 4; **5**, 131; **14**, 45; **44**, 240
Saxon, A. H., **31**, 188; **35**, 12n
Saxon, Rolf, **56**, 270
Saxony, Elector of, **22**, 121; **36**, 138
Saxony, King of, **14**, 112
Saxton, Christopher, **17**, 15; **50**, 143–5
Atlas, **1**, 70
Sayers, James, **38**, 69, 73
Sayle, Charles, **7**, 48; **55**, 64n
Sayle, R. T. D., **26**, 39n
Sbisà, Mariana, **50**, 19n
Sbragia, Giancarlo, **15**, 136; **16**, 136
Scacchi, Greta, **53**, 278
Scaliger, Joseph, **33**, 22; **37**, 13, 15
Scaliger, Julius Caesar, **15**, 97n; **20**, 20, 23; **39**, 128n; **50**, 144; **56**, 109, 110
Scallion, Simon, **55**, 327
Scammell, G. V., **17**, 22n
Scantlebury, Guy, **47**, 215
Scaramelli, Giovanni Carlo, **54**, 127n
Scarborough, Adrian, **50**, 227; **59**, 326
Scardifield, Simon, **57**, 265; **59**, 318
Scarfe, Gerald, **22**, 141
Scarisbrick, Diana, **47**, 173n, 175n, 178n
Scarisbrick, J. J., **52**, 168n, 177n; **54**, 126n
Scarisbrooke, J. J., **48**, 70n
Scarr, Richard, **56**, 336
Scarron, Paul, *Comical Romance of a Company of Stage Players*, **3**, 86; **12**, 32
Scarry, Elaine, **56**, 164; **57**, 97
Scase, David, **12**, 119, 121; **13**, 134, 136; **14**, 126, 128; **15**, 144, 146
Scattergood, John, **55**, 83n
Scéve, Maurice, **34**, 185
Schaaber, M. A., **59**, 40
Schaap, K., **15**, 128
Schaar, Claes, **19**, 139, 147; **23**, 72, 74; **26**, 173
Schabert, Ina, **26**, 176; **32**, 224; **37**, 156n, 158n; **41**, 198; **53**, 298–9
Schach, Leonard, **8**, 120
Schachar, Isaiah, **48**, 56n
Schad, Robert O., **6**, 63n
Schadewalt, W., **15**, 174
Schaefer, George, **57**, 147
Schafer, Elizabeth, **45**, 185; **53**, 321–2, 328; **57**, 327, 328
Schäfer, Jürgen, **23**, 119; 116; **24**, 176; **26**, 172; **27**, 59n; **30**, 208; **32**, 89n; **37**, 159n; **40**, 216
Schaferä, Jürgen, **51**, 316
Schaffeld, Norbert, **60**, 359–60, 361
Schalkwyk, David, **46**, 214; **49**, 295; **53**, 310; **57**, 162, 205, 307–9
Schall, Ekkehard, **48**, 176
Schalla, Hans, **4**, 127; **6**, 120; **8**, 119; **9**, 113; **10**, 119; **14**, 119; **15**, 138; **16**, 134; **18**, 124
Schaller, Henning, **40**, 58n
Schaller, Rudolf, **15**, 134; **16**, 63, 134; **20**, 117; **23**, 122; **37**, 160; **40**, 55; **48**, 178
Schamp, Dieter, **27**, 189
Schamp, Jutta, **53**, 309
Schanche, Ingolf, **3**, 113
Schanzer, Ernest, **9**, 136, 139, 143n; **10**, 4, 5, 9, 137, 140; **11**, 137–8, 140, 143, 147; **12**, 139; **14**, 153; **15**, 167, 170, 174; **18**, 162, 163; **19**, 138; **21**, 134; **22**, 62, 114, 118n, 153, 157; **23**, 148, 172, 182, 183; **24**, 152; **25**, 2, 5, 6n, 176; **26**, 97, 119n, 122, 126; **28**, 51n, 52–4; **29**, 6, 8, 67, 69, 77; **30**, 189; **31**, 107n, **32**, 129–30, 134n, 142n, 143; **33**, 120; **34**, 4; **40**, 28n; **41**, 35–7, 41–2, 92n; **44**, 69, 70; **48**, 27n; **51**, 72n; **59**, 41, 223
Shakespeare's Appian, **11**, 143
'The Marriage-Contracts in *Measure for Measure*', **13**, 81–9
'Shakespeare and the Doctrine of the Unity of Time', **28**, 57–61
Scharf, George, **20**, 110 and n
Recollections of the Scenic Effects of Covent Garden Theatre, 1838–9, **13**, 77
Scharf, **10**, 74
Scharf, H., **49**, 126
Schatoff, Fred A., **19**, 137
Schaufuss, Peter, **51**, 259
Schechner, Richard, **52**, 34–5, 37n, 39n; **60**, 147
Schechter, Abraham, **11**, 140
Scheer, Edward, **58**, 358
Scheffler, F. E., *Thomas Dekker als Dramatiker*, **14**, 12
Scheible, J., **36**, 139, 141
Scheil, Andrew, **51**, 45n
Scheil, Katherine West, **51**, 45–56; **53**, 301; **57**, 325
Schell, Edgar T., **23**, 168; **24**, 151; **28**, 154; **30**, 44; **55**, 234n
Schell, Maximilian, **15**, 134; **37**, 200; **43**, 252
Scheller, B., **26**, 164
Schelling, F. W. J. von, **58**, 183
Schelling, Felix E., **1**, 76; **6**, 2, 3; **7**, 97; **8**, 2, 8; **14**, 3; **20**, 24n; **42**, 2n
Elizabethan Drama, **14**, 1
The English Chronicle Play, **14**, 2
Schellner, Beverly E., **52**, 286
Schelp, H., **26**, 166n
Scherb, Victor I., **59**, 245
Scheyer, T. E., **28**, 161
Schiappalaria, Stefano, **10**, 34
Schiavonetti, Luigi, **13**, 76; **37**, 46
Schibler, Armin, **5**, 115
Schibsbye, K., **23**, 13n
Schick, Josef, **44**, 108n
Schickman, Allan, **32**, 236
Schifanoya, Il, **54**, 125n
Schiff, Gert, **37**, 45n; **49**, 122n, 123n
Schiffer, James, **46**, 208; **58**, 29; **60**, 351
Schikaneder, Emmanuel, **56**, 150
Schilders, Richard, **15**, 128
Schildkraut, Joseph, **7**, 116
Schiller, Adrian, **50**, 209–10; **52**, 239, 243; **54**, 256–7, 273, 281; **55**, 292, 309, 324; **56**, 281

Schiller, Gertrude, **57**, 243
Schiller, Johann Christoph Friedrich von, **4**, 118, 127; **5**, 10, 132; **10**, 119, 150; **12**, 85; **13**, 128; **14**, 119; **16**, 10, 14, 70, 134; **31**, 2; **35**, 13; **37**, 60, 71, 152; **40**, 58, 202; **43**, 112; **44**, 107, 109, 110; **45**, 95; **48**, 10, 177; **53**, 111; **54**, 141; **55**, 115; **56**, 315; **57**, 55, 56, 61, 62, 63, 64, 65, 116
Schilling, Mark, **60**, 135n17
Schimpf, Peter, **57**, 250
Schirmer, Walter F., **13**, 128
Schlaeger, Jürgen, **58**, 155
Schlapp, Otto, **18**, 52
Schlauch, Margaret, **20**, 164
Schlegel-Tieck-Baudissin translation of Shakespeare, **4**, 126–7, 128; **5**, 111; **7**, 111; **12**, 113; **13**, 131; **14**, 85; **15**, 15, 132, 134; **16**, 63, 65–7, 70, 134; **18**, 38, 104, 108–9, 114, 119; **20**, 117
Schlegel, August Wilhelm von, **4**, 109; **5**, 100, 105n; **6**, 1; **8**, 118, 120; **10**, 119; **23**, 122; **34**, 14, 51; **35**, 45; **37**, 143, 152, 155, 160, 161, 200; **39**, 139, 221; **40**, 51, 53, 58–9, 61; **42**, 113, 114, 116; **43**, 112; **45**, 6, 8, 15; **48**, 3–7, 9, 10, 11; **54**, 324
Schlegel, Friedrich von, **15**, 15; **28**, 107; **30**, 201; **37**, 152; **53**, 48; **55**, 344; **57**, 112, 115, 116; **59**, 194n7, 195
Schleiner, Louise, **39**, 232; **54**, 323–4.
Schleiner, Winifred, **29**, 174; **32**, 226; **39**, 226; **44**, 234; **46**, 117n; **56**, 88n
Schlesinger, Giselle, **34**, 180n
Schlesinger, Helen, **42**, 157; **43**, 206, 217; **46**, 202; **52**, 236–7, 240, 260, 265; **54**, 250
Schlesinger, John, **19**, 118; **34**, 154
Schless, H. H., **7**, 144
Schleuter, June, **45**, 188
Schlicke, Paul, **53**, 104n
Schlösser, Anselm, **15**, 140; **18**, 134; **19**, 153, 155–6; **21**, 132; **22**, 153; **23**, 141, 142–3; **25**, 176; **26**, 163; **32**, 216–17, 224; **48**, 183
Schlosser, Eric, **57**, 187
Schluchter, Wolfgang, **43**, 2n
Schlueter, June, **55**, 377; **58**, 237; **59**, 376n2; **60**, 237–49, 249n53
Schlüter, Kurt, **9**, 134; **46**, 242, 243; **53**, 2n
Shakespeares Dramatische Erzählkunst reviewed, **13**, 153
Schmid, E. E., **28**, 41n, 42
Schmid, Hans, **28**, 171; **35**, 6n
Schmid, Patric, **55**, 330
Schmidgall, Gary, **39**, 16n; **41**, 221; **45**, 187; **57**, 64, 67
Schmidt di Simoni, Karen, **23**, 117
Schmidt, A. V. C., **57**, 243
Schmidt, Alexander, **3**, 147; **23**, 22, 34; **30**, 87; **34**, 116; **37**, 85, 155; **44**, 100; **55**, 191–2
Lexicon, **7**, 2
Schmidt, Harvey, **45**, 157
Schmidt, Johann N., **56**, 315
Schmidt, L., **4**, 161
Schmitt, Car, **58**, 322
Schmitt, Jean-Claude, **55**, 241
Schmitt, Natalie Crohn, **24**, 160
Schmitt, Saladin, **4**, 126; **5**, 112; **8**, 152–3
Schmitz, L. D., **36**, 44n
Schmitzer, Renate, **44**, 195
Schmoller, Hans, **59**, 44
Schneider, Alan, **55**, 154n
Schneider, Ben Ross, Jr, **49**, 288; **51**, 179n; **54**, 231n
Schneider, Gary, **60**, 85n6, 183
Schneider, Jane, **55**, 373
Schneider, Joseph, **52**, 88n, 93n
Schneider, Rebecca, **60**, 176
Schneider, Reinhold, **12**, 139
Schneider, Robert, **54**, 315
Schneider, Romy, **15**, 133
Schnitzler, Arthur, **40**, 223
Schoch, Peter, **60**, 360
Schoch, Richard W., **56**, 120, 123n; **57**, 150, 250, 251, 326; **58**, 113
Schoeck, R.J., **54**, 322; **26**, 164; **55**, 182n
Schoell, F. L., **7**, 139
Schoenbaum, Samuel, **14**, 14n; **20**, 166–7; **21**, 65n; **23**, 171; **25**, 1n, 186–7, 191, 196n; **26**, 5; **29**, 138n, 168; **30**, 15n, 185, 191; **31**, 177; **32**, 103n, 223, 247; **34**, 111n, 164, 189; **35**, 179; **36**, 178n; **37**, 2, 217, **38**, 1, 15, 27n, 99n; **39**, 224; **40**, 212; **55**, 37n, 182, 367; 146n; **41**, 42n, 94, 202, 219; **42**, 63n, 64n, 185, 193, 195n; **43**, 144n, 231; **45**, 167, 185; **46**, 141, 235–6; **49**, 47n; **51**, 3, 7, 161n; **52**, 9n, 11n, 59n, 103n; **53**, 137n, 146n; **54**, 76n, 100n, 120n, 239, 241n, 242n, 243; **56**, 60n, 61n, 64n, 65n, 119n, 184n, 201; **57**, 234; **58**, 139, 149, 150; **59**, 5, 71n9, 108n2, 111n15, 112n21; **60**, 247
Middleton's Tragedies, **14**, 11
'*Richard* II and the Realities of Power', **28**, 1–13
Shakespeare's Lives, **46**, 235–6
Schoenfeldt, Michael, **51**, 296; **54**, 317–18
Schoepf, B. G., **35**, 66n
Schoff, Alfred, **9**, 134
Schoff, Francis F., **32**, 12
Schoff, Francis G., **9**, 139; **10**, 139; **14**, 147; **18**, 165
Schofield, Andrew, **44**, 203
Schofield, David, **38**, 203; **51**, 220–1; **52**, 259
Schofield, John, **55**, 374; **56**, 337
Schofield, Malcolm, **46**, 145n
Schofield, R. S., **38**, 26n, 29n
Scholar, Richard, **54**, 201n
Scholeheld, James, **54**, 36n
Scholes, Percy, **15**, 4, 5, 7
Scholes, Robert, **53**, 40n
Scholey, Annabel, **60**, 310
Scholfield, A. F., **48**, 142
Scholfield, Meriel, **44**, 202
Scholl, E. H., **7**, 4
Schollin, Christina, **14**, 123
Scholtes, Gertrud, **37**, 159n
Scholz, Professor Pieter, **57**, 166
Schön, Gerhard, **10**, 150n
Schondonk, Giles, **29**, 30n
Schöne, Albrecht, **26**, 117n
Schone, Richard, **49**, 129n
Schönemann, Horst, **48**, 174
Schönfeld, S. J., **31**, 182; **34**, 173
Schönlich, Christoph, **56**, 315
Schönmetzer, Adolphus, **32**, 132n
School of Night, The, **3**, 10; **4**, 16; **54**, 73
Schools, Elizabethan, **17**, 17, 53–63, 72, 115, 118
Schoop, Gunther, **11**, 148n
Schopenhauer, Arthur, **16**, 34; **24**, 97; **30**, 186; **40**, 82n

Schopenhauer, Joanna, **32**, 198
Schork, R. J., **52**, 279
Schrader, W., **26**, 156
Schramm, Percy Ernst, **60**, 113n46, 113n48
Schreiber-McGee, F., **43**, 47n, 67n
Schrevelius, Cornelius, **13**, 88; **32**, 136
Schreyvogel, F., **15**, 132
Schreyvogel, Josef, **35**, 22, 23, 24
Schrickx, Willem, **4**, 144n, 149; **6**, 159; **23**, 161; **27**, 157; **31**, 172, 192; **34**, 190; **35**, 175; **37**, 198; **38**, 99n, 227, 253; **40**, 214–15; **44**, 219; **54**, 25n, 40n; **57**, 216
'*Pericles* in a Book-List of 1619 from the English Jesuit Mission and Some of the Play's Special Problems', **29**, 21–32
Shakespeare's Early Contemporaries reviewed, **11**, 142
Schröder, Friedrich Ludwig, **9**, 110n; **15**, 132; **48**, 7
Schröder, Johann Friedrich, **57**, 56
Schrödes, Rudolf Alexander, **4**, 127; **5**, 112; **6**, 120; **7**, 111, 112; **9**, 113, 136; **12**, 113; **16**, 63, 66, 67, 134; **23**, 122; **26**, 166; **28**, 172; **35**, 23
Schroeder, Ernst, **55**, 154
Schroeder, H. J., **54**, 36n
Schroth, Christoph, **40**, 52; **52**, 284
Schubert, Franz, **5**, 112; **18**, 100
Schubert, Rosemarie, **12**, 116
Schuchter, J. D., **22**, 156
Schücking, Levin L., **1**, 14; **2**, 108, 119, 126, 140, 141; **3**, 3; **4**, 15, 16; **5**, 114; **6**, 4; **7**, 7; **9**, 10, 15; **10**, 6–7, 8, 50, 106n; **12**, 113, 132 and n; **13**, 32, 33; **18**, 41; **19**, 9; **21**, 9, 24, 25; **26**, 119; **29**, 137; **34**, 1; **35**, 99; **47**, 108; **59**, 78n15, 194n7
Schuckman, Christiaan, **60**, 237, 238–41, 242
Character Problems in Shakespeare's Plays, **13**, 10n, 39n
see also Ebisch, W.
Schüddekopf, **9**, 100n
Schuh, Fritz, **18**, 124
Schuler, Georg, **41**, 135
Schultz, Stephen C., **32**, 224; **35**, 9n
Schultze, Brigitte, **44**, 242; **48**, 4n
Schulz, Herbert C., **6**, 63n; **24**, 159
Curator of Manuscripts, Huntington Library, **8**, 105n
Schulz, Volker, **32**, 224; **37**, 158n
Schulze, Horst, **48**, 174
Schumach, Murray, **55**, 125n
Schumann, Hildegarde, **20**, 146; **26**, 157
Schumann, Robert, **45**, 173
Schürenberg, Siegfried, **3**, 119
Schuster, Louis A., **54**, 43n
Schut, Henk, **44**, 199; **57**, 291
Schutte, William M., *Joyce and Shakespeare*, **12**, 138 and n
Schütze, Johannes, **10**, 4; **34**, 191
Schwab, P., **11**, 121
Schwanenberger, J. G., **18**, 78
Schwanitz, Dietrich, **37**, 158n
Schwartz, Elias, **20**, 149
Schwartz, Joseph, **35**, 79n
Schwartz, Liz, **51**, 269
Schwartz, Murray M., **43**, 1n, 29n; **45**, 38n; **46**, 3, 76n, 95n, 101n, 117n; **50**, 44n, 49; **53**, 83n; **54**, 227n; **56**, 158n
Schwartz, Robert B., **35**, 87n; **38**, 154n; **44**, 222
Schwartz-Gastine, Isabelle, **57**, 327
Schwartzstein, Leonard, **43**, 83
Schwarz, Elias, **22**, 154; **25**, 181; **27**, 166
Schwarz, Hedwig, **11**, 147; **16**, 63; **26**, 166n
Schwarz, Kathryn, **56**, 67, 68
Schwarz, Marc L., **42**, 193
Schwarz, Mark, **57**, 250
Schwarz-Bostunitsch, Gregor, **48**, 62n
Schwarz, York-Wedigo M., **37**, 157n
Schwarze, Hans-Wilhelm, **37**, 158n
Schwarzenegger, Arnold, **45**, 12; **48**, 121; **54**, 314
Schweickart, Patrocinio P., **50**, 243
Schweikart, Hans, **4**, 127
Schwengl, Bruno, **55**, 322; **58**, 260
Schwertsik, Kurt, **44**, 197
Schwertz, M. M., **26**, 164
Schwob, Marcel, **2**, 121, 123; **9**, 67
Scobie, Alain, **54**, 288
Scofield, Martin, **35**, 163n; **36**, 44n; **51**, 27–43; **53**, 301
Scofield, Paul, **1**, 108, 110; **10**, 129, 130; **16**, 18; **18**, 125; **19**, 115–16, Pl. XA; **21**, 115, 119–22, 125; **28**, 171; **30**, 21; **31**, 158n; **33**, 45; **34**, 154; **37**, 168, 170; **39**, 39, 79, 81, 83; **40**, 40; **41**, 53; **44**, 194; **46**, 193; **50**, 30; **52**, 270, 309; **55**, 56–7, 174; **56**, 167; **57**, 147; **58**, 44
Scogins, John, **51**, 136
Scollins, Richard, **46**, 193
Scolnicov, Hanna, **45**, 161, 162; **48**, 61n, 117; **51**, 283
Scoloker, Anthony, **16**, 99; **18**, 35; **49**, 41
Diaphantus, **4**, 87–8
Scornful Lady, The, **52**, 81
Scorodonow, G., **49**, 118n
Scorsese, Martin, **58**, 189
Scot, Reginald, **8**, 150; **24**, 156; **28**, 119, 122; **34**, 188; **43**, 238; **50**, 188n; **57**, 32; **59**, 144, 145
Scot, Thomas, **42**, 189; **45**, 180
Scott, Bill, **53**, 274
Scott, Cherry, **45**, 146
Scott, Sir Clement, **9**, 16, 17, 56, 58n; **32**, 21, 33n; **35**, 7, 16n, 18n; **48**, 1, 11; **49**, 126; **57**, 92, 94
Scott, David, **37**, 47–9, 52; **41**, 224; **54**, 2n
Scott, F. R., **39**, 144n
Scott, Geoffrey, **54**, 52n
Scott, Sir Gilbert, **54**, 86
Scott, Grant, **51**, 300
Scott, Helen, **41**, 190
Scott, Inez, **34**, 195
Scott, J. G., **15**, 11, 14
Scott, J. W., **26**, 172
Scott, Linda Kerr, **44**, 183; **45**, 148; **46**, 188
Scott, Margaret, **37**, 186, 187
Scott, Mark W., **40**, 210n; **41**, 209; **42**, 169n; **43**, 231
Scott, Mary Augusta, **25**, 103
Scott, Matthew, **44**, 195; **45**, 151; **49**, 280; **50**, 227, 236
Scott, Michael, **38**, 237; **43**, 222; **49**, 97n; **56**, 316, 336
Scott, Nathan A., **15**, 123n
The Tragic Vision and the Christian Faith, **12**, 136
Scott, Paul, **34**, 4
Scott, Reginald, **13**, 39; **14**, 155; **17**, 52, 173; **19**, 4, 55, 57
Scott, Richard, **9**, 120; **10**, 123; **13**, 134
Scott, Steven, **51**, 259
Scott, Tom, **48**, 232; **49**, 269; **51**, 267

Scott, Sir Walter, **5**, 94, 99, 100, 103, 104; **9**, 102; **12**, 9; **14**, 79, 83, 86, 89n, 144; **16**, 10, 33; **18**, 19, 80; **19**, 57, 60; **26**, 70n; **38**, 9; **41**, 110; **44**, 135; **45**, 176; **46**, 142, 143; **51**, 112–14, 116, 117; **57**, 115, 126; **59**, 76, 263
Ancient British Drama, **14**, 82, 86
The Fortunes of Nigel, **17**, 7
Scott, W. I. D., **32**, 8
Scott, William, **13**, 136
Scott, William O., **18**, 171; **20**, 153; **32**, 215–16; **57**, 35, 36, 311
Scott-Giles, C. W., **4**, 151
Scott-Pearson, A. F., **17**, 125n
Scott-Siddons, Mary, **56**, 134
Scott-Warren, Jason, **59**, 113n23
Scotto, Giovanna, **10**, 120
Scottowe, John, **50**, 151, 161, 163–4
Scoufos, Alice Lyle, **21**, 152; **24**, 151; **25**, 174; **30**, 35n; **34**, 182–3; **36**, 172, 177; **38**, 14, 86n, 93n, 94, 95n, 97n, 98n; **48**, 70; **56**, 87n
Scouloudi, Irene, **60**, 238n9, 243
Scouten, Arthur H., **11**, 147; **30**, 184; **41**, 23 1n; **43**, 96n; **51**, 67n, 79n; **52**, 324; **53**, 217n; **55**, 3n
Scragg, Leah, **23**, 152; **28**, 5n; **33**, 200; **37**, 191, 192; **41**, 129n; **43**, 227; **46**, 17n, 24n; **47**, 224; **48**, 243–4; **52**, 130; **60**, 268n2
Discovery Shakespeare's Meaning, **48**, 244
'Iago, Vice or Devil?', **21**, 53–65
'Macbeth on Horseback', **26**, 81–8
'Shakespeare, Lyly and Ovid: The Influence of "Gallathea" on *A Midsummer Night's Dream*', **30**, 125–34
Studies on Shakespeare's Life, Times and Stage, *reviewed:* (1968), **22**, 167–76
(1969), **23**, 159–76
(1970), **24**, 154–69
Screech, M. A., **46**, 11n, 12n, 18n
Screen Shakespeare (ed. M. Skovmand), **48**, 262
Scribe, **22**, 2
Scrimgeour, Gary J., **22**, 165
Scriveners Company, *see under* London
Scudamore family, **11**, 107, 114
Scudamore, Frances, **11**, 107
Scudamore, Sir James, **11**, 107
Scudamore, Sir John (Viscount Scudamore) 1650–97, **11**, 107, 114n, 115n, 116n
Scudamore, Sir John, **35**, 130n
Scully, Paddy, **41**, 187
Scully, S. E., **41**, 209n
Scurfield, Matthew, **50**, 203; **51**, 214, 217
Scuro, Daniel, **56**, 19n
Sea Voyage, The, **50**, 255
Seale, Douglas, **1**, 109; **7**, 125; **8**, 124, 125; **9**, 120; **10**, 123, 124, 130; **11**, 134; **12**, 119, 120; **13**, 134, 135–6, 139; **14**, 117, 127; **16**, 26, 138; **38**, 17
Seale, Robert, **44**, 82
Seaman, John E., **22**, 161; **25**, 182
Searle, A., **38**, 31n
Searle, J. R., **44**, 215
Sears, Djanet, **54**, 340; **58**, 339; **60**, 349
Seary, Peter, **45**, 203n; **49**, 322; **51**, 7, 125n; **53**, 342; **59**, 30n46, 124n1
Seaton, Ethel, **1**, 122; **10**, 5; **25**, 128, 129n; **33**, 107n, 108n, 109n; **42**, 88n
Seaton, M. E., **17**, 41n
Seaton, Zoë, **51**, 266; **55**, 292; **56**, 288; **57**, 293; **58**, 306; **60**, 325
Seaward, Kate, **51**, 246
Seazer, J. A., **46**, 194
Sebeok, T. A., **46**, 43n
Sebonde, Raymond, **27**, 45n
Sebring, Jay, **57**, 155
Sebris, K., **39**, 83n
Secchi, Nicolò, **8**, 160; **9**, 141n; **14**, 153
Gl'Inganni and L'interesse, **9**, 142
L'Interesse, **13**, 157
Seccombe, T., **55**, 253n
Secford, Thomas, **50**, 143–5
Second Maiden's Tragedy, The, **3**, 51; **12**, 42; **43**, 242; **46**, 227
conjectural Shakespearian autograph, **8**, 159
Second Report of Doctor John Faustus, **1**, 70
Second Shepherds' Play (Wakefield), **52**, 298
Secord, A. W., **3**, 139–40
Secret of Secrets (1572), **3**, 6
Secrets, Jim, **50**, 199n
Sedge, Douglas, **43**, 270n; **46**, 225
Sedgewick, G. G., **6**, 33n; **40**, 124n, 126n
Sedgwick, Amy, **37**, 200
Sedgwick, Eve Kosofsky, **44**, 52; **46**, 4, 41n; **49**, 304; **50**, 20n; **51**, 295; **56**, 72, 73
Sedgwick, Fred, **53**, 154n, 156n; **54**, 339
Sedinger, Tracey, **51**, 276
Šedivý P., **9**, 101
Sedlak, Werner, **24**, 153; **37**, 157n
Sedley, Sir Charles, **55**, 361
Sedley, D. N., **46**, 145n
Seef, Adele, **39**, 230
Seeger, Kurt, **48**, 172n
Seehase, Georg, **25**, 186; **26**, 156; **32**, 218, 221
Seeley, J. R., **44**, 110n; **55**, 109n
Seeley, R. S. K., **10**, 111
Seely, Tim, **58**, 303
Segal, Charles, **39**, 126n; **40**, 74n
Segal, Jeffrey, **42**, 132–3
Segal, Miriam, **48**, 228
Segalle, Nick, **46**, 196
Segar, Sir William **44**, 141; **54**, 192n
Book of Honour and Arms, **3**, 17
Segelcke, Mrs Tore, **10**, 120
Sehrt, Ernst Theodore, **7**, 133; **8**, 9; **10**, 59n; **13**, 128; **14**, 147; **21**, 143; **23**, 115, 120; **28**, 172n; **37**, 157
Der dramatische Auftakt in der elisabethanischen Tragödie reviewed, **15**, 171
Shakespeare: Englische Essays aus drei Jahrhunderten zum Verständnis seiner Werke, **12**, 139 and n
Vergebung und Gnade bei Shakespeare reviewed, **7**, 132
Seide, Stuart, **50**, 33
Seiden, M., **25**, 177; **32**, 7
Seifert, Martin, **42**, 159
Seigel, Jerrold E., **43**, 63n
Seiler, R. M., **26**, 161
Seip, Didrik Arup, **43**, 15n; **48**, 11n
Sekacz, Ilona, **37**, 164, 170; **38**, 201; **42**, 150; **43**, 190, 200; **44**, 171, 193, 198; **45**, 152; **46**, 184, 198, 201; **47**, 209; **49**, 275; **53**, 285; **55**, 335

Sekgobela, Hope Sprinter, **57**, 292
Selbie, Christopher, **40**, 173, 181; **41**, 183, 189; **42**, 151, 153
Selby-Bigge, L. A., **37**, 150n
Selden, John, **1**, 64; **3**, 14; **4**, 80, 93; **6**, 54; **13**, 166; **17**, 86, 90; **20**, 28; **56**, 324
Table Talk, **12**, 95, 105n
Selden, Ramon, **49**, 37n
Selden, Samuel, **15**, 117, 118
Seldes, Gilbert, **13**, 145n
Selected Papers of the Shakespeare and Renaissance Association of West Virginia, **46**, 212
Selhn, Paul R., **33**, 92n
Selimus, **52**, 100; **55**, 21, 23, 29
Selişik, Çiğdem, **18**, 130
Selkane, Dorothy, **7**, 140
Sell, Colin, **42**, 150
Sell, Roger D., **24**, 159; **58**, 313
Sellars, Peter, **43**, 207; **49**, 274; **50**, 34; **52**, 287; **53**, 309; **57**, 328
Sellars, Susan, **53**, 235n
Seller, H., **26**, 162
Seller, Stuart, **45**, 155
Sellers, Peter, **39**, 197
Sellner, Gustav, **7**, 111; **9**, 113; **10**, 119; **52**, 284
Selous, H. C., **55**, 112
Seltzer, Daniel, **14**, 151; **21**, 155; **24**, 154; **29**, 2; **30**, 13n; **31**, 174; **32**, 220; **38**, 18; **39**, 51; **41**, 67–8, 70; **55**, 30n; **56**, 180; **59**, 41
'Prince Hal and Tragic Style', **30**, 13–27
Selver, Paul, **4**, 109
Selwyn, Don C., **60**, 355
Semak, Peter, **60**, 313
Semenov, Y., **2**, 127
Semmelroth, Wilhelm, **13**, 128; **15**, 134
Semon, K. A., **28**, 163
Semper, Gottfried, **12**, 11
Semper, Monsignor I. J., **3**, 5; **6**, 162; **7**, 143; **8**, 141; **9**, 8; **45**, 21, 22
Hamlet Without Tears, **2**, 137
Semple, Goldie, **40**, 157–8, 165, 168
Semple, Hilary, **43**, 230
Semprum, Francisco, **57**, 119
Sen Gupta, Subodh Chandra, **8**, 7; **21**, 129; **27**, 72n, 156; **32**, 225–6; **33**, 190; **38**, 4; **43**, 228–9
Shakespearian Comedy reviewed, **5**, 131
The Whirligig of Time reviewed, **16**, 163
Sen, Mohit, **19**, 120
Sen, Sailendra Kumar, **13**, 151; **16**, 180; **18**, 174; **31**, 194; **38**, 253; **41**, 213
Sen, Taraknath, **21**, 129n, 138, 158
Sen-Gupta, Rumu, **50**, 235
Senapati, Sukanya B., **56**, 336
Senda, Koreya, **12**, 115; **53**, 329
Seneca (the Elder), *Controversiae*, **10**, 41; **20**, 9
Seneca, Lucius Annaeus, **3**, 14, 67; **4**, 24; **7**, 95, 129; **8**, 59; **9**, 8, 9, 140; **10**, 2, 3, 5, 16, 17, 32, 36, 40, 48, 60, 64, 65, 106n, 136, 144; **11**, 143; **12**, 142; **15**, 23, 88n, 169, 174; **16**, 37–8; **19**, 3, 50, 82–3, 86–7, 88–90, 92, 93n; 20, 17–26; **22**, 109, 110–13, 151; **23**, 121, 169; **24**, 156; **27**, 16, 17, 19, 165, 173, 179; **28**, 40n; **29**, 80, 81, 87; **30**, 61, 62, 104, 109, 112, 192, 193; **31**, 7; **32**, 146; **33**, 22, 23, 25, 89, 90, 91, 95, 96, 195; **34**, 184, 188; **35**, 122, 177; **36**, 92; **38**, 216, 220; **40**, 75; **41**, 136; **42**, 55; **44**, 61, 66, 236–7; **46**, 214, 221, 222; **47**, 140–5, 151; **48**, 154; **50**, 247, 256; **51**, 40, 180, 190n; **52**, 298; **53**, 49, 52, 55, 58; **54**, 223, 318; **55**, 21, 23, 40, 65, 200, 202, 204, 206–8, 223, 229, 346–8, 368; **57**, 302; **58**, 45
De Beneficiis, **10**, 34, 38n
De Moribus, **20**, 22
De Quattuor Virtutibus, **20**, 22
De Remediis Fortuitorum, **10**, 146
Hercules Furens, **10**, 16, 18
Hercules Oetaeus, **10**, 144; **11**, 138, 143
Hippolytus, **15**, 83, 84
Medea, **20**, 21
Octavia, **20**, 25n
Phaedra, **20**, 24, 25n
Thyestes, **1**, 64; **20**, 20
Troas, **1**, 64
Senelick, Laurence, **37**, 201; **38**, 236; **45**, 67n; **54**, 142n; **55**, 239n; **60**, 335
Senellart, Michel, **50**, 65n
Senes, Daniel, **51**, 334
Senesi, Giorgia, **50**, 39n
Seng, Peter J., **13**, 161; **14**, 152; **15**, 9; **19**, 124, 147, 152; **20**, 151; **22**, 177; **26**, 111n; **36**, 112n
'Songs, Time, and the Rejection of Falstaff', **15**, 31–40
Senior, Matthew, **51**, 176n
Sennett, Mack, **54**, 267
Sennett, Richard, **56**, 182, 183n
Senoa, A., **4**, 117
Senoh, Kappa, **42**, 153
Sensabaugh, G. F., *The Tragic Muse of John Ford*, **14**, 12
Sequeira, Isaac, **19**, 133
Ser Giovanni, *Il Pecorone*, **7**, 106n
Serban, Andrei, **20**, 130
Serban, M., **15**, 140
Sergeant, Michael, **60**, 325
Sergent, Jan, **55**, 325
Serkis, Andy, **56**, 280; **57**, 295
Serlio, Sebastiano, **17**, 198; **33**, 144; **35**, 131–9 *passim*; **43**, 236; **45**, 110; **47**, 16, 17, 21, 22, 24; **51**, 283
Sermon on the Mount, **2**, 66–9, 79; **8**, 19
Sermons, Elizabethan, **2**, 70
Seronsy, Cecil C., **10**, 145; **15**, 170; **18**, 159; **33**, 59n; **55**, 263n; **60**, 84n2
Serpieri, Alessandro, **34**, 62n, 64; **40**, 87n, 88n; **59**, 362
Sérullaz, Maurice, **21**, 81, 82
Servetus, **17**, 148
Servius, **38**, 41, 42n; **53**, 13n, 19n
Serwouters, Johannes, **20**, 99, 104n
Šešplaukis, Alfonsas, **21**, 153n; **23**, 159
Sessions, Barbara F., **54**, 15n
Sessions, John, **44**, 194
Sethi, Simeon, **56**, 41
Sethna, K. D., **42**, 183–4
Settle, Dionyse, **17**, 31
Settle, Elkanah, *Il Pastor Fido*, **4**, 94
adaptation of *A Midsummer Night's Dream*, **9**, 85n
Seval, Mehlika, **54**, 37n
Sëve, Lucien, **34**, 30n
Seven Deadly Sins, The, **2**, 46, 51
(plot of), **3**, 50, 52

INDEX

Seven Lears, **44**, 194
Severs, J. Burke, **56**, 305
Severs, Kenneth, **3**, 136
Sevin, Nureddin, **8**, 122; **9**, 116; **12**, 117; **18**, 130
Julius Caezar reviewed, **13**, 154
Venedik Taciri reviewed, **13**, 154
Seward, Desmond, **38**, 56n
Seward, Frederick, W., **24**, 93n
Seward, J., **29**, 164
Seward, T., **16**, 31
Seward, William H., **24**, 92n
Sewell, A. C., **6**, 148; **7**, 2; **21**, 10n; **33**, 7–8; **34**, 30n, 136
Character and Society in Shakespeare reviewed, **6**, 149–50
Sewell, George, **5**, 51; **9**, 93; **46**, 41; **51**, 8; **52**, 303
Sewell, Rufus, **53**, 254–5; **54**, 287
Sex and Suicide, **49**, 278
Sexton, Joyce H., **33**, 193
Sexton, Nick, **44**, 198
Sexton, William, **21**, 103
Sextus Empiricus, **55**, 220
Seymour, Charles, **26**, 112n
Seymour, Di, **41**, 183, 187–8; **42**, 154, 156
Seymour, E. H., **30**, 96n
Seymour, Jane, **43**, 51; **52**, 170–1; **54**, 349
Seymour, Lynne, **49**, 278; **53**, 276
Seymour, M. C., **28**, 120n
Seymour, Mrs, **53**, 217
Seymour, William, **43**, 242
Seymour-Smith, Martin, **31**, 164; **42**, 112n
Seznec, Jean, **31**, 48n; **44**, 215; **54**, 15
Shaa, Robert, **33**, 158; **58**, 229
Shaaber, Matthias A., **3**, 27; **5**, 15n; **6**, 4, 8, 14, 16, 166, 171; **9**, 154–5; **11**, 153; **13**, 163; **15**, 39n; **20**, 49n; 173; **24**, 149; **25**, 183, 196, 199; **26**, 184; **31**, 189; **32**, 5; **38**, 14; **55**, 259–60, 262; **59**, 124n2
on the editing of Shakespeare, **3**, 143
'Unity of *Henry IV*', **2**, 139
Shaban, Nabil, **43**, 206
Shaban, Neil, **47**, 210
Shabbakah, Elias Abu, **36**, 7
Shackerly, Edward, **19**, 104
Shackford, Martha Hale, **10**, 4, 5; **22**, 116n; **56**, 44
Shadoian, J., **26**, 160
Shadwell, Charles, **18**, 94
Shadwell, Thomas, **3**, 44; **20**, 169; **24**, 167; **38**, 236; **51**, 19, 24n, 80; **54**, 199; **55**, 267, 344
adaptation of *The Tempest*, **9**, 85n
Shady, Raymond C., **35**, 175; **39**, 247; **42**, 209n
Shaffer, Brian W., **43**, 232
Shaffer, Elinor, **51**, 300
Shaffer, Peter, **38**, 225
Shaftesbury, Anthony Ashley, Third Earl of; *see under* Ashley, Anthony
Shahane, V. A., **19**, 126
Shahani, R. J., **15**, 26
Shahar, Shulamith, **55**, 37n
Shaheen, Naseeb, **23**, 155; **24**, 157; **34**, 185, 196; **36**, 194; **41**, 218; **48**, 86n; **54**, 7, 10, 41n, 189n; **57**, 241
Shairp, Ashley, **44**, 198
Shakerley, Sir Geoffrey, **13**, 92
Shakerley, Katherine, **13**, 92
Shakerley, Peter, **13**, 92, 94, 104n
Shakeshaft, William, **4**, 148n; **5**, 139n; **8**, 148; **28**, 166; **54**, 72, 121; **56**, 192
Shakespear, John, of Leicestershire, **1**, 85
Shakespeare Association, **5**, 46n
Shakespeare at the Tobacco Factory, **58**, 268, 298, 306
Shakespeare Memorial Theatre, Stratford-upon-Avon, *see under* Theatres
Shakespeare Society, the, **2**, 44
Shakespeare's Birthplace, **1**, 79–88
as a national memorial, **1**, 84–7
connection with Shakespeare family, **1**, 80
early history as a memorial, **1**, 80–2
literature, **1**, 79
restoration, **1**, 85
sale, **1**, 82–4; **3**, 2
library, **3**, 2
copy of Shakespeare's will, **4**, 69–77; **5**, 57
'Swan and Maidenhead', **1**, 79, 80, 82, 84, 85
Welcombe enclosures, **3**, 35
Shakespeare's England, **3**, 1, 5, 6, 7; **4**, 9; **7**, 2; **13**, 83, 88n
Shakespeare, Edmond, **58**, 230
Shakespeare, Edmund, **15**, 10; **30**, 199; **33**, 203
Shakespeare, Gilbert, **14**, 113; **44**, 208
Shakespeare, Hamnet, **1**, 39; **12**, 75; **27**, 94, 98; **37**, 190; **54**, 121
Shakespeare, Henry, **38**, 227
Shakespeare, Joan, *see* Hart, William, Joan, and family
Shakespeare, Joan, **13**, 39n
Shakespeare, John, **1**, 80, 123, 124; **6**, 160; **9**, 12; **10**, 12, 13; **12**, 98, **14**, 90, 92, 113; **17**, 14 and n, 126, 170; grant of arms, 117; **18**, 178; **22**, 167; **27**, 94, 98–104; **28**, 165; **38**, 227; **41**, 219; **43**, 248; **47**, 258; **52**, 103; **54**, 74, 116; **56**, 184–202; **60**, 13, 17
Shakespeare, Judith, *see* Quiney, Thomas and Judith
Shakespeare, Judith, **18**, 178; **54**, 121
Shakespeare, Mary, **13**, 39n; **27**, 98–104; **46**, 106
'Shakespeare, Mrs', **33**, 203
Shakespeare, Susanna, *see* Hall, Dr John, Susanna, and family
Shakespeare, Susanna, **54**, 121
Shakespeare, William, **58**, 237; **59**, 124n2
acting of his plays, **4**, 101–2, 105–7; **7**, 27, 82–9
actor–audience collaboration, **7**, 22–8
actors, **7**, 25–8, 33–4, 121–3; **8**, 69, 152
authorship, **4**, 7–8, 56–9, 158, 159–60
celestial imagery, **8**, 111–16
contemporary references, **1**, 44, 63
creation of myth, **4**, 142–3; **5**, 53, 55–6, 129, 137–9, 142, 149–50
critical studies, Elizabethan stage, **1**, 1–16
death, **1**, 61
deposition in Belott-Mountjoy suit, **3**, 11–12, 13; **4**, 69–77; **5**, 56–7
Editing the plays, earlier efforts, **5**, 1–2, 19–21, 25, 51
Essex's rebellion, **1**, 39–40, 65
family, **4**, 70–1; **5**, 56–7
financial interests, **1**, 47
for continental readers, **5**, 10–15; **7**, 51–6, 150–3; **8**, 153–8; **10**, 151–7
friendships, **3**, 11, 12; **4**, 59–66, 140, 149, 153–4
grammar, **7**, 1–3, 19–24, 35–6

handwriting and signatures, **1**, 61; **2**, 44, 54–8; **3**, 3, 4, 144, 152; **5**, 5, 34–5; **8**, 100, 104n, 148, 159; **10**, 153, 158
imagery, **2**, 59, 132, 136
in general, **7**, 12–34
in history plays, **6**, 11, 27–8, 31; **7**, 5, 8–11, 130, 132–3
in the history plays, **6**, 5–6; **8**, 158; **10**, 60, 119, 143
in the role of Hamlet, **9**, 16–23, 29, 54–8, 60–7, 107, 108, 112, 117–18; **10**, 72–6, 150
its use in characterization, **2**, 83–106; **3**, 132–4; **4**, 18–25, 54, 145; **5**, 132, 134–6, 138
language, vocabulary tests, **6**, 40, 47, 48n
modern editor's task, **5**, 1–9
nature and functions of, **5**, 62–5, 81–92; **6**, 101, 150–1
patterned language, **7**, 15–17
recent work on reviewed, **7**, 1–11
relations with Ben Jonson, **2**, 36–43; **3**, 53–4
Shakespeare's comedies, **8**, 1–13
Shakespeare's life and environment, **3**, 1–12
Shakespeare's Roman plays, **10**, 1–11
Shakespeare's style, **7**, 1–11
Shakespearian criticism, **4**, 1–25
Shakespearian production, **2**, 1–20
the history plays, **6**, 1–15
use of syncope and elision, **7**, 38–9
word-coinage, **7**, 18–19, 55, 56, 113–14, 115, 157, 159; **9**, 24, 26, 85, 104, 136; **10**, 60, 69
adaptations
of *All's Well That Ends Well*, *All's Well That Ends Well* (in modern dress), **8**, 79
of *Antony and Cleopatra*, *Cleopatra*, **53**, 274; *All for Love*, **55**, 322
of *As You Like It*, *As You Like it* (ballet), **55**, 322–3; *Call me Ganymede*, **52**, 255; *Rosalinda* (opera), **3**, 118; **8**, 75;
of *The Comedy of Errors*, **58**, 299; *Gli Equivoci*, **56**, 287; *Kyogen of Errors*, **56**, 288; *The Bomb-itty of Errors*, **57**, 290; *The Comedy of Errors* (Indian film), **59**, 370
of *Coriolanus*, **58**, 90; *Plebeians Rehearse the Uprising*, **56**, 288
of *Cymbeline*, *Cymbeline* (Kneehigh Theatre), **60**, 310–11, 312
of *Hamlet*, **56**, 289; **58**, 300; *A Hamlet of the Suburbs*, **54**, 285; *Act V*, **53**, 275; *The Al-Hal Summit*, **59**, 339; *Amiod's Journey*, **52**, 256; *Barbecuing Hamlet*, **56**, 289; *Death of Ophelia* (Japanese), **60**, 131; *Elsinore*, **52**, 255; *Elsinore* (almost solo), **51**, 259; *Fat Hamlet*, **54**, 28; film version, **14**, 120; *The Freethorpe Hamlet*, (made by children), **55**, 324; *Gertrude – The Cry*, **57**, 291; *Hamlet* (all female cast, with puppets), **52**, 255–6; *Hamlet* (ballet), **49**, 271; **60**, 321; *Hamlet* (ballet with traditional classical music), **51**, 259; *Hamlet* (eighty-minute production), **54**, 285; *Hamlet* (film), **55**, 324; *Hamlet* (film), **60**, 355; *Hamlet* (French), **60**, 217–18; *Hamlet* (Japanese popular), **60**, 131; *Hamlet* (Lithuanian), **54**, 285; *Hamlet* (played very fast), **52**, 255; *Hamlet* (solo, with puppets), **51**, 259; *Hamlet* (Welsh), **60**, 213, 321; *Hamlet: First Cut*, **54**, 285; *Hamlet: He Was A Grave Digger*, **60**, 359–60; *Hamlet in Mind*, **59**, 339; *Hamlet in the Mirror (Hamlet en el Espejo)*, **53**, 275; *Hamlet Project*, **54**, 285; *Hamlet, P'urhepecha*, **54**, 160–4; *Hamlet, the Dithering Dane*, **53**, 275; *Hamlet – the Panto*, **56**, 289; *Hamlet: The Actors' Quarto*, **54**, 284; *Hamlet – The Tragedy of Denmark*, **54**, 285; *Hamuletto yamato nishiki-e* (kabuki), **60**, 137n21; *Humble Boy*, **56**, 289; **57**, 291; **59**, 339; *I Hamlet* (three actors with masks and puppets), **51**, 259; *Kanadehon Hamlet*, **56**, 47, 289; *Kyo-tenshi (Evil Angel)* (Japanese), **60**, 133n13; *Last Action Hero* (film), **60**, 355; *Marowitz Hamlet*, **59**, 339; *One-Man Hamlet*, **53**, 275; *Ophelia*, **56**, 289; **57**, 291; *Ophelia* (amateur production, set in Elsinore), **51**, 259; *Prince of West End Avenue, The*, **52**, 256; Qui est là (fragment involving voices of past directors), **51**, 259; *Rosencrantz and Guildenstern are Dead*, **56**, 289; **57**, 291; **60**, 321; *Secret Love Life of Ophelia, The*, **56**, 289; **60**, 321; *Shamlet*, **55**, 324; *The Tragedy of Hamlet*, **56**, 289; *There is Nothing like a Dame*, **54**, 285; *Who Goes There?*, **57**, 291
of *Henry IV*, **53**, 1, 275; **58**, 301; **60**, 187; *At the Boar's Head* (chamber-opera, Holst), **60**, 185, 187, 189, 190–4, 195; *By Royal Command*, **55**, 335; *Chimes at Midnight*, **53**, 276; **60**, 111–12n39; *Henry IV* (single play), **60**, 116n63; *This England: The Histories*, **55**, 324
of *Henry V*, **58**, 301; *After Agincourt*, **60**, 322; *Battle of Agincourt, The*, **57**, 292; *Before Nell - After Agincourt*, **53**, 276; *Henry V* (French), **54**, 285; Oddsocks (Cast of Seven), **54**, 285; *This England: The Histories*, **55**, 324
of *1 Henry VI*, **18**, 74, 135–6; **19**, 79, 142; **20**, 178; *Rose Rage (Parts 1 and 2)* **56**, 290; **57**, 292; *Thoughts of Joan of Arc on the English as she Burns at the Stake, The*, **56**, 290
of *2 Henry VI*, **19**, 87, 89–90, 94n, 142; **20**, 77; *Rose Rage (Parts 1 and 2)* **56**, 290
of *3 Henry VI*, 89–91, 142, 160; *Rose Rage (Parts 1 and 2)* **56**, 291
of *Henry VIII*, **57**, 292
of *Julius Caesar*, *African Julius Caesar*, **53**, 276; *Dying of the Light, The*, **52**, 257; *Giulio Cesare*, **53**, 276; **54**, 286; *Julius Caesar* (includes Japanese kabuki), **52**, 256; *Julius Caesar* (Japanese), **59**, 370; *Rock Opera: Akatsuki no rooma (Rome at dawn)* (Japanese), **60**, 130–5, 140; *SeZar* (South African), **57**, 292; **60**, 332; Various productions including one experiment with gender reversal, **55**, 325
of *King John*, *La Vie et la Mort du Roi Jean* (French), **60**, 218n18
of *King Lear*, **58**, 90, 301; *Cordelia*, **51**, 260; *Edmund, son of Gloucester*, **51**, 260; *Executive Lear, The*, **56**, 291; *Kathakali King Lear*, **54**, 286–7; *King is Alive, The*, **56**, 291; *King Lear*, **51**, 260, 261; *King Lear* (for schools), **54**, 286; *King Lear* (opera), **43**, 222; **44**, 195; **55**, 325; *King Lear* (Russian), **60**, 313; *King Lear, the Panto*, **51**, 261; *Le Roi Lear*, **53**, 277; *Le Roi Lear* (French), **60**, 218n18; *Lear*, **57**, 293; **60**, 323; *Making the Nation*, **54**, 286; *Our Lear*, **60**, 323; *The Tale of Lear*, **50**, 34; Tate's version, **18**, 184, 186; *Thousand Acres, A* (film), **52**, 257; *Vision of Lear*, **57**, 293; *The Yiddish Queen Lear*, **54**, 286; **56**, 291
of *Love's Labour's Lost*, *The Big Life* (musical), **59**, 340; **60**, 323; *Love's Labour's Lost* (film), **55**, 325
of *Macbeth*, **58**, 302; Actors, puppets and masks, **55**, 326; *Akogun*, **52**, 258; *Barnam Vana (Birnam Wood)* (Hindi), **59**, 370; *Cumbrian Macbeth, A.*, **56**, 292; *The Dark: A Macbeth*, **51**, 262; Duncan's golden blood in, **19**, 34–44; film, **18**, 71 (Kurosawa's film) 73; *Euro-Macbeth*, **53**, 278; *From a Jack to a King*, **52**, 258; *Journey to Macbeth*, **54**, 288; *Lady Macbeth*, **51**, 262; *Lady Macbeth and Visions of Ophelia*, **51**, 262; *Lady Macbeth of Mtsensk*, **56**, 292; *Lady Macbeth of Mtsensk* (opera), **59**, 341; *Lady Macbeth Rewrites the Rulebook*, **56**, 292; *Macbeth*, **51**, 262; **56**, 292; **57**, 293;

Shakespeare, William (*cont.*)
Macbeth (1-hour touring production), **53**, 277; *Macbeth* (Custard factory), **52**, 258; *Macbeth* (Davenant's revision), **60**, 214; *Macbeth* (film), **59**, 63; *Macbeth* (film versions), **52**, 258–9; *Macbeth* (five actors), **52**, 258; *Macbeth* (for children), **55**, n 4–7, 327; **59**, 341; *Macbeth* (for schools), **54**, 288; *Macbeth* (French), **60**, 218n18; *Macbeth* (French teenagers), **53**, 278; *Macbeth* (in French and with mime), **53**, 278; *Macbeth* (in Japanese), **55**, 327; *Macbeth* (martial arts and voodoo ritual), **53**, 278; *Macbeth* (one-man performance), **55**, 327; *Macbeth* (opera), **60**, 324, 353, 356; *Macbeth* (radio), **55**, 327; *Macbeth* (schools tour), **52**, 258; **53**, 278; *Macbeth* (Scottish Opera), **54**, 288; *Macbeth* (seven actors), **55**, 327; *Macbeth* (seven-person version), **60**, 208–9; *Macbeth* (shortened version), **53**, 278; *Macbeth* (solo interpretation), **52**, 258; **60**, 324; *Macbeth* (three-man), **59**, 341; *Macbeth* (TV for schools), **53**, 278; *Macbeth – a Reworking*, **56**, 292; *Macbeth: Director's Cut*, **54**, 288; *Macbeth False Memory*, **55**, 326; *Macbeth from Manipur: Stage of Blood*, **52**, 258; *Macbeth: Information is Power*, **52**, 258; *Macbeth: Son of the Grave*, **56**, 292; *Macbeth the Panto*, **52**, 258; *Macbeth2* (modern warfare), **55**, 327; *Macbeth-Moment*, **55**, 327; *MacHomer*, **55**, 327; *Makbed blong William Sekspia*, **53**, 278; *Makinde*, **55**, 326; *Metal Macbeth* (Japanese), **60**, 130, 136Fig.21, 135–40; *Opera*, **54**, 288; *The Porter's Daughter*, **51**, 262; Puppet production, **55**, 326; *Scenes from Leviathan, a modern Macbeth*, **52**, 258; *Thirteenth Night*, **54**, 288; *Umabatha, the Zulu Macbeth*, **52**, 154–65, 258; **56**, 292; *Wyrd Sisters*, **60**, 324
of *Measure for Measure*, *A Millennium Measure for Measure*, **55**, 327; *Measure for Measure* (diverse), **52**, 259; *Measure for Measure Malaya*, **57**, 294; **59**, 185, 188–9; *Measure for Measure – restructured*, **56**, 293
of *The Merchant of Venice*, **18**, 72; **19**, 86, 112–14, 116–18, 146, 148, 150; **20**, 85, 90, 145, 152, 156–7, 165; Backbones Theatre production, **55**, 327; *The Merchant of Venice* (schools tour), **53**, 279; *Shylock*, **53**, 279; *Shylock* (one-man), **59**, 341; *Shylock: Four Hundred Years in the Life of a Legend*, **44**, 107; **52**, 99, 99n, 100n; *Shylock: Shakespeare's alien*, **56**, 293
of *The Merry Wives of Windsor*, **58**, 303; **60**, 184; *Die Lustigen Weiber von Windsor* (opera, Nicolai), **60**, 184, 192n24, 317; *Die Lustigen Weiber von Windsor* (opera, Ritter), **60**, 184; *Die Lustigen Weiber von Windsor* (opera, von Dittersdorf), **60**, 184; *Falstaff* (opera, Verdi), **55**, 328; *Falstaff*, **56**, 293; **57**, 294; **59**, 341; **60**, 184, 187, 189–90, 190, 192n24, 317, 324; *Falstaff* (operetta, J. P. Webber), **60**, 184; *Falstaff* (symphonic poem, Elgar), **60**, 185, 187, 194–5; *Falstaff, o le tre burle* (*opera buffa*, Salieri), **60**, 184, 190; *Herne le Chasseur* (opera), **60**, 184; 'In Windsor Forest' (cantata), **60**, 189n17; *Les Deux Amies, ou le Vieux Garçon* (opera), **60**, 184; *Merry Wives: Good Time Johnny* (musical), **60**, 184; *The Musical*, **60**, 184, 318Fig.59, 317–18, 319; *The Merry Wives* (in Elizabethan pronunciation), **8**, 122; *Sir John in Love* (opera, Vaughan Williams), **60**, 184, 185, 187, 188–91, 192, 192n24, 194, 195, 317
of *A Midsummer Night's Dream*, **51**, 264; **56**, 294; **58**, 303; **60**, 185; *The Dream* (ballet, Ashton), **60**, 325; *A Hard Midsummer Night's Dream*, **53**, 280; *A Midsummer Night's Dream* (ballet), **52**, 261; **53**, 280; **54**, 289; **59**, 342; **60**, 324; *A Midsummer Night's Dream* (Custard factory), **53**, 279; *A Midsummer Night's Dream* (cut text for cast of five), **52**, 261; *A Midsummer Night's Dream* (film), **52**, 262; **54**, 289; *A Midsummer Night's Dream* (for 8 actors), **55**, 329; *A Midsummer Night's Dream* (for children) **55**, n 4–7, 329; **59**, 342; *A Midsummer Night's Dream* (Japanese popular), **60**, 131; *A Midsummer Night's Dream* (on touring wagon), **55**, 329; *A Midsummer Night's Dream* (opera, Britten), **54**, 289; **59**, 342; **60**, 326; *A Midsummer Night's Dream* (Mendelssohn), **60**, 185; *A Midsummer Night's Dream* (schools), **53**, 279, 280; *A Midsummer Night's Dream* (versions for children), **52**, 261; *A Midsummer Night's Dream* (with Mendelssohn's music), **53**, 280; *Bottom's Dream*, **51**, 264; **53**, 280; *Brenddwyd Noswyl Ifan*, **55**, 328; *Children's Midsummer Night's Dream, The*, **56**, 294; Czechoslovakian versions, **12**, 145; **13**, 119, 167n; *Dear Brutus* (J. M. Barrie), **55**, 329; *Donkey Show, The*, **55**, 329; *Dream, The* (for children), **55**, 329; **56**, 294; *Dreaming, The*, **56**, 294; *Dream Nights*, **52**, 261; *Fairy Queen, The*, **57**, 294; *Get Over It*, **56**, 294; *Magical Midsummer Madness*, **53**, 280; *Oberon*, **53**, 279; *Pyramus and Thisbe* (opera), **59**, 342; *Release the Beast*, **59**, 342; Smith's *The Fairies*, **18**, 77–8; *The Wild Life*, **53**, 280; *Yume Shakespeare* (Japanese), **60**, 131n6, 162, 174, 177, 178
of *Much Ado About Nothing*, *Beatrice and Benedict*, **56**, 295; *Much Ado about Nothing* (film), **49**, 308; *Much Ado about Nothing* (Japanese), **60**, 131n6; *Much Ado about Nothing* (Rock Musical), **49**, 275–6; *Much Ado About Nothing (Three Weddings and a Funeral)*, **53**, 280
of *Othello*: **47**, 216; **56**, 295; **58**, 304; *Crazyblackmuthafuckin' self*, **57**, 295; *Desdemona: a play about a handkerchief*, **53**, 281; **56**, 295; **60**, 325; *Kaliyattam* (Hindi film), **59**, 370; *O* (film – **56**, update to US High School), 295; *O* (film), **60**, 165, 365; *Otello*, **56**, 295; **57**, 295, 313; *Otello* (Kirov opera), **56**, 295; *Otello* (opera, Verdi), **60**, 325; *Othello* (Arc Dance Company), **49**, 276; *Othello* (Custard Factory Adaptation), **49**, 276; *Othello* (French), **60**, 218n18, 221; *Othello* (ITV), **56**, 295; *Othellophobia*, **59**, 343; **60**, 163, 154–63, 167, 169; *Perfect Blackman – Othello*, **59**, 343; *William Shakespeare's Othello*, **54**, 290
of *Pericles*, *Islands*, **55**, 330; *The Legend of Pericles*, **51**, 265
of *The Rape of Lucrece*, **56**, 298
of *Richard II*, **58**, 90; *The Hollow Crown*, **60**, 329; *Richard II* (history of Lancaster), **55**, 330; *Shatranj Ke Khilari* (Hindi film), **59**, 370
of *Richard III*, **51**, 265; **59**, 343; *Bloody Richard*, **54**, 290; *The Goodbye Girl* (film), **60**, 356; *Little Richard*, **53**, 282; *Looking for Richard* (documentary film), **59**, 371, 372; **60**, 354–5; *Richard III* (London Fringe), **54**, 290; *Richard III* (ninety minute text), **52**, 262; *Richard III* (set in East End pub), **53**, 281–2; *Richard III* (shortened version), **55**, 330; *Richard III* (two people, music, text and mime), **52**, 262; *The African Company presents Richard III*, **53**, 282; *This England: The Histories*, **56**, 296
of *Romeo and Juliet*, **47**, 217; **51**, 266; **58**, 305; *Cut to the Chase*, **59**, 344; *Fatal Loins*, **56**, 296; *Forbidden Love – Romeo and Juliet*, **57**, 296; H & M cinema fashion commercial, **60**, 354; *I Capuleti e I Montecchi* (opera), **56**, 296; *Juliet and Romeo*, **59**, 344; *Mercutio Rising* (monologue), **60**, 326; *The Nurse's Story*, **54**, 291; *Rock'n*

Rolling Romeo (for primary schools), **52**, 263; *Rome and Jewels*, **56**, 296; **57**, 296; *Romeo and Juliet* (4 Kidztour), **54**, 291; *Romeo and Juliet* (ballet, Prokofiev), **52**, 263; **53**, 282; **54**, 291; **57**, 296; **59**, 344; **60**, 327; *Romeo and Juliet* (cast of eight), **54**, 291; *Romeo and Juliet* (English National), **56**, 296 *Romeo + Juliet* (film), **52**, 88–98, 197–8, 199, 200, 264; *Romeo + Juliet* (Baz Luhrmann), **53**, 163; *Romeo and Juliet* (film), **55**, 384; *Romeo and Juliet* (for schools), **52**, 263; *Romeo and Juliet* (Harvester), **46**, 238; *Romeo and Juliet* (industrial background), **54**, 291; *Romeo and Juliet* (Japanese popular), **60**, 131, 131n6; *Romeo and Juliet* (mime and music), **52**, 263; *Romeo and Juliet* (one-act ballet), **55**, 331; *Romeo and Juliet* (rehearsal), **54**, 291; *Romeo and Juliet* (schools tour – cast of 3), **53**, 282; *Romeo and Juliet* (Scottish ballet), **55**, 331; *Romeo and Juliet* (seven actors), **55**, 331; *Romeo and Juliet* (with young people and music group), **55**, 331; *Romeo and Juliette*, **50**, 36; *Romeo and Juliet Deceased*, **54**, 291; *Romeo and Juliet: the Musical*, **57**, 296; *Romeo and Tusi*, **55**, 175n; *Romeo et Giulietta*, **54**, 291; *Romeo et Juliette* (French), **60**, 218n18; *Romeo Must Die* (martial arts film), **55**, 331; *Romeu and Julieta* (in Portuguese), **55**, 331; *Shakespeare's R & J*, **59**, 344; *Tromeo and Juliet*, **53**, 282; *Tromeo and Juliet* (film), **60**, 355

of sonnets, *Dark Lady of the Sonnets* (film and live), **53**, 285; *Love's Fire*, **53**, 285

of *Taming of the Shrew*, **58**, 305, 306; 'A Bad Firangi Woman Brought to Sense' (Surat), **59**, 369; *Catherine and Petruchio*, **60**, 80n33; *'Katherine and Petruchio'*, **35**, 36, 38, 39; *Kiss Me, Kate*, **56**, 297; *Kiss Me Kate* (musical), **60**, 327, 354; *The Taming of the Shrew* (five actors), **52**, 264; *Shrew'd*, **56**, 297; *The Tamer Tamed*, **59**, 345; **60**, 327; **10** *Things I Hate About You* (Film), **54**, 292

of *The Tempest*, **51**, 267; **56**, 297; **58**, 306, 322; *Before the Tempest, After the Storm* (dance), **59**, 345; *Caliban*, **52**, 265; *Caliban and Miranda*, **55**, 333; *The Caliban's Island*, **52**, 264; *The Caribbean Tempest*, **54**, 293; Dryden's adaptation, **13**, 137–40; *Full of Noises*, **57**, 297; Frank Martin's operatic version, **11**, 117; *Maybe Tomorrow*, **54**, 292–3; *Ottra Tempestad*, **53**, 283; *Play for England*, **52**, 264; *Prospero's Children*, **53**, 283; *Prospero's Island*, **59**, 345; *Prospero – the Rough Magic of Doctor Dee*, **56**, 299; *Return to the Forbidden Planet*, **56**, 297; *Storm on the Lawn*, **53**, 283; *Strangest of Islands*, **52**, 264; *The Tempest* (abridged), **54**, 293; *The Tempest* (abridged for schools), **60**, 327; *The Tempest* (Ballet), **53**, 284; *The Tempest* (cast of six), **55**, 333; *The Tempest* (film), **60**, 199; *The Tempest* (for 3 actors), **54**, 292; *The Tempest* (for children), **52**, 264; *The Tempest* (gender-reversed), **60**, 327; *The Tempest* (opera), **59**, 345; *The Tempest* (Polka theatre for children), **55**, 333; *The Tempest* (TV film), **52**, 265; *The Tempest in Butetown* (community-based), **60**, 196, 197–9, 211; *The Tempest in Kowloon* (Japanese), **60**, 131n6, 133n12; *This Rough Magic*, **55**, 333; *Tossed*, **60**, 327; *Une Tempête* by Aime Cesaire, **53**, 283

of *Titus* Andronicus, *Titus Andronicus* (black comedy), **54**, 293; *Titus Andronicus* (criminal underworld), **54**, 293; *Titus Andronicus* (Joe Redner Films), **54**, 223; *Titus* (film – US release 1999), **54**, 223; Kaos *Titus Andronicus*, **57**, 297

of *Troilus and Cressida*, *Cressida*, **55**, 334

of *The Two Gentlemen of Verona*, *Two Gentlemen of Soho*, **51**, 269; *Say It Again* (Japanese), **60**, 131n6

of *Twelfth Night*, **57**, 297; **58**, 307; *Ballet*, **54**, 294–5; *The Deceived* (a related work), **54**, 295; *Malvolio's Revenge*, **56**, 298; **57**, 297; *On'na tachi no ju-ni-ya* (Japanese), **60**, 136n19; *Over the Edge*, **55**, 333; *Twelfth Night* (5 actors), **54**, 294; *Twelfth Night* (Ballet), **53**, 285; *Twelfth Night* (cut for young people), **53**, 284; *Twelfth Night* (for schools), **54**, 294; *Twelfth Night* (Japanese), **60**, 131n6, 133n12; *Twelfth Night* (schools' workshops), **53**, 284; *Twelfth Night – The 1960s San Francisco Psychedelic Musical*, **60**, 328; *Twelfth Night Fever*, **51**, 268; *Twelfth Night – The Musical – Five Go to Illyria*, **60**, 328; *Twelfth Night: Shakespeare Unplugged*, **52**, 265

of *The Winter's Tale*, **51**, 269; *The Winter's Tale* (Japanese), **60**, 131n6; *The Winter's Tale* (Riding Lights Company), **53**, 285

of *Venus and Adonis*, *Venus and Adonis* (with Bunraku puppet techniques), **59**, 346

general: *An, Act of Will, the Secret Life of William Shakespeare*, **55**, 334; *The All-New Super Shakespeare Show*, **53**, 286; *A Celebration Concert*, **55**, 335; *Dreams*, **55**, 335; *The Dresser*, **60**, 329; *Elizabeth Rex*, **57**, 298; *Enchantment*, **53**, 286; *Hallmarks*, **53**, 285; *Hollow Crown*, **57**, 298; *Jubilee*, **56**, 298–9; *The Loves of Shakespeare's Women* **57**, 298; *Madman William*, **55**, 335; *The Millennium Link Project*, 335; *My Son Will*, **55**, 335; *Nymphs and Shepherds (The Winter's Tale)*, **54**, 295; *The Plantagenets*, **43**, 171–81, 184, 212–13, 250, 255; *Romans*, **55**, 335; *Shakespeare d'good stuff*, **53**, 286; *Shakespeare in the Dark*, **53**, 285; *Shakespeare in Love* (film), **53**, 286; **54**, 296; **55**, 159; **60**, 49, 123, 160; *Shakespeare in the Year Tempo 12* (Japanese), **60**, 135–6n18; *Shakespeare Lives* (television workshop performances), **60**, 204; *Shakespeare on the Estate* (community-based), **60**, 196–7; *Shakespeare Translated: The Bard's 60 minutes of fame*, **55**, 335; *Shakespeare's End*, **54**, 76; *Shakespeare's Mums*, **53**, 286; *Shakespeare's Villains*, **53**, 285–6; *Shakespeare's Sisters – As Good As It Gets*, **60**, 324; *Shakespeare's Women*, **53**, 286; **56**, 299; *Shooting Shakespeare*, **59**, 346; *Stage Beauty*, **60**, 160; *Sweet William*, **60**, 329; *Theatre of Blood*, **60**, 329; *When the Cat's Away* (musical), **60**, 184

decay of rhetorical acting in recent years, **7**, 28–30, 123; **8**, 152–3; **10**, 112, 147–50

editions

Alexander, Peter, **7**, 55; **8**, 157; **9**, 48n; **22**, 92n; **23**, 27n, 49n; **26**, 69n, 95n, 181; **29**, 24n; **30**, 1n, 35n, 61n, 86n, 135n; **31**, 23n, 78n; **32**, 51, 73, 153n 154n, 158n; **33**, 56n, 69n, 89n, 113n, 116n; **34**, 23n; **35**, 88n, 119n; **36**, 86n, 108n; **44**, 25; **50**, 173n; **52**, 307; **59**, 5

Allen, Michael B. and Muir, Kenneth, **53**, 338

Applause, **59**, 89n34, 200–1

Arden, **3**, 73n; **5**, 80n, 148; **6**, 2, 5, 12, 148, 168; **7**, 2, 6, 103, 149; **8**, 6, 117n, 153, 157–8; **9**, 151; **10**, 1, 2, 3, 4, 6, 9, 10, 49n, 70n, 137, 141, 151–3; **11**, 150, 151, 155; **12**, 120, 122, 126; **13**, 41, 74, 105n, 116, 119–20, 120, 149, 150, 152, 156, 158, 160, 162, 164, 165–6, 172–3; **14**, 34, 73, 129n, 142, 147, 149 and n, 163; **15**, 80n, 102, 122, 125; **16**, 13, 14, 54, 83–94, 133–4, 163–4; **17**, 82n, 86, 126, 137, 145, 146, 157, 162, 164–5, 171, 192, 210, 236; **18**, 7, 48, 51, 52, 55, 63, 65, 94–5, 107, 112, 147–54, 158,

Shakespeare, William (*cont.*)
163, 168–9, 176; **21**, 27n; **22**, 26n, 77n, 92n; **23**, 51, 71n, 76n, 180; **24**, 52, 55n, 76n, 58, 106n, 113n, 172, 177; **25**, 4, 47n, 82, 84n, 85n, 87n, 126, 137n, 198; **26**, 5, 12, 13, 69, 71n, 72, 82n, 113n, 119n, 122n, 126n; **27**, 34n, 38n, 92n, 106n, 111n, 133; **28**, 39, 55, 90, 117, 121n; **29**, 1, 5, 11n, 22, 43n, 45n, 51n, 76n, 93n, 105n, 110, 139, 177; **30**, 29n, 35n, 47n, 73n, 61n, 193, 203, 204, 205; **31**, 13n, 25n, 29n, 65n, 87n, 93, 94, 136n; **32**, 1, 2, 37n, 38, 64n, 74n, 75, 85n, 98n, 103n, 116n, 118n, 124n, 128n, 234, 245, 246; **33**, 3, 7, 8, 13n, 15n, 17n, 29n, 35n, 44n, 69n, 70n, 75n, 79n, 99n; **34**, 25, 102n, 106n, 156n, 187, 189; **35**, 57, 80n, 81n, 119n, 121–7 *passim*, 178; **36**, 23n, 40n, 63, 98, 100n, 102n, 103n, 105, 116n, 119n, 161, 181, 184, 185, 186, 193n; **37**, 2, 5, 10, 20n, 23, 25, 33n, 59n, 90n, 92n, 100n, 161, 198, textual criticism of, 202–19 *passim*; **38**, 1, 12, 15, 18, 39, 44, 49, 50n, 62, 63, 85, 115n, 139, 146, 149, 156n, 167, 175, 238, 239, 241, 244, 247, 251; **39**, 67n, 123n, 127, 129n, 159n, 160n, 161n, 162n, 205, 238, 240–2, 244, 247; **40**, 55n, 63n, 78n, 107n, 119, 137, 193, 214, 219; **41**, 13n, 37, 69n, 70n, 89n, 134, 137, 153, 143n, 241; **42**, 25n, 39n, 40, 46n, 49n, 53, 101n, 181, 193, 203n, 204, 211n; **43**, 16n, 18n, 43n, 64n, 110, 113n, 132n, 135n, 267; **44**, 3, 23n, 139, 245; **45**, 10, 91, 197, 198; **46**, 11n, 84n, 89n, 93n, 104n, 131, 132, 149n; **47**, 131n, 140, 142, 267; **48**, 39n, 155; **49**, 3, 27, 33, 42n, 43, 70n, 75, 105, 129, 145, 164n, 310–13, 316, 317, 324n; **50**, 3, 20n, 22n, 110n, 268, 281; **51**, 142, 160n, 169n, 179n, 308, 309, 317, 331, 335–6; **52**, 130, 166, 189n, 276, 302, 303, 308, 316, 317; 3, 302–11; **53**, 2, 3, 85, 146n, 176n, 179n, 185–6, 188–93, 335–7, 339, 340, 342; **54**, 1, 3, 10, 34n, 115, 204, 208n, 210, 211, 343, 350, 352, 348–54; **55**, 3, 6n, 12, 13, 14n, 20n, 22, 25n, 36n, 46n, 117, 140, 181, 182, 187, 189, 191, 193, 196, 198, 210, 211, 257, 261, 280, 367; **56**, 9n, 14n, 23n, 39n, 41n, 64, 93, 94, 95, 101, 104n, 168, 169, 171, 173n, 174, 179, 235n, 330, 344, 349, 350, 352; **57**, 197, 217, 235, 239, 335, 340, 341, 342; **58**, 7, 51, 161, 208, 309, 313, 319, 327, 343, 354, 355, 357; **59**, 2–4, 21, 32n58, 37n87, 40, 43–4, 46, 47, 48, 52, 53–4, 55, 79, 83, 89, 89n34, 90, 102n15, 151, 152, 153, 375, 376, 378–9; **60**, 168n4.2, 169n6.5, 256n16, 272n13, 361, 363, 365, 366–8, 369
Ayscough's Edition, **57**, 341
Bankside, **45**, 40; **59**, 157n3
Bantam, **59**, 3
Barker, **53**, 226n
Barrington, David, **56**, 304
Bell, John, **34**, 14n; **37**, 43–5, 47, 148n; **43**, 105; **49**, 115n, 118; **51**, 88, 91, 109; **52**, 152; **53**, 214, 216–18, 225–6, 243, 343; **57**, 59; **59**, 57, 60n27
Bellamy, **53**, 343
Benson, John, sonnets (1640), **60**, 281
Bevington, David, **36**, 122n; **48**, 282; **51**, 302, 305; **52**, 320; **59**, 3, 5n15
Bobbs-Merrill, **38**, 245n
Booth, Lionel, **23**, 1n
Boswell-Malone Variorum (1821), **3**, 1; **4**, 56–8, 66, 80; **6**, 163; **7**, 41; **9**, 71; **10**, 26n
Bowers, Fredson, **53**, 338
Burby, Cuthbert, **60**, 258, 259
Cambridge CD-ROM, **59**, 169, 170–1
Cambridge Shakespeare in Production, **59**, 46–7, 87n29, 89n34, 201–2, 212, 371
Cambridge, **25**, 73; **26**, 181; **27**, 132n; **28**, 38n; **33**, 130n; **36**, 116n; **41**, 61n, 91n, 94n, 229; **42**, 211n; **43**, 267; **44**, 244–5; **48**, 268, 271; **49**, 311–12, 317; **50**, 114, 272; **51**, 307, 310, 312, 317; **52**, 134, 135n, 144, 303, 321; **54**, 334, 343; **56**, 227n, 228n; **57**, 329, 341; **58**, 115, 356; **59**, 3–4, 65n7, 98n10, 151–2
Cambridge (1863), **4**, 67n; **5**, 2, 3, 25, 50–1, 54; **7**, 41, 51–2, 55; **8**, 157; **9**, 48n
Cassell, **55**, 107
Clark and Wright, *see under* Cambridge (1863)
Clarendon, **30**, 206
Cliffs, **59**, 89n34
College Classics (Madras, 1900), **2**, 43n
Collins, **59**, 3
Cowden Clarke, **38**, 157n
Craig, Hardin, **26**, 111n; **30**, 47n
Craig, W. J., **23**, 15n; **31**, 48n
Craig-Parrott, **9**, 48n
Criterion, **52**, 185n
Crofts Classics, **2**, 153
Cumberland, **53**, 216, 228–30
Dicks, John, **58**, 110
Dolan, Francis, **55**, 193
Dolby, **53**, 216, 228–30
Dover Wilson, **55**, 280
Eighteenth Century Shakespeare, **24**, 171
Electronic, **52**, 323–5
Eric Sams, **51**, 315
Everyman, **59**, 55n17
Folger, **11**, 153; **12**, 4, 36, 61, 73, 134–6, 138, 142–3, 165; **14**, 20, 21–2, 28–9, 165, 166; **15**, 52, 131–3, 135, 137–9, 140, 142, 145, 174; **16**, 13, 65, 80, 132–3, 136, 138, 162, 174; **17**, 145–6, 151n, 209; **18**, 2, 11, 105, 148, 157, 163, 166; **19**, 8, 12, 20, 24, 28, 93, 118, 122, 134–6, 138, 140, 142, 146; **21**, 142; **22**, 116n, 169n; **28**, 172, 179, 180; **35**, 185; **41**, 106n, 216; **44**, 256; **49**, 122, 123; **50**, 143, 271, 273, 278, 288; **52**, 15, 185n; **53**, 213n, 216, 326, 333, 337; **54**, 2, 62n, 90n, 136n; **56**, 187n, 188; **57**, 314, 343; **59**, 2–3, 37–8n87, 89n34
Folios, **21**, textual studies of, 157–63; **22**, 109, 114; textual studies of, 176–83; **23**, 1, 18, 102, 121, 122, 143, 156; facsimiles of, 15n, 178, 186; copies of, 79, 80, 82, 86; textual studies of, 176–85; **24**, 52, 53, 54, 74n, 106, 150; Norton facsimile of, **24**, 170, 172; textual studies of, 170–9; **25**, 5, 6n, 7, 9, 49n–50n, 73–80, 85n; textual studies of, 193–200 *passim*; **26**, 12n, 177–84 *passim*; **27**, 49n, 105n, 106n, 108, 132, 135; editorial research on, 187–92; textual studies of, 179–92 *passim*; facsimiles of, 189; **28**, textual studies of, 173–81 *passim*; **29**, 24, 51, 77, 105n, 117–25 *passim*; textual studies of, 177–85 *passim*; **30**, 86n, 194, 198; textual studies of, 203–10 *passim*; **31**, 49n, 191, 193–4; **32**, 79, 106, 157n; textual studies of, 237–47; **33**, 1, 28–34, 45, 49, 50n, 64, 78n, 81, 116n, 158, 199, 204; textual studies of, 205–11; **34**, textual studies of, 188–96; **35**, 101, 119n, 120–7 *passim*, 166; textual studies of, 179–91; **36**, 47, 63, 79, 80, 83, 107, 108n, 109, 111n, 113, 114n, 116, 117, 118, 120, 143, 157; textual studies of, 182–94; **37**, 24, 34, 75, 82; **38**, 12, 85, 92, 103, 104n, 127, 155n, 166, 177, 239, 251, 253, 254;

39, 129, 138, 157, 168, 225, 236, 237, 238n, 239, 241, 242, 248–51; **40**, 66, 138, 146n, 147, 151n, 211, 216, 219, 224–6, 228–33, 235; **41**, 14, 16, 21, 26, 29, 37–8, 55–6, 60, 62, 69n, 87–9, 95n, 98, 123, 147n, 154–5, 202; **42**, 15, 46, 49n, 54n, 63, 108, 111, 119n, 123–5, 188, 189, 190, 193, 200–14; **43**, 43–4, 59, 99, 103, 155, 200, 225, 255–7, 266–70; **44**, 69n, 78, 79, 89, 113, 114, 116–18, 123, 125–9, 134n, 179, 182, 185, 232, 241; textual studies of, 244–56; **45**, 3, 27, 28, 29, 31, 33, 34, 54n, 60, 76, 79n, 80, 82, 84n, 86n, 87, 115, 186, 191, 193–9, 203; **46**, 47n, 63, 65, 94, 96, 134, 160, 192, 230, 237; textual studies of, 241–57; **47**, 45n, 149, 163, 165, 182, 217, 222; textual studies of, 259–87 *passim*; **48**, 28, 29, 42n, 231, 237, 266; textual studies of, 268–87; **49**, 22, 40, 129, 145, 217–23, 260, 299; textual studies of, 310–36 *passim*; **50**, 7n, 10n, 27n, 74n, 93n, 129, 142–4, 206, 215, 230; textual studies of, 272–88 *passim*; **51**, 67n, 83, 88, 92n, 129, 135, 137, 138, 165, 219, 229, 241, 247, 302–8, 311–22, 323, 324, 330–5; **52**, 4, 24, 69n, 70, 72–3, 76, 79, 84n, 87, 105–6, 117, 121, 134, 143–4, 154, 166n, 179, 197, 227, 229, 257, 259, 299, 308, 310, 312, 315n, 317, 321–2, 324–5; **53**, 47n, 49, 76, 78, 82, 166, 171, 187n, 214, 217, 218, 225–31, 239, 250, 295, 332–3, 336–14; **54**, 2, 210, 235n, 308, 310, 332, 343–57; **55**, 2–3, 36, 39, 40, 41, 45–9, 50, 51, 54n, 55, 58, 61, 150, 172, 184–5, 187, 189, 191–2, 194–5, 257–70, 286, 370, 381–2; **56**, 1n, 23n, 61, 81, 94, 95, 101, 168, 170, 171, 172, 174, 178, 179, 183, 227, 256, 276, 310, 320, 344, 352, 353, 354–5; **57**, 1, 3, 4, 5, 6, 69, 73, 96, 209, 212, 234, 274, 331, 333, 334, 337–43; **58**, 74, 78, 160, 207, 346, 348, 350, 352, 354, 356, 357; **59**, 1, 3, 4, 9, 11, 14, 15–16, 18–19, 44, 49–51, 62n31, 77, 79–90, 92, 93–4, 96–107, 128, 137, 140, 149, 155, 157–63, 170–1, 173–4, 198, 214, 356, 358, 382; **60**, 63n15, 107, 115n58, 201, 362, 363–5, 366, 367 *passim*

First Folio (1623), **1**, 13, 52, 57–60, 71, 77n, 128–9, 131, 133; **2**, 38–40, 109, 146, 148n, 150–1; **3**, 1, 12, 22, 28, 44, 47, 144–5, 148, 151; **4**, 57, 79, 85, 94, 139, 157–8, 160–1; **5**, 16–24; **6**, 4–5, 75, 81–2, 161, 165–72; **7**, 21, 45–6, 48, 51–5, 57, 91, 108, 148–9, 152–3; **8**, 28, 81, 90, 95, 98n, 153–7; **9**, 26–9, 43n, 44–5, 48n, 69, 74–5, 79, 82–3, 148–9, 151–2, 154–6; **11**, 21, 79, 81–2, 85–6, 123, 150–2, 154–5; **12**, 73, 147–52; **18**, 11, 12, 23, 27–8; **19**, 1, 155–60; **60**, 224n8, 237–8, 242, 249n53, 252, 263, 266, 268–9, 270, 277–8, 281, 358, 368
  advertisements of, **4**, 88–9
  Grenville copy in the British Museum, **9**, 84
  Holford copy in the Bibliotheca Bodmeriana, **9**, 83; **10**, 3, 12, 49n, 60, 69, 79, 83–4, 151–4, 156–7
  Tarbutt copy in the Bodleian Library, **4**, 82–5; **5**, 2–9, 12–13, 15n, 25, 50, 54, 80n, 144–7, 151

Second Folio (1632), **1**, 60, 67; **2**, 151; **3**, 48; **4**, 57, 80, 82, 85, 91, 94, 152; **5**, 9, 50–4; **7**, 21, 48–9, 53, 90–1, 152; **8**, 82, 120, 147; **12**, 125; **14**, 100n; **18**, 11, 12, 23, 177; **60**, 282
  Craven copy in the Bibliotheca Bodmeriana, **9**, 84

Third Folio (1663–4), **1**, 60; **3**, 48; **4**, 57, 80, 82, 85, 91, 94, 152; **5**, 9, 50–4; **7**, 21, 48–9, 53, 90, 91, 152; **9**, 84, 155; **11**, 30n; **18**, 23; **60**, 266n42

Fourth Folio (1685), **1**, 57, 60; **3**, 48; **4**, 57, 80, 82, 85, 91, 94, 152; **5**, 9, 50–4; **6**, 171; **7**, 21, 48–9, 53, 90, 91, 152; **11**, 30n; **18**, 11–13, 23
  Kerr copy in the Bibliotheca Bodmeriana, **9**, 84
  miniature editions of, **18**, 11, 20–1, 23–4
  street-ballad versions of plays, **19**, 95–100

French, **35**, 6; **53**, 228
Furness Variorum, **6**, 2, 4, 8, 110; **7**, 1–2, 6, 149
Furnivall, F. J. (1909), **10**, 151n
Ginn, **59**, 3
Griggs (facsimile), **22**, 181; **26**, 12, 13
Globe, **5**, 2, 3, 33, 46n, 68, 79n; **6**, 151; **7**, 2, 22, 41–2, 55; **23**, 1n; **25**, 73n; **34**, 192; **35**, 5; **59**, 46, 98n10, 151–2, 154n34, 160
Hailes, **53**, 228
Halliwell, James Orchard, **32**, 241
Hanmer, Sir Thomas, **4**, 85–6, 162; **10**, 28; **33**, 210; **37**, 43, 44, 213; **53**, 343
Harbage, Alfred, **32**, 163n
Harding, **53**, 343
Harrison, *see* Penguin
Harvester series, **48**, 268n, 271; **56**, 228n
Hemingway (Variorum), **1**, 128
Humphreys, A. R., **26**, 177
Hunter, G. K., **26**, 177–9
Internet, **58**, 354; **59**, 4, 173, 179, 180
Johnson, Dr Samuel, **4**, 56, 162–3; **10**, 24, 25n, 28; **37**, 100, 147, 149, 150; **53**, 343–4
Johnson and Steevens, George, **3**, 50; **4**, 80, 87; **34**, 14n; **37**, 45
Johnson-Steevens-Reed, Isaac, **59**, 115, 122n54, 125, 127–9, 130, 132–3, 134
Jonson, Ben, **54**, 334
Kemble, John Philip, **53**, 216, 225, 227–31
Kittredge, George Lyman, **9**, 48n
Kittredge-Ribner, Irving, **34**, 91n
Knight, Charles, **6**, 61
Lacey, **53**, 228
Lacy, **35**, 6
Laurel, **59**, 81
Leob, **53**, 26n, 27n; **54**, 31n, 33n, 202n, 207n, 209; **55**, 65n, 206n; **56**, 41n, 59n
Longman, **60**, 253
Macmillan, **30**, 206
Malone Society, **27**, 130n; **41**, 11; **44**, 256; **49**, 15n, 18n, 299; **50**, 19n; **51**, 315, 331; **52**, 84, 133n; **53**, 344; **54**, 136n; **58**, 353
Mercury, **59**, 66–8
Modern Standard Drama, **45**, 33
Munro, John, **26**, 44n
Necessary Shakespeare, **59**, 89n34
Neilson, William Allan and Charles Jarvis Hill, **31**, 106n
New Cambridge, **1**, 13, 127–9; **2**, 145; **3**, 32n, 33n, 73n, 143; **4**, 7, 12, 156–7, 162; **5**, 4, 139, 148, 150; **6**, 5, 8, 16, 35n, 92, 167, 169; **7**, 3, 6, 22, 82, 106, 139–40, 147–9; **8**, 26n, 27n, 157; **9**, 34n, 47n, 48n, 53n, 79, 79n, 150; **10**, 2–3, 5, 9–10, 25n, 49n, 70n, 152; **11**, 149–50; **12**, 36, 38, 44, 78, 131–2, 134, 136–7, 142–3, 145, 149, 158–9, 162; **15**, 2, 5, 9, 24, 27, 53, 85, 102, 114, 120, 121–2, 125, 132, 134, 137–42, 144, 146, 158–9, 161, 170, 172, 173, 174, 179–82; **16**, 13, 37–8, 55–6, 60–1, 64, 72–3, 74, 83, 88–9, 133, 136–7, 143–51, 156, 159, 166, 170, 177, 178–9; **17**, 7, 52, 86, 92n, 119, 137, 145–7, 151n, 157–8, 158n, 169, 171–2, 175–6, 209, 210, 214, 220–2, 233; **18**, 1, 4–6, 11,

Shakespeare, William (*cont.*)
47, 51, 54, 64, 100, 106, 116, 164–6, 174, 183, 159, 163; **25**, 2, 5, 9; **27**, 62n, 71n, 106n; **30**, 48n, 86n, 203, 208; **31**, 93; **32**, 85n, 145n, 151n, 152n, 153n, 156n; **33**, 1, 9; **34**, 189; **36**, 107n; **37**, 85, 90; **38**, 13, 18, 238–46; **40**, 228, 236; **41**, 37, 69n, 91n, 94n, 136, 139, 244; **42**, 53, 201, 205; **43**, 262; **44**, 247, 250, 251; **45**, 10n, 193n, 196; **46**, 63, 101n, 131, 132, 133, 240, 241, 242n, 243n, 245, 247, 250n, 251n, 256; **47**, 131n, 140, 264–6; **48**, 37n, 74n, 278, 281; **49**, 19n, 23, 145n, 163n, 314n, 328n; **50**, 82, 114n, 269, 289; **51**, 179n; **52**, 69, 185n, 291–2, 311–19; **53**, 185, 190; **54**, 352, 354; **55**, 181n, 184, 189, 190, 191, 193, 196, 198; **56**, 39n, 169, 171n, 172n; **57**, 146, 327, 328, 329, 337; **58**, 350, 356, 357; **59**, 2–3, 6, 9n37, 40, 52–3, 89n34, 89, 90, 147–8, 152–3, 154, 156, 161, 199; **60**, 368, 369

New Folger, **50**, 3; **51**, 330; **53**, 333

New Mermaid, **42**, 112n; **55**, 30n

New Oxford, **55**, 188, 305

New Pelican, **56**, 105n; **60**, 115n58

New Penguin, **21**, 157–8; **22**, 178–80; **23**, 181, 182; **24**, 172, 176; **26**, 177; **27**, 188, 190; **28**, 178–9; **29**, 6, 67; **30**, 203, 210; **31**, 118n, 153; **32**, 32, 79n, 85n, 86, 178n, 238–9; **33**, 1, 81, 83n, 172, 177; **34**, 152; **35**, 57, 80n, 83n, 84n, 119n, 121–7 *passim*, 182, 183; **36**, 117n, 171, 181, 182, 184, 186, 195n; **37**, 2, 6, 23, 38n, 75n, 120n, 161, 219; **38**, 12, 15, 18, 49n; **40**, 147, 230; **41**, 149n, 238, 242; **42**, 169, 193, 204n, 213n; **43**, 109, 201; **44**, 207, 245, 254; **46**, 160, 225, 242, 249; **47**, 131n, 154; **48**, 164n; **49**, 4n, 77, 129, 311, 320, 329n; **50**, 3, 270, 285, 289; **51**, 319; **53**, 46n, 176n; **55**, 196; **56**, 171; **60**, 163, 169

New Readers', **59**, 81, 86

New Riverside, **51**, 305

New Shakespeare, **21**, 114n, 146n, 147n; **24**, 52, 171, 172; **29**, 41n; **40**, 78n; **49**, 321

New Swan Advanced Series, **59**, 81

New Temple, **7**, 55

New Variorum, **1**, 128; **3**, 33n, 143; **8**, 11, 38n, 39n; **10**, 3, 59n, 151; **22**, 177; **23**, 69n; **31**, 17n, 127n; **33**, 13n, 17n, 18n, 209; **34**, 23n; **35**, 33n, 101n, 113n, 182, 183, 185; **36**, 61n, 63, 85n, 182n, 195n; **37**, 2, 156; **38**, 85, 185; **39**, 139n, 215; **41**, 56n, 83n, 143n, 240n; **45**, 3n, 193n, 196; **46**, 35n, 63n; **47**, 155n, 165n, 167n, 169n, 256; **49**, 100n; **50**, 51n; **52**, 131n, 276, 323; **53**, 187n; **54**, 28n, 101n, 115, 129n; **55**, 24n, 59, 259; **59**, 4, 41, 174–5, 179, 187–8

New Variorum supplement, **11**, 152–3

Nonesuch (ed. Herbert Farjeon), **8**, 158

Norton Critical Editions, **58**, 348–50, 356, 357

Norton, **32**, 239; **33**, 81; **51**, 302–6, 315, 330, 336; **52**, 143; **53**, 332, 341; **55**, 45n, 99n; **57**, 5, 137; **58**, 60; **59**, 3, 5n15, 49, 69n1, 89n34, 375; **60**, 113n47, 145n16, 224n8, 362

Oxberry, William, **35**, 6; **45**, 27n, 31; **53**, 220

Oxford, **7**, 41; **28**, 117n, 175; **34**, 189, 192n, 194; **37**, 2, 23, 34n, 202–5; **38**, 18, 46, 95, 238, 239, 245, 246; **39**, 251; **40**, 65, 74n, 78n, 156, 158, 166, 236; **41**, 37, 69n, 89n, 91n, 94n, 95n, 154, 228–45 *passim* (Oxford); **42**, 39n, 46n, 49n, 209 (Complete Oxford); 206n, 211n (Oxford); **43**, 11n, 12, 267; **44**, 55n, 119, 120, 167, 223; textual studies of, 244–56; **45**, 10n, 53, 79n, 82n, 194, 197, 199, 200, 203; **46**, 63, 241–2, 244–7, 248n, 251, 252–3, 255–7; **47**, 240, 241, 262, 266, 275; **48**, 75n, 155, 188, 268, 271–2, 276, 280–4; **49**, 10, 27, 49n, 181n, 311–12, 313n, 314n, 315, 317, 319, 320, 323, 334–6; **50**, 7n, 21n, 27, 267, 274, 278–83, 289; **51**, 302–3, 305, 307, 311, 312, 315, 324, 325, 331, 336; **52**, 66n, 69, 70, 80n, 100, 143–4, 166n, 306, 316, 319–23; **53**, 148n, 149n, 311, 331–2, 342–3; **54**, 25, 234n, 334, 344–5, 347, 350, 355; **55**, 2, 54n, 65n, 172, 182n, 184, 188, 189, 191, 194, 196, 198, 367, 368; **56**, 120, 169, 171n, 172, 174, 178–9, 228n, 244n, 302, 351; **57**, 81, 101, 238, 329, 335, 339, 340; **58**, 132, 309, 327, 343, 347, 354, 355, 356, 357; **59**, 2–4, 5–6, 11, 14–16, 44, 45–6, 47, 48, 69n1, 70, 71, 89, 153, 180, 196n14, 214, 215, 375–8, 382, 383; **60**, 126, 364, 365–6, 368, 369

Oxford Complete Sonnets and Poems, **60**, 256

Oxford Complete Works, **60**, 253, 364

Oxford World Classics, **56**, 39n, 80n; **57**, 23; **59**, 47, 53, 220; **60**, 191n22, 194n30

Panmun, **59**, 90n37

Pavier, Thomas, 266, 366

Pelican, **10**, 153; **12**, 4, 36–7, 38, 40, 48–50, 77, 79, 82–3, 85, 115, 119, 121, 134, 137–8, 142, 143, 146, 153; **13**, 156, 161, 163, 165, 167–9; 153; **24**, 172, 173–5; **26**, 55n; **31**, 55n, 128n, 191; **32**, 224; **34**, 42n, 133n, 136n, 189; **36**, 58n, 97n, 105, 116n, 182, 186n; **43**, 16n; **50**, 3; **58**, 356; **59**, 2–3, 4, 40–2, 43, 89n34

Pembroke, **59**, 139–40

Penguin, **2**, 153; **8**, 158; **9**, 48n, 152; **13**, 165; **14**, 96; **15**, 5, 71n 108, 109n, 118, 139, 142, 166, 169, 173, 180–1; **16**, 80–1, 132; **17**, 153, 172, 186–7, 215, 217–18, 233; **18**, 7, 172, 188; **19**, 2, 153; **20**, 91, 126, 151, 156; **32**, 100n; **47**, 131n; **52**, 303; **55**, 187; **56**, 173; **59**, 3, 4, 39–40, 45, 46, 47

Pléiade, **50**, 126n, 128n

Pope, Alexander, **33**, 209, 37, 71, 142

Pope (1723–5), **4**, 85–6; **10**, 27, 28

Quartos, **1**, 58, 128–31; **2**, 149, 153; **3**, 23–30, 44, 47, 82n, 144–5, 147–9, 150–2; **4**, 7–8, 57–9, 84, 94, 135, 157–63; **5**, 4–8, 11–12, 16–24, 25–6, 28, 31, 37, 39, 51–4, 144–6, 150–2; **6**, 4–5, 54, 58, 161, 164–72; **7**, 3, 36–47, 51–4, 90–1, 148–53; **8**, 28, 81–97, 98n, 99n, 153, 155–9; **9**, 7, 26–31, 33n, 43n, 44–7, 48n, 50, 69, 74–6, 79, 82–4, 150, 152–5; **10**, 80, 83–4, 151–2, 154–7; **11**, 80–1, 84–7, 149–52, 154–5; **12**, 152; **13**, 164–5; **18**, 11, 23, 26–33; **19**, 90, 120, 133, 142, 147, 155–60; **20**, 20, 30, 41–3, 47, 48, 71–2, 76, 85, 163, 176, 178; **21**, textual studies of, 157–63 *passim*; **22**, textual studies of, 176–83 *passim*; **23**, 121, 133, textual studies of, 176–85 *passim*; **24**, 52, 53, 74n, 106, textual studies of, 170–9 *passim*; **25**, 7, 8, 73–80, textual studies of, 193–200 *passim*; **26**, 33n, textual studies of, 177–84 *passim*; **27**, 45n, 113, 135; textual studies of, 179–92 *passim*; **28**, 109, textual studies of, 173–81 *passim*; **29**, 117–24 *passim*; textual studies of, 177–85 *passim*; **30**, 86n, textual studies of, 63n15, 107, 115n58, 145n16, 201, 203–10, 226, 252, 255, 255–6n16, 258–9, 361, 362, 363–5, 366, 368–9; **31**, 95–6, 137, 194; **32**, 105–6, 118, 128n, 153, 154n, 157n, 158n, 165n; textual studies of, 237–11; **35**, 101, 119n, 120–7 *passim*, 166, 177, 178; textual studies of, 179–91; **36**, 63, 79, 80, 108n, 112, 113, 157, 173, 174, 184, 185, 186; textual studies of, 184–94; **37**, 83, 120n, 142, 192 textual studies of, 202–19; **38**, 18, 85, 104, 155n, 248, 253, 254; **39**, 95, 99n, 129, 138, 195, 197, 217, 236, 237, 250; **40**, 65–6, 138, 146–7, 149, 151n,

152–3, 156, 158, 220, 231, 233–5; **41**, 13–22 *passim*, 26–7, 30, 37–8, 63n, 69n, 123, 150n; textual studies of, 228–45; **42**, 61, 93, 95, 101, 109, 124–5, 184, 188, 204–14; **44**, 78, 79, 115, 117, 118, 119n, 120, 121, 122, 123, 128, 151, 179; textual studies of, 244–56; **45**, 3, 27, 28, 29, 31–4, 61, 80, 82, 192, 194, 195, 198, 199, 203; **46**, 12n, 35, 40, 41, 63, 65, 159, 160, 162, 175, 227, 229, 230, 231, 237; textual studies of, 241–57; **47**, 45n, 149, 163, 182, 211, 222, 250; textual studies of, 259–76 *passim*; **48**, 42n, 50, 115, 166, 187, 231; textual studies of, 268–72, 278–81; **49**, 3, 7, 8, 10, 19, 21, 23, 24, 27–44, 50, 53, 55n, 59n, 61, 102n, 105n, 145, 167, 176, 216, 217–23, 231, 232, 240–2, 310–36 *passim*; **50**, 7n, 22, 140, 142, 144, 215, 270, 272–88 *passim*; **51**, 129, 137, 302–8, 310–16, 318–20, 324, 328, 330–6; **52**, 4, 24–5, 29, 65, 70, 76, 78n, 85, 105, 274, 289, 297, 304–6, 310, 311–13, 315, 316, 317, 318–19, 324–5; **53**, 14n, 41–4, 47, 48n, 238–9, 295, 310–11, 333–44; **54**, 19n, 285, 312, 322, 343–57; **55**, 2, 3n, 29n, 36, 39, 40, 45–51, 54n, 55, 58, 61, 86n, 150, 184–5, 187, 189, 237, 258, 263, 265, 305, 342, 370, 381–2; **56**, 1, 23n, 42n, 44n, 62n, 95, 101, 168, 170, 178, 310, 314, 320, 321, 349, 351, 354; **57**, 202–3, 222, 223, 228, 321, 331, 336–43; **58**, 350, 352, 353, 356, 357; **59**, 1, 6–9, 10, 11, 14, 15–16, 21–3, 44, 61, 97, 97n7, 154–5, 157–63, 170–1, 173–4, 382 *passim*; textual studies of, **54**, 356–7
Revels, **51**, 213n, 214n; **55**, 30n; **56**, 101n; **57**, 26, 57, 227; **59**, 70
Ridley, M.R., **32**, 239
Riverside, **28**, 173–7, 178; **29**, 184; **30**, 125n, 208; **31**, 4n, 34n; **32**, 129, 142, 177n, 239; **33**, 121; **34**, 55n; **35**, 102n, 119n, 120–7 *passim*, 184; **36**, 79; **37**, 15n, 70n, 85n; **38**, 63, 92, 101, 102n, 115n, 155n, 238, 241; **39**, 42n, 81n, 135n, 236n; **40**, 41n, 72n, 108n, 109n, 115n, 123n, 228n, 230; **41**, 89n, 231, 237; **42**, 39; **43**, 1n, 134n; **44**, 91; **45**, 128n, 197, 198; **46**, 51n; **47**, 162n; **48**, 42n, 86n; **50**, 3, 10n, 128; **51**, 302, 305, 315, 317; **52**, 66n, 99n, 143, 314; **53**, 12n, 29n, 227–8; **54**, 25n; **55**, 14n, 191, 226n, 260; **56**, 39n, 80n; **57**, 150; **59**, 3–4, 5n15, 23n14, 26n28, 46, 69n1, 159, 214
Riverside, 2, **60**, 63n14, 88n9, 102n1, 109n33, 253, 255n16
Rivington, **49**, 122
Rowe, Nicholas, **10**, 72; **27**, 191; **37**, 41, 42, 52, 71, 148, 149, 213; **42**, 19n, 20n; **43**, 88; **45**, 198n; **46**, 137; **48**, 270; **51**, 108n; **52**, 291; **53**, 218, 331–5, 342–4
RSC Complete Works, **60**, 366
Scolar, **22**, 181; **42**, 190
Signet, **41**, 89n; **49**, 129; **59**, 2–3, 4, 40, 41, 42, 43, 44, 45
Signet Classic, **22**, 67n; **27**, 34n; **33**, 35n; **35**, 119n, 121–7 *passim*; **37**, 143n; **38**, 18; **40**, 91n; **43**, 70n; **46**, 88n
Simply Shakespeare, **59**, 89n34
Sisson, C.J., **8**, 156–7; **9**, 48n; **10**, 3, 153
Stafford and Wright, **55**, 27, 30, 31
Staunton, Howard, **57**, 341
Steevens, George (1802), **6**, 61
Theobald, Lewis (1733), **10**, 28; (1757), **4**, 162–3; **33**, 209, 210; **37**, 43, 44, 203, 213
Thorpe, Thomas, sonnets, **60**, 253, 255, 259
Todd Press, **59**, 63–6, 67–8
Variorum, **21**, 27n; **22**, 116n; **27**, 28n, 29n, 43n, 69, 106, 107, 108n; **30**, 96n; **32**, 7n, 50n, 57n, 241, 242; **33**, 210; **40**, 70, 78n, 123n, 131n, 236; **45**, 38n, 39, 197; **46**, 10n, 45n, 51n, 57, 63n; **50**, 242; **52**, 303; **53**, 187, 228n, 232n, 344; **54**, 101n; **57**, 3, 197; **59**, 37n87, 53–4, 56–7n20, 57n21, 60, 98, 199
Variorum (Black, M.W.), **11**, 152
Walker's edition (1734), **18**, 15; **20**, 84–5, 89, 111, 126, 130, 153, 174, 175
Warburton, William (1747), **4**, 56, 57, 86, 162–3; **10**, 28; **33**, 202, 209, 210; **37**, 149, 213
White's Quarto, **55**, 29n
Windsor, **59**, 81
Witford, **45**, 32, 33n
Woodfall, **45**, 32
Yale, **2**, 153; **9**, 150, 151, 152; **10**, 152; **11**, 153; **12**, 2, 36, 46–7, 62, 73, 75, 78, 85, 134, 136–7, 142, 146; Yale Shakespeare edition reviewed, **15**, 178–9; **16**, 13, 38–40, 54–5, 78, 82–3, 132–3, 138, 160–1; **17**, 43, 47–50, 51n, 92n, 93, 139, 185, 210, 248n, 254n; **18**, 11, 52, 99, 161–2, 173, 175; **23**, 1n; **32**, 98n; **34**, 196; **50**, 272; **52**, 151n; **59**, 151, 153–4
literary influences
antithesis in, **19**, 25–33
attributed plays:
The London Prodigal, **54**, 295
Funeral Elegy, A, **51**, 326–7
attributed works:
Cardenio, **53**, 285
Edmund Ironside, **41**, 191, 233; **42**, 117, 127, 192; **52**, 266
Wars of the Roses, The, **31**, 149, 150, 152, 162; **46**, 162; **47**, 99, 211; **54**, 274; **55**, 293
comic prose, **8**, 57–68
costumes and illustration, **13**, 72–80
dialect, **7**, 3, 19–21; **8**, 56, 158–9
handwriting as source of corruption, **5**, 34–5
in the history plays, **6**, 4–6, 11; **7**, 1–11
of 'morality' framework, **3**, 69, 72–3
of Romance tradition, **4**, 143–4
of Shakespeare on Pushkin, **5**, 93–105
on the comedies, **8**, 2–4, 147–8
orthography generally, **7**, 35–47; **8**, 155, 159
printing of shakespeare's plays, **4**, 163; **5**, 5–7, 18, 21–2, 24, 28–35, 144–5, 146, 147, 150
pronunciation, **7**, 3–4, 35–47
punctuation, **1**, 131
recent work on, reviewed, **7**, 3–4
religion, **1**, 123;, **2**, 80, 134
reporting of plays, **5**, 17, 22–4, 26–8, 35–8, 40–1, 45, 151–2; 'piracy'
revision of plays, **3**, 131; **5**. 1–9, 16–17
Shakespeare's use of capital letters, **7**, 142–5;
sources, **1**, 62–3, 126; **2**, 139–40; **3**, 15–20, 24–6, 36, 38–9, 53–4, 136; **4**, 9, 26–34, 35–47, 141, 143; **5**, 66, 71, 134–5, 137, 140–2; **6**, 3–4, 33n, 34n, 79–90, 92, 153; **7**, 104, 140; **8**, 4–5, 52, 147–8; **10**, 4–6, 12, 29–35, 40, 42–8, 50–6, 144–5; *see also under titles of individual plays*
spelling, **2**, 57–8; **7**, 37–8
staging, **13**, 69–71, 75, 159, 161
style, **1**, 51–6; **10**, 47–8, 60–2, 64–70, 93–4, 135, 138, 144–5
theological significance in Shakespeare's plays, **5**, 66–80, 87, 141–2
use of Christian doctrine, **2**, 68, 79–80; **3**, 2, 5, 66–7, 70, 139

Shakespeare, William (*cont.*)
  use of familiar words, **4**, 52–5; **5**, 136–7
  variation, **1**, 54–6; **3**, 66–7, 72–3; **4**, 49–51
  miscellaneous:
    Fairies and Witches (*Macbeth* and *A Midsummer Night's Dream*), **54**, 295
    Monsters and Maidens (The Tempest), **54**, 295
    Mr Dickens and Mr Shakespeare, **54**, 295
    Shall I Die, **48**, 188
  plays
    All's Well That Ends Well, **1**, 54, 55, 114; **2**, 149; **3**, 29, 71, 119; **4**, 13, 14, 27, 126, 144; **5**, 3, 109, 120, 135–6; **6**, 155; **7**, 75, 96–7, 104, 105n, 107, 111, 112, 132; **8**, 2, 10–11, 75, 112, 119, 125, 128, 129, 138; **11**, 59n, 87, 123; **12**, 36, 136, 141; productions, Stratford-upon-Avon (1954), 86, elsewhere, 109; **13**, 31, 39n, 118, 147; productions, 128, Stratford-upon-Avon (1959), 140–2; New Arden edition reviewed, 163–4; **14**, 147; productions, 125; **15**, 84, 112, 134, 151, 167–8, 174, 180–1; **16**, 58, 83, 135, 138, 152; **17**, 41, 139, 146, 149n, 152 and n, 160, 178, 209, 233; **18**, 4, 60, 164, 184; opera version, 76; **19**, 133; **20**, 76, 85, 93n, 107, 109, 111, 154, 156, 164; **21**, 24, 127, 162; **22**, 79–92, 95, 138, 149, 160, 170; **23**, 71, 80, 140, 141, 151; **24**, 150, 172, 173, 176, 178; **25**, 1, 2, 3, 4, 45–61, 63, 66–7, 176; **26**, 119, 153, 154, 155n, 172; **27**, 106, 107, 108, 165n, 166; **28**, 39, 49n, 53, 54–5, 56, 102, 104, 141, 176; **29**, 43n, 157; **30**, 73–84, 153, 184, 192; **31**, 98, 116, 124, 144–6, 152, 165–6, 189; **32**, 63n, 211, 217, 230; **33**, 204, 205, 206n; **34**, 162, 175, 191; **35**, 3, 9n, 10; **36**, 60, 149, 155, 160, 161, 170, 176–7; **37**, 91–113 *passim*, 158n, 176–8, 180, 195, 200, 201, 213, 214; **38**, 29, 34, 59, 175n, 178n, 182, 218, 233; **39**, 14, 95, 98, 99, 108, 109, 230; **40**, 13, 16, 198, 223, 228–30; **41**, 197, 203–5, 235; **42**, 149, 167, 174, 181, 182, 186, 206; **43**, 75, 205, 219, 227, 230–1, 234, 270; **44**, 2n, 10, 11, 140, 158, 160, 161, 168, 191, 214, 218, 219, 240; **45**, 145; **46**, 8, 74, 109, 112, 116, 123, 125, 132, 165–8, 207, 211, 213, 223; **47**, 209, 224, 228–9, 241, 267–9; **48**, 227, 273; **49**, 181–200, 293; **50**, 5, 24, 54n, 140, 145, 225, 237, 241, 257; **51**, 148, 222–3, 257, 277, 280, 294; **52**, 76, 135, 254, 272; **53**, 3, 97, 110, 116, 175, 194, 218n, 237, 243, 288, 323, 343; **54**, 14n, 24n, 69, 239, 301, 321, 336; **55**, 13, 198n, 294, 322; **56**, 95, 287; **57**, 260, 316; **58**, 163–4, 166, 167, 265, 266, 269, 269–74, 271, 298, 350, 356; 59, 11, 47, 54, 55, 74, 141–2, 237; **60**, 367
    Antony and Cleopatra, **1**, 14, 52, 54, 59, 90–3, 104, 105, 114; **2**, 5, 14, 16, 121, 123, 127, 130; **3**, 30, 49, 130, 131, 133, 134, 139; **4**, 3, 4, 6, 15, 16, 17, 21, 22, 27, 48n, 51, 52–3, 54, 102, 118, 125, 147; **5**, 8, 26, 51, 64–5, 68, 89, 91n, 113, 116, 130, 132, 138, 142, 143, 148, 149; **6**, 26, 45, 91–3, 99, 101, 118, 121, 124, 140–2, 145, 151, 156; **7**, 9, 10, 46, 72–4, 76, 108, 125–6, 129, 130, 136, 145, 146; **8**, 54–5, 57, 112, 118, 120, 124, 125, 129, 152, 157; **9**, 110n, 134, 139; **10**, 1, 3, 4, 5, 6, 7, 8, 9–10, 11, 17, 25n, 8, 34, 58, 72, 73, 75, 77, 81, 82, 86n, 87n, 119, 137, 140, 141, 142, 146, 154; **11**, 31, 32, 56, 63, 118, 123, 140–1, 143, 154; **12**, 36–7, 47, 59, 65, 70, 88–94, 135, 137–8; productions, at Old Vic (1957), 84, elsewhere, 110, 111, 117–19; **13**, 1, 41, 50, 118, 133, 151, 158; productions, 132, 136; translation, 130; **14**, 139, 142, 154; productions, 116, 120, 123, 125; **15**, 27, 51, 73–80 *passim*, 87–8, 102, 116, 126, 131–2, 135–9, 142, 161, 174–7, 182; **16**, 15, 30–4, 56, 73–4, 80, 136, 138, 162, 168; **17**, 165, 199, 204, 215; **18**, 1, 3, 59, 60, 99, 100, 158, 163, 17–1, 173; film, 71; **19**, 2, 27, 121, 128–30, 146–7; **20**, 30, 76, 88, 145, 151, 156–7, 162; **21**, 14, 87, 108, 109, 128, 138, 139, 158; **22**, 32, 47, 98, 151, 156, 157, 162–3; **23**, 7, 10, 16, 25, 29, 35, 59–67, 118, 154, 159; **24**, 1–12, 23, 43, 138, 146–7, 153, 157, 168, 169, 175, 176; **25**, 2, 128–9, 174, 189; **26**, 16n, 58, 62–4, 95–101, 131n, 134, 141, 142, 146–8, 151, 158, 159, 165, 179; **27**, 3, 65, 131, 144, 146, 148, 156, 160, 162, 165, 167, 168, 169, **28**, 16, 29–36, 149, 150, 156, 157; **29**, 51n, 68, 82, 84, 115, 121, 165, 172, 185; **30**, 5, 7, 144, 182, 186, 187, 195; **31**, 2, 3, 6, 8, 9, 10, 33, 34, 45–52, 57, 58, 59–61, 65, 172, 183, 190, 197; **32**, 64n, 109, 112, 201, 220, 222, 223, 230, 238, 239, 245; **33**, 16n, 27, 32, 39n, 99–111, 113–22, 169, 177–8, 184, 189, 191, 193, 197, 204; **34**, 40, 48–50, 51, 62, 83, 135n, 139, 144, 164, 192, 193, 196; **35**, 24n, 47, 68, 76, 115, 157n, 166, 169, 171, 175; **36**, 2, 3, 4, 5–10, 14–15, 18, 58, 73, 81, 83, 115n, 162, 167, 179–80, 188; **37**, 115, 160n, 172, 173, 182, 195; **38**, 116, 128, 136, 175n, 176, 177, 182n, 201, 215, 216, 219–22, 236, 237; **39**, 10, 15, 90, 99, 170, 177, 178, 207, 218, 220, 223, 234; **40**, 169, 181–2, 209, 226, 233; **41**, 25, 45, 77–90, 134, 176–8, 180, 183, 204, 207, 238–9; **42**, 48, 149, 169, 196, 212; **43**, 19, 188, 205, 232; **44**, 8, 13n, 25, 191, 206, 207, 208, 211, 212, 226, 241; **45**, 59, 82, 83, 164–6, 168, 193–6, 197n; **46**, 61, 91, 100, 101n, 102, 103, 105, 106, 115, 173, 181, 184, 191, 207, 209, 217, 219, 220, 225; **47**, 113, 122, 209, 224, 234, 240, 241; **48**, 1, 27, 42n, 227, 239, 241, 242, 252, 276, 282, 284; **49**, 14, 67, 252–4, 269, 283, 289, 304, 310–15; **50**, 10, 14, 25n, 34, 43n, 126, 127, 147, 148, 225, 227; **51**, 29, 39, 137, 178n, 190, 257, 266, 279, 283, 284; **52**, 5, 7, 57, 76, 78, 185n, 250–3, 254, 271, 272; **53**, 1, 3, 4, 5, 7, 20, 75, 80, 174, 234n, 245–9, 274, 310, 322, 325, 327; **54**, 21, 26–9, 33, 283, 297, 301, 302, 303, 305, 307, 312, 313, 320; **55**, 13, 56, 175, 181n, 201, 212, 322, 335, 347, 355; **56**, 3, 9, 97, 237, 238, 249, 251, 256, 282, 345; **57**, 229, 244, 290, 313, 316; **58**, 11, 153, 157, 298, 339; **59**, 12, 41, 44, 48, 72, 74, 75, 76, 77, 77n12, 78, 130, 142, 143–4, 183, 190, 201, 257, 258, 330, 353–4, 362, 363, 364, 381, 383; **60**, 91, 270, 294, 293–4, 296, 299, 306–7, 320, 336, 341
    As You Like It, **1**, 8, 54, 58, 105, 106, 113, 115 (2), 116; **2**, 16, 116, 121, 124, 128–9, 151; **3**, 18, 19, 8, 50, 95, 109, 113, 116, 118; **4**, 14, 24, 42, 101, 110–13, 115n, 118, 119, 120, 123, 126, 127, 129; **5**, 13, 15n, 109, 112, 114, 115, 116, 119, 120; **6**, 44, 116, 117, 118, 119, 120, 125, 160; **7**, 107, 113, 114; **8**, 1, 3, 6–7, 8, 9, 40–51, 66–7, 68n, 75, 76, 119, 120, 121, 123, 124, 125; **9**, 111, 113, 114, 120, 122, 136, 152n; **10**, 19, 86n, 111, 117, 119, 121, 122, 123, 124, 125, 136, 146, 150; **11**, 38, 59n, 62, 66, 75, 118–19, 121–3, 142; Stratford-upon-Avon production, 134; **12**, 36, 72, 74, 79, 85–6; productions, Stratford-upon-Avon (1957), 86, elsewhere, 109–10, 113–14, 117, 119–20; **13**, 157, 168; productions, 124, 126, 128, 131, 134, 135; **14**, 22, 23, 34, 147, 152, 165; productions, 117, 122, 123; **15**, 84, 112, 118, 138–9, 141–2, 144–6, 162, 167, 169–70; **16**, 72, 78, 138; **17**, 61, 136, 170, 209, 233; **18**, 7–9, 47, 49, 100, 159–60, 180, 184; opera version, 78, 87; **19**, 95, 99–100, 137; **20**, 75–6, 83, 126, 128, 130; **21**, 131, 153,

162; **22**, 2, 7, 11, 12, 13, 46, 135, 139–40, 149, 150, 153, 177, 178; **23**, 2, 17, 23, 24, 80, 95, 99, 140, 144, 151, 158, 161; **24**, 149; **25**, 27, 50, 63, 101, 110, 171, 180; **26**, 111–17, 128, 154; **27**, 59, 69, 108, 130; **28**, 39, 75, 77, 78, 149, 160, 162; **29**, 6, 117, 138, 142; **30**, 5, 83, 183, 195, 199, 201; **31**, 116, 117, 146–7, 165, 182, 184, 189; **32**, 1–10 *passim*, 15–26 *passim*, 37–48, 49, 53, 54, 56n, 63–8, 155, 159, 160, 216, 217, 225–6, 229, 235, 237; **33**, 67–80, 81, 129, 169, 171n, 178–80, 189, 197, 199, 209; **34**, 35, 91, 143, 149–50, 162, 172, 173, 183, 190; **35**, 5, 36, 38, 39, 40, 41, 81, 87, 90–3, 150, 156–7, 158, 159, 167, 170, 179, 183; **36**, 9, 60, 63, 101, 104, 162, 167n, 170, 172, 177, 186n, 194; **37**, 1, 5, 34, 55, 57, 71, 86, 87, 161, 190, 191, 195, 219; **38**, 29, 34, 115, 199, 220, 224, 232, 253; **39**, 2, 15, 16, 95n, 96, 114, 119, 181, 191, 199, 200, 202, 203, 222; **40**, 1, 4, 11, 91–105, 169, 175, 186, 200, 216; **41**, 34, 183, 203–4, 222–3, 238; **42**, 8, 10, 57, 92, 107, 108, 129, 149, 181, 189, 200; **43**, 32, 115, 205, 253–4; **44**, 10, 106n, 134, 136n, 161, 173, 191, 223, 239; **45**, 93, 128, 129, 145, 160–2, 169; **46**, 6, 7, 9–21, 30, 113, 124, 155, 173, 177, 179, 180, 191, 192, 208, 212, 256n; **47**, 97, 106, 209, 222, 224, 227–8, 267, 273–5; **48**, 20, 164, 194–5, 227, 264, 276; **49**, 6, 153, 269, 291; **50**, 6, 33, 66, 80, 203–7, 225, 255; **51**, 10, 29, 37, 48, 52, 53, 121, 196, 201, 257, 265, 265, 272, 276, 297; **52**, 43, 76n, 135, 145, 215–17, 221–4, 228, 232–3, 251, 254–5, 264, 275, 280, 289; **53**, 3, 8, 14, 49, 57, 114, 115, 119, 235, 274–5, 288, 301, 306–7, 340; **54**, 15, 115–21, 152n, 154n, 155–6, 224, 225, 246, 265, 267–9, 271–3, 283, 284, 298, 307, 312, 339; **55**, 19, 25, 301, 322, 383, 384, 388–9; **56**, 56, 61, 65, 73, 79, 80, 84–9, 91, 95, 102, 105, 111, 118, 161–6, 248, 266, 287, 308; **57**, 213, 216, 258, 266, 267, 269, 276, 290, 302, 329, 330, 331; **58**, 2, 10, 13, 153, 154, 170, 298, 317, 330, 334, 337; **59**, 48, 71, 72, 73, 74, 76, 77, 184, 186, 201, 236, 257, 264n25, 310–13, 338, 357; **60**, 62, 66, 67, 94, 135n14, 262–3, 272n12, 320, 337, 338, 339, 363, 366–8, 369

Comedy of Errors, The **2**, 128, 149; **3**, 23–4, 95, 116, 117, 119; **4**, 9, 110, 118, 120, 125, 126, 127; **5**, 116, 117, 120; **6**, 124, 125; **7**, 131; **8**, 7, 63, 64, 121, 124, 126, 140; **9**, 101, 108, 112, 115, 117, 134; **10**, 64, 66, 86n, 116, 117, 125, 143, 155; **11**, 59n, 86, 120–3, 136, 145n, 146; **12**, 85, 143; productions, 119–20; **13**, 30, 39; **14**, 18, 20, 36; productions, 116, 118, 122, 124; **15**, 55, 134, 145; **16**, 64, 132, 136, 159, 167; **17**, 154, 171, 199; **18**, 99, 159, 179, 187, 188; opera version, 78; **19**, 112, 116–17, 136, 147, Pl. VIII; **20**, 76, 107, 125, 152–3, 165; **21**, 130, 139; **22**, 1, 15, 16, 17–18, 25, 39, 50, 127, 132, 137, 151, 152, 153, 167; **23**, 4–5, 8, 10, 17, 18, 35, 143, 161, 177n; **24**, 29, 142, 149; **25**, 60, 64, 81–91, 179; **26**, 140, 142; **27**, 2, 18, 93, 95, 163, 188, 189; **28**, 57–8, 76, 77, 159, 160; **29**, 8, 51; **30**, 6, 169, 176–7, 183; **31**, 4, 5, 6, 33n; **32**, 49, 50, 78; **33**, 39n, 56, 78, 208; **34**, 24, 25, 178; **35**, 3, 24n, 37, 41, 90, 160, 161n, 188–9; **36**, 81–2, 99n, 109, 160, 185; **37**, 1, 2, 5, 6, 13–17, 19, 21, 163, 164, 167–70, 179, 180, 193, 194n; **38**, 31, 182n, 201, 240; **39**, 7, 16, 220, 223, 224; **40**, 10, 205; **41**, 183, 193, 201, 213, 240; **42**, 150, 173, 200–2; **43**, 78, 205, 224, 230, 233, 266; **44**, 93, 136n, 155, 176, 192, 214, 218, 240, 256; **45**, 99, 145, 188, 201; **46**, 192, 198, 211, 240n, 241n, 242, 256; **47**, 210, 240, 254; **48**, 32, 184, 228, 234, 245, 273; **49**, 270, 276; **50**, 11, 14, 45, 49n, 74, 111–23, 215–19, 226, 244, 245, 263; **51**, 179, 181n, 182, 183, 258, 284, 324; **52**, 16, 26–7, 76, 144, 189, 231, 235, 255, 275, 278, 279, 289, 297, 299; **53**, 1, 8, 182, 261–3, 275 276; **54**, 37n, 38, 202–5, 206, 255, 266–7, 283–4; **55**, 189, 293, 323; **57**, 202, 250, 340; **58**, 209, 299, 324, 350, 356; **59**, 11, 12, 47, 71, 141, 233, 302, 299–304, 338, 367, 370, 376, 380; **60**, 272, 305, 320–1, 367

Coriolanus, **2**, 2, 59, 123, 138, 153; **3**, 19, 30, 34–42, 50, 105, 109, 117; **4**, 4, 5, 14, 18, 21, 24, 118, 147, 150–1, 152; **5**, 97, 113, 130, 146; **6**, 98, 151, 160; **7**, 24, 29, 46, 77, 111, 128–9, 136; **8**, 122, 132, 139, 143, 147, 154; **9**, 18, 77, 85n, 107, 112, 119, 134, 139, 144; **10**, 1, 3, 4, 5, 6, 7, 8, 9, 10–11, 27, 28, 32, 34–5, 37, 50, 52–7, 58, 59n, 72, 73, 74, 77, 86n, 118, 120, 142, 149; **11**, 56–7, 59n, 119, 120, 141, 145; Pelican edition, 153; **12**, 36, 38, 48–50, 79, 134; productions, 114, 145; **13**, 1, 151, 158; production, 145; translation, 130; **14**, 97, 139, 142, 153; production, 118; **15**, 161, 176–7; **16**, 55–6, 80, 83, 89, 92, 133, 135–6, 159; **17**, 158n, 224; **18**, 2, 48, 158, 163, 170, 174, 176, 184; **19**, 48, 121, 128, 130; **20**, 30, 117, 149, 165; **21**, 139, 156, 157, 158; **22**, 47, 156, 162, 163, 175; **23**, 16, 26, 33, 35, 138, 139, 144, 154, 159, 173; **24**, 16, 17, 27, 28, 140, 146, 148, 175; **25**, 127, 189; **26**, 38, 58, 60, 61–2, 92, 95–101, 141, 142–4, 146, 158, 159, 179; **27**, 60, 160, 179, 192; **28**, 22–3, 63–9, 157, 170; **29**, 8, 68, 83, 87, 119, 121, 122, 136, 158, 163, 165, 176; **30**, 5, 7, 85n, 90n, 135–46, 182, 187, 203–5; **31**, 2, 4, 6, 7, 8, 9, 10, 11, 12, 27, 55, 57, 58, 60, 61, 172, 175, 176, 195; **32**, 112, 212, 223, 227; **33**, 27, 185–6, 190, 192, 197, 198, 201; **34**, 3, 24, 62, 74–84, 135n, 136, 146, 175, 194, 196; **35**, 9, 18, 23n, 40, 41, 54, 166, 169; **36**, 2, 5, 61, 107, 115n, 159, 169, 172; **37**, 36, 39, 159n, 182, 189n; **38**, 28, 115–29 *passim*, 175, 176, 182n, 184n, 185, 191, 198, 216, 217, 222, 223, 244; **39**, 16, 17, 95, 108–10, 115, 120, 126n, 191–3, 197, 215, 216, 244; **40**, 6, 39; **41**, 46, 171, 183, 195, 197, 199, 204, 223, 238; **42**, 92, 150, 169, 170–2; **43**, 229, 233, 250; **44**, 5, 8, 17, 32, 72, 106n, 136n, 163, 190, 192, 206, 207, 208, 209, 241, 242; **45**, 100, 115, 130, 132, 133, 146, 156, 190; **46**, 91, 92, 93, 100, 102, 103, 105, 106, 184–7, 192, 206, 219; **47**, 113, 210, 222, 232, 241; **48**, 7–8, 11, 12, 175, 214–17, 228, 253, 273, 282, 285, 287; **49**, 252, 270, 290, 301; **50**, 30, 35, 226, 246, 247; **51**, 3, 19n, 24, 109, 258, 278, 282, 284, 331; **52**, 28n, 255, 279, 280, 291; **53**, 5, 6, 60–72, 75, 80, 83–7, 176, 275, 304, 342; **54**, 154n, 223, 226, 254–5, 335, 343, 254; **55**, 13, 19, 64, 116n, 260–2, 268–9, 338, 346, 353; **56**, 3, 52, 171, 173n, 221, 223, 240, 282, 288, 328, 341; **57**, 1, 227, 228, 229, 230, 231, 265, 285, 290, 316; **58**, 299, 320, 357, 358; **59**, 12, 41, 72, 73, 74, 75, 76, 77n12, 77, 78, 124–31, 132, 134n65, 141, 143, 185–6, 201, 286, 296, 360, 363; **60**, 170–1, 173–80, 182, 182n18, 291–2

Cymbeline, **1**, 47–9, 54, 55, 119; **2**, 58, 149; **3**, 1, 2, 22–3, 15–16, 18, 30, 109; **4**, 2, 6, 17, 24, 29–30, 48n, 88–9, 126, 144; **5**, 109; **6**, 78n, 98, 103, 123, 125, 148, 151; **7**, 32–3, 106n, 131; **8**, 35, 52–6, 76, 78–9, 126; **9**, 85n, 112, 140, 151–2; **10**, 86n, 118, 122, 141; **11**, 20, 23–4, 25, 30, 42–9, 50, 51, 57, 59n, 64, 66–7, 70, 74, 123, 135, 141, 144; Stratford-upon-Avon production noted 134; **12**, productions; Old Vic (1957), 80, elsewhere, 112–13, 118, 120, 127; **13**, 149; **14**, 96, 152; translation, 123; New Cambridge edition reviewed, 159, 163; **15**, 5, 9, 24, 27,

Shakespeare, William (*cont.*)
53, 102, 132, 134, 137, 142, 144, 173; **16**, 143–51; **17**, 157, 158n, 169, 209, 214; **18**, 4–5, 6, 100, 171; opera version, 76; **19**, 2, 150, 162; **20**, 85, 93n, 108–9, 111, 126, 128, 151, 167; **21**, 25, 127, 140; **22**, 99, 127, 132, 164, 174n, 177; **23**, 18, 28, 29, 31, 32, 155; **24**, 33, 34, 37, 105, 107, 151, 157, 172, 174; **25**, 178; **26**, 42, 44–5, 47, 64, 65, 66, 70, 106, 134n, 153, 156, 164, 179, 184; **27**, 133n; **28**, 141, 144, 148, 163, 180; **29**, 1, 2, 3, 4, 5, 6, 7, 8, 9, 41–9, 51–61, 65, 74, 123, 158, 169, 185; **30**, 7, 84, 154n, 195; **31**, 5n, 6, 8, 10, 23–32, 33n, 166; **32**, 63n, 64n, 72, 93n, 245; **33**, 80, 100, 111, 173–4, 188, 191, 193, 202; **34**, 91, 176, 183, 193; **35**, 8, 35, 37, 39, 156, 157, 179; **36**, 84, 88, 97–106, 111, 113, 114, 164, 167, 180; **37**, 6, 158n, 159n, 176–8, 195; **38**, 29, 30, 133, 136, 184n, 198, 217, 220, 224, 225, 227, 253; **39**, 17, 103, 104, 108–11, 118, 123, 127, 128, 132, 168n, 218; **40**, 155, 159–61, 164; **41**, 46, 92, 106, 111, 209, 214, 225, 236n; **42**, 9, 112, 118, 139–42, 148, 150, 170, 183; **43**, 26, 139n, 184, 189, 205, 224–5, 247, 261; **44**, 2n, 10, 83, 128n, 136n, 193, 222; **45**, 174, 189; **46**, 73–9, 83, 104n, 105, 115, 192, 210, 214, 247; **47**, 90, 112, 136, 224, 225, 230; **48**, 228, 245, 246, 255, 264, 273; **49**, 209n, 270, 291, 293, 294; **50**, 10, 149, 150, 226; **51**, 3, 30, 40, 228–30, 242, 247, 280, 330; **52**, 255, 271–2, 321–2; **53**, 1, 5, 6, 11, 36, 275, 297, 324, 344; **54**, 24, 26, 40–4, 199, 284, 298–9, 314, 315, 339; **55**, 19, 26, 45n, 286, 303, 309, 314–15, 348, 358, 371–2, 392; **56**, 52, 142, 215, 264, 272, 288, 321, 324, 355; **57**, 230, 259, 274, 276, 306–7, 316; **58**, 10, 103, 119, 171, 299; **59**, 44, 72, 74, 76, 77n12, 142, 184, 256, 258, 338, 358, 379–81, 383; **60**, 67, 189n17, 200, 206, 310–11, 312, 321, 331

Edward III, **41**, 117; **42**, 161, 166, 192; **52**, 310n, 314–15; **54**, 295, 351; **56**, 279–80; **57**, 233, 243, 291; **58**, 299, 320, 354; **59**, 5–6, 42, 214, 376–7

Hamlet, **1**, 10, 13, 14, 15, 42, 54, 70, 81, 90, 93–5, 105, 106, 113 (3), 114(2), 115 (5), 116, 119, 123, 124, 125, 131; **2**, 2, 3, 4, 5, 6, 10, 11, 12, 13, 14, 16, 18, 20, 36, 37, 42n, 58, 93, 116–17, 123, 129, 132, 135, 137–8, 140, 151, 153; **3**, 16, 19, 28, 29, 31, 44, 45, 47, 49, 50, 56, 57n, 58–64, 67, 74–82, 99, 100, 101, 108, 110, 111, 112, 113, 114, 117, 119, 130, 131, 137, 138, 140, 141, 147; **7**, 134; **4**, 3–4, 6, 7, 8, 10, 11, 13, 14, 17, 19, 22, 23–4, 44, 66, 80, 81, 94, 95, 109, 111, 120–2, 123, 124–5, 126, 128, 135, 139, 140–1, 142–3, 144, 147, 150, 151; **5**, 4, 21, 26, 37, 41, 51, 58–61, 72, 78, 84, 86, 89, 91n, 98, 107, 108, 109, 111, 112, 113, 114, 115, 117, 118, 119, 129, 131, 132–4, 140, 146, 149–50, 151–2; **6**, 44, 48n, 49, 54, 58, 106–11, 115, 116, 118, 119, 120, 121, 123, 124, 125, 141, 143, 149, 150, 151, 154, 156–7, 158, 159, 161, 162, 163 *and* n, 166, 167, 172; **7**, 3, 8, 9, 10, 25, 26, 28, 31, 33, 36, 39, 44, 46, 47, 51, 78, 82–4, 85, 87, 88, 91, 97, 105, 108, 109, 111, 112, 113, 114, 115, 121–2, 123, 128, 129, 130–1, 132, 134–5, 142, 145, 153; **8**, 37, 57, 63, 67, 95–6, 113, 114, 117n, 118, 119, 120, 121, 123, 124, 125, 132, 139, 140–2, 147, 155, 159; **9**, 1–15, 16–23, 24–34, 35–43, 44–8, 49–53, 54–8, 59–67, 60–7, 91–2, 94, 101, 102, 103, 105, 107, 108, 109, 110n, 111, 112, 113, 115, 116, 117–18, 137–8, 147, 148, 150, 152–3, 154–5; **10**, 23, 26n, 36, 83, 85, 86n, 88n, 110, 115, 116, 117, 118, 119, 120, 121, 123, 125, 128–30, 134, 138, 139, 142, 143, 147, 155, 156, 157; **11**, 23, 33, 56–7, 59n, 62–3, 66, 84, 88n, 118–24, 138, 139, 140, 143, 145–7, 154–5; Yale Shakespeare edition, 153; **12**, 2, 36, 46–7, 62, 73, 75, 78, 85, 134, 136–7, 142, 146; source in legend, 75; 1604–5 Quarto, 150; Q2, 152; productions, Strarford-upon-Avon (1956), 1, 4, Peter Brook production (Moscow, 1956), 85, elsewhere, 109, 110 (adaptation by Anne and Roger Bodart), 111–13, 115, 118, 120, 121; **13**, 1, 7–9, 30–1, 38, 39n, 49–50, 58, 64, 69, 78–80, 146, 148–9, 151–2, 156, 160–1, 167–8; productions, 124, 128, 132–6; translation, 130; **14**, 32, 44n, 45–55 *passim*, 72, 95, 96–7, 140–1, 145n, 148, 151, 155; productions, 116, 118–24, 160, 162, 164–5; film version, 120; translation, 124; **15**, 6, 17, 24, 84, 112, 115, 119, 121, 131–2, 134–5, 138–46, 159, 163, 171, 174, 179; **16**, 5, 11–13, 15–16, 37, 47, 53–9, 65, 72, 74–5, 95–6, 99–101, 133, 134, 156, 158–9, 168, 179; **17**, 86, 126, 151n, 153, 160n, 164, 176, 185–6, 191, 194, 210, 219, 234; **18**, 11, 34–45, 53, 65–6, 70–1, 73, 95, 104, 107, 109–14, 116, 157–8, 164, 166–7, 176, 180–1, 183–5, 187, 191; opera versions, 75, 80, 82–3; **19**, 13, 23, 33n, 48, 77, 79, 100n, 112–18, 122–5, 128, 151–2, 154, 162, Pls. XB, XI, XIIA; **20**, 1–3, 8, 10, 11, 33–9, 41, 109–10, 117–20,121–3, 126–7, 135, 140–1, 144, 146–8, 164–5, 169, 174; **21**, 1, 2–3, 10n, 26, 27n, 49, 87, 107, 133, 134, 146, 147, 149, 153, 154, 160, 163; **22**, 42, 125, 127, 130, 132, 133, 146, 147, 156, 158–9, 162, 165, 166, 167, 168, 175, 176, 183; **23**, 4, 9, 16, 17, 18, 20, 23, 31, 47, 64, 83, 97, 99n, 116, 120, 121, 122, 138–9, 140, 142, 147, 148, 149–50, 156, 161, 173, 174, 176, 179, 185; **24**, 15, 32, 40–1, 44, 49–50, 71–104, 118, 122–3, 128, 130, 139, 141, 142–5, 152, 153, 161, 167, 169, 170, 171, 175, 176, 178; **25**, 2, 4, 15, 63, 94, 110, 135, 172, 182, 184, 188, 189, 194, 196; **26**, 1, 3, 11–20, 21–31, 54, 56, 58, 59, 67, 73, 89, 99, 122n, 134n, 135n, 137, 159, 160–1, 162, 167, 175, 176, 179, 181, 184; **27**, 1n, 43–57, 59–69, 85, 90, 130, 132, 133, 136, 157, 161, 172, 173, 176, 181, 186; **28**, 6, 16, 19n, 30, 31, 36, 37, 38n, 39, 40–2, 45, 47, 49, 58, 107–15, 149, 153–4, 165, 176, 180, 181; **29**, 66, 82, 83, 86, 87, 88, 120, 121, 123, 137, 138–9, 140, 141–2, 143, 151–3, 156, 159, 161, 163, 164, 166, 171, 173, 174, 175, 176, 183, **30**, 1–12, 14–16, 21, 103–15, 117–23, 188, 190, 192, 193, 194, 200, 201, 202, 206n, 209, 210; **31**, 10, 20, 26, 34–6, 55, 57, 58, 77, 83, 115, 116, 119, 121, 169, 170, 171, 179, 181, 184, 190, 193, 195–6, 197; **32**, 127n, 151–61, 163–76, 212, 219–21, 227, 232, 235, 241, 245, 246; **33**, 7, 10, 16n, 36, 86, 87, 89–97, 113, 114, 160, 168, 182, 184, 186, 190, 197, 201, 203, 204, 210; **34**, 2, 3, 6, 12, 14, 29, 39, 40, 51–9, 62, 70, 74, 85, 101, 121, 136, 140, 147, 151, 165, 169, 170, 171–2, 174, 183, 185, 186, 195, 196; **35**, 2, 11, 23n, 28, 31, 36–41 *passim*, 45, 46–7, 49–54 *passim*, 87, 97–100, 106, 162–4, 169, 170, 172, 177, 182, 184, 185, 186; **36**, 2, 21–8, 32, 43–52, 53–6, 57, 122, 154–5, 159, 160, 163, 169, 186n, 189, 193; **37**, 159n, 161, 162, 168, 181, 183, 189, 190, 194, 198, 200, 201, 212, 214, 215, 218, 219; **38**, 10, 13, 30, 31, 37, 99, 145, 209, 210, 217, 218, 220, 221, 226, 230, 236, 237, 245, 246, 253; **39**, 3, 5, 7, 17–19, 39, 75, 77, 79, 100, 107, 114, 117, 119, 135–47 *passim*, 175, 194–7, 218, 221, 222, 230, 235, 238n, 241–3, 245, 246, 250; **40**, 1, 6, 12, 16, 34–5, 61, 63, 67, 70, 74n, 125, 147, 153, 183, 193, 199, 200, 202–4, 207–8, 211, 213, 217, 219, 221, 232–3, 234n, 235–6; **41**, 3, 8, 13, 35–43, 45, 53, 110, 127, 135, 141,

184, 191, 193, 195, 198, 200, 204, 206, 208–9, 217, 221, 225, 227, 229, 232, 237, 241–2; **42**, 39n, 41, 65, 100, 114–16, 124, 129, 150, 164–5, 170, 172–3, 176–9, 182, 193, 200, 210, 211; **43**, 16, 57, 88, 113, 184, 194, 196–7, 199, 202, 206–7, 217, 220, 222–3, 226, 229, 230, 232, 237, 241, 250–2, 266–7; **44**, 2n, 3n, 10n, 15, 25, 26, 83, 93, 94, 133, 134, 136n, 139, 193, 209–14, 216, 218, 221, 223, 240, 242, 243; **45**, 1–13, 15–26, 27–35, 37–51, 53–62, 63–74, 75–7, 91, 92, 146, 149, 160–2, 166, 172–4, 190, 200; **46**, 61, 103, 108, 110n, 113, 125, 158, 159, 160, 162, 192–3, 207, 208, 209, 217, 218, 227, 238, 254–6; **47**, 5, 7n, 11, 33, 39, 48, 62–4, 68, 69, 72, 74, 76, 97, 103, 105–6, 112, 162, 181–2, 185, 187, 189, 193, 199, 210–12, 219, 222, 232, 237, 242–3, 255n, 269; **48**, 3, 6, 10, 11, 34, 36n, 95, 99–121, 131, 165–6, 169, 171, 175, 178–83, 187, 191–4, 228, 241–2, 251–2, 264, 268–71, 274, 276, 281, 283; **49**, 27, 32, 36, 41, 48n, 67, 75, 145, 151, 153, 154, 176, 201n, 204n, 226, 231, 232, 235–40, 250, 270, 271, 282, 283, 286–8, 290, 308, 309, 327, 330–1; **50**, 22, 30, 33, 39, 46–7, 57–64, 126, 129, 151, 168, 171–86, 226–7, 231, 233, 236, 238, 241–2, 246–8, 257, 262, 272–3, 278–9, 286–9; **51**, 5, 12, 35, 40, 129, 136, 137, 138, 145, 172n, 175, 176, 182, 199, 200, 201, 208, 242–4, 258–9, 260, 272–2, 280, 281, 283, 284, 290, 294, 297, 300, 302, 303, 306, 318–19, 329, 336; **52**, 6, 21, 24, 28n, 41, 63–7, 68, 76, 78–80, 84–5, 87, 128, 135, 144–9, 185n, 249–50, 255–6, 275–7, 285, 287, 288–9, 292–3, 305–6, 310, 312–13, 323–4; **53**, 1, 2, 4, 6, 8, 14n, 19n, 25, 52, 80, 82n, 87, 97, 106, 108, 110, 111, 119, 170n, 186–8, 191, 217, 237–42, 252, 275, 284, 285, 292, 296, 299, 303, 306, 310, 320, 328, 332–5, 341; **54**, 9, 21, 28, 81, 108–14, 122–39, 140–51, 152–4, 160, 205–6, 240, 246, 259, 262–3, 277–8, 283, 284, 297, 298, 306, 308, 311, 313–14, 319–20, 323–4, 336, 344n; **55**, 1, 16, 19, 25–6, 43, 64, 106, 116n, 139, 141, 143, 159, 184, 186, 218n, 237, 251, 258, 265, 285, 292–303, 306, 308–9, 313–14, 323–4, 336–42, 346, 350, 355, 358, 360–2, 368, 370, 381–3, 390–1; **56**, 61, 80, 93–9, 101–3, 111, 118, 121n, 137–9, 141–3, 145, 247, 269, 280, 288–9, 301, 302, 305, 309, 316, 317, 329, 330, 341, 345–6, 347, 350, 354; **57**, 19, 22, 27, 40, 51, 115, 138, 142, 143, 162, 171, 194, 216, 228, 229, 249–56, 259, 284, 287, 288, 289, 291, 306, 311, 314, 316, 317–18, 319, 326, 327, 333, 339, 342, 343; **58**, 5, 6, 10, 11, 55, 95, 105, 112, 121, 128, 141, 148, 166, 186, 197, 209, 210, 218, 268, 299; **59**, 2, 6, 7, 9, 11, 14, 15, 34, 42, 43, 44, 47, 108, 141, 153, 157–67, 167n34, 173–4, 178, 180–1, 182, 184, 190–1, 200, 201, 237, 238, 258, 264n25, 291, 292, 297, 330, 335, 338–9, 347, 349, 350, 351–2, 360–1, 364, 365, 373, 374, 381, 382; **60**, 85n3, 102–3, 122–3, 124, 133n13, 135, 137n21, 145–7, 197, 204, 206, 213, 215–22, 223–35, 252, 270, 271, 278–82, 285–6, 291, 289–91, 292, 302, 307, 321, 334, 335, 338, 340, 345, 347, 349, 350, 351, 354, 355, 356, 358, 359–60, 361, 366, 369

Henry IV, **21**, 26, 128, 132, 152; **22**; **23**, 69, 70, 138, 145, 146–7; **25**, 111, 173, 174, 192; **26**, 105n, 156, 157, 179; **27**, 64, 94; **28**, 141n, 159; **29**, 68, 84, 171, 172, 185; **30**, 1–12, 14, 18, 21–7, 29–34, 35–45, 47, 49, 59, 68, 104, 192; **31**, 184; **32**, 219–20; **34**, 41, 105–10; **35**, 7, 25, 28, 41, 72, 141, 175n, 178, 221, 222, 237; **36**, 17, 25, 34, 58, 59, 149, 153–4, 164–5, 169, 192; **37**, 87, 88, 201; **39**, 40, 41, 43, 96, 216; **40**, 198, 200, 202; **41**, 185, 232, 242; **43**, 207, 217, 230, 240, 265n; **44**, 14, 123, 153, 219, 220, 244; **45**, 119, 142, 147, 153, 185; **46**, 43n, 211; **50**, 143, 219–24, 227, 251, 284; **51**, 259, 260, 303, 322; **52**, 148, 266, 280, 319; **53**, 46, 275, 311, 324, 335, 340, 341; **54**, 100–7, 225, 274, 304, 320–1; **55**, 290; **56**, 248, 341; **57**, 316, 319, 337; **58**, 11, 14, 31, 130, 171, 263; **60**, 102–17, 187, 193, 305, 318

1 Henry IV, **1**, 61, 62, 65, 83, 84, 114, 127–8; **2**, 10, 18, 84, 138, 153; **3**, 27, 32, 43, 44, 45, 47, 111, 135, 141, 143; **4**, 2, 10, 15, 23, 24, 37, 43, 81, 88, 94, 126, 127, 151; **5**, 51, 95, 96–7, 139; **6**, 2, 3, 4, 8, 9, 11, 12–14, 16–24, 35n, 121, 130, 134–8, 155; **7**, 10, 14, 107, 113, 131, 133; **8**, 61–3, 125, 132, 147, 156; **9**, 83, 85n, 102, 104, 108, 111, 113, 114, 115, 116, 133, 137, 151, 153–4, 155; **10**, 86n, 119, 121, 123, 142; **11**, 57, 74–5, 138, 148, 152–3; New Variorum supplement, 152–3; Pelican edition, 153; **12**, 115, 121, 134, 146; productions, Stratford-upon-Avon (1951) 80, elsewhere, 112, 118; **13**, 41, 120, 152, 163; productions, 124–5, 127, 134; **14**, 29, 32, 41, 95, 146, 147; production, 125; **15**, 51, 122, 132, 134, 138–9, 140–2, 144–5, 158, 166; **16**, 13, 42, 79, 80–1, 132–3, 136, 138, 161–2, 168–9; New Arden edition, 172–3; **17**, 146, 192, 236; **18**, 51, 65, 107, 112, 147–54, 163, 176; early quartos, 26–7; opera versions, 75, 80, 83, 87; **19**, 131, 146–7, 152; **20**, 41–3, 47–8, 61–73, 78, 80, 83–5, 91, 93n, 108, 126, 135–7, 139–40, 155, 169, 172, 178; **21**, 152; **22**, 54, 93, 125, 127, 131, 149, 155, 156, 173, 178, 179, 181; **23**, 1, 3, 6, 10, 11, 16, 30, 69, 95; **24**, 22, 23, 32, 151, 167, 178; **25**, 107, 110, 111, 192; **26**, 69, 99, 129, 132, 134n, 157n, 183; **27**, 24, 27n, 75, 160, 161; **28**, 39n, 173; **29**, 122, 160; **30**, 1–12, 30–1, 35, 37, 38, 50, 62, 65, 67, 69–70, 122, 185, 195; **31**, 57, 85–91, 115, 116, 189, 197; **32**, 93n, 165, 177, 219, 234, 238; **33**, 16n, 169, 182, 191, 206, 211; **34**, 63, 165, 107–8, 183; **35**, 23n, 26, 36, 39, 185, 186–7; **37**, 85, 87, 88, 190, 201, 209, 212, 215, 217; **38**, 1, 6, 7, 8, 9, 13–17, 19, 61–6 *passim*, 81, 85, 86, 87, 90, 92, 94n, 95–9, 134, 185, 192, 238n, 253; **39**, 19, 40, 42, 44, 45, 49, 51, 52, 113, 117, 119, 169, 173, 174, 215, 224, 246, 250, 251; **40**, 213, 232, 235; **41**, 25, 159, 161, 185, 212, 217, 239, 242; **42**, 31, 32n, 42, 94, 151, 160–2, 173, 192, 194; **43**, 8, 261; **44**, 3, 6, 9, 10n, 18, 28, 29, 216, 242, 247–9; **45**, 95, 139, 140, 164, 173, 175, 177, 187, 200; **46**, 156, 193, 211, 216; **47**, 125, 211; **48**, 21, 69–84, 92, 97n, 229, 242, 249, 274; **49**, 260, 284, 287, 328–9, 330–1; **50**, 12, 46, 143, 219–24, 250, 284; **51**, 259, 260, 263, 311, 314; **52**, 113–14, 119–21, 287, 310, 319; **53**, 324, 335, 340, 341; **54**, 28n, 40, 67, 89, 97–8, 154n, 239n, 240, 246, 274, 277, 279, 285, 335, 350; **55**, 324, 369; **56**, 100, 118, 126, 130, 136n, 279, 289, 325, 345, 347n, 349, 350–2, 354; **57**, 230, 236–47, 281, 291, 304, 332; **58**, 80, 130, 131, 132, 133, 135, 209, 263, 268, 356; **59**, 3, 10, 11, 12, 73, 142, 143, 186–7, 201, 258, 323–6, 339, 382; **60**, 102–6, 106n21, 107n23, 107, 108, 108n30, 109, 110, 111, 114, 114n54, 116n64, 117, 192, 193, 200–1, 206–7, 258–9, 305, 322, 334, 350, 366

2 Henry IV, **1**, 105, 114, 127–9; **2**, 57, 58, 84, 138; **3**, 27, 28–9, 32, 45, 56, 71–2, 141, 143; **4**, 4, 7, 8, 10, 37, 99; **5**, 51, 95, 96–7, 119, 139; **6**, 2, 3, 4, 8, 9, 11, 12–14, 16–24, 35n, 37, 38, 45, 85, 121, 124, 130, 134–8, 155, 166; **7**, 10, 14, 21, 82, 84, 107, 113, 131, 133–4; **8**, 61–3, 68, 68n, 155; **9**, 75, 82, 108, 113, 114, 115, 116, 119, 137, 151,

Shakespeare, William (*cont.*)
153–4, 155; **10**, 17, 86n, 119, 121, 123, 157; **11**, 138, 146; Pelican edition, 153; **12**, 119, 143; **13**, 156, 161, 163, 167–9; production, 134; **14**, 29, 32, 34, 41, 95, 146–7, 164–5; production, 125; **15**, 32–9 *passim*, 57–61, 61n, 122, 132, 134, 138, 140–2, 144, 158, 166; **16**, 13, 42, 79–81, 132–3, 136, 138, 161–2, 168–9; **17**, 79n, 136–7, 145, 149n, 151n, 156, 160, 232; **18**, 1, 15, 26–7, 149, 190; **19**, 131, 146–7, 162–3; **20**, 41, 43–5, 47–8, 76, 80, 85, 93n, 107, 111, 126, 135–6, 138–40, 155, 163, 172–4; **21**, 109, 112, 132, 160, **22**, 95, 149, 155, 156, 176, 181; **23**, 2, 3, 11, 19, 24, 69; **24**, 22, 23, 40; **25**, 63, 107, 110, 111, 192, 194, 196, 199; **26**, 131, 154n, 172, 173, 184; **27**, 132n, 135, 154, 161, 182, 191; **28**, 47, 152, 178; **29**, 155, 175; **30**, 1–12, 32–4, 35–45, 63, 65; **31**, 57, 99, 189, 198; **32**, 219, 235, 238, 239, 241; **33**, 16n, 56, 169, 182; **34**, 25, 35–7, 183, 196; **35**, 124, 177, 181–2, 185, 189, 190; **36**, 164; **37**, 86–8, 120n, 192, 201; **38**, 1, 5–11, 13–17, 44, 45, 61–7 *passim*, 71, 75, 86, 87, 90, 94n, 96, 97, 104, 115, 150, 176n, 240; **39**, 19, 41–52 *passim*, 151, 169, 173, 174, 216, 224, 242, 246, 250; **40**, 45–6, 213; **41**, 25, 159, 185, 212, 229, 230n; **42**, 94, 151, 161, 162, 192, 210; **43**, 35, 146; **44**, 3, 4, 6, 7, 12, 28, 29, 30, 247–9; **45**, 91, 139, 142, 175, 198; **46**, 193, 211, 216, 252; **47**, 125, 211; **48**, 21, 69–84, 97n, 229, 242, 249, 272, 274; **49**, 260, 262, 284, 328–9, 330–1; **50**, 143, 173n, 219–24, 250; **51**, 260, 277, 291, 333, 334; **52**, 76, 301, 319–20; **53**, 46, 311, 340; **54**, 67–8, 154n, 236, 246, 274, 277–8, 357; **55**, 57, 132, 184, 258n, 324, 369, 371; **56**, 97, 127, 130, 131, 279, 289, 325, 350–2; **57**, 230, 238, 240, 248, 291, 332, 337; **58**, 80, 131, 132, 133, 134, 135; **59**, 11, 46, 74, 186, 201, 326; **60**, 80n37, 104, 105–10, 110n36, 110n37, 111–12, 114, 114n54, 115, 116n64, 117, 188, 193, 194, 207, 271–2, 306, 323

Henry V, **1**, 71, 114, 116, 126, 127, 128, 129; **2**, 112; **3**, 4, 15, 27, 31, 37, 44, 47, 139; **4**, 148; **5**, 21, 51, 54, 97, 125–8, 135, 150; **6**, 1, 2, 3, 4, 6, 8, 9, 10, 11 12, 16–17, 18, 20, 21, 26, 35n, 80–1, 86–8, 132, 138–9; **7**, 52, 90, 91, 108, 109, 113, 129, 133; **8**, 54, 123, 124, 139, 157–8; **9**, 82, 109, 133, 143n, 153, 155–6; **10**, 19, 24, 25n, 77, 79, 86n, 125, 130, 156; **11**, 52, 57, 118, 138, 154; 'Table of Greene Fields' discussed, 138; Pelican edition, 153; **12**, 36–7, 79, 134; productions, Stratford-upon-Avon (1950), 86, elsewhere, 114, 119–20; **13**, 41; productions, 124, 134; **14**, 32, 153; Old Vic production, 134; **15**, 1, 56, 112, 132, 139, 141–2, 144–5, 158, 166; **16**, 43, 50, 56n, 132, 135, 168–9; **17**, 45, 108, 152, 164–5, 210, 230; **18**, 48, 74, 150–1, 169–70, 189; film, 71–3; **19**, 131–2; **20**, 41, 45–7, 71, 76–7, 88, 93n, 134–6, 138, 141, 155, 175, 178; **21**, 107–14, 119, 123, 132; **22**, 155, 173, 178, 179; **23**, 2, 3–4, 5, 6, 8, 9, 11, 19, 25, 26, 120, 132, 147; **24**, 139, 167; **25**, 110, 111n, 167, 168, 169, 174, 189, 198, 199; **26**, 131, 157; **27**, 71–9, 109, 186, 189; **28**, 9, 22, 39, 47, 58, 59, 159, 178; **29**, 83, 84, 123, 136, 143, 154, 155, 161, 171, 172, 185; **30**, 1, 4–5, 43, 47–59, 61–72, 121, 185, 209; **31**, 55, 56, 57, 58, 60, 88n, 93–104, 168, 194; **32**, 25, 212, 219, 230, 243; **33**, 16n, 187, 191, 200, 209, 211; **34**, 61, 157–8, 178, 189, 194, 196; **35**, 36, 39, 115, 155, 169, 178, 186, 189, 190; **36**, 62, 65, 159–60, 165, 166, 178, 185; **37**, 148, 190n, 202–4, 207, 208; **38**, 4–11, 13–19, 37, 43–6, 86, 87, 90, 95, 96, 142, 176, 204–7, 221, 222, 226, 227, 241, 247n; **39**, 2, 4–6, 13n, 19, 20, 40, 41, 75, 95, 96n 251; **40**, 11, 44, 47, 63–8, 188, 197, 216, 236; **41**, 14, 23–34 *passim*, 91, 95–7, 159, 161, 185, 204, 230, 232; **42**, 23n, 40, 101, 111, 123, 125, 128, 151, 161, 165, 181–2, 193, 194, 199, 213; **43**, 171–3, 180, 207, 217, 232, 237, 240, 251, 260, 265–6; **44**, 1, 4, 5, 6, 7n, 10n, 15, 32, 55, 61, 68, 107, 111, 137, 153, 155, 194, 209, 220, 242; **45**, 8, 64, 93, 147, 153, 161, 164, 185, 198, 199, 203; **46**, 108, 193, 205, 208, 210, 211, 215, 216, 228, 241, 251–4; **47**, 61n, 125, 185, 230–1, 241; **48**, 14, 21, 85–97, 207–11, 239, 242, 249–50, 263, 273; **49**, 23, 154, 271, 286, 308, 310–12, 321, 329, 330–1; **50**, 15, 35, 47, 227, 251, 256, 264, 286; **51**, 131, 178, 198, 206, 209–12, 217, 236–9, 292, 299; **52**, 44, 54–8, 63, 66, 70, 71, 76, 80, 85, 107–19, 192–4, 197, 217, 244, 256, 273, 287, 289, 294, 298; **53**, 175–6, 187, 234–5, 275–6, 292, 310, 324–5, 342; **54**, 14n, 40, 69, 102, 154n, 155n, 214, 220, 221, 235, 236, 240, 246, 274, 280–2, 285, 306, 314, 320–1, 344n; **55**, 34, 189, 286, 290, 324, 341, 358–9, 370, 389–90; **56**, 19, 61, 80, 97, 279–80, 290, 316, 320, 347, 351–2; **57**, 41, 231, 236, 248, 258, 259, 278, 279, 280, 283, 292, 316, 326, 327, 334; **58**, 10, 12, 30, 122, 185, 193, 209, 210, 301, 313, 317, 320, 328, 339; **59**, 6, 7, 12, 16, 41, 49, 72, 75, 97n7, 177, 183–4, 187, 201, 255, 256, 258, 321, 322, 348, 357, 365, 374; **60**, 22, 104, 106, 107, 110, 110n37, 111, 112, 115, 117, 123, 188, 200, 205, 206, 318, 322, 341, 347, 350, 354, 355

Henry VI (3 parts), **2**, 59, 68, 140; **3**, 23, 26, 27, 47, 110; **4**, 7, 49–50, 56–9, 62, 63–6, 97, 150, 160, 162–3; **5**, 7, 52, 132, 139; **6**, 2, 4–5, 6, 7, 8, 9, 11, 16, 25–6; 33n, 37; 43–4, 45, 148, 169; **7**, 15–16, 32, 77, 125, 139–40, 146, 147–52; **8**, 112, 120, 124, 125, 143; **9**, 73, 77, 85n, 104, 134, 137, 143, 151, 154; **10**, 64, 65, 66, 67, 69, 70, 77, 78, 79, 80, 82, 86n, 87n, 120, 122, 142, 145, 149, 155; **11**, 47, 59, 70, 123, 150, 155; *1 Henry VI*, 155; New Arden edition of *2 Henry VI* reviewed, 150; *2 Henry VI*, 151; *2* and *3 Henry VI*, 155; **12**, 120, 122, 126; **13**, 41, 116, 120, 156, 158, 165–6; **14**, 34; Penguin edition *of Henry VI, Parts One to Three* reviewed, 166; **15**, *1 Henry VI*, 109n; 71n, 118; **16**, 80–1, 132; New Arden edition of *1 Henry VI* reviewed, 173–4; **17**, *1 Henry VI*, 126, 145, 162, 171; *2 Henry VI*, 82n, 86, 210; *3 Henry VI*, 210; **18**, 52, 147, 152–4, 169; film, 71; Stratford-upon-Avon adaptation of, 74; **19**, *1 Henry VI*, 79, 142; *2 Henry VI*, 87, 89–90, 94n, 142; *3 Henry VI*, 89–91, 142, 160; **20**, *1 Henry VI*, 178; *2 Henry VI*, 77; Stratford-upon-Avon adaptation of, 135–6; **23**, 116, 142, 180; **26**, 108, 157n; **27**, 22, 79, 136; **28**, 46, 158, 171; **29**, 84, 87, 88, 160, 173; **30**, 182, 185; **31**, 148–51, 163; **32**, 223; **33**, 113n, 182, 186; **36**, 59, 113, 133, 164, 182, 186, 189; **37**, 26, 30n, 75–83; **38**, 4, 5, 40, 61, 83, 87, 91, 129; **39**, 92, 100, 105, 240n; **40**, 19, 216; **42**, 13, 20, 23, 32, 35, 86, 117; **43**, 171, 176, 181, 207, 255; **44**, 61, 153, 187, 211, 251; **45**, 164, 201; **47**, 211, 216, 231, 251–2, 264–6, 276; **49**, 19, 271, 277, 330–1; **50**, 33, 45, 228; **51**, 196, 281; **52**, 145, 323; **54**, 274, 346, 351–2; **55**, 18n; **56**, 240, 248 (trilogy), 260, 279 (trilogy), 346; **57**, 265, 311; **58**, 67, 156, 339; **59**, 41, 42; **60**, 207, 287–8, 340

1 Henry VI, **11**, 155; **21**, 108, 111, 131, 132; **22**, 93, 110, 138, 151, 155; **23**, 9, 10, 18, 81, 160; **24**, 29, 39, 152, 177; **27**, 1n, 182; **28**, 46; **29**, 122, 160; **30**, 7; **31**, 168, 185; **32**, 218; **33**, 197; **34**, 91n; **35**, 26; **36**, 183; **37**, 26, 27; **38**, 1, 2,

4, 6, 9, 12, 17, 37, 89, 122; **39**, 20, 101, 106n; **40**, 224–6; **41**, 61, 232–3, 236, 240n; **42**, 25, 30n, 33n, 34, 86, 112, 117, 118, 161, 193; **43**, 8, 9, 11, 17n, 255; **44**, 3, 4, 5n, 11, 13, 14n, 59, 133, 136n, 227, 244, 252; **46**, 115, 215, 235, 250; **48**, 242, 244, 264, 278; **49**, 271, 323, 330–1; **50**, 43; **51**, 37, 176, 316; **53**, 8, 175–7, 182, 293, 342; **54**, 66–7, 274, 320, 344, 346, 350–2; **55**, 19, 286, 381; **56**, 248, 280–1, 290, 312; **57**, 239, 292; **58**, 346–7; **59**, 5, 6, 72, 353; **60**, 112, 305, 322, 346–7

2 Henry VI, **21**, 107, 109, 111, 152; **22**, 93, 94, 105, 138, 151, 155, 173, 182; **23**, 2, 17, 24, 49–52, 54–5, 57, 58, 81; **24**, 137, 152, 177; **26**, 69, 98; **27**, 132n, 135, 154, 161, 182, 191; **29**, 121, 122; **30**, 201, 209; **31**, 167; **32**, 218, 230; **33**, 197; **35**, 122–3; **36**, 182, 183; **37**, 26, 212; **38**, 1, 4, 9, 12, 17, 37, 38, 42, 44, 103, 117, 137, 175n, 223, 247n, 253; **39**, 21, 105n, 106, 107, 110; **40**, 47; **41**, 13, 14n, 15–22, 150n, 222, 230, 232, 234–5, 239; **42**, 78, 86, 93, 117, 161, 193; **43**, 8, 255, 267; **44**, 3n, 10, 11n, 14, 15, 18, 19, 21, 24, 30, 131, 135; **46**, 52n, 113, 150, 215, 241, 250; **48**, 242, 244, 264, 278; **49**, 27, 271, 330–1; **50**, 278; **51**, 3, 297, 322, 332; **52**, 189, 287, 298; **53**, 175–6, 182–3, 291, 324, 334, 340, 342; **54**, 66, 274, 343, 344, 346, 351–3; **55**, 19, 22, 286, 381; **56**, 280, 290; **57**, 228, 292, 336, 339, 340; **59**, 7, 71, 76, 375; **60**, 113, 322, 352

3 Henry VI, **22**, 93, 96, 138, 151; **23**, 49, 50, 142; **24**, 43–4, 137, 152, 177; **25**, 37; **27**, 22, 23n, 132n, 135; **28**, 45; **29**, 118, 122; **30**, 7, 14, 209; **31**, 27, 167; **32**, 93n, 164; **33**, 30, 158, 197; **34**, 167; **35**, 121, 122; **36**, 182, 183; **37**, 26, 212; **38**, 1, 3, 4, 9, 12, 17, 42, 122, 133, 185n; **39**, 21; **40**, 48, 210n; **41**, 14n, 230, 234; **42**, 86, 94, 95, 116, 117, 161, 193; **43**, 267; **44**, 3, 6, 7, 11n, 13n, 25, 136n; **46**, 115, 215, 250; **48**, 46n, 73, 211–14, 242, 244, 278; **49**, 27, 29, 40, 259, 271, 330–1; **50**, 24; **51**, 322; **52**, 76, 323; **53**, 175–8, 181–3, 334, 340; **54**, 312, 344n, 346, 351, 353–4, 356; **55**, 21, 286, 392, 396; **56**, 290; **57**, 278, 292; **58**, 343; **59**, 7, 73, 257, 375; **60**, 176, 272, 352

Henry VIII, **1**, 49, 52, 112–13, 119, 124; **2**, 5, 11, 12, 15, 130; **3**, 30, 53, 120–9; **4**, 99–100, 159–60, 152, 161; **5**, 119; **6**, 1, 6, 35n, 36; **7**, 32, 57, 70–1, 79n, 109–10, 124–5, 145; **8**, 124, 129; **9**, 49, 51, 104, 146; **10**, 77, 86n, 87n, 155; **11**, 27–30, 43, 50, 51, 58, 70, 74, 150–1, 155, New Arden edition reviewed, 150–1; **12**, 47–8, 73, 122–6, 129n, 134, 142, 149; Old Vic production (1958), 122–6; New Arden edition, 129n, 149 and n; **13**, 74, 119–20, 149, 158, 160, 162; production, 135; New Arden edition, 105n; **14**, 163; productions, 116; **15**, 52, 109n, 134, 179; **16**, 168–9, 174–5; **17**, 157, 197, 202, 237; **18**, 63, 100, 186–7; **19**, 65; **20**, 93n, 109, 155n, 156; **21**, 130, 140, 153; **22**, 95, 155, 165, 177; **23**, 11, 79, 81, 83, 116, 121, 141, 144, 157; **26**, 33, 35, 47, 177, 184; **27**, 110, 170; **28**, 177, 180; **29**, 1, 6, 124, 165; **30**, 4; **31**, 98, 99; **32**, 213; **33**, 200; **34**, 176, 190; **35**, 3, 37, 38, 40, 121, 176, 185; **36**, 107, 108, 114, 157, 164, 165; **37**, 148, 149, 170, 171, 191; **38**, 1, 15, 16, 25, 74, 94n, 131–51 *passim*, 176n, 182n, 230; **39**, 21, 75, 95n, 96, 113, 132, 250; **40**, 47, 202, 210n; **41**, 23n, 25, 185, 233; **42**, 168–9, 208; **43**, 43–57, 59–68, 84–5, 87, 110n, 113n, 230, 232, 240, 257, 259, 268; **44**, 7, 11–14, 27n, 75, 244, 250; **45**, 93, 184, 189, 190, 200, 202; **46**, 106, 194, 257n; **47**, 85, 231–2; **48**, 135, 242, 265; **49**, 43, 323, 324, 325; **50**, 251, 268; **51**, 236, 239–41, 260, 327, 334; **52**, 166–82, 274, 323; **53**, 5, 175, 276, 289, 338–9, 344; **54**, 68, 234n, 237n, 238n, 239n, 234–45, 314, 315, 321, 343, 344, 348–50; **55**, 289, 348; **56**, 146, 173n, 215, 302, 339, 352, 354; **57**, 335; **58**, 10, 331; **59**, 6, 73, 94, 219, 220, 255, 258, 259–60, 266; **60**, 67–8, 91, 100–1, 186–7, 284, 356

Julius Caesar, **1**, 21, 104, 110, 114; **2**, 3, 5, 14, 59, 116, 123, 128; **3**, 28, 31, 38, 47, 109, 112, 117, 118, 137, 152; **4**, 5, 44, 88, 115n, 118, 119, 123, 128, 150, 152, 156–7; **5**, 24n, 97, 107, 109, 112, 113, 116, 119, 120, 130, 135, 143; **6**, 26, 33, 58, 94, 120, 121, 151, 157, 158; **7**, 3, 80–1n, 109, 111, 123–4, 128, 130; **8**, 109, 114, 117n, 118, 120, 121, 123, 124, 144, 154; **9**, 9–30, 32, 77, 83, 112, 114, 115, 116, 119, 133, 139, 143n; **10**, 3, 4, 5, 6, 7, 8, 9, 12, 24n, 27, 28, 32, 33, 34, 35–6, 37, 72, 73, 74, 75, 76n, 77, 83, 86n, 87n, 116, 117, 118, 119, 122, 124, 130, 140, 142, 152, 153, 155; **11**, 59n, 119–20, 122–3, 128, 138, 142 and n, 143, 145, 155; Stratford-upon-Avon production reviewed, 132–4; **12**, 36, 70, 83, 89, 126, 134, 142; productions, 112, 115, 117–20; **13**, 30, 41, 116, 118, 147, 160, 167; productions, 126, 131, 135; translations, 129–30, 132, 154; **14**, 37, 41–4, 84, 95, 124, 142, 145n, 151, 154; productions, 116, 125; translation, 123; Folger Library edition, 166; **15**, 52, 131–3, 135, 137–9, 140, 142, 145, 174; **16**, 13, 65, 80, 132–3, 136, 138, 162, 174; **17**, 145–6, 151n, 209; **18**, 2, 11, 105, 148, 157, 163; film, 74; **19**, 112, 128–30; **20**, 6, 7–8, 70, 77–8, 123–4, 144, 149, 151; **21**, 13, 14, 22, 25, 132, 142, 147, 157, 158; **22**, 109–15, 127, 132, 139, 140, 155, 156, 157, 171, 174; **23**, 16, 17, 57–8, 65, 95–7, 122, 140, 142, 144, 148, 149, 173, 183, 186; **24**, 146, 147–8, 152, 156, 167; **25**, 2, 15, 19, 94, 127, 171, 175; **26**, 97, 99, 131, 132n, 133, 137, 141, 142, 144–6, 151, 158, 182; **27**, 1, 159, 179, 191; **28**, 22, 39, 47, 156; **29**, 84, 86, 87, 103, 122, 124, 139, 158, 170, 176; **30**, 4, 5, 11, 186, 189; **31**, 1, 2, 6, 8, 9, 10, 27, 55, 57, 58, 172, 183; **32**, 103n, 238; **33**, 16n, 27, 160, 168, 176–7, 184, 190, 205; **34**, 4, 62, 97, 167, 182, 191, 192; **35**, 9, 10, 13, 14, 15, 16, 17, 19, 23n, 27, 28, 36, 38, 39, 120, 178, 186; **36**, 2, 5, 8, 14, 17, 57, 122, 127, 160, 162, 163, 170, 171–2, 186n; **37**, 143, 146, 160n, 172, 181, 200; **38**, 41, 46, 97, 116, 117, 128, 176n, 182n, 215, 216, 220–2, 231, 238, 250, 251; **39**, 9, 21–3, 40, 96, 115, 116, 120, 222, 251; **40**, 11, 63, 67, 69–89, 199, 202; **41**, 106, 117, 171–4, 185, 198, 201, 204, 211, 222, 238; **42**, 151, 165, 170, 205–6; **43**, 207, 219, 231, 233, 269; **44**, 2n, 5, 6, 8, 13n, 14n, 17, 32, 65–73, 88, 106, 194, 207, 208, 210, 220, 226; **45**, 107, 116, 119, 121, 147, 159, 161, 167, 173, 186; **46**, 148, 149, 184, 194, 206, 217; **47**, 43, 62, 108, 194–6, 211, 222, 241; **48**, 10, 35, 38, 106n, 124, 128, 229, 237, 252; **49**, 141, 250–2, 260, 272, 289; **50**, 30, 143, 228, 241, 246; **51**, 175, 258, 260, 274, 281, 282, 292, 334; **52**, 28n, 54–5, 58–64, 76n, 135, 143, 185n, 193, 228, 248–9, 256, 280, 295, 308; **53**, 58, 75, 80, 82n, 87, 189, 244–5, 276, 302–3, 340; **54**, 10, 21, 28n, 36, 108–14, 154n, 285–6, 297, 303, 314, 319–322, 335; **55**, 65, 116n, 209–12, 251, 292, 306, 308–9, 325, 335, 368, 381; **56**, 99, 219, 282, 291, 328, 341, 345; **57**, 138, 143, 227, 228, 229, 230, 252, 292, 332; **58**, 10, 12, 112, 131, 141, 157, 201, 301, 320, 340, 342; **59**, 18, 22n11, 41, 63, 72, 76, 77, 77n12, 78, 125, 130, 132, 189–90, 299, 328–30, 339, 353, 354–5, 363, 364, 370; **60**, 134, 130–5, 140, 171, 172–3, 176, 304–5, 322, 332

Shakespeare, William (*cont.*)
King John, **1**, 123, 125, 127; **2**, 1, 5, 120, 139–40; **3**, 26, 99, 117, 142; **4**, 6, 14, 59; **5**, 112, 114; **6**, 1, 2, 4, 6, 8, 10, 31–3, 33n, 35n, 36, 48n, 84; **7**, 16, 26, 107, 111; **8**, 117n, 124, 126, 132–3, 143; **9**, 55, 108, 113, 119, 137, 139, 143, 151, 153; **10**, 74, 77, 79, 82, 86n, 146; **11**, 87, 99, 119, 122, 137, 143; Stratford-upon-Avon production noted, 134; **12**, 122, 142; productions, Stratford-upon-Avon (1957), 84; elsewhere, 112, 119; **13**, 30; productions, 127, 134; **14**, 29, 30, 32, 41, 95, 151; productions, 117, 125; **15**, 52, 58, 142, 166, 172; **16**, 134–6, 168–9; **17**, 107, 138, 155; **18**, 169, 178, 184; **19**, 133; **20**, 51–9, 81n, 88, 108; **21**, 132, 148, 151, 152, 153; **22**, 127, 132, 155; **23**, 10, 17, 23, 56–7, 58, 79, 140, 145; **24**, 85n, 117, 118, 130, 142, 152, 174; **25**, 174; **26**, 96, 105n, 106, 132, 158, 183; **27**, 106n, 148, 180; **28**, 45, 47, 49, 138, 139, 140, 141, 166, 172, 172, 179, 180; **29**, 136, 140, 144; **30**, 7; **31**, 27, 153, 182; **32**, 165, 212, 213, 218; **33**, 200, 34, 26, 61, 63, 186; **35**, 5, 13, 18, 36, 39, 113n; **36**, 94, 113, 171, 173; **37**, 48, 147, 148; **38**, 4, 12, 13, 46, 94n, 99, 137, 176, 178n, 182, 183n, 191, 194, 196; **39**, 4, 23, 2n, 223; **40**, 216, 223; **41**, 23n, 212, 219n, 240n; **42**, 19n, 20, 37–52, 90, 95, 137–9, 151, 168–9, 193, 213; **43**, 184, 207, 230–2, 255; **44**, 3n, 5, 10n, 14n, 15, 18, 29, 136n, 137n, 194, 211, 217, 219, 244, 245, 252, 253; **45**, 93, 163, 190, 192; **46**, 257; **47**, 64, 93, 99, 105, 106, 225, 231, 241; **48**, 37, 79, 229, 264, 274, 283; **49**, 305; **50**, 13, 30, 43n; **51**, 116, 260, 331, 333; **52**, 76, 185n, 215, 227–8, 294, 323; **53**, 8, 175–83, 276, 308, 318; **54**, 2, 66–7, 213–22, 286; **55**, 19, 22, 24, 34, 285–6, 289–90, 292, 306, 308–10, 355; **56**, 146, 237, 249n, 252, 253, 279, 291, 312; **57**, 292, 300, 305; **58**, 4, 38, 353; **59**, 11, 42, 47, 73, 74, 260, 357, 360; **60**, 22, 309–10, 343
King Lear, **1**, 2, 60, 71, 98–102, 111, 112, 119, 131; **2**, 17, 19, 110, 118, 123, 128, 141, 153; **3**, 17, 18, 20, 30, 45, 50, 64, 71, 111, 112, 113, 117, 118, 130, 133, 134–5, 137, 140, 142, 147–9, 151, 152; **4**, 3, 4, 5, 6, 9, 10, 15, 17, 18, 19, 20, 21, 25, 27, 29, 32–3, 99, 115n, 120, 125, 135, 141–2, 151, 156, 157–8, 161; **5**, 52, 63, 68, 70, 71, 72, 85, 87, 90, 96, 109, 111, 112, 113, 115, 116, 118, 120, 131–2, 134, 141, 142, 144, 146–7, 151; **6**, 10, 47, 48n, 103, 117, 118, 119, 120, 124, 125, 144, 149, 150, 152, 153, 162, 166; **7**, 9, 10, 20–1, 26, 28, 29, 46, 53, 109, 125, 127, 129, 135–6, 149–50, 152–3; **8**, 36, 37, 41, 59, 67, 68, 69, 72, 109, 110, 113, 115, 118, 120, 123, 125, 140, 153, 155; **9**, 14, 38, 82, 83, 85n, 99, 101, 102, 107, 109, 110n, 113, 114, 115, 117, 119, 136, 138–9, 141, 144; **10**, 1, 44, 47, 59n, 83, 84, 86n, 88n, 89n, 90, 91, 92, 93–4, 94–5, 96–7, 117, 119, 120, 121, 122, 124, 130, 138, 139, 140, 143, 154, 156, 157; **11**, 32, 43, 46, 57, 59n, 121, 123, 140, 143–4, 154; **13**, 30, 39, 41–7, 107; **16**, 135, 159; **18**, 173, 189; **19**, 3, 13, 15, 16, 23, 29, 54n, 77, 79, 87, 91, 119–20, 121, 128, 137, 139, 147, 155, 162–3; **20**, 1, 8, 20, 28, 51, 71, 73n, 84, 88, 91, 92, 126, 145, 151, 157, 162, 169, 172, 178; **21**, 1, 2–3, 10n, 27n, 49, 87, 127, 128, 129, 133, 136, 145, 146, 149, 153, 160, 162; **22**, 46, 57, 63, 99, 127, 131, 132, 133, 136, 137, 139, 141–2, 156, 161–2, 165, 166, 168, 175, 182, 183; **23**, 8, 15, 17, 18, 19, 20, 25, 26, 31, 34, 35, 36, 50, 59, 64, 65, 85n, 88, 114, 117, 118, 120, 121, 123, 140, 141, 153, 159, 174, 175–6, 179; **24**, 17–18, 24, 25, 26, 27, 34–5, 41, 72, 76n, 77, 85n, 97, 127, 138, 139, 141, 145–6, 170, 171, 174, 175, 179; **25**, 163, 172, 175, 180, 181, 184, 194, 195, 196, 197, 200; **26**, 33–48, 54, 55, 56, 58, 59, 69–79, 89, 123, 130, 134, 151, 155, 159, 161, 162, 164, 165, 167, 171, 176, 177–9; **27**, 2, 3, 18n, 43, 59, 98, 109, 112n, 113, 127, 132, 133, 156, 158, 160, 168, 169, 172, 173, 174, 179, 182, 185, 186, 190, 192; **28**, 22, 30, 31, 32, 36, 39, 51, 122, 149, 155, 156, 157, 175, 176, 179; **29**, 6, 8, 23, 24, 82, 87, 88, 89, 111n, 124, 139, 141, 163, 164, 171, 176, 185; **30**, 5, 7, 21, 26–7, 90, 100n, 148, 149, 150, 152, 182, 186, 187, 188, 190, 192, 193, 194, 200, 202, 206, 207; **31**, 38–40, 56, 58, 60, 77, 115, 116, 117, 121–2, 169, 170, 171–2, 178, 187, 190; **32**, 57n, 112, 177n, 184n, 213, 220, 221–2, 226, 229, 230, 236; **33**, 1–12, 13–25, 27–34, 35–42, 43–53, 55–66, 67–80, 81–7, 120, 129, 136, 168, 190, 192, 195, 198, 201–2, 204, 208–9, 210; **34**, 5, 40, 47–8, 62, 136, 140, 144, 146, 165, 169–70, 175, 178, 179, 185, 193, 194; **35**, 3, 9, 11, 12n, 23n, 24–5, 26n, 27, 36, 40, 48, 59n, 60, 113n, 117n, 126, 161n, 166–7, 176, 177–8, 179–81, 184, 186, 189, 191; **36**, 2, 14–16, 32, 37, 45, 53n, 57, 58, 60, 63, 73, 78–9, 81, 82, 83, 88, 112, 122, 149, 152–3, 158, 159, 160, 169, 171, 176, 180, 189, 190, 191, 192; **37**, 36, 40, 69, 72, 87, 115, 128, 142, 151, 158n, 160n, 161, 162, 168, 185, 186, 192, 193, 201, 207–12, 213n, 214, 217, 218; **38**, 66, 75, 78, 89, 92, 93, 99, 112, 153–66 *passim*, 190, 196, 201, 202, 220, 222, 234, 245n, 251, 252, 254; **39**, 4–7, 9, 23, 24, 39, 75–89 *passim*, 100–2, 114, 116, 129, 208, 210, 219, 223, 230, 233–5, 248–50; **40**, 1, 2, 4, 5n, 6, 48, 122, 135–43, 146, 150, 152, 196, 198–9, 203, 205–7, 209, 210n, 213, 223, 230n, 232–3; **41**, 95, 126, 133–44, 145–57, 174–6, 185, 191, 194, 197, 200–2, 205–10, 223–9, 232, 239; **42**, 15, 17n, 111, 118, 151, 152, 165–7, 171–2, 174, 179, 182, 185, 193–4, 198, 199, 210, 211; **43**, 19, 39, 59, 78, 88, 110n, 135, 188, 207–8, 217, 222, 224–7, 229, 230, 232, 234, 237, 247, 251–3, 268n, 269; **44**, 2n, 7n, 18, 21, 42n, 75–83, 85–90, 95, 96, 136n, 153, 157, 178, 179, 183, 186, 194, 206, 210, 211, 212, 213, 216, 218, 222, 223, 233, 255; **45**, 51, 65, 67, 73, 76, 79–88, 100n, 147, 148, 151, 153, 164, 166, 167, 173, 187, 188; **46**, 7, 47, 48n, 61, 110, 113n, 129, 152, 153, 157, 188, 194, 198, 216, 217, 219, 224, 237, 239n, 254, 256; **47**, 11, 68, 99, 100, 106, 115, 187–8, 194, 199–201, 203, 211–12, 222, 224–5, 232–3, 235–6, 249–50, 255, 257, 259, 264, 269, 270–1, 275; **48**, 20, 49–50, 109, 133, 147, 187, 195–6, 230, 240, 252, 263, 274, 276, 278–81, 287; **49**, 48n, 145, 151n, 201n, 204n, 217–23, 227, 272, 285, 288, 290, 333–6; **50**, 4, 43n, 48n, 127, 142–4, 148, 225, 228, 236, 246, 249, 272, 274–5, 278, 281, 283; **51**, 3, 4, 21–2, 25, 31, 33, 36, 116, 148, 175, 183, 195, 199, 348, 245–52, 260, 266, 268, 272, 274, 282, 184, 189, 197, 300, 303, 306, 329, 330; **52**, 4, 46n, 59, 76, 78n, 86, 146, 149, 256–7, 270–2, 276–8, 284, 289–90, 295–6, 316, 324–5; **53**, 1, 2, 5–10, 80, 89, 103–13, 171, 175, 187, 189, 191, 217, 252, 276, 289, 295, 301, 304, 318, 320, 324, 332; **54**, 21–2, 25–6, 40, 60, 108, 118, 154, 237, 246–51, 286–7, 298, 303, 306, 308, 311, 312, 318, 322, 339, 344–5, 350; **55**, 1–180 *passim*, 226, 257, 303–4, 325, 338, 342, 356, 360, 371, 381–3, 392–3; **56**, 93, 99, 139, 161, 206, 215, 218, 221, 235, 237, 242, 247, 249, 254, 256, 280, 282–6, 291, 307, 311, 321, 324; **57**, 19, 42, 167, 270, 271, 284, 292, 302, 316, 329, 330, 340, 342; **58**, 4, 10, 11, 16, 17, 18–19, 21–2, 22, 31, 83, 95, 99, 154, 170, 185, 209, 268,

290, 301, 317, 320, 355, 358; **59**, 1, 3, 7, 9, 14–16, 20, 37n87, 41, 44, 71, 73, 74, 76, 77n12, 108, 114, 141, 169, 170–1, 178, 181, 200, 201, 202, 206n39, 239n1, 258, 295, 299, 327, 333–7, 339–40, 347, 348, 349, 351, 362, 364, 365, 366, 370–1, 375; **60**, 22, 123, 129, 211, 253, 313Fig.57, 312–13, 322–3, 334, 343–4, 350, 360

Love's Labour's Lost, **1**, 107, 108, 109, 124; **2**, 19, 58, 128, 149; **3**, 10, 17, 25, 29, 31, 45, 137; **4**, 16, 17, 54, 126, 129–35, 148; **5**, 4, 52, 116, 139, 144n; **6**, 44, 80, 99, 121–2, 124, 148, 169; **7**, 6, 98, 105, 111, 116; **8**, 3, 6, 8, 9, 43, 59, 60, 65, 66, 67, 80, 120, 124, 125, 139–40, 158; **9**, 44, 46, 47n, 82, 83, 110n, 116, 117, 121, 122, 151; **10**, 17, 64, 66, 67, 68, 86n; **11**, 47, 62, 84, 87, 120, 123, 142, 147; **12**, 73, 81, 141, 143; **13**, 167; production, 134; **14**, 19, 20, 22, 108n, 146–7, 154; productions, 116, 123, 125; **15**, 12, 20, 51, 64, 69, 72n, 126, 131, 168; **16**, 2, 4, 71–2, 121–4, 129, 131, 165, 167, 178; **17**, 57, 136, 165, 198–9, 209, 219, 239; **18**, 100, 160, 178, 180; **19**, 112, 116–17, 135, 144, 150, Pl. XIIb; **20**, 90–2, 110, 152–3, 178; **21**, 131, 143; **22**, 7, 11, 12, 13, 29, 39, 69–76, 82, 99, 151, 152, 153, 178, 181; **23**, 4, 5, 6, 7, 11, 12, 19, 34, 56, 90, 92, 118, 138, 140, 143, 172; **24**, 23, 24, 25, 50, 51–3, 55–62, 142, 149, 176; **25**, 64, 179, 188, 200; **26**, 16n, 90, 103, 105n, 109, 135, 136, 152, 153, 165, 179; **27**, 105, 106n, 107, 108, 131, 146, 148, 162, 163, 168, 191; **28**, 7, 39n, 46, 58, 75–6, 77, 78, 149, 161; **29**, 41, 45, 124, 162; **30**, 6, 7, 83, 125, 133, 201; **31**, 164–5, 179, 189, 194; **32**, 39, 49, 53, 54, 55n, 93n, 105–14, 184n, 201, 208–9, 215, 234, 244; **33**, 55, 56, 59n, 73, 199, 206–7; **34**, 5, 36–7, 71, 162, 165, 166; **35**, 40, 89, 91, 119, 120, 123, 124, 125, 126–7, 142, 176, 186; **36**, 74n, 89n, 123, 160, 161, 176, 181, 186–8, 190–1, 194; **37**, 1, 5, 7, 13, 17–19, 21, 181, 182, 191, 194, 215–17; **38**, 49–59 *passim*, 176, 182n, 184, 199, 211, 212, 233, 242, 253; **39**, 24, 108, 109, 188, 189, 215, 220, 223, 225, 237, 247; **40**, 146–7, 149, 151n, 152–3, 186, 210n, 217, 234n; **41**, 107, 203, 230, 236n, 239; **42**, 1, 5, 6n, 10–13, 51, 70, 72, 90, 92, 152, 194, 209; **43**, 85, 208, 230; **44**, 36, 37, 136n, 153, 155, 195, 232, 244, 253, 256; **45**, 93, 124, 125, 148, 160, 169, 186; **46**, 8, 74, 108, 122, 123, 126, 127n, 194, 209, 211, 235, 249, 256; **47**, 139, 153, 163, 205–7, 212, 226, 239, 252, 268, 275; **48**, 2, 230, 244, 246, 255; **49**, 55, 272, 293; **50**, 11, 26, 74, 128, 228, 244; **51**, 37, 48, 53, 137, 142, 176, 185, 189, 284, 285, 289, 308; **52**, 76, 141, 257, 272, 293, 309–11, 315; **53**, 278; **54**, 15, 117, 154n, 155n, 156n, 287, 298, 307, 331, 357; **55**, 182n, 247n, 309, 325, 384; **56**, 53, 105, 115, 291; **57**, 19, 196–206, 209–24, 262, 263, 264, 269, 301, 337; **58**, 123, 141, 150, 301, 355; **59**, 10, 22n11, 41, 71, 142, 143, 152–3, 255, 258, 263, 264n25, 340; **60**, 62, 64–5, 66, 188, 255, 257, 257–8, 259, 260, 262, 263, 264, 272n12, 323, 339, 354–5, 367

Macbeth, **1**, 54, 71, 114, 115 (2), 117; **2**, 2, 5, 6, 7, 10, 11, 15, 16, 90–3, 116, 123, 124, 128, 130, 131, 145–9; **3**, 18, 30, 31, 49, 50, 57n, 63–4, 67, 99, 105, 109, 113, 116, 117, 133, 135; **4**, 4, 5, 6, 7, 8, 10, 11, 12, 14, 15, 18, 19, 21, 22, 23, 24, 30–2, 35–47, 54, 80, 88, 101, 103, 104, 109, 110, 111, 120, 123, 126, 127, 150, 151, 161; **5**, 52, 63, 64, 71–2, 73, 75, 76, 82, 83–5, 86, 87, 89–90, 92n, 95–6, 109, 111, 112, 114, 116, 117, 119, 120, 130, 134, 136, 141, 144n, 147, 148; **6**, 17, 20, 26, 33, 45, 58, 66–8, 78–9, 94, 104, 112–13, 116, 117, 118, 119, 120, 121, 123, 124, 125, 148, 151, 157, 161–2, 163; **7**, 1, 2, 9, 10, 11, 26, 27, 33, 91, 107, 110, 111, 112, 113, 114, 115, 132, 136, 146n; **8**, 33, 53, 55, 113, 115, 117n, 118, 119, 120, 121, 123, 125, 132, 144, 147, 154; **9**, 38, 43n, 83, 85n, 99, 101, 102, 103, 104, 107, 109, 110n, 111, 113, 114, 116, 119, 120, 121, 122–31, 134, 137, 139, 140, 152; **10**, 1, 16, 23, 25n, 44, 67, 86n, 88n, 116, 117, 119, 120, 121, 122, 123, 124, 131, 136, 138, 140, 145, 146; **11**, 21, 33, 52, 57, 63, 70–1, 76, 87, 118, 119, 121–2, 140, 143, 148–9, 155; Pelican edition, 153; **12**, 4, 36, 40, 50, 77, 82–3, 85, 134, 137–8; productions, 109–11, 115, 118–20; **13**, 17, 20, 30, 37, 38, 40n, 49, 69, 81, 118, 146, 148, 151–2, 157, 160, 163; productions, 126–7, 130, 132, 134–6; Folger Library edition, 165; translation, 154; **14**, 66, 72, 84, 139, 145 and n, 152, 155–6; productions, 116, 117–21; **15**, 24, 112, 115–16, 121, 127, 131, 138–41, 145–6, 158–9, 161, 164, 174; **16**, 12, 37, 42–53, 55, 58, 64, 73–4, 81–4, 132–3, 137–8, 143–51, 153–4, 158–9, 175–6; Davenant's version, 181; **17**, 47n, 126, 156, 157, 159, 161, 164, 166, 171, 209; **18**, 3, 46–7, 49–53, 55–6, 104, 106–8, 116, 156–7, 168, 174; film, 71, (Kurosawa's film) 73; opera versions, 75–6, 82, 85–6; **19**, 121–2, 125–6, 128, 130, 141, 146–7; antithesis in, 25–33; the criminal as tragic hero in, 12–24; 'fiend-like queen' in, 75–94; Duncan's golden blood in, 34–44; hell-castle and its doorkeeper in, 68–74, Pls I, II; image and symbol in, 45–54; in street ballad, 95, 97–9; in twentieth-century criticism, 1–11; **20**, 1, 2–3, 8, 55, 75–6, 78, 89, 91, 92, 93n, 122–3, 144, 149–50, 164, 166, 169, 174; **21**, 24, 26, 27n, 47, 49, 107, 119–22, 127, 128, 133, 137, 138, 157, 158, 159–60, 162; **22**, 42, 99, 125, 127, 130–1, 133, 148, 156, 162, 174, 177; **23**, 15, 19, 50, 52–4, 57, 58, 64, 114, 116, 119, 120, 123, 138, 139, 147, 148, 153–4, 159, 173; **24**, 13n, 14, 32, 42, 77n, 138, 141, 145, 153, 156, 163, 167, 178, 179; **25**, 172, 180, 181n, 184, 185; **26**, 35, 40, 42, 53, 58, 60, 69, 70, 78, 81–8, 131, 132n, 133, 137, 151, 161, 172, 176, 177; **27**, 43, 47, 48n, 55, 145, 156, 158, 161, 172, 173, 179, 192; **28**, 5n, 118, 137, 151, 155, 157, 166, 171, 174, 176, 177, 179; **29**, 8, 9, 77, 82, 83, 88, 123, 135, 136, 139, 145–9, 165, 174; **30**, 5, 6, 21, 87, 95, 169, 170, 177–9, 182, 189, 190, 192, 198, 206n; **31**, 9, 33n, 40–2, 58, 77, 82, 83, 115, 152, 169, 173, 180, 188; **32**, 56n, 109, 112, 159, 220, 222, 225, 226, 230, 235, 242, 245; **33**, 10, 16n, 26, 46n, 67, 94, 120, 201, 204; **34**, 1, 5, 7, 53, 57, 61, 62, 81, 91, 94, 118n, 139, 142, 164, 175; **35**, 5, 10–11, 26, 27, 36–41 *passim*, 52, 54, 87, 103, 113n, 169, 178; **36**, 2, 5, 10, 26, 28, 31, 62, 63, 65–72, 75–6, 83, 84, 114, 127, 149, 151–2, 158, 160, 163, 166, 174; **37**, 36, 73n, 115n, 158n, 178, 184, 193, 199, 215; **38**, 156n, 175n, 182n, 184n, 185, 219, 220, 229, 231, 234, 236, 241; **39**, 3, 4, 8, 24–6, 40, 53, 67–74 *passim*, 75, 94, 100, 101, 115, 116, 119, 171, 175, 208, 209, 216, 222, 233, 234; **40**, 3, 48, 186, 193, 199, 202–3, 205, 21n, 213, 216; **41**, 8, 46, 134, 147, 170–1, 175, 185, 191, 196, 201, 205–8, 223, 227, 231, 238; **42**, 134, 136, 137, 152, 158, 170, 183, 192, 198; **43**, 9–11, 43, 110n, 111n, 114n, 190–1, 208–9, 223, 225–6, 232, 237, 251, 254; **44**, 2n, 4, 9, 13, 32, 36n, 95, 96, 136n, 195, 209, 213, 215, 221, 243, 244–7; **45**, 64, 79n, 82, 83, 148, 149, 157, 161, 162, 167, 173; **46**, 92, 115, 129n, 194, 195, 196, 205, 208, 210, 216, 222, 223, 237; **47**, 5, 6, 7, 9–11, 62, 68, 95, 101, 104–6, 112–13, 125–6, 153–9, 189–91,

Shakespeare, William (*cont.*)
212–14, 218–19, 223–4, 236, 240, 250; **48**, 20, 28, 36, 46–9, 111, 169, 183, 222–3, 230–1, 237, 255, 263, 270, 274, 276–7, 283; **49**, 67, 201n, 227, 234, 272–3, 278, 282–4, 288; **50**, 6, 14, 35, 101–10, 126, 197–211, 225, 228–9, 236, 246–7, 260, 262; **51**, 11, 79, 136, 137, 201, 261, 280–1, 282, 283, 284, 293, 297, 310–12, 330; **52**, 6, 47, 76n, 143–65, 185n, 257–9, 266, 270, 277, 291, 295, 322; **53**, 5, 6, 80, 90, 95, 98, 99n, 101, 102, 106, 108, 170n, 175, 187, 191, 252, 254–5, 278–9, 282, 285, 296, 304, 309, 318, 333; **54**, 14, 21, 22n, 154, 219, 246, 251–3, 283, 287–8, 290, 301, 305, 311, 317, 322, 335, 339, 341; **55**, 13, 64, 116n, 143n, 146, 182n, 212–13, 219–36, 257, 303, 305, 325–6, 358, 360, 370–1, 383; **56**, 3, 10n, 52, 97, 99, 101, 110, 111, 161, 215, 237, 239, 278, 280, 292, 309, 312, 315, 329, 339, 341, 342, 343, 348; **57**, 1–9, 147, 151, 173, 186–94, 284, 286, 287, 293, 299–302, 310, 312; **58**, 11, 106, 186, 186–97, 197, 213, 260, 261, 268, 287, 301, 318, 320, 324, 334, 337, 338, 342, 349, 356; **59**, 5, 12, 18, 41, 42, 63, 66n11, 130, 138, 142, 143, 144–5, 169, 171, 178, 183, 200, 201, 237, 238, 330–3, 340–1, 347, 348, 349, 360, 361, 364, 365, 366, 369, 370, 373; **60**, 123–9, 130, 136, 137n21, 135–7, 140, 141, 209, 208–9, 214, 271, 323–4, 334, 335, 337, 349, 353, 356

Measure for Measure, **1**, 54, 55, 107; **2**, 5, 66–82, 135, 151; **3**, 15, 29, 66–73, 117, 119, 137, 142, 151; **4**, 5, 6, 12, 13, 14–15, 16, 22, 24, 26–7, 33, 37, 51, 125, 126, 127, 129, 135–8, 144, 145n, 151, 152–3; **5**, 8, 43, 44, 68, 102, 108, 109, 117, 119, 136, 141, 142, 144n; **6**, 22, 23, 24, 45–7, 48n, 76, 98, 103, 118, 121, 152, 153, 155; **7**, 7, 104, 107, 111, 130, 132, 137, 142; **8**, 2, 10, 12–26, 66, 68n, 77, 121, 123, 136, 140, 147; **9**, 85n, 111, 112, 113, 115, 117, 133, 140, 148, 152; **10**, 86n, 119, 122, 124, 136; **11**, 52, 76, 87, 117–20, 122–3, 137, 143; Pelican edition, 153; **12**, 36, 142; productions, Stratford-upon-Avon (1950), 86, elsewhere, 110, 114, Connecticut, 117, 121; **13**, 31, 81–9, 116, 153; productions, 124, 131; translation, 130; **14**, 155–6; productions, 123, 125; translation, 122, 123; **15**, 58, 82, 132, 134, 137, 139, 142, 144, 162, 167–8, 174; **16**, 58, 83, 84, 93–4, 134, 136, 143–51, 163, 179; **17**, 81n, 83n, 92 and n, 112, 126, 140n, 163, 209; **18**, 2, 3, 6, 42, 49, 52, 95, 99, 148, 162–3, 177; opera version, 81; **19**, 112–14, 146, 150, 163; **20**, 76, 78–9, 81n, 89–90, 118, 126, 128, 144, 153, 165, 174, 178; **21**, 3, 24, 46n, 47, 52n, 127, 128, 134–5, 143, 162; **22**, 27, 29–30, 32, 88, 150, 160, 170, 176; **23**, 16, 23, 26, 31, 34, 42, 79, 82, 83, 118, 120, 140, 151, 176, 177n, 182, 183; **24**, 43, 123, 124, 125, 129, 149, 150, 155, 167, 173; **25**, 1, 2, 4, 5, 6, 7, 8, 27–35, 36–44, 45, 50, 60, 61, 63, 64–5, 101, 130n, 158, 175, 176, 177, 191; **26**, 119–28, 130, 136, 153, 155, 167, 172, 175; **27**, 81, 82–3, 84–92, 108, 109n, 145, 166, 167, 176, 177, 184, 189; **28**, 7, 38n, 39, 40, 51–6, 89–105, 137, 143, 146, 147, 162, 180; **29**, 52, 61, 67, 94, 95, 98, 123, 157, 158, 163, 166; **30**, 43, 83–4, 182, 184, 186, 187, 192, 193; **31**, 4, 21, 105–13, 115, 116, 117, 118, 119, 120, 121, 124, 166, 169, 189, 193, 197; **32**, 49, 53, 93n, 108, 129–44, 201, 205–7, 212, 217–18, 224, 229, 231, 234, 237, 246; **33**, 36, 67, 131, 187, 191, 200, 204; **34**, 23, 26, 37, 44–7, 163, 165, 173–4; **35**, 41, 45, 141, 151, 160n, 161, 168, 169, 170, 182, 183, 185; **36**, 4, 14, 102, 103, 109, 159, 160, 162, 163, 164, 170, 172, 176, 177; **37**, 38, 89–97 *passim*, 140, 158n, 159, 176, 179, 186, 187, 193, 194, 213, 214; **38**, 29, 34, 59, 99, 173, 182n, 201–4, 218, 219, 231, 236, 237, 253; **39**, 11, 26, 98, 202, 221, 223; **40**, 21–32, 107–22, 139, 210n, 229; **41**, 61, 65n, 110, 132, 151, 194, 197, 203–4, 212, 223, 231, 241n; **42**, 134, 135, 153, 167, 173, 180, 182, 183, 192, 199; **43**, 75, 93, 209, 232, 253–4, 261, 269; **44**, 7n, 10n, 128n, 134, 135n, 186n, 197, 226, 234, 240; **45**, 93, 99, 134–9, 149, 169; **46**, 8, 109, 113, 121, 122, 124n, 157, 196, 208, 211, 213, 241, 243–7, 253; **47**, 83, 161, 167–8, 214, 224, 229, 240; **48**, 20, 180, 191, 196, 217–22, 231, 244, 247, 264, 272, 274–6, 278; **49**, 183n, 252, 273, 274, 282, 284; **50**, 5, 230, 241, 243; **51**, 6, 29, 30, 31–2, 39, 40, 42, 69n, 147, 154–8, 224–7, 262–3, 276, 282, 294, 299, 325–6; **52**, 19–22, 24, 28n, 32, 76, 133–42, 225, 241–4, 259, 272, 274, 278, 297, 299, 301; **53**, 1, 3, 11, 80, 97, 176, 183n, 213–32, 239, 278, 288, 297, 299, 307, 319; **54**, 2, 38–9, 67n, 68, 69n, 116, 117n, 118, 154n, 165–81, 288, 301, 306, 308; **55**, 13, 24n, 195, 196n, 197, 327, 338, 347, 355, 358, 382, 390; **56**, 161, 162, 267, 292–3, 309, 318, 322, 339–40; **57**, 230, 269, 293, 326; **58**, 48–59, 81, 141, 199, 264, 269, 274–7, 275, 277, 302, 321, 354, 356; **59**, 5, 11, 12, 72, 73, 75, 78, 141, 143, 178, 183, 184, 185, 187–8, 201, 258, 286, 341, 352, 359, 362; **60**, 85n3, 99, 104n11, 107n25, 284–5, 313–14, 324, 339, 340–1, 368, 369

Merchant of Venice, The, **1**, 90, 95–6, 105, 107, 109, 115, 116 (2), 120; **2**, 3, 5, 15, 116, 123, 127, 128; **3**, 27, 31, 44, 71, 111, 112, 113, 141, 147; **4**, 12, 21, 94, 118, 120, 128, 149; **5**, 5, 24n, 52, 101, 107, 108, 109, 113–14, 115, 116, 119, 120, 122, 124–5; **6**, 116, 117, 118, 119, 121, 124; **7**, 2, 53, 91, 96, 97, 102–3, 104; 107, 109, 111, 112, 113, 116–17, 125, 132, 133; **8**, 3–6, 7, 8, 9, 63, 64, 65, 66, 75, 76, 78, 117n, 120, 121, 123, 124, 125, 143, 149; **9**, 50, 82, 83, 102, 103, 104, 107, 111, 112, 113, 114, 115, 119, 121, 131, 136, 143, 152–3; **10**, 21–3, 24, 75, 77, 82, 86n, 87n, 115, 116, 117, 119, 123, 124, 125, 151, 152, 155; **11**, 62, 68, 87, 89, 117–19, 122, 137; **12**, 74, 126, 132, 141 and n; productions, 109–10, 113, 115, 117, 119–21; **13**, 138, 166, 167n, 169n; productions, 124–5, 129–30, 132, 134–5; translation, 154; **14**, 23, 32, 34, 41–2, 44, 93, 151–2, 161; productions, 116, 120, 122–3; Stratford-upon-Avon production discussed, 135–7; **15**, 53–5, 57, 61, 131, 134–5, 139–41, 144–6, 162, 168, 170; Yale Shakespeare edition reviewed, 178–9; **16**, 13, 38–40, 54–5, 78, 82–3, 132–3, 138, 160–1; **17**, 43, 47–50, 51n, 92n, 93, 139, 185, 210, 248n, 254n; **18**, 52, 99, 161–2, 173, 175; cartoon, 72; **19**, 86, 112–14, 116–18, 146, 148, 150, Pl. VII; **20**, 85, 90, 145, 152, 156–7, 165; **21**, 130, 131, 141, 152, 157, 160, 162; **22**, 7, 11, 32, 93, 101, 113, 127, 131, 132, 133, 150, 154, 177; **23**, 17, 25, 30, 120, 138, 144; **24**, 128, 129, 131, 167, 169, 172, 176, 178; **25**, 95, 109, 110, 153–9, 164, 165–6, 179; **26**, 130n, 154, 179, 181, 182; **27**, 81, 82, 90, 91, 93–104, 107, 108, 131, 164, 181, 185, 186; **28**, 39n, 75–87, 89, 160, 171, 172, 176, 180; **29**, 51, 52, 93–101, 136, 139, 157, 158, 162, 178; **30**, 183, 195, 201; **31**, 9, 26, 115, 116, 117, 119, 165, 180, 182, 183, 184, 188; **32**, 5, 63n, 64n, 72n, 115–28, 201, 204–5, 216, 217, 234, 242; **33**, 16n, 73, 121, 166, 199; **34**, 39, 55, 162; **35**, 10, 11, 16, 18n, 19, 23n, 26, 27, 31–41 *passim* 52, 65, 67–71, 74, 75, 76, 88, 90, 98, 102, 141, 153–5, 169, 188; **36**, 2, 3, 10, 53n, 61, 73, 74–5, 83, 101,

164, 185, 186; **37**, 1, 2, 4, 10, 11, 55–68 *passim*, 116, 161, 182, 186, 190n; **38**, 34, 52, 85, 176n, 178n, 182, 183, 185, 191, 207, 209, 226, 231, 239; **39**, 26, 27, 94, 100, 114, 130, 185, 186, 189, 226; **40**, 11, 197, 199, 213, 216, 223; **41**, 23, 25, 134–5, 143n, 162–5, 168, 186, 188, 198, 204, 209, 213, 222, 236, 244; **42**, 8, 10, 34, 65, 67, 127, 153–4, 156, 173, 182; **43**, 30, 41, 184, 194, 202, 209, 225–7, 232; **44**, 41, 42n, 43, 45, 47, 49, 50, 51, 53, 106n, 136n, 155, 197, 218, 228; **45**, 57, 96, 130, 131, 150, 159, 162, 169, 173, 187; **46**, 5, 109, 138, 152, 196, 208, 211, 213, 220, 224, 240, 241n; **47**, 11, 93, 97–8, 105, 106, 161, 166, 196–9, 214, 223–4, 226–7, 267, 269, 270–1; **48**, 2, 23n, 37n, 46n, 54–8, 62–8, 106n, 124, 126, 142, 185, 196, 231, 240, 245–6, 264; **49**, 151n, 226, 272, 273–4, 283, 291, 292; **50**, 7–9, 11, 34, 127, 230, 243–4, 247, 261, 271, 276, 288; **51**, 8, 137, 159–73, 199, 201, 220–1, 263; **52**, 28n, 76, 99–106, 133, 137, 208, 211, 215–21, 228, 239–40, 259–60, 266, 270, 272, 280, 284, 287, 293–4, 297, 300; **53**, 1, 6, 81, 191, 235, 257, 267–71, 282, 285, 292, 296, 299, 306, 333, 335; **54**, 25n, 89–99, 118, 154, 236, 267, 288, 301, 308, 315–16; **55**, 19, 25–6, 114, 116, 181n, 200, 283–5, 327, 347, 368; **56**, 73, 74, 105, 220, 266, 293, 314, 315, 317, 341; **57**, 229, 265, 294, 300, 304, 318, 319–21, 326, 328, 330; **58**, 11, 97–9, 166, 167, 269, 279, 302, 309, 318, 320, 324, 338; **59**, 6–7, 10, 11, 61, 63–8, 68n19, 71, 72, 75, 76, 141, 183, 201, 233, 341, 352, 359, 361, 367, 369–70; **60**, 62, 63–4, 200, 209, 211–13, 337, 338–9, 341, 346, 355, 356, 367

Merry Wives of Windsor, The, **1**, 9, 113; **2**, 5, 10, 110, 151, 152; **3**, 14, 27, 28–9, 31, 44, 45, 56, 74, 111, 116; **4**, 94, 118, 119, 125, 126; **5**, 3, 52, 108, 109, 111, 113, 117, 120; **6**, 84, 117, 118, 125, 160, 169, 171–2; **7**, 52, 78, 108, 109, 113, 114; **8**, 4, 6, 7, 57, 59, 61, 62–3, 67, 78, 122; 158, **9**, 82, 83, 111, 114, 144; **10**, 13, 86n, 117, 118, 119, 120, 122, 124, 125, 130; **11**, 53, 57, 59n, 118, 122, 154; **12**, 43, 45, 102; productions, 110, 114, 118, 120; **13**, 153, 157; productions, 129, 132, 133; **14**, 23, 44n, 112, 160n; productions, 123, 125; translation, 123; **15**, 5, 40n, 132, 135–6, 140, 162, 173; **16**, 37, 54, 133, 135, 172; **17**, 45, 157 and n, 160, 209; **18**, 49, 188–9; opera versions, 76, 78, 81–2, 83–5, 87, 99; Walker's edition (1734), 15; **20**, 84–5, 89, 111, 126, 130, 153, 174, 175; **21**, 130; **22**, 139; **23**, 3, 4, 6, 177n, 178; **25**, 107–12, 192, 198, 199, 200; **27**, 108, 164, 165n, 177, 184, 185, 186; **28**, 77, 160, 178; **29**, 10, 51, 135, 137, 152, 154, 172, 183, 185; **30**, 2, 4, 87n, 209, 210; **31**, 194; **32**, 5, 64n, 85, 217, 225; **33**, 169, 199; **34**, 162, 165, 166, 182–3; **35**, 109, 119, 127, 186; **36**, 76–8, 83, 109, 113n, 170, 171; **37**, 1, 7, 8, 11, 88; **38**, 17, 31, 34, 73, 86, 90, 96, 122, 232; **39**, 27, 96, 97, 183, 186, 191, 196–8, 224, 246; **40**, 198, 202, 206; **41**, 14, 137, 187, 203, 213, 217, 219, 224, 242; **42**, 154, 173, 181, 203n; **43**, 217, 224, 230–1, 268n; **44**, 106n, 127, 133, 136n, 153, 155, 242, 244, 249; **45**, 151, 175, 178, 185; **46**, 30, 108, 141n, 173, 177, 180, 181, 196–7, 212, 255; **47**, 106, 161, 214, 227; **48**, 164, 189, 197–8, 232, 242, 266, 274; **49**, 260–3, 274, 285, 291, 293, 327, 329, 330, 331; **50**, 230–1, 286; **51**, 230, 234–6, 314, 318; **52**, 76, 85, 105n, 260, 266, 298, 310, 317; **53**, 279, 307; **54**, 117n, 288–9, 306, 307, 344, 353; **55**, 26, 69, 181n, 247n, 327–8, 335, 390; **56**, 53, 118, 127, 130, 237, 249n, 252, 293, 313, 339–40, 352; **57**, 113, 198, 211, 215, 265, 294, 305; **58**, 11, 131, 150, 269, 302, 324, 356; **59**, 6, 7–8, 9, 11, 18, 72, 141, 142, 186, 206, 211, 258, 341, 364, 365; **60**, 62, 65, 66, 114, 114n54, 115n58, 116n64, 184, 187, 188, 190, 317–18, 319, 324, 367

Midsummer Night's Dream, A, **1**, 2, 52, 113, 114, 115 (2), 116 (2), 124; **2**, 3, 5, 7, 8, 14, 19, 112, 118, 127, 128, 135; **3**, 26, 95, 97, 99, 110, 111, 113, 116, 117, 118; **4**, 5, 26, 42, 109, 111, 115n, 118, 119, 120, 126, 127, 128, 129, 159; **5**, 21, 52, 108, 109, 111, 112, 113, 116, 119, 120, 122, 132; **6**, 117, 118, 120, 121, 123, 124, 125; **7**, 53, 107, 108, 109, 111, 112, 113, 114, 115, 116; **8**, 2, 4, 40, 64, 76, 79, 80, 103, 112, 118, 119, 121, 125, 126, 136–8, 143, 147, 155; **9**, 83, 85n, 103, 110n, 111, 113, 115, 116, 119, 120, 142, 151; **10**, 21–2, 23, 25n, 26n, 28, 64, 66, 67, 71, 73, 86n, 111, 117, 120, 121, 122, 124, 137, 149, 150; **11**, 47, 52, 59n, 62, 70, 78, 80, 87, 118–23, 137; **12**, 73–4, 133, 141 productions, Stratford-upon-Avon (1954), 84, 86, elsewhere, 109–10, 113, 117–18, 120–1, Czecho-slovakian versions, 145; **13**, 119, 167n; productions, 125–8, 130–2, 135–6, at Stratford-upon-Avon (1959), 142–5; Folger Library edition, 165; **14**, 20, 21–2, 28–9; relationship with *John a Kent*, 92, 152, 155–6, 166; productions, 116–18, 120–5; **15**, 4, 5, 12, 53, 84, 112, 116, 118, 131–2, 134–5, 137–9, 141, 144–6, 148, 162, 170; **16**, 132–3, 134, 137–8, 143–51, 159–60, 164, 173, 178; **17**, 140n, 144, 169, 171, 192–3, 209–10, 210n; **18**, 31, 52, 63–4, 94, 97–9, 159, 179; Britten, 87; Purcell's *The Fairy Queen*, 77; Smith's *The Fairies*, 77–8; **19**, 59, 136, 150, 152; **20**, 93n, 109, 111, 122–3, 134, 152, 169, 179; **21**, 25, 87, 130, 157; **22**, 4, 7, 11, 12, 27, 30–1, 83, 151, 152, 153, 173; **23**, 4, 5, 7, 10, 16, 23, 92–3, 94, 120, 122, 132, 138, 143, 144, 161, 172, 173; **24**, 118, 119, 125–6, 128, 132–4, 156, 168, 178; **25**, 35, 158n, 164, 178, 179, 186; **26**, 92, 106, 135, 152, 153, 156, 172, 179; **27**, 7n, 59, 95, 107, 108, 162, 163, 164, 185, 186, 187; **28**, 7, 75, 76, 78, 161, 173, 176, 178; **29**, 48, 121, 122, 124, 138, 140, 141, 142, 151, 161, 162, 170, 173, 177, 184; **30**, 87n, 125–34, 183, 201, 206; **31**, 3, 4, 6, 33, 34, 77–83, 98, 141–4, 188, 198; **32**, 39, 42, 49, 53, 54, 112, 155, 201, 217, 228, 229, 244, 244; **33**, 56, 189, 191, 196, 200; **34**, 44, 103, 143, 158, 162, 165, 185, 187–9; **35**, 1, 2, 3, 9n, 12, 24n, 47, 57–63. 65, 67, 71–7, 141, 144, 146, 158, 175; **36**, 2, 10, 60, 65, 161, 167, 175, 181, 194; **37**, 1, 5, 8, 9, 11, 41–53 *passim*, 69, 70, 71, 87, 107, 158n, 159, 161, 162, 168–70, 179, 183, 187, 191, 194n, 200, 219; **38**, 34, 50, 134, 136, 171, 175n, 189, 193, 194, 199, 232, 235, 237; **39**, 1, 2, 13n, 27, 28, 60, 77, 95, 99, 108, 109, 115, 120, 124, 169, 182, 185, 219, 224, 225, 234, 238n, 240–2; **40**, 3, 8–9, 11, 51–61, 172–3, 175, 177, 193–4, 200, 210n, 223; **41**, 25, 84, 133–4, 137n, 187n, 194, 196, 219, 223, 225–6, 228; **42**, 13, 39n, 53, 57n, 60, 61, 63, 75, 154, 173–4, 196; **43**, 72, 74, 78, 85, 87, 93, 110n, 113, 184, 200–2, 210–12, 224, 232, 237, 269; **44**, 89, 95, 161, 198, 223, 236, 239, 256; **45**, 69, 71, 92, 115, 134, 151, 172, 195; **46**, 9, 106, 108, 114, 117n, 119, 121, 150, 168, 169, 187–9, 197–8, 206, 209, 211, 212, 240, 241; **47**, 92, 97, 101, 106, 112, 122, 139–51, 215, 219, 226, 227; **48**, 3n, 10, 20, 64, 109–10, 164, 183, 197, 200–4, 222, 232–3, 235, 237, 238, 246, 262; **49**, 9, 64, 74, 141, 274–5, 305, 306, 320; **50**, 14, 35–8, 89n, 227, 230–1, 235, 237–8, 244, 263; **51**, 21, 22, 48, 55, 79, 176n, 182,

Shakespeare, William (*cont.*)
219–21, 259, 263–4, 280, 284, 286, 294, 295, 300, 315, 332, 333; **52**, 76, 127, 145, 185n, 186, 208, 231–2, 260–1, 263, 270, 274, 276, 278–80, 288, 290, 293, 310; **53**, 2, 3, 4, 49–59, 159, 190, 271–3, 276, 279, 284, 288, 306, 335, 344; **54**, 37n, 154, 265, 289–90, 298–9, 301, 303, 306, 312, 321, 336, 339, 340–1; **55**, 25–6, 293, 309, 311–13, 328–9, 335, 383; **56**, 1–10, 14, 39, 40n, 41, 42, 45, 52, 53, 55, 56, 62, 63n, 65, 67–77, 81, 105, 106, 117–25, 135, 166, 237, 238n, 249, 251, 253, 255, 256, 264, 272, 293–4, 301, 328, 348; **57**, 227, 264, 265, 268, 294, 305, 306, 330, 334, 339; **58**, 6, 11, 49, 99, 185, 209, 212, 279–80, 303, 320, 339, 340, 341; **59**, 11, 12, 41, 47, 139, 140, 141, 183, 201, 237, 238, 298, 304–7, 341–2, 353, 369, 373; **60**, 62–3, 65, 104n11, 187, 189n17, 190, 270, 272, 272n12, 273, 274, 274n22, 276, 277n35, 300–1, 302, 306, 324–5, 339, 350, 360, 367

Much Ado, **1**, 62, 113, 114, 115 (2), 116 (2); **2**, 5, 79, 153; **3**, 27, 31, 95, 111, 116, 141, 147; **4**, 4, 18, 24, 88, 99–100, 110, 115n, 120, 126, 127, 143, 144, 161; **5**, 52, 109, 112, 113, 114, 116, 117; **6**, 41, 45, 117, 118, 120, 123, 124, 125, 153; **7**, 104, 109, 131, 133–4; **8**, 2, 4–5, 7, 9, 40, 58, 59, 65, 76, 77, 78, 80, 119, 120, 140; **9**, 82, 111, 114, 116, 117, 119, 120, 121, 136; **10**, 19, 86n, 117, 118, 124, 150; **11**, 62, 80, 118, 122, 123; **12**, 63n, 133, 141; 1600 quarto, 150; productions, 110, 117–18; **13**, 153, 157; productions, 125, 128, 131–2, 134–5; **14**, 22–3, 94–5, 97, 165; productions, 116, 117, 120, 123; **15**, 2, 126, 132, 135, 140, 144–5, 162, 168; **16**, 13, 72, 133–5, 170, 176; **17**, 81n, 92, 144n, 153, 163, 171, 195, 210, 237; **18**, 7–8, 52, 99–100, 158, 159, 176, 190–1; opera version, 85; 1600 quarto, 27–31; **19**, 25, 163; **20**, 75, 87, 91, 125, 128, 153, 157; **21**, 127, 130, 162; **22**, 7, 11, 31, 44, 133, 135, 139, 144n, 149, 153, 154, 178, 179; **23**, 9, 95, 144; **24**, 128, 149, 156, 173; **25**, 27, 93–105, 110, 161, 164, 165, 166, 169, 178, 180; **26**, 70, 129, 130, 134n, 154, 177, 179; **27**, 105–10, 162, 164, 180, 186, 191; **28**, 76, 77, 78, 160, 161; **29**, 8, 51, 52, 58, 141, 157, 162, 179, 181, 185; **30**, 7, 169, 171–2, 173, 169n, 201; **31**, 21, 34, 116, 122–4, 182; **32**, 1, 2, 3, 4, 6, 7, 11–12, 15–26 *passim*, 27–36, 38–9, 40, 49–61, 93n, 215, 216, 226–7, 235, 244; **33**, 128, 186, 193, 203, 210; **34**, 40, 44–7, 48, 49, 158–9, 162, 172, 173, 191, 196; **35**, 19, 24n, 31, 36, 38, 39, 88, 109, 115, 141, 150, 179; **36**, 152, 161, 169, 186, 187, 192; **37**, 1, 28, 85, 86, 176, 177, 190, 193, 218; **38**, 59, 182n, 184n, 237; **39**, 2n, 28, 29, 114, 131; **40**, 16, 203, 208, 223; **41**, 25, 188, 239; **42**, 38, 92, 96, 127, 130, 131, 133, 153–4, 156, 167, 203–4; **43**, 212, 225, 227, 231; **44**, 6, 13, 14, 17, 18, 50, 103, 106n, 136n, 141, 170, 198, 226; **45**, 90, 97, 152, 161, 169, 172; **46**, 8, 122, 129, 151, 158, 168, 169, 198, 238, 240n; **47**, 10, 96, 100, 106, 192, 198, 215–16, 226, 258, 267, 269, 271–2; **48**, 29, 164, 185, 233, 245, 256, 264; **49**, 75, 98, 176, 275–6, 293, 308; **50**, 74, 231–2; **51**, 29, 48, 53, 176n, 181, 197, 230–5, 264–5, 325; **52**, 28n, 76, 120, 135, 211n, 233–5, 261–2, 272, 274, 279, 291–2, 322; **53**, 1, 3, 4, 7, 8, 190, 194, 217, 280, 289, 294, 307, 311, 318; **54**, 68, 117n, 236n, 265, 290, 321; **55**, 19, 23, 188, 329; **56**, 62n, 161, 162, 166, 167, 169, 237, 253, 255–7, 267–8, 273, 282, 294–5, 307, 347; **57**, 19, 223, 227, 230, 294, 311, 326, 332, 339, 340; **58**, 11, 153, 185, 209, 280, 304, 323, 334; **59**, 10, 25, 41, 72, 74, 76, 141, 142, 152–3, 183, 187, 201, 233, 258, 264n25, 299, 307–10, 342–3, 373, 378–9, 383; **60**, 62, 65, 75, 302–3, 325, 335, 339, 355, 356

Othello, **1**, 21, 59, 113, 114 (2), 115, 116 (2); **2**, 58, 84–90, 116, 123, 128, 135, 150, 153; **3**, 15, 29, 32, 47, 53, 62–3, 64, 98–106, 109, 110, 111, 113, 116, 117, 118, 133, 135, 137; **4**, 3, 4, 10, 12, 17, 19, 21, 24, 27, 47, 88, 94, 95, 104, 111, 120, 125, 126, 128, 140–1, 150, 151, 152; **5**, 5, 6–7, 16–24, 41, 52, 54, 63, 64, 66–80, 89, 107, 108, 109, 111, 112, 113, 115, 116, 117, 118, 119, 120, 135, 147; **6**, 26, 94–105, 117, 118, 119, 120, 121, 122, 123, 124, 125, 145–6, 150, 153, 155, 157, 164, 166; **7**, 9, 10, 22, 27, 31, 46, 72, 75, 91, 96, 97, 102–3, 107, 108, 109, 111, 113, 114, 115, 130, 134, 135, 146n, 153; **8**, 36, 68, 110, 113, 114–15, 119, 120, 122, 132, 140, 142, 147, 155; **9**, 16, 38, 43n, 82, 83, 85n, 107, 110n, 111, 113, 117, 119, 121, 138; **10**, 77, 79, 83, 86n, 87n, 98–100, 103–5, 116, 117, 119, 120, 123, 125, 130, 131–4, 138, 139, 143, 154, 157; **11**, 23, 57, 59n, 63, 89, 117, 118, 120–3, 138, 140, 142–3, 149–50, 154; New Cambridge edition reviewed, 149–50; **12**, 36, 38, 78, 131–2, 134, 136–7, 142–3, 145; productions, 110–13, 117–19; **13**, 7, 9, 20, 49, 50, 58, 69, 116, 118, 148, 149, 151, 155, 158–9; productions, 125–6, 128–9, 132, 135; translation, 154; **14**, 34, 95, 144, 148, 151, 154; productions, 116, 119–24, 162, 165; translations, 120, 124; **15**, 1, 2, 3, 115–16, 119, 121, 132–5, 137–8, 140, 142, 151, 156, 158–9, 170; **16**, 12, 13, 15, 37, 46, 53–4, 83, 132–5, 158, 166, 179; **17**, 49–52, 92n, 95n, 126, 139, 145, 147, 150, 159, 209–10, 212, 216, 219; **18**, 1, 6, 7, 11, 23, 31, 36, 54–5, 71–4, 98, 105, 109, 116–17, 147, 154–5, 157, 176, 183–4; opera versions, 76, 80, 82, 84–5; **19**, 13, 15, 16, 23, 28, 54n, 95–7, 121–2, 126, 128, 148, 161–2; **20**, 1, 10, 75–6, 110, 121, 123, 126, 129, 145, 149, 166, 175; **21**, 1–12, 13–29, 31–8, 39–46, 47–52, 53–65, 67–77, 79–86, 87–96, 115, 136, 141, 149, 159, 160, 163; **22**, 97–8, 125, 127, 129–30, 133, 154, 156, 161, 167, 177, 178, 179, 180; **23**, 23, 25, 31, 32, 34, 35, 97–8, 116, 120, 140, 151–3, 162, 173, 176, 179; **24**, 41–2, 85n, 141, 146, 152, 153, 170, 171, 175, 178; **25**, 23, 69, 76n, 172, 181, 194, 196, 197; **26**, 56, 129, 151, 159, 162, 163n, 176, 179; **27**, 43, 143, 148n, 157, 172, 179; **28**, 149, 154–5, 167, 172, 175, 176, 180, 181; **29**, 8, 52, 58, 82, 88, 89, 118, 123, 139, 142, 164, 166, 169; **30**, 16, 17, 21, 100n, 187, 189, 192, 194, 200, 206, 207; **31**, 10, 26–8, 110–11, 115, 169, 172, 174, 175, 182, 183, 184, 190, 193, 198; **32**, 53, 211, 220, 222, 224, 230, 236, 241, 242, 244; **33**, 10, 16n, 36n, 55, 67, 73, 169, 174–6, 190, 193, 195, 202; **34**, 61–72, 74, 78, 134, 144, 146, 149, 154–5, 171, 176, 177, 178, 193, 196; **35**, 11, 24n, 26, 27, 31, 32–4, 36–41 *passim*, 45, 48, 52–3, 68, 101–11, 115, 167, 170, 184, 187, 188; **36**, 3, 8, 14, 53n, 58, 61, 62, 92, 99n, 140, 162, 166, 169, 170, 171, 175, 189, 193, 194n; **37**, 9, 36, 115–31 *passim*, 145, 158n, 160n, 161, 176–8, 180, 182, 184, 190, 207, 212, 214, 218; **38**, 10, 34, 112, 122, 156, 176n, 213, 232, 238n, 243, 245, 246; **39**, 3, 5, 29, 30, 53–5, 58, 60, 64, 65, 82, 98, 99, 149–58 *passim*, 205, 213, 247, 250, 251; **40**, 36, 123–33, 199, 205, 207–9, 217, 219, 221–3, 231–2, 234n, 236; **41**, 46, 72, 105n, 106, 119–44, 171, 188, 200, 209, 211, 225–9, 230n, 232, 235; **42**, 101n, 104, 156, 165, 182, 199, 210; **43**, 110n, 133, 183–4, 191, 193, 195, 203, 219, 221, 225, 232, 237, 251, 268; **44**, 42n, 83, 96, 136n, 141, 186, 199, 206, 210, 211, 212, 213, 217,

221, 222; **45**, 65, 74, 90, 134, 152, 159, 164, 167, 173, 198, 203; **46**, 7, 51–60, 61–8, 69–79, 108, 112, 116, 198, 207, 208, 209, 217, 218, 224, 256, 257n; **47**, 11, 12, 63, 65, 71–80, 93, 95, 106, 112, 136n, 140, 161, 162, 164–7, 216, 225, 232–3; **48**, 38, 123–33, 164, 165, 169, 173, 184, 189, 233–4, 239, 241, 243, 252, 255, 257, 262, 263, 274, 278; **49**, 22, 48n, 67, 75, 140n, 201–16, 226, 227, 229, 257, 281, 284, 288; **50**, 3–5, 12, 47, 91–9, 169n, 232, 240, 244, 246, 248–9, 268, 272–3, 275, 279, 281–3; **51**, 29, 31, 34, 57–66, 176, 177, 178n, 179, 184, 185, 186–7, 190–1, 199, 252–5, 265, 272–2, 279, 282–4, 296, 297, 306, 308; **52**, 78, 102, 120, 131–2, 134, 148, 189, 202–6, 262, 270, 274, 277–8, 290, 300; **53**, 3, 5, 6, 9, 11, 80, 108, 184–95, 252, 255–6, 281, 289, 291, 293, 300, 304, 306, 312, 318, 319; **54**, 28n, 154, 184–90, 287, 290, 300, 301, 312, 316, 321, 334, 337, 341; **55**, 13, 26, 61, 65, 116n, 143n, 258, 271–81, 329–30, 338, 341, 347, 359, 361, 368, 372, 379, 384, 390, 393; **56**, 53, 105–16, 118, 138, 247, 280, 295, 301, 322, 339–40; **57**, 22, 25, 54, 170, 174, 230, 258, 284, 295, 302, 307, 313, 317, 327, 333; **58**, 11, 30, 126, 156, 170, 185, 209, 244, 268, 281, 282, 285, 304, 340, 342, 349, 350, 352, 356, 357; **59**, 11–12, 14, 15–16, 21–3, 26, 37n87, 71, 72, 74, 76, 77n12, 142, 196, 200, 201, 236, 237n20, 257, 343–6, 347, 349, 350, 352, 353, 363, 364, 367, 370, 371, 381; **60**, 85n6, 137n21, 154–60, 162, 164, 165, 166, 167, 169, 190, 221, 286–7, 325, 330–1, 332, 334, 335, 341, 347–9, 350, 354, 356, 359, 365–6, 369

Pericles, **1**, 46, 55, 107, 108, 119; **3**, 30, 45, 94, 108, 111, 136, 150–2; **4**, 2, 7, 80, 84, 87, 147, 152; **5**, 25–8, 28–34, 35–8, 39–45, 47–9, 52, 120, 142, 147–9; **6**, 47, 160, 164–72; **7**, 46, 51, 66, 76, 81n, 136, 137, 144; **8**, 121, 144, 158, 159; **9**, 83, 104, 120, 140; **10**, 71, 86n, 141, 145; **11**, 21–5, 30, 58–9, 64, 66, 70, 74, 123, 149, 154; New Cambridge edition reviewed, 149; **12**, 44, 142; productions, 111, 117; **13**, 38, 58, 149, 162; production, 135; Penguin edition reviewed, 165; **14**, 96; **15**, 5, 108, 139, 142, 169, 173, 180–1; **17**, 153, 172, 186–7, 215, 217–18, 233; **18**, 7, 172, 188; **19**, 2, 153; **20**, 91, 126, 151, 156; **21**, 147, 150, 152, 162; **22**, 25, 43, 59, 61–5, 67, 95, 98, 145, 163, 164, 174, 176; **23**, 1n, 5, 10, 132, 133, 180; **24**, 28–30, 105–16, 150, 151, 155, 174; **25**, 85, 137, 145, 149, 150, 151, 158n, 177, 200; **26**, 33, 44, 46, 47, 64, 65, 66, 130n, 163, 179; **27**, 80, 175, 186; **28**, 59, 146, 167, 181; **29**, 2, 6, 7, 8, 11–20, 21–32, 67, 74, 165, 166, 171; **30**, 6, 147, 155, 185, 203, 205–6; **31**, 5, 6, 7n, 16, 28, 99, 166, 179, 192–3, 194; **32**, 213, 243; **33**, 138, 169, 171–3, 174, 178; **34**, 190, 191; **35**, 121, 127, 191; **36**, 2, 98, 99, 180; **37**, 158n, 159n, 193, 212n, 214; **38**, 99, 171, 175, 176, 198, 252; **39**, 30, 126n, 128, 130, 214, 250; **40**, 155–7, 210n, 234; **41**, 46, 92, 203, 213, 214n, 233, 235–6; **42**, 156, 170, 192, 212; **43**, 43, 78–9, 104n, 128, 131–40, 257, 261–2, 264; **44**, 10n, 18, 83, 155, 158, 160, 166, 168, 172, 175, 199, 233; **45**, 152, 200, 201, 202; **46**, 83, 105, 113, 134n, 177, 198, 213, 257n; **47**, 90; **48**, 213, 223–4, 228, 234, 237, 277; **49**, 199, 276, 323; **50**, 143, 147; **51**, 18, 32, 40, 67–77, 176n, 265, 290, 297, 317; **52**, 78n, 85, 262, 289, 298, 316–17; **53**, 5, 6, 8, 71n, 176, 281, 297, 301, 308–9; **54**, 23n, 24–6, 37–40, 199, 211, 290, 314; **55**, 104n, 330, 358, 390; **56**, 256, 269, 271–3, 354; **57**, 229, 259, 269, 270, 271, 272, 273, 274, 287, 295, 335, 342; **58**, 99, 304, 320, 343; **59**, 5, 5n12, 6, 7, 132, 214, 215, 216–17, 218, 219, 220, 221, 222, 223, 259, 318–19, 369; **60**, 136n19, 270, 326, 331, 366

Richard II, **1**, 39, 46, 60, 72, 105, 106, 107, 109, 127, 128; **2**, 5, 53, 59, 124, 127, 129, 140; **3**, 18, 26, 45, 47, 70, 117, 118, 137, 138, 141; **4**, 2, 20, 37, 81, 84, 88, 94, 126, 128, 143; **5**, 52, 86, 95, 96, 115, 119, 120, 135, 143; **6**, 2, 4, 6, 8, 11, 12, 14, 16, 30–1, 35n, 44, 58, 89–90n, 118, 119, 129–34, 143, 150, 159, 162; **7**, 16, 35, 36, 37–47 and n, 107, 115, 133, 145, 151; **8**, 71, 118, 120, 125, 143, 147, 159; **9**, 39, 77, 83, 85n, 99, 107, 113, 114, 120, 137, 151, 164, 174, 176, 177, 181, 184, 188, 190, 192–37, 212; **10**, 1, 18, 25n, 64, 65, 66, 67, 77, 79, 86n, 87n, 110, 123, 124, 137, 146n, 151; **11**, 81, 83, 119, 121, 137, 143, 150, 152, 155; New Arden edition reviewed, 150, 152; Variorum edition (Black, M.W.), 152; Pelican edition, 153; **12**, 134; productions, 112, 121; **13**, 41, 153, 156; productions, 124, 127, 131; **14**, 29, 34, 39, 40, 41, 44, 46, 162; production, 118; **15**, 32, 51, 96, 115, 131, 139, 142, 146, 166, 170; **16**, 79, 92, 133, 159, 162–3, 167; **17**, 91, 113n, 147, 155, 157, 209–10, 233, 238; **18**, 3–4, 54, 150, 169, 174, 180, 191–2; Q1 (1597), 27–33; **19**, 133, 142, 147; **20**, 30, 41–3, 47, 48, 71–2, 76, 85, 163, 176, 178; **21**, 13, 26, 108, 109, 115, 132, 141, 142, 147, 151, 152; **22**, 99, 148, 155; **23**, 8, 10, 18, 24, 25, 69–78, 120, 138, 142, 145, 146, 147, 182; **24**, 15, 21–2, 27, 49, 141, 142, 153; **25**, 64, 167, 168–9, 170, 173–4, 194, 195, 197, 198; **26**, 105n, 152, 155, 156, 175, 179; **27**, 1n, 21, 33–41, 144, 146, 151, 152, 161, 180, 186; **28**, 1–13, 46, 138, 141, 158–9; **29**, 160, 170, 175; **30**, 7, 18, 20, 65, 185, 199; **31**, 27, 153, 168, 175, 179, 181, 183, 187, 189; **32**, 37, 39, 93n, 165, 171n, 213, 219, 234, 237, 238, 245; **33**, 16n, 113, 114, 196, 206; **34**, 26, 37, 167; **35**, 18, 24n, 28, 47, 48, 52, 168–9, 178–36, **38**, 1–11, 17, 19, 20, 22, 24, 38, 42, 44, 62, 63, 66, 67, 91, 92n, 133–5, 183n, 191, 195, 221, 222, 225, 226; **39**, 30, 31, 40, 42, 44, 100, 105n, 119, 152, 217, 238, 240, 249; **40**, 19, 47, 67, 180–1, 188, 198, 203, 205, 221, 223; **41**, 2, 23n, 83, 159, 188, 223–4, 229, 230n, 245; **42**, 15, 17, 20, 39n, 65, 90, 93–5, 156, 160, 161, 169, 193, 194, 200; **43**, 54, 171, 173, 180, 184, 212–13, 226, 232, 241, 250, 259, 265n; **44**, 3, 6, 7, 9, 12, 15, 17, 18, 27, 28, 78, 83, 96, 134n, 135n, 136n, 200, 209, 217, 220, 229, 243; **45**, 116, 121, 125, 139, 147, 153, 163, 180; **46**, 61, 198, 208, 213, 240; **47**, 236; **48**, 21, 36, 46–7, 73, 212, 234, 273n; **49**, 19, 177, 263–7, 286, 325; **50**, 12, 29–31, 41–55, 232, 240, 250, 262; **51**, 48, 104, 148, 151, 152, 265, 296, 326; **52**, 28n, 76, 78n, 85, 111, 189, 262, 275, 289; **53**, 1, 5, 8, 175, 303, 309, 324; **54**, 28n, 154n, 205–6, 246, 254, 274–7, 301, 308, 319–21, 339, 357; **55**, 16, 19, 24, 262, 286, 290, 292, 330, 361, 381; **56**, 80, 121n, 295, 316, 349, 351–4; **57**, 143, 227, 230, 236, 305, 311, 316, 337, 339; **58**, 10, 11, 122, 131, 209, 210, 304, 320; **59**, 11, 12, 47, 71, 74, 77, 78, 185, 201, 258, 299, 321, 320–3, 343, 359, 364–5, 370, 373, 379, 381, 382; **60**, 104n10, 105, 109, 111, 113–14, 116–17, 188, 258–9, 281n49, 316–17, 326, 342, 356, 358, 366

Richard III, **1**, 52, 114, 115; **2**, 37, 113, 123; **3**, 18, 23, 26, 44, 45, 47, 64, 109, 112, 143, 147; **4**, 5, 32, 37, 50–1, 94, 124, 126, 128, 145; **5**, 23, 24n, 52, 95, 97, 102, 108, 109, 111, 114, 136, 137–8; **6**, 2, 4, 5, 7, 9, 11, 12, 16, 26–30, 31, 33n, 34n, 35n, 44, 50, 58, 117, 118, 119, 124, 156, 166; **7**, 25–6, 28, 55, 92, 103, 107, 113, 125, 146, 151,

Shakespeare, William (*cont.*)
153; **8**, 90, 119, 122, 123, 128, 129, 149, 155, 157, 158; **9**, 103, 107, 137, 143, 151, 153; **10**, 1, 20, 25n, 64, 65, 66, 77, 86n, 87n, 115, 123, 134, 147, 156, 157; **11**, 32, 59n, 120, 123, 152, 155; Old Vic production noted, 134; **12**, 122–3, 131–2, 135; productions, 110, 112, 113, 120; G. Baldini's translation, 114; S. Gerevini's *Il Testo del Riccardo III*, 114, 151; **13**, 41, 156; Shakespeare Quarto Facsimile reviewed, 164–5; production, 131; **14**, 29, 35, 37–8, 44 and n, 151, 154, 156, 159, 162, 164; productions, 120, 123; **15**, 71n, 109n, 118–19, 131–2, 134–5, 138, 140, 142–3, 158, 174; **16**, 56, 79–80, 81, 138, 152, 165, 167, 179; **18**, 3, 31, 71–3, 102, 105, 108, 174, 183–4; opera versions, 75, 86; **19**, 133, 151; **20**, 4, 27–8, 51–9, 76–7, 107, 110, 126, 154–5, 178; **21**, 141, 149, 159, 160; **22**, 125, 127, 128–9, 130, 132, 133, 148, 151, 155, 170, 176, 179, 181; **23**, 8, 56, 114, 142, 145, 158, 173, 179; **24**, 32, 42, 76, 83n, 106, 118, 119–20, 129, 171, 177; **25**, 102, 158n, 184, 185, 193–4, 195–6, 197–8; **26**, 69, 131n, 132n, 134n, 157, 158n, 179, 183; **27**, 1n, 18, 21–32, 132, 133, 135n, 186; **28**, 46, 141n, 151, 157, 158, 171; **29**, 84, 86, 87, 118, 121, 136, 153, 159, 160, 174, 176; **30**, 7, 16, 18, 206n, 209; **31**, 27, 41, 147–8, 177, 178, 197; **32**, 37, 145–50, 212, 218, 230, 242, 245; **33**, 10, 16n, 36, 67, 73, 94, 126, 187, 200; **34**, 19, 40, 42–4, 53, 63, 88, 168, 183, 184; **35**, 5, 11, 24n, 27, 31, 36, 38, 39, 40, 41, 47, 48, 50, 52, 53, 54, 184, 186; **36**, 2, 58, 129, 132, 160, 161, 163, 169, 171, 173, 176, 184, 185, 192, 193; **37**, 157, 190, 194, 212; **38**, 2–4, 8–10, 17, 18, 24, 38, 40n, 61, 99, 133, 134, 141, 156, 185, 205, 208, 209, 220, 225, 236; **39**, 31, 95, 100, 105, 106, 108n, 216, 217, 223, 240n; **40**, 4, 6, 17, 19, 41–9, 85, 180, 188, 205, 209, 215, 221, 235; **41**, 25, 34n, 147, 193, 212, 226, 230, 236n, 239, 240; **42**, 15, 16, 17, 20, 40n, 56n, 78, 86, 90, 93, 94, 104, 157, 161, 170, 194, 206; **43**, 78, 88, 172–3, 175–8, 180, 213, 217, 250, 255, 265; **44**, 3, 5, 6, 10n, 11, 12, 15, 17, 26, 27, 153, 186, 187, 189, 200, 211, 217, 219, 242; **45**, 23, 90, 149, 153, 157, 162, 164, 187n, 192, 201; **46**, 52n, 61, 120, 162, 164, 198, 210, 222; **47**, 11, 62, 63, 65, 66, 121–4, 126, 181, 185, 189, 193, 202, 211–12, 216; **48**, 3, 10, 15, 17, 19, 36n, 46, 73, 110, 175, 176–7, 188, 200, 234, 242, 264, 278; **49**, 36, 255, 258–60, 271, 276–7, 281, 332–3; **50**, 30, 104, 232, 260, 284–5; **51**, 3, 122n, 135, 265, 289, 300, 304, 311, 321–13, 316, 332; **52**, 76, 144–5, 148, 262, 264, 284, 289, 292, 294, 310; **53**, 4, 5, 6, 35, 113, 175–8, 180, 182, 183n, 243, 281–2, 302, 325, 340; **54**, 154n, 204, 238, 274, 290, 298, 303, 316, 319–20, 344–7; **55**, 16n, 19, 20, 21n, 22, 29, 34, 61, 116n, 155–6, 187, 189, 285–9, 330, 335, 344–5, 370, 382–3, 390; **56**, 3, 154, 236, 237n, 238n, 239n, 241, 249n, 250, 251, 276–8, 295–6, 301, 347; **57**, 143, 235, 276, 277, 278, 295, 305, 326, 329, 336; **58**, 7, 31, 185, 304, 320, 323, 340; **59**, 7, 9, 55, 72, 75, 182, 185, 201, 237, 256, 343, 371–2, 376n3; **60**, 22, 105, 204, 210, 258–9, 270, 274n22, 287–8, 289, 326, 334, 347, 351–2, 356, 366

Romeo and Juliet, **1**, 10, 52, 62, 81, 109, 114 (2), 116 (2); **2**, 14, 16, 57, 116, 123, 129, 131, 149, 153; **3**, 25–6, 44, 45, 65, 99, 100, 109, 111, 116, 118, 147, 149–50; **4**, 5, 14, 27, 83, 90, 94, 118, 119, 120, 125, 128, 147, 148, 158–9; **5**, 25, 26, 52, 54, 105n, 107, 108, 109, 111, 112, 113, 115, 116, 117, 119, 135, 139, 145, 146, 151; **6**, 17, 33, 82–3, 88n, 114, 115, 117, 118, 119, 120, 123, 124–5; **7**, 36, 37–46, 51, 72, 73, 76–7, 92, 100–2, 104, 107, 109, 110, 111, 114, 115, 116, 144, 149; **8**, 9, 68n, 81–99, 109, 112–13, 114, 117n, 118, 120, 121–2, 123, 125, 147, 153n, 154, 159; **9**, 43n, 69, 82, 83, 85n, 102, 107, 108, 110n, 111, 113, 114, 115, 119, 120, 121, 136, 146, 150, 151, 152, 154, 155; **10**, 25n, 64, 66, 77, 79, 80, 82, 86n, 87n, 115, 117, 118, 120, 121, 138; **11**, 80, 84, 87, 118, 120–2, 142n, 143, 146, 154–5; **12**, 2, 70, 73, 134–6, 141n, 143; productions, Stratford-upon-Avon (1954), 84, elsewhere, 110, 113–18; 1599 Quarto, 150; textual problem of Q2 (II, 1), 151–2; **13**, 7, 8, 58, 153; productions, 125–6, 129, 134–6; translations, 130, 154; **14**, 44n, 145n, 154, 165; productions, 117, 119, 123–5; translation, 123; Folger Library edition, 166; **15**, 8, 12, 20, 24, 28, 93, 118, 122, 134–6, 138, 140, 142, 146; Old Vic production (Zeffirelli) reviewed, 147–55, 158, 173, 182; **16**, 13, 46, 53, 121–2, 124–31, 133–5, 137–8, 147, 157–8; **17**, 92n, 153, 159–60, 165, 175, 195, 209–10, 219; **18**, 6, 49–50, 66, 68, 97, 100, 102, 110, 174, 178; opera versions; 75, 77, 78, 79, 80, 86; **19**, 127, 163; **20**, 10, 68, 75, 83, 87–92, 95–105, 110, 117, 121–2, 126, 150; **21**, 25, 40, 43, 107, 109, 128, 156, 157; **22**, 125–6, 127, 130, 131, 133, 151, 152, 156, 167, 182, 183; **23**, 1, 2, 3, 6–7, 8, 9, 10, 17, 18, 25, 27, 34, 35, 47, 80, 83, 95, 108, 117, 118, 120, 122, 142, 143, 167n; **24**, 40, 63–9, 85n, 128, 137, 142, 170, 174, 176; **25**, 7, 20, 51, 64, 73–80, 98, 127, 171, 182, 200; **26**, 41, 126, 131, 134n, 135, 137, 152, 163n, 172, 179, 184n; **27**, 1–9, 131, 135n, 137, 144, 146, 150, 191; **28**, 56, 149, 153, 174, 177, 180, 181; **29**, 52, 82, 120, 163, 164, 174; **30**, 7, 18, 169, 170, 179n, 193, 194, 200, 206, 208, 209; **31**, 11, 58, 112, 116, 118–19, 169, 174, 187, 195; **32**, 184n, 212, 217, 220, 229, 242, 244; **33**, 40n, 121, 131, 160, 167, 168, 183–4; **34**, 62, 82, 93–104, 185, 186, 187–9, 194; **35**, 19, 28, 36, 38, 39, 40, 44, 52, 58, 156, 178, 184, 185, 186, 188, 189; **36**, 1, 10, 14, 21, 25, 31n, 53n, 55, 61, 101, 121, 127, 128, 161, 169, 178, 190, 191, 195; **37**, 115, 193, 212, 213, 218, 219; **38**, 28, 29, 34, 171, 175n, 220, 221, 237, 238n, 241–3; **39**, 2, 31–3, 39, 76n, 95n, 105n, 119, 220, 246; **40**, 4, 6, 12–14, 51–2, 147, 152–3, 178–9, 211n, 228; **41**, 13, 110, 134, 188, 191, 211, 230n, 234, 239; **42**, 9, 11, 39, 40, 57n, 157, 158, 196, 199, 207, 213; **43**, 39, 79, 110n, 112, 184, 192, 196, 203, 213–14, 219, 227, 230–2, 269–70; **44**, 4, 13, 36, 89, 96, 106n, 135, 137n, 158, 200, 210, 211, 215; **45**, 53, 93, 116, 117, 119, 123, 153, 154, 157, 166, 171, 172, 173, 177, 186, 200; **46**, 113, 115, 134n, 154, 192, 198–9, 203, 208, 217, 237, 238, 240, 255, 256; **47**, 11, 62, 88–9, 95–6, 100–2, 105–6, 111, 211, 217, 219, 235, 239n; **48**, 3, 27, 164, 189, 229, 232, 234–5, 237, 251; **49**, 1–14, 15–25, 27–44, 204n, 240–5, 253, 273, 276, 277–8, 280, 284, 285, 330, 331; **50**, 3, 10, 16–17, 34, 36–7, 132n, 226–7, 232–3, 236, 244, 263, 272, 273n, 275, 286–7; **51**, 3, 25, 29, 30, 35, 39, 64, 196, 201, 266–7, 283, 285, 311, 328, 331, 332, 333, 336; **52**, 19, 76, 81, 86, 87, 90, 96n, 137, 140, 148, 200, 247–8, 263–4, 280, 284, 289, 292, 305–6, 310; **53**, 3, 7, 16n, 32, 39–48, 58, 96, 130, 159, 162, 279, 282–3, 300–5, 333; **54**, 28n, 68–9, 117n, 118, 154n, 184, 225, 234, 236, 239, 256–8, 283, 290–1, 301, 306, 317, 344, 347, 356; **55**, 57, 64, 116n, 159, 193, 262, 289, 305, 330–2, 346, 351–2, 355, 360, 382, 391–2; **56**, 62, 106,

107, 114, 122, 138, 141, 237, 249, 251, 296, 301, 311, 341, 347, 354, 356; **57**, 174, 216, 229, 250, 259, 284, 285, 287, 289, 295, 306, 326, 328, 330, 339; **58**, 11, 63, 100–101, 121, 141, 185, 201, 260, 268, 305, 314; **59**, 6, 7, 10, 11, 12, 22n11, 42, 47, 72, 74, 187, 201, 206n39, 233, 234, 238, 258, 293, 299, 327–8, 344, 347, 359–60, 362, 364, 369; **60**, 62, 63, 65, 66, 67, 75, 201–2, 203, 206, 212, 260, 262, 270, 272–4, 275–8, 285, 286, 326–7, 339, 355, 356

Sir Thomas More, **37**, 215; **38**, 101–14 *passim*, 117; **39**, 250; **40**, 225; **41**, 216, 233; **42**, 77–84, 119, 121, 127; **43**, 240, 262–3, 270; **45**, 157; **46**, 225, 257n; **49**, 323; **51**, 334; **52**, 315, 323; **53**, 71n; **54**, 90, 91, 96, 98–9, 303, 351; **57**, 225–35; **59**, 5, 6, 9, 10, 34, 69–78, 78n15, 151, 155, 214, 218, 320, 376, 377–8, 382; **60**, 327

Taming of the Shrew, The, **1**, 1, 52, 116 (2); **2**, 19, 112, 123, 129, 152; **3**, 24–5, 31, 47, 95, 113, 114, 116, 118, 150; **4**, 59, 94, 110, 113–14, 120, 123, 125, 126, 127, 128, 149, 162, 163; **5**, 52, 108, 109, 111, 112, 114, 115, 116, 117, 119, 120, 140; **6**, 117, 118, 119, 120, 121, 124, 125, 148; **7**, 96, 98, 99, 105, 108, 109, 110, 111, 115, 123, 125, 126–7, 151; **8**, 7, 43, 76, 79, 118, 119, 120, 123, 124, 142–3; **9**, 85n, 103, 104, 111, 113, 117, 119, 120, 121, 152, 153; **10**, 64, 66, 78, 79, 80, 83, 84, 86n, 87n, 115, 117, 119, 120, 121, 122, 124, 125, 139; **11**, 87, 119–22; **12**, productions, Connecticut, 118, elsewhere, 109–13, 115, 118; *Taming of a Shrew*, 141; **13**, 153, 167 and n; productions, 125, 128, 130–2, 135; **14**, 18, 32, 147, 152–3, 156; productions, 117, 119–20, 122–3; **15**, 126, 132–5, 137–9, 141, 145–6; **16**, 79, 132, 134–5, 137, 143–51, 153–4, 167, 175; **18**, 159–60, 170; **19**, 33n, 135–6, 146, 150; **20**, 86, 123–5, 128, 140, 152, 165, 176; **21**, 107, 130, 131, 147, 150–1; **22**, 125, 127, 129, 151, 152, 153, 178–9; **23**, 4, 10, 93–4, 143, 185; **24**, 142, 156; **25**, 179; **26**, 104, 106; **27**, 2, 106, 107, 108, 109, 132, 135, 136, 142, 146; **28**, 77, 78, 160, 172, 178; **30**, 183, 209; **31**, 5n, 116, 119, 165; **32**, 38, 64n, 201–2, 243; **33**, 36n, 55–56, 189; **34**, 91, 165, 171, 186; **35**, 2n, 3, 88, 123, 126, 127, 156, 158; **36**, 2, 82, 162, 173, 180, 184–6; **37**, 1, 2, 4, 6, 9, 11, 23–40 *passim*, 163, 165–8, 194, 203, 204, 207, 208, 211, 217; **38**, 31, 182n, 232, 238n; **39**, 4, 33, 34, 75, 79, 97, 99, 124n, 205, 213, 225, 236, 250; **40**, 6, 15, 19, 169–71, 173, 175, 211, 222–3, 228; **41**, 14, 168–70, 189, 196, 198, 203–4, 236; **42**, 13, 15, 108, 109n, 157, 193, 201; **43**, 22, 32, 37, 85, 214, 227, 230, 233, 237, 254, 268; **44**, 18, 23, 131, 135, 142, 158, 201, 210, 256; **46**, 76, 81, 85, 129, 173, 175, 177, 199, 208, 211, 221, 225, 240n, 241, 254n; **47**, 48, 95, 106, 162, 163n, 217, 224; **48**, 136, 164, 174, 189, 235–6, 241, 243, 273; **49**, 19, 168n, 255–7, 278–9, 292; **50**, 233–4, 245, 286; **51**, 47, 181, 182, 187, 267, 285, 318–19, 336; **52**, 73, 76, 229, 263–4, 279, 293, 297; **53**, 15n, 16n, 29, 181–3, 283, 294, 337–8; **54**, 28, 118, 154, 265, 265, 291–2, 303, 312; **55**, 19, 116n, 191–3, 194n, 285, 309, 348, 362, 378, 383; **56**, 45, 166, 247, 297, 314, 339–40, 344, 347; **57**, 229, 259, 261, 296, 312, 327, 330, 339; **58**, 4, 57, 130, 131, 143, 153, 305, 339, 340; **59**, 7, 74, 141, 186, 198, 201, 203, 207, 344–5, 350, 362, 367, 369, 381; **60**, 72–3, 77, 79, 81, 83, 84–101, 101n42, 203–5, 292–3, 305–6, 327, 335, 362, 367

Tempest, The, **1**, 9, 10, 47–9, 53, 54, 109, 113, 116, 119; **2**, 5, 112, 124, 127, 128; **3**, 17, 19, 30, 54, 56, 67, 109, 113, 116, 117; **4**, 8, 11, 15, 24, 42, 51, 80, 88, 111, 115n, 145, 147, 151, 152; **5**, 3, 52, 78, 112, 113, 115, 131–2; **6**, 114–15, 117, 118, 120; **7**, 10, 14, 22, 96, 97, 98, 99, 103–4, 106n, 108, 111, 115, 116, 129, 132, 137, 140; **8**, 37, 58, 61, 65, 74–5, 76–7, 78, 80, 113, 115–16, 117n, 123, 133, 140, 144; **9**, 79n, 82, 85n, 107, 110n, 115, 116, 119, 134, 140, 151; **10**, 20, 23, 25n, 76n, 77, 83, 86n, 110, 117, 118, 121, 124, 137, 141, 150; **11**, 25–7, 30, 42, 50–2, 56–7, 59n, 65–8, 70–1, 74, 76, 119, 122–3, 128, 142n; Frank Martin's operatic version, 117; Stratford-upon-Avon production noted, 134–5; **12**, 73–4, 85, 144–5; translation, 115; productions, 110, 112, 117; **13**, 30, 39n, 58–9, 61, 137–8, 139, 142; productions, 70, 127–8, 130; Dryden's adaptation, 137–40; translation, 154; **14**, 15, 20, 74, 148, 154, 156, 160n, 163; productions, 117, 119, 120, 122–3; translation, 122; **15**, 5, 6, 27, 100, 102, 106, 108, 116–17, 120, 135, 139, 145–6, 162, 173, 181; **16**, 11, 12, 14, 84, 136, 153–4, 170–1; **17**, 29n, 33 and n, 35–6, 36n, 42, 151 and n, 164, 171, 209, 215–16, 218, 233; **18**, 3, 4, 53, 97–9, 172, 174, 180; opera versions, 75–7, 79, 86, 94; **19**, 56, 59, 93n, 137, 148, 151; **20**, 75, 84, 107, 151, 154, 157, 166–7, 169; **21**, 25, 127, 128, 140, 153; **22**, 2, 29, 48–53, 56, 62, 98, 127, 164–5, 176, 178; **23**, 29, 80, 111, 149, 156, 157, 173, 175n, 177n; **24**, 30, 33, 46, 105, 106, 112, 117, 129, 130, 131, 150, 151, 167, 168, 178; **25**, 83, 91, 113–23, 125–35, 177–8; **26**, 33, 34, 42, 46, 48, 64, 66, 111n, 130, 153, 163, 168; **27**, 60, 88, 89, 108, 162, 167, 170, 172, 183, 184, 191; **28**, 36, 37, 38n, 54, 59, 117–23, 137, 159, 160, 161; **29**, 1, 2, 5, 6, 7, 9, 10, 63–7, 74, 77, 83, 138, 158, 159, 165, 169, 176, 184; **30**, 7, 27, 120, 121, 147–55, 182, 190, 191, 193, 195, 197, 202, 206n; **31**, 6, 33n, 56, 65, 77–83, 116, 117–18, 119–20, 124, 166, 167, 176, 180–1; **32**, 49, 53, 177–87, 201, 202–4, 212, 213, 218, 246; **33**, 36, 80, 130, 132, 188, 189, 191, 196, 202; **34**, 164, 174, 176, 177, 178, 183, 184; **35**, 12n, 27, 37, 39, 40, 47, 68, 106, 113–18, 185; **36**, 10, 31–7, 84, 104, 107–20, 154, 162, 164, 167–8, 170, 176, 177, 180, 189; **37**, 22, 73, 74, 133–40 *passim*, 193; **38**, 59, 143, 167–73 *passim*, 188, 220, 253; **39**, 34, 35, 95n, 96, 115, 116, 118, 123, 128, 130, 131, 159–68 *passim*, 171, 179, 182, 208, 210, 221, 223, 226; **40**, 6–7, 155, 186, 194, 199, 206, 209, 215; **41**, 3, 7, 9–11, 24–5, 46, 62, 91–102, 110, 189, 198, 204, 221, 224–5, 238–9, 240n, 243–4; **42**, 56n, 139, 144, 146, 148, 158, 163, 167, 170, 183, 192–3; **43**, 1–41, 69, 78, 91, 129, 184, 213–15, 220, 222, 227, 230–2, 241, 262; **44**, 17, 32, 77, 83, 96, 128n, 201, 209, 222, 224, 241; **45**, 63n, 67, 71, 72, 100n, 115, 130, 154, 155, 160, 162, 169–73, 189, 190; **46**, 70, 105, 106, 147, 157, 158, 199–200, 203, 207, 209, 210, 213, 214, 238, 244n; **47**, 101, 104, 106, 121, 124, 139, 202–5, 212, 217–19, 224, 229–30; **48**, 2, 32, 41n, 84, 123, 135–45, 147–54, 155–62, 169, 236, 241, 244, 247, 248, 273; **49**, 21n, 99, 245–50, 253, 260, 279, 282, 293, 294, 327, 333; **50**, 6, 16, 24, 35, 39, 82, 148, 187–99, 234, 239, 246, 262, 265, 267, 269; **51**, 14, 32, 33, 41, 42, 79–94, 101, 176n, 178, 179, 267, 272, 278, 279, 281, 283, 300, 320, 334; **52**, 24, 76, 82, 143, 145, 149, 185, 189, 190, 193, 197, 215, 237–8, 241, 255, 264–6, 270–2, 279–80, 286, 299, 310; **53**, 1, 3, 4, 6, 8, 17n, 39, 53, 57–8, 127–50, 164–74, 176, 186, 217, 266–7, 283–4, 289–91, 294, 297, 301, 321, 324–5, 332, 335–7; **54**, 15, 66n, 73,

Shakespeare, William (*cont.*)
154, 198–9, 207, 211, 223–33, 242, 263, 288, 292, 300, 301, 308, 311, 312, 314–15, 321, 323, 339, 340; **55**, 46n, 156, 191, 237, 243–56, 286, 309, 316, 335, 342–4, 348, 353, 358–9, 371, 380; **56**, 118, 146–60, 165, 166, 219, 256, 269, 271–3, 276, 297, 301, 303, 314, 315, 319, 327, 328, 339, 344, 348; **57**, 40, 264, 296, 306, 319, 337–8; **58**, 2, 10, 11, 99, 128, 141, 149, 160, 269, 306, 314, 328, 330, 348, 349, 357; **59**, 11, 41, 47, 79–90, 90n37, 91–105, 105n19, 143, 152, 184, 201, 202n25, 211, 239–53, 253n102, 257, 319–20, 345, 347, 352, 363, 367, 370; **60**, 67, 123, 197–200, 201, 270, 315, 314–15, 316, 327, 331, 347, 356

Timon of Athens, **1**, 52, 110, 113, 123; **3**, 8, 30, 117, 137; **4**, 7, 19, 21, 22, 24, 28, 111, 126, 127, 150; **5**, 2, 83, 89, 115, 130, 137, 142, 145; **6**, 75–8, 120, 152, 160, 171; **7**, 10, 114, 115, 135; **8**, 16, 143, 154; **9**, 111, 114, 143; **10**, 71, 77, 86n, 87n, 117, 121, 141, 149; **11**, 21, 56, 59n, 63, 66, 70, 123, 145; Old Vic production reviewed, 128–32; **12**, 36–8, 73, 134–5, 137; **13**, 1, 31, 49–50, 51–2, 158, 160; New Arden edition reviewed, 164; **14**, 73, 142; **15**, 80n, 102, 122, 125; **16**, 13, 14, 54, 83–94, 133–4; **17**, 137, 157, 154–5; **18**, 7, 48, 55, 63, 94–5, 158, 168–9; opera version, 78; **19**, 26, 114, 115–16, 117–18, 130, Pls. IX, Xa; **20**, 75, 84, 91, 150; **21**, 2, 3, 25, 88, 138, 146, 147, 148, 150, 152, 158; **22**, 156, 162; **23**, 4, 16, 24, 98–100, 119, 138, 140, 141, 154–5, 159, 180; **25**, 2, 63, 198; **26**, 8, 9, 58, 59, 60, 89–94, 106, 156, 160; **27**, 111–27; **28**, 157, 165; **29**, 84, 103–16, 119, 120, 122; **30**, 203, 207; **31**, 3, 5, 6, 7, 10, 12, 16, 169, 172–3, 174, 181, 182; **32**, 213, 236; **33**, 182, 187, 191, 201; **34**, 142, 153–4, 165, 175–6, 183, 184, 190; **35**, 76, 121, 176; **36**, 87n, 160, 164; **38**, 174n, 184n, 198, 220; **39**, 35, 235; **40**, 122, 226n; **41**, 25, 198, 204, 233, 237, 239; **42**, 158; **43**, 85, 138–9, 215, 230; **44**, 10n, 15, 18, 201, 210, 212, 234, 236; **45**, 91, 98–100, 134–7, 139, 185, 186, 200; **46**, 61, 91n, 130, 200, 257n; **47**, 232, 234, 241; **48**, 166, 180, 253, 277; **49**, 231, 279, 323; **50**, 20n, 21, 128, 247; **51**, 21–2, 24–5, 82, 304, 325; **52**, 76, 129, 265; **53**, 249–52, 301; **54**, 15, 154n, 202, 206–11, 293; **55**, 13, 40n, 160, 353, 370; **56**, 173n, 215–26, 227–35, 339, 356; **57**, 335; **58**, 141, 161, 306, 345–55, 357; **59**, 5, 6, 22n11, 75, 77, 130, 132, 381; **60**, 64, 66–7, 123, 206, 284, 314, 331, 358

Titus Andronicus, **1**, 9, 17–24, 58, 64, 75; **2**, 36, 134; **3**, 24, 47, 108, 131, 136, 138, 146–7; **4**, 59, 143, 145; **5**, 4, 53, 150–1; **6**, 54, 58, 155, 156, 160, 169; **7**, 6, 135; **8**, 55, 123, 143, 154, 157, 159; **9**, 41, 83, 85n, 104, 135, 151; **10**, 1–3, 9, 31, 32, 34, 39, 44–7, 40–8, 49n, 60, 61–2, 64–8, 69, 70–2, 78, 86n, 87n, 124, 126–8, 134, 149, 146n, 155, 157; **11**, 21, 59, 87, 123, 128, 135, 154, 155; **12**, 135–6, 145; productions, Peter Brook's, 78, Old Vic, 120; **13**, 30, 156; productions, 70, 124; **14**, 35–7, 44n, 102, 104–8, 109n, 158, 163; **15**, 23–5, 89, 115, 141, 151; **16**, 38, 165, 167; **17**, 51 and n, 140n; **18**, 149; Q1 (1594), 31; **19**, 90, 120, 142, 147; **20**, 20; **21**, 71, 88, 107, 150; **22**, 93, 94, 151, 167; **23**, 9, 10, 35, 121, 123, 138, 142–3, 161n, 180; **24**, 148, 153, 175; **25**, 176, 188; **26**, 98, 108, 141, 142, 148–50, 151, 152, 159, 160, 179; **27**, 1–9, 11–19, 135, 136, 159, 191; **28**, 71–4, 155, 180; **29**, 118, 121, 163, 170, 185; **30**, 18, 103, 104, 193, 203; **31**, 3, 7, 8, 9, 11, 12, 23–32, 152, 163, 172, 173, 185, 187, 198; **32**, 95, 230, 234; **33**, 186, 191, 203; **34**, 63, 71, 72, 91, 97, 155–7, 158, 163, 190, 193; **35**, 48, 120, 121, 122, 125, 142, 143, 144, 178, 186; **36**, 4, 14, 74, 164, 171, 173, 175, 190; **37**, 182–4, 190; 212, 217; **38**, 34, 217–223, 238n, 246, 247; **39**, 35, 104–8, 123–5, 215, 217, 237; **40**, 199, 205, 225–6; **41**, 111, 117, 133–5, 144, 159, 178–81, 193, 209, 211, 230, 233n, 238; **42**, 53, 57n, 168, 182, 208, 213; **43**, 203, 215, 268; **44**, 18, 136n, 201, 207, 208, 210, 220, 236; **45**, 160, 166, 180, 186, 188, 200; **46**, 110, 200, 201; **47**, 29, 111, 119, 121, 131, 136, 224; **48**, 24, 38, 39, 40–3, 46, 196, 236, 240, 241, 244, 250, 264; **49**, 6, 7, 15–19, 21, 36, 42, 88, 232, 247, 310–12, 316, 317, 319; **50**, 161, 234–5, 246, 287–8; **51**, 30, 40, 143, 177, 183, 201, 279, 283, 324; **52**, 61, 76, 78, 105, 141, 164, 189, 214, 265, 271, 279; **53**, 3, 36, 39, 175–6, 181–2, 328, 335; **54**, 26, 28, 34, 35, 44, 121, 293, 301, 302, 317, 318–19; **55**, 19, 24, 159, 163, 169, 199–208, 257, 271, 279–82, 333, 335, 349, 359, 381; **56**, 1–26, 138, 146, 219, 221, 297–8, 304, 305, 312, 329, 339; **57**, 221, 284, 297, 302, 330, 335, 336; **59**, 2, 5, 6, 41, 42, 73, 256, 347, 363, 367, 372, 376n2; **60**, 62, 64–5, 66, 303–4, 307–9, 358, 360, 366

Troilus and Cressida, **1**, 52, 59, 72; **2**, 11, 59, 141, 142, 151–2, 153; **3**, 19, 29, 31, 37, 44, 45, 50, 66, 118, 137, 139, 140; **4**, 6, 14, 19, 21, 22, 24, 51, 144, 149, 150, 152, 156; **5**, 5, 53, 89, 120, 144, 145; **6**, 18, 22, 23, 98, 120, 151, 155, 157, 170–1; **7**, 10, 24, 31, 46, 81n, 107, 111, 112, 132, 134, 149, 151–2; **8**, 2, 10, 11–12, 28–30, 33–4, 35, 55, 61, 67–8, 98n, 124, 136, 139, 146–7, 155; **9**, 11, 15, 77, 82, 83, 85n, 110n, 113, 115, 120, 134, 136–7, 142, 143, 144; **10**, 17, 86n, 115, 119, 123, 130–1, 134, 136, 146n, 155, 157; **11**, 59n, 62, 137, 144, 154; **12**, 44, 59–60, 74, 133–6, 146; translation, 115; production, 113; **13**, 31, 43, 156–8, 168; productions, 132, 135; **14**, 95–6, 139, 141–2, 164–5; productions, 116, 122; Stratford-upon-Avon production, 129–37 *passim*; **15**, 24, 85, 115, 125, 142, 145, 151, 167–8, 179; **16**, 72, 84, 94, 132, 136, 138, 147, 159, 179; **17**, 91, 114, 117, 137–8, 158n, 160, 164, 210, 215, 223–4, 237; **18**, 1, 42, 46, 49, 53, 163–4, 174; opera version, 76; **19**, 28–9, 133–5, 152–3, 161–2; **20**, 54, 81n, 90, 126, 129–30, 145, 154, 156–7, 164, 174; **21**, 11n, 113, 131, 134, 141, 150, 155, 160, 161; **22**, 5, 32, 137–8, 139, 142–4, 154, 156, 159–60, 164, 166, 168, 176; **23**, 6, 9, 13, 15, 17, 19, 20, 23, 24, 33, 55, 60, 97, 117, 140, 150, 161, 179; **24**, 148, 150, 152, 153, 170, 174, 175; **25**, 1, 2, 6, 7, 8, 9, 10, 11–25, 63, 64, 67–8, 69, 70, 174, 175, 176, 184, 196, 197; **26**, 7, 9, 38, 90, 100, 155, 159, 179; **27**, 22, 59n, 69, 119, 127, 166, 176; **28**, 39, 48, 49, 112, 162, 168, 177; **29**, 8, 9, 82, 83, 84, 87, 121, 162–3, 181, 184, 185; **30**, 6, 7, 87n, 88, 136, 174–6, 179n, 184, 186, 192; **31**, 3, 5, 6, 10, 26, 53–4, 60, 61, 99, 116, 124, 168, 169, 176, 181, 182–3, 189; **32**, 184n, 212, 215, 217, 220, 222, 229–30, 241; **33**, 200, 207; **34**, 7–8, 9n, 23, 26, 88, 163; **35**, 9n, 115, 141, 149, 160, 169, 185, 190; **36**, 4, 8, 85–95, 100, 159, 160, 164, 169, 185; **37**, 99, 144, 158n, 194, 195, 205, 207, 208; **38**, 49, 128, 177n, 182n, 184n, 222–39, 35, 58, 64, 113, 152, 191, 203, 205, 218n, 219n, 250; **40**, 77–8, 82, 207–8, 210, 223, 232; **41**, 63–76, 190, 199, 201, 203–5, 230n, 235, 237, 240n, 243, 245n; **42**, 15, 159, 173, 180, 181, 188, 210; **43**, 88, 101, 219, 220, 232, 238, 250, 269; **44**, 13n, 32, 49n, 134, 136n, 137n, 172, 183, 213, 217, 221; **45**, 76, 85n, 94, 155, 156, 161, 168, 188; **46**, 73,

75, 133, 151, 155, 157, 206, 207, 208, 210, 230, 256; **47**, 121–4, 202, 233, 241, 243, 274; **48**, 4, 174, 236–7, 243, 254, 255, 260, 278; **49**, 75, 279, 304; **50**, 22, 24, 30, 144, 211–15, 235, 238, 241, 277–9; **51**, 34, 149, 184, 185, 187, 267, 272, 294, 303, 305–6; **52**, 28n, 76, 135, 188, 271, 293–4, 304–7, 315n; **53**, 11, 39, 244, 257–61, 284, 293, 296, 323–4, 341–2; **54**, 28, 37n, 114, 253–4, 293, 306; **55**, 347, 355, 358, 369–70, 372, 382; **56**, 103–4, 356; **57**, 143, 215, 228, 231, 244, 305, 332, 337; **58**, 306, 324, 336; **59**, 15, 73, 74, 76, 141, 143, 201, 236, 237, 320, 347, 348, 371, 373; **60**, 85n3, 310, 328, 335, 356, 368–9

Twelfth Night, **1**, 83, 105, 109, 113, 114, 115 (3); **2**, 5, 7, 8, 122; **3**, 28, 32, 53, 54, 56, 80, 111, 113, 116, 117, 118; **4**, 29, 87, 118, 123, 126, 127, 162; **5**, 65, 107, 108, 109, 111, 112, 113, 115, 116, 117, 119, 120, 121–4, 142; **6**, 20, 44, 118, 120, 121, 122, 123, 124, 125, 160; **7**, 26, 99, 104, 108, 109, 110, 111, 113, 114, 116, 131; **8**, 2, 3, 4, 6, 7–8, 40, 41, 61, 67, 68n, 69–73, 76, 77, 80, 118, 119, 120, 123, 124, 125, 126, 132; **9**, 107, 111, 113, 114, 115, 116, 117, 119, 120, 122, 136, 141–2, 145, 152n; **10**, 86n, 111, 115, 117, 120, 121, 122, 123, 135, 146, 149n, 150; **11**, 21, 63, 66, 87, 117, 118, 120–2, 137, 148; **12**, 36, 63n, 126–7, 146; productions, Anouilh's adaptation, 112, others, 109–10, 113, 115–16, 118–19, 120–1, Stratford-upon-Avon (1958), 126–9, 130n; **13**, 30, 39, 153, 159; Pelican edition reviewed, 165; productions, 125 128, 131–2, 134–5; **14**, 15, 23, 148, 153–4; productions, 117, 119–25, 164; Stratford-upon-Avon production, 129–33 *passim*; translation, 123; **15**, 1, 5, 7, 9, 10, 55–6, 89, 112, 131, 133–5, 137, 140–1, 144–6, 162, 168; **16**, 56n, 71–2, 74, 78, 132–6, 138, 159; **17**, 28, 79, 140, 144 and n, 147, 157–8, 171, 175–6, 178, 192, 209; **18**, 52, 158–9, 160–1, 173, 178, 180; opera versions, 75, 86–7; **19**, 136–7; **20**, 76, 80, 85, 89, 125, 128, 134–5, 153, 169; **21**, 128, 130, 131, 139, 152; **22**, 7, 11, 12, 44, 150, 153, 154, 178; **23**, 7, 15, 28–9, 47, 71, 132, 133, 134–5, 140, 144, 151; **24**, 24, 29, 172; **25**, 50, 63, 64, 86, 109, 161, 164, 166–7, 171, 178, 179, 190; **26**, 111n, 135, 152, 154; **27**, 82, 91, 107n, 108, 110, 131, 141, 165, 166, 172, 189, 192; **28**, 77, 78, 79, 80, 137, 144, 159, 162; **29**, 42, 43, 44, 46, 137, 141, 143–4, 161, 162, 173, 175, 177, 179, 180; **30**, 5, 122, 182, 184, 206n; **31**, 30, 55, 56, 58, 116–17, 121, 124, 174, 177, 186, 189, 197; **32**, 1–10 *passim*, 15–26 *passim*, 39, 41, 49, 50, 53, 68–72, 73–8, 79–84, 85–104, 152, 155n, 216, 217, 230–1, 246; **33**, 16n, 73, 160, 166, 170–1, 196; **34**, 91, 111–19, 121–9, 142, 143, 149, 158, 162, 172, 173, 178; **35**, 1, 7, 13, 16, 17, 24n, 37, 40, 71, 79–86, 87, 90, 93–7, 98, 124, 127–150, 158, 159, 167–8; **36**, 65, 83, 92, 143n, 159, 160, 161, 166, 169; **37**, 1–5, 30n, 39, 55, 71, 161, 163–6, 188; **38**, 29, 59, 99, 175n, 182n, 239n, 252; **39**, 7, 35, 36, 64, 96, 114, 118, 119, 125, 251; **40**, 93, 129, 190, 199, 203, 206–7, 210, 213–14, 217, 219, 223, 228, 230–1; **41**, 25, 28, 55–62, 165–8, 190, 213, 221–2, 226; **42**, 159, 167; **43**, 34, 215–16, 219, 226, 232, 242; **44**, 10, 106n, 128n, 131, 138, 139, 141, 175, 201, 208, 223, 234; **45**, 115, 121, 123, 126, 156, 160, 178, 190; **46**, 6, 23–34, 119, 192, 203, 208, 211, 227, 247; **47**, 92–4, 96, 98, 102, 104, 106, 161, 169, 212, 218–19, 226, 228, 241; **48**, 4, 18n, 78, 135, 164, 167–9, 205–7, 233, 237, 245, 246, 249, 255, 283; **49**, 276, 278, 279–80, 306, 319; **50**, 4n, 10, 22, 65–80, 126, 231, 233, 235, 238, 245, 276; **51**, 29, 35, 37, 48, 260, 268, 280, 285, 324–4; **52**, 16, 25–6, 28n, 86, 120–32, 135, 235–7, 265, 272, 275, 285–6, 288, 296; **53**, 1, 3, 4, 6, 98, 262–3, 284–5, 297–8, 307, 325, 344; **54**, 67–8, 196, 239, 274, 294–5, 322; **55**, 159, 188–9, 309–10, 333–4, 337, 372, 376, 383, 390; **56**, 73, 84n, 95, 105, 106, 118, 172, 174, 176–9, 237, 256–61, 263, 272, 283, 298, 345, 347; **57**, 19, 39, 210, 220, 229, 268, 276, 297, 305, 329; **58**, 1, 11, 101–105, 125, 127, 199–207, 209, 264, 269, 277–9, 306, 324, 325, 342, 350, 351, 357; **59**, 47, 49–62, 62n31, 63, 72, 73, 76, 77, 143, 181, 186, 198–200, 200n15, 201, 203, 204, 206n39, 206, 207–8, 211, 234, 257, 299, 313–16, 345, 353; **60**, 135n14, 158, 202–3, 209–12, 270, 299–300, 328, 356

Two Gentlemen of Verona, The, **1**, 113, 114, 115, 116; **2**, 149, 150; **3**, 14, 25, 117; **4**, 51, 109, 127; **5**, 113, 141; **6**, 44, 117, 124, 125; **7**, 16–17, 96, 97–8, 99, 100, 104, 115, 129, 137; **8**, 3, 4, 7, 8, 47, 63, 64, 66, 77, 121, 123, 124, 142; **9**, 111, 116; **10**, 64, 66, 77, 84, 86n, 117, 121, 150; **11**, 87, 118, 122; **12**, productions, Old Vic (1957), 85, 145, elsewhere, 110, 117, 119; **13**, 167n; **14**, 20, 153, 156, productions, 119, 123; Stratford-upon-Avon production, 129–37 *passim*; translation, 122; **15**, 27, 113, 118, 132, 136, 144, 148, 163; **17**, 41n, 44, 46, 63 and n, 92n, 156, 209; **18**, 159; **20**, 83–4, 95, 107–8, 125, 128, 152–3; **21**, 131; **22**, 35–41, 151, 152, 153, 177; **23**, 6, 91, 138, 143, 177n, 178, 180–1; **24**, 120, 129, 149, 160n, 176; **25**, 179; **26**, 104, 106; **27**, 108, 109, 131, 142, 163, 184, 188, 189; **28**, 46, 75, 76, 77, 78–9, 80, 161, 174; **29**, 9, 162, 180; **30**, 83; **31**, 33n; **32**, 63n, 64n; **33**, 56; **34**, 44; **35**, 37, 40, 87, 88–90, 141, 142, 143, 144, 158, 179, 184; **36**, 109, 113, 119n; **37**, 1, 5, 6, 13, 19–22, 55, 57–59, 64, 70, 74, 187; **38**, 242; **39**, 36, 124, 125, 130, 189, 220, 237; **40**, 10; **41**, 213, 234, 236n; **42**, 5, 160, 169; **43**, 268, 277; **44**, 17, 93, 127, 136n, 202, 218, 220, 256; **45**, 126, 156; **46**, 65, 115, 117, 201–2, 241n, 242, 244n; **47**, 218, 227; **48**, 185, 237, 245, 266, 274; **49**, 280, 291; **50**, 45, 201–3; **51**, 37, 268–9, 324; **52**, 23–4, 27, 28n, 76, 225, 230–1; **53**, 190, 234, 285; **54**, 56, 68, 225, 295, 324, 350; **55**, 26, 61, 247n, 334; **56**, 78, 344; **57**, 262; **58**, 307, 347–8, 357; **59**, 11, 299, 345–6; **60**, 328, 367

Two Noble Kinsmen, The, **31**, 4, 6; **32**, 213, 229, 238; **33**, 204; **34**, 57n; **35**, 175; **36**, 107, 108, 111, 115; **37**, 211; **38**, 139, 234; **40**, 169, 175–6; **41**, 190, 227, 233, 238; **42**, 57n, 160, 208; **43**, 43, 69–79, 81, 84–5, 89, 257–9; **44**, 50, 52, 232; **45**, 184, 200; **46**, 107, 113, 115, 214, 221, 225; **47**, 238n; **48**, 273, 277; **49**, 323, 324; **50**, 147, 289; **51**, 95, 104, 181, 305, 309, 327, 331; **52**, 81, 214, 279; **53**, 300, 338; **54**, 17, 24n, 25–6, 28n, 37n, 263, 301, 306, 314–15, 350; **55**, 334, 390; **56**, 41, 48, 67–73, 75–8, 302, 308, 327, 354; **57**, 335; **58**, 2, 38, 44, 320, 324, 347, 356; **59**, 5, 6, 42, 213, 214, 215, 216, 218, 219, 221, 222, 259; **60**, 293

The Winter's Tale, The, **1**, 47–9, 53, 113, 119; **2**, 5, 7, 8, 138, 153; **3**, 30, 56, 116, 117; **4**, 16, 17, 22, 24, 88, 115n, 118; **5**, 63, 64, 65, 79, 107, 108, 109, 112, 114–15, 119, 120, 136; **6**, 45, 82, 120, 125, 142–5; **7**, 9, 106n, 107, 109, 111, 112, 137, 146; **8**, 64–5, 74, 75, 78, 80, 119, 121, 136, 144; **9**, 44, 86–9, 101, 108, 110n, 115, 122, 140, 142; **10**, 28, 71, 73, 86n, 121, 122, 123, 125, 130, 145, 148; **11**, 22, 24–6, 30, 31–41, 48, 50–2, 55, 57, 59n, 64–7, 70, 74, 121–2, 143, 146; Pelican edition, 153; Phoenix Theatre production (1951–2) discussed, 39; **12**, 83, 144, 146;

Shakespeare, William (*cont.*)
productions, 109, 112, 115–16, 118; **13**, 107, 119, 149; productions, 125–6, 131–2; **14**, 96, 152, 163; productions, 116, 117, 121, 123; **15**, 5, 85, 108, 112, 115, 118, 120, 122, 137, 139, 141–2, 145, 174; **16**, 35–7, 89, 133, 135–6; **17**, 172–3; **18**, 1, 4, 7, 52, 64, 171–2, 187–8; **19**, 29, 138, 151; **20**, 76–7, 79, 85, 93n, 126, 144, 153, 156–7, 178; **21**, 127, 131, 140, 141, 152, 153, 162; **22**, 25, 48, 49, 50, 59–60, 63–6, 93–107, 164, 176; **23**, 17, 19, 25, 26, 32, 35, 59, 99n, 133–4, 138, 139, 155–6, 182, 183, 186; **24**, 13n, 16, 33–5, 46, 105, 108, 138, 150, 151, 172, 173; **25**, 91, 95n, 177; **26**, 33, 34, 38, 42, 45–6, 47–8, 64, 65–6, 91, 106, 111n, 132, 136, 153, 163, 164n; **27**, 57, 86, 89, 103, 108, 137, 139, 167, 168, 179, 180, 184; **28**, 59, 163, 166, 180; **29**, 1, 2, 4, 6, 7, 8, 9, 51n, 65, 67–8, 123, 165, 169; **30**, 7, 19, 27, 79, 147, 148, 150, 154, 173–4, 179n, 184, 195, 202, 205; **31**, 4, 6, 16, 33n, 35n, 65–75, 98, 115, 116, 117, 166, 167, 190; **32**, 109, 113, 213, 229; **33**, 7, 80, 121, 123–38, 182, 188, 189, 191, 193, 202, 204n, 210; **34**, 166–7, 171, 176, 178; **35**, 1, 2, 16, 17, 24n, 37, 39, 40, 141, 157n, 188; **36**, 60, 88, 98, 101, 106, 109, 113, 114, 164, 167, 169, 173, 176, 193; **37**, 73, 86, 115, 121n, 124, 158n, 182, 190, 191, 193, 194, 199, 210; **38**, 24, 29, 55, 70, 136, 143, 184n, 224, 236; **39**, 36, 37, 60, 96, 100, 101, 104, 106, 127, 128, 130–2, 218, 230, 234; **40**, 38–9, 76, 128, 155, 163, 167–8, 177–8, 190, 223, 226; **41**, 25, 36, 46, 92, 191, 201, 226, 238, 245n; **42**, 7, 139, 142, 143, 160, 171, 173, 179, 180, 183, 186; **43**, 41, 74, 78–9, 116, 128, 206, 216, 231, 234, 261; **44**, 3n, 11, 13n, 18, 22, 23, 83, 106n, 127, 128, 135, 159, 203, 212, 215, 222, 239, 240; **45**, 82–4, 130, 156, 160, 161, 170, 173, 189; **46**, 17, 30, 74–9, 81–90, 92, 105, 114, 123, 128, 151, 156, 169, 170–3, 175, 202, 207, 208, 213, 214, 228, 244n; **47**, 26, 64n, 124, 140, 218–19, 225, 229, 230, 252n; **48**, 109, 169, 237, 240, 266, 273; **49**, 199, 209n, 280, 294; **50**, 4, 13, 52, 84, 111–23, 144n, 148, 150, 235, 245, 267–9; **51**, 4, 21–2, 42, 43, 136, 176, 206, 209, 210, 216, 223, 227–8, 269, 271, 285, 286; **52**, 73, 76, 266–7, 274, 284, 288; **53**, 1–8, 11, 39, 55, 108, 109, 118, 119, 120–5, 154, 158, 175–6, 262–7, 285, 299, 343; **54**, 9, 24, 29n, 37n, 40–4, 154n, 199, 225, 242, 244, 252, 268, 295, 297, 299, 306, 314–15, 318, 320–1, 249, 356; **55**, 67, 91, 285–6, 292, 294, 309, 317, 321, 346, 349; **56**, 3, 10n, 80, 161, 165, 248n, 257, 269–71, 273, 298, 306, 308, 311, 318, 322; **57**, 39, 41, 297, 302; **58**, 10, 247–59, 307, 314; **59**, 72, 73, 78, 142, 143, 158n5, 174, 184, 201, 257, 299, 316–18, 319, 346, 353, 364, 373; **60**, 67, 123, 295, 328–9, 331, 332, 336

Poems, **1**, 60; **3**, 44, 48; **4**, 153–4; **5**, 53–4; **6**, 58; **9**, 82, 85; **15**, 15–17, 41–61 *passim*, 62–72, 73–80, 81–8 *passim*, 91, 94, 142, 178; **16**, 135, 166; **17**, 136, 92; **18**, 172–3, 178, 180, 187; **19**, 139–40, 161; **20**, 127, 129, 145, 158, 161, 170–2; **59**, 5, 42, 94

Lover's Complaint, A, **19**, 139; **20**, 172, 173; **21**, 146; **27**, 178; **38**, 176n; **39**, 250; **40**, 236; **41**, 104–5, 112, 242n; **42**, 74n, 213n; **43**, 260–1; **46**, 247–9; **51**, 175, 327; **52**, 302, 303n, 305; **56**, 349; **58**, 26, 23–30, 31, 32, 33; **59**, 356, 359; **60**, 350–1

Passionate Pilgrim, The, **11**, 59; **13**, 161, 163; **18**, 189–90; **20**, 172; **22**, 176, 182; **26**, 103–9; **39**, 250; **40**, 228; **43**, 260n; 46, 247–9; **56**, 349–50; **60**, 252–66

Phoenix and Turtle, The, **3**, 31; **7**, 137; **8**, 121, 144; **9**, 135; **10**, 141, 142; **15**, 25–8, 29–30, 85, 99–110 *passim*, 178; **18**, 173, 189; **19**, 139; **20**, 158, 161, 172, 173; **21**, 140; **24**, 153; **26**, 164; **28**, 163; **34**, 183; **36**, 40–2; **43**, 235, 241–2; **46**, 247–9; **48**, 260; **51**, 296; **52**, 285; **56**, 349; **59**, 356

Rape of Lucrece, The, **1**, 60, 75; **2**, 149; **3**, 17, 25, 31, 44, 45, 48, 138, 144, 145; **4**, 45–7, 48n, 79–80, 85, 96n, 156; **5**, 53, 147; **6**, 44, 58, 72, 155; **7**, 3, 37, 40, 47, 130; **8**, 28, 29–30, 33; **10**, 16, 72; **12**, 141; **14**, 92, 145, 166; **15**, 12, 22–5; **22**, 151, 176, 181; **23**, 2, 10, 30, 54–6, 58, 71, 73, 76, 121, 157; **24**, 139, 169; **26**, 177; **27**, 2, 178; **29**, 166; **30**, 6, 185; **31**, 8, 11, 12, 13–22, 25, 164; **32**, 73; **34**, 85–92; **36**, 169, 170, 177; **37**, 175, 176, 179, 182, 191; **38**, 116, 183n, 217; **39**, 124, 217, 244, 250; **40**, 206, 232; **41**, 103–18, 133, 142, 197, 205, 239–41; **42**, 9, 17n, 66, 67, 185; **43**, 83, 260–1; **44**, 33–9; **45**, 161; **46**, 7, 202, 241, 247–9; **47**, 129n, 131, 136n; **48**, 123, 246, 255; **49**, 40, 55, 295; **50**, 23, 25, 135–41, 143, 145, 235, 244; **51**, 39, 40n, 41, 176n, 269, 280; **52**, 281; **53**, 19n, 39, 296; **54**, 32, 33n, 44, 295, 298, 318–19, **55**, 61, 205, 341, 358; **56**, 60, 349, 350; **57**, 230, 302, 309, 310; **58**, 6, 7, 28; **59**, 42, 238, 355–6, 363; **60**, 252, 258, 259, 340

Sonnets, **1**, 60, 115, 116, 123–4; **2**, 109, 127, 140, 153; **3**, 8, 9, 10, 31, 48, 53, 110, 111, 133, 138, 139; **4**, 8, 85, 147, 148, 153–6; **5**, 53, 136–8, 139, 148–9; **6**, 35n, 39, 42, 48n, 58, 82, 83–4, 88n, 118, 125, 142–3, 159; **7**, 10, 46, 100, 104, 113, 115, 139; **8**, 28–9, 30, 44, 145, 149–50; **9**, 82, 84–5, 103, 104, 135, 136, 139, 143n; **10**, 116, 141, 143; **11**, 143; translations, 118, 120, 141, 147; **12**, translations, 114; Sonnet LV, 142; **13**, 31, 155; translations, 126, 130, 154; **14**, 80, 119, 121, 139, 145; **15**, editions, 11; text, date and order, 11–13; sources, 13–15; interpretation, 15–17, 41–61 *passim*; translation, 142; **16**, 135, 166; **17**, 136, Sonnet CXL, 92; **18**, 172–3, 178, 180, 187; **19**, 139–40, 161; French translations, 140; **20**, 127, 129, 145, 158, 161; New Cambridge edition, 170–2; **30**, 58, 62, 84, 85, 127n, 140, 235, 269–71, 278; **31**, 99, 127–40, 163–4, 191; **32**, 213–15, 224, 231, 236; **33**, 56, 58, 121, 124n, 192, 198, 199, 207–8; **34**, 35, 165, 171; **35**, 167, 168; **36**, 7, 173, 176, 177, 190; **37**, 107, 108, 190, 191; **38**, 10, 176, 184n; **39**, 250; **40**, 41–2, 45, 47, 204, 208, 236; **41**, 104–5, 112, 117, 142, 193, 206, 219, 239, 242; **42**, 6, 64–76, 85, 113, 183–5, 212–13; **43**, 123, 128, 233, 234, 235, 246, 260–1; **44**, 36, 91, 218, 223, 254; **45**, 94, 157, 160, 185, 203; **46**, 4, 35–49, 73, 112n, 129n, 139, 141, 225, 241, 247–9, 257; **47**, 129, 135, 44, 171, 219, 246–7, 252, 267; **48**, 29, 132, 188, 237, 242, 253–4, 267, 270; **49**, 55, 57, 103n, 17n, 280, 294–5, 320, 326, 329; **51**, 35, 152, 175, 294–5, 315, 326, 327; **52**, 266, 268–9, 281, 302–5; **53**, 33, 34, 37, 42n, 43, 44, 78n, 146, 162, 189–94, 223–4, 275, 285, 310–11; **54**, 28n, 116, 121, 124n, 150, 239n, 256, 295; **55**, 197, 198, 350; **56**, 64, 65, 72, 78, 85, 111, 112, 137, 205, 310, 311, 349–50; **57**, 230, 303, 304, 307–10; **58**, 32, 156; **59**, 225–37, 256, 257, 258, 359, 362; **60**, 87n7, 253, 258, 259, 260, 283, 332–4

Venus and Adonis, **1**, 60, 75; **2**, 136, 149; **3**, 17, 25, 31, 44, 45, 48, 53, 144; **4**, 5, 6, 51, 54, 79, 81, 82, 84, 156; **5**, 50, 53, 137, 147, 149; **6**, 44, 58, 72, 125, 155; **7**, 3, 36–47, 113, 137; **8**, 53, 55, 56, 144, 157, 159; **9**, 24, 26, 85, 103, 136; **10**, 16, 25n, 47, 60, 69; **12**, 135; **14**, 90, 91–2, 145, 154, 166; **15**, 12, 19–22; **21**, 149, 153; **22**, 151, 176, 181;

23, 10, 71, 73, 121, 157, 186; **25**, 3, 102; **26**, 103–9, 164, 172–3; **27**, 2, 130n, 156, 178; **28**, 163; **29**, 45; **30**, 189; **31**, 6, 13, 16, 33n, 164; 32, 73, 93n, 213, 215, 231, 232; **33**, 199; **34**, 174; **35**, 167; **36**, 169, 177; **39**, 250; **40**, 108, 228; **41**, 103, 133, 142, 206, 240; **42**, 63, 65, 67; **43**, 83, 87, 217, 235, 260–1; **44**, 140, 232, 255; **45**, 200; **46**, 247, 249n; **47**, 156n, 219, 250n; **48**, 237, 254; **49**, 6, 55, 63, 295; **50**, 21–2, 52, 84, 236, 268; **51**, 176n, 269, 276, 286; **52**, 303; **53**, 12–24, 25–38, 317, 332; **54**, 37n, 319; **55**, 334, 349; **56**, 28, 32, 34, 35, 37, 61, 349, 350; **57**, 232, 233, 310; **59**, 42, 238, 346; **60**, 252, 258, 259, 260, 340
miscellaneous
biographical studies, **1**, 61–2, 122–3; **3**, 1–12, 13, 50–1; **4**, 149–50; **5**, 139–40; **6**, 158–60; **7**, 138–40; **11**, 100; **12**, 95–106; **17**, 13–14
acting, views on, **17**, 191–5
astronomy and astrology, **17**, 138–41, 144–6
bestiary, **17**, 151
childhood background, **17**, 167–70
of commonwealth, **17**, 119
emblem, use of, **17**, 180n, 185–7
fairy tale, use of, **17**, 170–2
family of, **17**, 13–14
games, **17**, 176
geography, **17**, 41
'Hand D', **17**, 45–6
handwriting, **17**, 211
ideas of kingship and Wars of the Roses, **17**, 107–8
language, **17**, 223–5, 228–30, 232, 237–9
law, **17**, 73, 81, 83, 85–6
London, **17**, 9–10, 12
medicine, **17**, 152–66 *passim*
music, **17**, 214–17
printing of, **17**, 205, 207, 209–10, 212–13
'pressing to death' in, **17**, 91–2, 92n
as producer, **17**, 195–7
and religion, **17**, 126
and satire, **17**, 136–7
and the sea, **17**, 33n, 35–6
of state, **17**, 113
Stratford-on-Avon, **17**, 13
'tent' imagery, **17**, 201
witchcraft in, **17**, 171, 173
education and learning, **2**, 36–7, 107, 109, 110–14, 134
library of, **3**, 4–6, 5–8, 14–21; **4**, 8–9
knowledge of French, **6**, 80–3, 84–8; **7**, 5–6, 104, 140
knowledge of poetic theory, **7**, 6–8, 14–15, 22–3; **8**, 146–7; **10**, 4–6, 12–24, 27–8, 33–5, 40
portraits, **1**, 59, 62, 75, 82, 86; **3**, 4–5; *Shakespeare's Portraiture*, **3**, 5
Ashbourne **1**, 62
Chandos **1**, 62
Cosway, **1**, 62
Dexter, **1**, 62
Droeshout, **1**, 59, 62, 124; **3**, 4–5; **4**, 85; **6**, 61
Ely Palace, **1**, 86
Fairthorne's engraving, **1**, 62
Felton, **1**, 62
Gunther, **1**, 62
Jannssen, **1**, 62
Lumley, **1**, 62
Marshall's engraving, **1**, 62
Page, **1**, 62
Zoust, **1**, 62
Zuccaro, **1**, 62
'"Shakespearian" Additions in *The Booke of Sir Thomas More*', **2**, 62–5
Shalcross, Alan, **39**, 105n
Shale, Kerry, **52**, 256; **54**, 285
Shalvi, Alice, **20**, 154; **23**, 138; **27**, 176
Shambroom, Paul, **60**, 177–9
Shammas, Sam, **53**, 281
Shand, G. B., **39**, 247; **41**, 229n; **42**, 209n; **53**, 295; **54**, 338; **59**, 383; **60**, 360
Shand, G. P., **55**, 43n
Shand, George, **24**, 160
Shand, Jan, **41**, 186
Shandy, Walter, **46**, 235
Shank, John, **47**, 173; **58**, 226, 227, 234, 242
Shankar, D. A., **54**, 341
Shanker, Sidney, **4**, 147, 150; **30**, 182
Shanks, Michael, **59**, 203n30; **60**, 154, 155
Shannon, Edgar F., **56**, 127n
Shannon, Laurie J., **51**, 310; **52**, 279; **56**, 69n, 75n, 308; **58**, 311, 333
Shannon, Mike, **41**, 185
Shapiro, H., **49**, 136n
Shapiro, I. A., **1**, 6; **4**, 98, 148; **5**, 149; **6**, 159; **10**, 144; **12**, 22; **13**, 156; **16**, 168, 177–8; **21**, 142, 145, 155; **23**, 172; **38**, 42n; **40**, 148n; **41**, 1, 3, 5, 6; **42**, 186n; **51**, 143–4; **52**, 3, 4; **53**, 201n, 202, 204n
'The Bankside Theatres: Early Engravings', **1**, 25–37
'An Original Drawing of the Globe Theatre', **2**, 21–3
'The Significance of a Date', **8**, 100–5
'Shakespeare and Mundy', **14**, 25–33
Shapiro, James, **44**, 220; **45**, 186–7; **50**, 54n, 261; **51**, 8, 161n; **52**, 101, 206n, 207, 280; **54**, 185n; **58**, 8, 9
Shapiro, Michael, **25**, 192; **33**, 196; **37**, 179; **42**, 116n; **44**, 227–8; **49**, 290–1; **53**, 147n, 234n, 325
Shapiro, Morris, **43**, 112n
Shapiro, Stephen A., **19**, 126; **21**, 138
Shapiro, Susan C., **32**, 235
Shaqui, Ahmad, **36**, 4, 5, 10
Sharma, Ghanshiam, **42**, 178
Sharma, R. C., **29**, 164
Sharman, Nancy, **58**, 117
Sharon-Zisser, Shirley, **60**, 350–1, 353
Sharp, Cecil, **60**, 186, 187–8, 189n17, 191
Sharp, Corona, **36**, 170n, 177
Sharpe, Ella Freeman, **5**, 131–2
Collected Papers on Psycho-Analysis, **13**, 30, 39n
Sharpe, J. A., **50**, 70n
Sharpe, Jim, **52**, 297; **54**, 166n, 173n
Sharpe, K. M., **54**, 166n, 170n
Sharpe, Kevin, **38**, 21n; **41**, 196n; **43**, 244; **44**, 10n; **48**, 257; **55**, 231n; **56**, 217n; **57**, 71, 126
Sharpe, Peter, **58**, 233
Sharpe, Richard, **58**, 233
Sharpe, Robert Boies, **14**, 148; **44**, 151, 152, 153
Sharpe, William, **53**, 109n
Sharpham, Edward, **32**, 95; **49**, 97n, 105n 303; **56**, 120n; **59**, 71, 72, 77; **60**, 276

Sharps, Tristan, **57**, 291
Sharratt, Bernard, **35**, 12n
Shatterel, Edward, **58**, 242
Shatterel, Robert, **58**, 242
Shattuck, Charles H., **18**, 184; **20**, 167n, 169; **24**, 100n, 168; **25**, 115n, 119n; **28**, 174; **30**, 199; **32**, 15n, 19n, 20n, 21n, 22n, 23n, 24n; **34**, 186; **35**, 5–6, 8n, 9, n, 12; **36**, 75n, 76, 79, 82, 83; **45**, 27n; **49**, 126n; **50**, 278; **51**, 59n; **53**, 216n, 231; **56**, 133n; **57**, 127, 128
Shatz-Jacobsen, Claus, **48**, 263
Shaughnessy, Robert, **50**, 249; **53**, 329; **58**, 161, 358; **60**, 168, 354, 355
Shaw, Catherine M., **37**, 193; **60**, 109n33
Shaw, Charles, **58**, 108, 109
Shaw, D. J., **23**, 163n
Shaw, Fiona, **39**, 200; **41**, 169–70, 188; **42**, 154, 156, 158, 200; **43**, 254; **44**, 191; **48**, 228; **49**, 263–4, 266–7; **50**, 232; **51**, 211; **52**, 262, 292; **54**, 270; **56**, 343; **57**, 330; **58**, 263; **59**, 328; **60**, 78, 79, 82n43, 322
Shaw, George Bernard, **1**, 104, 121; **2**, 130; **3**, 115; **4**, 12, 17–18, 102, 120; **5**, 131, 132; **6**, 12, 121; **7**, 27, 29–30, 116, 122; **8**, 38; **9**, 16, 23; **10**, 149; **11**, 121; **12**, 139 and n; **14**, 4, 129, 137n; **16**, 10, 14, 16, 25, 168; **18**, 2, 7, 131, 134, 184; **20**, 81n; **21**, 113; **22**, 2, 3, 4, 8, 79; **23**, 39, 175; **24**, 37, 38, 40, 42, 154, 168; **25**, 1, 11, 45, 117, 166; **26**, 3; **27**, 34n; **28**, 143; **29**, 133, 134, 137, 145; **30**, 83; **32**, 15, 18, 26; **34**, 146; **35**, 1, 6, 8, 9, 175; **36**, 2, 133; **37**, 33, 34, 85, 170, 178; **38**, 200; **39**, 158n, 213, 236; **40**, 11, 12, 19; **41**, 64, 73, 169, 245; **42**, 6, 25, 32n, 109; **43**, 228; **46**, 8, 9, 145; **47**, 93, 108; **48**, 192, 227; **49**, 2, 7, 126n, 128; **50**, 31; **52**, 224, 288, 323; **53**, 5; **54**, 42, 76n; **55**, 354, 362; **56**, 135, 241, 243, 244, 403; **57**, 256, 274; **58**, 141, 150; **59**, 149
  Back to Methuselah, **4**, 106
  Caesar and Cleopatra, **6**, 140, 141, 145
  The Dark Lady of the Sonnets, **3**, 9
Shaw, Glen Byam, **2**, 16; **5**, 120, 124, 125, 126–7; **6**, 138; **7**, 125, 126; **8**, 123, 124; **9**, 119, 120, 124, 127, 128; **10**, 124, 132; **11**, 128, 132, 134–5, 135n; **12**, 78, 86, 119, 120; **13**, 134, 135; **14**, 127; **15**, 152; **16**, 19, 26; **27**, 145; **31**, 152; **33**, 27, 34; **37**, 51; **50**, 262
Shaw, Guy, **49**, 115n; **51**, 10n
Shaw, Ian, **59**, 342
Shaw, James, **58**, 298–307; **60**, 320–9
Shaw, John, **9**, 136; **21**, 136, 139; **22**, 173; **28**, 157; **32**, 8; **33**, 11n; **52**; **55**, 58n
  'The Staging of Parody and Parallels in *1 Henry IV*', **20**, 61–74
Shaw, Kevin, **43**, 211; **51**, 264; **54**, 287
Shaw, Marjorie, **57**, 115
Shaw, Michael, **50**, 227
Shaw, Owen, **56**, 237
Shaw, Robert, **32**, 233; **52**, 254
Shaw, Roy, **44**, 97n, 100n
Shaw, Sebastian, **18**, 74; **22**, 138, 142, 143; **24**, 117, 122, 123; **25**, 65; **38**, 212; **58**, 50
Shaw, W. David, **58**, 71
Shaw, William P., **57**, 145
Shaw-Parker, David, **43**, 201
Shawcross, J., **15**, 61n
Shawe-Taylor, Desmond, **51**, 10, 11, 107–123; **53**, 300
Shaxper, Leigh, **58**, 145
Shcheglov, I. L., **20**, 35, 40n
Shchepkina-Kupernik, T. L., **5**, 117; **6**, 125
Shcherbina, Dmitry, **60**, 299
Sheader, Timothy, **60**, 328
Sheals, Helen, **57**, 293
Shealy, Daniel, **53**, 166n
Shearer, Norma, **9**, 114; **18**, 73; **40**, 4; **49**, 153–4
Shearing, Dinah, **11**, 117
Shearman, John, **28**, 153
Shearsmith, Reece, **59**, 310–11
Sheavyn, Phoebe, **22**, 169
Shebalin, V. Y., **18**, 87
Sheehan, Patrick, **39**, 75n
Sheen, Erica, **46**, 214
Sheen, Michael, **47**, 217; **51**, 237–9; **52**, 256, 292–3
Sheerin, Blaithin, **55**, 323
Sheets, George, **46**, 61n
Sheffield Theatre Company, **58**, 306
Sheidley, William E., **47**, 232
Shekspirovski Sbornik, **2**, 126
Shelby, Lon R., **33**, 145n
Sheldon (steward of Stratford Manor Court), **12**, 97
Sheldon, Andrew, **42**, 158
Sheldon, Esther K., **18**, 184; **22**, 174
Sheldon, Michael, **32**, 221
Shell, Alison, **54**, 15; **55**, 377; **57**, 4; **60**, 342
Shellard, D. M., **49**, 230n, 255n
Shelley, David, **52**, 232–3, 251, 253
Shelley, Jonathan, **56**, 298; **57**, 297
Shelley, Mary, **56**, 150–4, 160; **60**, 330
Shelley, Paul, **42**, 155, 160; **53**, 245, 247, 277; **54**, 283
Shelley, Percy Bysshe, **7**, 30, 115; **12**, 85; **14**, 83; **15**, 26; **39**, 73; **40**, 200–1; **43**, 121; **48**, 160–1; **52**, 273; **53**, 105; **58**, 92; **59**, 93n4
Shelly, Jonathan, **60**, 324
Shelly, Mary, **53**, 166
Shelton, Ron, **60**, 143n5, 146
Shelton, Thomas, **28**, 59; **51**, 95–105
Shelving, Paul, **8**, 77
Shen, Ruan, **45**, 89n
Shendrikova, V., **39**, 83n, 84
Shentall, Susan, **9**, 114; **49**, 156
Shepard, Alan, **56**, 334
Shepard, Paul, **48**, 265
Shepard, Richard F., **55**, 125
Shepard, Warren V., **11**, 139
Shephard, Guy, **1**, 100, 102
Shepherd, Edward, **47**, 15n
Shepherd, Geoffrey, **32**, 166n; **44**, 85n; **50**, 196n; **55**, 217n
Shepherd, Jack, **50**, 201; **51**, 260, 268; **52**, 225; **53**, 279; **56**, 247, 294; **57**, 293; **58**, 302
Shepherd, Mike, **60**, 311
Shepherd, R. H., **14**, 83, 87; **32**, 95n
Shepherd, Simon, **38**, 230; **42**, 164; **46**, 117n; **60**, 141–2, 151, 152
Shepley, J., **55**, 248n
Sheppard, Morgan, **25**, 169
Shepperd, John, **30**, 162
Shepphard, Nona, **55**, 330
Sher, Anthony, **54**, 251–3, 288; **55**, 271–2, 275, 279–84, 288, 293, 325, 345; **56**, 257, 278; **58**, 187, 206, 281, 282, 336; **60**, 161, 351; **36**, 152; **38**, 207, 208; **39**, 191, 249; **41**, 162–6, 168, 226; **42**, 86, 154, 160, 199; **43**, 216, 250; **44**,

184, 186, 187, 243; **45**, 192; **47**, 126; **50**, 235; **52**, 164n; **53**, 263–5, 285; **59**, 208n47, 343, 371, 373
Sher, Bartlett, **56**, 288
Sherbo, Arthur, **23**, 175n; **25**, 45n; **28**, 90n; **33**, 210; **34**, 104n; **35**, 178, 187n, 188n; **37**, 100n, 142n, 147n, 150n; **38**, 51n, 165; **40**, 137n; **41**, 245n; **46**, 236–7; **47**, 256; **49**, 5n; **51**, 7, 135; **53**, 213n, 226; **55**, 97n; **59**, 124n1, 127n22, 127, 128
Sherburn, George, **6**, 54; **43**, 83n
Sherburne, Edward, **30**, 161n
Sherek, Henry, **9**, 22
Shergold, N. D., **23**, 79n, 84n
Sheridan Alan, **40**, 110n; **44**, 43n; **46**, 3n; **48**, 40n; **49**, 58n; **55**, 240n; **56**, 138n
Sheridan, Michael, **48**, 229
Sheridan, Richard Brinsley, **3**, 53; **4**, 104, 120; **8**, 131; **13**, 38; **15**, 2; **16**, 109, 115; **18**, 98–100; **22**, 2; **38**, 70, 72, 73, 75; **42**, 85; **43**, 102n; **44**, 102; **47**, 62n; **51**, 89–90, 91n, 93, 114; **52**, 286, 291; **53**, 5; **54**, 255; **56**, 131
Sheridan, Thomas, **7**, 145; **10**, 72, 73; **18**, 37, 184; **22**, 174; **34**, 13, 15; **49**, 290; **51**, 4, 89; **57**, 86
Sheriff, W. E., **26**, 158
Sherley, Sir Anthony, **29**, 23–4, 32
Sherley, John, **25**, 148
Sherley, Lorraine, **21**, 156
Sherley, Robert, **29**, 24
Sherlock, Ceri, **41**, 190; **42**, 160; **43**, 206
Sherman, S. P., **26**, 4
Sherman, William H., **54**, 229n; **55**, 343; **56**, 314; **58**, 349, 357; **59**, 109n5; **60**, 269n4
Sherrin, Ned, **42**, 162
Sherry, Richard, **53**, 13n
Shershow, Scott, **55**, 341–2, 355
Sherwin, Charles, **49**, 118
Sherwin, Walter K., **29**, 174
Sherwood, Mr, **14**, 113
Sherwood, William, **47**, 96, 106
Sherzer, Jane, **18**, 118n
Shevtsova, Maria, **58**, 358
Shewring, Margaret, **47**, 19n, 118n, 237n, 249; **50**, 262; **51**, 205n; **52**, 12n, 13n, 14n, 39n, 107n; **53**, 325, 329; **54**, 194n; **55**, 247n; **60**, 26n9, 29n19, 29n20, 30n25, 32n29, 34n32, 34n32
Shiban, Theresa, **54**, 295
Shickman, Alan R., **46**, 219
Shield, H. A., **5**, 139n; **7**, 139; **8**, 148; **9**, 141; **11**, 142n; **12**, 140n
Shield, Malcolm, **45**, 156
Shifeng, Zheng, **42**, 157; **57**, 170, 171
Shih-chui, Liang, **6**, 115–16
Shilling, Eric, **44**, 195
Shillingford, Juliet, **53**, 281
Shillingsburg, Peter L., **37**, 218n; **51**, 321; **59**, 18
Shilo, Yizhak, **12**, 114
Shimizu, Kumiko, **53**, 280
Shimodate, **55**, 327
Shingler, Rebecca, **29**, 34, 37
Shingler, Thomas, **29**, 34, 37
Ships, Elizabethan, **17**, 21–36
Shiraishi, Kayoko, **57**, 270, 271
Shire, Helena Mennie, **48**, 135n
Shirley, Sir Anthony, **3**, 28; **6**, 160; **32**, 86, 87n
Shirley, Frances A., **18**, 183; **34**, 72; **41**, 22n; **42**, 169; **43**, 133; **59**, 371, 375
Shirley, J. W., **6**, 15n
Shirley, James, **1**, 64; **3**, 45; **8**, 66; **14**, 82; **15**, 135; **17**, 198, 199; **20**, 7; **26**, 5; **30**, 36n; **32**, 233; **33**, 197; **35**, 81n; **36**, 117; **41**, 112n; **43**, 244–5; **46**, 224; **47**, 247; **51**, 291; **52**, 82, 84, 296; **54**, 20, 62; **55**, 265; **56**, 121; **58**, 237, 241, 242; **60**, 105
Triumph of Peace, **11**, 116n
Shirley, John, **6**, 59; **38**, 101, 103n, 104
Shirley, Rae, **48**, 231
Shirley, Robert, **32**, 86, 87n
Shirley, Sir Thomas, **17**, 34, 176, 184
Shirley, W. W., **54**, 102n
Shivas, Mark, **57**, 147
Shlonsky, Abraham, **10**, 119
Shoaf, R. A., **46**, 104n
Shoemaker's Holiday, The, **52**, 296
Shoemaker, Neille, **19**, 145; **20**, 147
Shoham, Hanna, **32**, 127n
Shohet, Lauren, **57**, 310
Shore, Andrew, **56**, 293
Shore, Jane, **29**, 174; **49**, 260
Shorey, Paul, **31**, 7n
Shorey, Peter, **58**, 277
Short, Charles, **52**, 185n
Short, David, **47**, 217; **48**, 228; **54**, 286
Short, Peter, **26**, 183; **36**, 192; **40**, 235; **53**, 78n
Short, R. W., **15**, 27
Shortall, Tim, **42**, 155; **45**, 145
Shorter, Eric, **39**, 86
Shorter, Kingsley, **51**, 126n
Shostakovich, Dmitri, **39**, 83n; **55**, 383; **56**, 292; **57**, 113; **59**, 341, 359
Shottery, land disputes of 1584, **12**, 95–106
Show of Shows, The, **18**, 71
Show Within: Dramatic and Other Insets, The, **46**, 210
Showalter, Elaine, **40**, 190; **43**, 253; **45**, 40n; **51**, 300; **53**, 134, 136; **57**, 339
Showeman, Grant, **53**, 26n
Shrader, Ludwig, **57**, 215
Shrapnel, John, **36**, 154; **43**, 209; **47**, 182, 184; **59**, 328, 329
Shrapnel, Lex, **57**, 296
Shreiber, Flora Rheta, **39**, 9
Shreiber, Mordecai, **45**, 63n
Shrewsbury, Earl of, **53**, 67n
Shrewsbury, Francis Talbot, Fifth Earl of, *see under* Talbot
Shrewsbury, Gilbert, Seventh Earl of, *see under* Talbot
Shrewsbury, J. F. D., **50**, 19n
Shrimpton, Nick, **31**, 167
'Directing *The Tempest*', **29**, 63–7
Shriver, F. J., **54**, 1700
Shroeder, John, **14**, 153
The Great Folio of 1623 reviewed, **11**, 154–5; **13**, 163n, 164
Shuchter, J. D., **55**, 234n
Shudofsky, M. Maurice, **51**, 45n
Shuger, Debora Kuller, **51**, 296; **54**, 9, 10, 11, 12, 43n, 60, 61n, 69n, 73, 124n, 307; **55**, 229n, 230; **56**, 322
Shukla, Lalit, **45**, 89n
Shulman, Jeff, **35**, 179; **37**, 194; **51**, 180n
Shumake, Josie Slaughter, **50**, 43n

Shuman, S., **25**, 188
Shupe, Donald R., **32**, 219
Shurbanov, Alexander, **53**, 306; **54**, 148n; **56**, 341
Shurgot, Michael, **52**, 293–4
Shute, Anne, **5**, 53
Shute, John, **47**, 21, 23–4
Shutova, L., **16**, 138
Shütt, M., **38**, 110n
Shuttleworth, Bertram, **5**, 144n; **35**, 7n, 9n
Shvedov, Y., **12**, 118; **23**, 152
Shwartz, Kathryn, **52**, 279
Sian, Robert, **43**, 210
Sibbes, Richard, **54**, 68
Sibelius, Jean, **3**, 113; **10**, 117; **11**, 119; **18**, 121; **53**, 284
Siberry, Michael, **46**, 167, 178, 180; **48**, 222; **49**, 127–8, 129n; **50**, 234; **55**, 312; **56**, 293; **58**, 298
Sibilla, Mrs (Sibilla Gronaman), **51**, 83
Sibley, John, **21**, 143, 152
Sicherman, Carol Marks, **27**, 160; **39**, 251; **46**, 93n; **56**, 174n
Sickert, Walter, **49**, 127–8, 129n
Siddons, Mrs Sarah, **1**, 61; **2**, 19; **3**, 53; **4**, 86; **6**, 61, 172; **7**, 26, 34, 114; **10**, 73; **13**, 76; **18**, 104, 107; **19**, 75; **22**, 174; **24**, 43; **29**, 135, 146, 148; **35**, 51, 54, 55; **42**, 37, 38, 39n, 50; **45**, 43; **50**, 277–8; **51**, 11, 112–17; **52**, 149; **53**, 226n; **57**, 82
Sider, John W., **26**, 173; **27**, 162; **45**, 179
Sideris, Joannis, **19**, 145
Sideris, Yiannis, **58**, 217
Sidgwick, Frank, **8**, 4; **30**, 202
Sidgwick, Henry, **40**, 72
Sidnell, Michael J., **19**, 154
Sidney, George, **60**, 354
Sidney, Sir Henry, **17**, 227; **53**, 310
Sidney, Sir Herbert, **17**, 201; **55**, 110, 111n
Sidney, Lady Mary, **32**, 88; **39**, 231; **40**, 215; **42**, 188; **44**, 241; **45**, 197; **55**, 380
Sidney, Sir Philip, **1**, 119; **2**, 140; **3**, 18; **4**, 28, 143; **5**, 137; **6**, 152; **7**, 47n, 141; **8**, 17; **9**, 16, 25, 81; **10**, 15; **12**, 85; **14**, 17, 93, 146; **15**, 12, 26, 30, 41–3, 46–9, 86, 101–2; **16**, 12, 126; **17**, 118, 175, 218; **18**, 35; **20**, 9, 18; **21**, 48, 67; **22**, 38, 155, 170, 171; **23**, 92, 93, 99, 165–6; **24**, 24, 153, 159; **26**, 7, 174; **27**, 117n, 168, 169, 172; **28**, 49, 55, 57, 59, 66, 76; **29**, 4, 8, 170; **32**, 89, 166n, 222, 231, 236; **33**, 9, 13, 18, 19n, 48; **34**, 26, 28, 31, 34, 99n, 174, 188; **35**, 115, 116n, 164, 167; **36**, 172; **38**, 54, 122, 185, 233; **39**, 226; **40**, 46, 79n, 103, 195, 220, 227; **41**, 107, 195–6, 220; **42**, 71n, 111, 112, 166, 188, 194; **43**, 56, 228, 245–6; **44**, 1, 10, 85, 89, 131, 232, 239, 241, 252, 254; **45**, 11; **46**, 15, 19n, 40, 45, 56, 57, 99, 131n, 249; **47**, 130n, 133n, 259, 268; **48**, 124, 247, 257; **49**, 59n; **50**, 1, 120n, 196, 239; **51**, 136, 175, 178, 181; **53**, 24; **54**, 3, 9, 10, 15, 192n; **55**, 25n, 210, 215, 263n, 357; **56**, 44, 108, 109; **57**, 222, 223, 224, 314, 316; **59**, 32n61, 94, 229; **60**, 54, 188, 257–8, 262–3, 332–3
  Apologie for Poetrie, **4**, 9, 28; **15**, 48
  Arcadia, **13**, 30, 42, 44, 45; **14**, 80; **15**, 13, 14
  Arcadia, MS. of, **1**, 71; **2**, 103; **3**, 93; **4**, 4, 9, 32–3, 87, 142n, 143; **5**, 137; **6**, 60; **8**, 3, 48
  Astrophel and Stella, **4**, 156; **14**, 16; **15**, 42, 46–7, 86
  Defence of Poesie, **10**, 48
  Lady of May, The, **7**, 23; **10**, 65
Sidney, Robert, **38**, 93
Sidney, Robert, Earl of Leicester, **41**, 220; **42**, 188; **44**, 10, 240; **45**, 182; **46**, 225
Sidney, Robert, First Earl of Leicester (1563–1626), **7**, 61, 68n
Sidney, Sir Robert, **11**, 92, 97n; **17**, 127
  Sidney Papers, **11**, 97n
Sidney, Thomas, **42**, 193
Siebet, Harry, **56**, 40n
Siege of Rhodes, **54**, 199
Siegel, Paul N., **5**, 136; **8**, 140, 142, 143, 149; **9**, 139; **10**, 139–40, 146; **15**, 114, 165, 170; **16**, 158; **18**, 167; **19**, 141; **23**, 139; **27**, 81n, 91n; **28**, 159; **29**, 88n; **31**, 6n, 61n; **32**, 219; **33**, 3, 8, 200; **34**, 96n; **35**, 70n; **41**, 145, 198–9; **43**, 15n; **45**, 18n, 19n, 22n, 24n, 89; **50**, 171n; **54**, 123n
  Shakespearean Tragedy and the Elizabethan Compromise reviewed, **13**, 148
Siegmund-Schultze, Dorothea, **23**, 150
Siemens, Ray G., **59**, 170
Siemon, James Edward, **25**, 179; **27**, 162; **28**, 163; **29**, 67, 69; **31**, 171; **40**, 84n, 222
  'Noble Virtue in *Cymbeline*', **29**, 51–61
Siemon, James R., **46**, 63; **47**, 79n; **49**, 208n; **51**, 58, 150, 151n; **52**, 60n; **54**, 310, 326
Sieper, E., **57**, 218
Sierz, Aleks, **56**, 237n
Sievers, Eduard, **16**, 64; **44**, 110n
Sigismund III, King of Poland, **32**, 196; **33**, 168; **36**, 145
Sigüenza, **43**, 254
Silent Woman, The, **50**, 71n
Silhol, R., **19**, 138
Silk, Michael, **59**, 367
Sillars, Stuart, **32**, 234, 244; **60**, 353–4, 361
Silover, Brenda R., **58**, 118
Siluis Italicus, **31**, 45
Silva, Geno, **49**, 274
Silvain, Alexander, **54**, 96–7
  The Orator, **20**, 165
Silver Age, **54**, 356
Silver, George, **42**, 114, 118
Silverman, **54**, 323
Silverman, J. M., **27**, 166
Silverstein, Norman, **19**, 139
Silverstone, Catherine, **55**, 170n
Silvestre, **10**, 72
Silvestru, V., **20**, 131n
Silvette, Herbert, **32**, 102n
Silviria, Dale, **39**, 5; **45**, 50n
Sima, Jonas, **36**, 68n
Simeon, Charles, **54**, 50
Simić, **15**, 140, 142; **18**, 134
Simkins, Michael, **49**, 279
Šimko, Ján, **5**, 144n; **9**, 110n
  'Shakespeare in Slovakia', **4**, 109–16
Simmel, Georg, **50**, 73, 77; **56**, 140, 141n
Simmes, Valentine, **1**, 129; **14**, 165; **18**, 26–8; **26**, 177, 184; **27**, 180, 181, 186, 187; **29**, 182; **33**, 206; **36**, 192; **47**, 271; **57**, 25; **59**, 379
Simmons, Ernest J., **5**, 105n; **48**, 118
Simmons, J. L., **23**, 148; **24**, 147, 152; **26**, 165; **28**, 157, 169n; **31**, 4, 7n, 8, 51, 183; **33**, 100, 101n; **38**, 12, 40, 75n, 80n; **51**, 177n

INDEX

'*Antony and Cleopatra* and *Coriolanus*, Shakespeare's Heroic Tragedies: A Jacobean Adjustment', **26**, 95–101
Simmons, James, **39**, 169; **47**, 215; **55**, 324
Simmons, Jean, **45**, 49; **60**, 362
Simmons, Joseph, **22**, 128, 129–31
Simms, Stephen, **48**, 212
Simms, William Gilmore, **18**, 102
Simon, Barney, **55**, 271, 274
Simon, Hugh, **56**, 283
Simon, Jean Pierre, **49**, 121; **59**, 379
Simon, Josette, **38**, 211, 213; **42**, 134–5, 153; **50**, 234; **53**, 272–3; **54**, 289
Simon, Michel, **8**, 120
Simon, Myron, **55**, 132n
Simon, Neil, **60**, 356
Simonds, Peggy Muñoz, **37**, 195; **38**, 233; **43**, 234, 247; **44**, 222; **47**, 230; **48**, 253; **49**, 294; **54**, 26n
Simonetti, Gastone, **9**, 114
Simoni, Renato, **2**, 129
Simons, Jezz, **43**, 213
Simons, Joseph, **27**, 178
Simons, Mathew, **12**, 107
Simons, Nick, **47**, 197
Simons, Richard, **29**, 166; **59**, 339
Simonson, Lee, **35**, 13, 14, 18n
Simpson, A. W. B., **55**, 38n
Simpson, Aaron, **49**, 269
Simpson, Alan, **56**, 118
Simpson, Claude M., **55**, 87n
Simpson, David, **40**, 207; **55**, 7
Simpson, Evelyn, **33**, 79n, 137n, 139n; **36**, 117n, 188n; **38**, 132n; **41**, 119n; **43**, 4n; 46, 56n, 74n, 111n; **47**, 17n; **52**, 68n, 190n; **53**, 18n; **54**, 14n, 58n, 331–3; **55**, 84n, 244n; **57**, 19, 212; **59**, 212n62, 213n1, 223
Simpson, Frank, **6**, 159
'New Place: The Only Representation of Shakespeare's House, from an Unpublished Manuscript', **5**, 55–7
Simpson, J. A., **50**, 198
Simpson, Jacqueline, **55**, 53
Simpson, James, **59**, 261
Simpson, Lee, **60**, 329
Simpson, Michael, **51**, 180n
Simpson, Mrs, **40**, 159
Simpson, O., **41**, 119n
Simpson, O. J., **60**, 86, 348, 354, 365
Simpson, Percy, **1**, 11, 37n; **2**, 37; **5**, 2–3, 4, 140, 146, 152; **6**, 159 *and* n; **7**, 3, 8, 45; **9**, 134, 142; **10**, 9, 15, 24n, 26n; **11**, 71, 78, 115n; **14**, 8, 44; **15**, 29, 40n; **17**, 212n; **32**, 40n; **34**, and Evelyn, 134n; **35**, 79n, 137n, 139n; **36**, 117n, 188n; **41**, 95n, 220; **43**, 4n; **46**, 15n, 56n, 74n, 111n; **47**, 17n; 176n; **49**, 108n; **52**, 68n, 190n; **53**, 18n, 22n, 91n; **54**, 14n, 58n, 333–3; **55**, 84n, 244n, 263n; **57**, 19; **59**, 213n1, 223
see also under Herford, C. H.
Shakespearian Punctuation, **11**, 78; **14**, 5
Simpson, Percy and Evelyn, **25**, 100n; **26**, 39n; **27**, 112n, 118, 120, 123, 124, 125, 126; **44**, 175
Simpson, R., **32**, 156n; **44**, 83n
Simpson, R. R., **38**, 178, 184
Shakespeare and Medicine reviewed, **13**, 155; **17**, 258n
Simpson, Richard, **2**, 44, 58; **4**, 67n; **6**, 1, 5; **8**, 105n; **9**, 73, 79n; **45**, 172; **48**, 69; **54**, 94n, 116n; **56**, 192n
Simpson, Steven, **57**, 126, 127, 135
Simpson, Thomas, *Taffel Consort*, **11**, 65
Simuel, Lambert, **52**, 171
Sinatra, Frank, **57**, 155
Sincklo, John, **45**, 192
Sinclair, F. D., **7**, 114; **15**, 137
Sinclair, John D., **59**, 194n9
Sincler (Sincklo or Sinkler), John, **33**, 158; **36**, 147
Sinden, Sir Donald, **23**, 131, 132; **30**, 169, 172; **33**, 81–7, 175, 176; **39**, 230, 234; **40**, 223; **41**, 57; **43**, 194; **46**, 33; **49**, 235–6, 271; **56**, 249n; **58**, 206; **59**, 201n16, 208n47; **60**, 285, 286, 329
Sinfield, Alan, **30**, 188; **35**, 164n; **37**, 185, 201; **39**, 103n; **40**, 190, 212; **41**, 65n, 75n, 195; **43**, 1n, 15n, 16, 178–9, 253n; **44**, 68, 239; **46**, 3n, 205, 206; **47**, 9n; 48, 69n, 88n, 239–40; **49**, 58, 141n, 203n, 312; **50**, 110; **51**, 148n, 150, 326; **54**, 230n; **55**, 7n, 108, 113n, 161, 166–7, 352, 373; **56**, 67–78, 203, 204n, 205n; **57**, 1; **58**, 181, 184; **59**, 348; **60**, 167, 169, 173n8
Singer, **47**, 121
Singer, Charles, **55**, 61n
Singer, Herta, **35**, 22n
Singer, John, **33**, 158; **60**, 4, 21–2
Singer, S. W., **5**, 19; **18**, 108; **23**, 102; **39**, 238
Singh, G., **40**, 26n
Singh, Han, **55**, 332
Singh, Jyotsna, **45**, 168; **49**, 61n, 284, 301; **50**, 242; **51**, 276, 278; **52**, 279; **54**, 28n, 312
Singh, Sarup, **39**, 212, 213
Singh, Satyanarain, **19**, 139
Singham, Jeffrey L., **53**, 325
Singleton, Charles S., **27**, 56n; **40**, 98n, 126n
Sinklo, John, **1**, 8
Sinkovit, Imre, **18**, 125
Sinsheimer, Hermann, *Shylock* reviewed, **1**, 120
Sinyard, Neil, **55**, 384
Sion, Georgia, **50**, 232
Sipahigil, T., **25**, 181; **26**, 162, 172; **28**, 167; **30**, 202; **51**, 178n, 186n
Sipe, Dorothy L., **22**, 150
Sir Clyomon and Clamydes, **11**, 48; **13**, 157; **14**, 20
Sir Gregory Nonsense His Newes from no place, **3**, 54
Sir John Oldcastle, **3**, 45, 53, 112; **4**, 92; **6**, 170; **9**, 83, 84; **48**, 277
Sir John van Olden Barnavelt, **3**, 51
Sir Thomas More, **11**, 59, 80, 87n; **14**, 25, 29–33, 33n; **15**, 134, 179; **18**, 25; **31**, 184, 192, 193, 196; **48**, 278; **50**, 255; **52**, 72
the dating of, **8**, 102; **9**, 71–9, 120
Shakespeare's hand in, **3**, 3, 12, 50; **4**, 158; **6**, 5, 8, 60; **8**, 6, 100, 101, 103, 104, 157; **9**, 73–9, 133, 143; **10**, 144, 158
Shakespeare's share in, **2**, 44–61 *passim*; **3**, 3, 12, 19, 30–1, 50, 111, 152
see also under 'Booke of Sir Thomas More'
Sirett, Paul, **59**, 340
Sirli, Vasile, **50**, 234
Sirluck, Ernest, **10**, 144; **38**, 92n; **46**, 115n
Sirrett, Paul, **60**, 323
Sisk, John P., **23**, 144; **26**, 162; **32**, 219; **33**, 187; **38**, 15
Siska, Joachim, **44**, 197
Siskin, Clifford, **32**, 218; **30**, 147–55
Sisniega, Marcel, **54**, 154n

Sisson, Charles Jasper, **1**, 9; **2**, 60n, 66; **3**, 13; **4**, 7, 11, 149; **5**, 46n; **6**, 158; **8**, 6, 10; **9**, 34n, 48n, 132, 134, 145, 147, 152; **10**, 3; **11**, 82; **12**, 21n, 147, 150–1; **13**, 155; **14**, 117, 153, 157; **15**, 7, 174; **17**, 135n, 152n, 157n, 207n; **18**, 44, 157, 161, 180; **19**, 136, 161; **25**, 2, 4, 5, 94n; **26**, 170; **28**, 38n, 117; **29**, 22–3, 81; **32**, 152; **33**, 67, 161, 210; **38**, 99n, 101, 251; **40**, 214, 228; **46**, 32; **47**, 253; **50**, 143n; **51**, 142; **54**, 40n; **56**, 121n; **59**, 81n9

Le Goût Public et le Théâtre Elisabéthain, **3**, 7

Lost Plays of Shakespeare's Age, **11**, 102

'The Magic of Prospero', **11**, 70–7

The Mythical Sorrows of Shakespeare, **3**, 9

New Readings in Shakespeare, **11**, 105n; **12**, 151

New Readings in Shakespeare reviewed, **10**, 153

'The Red Bull Company and the Importunate Widow', **7**, 57–68

'Shakespeare's Friends: Hathaways and Burmans at Shottery', **12**, 95–106

'Studies in the Life and Environment of Shakespeare since 1900', **3**, 1–12

William Shakespeare: The Complete Works reviewed, **8**, 156–7

Sisson, Richard, **43**, 211

Sissons, Narelle, **41**, 191

Sissons, Neil, **41**, 186; **42**, 152, 157, 158; **43**, 206; **45**, 150; **46**, 121, 196; **47**, 211, 212; **48**, 228; **49**, 275; **52**, 259; **53**, 283; **55**, 333; **58**, 307

Sisyphus, **46**, 90

Sitwell family, **12**, 12

Sitwell, Dame Edith, **4**, 19; **5**, 73; **33**, 35n

A Notebook on William Shakespeare reviewed, **3**, 130, 133

Sitwell, Edith, and Walton, Sir William, *Façade*, **11**, 67

Sitwell, Osbert, **7**, 56n

Siwicka, Zofia, **10**, 120; **11**, 121; **15**, 137

Sixtus V, Pope, **4**, 148, 155

Siyang, Zhang, **45**, 89n

Sjöberg, Alf, **1**, 115; **10**, 121; **13**, 131; **14**, 123; **16**, 136; **18**, 128; **36**, 65; **58**, 313

Sjoberg, Elsa, **23**, 147

Sjöberg, Gunnar, **18**, 128

Sjögren, Gunnar, **15**, 167; **19**, 147; **20**, 165; **21**, 149, 163; **22**, 168; **24**, 166n; **37**, 198

'Thomas Bull and other "English Instrumentalists" in Denmark in the 1580s', **22**, 119–24

Skantze, P. A., **55**, 347

Skarsgaard, Stellan, **43**, 252

Skeaping, Roderick, **52**, 222

Skeat, Walter W., **10**, 33; **19**, 60; **29**, 104n; **52**, 186n

ed., *Shakespeare's Plutarch*, **12**, 94n

Skeele, David, **53**, 308–9

Skein, Valentinn, **22**, 120, 123

Skelton, John, **7**, 23; **17**, 46; **23**, 165; **28**, 21; **33**, 201; **48**, 257; **54**, 3, 8; **55**, 83; **59**, 364

Skelton, R. A., **17**, 32n, 34n; **35**, 133n; **53**, 202n

Skelton, Tom, **13**, 90–105; **15**, 172

Skemp, Arthur, **4**, 100n

Skene, Sir John, **19**, 3

Skeretkowicz, Victor, **32**, 245

Skillan, George, **20**, 82n

Skillern, David Lloyd, **45**, 155

Skills, Howard, **55**, 241n, 244

Skinner, B. F., **5**, 136; **15**, 17

Skinner, Claire, **44**, 203; **45**, 138, 152; **46**, 196; **51**, 253, 255; **52**, 262; **55**, 318, 321; **56**, 298; **59**, 346; **60**, 162, 168

Skinner, Paul, **54**, 284

Skinner, Quentin, **38**, 124n; **44**, 6n; **49**, 195n; **51**, 68, 136; **55**, 209n; **56**, 225n; **57**, 70

Skipp, V., **38**, 26n, 27n

Skipping, Tom, **45**, 152

Skipsey, Joseph, **58**, 112

Skipwith, Sir William, **42**, 186

Skjönberg, Espen, **8**, 120; **42**, 205

Sklar, Elizabeth S., **31**, 183

Skoda, Albin, **10**, 119; **11**, 117, 118

Skoda, Jan, **14**, 118

Skoloker, Anthony, **56**, 99

Skouloudis, M., **4**, 128; **5**, 112; **6**, 120

Skoumal, Aloys, **10**, 117; **16**, 133

Skovmand, Michael, **48**, 262; **57**, 149

Skretkowicz, Victor, **46**, 56n

Skulsky, Harold, **21**, 136–7; **24**, 143; **28**, 154; **31**, 169

Skura, Meredith Anne, **35**, 162; **40**, 110–11; **43**, 17, 27n, 222, 241; **48**, 242; **52**, 275; **54**, 232n; **55**, 19, 20, 24; **56**, 311; **58**, 3; **59**, 27n33, 37

Skuszanka, Krystyna, **60**, 335

Skybell, Steven, **51**, 213

Skyers, Michael, **44**, 199

Slack, Paul, **44**, 17n; **47**, 50n; **50**, 19n; **55**, 37n

Sládek, Josef Václav, **9**, 103–4, 105, 108; **11**, 118; **13**, 126; **14**, 118; **16**, 133; **18**, 121

Slaski, Christopher, **52**, 264

Slater, Ann Pasternak, **27**, 170; **32**, 231; **37**, 181, 182; **39**, 95; **41**, 8n; **49**, 76n; **55**, 242n

'Variations Within a Source: from Isaiah XXIX to *The Tempest*', **25**, 125–35

Slater, Daphne, **1**, 108, 109, 110; **47**, 112

Slater, Edward, **55**, 109n

Slater, Eliot, **27**, 178; **29**, 172, 185; **30**, 182; **31**, 189; **32**, 236; **40**, 225, 226n, 231; **41**, 232; **42**, 205; **43**, 261–2; **45**, 200, 201; **51**, 315

Slater, Guy, **44**, 198

Slater, Lucy, **49**, 277

Slater, Miriam, **35**, 73n

Slater, Simon, **55**, 324

Slaughter, Helena Robin, **41**, 57n

Slaughter, Richard, **48**, 227

Slavitt, David R., **55**, 228n

Sledd, James, **23**, 141n; **47**, 141n

Sleep, Wayne, **59**, 345

Slights, Camille Wells, **28**, 162; **35**, 154; **36**, 162–3, 166; **37**, 188; **38**, 218; **40**, 83n; **43**, 233; **47**, 226; **52**, 278; **54**, 97n; **57**, 200

Slights, Jessica, **56**, 304

Slights, William W. E., **31**, 172, 182; **36**, 166; **39**, 225; **50**, 65; **53**, 213n, 223; **56**, 336; **59**, 215n10

Slimp, Stephen, **57**, 320

Slinger, Jonathan, **51**, 208, 215; **54**, 268; **59**, 300, 306, 307

Sloan, Thomas O., **57**, 21

Sloane, Sir Hans, **3**, 43

Sloane, Steven, **55**, 328

Slotkin, Edgar M., **41**, 200n

Slovakia, Shakespeare and modern productions, **4**, 110–14
problems of translation, **4**, 114–15
translations, **4**, 109–10
see also under Czechoslovakia
Slowe, Georgia, **43**, 186–7, 213; **44**, 200; **59**, 293, 294
Slue, Errol, **34**, 156
Sly, Christopher, **38**, 239, 240; **40**, 171
Sly, Will, **45**, 113
Sly, William, **1**, 41, 42; **36**, 136
Small, Helen, **55**, 198n
Small, Ian, **46**, 256n; **51**, 128n; **59**, 17n69
Small, R. A., **1**, 50n; **27**, 122n
Small, S. A., **8**, 4
Smallwood, Robert L., **27**, 166; **28**, 178; **31**, 153; **36**, 171, 175; **37**, 201; **38**, 12, 17; **42**, 44n, 169, 193, 199; **43**, 185; **44**, 94n; **47**, 12, 236; **48**, 264; **51**, 219–55; **53**, 328; **56**, 113n; **57**, 172, 329, 330–1; **58**, 335, 342; **59**, 44, 47; **60**, 168
'The Design of *All's Well That Ends Well*', **25**, 45–61
Smart, Amy, **57**, 186
Smart, John S., **4**, 58; **10**, 14, 15, 24n; **20**, 160–1, 175, 176; **25**, 187
Smeaton, Oliphant, **13**, 48n
Smedley, W. T., **1**, 71
Smet, Robert de, '*Othello* in Paris and Brussels', **3**, 98–106
and see under Sanvic, Romain
Smetana, Bedřich, **9**, 107, 108; **18**, 75
Libuše, **9**, 103
Smethwicke, John, **1**, 57; **50**, 272n
Smidman, David, **35**, 153n
Smidt, Kristian, **5**, 134, 150; **19**, 163; **23**, 154, 179n; **24**, 163; **25**, 193–4; **37**, 202n; **38**, 4; **43**, 269; **44**, 28n, 256; **48**, 4n, 5; **56**, 321; **58**, 313
Smile, Jan, **52**, 222
Smiles, Samuel, **48**, 99, 100
Smiley, Jane, **51**, 306–7; **52**, 257; **53**, 110, 111; **54**, 311–12; **55**, 74, 132, 147, 148n; **56**, 302; **58**, 83, 84, 94, 95, 96, 99, 103, 106
Smillie, Robert, **58**, 112
Smirke, Robert, **7**, 92; **13**, 76; **49**, 119–20; **52**, 26; **59**, 132
Smirnov, A. A., **4**, 125; **5**, 117; **12**, 118; **13**, 133; **15**, 140; **16**, 15
Smith Bruce R., **53**, 325
Smith Jeffrey, **15**, 146
Smith, A. Hassell, **28**, 18n
Smith, A. J., **24**, 164; **39**, 218; **46**, 116, 124; **47**, 134n; **49**, 76n
Smith, Adam, **19**, 143; **46**, 43n
Smith, Agnes, **49**, 193
Smith, Alan G. R., **23**, 163n; **52**, 182; **56**, 292
Smith, Alexander, **45**, 150
Smith, Amy, **60**, 85, 96n33
Smith, Anna Deavere, **52**, 287
Smith, Arthur, **50**, 227
Smith, Barbara Herrnstein, **39**, 138; **48**, 242; **51**, 157n; **53**, 41n
Smith, Brian, **5**, 128
Smith, Bruce R., **30**, 192; **46**, 4n, 40n, 46n, 48; **47**, 246–7; **48**, 28n, 30, 44; **51**, 285; **54**, 322, 336n; **55**, 91n, 357; **56**, 70n, 71n, 72, 73, 303; **57**, 95; **59**, 351; **60**, 168n4.8, 357, 360
Smith, C. Gregory, **15**, 41; **18**, 176, 179
Smith, Caroline, **42**, 155; **43**, 210; **44**, 200; **45**, 147; **52**, 257
Smith, Cecil Harcourt, **55**, 137
Smith, Charles G., **32**, 163n, 166n, 168, 169n
Smith, Charles Hamilton, **20**, 108
Smith, Christopher, **41**, 225
Smith, Clarence, **47**, 217; **52**, 221, 225
Smith, David L., **54**, 169n; **55**, 40n
Smith, David Nichol, **9**, 100n, **10**, 38n; **18**, 12, 13, 16, 174; **33**, 46n; **37**, 142n, 143n, 147n, 148n, 149n; **42**, 99n; **51**, 4, 5, 14; **55**, 99n; **58**, 355; **60**, 194n31
Smith, Denzell S., **22**, 154; **26**, 158; **33**, 198
Smith, Derek, **27**, 147, 149
Smith, Edgar, **57**, 249
Smith, Elaine C., **52**, 261
Smith, Elizabeth, **55**, 217
Smith, Emma, **55**, 377; **56**, 317; **58**, 334; **59**, 372, 373; **60**, 353–61
Smith, Euan, **47**, 213
Smith, Fernanda, **3**, 118
Smith, G. C. Moore, **3**, 52; **6**, 2, 39; **9**, 25, 33n; **11**, 108; **29**, 111n
College Plays Performed in the University of Cambridge, **12**, 20n
Smith, G. Gregory, **6**, 2; **41**, 187; **42**, 55n, 66n; **44**, 199; 46, 222; **56**, 56n
Smith, Georgius D., **49**, 176n
Smith, Gordon Ross, **14**, 142; **18**, 34; **20**, 150; **31**, 168; **34**, 170, 172; **38**, 2
Smith, Gregory, **54**, 289; **56**, 298
Smith, Grover, **20**, 150; **43**, 128
Smith, H. H., **12**, 151; **18**, 183
Smith, Hallett, **4**, 153–4; **7**, 11n; **15**, 43; **18**, 172; **19**, 137; **22**, 167; **25**, 99n, 105, **26**, 112n; **27**, 168; **28**, 174; **29**, 4, 5, 8, 9, 11n; **30**, 148n, 201; **31**, 13n; **37**, 73n; **42**, 182
Smith, Henry, **2**, 70, 74; **28**, 166; **43**, 237; **50**, 246; **60**, 90n19, 90n21, 92
Memento for Magistrates, **2**, 70
Smith, Hugh, **17**, 32
Smith, Ian, **52**, 278; **55**, 342
Smith, India, **44**, 198; **46**, 192; **47**, 216
Smith, Irwin, **5**, 143; **7**, 143; **11**, 146; **20**, 167–8; **22**, 173; **23**, 158; **25**, 178; **36**, 116, 117, 118; **41**, 20n, 36; **52**, 2, 6, 183n
Shakespeare's Globe Playhouse, **12**, 143
Smith, Isabella, **15**, 136
Smith, Isobel, **43**, 210
Smith, J. C., composer, **18**, 77, 97, 98, 99, 100; **27**, 96n; **32**, 73n; **49**, 62n, 171n, 211n; **51**, 86–7, 91, 92; **53**, 13n
Smith, J. Oates, **22**, 159; **25**, 14n
Smith, J. Percy, **27**, 163; **35**, 6n
Smith, James, **4**, 24; **8**, 8–9; **28**, 160; **32**, 50n, 51n, 55n, 56n; **33**, 70, 75n; **35**, 33, 37; **37**, 3, 11; **42**, 181; **53**, 26n
Smith, Jean, **56**, 206n
Smith, John H., **42**, 208n; **43**, 268; **48**, 56n, 57n; **49**, 190, 194; **50**, 261
Smith, John Harrington, **13**, 156n
Smith, John Hazel, **18**, 190; **19**, 163; **33**, 198, 209; **40**, 110n
Smith, John, of Stratford-upon-Avon, **12**, 95–6, 98–106
Smith, Captain John, **1**, 69; **17**, 33
General History of Virginia (1624), **6**, 55
Smith, Sir John (*temp.* Henry VIII), **12**, 99
Smith, Jonathan, **23**, 156
Smith, Kirsten, **54**, 292
Smith, L. P., **15**, 15
Smith, Lacey B., **43**, 63n
Smith, Lucy Baldwin, **44**, 10n
Smith, Lucy Toulmin, **21**, 65n; **59**, 271, 272, 283
Smith, M., **34**, 104n
Smith, M. E., **33**, 203

Smith, M. W. A., **38**, 253; **39**, 250; **40**, 227n; **41**, 233n; **42**, 205n, 212; **43**, 261; **45**, 200, 201; **46**, 257n; **47**, 241n; **50**, 287
Smith, Dame Maggie, **18**, 154–5; **31**, 143, 144; **34**, 158, 159; **36**, 60, 81; **42**, 87; **57**, 269; **60**, 167
Smith, Margaret, **48**, 7n
Smith, Marion Bodwell, **21**, 128; **29**, 89
Smith, Mary, **58**, 108, 109, 111
Smith, Mary E., **31**, 185
Smith, Mathew, **58**, 224
Smith, Micha, **55**, 93–4
Smith, Micheal, **48**, 256
Smith, Molly, **45**, 165
Smith, Mrs, **51**, 89
Smith, N. C., **14**, 75n
Smith, Nichol D., **45**, 16n, 18n
Smith, Nigel, **42**, 182; **47**, 256
Smith, Paul, **46**, 4; **51**, 150n; **52**, 88n, 93n
Smith, Paul Julian, **56**, 40n
Smith, Peter, **45**, 148; **49**, 283; **53**, 307–8; **55**, 349
Smith, Peter D., **24**, 167
Smith, Peter J., **58**, 351
Smith, R. D., **38**, 50n
Smith, R. J., **19**, 134
Smith, R. M., **1**, 76; **4**, 96n, 140n; **5**, 51, 136; **6**, 39; **7**, 136; **9**, 84
Froissart and the English Chronicle Play, **14**, 3
Smith, Rae, **48**, 213, 229; **49**, 271; **56**, 264; **57**, 274; **59**, 312
Smith, Rebecca, **38**, 159n
Smith, Richard M., **55**, 37n, 39n
Smith, Richard Penn, **58**, 139
Smith, Rob, **52**, 254; **54**, 290; **55**, 328
Smith, Robert, **46**, 240n; **51**, 80
Smith, Robert A. H., **37**, 190
Smith, Robert Metcalf, **14**, 100n
Smith, Rochelle, **49**, 289
Smith, Ronan, **44**, 192
Smith, Sharon L., **19**, 147n
Smith, Sheila M., **19**, 129
Smith, Sidonie, **53**, 242n
Smith, Sol, **18**, 105, 117n
Smith, Stafford, **9**, 86, 89n
Smith, Steven R., **42**, 50n
Smith, Sydney (Canon), **56**, 127
Smith, Tenna Rochfort, **53**, 299
Smith, Sir Thomas, **7**, 19; **17**, 66n, 71, 75n, 76–8, 80n, 81, 82, 84n, 112–14, 117; **18**, 170; **28**, 63, 64, 68n; **29**, 93; **38**, 2; **41**, 12; **43**, 227, 238; **48**, 114
Smith, Thomasina, **46**, 194
Smith, Tom, **48**, 213; **54**, 267
Smith, Valerie, **41**, 67, 70n, 75
Smith, W. D., **31**, 96, 98n
Smith, W. G., *Oxford Dictionary of Proverbs*, **7**, 5
Smith, W. J., **25**, 137n
Smith, W., *The Commedia dell' Arte*, **14**, 3
Smith, Warren D., **4**, 147; **5**, 143; **7**, 7, 144–5; **8**, 144, 151; **9**, 155–6; **10**, 3; **11**, 49n, 138; **12**, 38; **13**, 155, **18**, 162; **19**, 136; **22**, 152; **24**, 67; **25**, 5; **30**, 197; **41**, 8n; **52**, 4
Smith, William, **1**, 61; **45**, 109n; **57**, 86; **59**, 165–6
Smith, William ('Gentleman' Smith), **10**, 72–3
Smith, William, *Chloris*, **15**, 101, 109n
Smith, William, of Stratford-upon-Avon, **12**, 105n
Smith, William C., **51**, 89n
Smith, Winifred, **8**, 3
Smith, Winston, **45**, 176
Smith-Howard, Alycia, **60**, 359, 361
Smithers, G. V., **25**, 184
'Guide-Lines for Interpreting the Uses of the Suffix "-ed" in Shakespeare's English', **23**, 27–37
Smithson, Harriet, **3**, 102; **20**, 164; **21**, 80; **30**, 200; **35**, 12; **38**, 234; **57**, 115
see also Berlioz
Smock, Ann, **55**, 71n
Smoktunovsky, Innokenti, **54**, 151
Smolenskin, Peretz, **54**, 184, 189n
Smollett, Tobias George, **16**, 16; **51**, 8
Smout, T. C., **57**, 126
Smuts, Jan C., **13**, 141
Smuts, Malcolm, **54**, 136n
Smyshlyaev, V., **54**, 146
Smyth, Francis, **7**, 66, 68n
Smyth, Francis, Alderman of Stratford-upon-Avon, **12**, 106n; **17**, 126
Smyth, Francis, of Wootton Wawen, **12**, 96–106
Smyth, George, of Wootton Wawen, **12**, 99
Smyth, H. W., **36**, 13n
Smyth, N., *History of Herodian, The*, **48**, 250
Smyth, Paul, **10**, 75
Smyth, Richard, **27**, 102
Smyth, Revd William, **17**, 57; **45**, 107
Smythe, Ian, **8**, 124
Smythe, John, **58**, 36, 134
Smythson, Robert, **47**, 17
Sneddon, Professor Elizabeth, **52**, 158–9; **57**, 164, 166
Snell, Jack, **57**, 277
Sneller, James, **58**, 224
Snider, Denton J., **58**, 144
Snitow, Ann, **45**, 45n
Snodin, David, **39**, 105, 110
Snow, Edward A., **35**, 187; **36**, 166; **37**, 117n, 125n; **44**, 217; **46**, 73n, 101n, 130n, 132n, 135n; **49**, 65n, 104n, 203n, 208n; **60**, 255n15
Snow, Stephen Eddy, **52**, 36, 37n, 38n, 40n
Snowden, John, **21**, 99–100, 105
Snowdon, George and Lionel, **37**, 211
Snyder, F. E., **28**, 170
Snyder, Richard C., **37**, 194
Snyder, Susan, **25**, 182; **33**, 189; **34**, 139n, 166; **35**, 159, 171; **37**, 72n, 186; **42**, 174, 187n; **44**, 215, 217; **47**, 267–8; **48**, 26n; **49**, 48n, 204n; **51**, 29n, 285; **54**, 306, 321; **56**, 99n, 102, 311; **59**, 54n14
Snyder, Ted, **57**, 250
Soans, Robin, **53**, 252
Soare, Soare Z., **20**, 126
Sobran, Joseph, **58**, 1
Société d'Histoire du Théâtre, **11**, 120; **12**, 112
Society for Theatre Research, **11**, 148; **12**, 55n
Socrates, **14**, 76; **20**, 26n; **22**, 3; **36**, 86, 88, 91, 92; **40**, 80, 207; **41**, 212; **49**, 61; **54**, 42, 304; **56**, 223
Söderwall, Margreta, **10**, 121; **18**, 128

Soellner, Rolf, **9**, 142; **10**, 146n; **13**, 155; **18**, 176; **23**, 141; **24**, 150; **31**, 13n; **34**, 165, 176; **37**, 191; **40**, 78n; **42**, 7n; **46**, 145n, 158n; **56**, 219n
Soens, Adolph L., **22**, 170; **23**, 143, 153, 172; **24**, 166; **25**, 181
Soest, Gerard, **15**, 130; **18**, 178
Sofaer, Abraham, **1**, 101, 102
Sofer, Andrew, **52**, 278; **60**, 227, 228
Sohm, Rudolf, **28**, 53
Sohmer, Steven, **51**, 334; **52**, 307; **54**, 335;
Sokol movement, **9**, 108
Sokol, B. J., **47**, 223–4; **49**, 294; **51**, 159–73; **53**, 306; **54**, 99; **55**, 39n; **56**, 105n; **58**, 319, 322, 333
Sokol, Mary, **55**, 39n; **58**, 319, 322, 333
Sokolova, Boika, **46**, 213; **49**, 308; **54**, 148n; **56**, 34n, 341
Sokolyansky, Mark, **54**, 151n; **55**, 383
Sole, Kelwyn, **57**, 159
Solich, Wolfgang, **38**, 237
Soliman and Perseda, **9**, 41; **55**, 23
Solly, Sir Henry Shaen, **38**, 187
Solomon, David, **44**, 192; **45**, 150
Solomon, Heather, **55**, 123n
Solomon, Julie Robin, **47**, 228–9
Solomon, King, **20**, 26n; **43**, 4
Solomon, Reb, **55**, 117
Solomon, Robert C., **37**, 122n; **51**, 153
Solomos, Alexis, **5**, 112; **7**, 112
Solon, **20**, 26n
Some Remarks on the Tragedy of Hamlet (1736), **18**, 36, 38
Some, Robert, **60**, 12n34
Somekawa, Ellen, **55**, 217
Somer, Paulus van, **7**, 114; **9**, 115
Somers, **21**, 103
Somers, William, **26**, 72
Somersalmi, Urho, **10**, 117; **11**, 119
Somerset House, *see under* London
Somerset, Alan, **39**, 247; **51**, 194n; **60**, 1, 1n1, 1n2, 2, 20
Somerset, Charles A., **46**, 142–3; **56**, 124; **58**, 138, 142
Somerset, Earl of, **27**, 100; **28**, 23
Somerset, Edward Seymour, Duke of, **38**, 23
Somerset, Edward, Earl of Worcester, **3**, 26; **7**, 60; **35**, 131; **36**, 142; **60**, 7
Somerset, J. Alan B., **30**, 192, 198; **32**, 219; **35**, 87, 89; **36**, 176n; **38**, 13; **40**, 218; **44**, 150n; **49**, 300; **50**, 168n, 187n; **52**, 24n
  'Falstaff, the Prince, and the Pattern of *2 Henry IV*', **30**, 35–45
Somerville, Geraldine, **47**, 217
Somerville, H., **13**, 39n
  Madness in Shakespearian Tragedy, **13**, 30
Somerville, John, of Edstone, **17**, 126; **54**, 116
Somma, **21**, 88
Sommer, Doris, **46**, 144; **51**, 19n
Sommer, H. O., **26**, 78n
Sommer, Thomas, **14**, 156
Sommers, Alan, **27**, 11n; **31**, 12n
Sommerville, C. John, **56**, 2n
Sommerville, Johann P., **44**, 75, 77n; **54**, 322; **56**, 216n; **57**, 247
Somogyvári, P., **14**, 120
Sondergard, Sidney L., **53**, 339–40; **54**, 14n
Sondheim, Moriz, **8**, 111
Songes and Sonettes (1557), *see under* 'Tottel's Miscellany'
Songmaker's Chair, The, **55**, 175
Sonnabend, Yolanda, **53**, 247; **54**, 283; **45**, 63n
Sonnenberg, Cecilia, **13**, 131
Sonnenfeld, Albert, **45**, 2
Sonnenschein, E. A., **7**, 4; **22**, 117n
Sonnenthal, Adolf von, **33**, 21, 22, 23, 25–6, 28, 29
Sonnenthal, Hermine von, **35**, 21n
Sonnets, **21**, 97–105, 128, 140, 147, 148, 153, 162; **22**, 79–92, 164, 165, 181, 182; **23**, 10, 69–78, 142, 157–8, 160, 176; **24**, 15, 16, 38, 138, 151, 153, 154, 157; **27**, 179; **28**, 49, 78, 80n, 149, 163; **29**, 175, 181–2; **30**, 6, 90, 100, 181–2
Sonnino, Lee, A., **23**, 164
Sonnino, Marc, **44**, 194
Sontag, Susan, **39**, 39n
Sophia Hedwig, of Brunswick-Wolfenbüttel, **33**, 166
Sophocles, **6**, 25; **10**, 36; **16**, 157; **20**, 22; **21**, 75, 77; **22**, 50, 158, 163, 164; **24**, 84n; **30**, 104, 105–6, 112, 113, 115; **32**, 220; **34**, 3; **38**, 87; **41**, 125, 205; **45**, 119; **46**, 55; **50**, 144; **53**, 54; **54**, 114; **55**, 153, 308; **56**, 241; **59**, 347, 352
  Antigone (ed. 1581), **1**, 69; **4**, 145n
  Antigone, **20**, 30
  Oedipus Rex, **4**, 31; **9**, 138; **13**, 9, 71; **20**, 4, 33–40
  Oedipus at Colonus, **8**, 109
  Philoctetes, **9**, 138
Sophonisba, The Wonder of Women, **50**, 110n; **52**, 297; **54**, 16, 17, 21
Šopor, A., **15**, 142
Sorabji, Richard, **42**, 89n
Sorano, Daniel, **16**, 133
Sorel, Cécile, **2**, 123
Sorelius, Gunnar, **21**, 156; **25**, 192; **28**, 179; **47**, 226; **48**, 159; 248, 254; **55**, 247n; **58**, 313, 334
Sorell, Walter, **12**, 144
Sorensen, Fred, **3**, 25
Sorge, Thomas, **32**, 217
Sorlien, Robert Parker, **31**, 177; **32**, 102n, 104n; **42**, 115n; **52**, 25n, 120n; **57**, 208
Sorsby, Arnold, **60**, 234n64
Sorsum, Baron de, **2**, 116
Sosanya, Nina, **47**, 216; **51**, 238; **57**, 267; **58**, 298
Soskin, Renée R., **8**, 124
Soteriou, Mia, **41**, 189; **42**, 159; **43**, 211; **54**, 283
Sotheby and Wilkinson, **13**, 68n
Sotheby, William, **24**, 44
Sotheby's, **4**, 81
Sotheran, Henry, and Co., **4**, 83
Sothern, E. H., **57**, 256
Soubise, Julius, **51**, 61
Souch, John, **60**, 226
Souglides, George, **44**, 197
Soule, Lesley Anne, **46**, 20n
Souleymane, Bah, **56**, 4n
Soulié, Frédéric, **30**, 200
Soulsby-Smith, **54**, 288, 291
'Sources of *Macbeth*', M. C. Bradbrook, **4**, 35–48
Sources of Shakespeare's plays, *see under* Shakespeare, literary influences, sources
Souriau, Etienne, **41**, 122
Sousa, Ronald, **51**, 297
South Africa, report on Shakespeare in, **1**, 112; **2**, 128; **5**, 112; **6**, 123; **7**, 114; **8**, 120–1; **9**, 115; **10**, 121; **11**, 122; **12**, 115–16; **13**, 131; **15**, 137; **18**, 127–8

South, Malcolm, **51**, 177n
Southall, Raymond, **15**, 174; **20**, 145; **25**, 13n, 15n; **41**, 74
Southam, B. C., **15**, 167
Southampton, Countess of, **32**, 235
Southampton, Henry Wriothesley, 3rd Earl of, **1**, 39; **2**, 53; **3**, 2, 10, 25, 138, 139; **4**, 148, 155–6; **5**, 137, 148; **6**, 159; **7**, 3, 37, 96, 105, 139; **14**, 91, 92; **15**, 12, 23, 27–8, 62, 71; **18**, 112, 178; **20**, 161, 172; **21**, 97, 104, 141; **23**, 43, 160; **24**, 151; **26**, 108; **27**, 129n; **28**, 165; **31**, 178; **33**, 195, 199; **35**, 168; **36**, 173; **41**, 107; **43**, 235; **44**, 34, 77, 232; **47**, 133, 161; **49**, 298; **53**, 317; **60**, 259, 282–3
Southampton, Mary, Countess, of, **21**, 97, 100, 103, 104; **23**, 160; **24**, 154
Southern, A. C., **7**, 106n; **17**, 121n; **32**, 103n; **54**, 91n, 95n
Southern, Clare, **44**, 196
Southern, Richard, merchant in Barbary, **11**, 90, 91
Southern, Richard, **3**, 85; **7**, 143; **8**, 152; **9**, 147; **10**, 85, 89n; **12**, 1, 20n; **13**, 123n, 160; **14**, 150; **17**, 194; **27**, 174–5; **28**, 130, 131n; **29**, 129, 130n, 131n; **41**, 3, 41n; **52**, 3–4, 6
Changeable Scenery reviewed, **7**, 144
The Medieval Theatre in the Round, **12**, 70n
The Open Stage, **12**, 36; **14**, 13
'On Reconstructing a Practicable Elizabethan Public Playhouse', **12**, 22–34
Southern, Thomas, **53**, 188; **56**, 107
Southey, Robert, **23**, 104
Southwark, *see under* London
Southwell, Lady Anne, **39**, 231
Southwell, Robert, **17**, 123–4, 124n; **28**, 166; **54**, 35, 96; **57**, 300, 301; **60**, 279n41, 342
Southworth, John, **52**, 262
Soviet Theatre, *see under* Theatre, Soviet
Sowards, J. K., **54**, 224n
Sowerbutts, Peter, **43**, 214; **45**, 155
Soyinka, Wole, **36**, 11–19; **38**, 217; **39**, 169–78 *passim*
Spacey, Kevin, **59**, 299, 320–1, 322–3; **60**, 326
Spacks, Patricia Meyer, **14**, 65n; **50**, 70n
Spadaro, Armando, **15**, 136
Spaeth, J. D., **4**, 140n
Spaethling, Robert, **56**, 151n
Spaggiari, Laura, **40**, 205
Spain, and relations between England and Barbary, **11**, 90–3, 96
Spain, Nancy, **56**, 131n
Spain, report on Shakespeare in, **1**, 116; **9**, 115–16
Spakowski, R. E., **25**, 176
Spalding, K. J., *The Philosophy of Shakespeare* reviewed, **8**, 145
Spalding, Mark, **47**, 214
Spalding, T. A., **19**, 66n; **29**, 79, 83
Spalinger, Adolf, **11**, 122
Spall, Timothy, **46**, 189; **47**, 215
Spangenberg, Heidemarie, **23**, 123; **37**, 159n
Spanish Tragedy, The, **50**, 35, 43; **54**, 13, 113, 313, 351
Spányik, E., **14**, 120
Spargo, J. W., **6**, 13, 15n; **19**, 11; **30**, 35
Sparling, H. H., **17**, 23n
Sparrow, John, **4**, 148, 155
Sparshott, F. E., **56**, 208n
Spate, O. K., **55**, 180n
Spathis, Dimitris, **58**, 209
Spaul, Richard, **45**, 63n
Speaight, George, **43**, 106n
Speaight, Robert, **1**, 121; **2**, 4, 127; **9**, 17, 18, 147; **10**, 59n; **12**, 118, 144; **16**, 172n; **18**, 131; **19**, 54n; **20**, 170; **23**, 174n; **24**, 167; **25**, 1n, 117n; **26**, 175, 176n; **29**, 87; **31**, 174, 178; **33**, 181; **35**, 11, 12; **41**, 59n; **47**, 85n; **49**, 128n; **50**, 30n; **52**, 17n, 18n; **53**, 235; **57**, 331
Nature in Shakespearian Tragedy reviewed, **10**, 137–8
Spear, Gary, **47**, 233
Spearing, A. C. and J. E., **30**, 206n
Spears, Monroe K., **36**, 30n
Speck, W. A., **51**, 70n
Spectator, The, **3**, 136
Spedding, James, **2**, 44, 58; **4**, 159–60; **6**, 5. 6; **9**, 73, 79n; **17**, 81n; **18**, 186; **28**, 16n; **32**, 23; **33**, 27; **38**, 145; **43**, 43–4, 49; **44**, 12n; **51**, 334; **57**, 201
Spedding, John, **54**, 82
Speed, John, **1**, 30; **5**, 149; **12**, 28; **15**, 172; **17**, 66; **30**, 163n; **38**, 97, 99; **42**, 35; **53**, 200; **54**, 100; **59**, 220
The History of Great Britain, **10**, 29; **11**, 45–6, 49n
Theatre of the Empire of Great Britain, **1**, 31, 35n
Speer, Albert, **35**, 164
Speght, Thomas, **11**, 145; **34**, 85; **54**, 25n
edition of *Chaucer*, **9**, 24, 81
Speidel, Ludwig, **35**, 21, 24, 25, 27n
Speirs, John, **20**, 73n
Spelman, Sir Henry, **51**, 136; **59**, 262
Spence, Joseph, **10**, 20; **14**, 80
Spence, Lewis, **17**, 175
Spence, Paul, **39**, 199; **41**, 165
Spence, Piers, **48**, 18n
Spencer, Brian, **13**, 151; **54**, 124n
Spencer, Charles, **50**, 34; **56**, 237n; **58**, 52
Spencer, Christopher, **16**, 181; **20**, 153, 169; **21**, 156; **24**, 167; **26**, 181; **32**, 38, 44; **43**, 91n; **46**, 138n; **51**, 23n; **52**, 151n; **55**, 96n; **57**, 56
Davenant's 'Macbeth' from the Yale Manuscript reviewed, **16**, 181
Spencer, Eric, **58**, 310
Spencer, Gabriel, **3**, 150; **4**, 158; **17**, 10, 88; **58**, 201
Spencer, Hazelton, **3**, 23; **6**, 7; **7**, 1; **15**, 29; **55**, 265
Art and Life of William Shakespeare, **3**, 8, 24
Spencer, Herbert, **55**, 258n; **56**, 206; **60**, 346
Spencer, Janet M., **46**, 213; **50**, 251
Spencer, John, **32**, 192n, 194, 197; **36**, 135, 138n
Spencer, Lois, **22**, 168
Spencer, Luke, **41**, 69
Spencer, Michael, **45**, 146
Spencer, Robert, **45**, 157
Spencer, Stanley, **46**, 173
Spencer, T. J. B. (Terence), **8**, 147; **10**, 1; **12**, 138; **16**, 166; **18**, 1, 56n, 129, 171, 179, 180; **19**, 125, 140, 143, 145; **20**, 105n; **21**, 129, 150, 157; **22**, 168; **23**, 141; **24**, 53, 64n; **26**, 89, 166; **29**, 115; **30**, 97n; **31**, 2n, 3–4, 5, 6, 11; **32**, 238; *33*, 181; **34**, 152n, 188, 189; **35**, 119n, 182–3, 189; **39**, 4n, 77n; **41**, 145; **49**, 4, 7n; **51**, 145, 155; **52**, 307; **53**, 46, 78n, 79, 81n, 84; **55**, 199n; **59**, 39–40, 42, 44, 45, 46, 47
'Shakespeare and the Elizabethan Romans', **10**, 27–38
'Shakespeare Learns the Value of Money', **6**, 75–8
The Tyranny of Shakespeare reviewed, **15**, 156
'Shakespeare *v.* The Rest: The Old Controversy', **14**, 76–89

Spencer, Theodore, **2**, 108; **3**, 29; **4**, 14; **6**, 8, 156; **7**, 135; **8**, 33, 34, 113; **11**, 59; **13**, 42; **14**, 100n; **25**, 8, 11n, 13n; **27**, 51n, 56n; **29**, 85, 86; **33**, 5; **44**, 205; **53**, 3
'The Elizabethan Malcontent', **2**, 143
Shakespeare and the Nature of Man, **3**, 7; **13**, 47n, 48n
Spencer, Thomas, **54**, 41n
Spender, Stephen, **4**, 19; **19**, 6, 51; **36**, 29, 30
Spengier, Oswald, **40**, 82n
Spens, Janet, **1**, 128; **3**, 25; **6**, 159; **8**, 3; **14**, 11; **15**, 112
Spenser, Benjamin T., **38**, 13
Spenser, Edmund, **1**, 63, 67; **2**, 54; **3**, 18, 19, 65; **4**, 49–50, 55n, 65, 143, 147; **5**, 50, 89, 138, 139n, 142; **6**, 54; **7**, 7, 8, 19, 141; **8**, 57; **9**, 24–5, 144; **10**, 17, 60; **12**, 133; **13**, 30, 110n; **14**, 80, 99, 100, 146; **15**, 19, 41, 43–4, 81, 83–4, 86–7, 96, 105; **16**, 12, 126, 165; **17**, 51, 114–15, 132, 171, 183; **18**, 35; **19**, 55–6, 58, 59; **20**, 20; **22**, 51, 166, 170; **23**, 21, 23, 61, 98, 166; **25**, 103, 105, 138; **26**, 107, 114n; **27**, 96, 99–100, 109, 117n, 169, 172, 191; **28**, 20, 41n, 76, 78, 122; **29**, 173; **31**, 13, 33, 108, 184, 191; **32**, 73, 74, 149, 150, 246; **33**, 17, 110, 193, 203; **34**, 87, 100; **35**, 79, 80; **36**, 93; **37**, 10; **38**, 22, 54, 122, 133, 178, 180–4, 191, 215, 232, 234; **39**, 219, 226; **40**, 48, 123–5, 128, 132, 227; **41**, 113, 142, 149, 196, 210; **42**, 29, 33, 35, **43**, 155n, 243, 255n; **44**, 62, 132–6, 140, 141, 239, 254; **45**, 54–6, 166, 182; **46**, 16, 40, 41n, 46n, 48n, 51n, 52, 57, 115, 125, 127n, 133; **48**, 124, 257; **49**, 62, 171, 295, 302; **51**, 18, 135; **52**, 114, 267, 287, 309; **53**, 13; **54**, 3, 4, 15, 32, 77, 320; **55**, 15, 21, 226n, 346, 360; **56**, 30, 44, 57n, 88, 217, 220, 308, 311; **57**, 242, 247, 314; **58**, 152, 157; **59**, 94, 259, 261, 267, 274, 275–6, 350–1, 355, 356; **60**, 262–3, 332–3, 344
Amoretti, **15**, 41–3
Colin Clouts Come Home Againe, **3**, 54; **14**, 163
Complaints, **10**, 25n
The Faerie Queene, **3**, 139; **4**, 4, 154; **5**, 146; **8**, 60; **9**, 81, 138, 142; **10**, 20; **11**, 107; **13**, 41, 44, 46, 157; **14**, 163; **15**, 83, 88n, 91, 176
Hymne in Honour of Beautie, **5**, 80n
Shepheards Calendar, **10**, 20
Thalia, **12**, 31
View of the Present State of Ireland (MS.), **1**, 71; **4**, 162
Spenser, Gabriel, **33**, 158
Spenser, Jeremy, **18**, 154
Spenser, T. J. B., **54**, 20n
Spenz, Liza, **43**, 210
Speratus, Julius, **15**, 98n
Sperli, Alessandro, **15**, 136
Speroni, Sperone, **15**, 89, 90
Spevack, Marvin, **22**, 157, 176; **23**, 176, 177; **25**, 94, 199; **28**, 177, 178; **29**, 183, 184; **30**, 89n, 90n, 95n, 209; **31**, 174; **33**, 184; **34**, 66n; **36**, 111n; **37**, 159; **40**, 147, 219, 228; **41**, 232–3; **42**, 127, 205–6, 212; **43**, 259; **45**, 30n, 193n, 194, 196–8, 203n; **48**, 243, 267; **52**, 188n; **53**, 133n; **54**, 15n, 28n; **55**, 181n, 192n; **59**, 257
Spewack, Sam and Bella, **42**, 157
Kiss Me, Kate, **4**, 123
Sphinx Theatre Company, **58**, 298
Spiekerman, Tim, **55**, 355–6
Spielberg, Stephen, **57**, 319
Spielmann, M. H., **1**, 59; **3**, 9; **5**, 57n
Spierenburg, Pieter, **46**, 235
Spies, Alfons, **15**, 97n
Spiker, S., **25**, 145n
Spikes, J. Doolin, **38**, 112n
Spikes, J. T., **41**, 145n
Spillane, Mickey, **27**, 177
Spiller, Elizabeth, **57**, 191; **58**, 358
Spiller, Jeremy, **51**, 47
Spiller, Michael, **48**, 253
Development of the Sonnet, An Introduction, The, **48**, 253
Spines, Christine, **52**, 94n
Spinetti, Victor, **18**, 153
Spingarn, J. E., **2**, 111; **7**, 89n; **21**, 46n
Spinner, Jonathan H., **31**, 194–5
Spinosa, Charles, **49**, 292; **50**, 249; **55**, 39n
Spinoza, Bruch de, **48**, 3; **49**, 138n
Spinrad, Phoebe S., **38**, 231
Spira, Theodor, **10**, 142
Spiro, Alison, **42**, 156
Spiro, Samantha, **54**, 269; **57**, 264
Spitz, Mark, **57**, 190–4
Spitzer, Leo, **57**, 308
Spivack, Bernard, **12**, 134; **21**, 3, 33, 53, 54, 57, 58, 61; **23**, 152; **26**, 7, 171; **27**, 23n; **30**, 36, 41n; **38**, 7, 155n
Shakespeare and the Allegory of Evil reviewed, **13**, 150–1
Spivack, Charlotte, **22**, 171
Spivak, Gayatri Chakravorty, **50**, 247; **54**, 323; **55**, 69n; **57**, 33
Splinter Group (New York), **58**, 305
Spock, Dr Benjamin, **57**, 138
Spolsky, Ellen, **57**, 307
Spon, Marian, **54**, 283
Spong, Andrew, **50**, 274; **51**, 333
Spooner, John, **48**, 236
Spoto, Donald, **49**, 233, 234n
Spotswood, Jerald W., **53**, 304; **55**, 6n; **56**, 328
Spottiswoode, Tracey, **41**, 189
Sprague, Arthur Colby, **1**, 4; **4**, 11; **8**, 140; **9**, 51, 53, 68n, 147; **10**, 149; **11**, 148n; **13**, 74; **14**, 12; **16**, 37; **18**, 40, 129, 184; **19**, 153; **20**, 72n, 152; **21**, 156; **22**, 133n, 165; **24**, 120; **25**, 185; **26**, 114n; **27**, 34n; **28**, 171; **30**, 91n; **32**, 23n, 31, 32n, 33n; **33**, 4–5, 7n, 11; **34**, 63n, 164; **36**, 119n; **39**, 17, 196; **40**, 37, 47; **41**, 56n; **42**, 37, 38n; **43**, 81n, 181n; **49**, 115n, 123n, 307; **56**, 97; **58**, 40; **60**, 116n61
Shakespearian Players and Performances, **13**, 80n
Shakespearian Players and Performances reviewed, **8**, 152
'Shakespeare's Unnecessary Characters', **20**, 75–82
Sprague, Richard S., **32**, 163n; **40**, 81n
Sprain, Patricia, **52**, 195n
Spranger, Barry, **51**, 11; **58**, 262
Spread of the Eagle, The, **39**, 9, 15, 16, 22, 94
Sprenger, J., **28**, 119
Sprenger, James, *see* Kramer, Heinrich
Sprengnether, Madelon, **40**, 92n; **50**, 247–8
Spriet, Pierre, **23**, 166–7; **38**, 222; **40**, 84n; **52**, 323
Spriggs, Elizabeth, **20**, 136; **22**, 139; **23**, 131; **25**, 166; **49**, 13
Sprinchorn, Evert, **24**, 166n; **47**, 32n, 38n, 88; **48**, 268–9; **50**, 151
Sprinkle-Jackson, Kathryn, **43**, 269
Sprott, S. E., **24**, 157n
Sproule, Albert F., **11**, 140
Spufford, Margaret, **55**, 37n

Spurgeon, Caroline, **1**, 120; **2**, 59; **3**, 132; **4**, 18, 19–20, 146, 160; **5**, 62, 81, 82–3, 84–5, 86, 87, 88, 91n, 92n; **6**, 150; **7**, 8–9; **8**, 8, 39n, 112; **9**, 14, 43n; **10**, 8; **11**, 53; **13**, 58, 66; **15**, 17, 123; **18**, 42, 46, 49, 52, 53, 55, 177; **19**, 6, 9, 35–6, 45, 54n, 62; **20**, 87, 127; **21**, 11n, 107; **22**, 162; **24**, 26; **28**, 30, 32, 35; **31**, 27; **33**, 113; **34**, 6; **36**, 174; **38**, 37, 57n; **41**, 103–4, 224; **42**, 179; **43**, 88; **44**, 2; **49**, 165; **51**, 167n; **54**, 202n; **56**, 243; **60**, 123
Shakespeare's Imagery, **2**, 83, 136; **13**, 45
Keats's Shakespeare, **13**, 68n
Spurgeon, Darrell, **53**, 209n
Spurgeon, Dickie A., **56**, 43n
Spurgeon, F. E., **25**, 8
Spurling, Hilary, **30**, 173n
Spurrier, Linda, **44**, 193
Spurzheim, Johann Kaspar, **60**, 234
Squarzina, Luigi, **7**, 112; **12**, 114; **20**, 130
Squire, J. C., **4**, 11–12; **9**, 75; **55**, 129
Squire, William Barclay, **3**, 55; **6**, 138; **7**, 124; **15**, 3, 6
Sreenivasan, B. R., **11**, 149n
Srigley, Michael, **34**, 185; **35**, 188; **48**, 151n, 248; **58**, 313
St Clair, William, **59**, 117n38
St George's, Southwark; St Mary Overie's; St Olave's, Southwark; St Paul's; *see under* London
St George, Julia, **41**, 24
St Germain, Christopher, **27**, 95, 96, 97; **29**, 93, 94n, 99
St John, Andrew, **59**, 344
St John, Christopher, **32**, 16n; **35**, 8n; **46**, 20n
St John, J. A., **14**, 98
St John, John, **59**, 194n8
St John, Oliver, **38**, 33
Stabler, Arthur P., **19**, 147n; **20**, 165; **21**, 152; **29**, 171
Stacey, Richard, **59**, 331
Stachniewski, John, **35**, 179
Stack, Richard, **34**, 12, 18n, 19, 20, 21
Stackhouse, Amy, **50**, 144n
Stacy, G., **31**, 182
Stading, Richard, **49**, 125n
Stadler, Edmund, **18**, 185; **29**, 176
Stadtbibliothek, Zürich, *see under* Libraries
Staebler, Warren, **4**, 144n; **29**, 164
Staël, Madame de (Anne Louise Germaine Necker), **3**, 100; **60**, 215, 222
Stafford, Earl of, **52**, 173
Stafford, Maeliosa, **53**, 280
Stafford, Simon, **55**, 27–35
Stafford, T. J., **26**, 154, 180n, 184n
Stafford, W. T., **18**, 118n
Stafford-Clark, Max, **47**, 187–8; **48**, 230; **59**, 340; **60**, 161
Stafford-Northcote, Julia, **53**, 283
Staford, Henry, **60**, 366
'Stage 49', Canada, **3**, 117
Stage Fright, **43**, 208
Stage, Elizabethan, *see under* Theatre, Elizabethan
Stagg, L. C., **36**, 174
Staging of Shakespeare's plays, *see under* Theatre, Elizabethan Theatres, productions of Shakespeare's plays, *and individual titles of plays*
Stahl, Ernst, **4**, 127; **35**, 23n
Shakespeare und das deutsche Theater reviewed, **3**, 117
Stahl, Hannelore, **9**, 134; **23**, 13n
Staiger, Emil, **7**, 115, 137–8; **37**, 152n
Staiger, Janet, **52**, 88n
Stalder, Verena, **23**, 156
Staley, Allen, **49**, 118n
Stalin, Josef, **48**, 189; **54**, 149; **55**, 165; **60**, 335
Stallo, J., **24**, 97
Stallworthy, Simon, **43**, 215; **53**, 277
Stallybrass, Oliver, **48**, 113n
Stallybrass, Peter, **37**, 184; **42**, 196; **44**, 22n, 217; **46**, 36n, 60, 71n, 131; **48**, 26n, 270–1; **49**, 70n; **50**, 58n, 141–2, 273–4; **51**, 274, 295, 332; **55**, 6n, 233n, 240n, 242, 250, 341–2, 371–3; **56**, 70n; **58**, 34, 40, 41, 70; **59**, 17n69, 20, 21, 108–9n3, 114n27; **60**, 73n3, 168, 228, 233n57, 255n14
Stalman, Julia, **41**, 27
Stamford Shakespeare Festival, **58**, 306
Stamford, 10th Earl of, *see* Grey, Roger
Stamm, Heinrich, **4**, 127
Stamm, Renate, **37**, 158n
Stamm, Rudolf, **5**, 112; **7**, 115; **8**, 121; **10**, 143, 146, 147; **13**, 131; **14**, 153; **18**, 129, 185; **19**, 135; **20**, 157; **22**, 159; **23**, 114; **25**, 12n, 14n, 23n, 24n, 174; **26**, 166n; **31**, 175; **32**, 224; **37**, 158, 161n; **38**, 225; **40**, 211n; **41**, 211, 245n; **44**, 210; **51**, 197n; **59**, 195
'Elizabethan Stage-Practice and the Tramsmutation of Source Material by the Dramatists', **12**, 64–70
Englische Literatur, **12**, 116, 139 and n
'Modern "Theatrical" Translations of Shakespeare', **16**, 63–9
Shakespeare's Word-Scenery, **12**, 70n
Shakespeare's Word-Scenery with Some Remarks on Stage-History and the Interpretation of his Plays reviewed, **8**, 145–6
Stamnitz, Suzanne, **37**, 158n
Stampfer, Judah, **15**, 158; **29**, 89; **33**, 8, 45; **41**, 145n; **45**, 81
'The Catharsis of *King Lear*', **13**, 1–10
Stanbridge, John, **1**, 68
Vulgaria, **1**, 67
Standen, Anthony, **57**, 201
Standidge, Eric, **43**, 208
Standing, Herbert, **49**, 116n
Stanford, Alan, **44**, 192; **45**, 152; **46**, 198; **47**, 210, 212; **48**, 233; **49**, 273; **58**, 260, 261, 262
Stanford, D., **26**, 165
Stanford, Henry, **28**, 174
Stanford, Peter, **57**, 51
Stanford, William Bedell, **44**, 85n
Stanhope, John, first Baron Stanhope of Harrington (? 1545–1621), accounts as Treasurer of the Chamber, **4**, 88, 91; **8**, 108
Stanhope, John Roddam Spencer, **49**, 125
Staniewski, Wlodzimierz, **58**, 358
Stanihurst, Richard, **57**, 43, 217
Stanislavsky, Konstantin, **3**, 106, 135–6; **4**, 101; **5**, 117; **6**, 118; **8**, 70; **12**, 79; **18**, 67; **23**, 174; **24**, 167; **26**, 140; **27**, 144; **29**, 153; **30**, 13n, 16, 26; **34**, 8; **36**, 70; **37**, 162, 201; **40**, 2; **41**, 129; **43**, 251; **45**, 67; **47**, 3; **48**, 108, 187, 189; **49**, 12; **50**, 38, 240; **54**, 142–5, 148–51, 309; **55**, 280; **56**, 346; **57**, 169, 171; **59**, 294
Stanivukovic, Goran, **56**, 34n
Stanley family, **44**, 232
Stanley, Arthur Penrhyn, **4**, 146n; **54**, 85
Stanley, Audrey, **45**, 27n
Stanley, Earls of Derby, **39**, 223

Stanley, Edward, Earl of Derby, **17**, 153
Stanley, Ferdinando, Earl of Derby, **3**, 23; **54**, 91
Stanley, Henry, Earl of Derby, **3**, 10
Stanley, Siobhan, **47**, 219
Stanley, Sir Thomas, **4**, 156; **34**, 95n
Stanley, William, Earl of Derby, **1**, 124–5; **3**, 11; **7**, 97, 138–9
Stanley, Sir William, **3**, 23; **35**, 72
Stannard, David E., **54**, 123n
Stansby, William, **15**, 128; **19**, 163; **51**, 291
Stansell, Christine, **45**, 45n
Stanton, Barry, **28**, 148; **39**, 79n; **42**, 161; **43**, 173, 180; **45**, 63n; **52**, 239; **55**, 310, 332; **56**, 293
Stanton, Sarah, **57**, 68, 171, 325
Stanton, Theodore, **45**, 44n
Stanton, Thomas, **5**, 55
Stanyhurst, Richard, **23**, 164–5; **57**, 217; **60**, 272n13
  translation of Virgil's *Aeneid*, **10**, 30
Stapers, Richard, **11**, 96
Stapfer, Paul, **31**, 2; **40**, 72
Stapleford, *see under* Rothwell, William
Staples, Jasper, **25**, 148
Staples, John, **6**, 73n
Stapleton, M. L., **48**, 254; **55**, 348
Stapleton, Thomas, **42**, 83
Star Chamber, the, **4**, 79; **8**, 7; **17**, 68, 76, 89
Star, Leonie, **31**, 186–7; **32**, 233
Stark, James, **22**, 133
Stark, Mrs James, **22**, 133
Starke, Michael, **44**, 203
Starkey, Colin, **42**, 154
Starkey, David, **60**, 61n8
Starkey, Thomas, **17**, 109
Starks, Lisa S., **54**, 311; **56**, 347; **57**, 145, 330; **59**, 354; **60**, 169n6.2
Starnes, De Witt T., **15**, 29; **19**, 88, 94n, 147; **26**, 112n; **31**, 33n; **32**, 168n
Starr, G. A., **20**, 165; **22**, 109
Startin, Simon, **57**, 295
Startup Papers: On Shakespeare's Friend, The (R. Hunt), **48**, 267
Staten, Henry, **50**, 172n, 181n
States, Bert O., **28**, 153; **40**, 126n; **49**, 203n; **55**, 239n; **57**, 29; **59**, 295; **60**, 104n12
Statham, Jonathan, **59**, 202
Stathan, Robert, **49**, 184
Stationers' Company, The, **4**, 78–9, 83; **7**, 36
Stationers' Company Records, **11**, 153; **17**, 68, 207–8, 213, 220
Statius, **10**, 48; **15**, 98n
Statman, Ingrid, **56**, 292
Staton, Walter, Jr, **42**, 63n
Staufer, Annegret, **37**, 159n
Stauffer, Donald A., **5**, 92n; **7**, 10; **8**, 9; **18**, 54; **27**, 22n
  Shakespeare's World of Images reviewed, **4**, 145
Staunford, J., **29**, 100
Staunton, Howard, **4**, 67n; **7**, 92; **8**, 153; **9**, 156; **53**, 336; **57**, 341; **59**, 53–4, 149
  Shakespeare, **13**, 80n
Staunton, William, **56**, 187n
Staves, Susan, **51**, 20n
Stavig, Mark, **23**, 171; **24**, 165; **50**, 244
Staviski, Aron Y., **24**, 153
Stavropoulos, Janet, **46**, 62n
Ste B.; *Counsel to the husband: to the wife instruction*, **60**, 89, 90, 91, 95
Steadman, Alison, **56**, 247
Steadman, John M., **14**, 154; **20**, 166; **54**, 322
Steafel, Sheila, **39**, 199
Steane, J. B., **47**, 129n, 132n; **48**, 27n; **57**, 231; **60**, 261n32
Stearns, David Patrick, **52**, 41n
Stebbings, Paul, **41**, 189
Steckel, Leonard, **6**, 124; **14**, 116
Stedder, James, **31**, 153
Stedefeld, G. F., **28**, 40, 41n
Stedman, Jane M., **41**, 225
Stedman-Jones, Gareth, **59**, 264n27
Steed, Maggie, **42**, 132; **43**, 212
Steedman, Tony, **16**, 150
Steegman, Mary G., **7**, 105n
Steel, David, **50**, 23n
Steel, Janet, **43**, 213; **44**, 200
Steele, Eugene, **55**, 247n
Steele, Jeffrey, **53**, 128n, 133
Steele, Miss M. S., **11**, 107, 108, 110, 113, 115n, 116n
  Plays and Masques at Court, **11**, 107, 115n
Steele, Sir Richard, **32**, 44; **34**, 11; **37**, 143n, 146
Steele, Robert R., **17**, 34n, 35n
Steen, Harald Heide, **14**, 122
Steen, Sara J., **42**, 192
Steenbergen, Paul, **18**, 127
Steer Matthew, **54**, 284
Steer, Aidan, **54**, 291
Steer, Barbara D. G., **7**, 139
Steer, Bartholomew, **44**, 18, 19
Steevens, George, **2**, 39; **3**, 43–4, 45, 47–8, 49, 57n; **4**, 80, 81, 87; **5**, 105n; **6**, 61; **7**, 82; **8**, 94; **18**, 17, 18, 19, 108; **19**, 78; **20**, 36, 90; **25**, 111n; **27**, 69, 111n, 112, 119; **29**, 111n; **32**, 85, 92–3, 96, 242; **33**, 210; **34**, 12, 13, 15, 16n, 18n, 192, 195; **35**, 178, 188n; **36**, 188, 193; **38**, 158n, 248; **39**, 128, 239; **41**, 35–7, **46**, 37, 39, 40n; **47**, 107, 246; **49**, 118–19, 165n; **50**, 280n; **51**, 7, 9, 134, 325; **53**, 60n, 187, 337; **54**, 56; **55**, 13, 388; **57**, 89, 112, 115; **58**, 353; **59**, 56–7n20, 57n21, 60, 93, 98, 114–15, 125, 127–9, 130, 132–4, 159, 216
Stefanović, S., **4**, 117
Stefansson, V. (ed.), **17**, 29n
Steggle, Matthew, **56**, 336; **58**, 200, 358
Stegner, Page, **50**, 125n
Stegner, Paul D., **58**, 26; **60**, 351
Stehlíková, Eva, **21**, 134
Steibelt, Daniel, **18**, 78
Steible, Mary, **58**, 358
Steiger, André, **10**, 118
Steiger, Rod, **55**, 243
Stein, Arnold, **23**, 150; **36**, 88n
Stein, Charles W., **57**, 250, 255
Stein, Dieter, **37**, 159n
Stein, Peter, **37**, 161, 162; **40**, 2; **44**, 94; **45**, 119; **48**, 229; **50**, 33; **51**, 193; **56**, 177; **58**, 150, 158; **59**, 298; **60**, 310
Stein, Walter, **33**, 12
Steinbach, Kari, **46**, 61n
Steinberg, Jonathan, **45**, 131
Steinbock, Rudolf, **18**, 119
Steiner, George, **30**, 88; **36**, 101; **48**, 2; **50**, 125n, 126, 132, 133n; **51**, 6; **55**, 72, 155; **58**, 169, 175, 176, 177, 182, 184

Steiner, Grundy, **21**, 142; **24**, 20
Steiner, Marcel, **51**, 262
Steiner, Rudolf, **51**, 284
Steinhausen, G., **33**, 156n
Steinsaltz, David, **58**, 313, 333
Stellmacher, Wolfgang, **21**, 149; **22**, 166
Stelter, Martina, **50**, 264
Stemhold, Thomas, **54**, 24
Stemmer, J. P., **13**, 131
Stempel, Daniel, **10**, 10, 140–1; **23**, 152
Sten, Maria, **54**, 152n
Stendhal (Henri Marie Beyle), **7**, 95; **16**, 54; **21**, 81, 82; **34**, 6, 9; **60**, 216
Stenning, H. J., **35**, 66n
Stenning, Stephen, **57**, 293
Stensgaard, Richard K., **26**, 172
Stent, Peter, **1**, 27; **50**, 169
Štěpánek, B., **9**, 104, 110n
Štěpanék, Vladimír, **21**, 140
Štěpánek, Zdeněk, **9**, 109, 111; **13**, 126
Stephanus, Robert, **24**, 53
Stephen, Leslie, **53**, 69n; **58**, 119, 128
Stephen, Pamela, **55**, 313
Stephen, Walter, **59**, 240n4
Stephens, Babette, **14**, 116
Stephens, Christopher, **55**, 248–9
Stephens, F. G., **38**, 70n
Stephens, James Brunton, **56**, 155
Stephens, Jenny, **51**, 263
Stephens, John C., **35**, 178
Stephens, Katy, **59**, 340
Stephens, Lyn, **47**, 223
Stephens, Peter, **46**, 194
Stephens, Sir Robert, **37**, 168, 170; **44**, 194, 198; **45**, 119, 143; **46**, 193; **47**, 199–203; **48**, 230; **54**, 248
Stephens, Rosemary, **19**, 123
Stephens, Thomas, **32**, 194
Stephens, Toby, **48**, 214–15, 217; **49**, 270; **55**, 326; **58**, 295; **59**, 339
Stephens, Walter, **57**, 31
Stephenson, A. A., **4**, 24; **8**, 39n
Stephenson, Gregory, **53**, 173n
Stephenson, Kristina, **42**, 150
Steppat, Michael, **35**, 164n; **37**, 160n
Stere, Bartholomew, **3**, 35
Sterling, Eric, **51**, 286
Sterling, John, **28**, 40; **54**, 82
Stern, Madeleine B., **53**, 166n
Stern, Tiffany, **55**, 375–6; **56**, 175–7, 179; **58**, 334, 341, 342; **59**, 12n52, 22; **60**, 360
Sternberg, Paul R., **45**, 197n
Sternbridge, Gerard, **48**, 228; **49**, 273
Sterne, Laurence, **18**, 37; **51**, 62
Sterne, Richard L., **23**, 174n
Sternfeld, Frederick W., **12**, 144; **13**, 161; **15**, 40n; **18**, 183; **19**, 152; **22**, 178; **23**, 183; **24**, 112n, 156; **26**, 173; **29**, 2; **34**, 189; **39**, 149n, 157; **44**, 238; **54**, 27n
 'Music and Ballads', **17**, 214–22
 'Twentieth-century Studies in Shakespeare's Songs, Sonnets, and Poems: 1, Songs and Music', **15**, 1–9
Sternfield, Moshe, **49**, 278
Sternlicht, Sanford, **21**, 134; **27**, 177
Stesichorus, **36**, 85
Stetner, S. C. V., **25**, 200
Stettin, Duke of, **36**, 147
Steuart, A. F., **38**, 71n
Steuart, David, **12**, 121
Stevens, Allan, **10**, 150
Stevens, David, **32**, 233; **41**, 1n; **45**, 151
Stevens, Denis, **15**, 8
Stevens, George Alexander, **55**, 90
Stevens, John, **15**, 8; **19**, 151; **34**, 27; **38**, 20; **44**, 238; **51**, 97n
Stevens, Martin, **24**, 160; **30**, 188; **31**, 171; **57**, 246
Stevens, Paul, **55**, 338; **60**, 282n51
Stevens, Philip, **58**, 300
Stevens, R. J. S., **18**, 98, 99, 100; **51**, 88
Stevens, Vicky, **57**, 209
Stevens, Wallace, **18**, 115
Stevenson, Adlai, **57**, 141
Stevenson, Allan H., **6**, 170
Stevenson, David Lloyd, **8**, 9; **11**, 137; **14**, 155–6; **15**, 16; **21**, 52n, 135; **25**, 7, 29; **28**, 93n; **56**, 215n
Stevenson, Gerda, **44**, 196, 199
Stevenson, J., **46**, 131n
Stevenson, Sir John, **18**, 99
Stevenson, Joseph, **55**, 53n
Stevenson, Juliet, **35**, 147; **38**, 202, 204; **39**, 191, 200–5; **41**, 68, 72–3, 75–6, 183, 190; **42**, 200; **43**, 254; **46**, 9, 11n; **54**, 270; **56**, 173, 343; **58**, 56
Stevenson, Karl, **45**, 152
Stevenson, Laura Caroline, **52**, 103
Stevenson, Lise, **51**, 225; **52**, 259
Stevenson, R., **54**, 120n
Stevenson, Randall, **57**, 126
Stevenson, Robert Louis, **53**, 169
Stevenson, Robert, **26**, 71, 72
Stevenson, Ruth, **49**, 143n, 284; **57**, 318
Stevenson, Warren, **20**, 146
Stevick, R. D., **18**, 169
Stewart of Bothwellhaugh, **24**, 156
Stewart, A., **54**, 223n
Stewart, Alan, **50**, 78n; **54**, 315; **57**, 207; **60**, 129
Stewart, Alice, **50**, 199n
Stewart, B. T., **26**, 161
Stewart, Carol, **48**, 24n
Stewart, Douglas J., **31**, 184; **38**, 14; **51**, 177n
Stewart, Eve, **42**, 158; **43**, 205
Stewart, Garrett, **36**, 167
Stewart, J. A., **8**, 116n
Stewart, J. I. M., **4**, 3, 13, 16–17; **6**, 13; **7**, 131; **10**, 8, 98, 106n; **12**, 134; **15**, 114; **19**, 9; **21**, 4, 9–10; **22**, 65; **27**, 45n, 159; **38**, 84; **46**, 65n; **56**, 102; **57**, 241
 Character and Motive in Shakespeare reviewed, **3**, 131–2
Stewart, Patrick, **24**, 117, 121; **26**, 143, 145, 157; **31**, 142; **32**, 205; **33**, 178; **35**, 141, 142, 143, 144, 148; **36**, 153; **38**, 238; **41**, 227; **45**, 60; **56**, 247, 293; **58**, 351; **60**, 293, 294, 295–6, 297, 315, 316
Stewart, R. J., **44**, 203
Stewart, Sara, **53**, 261
Stewart, Stanley, **56**, 147n
Stewart, Susan, **53**, 77n

Stewart, William, **19**, 3; **40**, 205
Buik of the Chroniclis of Scotland, **4**, 39–40
Sticcotti, Antonio, **59**, 288
Stickells, Robert, **33**, 142, 145
Stifter, Adalbert, **35**, 25
Stiles, George, **56**, 260
Stiles, Julia, **54**, 292
Still, Colin, **4**, 20; **7**, 8; **15**, 116, 117, 120; **29**, 9; **39**, 160, 165; **43**, 127
Still, Milly, **53**, 284
Stillinger, Jack, **41**, 108n, 112; **54**, 91n, 92n, 93n
Stillmark, Alexander, **48**, 174
Stilwell, Richard, **54**, 37n
Stirling, Brents, **3**, 41n; **5**, 135; **6**, 9; **7**, 134; **8**, 144; **10**, 8, 9; **13**, 167; **15**, 121, 167; **16**, 174; **18**, 54, 172; **19**, 6, 129, 139–40; **20**, 171; **21**, 22, 25; **23**, 157–8; **24**, 12; **27**, 39n; **31**, 127n, 129, 133; **33**, 205; **38**, 251; **40**, 85n, 86n
The Populace in Shakespeare reviewed, **4**, 150–1
Unity in Shakespearian Tragedy reviewed, **11**, 138
Stirling, Mrs, **49**, 128
Stöber, August, **9**, 95, 100n
Stochholm, Johanne H., **18**, 179; **49**, 113n
Stock, Angela, **57**, 339; **60**, 368
Stock, Brian, **59**, 261n16, 263
Stock, Jan van der, **60**, 238n11
Stockard, Emily, **52**, 281
Stockholder, Katherine S., **23**, 150; **24**, 148; **28**, 154
Stockholder, Kay, **46**, 3, 220; **49**, 64; **55**, 9
Stockholm, Janet M., **15**, 40n
Stockholm, Royal Library of, *see under* Libraries
Stocking, F. H., **26**, 164
Stockman, Jeff, **60**, 178
Stockton, Eric W., **19**, 141
Stockwood, John, **56**, 31
Stodder, Joseph H., **28**, 172
Stoeckel, Rudolph, **59**, 361
Stoedler, E., **10**, 5
Stoke-on-Trent Repertory Theatre Company, **58**, 306
Stoker, Bram, **32**, 33; **35**, 19; **58**, 193; **60**, 330–1
Stoker, Willard, **1**, 111; **8**, 126; **9**, 120; **10**, 125; **12**, 120; **13**, 134; **14**, 126; **15**, 145; **47**, 99, 100, 101, 106
Stokes, Adrian, **52**, 258
Stokes, E., **15**, 4
Stokes, James, **47**, 49n, 50n; **50**, 257; **51**, 290; **60**, 357
Stokes, John, **32**, 19n; **56**, 105n, 135n
Stokes, Simon, **42**, 162
Stoljar, S. J., **55**, 38n, 40n
Stoll, Edgar Elmer, **1**, 14, 15; **2**, 108; **4**, 3, 15, 16, 17, 23; **5**, 114, 135, 136; **6**, 6, 12, 13, 150, 153; **7**, 7, 8, 133, 135; **8**, 5–6, 9, 11, 139, 142, 149; **9**, 9–10, 15, 34n; **10**, 6–7, 98, 99, 106n; **15**, 33, 39n, 166; **18**, 40, 41, 54; **19**, 9, 67n; **21**, 9, 11n, 16, 24, 137; **22**, 146, 166; **23**, 159; **29**, 137; **30**, 109, 148n; **34**, 1; **37**, 11, 55; **45**, 15, 16, 18–20, 26; **52**, 99, 100; **54**, 101; **59**, 147, 147n2
critical attitude to Shakespeare, **4**, 12–13
John Webster, **14**, 11
Stoller, Jennie, **43**, 211
Stoller, Robert J., **46**, 95n
Stone, Alix, **60**, 116n62
Stone, E. D., **49**, 185n, 198n
Stone, Edward, **11**, 142, and n
Stone, Francis, **25**, 147
Stone, George Winchester Jr., **7**, 137; **10**, 150; **19**, 153; **48**, 54n, 55n; **51**, 6, 79n, 86n, 86; **53**, 217n; **54**, 46n, 47n, 56n; **55**, 96n, 97n; **56**, 97n; **57**, 59, 87
Stone, Harlan F., **27**, 104
Stone, Harry, **53**, 106n
Stone, Lawrence, **17**, 116n; **24**, 47n; **29**, 90; **33**, 6; **34**, 116n; **35**, 66n, 73n; **38**, 27n, 29n, 30, 32n, 33n; **39**, 213; **40**, 136n; **42**, 34; 44, 9n; **46**, 42n, 69; **47**, 46; **49**, 95n, 284; **51**, 41, 42, 70n, 71; **55**, 338; **56**, 2n, 68
Stone, P. W. K., **35**, 180; **36**, 189; **37**, 214; **39**, 248; **41**, 154, 157, 235n; **48**, 280; **55**, 2n, 3n, 55n
Stone, Rhashan, **51**, 232, 233; **53**, 267
Stone, Richard, **44**, 202
Stone, W. G., **8**, 149–50; **15**, 2
Stone-Fewings, Jo, **51**, 230, 235; **52**, 246; **55**, 291, 311; **56**, 291; **57**, 292; **58**, 335; **59**, 335
Stonehenge, **12**, 8
Stoner, Joanne, **47**, 216
Stonex, A. B., **52**, 102n
Stookey, Lorena, **32**, 214; **33**, 199
Stopes, Charlotte C., **3**, 2; **4**, 154; **41**, 42; **45**, 106n
Stopes, M. M., **7**, 88n
Stopes, Marie C., **2**, 151; **19**, 3
Stoppard, Edward, **59**, 330; **60**, 321
Stoppard, Tom, **26**, 175; **30**, 97; **36**, 21–8; **39**, 47; **40**, 6; **42**, 100, 150, 178; **43**, 222, 228; **45**, 10–12; **51**, 282; **53**, 286; **56**, 98, 289; **57**, 291; **58**, 150, 159; **60**, 49, 123, 321
Storace, Stephen, **18**, 78
Storer, Thomas, **20**, 24n
Thomas Wolsey, **3**, 54
Storey, David, **55**, 160
Storey, Graham, **15**, 160; **27**, 31n; **32**, 12; **53**, 103n
Storey, Robin, **59**, 263n24
Storin, Gheorghe, **20**, 126
Stormare, Peter, **42**, 150
Storozhenko, Nicolai Ilyich, **16**, 14; **23**, 175
Storr, F., **30**, 113n
Storry, Malcolm, **42**, 153; **44**, 165, 166, 192; **53**, 249; **55**, 317, 332, 335; **56**, 257, 271; **57**, 296; **59**, 305, 306–7; **60**, 324
Story, Alfred T., **37**, 48n
Story, Richard, **29**, 33
Stothard, Thomas, **13**, 76; **49**, 119; **59**, 132
Stott, Ken, **42**, 140, 144; **45**, 152; **55**, 327
Stovall, Floyd, **18**, 118n
Stovell, J., **27**, 98
Stow, James, **49**, 120
Stow, John, **3**, 18, 34, 35, 40n; **5**, 149; **6**, 65; **11**, 94–7, 97n; **14**, 30; **17**, 4, 39, 70n, 75n, 76n, 80n, 89 and n; **20**, 28; **23**, 45; **26**, 81n; **27**, 131; **28**, 1, 3; **30**, 69n, 164n; **33**, 16; **38**, 93, 94, 95n, 110; **42**, 27, 29, 34, 35, 114n; **43**, 248; **45**, 101, 105n, 106; **46**, 233; **47**, 16n; **49**, 79, 301; **51**, 135, 136; **52**, 174n, 178, 179; **53**, 200n, 202n, 204; **54**, 18, 34n, 91, 192n, 331; **60**, 67n17, 72–3n3, 226
The Annales of England, **8**, 107n; **11**, 97n
Chronicles, **4**, 159
edition of *Chaucer*, **9**, 81
Survey of London, **12**, 127, 129n; **14**, 30
Stow, Randolph, **53**, 111; **55**, 170–5, 178, 180
Stowe, Harriet Beecher, **53**, 136
Stowell, Sheila, **50**, 36n

Stoyle, J. D., **41**, 33
Strååt, Hans, **11**, 122
Strachan, Alan, **53**, 284; **54**, 265, 288; **55**, 312, 328; **56**, 294; **58**, 268; **59**, 339
Strachan, Bishop John, **10**, 111
Strachan, Kathy, **43**, 213; **47**, 209
Strachey, James, **37**, 106n; **39**, 144n; **40**, 94, 101n; **44**, 44n; **46**, 108n; **48**, 24n; **49**, 209n; **53**, 82n; **55**, 68n
Strachey, Lytton, **1**, 48; **4**, 2, 14; **5**, 122, 136; **29**, 138; **32**, 179n; **43**, 57n, 110, 117; **46**, 105; **53**, 265
Strachey, Ralph, **19**, 106n
Strachey, William, **1**, 71; **5**, 142; **11**, 103, 104; **17**, 33; **25**, 127n, 128, 131; **43**, 258; **48**, 148; **50**, 246
Stradling, Sir John, **33**, 22
Stradling, Robert, **60**, 187n13
Strafford, Earl of, *see under* Wentworth, Thomas
Straight, Beatrice, **39**, 81n
Straker, Peter, **35**, 151
Strakowski, Jerzy, **32**, 190
Strang, B. M. H., **23**, 23n
Strange, Ferdinando, Lord, **39**, 223, 228; **53**, 26; **54**, 121; **57**, 233
Strange, Lord, *see under* Stanley, Ferdinando, Earl of Derby
Strange's Men, *see under* Theatre, Elizabethan
Strange's-Admiral's Company, **55**, 28
Strasberg, Lee, **59**, 287
'Stratford-upon-Avon a Hundred Years Ago: extracts from the travel diary of the Reverend William Harness', **14**, 110–15
Stratford-upon-Avon, **1**, 38, 39, 59, 61, 75, 79ff.; **2**, 3; **3**, 1, 2, 3, 13, 20, 35, 40, 50; **4**, 101; **5**, 55–7, 140; **6**, 113, 158, 159–60
  Anne Hathaway's Cottage, **1**, 82, 86
  Grammar School, **2**, 23
  Holy Trinity Church, **1**, 58, 83
    Shakespeare's tomb, **5**, 55–7
  New Place, **1**, 61, 86; **5**, 55–7
Stratford-upon-Avon, Court Rolls of Manor of Old Stratford, **12**, 95–106; **17**, 13–14, 20, 59, 118, 126, 170
Stratford, Robert, **58**, 223, 224
Stratford, William, **58**, 224, 225
Strathcona, Lord, **4**, 84
Strathman, Ernest A., **3**, 25; **19**, 127; **38**, 53n
Stratmann, Francis Henry, **52**, 186
Stratton, Mark, **60**, 288
Stratton, Michael, **52**, 41n, 42n
Straumann, Heinrich, **6**, 156; **7**, 115, 137–8; **8**, 121; **15**, 28, 105, 108 and n; **18**, 129; **19**, 128; **28**, 172
  Phönix und Taube. Zur Interpretation von Shakespeares Gedankenwelt reviewed, 144
Strauss, Botho, **43**, 210
Strauss, David Friedrich, **48**, 3; **53**, 116
Strauss, Jennifer, **55**, 174n
Strauss, Leo, **41**, 198
Strauss, Richard, **37**, 207; **60**, 195
Stravinsky, Igor, **18**, 100
Straznicky, Marta, **46**, 226
Streder, James, **38**, 17
Streep, Meryl, **35**, 158; **56**, 256
Street, Carole, **48**, 229
Street, Edward, **45**, 109
Street, Elizabeth, **45**, 104, 109n, 113
Street, G. S., **55**, 133–4
Street, John, Sr, **45**, 101, 102
Street, John, Jr, **45**, 104, 113, 114
Street, Margaret, **45**, 104
Street, Martha, **45**, 104
Street, Peter, **7**, 143; **29**, 130; **33**, 139–51; **40**, 216; **43**, 236; **45**, 101–14; **47**, 15–19, 23, 24; **51**, 298; **52**, 8, 9, 12, 13, 21; **57**, 233; **60**, 29n18
Streett, J. B., **42**, 107n
Strehler, Giorgio, **2**, 129; **6**, 121; **12**, 114; **13**, 151; **31**, 152; **37**, 162; **38**, 234; **39**, 208; **40**, 2; **44**, 94; **48**, 15; **50**, 30, 37; **51**, 193; **55**, 380
Strehlow, John, **42**, 154; **43**, 214; **47**, 216; **48**, 227
Streinu, Vladimir, **20**, 127
Streitberger, W. R., **30**, 189; **41**, 216–17; **42**, 189–90; **46**, 233; **55**, 45n
Strelan, Rick, **54**, 37n
Strete, Richard, **45**, 101
Strete, William, **45**, 101
Stříbrný, Zdeněk, **16**, 133; **18**, 121, 131; **20**, 144, 167; **21**, 129, 153n; **22**, 166; **28**, 158; **29**, 90, 160; **31**, 168; **36**, 146n; **53**, 306; **54**, 308–9
  Shakespeare's History Plays reviewed, **13**, 152
Stride, John, **15**, 147; **27**, 138; **39**, 105
Strier, Richard, **43**, 16; **50**, 259; **51**, 296; **54**, 10, 50n, 73, 169n; **55**, 164n, 269; **59**, 351
Strindberg, August, **1**, 115; **3**, 115; **24**, 8; **34**, 7; **36**, 65; **40**, 58, 61, 202; **43**, 109–15, 117, 119; **44**, 215; **45**, 162; **47**, 3, 12; **52**, 273
Stringer, Gary A., **59**, 277n31
Stringer, Michael, **10**, 85
Stringer, Philip, **35**, 130, 131, 132, 136, 137
Stringer, Thomas, **37**, 187
Strode, William, **35**, 130; **54**, 62n
Stroedel, Wolfgang, **6**, 163n; **7**, 146n; **9**, 113, 147n; **10**, 119, 150n; **11**, 148n
Ström, Carl Johan, **14**, 123; **15**, 138; **36**, 65n, 68–9
Ström, Knut, **1**, 115; **41**, 223
Strömsted, Liv, **7**, 114
Strong, John, **19**, 106n
Strong, L. A. G., **9**, 133
Strong, Mark, **56**, 262, 263
Strong, Patience, **18**, 154
Strong, Sir Roy, **17**, 180n; **24**, 158n; **28**, 170; **30**, 157n, 167n; **32**, 227; **33**, 145n; **35**, 66n, 129n, 138n; **36**, 115n; **41**, 6, 107n; **42**, 83n; **43**, 162n; **46**, 16n, 111n, 115n, 117n; **47**, 17n; **54**, 126n, 136n, 195n, 197n; **55**, 243n; **60**, 7n13
Stroud, T. A., **13**, 151
Stroughair, Jeremy, **54**, 287
Stroup, T. B., **15**, 180; **19**, 128, 129; **26**, 17n; **33**, 203; **54**, 14n; **57**, 237
Stroupe, John H., **41**, 195n, 208n; **46**, 93n
Strout, Nathaniel, **56**, 328
Stroux, Karl-Heinz, **9**, 113; **10**, 119; **12**, 113; **13**, 128; **16**, 134
Strozza, Hercules, **7**, 101
Struijs, Jacob, *Romeo en Juliette*, **20**, 98–100
Strunk, William, **49**, 154
Strype, John, **6**, 64; **30**, 164n
Strzetelski, Jerzy, **53**, 3n
Stuart, Arabella, **42**, 192; **43**, 241; **57**, 13

Stuart, Betty Kantor, **22**, 162
Stuart, Ian, **59**, 81n9
Stuart, Ludovick, 2nd Duke of Lennox and Duke of Richmond, **11**, 92
Stuart, Simon, **33**, 186
Stuart-Wortley, Alice, **60**, 185
Stubbes, George, **34**, 116n
Stubbes, John, **57**, 29
Stubbes, Philip, **8**, 110; **38**, 29; **46**, 115n; **52**, 102, 104; **54**, 57–8, 69; **56**, 32, 34; **58**, 60; **60**, 73n4, 100n41, 114n55
Anatomie of Abuses, The, **1**, 70; **17**, 19–20, 83n, 128, 175, 178–9
Stubbs, Imogen, **40**, 177; **41**, 190; 43, 192–3; **44**, 199; **46**, 68; **47**, 12; **51**, 268; **58**, 164, 293; **59**, 321, 339
Stubbs, John, **46**, 251; **48**, 40–1, 43–4; **51**, 322
Stubbs, Una, **53**, 284
Stubbs, Professor William, **4**, 81
Stübner, Berndt, **40**, 54
Studies in Shakespeare, **11**, 59n
Studies in the Literary Imagination (1993), **48**, 242
Studing, Richard, **25**, 177; **47**, 257–8
Studley, John, **11**, 143; **15**, 84, 88n; **19**, 85–6, 88, 93n, 94n; **20**, 19, 21; **41**, 136; **42**, 55n; **47**, 140; **55**, 348
Stuhr, Jerzy, **51**, 261
Stukely, Dr, **12**, 8
Stukely, Sir Thomas (play), **17**, 51n, 88n
Stull, J. S., **8**, 147–8; **10**, 10, 141
Stuphen, Joyce, **57**, 309
Stupica, B., **15**, 140
Sturgess, Keith, **41**, 9–11; **52**, 296–7
Sturgess, Kim C., **58**, 316, 333
Sturluson, Snorri, **41**, 156n
Sturmer, J. R. van, **35**, 73n
Sturtevant, **53**, 71
Sturua, Robert, **47**, 211; **48**, 15, 188
Stürzl, Erwin A., **21**, 144; **34**, 167
Stutville, George, **58**, 224
Stuteville, Sir Martin, **46**, 31n; **54**, 136n
Styan, John L., **14**, 150; **22**, 173; **31**, 141, 151, 152, 188; **33**, 181; **35**, 1; **36**, 81n, 172; **38**, 153n; **39**, 6, 7n; **41**, 8n, 66; **43**, 230, 249–50; **47**, 74; **50**, 131; **51**, 57n; **52**, 32n; **53**, 233, 239n, 243; **54**, 336; **59**, 64n5
'The Actor at the Foot of Shakespeare's Platform', **12**, 56–63
Styles, Anthony, **45**, 150, 155
Styles, Philip, **17**, 117n; **32**, 95n
'The Commonwealth', **17**, 103–19
Styles, Sue, **42**, 156
Suard, Jean Baptiste A., **9**, 91; **54**, 48n
Suarès, André, **2**, 118–19
Suarez, Franciscus, **44**, 62n
Subbotina, E., **2**, 126
Subramaniam, L., **45**, 154
Such, Susie Speakman, **54**, 92n
Suchet, David, **27**, 149, 151; **28**, 140, 142; **32**, 202, 203; **35**, 141, 149; **38**, 238; **39**, 204, 205; **41**, 188; **42**, 200; **45**, 135; **46**, 200; **47**, 270; **56**, 113
Suci, G., **40**, 36n
Suckling, Sir John, **10**, 14; **17**, 175, 199; **60**, 75n15, 281
Aglaura, **3**, 51
Suckling, Norman, **19**, 140
Sucksmith, Harvey Peter, **53**, 108n
Sudbury, John, **53**, 201n
Suddard, S. J. Mary, **8**, 12; **27**, 18
Sudhoff, C., **19**, 43
Sueki, Toshifumi, **56**, 289
Suerbaum, E., **26**, 157, 166n
Suerbaum, Ulrich, **30**, 208; **37**, 156n
Suetonius, **10**, 31, 35, 38; **22**, 109; **27**, 119; **53**, 78, 79, 83; **55**, 205
Suffolk Place, *see under* London
Suffolk, Duke of (Charles Brandon), **60**, 69–70
Suffolk, Thomas Howard, 1st Earl of, **32**, 227; **35**, 131–7 *passim*; **36**, 140
Sugden, Edward H., **5**, 80n; **32**, 93n, 103n
Sugnet, Charles J., **32**, 220
Sullivan, Anita, **55**, 330
Sullivan, Sir Arthur, **12**, 85; **16**, 103; **18**, 81, 100; **41**, 24–5, 225
Sullivan, Barry, **35**, 37
Sullivan, Sir Edward, **7**, 98–9; **50**, 69n
Sullivan, Garrett A., **53**, 324; **54**, 321
Sullivan, Henry W., **55**, 239n
Sullivan, Maxine, **13**, 142
Sullivan, Vickie, **51**, 282
Sully, James, **49**, 138n
Summer, David, **47**, 194–5
Summers, Claude J., **48**, 254; **50**, 43n
Summers, David, **53**, 303
Summers, Joseph H., **32**, 7, 68; **34**, 117, 121n, 169–70; **35**, 97; **41**, 147n; **43**, 16n; **45**, 7
Summers, Montague, **10**, 88n; **20**, 169; **28**, 119n; **43**, 96
Summers, Toby, **52**, 259
Summers, Will, **13**, 100–2, 105n; **42**, 87, 88, 92; **44**, 81
Summerscale, David, **15**, 136; **16**, 135
Summerson, Sir John, **20**, 21; **30**, 158n; **33**, 140n, 142n, 145n; **35**, 133n; **47**, 17, 21n
Summit, Jennifer, **51**, 293
Sumpter, Donald, **41**, 167, 179; **42**, 140, 150; **53**, 252, 277; **54**, 284
Sunde, Karen, **43**, 217
Sundelson, David, **43**, 1n, 31; **46**, 3; **54**, 227n
Sunderland, Adam, **56**, 253
Sunderlin, Lord, **4**, 80
Sundström, Frank, **14**, 123; **15**, 138; **16**, 137; **18**, 128
Supervielle, Jacques, **7**, 110
Supervielle, Jean-Louis, **13**, 127; **14**, 118
Supervielle, Jules, **2**, 121; **13**, 127; **14**, 118; **18**, 122
Supple, Tim, **46**, 184, 185, 187; **47**, 210; **50**, 215–19; **51**, 258; **52**, 235; **53**, 284; **54**, 38; **55**, 305–6, 331; **58**, 103; **60**, 300–1, 302
Supposes, **50**, 115
Surman, John, **42**, 159; **47**, 218
Surmount, **53**, 226n
Surrealism, and stage settings, **12**, 12
Surrey, Henry Howard, Earl of, *see under* Howard, Henry
Surrey, Kit, **41**, 162, 166; **42**, 150, 154, 160; **44**, 170; **45**, 152; **47**, 214; **48**, 233, 236; **51**, 262; **55**, 328, 329; **56**, 291, 294; **60**, 305–6
A Survey of History: or, A Nursery for Gentry, **60**, 275n30
Surrey, Meg, **44**, 203; **46**, 197; **47**, 214, 218; **48**, 235
Survivor, **55**, 75n
Susa, Conrad, **45**, 172
Susenbrotus, **53**, 13

Sussex, Countess of, **32**, 88, 89
Sussex, Earl of, **46**, 142
Sussex's Men, *see* Theatre, Elizabethan
Sutchffe, M., **54**, 169n
Sutcliffe, Alison, **42**, 155; **45**, 154
Sutcliffe, Matthew, **30**, 63, 64; **38**, 94; **58**, 36
Sutherland, Graham, **12**, 12
Sutherland, James, **18**, 21n; **19**, 127, 141, 146n; **20**, 131n; **29**, 41, 46n; **46**, 105n
Sutherland, Jim, **51**, 263
Sutherland, John, **56**, 114n, 128n
Sutherland, Malcolm, **47**, 219
Sutherland, Martin, **42**, 159; **43**, 211
Sutherland, R. C., **18**, 178
Sutherland, Sarah P., **38**, 230
Sutherland, W. O. S., **7**, 145
Sutro, Edward, **49**, 232
Sutton, Anne F., **60**, 112n41
Sutton, Dana F., **54**, 61n
Sutton, E. W., **42**, 88n
Sutton, Nicholas, customs farmer, **17**, 9
Sutton, Shaun, **39**, 86n, 94, 95n; **41**, 227; **45**, 188
Sutton, Thomas, **17**, 56–7; **36**, 140
Sutton, Tim, **59**, 312
Suvin, Darko, **53**, 101n
Suzman, Arthur, **11**, 137; **12**, 115; **33**, 113, 114
Suzman, Janet, **20**, 134; **22**, 138–9; **26**, 147, 149; **36**, 81; **43**, 212, 230; **46**, 183; **52**, 290; **53**, 290; **55**, 271–9, 283–4; **56**, 175; **57**, 40; **58**, 350; **59**, 298, 371; **60**, 285–6, 289–91, 292, 302, 359
Suzuki, Tadashi, **53**, 329; **47**, 3; **48**, 109; **49**, 272; **50**, 34
Suzuki, Toshiaki, **43**, 215
Švanda, P., **9**, 108
Svartengren, T. Hilding, **4**, 18
Svartik, Jan, **53**, 14n
Svendsen, Clara, **43**, 110n, 117n
Svensson, K. A., **18**, 128
Sverdlin, Y., **15**, 140
Svigley, Michael, **55**, 247n
Svoboda, Josef, **14**, 118; **40**, 37
Swaczynna, Wolfgang, **37**, 160
Swain, Barbara, **37**, 135n
Swain, Joanna, **56**, 252
Swain, Rob, **49**, 274; **51**, 261, 266
Swales, Martin, **53**, 167n
Swallow, tenant at Shottery, **12**, 100
Swaminathan, S. R., **24**, 156
Swan Theatre, *see under* Theatres, Elizabethan
Swander, Homer D., **24**, 168; **29**, 5, 53n, 55n–6n, 60n; **31**, 173; **32**, 223; **36**, 59n, 103; **38**, 17; **40**, 233; **42**, 35n, 116n; **43**, 171n; **44**, 236; **51**, 285
Swann, Martha, **58**, 298
Swann, Robert, **51**, 219
Swanston, Ellyard, **11**, 109
Swanston, Hamish F. G., **12**, 133
Swart, J., **16**, 159; **18**, 126
Swatkins, Mark, **50**, 226
Sweden, report on Shakespeare in, **1**, 115; **5**, 114; **6**, 123–4; **7**, 114–15; **8**, 121; **9**, 116; **10**, 121; **11**, 122; **12**, 116; **13**, 131; **14**, 123; **15**, 138; **16**, 136–7; **18**, 128–9
Swedenberg, H. T., Jr, **36**, 114n; **50**, 147n; **57**, 213
Swedenborg, Emanuel, **41**, 24
Swetnam, Joseph, **42**, 118; **50**, 159; **60**, 121n6
  Araignment of . . . Women, **1**, 70
Swier, C. S., **60**, 184
Swift, Carolyn Ruth, **39**, 231
Swift, Clive, **16**, 148; **25**, 48; **41**, 185
Swift, David, **31**, 148
Swift, Jonathan, **6**, 55, 63n; **8**, 66; **9**, 94; **26**, 92; **31**, 184; **34**, 114, 128; **39**, 69; **41**, 203; **51**, 170
Swift, Julia, **35**, 144; **43**, 217
Swift, Phil, **42**, 155; **44**, 192, 194
Swigg, R., **22**, 162
Swinarski, Konrad, **31**, 152; **47**, 3
Swinburne, Algernon Charles, **1**, 73, 118; **4**, 1, 5, 24, 146; **6**, 12, 46, 48n; **8**, 28; **10**, 50; **11**, 48; **15**, 11, 19; **16**, 32; **18**, 2; **21**, 3; **23**, 94, 95; **24**, 154; **26**, 3; **40**, 127n, 200; **56**, 136n, 206; **59**, 153; **60**, 252, 253
  on the authorship of *Edward III*, **6**, 39
Swinburne, Henry, **13**, 84–6; **28**, 52, 53; **32**, 136, 140n; **49**, 181–3, 186–94, 197; **52**, 322
  Brief Treatise of Testaments, **12**, 142
  Treatise on Spousals, **13**, 83, 88n, 89n
Swindell, Julia, **59**, 374
Swinden, Patrick, **28**, 160; **29**, 6; **32**, 5, 7, 11; **42**, 200
Swinley, Ion, **45**, 76; **55**, 135
Swinnerton, Thomas, **7**, 60; **33**, 164
Swinstead, Joan, **8**, 125
Swinton, Rob, **45**, 150; **48**, 232; **49**, 271; **50**, 225
Switzerland, report on Shakespeare in, **1**, 115; **2**, 127, 128; **3**, 119; **5**, 114–15; **6**, 124; **7**, 115; **8**, 121; **9**, 116; **10**, 121; **11**, 122; **12**, 116–17; **13**, 131; **14**, 123; **15**, 138; **18**, 129–30
Swynnerton, John, **54**, 95
Swynnerton, Thomas, **54**, 8
Syal, Rajeev, **50**, 33n
Sybant, Abraham, **28**, 172
Sydow, Karl, **54**, 287
Sykes, Barbara, **15**, 144
Sykes, Dugdale, **25**, 137n, 138n
Sykes, H. Dugdale, **4**, 7; **11**, 51
Sykes, Peter, **42**, 158, 159
Sylbert, Richard, **57**, 153
Sylvain, Le (A. van den Busche), *Orator*, **3**, 54
Sylvester, Joshua, **9**, 24; **17**, 203; **60**, 278n37
  translation from Du Bartas, **8**, 147
Sylvester, Richard S., **43**, 50n
Sylvester, Suzan, **41**, 188; **44**, 160, 168–70, 199; **46**, 192; **47**, 212
Sylvester, Victor, **46**, 206
Sylvius, Aeneas, **10**, 145
Symcocke, Thomas, **38**, 249n
Symeoni, Gabriello, **17**, 187
Symmons, Charles, **14**, 98
Symonds, John Addington, **3**, 19; **6**, 39; **19**, 143; **20**, 24n; **26**, 3; **56**, 206, 209, 210, 211n
Symons, A. J. A., **3**, 144; **53**, 148n, 229, 230n
Symphosius, **15**, 109n
Syms, Richard, **45**, 150
Syms, Sylvia, **44**, 193; **46**, 191
Synesius, **20**, 22 and n; **47**, 26
Synge, John Millington, **26**, 139, 140; **50**, 31

Sypher, F. Wylie, **38**, 10; **40**, 212; **49**, 208n
Sypher, Willie, **5**, 136
Syrus, Publius, **18**, 176; **20**, 22, 25n
Syson, Luke, **52**, 187n
Szabo, Lörinc, **12**, 114; **16**, 135
Szabó, Magda, **54**, 55
Szabó, Otto, **14**, 120
Szatek, Karoline, **57**, 320
Szenczi, Miklos J., **15**, 135; **21**, 129
Szendró, J., **14**, 120; **16**, 135
Szigligeti family, **59**, 126
Szondi, Peter, **51**, 148; **56**, 315
Szyfman, Arnold, '*King Lear* on the Stage: A Producer's Reflections', **13**, 69–71

A true credible report of a great fight at sea between England and Spain (1600), **17**, 34
'T.B.', **21**, 48
Tablic, Bohuslav, *Poezye*, **4**, 109
Tabori, George, **37**, 162
Taborski, Boleslaw, **22**, 159; **25**, 19n; **38**, 145n; **39**, 57n; **42**, 18n; **55**, 153n; **57**, 149
Tabukashvili, Rezo, **48**, 188n
Tacitus, **10**, 29, 31, 35, 38n; **20**, 28; **28**, 67; **33**, 14, 22, 23; **44**, 6; **55**, 23
Tacuinus, J., **15**, 97n
Tadashi, Suzuki, **51**, 193
Taddei, Tresy, **56**, 4n
Tadema, Sir Lawrence Alma-, **10**, 75
Tadmoor, Naomi, **55**, 198n
Taft, Edmund, **41**, 213
Tagg, Alan, **7**, 123; **10**, 131
Tagore, Rabindranath, **29**, 167
Tailor, Robert, *The Hog hath lost his Pearl*, **12**, 55n
Taine, Hippolyte Adolphe, **2**, 116, 117; **3**, 110; **44**, 109n; **55**, 143
Tait, A. A., **35**, 135
Tait, J., *Parish Registers of Wigan*, **13**, 104n
Taiwo, Olu, **59**, 343
Takahashi, Yasunari, **56**, 288
Takakuwa, Yoko, **53**, 329
Takamiya, Toshiyuki, **56**, 168n
Takata, Keitoku, **46**, 194
Takeda, Chimaki, **60**, 304
Takei, N., **26**, 160
Tal, Ada, **6**, 121
Talbert, E. M., **38**, 2
Talbert, Ernest William, **18**, 180; **19**, 88, 94n, 142; **22**, 148, 155; **26**, 112n; **41**, 145n; **43**, 54n
Talbot, Lady Anne, **32**, 88, 89
Talbot, C. (ed.), **17**, 90n
Talbot, Francis, Fifth Earl of Shrewsbury, **6**, 73n
Talbot, Gilbert, 7th Earl of Shrewsbury, **11**, 114n; **14**, 109n
Talbot, Ian, **42**, 155, 160; **43**, 210, 212; **44**, 202; **46**, 197; **47**, 215; **51**, 258; **52**, 260; **53**, 279; **59**, 341
Talbot, Lord, **42**, 30
Talbot, Peter, **54**, 284; **55**, 334
Talbot, T. H., **32**, 198n
Tales, A C. Mery, **1**, 62
Talfourd, Thomas Noon, **35**, 54–5
Tallis, John, **32**, 241
Tallis, Thomas, **3**, 56; **24**, 158; **46**, 18
Tallós, E., **14**, 120
Talma, François Joseph, **3**, 100, 101, 103; **9**, 60, 62; **10**, 74; **20**, 164; **21**, 79; **24**, 85, 86; **60**, 218n17, 219n21, 221, 222
Talon, Omer, **48**, 31n
Talvi, Aino, **12**, 118; **16**, 15
Tamaizumi, Yasuo, **35**, 160n; **54**, 305
Tamar Cam, **3**, 52; **7**, 82, 85; **17**, 51
Tamberlani, Carlo, **10**, 120
Tambling, Jeremy, **57**, 306
Tamburlaine, **52**, 79; **50**, 55n, 153; **54**, 207n, 357
Tamer Tamed, The, **52**, 73, 81
Taming of a Shrew, The, **1**, 52–3; **2**, 152; **3**, 24, 47, 150; **4**, 87; **6**, 58; **8**, 142; **9**, 152; **10**, 80, 83, 87n; **14**, 32, 153; **16**, 175, 177; **50**, 286
Taming of the Shrew: A Comparative Study of Oral and Literary Versions, **46**, 221n
Tanaka, Yuko, **57**, 271
Tancred and Ghismonda (MS.), **3**, 52; **11**, 48
Tandler, J., **9**, 101
Tandy, Philip, **60**, 255–6n16, 259n25
Tang, Xianzu, **36**, 54
Tannen, Deborah, **50**, 93n; **60**, 80n35
Tannenbaum, Percy, **40**, 36n
Tannenbaum, Samuel A., **2**, 45, 46, 56, 58, 148; **3**, 3, 25; **8**, 6; **15**, 40n; **26**, 81, 82, 83, 85n, 86; **28**, 37n, 38; **34**, 196
Tanner, Alice, **25**, 143
Tanner, I. E., **54**, 125n
Tanner, J. R., **17**, 112n; **57**, 247
Tanner, John, **47**, 18n
Tanner, Lawrence E., **6**, 73n; **12**, 20n
Tanner, Leon, **42**, 158
Tanner, Michael, **50**, 180n
Tanner, Bishop Thomas
  Bibliotheca Britannico-Hibernica, **4**, 86
  his library, **4**, 86–7
Tanner, Tony, **58**, 85
Tanselle, G. Thomas, **18**, 170; **19**, 127; **24**, 177; **26**, 180; **37**, 218; **40**, 236n; **45**, 1n; **50**, 277n; **51**, 131; **59**, 17n71, 20–1, 28, 31, 32n59, 37; **60**, 254n12
Tansey, Andrew, **42**, 158; **46**, 202
Tansley, Charles, **58**, 120
Tante, Alice, **49**, 198
Taranow, Gerda, **51**, 299–300
Tarantino, Quentin, **52**, 94n; **56**, 304–5
Tardiff, Joseph C., **57**, 85, 87, 88, 90, 92
Targoff, Ramie, **54**, 69n; **57**, 308
Tarlinskaja, Marina, **41**, 233n; **42**, 174; **43**, 227
Tarl(e)ton, Richard, **1**, 128; **6**, 74n, 157; **7**, 123; **9**, 147n; **15**, 68, 72n; **17**, 193–4, 196; **20**, 64, 73n; **22**, 38, 39, 40, 42; **23**, 114; **27**, 133, 136; **28**, 133n; **40**, 216; **41**, 39; **42**, 105n, 113; **43**, 81, 149, 230, 247; **47**, 39, 115; **48**, 245; **50**, 151, 161, 163–4; **56**, 62, 95n; **58**, 63, 230; **60**, 4, 9, 21–2, 54
  2 Seven Deadly Sins, **12**, 47
  Tarlton's News out of Purgatory, **15**, 72n
Tarnawski, Wladyslaw, **1**, 113; **10**, 120 142; **11**, 121; **14**, 122
  Burza reviewed, **13**, 154
'Tarras' at the Globe Theatre, **7**, 72, 75, 76, 77, 80n
  use of Carpenters' Hall as a theatre, **6**, 65
  use of Trinity Hall as a theatre, 1557–68, **6**, 65–74

Tarry, Isaac, **47**, 92
Tassencourt, Marcelle, **18**, 123
Tasso, E. and T., **46**, 126n
Tasso, Torquato, **3**, 15; **32**, 183n; **35**, 177; **50**, 243
Tassoni, Alessandro, *La Secchia Rapita*, **8**, 67
Tatarinova, G. and T., **42**, 150
Tate, Allen, **15**, 123n
Tate, Nahum, **2**, 15; **7**, 1; **10**, 27; **13**, 73, 74; **18**, 106, 184; **20**, 133, 145, 169; **22**, 131; **23**, 153; **26**, 34; **28**, 138; **30**, 194; **31**, 1, 3, 187; **32**, 38; **33**, 3, 40–1; **35**, 47; **36**, 175, 180; **38**, 163, 165, 254; **39**, 233; **41**, 226; **42**, 152, 181, 198; **46**, 237–8; **47**, 257, 262; **48**, 7; **49**, 290, 302; **51**, 3, 19, 22–3, 129, 306; **52**, 24, 291; **53**, 217, 323; **54**, 340; **55**, 69, 80, 81, 96–100, 103–5, 106, 110, 130, 145, 159, 257, 265, 269; **56**, 121, 122; **59**, 171; **60**, 170, 182
  adaptations of *Richard II*, *King Lear*, and *Coriolanus*, **9**, 85n
  Constant Gallant, **1**, 66
  Ingratitude of the Commonwealth, The, **48**, 7
Tate, Sharon, **39**, 71n; **57**, 145, 155
Tatian, **54**, 80
Tatlock, J. S. P., **8**, 10; **25**, 9; **59**, 243n33
Tatlow, Antony, **57**, 169
Tatrinov, V., **54**, 146
Tatspaugh, Patricia, **55**, 383
Tatum, Sally, **59**, 314
Tauber, Anne-Marie, **23**, 115
Taubert, **25**, 116
Taubert, W., **18**, 86
Taubin, Amy, **52**, 96n
Taunton, Nina, **58**, 321, 333
Taupin, René, **8**, 139; **9**, 148; **45**, 4, 5n
Taussig, Michael, **55**, 238n, 239n
Tave, Stuart M., **7**, 133
Taverner, Richard, **32**, 168n, 174; **54**, 63n
Tawney, R. H., **2**, 144; **3**, 41n; **17**, 120; **33**, 5; **37**, 170; **44**, 20n
Tawyer (Toyer), William, **19**, 104
Tayler, Frederick, **49**, 123
Taylerson, Marilyn, **30**, 173, 174
Taylor, **55**, 265
Taylor, A. B., **23**, 161n, 166; **24**, 162; **55**, 203, 349; **56**, 27n, 29n, 55–66; **59**, 366–7, 368
Taylor, A. E., **53**, 25n
Taylor, A. J. P., **40**, 21
Taylor, Anthony, **45**, 203; **46**, 221; **50**, 251
Taylor, Anthony Brian, **32**, 230–1
Taylor, Barry, **46**, 107n
Taylor, Charles, **51**, 151, 156, 157n; **53**, 81, 91, 311; **55**, 338; **56**, 210
Taylor, Dick, Jr., **13**, 155
Taylor, Don, **42**, 152
Taylor, Donn Ervin, **37**, 195
Taylor, E. G. R., **17**, 27n, 28 and n, 39n
Taylor, E. M. M., **10**, 140
Taylor, Edward, **45**, 167
Taylor, Elizabeth, **18**, 132; **44**, 173; **48**, 227; **54**, 312, 345; **57**, 155, 261
Taylor, G. C., **28**, 37n, 38n, 40n, 41; **29**, 79, 81
Taylor, G. F., **8**, 10
Taylor, G. L., **7**, 79n
Taylor, Gary, **32**, 246; **33**, 204, 210–11; **34**, 189, 194; **35**, 166, 179, 184, 185–6, 189; **36**, 189, 192–3; **37**, 192, 202, 203, 205, 208, 209, 214, 215n; **38**, 18, 46, 89n, 92n, 244n, 245; **39**, 126n, 238–40, 242, 246, 248, 250, 251; **40**, 65n, 66n, 67n, 78n, 138, 139n, 140n, 156, 206, 212, 226n, 227–8, 230n, 232, 234; **41**, 13n, 14, 26, 154, 217, 219, 228, 230–2, 234, 237–41, 243; **42**, 25n, 33, 93n, 202, 206–7, 210; **43**, 43n, 91n, 262–4, 265n, 266, 268, 270; **44**, 55n, 69, 79n, 81n, 113, 114, 128n, 166, 179, 222, 244, 248, 253, 255; **45**, 37n, 79n, 80n, 82n, 186n, 193n, 198–200, 203; **46**, 41, 45n, 61n, 244, 246, 252–3; **47**, 260–1, 264, 268–9; **48**, 74n, 75n, 188, 208, 272–80, 286; **49**, 21n, 27, 28n, 141n, 164n, 165n, 219, 242, 288, 311n, 313–14, 323, 328, 334–6; **50**, 153n, 160, 279–81, 289n; **51**, 2, 14, 67n, 71n, 72n, 112, 125, 130, 167n, 305, 324; **52**, 69n, 120n, 143, 166n, 213n, 306, 316n, 317n, 320; **53**, 71n, 238n, 300, 332–3, 341, 343; **54**, 13n, 17n, 19n, 20n, 21n, 22n, 23n, 26n, 28n, 68n, 72n, 96n, 97n, 98n, 100n, 203n, 206n, 208n, 210, 235n, 312; **55**, 2–4, 54n, 55n, 56, 184n, 189, 194–5, 210n, 257n, 270, 280n, 361–2, 390; **56**, 55n, 95n, 170n, 171n, 176, 243n, 244–5, 314, 349n; **57**, 79, 95, 325; **58**, 16, 19, 176, 343, 349, 357; **59**, 5n17, 5n18, 6n22, 8n33, 11, 12n51, 14n59, 15, 20n2, 23n14, 46, 46n8, 54n14, 69n1, 70n5, 78, 124n1, 124n2, 140, 151n20, 213, 213n5, 216, 217–18, 223n38, 255n5, 272, 282–3, 368, 375, 376, 378, 381, 382, 383; **60**, 140, 253, 358, 361
Taylor, Gary and Julia Jowett, *Shakespeare Reshaped*, **48**, 272, 274, 276, 281n
Taylor, George, **56**, 123n
Taylor, George C., **2**, 152; **4**, 9; **51**, 177, 278n
Taylor, Gerald, **47**, 173n, 175n, 178n
Taylor, Gwen, **49**, 236, 271
Taylor, James O., **47**, 232
Taylor, Jeffrey, **42**, 157
Taylor, Jeremy, **36**, 162; **43**, 61n
Taylor, Jerome, **57**, 245
Taylor, Joanna, **48**, 228
Taylor, John, **25**, 188; **32**, 103n; **41**, 103n, 112n; **50**, 188, 199; **56**, 119, 120; **57**, 239
Taylor, John, the Water Poet, **3**, 14; **17**, 88 and n, 89–90, 99n; **60**, 46, 270n5, 270n7, 283
Taylor, John Russell, **39**, 4, 8, 9, 77, 128
Taylor, Joseph, **11**, 109, 110; **17**, 197 and n; **58**, 233
Taylor, Kate, **58**, 157
Taylor, Mrs Maria, **22**, 128–32
Taylor, Marion A., **32**, 86n
Taylor, Mark, **47**, 154n, 230; **48**, 247; **57**, 306; **58**, 52, 99
Taylor, Michael, **23**, 143; **24**, 143; **25**, 181, 182; **26**, 163; **27**, 164, 165; **28**, 152, 156; **37**, 9; **38**, 224, 225; **56**, 303; **58**, 346–7, 356; **59**, 156n42; **60**, 330–53
Taylor, Mr, **14**, 112
Taylor, Myron, **23**, 149; **31**, 1n
Taylor, Neil, **25**, 179; **26**, 184; **27**, 188; **38**, 234; **41**, 227; **47**, 8n; **52**, 276; **55**, 383; **56**, 94; **57**, 342; **58**, 355, 357; **60**, 225n14, 361, 369
Taylor, Paul, **43**, 188–9; **46**, 167, 168, 173, 180; **47**, 203; **48**, 205, 223; **49**, 245, 251; **50**, 35n; **52**, 116n, 118n; **56**, 250; **58**, 344; **60**, 171, 171n4
Taylor, R. K. S., **41**, 65n, 67n
Taylor, Ray, **10**, 125
Taylor, Richard, **51**, 267

Taylor, Robert, **29**, 32n; **41**, 190
Taylor, Roberta, **49**, 242
Taylor, Rupert, **3**, 25; **8**, 6; **27**, 132n; **53**, 180
Taylor, Sam, **39**, 4, 79
Taylor, Sion, **47**, 213
Taylor, Timothy, **53**, 326
Taylor, Tom, **40**, 33; **41**, 24–5
Taylor, Valerie, **1**, 108
Taylor, William, **45**, 103n
Taymor, Julie, **54**, 293; **56**, 4, 5, 10–26; **57**, 330; **58**, 185, 325; **60**, 360
Tazel, Erica, **56**, 288
Tazi, Nadia, **55**, 240n, 241n
Tchabukiani, V., **12**, 118
Tchaikovsky, André, **58**, 336; **60**, 229
Tchaikovsky, Peter Ilitch, **9**, 22; **18**, 75; **46**, 170; **49**, 4, 153, 240
Tchertkoff, V., **23**, 39
Tchkhikvadze, Ramaz, **43**, 217
Teague, Frances N., **32**, 241; **40**, 236; **46**, 210, 218; **48**, 245; **51**, 292; **54**, 152n; **60**, 229–30
Teale, Leonard, **12**, 109
Teale, Owen, **44**, 192; **45**, 121, 140, 143; **46**, 194; **47**, 198, 202, 206; **49**, 280; **54**, 287
Teare, Jeff, **43**, 216
Tearle, Sir Godfrey, **2**, 130; **6**, 141; **7**, 73; **49**, 230
Tearle, John, **46**, 237
Tearle, Osmond, **47**, 92
Tebbutt, Gerry, **44**, 197
Tedeschi, Gianrico, **9**, 114
Tedii, Perihan, **15**, 139
Tedü, Suavi, **9**, 116
Tegg, Thomas, **18**, 19
Telbin, William, **20**, 109; **41**, 26, 30; **49**, 126
Telesius, Bernardinus, **38**, 182n, 183
Television Shakespeare, *An Age of Kings*, **18**, 70
The Spread of the Eagle, **18**, 70
Telfer, John, **55**, 325
Telfer, Matthew, **52**, 266
Teliver, Harold E., **21**, 144
Tellefsen, Rut, **14**, 122
Tempera, Mariangela, **48**, 257; **54**, 318; **59**, 372
Temperley, Nicholas, **54**, 20n, 24n
Temple, Frederick (Archbishop of Canterbury), **54**, 80
Temple, Peter, **6**, 59
Temple, Sir Thomas, **6**, 59
Templeman, Simon, **35**, 147; **47**, 102–3
Templer, Sir Gerald, **7**, 113
Tena, Don Torcuato Luca de, **18**, 127
Tennant, David, **50**, 206; **53**, 328; **54**, 250, 255–8, 266–7; **55**, 313, 331; **56**, 168, 296
Tennant, Emma, **58**, 95
Tennant, Nicolas, **54**, 248; **57**, 259
Tennenhouse, Leonard, **40**, 139; **41**, 3n, 195; **43**, 45n; **44**, 89; **46**, 93n, 220; **51**, 285; **52**, 325; **53**, 16n; **55**, 6, 240n; **58**, 173
Tennison, Helen, **59**, 339
Tennyson, Alfred, Lord, **4**, 156; **6**, 39; **7**, 30; **10**, 15–16, 17; **15**, 181; **24**, 39; **31**, 191; **44**, 135; **52**, 322; **53**, 125; **54**, 82; **56**, 127, 131, 135
Tenschert, Joachim, **42**, 159; **48**, 175, 176n
Teodor, Jacob, **36**, 138
Teomi, Oded, **44**, 197
Tephany, Arlette, **18**, 122
Terajama, Shuji, **46**, 194
Terence, **1**, 68, 73, 126; **3**, 15, 86, 87; **4**, 8, 9; **5**, 53; **8**, 2; **11**, 21; **14**, 15, 17, 19, 21, 22; **17**, 61; **18**, 159, 188; **20**, 21; **22**, 3, 4; **24**, 150; **30**, 192; **32**, 233
Terence, David, **52**, 264
Terence, Treschel, **43**, 146n, 158, 160, 167; **44**, 236; **50**, 144, 152
Terera, Gilz, **55**, 316
Teresa, Mother, **44**, 78
Teresa, St, **59**, 236
Terfel, Bryn, **58**, 303
Terre'Blanche, Eugene, **55**, 272, 279
Terrent, Thomas, **54**, 58n
Terris, Olwen, **52**, 185n
Terriss, William, **41**, 224
Terrors of the Night, The, **52**, 121n
Terry, Dame Ellen, **1**, 61, 72; **2**, 1, 19; **4**, 105; **7**, 26, 29, 33–4, 92; **8**, 69, 74; **9**, 20; **18**, 63; **19**, 75; **28**, 143; **32**, 16, 21, 22, 27, 29, 30, 32, 33, 35; **33**, 86; **35**, 8, 10; **40**, 12; **41**, 224; **42**, 38, 47, 49n; **44**, 103; **46**, 20; **49**, 128, 136; **52**, 292, 322–3; **53**, 92; **55**, 318; **56**, 130, 136; **57**, 93, 94; **58**, 337; **59**, 66
Terry, Fred, **32**, 28
Terry, Kate, **32**, 33; **35**, 18; **42**, 38
Terry, Marion, **38**, 200
Terry, Nigel, **41**, 187–8; **42**, 154, 156; **44**, 169, 199; **45**, 152
Terry, Reta, **59**, 215n10
Tertullian, **15**, 90, 97n; **33**, 99n; **46**, 98; **54**, 80
Tervarent, Guy de, **56**, 45n
Tesauro, Emmanuele, **17**, 183
Tessitore, Maria Vittoria, **44**, 214
Tetauer, F., **16**, 133
Tethys' Festival, **54**, 197
Tetzeli von Rosador, Kurt, **37**, 157n; **39**, 220; **40**, 202; **43**, 223, 263n; **50**, 47n
Textor, J. Ravisius, **42**, 66n
Textual problems, *see under* Shakespeare
Tezuka, Osamu, **60**, 135n14
Thacker, David, **41**, 185, 187–8; **42**, 153, 157; **44**, 96, 102, 158, 166, 167, 170, 172, 175, 197, 199; **45**, 126, 127; **46**, 173, 177, 180, 202; **47**, 193, 195–9, 209, 214; **48**, 214–16, 229, 231; **49**, 245–7, 250, 253, 270, 272; **50**, 203; **52**, 317; **53**, 149n; **57**, 332; **59**, 299
Thacker, Kit, **43**, 206
Thackeray, William Makepeace, **13**, 77; **16**, 16, 108; **56**, 127, 128
Thalbach, Katherina, **46**, 195
Thaler, Alwin, **1**, 9; **2**, 140; **4**, 9; **7**, 5, 6; **11**, 139; **19**, 120n; **20**, 163; **23**, 93n, 99n; **37**, 36n; **60**, 84n2
Thaler, Brigitte, **23**, 115
Thám, K. H., **4**, 115n; **9**, 101
Thamara, Francisco, **32**, 90–1
Thane, Pat, **55**, 37n
Thanhauser, Edwin, **39**, 76, 79, 83
Thare (Thayer), John, **33**, 163, 164n
Tharia, Zahid, **43**, 212
That Way Madness Lies, **47**, 212
Thatcher, David, **45**, 149; **47**, 232; **48**, 254; **49**, 293; **51**, 4, 81n; **54**, 306
Thatcher, Lady Margaret, **37**, 170; **44**, 58; **45**, 149; **56**, 166; **57**, 41
Thate, Hilmar, **48**, 176

Thauer, Friedrich, **32**, 134n
Thavomis, Yannis, **53**, 274
Thaw, Abigail, **55**, 314
Thaw, John, **37**, 164, 166, 170, 171
Thaw, Melanie, **45**, 152
Thayer, C. G., **38**, 5, 221–2
Theaker, Jo, **58**, 279
Theater of Envy, A, **46**, 206
Theatre Set-Up, **58**, 307
Theatre, Elizabethan, **1**, 1–16, 21, 23–4, 25–37, 38–49, 59, 75, 89, 93, 94, 97; **2**, 17, 21–3, 24, 25, 26, 29, 30, 120, 141–2; **3**, 120, 140; **17**, 198–204, 207–8
  acting, **1**, 8, 114
    conditions, **2**, 4, 8, 16; **3**, 140
    acting style in, **7**, 27, 82–9
  actors, **1**, 7 (*see also individual actors*)
  actors responsible for 'bad' quartos, **3**, 74–82, 147–8, 149–50
  'arena' theory, the, discussed, **10**, 147
  as the context for Shakespeare study, **1**, 38–50
  audiences, **1**, 7, 43; **3**, 7, 140
  buildings, construction of, **2**, 22, 23n, 30
  companies (*see also individual companies*), **2**, 31, 51–4
  compared with modern theatres, **1**, 89–97
  costume, **1**, 8, 21
  court performances, **1**, 10
  documents relating to, **1**, 9, 64–8
  early engravings, **1**, 25–37
  effect of research on criticism, **1**, 12, 14
  external structure, **1**, 25–37
  history of Queen Anne's Men at the Boar's Head, Cockpit and Red Bull Theatres, **7**, 57–68
  influence of *Commedia dell'arte*, **1**, 8
  internal structure, **1**, 5, 6, 34
  length of plays, **1**, 12–13
  masques, **1**, 11, 43, 54–5
  performances on the ship 'Dragon', **6**, 162
  physical features of Playhouses, **3**, 95–6
    influence of street theatre, **3**, 85
    inn-yard tradition, **3**, 85
    tiring-house, **3**, 83
  private theatres, **1**, 10–11
  provincial companies, **1**, 9
  public playhouse, the, **8**, 109
  public theatres, **1**, 3–9, 59
  reconstructions, **1**, 2, 15, 59, 93, 95–7
  research needed, **1**, 14–16
  respectability, **1**, 40
  Shakespeare's use of a gallery, **10**, 177–85
  shape of, **2**, 21–3
  situation of individual theatres, **1**, 25–37
  staging, **3**, 83–94; **4**, 151–2; **5**, 103, 143–4, 151; **7**, 69–81
    multiple staging, **2**, 113
    medieval platform stages, **3**, 86–8
    area beneath stage, **3**, 89, 90
    stage-draperies, **3**, 92–3
    private stages, **5**, 139
    public stages, **5**, 143
    stage-rails and yard-alleys, **7**, 69–81
    effect of stage conditions on comedies, **8**, 5

COMPANIES

Admiral's Men, **2**, 51, 52, 53; **3**, 52; **7**, 83, 84, 149; **8**, 102; **12**, 18; **14**, 25, 31, 106; **27**, 130, 133, 134n, 136, 315; **32**, 194, 196, 197, 198; **33**, 153, 157–9, 160, 168; **36**, 136; **41**, 38–9, 215–16; **42**, 114; **44**, 146, 149, 151–4, 230; **45**, 107, 108; **46**, 65, 231; **47**, 17, 171, 177, 239; **49**, 20, 104; **51**, 194, 291; **52**, 73–4, 315; **53**, 329; **55**, 34; **57**, 232
Boys' companies, **1**, 40; **3**, 52; **9**, 27–9
Children of the Chapel, **11**, 100, 102
Children of the Queen's Revels, **1**, 42; **11**, 100, 102–3
Lord Chomley's Men, **52**, 78n; **56**, 121n
Derby's Men, **3**, 145; **10**, 69; 14, 105–6; 27, 133n, 135, 136; **32**, 195, 238; **33**, 160–1; **37**, 196; **44**, 150
Duke of Richmond's, **11**, 72
Globe Theatre (London), **58**, 305
Henrietta Maria's, **11**, 72
Hunsdon's Men, **3**, 149; **49**, 34
King's, **11**, 63, 109
Leicester's Men, **3**, 24; **33**, 98; **44**, 146, 147; **47**, 52, 115, 258
Lord Chamberlain–King's Men, **1**, 4, 8, 38–50, 124; **2**, 40, 144–5, 149; **3**, 17, 28, 51, 74, 82, 140, 146, 150, 151; **4**, 95, 100n, 158; **5**, 142, 143, 148; **6**, 163; **7**, 50, 54, 83, 148, 152; **8**, 158; **9**, 28, 86; **10**, 150; **11**, 82, 100, 149, 154; **12**, 36, 140, 150; **13**, 117–19, 167; **14**, 106, 158; **17**, 195, 207–8; **27**, 134n, 136, 173, 178; **28**, 6, 169, 180; **30**, 208; **32**; 6, 194, 243; **33**, 157, 160, 162; **34**, 131n; **36**, 62, 83, 107, 136; **41**, 9, 10, 37, 61, 98, 120, 127–8, 215, 220; **42**, 63, 64n, 92, 188, 194, 202; **43**, 55n, 63, 66, 72, 146, 148–53, 155, 240, 242, 264; **44**, 66, 72, 83, 114, 124–9, 146, 148–53, 150, 154, 155, 231; **45**, 108, 113, 172, 180; **46**, 62, 196, 106, 231, 232n; **47**, 16, 45–60, 112, 173, 175, 239, 240; **48**, 148, 273; **49**, 19, 20, 34, 327, 332; **50**, 19, 160, 169n, 262, 282; **51**, 95, 144, 194n, 216, 276, 313, 327; **52**, 68, 72–81, 82, 84, 86, 133–6, 140n, 148, 190, 294, 297, 312; **53**, 329, 335; **54**, 18, 20, 21, 28, 30, 193, 198–9, 346; **55**, 13, 18, 28, 34, 44–5, 47, 49, 251, 252, 330, 369, 381, 387, 390; **56**, 60, 62, 66, 95, 97, 99, 217, 218, 225, 253, 324, 355; **57**, 5, 137, 202–3, 227, 333
King's Men, The, **28**, 169, 180; **33**, 162; **34**, 131n; **36**, 62, 83, 107; **41**, 9, 10, 61, 98, 120, 127–8, 215, 220; **42**, 188, 194, 202; **43**, 55n, 63, 242, 264; **44**, 83, 114, 124–9, 150, 154, 155, 231; **45**, 113, 172; **46**, 62, 106, 231, 232n; **47**, 45–60, 112, 173, 175, 239, 240; **48**, 148, 273; **49**, 19; **50**, 19, 160, 169n, 262, 282; **51**, 95, 144, 194n, 216, 276, 327; **52**, 68, 72–81, 84, 86, 133–6, 140n, 148, 190, 297, 312; **53**, 329, 335; **54**, 18, 20, 21, 28, 30, 198–9; **55**, 13, 44–5, 47, 49, 251, 252, 369, 387, 390; **56**, 217, 218, 225; **57**, 5, 137
  and Shakespeare, **1**, 38–50
  acquisition of Blackfriars, **1**, 40–50
  connection with *Sir Thomas More*, **2**, 53
  Essex rebellion, **1**, 39
  origins, **1**, 39
  performances at court, **1**, 40
  possible link with Amphitheatre, **2**, 31
  receipts, **1**, 47
  repertory, **1**, 43
  'War of the Theatres', **1**, 41
Oxford's Men, **4**, 95; **14**, 27; **32**, 238; **33**, 161
Paul's Boys, **11**, 102; **13**, 120; **17**, 202, 206, 208
Pembroke's Men, **3**, 2, 24, 145, 150; **4**, 158; **6**, 170, **7**, 148, 149; **10**, 69; **11**, 151; **14**, 106; **17**, 208; **27**, 129–36; **30**,

196; **32**, 243; **33**, 157, 159; **36**, 173; **44**, 149n, 150, 153; **46**, 251; **47**, 265; **49**, 19; **55**, 18, 394
Players of the Revels, **7**, 86
Prince Charles's Men, **4**, 91; **7**, 67n; **50**, 44n
Prince Henry's Men, **41**, 216; **52**, 215
Queen Elizabeth's Men, **51**, 291
Queen Henrietta's, **7**, 86
Queen's Men, The, **3**, 31; **6**, 159, 170; **9**, 143; **11**, 148; **14**, 206; **17**, 198, 208; **27**, 129–36; **30**, 196; **44**, 146, 149, 150; **47**, 30, 45n, 52, 55; **49**, 17–19; **50**, 163; **52**, 82, 85, 294; **53**, 179; **55**, 12, 13, 18, 19n, 21, 27–35, 47, 52, 367
Strange's Men, **2**, 51, 52; **3**, 24, 31, 52, 145; **6**, 158; **7**, 147, 148, 149; **8**, 102; **13**, 167; **27**, 129, 134, 136; **30**, 202; **32**, 194, 227; **33**, 154, 159, 160; **41**, 216; **42**, 114; **44**, 149n, 150, 230, 251; **46**, 251; **47**, 46, 251, 265; **49**, 19; **54**, 121, 353; **55**, 18; **57**, 227, 232, 233
Sussex's Men, **3**, 145; **10**, 69–72; **14**, 105, 106; **17**, 208; **27**, 134, 135, 136; **3**, 156; **55**, **18**, 27
Westminster Boys, **1**, 65; **3**, 52
Worcester's Company, **52**, 74–5, 137
Worcester's Men, **33**, 154, 161, 162, 167n, 168; **41**, 216, 218; **44**, 150, 154; **47**, 38, 52, 171; **51**, 291
THEATRES
Banqueting House, Whitehall, **11**, 107, 110–11, 114
Bear Garden, **8**, 106
Blackfriars, **1**, 10, 38–50, 61, 65; **4**, 100n; **6**, 65, 161 165; **10**, 87n; **11**, 110, 102, 104–5, 109; **12**, 36; **13**, 113, 115–19, 121–3, 160; **15**, 10; **16**, 8, 9, 33, 95–101; **17**, 198–9, 202, 203
acquisition by King's Men, **1**, 40–9
characteristics of performances, **11**, 41–5
influence on Shakespeare's development, **1**, 41, 46–9
receipts, **1**, 47
Boar's Head Inn, **7**, 60, 61, 63, 64, 66, 67n; **12**, 17
Bull Inn, **12**, 20n
Cockpit, **6**, 163; **7**, 65, 67n, 68n, 86; **11**, 115n; **16**, 95–101; **17**, 198, 202, 203
Cockpit-in-Court, **11**, 109, 114, 115n
Curtain, **1**, 68; **2**, 51; **3**, 24, 85; **4**, 91; **6**, 72; **10**, 87n; **12**, 16
Fortune, **1**, 7, 45, 46; **2**, 30, 53; **3**, 84, 85, 88, 90, 91–2, 94; **7**, 60–1, 76, 79, 82, 143; **8**, 106; **10**, 80; **11**, 123; **12**, 22–4, 27–8, 46
contract for, **12**, 11, 22–5, 56
Tieck's reconstruction of, **12**, 11; **13**, 112, 119; **15**, 172; **16**, 95–101; **17**, 208
Globe, **1**, 1, 10, 25, 28, 36n, 41, 42, 82; **2**, 21–3, 141, 142; **3**, 30, 53, 74, 85, 89, 90, 91–2; **4**, 88, 97–9; **5**, 143; **6**, 161, 165; **7**, 71, 73–6, 79, 80n, 82, 84, 99, 109, 117, 143, 144; **8**, 106, 151; **9**, 28, 49–53, 117, 148; **10**, 75, 77, 84, 87n, 88n, 89n, 114, 148; **11**, 34, 83, 109, 146; **12**, 8, 9, 12, 13, 16, 28, 30, 35–8, 41, 43–6, 49, 143–4; **13**, 113–23, 158, 160; **15**, 114; **16**, 8, 9, 95–101, 152; **17**, 198, 200, 203, 208; **58**, 269, 280, 304
audiences at, **1**, 45
building of, **1**, 39
destruction of, in 1644, **1**, 34
influence on Tieck, **1**, 2
performances at, **1**, 13
recepits, **1**, 47
shape of exterior, **1**, 6, 27ff
shape of stage, **1**, 6, 34
site of, **1**, 6, 28–9, 32
size of, **1**, 6–7
types of plays popular, **1**, 43, 46
Globe, the Second, **2**, 30
Hope, **1**, 44; **3**, 89, 92, 93, 94; **7**, 79; **8**, 106
Masquing House, Whitehall, **11**, 111–13, 114
Newington Butts
Red Bull, **1**, 4, 5, 10, 45, 46, 128; **3**, 93; **4**, 97; **7**, 57–68, 82; **9**, 147; **10**, 77, 87n; **11**, 72; **13**, 113, 116, 119; **16**, 95–101; **52**, 5
Red Lion Inn, **7**, 57
Rose, The, **1**, 24, 25, 27, 29, 32; **2**, 51, 53; **3**, 23, 24, 145; **7**, 50, 60, 73, 80n, 82, 84; **10**, 77; **11**, 112; **14**, 106; **15**, 172; **17**, 201, 203, 207; **52**, 10, 11, 13, 78, 183
shape of, **1**, 25–37 *passim*
site of, **1**, 31
Salisbury Court, **7**, 86
Swan, **1**, 2, 9, 21, 23–4, 25, 27, 28, 31; **2**, 22, 119; **3**, 83–4, 90, 92, 93, 113; **4**, 96; **5**, 143; **6**, 160, 161; **7**, 75, 79, 129, 143; **10**, 77, 80, 84, 86n, 87n; **11**, 146; **12**, 16, 18, 19, 27, 144; **52**, 3–8, 14, 21, 227; **58**, 268, 269, 274
drawing of, *see* de Will, Johannes, **13**, 112–13, 116, 119; **17**, 203
Theatre, **1**, 68; **2**, 22, 51; **3**, 24, 85; **6**, 64–5, 72; **7**, 143; **12**, 16, 18, 31; **16**, 8
Theatre Royal (Cockpit-in-Court), **11**, 115n
Whitefriars, **1**, 10; **13**, 120
Theatre, French, **2**, 122–4; **3**, 98–106
Theatre, German, **3**, 95–7
Theatre, Soviet, **2**, 83, 106n, 126
Theatres
Albany, **58**, 301
Albery, **58**, 269, 277
Aldwych, **16**, 28
American Repertory Theatre, **1**, 112
American Shakespeare Festival Theatre, **11**, 122, 148
Arcola, **58**, 268, 302
Birmingham Repertory, **1**, 110; **2**, 10–11; **6**, 122; **58**, 300; **11**, 134
productions of *2* and *3 Henry VI*, **6**, 49–52; **7**, 107, 146
production of *Henry VI* reviewed, **7**, 125; **8**, 78–9, 124–5; **10**, 124
Blue Mountain, **58**, 301
Bochum Theatre, **4**, 126
Bristol Old Vic, **1**, 99–100; **58**, 268, 299, 303
Comédie Française, **2**, 123; **3**, 99, 101, 102, 103, 105; **11**, 119; **12**, 112
Compagnie des Quinze, La, **4**, 101
Complicité, Théâtre de, **46**, 170, 171; **58**, 269, 274, 277
Covent Garden, **9**, 17, 55, 61; **10**, 72, 73, 74; **16**, 109, 112–13
Crucible, Sheffield, **58**, 301, 303
Dengate Theatre, Northampton, **58**, 304
Derby Playhouse Theatre, **58**, 279
Drury Lane, **9**, 16, 55, 61, 90, 98; **10**, 72, 73, 75, 76, 88n 150; **11**, 123–4, 128; **12**, 9; **16**, 112–13
Dundee Repertory Theatre, **58**, 307
Earle Grey Players, the, **3**, 116
English Touring Theatre, **58**, 269, 278, 301, 305
Gate Theatre, Dublin, **1**, 89–97
Gielgud Theatre, **58**, 269, 274
Greenwich Theatre, **58**, 204

Theatres (*cont.*)
Habima Players, **2**, 15
Harz Mountain, **3**, 96
Haymarket, **5**, 107; **7**, 92; **9**, 18, 19; **11**, 123–4; **16**, 113; **58**, 364
Helsinki Popular Theatre, **11**, 119
Her Majesty's, **10**, 75
His Majesty's, **8**, 76
Jermyn Street Theatre, London, **58**, 307
King's, Hammersmith, **8**, 123, 125–6, 132
Kingsway, **9**, 57
Liverpool Repertory Theatre, **1**, 100–1
Lyceum, **8**, 69; **9**, 56; **11**, 124
Lyric, Hammersmith, **58**, 304
Maddermarket, **2**, 4, 18; **12**, 71, 72, 75; **58**, 300, 303
Mayakovski Theatre, Moscow, **12**, 118
Mermaid, **8**, 124–5; **9**, 49; **10**, 85, 89n
National Populaire, **12**, 1, 112
Northern Ballet Theatre, **58**, 303, 305
Old Vic, **1**, 13, 98–9, 103–5; **2**, 1, 10–11, 15, 18, 131; **3**, 114, 135; **4**, 101, 106, 113; **8**, 134–6; **9**, 109, 111, 114, 117, 134, 142; **10**, 86n, 121, 136, 149; **11**, 117–18, 123, 128–32, 134, 135; **12**, 36–8, 73, 80, 85, 86, 112–6, 119–21, 131–2, 134–5, 137, 145; **13**, 1, 30, 31, 49–50, 51–2, 156, 158, 160; **15**, 1, 56, 112, 132, 139, 141–2, 144–5, 147–55, 158, 166, 173, 182; **16**, 13, 43, 50, 53, 56n, 121–2, 124–31, 132, 133–5, 137–8, 147, 157–8, 168–9; **17**, 45, 92n, 108, 152, 153, 159–60, 164–5, 175, 195, 209–10, 219, 230; **18**, 6, 48, 49–50, 66, 68, 74, 97, 100, 102, 110, 150–1, 169–70, 174, 178, 189; **20**, 84
production of *Love's Labour's Lost*, **4**, 129–35; **5**, 115, 119, 120, 121
production of *Twelfth Night*, **5**, 121–4
production of *Henry V*, **5**, 125–8; **6**, 49, 117, 119, 123, 124, 138–9; **7**, 31, 107, 109, 113, 114, 115
1952–3 Shakespeare production reviewed, **7**, 123–5; **8**, 123–6, 127, 131, 132–6; **9**, 18, 19–20, 21, 22, 23, 122–31; **10**, 123–5, 130, 133, 148, 149
of *Henry VIII* (1958), **12**, 122–6; **13**, 79, 125, 137–9, 160
productions of *Winter's Tale* (1956), **12**, 83
Olivier, **58**, 301
Olympic, **16**, 103
Oskaras Korsunovas Theatre, Brighton, **58**, 303
Phoenix Theatre, **11**, 39; **12**, 83, 144, 146
Playbox Theatre, Warwick, **58**, 303, 306
Playhouse Theatre, London **58**, 268
Princess', **9**, 55, **11**, 124; **16**, 113, 116
Queen's, **9**, 20
Queen's Theatre, Hornchurch, **58**, 30
Richmond Theatre, **58**, 301
Römerberg, Frankfurt, **3**, 96
Royal Exchange, Manchester, **58**, 307
Royal Lyceum, Edinburgh, **58**, 301
Royal National Theatre, **58**, 269, 300, 301, 306
Royal Netherlands, Antwerp, **5**, 107–8, 109
Royal Opera House, **58**, 300, 303
Royal Theatre, Northampton, **58**, 304
Sadler's Wells, **10**, 74, 75; **16**, 33, 113
Savoy, **8**, 80
Stratford-upon-Avon, **11**, 132–5; **12**, 1, 4, 36, 70, 73–4, 80, 83, 84, 85, 86, 89, 122, 123, 129–33 *passim*, 134, 142, 144–5; **13**, 49–57; **14**, 135–7; **15**, 1, 5, 7, 9, 10, 53–5, 55–6, 57, 61, 89, 112, 131, 133–5, 137, 139–41, 144–6, 162, 168, 170; **16**, 56n, 71–2, 74, 78, 132–6, 138, 159; **17**, 28, 79, 140, 144 and n, 147, 157–8, 171, 175–6, 178, 192, 209; **18**, 52, 158–9, 160–1, 173, 178, 180; 129–37, *passim*; **15**, 24, 85, 115, 125, 142, 145, 151, 167–8, 179; **16**, 72, 84, 94, 132, 136, 138, 147, 159, 179; **17**, 91, 114, 117, 137–8, 158n, 160, 164, 210, 215, 223–4, 237; **18**, 1, 42, 46, 49, 53, 163–4, 174; 129–37 *passim*; translation, 122; **15**, 27, 113, 118, 132, 136, 144, 163; **17**, 41n, 44, 46, 63 and n, 92n, 156, 209; **18**, 159; **20**, 83–4, 95, 107–8, 125, 128, 134, 152–3; **12**, 36, 72, 74, 79, 85–6
Schiller Theatre, Berlin, **12**, 112
Setagaya Public Theatre, **58**, 300
Shakespeare Memorial Theatre, Stratford-upon-Avon, **1**, 107–11; **2**, 10–11, 15; **3**, 120, 135, 141, 150–1; **11**, 123, 128, 132–4; **14**, 70, 74–5, 79, 137, 140, 145, 160; **52**, 20
production of *Henry VIII*, reviewed, **3**, 120–9; **4**, 99–100, 113
production of *Measure for Measure* reviewed, **4**, 135–8; **5**, 58, 115, 119, 120, 121; **6**, 49, 117
1951 productions of history plays reviewed, **6**, 129–39; **7**, 31, 113, 123, 124, 146
1953 season reviewed, **7**, 125–7; **8**, 76, 77, 123–5, 131, 132, 136–8; **9**, 22, 124–31; **10**, 123–4, 126, 133, 148, 149
Sheffield Theatres, **58**, 301, 303
Smock Alley Theatre, Dublin, **4**, 142
Stoll, **11**, 128
Stratford Theatre, Connecticut, **10**, 149; **12**, 145
Stratford Theatre, Ontario, Canada, **10**, 85, 89n, 111–14, 149; **11**, 118; **12**, 11, 145
Surrey, **9**, 56; **11**, 124
Teatre Romea, **58**, 302
Théâtre des Bouffes du Nord/CICT, **58**, 300
Theatre Royal (Restoration), **16**, 133
Theatre Royal, Bath, **4**, 107
Theatre Royal, Bristol, **4**, 107
Theatre Royal, Liverpool, **1**, 85
Theatre Royal, Manchester, **1**, 84
Theatre Royal, Plymouth, **58**, 305
Theatre Vesturport (Reykjavik), **58**, 305
West Riding Repertory Company, **1**, 99, 102
Wundsiedl Theatre, **3**, 96
Young Vic Company, production of *Merchant of Venice*, reviewed, **5**, 120, 124–5
Zürich Repertory Company, **1**, 115
Theile, Wolfhard, **48**, 182n
Theilgaard, Alice, **49**, 308
Theis, Jeffrey, **56**, 313
Theobald, Lewis, **1**, 60; **2**, 109; **3**, 47, 49, 50; **4**, 56, 57, 59, 67n, 85, 161, 162–3; **5**, 1–2, 16, 20, 21, 50, 51, 52, 80n; **6**, 77, 164; **7**, 91; **8**, 51n; **9**, 93; **10**, 28; **13**, 157, 168; **14**, 80; **15**, 181; **18**, 14, 16, 36; **20**, 84; **24**, 155, 178; **25**, 187, 198; **26**, 71, 72, 181, 182, 184; **27**, 187, 192; **28**, 177; **29**, 124, 179; **31**, 195, 196, 198; **32**, 239; **33**, 198, 209, 210; **34**, 11, 45n, 194; **35**, 125; **36**, 175; **38**, 98n; **39**, 251; **40**, 234, 236; **41**, 99; **42**, 123–4, 203, 207; **43**, 81–4, 88–9, 269; **45**, 3; **46**, 137; **48**, 277, 279, 284; **49**, 113, 316, 322; **51**, 4, 5, 7, 8, 48n, 86, 88, 90, 95–7, 99, 101, 104, 105, 129–39, 321; **53**, 49, 301–2, 337, 342; **54**, 56; **55**, 12, 205–6, 388; **56**, 81; **59**, 30n46, 32n58, 49, 56n20, 56–7, 57n20, 58–9, 93, 100n12, 128, 131

Theocritus, **8**, 46; **11**, 71; **15**, 21, 29; **37**, 69; **42**, 66
Theodorus, **3**, 20
Theophrastus, **15**, 97n; **51**, 171
Theotokas, George, **10**, 119; **11**, 121; **12**, 113
Theotokis, Constantin, **6**, 120
Therborn, Goran, **49**, 89n, 95
Thesiger, Ernest, **10**, 129
Thevet, André, **17**, 39
Thibaudet, Albert, **28**, 44n; **57**, 117
Thibault, John C., **56**, 29n
Thielgaard, Alice, **59**, 295
Thieme, Hans Otto, **37**, 157n
Thieme, Thomas, **60**, 287
Thienen, F. W. S. van, **18**, 126
Thiess, Frank, **4**, 127
Thiong'o, Ngûgîwa, **53**, 291
Thirlby, Styan, **26**, 181n, 182; **33**, 198–9, 209; **59**, 165, 166
Thirsk, Joan, **38**, 27n; **55**, 37n, 373
This Island's Mine, **43**, 215; **54**, 340
Thiselton, Alfred, **5**, 3, 8–9, 146; **7**, 3; **16**, 32
Thisted, Ronald, **40**, 228
Thistleton, A. E., **32**, 239
Thody, Liz, **44**, 191
Thomas Lord Cromwell, **3**, 45; **4**, 92; **6**, 58; **12**, 43, 45, 50
Thomas of Woodstock, see *Woodstock*
Thomas, *Rules of Italian Grammar*, **1**, 128
Thomas, Amboise, **3**, 100; **18**, 83; **20**, 164; **45**, 174; **56**, 289; **58**, 300
Thomas, Bardy, **43**, 217
Thomas, Ben, **48**, 195–6; **49**, 272; **52**, 262
Thomas, Charles, **19**, 113; **23**, 131, 132
Thomas, Christopher, **53**, 279; **58**, 107
Thomas, D. L., **52**, 103n
Thomas, David, **47**, 27n; **51**, 107n; **56**, 200n
Thomas, Debora, **57**, 152
Thomas, Dylan, **18**, 46; **48**, 50; **54**, 345
  Under Milk Wood, **11**, 19
Thomas, Edward, **55**, 135
Thomas, Ellen, **44**, 202
Thomas, Gail H., **19**, 131n
Thomas, Gareth, **33**, 170; **44**, 194
Thomas, Helen, **24**, 161
Thomas, Sir Henry, **3**, 55; **4**, 147; **5**, 46n
Thomas, Jez, **45**, 147
Thomas, Keith, **28**, 118; **31**, 106n; **39**, 218, 232; **43**, 2n; **46**, 131n; **48**, 232; **51**, 167; **54**, 5, 29, 36n; **55**, 37n; **56**, 2n; **57**, 30; **59**, 247, 247n62, 252n98
Thomas, Lord Cromwell, **48**, 277
Thomas, Mark, **53**, 285
Thomas, Mary Olive, **18**, 170; **26**, 157; **41**, 87n
Thomas, Max W., **60**, 263
Thomas, Merlin, **15**, 144
Thomas, Michael, **51**, 268; **54**, 266
Thomas, Powys, **5**, 125
Thomas, R. George, **55**, 135n
Thomas, Sara M., **42**, 153
Thomas, Sian, **40**, 171; **54**, 248; **56**, 247n; **58**, 287; **59**, 339, 340; **60**, 78, 323
Thomas, Sidney, **3**, 25, 26; **4**, 158–9; **6**, 159; **8**, 83, 97n, 98n; **11**, 136, 145; **13**, 103, 105n; **21**, 148; **28**, 181; **30**, 208; **32**, 242; **38**, 252; **39**, 249; **40**, 216; **41**, 219n; **43**, 131n; **46**, 254n; **49**, 33n; **50**, 283, 287; **51**, 331; **55**, 3n
  First Two Quartos of 'Romeo & Juliet' reviewed, **3**, 150
  'The Queen Mab Speech in *Romeo and Juliet*', **25**, 73–80
Thomas, Thomas, **52**, 185n; **56**, 40
Thomas, Vivian, **41**, 204–5; **44**, 8n, 71n, 207–8; **46**, 217, 220; **48**, 255; **54**, 228n; **58**, 50, 52; **59**, 354
Thomas, William, **48**, 70n
Thomlinson, Richard, **45**, 112
Thompson, A. R., **6**, 33n
Thompson, Ann, **30**, 193, 195–6; **31**, 189; **32**, 229–30, 236; **33**, 191, 204; **36**, 173, 185; **38**, 239, 240; **40**, 70; **41**, 74, 199; **42**, 61n, 168; **43**, 70–1; **44**, 119n, 217; **45**, 162; **46**, 123n, 151n, 241n; **47**, 139n; **49**, 310; **51**, 6, 279–80, 284, 293; **52**, 276; **53**, 299, 344; **54**, 42n; **55**, 183n, 191, 193, 258, 265, 352, 353–4; **56**, 93–104, 147n, 330; **57**, 188, 194, 327, 328, 339, 341, 342; **58**, 96, 355, 357; **59**, 21, 87n25, 87n26, 87n27, 212n61, 259n11, 381, 383; **60**, 361, 369
Thompson, Cargill, **50**, 227
Thompson, Constance, **11**, 97n
Thompson, Craig R., **17**, 59n; **46**, 112n; **56**, 43n
Thompson, D'Arcy, **44**, 136n
Thompson, David, **8**, 123
Thompson, David Mark, **55**, 333; **56**, 288
Thompson, Denys, **40**, 30
Thompson, Dr, **14**, 110, 114
Thompson, E. N. S., *The Controversy between the Puritans and the Stage*, **12**, 21n
Thompson, E. P., **51**, 51n, 52; **55**, 37n
Thompson, Sir Edward Maunde, **2**, 52; **3**, 4; **4**, 86; **6**, 5; **8**, 104n, 105n; **9**, 70–1, 73–4, 75, 76, 77; **10**, 153; **14**, 32, 33; **16**, 168; **28**, 38n; **31**, 193, **42**, 131; **43**, 206; **44**, 162, 192; **47**, 209; **50**, 264; **57**, 331; **58**, 277; **59**, 341
  Shakespeare's Handwriting, **2**, 44, 55–6; **3**, 3; **14**, 5
Thompson, Emma, **44**, 194; **45**, 151; **47**, 258; **48**, 233; **52**, 303
Thompson, Flora, **17**, 178
Thompson, Fran, **41**, 185, 189; **42**, 149, 157; **43**, 216; **44**, 197, 199; **47**, 194; **48**, 229; **49**, 270
Thompson, Gregory, **50**, 225, 235; **52**, 259; **53**, 284; **55**, 330; **57**, 266, 267, 269; **58**, 298
Thompson, Helena, **56**, 289; **57**, 291, 293
Thompson, Ian, **41**, 184
Thompson, John, **42**, 107n; **58**, 227–8, 233, 234
Thompson, John B., **50**, 91n; **52**, 190n
Thompson, John O., **41**, 199; **59**, 381, 383
Thompson, Karl F., **7**, 130; **11**, 137; **12**, 142; **21**, 134; **22**, 160; **26**, 159–60
Thompson, Laura, **43**, 206; **44**, 195, 200
Thompson, Leslie, **55**, 24, 25n; **57**, 316
Thompson, Mark, **42**, 131, 134, 153; **43**, 212; **44**, 177, 198; **45**, 146; **48**, 224; **51**, 243; **52**, 255; **59**, 325
Thompson, Marvin, **43**, 250n; **47**, 149n; **49**, 171n
Thompson, Miles, **56**, 317
Thompson, Peter E., **42**, 28n
Thompson, Robert, **57**, 41, 51
Thompson, Ruth, **43**, 250n; **47**, 149n; **49**, 171n
Thompson, Sharon, **45**, 45n
Thompson, Sophie, **42**, 131; **43**, 206; **44**, 162, 192; **46**, 168; **47**, 209; **57**, 331; **58**, 277; **59**, 341
Thompson, Stith, **44**, 45n; **49**, 190n
Thomsen, Kerri, **50**, 251

Thomson, A. Landesborough, **21**, 142n
Thomson, David Mark, **53**, 277; **57**, 294
Thomson, Elbert Nevius Sebring, **32**, 70n
Thomson, George, **49**, 332
Thomson, I., **42**, 58–60
Thomson, J., **56**, 64
Thomson, J. A. K., **4**, 67n, 68n; **6**, 155; **10**, 6, 15, 16, 18, 25n, 59n; **15**, 29; **31**, 6; **35**, 119; **40**, 73; **42**, 53n, 54
Thomson, J. O., **17**, 43n
Thomson, James, **18**, 184; **24**, 17; **44**, 242; **48**, 8; **49**, 290; **52**, 291
Thomson, James (1700–48), version of *Coriolanus*, **10**, 72
Thomson, John A. F., **52**, 168n
Thomson, Kim, **44**, 194
Thomson, Leslie, **43**, 265n, 266; **46**, 26n; **49**, 22n, 24; **54**, 16n, 18n, 20n, 23n, 27n, 28n, 356; **56**, 333–48; **60**, 109n31
Thomson, Mark, **54**, 291; **58**, 301; **59**, 343; **60**, 320
Thomson, Mark A., **57**, 74
Thomson, Mervyn, **55**, 172
Thomson, Patricia, **21**, 147; **23**, 150; **25**, 8; **44**, 46n
Thomson, Peter, **35**, 3n, 9n; **37**, 182, 195, 196; **41**, 9, 224; **42**, 86n; **43**, 249; **47**, 1n, 251–2; **50**, 164; **51**, 194n; **52**, 52n, 81; **56**, 62n, 63n, 177, 183; **57**, 88
 The Royal Shakespeare Season 1970, reviewed, **24**, 117–26
 'No Rome of Safety': The Royal Shakespeare Season 1972, *reviewed*, **26**, 139–50
 'Shakespeare Straight and Crooked': a Review of the 1973 Season at Stratford, **27**, 143–54
 'The Smallest Season': The Royal Shakespeare Company at Stratford in 1974, *reviewed*, **28**, 137–48
 'Towards a Poor Shakespeare': the Royal Shakespeare Company at Stratford in 1975, *reviewed*, **29**, 151–6
Thomson, Dr Thomas, **1**, 83
Thomson, Virgil, **39**, 81n, 82; **43**, 18; **44**, 243
Thomson, W. G., **60**, 247n43, 247n44
Thomson, W. H., **6**, 157
Thomson, Sir William (Lord Kelvin), **52**, 183
Thomte, Reidar, **57**, 102
Thorby, Philip, **41**, 188
Thoreau, Henry David, **24**, 87, 88, 103, 104; **53**, 131n
Thorent, André, **7**, 110, 115
Thornber, Kraig, **44**, 201
Thornberry, Richard T., **32**, 231
Thorndike, Ashley H., **1**, 4, 48; **3**, 31; **4**, 2, 11; **7**, 8; **8**, 1, 2, 3; **18**, 186; **20**, 24n; **35**, 15n; **37**, 11; **45**, 20; **47**, 26n
 English Comedy, **14**, 3
 The Influence of Beaumont and Fletcher on Shakespeare, **14**, 12; **20**, 18
Thorndike, Daniel, **45**, 146
Thorndike, Dame Sybil, **2**, 11, 14; **4**, 105; **8**, 130; **32**, 28, 32; **34**, 8; **42**, 40
Thorne, Alison, **56**, 315; **57**, 316
Thorne, Angela, **51**, 219, 264
Thorne, J. P., **26**, 164
Thorne, S. E., **17**, 251n; **29**, 93n
Thorne, William Barry, **23**, 155; **25**, 177; **26**, 153; **29**, 11n; **42**, 1n
Thornton, Frank, **28**, 144, 145
Thornton, R. K. R., **24**, 165
Thornton, Tamara Plakins, **59**, 116n35
Thorp, Margaret Farrand, **13**, 161; **31**, 15
Thorpe, James, **26**, 180; **59**, 15n64
Thorpe, John, **33**, 145
Thorpe, Thomas, **5**, 148; **15**, 11, 13, 53; **20**, 170, 171; **21**, 97, 102, 104; **22**, 182; **23**, 160; **37**, 218; **41**, 219; **46**, 37; **51**, 286, 328; **52**, 304; **53**, 78n; **60**, 253, 255, 259, 261
Thorssen, Marilyn J., **46**, 5
Thorvaldsen, B., **29**, 145, 146
Thrale, Mrs Hester, **12**, 8; **26**, 168; **46**, 237; **52**, 1
Thrall, W. F., **3**, 21n
Three Kings of Colchester, **17**, 172, and n
Three Ladies of London, The, **50**, 255; **52**, 100
Three Marriage Plays, **50**, 256
Three Renaissance Travel Plays, **50**, 255
Threlfall, David, **33**, 169; **40**, 183; **41**, 184; **43**, 209, **49**, 267
Throckmorton family, **14**, 115
Throckmorton, Job, **54**, 118; **60**, 11, 12
Throckmorton, Sir Robert, of Coughton Court, **12**, 99
Throne of Blood, **43**, 251; **47**, 112
Thucydides, **56**, 223, 225
Thuillier, Emilio, **54**, 154
Thum, Hans W., **37**, 157n
Thumboo, Edwin, **25**, 181
Thurber, James, **43**, 228
Thurlow, Edward, **38**, 71
Thurman, Judith, **43**, 110n, 119n
Thurn, David H., **50**, 43n
Thurnher, Eugen, **18**, 119
Thurston, Herbert, **1**, 123; **54**, 92n; **56**, 188
Thurston, John, **10**, 73; **13**, 76
Thürwächter, Sabine, **50**, 264
Thynne, Francis, **24**, 66n; **42**, 28; **57**, 11, 71; **59**, 275–6
 Animadversions, **6**, 60
Thynne, Henry, 6th Marquis of Bath, **13**, 104n
Thynne, William, **1**, 23
 edition of *Chaucer*, **9**, 81
Tian, Han, **36**, 53
Tian, Mansha, **57**, 182, 183–4
Tibbetts, Chris, **60**, 180
Tibbetts, Michael, **57**, 295
Tibet, Kartal, **12**, 117; **14**, 123; **15**, 138
Tibullus, **15**, 97n
Tidblad, Inga, **12**, 116; **14**, 123
Tiddy, R. J. E., **15**, 113
Tide, Andreas, **22**, 123
Tieck, Dorothea, **26**, 166; **48**, 3, 8; **53**, 299
Tieck, Ludwig, **1**, 2, 3; **3**, 49; **8**, 118; **10**, 119; **12**, 11, 12; **14**, 85; **15**, 132, 134; **23**, 122; **29**, 175; **37**, 155, 160, 161, 200; **41**, 225; **47**, 88, 89; **48**, 3, 4, 7, 10, 116; **57**, 112, 115; **58**, 142; **59**, 194n7, 195
 see also under Schlegel
Tiedge, C. A., **54**, 183
Tieghem, Paul van, **9**, 97, 100n
 Le préromantisme reviewed, **3**, 136
Tiepolo, Giovanni Battista, **10**, 75; **37**, 176
Tiernan, Andrew, **57**, 45
Tierney, Colin, **51**, 255; **54**, 284
Tierney, Malcolm, **46**, 191
Tierney, Margaret, **26**, 141n
Tierney, Moira, **57**, 186
Tietze, H., *Dürer Catalogue*, **13**, 80n
Tiffany, Grace, **47**, 227, 233; **49**, 291; **57**, 320; **58**, 1
Tiffin, Helen, **48**, 157n

Tiger, The, **11**, 76
Till, Lawrence, **43**, 209; **48**, 236; **50**, 228
Tiller, Kenneth J., **59**, 241–2n19
Tilley, Morris Palmer, **8**, 8; **9**, 43n; **18**, 176, 179; **27**, 189; **32**, 163n, 164n, 166, 168n, 171n; **33**, 19, 20n; **35**, 83; **38**, 37, 44n; **40**, 78n; **46**, 130n; **47**, 153n, 162–3; **49**, 165n, 166n, 169n; **55**, 23n, 207n
English Proverbs of the Sixteenth and Seventeenth Centuries, **7**, 5
Tillotson, Geoffrey, **46**, 62n; **52**, 78n
Tillotson, Kathleen, **29**, 182; **38**, 97n; **53**, 103n
Tillyard, E. M. W., **1**, 121, 126, 127–8; **2**, 108; **3**, 27; **4**, 6, 14–15, 144; **6**, 8, 10, 11, 12, 13, 14, 16, 17, 24, 33n, 37, 151, 156; **7**, 8, 9; **8**, 11, 12, 37, 38, 111, 143; **9**, 11; **10**, 3, 40, 44, 49n; **11**, 60, 69n; **12**, 129n; **13**, 153; **14**, 98, 101n, 138, 143; **15**, 122, 124n; **16**, 84, 160; **18**, 9, 42, 159, 160; **19**, 8, 65, 131, 136; **20**, 152–3, 165; **21**, 135; **22**, 10, 14n, 72, 79, 80, 84, 148, 155, 159; **23**, 145; **24**, 55n, 56n; **25**, 2, 3, 6; **27**, 11n, 12n; **28**, 2, 89; **29**, 84, 85, 88; **30**, 47; **31**, 85n; **32**, 3; **35**, 65, 118, 178; **36**, 159, 160; **37**, 5; **38**, 1–5, 10, 11, 18, 46, 226; **39**, 139n, 226; **40**, 63, 187, 192; **41**, 70, 198–9; **42**, 6n, 168–9; **43**, 8n, 238–9; **44**, 2, 3, 4, 49n, 206; **45**, 159, 163, 188; **46**, 215; **47**, 113, 256; **48**, 69, 70, 78n; **52**, 111, 277; **53**, 179, 181; **54**, 352; **55**, 345; **56**, 320, 323, 351
Shakespeare's History Plays, **3**, 7; **12**, 139; **14**, 3
reviewed, **6**, 9, 36
Shakespeare's Problem Plays reviewed, **4**, 144–5
The Elizabethan World Picture, **3**, 7
Tilmouth, Michael, **51**, 80n
Tilney, Charles, **9**, 85n
Tilney, Sir Edmund, **2**, 45, 48, 50–1, 54, 60n; **3**, 51; **5**, 139; **9**, 71–2; **40**, 218; **41**, 216–17, 220; **43**, 249; 44, 228–9; **46**, 232, 233; **52**, 72–5, 294; **53**, 71n; **55**, 44–5, 52; **56**, 43; **60**, 7
Time magazine, **59**, 68
Times Literary Supplement, The, **2**, 44
Timings, E. K., **11**, 107
Timmins, Samuel, **7**, 90
Timor, Rachel, **6**, 121
Ting, Shao, **6**, 115
Tinkler, F. C, **4**, 24; **15**, 122; **36**, 100n
Tintoretto, Jacopo, **4**, 102; **26**, 49, 50, 51, 52, 53, 55, 64, 65
Tipton, Anne, **60**, 292–3
Tiramani, Jenny, **42**, 131; **43**, 205–6, 208, 212; **45**, 151; **46**, 200; **50**, 229, 236; **52**, 256; **53**, 244, 246, 279; **54**, 283, 286; **55**, 323
'Tis Pity She's a Whore, **52**, 300
Tison, John L., **15**, 174
Titanic, **52**, 90, 93
Titherley, A. W., **7**, 138–9
Titian, Vecellio, **10**, 71, 76n; **15**, 19; **26**, 52; **27**, 55; **31**, 18; **36**, 170
Titmarsh, Belgrave, **60**, 223, 234–5
Titmarsh, M. A., **56**, 128n
Tittler, Robert, **49**, 16; **52**, 78n; **60**, 3, 9
To Wong Foo, With Love, **52**, 90
Titunik, Irwin R., **44**, 67n; **60**, 228n30
Titus and Vespasian, **3**, 24; **10**, 2
Tkhapsayev, Vladimir, **5**, 117
Toad of Toad Hall, **55**, 310
Toba, Christopher, **47**, 216, 217
Tobias, Richard C., **29**, 165; **31**, 12n
Tobin, John J. M., **31**, 34n, 183; **32**, 230, 234, 235; **33**, 191; **34**, 185, 194–5; **35**, 179, 184; **36**, 175, 176; **37**, 190, 215; **38**, 232, 242; **40**, 69; **43**, 269
Tobin, Terence, **23**, 173n
Tocilescu, Alexandru, **45**, 146; **48**, 119n
Todd, Ann, **9**, 124
Todd, Carole, **60**, 328
Todd, D. K. C., **29**, 164; **40**, 197
Todd, Henry John, **57**, 236
Todd, J., **55**, 108n
Todd, Jane, **53**, 27n
Todd, Richard, **47**, 213; **52**, 256
Todd, Susan, **56**, 343
Todd, William B., **7**, 152; **58**, 356; **59**, 281n46
Todorov, Tzvetan, **34**, 33; **46**, 92; **48**, 32n; **55**, 272n, 280
Tofan, Mihai, **20**, 129
Tofano, Gilberto, **12**, 114
Tofeh, Bryan, **55**, 330
Tofte, Robert, **38**, 52; **46**, 126n, 127; **60**, 273n15
Tohyama, Shizuo, **42**, 162
Toksvig, Sandy, **46**, 197–8
Toland, John, **48**, 54n
Tolbert, James M., **15**, 29
Toliver, Harold E., **20**, 155, 159; **27**, 27n; **38**, 8; **44**, 212
Tolkien, J. R. R., **30**, 82
Tolles, Frederick B., **6**, 62
Tollet, **32**, 245
Tollett, George, **55**, 264
Tolman, Albert H., **6**, 13; **9**, 2; **10**, 7; **18**, 39; **27**, 106–7, 108
Tolson, Francis, **55**, 93
Tolstoy, Count Alexis, **4**, 120; **5**, 104
Tolstoy, Count Lev Nikolaevich, **53**, 187; **55**, 115
Tolstoy, Leo, **14**, 144; **16**, 10; **21**, 113; **22**, 147; **28**, 30, 55; **39**, 236; **51**, 39; **54**, 140–2, 145–6; **56**, 303
Tomalin, Claire, **51**, 4; **58**, 84, 91
Tomarken, Edward, **46**, 236–7; **52**, 275
Tomelty, Frances, **38**, 209
Tomkins, F. G., **47**, 61n
Tomkis, Thomas, **39**, 214; **49**, 300; **59**, 72, 73
Albumazar, **13**, 169; **16**, 96
Lingua, **17**, 196n
Tomlin, Karen, **55**, 311
Tomlins, F. G., **1**, 83
Tomlinson, Gary, **48**, 141n; **55**, 342
Tomlinson, H., **54**, 170n
Tomlinson, Maggie, **38**, 8
Tomlinson, Michael, **38**, 226
Tomlinson, Philip, **24**, 38n
Tomlinson, T. B., **13**, 151; **26**, 7, 8
Tompkins, Eugene, **24**, 99n
Tompkins, J. M. S., **7**, 136; **31**, 7n
Tompkinson, Stephen, **47**, 212
Tompson, John, **58**, 225
Toms, Carl, **43**, 213
Tomson, Arnold, **11**, 90
Tomson, Bob, **43**, 211
Tomson, George, **11**, 90, 91–2, 96
Tomson, Jasper, **11**, 90, 91
Tomson, L., **51**, 164n
Tomson, Richard, **11**, 90, 91
Tongue, Ruth, **17**, 169–70, 170n

Tonson, J. & R., **51**, 2, 14n, 86
Tonson, Jacob, **3**, 47, 50; **4**, 85, 91; **7**, 91; **10**, 72, 76n; **11**, 147; **12**, 150; **14**, 157; **18**, 13–16, 19; **20**, 163; **27**, 191; **37**, 41, 42; **53**, 216, 217, 218, 335, 342–3; **55**, 267–9; **59**, 159, 214
Tooke, Andrew, **10**, 20
Tooker, William, **43**, 3
Toole, J. L., **41**, 24
Toole, William B., **22**, 159; **25**, 2; **26**, 160; **29**, 160
'The Motif of Psychic Division in *Richard III*', **27**, 21–32
Tooley, Nicholas, **46**, 231; **47**, 173; **58**, 230
Toomey, Patrick, **45**, 129
Top of the World Company, **58**, 299
Topcliffe, Richard, **2**, 53; **42**, 82; **54**, 90, 94, 95
Topham, Forrest, reconstruction of stage, **12**, 22
Topographical Descriptions, Regiments and Policies, **46**, 233
Topol, Josef, **16**, 133
Toppen, W. H., **21**, 137
Topping, Richard, **60**, 52
Topsell, Edward, **6**, 60; **17**, 150–1; **56**, 234n
Torbarina, Josip, **4**, 118, 119; **15**, 138, 142; **18**, 134
Torelli, Giacomo, **10**, 72, 76n
Tornea, Florin, **20**, 131n
Törocsik, Mari, **16**, 135
Torrance, Robert M., **38**, 65
Torre, Pierre della, **18**, 123
Torsslow, **5**, 114
Toshioka, Fumio, **48**, 252
Toso, Otello, **15**, 136
Toto, Anthony, **53**, 326
Tottel's *Songs and Sonnets*, **15**, 6
'Tottel's Miscellany', **4**, 86
Toucatt, Ralph, **36**, 25n
Tough, A. J., **26**, 162
Toulmin-Smith, L., **19**, 70
Toulouse-Lautrec, Henri de, **36**, 149
Tourneur, Cyril, **7**, 6, 96, 142; **9**, 144; **11**, 64; **14**, 8, 11, 143; **22**, 137, 171; **26**, 7, 41, 55, 57, 153; **29**, 170; **36**, 174; **37**, 189; **40**, 215; **42**, 12; **43**, 260; **45**, 75; **46**, 124n; 47, 244n; **60**, 231
The Atheist's Tragedy, **4**, 150; **5**, 66, 69–70, 132; **12**, 54
The Revenger's Tragedy, **12**, 44–5, 48–50, 53; **14**, 11; **15**, 113, 137; **16**, 90; **17**, 46; **20**, 167
Tourneur, P. le, *see* Letourneur, P.
Tournier, Jacques, **10**, 118
Tours, Guy de, **15**, 98n
Tout, T. F., **6**, 53
Toutougi, Emmanuel, **51**, 260
Tovell, James, **59**, 339
Tovey, Barbara, **51**, 282
Towards Macbeth - A Prologue, **43**, 209
Towers, Geoffrey, **45**, 148
Towne, Susannah, **50**, 226
Towne, Thomas, **33**, 158
Towneley Plays, **6**, 59; **7**, 69
Processus Noe Cum Filiis, **20**, 66
Secunda Pastorum, **20**, 66
Towns, Colin, **52**, 256
Townsend, F. L., **14**, 56–7, 65n
Townshend, Aurelian, *Albion's Triumph*, **11**, 116n; **28**, 169
Townshend, Charles, 1st Baron Bayning, **38**, 171
Townshend, Matthew, **54**, 290
Toye, Wendy, **14**, 127
Toynbee, Arnold, **56**, 206n
Toynbee, Paget, **4**, 93
Toynbee, William, **35**, 8; **57**, 90
Toyne, Gabriel, **1**, 99, 102
Trace, Jacqueline, **36**, 169
Trachey, Ralph, **19**, 102, 106n, 107n
Traci, P. J., **26**, 158–9
Tracy, Robert, **20**, 164
Tracy, Susan, **45**, 152
Trafalgar, Studios, **58**, 268
Trafton, Dain, **36**, 164
Tragedie of Antonie, **55**, 380
Tragedie of Dido, The, **54**, 207n
Tragedie of Lodovick Sforza Duke of Milan, **54**, 62
Tragedy of Ferrex and Porrex, The; or, Gorboduc, **54**, 27–8
Tragedy of Mariam, The Fair Queen of Jewry, The (M. Cary), **46**, 226; **48**, 265, 284
Tragelehn, B. K., **48**, 176, 177, 178, 182
Tragical History, Admirable Atchievements and various events of Guy earl of Warwick, The, **60**, 342–3
Tragicomedy of the Witch, The, **54**, 14
Traherne, Susan, **55**, 180
Traherne, Thomas, **17**, 167; **23**, 167; **60**, 337, 338
Traill and Mann, editors, **17**, 45n
Trainer, James, **14**, 148
Trainspotting, **52**, 90
Traister, Barbara Howard, **39**, 231, 232; **43**, 1n; **54**, 228n
Trajan, Emperor, **10**, 31
Tranquillius, C. Suetonius, **44**, 66n
Translations of Shakespeare, problems of translation, **1**, 116; **2**, 116, 121–2, 127; **3**, 98–106, 108, 111–12, 116, 117–19; **4**, 114–15, 118–19, 126–7; **5**, 50, 51, 52, 111, 112–15, 117–18
Afrikaans, **5**, 112
Chinese, **6**, 112–16
Hebrew, **5**, 52; **6**, 106–11, 118–19, 120–2, 124–5
Spanish, **6**, 106–11; **7**, 93, 108, 110–13, 115–16; **8**, 118, 120–1; **9**, 59–67, 85n, 92–4, 101–5, 108, 110n, 112–16, 118, 152; **10**, 115–21, 142–3; *see also under names of individual authors and countries*
Trapani, Sal, **60**, 328
Trapido, Barbara, **56**, 302
Trapnel, Anna, **49**, 303
Trapp, J. B., **42**, 82n
Trapp, Simon, **4**, 70, 75
Trappolin Supposed a Prince, **12**, 142
Trask, Willard R., **40**, 124n
Traub, Valerie, **44**, 220; **45**, 160; **46**, 3, 5, 6, 207, 208; **47**, 247; **49**, 202, 212n, 216; **51**, 276; **52**, 279, 293n; **53**, 86n; **54**, 342; **55**, 352; **56**, 69n, 71, 73, 75n, 156n; **58**, 184; **60**, 114n54, 169n9.4
Trautmann, K., **33**, 156n, 164n; **36**, 138n
Trautvetter, Christine, **24**, 149; **27**, 189
Traux, Elizabeth, **51**, 180n
Travels of the Three English Brothers, The, **50**, 255; **52**, 78n
Travers, Peter, **52**, 94n
Travers, Walter, **17**, 125
Traversi, Derek A., **2**, 139; **4**, 24, 147; **5**, 135; **6**, 12; **7**, 9, 135; **8**, 11, 33, 140; **9**, 136, 140; **10**, 11; **11**, 46, 47; **15**, 59, 124n; **16**, 48, 156; **18**, 3–4, 8–9, 42; **19**, 128–9, 131; **21**, 142; **22**,

158; **23**, 132, 133, 140–1; **25**, 1n, 2, 5, 8, 12n, 13n; **27**, 72; **29**, 59; **30**, 52n; **32**, 180n, 181n, 182; **33**, 4; **34**, 140n; **35**, 178; **37**, 5, 30n; **38**, 5; **39**, 59; **40**, 72, 187; **43**, 16n; **46**, 93n; **47**, 235; **57**, 31
Travitsky, Betty S., **39**, 230; **45**, 160; **51**, 293; **52**, 178n
Trawick, Buckner B., **33**, 192
Treatise of Treasons, A, **1**, 125
Tree, Ellen, **18**, 106; **56**, 134
Tree, Sir Herbert Beerbohm, **1**, 106; **2**, 1, 2, 3, 5–6; **4**, 105; **8**, 76–7; **9**, 57; **10**, 75, 149, 150; **11**, 124; **18**, 185; **25**, 113, 118–23; **26**, 142; **27**, 34n; **28**, 172; **29**, 134, 135, 139, 143; **30**, 200; **31**, 188; **32**, 25, 27, 28, 30, 35n; **35**, 2, 7, 9–10, 19; **36**, 74, 181; **37**, 85; **39**, 4, 75, 109; **40**, 1, 12; **41**, 224; **44**, 108; **46**, 218; **47**, 231; **48**, 265, 282; **52**, 162n, 163n, 203n; **54**, 312; **55**, 380; **56**, 130, 245; **59**, 150; **60**, 186–7
Tree, Marion, **32**, 22
Tree, Maud, **55**, 135
Tree, Viola, **25**, 119; **55**, 135
Trefethan, Mrs Florence, **4**, 47n
Tregear, Lucy, **47**, 217
Treglown, Jeremy, **59**, 201
Trehern, E. M., **9**, 144
Treichler, Paula A., **18**, 132; **56**, 70n
Treilhou-Balaudé, Catherine, **52**, 285
Trench, Archbishop Richard Chenevix, **40**, 72; **54**, 82–8
Trench, W. F., **9**, 3, 4
Trent, W. P., **9**, 110n
Tresham, Sir Thomas, **17**, 73; **47**, 24
Treswell, Ralph, **55**, 375
Tretiak, A., **8**, 6
Trevelyan, C. E., **23**, 44n
Trevelyan, Sir George, **46**, 200
Trevelyan, W. C., **23**, 44n
Trevelyon, Thomas, **1**, 72
Treves, Frederick, **39**, 193–5
Trevet, Nicholas, **59**, 244, 250
Trevis, Di, **40**, 171; **41**, 189; **42**, 131; **43**, 212; **47**, 121
Trevisa, **17**, 39
Trevor, Douglas, **59**, 350–1, 368
Trevor-Roper, Hugh R., **11**, 107, 114n; **17**, 81n; **29**, 90; **31**, 58n; **35**, 130n; **54**, 61n; **59**, 250n58
The Gentry, 1540–1640, **14**, 95
Trewin, J. C., **7**, 146n; **18**, 185; **23**, 131; **25**, 1n, 115n; **31**, 174; **32**, 31, 32–3; **33**, 196; **35**, 4n, 7–8, 9, 10; **36**, 79n, 81n; **38**, 17, 50n; **49**, 307; **53**, 104n, 241; **56**, 5n
Trial of Treasure, **17**, 219–20
Tricomi, Albert H., **26**, 173; **29**, 163; **31**, 24n, 30, 172; **34**, 174; **38**, 53, 54, 55n, 58n, 59; **42**, 188; **44**, 10n; **51**, 294
'The Aesthetics of Mutilation in *Titus Andronicus*', **27**, 11–19
Trienens, Roger J., **8**, 144; **9**, 144
Trigge, Randall, **58**, 226, 227
Trigge, Robert, **58**, 227
Trigge, William, **58**, 225, 226–7, 227, 234
Triggs, Jeffery A., **52**, 323; **59**, 157n1, 161–2n17, 164, 165, 167
Trill, Suzanne, **51**, 293
Trilling, Lionel, **7**, 10; **46**, 131n; **58**, 85
Trimble, William Raleigh, **54**, 96n
Trinder, Simon, **57**, 275
Trinity College, Cambridge, **11**, 108, 114
Trinity House, Deptford, **17**, 27–8
Trintignant, Jean-Louis, **14**, 119
Tristan L'Hermite, **16**, 53
Tristram, E. W., **26**, 74, 75n
'Triumph of Isabella', **3**, 87
Triumph of the Will, **52**, 193
Trivedi, Harish, **50**, 264
Trivedi, Poonam, **57**, 171; **58**, 53; **59**, 369–70, 375
Trnka, Jiří, **12**, 110; **13**, 126; **14**, 118; **16**, 133
Troeber, Hans-Joachim, **37**, 159n
Troilus and Cressida (MS. ? by Chettle and Dekker), **3**, 52
Trollope, Anthony, **10**, 33; **57**, 113
Trollope, T. A., **59**, 264
Trombley, Stephen, **48**, 113
Tromeo and Juliet, **52**, 90
Tromley, F. B., **29**, 165; **32**, 8
Trompf, G. W., **48**, 83n
Tronch-Pérez, Jesús, **56**, 101n; **58**, 348, 357; **59**, 161, 162, 163
Trott, C. J. F., **8**, 123
Trotter, Catherine, **43**, 254
Troublesome Raigne of John, King of England, The, **1**, 123, 127; **3**, 26, 31, 47, 57n; **4**, 59, 87; **6**, 4, 11, 35n, 36, 58, 170; **7**, 148; **9**, 84, 151; **10**, 70n; **12**, 142; **14**, 30, 32, 41; **16**, 169, 173, 177; **20**, 24; **54**, 213, 214, 216, 221; **55**, 18, 22, 23
Troughton, Ali, **56**, 247n
Troughton, David, **43**, 190, 201; **44**, 173, 181, 193, 198; **45**, 125, 148, 156; **47**, 204–5; **49**, 258–9; **50**, 32; **53**, 329; **54**, 275–7, 279; **55**, 324, 330; **56**, 289, 290, 295, 343; **57**, 278; **58**, 275; **59**, 341; **60**, 285
Troughton, Henry, **13**, 94
Troughton, Sam, **55**, 289, 290
Trousdale, Jacqueline, **48**, 235
Trousdale, Marion, **28**, 168; **36**, 180; **37**, 180, 181; **38**, 49n; **40**, 97n, 98; **43**, 18n, 265n; **45**, 190, 194n; **52**, 71n; **55**, 3n; **59**, 17n69
Trowbridge, Alexander B., **1**, 58
Troyat, Henri, **48**, 118
Trubowitz, Rachel, **45**, 167
Truchet, Sybil, **38**, 231
Trudgill, E., **51**, 77n
True Chronicle History of King Leir, **60**, 253
True reporte of the death and martyrdome of M. Campion . . ., **8**, 103
True Rites and Maimed Rites: Ritual and Anti-Ritual in Shakespeare and his Age, **46**, 208
True Tragedie of Richard Duke of York, The, see under 'Richard, Duke of York'
Trueman, Pat, **44**, 201; **46**, 198; **49**, 274; **50**, 235; **52**, 254
Truffaut, François, **26**, 175
Trumbach, Randolph, **49**, 181n
Trumbull, William, **33**, 167; **54**, 197
Trundle, John, **36**, 142; **38**, 245–6; **50**, 156
Trussell, John, **59**, 245; **39**, 234, 235
Truth brought to light (1651), **17**, 203–4
Try all of Chevalry, The, **1**, 64
Tsarev, M., **13**, 133
Tschischwitz, Benno, **6**, 110
Tschopp, Elizabeth, *Zur Verteilung von Vers und Prosa in Shakespeares Dramen*, **12**, 116
Tschumi, Raymond, **18**, 129
Tse, David KS, **47**, 217; **58**, 301
Tse, Elaine, **49**, 274
Tsetung, Mao, **57**, 171, 173
Tsubouchi, Shōyō, **48**, 102, 106–7, 110; **54**, 110–11; **60**, 132n9

Tsukayama, Masane, **42**, 153
Tsutsumi, Harue, **48**, 102n
Tsyavlovsky, M. A., **5**, 104n, 105n
Tuck, Richard, **59**, 264n27
Tucker, Antony, **50**, 226
Tucker, E. F. J., **31**, 180
'The Letter of the Law in *The Merchant of Venice*', **29**, 93–101
Tucker, James, **59**, 318
Tucker, Patrick, **45**, 157; **48**, 237; **52**, 39, 227; **53**, 276; **54**, 284; **55**, 323; **56**, 176, 177n, 344
Tucker, T. G., **15**, 11, 12, 16
Tucker-Brooke, C. F., **23**, 51n, 69, 72n
Tuckey, Antony, **41**, 183; **42**, 149, 154; **44**, 197
Tuckey, John S., **11**, 138
Tuckley, Emily, **47**, 96
Tudeau-Clayton, Margaret, **53**, 18n, 20n, 321; **55**, 349; **56**, 30n; **57**, 221
Tuke, Sir Brian, **17**, 227
Tukur, Uli, **60**, 197
Tullye, Mark, **40**, 79, *see* Cicero, Marcus Tullus
Tumanishvili, Michail, **48**, 232; **49**, 275
Tumstall, Robert, **41**, 190
Tunmer, Raymond, **14**, 127
Tunney, Russ, **57**, 297
Tunstall [Dunstan], James, **60**, 21
Tupper, Martin Farquhar, *Proverbial Philosophy*, **10**, 33
Turan, Kenneth, **52**, 91n
Turberville, George, **17**, 31; **41**, 140; **42**, 54n; **44**, 139n, 140, 141, 142n; **46**, 30; **57**, 218; **60**, 274n22
Turbutt, G. M. R., **4**, 82–4, 85
Turchaninova, Anna, **48**, 117
Türck, Susanne, **28**, 37n, 39, 40n, 41
Turgenev, Ivan Sergeevitch, **20**, 127; **45**, 3, 4; **49**, 285; **53**, 111; **55**, 140, 141; **56**, 303
Turkey, report on Shakespeare in, **7**, 115–16; **8**, 121–2; **9**, 116; **12**, 117; **13**, 132; **14**, 123; **15**, 138; **16**, 137; **18**, 130
Turkle, Sherry, **52**, 93n
Turks, **17**, 40 and n, 144n
Turler, Jerome, **17**, 43
Turley, David, **52**, 154n
Turnage, Mark Anthony, **55**, 335
Turnbull, Alexander, **55**, 171
Turner, Anthony, **58**, 238
Turner, Bryan S., **55**, 240
Turner, Cathy, **48**, 237
Turner, Celeste, **8**, 105n; **54**, 89n, 90n, 95n, 98n
Anthony Mundy, **14**, 33n
Turner, Charles, **1**, 32
Turner, David, **5**, 120
Turner, Dawson, **3**, 49; **49**, 122n
Turner, Frederick, **26**, 151; **32**, 9
Turner, George, **54**, 136n
Turner, Godfrey, **26**, 114
Turner, Graham, **43**, 201–2; **44**, 176, 178; **45**, 146; **46**, 173; **59**, 341
Turner, Helen, **44**, 196; **46**, 191
Turner, James Grantham, **46**, 126n, 128n; **49**, 302; **51**, 32n
Turner, Jane, **49**, 303; **58**, 358
Turner, John, **43**, 225; **45**, 160; **50**, 243; **55**, 5
Turner, Joseph Mallord William, **49**, 123, 125
Turner, Liz, **48**, 237
Turner, Martin, **41**, 187; **53**, 261
Turner, Mrs, **11**, 72, 73
Turner, Myron, **26**, 174n
Turner, Nick, **45**, 160
Turner, Niki, **53**, 279; **54**, 271; **56**, 287
Turner, Patrick, **52**, 183n
Turner, R., **57**, 215
Turner, R. W., **29**, 97n
Turner, Robert Kean, **13**, 169; **14**, 165; **16**, 178; **17**, 210 n; **19**, 163; **32**, 98n, 237; **40**, 230; **41**, 91n; **46**, 226; **50**, 277; **59**, 24n20, 158n5
Turner, Robert Y., **15**, 167; **19**, 132–3; **20**, 49n; **25**, 3n; **29**, 159–60; **37**, 195; **38**, 5; **42**, 1
Turner, Thomas, **6**, 61; **13**, 93–5
Turner, Tony, **45**, 149; **47**, 216
Turner, Victor, **29**, 18n; **49**, 57; **50**, 246; **56**, 1n
Turner, William, **13**, 106; **23**, 45
Turner, Zatella R., **18**, 131
Turph, Peter, **44**, 210
Turturro, John, **53**, 102
Turville, **12**, 99
Tussaud, Madame, **31**, 188
Tutin, Dorothy, **5**, 126; **12**, 129; **14**, 130, 133, 136; **15**, 150; **16**, 23; **20**, 134; **22**, 140; **28**, 144; **31**, 152; **32**, 79; **34**, 8; **37**, 184; **39**, 89n, 90; **41**, 67; **45**, 157; **46**, 194
Tuve, Rosemond, **4**, 9, 19; **5**, 83, 86, 91n; **6**, 152; **7**, 7, 11; **18**, 53, 55; **21**, 145n; **23**, 87; **49**, 208n; **54**, 128
Twain, Mark, **18**, 103, 107, 112; **19**, 144; **24**, 99; **40**, 201–2; **43**, 228
Tweedie, Eleanor M., **31**, 185
Tweedy, Carole, **48**, 236
Tweg, Sue, **53**, 301
Tweit, Terj, **54**, 285
Twentyman, Robert, **45**, 112, 113
Twice, Anne, **9**, 89n
Twigg, Graham, **50**, 19n
Twine, Laurence, **24**, 108, 111; **29**, 30; **33**, 173; **41**, 235; **43**, 132; **54**, 38; **57**, 340; **59**, 223
Pattern of Painfull Adventures, **3**, 30, 151; **4**, 87; **5**, 39
Twiss, Horace, **38**, 69n
Twist, Benjamin, **51**, 267; **52**, 261; **59**, 344
Twist, Susan, **47**, 214
Two Maids of Mortlake, The, **52**, 148n
Two Minds Theatre Company, **58**, 299
Two New Plays, **50**, 284
Two Noble Kinsmen, The, **1**, 47–9; **3**, 30; **4**, 7; **9**, 84, 89n, 133; **10**, 77, 86n; **54**, 17, 24n, 25, 26, 28n, 37n
Two Noble Ladies, The (MS.), **3**, 51, 52
Twycross, Meg, **36**, 180; **50**, 237; **56**, 338–9; **58**, 222
Tyacke, Nicholas, **54**, 1n, 5n, 170; **59**, 252n95
Tybbes, William, **23**, 144
Tydeman, William, **54**, 228n
Tyl, J. K., **7**, 109; **9**, 102, 110n
Tyler, Margaret, **46**, 133
Tyler, Richard, **47**, 174n
Tyler, Sharon, **42**, 194, 195n
Tyler, T., **18**, 187
Tyler, Wat, **44**, 18, 19
Tylney, Edmund, **42**, 189; **56**, 45n
Tymme, Thomas, **50**, 197n
Tynan, J. L., **8**, 3

Tynan, Kathleen, **57**, 148
Tynan, Kenneth, **16**, 28; **18**, 160; **30**, 21–2, 23, 26; **36**, 21n, 61n; **39**, 47, 49n; **45**, 141; **49**, 225, 231–2; **52**, 309; **57**, 81, 90, 119, 145–58
Tyndale, William, **1**, 68; **17**, 105–6, 107; **34**, 85; **36**, 50, 51; **37**, 176; **38**, 94, 218; **44**, 234; **54**, 3–12, 43, 102n; **58**, 51; **59**, 249, 249n76, 251
Tynjanov, Juri, **31**, 56n
Tyrwhitt, Jessica, **46**, 195
Tyrwhitt, Thomas, **2**, 39, 40; **3**, 23, 28; **4**, 56, 57, 59; **47**, 256
Tysdahl, Bjørn, **49**, 328n; **53**, 39n
Tyson, Brian F., **33**, 202
Tyson, Cathy, **43**, 206; **48**, 236; **51**, 221; **52**, 251, 259; **53**, 274; **54**, 289
Tytler, P. F., **38**, 24n
Tyzack, Margaret, **26**, 144, 149; **31**, 144, 147–8

U.S.A., report on Shakespeare in, **1**, 112; **2**, 129, 130–1; **4**, 123–5; **5**, 115–16; **6**, 124; **7**, 116–17; **8**, 122; **9**, 116–17; **10**, 121–2; **11**, 122–3; **12**, 117–18; **13**, 132; **14**, 124; **15**, 139; **16**, 137–8; **18**, 130–3
U.S.S.R., report on Shakespeare in, **1**, 114; **2**, 126–7; **4**, 125–6; **5**, 117–18; **6**, 124–5; **9**, 117–18; **12**, 118; **13**, 132; **15**, 139; **16**, 15, 18, 138–9; **18**, 135
Ubaldini, Petruccio, **5**, 149; **17**, 34
Uccello, **49**, 157
Uchigama, Takato, **22**, 155
Uchino, Masaaki, **60**, 136, 138
Udall, John, **17**, 126
Udall, Nicholas, **17**, 195; **18**, 176; **42**, 187; **53**, 326; **56**, 44
Floures for Latine Spekynge, **1**, 68
Ralph Roister Doister, **7**, 141; **15**, 135
Udovicki, Lenka, **54**, 263–4; **55**, 332
Udriste, I. Popescu, **20**, 129
Udwin, Leslee, **42**, 136, 153
Uéno, Yoshiko, **50**, 248
Uffenback, Zacharias von, **30**, 165
Uhler, John Earle, **8**, 144
Uhlig, Claus, **22**, 168; **23**, 119, 144, 161; **29**, 184n; **54**, 323; **56**, 82n, 322, 325; **60**, 369n8
Ukino, Masaaki, **57**, 270, 271
Ulanova, Galina, **12**, 118; **16**, 15
Ulbright, Walter, **48**, 178
Ulh, Friedrich, **35**, 27n
Ullmann, Stephen, **16**, 77
Ullrich, Peter, **48**, 179n
Ullyart, Kendra, **47**, 215; **49**, 243; **50**, 233
Ulmer, Gregory, **50**, 59
Ulrich, Leon, **10**, 120; **14**, 123; **15**, 137
Ulrichi, H., **48**, 6n
Ulrici, D. Hermann, **36**, 44–5, 49; **37**, 46; **43**, 112n; **44**, 110n
Ulrici, H., **3**, 110; **18**, 109
Ultz, **38**, 207; **39**, 109n; **44**, 192; **45**, 122; **46**, 201; **58**, 299
Ulyanov, Vladimir (Lenin), **54**, 144–5, 146
Ulysses Redux, **54**, 62
Umabatha, **47**, 112; **54**, 340
Umbers, Mark, **53**, 269
Un re in Ascolto, **44**, 201
Underdown, David E., **46**, 28, 33, 131n; **58**, 251, 256
Underdown, Thomas, **56**, 29n; **13**, 83
Underhill, Arthur, **32**, 129n
Underhill, Evelyn, **59**, 236, 236n16
Underhill, Nicholas, **19**, 103, 104, 106 n; **58**, 233
Underhill, Samuel, **19**, 103
Underhill, William, **17**, 126; **31**, 177
Underwood, R. A., **28**, 163
Unfortunate Traveller, The, **52**, 100, 101
Ungaretti, Giuseppe, **1**, 116
Unger, Gil, **54**, 292
Ungerer, Freidrich, **32**, 91n; **23**, 116
Ungerer, Gustav, **14**, 108 n; **16**, 165; **18**, 180; **31**, 178–9; **34**, 173; **39**, 251; **40**, 216
Anglo-Spanish Relations in Tudor Literature, **12**, 140–1 and n
'An Unrecorded Elizabethan Performance of *Titus Andronicus*', **14**, 102–9
Ungváry, Lázló, **18**, 125
Uniformity, Bill of, **17**, 121
Universities, in sixteenth century, **17**, 57, 63–6, 115–16, 121–2, 197, 200
'University Wits', **17**, 129–30
Unverfehrt, Gerd, **51**, 300
Unwin, Fisher, **14**, 87
Unwin, George, **17**, 6
Unwin, Paul, **45**, 152; **46**, 192
Unwin, Stephen, **42**, 162; **48**, 194, 228, 232; **49**, 270; **50**, 219–24, 229; **52**, 229; **53**, 283; **56**, 282, 284, 291; **57**, 285, 292; **58**, 278, 301, 305; **59**, 330, 345; **60**, 321
Unwin, William, **54**, 54
Updike, John, **57**, 339; **58**, 95, 96, 103, 261
Upham, A. H., **28**, 39n, 40n
Uphaus, R., **26**, 163
Upor, T., **14**, 120
Upton, John, **3**, 14; **34**, 11; **47**, 154–5; **51**, 129, 134, 135, 137, 139, 321; **55**, 102n; **58**, 80
Ur-Hamlet, The, **3**, 28; **4**, 8, 150
Ur-Pericles, **11**, 149
Uray, Tibor, **14**, 120
Urban, Raymond A., **30**, 202
Urbánek, Zdeněk, **12**, 110; **14**, 118; **16**, 133
Ure, Gudrun, **6**, 146
Ure, Mary, **13**, 144
Ure, Peter, **6**, 161; **8**, 147; **10**, 137; **11**, 138, 151; **14**, 40, 44 n, 65 n; **18**, 31, 33; **19**, 141; **20**, 17, 164; **21**, 134, 151; **22**, 71n; **24**, 165; **25**, 2; **26**, 5, 9; **27**, 33n, 34n, 38n; **28**, 46; **34**, 54; **38**, 39; **39**, 238, 239; **50**, 50, 54n; **51**, 145; **57**, 236
New Arden *Richard II* reviewed, **11**, 152
Shakespeare and the Inward Self of the Tragic Hero reviewed, **15**, 161
Uricchio, William, **52**, 194; **60**, 355
Urkowitz, Steven, **33**, 28n, 34n; **34**, 194; **35**, 179, 180, 186; **36**, 189; **37**, 208, 210; **38**, 155n, 254; **40**, 232–3; **41**, 154, 230n; **43**, 230, 266–7; **45**, 28; **46**, 255; **49**, 27n, 43, 330, 334, 336; **50**, 278; **51**, 332; **52**, 317; **55**, 2, 3n, 4; **57**, 343; **59**, 8n32
Urmson, J. O., **50**, 19n
Urquhart, Sir Thomas, **46**, 14n; **49**, 77
Urry, William, **45**, 192n; **46**, 236
Urspruch, A., **18**, 86
Usher, Roland G., **28**, 65
Usher, Simon, **43**, 215; **45**, 152; **46**, 202; **50**, 227
Usluer, Kâmiran, **18**, 130
Ustinov, Peter, **40**, 212

Usuda, Kenji, **48**, 107n
Usurer, William, **29**, 33, 34
Usurer's Daughter: Male Friendship and Fictions of Women in Sixteenth Century England, The (L. Hutson), **48**, 259
Uter, Elizabeth, **45**, 152
Uther Pendragon, **11**, 49n
Utley, Francis Lee, **56**, 40n
Utterback, R. V., **28**, 153; **30**, 202
Uzaki, Ryudo, **43**, 215; **51**, 264; **54**, 286
Uzin, V., **2**, 126

Vacalo, George, **16**, 134
Vacci, N., **18**, 80
Vachnadze, Vakhtang, **48**, 189
Vackár, D. C., **11**, 118
Vaghan (Vaughan), Justice, **25**, 144
Vahtanghov, Eugene, **40**, 2
Vajansky, H., **4**, 115n
Vakhtangov, E., **5**, 117; **54**, 145
Valère, Simone, **10**, 118; **15**, 132; **18**, 122
Valakou, Antigone, **16**, 134
Valck, Gerard, **23**, 165n
Valdés, Mario, J., **51**, 126n
Vale, Malcolm, **38**, 11
Vale, Michael, **49**, 217
Valency, Maurice, **28**, 76n
Valentine, C. W., **5**, 92n
Valenza, Robert J., **51**, 316, 326–8; **59**, 69
Valeri, Valeria, **12**, 114
Valeriano, Piero, **31**, 47
Valerius, Maximus, **15**, 90
Valéry, Paul, **1**, 104; **10**, 59n; **23**, 176; **45**, 5, 6, 8, 12; **49**, 206n
Valk, A.M., **54**, 163n
Valk, Diana, *Shylock for a Summer*, **13**, 126
Valk, Frederick, **10**, 116; **13**, 126
Valk, Gerhard, **8**, 116n
Valla, Lorenzo, **54**, 43
Vallee, Lillian, **43**, 18n
Valli, Romolo, **13**, 129; **16**, 136
Vallone, A., **24**, 162n
Valpy, Dr Richard, **42**, 47
Valverde, José María, **54**, 155n
Vámos, L., **16**, 135; **18**, 125
Van, Billy, **57**, 154
van Bleeck, Peter, **51**, 10
Van Boxel, Piet, **52**, 297
Vanbrugh, Violet, **18**, 72; **32**, 28, 33
van Buchell, Arend (Aernout), **36**, 179; **42**, 190; **43**, 143–4, 149; **50**, 169; **52**, 5
Vančura, Zdeněk, **21**, 129
Van Dam, B. A. P., **25**, 77
Van den Berg, Kent T., **40**, 216–17; **41**, 42–3
Van den Berg, Kent Talbot, **30**, 183
Van den Berg, Sara, **33**, 199; **49**, 301
Van den Branden, L., **29**, 32n
Vandenbrouke, Russell, **52**, 157n
van den Busche, Alexandre, **54**, 96–7
Vandenhoff, George, **16**, 104; **57**, 127
Vandenhoff, Hess, **49**, 126
Van den Wyngaerde, Antony, **2**, 23
Van de Passe brothers, **43**, 155, 161–2
Vander Gucht, Gerard, **49**, 113; **59**, 131
Vanderhoof, Mary B., **24**, 80n; **60**, 218n17, 221n23
van der Horst, Dr Koert, **53**, 196n
Van der Keere, Peter, **32**, 190n
Vandermeulen, Gaston, **5**, 108; **12**, 110
Vander Motten, J. P., **40**, 215, 236; **60**, 249n53
Van Der Niss, I. W., **23**, 186
Vandersall, Stanley T., **47**, 147n; **53**, 33n
Vandersee, Charles, **24**, 87ff, 93n; **26**, 116
'The Hamlet in Henry Adams', **24**, 87–104
Van der Weyden, Roger, **33**, 99n
Van Dijk, Maarten, **29**, 176; **37**, 198; **56**, 342
Van Doren, Mark, **23**, 148; **24**, 4n; **28**, 10; **30**, 47, 58n; **36**, 34n; **38**, 167; **40**, 63; **52**, 120n
Van Dorsten, J. A., **40**, 46n
van Dorsten, Jan, **45**, 11n
Van Dyck, Sir Anthony, **9**, 54, 55; **11**, 36; **13**, 74; **24**, 158; **28**, 24
'Van Dyck' costume, **11**, 124
Van Dyke, Joyce, **32**, 223
'Making a Scene: Language and Gesture in *Coriolanus*', **30**, 135–46
Vanek, Joe, **51**, 261
Van Eerde, Katherine S., **23**, 162
Van Emden, W. G., **29**, 170
Van Eyck, **47**, 29
Van Fossen, R. W., **34**, 138n; **54**, 64n; **56**, 101n
Van Gogh, Vincent, **22**, 99
Van Hasselt, G., **33**, 155n
Vanita, Ruth **48**, 252; **55**, 346; **60**, 84–101
Van Kampen, Claire, **44**, 200; **46**, 200; **47**, 210; **50**, 229, 236; **51**, 268; **52**, 217, 266; **53**, 279; **55**, 323; **54**, 283
Van Laan, Thomas F., **21**, 133; **32**, 212; **34**, 25; **37**, 3; **38**, 162n; **40**, 86n; **48**, 11n
Van Langeren, Jacob, **8**, 116n
van Laun, H., **44**, 109n
van Lennep, William, **43**, 96n; **51**, 79n; **53**, 217n
Van Loock, Sara, **41**, 191
Van Maanen, W., **12**, 115; **18**, 127
van Mander, Karel, **55**, 348
Van Nassau-Sarolea, Annie, **28**, 172
van Oldenbarnavelt, Sir John, **44**, 125
Van Peer, Willie, **49**, 94n
Vanrigh, Anny Crunelle, **47**, 234
Van Sant, Gus, **51**, 278; **58**, 349
Van Somer, Paul, **43**, 161; **53**, 201n
Van Tieghem, Ph., **24**, 85n
van Veen, Otto, **49**, 83–5
Van Winghe, Joos, **49**, 83
Var Turgut, **50**, 32n
Varchi, B., **46**, 126
Vardac, A. Nicholas, **39**, 1, 75n
Vardi, Dov, **12**, 146
Varesi, Felice, **57**, 66, 116
Varey, J. E., **23**, 79n, 84n
Varga, M., **14**, 120
Vargo, Lisa, **56**, 154n
Varla, Zubin, **48**, 234; **49**, 243; **50**, 233; **55**, 316; **59**, 328
Varma, R. S., **27**, 190
Varndell, Teddy, **50**, 199n
Varney, Kate, **58**, 302, 304

Varnom, Steve, **47**, 211
Vas, I., **14**, 120
Vasari, Giorgio, **26**, 112n; **31**, 16; **35**, 167
Vasary, Mladen, **50**, 38, 39n
Vasey, Linden, **45**, 2n
Vassiliou, S., **7**, 112
Vasvari, Louise O., **56**, 40n
Vaughan, Alden T., **42**, 192; **43**, 222, 241; **51**, 8, 57n; **53**, 133n, 164n, 168n, 335–7; **56**, 147n, 344n
Vaughan, Henry Halford, **15**, 40n; **39**, 83; **46**, 115n
Vaughan, Percival, **50**, 63n
Vaughan, Robert, **43**, 162
Vaughan, Stephen, **59**, 207
Vaughan, Virginia Mason, **46**, 214, 218; **49**, 202n, 288; **50**, 93n; **51**, 6, 8, 57–66, 279; **52**, 188n; **53**, 133n, 164n, 168n, 291–2, 335–7; **54**, 37n; **56**, 147n, 344n; **60**, 161, 168, 349, 365
Vaughan, Virginia Mason and Alden T., **59**, 79, 246n51, 253n100
Vaughan Williams, Sir Ralph, **18**, 87; **45**, 171; **56**, 130; **60**, 184, 185, 186, 187, 188–91, 191, 192, 192n24, 194, 195, 317
Vautrollier, Thomas, **7**, 36; **57**, 233
Vaux, Lady, **56**, 200n
Vaux, Thomas, Lord, **3**, 56
Vavasour, Anne, **53**, 323–4; **60**, 351
Vawter, Marvin L., **28**, 156; **31**, 10n, 172, 183
Vazquez, Yolanda, **45**, 153; **47**, 102; **53**, 261; **58**, 280; **59**, 342
Veakis, Elena, **20**, 128
Veakis, Iannis, **20**, 128
Vecellio, Cesare, **10**, 71, 76n
Vedel, Valdemar, **3**, 109
Vedia y Mitre, Mariano de, **9**, 135
Vedrenne, John, **59**, 149
Veeser, H. Aram, **52**, 109n
Vega, Lope de, **5**, 94; **6**, 106; **16**, 11, 14, 118–20; **18**, 179
  Castelvines y Monteses, **20**, 95–105
  Fuenteovejuna, **20**, 97
  La Arcadia, **20**, 101, 104n
  La Dorotea, **20**, 101, 102, 104n
  La Gatomaquia, **20**, 102, 104n
  El Gran Duque de Moscovia, **20**, 103n
  La nueva ira de Dios y Gran Tamorlán de Persia, **20**, 99, 104n
  Lo fingido verdadero, **20**, 103n
  Peribáñez, **20**, 97
Vega, Ventura de la, **58**, 139
Veinstein, André, **13**, 160
Veit, Paulita, **6**, 34n
Velasquez, Diego Rodriguez, **53**, 186; **57**, 30, 31
Vele, Abraham, **32**, 97
Veltrusky, Jiri, **31**, 54n; **60**, 228
Velz, John W., **20**, 146; **22**, 174; **23**, 149, 169, 174, 186; **24**, 156, 167, 168; **25**, 175; **26**, 181; **27**, 59n, 160, 179; **29**, 170, 176; **31**, 7n, 33n, 190, 192; **32**, 226, 241; **33**, 170–1; **35**, 177; **37**, 189; **38**, 41n, 119n, 217; **40**, 69, 71n, 75n, 236; **43**, 262, 269; **53**, 60n; **54**, 322; **55**, 349, 350; **56**, 27n; **60**, 342
  'Clemency, Will, and Just Cause in *Julius Caesar*', **22**, 109–18
Velz, Sarah C., **27**, 167; **28**, 91n; **29**, 170, 176
  'Man's Need and God's Plan in *Measure for Measure* and Mark iv', **25**, 37–44
Venable, Emerson, **2**, 138
Venables, Clare, **43**, 210; **45**, 146; **57**, 272
Venables, Jon, **57**, 41, 51
Venables, Paul, **44**, 160, 161, 191
Venantius Fortunatus, **15**, 98n
Vendenheym, H. J. Wurmsser von, **3**, 53
Vendler, Helen, **48**, 241; **52**, 268–9, 281; **54**, 28n; **56**, 310–11; **58**, 32; **59**, 234
Vendryes, J., **23**, 28n
Venet, Gisèle, **32**, 223
Venezky, Alice S., **6**, 163n; **15**, 112; **38**, 2
Venice, **11**, 89, 91; **17**, 46–7
Venn, John, **17**, 57
Vennar, Richard, **12**, 42
Venne, van der, **12**, 32, 34; **13**, 123n
Venner, Richard, **3**, 93
Venora, Diane, **45**, 43; **52**, 95
Venosa, Gesualdo de, **15**, 133
Ventadorn, Bernart de, **15**, 98n
Ventimiglia, Peter J., **35**, 6n, 10
Ventry, Laurie, **42**, 156
Ventura, Stephen, **51**, 226
Venus and Adonis (opera), **52**, 215
Venus and Lucrece, **43**, 217
Veracini, F. M., **18**, 78
Verdi, Giuseppe, **5**, 117; **11**, 148; **13**, 128; **15**, 134; **18**, 75, 80, 82–5, 128, 131; **19**, 151; **21**, 6, 87–96; **35**, 111; **39**, 232, 233; **40**, 203; **43**, 192; **45**, 173–5, 187; **46**, 218; **54**, 285, 288; **55**, 328; **56**, 130, 292, 293, 295; **57**, 56, 64, 65, 66, 67, 68, 112, 113, 115, 116, 124, 294, 295, 313; **58**, 302, 303; **59**, 341; **60**, 184, 187, 189–90, 190, 192n24, 317, 349, 353, 356
  Macbeth, **10**, 120
Vere, Edward de, 17th Earl of Oxford, **3**, 11; **7**, 139; **10**, 143; **14**, 27; **60**, 262–3
Vere, Elizabeth, **35**, 72
Verecundia, Doña Teresa, **20**, 104n
Vereen, Ben, **52**, 98n
Verey (18th-century London bookseller), **59**, 117
Verger, Pierre, **39**, 176n
Vergil, Polydore, **2**, 139; **4**, 27; **6**, 7; **22**, 147; **23**, 36, 65; **24**, 174; **25**, 125, 128, 172; **27**, 28n; **29**, 5; **30**, 61; **33**, 16; **38**, 94; **42**, 26, 35; **52**, 172, 174; **54**, 107n; **59**, 379–80
Verity, A. W., **8**, 148–9; **18**, 39; **19**, 2
Verma, Jatinder, **48**, 236; **52**, 260; **60**, 324
Verma, Rajiva, **41**, 207; **45**, 159; **59**, 370
Vermeer, Jan, **39**, 109
Vermeer, Johannes, **50**, 3
Verney, Francis, **45**, 185
Verney, Guy, **5**, 119
Vernon, Elizabeth, **32**, 87n
Vernon, J., **15**, 3
Vernon, James, **58**, 116
Vernon, John, **44**, 195
Vernon, Joseph, **51**, 89
Veronese, Paolo, **4**, 102; **10**, 75, 76, 130; **15**, 136; **21**, 52n; **37**, 99; **39**, 95, 100
Veronesi, Alberto, **60**, 190n20
Verplanck, Gulian, **18**, 102, 108; **27**, 106n
Verreiken, Lodovick, **38**, 90
Verrey, David, **46**, 200
Verrocchio, **26**, 116n
Verstegan, Richard, **46**, 46n; **48**, 72n; **54**, 95n

Vertsman, I., **15**, 140
Vertue, George, **31**, 177; **33**, 198; **51**, 14
account of New Place, **5**, 55–7; **6**, 160
Vertumnus, sive Annus Recurrens, **11**, 114n
Verulam, Earl of, **4**, 84
Very, Alice, **59**, 141n14
Vesalius, Andreas, **17**, 148, 157; **47**, 202; **48**, 25, 26; **60**, 227
Vespucci, Amerigo, **30**, 194
Vesseur, Wim, **14**, 122
Vest, James M., **44**, 240
Vesterian controversy, **17**, 124–5
Vestris, Madame Lucia Elizabeth, **20**, 110, 111; **35**, 10, 12; **36**, 181; **52**, 290; **53**, 328; **60**, 190
Vesturport, Icelandic company, **57**, 259, 289
Vezey, Desmond I., **55**, 180n
Vezin, Hermann, **2**, 4; **9**, 56; **11**, 124
Vianu, Tudor, **20**, 127
Vibrans, Mark, **41**, 187; **43**, 211; **44**, 167, 192, 199; **45**, 149; **47**, 217; **48**, 229; **52**, 256
Vicary, Thomas, **17**, 157; **38**, 180; **46**, 114, 126
Vice, the, **17**, 191–2
Vicinus, Martha, **46**, 4n
Vick, Graham, **44**, 201; **55**, 328; **56**, 293; **58**, 303
Vickerage, Lesley, **52**, 230
Vickers, Brian, **22**, 149–50, 168; **24**, 40, 173; **27**, 83; **28**, 164; **29**, 167; **30**, 189, 200; **32**, 5, 226; **33**, 190; **34**, 11n, 13n, 171; **36**, 168; **37**, 8, 30, 31n, 141n; **38**, 7; **40**, 72n; **42**, 89n, 195; **43**, 2n, 3n; **44**, 20n, 214; **45**, 2n; **46**, 236n; **47**, 221, 223, 235; **48**, 240, 268–9, 271, 276; **49**, 47; **50**, 287n; **51**, 5, 8, 250n; **52**, 273; **53**, 4n, 12n, 188n, 214n; **54**, 42n, 50n, 134n, 311; **55**, 96n, 97n, 102n, 105n, 182; **56**, 232n, 310; **57**, 300, 305, 308, 309, 335–6; **58**, 75, 321; **59**, 5n15, 5n19, 6n22, 69n1, 376; **60**, 254, 265n37, 351, 368
Vickers, Nancy J., **34**, 185; **40**, 190; **41**, 106n; **43**, 224; **44**, 33; **46**, 7, 71n, 123n, 134n; **47**, 131n; **48**, 26n; **49**, 312; **50**, 195n; **55**, 8n, 117n, 240n; **58**, 254
Vickery, John B., **15**, 123n
Vico, Giovanni Battista, **59**, 265
Victor, Benjamin, **9**, 93; **32**, 42
Victoria, Queen, **16**, 112; **37**, 47; **44**, 158; **53**, 125; **54**, 76; **56**, 126–7, 131, 132
Victoria, University of, *Internet Shakespeare Editions*, **59**, 173, 180
Victory, Fiona, **43**, 211
Vida, M. G., **23**, 83
Vidal, Gore, **56**, 348
Vielhaber, Christiane, **37**, 159n
Vienne-Guerrin, Nathalie, **58**, 340; **59**, 371–2
Vietor, Wilhelm, **7**, 3; **59**, 157n3
Vigarello, Georges, **55**, 240, 245n, 250n
Vigenere, Blaise de, **31**, 17
Vigny, Alfred de, translations of Shakespeare, **2**, 116; **3**, 98; **16**, 54
Vilar, Jean, **2**, 124, 129; **8**, 120, 125; **9**, 113; **10**, 117, 118; **11**, 119; **12**, 1, 112; **13**, 127; **14**, 118, 119; **16**, 54; **18**, 123; **50**, 29–30
Viles, Edward, **44**, 21n; **55**, 82n
Villa, Carlo, **6**, 160 *and* n
Villa, Pancho, **18**, 131
Villarejo, Oscar M., **20**, 103n; **22**, 167
'Shakespeare's *Romeo and Juliet*: its Spanish Source', **20**, 95–106
Villaurrutia, Xavier, **3**, 118
Villegaignon, **48**, 152
Villey, Pierre, **3**, 19; **28**, 37, 38n, 40n; **38**, 148n
Villiers, Christopher, **42**, 160
Villiers, Sir Edward, **60**, 55
Villiers, George, Duke of Buckingham, **13**, 110; **14**, 159; **28**, 23; **55**, 374; **56**, 71
Villiers, George, Second Duke of Buckingham, **2**, 26
The Rehearsal, **10**, 48
Villiers, J. I. de, **12**, 115
Villiers, Jay, **42**, 131; **57**, 296
Vinaver, Eugene, **41**, 156n
Vince, Ronald W., **38**, 226, 227
Vincent, Andrew, **56**, 253; **57**, 293
Vincent, Augustine, **1**, 60
A Discovery of Errors, **13**, 166
Vincent, Charles, **15**, 3
Vincent, David, **58**, 115, 116
Vincent, E. R. P., **27**, 46n
Vincent, George, **36**, 139, 140, 141, 142, 144, 145, 147; **38**, 227
Vincent, Seddon, **14**, 116
Vincent, Thomas, **36**, 147; **52**, 72
Vincentio Saviolo His Practice, **48**, 251
Vincenzi, Simon, **52**, 257
Viner, Frances, **44**, 196
Vining, Edward P., **45**, 39–51
Vining, Frederick, **32**, 29
Vining, Joyce, **45**, 4n; **56**, 98n
Viola, Bill, **60**, 355
Virdestam, Bengt, **15**, 138
Virgil, **1**, 51; **3**, 14; **4**, 68n; **5**, 53; **6**, 152; **7**, 23; **8**, 43, 51n; **10**, 48; **11**, 76, 146; **14**, 76, 154; **15**, 24, 87, 90, 95; **17**, 61, 64; **19**, 55–7; **31**, 5, 7, 8, 12, 13, 17, 18, 37, 50–1; **32**, 230; **34**, 35; **35**, 122, 178; **36**, 41; **37**, 144; **38**, 40–7, 119n, 215, 217, 233; **39**, 124, 143, 159, 160, 161n, 163, 164, 168, 221; **40**, 74–5; **41**, 133n; **42**, 66; **43**, 158, 160–1, 164; **44**, 38, 222, 238; **45**, 170–1, 181; **46**, 16, 40, 46n; **47**, 26; **48**, 5, 154; **51**, 53n, 180; **53**, 13, 19, 20, 21, 23, 39, 321; **54**, 41n; **55**, 21, 199–206, 208, 218n; **56**, 30, 40, 41, 48; **57**, 217, 221, 302; **58**, 45; **59**, 355, 367
Aeneid, **4**, 31; **10**, 17, 20, 30; **11**, 76; **15**, 92, 94–6, 98n
Virgil, III, **52**, 271
Virgin Martyr, **55**, 358
Virginia Company, **17**, 12, 27, 33
Virginia University Library, *see under* Libraries
Virkus, Daniel, **52**, 210
Visconti, Luchino, **3**, 118; **15**, 133; **50**, 30
Vision of Ophelia/Lady Macbeth, A, **42**, 162
Visscher, Cornelius, **41**, 1, 6
Visscher, Jan Claes, **32**, 190n; **33**, 148; **50**, 151; **52**, 1–3; **53**, 197, 205
View of London, **1**, 27, 30–1, 32, 36n, 75
Visser, Colin, **49**, 115n
Visser, Nicolas, **51**, 284
Viswanath, S., **42**, 181
Viswanathan, S., **24**, 152; **30**, 201; **31**, 10n; **33**, 204; **35**, 171, 173; **59**, 373, 375
Vitaliani, Signor, **38**, 197
Vitaly, Georges, **7**, 108; **12**, 111
Vitez, Antoine, **52**, 285
Vitkus, Daniel, **51**, 279; **52**, 202, 204n, 207n, 210n, 213

Vitoria, Francisco de, **44**, 62n
Vitruvius Pollio, Marcus, **7**, 77; **24**, 166; **33**, 140, 142; **35**, 137; **43**, 236; **47**, 20–4
Vittore-Pomar, Company of, **54**, 154
Vittorini, Elio (pseudonym Giovanni Rota), **8**, 120; **9**, 144
Vivaldino, Ottaviano, **54**, 125n
Vives, Jaime Vincens, **31**, 33; **38**, 53, 57n
Vives, Juan Luis, **29**, 159; **39**, 214; **56**, 43
Vivis, Anthony, **23**, 174n; **43**, 210
Vizitelly, Edward, **14**, 87, 88
Vlad, Roman, **9**, 114
Vladislaus IV, King of Poland, **32**, 190
Vladislav, Jan, **6**, 118; **10**, 116; **13**, 126
Vlasopolus, Anca, **32**, 228
Vlastos, **15**, 9
Vlĉek, J., **4**, 115n
Vleteren, Timotheus van, **60**, 240, 251
Voadicia, **11**, 49n
Vočadlo, Otakar, **6**, 119; **10**, 116; **11**, 118, 141; **13**, 126; **14**, 118, **16**, 133; **18**, 121; **20**, 164; **21**, 142; **48**, 165
'*Shakespeare and Bohemia*', **9**, 101–10
Vocht, Henry de, **5**, 110n; **14**, 6
Vocovits, Stelios, **16**, 134
Vodák, Jindřich, **9**, 105
Voege, E., **15**, 17
Voet, L., **55**, 265–6
Voeten, Bert, **7**, 113; **13**, 125, 130; **14**, 122
Vogel, Paul, **54**, 312, 340
Vogel, Paula, **53**, 281; **56**, 295; **60**, 325, 349
Vogt, Herr, **45**, 95–6
Voitl, Herbert, **24**, 153
Vojan, Edward, **9**, 107, 108, 109
Vokach, A., **39**, 83n
Vokins, Joan, **49**, 303
Volchek, G., **39**, 83n
Volenté, Gian Maria, **15**, 136
Volkenshtein, V., **54**, 145
Vollardt, W., **8**, 4
Völlenklee, Markus, **46**, 195
Volonakis, Minos, **18**, 124
Volosinov, V. N., **40**, 78n; **44**, 67, 68n
Volpone, **52**, 120; **43**, 206; **54**, 61
Volska, Anna, **58**, 59
Volt, Jim, **44**, 93n
Voltaire (François-Marie Arouet), **2**, 115, 124n; **3**, 98–9, 136; **5**, 93; **9**, 59, 65, 92–4, 96, 97, 100n; **16**, 53, 70, 75; **18**, 108, 112; **19**, 143; **20**, 164; **24**, 79, 81, 84; **25**, 185; **28**, 30; **37**, 146, 147; **47**, 257n; **50**, 175; **51**, 5n, 14; **52**, 323; **53**, 187; **55**, 97; **56**, 97; **57**, 89, 112, 113, 114, 176; **60**, 215, 216–17, 218, 222
von Baeske, Wilhelm, **54**, 107n
Von Buchenbach, Hans Jacob Breuning, **49**, 328
Von Bülow, Eduard, **58**, 142
Von Erffa, Helmut, **49**, 118n
von Friesen, Hermann, **55**, 20
Von Hoschenperg, Stephan, **33**, 145
von Humboldt, Wilhelm, **56**, 207
von Kampen, Clare, **43**, 206
von Ledebur, Ruth, **45**, 162; **48**, 61n
von Rad, Gerhard, **48**, 86n, 87
Von Rothkirch, A., **57**, 165
von Schlegel, August Wilhelm, **45**, 91
von Sydow, Max, **43**, 215
von Westphalen, Eduard, **45**, 90, 91
von Winterstein, Eduard, **45**, 43n
Von Wright, G. H., **40**, 28n; **57**, 107
Voorbergh, Cruys, **13**, 130
Vorberg, Gaston, **32**, 100n
Vörösmarty, Mihály, **3**, 117; **53**, 319; **59**, 125
Vorster, B. J., **55**, 272, 274n
Vortigern, **3**, 53; **52**, 266
Vos, Erik, **13**, 130
Vos, Jan, **24**, 156
Voskerchian, Haig, **24**, 169n
Vosper, Frank, **9**, 19
Voss, Gert, **48**, 229; **49**, 269; **50**, 230
Voss, Jürgen, **59**, 262n21
Voss, Paul J., **56**, 330
Voss, Philip, **44**, 194; **45**, 143; **48**, 204, 215; **50**, 212, 215; **52**, 237, 239–40, 260, 265; **55**, 316, 332; **56**, 297; **57**, 262, 267; **58**, 298, 335; **59**, 307
Voth, Grant L., **31**, 168; **41**, 69, 70n, 74
voyage literature, **17**, 31–4, 39–42
Vraca, George, **20**, 126
Vrchlicky, Jaroslav (Emil Frida), **4**, 109; **9**, 103, 106, 107; **10**, 116
Vyazemsky, Prince Peter, **5**, 105n
Vygotosky, Lev Semenovich, **54**, 145n, 146n
Vyvyan, John, *Shakespeare and the Rose of Love* reviewed, **15**, 163; **23**, 83; **28**, 80; **29**, 91; **32**, 5; **36**, 85, 91n, 92n; **45**, 18n, 22n; **50**, 176; **59**, 362
The Shakespearean Ethic reviewed, **13**, 149–50
Shakespeare and Platonic Beauty reviewed, **16**, 159–60, 161

Waad, Armigail, **25**, 15n
Waage, Frederick O., Jr, **38**, 16; **43**, 55n
Wachsmann, Michael, **43**, 223
Wack, Henry Wellington, **58**, 144
Waddel, Ginette, **1**, 96
Waddington, Martin, **41**, 183; **47**, 102
Waddington, Raymond B., **21**, 138; **23**, 59n, 170n; **48**, 254; **50**, 254; **56**, 39n
Wade, A., **34**, 65n
Wade, Allan, **49**, 4n; **57**, 92
Wade, Andrew, **54**, 291
Wadmore, John, **44**, 195
Wadoll, Nicholas, **19**, 103
Wadsworth, Frank W., **14**, 55n; **21**, 156; **39**, 9
The Poacher from Stratford reviewed, **14**, 152
Waelder, R., **45**, 77n
Wagenaer, L. J., *The mariners mirrour*, **17**, 28 and n
Wager, William, **39**, 221; **42**, 116; **55**, 86n
Waggoner, G. R., **8**, 150
Wagner Book (1594), **3**, 92
Wagner, Alice, **17**, 210 nn.
Wagner, Bernard M., *The Appreciation of Shakespeare* reviewed, **4**, 146; **32**, 183n
Wagner, Erica, **56**, 159n
Wagner, H. R., **17**, 29n
Wagner, Heinrich Leopold, **57**, 62
Wagner, Joseph B., **56**, 330
Wagner, Linda, **18**, 167

Wagner, Richard, **12**, 1; **18**, 76, 81; **56**, 315
Wagner, Wilhelm Richard, **44**, 215
Wagonheim, Sylvia, **45**, 185; **59**, 71n9
Wahl, Anders de, **3**, 113
Wain, John, **10**, 140n, 142n; **15**, 27, 108n; **20**, 156; **23**, 132; **32**, 11; **34**, 168; **35**, 102n; **43**, 39n; **48**, 255; **50**, 102n
Waingrow, Marshall, **13**, 152
Wainwright, Jeffrey, **49**, 253; **56**, 237n, 250
Waite, James, **13**, 94
Waite, Ralph, **13**, 93, 94
Waites, Ailine, **41**, 187
Waites, Zoe, **52**, 247–8, 263; **53**, 256; **54**, 290; **55**, 310; **56**, 298; **59**, 335
Waith, Eugene M., **7**, 142; **9**, 134, 152; **10**, 10; **12**, 136; **19**, 2, 6; **20**, 5; **25**, 189; **26**, 6, 99; **27**, 11n, 16, 111n; **31**, 9n, 10n, 26, 29; **33**, 200; **38**, 13, 141n, 246–50; **39**, 215n; **41**, 204; **43**, 70, 73n, 257–8; **44**, 50n; **45**, 190; **51**, 324; **54**, 17n; **56**, 41n; **59**, 259n12
  The Herculean Hero reviewed, **16**, 157
  'The Metamorphosis of Violence in *Titus Andronicus*', **10**, 39–49
  The Pattern of Tragi-Comedy in Beaumont and Fletcher, **14**, 12
Wajda, Andrej, **50**, 37
Wake, Isaac, **35**, 130n, 131, 134, 135, 136, 137, 139
Wakefield Cycle, **21**, 55
  Mactatio Abel, **20**, 25n
  The Second Shepherd's Play, **60**, 108
Wakeman, Rick, **47**, 211
Wakhevitch, Georges, **10**, 128
Walbrook, H. M., **2**, 8; **32**, 22
Walch, Eva, **48**, 178
Walch, Günter, **42**, 165; **44**, 71n; **53**, 303, 308
Walcott, Derek, **57**, 313
Walcutt, Charles C., **21**, 133
Waldeck, P. B., **40**, 35n
Walden, Ben, **53**, 246
Walden, Lord Howard de, **4**, 106
Waldhorn, Gary, **43**, 216; **49**, 274; **50**, 220–1; **56**, 267; **58**, 272
Waldman, Guido, **50**, 23n
Waldo, T. M., **48**, 136n
Waldo, Tommy Ruth, **13**, 167; **14**, 152; **15**, 9; **29**, 166; **35**, 172
Waldock, A. J. A., **3**, 21n; **9**, 11; **14**, 47; **18**, 41; **34**, 3; **36**, 46n
  Hamlet: a Study in Critical Method, **14**, 55n
Waldron, John, **9**, 138
Walentin, Arne, **3**, 118
Wales, Katie, **55**, 183n, 354
Walford, Glen, **41**, 186; **42**, 157; **43**, 206; **44**, 203; **45**, 145; **52**, 261; **53**, 275; **54**, 289
Walkeley, Thomas, **26**, 181
Walken, Christopher, **58**, 194
Walker, Alice, **5**, 10, 144–5; **7**, 5, 149; **8**, 11, 81, 90, 91, 98n, 99n, 154–6, 157; **9**, 6–7, 151, 152, 154–5; **10**, 70n, 151, 156; **12**, 147–9; **14**, 5, 159; **15**, 179; **16**, 180; **18**, 17, 25, 26; **19**, 159n; **20**, 173, 175; **23**, 177; **24**, 172; **25**, 9, 13n, 67, 196, 198; **27**, 183; **29**, 118n, 181; **32**, 238, 241, 242; **33**, 2, 206; **34**, 189; **36**, 194; **37**, 206, 209, 213, 214; **38**, 243–5, 254; **40**, 87n, 229; **41**, 63n, 65, 69n, 70, 73, 229, 235; **42**, 66n, 101n; **44**, 46n; **50**, 60n, 135n; **53**, 13n, 22n; **55**, 390; **58**, 352; **59**, 2, 2n5, 30n46, 212n62, 382
  New Cambridge *Othello* reviewed, **11**, 149
  textual articles on *2 Henry IV*, *Othello* and *Hamlet* reviewed, **6**, 165–7
  Textual Problems in the First Folio, **11**, 149, 150; **12**, 148
  Textual Problems of the First Folio reviewed, **7**, 152–3
  'The 1622 Quarto and the First Folio Texts of *Othello*', **5**, 16–24
Walker, Anthony, **32**, 228; **49**, 116–18
Walker, C. F., **17**, 22n
Walker, Catherine, **53**, 261; **58**, 278
Walker, Christopher, **57**, 187, 190
Walker, D. P., **17**, 216n; **43**, 2n; **44**, 36n
Walker, Elizabeth, **32**, 228
Walker, Elsie, **60**, 354–5
Walker, Frank, **21**, 96n
Walker, Gilbert, **52**, 125–6
Walker, Greg, **53**, 25n, 325–6; **56**, 215n; **60**, 61n8
Walker, Henry, **3**, 50
Walker, Isabel, **49**, 184
Walker, J. D. (ed.), **17**, 79n
Walker, James, **49**, 320
Walker, Janet, **55**, 239n
Walker, Julia M., **52**, 114n; **53**, 297–8; **54**, 134
Walker, Leslie J., **44**, 57n; **48**, 88n; **55**, 209n
Walker, Lewis, **31**, 172; **34**, 175–6
Walker, R. F., **19**, 23n
Walker, Ralph S., **22**, 118n; **54**, 51n
Walker, Randolph, **38**, 213
Walker, Robert, **7**, 91; **12**, 150; **14**, 157; **18**, 15, 16, 19; **43**, 211; **60**, 223–4
Walker, Roy, **4**, 24, 43; **5**, 87; **6**, 159; **7**, 10; **8**, 51n, 117n, 152; **9**, 14; **10**, 8, 142; **12**, 129n; **13**, 160; **15**, 115; **18**, 44; **19**, 7, 54n, 78; **22**, 116n; **47**, 154n, 157n, 159n; **57**, 28
  'The Celestial Plane in Shakespeare', **8**, 109–17
  The Time is Free reviewed, **4**, 139–40
  The Time is Out of Joint, **2**, 137
  'Unto Caesar: A Review of Recent Productions', **11**, 128–35
  'The Whirligig of Time: A Review of Recent Productions', **12**, 122–30
Walker, Rudolph, **43**, 208; **44**, 166; **52**, 317
Walker, Saxon, **11**, 148
Walker, Sue, **59**, 117n37
Walker, Timothy, **42**, 136; **43**, 215; **45**, 146; **52**, 249; **53**, 267
Walker, William (engraver), **49**, 118, 184, 190
Walker, William Sidney, **6**, 110; **43**, 256–7; **59**, 216
Walker, Zena, **8**, 138
Walkington, Andrew, **49**, 275
Walkinson, Juliette, **48**, 235
Walkley, A. B., **6**, 140; **12**, 148; **18**, 40; **56**, 134n
Walkley, Thomas, **11**, 150, 154; **17**, 212; **50**, 169n, 282; **58**, 350; **59**, 24n20; **60**, 369
Walkling, Andrew R., **49**, 302
Wall, Alison, **44**, 228
Wall, Geoffrey, **44**, 67n
Wall, John N., **34**, 177
Wall, Kim, **47**, 102
Wall, Stephen, **36**, 152; **39**, 193
Wall, Wendy, **53**, 307; **57**, 305; **58**, 25, 27
Wallace, Bill, **60**, 211
Wallace, Charles W., **1**, 3, 9, 10; **3**, 3, 11, 13; **7**, 68n; **11**, 104–5, 105n; **25**, 138; **31**, 185; **32**, 128n; **33**, 145n, 146n; **44**, 145, 146, 151n; **52**, 12n

Wallace, David L., **40**, 225n; **60**, 81n39
Wallace, Dewey D., **57**, 237
Wallace, Gavin, **57**, 126
Wallace, John M., **55**, 40n; **56**, 218n, 223n, 224n, 225n
Wallace, Karl, **54**, 291
Wallace, Naomi Claire, **58**, 154
Wallace, Nathaniel, **45**, 166; **49**, 96n
Wallack, J. W., **16**, 104; **20**, 111; **21**, 80
Waller, A. R., **14**, 8; **15**, 40n; **32**, 93n; **54**, 66n
Waller, D., **22**, 133
Waller, David, **12**, 125; **20**, 139; **22**, 142; **24**, 119, 122; **28**, 144, 145; **30**, 170, 175; **37**, 167; **41**, 173; **42**, 132–3, 151; **44**, 177; **45**, 153
Waller, Edmund, **51**, 87
Waller, Emma, **22**, 133
Waller, F. O., **12**, 150
Waller, G. F., **25**, 177; **38**, 10
Waller, Gary, **46**, 220
Waller, J. J., **55**, 333
Waller, Lewis, **29**, 136, 142; **49**, 230
Waller, Marguerite, **48**, 129
Waller, R. D., **6**, 7; **14**, 8
Wallerstein, Emmanual, **52**, 203n
Walley, H. R., **9**, 34n
Walley, Harold G., **31**, 13n
Walley, Henry, **6**, 171; **11**, 154; **14**, 44n; **16**, 159; **21**, 161; **25**, 7; **26**, 33n; **29**, 184; **60**, 369
Walling, Michael, **44**, 192; **45**, 157
Wallis, Albany, **59**, 122n54
Wallis, Bill, **45**, 122
Wallis, Charles G., **32**, 170n
Wallis, Helen M., **17**, 28n
Wallis, John, **17**, 66n
Wallis, Mick, **55**, 238n
Walls, Peter, **50**, 261–2
Walmesley, Gilbert, **54**, 46
Walpole, Horace, **5**, 55; **32**, 42; **34**, 18n; **37**, 45; **38**, 70; **49**, 121; **51**, 5; **52**, 291
British Traveller, **1**, 81
Walpole, Lord, **51**, 51, 69, 70, 72, 73, 76; **53**, 219; **56**, 242n
Walpole, Robert, actor, **7**, 58, 60, 67n
Walpole Society, **5**, 57n
Walser, Martin, **20**, 117, 120n
Walsh, Colin, **49**, 277
Walsh, David, **53**, 280
Walsh, John, **51**, 87
Walsh, Marcus, **46**, 256n; **51**, 2, 8, 125–39, 320–1; **53**, 302; **55**, 264n; **59**, 114n25, 124n2
Walsh, Martin W., **42**, 178; **47**, 230
Walsh, P. G., **31**, 33n, 36n
Walsh, Sandra, **55**, 325
Walsh, W., **24**, 1n
Walsham, Alexandra, **54**, 34n, 166n, 177n
Walsingham, Lord, **23**, 41; **28**, 20, 23
Walsingham, Sir Francis, **17**, 31, 109, 127; **38**, 94, 95n; **44**, 149; **52**, 294; **54**, 99; **57**, 15; **60**, 7
Walsingham, Sir Thomas, **10**, 143
Walt, Trevor, **59**, 292
Walter of Henley, **17**, 19
Walter, Gérard, **53**, 74n
Walter, Harriet, **35**, 147; **36**, 150; **41**, 166–7; **42**, 140, 142, 150, 154, 160; **43**, 254; **54**, 251–3, 266, 288; **55**, 306, 325, 335; **56**, 257, 267–8, 345; **57**, 294; **58**, 189; **60**, 293, 294, 297, 329
Walter, J. H., **3**, 27; **5**, 150; **12**, 146; **15**, 141; **19**, 147; **21**, 111, 113; **23**, 161n; **25**, 147; **30**, 47n, 48n, 53n, 56n, 58n, 61n, 64n, 71; **31**, 93, 95n; **37**, 202; **38**, 95n; **40**, 63n, 65n; **44**, 19n; **52**, 173n
'New Arden' edition of *Henry V*
reviewed, **8**, 157–8
'Shakespeare in Schools', **10**, 107–10
'With Sir John in It' reviewed, **1**, 130
Walter, Julia C. Van de, **38**, 13
Walter, Wilfrid, **32**, 31
Wälterlin, Oskar, **12**, 144
Walters, Sam, **39**, 193, 194, 197; **53**, 277
Waltham Black Act, **17**, 83
Walton, Anne, **23**, 43
Walton, George, **25**, 147
Walton, Izaak, **54**, 207n; **55**, 82, 92; **59**, 277
Walton, J. K. **14**, 144; **15**, 159; **19**, 123; **20**, 144; **25**, 193, 194–8; **26**, 184; **33**, 1, 2, 8, 45; **38**, 243, 244; **39**, 135n; **41**, 145n; **59**, 11n47
The Copy for the Folio Text of Richard III, **14**, 164, and n
The Copy for the Folio Text of Richard III with a Note on the Copy for the Folio Text of King Lear reviewed, **10**, 157
'Lear's Last Speech', **13**, 11–19
Textual Studies *reviewed* (1967) **21**, 157–63
Walton, Judyth, **25**, 147
Walton, Kendall L., **51**, 148n; **53**, 95n
Walton, Sir William, **45**, 50, 147
Walvin, James, **51**, 57n
Wambus, Francis, **47**, 54
Wanamaker, Sam, **38**, 201; **40**, 169; **43**, 184; **46**, 228; **51**, 205, 298; **52**, 1, 8, 10, 12–16, 41n, 43n, 219, 228; **54**, 316, 336; **55**, 390
Wanamaker, Zoë, **37**, 165, 168; **43**, 194; **44**, 199; **60**, 205
Wandsworth, Matthew, **42**, 157
Wang, Deming, **57**, 176
Wangenheim, Gustav von, **48**, 171
Wangenheim, Inge von, **48**, 172
Wanieck, Herbert, **2**, 128
Wanshel, Jeff, **47**, 211
Wapner, S., **51**, 153n
Wapull, George, **42**, 116
Warbeck, Stephen, **45**, 147; **50**, 234; **52**, 263; **53**, 283; **55**, 331, 335
Warburton, John, **5**, 51
Warburton, Justice, **57**, 20
Warburton, William, **3**, 49, 50; **4**, 56, 57, 67n, 86, 162, 163; **8**, 6; **9**, 93; **10**, 17, 28; **16**, 31, 32; **18**, 8, 14, 16; **23**, 61n; **26**, 181; **31**, 77; **33**, 202, 209, 210; **34**, 11; **38**, 98; **39**, 245; **41**, 240; **42**, 99, 204, 207; **46**, 10n, 237; **49**, 322; **51**, 4, 7; **52**, 8, 129, 133, 137, 138, 321; **53**, 60n, 61n, 92, 337, 342–3; **55**, 389; **59**, 56–7n20, 59
Warchus, Matthew, **47**, 192–3; **48**, 207–11, 214, 233; **49**, 271; **51**, 242–4; **52**, 249, 255; **56**, 248n, 269–71, 293; **57**, 298, 332; **58**, 335
Warcope, Thomas, **21**, 98
Ward bust of Shakespeare, **1**, 62
Ward Howe, Julia, **24**, 100

Ward, A. C., **9**, 136; **58**, 146
Ward, A. W., **6**, 39, **36**, 143; **51**, 75n
A History of English Literature, **14**, 65n
Ward, Anthony, **42**, 158; **44**, 192; **45**, 155–6; **46**, 174; **47**, 124, 199, 201, 204, 219; **48**, 202, 204, 230, 236; **49**, 275; **51**, 229, 252; **52**, 255, 262, 265; **53**, 283; **56**, 260
Ward, B. M., **54**, 94n
Ward, Chris, **46**, 195
Ward, David, **42**, 183
Ward, E. M., **49**, 123
Ward, Edward, **51**, 97n
Ward, H. Snowden, **52**, 29n
Ward, J. (ed.), **17**, 219n
Ward, John, **6**, 172; **15**, 8, 9; **17**, 71n, 72n; **54**, 76; **55**, 241n, 243n, 255n, 265n; **58**, 10
Ward, Reverend John, **1**, 61
Ward, John Powell, **46**, 212
Ward, John Woodruff, **54**, 62n
Ward, Lauren, **56**, 271, 273
Ward, P., **60**, 46n55
Ward, R. H., **5**, 119; **9**, 119
Ward, Trisha, **41**, 186
Warde, Ernest, **39**, 76, 78–81
Warde, Frederick, **25**, 117, 118; **35**, 95; **39**, 76–9, 82, 83, 88, 90; **51**, 266
Warde, James Prescott, **10**, 73; **16**, 104
Warde, Luke, **17**, 30, 32
Warden, John, **39**, 126n; **41**, 185, 187
Wardle, Ed, **49**, 279
Wardle, Irving, **31**, 151; **37**, 182, 183; **38**, 203; **39**, 181, 185, 202; **40**, 168; **43**, 189, 200; **46**, 162, 165, 168, 169n, 187; **47**, 7n; **48**, 215, 222; **49**, 250; **50**, 114n; **56**, 236, 238n, 249
Wardman, Alan, **53**, 74n, 77n
Wardman, Judith, **59**, 45
Wardrop, Sir Oliver, **48**, 187
Wardroper, John, **23**, 165; **38**, 69n
Wardropper, B. W., **23**, 84n, 88n
Ware, M. W., **15**, 181
Wareing, Alfred J., **52**, 28n
Waren, Jim, **50**, 234
Warhaft, Sidney, **16**, 9n; **18**, 166
Warhol, Andy, **39**, 77; **51**, 282
Waring, Amanda, **41**, 184
Waring, John, **11**, 90
Waring, Nick, **46**, 199
Wark, Penny, **52**, 43n
Wark, Robert R., **49**, 116n, 118n
Warley, Christopher, **58**, 28; **60**, 332–4, 353
Warley, Thomas, **17**, 237, 239
Warlock, Peter, **15**, 6
Warmington, Neil, **47**, 192, 215; **48**, 208, 233; **49**, 271; **51**, 267; **56**, 291
Warmington, William, **17**, 90n
Warner, A., **60**, 42n22
Warner, Alan, **11**, 140
Warner, B. E., **6**, 1
Warner, David, **18**, 150, 151; **19**, 113, 115, 118; **20**, 135–6, 140, 141; **23**, 132; **24**, 43; **27**, 34n; **31**, 150; **41**, 46, 52; **45**, 9, 58; **59**, 334, 333–7; **60**, 322
Warner, Deborah, **41**, 178–9, 184; **42**, 37, 40, 47n, 48n, 50n, 137, 139, 159; **43**, 194, 202–3, 207, 255; **44**, 178, 179, 183–6; **45**, 148; **47**, 119, 121; **49**, 263–7, 305, 311; **50**, 50, 232, **52**, 262, 289; **54**, 36; **55**, 295; **56**, 5, 279; **57**, 284; **59**, 183, 295, 299, 328–30; **60**, 171, 172–3, 322
Warner, Florence May, **52**, 24n
Warner, George F., **8**, 107n; **23**, 111; **29**, 34n; **36**, 144; **47**, 172n, 174n, 254; **60**, 47n59, 51n10, 51n11, 52n17, 52n18, 52n19, 52n20
Catalogue of the Manuscripts and Muniments of Alleyn's College of God's Gift at Dulwich, **13**, 112n
Warner, John, **41**, 185
Warner, Marina, **46**, 110; **53**, 54n, 172n; **55**, 344; **56**, 146, 155–7, 302; **57**, 41
Warner, Rex, **56**, 225n
Warner, Richard, **3**, 50; **4**, 94; **51**, 137, 179
Warner, Robert, **41**, 190
Warner, William, **9**, 24; **15**, 12; **33**, 16; **39**, 251; **42**, 66; **54**, 203; **59**, 73, 75
Albions England, **1**, 67
translation of *Menaechmi*, **3**, 54; **11**, 146; **12**, 141
Warning for Fair Women, A, **3**, 92; **12**, 36–8, 40, 46, 51–2; **13**, 118; **20**, 23, **52**, 6
Warnke, Frank J., **49**, 164n
Warnke, K., **44**, 83n
Warr, Michael, **27**, 142
Warrack, John, **53**, 279; **60**, 191n23
Warre, Michael, **13**, 130; **14**, 122
Warren, Austin, **24**, 91n; **28**, 150; **51**, 104n
Warren, Charles, **41**, 200
Warren, Florence, **49**, 79n
Warren, Huw, **55**, 335
Warren, Jason Scott, **60**, 122n7
Warren, Michael J., **25**, 200; **33**, 2, 28n, 34n, 208–9; **34**, 194; **35**, 179, 188; **36**, 189; **37**, 208, 218; **38**, 89n, 155n, 254; **39**, 249; **40**, 138n, 230n, 233; **41**, 154n, 209; **44**, 255–6; **45**, 17n, 80n, 81n; **46**, 61n, 254; **47**, 263; **48**, 270; **49**, 219n, 334n; **53**, 334, 341; **55**, 2, 3n, 4, 36n, 45n, 55n, 185n; **56**, 170; **58**, 352, 357; **59**, 14n59, 20n2, 37n86, 157; **60**, 348
Warren, Nicholas, **53**, 118n
Warren, Robert P., **40**, 201
Warren, Roger, **23**, 143–4; **24**, 150, 151; **25**, 179; **27**, 165; **31**, 166–7; **32**, 223; **34**, 173; **35**, 81n; **36**, 175; **37**, 107n, 208; **38**, 237; **39**, 230; **41**, 71, 73; **44**, 79; **45**, 189, 190; **47**, 6n, 7n; **49**, 319–20, 334; **50**, 114n; **52**, 317, 321–3; **55**, 188; **56**, 172, 174, 179, 181, 279, 290, 291; **57**, 276, 292, 329, 339–40; **58**, 343–5, 357; **59**, 47, 53, 381
'Why Does it End Well? Helena, Bertram, and The Sonnets', **22**, 79–92
'Theatrical Virtuosity and Poetic Complexity in *Cymbeline*', **29**, 41–9
'Theory and Practice': Stratford 1976, **30**, 169–70
Warren, William, **32**, 21n
Warrin, Thomas, **22**, 120–1, 123
Warrington, Don, **51**, 220–1
Wars of the Roses, The, **39**, 20, 21, 31, 105; **40**, 17, 19, 223; **41**, 45–6; **42**, 151, 157, 160, 161; **43**, 171–81, 184; **45**, 130, **51**, 270; **54**, 274
Warton, Joseph, **18**, 3, 47; **34**, 11; **51**, 4
Warton, Thomas, **14**, 98, 101n; **15**, 1; **20**, 33; **35**, 188n; **45**, 202n; **54**, 56; **57**, 211; **59**, 263, 264n27
Observations, **14**, 89n
Warwick, Countess of, **32**, 88, 89

Warwick, Earl of (Lord Rich), **53**, 200n
Warwick, Earl of, *see under* Dudley, Ambrose,
Warwick, Earl of, **44**, 147
Warwick, Earl of, **4**, 70
Warwickshire, **3**, 2, 35, 40; **17**, 14–15
Saxton's map, **17**, 15
Weston-in-Arden, **8**, 7
words peculiar to, **6**, 158
see also under Libraries, Huntington
Washington, Denzel, **48**, 233; **52**, 211n, 279
Washington, George, **24**, 99
Wassberg, Goran, **42**, 150
Wasserman, Bryna, **55**, 115, 123, 124–5
Wasserman, Rena, **55**, 123
Wassermann, Earl R., **20**, 160
Wasson, John, **15**, 164, 167; **24**, 150, 155; **25**, 6n; **42**, 195; **44**, 150n; **60**, 2n4
Watching Shakespeare on Television (H. Coursen), **48**, 263
Water, Julia C. Van de, **15**, 166
Waterhouse, Ellis, *Painting in Britain*, **13**, 80n
Waterhouse, Osborn, **21**, 65n; **24**, 159
Waterman, Anthony, **42**, 151
Watermeier, Daniel J., **25**, 192; **35**, 7; **42**, 199
Waters, D. W., **17**, 21n, 25n, 27n, 28 and n, 29n
Waters, Damien, **51**, 269
Waters, John, **33**, 168
Waters, William, **58**, 33
Waterschoot, W., **29**, 26n
Waterson, Simon, **55**, 263n
Waterson, Revd Will, **51**, 52
Wateson, George, **17**, 25
Watford, Glen, **50**, 233
Watford, Gwen, **44**, 161
Watkin, E. I., **24**, 71n
Watkins, Graham, **44**, 196; **46**, 198; **47**, 210
Watkins, Juliet, **42**, 158
Watkins, Roger, **51**, 224
Watkins, Ronald, **5**, 120; **7**, 72; **8**, 124; **9**, 120; **10**, 89n, 124, 148; **12**, 70n; **13**, 135; **14**, 127; **15**, 10, 145; **19**, 31, 33n; **28**, 150; **30**, 185
On Producing Shakespeare, **12**, 60
On Producing Shakespeare reviewed, **5**, 143
Watkins, W. B. C., **5**, 142; **7**, 8; **22**, 166
Watkinson, Juliet, **44**, 193; **47**, 214
Watling, Dilys, **47**, 213
Watling, E. F., **30**, 113n
Watson, Curtis Brown, **19**, 143; **31**, 86n
Shakespeare and the Renaissance Concept of Honour reviewed, **15**, 173
Watson, Donald, **57**, 119
Watson, Donald C., **44**, 211
Watson, Donald G., **32**, 213, 232; **33**, 192; **53**, 30n
Watson, Douglas, **5**, 116
Watson, Emily, **56**, 257, 260, 262–3
Watson, Emma, **38**, 204
Watson, Foster, **17**, 44n; **55**, 245n; **56**, 42n
Watson, George, **25**, 192, 193; **31**, 180; **49**, 12n; **53**, 31n
Watson, Gilbert, **33**, 204
Watson, Ian, **39**, 169, 171, 172
Watson, J. D., **41**, 25, 28
Watson, June, **42**, 161; **45**, 146, 156
Watson, Nicola J., **43**, 99n; **46**, 137n, 143n; **56**, 117, 124n; **57**, 129; **58**, 138, 144, 145, 330, 331
Watson, Philip S., **33**, 92n
Watson, Ralph, **52**, 225
Watson, Robert, **51**, 296; **53**, 297
Watson, Robert N., **42**, 171, 198; **45**, 184; **49**, 282–3, 288; **54**, 124n, 130; **56**, 79–92; **60**, 107n24, 337–9, 352, 353
Watson, Robert Spence, **58**, 112
Watson, Sara Rith, **10**, 147n; **32**, 152
Watson, Thomas, **1**, 68; **4**, 156; **6**, 74n; **9**, 24, 25, 33n; **17**, 88; **25**, 188; **36**, 85n; **42**, 69, 70, 72, 75, 198
Passionate Century of Love, **7**, 101
Watson, William, **24**, 72, 75, 76; **57**, 13
Watt, Ian, **24**, 48; **42**, 93n
Watt, R. J. C., **40**, 234; **41**, 141n; **50**, 288
Watt, Tessa, **50**, 156n; **55**, 92n; **56**, 36n
Watt, Tom, **47**, 211
Watteau, Jean Antoine, **4**, 101; **8**, 71, 80; **13**, 73; **14**, 19; **39**, 109
Wattenberg, Daniel, **57**, 136
Watters, Alison, **46**, 196
Watters, Jack, **60**, 179
Watterson, William C., **51**, 187n
Wattie, Nelson, **55**, 175n
Watts, Cedric T., **33**, 187–8; **43**, 229; **46**, 217; **49**, 172n; **50**, 275–6; **56**, 114n
Watts, Graham, **48**, 235; **52**, 259; **53**, 280
Watts, Isaac, **51**, 133
Watts, John, **43**, 214
Watts, Richard, **39**, 1
Watts, Robert A., **23**, 153
Waugh, Arthur, **55**, 129–30
Waugh, Evelyn, **40**, 29
Waugh, Margaret, **54**, 35n
Waugh, W. T., **42**, 25, 26n, 28
Waverly, William, **58**, 235
Way, A. S., **36**, 14n
Way, Brian, **9**, 120
Wayburn, Ned, **57**, 249
Wayd, John, **36**, 140
Waymouth, George, **17**, 32–3
Wayne, Don E., **42**, 163; **54**, 307; **58**, 173, 179
Wayne, Valerie, **45**, 160; **46**, 3n; **53**, 331, 337; **55**, 7n, 359; **56**, 43n; **59**, 17n72, 80, 81, 83–5, 86, 88, 89; **60**, 96n33
Wayne, Wayne, **52**, 290
Wayte, Antony, **17**, 231, 238
Wayte, William, **3**, 28; **8**, 6
Weakest Goeth to the Wall, The, **52**, 298; **54**, 14n
Wear, Andy, **53**, 262; **56**, 254
Wearing, J. P., **44**, 106n; **52**, 29n
Weart, Spencer R., **55**, 156n
Weatherall, Jack, **31**, 144
Weaver, Robin, **49**, 280; **54**, 248
Weaver, William, **39**, 233; **57**, 65, 115
Webb, Alan, **9**, 19; **15**, 151; **39**, 79n
Webb, Daniel, **44**, 193; **56**, 278
Webb, Henry J., **6**, 157; **7**, 135; **12**, 132
Webb, J. Barry, **56**, 39n
Webb, John, **23**, 125–9; **30**, 166, 167n; **33**, 145n; **35**, 135n, 139n; **39**, 227; **42**, 194; **47**, 21; **49**, 17n
Webb, Josephine, **56**, 317

Webb, Troy, **46**, 195
Webb, William, **42**, 55; **56**, 30–1
Webbe, Agnes, **21**, 148
Webbe, Thomas, **31**, 112n-113n; **44**, 80
Webbe, William, *Discourse of English Poetry*, **8**, 4
Webber, Andrew Lloyd, **50**, 33
Webber, David, **48**, 196
Webber, J. P., **60**, 184
Webber, Joan, **18**, 169; **23**, 167n
Webber, Mark, **55**, 248–9
Webber, Nan, **49**, 271
Weber, *Oberon*, **16**, 103
Weber, Carl Maria, **57**, 65
Weber, Carl von, **42**, 150; **45**, 174
Weber, Elizabeth, **23**, 117
Weber, Harold, **48**, 152n, 248; **51**, 167n
Weber, Henry, **14**, 82–4, **43**, 84n
Weber, Klaus-Rudolf, **40**, 54
Weber, Max, **43**, 2; **54**, 29; **55**, 360–1
websites, **59**, 17n72, 80, 81, 83–5, 86, 88, 89
Backstage, **59**, 180
Bartleby.com, **59**, 180
Biographical Index to the Elizabethan Theater, **59**, 180
Birmingham University Shakespeare Institute Library, **59**, 172, 179
British Library *Treasures in Full: Shakespeare in Quarto*, **59**, 173, 180
Canadian Adaptations of Shakespeare, **59**, 180
Cleveland Press Shakespeare Photos, **59**, 180
Designing Shakespeare: An Audio-visual Archive 1960–2000, **59**, 176–7, 180
Early English Books Online (EEBO), **60**, 271n9
FESTE Database, **59**, 180
Folger Library, **59**, 172, 179
hamletworks, **59**, 163–7; **60**, 218n17
'Literature Online' electronic database, **59**, 69–78, 172, 179, 221; **60**, 271, 278
Massachusetts Institute of Technology *Complete Works*, **59**, 172, 179
Mr William Shakespeare and the Internet, **59**, 172, 179, 180
Open Source Shakespeare's Concordance, **59**, 180
Oxford Text Archive, **59**, 179
Pennsylvania University Quarto and Folio fascimile, **59**, 173, 180
Royal Shakespeare Company, **59**, 177, 178, 180
Sh:in:E (Shakespeare in Europe), **59**, 172
Shakespeare Centre Library, Stratford-upon-Avon, **59**, 172, 179
Shakespeare Concordance, **59**, 180
Stagework website, **59**, 177
Toronto University Renaissance Electronic Texts, **59**, 180
Touchstone, **59**, 172, 179, 180, 338; **60**, 320–9
Virginia University Electronic Text Center, **59**, 172, 180
Virtual Library, **59**, 180
Works of the Bard, **59**, 180
Webster, Benjamin, **1**, 1; **2**, 19
Webster, George, **32**, 195
Webster, John, **1**, 42, 52; **3**, 19, 45; **4**, 29; **6**, 72; **7**, 1, 27, 86–7, 89n, 95–6, 131, 136, 142; **9**, 144; **10**, 35; **11**, 64; **13**, 33, 116, 119; **14**, 11, 45–55, 82, 83; **16**, 47, 97, 168; **17**, 207–8, 210, 212; **19**, 37, 39, 63–4; **20**, 18, 22; **21**, 44–5; **23**, 160, 171; **24**, 164–5; **25**, 162, 163, 164; **26**, 1, 2, 4, 8, 9, 39, 57, 90, 168, 174, 175; **27**, 177, 184; **28**, 38; **29**, 173; **32**, 138; **33**, 91, 203; **34**, 53; **35**, 3, 175, 190, 191; **36**, 133, 142, 174, 175, 176, 177, 180; **37**, 215; **39**, 152, 218n; **40**, 19; **41**, 7; **42**, 3n, 103, 104, 187, 188, 197, 212; **43**, 223, 252, 260, 262; **44**, 127, 128, 210, 227n, 237; **45**, 114, 191; **46**, 125, 210, 235; **47**, 110, 240, 249; **48**, 37n, 258, 275; **49**, 40; **50**, 243; **51**, 289, 294; **52**, 69, 80, 82, 208, 297; **53**, 295, 300; **54**, 301; **55**, 57, 350; **56**, 4; **58**, 227, 233; **59**, 2, 71, 72, 73, 75, 217; **60**, 109n33, 358–9
Devil's Law-Case, **7**, 100
The Duchess of Malfi, **2**, 124; **4**, 150; **6**, 157; **13**, 38; **14**, 8, 49–55, 83; **17**, 199–200
The Thracian Wonder (with Rowley, William), **13**, 115
Westward Ho!, **8**, 150; **9**, 86
The White Devil, **1**, 103, 105; **4**, 40, 47n, 97, 151; **6**, 20, 157; **7**, 57, 59, 87; **8**, 150; **12**, 54; **13**, 38; **14**, 8, 14n, 49–55, 77
see also under Dekker, Thomas, *Northward Ho!*
Webster, Margaret, **1**, 112; **3**, 116; **4**, 123–4; **5**, 116; **6**, 124; **8**, 122; **10**, 89n, 131; **12**, 121; **18**, 131; **20**, 113; **37**, 33n; **51**, 57; **59**, 203
Shakespeare Today, **12**, 86–7; **13**, 69
Webster, Paul, **36**, 154; **39**, 198; **42**, 154; **43**, 201; **45**, 152
Wechesler, E., **15**, 98n
Weckherlin, Georg Rudolph, **11**, 110–11, 115n, 116n
Weckmann, Luis, **17**, 41n
Wedderborn, Richard, **22**, 121
Wedekind, Frank, **40**, 58
Wedel, Lupold von, **60**, 44, 45
Wedgwood, Miss C. V., **18**, 21n; **19**, 149; **22**, 151
Wedmore, Frederick, **57**, 94
Wee, David L., **57**, 245
Weedin, E. K., Jr, **29**, 164
Weeks, Honeysuckle, **59**, 315, 316; **60**, 328
Weeks, John, **30**, 195
Weelkes, Thomas, **1**, 68; **13**, 107; **60**, 260n30
Ballets and Madrigals, **1**, 69, 70
Weever, John, **32**, 232; **34**, 51, 87; **38**, 93, 97, 98; **43**, 263; **46**, 226
Epigrammes, **4**, 87
Wegener, Paul, **48**, 172
Wehmeyer, Jörg, **37**, 161
Wei, Minglun, **57**, 185
Weidhorn, Manfred, **18**, 165; **23**, 148; **24**, 152
Weigand, Hermann J., **20**, 147, 159
Weigel, Alexandra, **48**, 179
Weigelin, Ernst, **5**, 134
Weightman, Doreen, **35**, 66n
Weightman, John, **35**, 66n; **49**, 211n
Weil, Herbert S., Jr, **24**, 149, 150; **25**, 6; **26**, 175; **27**, 167; **32**, 4; **36**, 169, 171; **44**, 247; **52**, 319; **56**, 165
'Comic Structure and Tonal Manipulation in Shakesheare and some Modern Plays', **22**, 27–33
'The Options of the Audience: Theory and Practice in Peter Brook's *Measure for Measure*', **25**, 27–35
Weil, Judith, **52**, 319; **59**, 348–9, 350, 368
Weilen, Alexander von, **35**, 28n
Weilgart, Wolfgang J., **19**, 23n
Shakespeare Psychognostic. Character Evolution and Transformation reviewed, **8**, 145

Weill, Kurt, **37**, 170; **39**, 205; **55**, 310
Weimann, Robert, **20**, 144n; **21**, 156; **22**, 166, 172, 175; **23**, 114, 143, 171, 174n; **24**, 149, 160; **25**, 179; **26**, 158; **27**, 171–2, 179; **29**, 90, 167; **31**, 54n, 61n, 175; **35**, 66n, 87n, 89–90; **36**, 168; **38**, 153, 154, 156n; **39**, 230; **40**, 60n, 61n, 136, 187, 190, 198; **41**, 8, 121; **43**, 65, 232, 239; **44**, 20n, 68; **45**, 89, 190n; **47**, 236; **48**, 176; **49**, 208n; **50**, 242; **51**, 126, 145, 278; **52**, 112, 119, 283; **54**, 321; **55**, 92n, 237–8, 242, 346, 370; **58**, 64; **59**, 36n80, 373–4; **60**, 123, 335
'Laughing with the Audience: *The Two Gentlemen of Verona* and the Popular Tradition of Comedy', **22**, 35–42
'Shakespeare on the Modern Stage: Past Significance and Present Meaning', **20**, 113–20
Weinberg, Gail S., **23**, 165n
Weinbrot, Howard D., **51**, 18n
Weinburg, Joanna, **43**, 212
Weiner, A. B., **18**, 183, 191; **19**, 153n; **52**, 312
Weiner, A. D., **26**, 153
Weiner, E. S. C., **50**, 198n
Weiner, Randy, **55**, 329
Weingarten, Samuel, **21**, 132
Weinglass, David H., **49**, 122n
Weingott, Owen, **12**, 109
Weinheimer, Horst, **40**, 57
Weinreb, Ben, **53**, 209n
Weinsheimer, Joel C., **40**, 82n; **51**, 126
Weinstein, P. M., **25**, 177
Weinstock, Horst, **21**, 151; **23**, 117
Weintraub, Stanley, **56**, 126n, 131
Weir, Anthony, **9**, 119
Weis, René, **45**, 167; **47**, 263–4; **48**, 279–81; **49**, 219n; **50**, 283; **52**, 319–22; **54**, 44–5; **55**, 3n, 36n, 184–7
Weiser, David K., **33**, 192; **42**, 184
Weisinger, Herbert, **10**, 137; **15**, 116, 121
Weismiller, Edward R., **59**, 94n6
Weiss, Adrian, **42**, 195n; **43**, 264; **51**, 322
Weiss, John, **45**, 39
Weiss, Peter, **59**, 293
Weiss, Robert, **20**, 26n
Weiss, Samuel A., **13**, 167; **14**, 165
Weiss, Theodore, **26**, 152; **35**, 83n
Weiss, Wolfgang, **32**, 222; **37**, 156n; **42**, 183; **48**, 253
Weisser, David K., **32**, 218
Weissman, Ronald F. E., **54**, 126n
Weitz, Morris, **19**, 124; **20**, 146–7; **21**, 134; **25**, 181; **28**, 41n; **30**, 186
'Literature Without Philosophy: *Antony and Cleopatra*', **28**, 29–36
Weitzmann, Kurt, **33**, 99n
Weixlmann, Joseph, **28**, 170
Wekin, Roy, **44**, 203
Wekwerth, Manfred, **42**, 189; **48**, 175–7
Welch, Christopher, **15**, 6, 164
Welch, Clare, **47**, 102–3
Welch, Elizabeth, **45**, 73
Welch, Robert, **54**, 77n, 313
Weld, John S., **11**, 136–7, 146; **30**, 182–3
Welde, Humphrey, **1**, 28
Weldon, Anthony, **55**, 93n; **56**, 221, 222
Weldon, John, **18**, 95, 100; **51**, 80–2, 85, 87–93
Wellek, René, **28**, 150; **30**, 189; **33**, 187n; **51**, 5, 104n
Weller, Barry, **37**, 187; **48**, 265; **51**, 331
Welles, Orson, **2**, 131; **7**, 146n; **10**, 121, 122; **11**, 132; **12**, 117; **34**, 182; **36**, 165; **38**, 18; **39**, 3, 13, 39–57, 61–71 *passim*, 79, 81–3, 86; **41**, 206, 227; **43**, 251; **45**, 63–5, 74; **48**, 262–3; **49**, 288; **52**, 290; **53**, 102, 276; **55**, 293, 306–7, 383; **56**, 107, 348; **57**, 146; **59**, 63–8; **60**, 111–12n39, 167, 194
Chimes at Midnight, **39**, 19, 39, 40–5 *passim*, 50, 52–3; **41**, 227; **43**, 251
production of *Othello* reviewed, **6**, 145–6
Wellington, Duke of, **3**, 100
Wellman, James, **47**, 99
Wells, Byron R., **45**, 159
Wells, Dee, **48**, 232
Wells, Henry W., **4**, 18; **5**, 81, 83, 86, 89; **10**, 3; **18**, 53
Wells, Marion, **58**, 247
Wells, Meri, **45**, 154
Wells, Robin Headlam, **41**, 195, 212; **44**, 2n, 27n, 227; **48**, 249, 261; **49**, 309; **55**, 211n, 218n, 357–8; **60**, 125, 344–5, 346, 353
Elizabethan Mythologies: Studies in Poetry, Drama and Music, **48**, 249, 261
Wells, Stanley, **16**, 170; **18**, 159, 184; **19**, 125, 153; **21**, 130–1, 139, 143, 145, 157; **22**, 175; **23**, 137, 181, 182; **25**, 189–90; **26**, 170; **27**, 39, 162, 188; **28**, 164; **29**, 4, 177; **30**, 148n; **31**, 176, 191, 198; **32**, 22, 247; **33**, 161n, 190; **34**, 164, 189–90, 191, 194, 196; **35**, 6n, 12, 57, 90n, 167; **36**, 55n, 57n, 61, 190–1; **37**, 5, 19n, 168, 185, 199, 201–3, 208, 210, 216; **38**, 17, 18, 54n, 238n, 245, 249n, 253; **39**, 10, 11, 94n, 95, 105, 106n, 111, 236–8, 242, 246, 247, 249; **40**, 146n, 147, 156n, 190n, 210, 214, 216, 222, 226n, 231, 235, 236n; **41**, 13n, 14n, 46, 57n, 67n, 103n, 202, 213, 227, 228n, 229, 231, 234–5, 237, 240–1; **42**, 11n, 25n, 39n, 43n, 44n, 93n, 94n, 186, 202n, 208n, 209n, 210, 213; **43**, 23, 43n, 91n, 99n, 232, 264n, 268; **44**, 69n, 113n, 119n, 158, 161, 179, 217; **45**, 37n, 61n, 79n, 82n, 83n, 115n, 121n, 134, 162, 186n, 190, 193n, 204n; **46**, 165n, 228; **47**, 12, 64n, 139–40, 261n; **48**, 11n, 75n, 184n, 188, 244; **49**, 1n, 21n, 27, 28n, 146n, 153n, 159n, 163n, 165n, 308, 311n, 313n, 314n, 319–20; **50**, 160n, 262, 280, 287n; **51**, 71n, 72n, 96, 145–6, 167n, 285, 319; **52**, 69n, 120n, 143, 166n, 288, 303n, 306n, 309n; **53**, 71n, 332; **54**, 17n, 20n, 66, 96n, 98n, 152n, 203n, 206n, 208n, 210, 242n, 243n, 306, 310, 344–5; **55**, 2–3, 12, 13, 17–18, 19, 54n, 56, 87n, 93n, 163, 184n, 188, 194–5, 210n, 211n, 212n, 219n, 257n, 259n, 280n, 305, 381, 382, 390; **56**, 55n, 170–4, 179, 181, 182n, 184n, 204n; **57**, 68, 79, 171, 250, 321, 325, 329; **58**, 2, 27, 324, 333, 334; **59**, 2n7, 3, 9, 15, 23n14, 46n8, 39–46, 48, 53, 68n19, 69n1, 78, 193, 196, 223n38, 272, 282–3, 359, 368, 376, 378, 383; **60**, 1n2, 168, 188n15, 193n27, 229, 253, 259n26, 341
Shakespeare; a Dramatic Life, **48**, 244
'Shakespeare in Max Beerbohm's Theatre Criticism', **29**, 132–44
'Shakespeare in Planché's Extravaganzas', **16**, 103–17
Wells, William, **34**, 190; **59**, 275n21
Wellstood, F. C., **1**, 86
Catalogue of . . . Shakespeare's Birthplace, **3**, 2
Welsford, Enid, **4**, 19; **6**, 13; **10**, 135; **15**, 112; **27**, 59n; **29**, 1, 91; **35**, 70n, 87n; **37**, 9; **54**, 194–5; **60**, 59n3, 60n7, 61n9, 62n10, 62n11, 62n12
The Fool, **2**, 143, **13**, 39n, 104n

Welsh, Alexander, **32**, 217; **53**, 107; **58**, 45
Welsh, C., **1**, 35n
Welsh, Dr David, **57**, 163
Welsh, James M., **29**, 184; **39**, 85n
Welsh, Robert F., **34**, 193
Welth, and Helth, Enterlude of, **3**, 45
Weltje, Louis, **38**, 71
Welton, Timothy, **44**, 200
Welton, Wendy, **45**, 154
Welz, John W., **42**, 196
Wendel, Karl-Heinz, **23**, 117; **37**, 19n
Wendell, Barrett, **2**, 119; **27**, 106n; **43**, 112n
Wendler, Helen, **53**, 311
Wendt, Albert, **55**, 170, 175–7, 178, 180
Wenger, B. V., **8**, 4
Wentersdorf, Karl P., **6**, 159, 160, 170; **8**, 142–3; **20**, 162; **27**, 129n, 179, 192; **28**, 167; **31**, 168; **32**, 242–3, 244–5; **33**, 186–7, 203, 210; **34**, 173–4; **36**, 185; **37**, 204; **38**, 15, 231, 252; **39**, 124n, 251; **40**, 205; **42**, 206; **51**, 316; **53**, 8n; **54**, 41n, 116n; **55**, 17, 18
Wentworth, F., **57**, 115
Wentworth, Sir Peter, *A Pack of Puritans*, **12**, 107
Wentworth, Thomas, Earl of Strafford, **11**, 113, 116n
Wenzel, Peter, **37**, 160n
Werder, Karl, **9**, 2, 4; **18**, 39
Wergeland, Henrik, **58**, 208
Werk, Sein, **41**, 198
Werner, Sarah, **51**, 276–7; **56**, 342, 343–4; **60**, 167Fig.30, 169n9.2
Wernham, R. B., **42**, 34; **51**, 185; **55**, 210n
Werstine, Paul, **33**, 206–7, 208; **34**, 193, 196–7; **35**, 185, 186, 188–9; **36**, 187n, 188, 191; **37**, 209, 218; **38**, 229; **39**, 247, 248n, 249n; **40**, 146, 149–53, 230, 235; **41**, 219n; **42**, 194, 202, 209, 211; **43**, 265–6, 269; **44**, 150n; **45**, 194, 195, 199; **46**, 252n; **48**, 271, 272n; **50**, 3, 93n, 271–3, 276n, 289; **51**, 290, 330, 331; **52**, 71n, 85n, 310–11; **53**, 312, 334, 344; **54**, 323; **55**, 30n; **56**, 330, 355; **57**, 19, 227, 228, 231, 337; **58**, 352, 353, 357; **59**, 8, 10, 12–13, 26, 32–6, 37, 37–8n87, 70n2, 77n13, 84n16, 89n34, 124n1, 125, 128, 174, 213n5, 218
Wertham, Frederic, **9**, 13
Wertham, James, **4**, 11
Wertheim, Albert, **27**, 164; **32**, 226
Wertheim, Ursula, **25**, 186
Wertheim, W. F., **44**, 25n
Wertzman, W., **23**, 175
Wesker, Arnold, **16**, 19; **43**, 222; **53**, 1; **55**, 160; **56**, 246, 314
Weskin, Roy, **46**, 160–1
Wesley, Samuel, **18**, 98
West Riding Repertory Company, *see under* Theatres
West Scheil, Katherine, **51**, 45–55
West Side Story, **52**, 90
West, Alick, **20**, 145; **22**, 166
West, Anthony James, **49**, 321–2; **50**, 288; **55**, 386–8
West, Benjamin, **6**, 61; **13**, 61, 62, 75; **49**, 118, 120, 121n; **53**, 109; **59**, 131n47
West, Cornel, **51**, 57n
West, Diana, **35**, 177; **41**, 191; **42**, 153, 156
West, E. J., **10**, 150; **35**, 9n
West, Gillian, **30**, 185; **32**, 234; **34**, 189; **38**, 253; **43**, 234; **44**, 86n, 218
West, Grace Starry, **36**, 175
West, Hon. James, **4**, 72–3; **5**, 57
West, M., **28**, 160
West, Mae, **36**, 81
West, Michael, **31**, 133n
West, Peter, **43**, 210
West, R. H., **15**, 160; **19**, 126, 138, 151; **20**, 160; **24**, 140–1; **28**, 118; **29**, 89, 90; **34**, 182
West, Rebecca, **36**, 53n; **40**, 24n
The Court and the Castle reviewed, **13**, 148
West, Richard, **54**, 58n; **55**, 83
West, Robert H., **8**, 150; **10**, 138; **45**, 21, 22n, 24; **54**, 123n
West, Russell, **56**, 337
West, Samuel, **50**, 221–2; **51**, 260; **52**, 253; **54**, 274–5, 277; **55**, 292, 295, 297–302, 324, 330; **56**, 97, 288, 295; **57**, 291; **59**, 307, 308, 309, 310; **60**, 325
West, Shearer, **49**, 115n, 119n; **51**, 4; **55**, 241n; **59**, 291
West, Thomas G., **36**, 164n; **56**, 222n
West, Timothy, **45**, 146, 157; **47**, 212; **49**, 273; **50**, 221–2, **51**, 251, 260; **53**, 280; **56**, 283, 284; **57**, 292; **58**, 301
West, William, **27**, 95, 96, 97; **55**, 36–8, 41, 370
Symbolaeographie, **4**, 41–2
Westall, **10**, 73
Westall, Richard, **59**, 132
Westaway, Alan, **57**, 295
Westbrook, David, **42**, 157; **45**, 150; **46**, 121
Westbrook, P. D., **2**, 140n; **10**, 5
Westcote, Sebastian, **17**, 195
Westcott, Jim, **60**, 180
Westermarck, Edward, **60**, 76n21
Westerweel, Bart, **53**, 15n
Westfall, A. V. R., **18**, 117n
Westfall, Suzanne R., **44**, 229–30, 240; **51**, 290; **57**, 333; **60**, 7n11, 54n27
Westfelt, Mäns, **18**, 128
Westlake, Michael, **45**, 49n
Westlund, Joseph, **22**, 153
Westminster Boys, *see under* Theatre, Elizabethan, companies
Westmorland, Mildmay Fane, Duke of, *see under* Fane, Mildmay
Weston, David, **52**, 266
Weston, Jessie L., **18**, 117
Weston, Sir Richard, **60**, 69–70
Westrup, Jack, **17**, 214n; **45**, 172
Westward Ho!, see under Webster, John
Westwell, Raymond, **12**, 120; **15**, 145; **26**, 143, 144; **32**, 207
Wetherall, Jack, **34**, 157; **36**, 60
Wetz, W., **37**, 152n
Wexler, Joyce, **46**, 85–7, 89
Weyer, John, **28**, 119
'W. Har.', **34**, 86
W. H., Mr, **22**, 165; **23**, 157, 160; **28**, 165; **34**, 5, 161; **35**, 167, 168; **36**, 190
Whalley, Joyce I., **20**, 168
Whalley, Peter, **51**, 17n; **53**, 63n
Wharton, Edward, **32**, 103n
Wharton, George, **45**, 109, **48**, 27n
Wharton, Joseph, **13**, 34; **43**, 104n
Wharton, Philip, Duke of, **51**, 55
Wharton, Robert, **45**, 108, 109, 113
Wharton, T. F., **38**, 17, 237; **56**, 335, 336; **58**, 54, 58
Wharton, William, **45**, 108

Whateley, Anne, **3**, 9, 139; **5**, 139n; **7**, 139; **15**, 12; **45**, 191
Whateley, Thomas, **2**, 109; **18**, 3; **25**, 185; **34**, 11, 12, 17–18; **37**, 142; **57**, 89, 94
Whately, Richard, **53**, 131n; **54**, 83
Whately, William, **53**, 36n
Whatley, J., **29**, 165; **59**, 113–14
Wheale, Nigel, **45**, 70; **46**, 205, 206, 239; **49**, 142n; **50**, 247–8; **55**, 9n; **57**, 46
Wheater, Isabella, **47**, 227
Wheatley, Brian, **49**, 276
Wheatley, Francis, **13**, 108; **58**, 278
Wheatley, H. B., **1**, 2, 35n, 36n; **38**, 69n; **42**, 58n; **55**, 83n
Wheeler, Andrew C., **35**, 7n
Wheeler, Charles B., **9**, 135
Wheeler, David, **49**, 290
Wheeler, Richard P., **37**, 101n, 102, 107n, 110n; **40**, 110n, 117n; **41**, 193; **42**, 10n, 12, 13, 191; **44**, 208; **46**, 92n, 111n; **55**, 362
Wheeler, Thomas, **44**, 246n; **46**, 220
Wheeler, Wendy, **55**, 80n
Wheelwright, Philip, **15**, 114, 121
Whelan, Andy, **55**, 324
Whelan, Peter, **48**, 237; **51**, 269; **54**, 73; **58**, 1, 151–2, 154, 156–7
Whelehan, Imelda, **56**, 317
Wheler, Robert Bell (Wheeler), **1**, 82, 86, 87n; **9**, 100n; **14**, 111, 113, 114; **56**, 185n
When You See Me You Know Me, **52**, 24, 28n; **54**, 244n
Whetham, Alan, **55**, 325
Whetson, Robert, **56**, 200
Whetstone, George, **3**, 15; **7**, 104; **12**, 55n; **13**, 84; **15**, 181; **17**, 206; **19**, 146; **21**, 135; **25**, 31, 45; **28**, 94; **35**, 183; **40**, 107; **47**, 167, 168, 169; **48**, 72n; **51**, 155, 156; **52**, 134; **55**, 23, 24n; **60**, 272n13
  An Heptameron of Ciuill Discourses, **13**, 88n
  Promos and Cassandra, **3**, 54, 73; **4**, 26–7, **15**, 181
  tale of Rinaldo and Giletta, **8**, 4
Whewell, William, **53**, 165
Whibley, Charles, **23**, 61n; **31**, 39n
Which Shakespeare? A User's Guide to Editions, **46**, 241n
Whigham, Frank, **35**, 154; **41**, 115n; **50**, 65, 258; **55**, 240
Whipple, E. P., **18**, 113
Whishaw, Ben, **58**, 293; **59**, 339
Whistler, James Abbot McNeill, **10**, 75
Whistler, Rex, **12**, 12
Whitaker, Virgil K., **9**, 132; **10**, 5, 25n; **11**, 132, 135n; **16**, 172n; **19**, 120–1; **20**, 157; **22**, 148; **25**, 7; **28**, 156; **29**, 51n, 86; **33**, 9; **34**, 97n; **38**, 3, 229; **45**, 22n
  Shakespeare's Use of Learning reviewed, **8**, 146–7
  Shakespeare's Use of Learning, **11**, 135n
Whitbread, Peter, **42**, 162
White, **10**, 73
White Devil, The, **52**, 208
White, Allon, **44**, 22n; **49**, 70n
White, Anne, **41**, 187; **42**, 136; **44**, 193
White, Beatrice, **14**, 145n; **49**, 79n
White, Bruce, **45**, 154
White, Colin, **51**, 188n
White, D. M., **3**, 33
White, Diana, **43**, 112n
White, Edward (the younger), **54**, 92n; **55**, 27–35
White, H. B., **26**, 156
White, Hayden, **46**, 52; **53**, 73, 76; **55**, 210, 217; **57**, 11, 12; **59**, 27n32, 27n34, 28; **52**, 202
White, Howard B., **31**, 6
White, Jon, **51**, 184
White, Martin, **46**, 200; **47**, 243–4; **52**, 30n, 47n; **53**, 328; **55**, 237n; **59**, 372
White, Melanie, **53**, 285
White, Patrick, **26**, 8; **55**, 174
White, Paul Whitfield, **47**, 237, 239; **54**, 57n, 60, 99n; **56**, 34n; **57**, 333; **60**, 7n11, 54n27
White, R. G., **16**, 32; **18**, 102–3, 109–13; **25**, 76n, 93; **32**, 21n, 24n, 49n, 241
White, R. S., **31**, 164, 182; **32**, 22; **38**, 49n, 55n; **40**, 185, 198n; **41**, 103n, 112n, 193, 200n, 223–4; **42**, 163; **43**, 219–34, 268; **46**, 212; **49**, 296; **51**, 285; **52**, 273; **53**, 296; **54**, 322; **56**, 204n, 205n
White, Robert, **43**, 266
White, Rowland, **11**, 92, 93, 96
White, Sidney H., **19**, 132
White, Theodore H., **57**, 152
White, Thomas, **36**, 140
  A Sermon Preached at Pawles Crosse, **1**, 68
White, W. A., **1**, 58, 69
White, Willard, **43**, 192–3; **44**, 199; **46**, 68; **47**, 12; **60**, 365–6
White, William, **32**, 106; **33**, 206, 207; **39**, 247; **40**, 147, 149, 150, 152, **42**, 209; **52**, 72n
Whitefriars Theatre, *see under* Theatres, Elizabethan
Whitehall, *see under* London
Whitehead, A. N., **11**, 79
Whitehead, Andrew, **56**, 237, 238
Whitehead, Paxton, **15**, 144
Whitehouse, Lorna, **1**, 101, 102
Whitelaw, John, **48**, 236
Whiteley, Jane, **45**, 89n
Whiteley, Steve, **44**, 195
Whitelock, James, **17**, 80n
Whitelocke, B., **19**, 101
Whiter, Walter, **4**, 18, 19; **7**, 8; **8**, 30; **15**, 24; **18**, 47–51, 174; **22**, 145, 163; **23**, 50; **25**, 39, 127; **34**, 99n; **50**, 102–3
  Dissertation on the Disorder of Death, A, **20**, 89, 92
  Etymologicon Universale, **20**, 92
  Nova Tentamina Mythologica, **20**, 92
  Specimen of a Commentary on Shakespeare, **20**, 83–94
Whitfield, Andy, **42**, 155; **43**, 205
Whitfield, Christopher, **16**, 164–5; **18**, 178; **19**, 146; **21**, 147–8; **29**, 34n
Whitfield, J. H., **38**, 123n
Whitfield, Nich, **43**, 208
Whitfield, Nicholas, **15**, 146
Whitfield, Peter, **52**, 187n
Whitfield, Simon, **43**, 208
Whitford, Margaret, **56**, 146n
Whitforde, Richard, **32**, 133
Whitgift, John, Archbishop of Canterbury, **8**, 101–2; **17**, 109, 125; **27**, 135; **33**, 93; **54**, 170; **60**, 13
Whiting, B. J., **32**, 163n, 164n, 166, 168, 169n, 171n
Whiting, George, **57**, 250
Whiting, John, **40**, 223
Whiting, Leonard, **49**, 172

Whitman, Cedric H., **20**, 35, 40n
Whitman, Peter, **47**, 214
Whitman, Walt, **16**, 179; **18**, 103, 105–7, 111–15; **45**, 41; **53**, 293; **54**, 302; **56**, 203
Leaves of Grass, **14**, 160 and n
Whitman, Walter, **35**, 32
Whitmore, Walter, **55**, 289
Whitney, Charles, **49**, 287; **54**, 322; **55**, 339, 341
Whitney, Cynthia, **19**, 130
Whitney, Geoffrey, **1**, 63; **24**, 66n; **25**, 99; **29**, 171; **30**, 194; **32**, 167n, 171n; **34**, 185; **39**, 127n; **43**, 246; **44**, 236; **53**, 24n; **55**, 25n; **57**, 211, 212, 221; **58**, 247
Choice of Emblemes, A **13**, 73; **17**, 180n, 182, 185–6, 187
Whitrow, Benjamin, **46**, 180–1
Whittaker, Herbert, **36**, 84n
Stratford, the First Five Years, **13**, 126
Whittaker, Samantha, **59**, 339
Whittaker, Steve, **54**, 289
Whittier, Gayle, **49**, 57, 65n, 99n
Whittingham, Charles, **18**, 19
Whittington, Robert, **1**, 68
Whittington, Thomas, **36**, 174
Whitworth, Charles, **46**, 256; **57**, 340–1
Whitworth, David, **38**, 237
Whitworth, Geoffrey, **44**, 107n
Whitworth, Paul, **35**, 149; **45**, 27n
Whitworth, Stephen, **60**, 350–1
Who's Afriad of Virginia Woolf?, **54**, 252
Whole contention betweene the two famous houses Lancaster and Yorke, The, see under *'Contention betweene the two famous houses Lancaster and Yorke, The Whole'*
Whole Duty of Man, The, **14**, 113
Whore of Babylon, **54**, 66
Whorf, Richard, **4**, 123; **8**, 122
Whybrow, John, **54**, 37n
Whybrow, Lucy, **49**, 148, 243, 245; **50**, 233; **58**, 301
Whymark, Pat, **45**, 151
Whyte, Roland, **38**, 90
Whythorne, Thomas, **24**, 158; **44**, 228; **50**, 66–9, 72, 74
Wicherek, Michael, **45**, 152; **53**, 279, 282; **54**, 294
Wicht, Wolfgang, **20**, 160; **21**, 139
Wickert, Maria, **8**, 145; **10**, 5
Wickham, Chris, **52**, 55n, 62
Wickham, Glynne, **9**, 133; **13**, 162; **18**, 181–2; **20**, 72n, 168; **21**, 137, 139, 156; **22**, 35; **23**, 138–9; **26**, 169–70; **28**, 163, 169–70; **29**, 3, 4, 158; **30**, 157, 168, 164n; **31**, 62n, 103; **33**, 162n; **34**, 103n, 179; **35**, 131n, 174, 175; **36**, 178; **39**, 225; **40**, 70, 218; **41**, 6–8, 60n, 219; **42**, 114, 115; **43**, 51n, 70n, 74n, 77n, 144n, 149, 158, 168; **44**, 243, 254; **47**, 34, 59n, 111; **50**, 42n; **51**, 311; **52**, 7–8; **53**, 196, 197n; **55**, 96n, 242n; **57**, 238; **60**, 45n41
Early English Stages, Vol. 1, reviewed, **13**, 159–60; **14**, 3, 13
'From Tragedy to Tragi-Comedy: *King Lear* as Prologue', **26**, 33–48
'Hell-Castle and its Door-Keeper', **19**, 68–74
Wickham, Rupert, **49**, 277; **54**, 284; **55**, 326, 327; **57**, 281, 295
Wickington, Pamela, **45**, 151
Wicks, Victoria, **47**, 209
Widdowson, P., **39**, 103n
Widgren, Olof, **13**, 131
Widmann, Ruth I., **27**, 187; **29**, 184
Widmann, W., **9**, 110n
Widmayer, Martha, **50**, 249
Wieland, Christoph Martin, **4**, 126, 127; **9**, 94, 96, 97, 100n; **14**, 151; **40**, 58, 61; **57**, 56, 62
Wieland, Theodore, **57**, 132, 135
Wieler, J. W., *George Chapman*, **14**, 11
Wiesenfarth, J., **49**, 133n
Wiesner, C. U., **48**, 182
Wiesner-Hanks, Merry E., **46**, 161n; **54**, 341–2
Wietfield, A., **15**, 12
Wife for a Month, **54**, 15
Wigan Public Library, *see under* Libraries
Wigert, Knut, **7**, 114; **14**, 122
Wigfall, A., **27**, 114n
Wiggins, Martin, **46**, 210; **49**, 287; **50**, 156n, 289; **55**, 368–9; **56**, 303, 305
Journeymen in Murder, **46**, 210
Wiggins, Michelle, **59**, 342
Wight, Peter, **43**, 198
Wight, Thomas, **55**, 37n
Wigpitt, Thomas, **47**, 18n
Wikander, Matthew H., **40**, 202; **41**, 213, 223; **43**, 100n; **46**, 6; **47**, 231
Wilberforce, Bishop Samuel, **54**, 82–3
Wilberforce, William, **54**, 82, 85
Wilberg, Wolff Rainer, **29**, 176
Wilbraham, William, **58**, 238
Wilbur, Richard, **24**, 174
Wilbye, John, **1**, 68
Wilcher, Robert, **41**, 68, 73
Wilcken, Franzisk, **50**, 229
Wilcox, G. D., **50**, 60n
Wilcox, Helen, **51**, 293; **57**, 342
Wilcox, John, **1**, 8; **4**, 141n; **10**, 10
Wilcox, Lance, **52**, 117n
Wilcox, Paula, **49**, 270
Wilcox, Thomas, **17**, 125
Wilcox, Toyah, **43**, 211; **45**, 63n, 72, 154; **50**, 230; **52**, 261
Wild Thyme Theatre Company, **58**, 299
Wild, Christopher, **44**, 200
Wild, Peter Leslie, **46**, 203
Wilde, Oscar, **4**, 104; **6**, 136; **8**, 131; **10**, 141; **22**, 2, 5, 141; **23**, 91; **29**, 133; **32**, 25, 26n; **36**, 21; **38**, 213; **42**, 147, 184; **43**, 228; **45**, 41, 42; **46**, 82; **48**, 186; **50**, 31; **53**, 138–40, 143, 146–9; **54**, 76; **55**, 343; **56**, 135, 136n, 137–8, 206
Wilde, Patrick, **44**, 191
Wilder, Billy, **56**, 241n
Wilder, Thornton, **1**, 97; **26**, 90
Wilders, John, **31**, 165; **33**, 187; **37**, 200; **38**, 10, 47, 134n; **39**, 9, 11, 92, 96, 106; **40**, 63n; **42**, 1n, 175; **45**, 172; **49**, 143n, 160, 161, 310–15; **58**, 334, 337, 342
Wildgoose, William, **4**, 82, 83
Wildgruber, Ulrich, **60**, 166, 169n8.9
Wildhagen, Heinz D., **6**, 120
Wildi, Max, **7**, 115; **18**, 129
Wilding, Michael, **21**, 148
Wildman, R. I., **24**, 178
Wilds, Lilian, **29**, 166; **39**, 80
Wiles, David, **41**, 127n, 216–17, 220; **48**, 246, 261; **52**, 274, 280; **55**, 247, 250; **56**, 62n, 63n, 95n, 97, 99; **60**, 114

Shakespeare's Almanac: 'A Midsummer Night's Dream', Marriage and the Elizabethan Calendar, **48**, 246, 261
Wiles, R. M., **3**, 137
Wilhams, Michael, E., **54**, 91
Wilhelm II, Emperor of Germany, **44**, 108; **48**, 176
Wilkes, G. A., **16**, 165; **30**, 64n; **34**, 171; **36**, 188; **44**, 218; **48**, 252; **50**, 58n; **51**, 67n
Wilkes, John, **24**, 100
Wilkie, Allan (theatre company), **11**, 117; **20**, 80
Wilkins (Wilkinson), Alice, **25**, 143
Wilkins, Bartholomew, **25**, 143
Wilkins, Edward G. P., **35**, 7n
Wilkins, George (Wilkinson), **3**, 30; **5**, 39; **6**, 165; **7**, 65–6; **8**, 56; **11**, 96, 149; **15**, 180, **18**, 188; **21**, 150, 152; **23**, 133; **24**, 107, 113n, 155; **25**, 127–52, 142–3; **26**, 44; **29**, 22, 23, 25, 26, 29n, 31, 32, 33–9; **30**, 205; **31**, 179, 192–3; **32**, 138; **33**, 172, 173; **34**, 190; **37**, 192; **38**, 252; **40**, 156, 158; **41**, 233, 235–6; **42**, 212; **43**, 261, 264; **44**, 155, 166, 233; **45**, 201–2; **48**, 278; **50**, 160; **57**, 335; **58**, 343; **59**, 5, 72, 74, 75, 214, 216–17, 219, 220, 221, 223–4, 259n13
The Painfull Adventures of Pericles Prince of Tyre, **3**, 45, 151–2; **5**, 26, 39–45; **8**, 158; **13**, 162
The Miseries of Enforced Marriage, **1**, 46, **12**, 36, 40–1
The Three Miseries of Barbary, **11**, 96
Wilkins, Katherine, **29**, 33
Wilkinson, *see* Sotheby and Wilkinson
Wilkinson, Allan, **5**, 150
Wilkinson, Andrew M., **21**, 132
Wilkinson, C. H., **4**, 96n; **23**, 125
Wilkinson, Edward, **47**, 26
Wilkinson, Helen, **47**, 101, 106
Wilkinson, Jane, **57**, 302
Wilkinson, John, **19**, 103
Wilkinson, L. P., **10**, 146n; **31**, 37; **38**, 40n; **56**, 33n, 34n
Wilkinson, Marc, **43**, 213
Wilkinson, Naomi, **47**, 218
Wilkinson, Norman, **2**, 75; **8**, 80
Wilkinson, Robert, **53**, 63
Wilkinson, Tate, **18**, 17; **51**, 86, 115
Wilkinson, Tom, **34**, 149, 153; **47**, 188–9; **48**, 230
Wilkinson, Valentine, **29**, 32
Wilkock, Gladys Doidge, **53**, 13n, 22n
Wilks, John S., **44**, 210
Wilks, Robert, **24**, 167; **32**, 42
Will of Whitbeck, **13**, 97
Willan, Brian, **57**, 159
Willbern, David, **32**, 217; **33**, 186; **41**, 207; **46**, 101n, 117n; **52**, 270, 281; **55**, 203n; **59**, 355
Willcock, Gladys Doidge, **4**, 9; **7**, 5, 11n; **9**, 134, 141; **10**, 135; **17**, 224; **23**, 11; **40**, 87n; **42**, 66n; **44**, 46n; **50**, 65n, 135n
'Shakespeare and Elizabethan English', **7**, 12–24
Willcox, Pip, **53**, 25n
Willeford, William, **24**, 162n; **32**, 6; **35**, 87
Willemen, Paul, **45**, 49n
Willems, Michèle, **34**, 181; **41**, 227; **49**, 308; **50**, 257; **53**, 167n; **55**, 383; **60**, 214–22
Willems, Raymond, **41**, 228
Willer, Peter, **32**, 190, 195n, 199
Willes, Richard, **17**, 51
Willet, Andrew, *Ecclesia Triumphans*, **2**, 70
Willets, Shelly, **44**, 195
Willett, Andrew, **17**, 183
Willett, John, **42**, 102n, 103n; **45**, 133n; **48**, 10n; **50**, 41n; **58**, 133; **60**, 174n10
Willey, Basil **19**, 131n
The Seventeenth-Century Background, **3**, 7
Willey, Edward P., **59**, 126, 127, 129n33, 134n61
Willey, Elizabeth, **53**, 173n
Willey, Margaret, **24**, 2n
William and Mary, English Monarchs, **57**, 74
William III, King, **14**, 30; **17**, 123; **29**, 26; **51**, 73
William IV, King, **56**, 127
William Shakespeare's Romeo + Juliet, **52**, 88–98
William, David, **18**, 185; **19**, 116; **40**, 163, 165
William, Michael, **51**, 239
Williams, Alan Vaughan, **43**, 210; **58**, 278
Williams, Andy, **52**, 236
Williams, Bishop, **29**, 94
Williams, C., **38**, 73, 74
Williams, C. H., **54**, 170n
Williams, Carolyn, **51**, 291
Williams, Charles, **4**, 6, 146; **8**, 9, 12, 36; **18**, 3; **35**, 83n; **36**, 30; **58**, 146
Williams Clare **30**, 164; **54**, 191n
The Image of the City and Other Essays reviewed, **13**, 148
Williams, Clifford, **12**, 119; **18**, 149; **19**, 117, 118; **20**, 134; **22**, 137; **23**, 132; **25**, 163; **30**, 176, 177; **31**, 159; **32**, 201, 202–3; **38**, 17; **43**, 184, 213; **44**, 200; **45**, 128
Williams, D. E., **51**, 119n
Williams, David, **10**, 124; **39**, 235n; **48**, 14n; **52**, 162
Williams, Deanne, **59**, 364–5, 368
Williams, Edith, **28**, 167
Williams, Edward, **48**, 160
Williams, Emlyn, **10**, 131, 133–4
Williams, Faynia, **43**, 212
Williams, Frank, **51**, 220
Williams, Franklin, B., Jr, **22**, 180; **23**, 160
Williams, Frayne, *Mr Shakespeare of the Globe*, **3**, 9
Williams, G., **29**, 160
Williams, Gary J., **34**, 165n; **35**, 10
Williams, Gary Jay, **52**, 290–1
Williams, George Walton, **4**, 161, 163; **5**, 134; **10**, 155; **11**, 155; **12**, 149; **15**, 181, 182; **17**, 210n; **19**, 163; **20**, 148; **23**, 146–7; **25**, 73n; **27**, 179; **30**, 203, 210; **31**, 198; **33**, 211; **37**, 217, 218; **38**, 11n, 87n; **39**, 222; **40**, 235; **41**, 154n; **42**, 1832, 209n; **44**, 123n; **46**, 226; **50**, 143n, 272n; **51**, 331, 332; **52**, 71n; **53**, 332; **54**, 306, 350–1; **55**, 84n; **57**, 342, 343; **59**, 40
Williams, Gordon, **25**, 188; **49**, 302; **50**, 240; **51**, 325–6; **60**, 103n7
Williams, Guy, **43**, 215; **57**, 265
Williams, Gweno, **19**, 136; **37**, 16n; **43**, 208; **55**, 379–80
Williams, Harcourt, **2**, 14, 16; **9**, 20; **10**, 75; **23**, 132; **41**, 55–7; **47**, 90
Williams, Haydn M., **19**, 133
Williams, Heathcote, **45**, 63n, 72
Williams, Ioan, **56**, 134n
Williams, Iolo A., **2**, 21; **33**, 148n
Williams, Jane, **48**, 160
Williams, Jano, **60**, 131n3
Williams, John, **2**, 24, 25, 26, 27, 32, 34; **13**, 104n; **58**, 239

Williams, John Antony, **21**, 140
Williams, Kaz, **45**, 148
Williams, Kelly, **59**, 345
Williams, Kenneth, **50**, 212; **58**, 264
Williams, Lee, **57**, 50
Williams, Lia, **47**, 189, **59**, 313, 314; **60**, 320
Williams, Mark, **44**, 192
Williams, Mary C., **27**, 176
Williams, Michael, **22**, 137; **25**, 164; **27**, 139; **30**, 174; **44**, 194
Williams, Neville, **52**, 168n
Williams, Olivia, **57**, 262
Williams, Patricia, **57**, 163, 164
Williams, Penry, **48**, 70n; **55**, 210n
Williams, Philip, **3**, 152; **4**, 157, 162, 163; **5**, 144, 145; **7**, 149; **8**, 11, 154, 155; **10**, 155; **11**, 154; **12**, 134; **13**, 166; **14**, 158 and n, 159, 162; **20**, 178; **30**, 37n; **38**, 243
Williams, Philippa, **42**, 156
Williams, Porter, Jr, **32**, 8
Williams, Ralph G., **57**, 136
Williams, Ralph J., **54**, 30n
Williams, Raymond, **22**, 148; **39**, 103; **40**, 78n, 198; **41**, 131; **48**, 113n; **49**, 301; **50**, 248; **55**, 272, 359; **60**, 59n3, 60n7
Williams, Richard, **40**, 183; **41**, 184; **43**, 217, **51**, 264
Williams, Robert D., **14**, 88n
Williams, Roger, **17**, 32n
Williams, Sarah, **23**, 44n
Williams, Sheila, **15**, 71n
Williams, Simon, **37**, 199; **41**, 225; **57**, 55, 68
Williams, Tad, **53**, 169n, 173n
Williams, Tam, **59**, 316–18, 319
Williams, Tenessee, **6**, 140; **10**, 100; **16**, 19; **22**, 3; **53**, 111
Cat on a Hot Tin Roof, **12**, 1
Streetcar Named Desire, **12**, 7
Williams, Thomas L., **56**, 194n
Williams, Walter, **58**, 239
Williams, William P., **24**, 178; **34**, 197
Williamson, Arthur H., **57**, 70
Williamson, Audrey, **6**, 163n; **27**, 34n
Williamson, C. F., **23**, 167n; **30**, 182; **31**, 136; **32**, 214; **41**, 154n, 157n
Williamson, David, **51**, 269; **58**, 153–4, 158, 300
Williamson, G. A., **54**, 39n
Williamson, George C., **17**, 29n; **56**, 32n
Williamson, Hugh Ross, **4**, 148, 156
Williamson, J. A., **17**, 29n; **38**, 20
Williamson, J. C., **14**, 116; **35**, 32
Williamson, Jane, **35**, 9; **51**, 108n, 116n; **53**, 213n, 232n
Williamson, Marilyn L., **23**, 147, 154; **25**, 175; **32**, 10; **36**, 170n; **43**, 1n; **49**, 66n, 88
Williamson, Nicol, **28**, 137, 144, 145; **29**, 153; **39**, 102; **43**, 35, 53, 56–9, 62; **56**, 269, 291
Williamson, Robert J., **50**, 231, 235; **51**, 257, 265; **52**, 263, 264; **53**, 276, 279; **54**, 283, 284; **55**, 329, 333; **58**, 298; **59**, 343, 345
Williamson, Sandra, L., **43**, 231
Williamson, Sarah, **51**, 263
Willichius Iodocus, **30**, 61n; **38**, 41, 42n, 43, 44
Willis, Bev, **41**, 190; **47**, 214
Willis, Bill, **55**, 325
Willis, Deborah, **43**, 241; **46**, 208; **50**, 260; **57**, 30
Willis, John, *Stenographie*, **5**, 151
Willis, Mervyn, **42**, 157
Willis, Paul J., **56**, 83n, 85n, 92n
Willis, Ralph, **33**, 204
Willis, Raymond, **47**, 57n, 113
Willis, Richard, **17**, 51, 167–8, 169
Willis, Susan, **37**, 200; **45**, 188; **47**, 10n
Willman, Noel, **10**, 123
Willmington, Sue, **55**, 330
Willmott, Phil, **47**, 216; **57**, 292, 294; **59**, 188–9
Willobie, Henry, **34**, 86, 89
Willoughby, Sir Ambrose, **8**, 7
Willoughby, Edwin E., **1**, 75, 77n; **4**, 88; **5**, 47, 144, 147; **7**, 152; **8**, 153, 154; **10**, 88n; **11**, 154; **38**, 14n, 91n; **41**, 20n; **52**, 4n; **60**, 256
Willoughby, Francis, **47**, 273
Willoughby, Henry, *Willobie his Avisa*, **3**, 10, 54; **4**, 88
Willoughby, Sir Hugh, **17**, 32
Willoughby, John, **23**, 44
Wills, Garry, **49**, 288; **52**, 102; **57**, 29
Wills, M. M., **42**, 55n
Wills, W. G., **29**, 136
Willson, D. Harris, **17**, 118n; **44**, 227n; **38**, 21n; **54**, 133n, 134n; **56**, 217n, 221n
Willson, John, **45**, 114
Willson, Robert F., Jr, **23**, 171n; **24**, 156; **28**, 161; **30**, 201; **32**, 211, 222; **33**, 192, 201
Willymat, William, **2**, 70, 72; **19**, 67n
A Loyal Subject's Looking-Glasse, **2**, 70; **4**, 40
A Prince's Looking-Glass, **4**, 40
Wilmanns, W., **23**, 28n
Wilmeth, Don B., **28**, 171; **35**, 8
Wilmington, Sue, **46**, 191
Wilmot, John, **53**, 27–9, 31, 36, 37
Wilmot, R., **22**, 152
Wilmott, Phil, **56**, 267, 298
Wilshire, Bruce, **55**, 239n
Wilson, A., *The History of Great Britain*, **13**, 110n
Wilson, A. N., **54**, 83n, 88
Wilson, Alan, **45**, 63n
Wilson, Angus, **55**, 150–1
Wilson, Arthur, **28**, 28n; **58**, 234
The Swisser (MS.), **3**, 52
Wilson, Benjamin, **13**, 74, 80n; **49**, 114–16, 122n; **58**, 40, 174
Wilson, Charles, **38**, 57n
Wilson, Christopher R., **44**, 238; **60**, 356, 361
Wilson, Daniel, **25**, 114
Wilson, David Henry, **50**, 228–9
Wilson, E. C., 'Shakespeare's Enobarbus', **2**, 135
Wilson, Edward, **41**, 186
Wilson, Edward M., **20**, 104n
'Shakespeare and Christian Doctrine: Some Qualifications', **23**, 79–89
Wilson, Edwin, **25**, 45n, 117n; **27**, 34n; **31**, 23n; **32**, 15n; **35**, 6, 8n; **37**, 34n; **41**, 169n; **46**, 8n; **49**, 2n; **52**, 224n
Wilson, Emily R., **59**, 365–6, 368
Wilson, F. P., **1**, 12, 122; **2**, 152; **3**, 69; **4**, 9, 25, 50, 67n, 88, 149; **5**, 137; **6**, 57, 63n; **7**, 5, 51, 55n, 132, 142, 147; **8**, 2, 11, 18; **9**, 32, 34n, 138n, 146; **10**, 14, 15; **11**, 82, 87n, 106n; **14**, 7, 9, 13, 34; **16**, 162, 178; **17**, 32n, 98n, 165 and n, 224; **18**, 24–5, 181; **19**, 8; **23**, 40, 47, 137–8, 143, 167–8;

24, 168, 171; **26**, 70, 72; **27**, 83n; **28**, 4n, 38, 41n; **32**, 2, 6, 7, 10; **33**, 7; **36**, 109–10; **37**, 5, 7; **38**, 7; **42**, 20, 23, 78n; **46**, 127n; **47**, 131n; **50**, 19n, 78n; **51**, 142; **54**, 63n; **58**, 353; **59**, 1n1, 28n38
Elizabethan and Jacobean, **14**, 2
Elizabethan and Jacobean Studies presented to F. P. Wilson reviewed, **14**, 145
'Illustrations of Social Life': 'I, The Funeral Obsequies of Sir All-in-New-Fashions', **11**, 98–9
'II, A Butcher and some Social Pests', **12**, 107–8
'III, Street Cries', **13**, 106–10
'IV, The Plague', **15**, 125–9
Marlowe and the Early Shakespeare, **14**, 10, 44n
The Plague in Shakespeare's London, **3**, 6, **11**, 106n
'Shakespeare's Reading', **3**, 14–21
Wilson, Gayle Edward, **23**, 170
Wilson, Georges, **13**, 128; **18**, 123
Wilson, H. A. (ed.), **17**, 59n
Wilson, H. Schütz, **35**, 18n
Wilson, Harold S., **8**, 140; **16**, 45; **21**, 149; **23**, 166; **24**, 12; **25**, 3; **45**, 18n; **50**, 181n
On the Design of Shakespearian Tragedy, **12**, 134, and n, 135; **13**, 10n
Wilson, Henry, **19**, 102–4
Wilson, Holly, **42**, 156
Wilson, J., **27**, 61
Wilson, J. H., **14**, 12
Wilson, Jack, **15**, 2
Wilson, James, **55**, 90
Wilson, Jennifer, **55**, 334
Wilson, John, *Belphegor*, **1**, 66; **11**, 65, 66; **19**, 102, 105; **21**, 16, 27n; **23**, 183; **32**, 17n; **51**, 132, 133n, 136; **54**, 333; **56**, 114
Cheerful Ayres **3**, 56
Wilson, John Dover, **1**, 9, 10, 12, 13, 94, 114; **2**, 57, 58, 84, 108, 113, 140, 148; **3**, 3, 6, 10, 18, 21n, 23, 24, 26, 27, 28, 75, 80, 82, 137, 141, 152; **4**, 8, 10, 36, 44, 88, 161, 162; **5**, 4–5, 61, 139, 148, 150, 152; **6**, 7, 10, 11, 12, 13, 14, 18, 155, 157, 159, 168, 169; **7**, 3, 6, 8, 82–3, 107, 136, 151; **8**, 2, 14, 22, 23, 101–2, 110; **9**, 4–6, 7–9, 12, 13, 15, 26, 27, 31, 32, 33n, 44–5, 48n, 50, 51, 150, 152, 153; **10**, 2, 3, 5, 9, 10, 39, 49n, 70n, 71–2, 138, 158; **11**, 33–4, 41n, 88n, 132, 141, 149; **12**, 92, 94n, 129n, 132, 142–3, 150; **14**, 109n, 155, 158–9; **15**, 7, 29, 33, 39n, 64, 71n, 113, 176–8; **16**, 64, 100, 173, 178; **17**, 89n, 160n; **18**, 20, 25, 31, 33n, 34, 40–1, 127, 159, 178, 187; **19**, 1, 3, 31, 94n, 161; **20**, 39, 120n, 127, 146, 170–2; **21**, 4, 23, 27n, 28n, 107, 110, 113, 147; **22**, 35, 75, 180; **23**, 56n, 145; **24**, 2n, 52, 53, 171; **25**, 3, 5, 73n, 75n, 94n; **26**, 3, 81, 82, 85n, 97, 98, 137, 182; **27**, 11n, 51n, 62, 71n, 106n, 132n, 135, 192; **28**, 3, 4n, 38n, 58, 107; **29**, 82, 83, 86, 166, 179, 180, 181; **30**, 36, 38n, 42–3, 48n, 71, 86n, 91n, 96n, 98n, 112, 181, 193, 208; **31**, 93–4, 94–5; **32**, 1, 7, 11, 50n, 96n, 106–7, 108, 145n, 151, 152, 153, 155n, 156, 158n, 239, 242; **33**, 1, 2n, 121, 130n, 205, 207, 208; **34**, 93n; **36**, 49n, 107n, 182; **37**, 5, 9, 85, 90, 202; **38**, 13, 17, 49n, 51, 83, 88, 95n, 96, 175, 176, 218; **39**, 136n, 145, 146, 243n; **40**, 39n, 185, 187, 189, 192, 228; **41**, 86, 94; **42**, 25n, 30, 33, 53n, 54, 77n, 114, 119, 199, 212; **43**, 252, 267; **44**, 28n, 66, 135n; **45**, 7, 19n, 21, 22n, 24, 193, 194; **46**, 226, 228, 257; **47**, 109, 113, 275; **48**, 109, 277, 284; **50**, 271, 277; **51**, 142; **52**, 5, 112, 116; **53**, 68n, 179, 181, 334; **55**, 20, 28, 280n, 338; **56**, 95n, 96, 98, 99n, 218n; **57**, 227, 238; **58**, 204, 353; **59**, 1, 2–3, 28, 40, 43, 147–8, 152–3, 154–5, 156, 161, 166, 198n4, 382; **60**, 58, 111n39, 364
'Ben Jonson and *Julius Caesar*', **2**, 36–43
edition of *King Henry VI* (3 parts) reviewed, **7**, 139–40, 147–9
edition of *Titus Andronicus* reviewed, **3**, 143–4, 145
Henry IV and *Henry V* reviewed, **1**, 127–30
Macbeth, **2**, 145–8
'Malone and the Upstart Crow', **4**, 56–68
New Cambridge edition of *Julius Caesar* reviewed, **4**, 156–7
New Cambridge edition of *Richard III* reviewed, **8**, 157
New Cambridge editions of history plays, **6**, 5, 8, 16, 35n
New Cambridge edition of *Othello* reviewed, **11**, 149
New Cambridge Shakespeare, **2**, 145
'The New Way with Shakespeare's Texts: An Introduction for Lay Readers I. The Foundations', **7**, 48–56; **11**, 78–88
'The New Way with Shakespeare's Texts. II. Recent Work on the Text of *Romeo and Juliet*', **8**, 81–99
'The New Way with Shakespeare's Texts. III. In Sight of Shakespeare's Manuscripts', **9**, 69–80
The Essential Shakespeare, **3**, 9, 29
The Manuscript of Shakespeare's 'Hamlet', **11**, 88n
'*Titus Andronicus* on the Stage in 1595', **1**, 17–22
'Shakespeare's "small Latin"—how much?', **10**, 12–26
What Happens in 'Hamlet', **14**, 55n
Wilson, Josephine, **9**, 49, 147; **10**, 89n
Wilson, Katharine M., **31**, 129, 135; **46**, 45n
Wilson, Katie, **44**, 192
Wilson, Lois Hawley, **54**, 92n
Wilson, Luke, **47**, 232; **53**, 87n; **56**, 224n
Wilson, M. Glen, **35**, 7
Wilson, Philip, **15**, 6
Wilson, R. Rawdon, **42**, 185; **49**, 285; **53**, 1n
Wilson, Richard, **41**, 197–8, 222; **44**, 20n, 69n; **45**, 168–9; **46**, 212, 219, 220; **47**, 222–3; **50**, 66, 110n, 243; **51**, 279; **52**, 285n, 298, 307; **53**, 54, 72n, 317–18; **54**, 91, 314; **55**, 7, 39n, 251, 341; **56**, 184n, 192n; **57**, 301; **58**, 4, 5, 172; **59**, 357–8, 368
Wilson, Rob, **55**, 180n
Wilson, Robert, actor, **6**, 74n; **15**, 68–70; **17**, 193; **27**, 130n; **29**, 162; **30**, 38; **32**, 106n, 109; **36**, 176; **39**, 224, 225; **40**, 198, 204; **42**, 150, 187; **44**, 232, 253; **47**, 3; **56**, 345–6; **57**, 336; **58**, 13, 62; **59**, 71, 72, 74, 75, 77, 78, 78n15; **60**, 21–2, 54
The Cobbler's Prophecy, **15**, 69, 72n
The Three Ladies of London, **13**, 103, 107; **15**, 72n; **17**, 44, 46–7, 49, 50, 51n, 52
The Three Lords and Three Ladies & London, **15**, 72n
see also Mundy, Anthony
Wilson, Roderick, **49**, 143n
Wilson, Scott, **44**, 44n; **50**, 243
Wilson, Snoo, **42**, 162; **54**, 73; **56**, 297; **58**, 150
Wilson, Stuart, **56**, 256, 282; **57**, 290
Wilson, Thomas, **9**, 143; **17**, 43, 78 and n, 80 and n, 81n, 225; **26**, 103, 112n; **32**, 163n, 164n, 171n, 174n; **37**, 180; **40**, 81, 97n; **41**, 103n; **43**, 238; **46**, 42, 45; **48**, 257; **49**, 46n; **53**, 13; **54**, 5, 8; **55**, 24n; **56**, 79; **57**, 197, 198
Arte of Rhetorique, **3**, 6, 15; **4**, 86; **7**, 14; **10**, 69, 144; **15**, 14
Wilson, Violet, **3**, 28
Wilson-Okamura, David Scott, **58**, 328, 333

Wiltenburg, Robert, **44**, 236
Wilton's Music Hall, **58**, 268
Wilton, Jack, **11**, 19
Wilton, Penelope, **35**, 151; **39**, 86n, 87
Wilton, Terence, **51**, 227
Wiltshire, Earl of (Henry Stafford), **60**, 68
Wiltshire, John, **58**, 83, 85
Wily Beguilde, **60**, 272n14
Wiman, Dwight D., **5**, 116
Wimsatt, James I., **24**, 143; **32**, 168n
Wimsatt, W. K. Jnr., **15**, 123; **18**, 158 (ed.); **28**, 57n; **33**, 53n; **39**, 135n; **44**, 207; **60**, 214n1
  English Stage Comedy, **14**, 4; **42**, 38n, 40n; **45**, 18n
Winch, Peter, **40**, 29n; **57**, 107
Winchester House, *see under* London
Winchester, Marquis of, **1**, 34
Winckelmann, J. J., **20**, 22
Winckelmann, Johannes, **43**, 2n
Wincor, Richard, **5**, 136; **15**, 120
Wind, Edgar, **24**, 66, 67; **25**, 103n, 104n; **26**, 116n; **28**, 76n; **29**, 91; **31**, 45, 46, 49, 51n; **34**, 95, 96; **37**, 99, 100n, 106; **44**, 215; **46**, 127n, 128n; **47**, 23n; **50**, 65, 118n; **53**, 29n; **56**, 35, 45
Windeatt, Barry, **53**, 174n
Windebank, Francis, **2**, 34
Windet, John, **15**, 128
Windhem, John, **11**, 90
Windsor, Barbara, **48**, 225
Windsor, Thomas, **11**, 72–3, 77n
Windt, Valentine, **4**, 123
Wine, M. L., **28**, 167, 179; **36**, 121, 123n, 129n; **49**, 210n; **52**, 83n
Winfield, Frank, **14**, 128
Wing, Donald, *Short-Title Catalogue, 1641–1700*, **6**, 57
Wingate, Charles E. L., **35**, 33n
Winger, Carsten, **14**, 122
Wingfield, **6**, 140
Wingfield, A., **27**, 112
Wingfield, Sir Edward, **14**, 104
Wingfield, Lewis Strange, The Hon., **31**, 187; **32**, 19; **41**, 24; **49**, 128
Wingfield, Sir Richard, **60**, 69–70
Wingfield, Sir Robert, **60**, 69–70
Winifrid, Saint, **56**, 198, 200
Winkler, Angela, **54**, 263; **55**, 323
Winman, Sarah, **45**, 152
Winn, James Anderson, **43**, 96–7; **55**, 267
Winny, James, **23**, 145, 158; **27**, 45n, **31**, 127n, 128, 130; **38**, 5, 64; **60**, 108n30
Winslow, Colin, **46**, 198
Winstanley, Eliza, **22**, 128, 130
Winstanley, Humphrey, **49**, 189n
Winstanley, Lilian, **9**, 12; **21**, 52n; **43**, 57n
Winstanley, Mr, **22**, 130
Winston, James, **35**, 8
Winston, Matthew, **36**, 172
Winstone, Ray, **57**, 45
Winter, Carl, **40**, 236n
Winter, June, **33**, 204
Winter, Michael, **47**, 190; **43**, 214; **46**, 192; **52**, 255; **56**, 298
Winter, S., **1**, 81
Winter, William, **9**, 68n; **20**, 81n; **21**, 103; **25**, 192; **32**, 19n, 24, 26, 37; **35**, 4, 7n, 10; **37**, 85n, 87n; **41**, 56n; **45**, 32n, 34n; **53**, 70; **58**, 40; **60**, 116n59, 116n60
Winters, Yvor, **24**, 91; **31**, 164; **32**, 214; **38**, 6
Wintershall, William, **58**, 241, 244
Winterson, Jeanette, **44**, 41, 43
Winterton, J. B., **24**, 179
Wintle, Sarah, **45**, 167
Winton, Roger, **8**, 123, 125; **9**, 121; **10**, 125
Winwood, Ralph, **11**, 92; **17**, 233n; **29**, 23n; **33**, 166; **35**, 130n; **44**, 154
Wiren, Dag, **10**, 121; **16**, 137
Wirgman, Charles, **48**, 100
Wirth, Franz Peter, **15**, 134
Wirthner, Naomi, **44**, 193
Wisbey, R. A., **27**, 187
Wisdom of Doctor Dodipol, The, **2**, 37; **16**, 170; **17**, 169
Wise Children, **50**, 264
Wise, Andrew, **25**, 194; **60**, 258–9
Wise, Ernie (Ernest Wiseman), **60**, 228
Wise, Herbert, **8**, 123
Wise, Thomas J., **3**, 45
Wisely, Willie, **53**, 283
Wiseman, Cardinal, **54**, 87–8
Wiseman, Polly, **55**, 333
Wiseman, Susan J., **52**, 290; **55**, 242n; **58**, 349; **60**, 129n33
Wisker, Stephen, **55**, 330
Wislicenus, Paul, **16**, 164; **31**, 5n
Wiss, Adrian, **42**, 194
Wisten, Fritz, **11**, 120
Wit at Several Weapons, **54**, 29
Witch of Edmonton, The, **17**, 175; **52**, 143, 147–8; **54**, 357
Witchcraft
  in *Macbeth*, **4**, 41–3
  North Berwick witches, **4**, 35, 42
  trials of witches, **4**, 35, 41–2
Wither, George, **1**, 63; **16**, 96; **17**, 91, 100n, 175, 207; **41**, 38; **56**, 32; **60**, 283
Witherington, R., *English Pageantry*, **14**, 3
Withington, R., **17**, 51
Withycombe, E. G., **47**, 262n
Witt, Anne E., **56**, 39n
Witt, Johan de, **60**, 45
Witt, Johannes de, *see* De Witt, Johannes
Witt, Robert W., **33**, 192; **53**, 303, 305
Wittgenstein, Ludwig Josef Johann, **24**, 105; **35**, 65; **36**, 21, 22, 23, 24, 25, 26, 27; **40**, 25–32, 188, 193; **42**, 165; **44**, 213; **46**, 146n; **48**, 120, 241; **52**, 269; **53**, 310; **57**, 107, 308
Wittkower, Rudolf, **17**, 39–40, 40n; **28**, 168; **30**, 158n; **46**, 117n
Wittmann, Henri, **53**, 1
Witton (Chester) grammar school, **17**, 53
Wittreich, Joseph, **39**, 219; **55**, 11; **59**, 239n1
Witzmann, Thomas, **49**, 278
Wivell, Abraham, **16**, 171
Wixson, Douglas C., **36**, 171; **38**, 13
Wladyslav, IV Vasa, Crown Prince of Poland, **36**, 145, 146–7
'W. N.', **34**, 12
Woddis, Carole, **56**, 237n
Wodehouse, P. G., **22**, 3; **34**, 181; **45**, 127; **51**, 219; **55**, 310
Woffington, Peg, **58**, 262
Wojcik, Jan, **46**, 218

Wojtczak, Tessa, **44**, 201
Woldan, Erich, **17**, 39n
Wolf, Amy, **58**, 18
Wolf, Christa, **44**, 217; **48**, 183
Wolf, Lucie, **43**, 115n
Wolf, Lucien, **51**, 161n
Wolf, Matt, **49**, 238
Wolfe, Don M., **57**, 70
Wolfe, George C., **52**, 34
Wolfe, John, **5**, 146; **6**, 79; **10**, 144; **13**, 109, 110n; **15**, 128; **21**, 148; **32**, 91n; **43**, 268–9; **52**, 129
Wolfe, Nicholas, **47**, 56n
Wolfensperger, Peter, **48**, 245
Shakespeare; Impartial and Partial, Strategies of Persuasion in the Comedies, **48**, 2
Wolff, Cynthia Griffin, **23**, 165
Wolff, E., **10**, 6
Wolff, Kurt H., **50**, 73n; **56**, 141n
Wolff, M. J., **1**, 9; **8**, 3; **15**, 13–15; **51**, 77n
Wolff, T., **26**, 167
'Shakespeare's Influence on Pushkin's Dramatic Work', **5**, 93–105
Wölfflin, Heinrich, **8**, 149; **20**, 5; **26**, 49
Wolfit, Sir Donald, **1**, 105–6; **5**, 120; **8**, 123, 125, 126, 132, 138; **16**, 27; **23**, 131; **24**, 37; **33**, 84, 85; **36**, 81; **47**, 48, 90; **49**, 225; **57**, 147
Wolfit, Margaret, **44**, 203
Wolfson, Susan J., **45**, 39n, 48n
Wolk, A., **26**, 154
Wolk, Emil, **45**, 155
Wollaton Hall, **12**, 11
Wollenberg, Susan, **44**, 238; **45**, 162
Wolley, Hannah, **49**, 302
Wollstonecraft, Mary, **55**, 108; **58**, 89
Wolper, Roy S., **48**, 57n
Wolpers, Theodore, **43**, 223
Wolsey, Cardinal Thomas, **13**, 100, 105n; **20**, 21, 22; **28**, 20, 21; **29**, 94; **43**, 63; **52**, 167–8, 173–5, 181; **54**, 242
Wolsey, Thomas, **38**, 25
Womack, Mark, **58**, 318, 324, 333
Womack, Peter, **50**, 250; **53**, 294
Woman Killed with Kindness, A, **52**, 296; **50**, 147
Woman's Prize; or The Tamer Tamed, The, **52**, 73; **54**, 340
Women Beware Women, **50**, 284; **54**, 15
Women's Theatre Group, **55**, 132; **58**, 298, 301
Womersley, David, **44**, 219; **50**, 251; **53**, 105n; **56**, 138n
Wonder of Women, The, **52**, 143
Wong, Benedict, **53**, 245
Wong, Denise, **42**, 155
Woo, John, **52**, 90
Wood, A. C., **13**, 104n
Wood, Andrew, **50**, 233; **52**, 261
Wood, Anne-Marie, **58**, 266
Wood, Anthony à, **4**, 78, 93; **16**, 119; **35**, 130; **54**, 350
Athenae Oxonienses, **4**, 86
Wood, Beth, **46**, 200
Wood, Briar, **55**, 175n
Wood, C., **15**, 17
Wood, Charles, **23**, 39; **43**, 172
Wood, Christopher John, **44**, 203
Wood, Clive, **36**, 152; **48**, 207–9; **55**, 288; **56**, 267; **59**, 314, 339
Wood, D., **46**, 82n
Wood, David, **55**, 75n
Wood, E. R., **13**, 166
Wood, Grant, **57**, 52
Wood, H. Harvey, **9**, 34n; **28**, 41n; **32**, 104n
Wood, Helen Atkinson, **43**, 216
Wood, J. T., **54**, 36, 37n
Wood, James O., **18**, 180; **19**, 147; **21**, 147, 163; **25**, 177, 188; **27**, 160, 191; **28**, 167, 181; **34**, 190–1; **53**, 274
Wood, John, **8**, 123; **26**, 145, 147, 148, 149; **37**, 52, 53; **42**, 147; **43**, 215; 44, 180–4; **45**, 125, 148; **47**, 199; **59**, 326, 327; **60**, 322
Wood, John Christopher, **41**, 186; **43**, 208; **58**, 302
Wood, Jon, **42**, 159
Wood, Juliette, **57**, 126
Wood, Manley, **59**, 134
Wood, Matthew, **47**, 216
Wood, Michael, **58**, 5, 6–7; **60**, 355
Wood, N. H., (ed.) *The Plays of John Marston*, **14**, 9
Wood, Nigel, **46**, 43n; **50**, 243, 248, 249, 250; **56**, 317
Wood, Peter, **9**, 120; **10**, 123; **15**, 145; **24**, 3n
Wood, Robert E., **33**, 200; **49**, 287
Wood, Roger, **42**, 37
Wood, Terry, **35**, 149
Woodall, Andrew, **59**, 311–12
Woodbridge, L. T., **37**, 190
Woodbridge, Linda, **42**, 213; **46**, 71n, 123n, 208; **47**, 224; **49**, 98n, 203n, 303; **53**, 75; **57**, 30; **58**, 310, 330, 334; **59**, 354; **60**, 81n40, 84n2, 114n49
Wooden, Rod, **52**, 258
Woodes, Nathaniel, **55**, 233
Woodeson, Nicholas, **42**, 41n, 137–8; **43**, 207; **44**, 202; **48**, 264
Woodfill, Walter L., **15**, 8; **19**, 101, 105n
Woodford, Donna, **58**, 358
Woodford, Thomas, **11**, 102, 103; **19**, 103; **40**, 218
Woodhall, Andrew, **51**, 248
Woodhead, M. R., **32**, 235; **34**, 174; **36**, 176; **51**, 178n
Woodhouse, Henry, **7**, 58
Woodhouse, Richard, **35**, 46n; **41**, 103n, 105n, 111, 112n
Woodhouse, Trish, **45**, 150
Woodington, Albie, **43**, 141, 142
Woodliffe, Oliver, **7**, 60; **40**, 214; **47**, 241
Woodman, Penelope, **59**, 343, 345
Woodmason, James, **37**, 45
Woodrow, Alan, **44**, 195
Woods, Alan, **39**, 76n
Woods, Charles P., **26**, 9
Woods, Karen, **42**, 188
Woods, Leigh, **35**, 177; **39**, 230, 233; **46**, 170n
Woods, William S., **53**, 14n
Woodson, William C., **32**, 236, 241–2; **33**, 210; **40**, 236
Woodstock, **3**, 18, 26, 51, 52, 94, 138; **4**, 143, 150; **6**, 4, 10, 36; **12**, 48; **14**, 44n; **15**, 169; **20**, 162; **55**, 21
Woodstock, Thomas of, **28**, 1, 4, 5, 8
Woodthorpe, Peter, **25**, 166, 168
Woodvine, John, **30**, 171, 172, 178; **33**, 169, 170, 176; **41**, 161, 185; **42**, 161; **45**, 131, 150; **47**, 218; **48**, 21; **50**, 206; **51**, 269; **53**, 250; **58**, 300; **60**, 209
Woodwall, William, **53**, 65, 67, 68
Woodward (Stratford Manor Court), **12**, 100
Woodward, Daniel H., **23**, 166n

Woodward, E. L., *see* McManaway, James G.
Woodward, Fraunces, **27**, 99
Woodward, George, **49**, 115
Woodward, Henry, **14**, 113; **49**, 116
Woodward, James, **57**, 74
Woodward, Jennifer, **54**, 134
Woodward, Joan (*later* Alleyn), **47**, 172; **60**, 51
Woodward, Kirsty, **60**, 311
Woodward, Peter, **41**, 191; **42**, 140–1, 157; **44**, 191, 196; **46**, 195
Woodward, Sarah, **41**, 188; **43**, 217; **47**, 204
Woodward, Steve, **42**, 157
Woodward, Tara, **49**, 277
Woodward, Tim, **42**, 157; **52**, 233, 251; **53**, 274; **54**, 262; **55**, 323
Woodward, Victoria, **52**, 232–3
Woof, Emily, **49**, 148, 240, 242; **50**, 233
Wooland, Norman, **6**, 145
Woolcock, Penny, **57**, 40, 45, 46, 47, 48, 51, 52
Wooldridge, H. E., **15**, 2, 3, 7
Wooldridge, Hugh, **46**, 195
Wooldridge, Ian, **41**, 187; **42**, 154; **44**, 199; **46**, 199; **47**, 217
Wooley, Robert, **42**, 156
Wooley, Sarah, **54**, 288
Woolf, Rosemary, **30**, 192
Woolf, Virginia, **6**, 102; **33**, 189; **37**, 13; **40**, 190, 210; **44**, 206, 241; **45**, 115, 144; **47**, 110; **52**, 288; **58**, 118–29, 148; **60**, 186n11
Woolfe, John, **25**, 148
Woolfenden, Guy, **30**, 176; **38**, 207; **42**, 151, 154; **44**, 199; **45**, 148, 172; **46**, 202; **47**, 209, 211; **50**, 228, 230; **55**, 335
Woolgar, Fenella, **54**, 270; **56**, 264, 266
Woolland, Brian, **53**, 321–2
Wooton, Sir Henry, **54**, 348–9
Wootton, David, **59**, 250n82
Wootton, John, **60**, 353–4
Worall, Jessica, **53**, 262
Worcester, 3rd Earl of (William Somerset), **60**, 7
Worcester, Earl of, **17**, 10, 168
Worcester, Edward Somerset, Earl of, *see under* Somerset, Edward
Worde, Winkyn de, **56**, 30; **1**, 67; **59**, 243, 244n38, 246n58
Scala Perfectionis, **1**, 67
Worden, Blair, **44**, 6n, 11n; **49**, 302; **54**, 333; **55**, 211n; **56**, 215n, 217n; **60**, 342
Wordsworth, Bishop Charles, **54**, 54, 87
Wordsworth, Elizabeth, **55**, 113n
Wordsworth, Richard, **15**, 146
Wordsworth, William, **4**, 10, 50, 52; **7**, 30; **9**, 134, 138; **13**, 63; **14**, 82; **15**, 11, 15, 48; **21**, 68; **40**, 200–1; **43**, 121; **49**, 139; **53**, 106, 115; **56**, 119, 140
Worke for Cutlers, **4**, 95
Worlock, Gloucester, **39**, 81n
Wormald, Jenny, **57**, 4, 9
Wormuth, F. D., **53**, 69n
Worpole, Ken, **56**, 243n, 244n
Worrall, Jessica, **48**, 201; **50**, 225; **54**, 294; **56**, 291
Worsley, Alice, **49**, 189n
Worsley, Joyce, **12**, 119
Worsley, Robert, **8**, 148
Worsley, T. C., **7**, 146n; **38**, 17; **44**, 28n
Worsop, Edward, **33**, 142, 143n
Worth *v.* Baskervile (Worth, Ellis, *versus* Baskervile, Susan), Chancery suit of 1623 discussed, **7**, 57–68
Worth, Blandina, **7**, 67n
Worth, Ellis, junior, **7**, 67n
Worth, Ellis, senior, actor, **7**, 59, 60, 62, 63, 65, 67n; **40**, 219; **58**, 224
Worth, Irene, **7**, 114; **8**, 129; **16**, 148–50; **24**, 3n, 4, 8; **39**, 79n, 191, 193, 194
Worth, Katharine, **48**, 4n
Worth, Katherine, junior, **7**, 67n
Worth, Roland H., **54**, 43n
Wortham, Christopher, **40**, 215, 219; **49**, 289
Worthen, Christopher, **51**, 284
Worthen, John, **45**, 2n
Worthen, William, B., **47**, 8; **48**, 202; **52**, 88n, 89, 287–8; **53**, 294; **54**, 316; **56**, 342; **57**, 42; **58**, 61, 160, 161; **59**, 212n63; **60**, 148, 150, 151, 152, 156, 360
Wortley, Sir Francis, **55**, 92
Wotton, Henry, **52**, 166n
Cupid's Cautels, **8**, 4
Wotton, Sir Henry, **23**, 171; **28**, 131; **36**, 144; **43**, 55n, 64n; **44**, 75; **51**, 239; **56**, 137–8
Wotton, Thomas, **43**, 67
Woudhuysen, Henry R., **38**, 230; **40**, 173; **44**, 207, 256; **45**, 195n; **46**, 237n; **51**, 332; **52**, 309–11, 321; **53**, 25n, 26n; **57**, 197, 207, 210, 217, 218, 222, 341; **58**, 353, 357; **59**, 23, 23n18, 27, 116n33, 118, 122n53; **60**, 256n16
Wrangham, Francis, **59**, 279n34, 280n35
Wrather, Jonathan, **49**, 278
Wraxhall, Nathaniel, **38**, 69
Wray, Ramona, **52**, 286; **55**, 384; **56**, 4n; **60**, 355, 356, 360
Wreford, Edgar, **7**, 125
Wren, Christopher, **53**, 204n
Wren, Robert M., **24**, 166n
Wright, Angus, **51**, 219; **58**, 275; **60**, 285
Wright, Bernard, **45**, 148
Wright, Celeste Turner, **46**, 117n; **54**, 91, 96n
Wright, Chris, **47**, 217
Wright, Edward, **11**, 91; **17**, 28, 144; **19**, 106n; **32**, 86; **55**, 32
Wright, Ernest Hunter, **29**, 107n, 111n
Wright, George T., **35**, 177; **43**, 18n, 21n, 227–8; **46**, 100, 103, 105n; **50**, 95n, 149, 150; **53**, 310–11; **54**, 128; **55**, 354; **56**, 309, 311; **58**, 318; **59**, 94n6
Wright, Graeme, **14**, 126
Wright, H. G., **9**, 142
Wright, James, **5**, 53; **16**, 95; **58**, 235, 240–3
Wright, Joanne, **51**, 10
Wright, John, **33**, 208; **52**, 304; **54**, 284; **55**, 28–35; **58**, 223, 224, 226
Wright, John, actor, **7**, 67n
Wright, Joseph, **9**, 119; **47**, 96, 106; **49**, 120, 121, 122n
Dialect Dictionary **7**, 3
Wright, Jules, **41**, 186; **59**, 204–6
Wright, L., **7**, 79n
Wright, Laurence, **44**, 222; **46**, 224
Wright, Louis B., **1**, 8, 10; **6**, 10; **9**, 132; **11**, 106n, 153; **13**, 122, 165; **14**, 166n; **15**, 7; **17**, 34, 41n, 111n; **18**, 175; **19**, 148; **20**, 26n; **24**, 169; **32**, 97n; **41**, 22n
'An Obligation to Shakespeare and the Public', **16**, 1–9
Wright, Lyle H., **6**, 61, 63n
Wright, Marmaduke, **58**, 224
Wright, Matthew, **51**, 258

Wright, Michael, **56**, 237n
Wright, Norman, **1**, 109
Wright, Peter M., **55**, 381
Wright, Richard, **60**, 330
Wright, Rosemary, **39**, 225; **55**, 250n
Wright, Susan, **39**, 184, 185; **40**, 159, 166–7
Wright, Thomas, **17**, 216; **50**, 70; **55**, 62, 93n; **56**, 83n; **57**, 21
The Passions of the Minde in Generall, **4**, 27
Wright, Tom, **60**, 327
Wright, Trevelyan, **54**, 292
Wright, W., **21**, 148
Wright, William Aldis (*see also* Clark, W. G.), **2**, 39, 41; **4**, 67n; **5**, 50, 54; **7**, 49, 51–2, 55; **19**, 1, 2, 81n; **32**, 95n; **47**, 154; **52**, 183n; **55**, 388; **59**, 53–4, 160n12
Wright, W. S., **47**, 172n
Wrightson, Keith, **38**, 26n, 29n, 30n, 31n, 32n; **40**, 137n
Wrightson, Nigel, **52**, 256
Wrigley, E. A., **38**, 26n, 29n
Wrigley, Steven, **46**, 199
Wringer, Leo, **42**, 151; **50**, 216, 218; **53**, 252; **57**, 295; **58**, 304; **60**, 162
Wriothesley, Henry, *see* Southampton, Third Earl of
Wriothesley, Thomas, **17**, 235–7
Wriothesley, William, **41**, 107
Wroth, Lady Mary, **39**, 231, 235; **44**, 227; **46**, 131n; **51**, 279; **54**, 301; **55**, 380; **58**, 221; **60**, 344
Wroth, Sir Robert, **37**, 190; **39**, 235; **57**, 213
Wrottesley, Mrs George, **18**, 99
Wroughton, Richard, **35**, 48n
'W. S.', anon., **59**, 362
Locrine, **59**, 72, 73
Thomas Lord Cromwell, **59**, 71, 73, 76, 77n12, 78n15
Wulf, Joseph, **48**, 62n
Wulfstan, **59**, 242, 249, 252
Wulstan, David, **58**, 222
Wunsche, Janine, **56**, 297
Wurfl, G., **18**, 118n
Württemberg, Louis Frederick, Duke of, **3**, 53
Würzbach, Natasha, **55**, 91n, 92
Wurzbach, Wolfgang von, **20**, 98, 104n
Wyat, **55**, 265
Wyatt, Colin, **45**, 146
Wyatt, Mr, **22**, 132
Wyatt, Peter, **39**, 194; **47**, 97
Wyatt, R. O., **28**, 167
Wyatt, Sir Thomas, **3**, 65; **14**, 146; **15**, 167; **23**, 165; **38**, 24; **43**, 228; **44**, 1, 10; **46**, 46n, 238; **51**, 135
Wycherley, William, **36**, 82; **37**, 125; **47**, 193n; **53**, 194
Plain Dealer, **6**, 55
Wyck, Thomas, **1**, 36n
Wycliff, John, **6**, 59; **52**, 186; **54**, 100
Wyfe, Lynn, **44**, 200
Wyld, H. C., **7**, 3, 4, 24n; **17**, 223–4
Wylde, David, **41**, 185, 191
Wylde, Humphrey, *see* Welde, Humphrey
Wylie, J. H., **44**, 56n, 59n, 60n
Wylton, Tim, **29**, 154; **49**, 261
Wymark, Patrick, **9**, 129; **11**, 135; **12**, 128; **14**, 129
Wymer, Roland, **40**, 199
Wynder, Malcolm, **42**, 156
Wynder, Rowland, **45**, 177–8
Wyndham, Francis, **57**, 147
Wyndham, George, **4**, 9; **7**, 42; **15**, 11, 19, 22; **40**, 73n, 86n; **41**, 196n
Wyndham, Lewis, **40**, 193
Wyndham, Marivic, **55**, 180n
Wyndham, W., **18**, 187
Wyngaerde, Anthonis, **53**, 197, 198, 203n, 209n
Wynne, Alison, **45**, 155
Wynne, Gilbert, **47**, 101
Wynne, Ken, **45**, 119
Wynne-Davies, Marion, **45**, 160; **50**, 256; **60**, 100n40
Wynyard, Diana, **3**, 122, 124–8; **6**, 143; **16**, 20; **18**, 119; **32**, 29, 32
Wynyard, Melanie, **47**, 216
Wyrick, Deborah Baker, **37**, 194; **51**, 181n, 182
Wyver, John, **39**, 104n
Wyzniewski, Arno, **48**, 180

Xavier, Francis, **52**, 211n
Xenophon, **4**, 27; **25**, 99, 100n; **31**, 45, 46; **33**, 23
Xiaoyang, Zhang, **57**, 169
Xing, Yunfei, **57**, 174
Xu Xiaozhong, **58**, 338; **57**, 169, 171, 173

Yachnin, Paul, **35**, 178, 179; **45**, 180; **46**, 219; **56**, 342; **58**, 349
Yadin, Yosef, **14**, 121
Yaeger, Patricia, **46**, 144n; **51**, 19n
Yale Elizabethan Club publications, **18**, 189–90
Yale, D. E. C., **29**, 93n, 97n, 98n
Yale, Department of Drama at, **1**, 13
Yalman, Tunç, **18**, 130
Yalton, Jaron, **49**, 270
Yamada, Akihiro, **22**, 171; **24**, 161, 167; **55**, 181n
Yamada, Naomi, **41**, 211
Yamada, Yumiko, **54**, 304
Yamagishi, Masayuki, **47**, 241
Yamaguchi, Hideo, **19**, 137
Yang, Daniel S. P., **48**, 2; **56**, 165
Yang, Tom, **48**, 225
Yang, Zhouhan, **36**, 55
Yannopoulos, Dinos, **11**, 121
Yano, Masato, **19**, 132
Yao, Li Jia, **42**, 152
Yardley, May, **3**, 21n
Yarmolinsky, Avrahm, **5**, 105n; **35**, 153n
Yarrow, Duncan, **11**, 124
Yarrow, Ralph, **50**, 30n
Yarvet, Yuri, **39**, 83, 84
Yarwood, Brian, **54**, 284
Yate, Anne, **49**, 185
Yates, Donald A., **34**, 161n
Yates, Dame Frances A., **4**, 16; **6**, 80, 84, 88n, 168; **7**, 6, 106n; **8**, 6; **17**, 216n; **20**, 167; **21**, 155; **23**, 172; **24**, 48, 166; **27**, 45n; **28**, 39; **29**, 26n, 158, 173; **30**, 166; **31**, 185; **33**, 140n, 163n; **37**, 196; **38**, 49n, 51, 53n, 56; **39**, 139n, 140n, 232; **40**, 216; **41**, 41; **42**, 89n; **43**, 45n, 53n, 236; **44**, 37; **46**, 111n; **47**, 111; **52**, 51, 65n, 194n; **54**, 126n; **55**, 247n; **57**, 203, 210, 218; **59**, 229n7, 362
A Study of 'Love's Labour's Lost', **3**, 10, 25

Yates, Julian, **57**, 17, 18
Yates, Marjorie, **33**, 180; **45**, 153
Yates, Mary Ann, **53**, 223, 226n
Yates, Peter, **39**, 76
Yaw, Sandra, **42**, 152; **47**, 214
Ye, Zhongmin, **57**, 180
Yearsley, Macleod, **17**, 258n
Yeats, William B., **4**, 2; **6**, 12; **7**, 4, 6, 10, 30; **9**, 133; **12**, 72; **14**, 145; **15**, 50, 61; **16**, 34, 38; **21**, 141; **24**, 11, 46, 169; **26**, 139; **28**, 10; **29**, 26; **30**, 1, 90, 104; **34**, 178; **36**, 1, 29–30, 51; **39**, 168, 240; **40**, 107; **45**, 8, 12; **46**, 81, 88; **47**, 81; **49**, 212; **50**, 31; **52**, 161, 162n; **53**, 55; **55**, 302; **58**, 122
Lapis Lazuli, **8**, 121
Yelland, David, **51**, 248; **52**, 245
Yellow Earth Theatre Company, **58**, 301
Yelverton, Henry, **28**, 68
Yeobright, Clym, **36**, 95n
Yeomans, David, **11**, 102, 103
Yershon, Gary, **41**, 187–8; **44**, 192; **45**, 156; **46**, 178; **47**, 209; **52**, 255
Yerushalmi, Rina, **49**, 278
Yip, David, **42**, 151
Yockney, John, **58**, 224
Yoder, Audrey, **8**, 35
Animal Analogy, **2**, 136
Yoder, R. Audrey, **27**, 158, 166; **28**, 156; **41**, 69, 73–4
'"Sons and Daughters of the Game": an Essay on Shakespeare's *Troilus and Cressida*', **25**, 11–25
Yogev, Michael, **49**, 284; **53**, 296
Yoklavich, J., **7**, 145
Yong, Bartholomew, **22**, 168
Yonge, Walter, **58**, 17, 18, 20
York cycle, **7**, 69, 70; **21**, 54, 55; **23**, 120
York Cycle: *Sacrificium Cayme and Abell*, **20**, 73n
York House, *see under* London
York, Duke of, **43**, 95, 97–8; **54**, 197
York, Edward, **49**, 271; **51**, 261
York, Michael, **39**, 105
York, Neil L., **47**, 232
York, Philip, **41**, 185
York, Susannah, **51**, 234, 235, 244; **57**, 298; **58**, 307
Yorke, Oliver, **56**, 128n
Yorkshire Tragedy, A, **52**, 84–5; **1**, 46; **4**, 92; **7**, 95; **12**, 36; **15**, 38; **42**, 162; **43**, 217; **48**, 277; **55**, 390; **60**, 266, 266n42
Yörükaslan, Aytaç, **18**, 130
Yoshida, Kotaro, **57**, 288; **60**, 303
Yoshihara, Yukari, **60**, 130–40, 140n34
Yoshimi, Chisato, **58**, 264
Yoshioka, Fumio, **44**, 221; **46**, 219; **54**, 321
Yoshitomi, Sakae, **45**, 168
Young, Abigail, **47**, 49n
Young, Alan R., **29**, 164, 171; **33**, 16n; **41**, 3n, 223; **43**, 60n, 246; **52**, 298n; **53**, 343; **57**, 314–15, 343
Young, B. A., **31**, 151n; **45**, 9n
Young, Bartholomew, **45**, 69n
Young, Bruce W., **43**, 232; **46**, 209
Young, Charles, **35**, 35
Young, Charles Mayne, **9**, 55; **10**, 74; **35**, 44; **56**, 111
Young, Christopher, **12**, 147; **26**, 85; **60**, 144n12
Young, David P., **22**, 153; **27**, 167, 168; **29**, 6, 8, 90; **30**, 128, 131n; **32**, 10; **33**, 189; **37**, 4, 9, 72n; **40**, 91n, 94n 103; **44**, 213; **56**, 89n
Young, Edward, **9**, 94, 97; **16**, 31; **21**, 67
Young, Miss Esther, **51**, 83
Young, Filson, **39**, 8
Young, Freda Jackson, **47**, 95
Young, G. M., **6**, 162; **9**, 141; **13**, 39n
Shakespeare and the Termers, **2**, 144
Young, Hugh, **49**, 200
Young, Isabella, **51**, 88
Young, Karl, **19**, 69; **57**, 237
Young, Nicholas, **46**, 196; **50**, 229; **54**, 283, 291
Young, Richard B., **15**, 46, 49n
Young, Sir Richard, **2**, 34
Young, Robert, **46**, 96n; **47**, 93, 94, 99, 105–6
Young, Stark, **35**, 2
Young, Stephen Blase, **47**, 244n
Young, Steven C., **23**, 168
Young, Susan, **50**, 264
Young, Thomas, *England's Bane*, **15**, 38
Young, W., **36**, 147n
Young, William, **8**, 107n; **47**, 18n; **55**, 109n; **58**, 224
Young, Sir William, **56**, 97n
Younge, Richard, **35**, 32, 35
Younger, Mrs Elizabeth, **51**, 55
Younger, Joseph, **53**, 218
Youngs, Tim, **53**, 168n
Yu, N. C., **6**, 114
Yu, Weijie, **57**, 169
Yugoslavia, report on Shakespeare in, **15**, 140; **18**, 133–5
Yugoslavia, Shakespeare and difficulty of translating, **4**, 118–19
recent productions, **4**, 120–2
translations, **4**, 117–19
Yuill, Jimmy, **42**, 130; **46**, 187; **55**, 325
Yutkevich, Sergei, **39**, 5, 85; **54**, 147n
Yuzovski, Y., **2**, 126

Záborský, J., **4**, 115n
Zabus, Chantal, **56**, 158n
Zacconi, Ermete, **20**, 121
Zacharias, John, **10**, 121
Zachrisson, R. E., **7**, 3, 4
Zadek, Peter, **37**, 162; **44**, 94; **49**, 269; **50**, 33, 34, 35, 39, 230; **54**, 263; **55**, 323; **60**, 166
Zadorovna, Velta, **31**, 174–5
Zaehner, R. C., **59**, 235–6
Zagorin, Perez, **54**, 97n
Zagorski, M., **2**, 126
Zähringer, Georg, **48**, 61n
Zaim, Turgut, **9**, 116
Zaimoglu, Feridun, **60**, 287
Zaïre, **3**, **98**, 104
Zajko, Vanda, **59**, 367
Zak, William F., **55**, 9
Zalce, Alfredo, **54**, 160–1
Zalkinson, Isaac E., **5**, 113
Zampari, Franco, **20**, 122

Zander, Horst, **37**, 159n; **38**, 225; **59**, 353, 354–5, 368; **60**, 132n10
Zandvoort, R. W., **7**, 138; **10**, 5; **11**, 140, 141; **18**, 127
Zandwijk, Alize, **57**, 293
Zankevich, M., **5**, 117
Zaradin, John, **43**, 213
Zaradski, Iu., **13**, 133
Zareschi, Elena, **7**, 112; **15**, 136
Zarian, Rouben, **24**, 169
Zarrilli, Philip B., **55**, 281n; **60**, 147n19
Zaslavsky, Robert, **49**, 292
Zasukin, N., **16**, 138
Zavadsky, Yuri, **2**, 106; **5**, 117
Zbierski, Henryk, *Shakespeare and the 'War of the Theatres'*, **12**, 140 and n
Zeami, Motokiyo, **56**, 346
Zeeveld, H. G., **18**, 170
Zeeveld, W. Gordon, **6**, 7; **7**, 133; **26**, 98; **28**, 63n, 68; **29**, 84, 157–8; **38**, 11; **53**, 69n
Zeffirelli, G. Franco, **15**, 146, 147–55; **16**, 23, 135, 147; **18**, 126; **24**, 65, 128; **37**, 88; **38**, 243; **39**, 39, 65, 75; **42**, 199; **45**, 12, 53, 61, 63; **46**, 193; **47**, 10; **48**, 263; **49**, 3, 4, 74, 87, 142, 153, 157, 158–79; **50**, 30, 262; **52**, 90, 91n; **55**, 382–3; **56**, 347; **58**, 47
Zeifman, Hersh, **36**, 23n, 25n
Zeitlin, Jacob, **46**, 14n
Zelénski, Tadeusz Boy, **13**, 69
Želenský, Drahõs, **4**, 114
Zelauto, **54**, 90–6, 99
Zelený, Jendřich, **35**, 76
Zelinsky-Zelinsky, V. A., **5**, 104n
Zeller, Gaston, **44**, 60n
Zeller, Hans, **38**, 89n
Zellwecker, Edwin, **4**, 128; **5**, 111
Zender, Karl F., **48**, 247, 252; **55**, 352
Zeno, **33**, 23; **35**, 162
Zesmer, David M., **31**, 176
Zeyer, Julius, **9**, 103
Zeyneck, Theodor von, **8**, 118; **15**, 134; **16**, 63
Zglinicki, Simone V., **40**, 56
Zhang Qihong, **58**, 338
Zhang, Xiao Yang, **50**, 264
Zheng, Shifeng, **57**, 170, 171
Zhenghua, Ji, **42**, 152
Zhong, Mingde, **57**, 181
Zhouhan, Yan, **42**, 179
Zhu Shenghao, **36**, 55
Zhukovsky, V. A., **5**, 99
Ziablikova, Aida, **58**, 340
Ziegel, Erich, **1**, 115
Ziegler, Georgianna, **39**, 225; **40**, 232n; **44**, 33; **46**, 71n; **51**, 286, 300; **54**, 311; **57**, 128
Ziegler, Joseph, **39**, 188, 189; **40**, 158, 160, 162–4, 168
Ziegler, Matilda, **44**, 194; **55**, 311
Ziegler, Philip, **50**, 19n
Ziellenbach, Annette, **59**, 342
Zillich, Winifred, **6**, 120
Zimansky, Curt A., **21**, 27n, 67, 68, 73; **26**, 9; **37**, 124n, 145n; **46**, 66n; **49**, 210
Rymer's *Critical Works*, **11**, 141
Zimara, Mercantonio, **40**, 79
Zimbardo, R. A., **27**, 163–4; **38**, 8; **41**, 204; **43**, 11n; **45**, 167
Zimmerman, Heiner O., **49**, 287
Zimmerman, Susan, **40**, 235; **46**, 5; **47**, 228, 247–8; **49**, 104n, 213n; **51**, 328–9; **53**, 234n; **54**, 126n
Zimmermann, Franklin B., **51**, 81n
Zimmermann, Heinz, **30**, 189; **37**, 158n
Zimmermann, P., **33**, 155n, 161n
Zingarelli, N. A., **18**, 78
Zinkernagel, Franz, **9**, 100n
Zins, H., **32**, 198n
Zirotin, Baron von, **14**, 109n
Zitner, Sheldon P., **13**, 159; **22**, 156, 183; **24**, 144; **27**, 179; **32**, 177n; **38**, 166n; **39**, 10, 86n, 215, 216, 247; **40**, 233; **41**, 61n, 133n; **42**, 109n; **43**, 8n; **44**, 214, 215; **46**, 29n; **47**, 8, 271–3; **51**, 325; **52**, 6n; **55**, 43n, 188–9; **58**, 358
Živanović, M., **4**, 121, **15**, 141
Živojinović, B., **18**, 134
Živojinović, V., **4**, 118, 119; **15**, 142; **18**, 134
Žižek, Slavoj, **51**, 284; **53**, 75; **55**, 340; **56**, 141, 347; **58**, 180, 183, 187; **59**, 353; **60**, 345–6
Zoega, Mathias, **22**, 119–20
Zoffany, Johann, **13**, 74, 80n; **16**, 110; **49**, 155; **51**, 107–13, 121–3; **57**, 85
Zohar, Miriam, **10**, 119
Zohn, Harry, **39**, 53n
Zola, Émile, **14**, 87; **55**, 143, 145–7
La Terre, **14**, 87
Zolbrod, Paul G., **26**, 158; **29**, 165; **31**, 12n
Zolchow, Heiko, **40**, 55n
Zoob, David, **45**, 150
Zook, Kristen, **46**, 90n
Zorn, Harry, **56**, 77n, 140n
Zornov, Edith, **56**, 5n
Zouche, Sir Edward, **55**, 93n
Zoust portrait of Shakespeare, *see under* Shakespeare, William, portraits
Zubov, K., **13**, 133
Zubova, N., **15**, 140; **16**, 139
Zuccaro portrait of Shakespeare, *see under* Shakespeare, William, portraits
Zucker, Carole, **56**, 173n
Zucker, David Hard, **27**, 176; **44**, 65
Zuger, Harry, **31**, 167
Zukav, Gary, **40**, 145, 148n, 151; **42**, 208
Zuolin, Huang, **42**, 152
Župančić, O., **4**, 117–18, 119; **15**, 142
Zwicker, Steven N., **41**, 196n; **43**, 97; **49**, 302; **55**, 231n; **57**, 71, 126
Zwingli, Ulrich, **54**, 44, 139
Zylbercwaig, Zalmen, **55**, 116, 125n
Zyvatkauskas, Betty, **57**, 321
Zyvatkauskas, Sonia, **57**, 321